CAPTAIN JOHN SMITH
WITH OTHER NARRATIVES

Captain John Smith

WRITINGS
WITH OTHER NARRATIVES OF
ROANOKE, JAMESTOWN, AND THE
FIRST ENGLISH SETTLEMENT
OF AMERICA

THE LIBRARY OF AMERICA

The paper used in this publication meets the
minimum requirements of the American National Standard for
Information Sciences—Permanence of Paper for Printed
Library Materials, ANSI Z39.48—1984.

Distributed to the trade in the United States
by Penguin Putnam Inc.
and in Canada by Penguin Books Canada Ltd.

Library of Congress Catalog Number: 2006050239
For cataloging information, see end of Index.
ISBN 978–1–59853–001–8

First Printing
The Library of America—171

Manufactured in the United States of America

JAMES HORN
SELECTED THE TEXTS AND WROTE THE NOTES
FOR THIS VOLUME

Captain John Smith: Writings
with Other Narratives of Roanoke, Jamestown,
and the First English Settlement of America
is published with support from the
National Endowment for the Humanities.

Contents

A TRUE RELATION

of such occurrences and
accidents of noate as hath hapned
in Virginia since the first planting of
that Collony, which is now resident
in the South part thereof, till the
last returne from thence.

Written by Captaine Smith
one of the said Collony, to a
worshipfull friend of his in England.

1608

TO THE COURTEOUS READER.

Courteous, Kind and indifferent Readers, whose willing-nesse to reade and heare this following discourse, doth ex-plaine to the world your hearty affection, to the prosecuting and furtherance of so worthy an action: so it is, that like to an unskilfull actor, who having by misconstruction of his right Cue, over-slipt himselfe, in beginning of a contrary part, and fearing the hatefull hisse of the captious multitude, with a modest blush retires himselfe in private; as doubting the repre-hension of his whole audience in publicke, and yet againe upon further deliberation, thinking it better to know their censures at the first, and upon submission to reape pardon, then by seeking to smother it, to incurre the danger of a secret scandall: Imboldening himselfe upon the curteous kindnesse of the best, and not greatly respecting the worst, comes fourth againe, makes an Apollogie for himselfe, shewes the cause of his error, craves pardon for his rashnes, and in fine, receives a generall applauditie of the whole assemblie: so I gentle Readers, hap-pening upon this relation by chance (as I take it, at the second or third hand) induced thereunto by divers well willers of the action, and none wishing better towards it then my selfe, so farre foorth as my poore abilitie can or may stretch too, I thought good to publish it: but the Author being absent from the presse, it cannot be doubted but that some faults have es-caped in the printing, especially in the names of Countries, Townes, and People, which are somewhat strange unto us: but most of all, and which is the chiefe error, (for want of knowl-edge of the Writer) some of the bookes were printed under the name of Thomas Watson, by whose occasion I know not, un-lesse it were the over rashnesse, or mistaking of the workemen, but since having learned that the saide discourse was written by Captaine Smith, who is one of the Counsell there in Virginia: I

thought good to make the like Apollogie, by shewing the true
Author so farre as my selfe could learne, not doubting, but
that the wise noting it as an error of ignorance, will passe it
over with patience, and if worthy an applauditie, to reserve it
to the Author, whose paines in my judgement deserveth commendations; somewhat more was by him written, which being
as I thought (fit to be private) I would not adventure to make
it publicke. What more may be expected concerning the scituation of the Country, the nature of the clime, number of our
people there resident, the manner of their government, and
living, the commodities to be produced, and the end and effect it may come too, I can say nothing more then is here written, only what I have learned and gathered from the generall
consent of all (that I have conversed withall) aswell marriners
as others, which have had imployment that way; is that the
Country is excellent and pleasant, the clime temperate and
healthfull, the ground fertill and good, the commodities to be
expected (if well followed) many, for our people, the worst being already past, these former having indured the heate of the
day, whereby those that shall succeede, may at ease labour for
their profit, in the most sweete, coole, and temperate shade:
the action most honorable, and the end to the high glory of
God, to the erecting of true religion among Infidells, to the
overthrow of superstition and idolatrie, to the winning of
many thousands of wandring sheepe, unto Christs fold, who
now, and till now, have strayed in the unknowne paths of
Paganisme, Idolatrie, and superstition: yea, I say the Action
being well followed, as by the grave Senators, and worthy ad-
venturors, it hath beene worthily begunne: will tend to the
everlasting renowne of our Nation, and to the exceeding good
and benefit of our Weale publicke in generall: whose Counsells, labours, godly and industrious endevours, I beseech the
mightie Jehovah to blesse, prosper, and further, with his heavenly ayde, and holy assistance.

Farewell.
I.H.

A TRUE RELATION

of such occurrences and accidents
of note, as hath hapned in Virginia,
since the first planting of that Collony,
which is now resident in the
South part thereof, till the
last returne.

KINDE SIR, commendations remembred, etc. You shall
understand that after many crosses in the downes by tempests, wee arrived safely uppon the Southwest part of the great
Canaries: within foure or five daies after, we set saile for Dominica, the 26. of Aprill: the first land we made, wee fell with
Cape Henry, the verie mouth of the Bay of Chissiapiacke,
which at that present we little expected, having by a cruell
storme bene put to the Northward: anchoring in this Bay
twentie or thirtie went a shore with the Captain, and in comming aboard, they were assalted with certaine Indians, which
charged them within Pistoll shot: in which conflict, Captaine
Archer and Mathew Morton were shot: wherupon Captaine
Newport seconding them, made a shot at them, which the Indians little respected, but having spent their arrowes retyred
without harme. And in that place was the Box opened, wherin
the Counsell for Virginia was nominated: and arriving at the
place where wee are now seated, the Counsell was sworne, the
President elected, which for that yeare was Maister Edward
Maria Wingfield, where was made choice for our scituation, a
verie fit place for the erecting of a great cittie, about which
some contention passed betwixt Captaine Wingfield and Captaine Gosnold. Notwithstanding all our provision was brought
a shore, and with as much speede as might bee wee went about
our fortification.

The two and twenty day of Aprill, Captain Newport and my
selfe with divers others, to the number of twenty two persons,
set forward to discover the River, some fiftie or sixtie miles,
finding it in some places broader, and in some narrower; the
Countrie (for the moste part) on each side plaine high ground,

with many fresh Springes, the people in all places kindely intreating us, daunsing and feasting us with strawberries, Mulberies, Bread, Fish, and other their Countrie provisions wherof
we had plenty: for which Captaine Newport kindely requited
their least favours with Bels, Pinnes, Needles, beades or Glasses,
which so contented them that his liberallitie made them follow
us from place to place, and ever kindely to respect us. In the
midway staying to refresh our selves in a little Ile foure or five
savages came unto us which described unto us the course of
the River, and after in our journey, they often met us, trading
with us for such provision as wee had, and ariving at Arsatecke,
hee whom we supposed to bee the chiefe King of all the rest,
moste kindely entertained us, giving us a guide to go with us
up the River to Powhatan, of which place their great Emperor
taketh his name, where he that they honored for King used us
kindely. But to finish this discoverie, we passed on further,
where within a mile we were intercepted with great craggy
stones that in midst of the river, where the water falleth so
rudely, and with such a violence, as not any boat can possibly
passe, and so broad disperseth the streame, as there is not past
five or sixe Foote at a low water, and to the shore scarce passage with a barge, the water floweth foure foote, and the
freshes by reason of the Rockes have left markes of the inundations 8. or 9. foote: The south side is plaine low ground, and
the north side high mountaines, the rockes being of a gravelly
nature, interlaced with many vains of glistring spangles.

That night we returned to Powhatan: the next day (being
Whitsunday after dinner) we returned to the fals, leaving a
mariner in pawn with the Indians for a guide of theirs. Hee
that they honoured for King followed us by the river. That
afternoone we trifled in looking upon the Rockes and river
(further he would not goe) so there we erected a crosse, and
that night taking our man at Powhatans, Captaine Newport
congratulated his kindenes with a Gown and a Hatchet: returning to Arsetecke, and stayed there the next day to observe
the height therof, and so with many signes of love we departed. The next day the Queene of Apamatuck kindely intreated us, her people being no lesse contented then the rest,
and from thence we went to another place, (the name whereof

I doe not remember) where the people shewed us the manner of their diving for Mussels, in which they finde Pearles.

That night passing by Weanock some twentie miles from our Fort, they according to their former churlish condition, seemed little to affect us, but as wee departed and lodged at the point of Weanocke, the people the next morning seemed kindely to content us. Yet we might perceive many signes of a more Jealousie in them then before, and also the Hinde that the King of Arseteck had given us, altered his resolution in going to our Fort, and with many kinde circumstances left us there. This gave us some occasion to doubt some mischiefe at the Fort, yet Captaine Newport intended to have visited Paspahegh and Tappahanocke, but the instant change of the winde being faire for our return we repaired to the fort with all speed, where the first we heard was that 400. Indians the day before had assalted the fort, and supprised it. Had not God (beyond al their expectations) by meanes of the shippes at whom they shot with their Ordinances and Muskets, caused them to retire, they had entred the fort with our own men, which were then busied in setting Corne, their armes beeing then in drie-fats and few ready but certain Gentlemen of their own, in which conflict, most of the Counsel was hurt, a boy slaine in the Pinnas, and thirteene or fourteene more hurt. With all speede we pallisadoed our Fort: (each other day) for sixe or seaven daies we had alarums by ambuscadoes, and foure or five cruelly wounded by being abroad: the Indians losse wee know not, but as they report three were slain and divers hurt.

Captaine Newport having set things in order, set saile for England the 22 of June, leaving provision for 13. or 14 weeks. The day before the Ships departure, the King of Pamaunke sent the Indian that had met us before in our discoverie, to assure us peace, our fort being then palisadoed round, and all our men in good health and comfort, albeit, that throgh some discontented humors, it did not so long continue, for the President and Captaine Gosnold, with the rest of the Counsell, being for the moste part discontented with one another, in so much, that things were neither carried with that discretion nor any busines effected in such good sort as wisdome would, nor our owne good and safetie required thereby, and through the hard dealing of our President, the rest of the counsell beeing diverslie affected through his audacious commaund, and for Captaine Martin, (albeit verie honest) and wishing the best good, yet so sicke and weake, and my selfe so disgrac'd through others mallice, through which disorder God (being angrie with us) plagued us with such famin and sicknes, that the living were scarce able to bury the dead: our want of sufficient and good victualls, with continuall watching, foure or five each night at three Bulwarkes, being the chiefe cause: onely of Sturgion wee had great store, whereon our men would so greedily surfet, as it cost manye their lives; the Sack, Aquavitie, and other preservatives for our health, being kept onely in the Presidents hands, for his owne diet, and his few associates: shortly after Captaine Gosnold fell sicke, and within three weekes died, Captaine Ratcliffe being then also verie sicke and weake, and my selfe having also tasted of the extremitie therof, but by Gods assistance being well recovered. Kendall about this time, for divers reasons deposed from being of the Councell: and shortly after it pleased God (in our extremity) to move the Indians to bring us Corne, ere it was halfe ripe, to refresh us, when we rather expected when they would destroy us: about the tenth of September there was about 46. of our men dead, at which time Captaine Wingefield having ordred the affaires in such sort that he was generally hated of all, in which respect with one consent he was deposed from his presidencie, and Captaine Ratcliffe according to his course was elected.

Our provision being now within twentie dayes spent, the Indians brought us great store both of Corne and bread ready made: and also there came such aboundance of Fowles into the Rivers, as greatly refreshed our weake estates, whereuppon many of our weake men were presently able to goe abroad. As yet we had no houses to cover us, our Tents were rotten, and our Cabbins worse than nought: our best commoditie was Yron which we made into little chissels, the president, and Captaine Martins sicknes, constrayned me to be Cape Marchant, and yet to spare no paines in making houses for the company, who notwithstanding our misery, little ceased their mallice, grudging and muttering. As at this time were most of our chiefest men either sicke or discontented, the rest being in such dispaire, as they would rather starve and rot with idlenes, then be per-

swaded to do anything for their owne reliefe without constraint: our victualles being now within eighteene dayes spent,
and the Indians trade decreasing, I was sent to the mouth
of the river, to Kegquouhtan, an Indian Towne, to trade for
Corne, and try the river for Fish, but our fishing we could not
effect by reason of the stormy weather. The Indians thinking
us neare famished, with carelesse kindnes offred us little pieces
of bread and small handfulls of beanes or wheat, for a hatchet
or a piece of copper: In the like maner I entertained their
kindnes, and in like scorne offered them like commodities, but
the Children, or any that shewed extraordinary kindenes, I liberally contented with free gifte, such trifles as wel contented
them; finding this colde comfort, I anchored before the Towne,
and the next day returned to trade, but God (the absolute dis-
poser of all heartes) altered their conceits, for now they were
no lesse desirous of our commodities then we of their Corne:
under colour to fetch fresh water, I sent a man to discover the
Towne, their Corne, and force, to trie their intent, in that they
desired me up to their houses: which well understanding with
foure shot I visited them. With fish, oysters, bread and deere,
they kindly traded with me and my men, beeing no lesse in
doubt of my intent, then I of theirs, for well I might with
twentie men have fraighted a Shippe with Corne: The Towne
conteineth eighteene houses, pleasantly seated upon three
acres of ground, uppon a plaine, halfe invironed with a great
Bay of the great River, the other parte with a Baye of the other
River falling into the great Baye, with a little Ile fit for a Castle
in the mouth thereof, the Towne adjoyning to the maine by a
necke of Land of sixtie yardes. With sixteene bushells of Corne
I returned towards our Forte: by the way I encountred with
two Canowes of Indians, who came aboord me, being the inhabitants of Waraskoyack, a kingdome on the south side of the
river, which is in breadth 5. miles and 20 mile or neare from the
mouth: with these I traded, who having but their hunting provision requested me to returne to their Towne, where I should
load my boat with corne, and with near thirtie bushells I returned to the fort, the very name wherof gave great comfort to
our desparing company:

Time thus passing away, and having not above 14. daies vituals left, some motions were made about our presidents and

Captaine Archers going for England, to procure a supply, in which meane time we had reasonablly fitted us with houses, and our President and Captaine Martin being able to walk abroad, with much ado it was concluded that the pinnace and barge should goe towards Powhatan, to trade for corne: Lotts were cast who should go in her. The chance was mine, and while she was a rigging, I made a voiage to Topohanack, where ariving, there was but certain women and children who fled from their houses, yet at last I drew them to draw neere. Truck they durst not, corne they had plenty, and to spoile I had no commission: In my returne to Paspahegh, I traded with that churlish and trecherous nation: having loaded 10 or 12 bushels of corne, they offred to take our pieces and swords, yet by stelth, but seeming to dislike it, they were ready to assault us, yet standing upon our guard in coasting the shore, divers out of the woods would meet with us with corn and trade. But least we should be constrained, either to indure overmuch wrong or directly fal to revenge, seeing them dog us, from place to place, it being night, and our necessitie not fit for warres, we tooke occasion to returne with 10 bushells of corne: Captaine Martin after made 2 journies to that nation of Paspahegh but eache time returned with 8. or 10. bushells.

All things being now ready for my journey to Powhatan, for the performance thereof, I had 8. men and my selfe for the barge, as well for discoverie, as trading; the Pinnace, 5. Marriners, and 2. landmen to take in our ladings at convenient places. The 9 of November I set forward for the discovery of the country of Chikhamania, leaving the pinnace the next tide to followe and stay for my comming at Point Weanock, 20 miles from our fort: the mouth of this river falleth into the great river at Paspahegh, 8 miles above our fort: that afternoone I stayed the eb, in the bay of Paspahegh with the Indians: towards the evening certaine Indians haled me, one of them being of Chikahamania, offred to conduct me to his country, the Paspahegheans grudged therat: along we went by moonelight, at midnight he brought us before his Towne, desiring one of our men to go up with him, whom he kindely intertained, and I returned back to the barge: the next morning I went up to the towne, and shewed them what copper and hatchets they shold have for corne, each family seeking to give me most content: so long they caused me to stay that 100 at least was expecting my comming by the river with corne. What I liked I bought, and least they should perceive my too great want I went higher up the river:

This place is called Manosquosick a quarter of a mile from the river, conteining thirtie or fortie houses, uppon an exceeding high land: at the foote of the hill towards the river, is a plaine wood, watered with many springes, which fall twentie yardes right downe into the river: right against the same is a great marsh, of 4. or 5. miles circuit, devided in 2 ilands, by the parting of the river, abounding with fish and foule of all sorts; a mile from thence is a Towne called Oraniocke; I further discovered the Townes of Mansa, Apanaock, Werawahone, and Mamanahunt at eche place kindely used, especially at the last, being the hart of the Country, where were assembled 200. people with such aboundance of corne, as having laded our barge, as also I might have laded a ship: I returned to Paspah-hegh, and considering the want of Corne at our Fort, it being night, with the ebb, by midnight I arived at our fort, where I found our Pinnis run aground: the next morning I unladed seaven hogsheds into our store.

The next morning I returned againe: the second day I arived at Mamanahunt, wher the people having heard of my comming, were ready with 3 or 400. baskets litle and great, of which having laded my barge, with many signes of great kindnes I returned: at my departure they requested me to hear our pieces, being in the midst of the river, which in regard of the eccho seemed a peale of ordnance. Many birds and fowles they see us dayly kil that much feared them, so desirous of trade wer they, that they would follow me with their canowes, and for any thing give it me, rather then returne it back, so I unladed again 7 or 8. hogsheads at our fort. Having thus by Gods assistance gotten good store of corne, notwithstanding some bad spirrits not content with Gods providence still grew mutinous, in so much, that our president having ocasion to chide the smith for his misdeamenor, he not only gave him bad language, but also offred to strike him with some of his tooles, for which rebellious act the smith was by a Jury condemned to be hanged. But being uppon the ladder continuing verry obstinate, as hoping upon a rescue, when he saw no other way but death with him, he became penitent, and declared a dangerous conspiracy, for which Captaine Kendall as principal, was by a Jury condemned and shot to death. This conspiracy appeased, I set forward for the discovery of the River of Chickahominy: this third time I discovered the Townes of Matapamient, Morinogh, Ascacap, Moysenock, Righkahauck, Nechanichock, Mattalunt, Attamuspincke, and divers others. Their plenty of corne I found decreased, yet lading the barge, I returned to our fort: our store being now indifferently wel provided with corne, there was much adoe for to have the pinace goe for England, against which Captain Martin and my selfe, standing chiefly against it, and in fine after many debatings, pro et contra, it was resolved to stay a further resolution:

This matter also quieted, I set forward to finish this discovery, which as yet I had neglected in regard of the necessitie we had to take in provision whilst it was to be had: 40. miles I passed up the river, which for the most part is a quarter of a mile broad, and 3. fatham and a half deep, exceeding osey, many great low marshes, and many high lands, especially about the midst at a place called Moysonicke, a Peninsule of 4. miles circuit, betwixt two rivers joyned to the main, by a neck of 40. or 50. yards, and 40. or 50 yards from the high water marke: on both sides in the very necke of the maine, are high hills and dales, yet much inhabited, the Ile declining in a plaine fertile corne field, the lower end a low marsh. More plentie of swannes, cranes, geese, duckes, and mallards and divers sorts of fowles none would desire: more plaine fertile planted ground, in such great proportions as there, I had not seene, of a light blacke sandy mould, the cliffes commonly red, white and yellowe coloured sand, and under, red and white clay, fish great plenty, and people aboundance, the most of their inhabitants, in view of the neck of Land, where a better seat for a towne cannot be desired:

At the end of forty miles this river invironeth many low ilands, at each high water drowned for a mile, where it uniteth it selfe at a place called Apokant the highest Towne inhabited. 10. miles higher I discovered with the barge in the mid way, a great tree hindred my passage which I cut in two: heere the river became narrower, 8.9 or 10. foote at a high water, and 6. or 7. at a lowe: the streame exceeding swift, and the bottom hard channell, the ground most part a low plaine, sandy soyle. This occasioned me to suppose it might issue from some lake or some broad ford, for it could not be far to the head, but rather then I would endanger the barge, yet to have beene able to re-solve this doubt, and to discharge the imputation of malicious tungs, that halfe suspected I durst not for so long delaying, some of the company as desirous as my self, we resolved to hier a Canow, and returne with the barge to Apocant, there to leave the barge secure, and put our selves uppon the adventure: the country onely a vast and wilde wildernes, and but onely that Towne: within three or foure mile we hired a Canow, and 2. Indians to row us the next day a fowling: having made such provision for the barge as was needfull, I left her there to ride, with expresse charge not any to go ashore til my returne. Though some wise men may condemn this too bould attempt of too much indiscretion, yet if they well consider the friend-ship of the Indians in conducting me, the desolatenes of the country, the probabilitie of some lacke, and the malicious judges of my actions at home, as also to have some matters of worth to incourage our adventurers in England, might well have caused any honest minde to have done the like, as wel for his own discharge as for the publike good:

Having 2 Indians for my guide and 2 of our own company, I set forward, leaving 7 in the barge: having discovered 20 miles further in this desart, the river stil kept his depth and bredth, but much more combred with trees: here we went ashore (being some 12 miles higher then the barge had bene) to re-fresh our selves. During the boyling of our vituals, one of the Indians I tooke with me, to see the nature of the soile, and to crosse the boughts of the river, the other Indian I left with Master Robbinson and Thomas Emry, with their matches light and order to discharge a peece, for my retreat at the first sight of any Indian. But within a quarter of an houre I heard a loud cry, and a hollowing of Indians, but no warning peece; sup-posing them surprised, and that the Indians had betraid us, presently I seazed him and bound his arme fast to my hand in a garter, with my pistoll ready bent to be revenged on him: he advised me to fly, and seemed ignorant of what was done, but as we went discoursing, I was struck with an arrow on the right thigh, but without harme: upon this occasion I espied

2 Indians drawing their bowes, which I prevented in discharging a French pistoll:

By the time that I had charged againe 3 or 4 more did the like, for the first fell downe and fled: at my discharge they did the like; my hinde I made my barricado, who offered not to strive. 20. or 30. arrowes were shot at me, but short, 3 or 4 times I had discharged my pistoll ere the king of Pamaunck called Opeckankenough with 200 men, invironed me, eache drawing their bowe, which done they laid them upon the ground, yet without shot; my hinde treated betwixt them and me of conditions of peace. He discovered me to be the Captaine. My request was to retire to the boate; they demaunded my armes, the rest they saide were slaine, onely me they would reserve: the Indian importuned me not to shoot. In retiring being in the midst of a low quagmire, and minding them more then my steps, I stept fast into the quagmire, and also the Indian in drawing me forth: thus surprised, I resolved to trie their mercies, my armes I caste from me, till which none durst approch me: being ceazed on me, they drew me out and led me to the king. I presented him with a compasse diall, describing by my best meanes the use therof, whereat he so amazedly admired, as he suffered me to proceed in a discourse of the roundnes of the earth, the course of the sunne, moone, starres and plannets. With kinde speeches and bread he requited me, conducting me where the Canow lay and John Robbinson slaine, with 20 or 30. arrowes in him. Emry I saw not, I perceived by the aboundance of fires all over the woods, at each place I expected when they would execute me, yet they used me with what kindnes they could: approaching their Towne, which was within 6 miles where I was taken, onely made as arbors and covered with mats, which they remove as occasion requires: all the women and children, being advertised of this accident, came foorth to meet them, the King well guarded with 20 bowmen 5 flanck and rear, and each flanck before him a sword and a peece, and after him the like, then a bowman, then I on each hand a boweman, the rest in file in the reare, which reare led foorth amongst the trees in a bishion, eache his bowe and a handfull of arrowes, a quiver at his back grimly painted: on eache flanck a sargeant, the one running alwaies towards the front the other towards the reare, each a true pace

and in exceeding good order. This being a good time continued, they caste themselves in a ring with a daunce, and so
eache man departed to his lodging, the Captain conducting
me to his lodging; a quarter of Venison and some ten pound of
bread I had for supper, what I left was reserved for me, and
sent with me to my lodging: each morning 3. women presented me three great platters of fine bread, more venison then
ten men could devour I had; my gowne, points and garters,
my compas and a tablet they gave me again. Though 8 ordinarily guarded me, I wanted not what they could devise to
content me: and still our longer acquaintance increased our
better affection: much they threatned to assault our forte, as
they were solicited by the King of Paspahegh who shewed at
our fort great signes of sorrow for this mischance: the King
tooke great delight in understanding the manner of our ships,
and sayling the seas, the earth and skies and of our God: what
he knew of the dominions he spared not to acquaint me with,
as of certaine men cloathed at a place called Ocanahonan,
cloathed like me, the course of our river, and that within 4 or 5
daies journey of the falles was a great turning of salt water: I
desired he would send a messenger to Paspahegh, with a letter
I would write, by which they shold understand, how kindly
they used me, and that I was well, least they should revenge
my death: this he granted and sent three men, in such weather,
as in reason were unpossible by any naked to be indured: their
cruell mindes towards the fort I had deverted, in describing
the ordinance and the mines in the fields, as also the revenge
Captain Newport would take of them at his returne. Their
intent, I incerted the fort, the people of Ocanahonum and
the back sea, this report they after found divers Indians that
confirmed.

The next day after my letter, came a salvage to my lodging,
with his sword to have slaine me, but being by my guard intercepted, with a bowe and arrow he offred to have effected his
purpose: the cause I knew not, till the King understanding
thereof came and told me of a man a dying, wounded with my
pistoll: he tould me also of another I had slayne, yet the most
concealed they had any hurte: this was the father of him I had
slayne, whose fury to prevent, the King presently conducted
me to another Kingdome, upon the top of the next northerly

river, called Youghtanan. Having feasted me, he further led me
to another branch of the river, called Mattapanient; to two
other hunting townes they led me, and to each of these Countries, a house of the great Emperour of Powhatan, whom as
yet I supposed to bee at the Fals, to him I tolde him I must
goe, and so returne to Paspahegh. After this foure or five dayes
march, we returned to Rasaweack, the first towne they brought
me too, where binding the Mats in bundels, they marched two
dayes journey, and crossed the River of Youghtanan, where it
was as broad as Thames: so conducting me to a place called
Menapacute in Pamaunke, where the King inhabited: the next
day another King of that nation called Kekataugh, having received some kindnes of me at the Fort, kindly invited me to
feast at his house; the people from all places flocked to see me,
each shewing to content me.

By this the great King hath foure or five houses, each containing fourescore or an hundred foote in length, pleasantly
seated upon an high sandy hill, from whence you may see
westerly a goodly low Country, the river before the which his
crooked course causeth many great Marshes of exceeding
good ground. An hundred houses, and many large plaines are
here togither inhabited, more abundance of fish and fowle,
and a pleasanter seat cannot be imagined: the King with fortie
Bowmen to guard me, intreated me to discharge my Pistoll,
which they there presented me, with a mark at six score to strike
therwith but to spoil the practice I broke the cocke, whereat
they were much discontented though a chaunce supposed.

From hence this kind King conducted mee to a place called
Topahanocke, a kingdome upon another River northward: the
cause of this was, that the yeare before, a shippe had beene in
the River of Pamaunke, who having beene kindly entertained
by Powhatan their Emperour, they returned thence, and discovered the River of Topahanocke, where being received with
like kindnesse, yet he slue the King, and tooke of his people,
and they supposed I were hee. But the people reported him a
great man that was Captaine, and using mee kindly, the next
day we departed. This River of Topahanock seemeth in breadth
not much lesse then that we dwell upon. At the mouth of the
River is a Countrey called Cuttatawomen; upwards is Mar-
raughtacum, Tapohanock, Appamatuck, and Nantaugstacum;

at Topmanahocks, the head issuing from many Mountaines. The next night I lodged at a hunting town of Powhatans, and the next day arrived at Werowocomoco upon the river of Pamauncke, where the great king is resident: by the way we passed by the top of another little river, which is betwixt the two, called Payankatank. The most of this Countrey though Desert, yet exceeding fertil, good timber, most hils and dales, in each valley a cristall spring.

Arriving at Werawocomoco, their Emperour proudly lying uppon a Bedstead a foote high upon tenne or twelve Mattes, richly hung with manie Chaynes of great Pearles about his necke, and covered with a great Covering of *Rahaughcums*. At his heade sat a woman, at his feete another, on each side sitting uppon a Matte uppon the ground were raunged his chiefe men on each side the fire, tenne in a ranke, and behinde them as many yong women, each a great Chaine of white Beades over their shoulders, their heades painted in redde, and he with such a grave and Majesticall countenance, as drave me into admiration to see such state in a naked Salvage, hee kindly welcomed me with good wordes, and great Platters of sundrie Victuals, assuring me his friendship, and my libertie within foure dayes; hee much delighted in Opechancanoughs relation of what I had described to him, and oft examined me upon the same. Hee asked mee the cause of our comming; I tolde him, being in fight with the Spaniards our enemie, beeing over powred, neare put to retreat, and by extreame weather put to this shore, where landing at Chesipiake, the people shot us, but at Kequoughtan they kindly used us; we by signes demaunded fresh water; they described us up the River was all fresh water; at Paspahegh, also they kindly used us; our Pinnasse being leake wee were inforced to stay to mend her, till Captaine Newport my father came to conduct us away. He demaunded why we went further with our Boate; I tolde him, in that I would have occasion to talke of the backe Sea, that on the other side the maine, where was salt water, my father had a childe slaine, whiche wee supposed Monocan his enemie had done whose death we intended to revenge.

After good deliberation, hee began to describe mee the Countreys beyonde the Falles, with many of the rest, confirming what not onely Opechancanoyes, and an Indian which had beene prisoner to Powhatan had before tolde mee, but some called it five dayes, some sixe, some eight, where the sayde water dashed amongest many stones and rockes, each storme which caused oft tymes the heade of the River to bee brackish: Anchanachuck he described to bee the people that had slaine my brother, whose death hee would revenge. Hee described also upon the same Sea a mighty Nation called Pocoughtronack, a fierce Nation that did eate men, and warred with the people of Moyaoncer, and Pataromerke, Nations upon the toppe of the heade of the Bay, under his territories, where the yeare before they had slain an hundred; he signified their crownes were shaven, long haire in the necke, tied on a knot, Swords like Pollaxes.

Beyond them he described people with short Coates, and Sleeves to the Elbowes, that passed that way in Shippes like ours. Many Kingdomes hee described mee to the heade of the Bay, which seemed to bee a mightie River, issuing from mightie Mountaines betwixt the two Seas. The people cloathed at Ocanahonan he also confirmed, and the Southerly Countries also, as the rest, that reported us to be within a day and a halfe of Mangoge, two dayes of Chawwonock, 6. from Roanoke, to the south part of the backe sea: he described a countrie called Anone, where they have abundance of Brasse, and houses walled as ours. I requited his discourse, seeing what pride hee had in his great and spacious Dominions, seeing that all hee knewe were under his Territories.

In describing to him the territories of Europe, which was subject to our great King whose subject I was, and the innumerable multitude of his ships, I gave him to understand the noyse of Trumpets, and terrible manner of fighting were under captain Newport my father, whom I intituled the Meworames which they call King of all the waters. At his greatnesse hee admired, and not a little feared: hee desired mee to forsake Paspahegh, and to live with him upon his River, a Countrie called Capahowasicke: hee promised to give me Corne, Venison, or what I wanted to feede us, Hatchets and Copper wee should make him, and none should disturbe us. This request I promised to performe: and thus having with all the kindnes hee could devise, sought to content me: hee sent me home with 4.

men, one that usually carried my Gowne and Knapsacke after me, two other loded with bread, and one to accompanie me.

This River of Pamaunke is not past twelve mile from that we dwell on, his course northwest and westerly, as the other. Weraocomoco is upon salt water, in bredth two myles, and so keepeth his course without any tarrying some twenty miles, where at the parting of the fresh water and the salt, it divideth it selfe into two partes, the one part to Goughland, as broad as Thames, and navigable, with a Boate threescore or fourescore miles, and with a Shippe fiftie, exceeding crooked, and manie low grounds and marishes, but inhabited with aboundance of warlike and tall people. The Countrey of Youghtanand, of no lesse worth, onely it is lower, but all the soyle, a fatte, fertill, sandie ground. Above Menapacunt, many high sandie Mountaines. By the River is many Rockes, seeming if not of severall Mines: The other branch a little lesse in breadth, yet extendeth not neare so farre, nor so well inhabited; somewhat lower, and a white sandie, and a white clay soyle: here is their best Terra Sigillata: The mouth of the River, as I see in the discoverie therof with captain Newport, is halfe a mile broad, and within foure miles not above a Masket shot: the channell exceeding good and deepe, the River straight to the devisions. Kiskirk the nearest Nation to the entrances.

Their religion and Ceremonie I observed was thus: three or foure dayes after my taking seven of them in the house where I lay, each with a rattle began at ten a clocke in the morning to sing about the fire, which they invironed with a Circle of meale, and after, a foote or two from that, at the end of each song, layde downe two or three graines of wheate, continuing this order till they have included six or seven hundred in a halfe Circle, and after that two or three more Circles in like maner, a hand bredth from other: That done, at each song, they put betwixt everie three, two or five graines, a little sticke, so counting as an old woman her Pater noster.

One disguised with a great Skinne, his head hung round with little Skinnes of Weasels, and other vermine, with a Crownet of feathers on his head, painted as ugly as the divell, at the end of each song will make many signes and demonstrations, with strange and vehement actions; great cakes of Deere suet, Deare, and Tobacco he casteth in the fire. Till sixe a clocke in the Evening, their howling would continue ere they would depart. Each morning in the coldest frost, the principall to the number of twentie or thirtie, assembled themselves in a round circle, a good distance from the towne, where they told me they there consulted where to hunt the next day: so fat they fed mee, that I much doubted they intended to have sacrificed mee to the *Quiyoughquosicke*, which is a superiour power they worship; a more uglier thing cannot be described: one they have for chief sacrifices, which also they call *Quiyoughquosicke*: to cure the sick, a man with a Rattle and extreame howling, showting, singing, and such violent gestures, and Anticke actions over the patient will sucke out blood and flegme from the patient out of their unable stomacke, or any diseased place, as no labour will more tire them. Tobacco they offer to the water in passing in fowle weather. The death of any they lament with great sorrow and weeping: their Kings they burie betwixt two mattes within their houses, with all his beads, jewels, hatchets, and copper: the other in graves like ours. They acknowledge no resurrection.

Powhatan hath three brethren, and two sisters, each of his brethren succeeded other. For the Crowne, their heyres inherite not, but the first heyres of the Sisters, and so successively the weomens heires: For the Kings have as many weomen as they will, his Subjects two, and most but one.

From Weramocomoco is but 12. miles, yet the Indians trifled away that day, and would not goe to our Forte by any perswasions: but in certaine olde hunting houses of Paspahegh we lodged all night. The next morning ere Sunne rise, we set forward for our Fort, where we arrived within an houre, where each man with the truest signes of joy they could expresse welcommed mee, except Master Archer and some 2. or 3. of his, who was then, in my absence, sworne Counsellour, though not with the consent of Captaine Martin: great blame and imputation was laide upon mee by them for the losse of our two men which the Indians slew, insomuch that they purposed to depose me; but in the midst of my miseries, it pleased God to send Captaine Nuport, who arriving there the same night, so tripled our joy, as for a while these plots against me were deferred, though with much malice against me, which captain

Newport in short time did plainly see. Now was maister Scrivener, captaine Martin, and my selfe, called Counsellers.

Within five or sixe dayes after the arrivall of the Ship, by a mischaunce our Fort was burned, and the most of our apparell, lodging and private provision, many of our old men diseased, and of our new for want of lodging perished. The Emperour Powhatan each weeke once or twice sent me many presents of Deare, bread, *Raugroughcuns*, halfe alwayes for my father, whom he much desired to see, and halfe for me: and so continually importuned by messengers and presents, that I would come to fetch the corne, and take the Countrie their King had given me, as at last Captaine Newport resolved to go see him. Such acquaintance I had amongst the Indians, and such confidence they had in me, as neare the Fort they would not come till I came to them, every of them calling me by my name, would not sell any thing till I had first received their presents, and what they had that I liked, they deferred to my discretion: but after acquaintance, they usually came into the Fort at their pleasure: The president, and the rest of the Councell, they knewe not, but Captaine Newports greatnesse I had so described, as they conceyved him the chiefe, the rest his children, Officers, and servants. We had agreed with the king of Paspahegh to conduct two of our men to a place called Panawicke, beyond Roanoke, where he reported many men to be apparelled. Wee landed him at Warraskoyack, where playing the villaine, and deluding us for rewards, he returned within three or foure dayes after without going further.

Captaine Newport, maister Scrivener, and my selfe, found the mouth of Pamuncks river, some 25. or 30. miles northward from Cape Henrie, the chanell good as before expressed.

Arriving at Weramocomoca, being jealous of the intent of this politick salvage, to discover his intent the better, I with 20. shot armed in Jacks went a shore; the Bay where he dwelleth hath in it 3. cricks, and a mile and a halfe from the chanel all os. Being conducted to the towne, I found my selfe mistaken in the creeke, for they al there were within lesse then a mile; the Emperors sonne called Naukaquawis, the captaine that tooke me, and diverse others of his chiefe men, conducted me to their kings habitation, but in the mid way I was intercepted by a great creek over which they had made a bridge of grained stakes and railes. The king of Kiskieck, and Namontack, who all the journey the king had sent to guide us, had conducted us this passage, which caused me to suspect some mischiefe: the barge I had sent to meet me at the right landing, when I found my selfe first deceyved, and knowing by experience the most of their courages to proceede from others feare, though fewe lyked the passage, I intermingled the Kings sonne, our conductors, and his chiefe men amongst ours, and led forward, leaving halfe at the one ende to make a guard for the passage of the Front. The Indians, seeing the weaknesse of the Bridge, came with a Canow, and tooke me in of the middest with foure or five more, being landed wee made a guard for the rest till all were passed. Two in a ranke we marched to the Emperors house. Before his house stood fortie or fiftie great Platters of fine bread; being entred the house, with loude tunes they all made signes of great joy. This proude salvage, having his finest women, and the principall of his chiefe men assembled, sate in rankes as before is expressed, himselfe as upon a Throne at the upper ende of the house, with such a Majestie as I cannot expresse, now yet have often seene, either in Pagan or Christian; with a kinde countenance hee bad mee welcome, and caused a place to bee made by himselfe to sit. I presented him a sute of red cloath, a white Greyhound, and a Hatte; as Jewels he esteemed them, and with a great Oration made by three of his Nobles, if there be any amongst Salvages, kindly accepted them, with a publike confirmation of a perpetuall league and friendship.

After that, he commaunded the Queene of Appomattoc, a comely yong Salvage, to give me water, a Turkie-cocke, and breade to eate: being thus feasted, hee began his discourse to this purpose.

Your kinde visitation doth much content mee, but where is your father whom I much desire to see, is he not with you.

I told him he remained aboord, but the next day he would come unto him; with a merrie countenance he asked me for certaine peeces which I promised him, when I went to Paspahegh. I told him according to my promise, that I proffered the man that went with me foure Demy Culverings, in that he so desired a great Gunne, but they refused to take them; whereat

with a lowde laughter, he desired me to give him some of lesse
burthen, as for the other I gave him them, being sure that none
could carrie them:

But where are these men you promised to come with you.

I told him without, who therupon gave order to have them
brought in, two after two, ever maintaining the guard without.
And as they presented themselves ever with thankes, he would
salute me, and caused each of them to have foure or five
pound of bread given them. This done, I asked him for the
corne and ground he promised me. He told me I should have
it, but he expected to have all these men lay their armes at his
feet, as did his subjects. I tolde him that was a ceremonie our
enemies desired, but never our friends, as we presented our
selves unto him, yet that he should not doubt of our friendship: the next day my Father would give him a child of his, in
full assurance of our loves, and not only that, but when he
should thinke it convenient, wee would deliver under his subjection the Country of Manacam and Pocoughtaonack his
enemies.

This so contented him, as immediatly with attentive silence,
with a lowd oration he proclaimed me a werowanes of Powhatan, and that all his subjects should so esteeme us, and no
man account us strangers nor Paspaheghans, but Powhatans,
and that the Corne, weomen and Country, should be to us as
to his owne people: this proffered kindnes for many reasons
we contemned not, but with the best languages and signes of
thankes I could expresse, I tooke my leave.

The King, rising from his seat, conducted me foorth, and
caused each of my men to have as much more bread as hee
could beare, giving me some in a basket, and as much he sent
a board for a present to my Father: victuals you must know is
all there wealth, and the greatest kindnes they could shew us:
arriving at the River, the Barge was fallen so low with the ebbe,
though I had given order and oft sent to prevent the same, yet
the messengers deceived mee. The Skies being very thicke and
rainie, the King understanding this mischance, sent his Sonne
and Namontack, to conduct mee to a great house sufficient to
lodge mee, where entring I saw it hung round with bowes and
arrowes.

The Indians used all diligence to make us fires, and give us content: the kings Orators presently entertained us with a kinde oration, with expresse charge that not any should steale, or take out bowes or arrowes, or offer any injury.

Presently after he sent me a quarter of Venizon to stay my stomacke: in the evening hee sent for mee to come onely with two shot with me: the company I gave order to stand upon their guard, and to maintaine two sentries at the ports all night. To my supper he set before me meate for twenty men, and seeing I could not eate, hee caused it to be given to my men: for this is a generall custome, that what they give, not to take againe, but you must either eate it, give it away, or carry it with you: two or three houres we spent in our auncient discourses, which done, I was with a fire stick lighted to my lodging.

The next day the King, conducting mee to the River, shewed me his Canowes, and described unto me how hee sent them over the Baye, for tribute Beades, and also what Countries paide him Beads, Copper or Skins. But seeing Captaine Nuport, and Maister Scrivener, comming a shore, the King returned to his house, and I went to meete him. With a trumpet before him, wee marched to the King: who after his old manner kindly received him, especially a Boy of thirteen yeares old, called Thomas Salvage, whom he gave him as his Sonne: he requited this kindnes with each of us a great basket of Beanes, and entertaining him with the former discourse, we passed away that day, and agreed to bargaine the next day, and so returned to our Pinnis: the next day comming a shore in like order, the King having kindly entertained us with a breakfast, questioned with us in this manner.

Why we came armed in that sort, seeing hee was our friend, and had neither bowes nor arrowes, what did wee doubt? I told him it was the custome of our Country, not doubting of his kindnes any waies. Wherewith, though hee seemed satisfied, yet Captaine Nuport caused all our men to retire to the water side, which was some thirtie score from thence: but to prevent the worst, Maister Scrivener or I were either the one or other by the Barge. Experience had well taught me to beleeve his friendship, till convenient opportunity suffred him to betray us; but quickly this polititian had perceived my absence, and cunningly sent for mee; I sent for Maister Scrivener to supply my place, the King would demaund for him, I would againe releeve him, and they sought to satisfie our suspition with kind Language, and not being agreed to trade for corne, hee desired to see all our Hatchets and Copper together, for which he would give us corne; with that auncient tricke the Chickahomaniens had oft acquainted me: his offer I refused, offering first to see what hee would give for one piece. Hee seeming to despise the nature of a Merchant, did scorne to sell, but we freely should give him, and he liberally would requite us.

Captaine Nuport would not with lesse then twelve great Coppers try his kindnes, which he liberally requited with as much corne as at Chickahamania, I had for one of lesse proportion: our Hatchets hee would also have at his owne rate, for which kindnes hee much seemed to affect Captaine Nuport. Some few bunches of blew Beades I had, which he much desired, and seeing so few, he offred me a basket of two pecks, and that which I drew to be three pecks at the least, and yet he seemed contented and desired more: I agreed with him the next day for two bushells, for the ebbe now constrained us to returne to our Boate, although he earnestly desired us to stay for dinner which was a providing, and being ready he sent aboard after us, which was bread and venizon, sufficient for fiftie or sixtie persons.

The next day hee sent his Sonne in the morning not to bring a shore with us any pieces, least his weomen and children should feare. Captaine Nuports good beliefe would have satisfied that request, yet twentie or twentie five shot we got a shore: the King importuning mee to leave my armes a board, much misliking my sword, pistol and target, I told him the men that slew my Brother with the like tearmes had perswaded me, and being unarmed shot at us, and so betraide us.

He oft entreated Captaine Nuport that his men might leave their armes, which still hee commanded to the water side, this day we spent in trading for blew Beads, and having neare fraighted our Barge.

Captaine Nuport returned with them that came abord, leaving me and Maister Scrivener a shore, to follow in Canowes; into one I got with six of our men, which beeing lanched a stones cast from the shore stuck fast in the Ose:

Maister Scrivener seeing this example, with seven or eight more passed the dreadfull bridge, thinking to have found deeper water on the other creeke, but they were inforced to stay with such entertainment as a salvage, being forced ashore with wind and raine, having in his Canow, as commonly they have, his house and houshold, instantly set up a house of mats which succoured them from the storme.

The Indians seeing me pestred in the Ose, called to me; sixe or seven of the Kings chiefe men threw off their skins, and to the middle in Ose, came to bear me out on their heads. Their importunacie caused me better to like the Canow then their curtesie, excusing my deniall for feare to fall into the Ose, desiring them to bring me some wood, fire, and mats, to cover me, and I would content them: each presently gave his helpe to satisfie my request, which paines a horse would scarce have indured, yet a couple of bells richly contented them.

The Emperor sent his Seaman Mantiuas in the evening with bread and victuall for me and my men; he no more scripulous then the rest seemed to take a pride in shewing how litle he regarded that miserable cold and durty passage, though a dogge would scarce have indured it. This kindnes I found, when I litle expected lesse then a mischiefe, but the blacke night parting our companies, ere midnight the flood tide served to carry us aboard: the next day we came ashore, the King with a solemne discourse, causing all to depart, but his principall men, and this was the effect when as hee perceived that we had a desire to invade Monacum, against whom he was no professed enemy, yet thus farre hee would assist us in this enterprise: First hee would send his spies, perfectly to understand their strength and ability to fight, with which he would acquaint us himselfe.

Captaine Nuport would not be seene in it himselfe, being great Werowances, they would stay at home, but I, Maister Scrivener, and two of his Sonnes, and Opechankanough, the King of Pamaunke, should have 100. of his men to goe before as though they were hunting, they giving us notise where was the advantage we should kill them. The weomen and young children he wished we should spare, and bring them to him. Only 100. or 150. of our men he held sufficient for this exploit: our boats should stay at the falls, where we might hew timber, which we might convey each man a piece till we were past the stones, and there joyne them, to passe our men by water; if any were shot, his men should bring them backe to our boats. This faire tale had almost made Captaine Nuport undertake, by this meanes to discover the South sea, which will not be without trecherie, if wee ground our intent upon his constancie.

This day we spent in trading, dancing, and much mirth. The King of Pamaunke sent his messenger, as yet not knowing Captaine Nuport, to come unto him, who had long expected mee, desiring also my Father to visite him: the messenger stayed to conduct us, but Powhatan understanding that we had Hatchets lately come from Paspahegh, desired the next day to trade with us, and for us not to go further.

This new tricke he cunningly put upon him, but onely to have what hee listed, and to try whether we would go or stay. Opechankenoughs messenger returned saying that wee would not come: the next day his Daughter came to entreate me, shewing her Father had hurt his legge, and much sorrowed he could not see me.

Captaine Nuport being not to bee perswaded to goe, in that Powhatan had desired us to stay, sent her away with the like answer. Yet the next day upon better consideration intreatie prevailed, and wee anchored at Cinquoateck, the first towne above the parting of the river, where dwelled two Kings of Pamaunke, Brothers to Powhatan: the one called Opitchapam, the other Katatough. To these I went a shore, who kindly intreated mee and Maister Scrivener, sending some presents aboard to Captaine Nuport, whilst we were trucking with these Kings.

Opechankanough his wife, weomen, and children came to meete me with a naturall kind affection, hee seemed to rejoyce to see me.

Captaine Nuport came a shore. With many kind discourses wee passed that forenoone: and after dinner, Captaine Nuport went about with the Pinnis to Menapacant which is twenty miles by water, and not one by land: Opechankanough conducted me and Maister Scrivener by land, where having built a feasting house a purpose to entertaine us with a kind Oration, after their manner and his best provision, kindly welcomed us. That day he would not trucke, but did his best to delight us with content: Captaine Nuport arrived towards evening, whom the King presented with six great platters of fine bread, and *Pansarowmana*. The next day till noone wee traded: the King feasted all the company, and the afternoone was spent in playing, dauncing, and delight; by no meanes hee would have us depart till the next day, he had feasted us with venizon, for which he had sent, having spent his first and second provision in expecting our comming: the next day he performed his promise, giving more to us three, then would have sufficed 30. and in that we carried not away what we left, hee sent it after us to the Pinnis. With what words or signes of love he could expresse, we departed.

Captaine Nuport in the Pinnis, leaving mee in the Barge to digge a rocke, where wee supposed a Mine at Cinquaoteck, which done, ere midnight I arrived at Weracomoco, where our Pinnis anchored, being 20. miles from Cinquaotecke. The next day we tooke leave of Powhatan, who in regard of his kindnes gave him an Indian, he well affected to goe with him for England in steed of his Sonne, the cause I assure me was to know our strength and countries condition: the next day we arrived at Kiskiack, the people so scornefully entertained us, as with what signes of scorne and discontent we could, we departed and returned to our Fort with 250. bushells of Corne. Our president being not wholy recovered of his sicknes, in discharging his Piece brake and split his hand, of which he is not yet well recovered.

At Captaine Nuports arrivall, wee were victualled for twelve weekes, and having furnished him of what hee thought good, hee set saile for England the tenth of Aprill: Maister Scrivener and my selfe with our shallop, accompanied him to Cape Henrie.

Powhatan having for a farrewell, sent him five or sixe mens loadings, with Turkeyes for swords, which hee sent him in our return to the fort: we discovered the river of Nansemond, a proud warlike Nation, as well we may testified, at our first arrivall at Chesiapiack: but that injury Captaine Nuport well revenged at his returne, where some of them intising him to their Ambuscadoes by a daunce, hee perceiving their intent, with a volley of musket shot, slew one, and shot one or two more, as themselves confesse. The King at our arivall sent for me to come unto him: I sent him word what commodities I had to exchange for wheat, and if he would, as had the rest of his Neighbours, conclude a Peace, we were contented. At last he came downe before the Boate which rid at anchor some fortie yards from the shore; he signified to me to come a shore, and sent a Canow with foure or five of his men, two whereof I desired to come aboard and to stay, and I would send two to talke with their King a Shore. To this hee agreed: the King wee presented with a piece of Copper, which he kindly accepted, and sent for victualls to entertaine the messengers.

Maister Scrivener and my selfe also, after that, went a shore: the King kindly feasted us, requesting us to stay to trade till the next day, which having done, we returned to the Fort. This river is a musket shot broad, each side being should bayes, a narrow channell, but three fadom, his course for eighteene miles, almost directly South, and by West, where beginneth the first inhabitants; for a mile it turneth directly East, towards the West, a great bay and a white chaukie Iland, convenient for a Fort: his next course South, where within a quarter of a mile, the river divideth in two, the neck a plaine high Corne field, the wester bought a high plaine likewise, the Northeast answerable in all respects: in these plaines are planted aboundance of houses and people. They may containe 1000. Acres of most excellent fertill ground, so sweete, so pleasant, so beautifull, and so strong a prospect, for an invincible strong Citty, with so many commodities, that I know as yet I have not seene: This is within one daies journey of Chawwonocke. The river falleth into the Kings river, within twelve miles of Cape Henrie.

At our Fort, the tooles we had were so ordinarily stolen by the Indians, as necessity inforced us to correct their braving theeverie: for he that stole to day, durst come againe the next day. One amongst the rest, having stolen two swords, I got the Counsels consent to set in the bilboes: the next day with three more, he came with their woodden swords in the midst of our men to steale, their custome is to take any thing they can ceaze off, onely the people of Pamunke, wee have not found stealing: but what others can steale, their King receiveth.

I bad them depart, but flourishing their swords, they seemed to defend what they could catch but out of our hands. His pride urged me to turne him from amongst us, whereat he offred to strike me with his sword, which I prevented, striking him first: the rest offring to revenge the blow, received such an incounter, and fled; the better to affright them, I pursued them with five or sixe shot, and so chased them out of the Iland: the beginning of this broyle, litle expecting by his carriage, we durst have resisted, having even till that present not beene contradicted, especially them of Paspahegh: these Indians within one houre, having by other Salvages, then in the Fort, understood that I threatned to be revenged, came presently of themselves, and fell to working upon our wears, which were then in hand by other Salvages, who seeing their pride so incountred, were so submissive, and willing to doe any thing as might be, and with trembling feare, desired to be friends within three daies after: From Nansemond which is 30. miles from us, the King sent us a Hatchet which they had stollen from us at our being there: the messenger as is the custome, also wee well rewarded and contented.

The twenty of Aprill, being at worke, in hewing downe Trees, and setting Corne, an alarum caused us with all speede to take our armes, each expecting a new assault of the Salvages: but understanding it a Boate under saile, our doubts were presently satisfied, with the happy sight of Maister Nelson, his many perrills of extreame stormes and tempests passed. His ship well, as his company could testifie, his care in sparing our provision, was well: but the providence thereof, as also of our stones, Hatchets, and other tooles, onely ours excepted, which of all the rest was most necessary, which might inforce us, to think either a seditious traitor to our action, or a most unconscionable deceiver of our treasures. This happy arrivall of Maister Nelson in the *Phenix*, having beene then about three monethes missing, after Captaine Nuports arrivall, being to all our expectations lost: albeit, that now at the last, having beene long crossed with tempestuous weather, and contrary winds, his so unexpected comming, did so ravish us with exceeding joy, that now we thought our selves as well fitted, as our harts could wish, both with a competent number of men, as also for all other needfull provisions, till a further supply should come unto us: whereupon the first thing that was concluded, was that my selfe and Maister Scrivener should with 70. men goe with the best meanes we could provide, to discover beyond the Falls, as in our judgements conveniently we might: six or seaven daies we spent only in trayning our men to march, fight, and scirmish in the woods. These willing minds to this action, so quickned their understanding in this exercise, as in all judgements wee were better able to fight with Powhatans whole force in our order of battle amongst the Trees, (for Thicks there is few) then the Fort was to repulse 400. at the first assault, with some tenne or twenty shot, not knowing what to doe, nor how to use a Piece: our warrant being sealed, Maister Nelson refused to assiste us with the voluntary Marriners, and himselfe, as he promised, unlesse we would stand bound to pay the hire for shippe and Marriners for the time they stayed: and further there was some contraversie, through the diversitie of Contrary opinions, some alleadging that, how profitable and to what good purpose soever our journey should portend, yet our commission, commanding no certaine designe, we should be taxed for the most indiscreete men in the world, besides the wrong we should doe to Captaine Nuport, to whom only all discoveries did belong, and to no other:

The meanes for guides, beside the uncertaine courses of the river, from which we could not erre much, each night would fortifie us in two houres, better then that they first called the Fort. Their Townes upon the river, each within one dayes journey of other, besides our ordinary provision, might well be supposed to adde reliefe, for truck and dealing only, but in love and peace, as with the rest. If they assalted us, their Townes they cannot defend, nor their luggage so convey that we should not share; but admit the worst, 16. daies provision we had of Cheese, Oatmeale, and bisket besides, our randevous, we could and might have hid in the ground. With sixe men, Captaine Martin, would have undertaken it himselfe, leaving the rest to defend the Fort, and plant our Corne: yet no reason could be reason to proceede forward, though we were going aboard to set saile. These discontents caused so many doubts to some, and discouragement to others, as our journey ended: yet some of us procured petitions to set us forward, only with hope of our owne confusions. Our next course was to turne husbandmen, to fell Trees and set Corne. Fiftie of our men, we imployed in this service, the rest kept the Fort, to doe the command of the president, and Captaine Martin, while 30. dayes the ship lay expecting the triall of certain matters which for some cause I keepe private: the next exploit was an Indian, having stolen an Axe, was so pursued by Maister Scrivener, and them next him, as he threw it downe, and flying drew his bow at any that durst incounter him: within foure or five dayes after, Maister Scrivener and I, being a litle from the Fort among the Corne, two Indians, each with a cudgell, and all newly painted with Terrasigillata, came circling about mee, as though they would have clubed me like a hare: I knew their faining love is towards me, not without a deadly hatred, but to prevent the worst, I calling maister Scrivener retired to the Fort: the Indians seeing me suspect them, with good tearmes, asked me for some of their men whom they would beate, and went with me into our Fort, finding one that lay ordinarily with us, only for a spie: they offered to beat him. I in perswading them to forbeare, they offered to beginne with me, being now foure, for two other arrayed in like manner, came in on the other side the Fort: whereupon I caused to shut the Ports, and apprehend them. The president and Counsell, being presently acquainted, remembring at the first assault, they came in like manner, and never else but against some villanie, concluded to commit them to prison, and expect the event; eight more we ceazed at that present. An houre after, came three or foure other strangers, extraordinarily fitted with arrowes, skinnes, and shooting gloves; their jealousie and feare bewrayed their bad intent, as also their suspitious departure.

The next day came first an Indian, then another, as Embassadors for their men; they desired to speake with me. Our discourse was, that what Spades, Shovells, swords, or tooles they had stolne, to bring home (if not the next day, they should hang). The next newes was, they had taken two of our men, ranging in the woods, which mischiefe no punishment will prevent but hanging, and these they would should redeeme their owne 16. or 18. thus braving us to our doores. We desired the president, and Captaine Martin, that afternoone to sally upon them, that they might but know, what we durst to doe, and at night mand our Barge, and burnt their Townes, and spoiled, and destroyed, what we could, but they brought our men, and freely delivered them: the president released one, the rest we brought well guarded, to Morning and Evening prayers. Our men all in armes, their trembling feare, then caused them to much sorrow, which till then scoffed and scorned at what we durst doe. The Counsell concluded that I should terrifie them with some torture, to know if I could know their intent. The next day I bound one in hold to the maine Mast, and presenting sixe Muskets with match in the cockes, forced him to desire life, to answere my demaunds he could not, but one of his Comouodos was of the counsell of Paspahegh, that could satisfie me: I, releasing him out of sight, I affrighted the other, first with the rack, then with Muskets, which seeing, he desired me to stay, and hee would confesse to this execution: Maister Scrivener come, his discourse was to this effect, that Paspahegh, the Chickahamanian, Youghtanum, Pamunka, Mattapanient, and Kiskiack, these Nations were altogether a hunting that tooke me; Paspahegh, and Chicahamanya, had entended to surprise us at worke, to have had our tools: Powhatan, and al his would seeme friends till Captaine Nuports returne, that he had againe his man, which he called Namontack, where with a great feast hee would so enamor Captain Nuport and his men, as they should ceaze on him, and the like traps would be laied for the rest.

This trap for our tooles, we suspected the chiefe occasion was foure daies before Powhatan had sent the boy he had to us, with many Turkies to Maister Scrivener, and mee, understanding I would go up into his Countries to destroy them, and he doubted it the more, in that I so oft practised my men, whose shooting he heard to his owne lodging, that much feared his wives, and children; we sent him word, we entended no such thing, but only to goe to Powhatan to seeke stones to make Hatchets, except his men shoot at us, as Paspahegh had told us they would, which if they did shoote but one arrowe, we would destroy them, and least this mischiefe might happen, sent the boy to acquaint him thus much, and request him to send us Weanock, one of his subjects for a guide. The boy he returned backe with his Chest, and apparell, which then we had given him, desiring another for him, the cause was, he was practising with the Chikahamanias, as the boy suspected some villanie, by their extraordinary resort, and secret conference from whence they would send him. The boy we keepe, now we would send him many messengers, and presents. The guide we desired he sent us, and withall requested us to returne him either the boy, or some other, but none he could have, and that day these Indians were apprehended, his sonne with others that had loaded at our Fort returned, and being out of the Fort, rayled on me, to divers of our men, to be enemies to him, and to the Chikamanias. Not long after Weanock that had bin with us for our guide, whom wee kept to have conducted us in another journy, with a false excuse returned, and secretly after him, Amocis the Paspaheyan, who alwaies they kept amongst us for a spie, whom the better to avoide suspition presently after they came to beate away: these presumptions induced me to take any occasion, not onely to try the honesty of Amocis, the spie, but also the meaning of these cunning trickes of their Emperour of Powhatan; whose true meaning Captaine Martin most confidently pleaded.

The confession of Macanoe, which was the counseller of Paspahegh: first I, then Maister Scrivener, upon their severall examinations, found by them all confirmed, that Paspahegh, and Chickahammania did hate us, and intended some mischiefe, and who they were that tooke me, the names of them that stole our tooles, and swords, and that Powhatan received them, they all agreed: certaine vollies of shot we caused to be discharged, which caused each other to thinke that their fellowes had beene slaine.

Powhatan, understanding we detained certaine Salvages, sent his Daughter, a child of tenne yeares old, which not only for feature, countenance, and proportion, much exceedeth any of the rest of his people, but for wit, and spirit, the only Nonpariel of his Country: this hee sent by his most trustie messenger, called Rawhunt, as much exceeding in deformitie of person, but of a subtill wit and crafty understanding. He with a long circumstance told mee how well Powhatan loved and respected mee, and in that I should not doubt any way of his kindnesse, he had sent his child, which he most esteemed, to see me, a Deere and bread besides for a present: desiring me that the Boy might come againe, which he loved exceedingly, his litle Daughter hee had taught this lesson also: not taking notice at all of the Indeans that had beene prisoners three daies, till that morning that she saw their fathers and friends come quietly, and in good tearmes to entreate their libertie.

Opechaukanough sent also unto us, that for his sake, we

would release two that were his friends, and for a token sent me his shooting Glove and Bracer, which the day our men was taken upon, separating himselfe from the rest a long time, intreated to speake with me, where in token of peace, he had preferred me the same: now all of them having found their peremptorie conditions, but to increase our malice, which they seeing us begin to threaten to destroy them, as familiarly as before, without suspision or feare, came amongst us to begge libertie for their men: In the afternoone, they being gone, we guarded them as before to the Church, and after prayer, gave them to Pocahuntas, the Kings Daughter, in regard of her fathers kindnesse in sending her: after having well fed them, as all the time of their imprisonment, we gave them their bowes, arrowes, or what else they had, and with much content, sent them packing: Pocahuntas also we requited, with such trifles as contented her, to tel that we had used the Paspaheyans very kindly in so releasing them. The next day we had suspition of some other practise for an Ambuscado, but perfectly wee could not discover it; two daies after, a Paspaheyan came to shew us a glistering Minerall stone: and with signes demonstrating it to be in great aboundance, like unto Rockes. With some dozen more, I was sent to seeke to digge some quantitie, and the Indean to conduct me: but suspecting this some tricke to delude us for to get some Copper of us, or with some ambuscado to betray us, seeing him falter in his tale, being two miles on our way, led him ashore, where abusing us from place to place, and so seeking either to have drawne us with him into the woods, or to have given us the slippe: I shewed him Copper, which I promised to have given him if he had performed his promise, but for his scoffing and abusing us, I gave him twentie lashes with a Rope, and his bowes and arrowes, bidding him shoote if he durst, and so let him goe.

In all this time, our men being all or the most part well recovered, and we not willing to trifle away more time then necessitie enforced us unto, we thought good for the better content of the adventurers in some reasonable sort to fraight home Maister Nelson with Cedar wood, about which, our men going with willing minds, was in very good time effected, and the ship sent for England; wee now remaining being in good health, all our men wel contented, free from mutinies, in love one with another, and as we hope in a continuall peace with the Indians, where we doubt not but by Gods gracious assistance, and the adventurers willing minds and speedie furtherance to so honorable an action in after times, to see our Nation to enjoy a Country, not onely exceeding pleasant for habitation, but also very profitable for comerce in generall, no doubt pleasing to almightie God, honourable to our gracious Soveraigne, and commodious generally to the whole Kingdome.

FINIS.

THE PROCEEDINGS OF THE ENGLISH COLONIE IN

Virginia since their first beginning from
England in the yeare of our Lord 1606,
till this present 1612, with all their
accidents that befell them in their
Journies and Discoveries.

Also the Salvages discourses, orations and relations
of the Bordering neighbours, and how they
became subject to the English.

*Unfolding even the fundamentall causes from whence have sprang so many
miseries to the undertakers, and scandals to the businesses taken
faithfully as they were written out of the writings of Thomas
Studley the first provant maister, Anas Todkill, Walter
Russell Doctor of Phisicke, Nathaniell Powell,
William Phettyplace, Richard Wyffin, Thomas
Abbay, Tho: Hope, Rich: Polts and the
labours of divers other diligent
observers, that were
residents in Virginia.*

*And perused and confirmed by diverse now resident in
England that were actors in this busines.*

1612

TO THE READER.

Long hath the world longed, but to be truely satisfied what Virginia is, with the truth of those proceedings, from whence hath flowne so manie reports of worth, and yet few good effects of the charge, which hath caused suspition in many well willers that desire yet but to be truely satisfied therein. If any can resolve this doubt it is those that have lived residents in the land: not salers, or passengers, nor such mercinary contemplators, that only bedeck themselves with others plumes. This discourse is not from such, neither am I the author, for they are many, whose particular discourses are signed by their names. This solid treatise, first was compiled by Richard Pots, since passing the hands of many to peruse, chancing into my hands, (for that I know them honest men, and can partly well witnesse their relations true) I could do no lesse in charity to the world then reveale; nor in conscience, but approve. By the advise of many grave and understanding gentlemen, that have pressed it, to the presse, it was thought fit to publish it, rather in its owne rude phrase then other waies. For that nothing can so purge that famous action from the infamous scandal some ignorantly have conceited, as the plaine simple and naked truth. For defect whereof the businesse is still suspected, the truth unknowne, and the best deservers discouraged, and neglected, some by false reports, others by conjecture, and such power hath flattry to ingender of those, hatred and affection, that one is sufficient to beguile more, then 500 can keepe from being deceived.

But this discourse is no Judge of mens manners, nor catalogue of their former courses; only a reporter of their actions in Virginia, not to disgrace any, accuse any, excuse any, nor flatter any; for which cause there is no wrong done but this, shortnesse in complaining, and so sparing in commending as only the reader may perceive the truth for his paines, and the action purged of foule slander; it can detract from none that intendeth there to adventure their fortunes; and to speake truly of the first planters, that brake the yce and beate the path, howsoever many difficulties obscured their indevours, he were worse then the worst of Ingrates, that would not spare them memory that have buried themselves in those forrain regions. From whose first adventures may spring more good blessings then are yet conceived. So I rest thine, that will read, peruse, and understand me. If you finde false orthography or broken English, they are small faultes in souldiers, that not being able to write learnedly, onlie strive to speake truely, and be understood without an Interpreter.

T. Abbay.

THE PROCEEDINGS
of the English Colony in Virginia,
taken faithfully out of the writings of
Thomas Studly Cape-marchant,
Anas Todkill, Doctor Russell,
Nathaniel Powell, William Phetiplace,
and Richard Pot, with the laboures
of other discreet observers, during
their residences.

Chapter 1.

IT might wel be thought, a countrie so faire (as Virginia is) and a people so tractable, would long ere this have beene quietly possessed, to the satisfaction of the adventurers, and the eternizing of the memorie of those that affected it. But because all the world doe see a defailement; this following Treatise shall give satisfaction to all indifferent readers, how the businesse hath beene carried, where no doubt they will easily understand and answer to their question, howe it came to passe there was no better speed and successe in those proceedings.

The first mover of the action. Captaine Bartholomew Gosnold, the first mover of this plantation, having many yeares solicited many of his friends, but found small assistants; at last prevailed with some Gentlemen, as Master Edward Maria Wingfield, Captaine John Smith, and diverse others who depended a yeare upon his projects, but nothing could be effected, till by their great charge and industrie it came to be apprehended by certaine of the Nobilitie, Gentrie, and Marchants, so that his Majestie by his letters patents, gave commission for establishing Councels, to direct here, and to governe, and to execute there; to effect this, was spent another yeare, and by that time, three ships were provided, one of 100 Tonns, another of 40. and a Pinnace of 20. The transportation of the company was committed to Captaine Christopher Newport, a Marriner well practised for the westerne parts of America. But their orders

Orders for
government.
for governement were put in a box, not to be
opened, nor the governours knowne untill they
arived in Virginia.

On the 19 of December, 1606. we set saile, but by unprosperous winds, were kept six weekes in the sight of England; all
which time, Master Hunt our Preacher, was so weake and sicke,
that few expected his recoverie. Yet although he were but 10 or
12 miles from his habitation (the time we were in the downes)
and notwithstanding the stormie weather, nor the scandalous
imputations (of some few, little better then Atheists, of the
greatest ranke amongst us) suggested against him, all this could
never force from him so much as a seeming desire to leave the
busines, but preferred the service of God, in so good a voyage,
before any affection to contest with his godlesse foes, whose
disasterous designes (could they have prevailed) had even then
overthrowne the businesse, so many discontents did then arise,
had he not with the water of patience, and his godly exhortations (but chiefly by his true devoted examples) quenched
those flames of envie, and dissention.

Wee watred at the Canaries, wee traded with the Salvages at
Dominica; three weekes we spent in refreshing our selvs
amongst these west-India Iles; in Gwardalupa we found a bath
so hot, as in it we boiled porck as well as over the fire. And at
a little Ile called Monica, we tooke from the bushes with our
hands, neare 2 hogsheads full of birds in 3 or 4 houres.
In Mevis, Mona, and the Virgin Iles, we spent some
time, where with a lothsome beast like a Crocadil,
called a Gwayn, Tortoses, Pellicans, Parrots, and fishes, we
daily feasted. Gone from thence in search of Virginia, the company was not a little discomforted, seeing the Marriners had
three daies passed their reckoning and found no land, so that
Captaine Ratcliffe (Captaine of the Pinnace) rather desired to
beare up the helme to returne for England, then make further
search. But God the guider of all good actions, forcing them
by an extream storme to hul all night, did drive them by his
providence to their desired port, beyond all their expectations,
for never any of them had seene that coast. The first
land they made they called Cape Henry; where anchoring, Master Wingfeild, Gosnoll, and Newport,
with 30 others, recreating themselves on shore, were assalted

Monica an
unfrequented
Ile full of
birds.

Their first
landing.

by 5 Salvages, who hurt 2 of the English very dangerously.
That night was the box opened, and the orders read, in which
Bartholomew Gosnoll, Edward Wingfeild, Christopher Newport, John Smith, John Ratliffe, John Martin, and George
Kendall, were named to bee the Councell, and to choose a
President amongst them for a yeare, who with the
Councell should governe. Matters of moment were
to be examined by a Jurie, but determined by the
major part of the Councell in which the Precedent had 2
voices. Untill the 13 of May they sought a place to plant in,
then the Councell was sworne, Master Wingfeild was chosen
Precident, and an oration made, whie Captaine Smith was not
admitted of the Councell as the rest.

Matters of government.

Now falleth every man to worke, the Councell contrive the
Fort, the rest cut downe trees to make place to pitch their
Tents; some provide clapbord to relade the ships, some make
gardens, some nets, etc. The Salvages often visited us kindly.
The Precidents overweening jealousie would admit no exercise
at armes, or fortification, but the boughs of trees cast together
in the forme of a halfe moone by the extraordinary paines and
diligence of Captaine Kendall. Newport, with Smith,
and 20 others, were sent to discover the head of the
river: by divers smal habitations they passed, in 6 daies
they arrived at a towne called Powhatan, consisting of some
12 houses pleasantly seated on a hill; before it 3 fertil Iles, about
it many of their cornefields. The place is very pleasant, and
strong by nature. Of this place the Prince is called Powhatan,
and his people Powhatans, to this place the river is navigable;
but higher within a mile, by reason of the Rockes and Iles,
there is not passage for a smal boate, this they call the Falles.
The people in al parts kindly intreated them, til being returned
within 20 miles of James towne, they gave just cause of jealousie, but had God not blessed the discoverers otherwise then
those at the fort, there had then beene an end of that plantation; for at the fort, where they arived the next day, they found
17 men hurt, and a boy slaine by the Salvages, and had it not
chanced a crosse barre shot from the ships strooke
down a bough from a tree amongst them that caused
them to retire, our men had all been slaine, being securely all at worke, and their armes in drie fats.

The discovery of the Falles and Powhatan.

The Fort assalted by the Salvages.

Hereupon the President was contented the Fort should be pallisadoed, the ordinance mounted, his men armed and exercised, for many were the assaults, and Ambuscadoes of the Salvages, and our men by their disorderly stragling were often hurt, when the Salvages by the nimblenesse of their heeles well escaped. What toile wee had, with so smal a power to guard our workmen adaies, watch al night, resist our enimies and effect our businesse, to relade the ships, cut downe trees, and prepare the ground to plant our corne, etc. I referre to the readers consideration. Six weekes being spent in this manner, Captaine Newport (who was hired only for our transportation) was to return with the ships. Now Captaine Smith, who all this time from their departure from the Canaries was restrained as a prisoner upon the scandalous suggestions of some of the chiefe (envying his repute) who fained he intended to usurpe the governement, murder the Councell, and make himselfe king, that his confederats were dispearsed in all the three ships, and that divers of his confederats that revealed it, would affirme it, for this he was committed. 13 weekes he remained thus suspected, and by that time the ships should returne they pretended out of their commisserations, to referre him to the Councell in England to receave a check, rather then by particulating his designes make him so odious to the world, as to touch his life, or utterly overthrowe his reputation; but he much scorned their charitie, and publikely defied the uttermost of their crueltie. Hee wisely prevented their pollicies, though he could not suppresse their envies, yet so wel he demeaned himselfe in this busines, as all the company did see his innocencie, and his adversaries malice, and those suborned to accuse him, accused his accusers of subornation; many untruthes were alleaged against him; but being so apparently disproved begat a generall hatred in the harts of the company against such unjust commanders; many were the mischiefes that daily sprong from their ignorant (yet ambitious) spirits; but the good doctrine and exhortation of our preacher Master Hunt reconciled them, and caused Captaine Smith to be admitted of the Councell; the next day all received the Communion, the day following the Salvages voluntarily desired peace, and Captaine Newport returned for England with newes; leaving in Virginia 100. the 15 of June 1607.

Captaine Newports returne for England.

The names of them that were the first planters,
were these following.

Master Edward Maria Wingfield.
Captaine Bartholomew Gosnoll.
Captaine John Smyth.
Captaine John Ratliffe.
Captaine John Martin.
Captaine George Kendall.
Master Robert Hunt *Preacher*.

Councell.

Master George Percie.
Anthony Gosnoll.
Captaine Gabriell Archer.
Robert Ford.
William Bruster.
Dru Pickhouse.
John Brookes.
Thomas Sands.
John Robinson.
Ustis Clovill.
Kellam Throgmorton.
Nathaniell Powell.
Robert Behethland.
Jeremy Alicock.
Thomas Studley.
Richard Crofts.
Nicholas Houlgrave.
Thomas Webbe.
John Waler.
William Tankard.
Francis Snarsbrough.
Edward Brookes.
Richard Dixon.
John Martin.
George Martin.
Anthony Gosnold.
Thomas Wotton, *Sierg*.
Thomas Gore.
Francis Midwinter.

Gentlemen.

William Laxon.
Edward Pising.
Thomas Emry.   } *Carpenters.*
Robert Small.
Anas Todkill.
John Capper.
James Read, *Blacksmith.*
Jonas Profit, *Sailer.*
Thomas Couper, *Barber.*
John Herd, *Brick layer.*
William Garret, *Bricklayer.*
Edward Brinto, *Mason.*
William Love, *Taylor.*
Nicholas Skot, *Drum.*
John Laydon.
William Cassen.
George Cassen.
Thomas Cassen.
William Rods.
William White.
Ould Edward.   } *Labourers.*
Henry Tavin.
George Golding.
John Dods.
William Johnson.
William Unger.
William Wilkinson. *Surgeon.*
Samuell Collier.
Nathaniel Pecock.   } *Boyes.*
James Brumfield.
Richard Mutton.
with diverse others to the number of 105.

Chapter 2.
What happened till the first supply.

BEING thus left to our fortunes, it fortuned that within tenne
daies scarse ten amongst us coulde either goe, or well

The occasion of sicknesse. stand, such extreame weaknes and sicknes oppressed
us. And thereat none need mervaile, if they consider
the cause and reason, which was this; whilest the ships staied,
our allowance was somewhat bettered, by a daily

The sailers abuses. proportion of bisket which the sailers would pilfer to
sell, give or exchange with us, for mony, saxefras,
furres, or love. But when they departed, there remained neither
taverne, beere-house nor place of relief but the common kettell.
Had we beene as free from all sinnes as gluttony, and drunk-
ennes, we might have bin canonized for Saints; But our President would never have bin admitted, for ingrossing to his
privat, Otemeale, sacke, oile, aquavitæ, beefe, egs, or what not;
but the kettel, that indeede he allowed equally to be distributed, and that was halfe a pinte of wheat and as much barly
boyled with water for a man a day, and this having fryed some
26. weeks in the ships hold, contained as many wormes as
graines; so that we might truely call it rather so much bran
then corne, our drinke was water, our lodgings castles in aire.
With this lodging and diet, our extreame toile in bearing and
planting pallisadoes, so strained and bruised us, and our continuall labour in the extremity of the heate had so weakened us,
as were cause sufficient to have made us as miserable in our native country, or any other place in the world. From May, to
September, those that escaped lived upon Sturgion, and sea-

A bad Precident. Crabs, 50. in this time we buried. The rest seeing the
Presidents projects to escape these miseries in our
Pinnas by flight (who all this time had neither felt
want nor sicknes) so moved our dead spirits, as we deposed
him; and established Ratcliffe in his place. Gosnoll being dead,
Kendall deposed, Smith newly recovered, Martin and Ratliffe
was by his care preserved and relieved, but now was all our
provision spent, the Sturgeon gone, all helps abandoned, each
houre expecting the fury of the Salvages; when God the patron of all good indeavours in that desperate extreamity so

Plentie
unexpected.
changed the harts of the Salvages, that they brought such plenty of their fruits, and provision as no man wanted.

And now where some affirmed it was ill done of the Councel to send forth men so badly provided, this incontradictable reason will shew them plainely they are too ill advised to nourish such il conceipts; first the fault of our going was our owne, what coulde bee thought fitting or necessary wee had, but what wee should finde, what we should want, where we shoulde be, we were all ignorant, and supposing to make our passage in two monthes, with victuall to live, and the advantage of the spring to worke; we weare at sea 5. monthes where we both spent our victuall and lost the opportunity of the time, and season to plant.

Such actions have ever since the worlds beginning beene subject to such accidents, and every thing of worth is found full of difficulties, but nothing so difficult as to establish a common wealth so farre remote from men and meanes, and where mens mindes are so untoward as neither do well themselves nor suffer others; but to proceed.

The new President, and Martin, being little beloved, of weake judgement in dangers, and lesse industry in peace, committed the managing of all things abroad to captaine Smith: who by his owne example, good words, and faire promises, set some to mow, others to binde thatch, some to build houses,

The building
of James
Towne.
others to thatch them, himselfe alwaies bearing the greatest taske for his own share, so that in short time, he provided most of them lodgings neglecting any for himselfe. This done, seeing the Salvages superfluity beginne to decrease (with some of his workemen) shipped himselfe in the shallop to search the country for trade. The want of the language, knowledge to mannage his boat with out sailers, the want of a sufficient power, (knowing the multitude of the Salvages) apparell for his men, and other necessaries, were infinite impediments, yet no discouragement. Being but 6 or 7 in company he went down the river to Kecoughtan, where at first they scorned him, as a starved man, yet he so dealt with them,

The
beginning of
trade abroad.
that the next day they loaded his boat with corne, and in his returne he discovered and kindly traded with the Weraskoyks. In the meane time those at the

fort so glutted the Salvages with their commodities as they became not regarded.

Smith perceiving (notwithstanding their late miserie) not
any regarded but from hand to mouth, (the company being
well recovered) caused the Pinas to bee provided with things
fitting to get provision for the yeare following; but in the in-
The   terim he made 3. or 4. journies and discovered the
discoverie of   people of Chickahamine. Yet what he carefully pro-
Chickahamine.   vided the rest carelesly spent. Wingfield and Kendall
living in disgrace, seeing al things at randome in the absence of
Smith, The companies dislike of their Presidents weaknes, and
their small love to Martins never-mending sicknes, strengthened themselves with the sailers, and other confederates to regaine their former credit and authority, or at least such meanes
abord the Pinas, (being fitted to saile as Smith had appointed
for trade) to alter her course and to go for England. Smith unexpectedly returning had the plot discovered to him, much
trouble he had to prevent it till with store of fauken and musket shot he forced them stay or sinke in the river, which action
cost the life of captaine Kendall. These brawles are so disgustfull, as some will say they were better forgotten, yet all men of
good judgement will conclude, it were better their basenes
should be manifest to the world, then the busines beare the
scorne and shame of their excused disorders. The President
Another   and captaine Archer not long after intended also to
project to   have abandoned the country, which project also was
abandon   curbed, and suppressed by Smith. The Spanyard
the Country.   never more greedily desired gold then he victuall, which finding
so plentiful in the river of Chickahamine where hundreds of
Salvages in divers places stood with baskets expecting his comming. And now the winter approaching, the rivers became so
covered with swans, geese, duckes, and cranes, that we daily
feasted with good bread, Virginia pease, pumpions, and
putchamins, fish, fowle, and diverse sorts of wild beasts as fat
as we could eat them: so that none of our Tuftaffaty humorists
desired to goe for England. But our comædies never endured
long without a Tragedie; some idle exceptions being muttered
against Captaine Smith, for not discovering the head of Chickahamine river, and taxed by the Councell, to bee too slowe in
so worthie an attempt. The next voyage hee proceeded so farre

that with much labour by cutting of trees in sunder he made his passage, but when his Barge could passe no farther, he left her in a broad bay out of danger of shot, commanding none should goe ashore till his returne, himselfe with 2 English and two Salvages went up higher in a Canowe, but hee was not long absent, but his men went ashore, whose want of government, gave both occasion and opportunity to the Salvages to surprise one George Casson, and much failed not to have cut of the boat and all the rest. Smith little dreaming of that accident, being got to the marshes at the rivers head, 20 myles in the desert, had his 2 men slaine (as is supposed) sleeping by the Canowe, whilst himselfe by fowling sought them victuall, who finding he was beset with 200 Salvages, 2 of them hee slew, stil defending himselfe with the aid of a Salvage his guid, (whome hee bound to his arme and used as his buckler,) till at last slipping into a bogmire they tooke him prisoner: when this newes came to the fort much was their sorrow for his losse, fewe expecting what ensued. A month those Barbarians kept him prisoner, many strange triumphes and conjurations they made of him, yet hee so demeaned himselfe amongst them, as he not only diverted them from surprising the Fort, but procured his owne liberty, and got himselfe and his company such estimation amongst them, that those Salvages admired him as a demi-God. So returning safe to the Fort, once more staied the Pinnas her flight for England, which til his returne, could not set saile, so extreame was the weather, and so great the frost.

The 3 projects to abandon the fort.

His relation of the plentie he had seene, especially at Werowocomoco, where inhabited Powhatan (that till that time was unknowne) so revived againe their dead spirits as all mens feare was abandoned. Powhatan having sent with this Captaine divers of his men loaded with provision, he had conditioned, and so appointed his trustie messengers to bring but 2 or 3 of our great ordenances, but the messengers being satisfied with the sight of one of them discharged, ran away amazed with feare, till meanes was used with guifts to assure them our loves. Thus you may see what difficulties still crossed any good indeavour, and the good successe of the businesse, and being thus oft brought to the very period of destruction, yet you see by what strange meanes God hath still delivered it.

As for the insufficiencie of them admitted in commission, that errour could not be prevented by their electors, there being no other choice, and all were strangers to each others education, quallities, or disposition; and if any deeme it a shame to our nation, to have any mention made of these enormities, let them peruse the histories of the Spanish discoveries and plantations, where they may see how many mutinies, discords, and dissentions, have accompanied them and crossed their attempts, which being knowne to be particular mens offences, doth take away the generall scorne and contempt, mallice, and ignorance might else produce, to the scandall and reproach of those, whose actions and valiant resolution deserve a worthie respect. Now whether it had beene better for Captaine Smith to have concluded with any of their severall projects to have abandoned the Countrie with some 10 or 12 of them we cal the better sort, to have left Master Hunt our preacher, Master Anthony Gosnoll, a most honest, worthie, and industrious gentleman, with some 30 or 40 others his countrie men, to the furie of the Salvages, famin, and all manner of mischiefes and inconveniences, or starved himselfe with them for company, for want of lodging, or but adventuring abroad to make them provision, or by his opposition, to preserve the action, and save all their lives, I leave to the censure of others to consider.

A true proofe of Gods love to the action.

Of two evils the lesser was chosen.

Thomas Studley.

Chapter 3.
The arrivall of the first supply with their proceedings and returne.

All this time our cares were not so much to abandon the Countrie, but the Treasurer and Councell in England were as diligent and carefull to supplie us. Two tall ships they sent us, with neere 100 men, well furnished with all things could be imagined necessarie, both for them and us. The one commanded by Captaine Newport: the other by Captaine Nelson, an honest man and an expert marriner, but such was the

leewardnesse of his ship, that (though he were within sight of
Cape Henry) by stormy contrarie windes, was forced
so farre to sea, as the West Indies was the next land
for the repaire of his Masts, and reliefe of wood and
water. But Captaine Newport got in, and arived at
James towne, not long after the redemption of Captaine Smith,
to whome the Salvages every other day brought such plentie of
bread, fish, turkies, squirrels, deare, and other wild beasts, part
they gave him as presents from the king; the rest, hee as their
market clarke set the price how they should sell.

The Phenix from Cape Henry forced to the west Indies.

So he had inchanted those poore soules (being their prisoner) in demonstrating unto them the roundnesse of the
world, the course of the moone and starres, the cause of the
day and night the largenes of the seas the qualities of our ships,
shot and powder, The devision of the world, with
the diversity of people, their complexions, customes
and conditions. All which hee fained to be under the
command of Captaine Newport, whom he tearmed to them
his father; of whose arrival, it chanced he so directly prophe-
cied, as they esteemed him an oracle; by these fictions he not
only saved his owne life, and obtained his liberty, but had them
at that command, he might command them what he listed.
That God that created al these things; they knew he adored for
his God, whom they would also tearme in their discourses, the God of captaine Smith. The President
and Councel so much envied his estimation amongst
the Salvages (though wee all in generall equally participated
with him of the good therof) that they wrought it into their
understandings, by their great bounty in giving 4. times more
for their commodities then he appointed, that their greatnesse
and authority, as much exceeded his, as their bounty, and lib-
erality; Now the arrivall of this first supply, so overjoyed us,
that we could not devise too much to please the mariners. We
gave them liberty to truck or trade at their pleasures. But in a
short time, it followed, that could not be had for a pound of
copper, which before was sold for an ounce. Thus ambition,
and sufferance, cut the throat of our trade, but confirmed their
opinion of Newports greatnes, (wherewith Smith had possessed Powhatan) especially by the great presents Newport
often sent him, before he could prepare the Pinas to go and visit

How Captaine Smith got his liberty.

Their opinion of our God.

him; so that this Salvage also desired to see him. A great bruit there was to set him forwarde: when he went he was accompanied, with captaine Smith, and Master Scrivener a very wise understanding gentleman newly arrived, and admitted of the Councell, and 30. or 40. chosen men for their guarde. Arriving at Werowocomo Newports conceipt of this great Salvage, bred many doubts, and suspitions of treacheries; which Smith, to make appeare was needlesse, with 20. men well appointed, undertooke to encounter (with that number) the worst that could happen there names were.

Smiths revisiting Powhatan.

Nathaniell Powell.	John Taverner.
Robert Beheathland.	William Dier.
William Phettiplace.	Thomas Coe.
Richard Wyffin.	Thomas Hope.
Anthony Gosnoll.	Anas Todkell.

with 10. others whose names I have forgotten. These being kindly received a shore, with 2. or 300. Salvages were conducted to their towne; Powhatan strained himselfe to the uttermost of his greatnes to entertain us, with great shouts of Joy, orations of protestations, and the most plenty of victuall hee could provide to feast us. Sitting upon his bed of mats, his pillow of leather imbroydred (after their rude manner) with pearle and white beades, his attire a faire Robe of skins as large as an Irish mantle, at his head and feet a handsome young woman; on each side his house sate 20. of his concubines, their heads and shoulders painted red, with a great chaine of white beads about their necks. Before those sate his chiefest men in like order in his arbor-like house. With many pretty discourses to renue their olde acquaintaunce; the great kinge and our captaine spent the time till the ebbe left our Barge aground, then renuing their feasts and mirth we quartred that night with Powhatan: the next day Newport came a shore, and received as much content as those people could give him, a boy named Thomas Savage was then given unto Powhatan who Newport called his son, for whom Powhatan gave him Namontacke his trusty servant, and one of a shrewd subtill capacity. 3. or 4. daies were spent in feasting dancing and trading, wherin Powhatan carried

Powhatans first entertainement of our men.

The exchange of a Christian for a Salvage.

himselfe so prowdly, yet discreetly (in his Salvage manner) as made us all admire his natural gifts considering his education; as scorning to trade as his subjects did, he bespake Newport in this manner.

Captain Newport it is not agreeable with my greatnes in this pedling manner to trade for trifles, and I esteeme you a great werowans. Therefore lay me down all your commodities togither, what I like I will take, and in recompence give you that I thinke fitting their value.

Captaine Smith being our interpreter, regarding Newport as his father, knowing best the disposition of Powhatan, told us his intent was but to cheat us; yet captaine Newport thinking to out brave this Salvage in ostentation of greatnes, and so to bewitch him with his bounty, as to have what he listed, but so it chanced Powhatan having his desire, valued his corne at such a rate, as I thinke it better cheape in Spaine, for we had not 4. bushels for that we expected 20. hogsheads. This bred some unkindnes betweene our two captaines, New- port seeking to please the humor of the unsatiable Salvage; Smith to cause the Salvage to please him, but smothering his distast (to avoide the Salvages suspition) glaunced in the eies of Powhatan many Trifles who fixed his humour upon a few blew beads; A long time he importunatly desired them, but Smith seemed so much the more to affect them, so that ere we departed, for a pound or two of blew beads he brought over my king for 2 or 300 bushels of corne, yet parted good friends. The like entertainement we found of Opechanchynough king of Pamaunke whom also he in like manner fitted, (at the like rates) with blew beads: and so we returned to the fort. Where this new supply being lodged with the rest, accidently fired the quarters, and so the Towne, which being but thatched with reeds the fire was so fierce as it burnt their pallizadoes (though 10. or 12 yardes distant) with their armes, bedding, apparell, and much private provision. Good Master Hunt our preacher lost all his library, and al that he had (but the cloathes on his backe,) yet none ever see him repine at his losse. This hapned in the winter, in that extreame frost, 1607. Now though we had victuall sufficient, I meane only of Oatemeale, meale, and corne, yet the ship staying there 14. weeks when shee

might as well have been gone in 14. daies, spent the beefe, porke, oile, aquavitæ, fish, butter, and cheese, beere and such like; as was provided to be landed us. When they departed, what their discretion could spare us, to make a feast or two with bisket, pork, beefe, fish, and oile, to relish our mouths, of each somwhat they left us, yet I must confess those that had either mony, spare clothes, credit to give bils of payment, gold rings, furres, or any such commodities were ever welcome to this removing taverne, such was our patience to obay such vile commanders, and buy our owne provision at 15 times the valew, suffering them feast (we bearing the charge) yet must not repine, but fast; and then leakage, ship-rats, and other casualties occasioned the losse, but the vessell and remnants (for totals) we were glad to receive with all our hearts to make up the account, highly commending their providence for preserving that. For all this plentie our ordinarie was but meale and water, so that this great charge little relieved our wants, whereby with the extreamity of the bitter cold aire more then halfe of us died, and tooke our deathes, in that piercing winter I cannot deny, but both Skrivener and Smith did their best to amend what was amisse, but with the President went the major part, that their hornes were too short. But the worst mischiefe

was, our gilded refiners with their golden promises, made all men their slaves in hope of recompence; there was no talke, no hope, no worke, but dig gold, wash gold, refine gold, load gold, such a brute of gold, as one mad fellow desired to bee buried in the sandes, least they should by their art make gold of his bones. Little need there was and lesse reason, the ship should stay, their wages run on,

our victuall consume, 14 weekes, that the Marriners might say, they built such a golden Church, that we can say, the raine washed neare to nothing in 14 daies. Were it that Captaine Smith would not applaud all those golden inventions, because they admitted him not to the sight of their trials, nor golden consultations I knowe not; but I heard him question with Captaine Martin and tell him, except he would shew him a more substantiall triall, hee was not inamored with their durtie skill, breathing out these and many other passions, never any thing did more torment him, then to see all necessarie businesse neglected, to fraught such a drunken ship with so much gilded durt; till then wee never accounted Captaine Newport a refiner; who being fit to set saile for England, and wee not having any use of Parliaments, plaies, petitions, admirals, recorders, interpreters, chronologers, courts of plea, nor Justices of peace, sent Master Wingfield and Captaine Archer with him for England to seeke some place of better imploiment.

A returne to England.

Chapter 4.
The arivall of the Phœnix, her returne, and other accidents.

THE authoritie nowe consisting in refining, Captaine Martin and the still sickly President, the sale of the stores commodities maintained their estates as inheritable revenews. The spring approching, and the ship departed, Master Skrivener and Captaine Smith divided betwixt them, the rebuilding our towne, the repairing our pallisadoes, the cutting downe trees, preparing our fields, planting our corne, and to rebuild our Church, and recover our store-house; al men thus busie at their severall labours, Master Nelson arived with his lost *Phœnix* (lost I say, for that al men deemed him lost) landing safely his men; so well hee had mannaged his ill hap, causing the Indian Iles to feed his company that his victuall (to that was left us before) was sufficient for halfe a yeare. He had nothing but he freely imparted it, which honest dealing (being a marriner) caused us admire him, wee would not have wished so much as he did for us. Nowe to relade this ship with some good tidings, the President (yet notwithstanding with his dignitie to leave the fort) gave order to Captaine Smith and Master Skrivener to discover and search the commodities of Monacans countrie beyound the Falles, 60 able men was allotted their number, the which within 6 daies exercise, Smith had so well trained to their armes and orders, that they little feared with whome they should encounter. Yet so unseasonable was the time, and so opposite was

The repairing of James towne.

60 appointed to discover Monacan.

Captaine Martin to every thing, but only to fraught this ship also with his phantasticall gold, as Captaine Smith rather desired to relade her with Cedar, which was a present dispatch; then either with durt, or the reports of an uncertaine discoverie. Whilst their conclusion was resolving, this hapned.

Powhatan to expresse his love to Newport, when he departed, presented him with 20 Turkies, conditionally to returne him 20 Swords, which immediatly were sent him. Now after his departure hee presented Captaine Smith with the like luggage, but not finding his humor obaied in sending him weapons, he caused his people with 20. devises to obtain them, at last by ambuscadoes at our very ports they would take them per force, surprise us at work, or any way, which was so long permitted that they became so insolent, there was no rule, the command from England was so straight not to offend them as our authority bearers (keeping their houses) would rather be any thing then peace breakers: this charitable humor prevailed, till well it chaunced they medled with captaine Smith, who without farther deliberation gave them such an incounter, as some he so hunted up and downe the Ile, some he so terrified with whipping, beating and imprisonment, as for revenge they surprised two of his forraging disorderly souldiers, and having assembled their forces, boldly threatned at our ports to force Smith to rediver 7. Salvages which for their villanies he detained prisoners, but to try their furies, in lesse then halfe an houre he so hampered their insolencies, that they brought the 2. prisoners desiring peace without any farther composition for their prisoners, who being threatned and examined their intents and plotters of their villanies confessed they were directed only by Powhatan, to obtaine him our owne weapons to cut our own throats, with the manner how, where, and when, which wee plainely found most true and apparrant, yet he sent his messengers and his dearest Daughter Pocahuntas to excuse him, of the injuries done by his subjects, desiring their liberties, with the assuraunce of his love. After Smith had given the prisoners what correction hee thought fit, used them well a day or two after, and then delivered them Pocahuntas, for whose sake only he

Marginal notes:

An ill example to sell swords to Salvages.

Powhatans trecherie.

The governours weaknesse.

Smiths attempt to suppresse the Salvages insolencies.

Powhatans excuses.

fained to save their lives and graunt them liberty. The patient councel, that nothing would move to warre with the Salvages, would gladly have wrangled with captaine Smith for his cruelty, yet none was slaine to any mans knowledge, but it brought them in such feare and obedience, as his very name wold sufficiently affright them. The fraught of this ship being concluded to be Cedar, by the diligence of the Master, and captaine Smith shee was quickly reladed; Master Scrivener was neither Idle nor slow to follow all things at the fort; the ship falling to the Cedar Ile, captaine Martin having made shift to be sicke neare a yeare, and now, neither pepper, suger, cloves, mace, nor nutmegs, ginger nor sweet meates in the country (to injoy the credit of his supposed art) at his earnest request, was most willingly admitted to returne for England, yet having beene there but a yeare, and not past halfe a year since the ague left him (that he might say somewhat he had seene) hee went twice by water to Paspahegh a place neere 7. miles from James towne, but lest the dew should distemper him, was ever forced to returne before night, Thus much I thought fit to expresse, he expresly commanding me to record his journies, I being his man, and he sometimes my master.

Thomas Studly. Anas Todkill.

A ship fraught with Cedar.

The adventures of Captaine Martin.

Their names that were landed in this supply;
Matthew Scriviner, *appointed to be of the Councell.*

Michaell Phetyplace.
William Phetyplace.
Ralfe Morton.
William Cantrill.
Richard Wyffin.
Robert Barnes.
George Hill.
George Pretty.
John Taverner.
Robert Cutler.
Michaell Sickelmore.
Thomas Coo.
Peter Pory.

} *Gentlemen.*

Richard Killingbeck.
William Causey.
Doctor Russell.
Richard Worley.
Richard Prodger.
William Bayley.
Richard Molynex.
Richard Pots.   *Gentlemen.*
Jefrey Abots.
John Harper.
Timothy Leds.
Edward Gurganay.
George Forest.
John Nickoles.
William Gryvill.

Daniell Stalling *Jueller.*
William Dawson *Refiner.*
Abraham Ransacke *Refiner.*
William Johnson *Goldsmith.*
Peter Keffer *a Gunner.*
Robert Alberton *a Perfumer.*
Richard Belfield *Goldsmith.*

Raymond Goodyson.
John Speareman.
William Spence.
Richard Brislow.
William Simons.
John Bouth.
William Burket.
Nicholas Ven.
William Perce.   *Labourers.*
Francis Perkins.
Francis Perkins.
William Bentley.
Richard Gradon.
Rowland Nelstrop.
Richard Salvage.
Thomas Salvage.

Richard Miler.
William May.
Vere.   } *Labourers.*
Michaell.
Bishop Wyles.
John Powell.
Thomas Hope.
William Beckwith.   } *Tailers.*
William Yonge.
Laurence Towtales.
William Ward.

Christopher Rodes.
James Watkings.
Richard Fetherstone.
James Burne.
Thomas Feld.   } *Apothecaries.*
John Harford.
Post Gittnat *a Surgion.*
John Lewes *a Couper.*
Robert Cotten *a Tobaco-pipe-maker.*
Richard Dole *a blacke Smith.*
And divers others to the number of 120.

Chapter 5.
The accidents that happened in the
Discoverie of the bay.

THE prodigality of the Presidents state went so deepe in the store that Smith and Scrivener had a while tyed both Martin and him to the rules of proportion, but now Smith being to depart, the Presidents authoritie so overswayed Master Scriveners discretion as our store, our time, our strength and labours was idlely consumed to fulfill his phantasies. The second of June 1608. Smith left the fort to performe his discoverie; with this company.

Walter Russell *Doctour of Physicke.*

Ralph Morton.
Thomas Momford.
William Cantrill.
Richard Fetherstone.   } *Gentlemen.*
James Bourne.
Michael Sicklemore.

Anas Todkill.
Robert Small.
James Watkins.   } *Souldiers.*
John Powell.

James Read *blackesmith.*
Richard Keale *fishmonger.*
Jonas Profit *fisher.*

These being in an open barge of two tunnes burthen leaving the *Phenix* at Cape-Henry we crossed the bay to the Easterne shore and fell with the Iles called Smiths Iles. The first people we saw were 2 grimme and stout Salvages upon Cape-Charles with long poles like Javelings, headed with bone, they boldly demanded what we were, and what we would, but after many circumstances, they in time seemed very kinde, and directed us to Acawmacke the habitation of the Werowans where we were kindly intreated; this king was the comliest proper civill Salvage wee incountred: his country is a pleasant fertill clay-soile. Hee tolde us of a straunge accident lately happened him, and it was. Two dead children by the extreame passions of their parents, or some dreaming visions, phantasie, or affection moved them againe to revisit their dead carkases, whose benummed bodies reflected to the eies of the beholders such pleasant delightfull countenances, as though they had regained their vital spirits. This as a miracle drew many to behold them, all which, (being a great part of his people) not long after died, and not any one escaped. They spake the language of Powhatan wherein they made such descriptions of the bay, Iles, and rivers that often did us exceeding pleasure. Passing along the coast, searching every inlet, and bay fit for harbours and habitations seeing many Iles in the midst of the bay, we bore up for them, but ere wee could attaine them, such an extreame gust of wind, raine, thunder, and lightning

Cape Charles.

Acawmacke.

A strange mortalitie of Salvages.

An extreame gust.

happened, that with great daunger we escaped the unmercifull raging of that ocean-like water. The next day searching those

inhabitable Iles (which we called Russels Iles) to provide fresh water, the defect whereof forced us to follow the next Easterne channell, which brought us

to the river Wighcocomoco. The people at first with great furie, seemed to assault us, yet at last with songs, daunces, and much mirth, became very tractable, but

searching their habitations for water, wee could fill but 3, and that such puddle that never til then, wee ever knew the want of good water. We digged and searched many places but ere the end of two daies wee would have refused two barricoes of gold for one of that puddle water of Wighcocomoco. Being past these Iles, falling with a high land upon the maine wee found a great pond of fresh water, but so exceeding hot, that we supposed it some bath: that place we called Point Ployer. Being thus refreshed in crossing over from the maine to other Iles, the wind and waters so much increased with thunder, lightning, and raine, that our fore-mast blew overbord and such mightie waves over-

wrought us in that smal barge, that with great labour wee kept her from sinking by freeing out the water, 2 daies we were inforced to inhabit these uninhabited Iles, which (for the extremitie of gusts, thunder, raine, stormes, and il weather) we called Limbo. Repairing our fore saile with our shirts, we set saile for the maine and fel with a faire river on the East called Kuskarawaocke, by it inhabit the people of So-

raphanigh, Nause, Arsek, and Nautaquake that much extolled a great nation called Massawomekes, in search of whome wee returned by Limbo, but finding this easterne shore shallow broken Iles, and the maine for most part without fresh water, we passed by the straights of Limbo for the weasterne shore. So broad is the bay here, that we could scarse perceive the great high Cliffes on the other side; by them wee ancored that night, and called them Richards Cliffes. 30 leagues we sailed more Northwards, not finding any inhabitants, yet the coast well watred, the mountaines very barren, the vallies very fertil, but the woods extreame thicke, full of Woolves, Beares, Deare, and other wild beasts. The first inlet we found, wee called Bolus, for that the clay (in many

Bolus river. places) was like (if not) Bole-Armoniacke: when we first set saile, some of our gallants doubted nothing, but that our Captaine would make too much hast home; but having lien not above 12 daies in this smal Barge, oft tired at their oares, their bread spoiled with wet, so much that it was rotten (yet so good were their stomacks that they could digest it) did with continuall complaints so importune him now to returne, as caused him bespeake them in this manner.

Smiths speech to his souldiers. Gentlemen if you would remember the memorable historie of Sir Ralfe Lane, how his company importuned him to proceed in the discoverie of Morattico, alleaging, they had yet a dog, that being boyled with Saxafras leaves, would richly feed them in their returnes; what a shame would it be for you (that have beene so suspitious of my tendernesse) to force me returne with a months provision scarce able to say where we have bin, nor yet heard of that wee were sent to seeke; you cannot say but I have shared with you of the worst is past; and for what is to come of lodging, diet, or whatsoever, I am contented you allot the worst part to my selfe; as for your feares, that I will lose my selfe in these unknowne large waters, or be swallowed up in some stormie gust, abandon those childish feares, for worse then is past cannot happen, and there is as much danger to returne, as to proceed forward. Regaine therefore your old spirits; for return I wil not, (if God assist me) til I have seene the Massawomekes, found Patawomeck, or the head of this great water you conceit to be endlesse.

3 or 4 daies wee expected wind and weather, whose adverse extreamities added such discouragements to our discontents as 3 or 4 fel extreame sicke, whose pittiful complaints caused us to returne, leaving the bay some 10 miles broad at 9 or 10 fadome water.

The 16 of June we fel with the river of Patawomeck: feare The discovery of Patawomeck. being gon, and our men recovered, wee were all contented to take some paines to knowe the name of this 9 mile broad river, we could see no inhabitants for 30 myles saile; then we were conducted by 2 Salvages up a little bayed creeke toward Onawmament where all the woods were Ambuscados of Salvages. laid with Ambuscadoes to the number of 3 or 400 Salvages, but so strangely painted, grimed, and disguised, showting, yelling, and crying, as we rather supposed them so many divels. They made many bravadoes, but to appease their furie, our Captaine prepared with a seeming willingnesse (as they) to encounter them, the grazing of the bullets upon the river, with the ecco of the woods so amazed them, as down went their bowes and arrowes; (and exchanging hostage) James Watkins was sent 6 myles up the woods to their kings habitation: wee were kindly used by these Salvages, of whome wee understood, they were commaunded to betray us, by Powhatans direction, and hee so directed from the discontents of James towne. The like incounters we found at Patawomeck, Cecocawone and divers other places, but at Moyaones, Nacothtant and Taux, the people did their best to content us. The cause of this discovery, was to search a glistering mettal, the Salvages told us they had from Patawomeck, (the which Newport assured that he had tryed to hold halfe silver) also to search what furres, metals, rivers, Rockes, nations, woods, fishings, fruits, victuals and other commodities the land afforded, and whether the bay were endlesse, or how farre it extended. The mine we found 9 or 10 myles up in the country from the river, but it proved of no value: Some Otters, Beavers, Martins, Luswarts, and sables we found, and in diverse places that abundance of fish lying so thicke with their heads above the water, as for want of nets (our barge driving amongst them) we attempted to catch them with a frying pan, but we found it a bad instrument to catch fish with. Neither better fish more plenty or variety had any of us ever seene, in any place swimming in the water, then in the bay of Chesapeack, but they are not to be caught with frying-pans. To expresse al our quarrels, treacheries and incounters amongst those Salvages, I should be too tedious; but in briefe at al times we so incountred them and curbed their insolencies, as they concluded with presents to purchase peace, yet wee lost not a man, at our first meeting our captaine ever observed this order to demaunde their bowes and arrowes swords mantles or furres, with some childe for hostage, wherby he could quickly perceive when they intended any villany. Having finished this discovery (though our victuall was neare spent) he intended to have seene his imprisonment-acquaintances upon the river of Toppahannock. But our boate

A treacherous project.

Antimony

An abundant plentie of fish.

How to deale with the Salvages.

(by reason of the ebbe) chansing to ground upon a many shoules lying in the entrance, we spied many fishes lurking amongst the weedes on the sands, our captaine sporting himselfe to catch them by nailing them to the ground with his sword, set us all a fishing in that manner, by this devise, we tooke more in an houre then we all could eat; but it chanced, the captaine taking a fish from his sword (not knowing her condition) being much of the fashion of a Thornebacke with a longer taile, whereon is a most poysoned sting of 2. or 3. inches long, which shee strooke an inch and halfe into the wrist of his arme the which in 4. houres had so extreamly swolne his hand, arme, shoulder, and part of his body, as we al with much sorrow concluded his funerall, and prepared his grave in an Ile hard by (as himselfe appointed) which then wee called Stingeray Ile after the name of the fish. Yet by the helpe of a precious oile Doctour Russell applyed, ere night his tormenting paine was so wel asswaged that he eate the fish to his supper, which gave no lesse joy and content to us, then ease to himselfe. Having neither Surgeon nor surgerie but that preservative oile, we presently set saile for James Towne; passing the mouth of Pyankatanck, and Pamaunke rivers, the next day we safely arrived at Kecoughtan. The simple Salvages, seeing our captaine hurt, and another bloudy (which came by breaking his shin) our number of bowes, arrowes, swords, targets, mantles and furs; would needs imagine we had bin at warres, (the truth of these accidents would not satisfie them) but impaciently they importuned us to know with whom wee fought. Finding their aptnes to beleeve, we failed not (as a great secret) to tel them any thing that might affright them, what spoile wee had got and made of the Masawomeckes. This rumor went faster up the river then our barge; that arrived at Weraskoyack the 20. of Julie, where trimming her with painted streamers, and such devises we made the fort jealous of a Spanish frigot; where we all safely arrived the 21. of July. There wee found the last supply, al sicke, the rest, some lame, some bruised, al unable to do any thing, but complain of the pride and unreasonable needlesse cruelty of their sillie President, that had riotously consumed the store, and to fulfill his follies about building him an unnecessarie pallace in

A Stingray very hurtfull.

The Salvages affrighted with their owne suspition.

A needlesse miserie.

the woods had brought them all to that miserie; That had not we arrived, they had as strangely tormented him with revenge. But the good newes of our discovery, and the good hope we had (by the Salvages relation) our Bay had stretched to the South-sea, appeased their fury; but conditionally that Ratliffe should be deposed, and that captaine Smith would take upon him the government; their request being effected, hee Substituted Master Scrivener his deare friend in the Presidencie, equally distributing those private provisions the other had ingrossed; appointing more honest officers to assist Scrivener, (who then lay extreamelie tormented with a callenture) and in regard of the weaknes of the company, and heat of the yeare they being unable to worke; he left them to live at ease, but imbarked himselfe to finish his discovery.

The company left to live at ease.

Written by Walter Russell and Anas Todkill.

Chapter 6.
What happened the second voyage
to discover the Bay.

THE 20 of July Captaine Smith set forward to finish the discovery with 12. men their names were

Nathaniel Powell.	
Thomas Momford.	
Richard Fetherstone.	*Gentlemen.*
Michaell Sicklemore.	
James Bourne.	
Anas Todkill.	
Edward Pysing.	
Richard Keale.	
Anthony Bagnall.	*Souldiers.*
James Watkins.	
William Ward.	
Jonas Profit.	

The winde beeing contrary caused our stay 2. or 3. daies at Kecoughtan the werowans feasting us with much mirth, his

people were perswaded we went purposely to be revenged of the Massawomeckes. In the evening we
firing 2. or 3. rackets, so terrified the poore Salvages,
they supposed nothing impossible wee attempted, and desired
to assist us. The first night we ancored at Stingeray Ile, the
nexte day crossed Patawomecks river, and hasted for the river
Bolus, wee went not much farther before wee might
perceive the Bay to devide in 2. heads, and arriving
there we founde it devided in 4, all which we searched
so far as we could saile them; 2. of them wee found uninhabited, but in crossing the bay to the other, wee incountered 7. or 8. Canowes-full of Massawomecks.
We seeing them prepare to assault us, left our oares
and made way with our saile to incounter them, yet were we
but five (with our captaine) could stand; for within 2. daies
after wee left Kecoughtan, the rest (being all of the last supply)
were sicke almost to death, (untill they were seasoned to the
country) having shut them under our tarpawling, we put their
hats upon stickes by the barge side to make us seeme many,
and so we thinke the Indians supposed those hats to be men,
for they fled with all possible speed to the shoare, and there
stayed, staring at the sailing of our barge, till we anchored
right against them. Long it was ere we could drawe them to
come unto us, at last they sent 2 of their company unarmed in
a Canowe, the rest all followed to second them if need required; These 2. being but each presented with a bell, brought
aborde all their fellowes, presenting the captain with venison,
beares flesh, fish, bowes, arrows, clubs, targets, and beare-skins;
wee understood them nothing at all but by signes, whereby
they signified unto us they had been at warres with the Tockwoghs the which they confirmed by shewing their green
wounds; but the night parting us, we imagined they appointed
the next morning to meete, but after that we never saw them.
Entring the River of Tockwogh the Salvages all
armed in a fleete of Boates round invironed us; it
chanced one of them could speake the language of
Powhatan who perswaded the rest to a friendly parly: but
when they see us furnished with the Massawomeckes weapons,
and we faining the invention of Kecoughtan to have taken
them perforce; they conducted us to their pallizadoed towne,

mantelled with the barkes of trees, with Scaffolds like mounts, brested about with Barks very formally, their men, women, and children, with dances, songs, fruits, fish, furres, and what they had kindly entertained us, spreading mats for us to sit on, stretching their best abilities to expresse their loves.

Hatchets from Sasquesa-hanock.   Many hatchets, knives, and peeces of yron, and brasse, we see, which they reported to have from the Sasquesahanockes a mighty people, and mortall enimies with the Massawomeckes; the Sasquesahanocks, inhabit upon the chiefe spring of these 4. two daies journey higher then our Barge could passe for rocks. Yet we prevailed with the interpreter to take with him an other interpreter to perswade the Sasquesahanocks to come to visit us, for their language are different: 3. or 4. daies we expected their returne then 60. of these giantlike-people came downe with presents of venison, Tobacco pipes, Baskets, Targets, Bowes and Arrows. 5 of their Werowances came boldly abord us, to crosse the bay for Tockwogh, leaving their men and Canowes, the winde being so violent that they durst not passe.

Our order was, dayly to have prayer, with a psalm, at which solemnitie the poore Salvages much wondered: our prayers being done, they were long busied with consultation till they had contrived their businesse; then they began in most passionate manner to hold up their hands to the sunne with a most The Sasquesa-hanocks offer to the English. feareful song, then imbracing the Captaine, they began to adore him in like manner, though he rebuked them, yet they proceeded til their song was finished, which don with a most strange furious action, and a hellish voice began an oration of their loves; that ended, with a great painted beares skin they covered our Captaine, then one ready with a chaine of white beads (waighing at least 6 or 7 pound) hung it about his necke, the others had 18 mantles made of divers sorts of skinnes sowed together, all these with many other toyes, they laid at his feet, stroking their ceremonious handes about his necke for his creation to be their governour, promising their aids, victuals, or what they had to bee his, if he would stay with them to defend and revenge them of the Massawomecks; But wee left them at Tockwogh, they much sorrowing for our departure, yet wee promised the next yeare againe to visit them; many descriptions and discourses

they made us of Atquanahucke, Massawomecke, and
Cannida. other people, signifying they inhabit the river of Cannida, and from the French to have their hatchets,
and such like tooles by trade, these knowe no more of the territories of Powhatan then his name, and he as little of them.

Thus having sought all the inlets and rivers worth
Pawtuxunt
River. noting, we returned to discover the river of Pawtuxunt, these people we found very tractable, and more
civill then any. Wee promised them, as also the Patawomecks,
the next yeare to revenge them of the Massawomecks. Our
purposes were crossed in the discoverie of the river
Toppahanock
River. of Toppahannock, for wee had much wrangling with
that peevish nation; but at last they became as tractable as the rest. It is an excellent, pleasant, well inhabited, fertill, and a goodly navigable river, toward the head thereof; it
pleased God to take one of our sicke (called Master
Fetherstone
buried. Fetherstone) where in Fetherstons bay we buried him
in the night with a volly of shot; the rest (notwithstanding their ill diet, and bad lodging, crowded in so small a
barge in so many dangers, never resting, but alwaies tossed to
and againe) al well recovered their healthes; then we
Payankatanke
discovered. discovered the river of Payankatank, and set saile for
James Towne; but in crossing the bay in a faire calme,
such a suddaine gust surprised us in the night with thunder
and raine, as wee were halfe imployed in freeing out water,
never thinking to escape drowning. Yet running before the
winde, at last we made land by the flashes of fire from heaven,
by which light only we kept from the splitting shore, until it
pleased God in that black darknes to preserve us by that light
Their
proceedings
at James
Towne. to find Point Comfort, and arived safe at James
Towne, the 7 of September, 1608. where wee found
Master Skrivener and diverse others well recovered,
many dead, some sicke. The late President prisoner for
muteny, by the honest diligence of Master Skrivener the harvest gathered, but the stores, provision, much spoiled with
raine. Thus was that yeare (when nothing wanted) consumed
and spent and nothing done; (such was the government of
Captain Ratliffe) but only this discoverie, wherein to expresse
all the dangers, accidents, and incounters this small number
passed in that small barge, with such watrie diet in these great

waters and barbarous Countries (til then to any Christian utterly unknowne) I rather referre their merit to the censure of
the courteous and experienced reader, then I would be tedious, or partiall, being a partie;

By Nathaniell Powell, and Anas Todkill.

Chapter 7.
The Presidencie surrendred to Captaine Smith,
the arrivall and returne of the second supply:
and what happened.

THE 10. of September 1608. by the election of the Councel,
and request of the company Captaine Smith received the letters
patents, and tooke upon him the place of President, which till
then by no meanes he would accept though hee were often
importuned thereunto. Now the building of Ratcliffes pallas
staide as a thing needlesse; The church was repaired, the store-
house recovered; buildings prepared for the supply we expected. The fort reduced to the forme of this figure, the order
of watch renued, the squadrons (each setting of the
QUERE, 8.   watch) trained. The whole company every Satturday
exercised in a fielde prepared for that purpose; the
boates trimmed for trade which in their Journey encountred
the second supply, that brought them back to discover the
country of Monacan. How, or why, Captaine Newport obtained such a private commission as not to returne without a
lumpe of gold, a certainty of the south sea or one of the lost
company of Sir Walter Rawley I know not, nor why he brought
such a 5 pieced barge, not to beare us to that south sea, till we
had borne her over the mountaines: which how farre they extend is yet unknowne. As for the coronation of Powhatan and
his presents of Bason, Ewer, Bed, Clothes, and such costly
novelties, they had bin much better well spared, then so ill
Powhatans   spent. For we had his favour much better, onlie for a
scorne when   poore peece of Copper, till this stately kinde of solic-
his curtesie   iting made him so much overvalue himselfe, that he
was most   respected us as much as nothing at all; as for the
deserved.

hiring of the Poles and Dutch to make pitch and tarre, glasse milles, and sope-ashes, was most necessarie and well. But to send them and seaventy more without victuall to worke, was not so well considered; yet this could not have hurt us, had they bin 200. (though then we were 130 that wanted for our selves.) For we had the Salvages in that Decorum, (their harvest beeing newly gathered) that we feared not to get victuall

No way but one to overthrowe the busines.

sufficient had we bin 500. Now was there no way to make us miserable but to neglect that time to make our provision, whilst it was to be had; the which was done to perfourme this strange discovery, but more strange coronation; to loose that time, spend that victuall we had, tire and starve our men, having no means to carry victuall, munition, the hurt or sicke, but their owne backs. How or by whom they were invented I know not; But Captaine Newport we only accounted the author, who to effect these projects had so gilded all our hopes, with great promises, that both company and Councel concluded his resolution. I confesse we little understood then our estates, to conclude his conclusion, against al the inconveniences the foreseeing President alleadged. There was added to the councell one Captaine Waldo, and Captaine Winne two ancient souldiers and valiant gentlemen, but ignorant of the busines (being newly arrived). Ratcliffe was also permitted to have his voice, and Master Scrivener desirous to see strange countries, so that although Smith was President, yet the Councell had the authoritie, and ruled it as they listed; as for cleering Smiths objections, how pitch, and tarre, wanscot, clapbord, glasse, and sope ashes, could be provided to relade the ship; or provision got to live withal, when none was in the Country and that which we had, spent before the ships departed; The answer was, Captaine Newport undertook to fraught the Pinnace with corne, in going and returning in his discoverie, and to refraught her againe from Werawocomoco; also promising a great proportion of victuall from his ship, inferring that Smiths propositions were only devises to hinder his journey, to effect it himselfe; and that the crueltie Smith had used to the Salvages, in his absence, might occasion them to hinder his designes; For which, al workes were left; and 120 chosen men were appointed for his guard, and Smith, to make cleere these seeming suspicions, that the

Salvages were not so desperat, as was pretended by Captaine

Captaine
Smith with
4 goeth to
Powhatan.

Newport, and how willing he was to further them to effect their projects, (because the coronation would consume much time) undertooke their message to Powhatan, to intreat him to come to James Towne to receive his presents. Accompanied only with Captaine Waldo, Master Andrew Buckler, Edward Brinton, and Samuell Collier; with these 4 hee went over land, against Werawocomoco, there passed the river of Pamaunke in the Salvages Canowes, Powhatan being 30 myles of, who, presently was sent for, in the meane time his women entertained Smith in this manner.

The womens
entertaine-
ment at
Werawoco-
moco.

In a faire plaine field they made a fire, before which he sitting uppon a mat; suddainly amongst the woods was heard such a hideous noise and shriking, that they betooke them to their armes, supposing Powhatan with all his power came to surprise them; but the beholders which were many, men, women, and children, satisfied the Captaine there was no such matter, being presently presented with this anticke, 30 young women came naked out of the woods (only covered behind and before with a few greene leaves) their bodies al painted, some white, some red, some black, some partie colour, but every one different; their leader had a faire paire of stagges hornes on her head, and an otter skinne at her girdle, another at her arme, a quiver of arrowes at her backe, and bow and arrowes in her hand, the next in her hand a sword, another a club, another a pot-stick, all hornd alike, the rest every one with their severall devises. These feindes with most hellish cries, and shouts rushing from amongst the trees, cast themselves in a ring about the fire, singing, and dauncing with excellent ill varietie, oft falling into their infernall passions, and then solemnely againe to sing, and daunce. Having spent neere an houre, in this maskarado; as they entered; in like manner departed; having reaccommodated themselves, they solemnely invited Smith to their lodging, but no sooner was hee within the house, but all these Nimphes more tormented him then ever, with crowding, and pressing, and hanging upon him, most tediously crying, love you not mee? This salutation ended, the feast was set, consisting of fruit in baskets, fish, and flesh in wooden platters, beans and pease there wanted not (for 20 hogges) nor any Salvage daintie their invention could devise; some attending, others singing and dancing about them; this mirth and banquet being ended, with firebrands (instead of torches) they conducted him to his lodging.

Captain Smiths message.

The next day came Powhatan; Smith delivered his message of the presents sent him, and redelivered him Namontack, desiring him come to his Father Newport to accept those presents, and conclude their revenge against the Monacans, whereunto the subtile Salvage thus replied.

Powhatans answer.

If your king have sent me presents, I also am a king, and this my land, 8 daies I will stay to receave them. Your father is to come to me, not I to him, nor yet to your fort, neither will I bite at such a baite: as for the Monacans, I can revenge my owne injuries, and as for Atquanuchuck, where you say your brother was slain, it is a contrary way from those parts you suppose it. But for any salt water beyond the mountaines, the relations you have had from my people are false.

Wherupon he began to draw plots upon the ground (according to his discourse) of all those regions; many other discourses they had (yet both desirous to give each other content in Complementall courtesies) and so Captaine Smith returned with this answer.

Powhatans Coronation.

Upon this Captaine Newport sent his presents by water, which is neare 100 miles; with 50 of the best shot, himselfe went by land which is but 12 miles, where he met with our 3 barges to transport him over. All things being fit for the day of his coronation, the presents were brought, his bason, ewer, bed and furniture set up, his scarlet cloake and apparel (with much adoe) put on him (being perswaded by Namontacke they would doe him no hurt.) But a fowle trouble there was to make him kneele to receave his crowne, he neither knowing the majestie, nor meaning of a Crowne, nor bending of the knee, indured so many perswasions, examples, and instructions, as tired them all. At last by leaning hard on his shoulders, he a little stooped, and Newport put the Crowne on his head. When by the warning of a pistoll, the boates were prepared with such a volly of shot, that the king start up in a horrible feare, till he see all was well, then remembring himselfe, to congratulate their kindnesse, he gave his old shoes and his mantle to Captain Newport. But perceiving his purpose was to discover the Monacans, hee laboured to divert his resolution, refusing to lend him either men, or guids, more then Namontack, and so (after some complementall kindnesse on both sides) in requitall of his presents, he presented Newport with a heape of wheat eares, that might contain some 7 or 8 bushels, and as much more we bought ready dressed in the towne, wherewith we returned to the fort.

The ship having disburdened her selfe of 70 persons, with the first gentlewoman, and woman servant that arrived in our Colony; Captaine Newport with al the Councell, and 120 chosen men, set forward for the discovery of Monacan, leaving the President at the fort with 80. (such as they were) to relade the shippe. Arriving at the falles, we marched by land some forty myles in 2 daies and a halfe, and so returned downe the same path we went. Two townes wee discovered of the Monacans, the people neither using us well nor ill, yet for our securitie wee tooke one of their pettie Werowances, and lead him bound, to conduct us the way. And in our returne searched many places wee supposed mynes, about which we spent some time in refining, having one William Callicut a refiner, fitted for that purpose. From that crust of earth wee digged hee perswaded us to beleeve he extracted some smal quantitie of silver (and not unlikely better stuffe might bee had for the digging) with this poore trial being contented to leave this faire, fertill, well watred countrie. Comming to the Falles, the Salvages fained there were diverse ships come into the Bay to kill them at James Towne. Trade they would not, and find their corn we could not, for they had hid it in the woods, and being thus deluded we arrived at James Towne, halfe sicke, all complaining, and tired with toile, famine, and discontent, to have only but discovered our gilded hopes, and such fruitlesse certaineties, as the President foretold us.

No sooner were we landed, but the President dispersed many as were able, some for glasse, others for pitch, tarre and sope ashes, leaving them, (with the fort) to the Councels oversight. But 30 of us he conducted 5. myles from the fort to learn

The discovery of Monacan.

to make clapbord, cut downe trees, and ly in woods; amongst
the rest he had chosen Gabriell Beadell, and John Russell the
only two gallants of this last supply, and both proper gentlemen: strange were these pleasures to their conditions, yet
lodging eating, drinking, working, or playing they doing but
as the President, all these things were carried so pleasantly, as
within a weeke they became Masters, making it their delight to
heare the trees thunder as they fell, but the axes so oft blistered
there tender fingers, that commonly every third blow had a
lowd oath to drowne the eccho; for remedy of which sin the
President devised howe to have everie mans oathes
numbred, and at night, for every oath to have a can
of water powred downe his sleeve, with which every
offender was so washed (himselfe and all) that a man should
scarse heare an oath in a weeke.

A punishment for swearing.

By this, let no man think that the President, or these gentlemen spent their times as common wood-hackers at felling of
trees, or such like other labours, or that they were pressed to
any thing as hirelings or common slaves, for what they did
(being but once a little inured) it seemed, and they conceited
it only as a pleasure and a recreation. Yet 30 or 40 of
such voluntary Gentlemen would doe more in a day
then 100 of the rest that must bee prest to it by compulsion. Master Scrivener, Captaine Waldo, and Captaine
Winne at the fort, every one in like manner carefully regarded
their charge. The President returning from amongst the woodes,
seeing the time consumed, and no provision gotten, (and the
ship lay Idle, and would do nothing) presently imbarked himselfe in the discovery barge, giving order to the Councell, to
send Master Persey after him with the next barge that arrived
at the fort; 2. barges, he had himselfe, and 20. men, but arriving at Chickahamina, that dogged nation was too wel acquainted with our wants, refusing to trade, with as much
scorne and insolencie as they could expresse. The President
perceiving it was Powhatans policy to starve us, told them he
came not so much for their corne, as to revenge his
imprisonment, and the death of his men murdered
by them, and so landing his men, and ready to
charge them, they immediatly fled; but then they sent their
imbassadours, with corne, fish, fowl, or what they had to make

One gentleman better then 20 lubbers.

The Chickaha-mines forced to contribution.

their peace, (their corne being that year bad) they complained extreamly of their owne wants, yet fraughted our boats with 100 bushels of corne, and in like manner Master Persies, that not long after us arrived; they having done the best they could to content us, within 4. or 5. daies we returned to James Towne.

Though this much contented the company (that then feared nothing but starving) yet some so envied his good successe,

A bad
reward for
well doing. that they rather desired to starve, then his paines should prove so much more effectuall then theirs; some projects there was, not only to have deposed him but to have kept him out of the fort, for that being President, he would leave his place, and the fort without their consents; but their hornes were so much too short to effect it, as they themselves more narrowly escaped a greater mischiefe.

A good
taverne in
Virginia. All this time our old taverne made as much of all them that had either mony or ware as could bee desired; and by this time they were become so perfect on all sides (I meane Souldiers, Sailers, and Salvages,) as there was ten-times more care to maintaine their damnable and private trade, then to provide for the Colony things that were necessary. Neither was it a small pollicy in the mariners, to report in England wee had such plenty and bring us so many men without victuall, when they had so many private factors in the fort, that within 6. or 7. weekes after the ships returne, of

A bad trade
of masters
and sailers. 2. or 300. hatchets, chissels, mattocks, and pickaxes scarce 20 could be found, and for pike-heads, knives, shot, powder, or any thing (they could steale from their fellowes) was vendible; They knew as well (and as secretly) how to convay them to trade with the Salvages, for furres, baskets, mussaneekes, young beastes or such like commodities, as exchange them with the sailers, for butter, cheese, biefe, porke, aquavitæ, beere, bisket, and oatmeale; and then faine, all was sent them from their friends. And though Virginia afford no furs for the store, yet one mariner in one voyage hath got so many, as hee hath confessed to have solde in England for 30^l.

Those are the Saint-seeming worthies of Virginia, that have notwithstanding all this, meate, drinke, and pay, but now they begin to grow weary, their trade being both perceived and prevented; none hath bin in Virginia (that hath observed any thing) which knowes not this to be true, and yet the scorne, and shame was the poore souldiers, gentlemen and carelesse governours, who were all thus bought and solde, the adventurers cousened, and the action overthrowne by their false excuses, informations, and directions, by this let all the world Judge, how this businesse coulde prosper, being thus abused by such pilfering occasions.

The proceedings and accidents,
with the second supply.

Master Scrivener was sent with the barges and Pinas to Werawocomoco, where he found the Salvages more ready to fight then trade, but his vigilancy was such, as prevented their projectes, and by the meanes of Namontack got 3. or 4. hogshead of corne, and as much Red paint which (then) was esteemed an excellent die.

Skriveners voiage to Werawoco-moco.

Captaine Newport being dispatched with the tryals of pitch, tarre, glasse, frankincense, and sope ashes, with that clapbord and wainscot could bee provided met with Master Scrivener at point Comfort, and so returned for England, leaving us in all 200. with those hee brought us.

The names of those in this supply are these.

Captaine Peter Winne.	*were appointed to bee*
Captaine Richard Waldo.	*of the Councell.*
Master Francis West.	
Thomas Graves.	
Rawley Chroshaw.	
Gabriell Bedle.	
John Russell.	
John Bedle.	
William Russell.	
John Gudderington.	*Gentlemen.*
William Sambage.	
Henry Collings.	
Henry Ley.	
Harmon Haryson.	
Daniell Tucker.	
Hugh Wollystone.	

John Hoult.
Thomas Norton.
George Yarington.
George Burton.
Henry Philpot.
Thomas Maxes.
Michaell Lowicke.   } *Gentlemen.*
Master Hunt.
Thomas Forest.
William Dowman.
John Dauxe.
Thomas Abbay.

Thomas Phelps.
John Prat.
John Clarke.
Jefry Shortridge.
Dionis Oconor.
Hugh Wynne.
David ap Hugh.
Thomas Bradley.   } *Tradesmen.*
John Burras.
Thomas Lavander.
Henry Bell.
Master Powell.
David Ellys.
Thomas Gipson.

Thomas Dowse.
Thomas Mallard.
William Taler.
Thomas Fox.
Nicholas Hancock.
Walker.   } *Laborers.*
Williams.
Morrell.
Rose.
Scot.
Hardwin.

Milman.   } *Boyes.*
Hellyard.

Mistresse Forest and Anne Buras her maide, 8. Dutchmen, and Poles with divers to the number of 70. persons.

Those poore conclusions so affrighted us all with famine; that the President provided for Nansamund, tooke with him Captaine Winne and Master Scrivener (then returning from Captaine Newport). These people also long denied him trade, (excusing themselves to bee so commanded by Powhatan) til we were constrained to begin with them perforce, and then they would rather sell us some, then wee should take all; so loading our boats, with 100. bushels we parted friends, and came to James Towne, at which time, there was a marriage betweene John Laydon and Anna Burrowes, being the first marriage we had in Virginia.

Nansamund forced to contribution.

Long he staied not, but fitting himselfe and captaine Waldo with 2 barges, from Chawopo, Weanocke and all parts there, was found neither corne nor Salvage, but all fled (being Jealous of our intents) till we discovered the river and people of Appametuck, where we founde little that they had, we equally devided, betwixt the Salvages and us (but gave them copper in consideration). Master Persie and Master Scrivener went also abroad but could finde nothing.

Appamatucke discovered.

The President seeing this procrastinating of time, was no course to live, resolved with Captaine Waldo, (whom he knew to be sure in time of need) to surprise Powhatan, and al his provision, but the unwillingnes of Captaine Winne, and Master Scrivener (for some private respects) did their best to hinder their project: But the President whom no perswasions could perswade to starve, being invited by Powhatan to come unto him, and if he would send him but men to build him a house, bring him a grinstone, 50. swords, some peeces, a cock and a hen, with copper and beads, he would loade his shippe with corne. The President not ignoraunt of his devises, yet unwilling to neglect any opportunity, presently sent 3. Dutch-men and 2. English (having no victuals to imploy them, all for want therof being idle) knowing there needed no better castel, then that house to surprize Powhatan, to effect this project he took order with Captaine Waldo to second him if need required; Scrivener he left his substitute; and set forth with the Pinnas 2. barges

and six and forty men which only were such as voluntarily
offered themselves for his journy, the which (by reason of Master Scriveners ill successe) was censured very desperate, they all
knowing Smith would not returne empty howsoever, caused
many of those that he had appointed, to finde excuses to stay
behinde.

Chapter 8.
Captaine Smiths journey to Pamaunke.

THE 29 of December hee set forward for Werawocomoco, his
company were these.

In the Discovery barge, himselfe.

Robert Behethland.
Nathaniell Powell.
John Russell.
Rawly Crashaw.   } *Gentlemen.*
Michaell Sicklemore.
Richard Worlie.

Anas Todkill.
William Love.
William Bentley.
Geoffery Shortridge.   } *Souldiers.*
Edward Pising.
William Warde.

In the Pinnace.

Master George Persie, *brother to the Earle of
    Northumberland,*
Master Frauncis West, *brother to the Lord De-la-Ware.*
William Phetiplace *Captaine of the Pinnas.*
Jonas Profit *Master.*
Robert Ford *clarcke of the councell.*

Michaell Phetiplace.
Geoffery Abbot *Sergeant.* } *Gentlemen.*
William Tankard.
George Yarington.

James Bourne.
George Burton.   } *Gentlemen.*
Thomas Coe.
John Dods.
Edward Brinton.
Nathaniel Peacocke.
Henry Powell.
David Ellis.
Thomas Gipson.
John Prat.   } *Souldiers.*
George Acrigge.
James Reade.
Nicholas Hancocke.
James Watkins.
Anthony Baggly *Serg.*
Thomas Lambert.
Edward Pising. *Sergeant.*

4. Dutchmen and Richard Salvage were sent by land, to build the house for Powhatan against our arrivall.

This company being victualled but for 3. or 4. daies lodged the first night at Weraskoyack, where the President tooke sufficient provision. This kind Salvage did his best to divert him from seeing Powhatan, but perceiving he could not prevaile, he advised in this maner.

The good
counsell of
Weraskoyack.
Captaine Smith, you shall finde Powhatan to use you kindly, but trust him not, and bee sure hee hath no opportunitie to seaze on your armes, for hee hath sent for you only to cut your throats.

The Captaine thanked him for his good counsell, yet the better to try his love, desired guides to Chowanoke, for he would send a present to that king to bind him his friend. To performe this journey, was sent Michael Sicklemore, a very honest, valiant, and painefull souldier, with him two guids, and directions howe to search for the lost company of Sir Walter Rawley, and silke grasse: then wee departed thence, the President assuring the king his perpetuall love, and left with him Samuell Collier his page to learne the language.

The next night being lodged at Kecoughtan 6 or 7 daies, the extreame wind, raine, frost, and snowe, caused us to keepe

Christmas amongst the Salvages, where wee were never more
merrie, nor fedde on more plentie of good oysters,
fish, flesh, wild foule, and good bread, nor never had
better fires in England then in the drie warme smokie
houses of Kecoughtan. But departing thence, when we found
no houses, we were not curious in any weather, to lie 3 or 4
nights together upon any shore under the trees by a
good fire. 148 fowles the President, Anthony Bagly,
and Edward Pising, did kill at 3 shoots. At Kiskiack
the frost forced us 3 or 4 daies also to suppresse the insolencie
of those proud Salvages; to quarter in their houses, and guard
our barge, and cause them give us what wee wanted, yet were
we but 12 with the President, and yet we never wanted harbour
where we found any houses. The 12 of Januarie we arrived at
Werawocomoco, where the river was frozen neare halfe a mile
from the shore; but to neglect no time, the President with his
barge, so farre had approached by breaking the Ice as the eb
left him amongst those oozie shoules, yet rather then to lie
there frozen to death, by his owne example hee taught
them to march middle deepe, more then a flight shot
through this muddie frore ooze; when the barge
floted he appointed 2 or 3 to returne her abord the Pinnace,
where for want of water in melting the salt Ice they made fresh
water, but in this march Master Russell (whome none could
perswade to stay behind) being somewhat ill, and exceeding
heavie, so overtoiled him selfe, as the rest had much adoe (ere
he got a shore) to regaine life, into his dead benummed spirits.
Quartering in the next houses we found, we sent to Powhatan
for provision, who sent us plentie of bread, Turkies, and Venison. The next day having feasted us after his ordinarie manner,
he began to aske, when we would bee gon, faining hee sent not
for us, neither had hee any corne, and his people much lesse,
yet for 40 swords he would procure us 40 bushels. The President shewing him the men there present, that brought him the
message and conditions, asked him how it chaunced
he became so forgetful, thereat the king concluded
the matter with a merry laughter, asking for our
commodities, but none he liked without gunnes and swords,
valuing a basket of corne more pretious then a basket of copper,
saying he could eate his corne, but not his copper.

Plentie of victuall.

148 Fowles killed at 3 shoots.

An ill march.

Powhatans subteltie.

Captaine Smith seeing the intent of this subtil Salvage began to deale with him after this manner,

Captaine Smithes discourse to Powhatan. Powhatan, though I had many courses to have made my provision, yet beleeving your promises to supply my wants, I neglected all, to satisfie your desire, and to testifie my love, I sent you my men for your building, neglecting my owne: what your people had you have engrossed, forbidding them our trade, and nowe you thinke by consuming the time, wee shall consume for want, not having to fulfill your strange demandes. As for swords, and gunnes, I told you long agoe, I had none to spare. And you shall knowe, those I have, can keepe me from want, yet steale, or wrong you I will not, nor dissolve that friendship, wee have mutually promised, except you constraine mee by your bad usage.

The king having attentively listned to this discourse; promised, that both hee and his Country would spare him what they could, the which within 2 daies, they should receave.

Powhatans reply and flattery. Yet Captaine Smith, (saith the king) some doubt I have of your comming hither, that makes me not so kindly seeke to relieve you as I would; for many do informe me, your comming is not for trade, but to invade my people and possesse my Country, who dare not come to bring you corne, seeing you thus armed with your men. To cleere us of this feare, leave abord your weapons, for here they are needlesse we being all friends and for ever Powhatans.

With many such discourses they spent the day, quartring that night in the kings houses. The next day he reviewed his building, which hee little intended should proceed; for the Dutchmen finding his plenty, and knowing our want, and perceived his preparation to surprise us, little thinking wee could escape both him and famine, (to obtaine his favour) revealed to him as much as they knew of our estates and projects, and how to prevent them; one of them being of so good a judgement, spirit, and resolution, and a hireling that was certaine of wages for his labour, and ever well used, both he and his countrimen, that the President knewe not whome better to trust, and not knowing any fitter for that imploiment, had sent him as a spie to discover Powhatans intent, then little doubting his honestie, nor could ever be certaine of his villany, till neare halfe a yeare after.

Whilst we expected the comming in of the countrie, we wrangled out of the king 10 quarters of corne for a copper kettle, the which the President perceived him much to affect, valued it at a much greater rate, but (in regard of his scarcety) hee would accept of as much more the next yeare, or else the country of Monacan, the king exceeding liberall of that hee had not yeelded him Monacan. Wherewith each seeming well contented; Powhatan began to expostulate the difference betwixt peace and war, after this manner.

Powhatans
discourse of
peace and
warre. Captaine Smith you may understand, that I, having seene the death of all my people thrice, and not one living of those 3 generations, but my selfe, I knowe the difference of peace and warre, better then any in my Countrie. But now I am old, and ere long must die, my brethren, namely Opichapam, Opechankanough, and Kekataugh, my two sisters, and their two daughters, are distinctly each others successours, I wish their experiences no lesse then mine, and your love to them, no lesse then mine to you; but this brute from Nansamund that you are come to destroy my Countrie, so much affrighteth all my people, as they dare not visit you; what will it availe you, to take that perforce, you may quietly have with love, or to destroy them that provide you food? what can you get by war, when we can hide our provision and flie to the woodes, whereby you must famish by wronging us your friends; and whie are you thus jealous of our loves, seeing us unarmed, and both doe, and are willing still to feed you with that you cannot get but by our labours? think you I am so simple not to knowe, it is better to eate good meate, lie well, and sleepe quietly with my women and children, laugh and be merrie with you, have copper, hatchets, or what I want, being your friend; then bee forced to flie from al, to lie cold in the woods, feed upon acorns, roots, and such trash, and be so hunted by you, that I can neither rest, eat, nor sleepe; but my tired men must watch, and if a twig but breake, everie one crie there comes Captaine Smith, then must I flie I knowe not whether, and thus with miserable feare end my miserable life; leaving my pleasures to such youths as you, which through your rash unadvisednesse, may quickly as miserably ende, for want of that you never knowe how to find? Let this therefore assure you of our loves and everie yeare our friendly trade shall furnish you with corne, and now also if you would come in friendly manner to see us, and not thus with your gunnes and swords, as to invade your foes.

To this subtil discourse the President thus replied.

Captaine
Smiths reply. Seeing you will not rightly conceave of our words, wee strive to make you knowe our thoughts by our deeds. The vow I made you of my love, both my selfe and my men have kept. As for your promise I finde it everie daie violated, by some of your subjects, yet wee finding your love and kindnesse (our custome is so far from being ungratefull) that for your sake only, wee have curbed our thirsting desire of revenge, else had they knowne as wel the crueltie we use to our enimies as our true love and curtesie to our friendes. And I thinke your judgement sufficient to conceive as well by the adventures we have undertaken, as by the advantage we have by our armes of yours: that had wee intended you anie hurt, long ere this wee coulde have effected it; your people comming to me at James towne, are entertained with their bowes and arrowes without exception; we esteeming it with you, as it is with us, to weare our armes as our apparell. As for the dangers of our enimies, in such warres consist our chiefest pleasure, for your riches we have no use, as for the hiding your provision, or by your flying to the woods, we shall so unadvisedly starve as you conclude, your friendly care in that behalfe is needlesse; for we have a rule to finde beyond your knowledge.

Manie other discourses they had, til at last they began to trade, but the king seing his will would not bee admitted as a lawe, our gard dispersed, nor our men disarmed, he (sighing) breathed his mind, once more in this manner.

Powhatans
importunitie
for to
have them
unarmed, to
betray them. Captaine Smith, I never used anie of Werowances, so kindlie as your selfe; yet from you I receave the least kindnesse of anie. Captaine Newport gave me swords, copper, cloths, a bed, tooles, or what I desired, ever taking what I offered him, and would send awaie his gunnes when I intreated him: none doth denie to laie at my feet (or do) what I desire, but onelie you, of whom I can have nothing, but what you regard not, and yet you wil have whatsoever you demand. Captain Newport you call father, and so you call me, but I see for all us both, you will doe what you list, and wee must both seeke to content you: but if you intend so friendlie as you saie, sende hence your armes that I may beleeve you, for you see the love I beare you, doth cause mee thus nakedlie forget my selfe.

Smith seeing this Salvage but trifled the time to cut his throat: procured the Salvages to breake the ice, (that his boat might come to fetch both him and his corne) and gave order for his men to come ashore, to have surprised the king, with whom also he but trifled the time till his men landed, and to keepe him from suspition, entertained the time with this reply.

Captaine Smiths discourse to delay time, that hee might surprise Powhatan.

Powhatan, you must knowe as I have but one God, I honour but one king; and I live not here as your subject, but as your friend, to pleasure you with what I can: by the gifts you bestowe on me, you gaine more then by trade; yet would you visite mee as I doe you, you should knowe it is not our customes to sell our curtesie as a vendible commoditie. Bring all your Country with you for your gard, I will not dislike of it as being over jealous. But to content you, to morrow I will leave my armes, and trust to your promise. I call you father indeed, and as a father you shall see I will love you, but the smal care you had of such a child, caused my men perswade me to shift for my selfe.

Powhatans plot to have murdered Smith.

By this time Powhatan having knowledge, his men were readie: whilst the ice was breaking, his luggage women, and children fledde, and to avoid suspition, left 2 or 3 of his women talking with the Captaine, whilst he secretly fled, and his men as secretlie beset the house, which being at the instant discovered to Captaine Smith, with his Pistol, Sword and Target, he made such a passage amongst those naked divels, that they fled before him some one waie some another, so that without hurt he obtained the Corps du-guard; when they perceived him so well escaped, and with his 8 men (for he had no more with him), to the uttermost of their skill, they sought by excuses to dissemble the matter, and Powhatan to excuse his flight, and the suddaine comming of this multi-

A chain of perle for a present.

tude, sent our Captaine a greate bracelet, and a chaine of pearle, by an ancient Orator that bespoke us to this purpose, (perceiving them from our Pinnace, a barge and men departing and comming unto us.)

His excuse.

Captaine Smith, our Werowans is fled, fearing your guns, and knowing when the ice was broken there would come more men, sent those of his to guard his corne from the pilfrie, that might happen without your knowledge: now though some bee hurt by your misprision, yet he is your friend, and so wil continue: and since the ice is open hee would have you send awaie your corne; and if you would have his companie send also your armes, which so affrighteth his people, that they dare not come to you, as he hath promised they should.

Nowe having provided baskets for our men to carrie the corne, they kindlie offered their service to gard our armes, that none

Pretending to kill our men loded with baskets we forced the Salvages carrie them.

should steale them. A great manie they were, of goodlie well appointed fellowes as grim as divels; yet the verie sight of cocking our matches against them, and a few words, caused them to leave their bowes and arrowes to our gard, and beare downe our corne on their own backes; wee needed not importune them to make quick dispatch. But our own barge being left by the ebb, caused us to staie, till the midnight tide carried us safe abord, having spent that halfe night with such mirth, as though we never had suspected or intended any thing, we left the Dutch-men to build, Brinton to kil fowle for Powhatan (as by his messengers he importunately desired) and left directions with our men to give Powhatan all the content they could, that we might injoy his company at our returne from Pamaunke.

Chapter 9.
How we escaped surprising at Pamaunke.

The dutchmen deceave Captaine Smith.

WEE had no sooner set saile, but Powhatan re-turned, and sent Adam and Francis (2. stout Dutch men) to the fort, who faining to Captaine Winne that al things were well, and that Captaine Smith had use for their armes, wherefore they requested newe (the which were given them) they told him their comming was for some ex-traordinary tooles and shift of apparell; by this colourable ex-cuse, they obtained 6. or 7. more to their confederacie, such expert theefes, that presently furnished them with a great many swords, pike-heads, peeces, shot, powder and such like. They had Salvages at hand ready to carry it away, the next day they returned unsuspected, leaving their confederates to follow, and in the interim, to convay them a competencie of all things they could, for which service they should live with Powhatan as his chiefe affected: free from those miseries that would happen the Colony. Samuell their other consort, Powhatan kept for their pledge, whose diligence had provided them, 300. of their kinde of hatchets, the rest, 50. swords, 8. peeces, and 8. pikes: Brinton, and Richard Salvage seeing the Dutch-men so strangly diligent to accommodate the Salvages these weapons attempted to have got to James Towne; but they were apprehended; within 2. or 3. daies we arrived at Pamaunke: the king as many daies, entertained us with feasting and much mirth: and the day he appointed to begin our trade, the President, with Master Persie, Master West, Master Russell, Master Beheathland, Master Powell, Master Crashaw, Master Ford, and

Opechanca-
noughs
abandoned. some others to the number of 15. went up to Opechancanougs house (near a quarter of a mile from the river,) where we founde nothing, but a lame fellow and a boy, and all the houses about, of all things abandoned; not long we staide ere the king arrived, and after him came divers of his people loaded with bowes and arrowes, but such pinching commodities, and those esteemed at such a value, as our Captaine beganne with him in this manner.

Smiths
speech to
Opechanca-
nough. Opechancanough the great love you professe with your tongue, seemes meere deceipt by your actions; last yeare you kindly fraughted our ship, but now you have invited me to starve with hunger. You know my want, and I your plenty, of which by some meanes I must have part, remember it is fit for kings to keepe their promise. Here are my commodities, wherof take your choice; the rest I will proportion, fit bargaines for your people.

The king seemed kindly to accept his offer; and the better to colour his project, sold us what they had to our own content; promising the next day, more company, better provided; (the barges, and Pinnas being committed to the charge of Master Phetiplace) the President with his old 15 marched up to the kings house, where we found 4 or 5 men newly come with great baskets, not long after came the king, who with a strained cheerefulnes held us with discourse, what paines he had taken to keepe his promise; til Master Russell brought us in news

700 Salvages
beset the
English
being but 16. that we were all betraied: for at least 6. or 700. of well appointed Indians had invironed the house and beset the fields. The king conjecturing what Russell related, we could wel perceive how the extremity of his feare

bewrayed his intent: whereat some of our companie seeming dismaide with the thought of such a multitude; the Captaine incouraged us after this manner.

Smiths speech
to his
company.
Worthy countrymen were the mischiefes of my seeming friends, no more then the danger of these enemies, I little cared, were they as many more, if you dare do, but as I. But this is my torment, that if I escape them, our malicious councell with their open mouthed minions, will make mee such a peace-breaker (in their opinions) in England, as wil break my neck; I could wish those here, that make these seeme Saints, and me an oppressor. But this is the worst of all, wherin I pray aide me with your opinions; should wee begin with them and surprize this king, we cannot keep him and defend well our selves. If we should each kill our man and so proceede with al in this house; the rest will all fly, then shall we get no more, then the bodies that are slaine, and then starve for victuall: as for their fury it is the least danger; for well you know, (being alone as-saulted with 2 or 300 of them) I made them compound to save my life, and we are now 16 and they but 700. at the most, and assure your selves God wil so assist us, that if you dare but to stande to discharge your peeces, the very smoake will bee sufficient to affright them; yet howsoever (if there be occasion) let us fight like men, and not die like sheep; but first I will deale with them, to bring it to passe, we may fight for some thing and draw them to it by conditions. If you like this motion, promise me youle be valiant.

The time not permitting any argument, all vowed to execute whatsoever he attempted, or die; whereupon the captaine, ap-proaching the king bespoke him in this manner.

Smiths
offer to
Opechanca-
nough.
I see Opechancanough your plot to murder me, but I feare it not, as yet your men and mine, have done no harme, but by our directions. Take therefore your arms; you see mine; my body shalbe as naked as yours; the Ile in your river is a fit place, if you be contented: and the conqueror (of us two) shalbe Lord and Master over all our men; otherwaies drawe all your men into the field; if you have not enough take time to fetch more, and bring what number you will, so everie one bring a basket of corne, against all which I will stake the value in copper; you see I have but 15 men, and our game shalbe the conquerer take all.

Opechanca-
noughs devise
to betray
Smith.
The king, being guarded with 50 or 60 of his chiefe men, seemed kindly to appease Smiths suspi-tion of unkindnesse, by a great present at the dore,

they intreated him to receive. This was to draw him without
the dore where the present was garded with at the least 200
men and 30 lying under a greate tree (that lay thwart as a Barricado) each his arrow nocked ready to shoot; some the President commanded to go and see what kinde of deceit this was,
and to receive the present, but they refused to do it, yet divers
offered whom he would not permit; but commanding Master
Persie and Master West to make good the house, tooke Master
Powell and Master Beheathland to guard the dore, and in such
a rage snatched the king by his vambrace in the midst of his
men, with his pistoll ready bent against his brest: thus he led
the trembling king, (neare dead with feare) amongst all his
people, who delivering the Captaine his bow and arrowes, all
his men were easily intreated to cast downe their armes, little
dreaming anie durst in that manner have used their king; who
then to escape himselfe, bestowed his presents in goodsad-
nesse. And having caused all his multitude to approach disarmed; the President argued with them to this effect.

Smiths
discourse
to the
Pamaunkies.   I see you Pamaunkies the great desire you have to cut
my throat; and my long suffering your injuries, have in-
boldened you to this presumption. The cause I have forborne your insolencies, is the promise I made you (before
the God I serve) to be your friend, till you give me just cause to bee
your enimie. If I keepe this vow, my God will keepe me, you cannot
hurt me; if I breake it he will destroie me. But if you shoot but one arrow, to shed one drop of blood of any of my men, or steale the least
of these beades, or copper, (I spurne before me with my foot) you
shall see, I wil not cease revenge, (if once I begin) so long as I can
heare where to find one of your nation that will not deny the name of
Pamaunke; I am not now at Rasseweac (halfe drownd with mire)
where you tooke me prisoner, yet then for keeping your promise, and
your good usage, and saving my life, I so affect you, that your denials
of your treacherie, doth half perswade me to mistake my selfe. But if I
be the marke you aime at, here I stand, shoote hee that dare. You
promised to fraught my ship ere I departed, and so you shall, or I
meane to load her with your dead carkases; yet if as friends you wil
come and trade, I once more promise not to trouble you, except you
give me the first occasion.

Upon this awaie went their bowes and arrowes, and men,
women, and children brought in their commodities, but 2 or
three houres they so thronged about the President, and so

The Salvages
dissemble
their intent.
overwearied him, as he retired himself to rest, leaving Master Beheathland and Master Powel to accept
their presents; but some Salvage perceiving him fast
asleepe, and the guard carelesly dispersed, 40 or 50 of their
choice men each with an English sword in his hand, began to
enter the house, with 2 or 300 others that pressed to second
them. The noise and hast they made in, did so shake the house,
as they awoke him from his sleep, and being halfe amazed with
Their excuse
and reconcile-
ment.
this suddaine sight, betooke him straight to his
sword and target, Master Crashaw and some other
charging in like manner, they thronged faster backe,
then before forward. The house thus clensed, the king and his
ancients, with a long oration came to excuse this intrusion.
The rest of the day was spent with much kindnesse, the company againe renuing their presents of their best provision. And
what soever we gave them, they seemed well contented with it.

Now in the meane while since our departure, this hapned at
the fort, Master Scrivener willing to crosse the surprizing of
Powhatan; 9 daies after the Presidents departure, would needs
visit the Ile of hogges, and took with him Captaine Waldo
(though the President had appointed him to bee readie to second his occasions) with Master Anthony Gosnoll and eight
others; but so violent was the wind (that extreame frozen time)
that the boat sunke, but where or how, none doth knowe, for
they were all drowned; onlie this was knowne, that the Skiffe
The losse
of Master
Skrivener
and others
with a Skiffe.
was much overloaded, and would scarse have lived in
that extreame tempest, had she beene emptie; but by
no perswasion hee could bee diverted, though both
Waldo and 100 others doubted as it hapned. The Salvages were the first that found their bodies, which so much the
more encouraged them to effect their projects. To advertise the
President of this heavie newes, none could bee found would
undertake it, but the journey was often refused of all in the
Master Wiffin
his journey to
the President.
fort, untill Master Wiffin undertooke alone the performance thereof; wherein he was encountred with
many dangers and difficulties, and in all parts as hee
passed (as also that night he lodged with Powhatan) perceived
such preparation for warre, that assured him, some mischiefe
was intended, but with extraordinarie bribes, and much trouble, in three daies travell at length hee found us in the midst of

these turmoiles. This unhappie newes, the President swore him to conceale from the rest, and so dissembling his sorrow, with the best countenance he could, when the night approached, went safely abord with all his companie.

Now so extreamely Powhatan had threatned the death of his men, if they did not by some meanes kill Captaine Smith, that the next day they appointed the Countrie should come to trade unarmed: yet unwilling to be treacherous, but that they were constrained, hating fighting almost as ill as hanging, such feare they had of bad successe. The next morning the sunne had not long appeared, but the fieldes appeared covered with people, and baskets to tempt us ashore. The President determined to keepe abord, but nothing was to bee had without his presence, nor they would not indure the sight of a gun; then the President seeing many depart, and being unwilling to lose such a booty, so well contrived the Pinnace, and his barges with Ambuscadoes, as only with Master Persie, Master West, and Master Russell armed, he went ashore, others unarmed he appointed to receive what was brought; the Salvages flocked before him in heapes, and (the bancke serving as a trench for retreat) hee drewe them faire open to his ambuscadoes, for he not being to be perswaded to go to visit their king, the King came to visit him with 2 or 300 men, in the forme of two halfe moons, with some 20 men, and many women loaded with great painted baskets; but when they approached somewhat neare us, their women and children fled; for when they had environed and beset the fieldes in this manner, they thought their purpose sure; yet so trembled with fear as they were scarse able to nock their arrowes; Smith standing with his 3 men readie bent beholding them, till they were within danger of our ambuscado, who, upon the word discovered themselves, and he retiring to the banke; which the Salvages no sooner perceived but away they fled, esteeming their heeles for their best advantage.

That night we sent to the fort Master Crashaw and Master Foard, who (in the mid-way betweene Werawocomoco and the fort) met 4 or 5. of the Dutch mens confederates going to Powhatan, the which (to excuse those gentlemens Suspition of their running to the Salvages) returned to the fort and there continued.

Powhatan constraineth his men to be trecherous.

Their third attempt to betray us.

The Salvages hearing our barge depart in the night were so terriblie aifraide, that we sent for more men, (we having so much threatned their ruine, and the rasing of their houses, boats, and canowes) that the next day the king sent our Captaine a chaine of pearle to alter his purpose; and stay his men, promising (though they wanted themselves) to fraught our ship, and bring it abord to avoid suspition, so that 5 or 6 daies after, from al parts of the countrie within 10 or 12 miles, in the extreame cold frost, and snow, they brought us provision on their naked backes.

A chaine of pearle sent to obtaine peace.

Yet notwithstanding this kindnesse and trade; had their art and poison bin sufficient, the President with Master West and some others had been poysoned; it made them sicke, but expelled it selfe; Wecuttanow a stout yong fellow, knowing hee was suspected for bringing this present of poison, with 40 or 50. of his choice companions (seeing the President but with a few men at Potauncac) so prowdlie braved it, as though he expected to incounter a revenge; which the President perceiving in the midst of his companie did not onlie beat, but spurned him like a dogge, as scorning to doe him anie worse mischiefe; whereupon all of them fled into the woods, thinking they had done a great matter, to have so well escaped; and the townsmen remaining, presentlie fraughted our barge, to bee rid of our companies, framing manie excuses to excuse Wecuttanow (being son to their chiefe king but Powhatan) and told us if we would shew them him that brought the poyson, they would deliver him to us to punish as wee pleased.

The President Poysoned. The offender punished.

Men maie thinke it strange there should be this stir for a little corne, but had it been gold with more ease we might have got it; and had it wanted, the whole collonie had starved. We maie be thought verie patient, to indure all those injuries; yet onlie with fearing them, we got what they had. Whereas if we had taken revenge, then by their losse we should have lost our selvs. We searched also the countries of Youghtanund and Mattapamient, where the people imparted that little they had, with such complaints and tears from women and children; as he had bin too cruell to be a Christian that would not have bin satisfied, and moved with compassion. But had this happened in October, November, and

The Salvage want and poverty.

December, when that unhappie discoverie of Monacan was made we might have fraughted a ship of 40 tuns, and twice as much might have bin had from the rivers of Toppahannock, Patawomeck, and Pawtuxunt. The maine occasion of our temporizing with the Salvages was to part friends, (as we did) to give the lesse cause of suspition to Powhatan to fly; by whom

The Dutchmen did much hurt.

we now returned, with a purpose, to have surprised him and his provision. For effecting whereof, (when we came against the towne) the President sent Master Wiffin and Master Coe ashore to discover and make waie for his intended project. But they found that those damned Dutch-men had caused Powhatan to abandon his new house, and Werawocomoco, and to carrie awaie all his corne and provision; and the people, they found (by their means so ill affected), that had they not stood well upon their guard, they had hardlie escaped with their lives. So the President finding his intention thus frustrated, and that there was nothing now to be had, and therefore an unfit time to revenge their abuses, helde on his course for James Towne; we having in this Jornie (for 25^l of copper 50^l of Iron and beads) kept 40 men 6. weekes, and dailie feasted with bread, corne, flesh, fish, and fowle, everie man having for his reward (and in consideration of his commodities) a months provision; (no trade being allowed but for the store,) and we delivered at James Towne to the Cape-Marchant 279 bushels of corne.

Those temporall proceedings to some maie seeme too charitable; to such a dailie daring trecherous people: to others unpleasant that we washed not the ground with their blouds, nor shewed such strange inventions, in mangling, murdering, ransaking, and destroying, (as did the Spaniards) the simple bodies of those ignorant soules; nor delightful because not stuffed with relations of heaps, and mines of gold and silver, nor such rare commodities as the Portugals and Spaniards found in the East and West Indies. The want wherof hath begot us (that were the first undertakers) no lesse scorne and contempt, then their noble conquests and valiant adventures (beautified with it) praise and honor. Too much I confesse the world cannot attribute to their ever memorable merit. And to cleare us from the worlds blind ignorant censure, these fewe words may suffise to any reasonable understanding.

It was the Spaniards good hap to happen in those parts, where were infinite numbers of people, whoe had manured the ground with that providence, that it afforded victuall at all times: and time had brought them to that perfection, they had the use of gold and silver, and the most of such commodities, as their countries afforded, so that what the Spaniard got, was only the spoile and pillage of those countrie people, and not the labours of their owne hands. But had those fruitfull Countries, beene as Salvage, as barbarous, as ill peopled, as little planted, laboured and manured as Virginia, their proper labours (it is likely) would have produced as small profit as ours. But had Virginia bin peopled, planted, manured, and adorned, with such store of pretious Jewels, and rich commodities, as was the Indies: then, had we not gotten, and done as much as by their examples might bee expected from us, the world might then have traduced us and our merits, and have made shame and infamy our recompence and reward.

But we chanced in a lande, even as God made it. Where we found only an idle, improvident, scattered people; ignorant of the knowledge of gold, or silver, or any commodities; and carelesse of any thing but from hand to mouth, but for bables of no worth; nothing to encourage us, but what accidentally wee found nature afforded. Which ere wee could bring to recompence our paines, defray our charges, and satisfie our adventurers, we were to discover the country, subdue the people, bring them to be tractable, civil, and industrious, and teach them trades, that the fruits of their labours might make us recompence, or plant such colonies of our owne that must first make provision how to live of themselves, ere they can bring to perfection the commodities of the countrie, which doubtles will be as commodious for England, as the west Indies for Spaine, if it be rightly managed; notwithstanding all our home-bred opinions, that will argue the contrarie, as formerly such like have done against the Spaniards and Portugals. But to conclude, against all rumor of opinion, I only say this, for those that the three first yeares began this plantation, notwithstanding al their factions, mutenies, and miseries, so gently corrected, and well prevented: peruse the Spanish Decades, the relations of Master Hacklut, and tell mee how many ever with such smal meanes, as a barge of 2 Tunnes; sometimes with 7. 8. 9, or but at most 15 men did ever discover so many faire and navigable rivers; subject so many severall kings, people, and nations, to obedience, and contribution with so little bloud shed.

And if in the search of those Countries, wee had hapned where wealth had beene, we had as surely had it, as obedience and contribution, but if wee have overskipped it, we will not envy them that shall chance to finde it. Yet can wee not but lament, it was our ill fortunes to end, when wee had but only learned how to begin, and found the right course how to proceed.

By Richard Wiffin, William Phettiplace
and Anas Todkill.

Chapter 10.
How the Salvages became subject to the English.

WHEN the shippes departed, al the provision of the store (but that the President had gotten) was so rotten with the last somers rain, and eaten with rats, and wormes, as the hogs would scarsely eat it, yet it was the souldiers diet, till our returnes: so that wee found nothing done, but victuall spent, and the most part of our tooles, and a good part of our armes convayed to the Salvages. But now, casting up the store, and finding sufficient till the next harvest, the feare of starving was abandoned; and the company divided into tennes, fifteenes, or as the businesse required, 4 houres each day was spent in worke, the rest in pastimes and merry exercise; but the untowardnesse of the greatest number, caused the President to make a generall assembly, and then he advised them as followeth.

The
Presidents
advise to
the company.
Countrimen, the long experience of our late miseries, I hope is sufficient to perswade every one to a present correction of himselfe; and thinke not that either my pains, or the adventurers purses, will ever maintaine you in idlenesse and sloth; I speake not this to you all, for diverse of you I know deserve both honor and reward, better then is yet here to bee had: but the greater part must be more industrious, or starve, howsoever you have bin

heretofore tolerated by the authoritie of the Councell from that I have often commanded you, yet seeing nowe the authoritie resteth wholly in my selfe, you must obay this for a law, that he that will not worke shall not eate (except by sicknesse he be disabled) for the labours of 30 or 40 honest and industrious men shall not bee consumed to maintaine 150 idle varlets. Now though you presume the authoritie here is but a shaddow, and that I dare not touch the lives of any, but my own must answer it; the letters patents each week shall be read you, whose contents will tell you the contrary. I would wish you therefore without contempt seeke to observe these orders set downe: for there are nowe no more Councells to protect you, nor curbe my indeavors. Therefore hee that offendeth let him assuredly expect his due punishment.

Hee made also a table as a publike memoriall of every mans deserts, to encourage the good, and with shame to spurre on the rest to amendment. By this many became very industrious, yet more by severe punishment performed their businesse; for all were so tasked, that there was no excuse could prevaile to deceive him, yet the Dutchmens consorts so closely still convaid powder, shot, swords, and tooles, that though we could find the defect, we could not find by whom it was occasioned, till it was too late.

The Dutchmens plot to murder Captaine Smith.   All this time the Dutchmen remaining with Powhatan, received them, instructing the Salvages their use. But their consorts not following them as they expected, to knowe the cause, they sent Francis their companion (a stout young fellow) disguised Salvage like to the glasse-house, (a place in the woods neere a myle from James Towne) where was the randavus for all their unsuspected villany. 40 men they procured of Powhatan to lie in Ambuscadoe for Captaine Smith, who no sooner heard of this Dutchman, but hee sent to apprehend him, who found he was gon, yet to crosse his returne to Powhatan, Captaine Smith presently dispatched 20 shot after him, and then returning but from the glasse-house alone, hee incountred the king of Paspaheigh, a most strong stout Salvage, whose perswasions not being able to perswade him to his ambush, seeing him only armed but with a fauchion, attempted to have shot him; but the President prevented his shot by grapling with him, and the Salvage as well prevented him for drawing his fauchion, and perforce

bore him into the river to have drowned him; long they strug-
gled in the water, from whence the king perceiving two of the
Smith taketh
the king of
Paspaheigh
prisoner.
Poles upon the sandes would have fled; but the President held him by the haire and throat til the Poles
came in; then seeing howe pittifully the poore Salvage begged his life, they conducted him prisoner to the fort.
The Dutchman ere long was also brought in, whose villany,
though all this time it was suspected, yet he fained such a formall excuse, that for want of language, Win had not rightly
understood them, and for their dealings with Powhatan, that
to save their lives they were constrained to accommodate his
armes, of whome he extreamely complained to have detained
them perforce; and that hee made this escape with the hazard
of his life, and meant not to have returned, but only walked in
the woods to gather walnuts: yet for all this faire tale (there
was so smal appearance of truth) hee went by the heeles; the
king also he put in fetters, purposing to regaine the Dutch-
men, by the saving his life; the poore Salvage did his best, by
his daily messengers to Powhatan, but all returned that the
Dutchmen would not returne, neither did Powhatan stay them,
and bring them fiftie myles on their backes they were not able;
daily this kings wives children, and people, came to visit him
with presents, which hee liberally bestowed to make his peace,
much trust they had in the Presidents promise, but the king
finding his gard negligent (though fettered) yet escaped. Captaine Win thinking to pursue him, found such troopes of Salvages to hinder his passages, as they exchanged many volies of
shot for flights of arrowes. Captaine Smith hearing of this, in
returning to the fort tooke two Salvages prisoners, the one
called Kemps, the other Kinsock, the two most exact villaines
in the countrie; with those, Captaine Win, and 50 chosen men
attempted that night to have regained the king, and revenged
his injurie and so had done if he had followed his directions, or
bin advised by those two villaines, that would have betraied
both their king and kindred for a peece of copper, but hee trifling away the night, the Salvages the next morning by the
rising of the sunne, braved him come a shore to fight, a good
time both sides let flie at other, but wee heard of no hurt, only
they tooke two Canows, burnt the kings house and so returned.

The President fearing those bravadoes would but incourage the Salvages, begun himselfe to trie his conclusions; whereby 6 or 7 Salvages were slaine, as many made prisoners; burnt their houses, tooke their boats with all their fishing weares, and planted them at James Towne for his owne use; and nowe resolved not to cease till he had revenged himselfe upon al that had injured him. But in his journey passing by Paspaheigh towards Chickahamina, the Salvages did their best to draw him to their ambuscadoes; but seeing him regardlesly passe their Countrey, all shewed themselves in their bravest manner, to trie their valours; he could not but let flie, and ere he could land, the Salvages no sooner knewe him, but they threw downe their armes and desired peace; their Orator was a stout young man called Ocanindge, whose worthie discourse deserveth to be remembred; and this it was.

The Salvages desire peace.

Captaine Smith, my master is here present in this company thinking it Captaine Win, and not you; and of him hee intended to have beene revenged, having never offended him: if hee have offended you in escaping your imprisonment; the fishes swim, the fowles flie, and the very beastes strive to escape the snare and live; then blame not him being a man, hee would entreat you remember, your being a prisoner, what paines he tooke to save your life; if since he hath injured you he was compelled to it, but howsoever, you have revenged it with our too great losse. We perceive and well knowe you intend to destroy us, that are here to intreat and desire your friendship, and to enjoy our houses and plant our fields, of whose fruit you shall participate, otherwise you will have the worst by our absence, for we can plant any where, though with more labour, and we know you cannot live if you want our harvest, and that reliefe wee bring you; if you promise us peace we will beleeve you, if you proceed in reveng, we will abandon the Countrie.

Ocanindge his Oration.

Upon these tearmes the President promised them peace, till they did us injurie, upon condition they should bring in provision, so all departed good friends, and so continued till Smith left the Countrie.

Ariving at James Towne, complaint was made to the President that the Chickahaminos, who al this while continued trade, and seemed our friendes, by colour thereof were the only theeves, and amongst other things, a

A Salvage smothered at James Towne, and was recovered.

pistol being stolne, and the theefe fled, there were apprehended 2 proper young fellows that were brothers, knowne to
be his confederats. Now to regain this pistoll, the one we imprisoned, the other was sent to returne againe within 12 houres,
or his brother to be hanged, yet the President pittying the
poore naked Salvage in the dungeon, sent him victuall and
some charcole for fire; ere midnight his brother returned with
the pistoll, but the poore Salvage in the dungeon was so
smothered with the smoke he had made, and so pittiously
burnt, that wee found him dead, the other most lamentably
bewailed his death, and broke forth in such bitter agonies, that
the President (to quiet him) told him that if herafter they
would not steal, he wold make him alive againe, but little
thought hee could be recovered, yet (we doing our best with
aquavitæ and vineger) it pleased God to restore him againe to
life, but so drunke and affrighted that he seemed lunaticke,
not understanding any thing hee spoke or heard, the which as
much grieved and tormented the other, as before to see him
dead; of which maladie (upon promise of their good behaviour
afterward) the President promised to recover him and so
caused him to be laid by a fire to sleepe, who in the morning
(having well slept) had recovered his perfect senses; and then
being dressed of his burning, and each a peece of copper given
them, they went away so well contented, that this was spread
amongst all the Salvages for a miracle, that Captaine Smith
could make a man alive that is dead; these and many other
such pretty accidents, so amazed and affrighted both
Powhatan and all his people that from all parts with presents
they desired peace, returning many stolne things which wee
neither demaunded nor thought of. And after that, those that
were taken stealing (both Powhatan and his people) have sent
them backe to James Towne to receive their punishment, and
all the countrie became absolutely as free for us, as for themselves.

Chapter 11.
What was done in three monthes having victuall.
The store devoured by rats, how we lived 3 monthes
of such naturall fruits as the countrie afforded.

Now wee so quietly followed our businesse, that in 3 monthes
we made 3 or 4 last of pitch and tarre, and sope ashes, produced
a triall of glasse, made a well in the forte of excellent sweete
water (which till then was wanting) built some 20 houses, recovered our Church, provided nets and weares for
fishing (and to stop the disorders of our disorderly
theeves and the Salvages) built a blocke house in the
necke of our Ile, kept by a garrison, to entertaine the Salvages
trade, and none to passe nor repasse, Salvage, nor Christian,
without the Presidents order. 30 or 40 acres of ground we
digged, and planted; of 3 sowes in one yeare increased 60 and
od pigges, and neere 500 chickens brought up themselves
(without having any meate given them) but the hogges were
transported to Hog Ile, where also we built a blocke house
with a garrison, to give us notice of any shipping, and for their
exercise they made clapbord, wainscot, and cut downe trees
against the ships comming. We built also a fort for a retreat,
neare a convenient river upon a high commanding hill, very
hard to be assaulted, and easie to be defended; but ere it was
halfe finished this defect caused a stay; in searching our casked
corne, wee found it halfe rotten, the rest so consumed with the
many thousand rats (increased first from the ships) that we
knewe not how to keepe that little wee had. This did drive us
all to our wits ende, for there was nothing in the countrie but
what nature afforded. Untill this time Kemps and Tassore,
were fettered prisoners, and daily wrought, and taught us how
to order and plant our fields. Whome now (for want of victuall) we set at libertie, but so wel were they used, that they
little desired it; and to express their loves, for 16 daies continuance, the Countrie brought us (when least) 100 a daie of squirrils, Turkies, Deare, and other wild beastes; but this want of
corne occasioned the end of all our workes, it being worke sufficient to provide victuall. 60 or 80 with Ensigne Laxon were
sent downe the river to live upon oysters, and 20 with leiftenant

More done in 3 monthes then 3 yeares.

Percie to trie for fishing at Point-Comfort, but in 6 weekes, they would not agree once to cast out their net. Master West with as many went up to the falles, but nothing could bee found but a fewe berries and acornes; of that in the store every one had their equall proportion. Till this present (by the hazard and endeavour of some 30 or 40) this whole number had ever been fed. Wee had more Sturgeon then could be devoured by dogge and man; of which the industrious, by drying and pownding, mingled with caviare, sorrel, and other wholsome hearbs, would make bread and good meate; others would gather as much *Tockwough* roots in a day, as would make them bread a weeke, so that of those wilde fruites, fish and berries, these lived very well, (in regard of such a diet). But such was the most strange condition of some 150, that had they not beene forced nolens volens perforce to gather and prepare their victuall they would all have starved, and have eaten one another. Of those wild fruites the Salvages often brought us: and for that the President would not fulfill the unreasonable desire of those distracted lubberly gluttons, to sell, not only our kettles, howes, tooles, and Iron, nay swords, peeces, and the very ordenance, and houses, might they have prevailed but to have beene but idle, for those salvage fruits they would have imparted all to the Salvages; especially for one basket of corne they heard of, to bee at Powhatans, 50 myles from our fort, though he bought neere halfe of it to satisfie their humours, yet to have had the other halfe, they would have sold their soules, (though not sufficient to have kept them a weeke). Thousands were their exclamations, suggestions, and devises, to force him to those base inventions, to have made it an occasion to abandon the Countrie. Want perforce constrained him to indure their exclaiming follies till he found out the author, one Dyer, a most craftie knave, and his ancient maligner, whom he worthely punished, and with the rest he argued the case in this manner.

The pains of 40 fed 150.

Their desire to destroy themselves.

Fellow souldiers, I did little thinke any so false to report, or so many so simple to be perswaded, that I either intend to starve you, or that Powhatan (at this present) hath corne for himselfe, much lesse for you; or that I would not have

The Presidents speech to the drones.

it, if I knewe where it were to be had. Neither did I thinke any so malitious as nowe I see a great many, yet it shall not so much passionate me, but I will doe my best for my worst maligner. But dreame no longer of this vaine hope from Powhatan; nor that I wil longer forbeare to force you from your Idlenesse, and punish you if you raile. You cannot deny but that by the hazard of my life, many a time I have saved yours, when, might your owne wils have prevailed, you would have starved, and will doe still whether I will or no. But I protest by that God that made me, since necessitie hath not power to force you to gather for your selvs those fruits the earth doth yeeld, you shall not only gather for your selves, but for those that are sicke: as yet I never had more from the store then the worst of you; and all my English extraordinarie provision that I have, you shall see mee devide among the sick. And this Salvage trash, you so scornfully repine at, being put in your mouthes your stomacks can digest it, and therefore I will take a course you shall provide it. The sicke shal not starve, but equally share of all our labours, and every one that gathereth not every day as much as I doe, the next daie shall be set beyond the river, and for ever bee banished from the fort, and live there or starve.

This order many murmured, was very cruell, but it caused the most part so well bestir themselves, that of 200 men (except they were drowned) there died not past 7 or 8. As for Captaine Win, and Master Ley, they died ere this want happened, and the rest died not for want of such as preserved the rest. Many were billitted among the Salvages, whereby we knewe all their passages, fieldes, and habitations, howe to gather and use their fruits, as well as themselves.

But 7 of 200 died in 9 months.

So well those poore Salvages used us, (that were thus Billited) as divers of the souldiers ran away, to search Kemps our old prisoner. Glad was this Salvage to have such an occasion to testifie his love. For insteed of entertaining them, and such things as they had stolne, with all the great offers and promises they made them, to revenge their injuries upon Captaine Smith, First he made himselfe sport, in shewing his countrymen (by them) how he was used; feeding them with this law who would not worke must not eat, till they were neere starved, continuallie threatning to beate them to death, neither could they get from him, til perforce he brought them to our Captaine, that so well contented him, and punished them: as manie others that intended also to have followed them, were rather contented to labour at home, then

The Salvages returne our fugitives.

adventure to live Idle among the Salvages, (of whom there was more hope to make better christians and good subjects, then the one halfe of those that counterfeited themselves both.) For so afeard were all those kings and the better sorte of their people, to displease us, that some of the baser sort that we have extreamelie hurt and punished for their villanies, would hire us, we should not tell it to their kings or countrymen, who would also repunish them, and yet returne them to James Towne to content the President, by that testimonie of their loves.

Search for them sent by Sir Walter Rawley. Master Sicklemore well returned from Chawo-nock, but found little hope and lesse certainetie of them were left by Sir Walter Rawley. So that Nathaniell Powell and Anas Todkill, were also, by the Quiy-oughquohanocks, conducted to the Mangoages to search them there. But nothing could we learne but they were all dead. This honest, proper, good promis-keeping king, of all the rest did ever best affect us, and though to his false Gods he was yet very zealous, yet he would confesse, our God as much exceeded his, as our guns did his bowe and arrowes, often sending our President manie presents to praie to his God for raine, or his corne would perish, for his Gods were angrie. All this time to reclaime the Dutchmen, and one Bentley an other fugitive, we imploied one William Volda (a Switzer by birth) with pardons and promises to regaine them. Litle we then suspected this

The Dutchmens projects. double villaine, of anie villanie, who plainlie taught us, in the most trust was the greatest treason. For this wicked hypocrit, by the seeming hate he bore to the lewd condition of his cursed countrimen, having this opportu-nitie by his imploiment to regaine them, conveighed them everie thing they desired to effect their project to destroie the colonie. With much devotion they expected the Spanyard, to whom they intended to have done good service. But to begin with the first oportunitie, they seeing necessitie thus inforced us to disperse our selves; importuned Powhatan to lend them but his forces, and they would not onlie destroie our hogs, fire our towne, and betraie our Pinnas; but bring to his service and subjection the most part of our companies. With this plot they had acquainted manie discontents and manie were agreed to their divelish practise. But on Thomas Dowse and Thomas

Mallard, whose christian harts much relenting at such an unchristian act, voluntarily revealed it to Captaine Smith: who
did his best it might be concealed, perswading Dowse and
Malard to proceed in the confederacie: onlie to bring the irreclamable Dutch men, and inconstant Salvages in such a maner
amongst his ambuscadoes as he had prepared, as not manie of
them shoulde ever have returned from out our peninsula. But
this brute comming to the ears of the impatient multitude,
they so importuned the President to cut of those Dutchmen,
as amongst manie that offered to cut their throates before the
face of Powhatan. Master Wiffin and Jefra Abot were sent to
Two gentlemen sent to kill them. stab or shoot them; but these Dutch men made such
excuses accusing Volday whom they supposed had
revealed their project, as Abbot would not, yet Wiffin would, perceiving it but deceipt. The king understanding
of this their imploiment, sent presentlie his messengers to
Captaine Smith to signifie it was not his fault to detaine them,
nor hinder his men from executing his command, nor did he
nor would he maintaine them, or anie to occasion his displeasure. But ere this busines was brought to a point, God having
seene our misery sufficient, sent in Captaine Argall to fish for
Sturgion with a ship well furnished with wine and bisket,
which though it was not sent us, such were our occasions we
tooke it at a price, but left him sufficient to returne for England, still dissembling Valdo his villany, but certainlie hee had
not escaped had the President continued.

Note these inconven-iences. By this you may see, for all those crosses, treacheries, and dissentions, howe he wrastled and over-
came (without bloud shed) all that hapned. Also what
good was done, how few died, what food the country naturally
affordeth, what small cause there is men shoulde starve, or be
murdered by the Salvages, that have discretion to manage this
courage and industry. The 2. first years though by his adventures he had oft brought the Salvages to a tractable trade, yet
you see how the envious authority ever crossed him, and frustrated his best endeavours. Yet this wrought in him that experience and estimation among the Salvages, as otherwaies it
had bin impossible he had ever effected that he did; though
the many miserable yet generous and worthy adventures he
had long and oft indured as wel in some parts of Africa, and

America, as in the most partes of Europe and Asia by land or sea had taught him much, yet in this case he was againe to learne his Lecture by experience. Which with thus much a doe having obtained, it was his ill chance to end, when hee had but onlie learned how to begin. And though hee left these unknowne difficulties, (made easie and familiar) to his unlawfull successors, whoe onlie by living in James Towne, presumed to know more then al the world could direct them; though they had all his souldiers with their triple power, and twise triple better meanes, by what they have done in his absence, the world doth see: and what they would have done in his presence, had he not prevented their indiscretions: it doth justlie approve what cause he had to send them for England. But they have made it more plaine since their returne, having his absolute authoritie freely in their power, with all the advantages, and opportunity that his labours had effected. As I am sorry their actions have made it so manifest, so I am unwilling to say what reason doth compell me to make apparant the truth, least I should seeme partial, reasonlesse, or malitious.

Chapter 12.
The Arivall of the third supply.

To redresse those jarres and ill proceedings, the Councell in England altered the governement and devolved the authoritie to the Lord De-la-ware. Who for his deputie, sent Sir Thomas Gates, and Sir George Somers, with 9 ships and 500 persons, they set saile from England in May 1609. A smal catch perished at sea in a Herycano. The Admirall, with 150 men, with the two knights, and their new commission, their bils of loading with al manner of directions, and the most part of their provision arived not. With the other 7 (as Captaines) arived Ratliffe, whose right name was Sickelmore, Martin, and Archer. Who as they had been troublesome at sea, beganne againe to marre all ashore. For though, as is said, they were formerly deposed and sent for England: yet now returning againe, graced by

The alteration of the governement.

The losse of Virginia.

the title of Captaines of the passengers, seeing the admirall wanting, and great probabilitie of her losse, strengthned themselves with those newe companies, so railing and exclaiming against Captaine Smith, that they mortally hated him, ere ever they see him. Who understanding by his scouts the arivall of such a fleet (little dreaming of any such supply) supposing them Spaniards, hee so determined and ordered his affaires, as wee little feared their arivall, nor the successe of our incounter, nor were the Salvages any way negligent or unwilling, to aide and assist us with their best power. Had it so beene, wee had beene happy. For we would not have trusted them but as our foes, whereas receiving those as our countriemen and friends, they did their best to murder our President, to surprise the store, the fort, and our lodgings, to usurp the governement, and make us all their servants, and slaves to our owne merit. To 1000 mischiefes those lewd Captaines led this lewd company, wherein were many unruly gallants packed thether by their friends to escape il destinies, and those would dispose and determine of the governement, sometimes one, the next day another, to day the old commission, to morrow the new, the next day by neither. In fine, they would rule all or ruine all; yet in charitie we must endure them thus to destroy us, or by correcting their follies, have brought the worlds censure upon us to have beene guiltie of their bloods. Happy had we bin had they never arrived; and we for ever abandoned, and (as we were) left to our fortunes, for on earth was never more confusion, or miserie, then their factions occasioned.

The Salvages offer to fight under our colours.

Mutinie.

The President seeing the desire those braves had to rule, seeing how his authoritie was so unexpectedly changed, would willingly have left all and have returned for England, but seeing there was smal hope this newe commission would arive, longer hee would not suffer those factious spirits to proceed. It would bee too tedious, too strange, and almost incredible, should I particularly relate the infinite dangers, plots, and practises, hee daily escaped amongst this factious crue, the chiefe whereof he quickly laid by the heeles, til his leasure better served to doe them justice; and to take away al occasions of further mischiefe, Master Persie had his request granted to returne for England, and Master West

The planting Nansamund.

A plantation of the falles.

with 120 went to plant at the falles. Martin with neare as many to Nansamund, with their due proportions, of all provisions, according to their numbers.

Now the Presidents yeare being neere expired, he made Martin President, who knowing his own insufficiencie, and the companies scorne, and conceit of his unworthinesse, within 3 houres resigned it againe to Captaine Smith, and at Nansa-

The breach of peace with the Salvages.

mund thus proceeded. The people being contributers used him kindly: yet such was his jealous feare, and cowardize, in the midst of his mirth, hee did surprize this poore naked king, with his monuments, houses, and the Ile he inhabited; and there fortified himselfe, but so apparantly distracted with fear, as imboldned the Salvages to assalt him, kill his men, redeeme their king, gather and carrie away more then 1000 bushels of corne, hee not once daring to intercept them. But sent to the President then at the Falles for 30 good shotte, which from James towne immediatly were sent him, but hee so well imploid them, as they did just nothing, but returned, complaining of his childishnesse, that with them fled from his company, and so left them to their fortunes.

Master West having seated his men at the Falles, presently returned to revisit James Towne, the President met him by the way as he followed him to the falles: where he found this company so inconsiderately seated, in a place not only subject to

Powhatan sold for copper.

the rivers inundation, but round invironed with many intollerable inconveniences. For remedy whereof, he sent presently to Powhatan to sell him the place called Powhatan, promising to defend him against the Monacans, and these should be his conditions (with his people) to resigne him the fort and houses and all that countrie for a proportion of copper: that all stealing offenders should bee sent him, there to receive their punishment: that every house as a custome should pay him a bushell of corne for an inch square of copper, and a proportion of *Pocones* as a yearely tribute to King James, for their protection as a dutie: what else they could spare to barter at their best discreation.

Mutinies.

But both this excellent place and those good conditions did those furies refuse, contemning both him, his kind care and authoritie. The worst they could to shew their spite, they did. I doe more then wonder to thinke

how only with 5 men, he either durst, or would ad-
5 suppresse
120.
venture as he did, (knowing how greedy they were
of his blood) to land amongst them and commit to
imprisonment the greatest spirits amongst them, till by their
multitudes being 120. they forced him to retire; yet in that
retreate hee surprised one of the boates, wherewith hee returned to their shippe, wherein was their provisions, which
also hee tooke. And well it chaunced hee found the marriners
so tractable and constant, or there had beene small possibility
he had ever escaped. Notwithstanding there were many of the
best, I meane of the most worthy in Judgement, reason or experience, that from their first landing hearing the generall good
report of his old souldiers, and seeing with their eies his actions so wel managed with discretion, as Captaine Wood, Captaine Web, Captaine Mone, Captaine Phitz-James, Master
Partridge, Master White, Master Powell and divers others.
When they perceived the malice and condition of Ratliffe,
Martin, and Archer, left their factions; and ever rested his faithfull friends: But the worst was, the poore Salvages that dailie
brought in their contribution to the President. That disorder-
lie company so tormented those poore naked soules, by stealing
The breach
of peace with
the Salvages
at the Falles.
their corne, robbing their gardens, beating them,
breaking their houses, and keeping some prisoners;
that they dailie complained to Captaine Smith he had
brought them for protectors worse enimies then the Monocans themselves; which though till then, (for his love) they had
indured: they desired pardon, if hereafter they defended themselves, since he would not correct them, as they had long expected he would: so much they importuned him to punish their
misdemeanores, as they offered (if hee would conduct them)
to fight for him against them. But having spent 9. daies in
seeking to reclaime them, shewing them how much they did
abuse themselves with their great guilded hopes of seas, mines,
commodities, or victories they so madly conceived. Then
(seeing nothing would prevaile with them) he set saile for James
Towne: now no sooner was the ship under saile but the Salvages assaulted those 120 in their fort, finding some
An assault by
the Salvages.
stragling abroad in the woods they slew manie, and
so affrighted the rest, as their prisoners escaped, and
they scarse retired, with the swords and cloaks of these they

had slaine. But ere we had sailed a league our shippe grounding, gave us once more libertie to summon them to a parlie. Where we found them all so stranglie amazed with this poore simple assault, as they submitted themselves upon anie tearmes to the Presidents mercie. Who presentlie put by the heeles 6 or 7 of the chiefe offenders, the rest he seated gallantlie at Powhatan, in their Salvage fort they built and pretilie fortified with poles and barkes of trees sufficient to have defended them from all the Salvages in Virginia, drie houses for lodgings 300

The planting of Nonsuch. acres of grounde readie to plant, and no place so strong, so pleasant and delightful in Virginia, for which we called it Nonsuch. The Salvages also he presentlie appeased; redelivering to every one their former

New peace concluded. losses. Thus al were friends, new officers appointed to command, and the President againe readie to de-part. But at that Instant arrived Master West, whose good na-ture with the perswasions and compassion of those mutinous prisoners was so much abused, that to regaine their old hopes new turboiles arose. For the rest being possessed of al their victuall munition and everie thing, they grew to that height in their former factions, as there the President (left them to their fortunes, they returning againe to the open aire at West Fort, abandoning Nonsuch, and he to James Towne with his best expedition, but this hapned him in that Journie.

Captaine Smith blowne up with powder. Sleeping in his boat, (for the ship was returned 2 daies before,) accidentallie, one fired his powder bag, which tore his flesh from his bodie and thighes, 9. or 10. inches square in a most pittifull manner; but to quench the tormenting fire, frying him in his cloaths he leaped over bord into the deepe river, where ere they could recover him he was neere drownd. In this estat, without either Chirurgion, or chirurgery he was to go neare 100. miles. Ariving at James Towne causing all things to bee prepared for peace or warres to obtain provision, whilest those things were providing, Martin, Ratliffe, and Archer, being to have their trials, their guiltie consciences fearing a just reward for their deserts, seeing the President unable to stand, and neare bereft of his senses by reason of his torment, they had plotted to have mur-

A bloody intent. dered him in his bed. But his hart did faile him that should have given fire to that mercilesse pistol. So, not finding that course to be the best they joined togither to usurp the government, thereby to escape their punishment, and excuse themselves by accusing him. The President, had notice of their projects: the which to withstand, though his old souldiers importuned him but permit them to take of their heads that would resist his commaund, yet he would The governe-ment usurped. not permit them, But sent for the masters of the ships and tooke order with them for his returne for England. Seeing there was neither chirurgion, nor chirurgery in the fort to cure his hurt, and the ships to depart the next daie, his commission to be suppressed he knew not why, himselfe and souldiers to be rewarded he knew not how, and a new commission graunted they knew not to whom, the which so disabled that authority he had, as made them presume so oft to those mutinies and factions as they did. Besides so grievous were his wounds, and so cruell his torment, few expected he could live, nor was hee able to follow his businesse to regaine what they had lost, suppresse those factions and range the countries for provision as he intended, and well he knew in those affaires his owne actions and presence was as requisit as his experience, and directions, which now could not be; he went presently abord, resolving there to appoint them governours, and to take order for the mutiners and their confederates. Who seeing him gone, perswaded Master Persie (to stay) and be their President, and within lesse then an howre was this mutation begun and concluded. For when the company understood Smith would leave them, and see the rest in Armes called Presidents and councellors, divers began to fawne on those new commanders, that now bent all their wits to get him resigne them his commission, who after many salt and bitter repulses, that their confusion should not be attributed to him for leaving the country without government and authority; having taken order to bee free from danger of their malice; he The causes why Smith left the countrie and his commission. was not unwilling they should steale it from him, but never consented to deliver it to any. But had that unhappy blast not hapned, he would quickly have qualified the heate of those humors and factions, had the ships but once left them and us to our fortunes, and have made that provision from among the Salvages, as we neither feared Spanyard, Salvage, nor famine: nor would have left

Virginia, nor our lawfull authoritie, but at as deare a price as
we had bought it, and paid for it. What shall I say? but thus we
lost him, that in all his proceedings, made Justice his first guid,
and experience his second; ever hating basenesse, sloth, pride,
and indignitie, more then any dangers; that never allowed
more for himselfe, then his souldiers with him; that upon no
danger would send them where he would not lead them himselfe; that would never see us want what he either had, or
could by any meanes get us; that would rather want then borrow, or starve then not pay; that loved actions more then
wordes, and hated falshood and cousnage worse then death:
whose adventures were our lives, and whose losse our deathes.
Leaving us thus with 3 ships, 7 boates, commodities ready to
trade, the harvest newly gathered, 10 weekes provision in the
store, 490 and odde persons, 24 peeces of ordinances, 300
muskets, snaphances and fire lockes, shot, powder, and match
sufficient, curats, pikes, swords, and moryons more then men:
the Salvages their language and habitations wel knowne to 100
well trained and expert souldiers; nets for fishing, tooles of all
sortes to worke, apparell to supply our wants, 6 mares and a
horse, 5 or 600 swine, as many hens and chickens; some goates,
some sheep; what was brought or bread there remained, but
they regarded nothing but from hand to mouth, to consume
that we had, tooke care for nothing but to perfit some colourable complaints against Captaine Smith, for effecting whereof,
3 weekes longer they stayed the 6 ships til they could produce
them. That time and charge might much better have beene
spent, but it suted well with the rest of their discreations.

Their
complaints
and proofe
against him.   Now all those Smith had either whipped, punished, or any way disgraced, had free power and liberty to say or sweare any thing, and from a whole
armefull of their examinations this was concluded.

The mutiners at the Falles, complained hee caused the Salvages assalt them, for that hee would not revenge their losse,
they being but 120, and he 5 men and himselfe, and this they
proved by the oath of one hee had oft whipped for perjurie
and pilfering. The dutch-men that he had appointed to bee
stabd for their treacheries, swore he sent to poison them with
rats baine. The prudent Councel, that he would not submit
himselfe to their stolne authoritie. Coe and Dyer, that should

have murdered him, were highly preferred for swearing, they heard one say, he heard Powhatan say, that he heard a man say: if the king would not send that corne he had, he should not long enjoy his copper crowne, nor those robes he had sent him: yet those also swore hee might have had corne for tooles but would not. The truth was, Smith had no such ingins as the king demanded, nor Powhatan any corne. Yet this argued he would starve them. Others complained hee would not let them rest in the fort (to starve) but forced them to the oyster bankes, to live or starve, as he lived himselfe. For though hee had of his owne private provisions sent from England, sufficient; yet hee gave it all away to the weake and sicke, causing the most untoward (by doing as he did) to gather their food from the unknowne parts of the rivers and woods, that they lived (though hardly) that otherwaies would have starved, ere they would have left their beds, or at most the sight of James Towne to have got their own victuall. Some propheticall spirit calculated hee had the Salvages in such subjection, hee would

Pocahontas Powhatans daughter.

have made himselfe a king, by marrying Pocahontas, Powhatans daughter. It is true she was the very nomparell of his kingdome, and at most not past 13 or 14 yeares of age. Very oft shee came to our fort, with what shee could get for Captaine Smith, that ever loved and used all the Countrie well, but her especially he ever much respected: and she so well requited it, that when her father intended to have surprized him, shee by stealth in the darke night came through the wild woods and told him of it. But her marriage could no way have intitled him by any right to the kingdome, nor was it ever suspected hee had ever such a thought, or more regarded her, or any of them, then in honest reason, and discreation he might. If he would he might have married her, or have done what him listed. For there was none that could have hindred his determination. Some that knewe not any thing to say, the Councel instructed, and advised what to sweare. So diligent they were in this businesse, that what any could remember, hee had ever done, or said in mirth, or passion, by some circumstantiall oath, it was applied to their fittest use, yet not past 8 or 9 could say much and that nothing but circumstances, which all men did knowe was most false and untrue. Many got their passes by promising in England to say much

against him. I have presumed to say this much in his behalfe
for that I never heard such foule slaunders, so certainely
beleeved, and urged for truthes by many a hundred, that doe
still not spare to spread them, say them and sweare them, that
I thinke doe scarse know him though they meet him, nor have
they ether cause or reason, but their wills, or zeale to rumor or
opinion. For the honorable and better sort of our Virginian
adventurers I think they understand it as I have writ it. For instead of accusing him, I have never heard any give him a better
report, then many of those witnesses themselves that were sent
only home to testifie against him.

Richard Pots, W. P.

When the ships departed Captaine Davis arived in
a smal Pinnace with some 16 proper men more, to
those were added a company from James Towne
under the command of Captaine Ratliffe to inhabit Point-
Comfort. Martin and Master West having lost their boates,
and neere halfe their men amongst the Salvages, were returned
to James Towne, for the Salvages no sooner understood of
Captaine Smiths losse, but they all revolted, and did murder
and spoile all they could incounter. Now were we all constrained to live only of that which Smith had only for his owne
company, for the rest had consumed their proportions. And
now have we 20 Presidents with all their appurtenances, for
Master Persie was so sicke he could not goe nor stand. But ere
all was consumed, Master West and Ratliffe each with a pinnace, and 30 or 40 men wel appointed, sought abroad to trade,
how they carried the businesse I knowe not, but Ratliffe and
his men were most slaine by Powhatan, those that escaped returned neare starved in the Pinnace. And Master
West finding little better successe, set saile for England. Now wee all found the want of Captaine
Smith, yea his greatest maligners could then curse his losse.
Now for corne, provision, and contribution from the Salvages;
wee had nothing but mortall wounds with clubs and arrowes.
As for our hogs, hens, goats, sheep, horse, or what lived, our
commanders and officers did daily consume them, some small
proportions (sometimes) we tasted till all was devoured, then
swords, arrowes, peeces, or any thing we traded to the Sal-

The planting at Point Comfort.

Ratliffe slain by Powhatan.

vages, whose bloody fingers were so imbrued in our bloods, that what by their crueltie, our Governours indiscreation, and the losse of our ships; Of 500, within 6 monthes after there remained not many more then 60. most miserable and poore creatures. It were to vild to say what we endured; but the occasion was only our owne, for want of providence, industrie, and governement, and not the barrennesse and defect of the countrie, as is generally supposed, for till then in 3 yeares (for the numbers were landed us) we had never landed sufficient provision for 6 months; such a glutton is the sea, and such good fellowes the marriners, wee as little tasted of those great proportions for their provisions, as they of our miseries, that notwithstanding ever swaid and overruled the businesse: though we did live as is said, 3 yeares chiefly of what this good countrie naturally affordeth: yet now had we beene in Paradice it selfe (with those governours) it would not have beene much better with us, yet was there some amongst us, who had they had the governement, would surely have kept us from those extremities of miseries, that in 10 daies more would have supplanted us all by death.

The fruits of improvidences.

But God that would not it should bee unplanted, sent Sir Thomas Gates, and Sir George Sommers, with a 150 men, most happily preserved by the Berondoes to preserve us. Strange it is to say how miraculously they were preserved, in a leaking ship, in those extreame stormes and tempests in such overgrowne seas 3 daies and 3 nights by bayling out water. And having given themselvs to death, how happily when least expected that worthy Captaine Sir George Somers, having line all that time cuning the ship before those swalowing waves, discovered those broken Iles, where how plentifully they lived with fish and flesh, what a paradice this is to inhabit, what industrie they used to build their 2 ships, how happily they did transport them to James Towne in Virginia, I refer you to their owne printed relations.

The arivall of Sir Thomas Gates with 150.

But when those noble knights did see our miseries (being strangers in the country) and could understand no more of the cause but by their conjecture, of our clamors and complaints, of accusing or excusing one an other, they imbarked us with themselves, with the best means they could, and abandoning James Towne set saile for England.

James Towne abandoned.

The arival
of the Lord
La-ware. But yet God would not so have it, for ere wee left
the river we met the Lord de-la-ware, then governour for the countrie, with 3 ships exceeding well
furnished with al necessaries fitting, who againe returned them
to the abandoned James Towne, the 9. of June, 1610. accompanied with Sir Ferdinando Wainman, and divers other gentlemen of sort. Sir George Somers, and Captaine Argall he
presentlie dispatcheth to require the Bermondas to furnish
them with provision: Sir Thomas Gates for England to helpe
forward their supplies: himselfe neglected not the best was in
his power for the furtherance of the busines and regaining
what was lost. But even in the beginning of his proceedings,
his Lordship had such an incounter with a scurvy sickenesse,
that made him unable to weld the state of his body, much lesse
the affaires of the colonie, so that after 8. monthes sicknesse,
he was forced to save his life by his returne for England.

2 Ships sent
to the
Bermundas. In this time Argall not finding the Bermondas,
having lost Sir George Somers at sea, fell on the
coast of Sagadahock, where refreshing himselfe,
found a convenient fishing for Cod. With a tast whereof hee
returned to James towne, from whence the Lord De-la-ware
sent him to trade in the river of Patawomecke, where finding
an English boy those people had preserved from the furie of
Powhatan, by his acquaintance had such good usage of those
kind Salvages, that they fraughted his ship with corne, wherewith he returned to James Towne, and so for England with the
Lord governour; yet before his returne, the adventurers had
The arival of
Sir Thomas
Dale. sent Sir Thomas Dale with 3 ships, men and cattell,
and all other provisions necessarie for a yeare, all
which arived the 10 of May, 1611.

Againe, to second him with all possible expedition there was
prepared for Sir Thomas Gates, 6 tall ships with 300 men, and
100 kyne, with other cattel, with munition and all manner of
provision could bee thought needfull, and they arived about
the 1 of August next after safely at James towne.

Sir George
Somers
arivall at the
Bermondas
and dieth. Sir George Somers all this time was supposed lost:
but thus it hapned, missing the Bermondas, hee fell
also as did Argall with Sagadahock, where being refreshed, would not content himselfe with that repulse, but
returned againe in the search; and there safely arived. But over-

toiling himselfe on a surfeit died. And in this Cedar ship built by his owne directions, and partly with his owne hands, that had not in her any iron but only one bolt in her keele, yet well endured thus tossed to and againe in this mightie Ocean, til with his dead body she arived in England at fine, and at Whitchurch in Dorsetshire, his body by his friends was honourably buried, with many volies of shot, and the rights of a souldier. And upon his Tombe was bestowed this Epitaph

His Epitaph.

Hei mihi Virginia, quod tam cito præterit æstas,
Autumnus sequitur, sæviet inde & hyems.
At ver perpetuum nascetur, & Anglia læta,
Decerpit flores, Floryda terra tuos.

Alas *Virginia* Somer so soone past
Autume succeeds and stormy winters blast,
Yet Englands joyfull spring with Aprill shewres,
O *Floryda*, shall bring thy sweetest flowers.

Since there was a ship fraughted with provision, and 40 men, and another since then with the like number and provision to stay in the Countrie 12 months with Captaine Argall.

The Lord governour himselfe doth confidently determine to goe with the next, or as presently as hee may in his owne person, with sundry other knights and gentlemen, with ships and men so farre as their meanes will extend to furnish: as for all their particular actions since the returne of Captaine Smith, for that they have beene printed from time to time, and published to the world, I cease farther to trouble you with any repetition of things so well knowne, more then are necessarie. To conclude the historie, leaving this assurance to all posteritie, howe unprosperously things may succeed, by what changes or chances soever. The action is honorable and worthie to bee approved, the defect whereof hath only beene in the managing the businesse; which I hope now experience hath taught them to amend, or those examples may make others to beware, for the land is as good as this booke doth report it.

FINIS.

Captaine Smith I returne you the fruit of my labours, as Master Croshaw requested me, which I bestowed in reading the discourses, and hearing the relations of such which have walked, and observed the land of Virginia with you. The pains I took was great: yet did the nature of the argument, and hopes I conceaved of the expedition, give me exceeding content. I cannot finde there is any thing, but what they all affirme, or cannot contradict: the land is good: as there is no citties, so no sonnes of Anak: al is open for labor of a good and wise inhabitant: and my prayer shall ever be, that so faire a land, may bee inhabited by those that professe and love the Gospell.

Your friend
W. S.

A DESCRIPTION OF NEW ENGLAND:

or

The observations, and discoveries, of
Captain John Smith (Admirall of that Country)
in the North of America, in the year of our
Lord 1614: with the successe of sixe Ships,
that went the next yeare 1615; and the
accidents befell him among the
French men of warre:

With the proofe of the present benefit this
Countrey affoords: whither this present yeare,
1616, eight voluntary Ships are gone
to make further tryall.

1616

NEW ENGL

The most remarqueable parts thus named
by the high and mighty Prince CHARLE
Prince of great Britaine

THE PORTRAICTUER OF CAPTAYNE IOHN SMITH ADMIRALL OF NEW ENGLAND .

Æta 37
A° 1616

These are the Lines that shew thy Face; but those
That shew thy Grace and Glory, brighter bee:
Thy Faire-Discoueries and Fowle-Overthrowes
Of Salvages, much Civiliz'd by thee
Best shew thy Spirit; and to it Glory Wyn;
So, thou art Brasse without, but Golde within.

If so; in Brasse, (too soft smiths Acts to beare)
43 I fix thy Fame, to make Brasse steele out weare.

Thine, as thou art Virtues,
John Dauies. Heref:

Can
The

Schooters hill
Sandwich
Dartmouth
P. Kent
Iswich
Snadoun hill
Bostou
Poynt Dauies
Hull
Smith Iles
SouthHampton
Bristow
Bastable
Cape ANNA
Talbotts Bay
Fawmouth
Fullerton Ils
The River CHARLES
Cary Ils
Cheuyot hills
P. Murry
London
Oxford
Poynt Suttliff
Poynt Gorge
Cape IAMES
6 Plimouth
STUARDS
Bay
Barwick

42

Simon Passæus sculpsit.
Robert Clerke excudit .

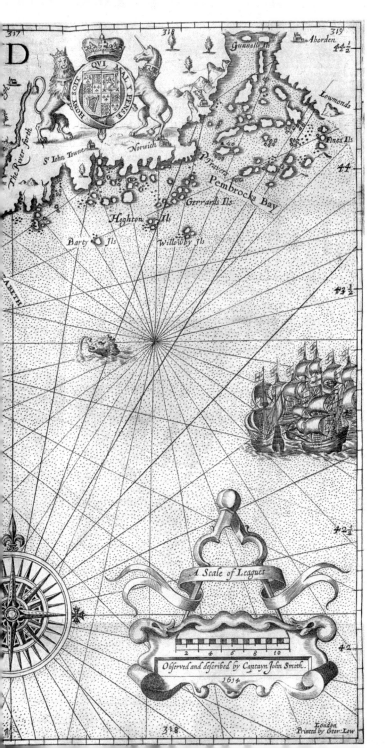

D

317   318   319

Ahorden

44½

QVI MALY PENSE
HONI SOIT

Gunnell: Ils

The River forth

Pemaquid Cape

St Iohn Towne

Norwich

Lowmonds

Fines Ils

44

Pentaway

Pembrocks Bay

Gerrards Ils

Heghton   Ils

Barty   Ils   Willowby Ils

SMITH

43½

43¼

A Scale of Leagues

2   4   6   8   10

Observed and described by Captayn John Smith.

1614

42¼

42

London
Printed by Geor: Low

318

BECAUSE THE BOOKE WAS PRINTED ERE
the Prince his Highnesse had altered
the names, I intreate the Reader, peruse
this schedule; which will plainely shew him the
correspondence of the old names to the new.

The old names.	The new.
Cape Cod	Cape James
	Milford haven
Chawum	Barwick
Accomack	Plimouth
Sagoquas	Oxford
Massachusets Mount	Chevit hill
Massachusets River	Charles River
Totant	Fawmouth
A Country not discovered	Bristow
Naemkeck	Bastable
Cape Trabigzanda	Cape Anne
Aggawom	Southhampton
Smiths Iles	Smiths Iles
Passataquack	Hull
Accominticus	Boston
Sassanowes Mount	Snodon hill
Sowocatuck	Ipswitch
Bahana	Dartmouth
	Sandwich
Aucociscos Mount	Shooters hill
Aucocisco	The Base
Aumoughcawgen	Cambridge
Kinebeck	Edenborough
Sagadahock	Leeth
Pemmaquid	S. Johns towne
Monahigan	Barties Iles
Segocket	Norwich
Matinnack	Willowby's Iles
Metinnicut	Hoghton's Iles
Mecadacut	Dunbarton
Pennobscot	Aborden
Nusket	Lowmonds

TO THE HIGH
Hopeful Charles,
Prince of Great Britaine.

Sir:

So favourable was your most renowned and memorable Brother, Prince Henry, to all generous designes; that in my discovery of Virginia, I presumed to call two namelesse Headlands after my Soveraignes heires, Cape Henry, and Cape Charles. Since then, it beeing my chance to range some other parts of America, whereof I heere present your Highness the description in a Map; my humble sute is, you would please to change their Barbarous names, for such English, as Posterity may say, Prince Charles was their Godfather. What here in this relation I promise my Countrey, let mee live or die the slave of scorne and infamy, if (having meanes) I make it not apparent; please God to blesse me but from such accidents as are beyond my power and reason to prevent. For my labours, I desire but such conditions as were promised me out of the gaines; and that your Highnesse would daigne to grace this Work, by your Princely and favourable respect unto it, and know mee to be
Your Highnesse true and faithfull servant,
John Smith.

TO THE RIGHT HONOURABLE
and worthy Lords, Knights, and
Gentlemen, of his Majesties Councell,
for all Plantations and discoveries;
especially, of New England.

Seeing the deedes of the most just, and the writings of the most wise, not onely of men, but of God himselfe, have beene diversly traduced by variable judgements of the Times opinionists; what shall such an ignorant as I expect? Yet reposing my selfe on your favours, I present this rude discourse, to the worldes construction; though I am perswaded, that few do think there may be had from New England Staple commodities, well worth 3 or 400000 pound a yeare, with so small charge, and such facilitie, as this discourse will acquaint you. But, lest your Honours, that know mee not, should thinke I goe by hearesay or affection; I intreat your pardons to say thus much of my selfe: Neere twice nine yeares, I have beene taught by lamentable experience, aswell in Europe and Asia, as Affrick, and America, such honest adventures as the chance of warre doth cast upon poore Souldiers. So that, if I bee not able to judge of what I have seene, contrived, and done; it is not the fault either of my eyes, or foure quarters. And these nine yeares, I have bent my endeavours to finde a sure foundation to begin these ensuing projects: which though I never so plainely and seriously propound; yet it resteth in God, and you, still to dispose of. Not doubting but your goodnesse will pardon my rudenesse, and ponder errours in the balance of good will; No more: but sacring all my best abilities to the good of my Prince, and Countrey, and submitting my selfe to the exquisit judgements of your renowned vertue, I ever rest

Your Honours, in all honest service,

J. S.

TO THE RIGHT WORSHIPFULL
Adventurers for the Countrey of
New England, in the Cities of
London, Bristow, Exceter, Plimouth,
Dartmouth, Bastable, Totneys, etc.
and in all other Cities and Ports,
in the Kingdome of England.

If the little Ant, and the sillie Bee seek by their diligence the good of their Commonwealth; much more ought Man. If they punish the drones and sting them steales their labour; then blame not Man. Little hony hath that hive, where there are more Drones then Bees: and miserable is that Land, where more are idle then well imployed. If the indeavours of those vermin be acceptable, I hope mine may he excuseable; Though I confesse it were more proper for mee, To be doing what I say, then writing what I knowe. Had I returned rich, I could not have erred: Now having onely such fish as came to my net, I must be taxed. But, I would my taxers were as ready to adventure their purses, as I, purse, life, and all I have: or as diligent to furnish the charge, as I know they are vigilant to crop the fruits of my labours. Then would I not doubt (did God please I might safely arrive in New England, and safely returne) but to performe somewhat more then I have promised, and approve my words by deeds, according to proportion.

I am not the first hath beene betrayed by Pirats: And foure men of warre, provided as they were, had beene sufficient to have taken Sampson, Hercules, and Alexander the great, no other way furnisht then I was. I knowe not what assurance any have do passe the Seas, Not to bee subject to casualty as well as my selfe: but least this disaster may hinder my proceedings, or ill will (by rumour) the behoofefull worke I pretend; I have writ this little: which I did thinke to have concealed from any publike use, till I had made my returnes speake as much, as my pen now doth.

But because I speake so much of fishing, if any take mee for such a devote fisher, as I dreame of nought else, they mistake mee. I know a ring of golde from a graine of barley, aswell as a goldesmith: and nothing is there to bee had which fishing doth hinder, but furder us to obtaine. Now for that I have made knowne unto you a fit place for plantation, limited within the bounds of your Patent and Commission; having also received meanes, power, and authority by your directions, to plant there a Colony, and make further search, and discovery in those parts there yet unknowne: Considering, withall, first those of his Majesties Councell, then those Cities above named, and diverse others that have beene moved to lend their assistance to so great a worke, doe expect (especially the adventurers) the true relation or event of my proceedings which I heare are so abused; I am inforced for all these respects, rather to expose my imbecillitie to contempt, by the testimonie of these rude lines, then all should condemne me for so bad a Factor, as could neither give reason nor account of my actions and designes.

Yours to command,
John Smith.

IN THE DESERVED
Honour of the Author,
Captaine John Smith,
and his Worke.

Damn'd Envie is a sp'ite, that ever haunts
Beasts, mis-nam'd Men; Cowards, or Ignorants.
But, onely such shee followes, whose deere WORTH
(Maugre her malice) sets their glorie forth.
    If this faire Overture, then, take not; It
    Is Envie's *spight (dear friend) in men-of-wit;*
Or Feare, *lest morsels, which our mouthes possesse,*
Might fall from thence; or else, tis Sottishnesse.
    If either; (I hope neither) thee they raise;
    Thy* Letters are as Letters in thy praise;
Who, by their vice, improve *(when they* reproove*)*
Thy vertue; so, in hate, procure thee Love.
    Then, On firme Worth: this Monument I frame;
    Scorning for any Smith to forge *such* fame.
                    Jo: Davies, Heref:
*Hinderers.

TO HIS WORTHY
Captaine the Author.

That which wee call the subject of all Storie,
Is Truth: which in this Worke of thine gives glorie
To all that thou hast done. Then, scorne the spight
Of Envie; which doth no mans merits right.
    My sword may helpe the rest: my Pen no more
    Can doe, but this; I'ave said enough before.
             Your sometime souldier,
             J. Codrinton, now Templer.

TO MY WORTHY
friend and Cosen,
Captaine John Smith.

It over-joyes my heart, when as thy Words
Of these designes, with deeds I doe compare.
Heere is a Booke, such worthy truth affords,
None should the due desert thereof impare;
Sith thou, the man, deserving of these Ages,
Much paine hast ta'en for this our Kingdoms good,
In Climes unknowne, Mongst Turks and Salvages,
T'inlarge our bounds; though with thy losse of blood.
Hence damn'd Detraction: stand not in our way.
Envie, it selfe, will not the Truth gainesay.

N. Smith.

TO THAT WORTHY
and generous Gentleman,
my verie good friend,
Captaine Smith.

May Fate thy Project prosper, that thy name
May be eternised with living fame:
Though foule Detraction Honour would pervert,
And Envie ever waits upon desert:
In spight of Pelias, when his hate lies colde,
Returne as Jason with a fleece of Golde.
Then after-ages shall record thy praise,
That a New England to this Ile didst raise:
And when thou dy'st (as all that live must die)
Thy fame live heere; thou, with Eternitie.

R: Gunnell.

TO HIS FRIEND
Captaine Smith, upon his
description of New England.

Sir; your Relations I have read: which shewe,
Ther's reason I should honour, them *and you:*
And if their meaning I have understood,
I dare to censure, thus: Your Project's *good;*
And may (if follow'd) doubtlesse quit the paine,
With honour, pleasure and a trebble gaine;
Beside the benefit that shall arise
To make more happie our Posterities.

    For would we daigne to spare, though 'twere no more
Then what o're-filles, and surfets us in store,
To order Nature's *fruitfulnesse a while*
In that rude Garden, *you* New England *stile;*
With present good, ther's hope in after-daies
Thence to repaire what Time *and* Pride *decaies*
In this rich kingdome. And the spatious West
Beeing still more with English *blood possest,*
The Proud Iberians *shall not rule those Seas,*
To checke our ships from sayling where they please;
Nor future times make any forraine power
Become so great to force a bound to Our.

    Much good my minde fore tels would follow hence
With little labour, and with lesse expence.
Thrive therefore thy Designe, *who ere envie:*
England *may joy in* England's *Colony,*
Virginia seeke *her Virgine sisters good,*
Be blessed in such happie neighbourhood:
    Or, what-soere Fate pleaseth to permit,
    Be thou still honor'd for first mooving it.
                  George Wither, è societate Lincol.

MICHAEL PHETTIPLACE,
William Phettiplace, and Richard Wiffing,
Gentlemen, and Souldiers under
Captaine Smiths Command:
In his deserved honor for
his Worke, and worth.

Why may not we in this Worke have our Mite,
That had our share in each black day and night,
When thou Virginia *foild'st, yet kept'st unstaind;*
And held'st the King of Paspeheh *enchaind.*
Thou all alone this Salvage *sterne didst take.*
    Pamunkes *king wee saw thee captive make.*
Among seaven hundred of his stoutest men,
To murther thee and us resolved; when
Fast by the hand thou ledst this Salvage grim,
Thy Pistoll at his breast to governe him:
Which did infuse such awe in all the rest
(Sith their drad Soveraigne thou had'st so distrest)
That thou and wee (poore sixteene) safe retir'd
Unto our helplesse ships. *Thou (thus admir'd)*
Didst make proud Powhatan, *his subjects send*
To James *his Towne, thy censure to attend:*
And all Virginia's *Lords, and pettie Kings,*
Aw'd by thy vertue, crouch, and Presents brings
To gaine thy grace; so dreaded thou hast beene:
And yet a heart more milde is seldome seene;
So, making Valour Vertue, really;
Who hast nought in thee counterfet, or slie;
If in the sleight bee not the truest art,
That makes men famoused for faire desert.
    Who saith of thee, this savors of vaine-glorie,
Mistakes both thee and us, and this true storie.
If it bee ill in Thee, so well to doe;
Then, is it ill in Us, to praise thee too.
But, if the first bee well done; it is well,
To say it doth (if so it doth) excell!
Praise is the guerdon of each deere desert,

Making the praised act the praised part
With more alacritie: Honours *Spurre is* Praise;
Without which, it (regardlesse) soone decaies.
    And for this paines of thine wee praise thee rather,
That future Times may know who was the father
Of this rare Worke (New Engand) *which may bring*
Praise to thy God, and profit to thy King.

A DESCRIPTION OF

New-England, by Captaine John Smith.

IN the moneth of Aprill, 1614. with two Ships from London, of a few Marchants, I chanced to arrive in New-England, a parte of Ameryca, at the Ile of Monahiggan, in 43½ of Northerly latitude: our plot was there to take Whales and make tryalls of a Myne of Gold and Copper. If those failed, Fish and Furres was then our refuge, to make our selves savers howsoever: we found this Whale-fishing a costly conclusion: we saw many, and spent much time in chasing them; but could not kill any: They beeing a kinde of Jubartes, and not the Whale that yeeldes Finnes and Oyle as wee expected. For our Golde, it was rather the Masters device to get a voyage that projected it, then any knowledge hee had at all of any such matter. Fish and Furres was now our guard: and by our late arrival, and long lingring about the Whale, the prime of both those seasons were past ere wee perceived it; we thinking that their seasons served at all times: but wee found it otherwise; for, by the midst of June, the fishing failed. Yet in July and August some was taken, but not sufficient to defray so great a charge as our stay required. Of dry fish we made about 40000. of Cor fish about 7000. Whilest the sailers fished, my selfe with eight or nine others of them might best bee spared; Ranging the coast in a small boat, wee got for trifles neer 1100 Bever skinnes, 100 Martins, and neer as many Otters; and the most of them within the distance of twenty leagues. We ranged the Coast both East and West much furder; but Eastwards our commodities were not esteemed, they were so neare the French who affords them better: and right against us in the Main was a Ship of Sir Frances Popphames, that had there such acquaintance, having many yeares used onely that porte, that the most parte there was had by him. And 40 leagues westwards were two French Ships, that had made there a great voyage by trade, during the time wee tryed those conclusions, not knowing the Coast, nor

My first voyage to new-England.

Salvages habitation. With these Furres, the Traine, and Cor-
fish I returned for England in the Bark: where within six
monthes after our departure from the Downes, we safe arrived
back. The best of this fish was solde for five pound the hundreth, the rest by ill usage betwixt three pound and fifty
shillings. The other Ship staied to fit herselfe for Spaine with
the dry fish which was sould, by the Sailers reporte that returned, at forty ryalls the quintall, each hundred weighing two
quintalls and a halfe.

The situation of New England.   New England is that part of America in the Ocean
Sea opposite to Nova Albyon in the South Sea; dis-
covered by the most memorable Sir Francis Drake in
his voyage about the worlde. In regarde whereto this is stiled
New England, beeing in the same latitude. New France, off it,
is Northward: Southwardes is Virginia, and all the adjoyning
Continent, with New Granado, New Spain, New Andolosia and
the West Indies. Now because I have beene so oft asked such
strange questions, of the goodnesse and greatnesse of those
spatious Tracts of land, how they can bee thus long unknown,
or not possessed by the Spaniard, and many such like demands; I intreat your pardons, if I chance to be too plaine, or
tedious in relating my knowledge for plaine mens satisfaction.

Notes of Florida.   Florida is the next adjoyning to the Indes, which
unprosperously was attempted to bee planted by the
French. A Country farre bigger then England, Scotland, France and Ireland, yet little knowne to any Christian,
but by the wonderful endevours of Ferdinando de Soto a
valiant Spaniard: whose writings in this age is the best guide
knowne to search those parts.

Notes of Virginia.   Virginia is no Ile (as many doe imagine) but part
of the Continent adjoyning to Florida; whose
bounds may be stretched to the magnitude thereof
without offence to any Christian inhabitant. For from the degrees of 30. to 45 his Majestie hath granted his Letters patents,
the Coast extending South-west and North-east aboute 1500
miles; but to follow it aboard, the shore may well be 2000. at
the least: of which, 20. miles is the most gives entrance into the
Bay of Chisapeak, where is the London plantation: within
which is a Country (as you may perceive by the description in
a Booke and Map printed in my name of that little I there dis-

covered) may well suffice 300000 people to inhabit. And Southward adjoyneth that part discovered at the charge of Sir Walter Rawley, by Sir Ralph Lane, and that learned Mathematician Master Thomas Heryot. Northward six or seaven degrees is the River Sagadahock, where was planted the Westerne Colony, by that Honourable Patrone of vertue Sir John Poppham, Lord chief Justice of England. Ther is also a relation printed by Captaine Bartholomew Gosnould, of Elizabeths Iles: and an other by Captaine Waymoth, of Pemmaquid. From all these diligent observers, posterity may be bettered by the fruits of their labours. But for divers others that long before and since have ranged those parts, within a kenning sometimes of the shore, some touching in one place some in another, I must entreat them pardon me for omitting them; or if I offend in saying that their true descriptions are concealed, or never well observed, or died with the Authors: so that the Coast is yet still but even as a Coast unknowne and undiscovered. I have had six or seaven severall plots of those Northren parts, so unlike each to other, and most so differing from any true proportion, or resemblance of the Countrey, as they did mee no more good, then so much waste paper, though they cost me more. It may be it was not my chance to see the best; but least others may be deceived as I was, or throgh dangerous ignorance hazard themselves as I did, I have drawen a Map from Point to Point, Ile to Ile, and Harbour to Harbour, with the Soundings, Sands, Rocks, and Land-marks as I passed close aboard the Shore in a little Boat; although there be many things to bee observed which the haste of other affaires did cause me omit: for, being sent more to get present commodities, then knowledge by discoveries for any future good, I had not power to search as I would: yet it will serve to direct any shall goe that waies, to safe Harbours and the Salvages habitations: What marchandize and commodities for their labour they may finde, this following discourse shall plainely demonstrate.

Thus you may see, of this 2000. miles more then halfe is yet unknowne to any purpose: no not so much as the borders of the Sea are yet certainly discovered. As for the goodnes and true substances of the Land, wee are for most part yet altogether ignorant of them, unlesse it bee those parts about the Bay of Chisapeack and Sagadahock: but onely here and there

wee touched or have seene a little the edges of those large dominions, which doe stretch themselves into the Maine, God
doth know how many thousand miles; whereof we can yet no
more judge, then a stranger that saileth betwixt England and
France can describe the Harbors and dangers by landing here
or there in some River or Bay, tell thereby the goodnesse and
substances of Spaine, Italy, Germany, Bohemia, Hungaria and
the rest. By this you may perceive how much they erre, that
think every one which hath bin at Virginia understandeth or
knowes what Virginia is: Or that the Spaniards know one halfe
quarter of those Territories they possesse; no, not so much as
the true circumference of Terra Incognita, whose large dominions may equalize the greatnesse and goodnes of America, for
any thing yet known. It is strange with what small power hee
hath raigned in the East Indes; and few will understand the
truth of his strength in America: where he having so much to
keepe with such a pampered force, they neede not greatly feare
his furie, in the Bermudas, Virginia, New France, or New England; beyond whose bounds America doth stretch many
thousand miles: into the frozen partes whereof one Master
Hutson an English Mariner did make the greatest discoverie of
any Christian I knowe of, where he unfortunately died. For
Affrica, had not the industrious Portugales ranged her unknowne parts, who would have sought for wealth among
those fryed Regions of blacke brutish Negers, where notwithstanding all the wealth and admirable adventures and endeavours more then 140 yeares, they knowe not one third of those
blacke habitations. But it is not a worke for every one, to manage such an affaire as makes a discoverie, and plants a Colony:
It requires all the best parts of Art, Judgement, Courage,
Honesty, Constancy, Diligence and Industrie, to doe but neere
well. Some are more proper for one thing then another; and
therein are to be imployed: and nothing breedes more confusion then misplacing and misimploying men in their undertakings. Columbus, Cortez, Pitzara, Soto, Magellanes, and the
rest served more then a prentiship to learne how to begin their
most memorable attempts in the West Indes: which to the
wonder of all ages succesfully they effected, when many hundreds of others farre above them in the worlds opinion, beeing
instructed but by relation, came to shame and confusion in ac-

tions of small moment, who doubtlesse in other matters, were both wise, discreet, generous, and couragious. I say not this to detract any thing from their incomparable merits, but to answer those questionlesse questions that keep us back from imitating the worthinesse of their brave spirits that advanced themselves from poore Souldiers to great Captaines, their posterity to great Lords, their King to be one of the greatest Potentates on earth, and the fruites of their labours, his greatest glory, power and renowne.

The descrip-
tion of New
England. That part wee call New England is betwixt the degrees of 41. and 45: but that parte this discourse speaketh of, stretcheth but from Pennobscot to Cape Cod, some 75 leagues by a right line distant each from other: within which bounds I have seene at least 40. severall habitations upon the Sea Coast, and sounded about 25 excellent good Harbours; In many whereof there is ancorage for 500. sayle of ships of any burthen; in some of them for 5000: And more then 200 Iles overgrowne with good timber, of divers sorts of wood, which doe make so many harbours as requireth a longer time then I had, to be well discovered.

The
particular
Countries or
Governments The principall habitation Northward we were at, was Pennobscot: Southward along the Coast and up the Rivers we found Mecadacut, Segocket, Pemmaquid, Nusconcus, Kenebeck, Sagadahock, and Aumoughcawgen; And to those Countries belong the people of Segotago, Paghhuntanuck, Pocopassum, Taughtanakagnet, Warbigganus, Nassaque, Masherosqueck, Wawrigweck, Moshoquen, Wakcogo, Passharanack, etc. To these are allied the Countries of Aucocisco, Accominticus, Passataquack, Aggawom, and Naemkeck: all these, I could perceive, differ little in language, fashion, or government: though most be Lords of themselves, yet they hold the Bashabes of Pennobscot, the chiefe and greatest amongst them.

The next I can remember by name are Mattahunts; two pleasant Iles of groves, gardens and corne fields a league in the Sea from the Mayne. Then Totant, Massachuset, Pocapawmet, Quonahassit, Sagoquas, Nahapassumkeck, Topeent, Seccasaw, Totheet, Nasnocomacack, Accomack, Chawum; Then Cape Cod by which is Pawmet and the Ile Nawset, of the language, and alliance of them of Chawum: The others are called

Massachusets; of another language, humor and condition: For
their trade and marchandize; to each of their habitations they
have diverse Townes and people belonging; and by their relations and descriptions, more then 20 severall Habitations and
Rivers that stretch themselves farre up into the Countrey, even
to the borders of diverse great Lakes, where they kill and take
most of their Bevers and Otters. From Pennobscot to Sagadahock this Coast is all Mountainous and Iles of huge Rocks,
but overgrowen with all sorts of excellent good woodes for
building houses, boats, barks or shippes; with an incredible
abundance of most sorts of fish, much fowle, and sundry sorts
of good fruites for mans use.

The mixture   Betwixt Sagadahock and Sowocatuck there is but
of an
excellent   two or three sandy Bayes, but betwixt that and Cape
soyle.   Cod very many: especialy the Coast of the Massachusets is so indifferently mixed with high clayie or sandy cliffes
in one place, and then tracts of large long ledges of divers
sorts, and quarries of stones in other places so strangely divided with tinctured veines of divers colours: as, Free stone for
building, Slate for tiling, smooth stone to make Fornaces and
Forges for glasse or iron, and iron ore sufficient, conveniently
to melt in them: but the most part so resembleth the Coast of
Devonshire, I thinke most of the cliffes would make such lime-
stone: If they be not of these qualities, they are so like, they
may deceive a better judgement then mine; all which are so
neere adjoyning to those other advantages I observed in these
parts, that if the Ore prove as good iron and steele in those
parts, as I know it is within the bounds of the Countrey, I dare
engage my head (having but men skilfull to worke the simples
there growing) to have all things belonging to the building
and the rigging of shippes of any proportion, and good marchandize for the fraught, within a square of 10 or 14 leagues:
and were it for a good rewarde, I would not feare to proove it
in a lesse limitation.

A proofe of   And surely by reason of those sandy cliffes and
an excellent   cliffes of rocks, both which we saw so planted with
temper.   Gardens and Corne fields, and so well inhabited with
a goodly, strong and well proportioned people, besides the
greatnesse of the Timber growing on them, the greatnesse of
the fish and the moderate temper of the ayre (for of twentie

five, not any was sicke, but two that were many yeares diseased before they went, notwithstanding our bad lodging and accidentall diet) who can but approove this a most excellent place, both for health and fertility? And of all the foure parts of the world that I have yet seene not inhabited, could I have but meanes to transport a Colonie, I would rather live here then any where: and if it did not maintaine it selfe, were wee but once indifferently well fitted, let us starve.

A proofe of health.

The maine Staple, from hence to bee extracted for the present to produce the rest, is fish; which however it may seeme a mean and a base commoditie: yet who will but truely take the pains and consider the sequell, I thinke will allow it well worth the labour. It is strange to see what great adventures the hopes of setting forth men of war to rob the industrious innocent, would procure; or such massie promises in grosse: though more are choked then well fedde with such hastie hopes. But who doth not know that the poore Hollanders, chiefly by fishing, at a great charge and labour in all weathers in the open Sea, are made a people so hardy, and industrious? and by the venting this poore commodity to the Easterlings for as meane, which is Wood, Flax, Pitch, Tarre, Rosin, Cordage, and such like (which they exchange againe, to the French, Spaniards, Portugales, and English, etc. for what they want) are made so mighty, strong and rich, as no State but Venice, of twice their magnitude, is so well furnished with so many faire Cities, goodly Townes, strong Fortresses, and that aboundance of shipping and all sorts of marchandize, as well of Golde, Silver, Pearles, Diamonds, Pretious stones, Silkes, Velvets, and Cloth of golde; as Fish, Pitch, Wood, or such grosse commodities? What Voyages and Discoveries, East and West, North and South, yea about the world, make they? What an Army by Sea and Land, have they long maintained in despite of one of the greatest Princes of the world? And never could the Spaniard with all his Mynes of golde and Silver, pay his debts, his friends, and army, halfe so truly, as the Hollanders stil have done by this contemptible trade of fish. Divers (I know) may alledge many other assistances: But this is their Myne; and the Sea the source of those silvered streames of all their vertue; which hath made them now the very miracle of industrie, the pattern of perfection for

Staple commodities present.

The Hollanders fishing.

these affaires: and the benefit of fishing is that Primum mobile that turnes all their Spheres to this height of plentie, strength, honour and admiration.

Herring, Cod, and Ling, is that triplicitie that makes their wealth and shippings multiplicities, such as it is, and from which (few would thinke it) they yearly draw at least one million and a halfe of pounds starling; yet it is most certaine (if records be true): and in this faculty they are so naturalized, and of their vents so certainely acquainted, as there is no likelihood they will ever bee paralleld, having 2 or 3000 Busses, Flat bottomes, Sword pinks, Todes, and such like, that breedes them Saylers, Mariners, Souldiers and Marchants, never to be wrought out of that trade, and fit for any other. I will not deny but others may gaine as well as they, that will use it, though not so certainely, nor so much in quantity; for want of experience. And this Herring they take upon the Coast of Scotland and England; their Cod and Ling, upon the Coast of Izeland and in the North Seas.

Which is fifteen hundred thousand pound.

Hamborough, and the East Countries, for Sturgion and Caviare, gets many thousands of pounds from England, and the Straites: Portugale, the Biskaines, and the Spaniards, make 40 or 50 Saile yearely to Cape-blank, to hooke for Porgos, Mullet, and make Puttargo: and New found Land, doth yearely fraught neere 800 sayle of Ships with a sillie leane skinny Poore-John, and Corfish, which at least yearely amounts to 3 or 400000 pound. If from all those parts such paines is taken for this poore gaines of fish, and by them hath neither meate, drinke, nor clothes, wood, iron, nor steele, pitch, tarre, nets, leades, salt, hookes, nor lines, for shipping, fishing, nor provision, but at the second, third, fourth, or fift hand, drawne from so many severall parts of the world ere they come together to be used in this voyage: If these I say can gaine, and the Saylers live going for shares, lesse then the third part of their labours, and yet spend as much time in going and comming, as in staying there, so short is the season of fishing; why should wee more doubt, then Holland, Portugale, Spaniard, French, or other, but to doe much better then they, where there is victuall to feede us, wood of all sorts, to build Boats, Ships, or Barks; the fish at our doores, pitch, tarre, masts, yards, and most of other necessaries onely for making? And here are no hard Landlords to racke us with high rents, or extorted fines to consume us, no tedious pleas in law to consume us with their many years disputations for Justice: no multitudes to occasion such impediments to good orders, as in popular States. So freely hath God and his Majesty bestowed those blessings on them that will attempt to obtaine them, as here every man may be master and owner of his owne labour and land; or the greatest part in a small time. If hee have nothing but his hands, he may set up this trade; and by industrie quickly grow rich; spending but halfe that time wel, which in England we abuse in idlenes, worse or as ill. Here is ground also as good as any lyeth in the height of forty one, forty two, forty three, etc.

Examples of the altitude comparatively which is as temperate and as fruitfull as any other paralell in the world. As for example, on this side the line West of it in the South Sea, is Nova Albion, discovered as is said, by Sir Francis Drake. East from it, is the most temperate part of Portugale, the ancient kingdomes of Galazia, Biskey, Navarre, Arragon, Catalonia, Castilia the olde, and the most moderatest of Castilia the new, and Valentia, which is the greatest part of Spain: which if the Spanish Histories bee true, in the Romanes time abounded no lesse with golde and silver Mines, then now the West Indies; the Romanes then using the Spaniards to work in those Mines, as now the Spaniard doth the Indians.

In France, the Provinces of Gasconie, Langadock, Avignon, Province, Dolphine, Pyamont, and Turyne, are in the same paralel: which are the best and richest parts of France. In Italy, the provinces of Genua, Lumbardy, and Verona, with a great part of the most famous State of Venice, the Dukedoms of Bononia, Mantua, Ferrara, Ravenna, Bolognia, Florence, Pisa, Sienna, Urbine, Ancona, and the ancient Citie and Countrey of Rome, with a great part of the great Kingdome of Naples. In Slavonia, Istrya, and Dalmatia, with the Kingdomes of Albania. In Grecia, that famous Kingdome of Macedonia, Bulgaria, Thessalia, Thracia, or Romania, where is seated the most pleasant and plentifull Citie in Europe, Constantinople. In Asia also, in the same latitude, are the temperatest parts of Natolia, Armenia, Persia, and China, besides divers other large Countries and Kingdomes in these most milde and temperate Regions of Asia. Southward, in the same height, is the richest of golde Mynes, Chily and Baldivia, and the mouth of the great River of Plate, etc: for all the rest of the world in that height is yet unknown. Besides these reasons, mine owne eyes that have seene a great part of those Cities and their Kingdomes, as well as it, can finde no advantage they have in nature, but this, They are beautified by the long labour and diligence of industrious people and Art. This is onely as God made it, when he created the worlde. Therefore I conclude, if the heart and intralls of those Regions were sought: if their Land were cultured, planted and manured by men of industrie, judgement, and experience; what hope is there, or what neede they doubt, having those advantages of the Sea, but it might equalize any of those famous Kingdomes, in all commodities, pleasures, and conditions? seeing even the very edges doe naturally afford us such plenty, as no ship need returne away empty: and onely use but the season of the Sea, fish will returne an honest gaine, beside all other advantages; her treasures having yet never beene opened, nor her originalls wasted, consumed, nor abused.

The particular staple commodities that may be had.

And whereas it is said, the Hollanders serve the Easterlings themselves, and other parts that want, with Herring, Ling, and wet Cod; the Easterlings, a great part of Europe, with Sturgion and Caviare; Cape-blanke, Spaine, Portugale, and the Levant, with Mullet, and Puttargo; New found Land, all Europe, with a thin Poore John: yet all is so overlaide with fishers, as the fishing decayeth, and many are constrained to returne with a small fraught. Norway, and Polonia, Pitch, Tar, Masts, and Yardes; Sweathland, and Russia, Iron, and Ropes; France, and Spaine, Canvas, Wine, Steele, Iron, and Oyle; Italy and Greece, Silks, and Fruites. I dare boldly say, because I have seen naturally growing, or breeding in those parts the same materialls that all those are made of, they may as well be had here, or the most part of them, within the distance of 70 leagues for some few ages, as from all those parts; using but the same meanes to have them that they doe, and with all those advantages.

The nature of ground approoved.

First, the ground is so fertill, that questionless it is capable of producing any Grain, Fruits, or Seeds you will sow or plant, growing in the Regions afore named: But it may be, not every kinde to that perfection of delicacy; or some tender plants may miscarie, because the Summer is not so hot, and the winter is more colde in those parts wee have yet tryed neere the Sea side, then we finde in the same height in Europe or Asia; Yet I made a Garden upon the top of a Rockie Ile in 43.½, 4 leagues from the Main, in May, that grew so well, as it served us for sallets in June and July. All sorts of cattell may here be bred and fed in the Iles, or Peninsulaes, securely for nothing. In the Interim till they encrease if need be (observing the seasons) I durst undertake to have corne enough from the Salvages for 300 men, for a few trifles; and if they should bee untoward (as it is most certaine they are) thirty or forty good men will be sufficient to bring them all in subjection, and make this provision; if they understand what they doe: 200 whereof may nine monethes in the yeare be imployed in making marchandable fish, till the rest provide other necessaries, fit to furnish us with other commodities.

The seasons
for fishing
approoved. In March, Aprill, May, and halfe June, here is Cod in abundance; in May, June, July, and August Mullet and Sturgion; whose roes doe make Caviare and Puttargo. Herring, if any desire them, I have taken many out of the bellies of Cods, some in nets; but the Salvages compare their store in the Sea, to the haires of their heads: and surely there are an incredible abundance upon this Coast. In the end of August, September, October, and November, you have Cod againe, to make Cor fish, or Poore John: and each hundred is as good as two or three hundred in the New-found Land. So that halfe the labour in hooking, splitting, and turning, is saved: and you may have your fish at what Market you will, before they can have any in New-found Land; where their fishing is chiefly but in June and July: whereas it is heere in March, Aprill, May, September, October, and November, as is said. So that by reason of this plantation, the Marchants may have fraught both out and home: which yeelds an advantage worth consideration.

Your Cor-fish you may in like manner transport as you see cause, to serve the Ports in Portugale (as Lisbon, Avera, Porta port, and divers others, or what market you please) before your Ilanders returne: They being tyed to the season in the open Sea; you having a double season, and fishing before your doors, may every night sleep quietly a shore with good cheare and what fires you will, or when you please with your wives and familie: they onely, their ships in the maine Ocean.

The Mullets heere are in that abundance, you may take them with nets, sometimes by hundreds, where at Cape blank they hooke them; yet those but one foot and a halfe in length; these two, three, or foure, as oft I have measured: much Salmon some have found up the Rivers, as they have passed: and heer the ayre is so temperate, as all these at any time may well be preserved.

Imployment for poore people and fatherlesse children.

Now, young boyes and girles Salvages, or any other, be they never such idlers, may turne, carry, and return fish, without either shame, or any great paine: hee is very idle that is past twelve yeares of age and cannot doe so much: and she is very olde, that cannot spin a thred to make engines to catch them.

The facility of the plantation.

For their transportation, the ships that go there to fish may transport the first: who for their passage will spare the charge of double manning their ships, which they must doe in the New-found Land, to get their fraught; but one third part of that companie are onely but proper to serve a stage, carry a barrow, and turne Poor John: notwithstanding, they must have meate, drinke, clothes, and passage, as well as the rest. Now all I desire, is but this; That those that voluntarily will send shipping, should make here the best choise they can, or accept such as are presented them, to serve them at that rate: and their ships returning leave such with me, with the value of that they should receive comming home, in such provisions and necessarie tooles, armes, bedding and apparell, salt, hookes, nets, lines, and such like as they spare of the remainings; who till the next returne may keepe their boates and doe them many other profitable offices: provided I have men of ability to teach them their functions, and a company fit for Souldiers to be ready upon an occasion; because of the abuses which have beene offered the poore Salvages, and the liberty both French, or any that will, hath to deale with them as they please: whose disorders will be hard to reforme; and the longer the worse. Now such order with facilitie might be taken, with every port Towne or Citie, to observe but this order, With free power to convert the benefits of their fraughts to what ad-vantage they please, and increase their numbers as they see occasion; who ever as they are able to subsist of themselves, may beginne the new Townes in New England in memory of their olde: which freedome being confined but to the necessity of the generall good, the event (with Gods helpe) might produce an honest, a noble, and a profitable emulation.

Salt upon salt may assuredly he made; if not at the first in ponds, yet till they bee provided this may be used: then the Ships may transport Kine, Horse, Goates, course Cloath, and such commodities as we want; by whose arrivall may be made that provision of fish to fraught the Ships that they stay not: and then if the sailers goe for wages, it matters not. It is hard if this returne defray not the charge: but care must be had, they arrive in the Spring, or else provision be made for them against the Winter.

Present commodities.

Of certaine red berries called Alkermes which is worth ten shillings a pound, but of these hath been sould for thirty or forty shillings the pound, may yearely be gathered a good quantitie.

Of the Musk Rat may bee well raised gaines, well worth their labour, that will endevor to make tryall of their goodnesse.

Of Bevers, Otters, Martins, Blacke Foxes, and Furres of price, may yearely be had 6 or 7000: and if the trade of the French were prevented, many more: 25000 this yeare were brought from those Northren parts into France; of which trade we may have as good part as the French, if we take good courses.

Of Mynes of Golde and Silver, Copper, and probabilities of Lead, Christall and Allum, I could say much if relations were good assurances. It is true indeed, I made many trials according to those instructions I had, which doe perswade mee I need not despaire, but there are metalls in the Countrey: but I am no Alchymist, nor will promise more then I know: which is, Who will undertake the rectifying of an Iron forge, if those that buy meate, drinke, coals, ore, and all necessaries at a deer rate gaine; where all these things are to be had for the taking up, in my opinion cannot lose.

Of woods seeing there is such plenty of all sorts, if those that build ships and boates, buy wood at so great a price, as it is in England, Spaine, France, Italy, and Holland, and all other provisions for the nourishing of mans life; live well by their trade:

when labour is all required to take those necessaries without any other tax; what hazard will be here, but doe much better? And what commoditie in Europe doth more decay then wood? For the goodnesse of the ground, let us take it fertill, or barren, or as it is: seeing it is certaine it beares fruites, to nourish and feed man and beast, as well as England, and the Sea those severall sorts of fish I have related. Thus seeing all good provisions for mans sustenance, may with this facility be had, by a little extraordinarie labour, till that transported be increased; and all necessaries for shipping, onely for labour: to which may bee added the assistance of the Salvages, which may easily be had, if they be discreetly handled in their kindes; towards fishing, planting, and destroying woods. What gaines might be raised if this were followed (when there is but once men to fill your store houses, dwelling there, you may serve all Europe better and farre cheaper, then can the Izeland fishers, or the Hollanders, Cape blank, or New found Land: who must be at as much more charge, then you) may easily be conjectured by this example.

An example of the gains upon every yeare or six monethes returne.   2000. pound will fit out a ship of 200. and 1 of a 100 tuns: If the dry fish they both make, fraught that of 200. and goe for Spaine, sell it but at ten shillings a quintall; but commonly it giveth fifteen, or twentie: especially when it commeth first, which amounts to 3 or 4000 pound: but say but tenne, which is the lowest, allowing the rest for waste, it amounts at that rate, to 2000 pound, which is the whole charge of your two ships, and their equipage: Then the returne of the money, and the fraught of the ship for the vintage, or any other voyage, is cleere gaine, with your shippe of a 100 tuns of Train oyle, besides the bevers, and other commodities; and that you may have at home within six monethes, if God please but to send an ordinarie passage. Then saving halfe this charge by the not staying of your ships, your victual, overplus of men and wages; with her fraught thither of things necessarie for the planters, the salt being there made: as also may the nets and lines, within a short time: if nothing were to bee expected but this, it might in time equalize your Hollanders gaines, if not exceed them: they returning but wood, pitch, tarre, and such grosse commodities; you wines, oyles, fruits, silkes, and such Straits commodities, as you please to provide by your Factors, against such times as your shippes arrive with them. This would so increase our shipping and sailers, and so employ and encourage a great part of our idlers and others that want imployments fitting their qualities at home, where they shame to doe that they would doe abroad; that could they but once taste the sweet fruites of their owne labours, doubtlesse many thousands would be advised by good discipline, to take more pleasure in honest industrie, then in their humours of dissolute idlenesse.

A description of the Countries in particular, and their situations. But, to returne a little more to the particulars of this Countrey, which I intermingle thus with my projects and reasons, not being so sufficiently yet acquainted in those parts, to write fully the estate of the Sea, the Ayre, the Land, the Fruites, the Rocks, the People, the Government, Religion, Territories, and Limitations, Friends, and Foes: but, as I gathered from the niggardly relations in a broken language to my understanding, during the time I ranged those Countries etc. The most Northren part I was at, was the Bay of Pennobscot, which is East and West, North and South, more then ten leagues: but such were my occasions, I was constrained to be satisfied of them I found in the Bay, that the River ranne farre up into the Land, and was well inhabited with many people, but they were from their habitations, either fishing among the Iles, or hunting the Lakes and Woods, for Deer and Bevers. The Bay is full of great Ilands, of one, two, six, eight, or ten miles in length, which divides it into many faire and excellent good harbours. On the East of it, are the Tarrantines, their mortall enemies, where inhabit the French, as they report that live with those people, as one nation or family. And Northwest of Pennobscot is Mecaddacut, at the foot of a high mountaine, a kinde of fortresse against the Tarrantines, adjoyning to the high mountaines of Pennobscot, against whose feet doth beat the Sea: But over all the Land, Iles, or other impediments, you may well see them sixteene or eighteene leagues from their situation. Segocket is the next; then Nusconcus, Pemmaquid, and Sagadahock. Up this River where was the Westerne plantation are Aumuckcawgen, Kinnebeck, and divers others, where there is planted some corne fields. Along this River 40 or 50 miles, I saw nothing but great high cliffes of barren Rocks, overgrowne with wood: but where the Salvages dwelt there the ground is exceeding fat and fertill. Westward of this River, is the Countrey of Aucocisco, in the bottome of a large deepe Bay, full of many great Iles, which divides it into many good harbours. Sowocotuck is the next, in the edge of a large sandy Bay, which hath many Rocks and Iles, but few good harbours, but for Barks, I yet know. But all this Coast to Pennobscot, and as farre I could see Eastward of it is nothing but such high craggy Cliffy Rocks and stony Iles that I wondered such great trees could growe upon so hard foundations. It is a Countrie rather to affright, then delight one. And how to describe a more plaine spectacle of desolation or more barren I knowe not. Yet the Sea there is the strangest fishpond I ever saw; and those barren Iles so furnished with good woods, springs, fruits, fish, and foule, that it makes mee thinke though the Coast be rockie, and thus affrightable; the Vallies, Plaines, and interior parts, may well (notwithstanding) be verie fertile. But there is no kingdome so fertile hath not some part barren: and New England is great enough, to make many Kingdomes and Countries, were it all inhabited. As you passe the Coast still Westward, Accominticus and Passataquack are two convenient harbors for small barks; and a good Countrie, within their craggie cliffs. Angoam is the next; This place might content a right curious judgement: but there are many sands at the entrance of the harbor: and the worst is, it is inbayed too farre from the deepe Sea. Heere are many rising hilles, and on their tops and descents many corne fields, and delightfull groves. On the East, is an Ile of two or three leagues in length; the one halfe, plaine morish grasse fit for pasture, with many faire high groves of mulberrie trees and gardens: and there is also Okes, Pines, and other woods to make this place an excellent habitation, beeing a good and safe harbor.

Naimkeck though it be more rockie ground (for Angoam is sandie) not much inferior; neither for the harbor, nor any thing I could perceive, but the multitude of people. From hence doth stretch into the Sea the faire headland Tragabigzanda, fronted with three Iles called the three Turks heads: to the North of this, doth enter a great Bay, where wee founde some habitations and corne fields: they report a great River, and at least thirtie habitations, doo possesse this Countrie. But because the French had got their Trade, I had no leasure to discover it. The Iles of Mattahunts are on the West side of this Bay, where are many Iles, and questionlesse good harbors: and then the Countrie of the Massachusets, which is the Paradise of all those parts: for, heere are many Iles all planted with corne; groves, mulberries, salvage gardens, and good harbors: the Coast is for the most part, high clayie sandie cliffs. The Sea Coast as you passe, shewes you all along large corne fields, and great troupes of well proportioned people: but the French having remained heere neere six weekes, left nothing, for us to take occasion to examine the inhabitants relations, viz. if there be neer three thousand people upon these Iles; and that the River doth pearce many daies journeies the intralles of that Countrey. We found the people in those parts verie kinde; but in their furie no lesse valiant. For, upon a quarrell wee had with one of them, hee onely with three others crossed the harbor of Quonahassit to certaine rocks whereby wee must passe; and there let flie their arrowes for our shot, till we were out of danger.

Then come you to Accomack, an excellent good harbor, good land; and no want of any thing, but industrious people. After much kindnesse, upon a small occasion, wee fought also with fortie or fiftie of those: though some were hurt, and some slaine; yet within an houre after they became friendes. Cape Cod is the next presents it selfe: which is onely a headland of high hils of sand, overgrowne with shrubbie pines, hurts, and such trash; but an excellent harbor for all weathers. This Cape is made by the maine Sea on the one side, and a great Bay on the other in forme of a sickle: on it doth inhabit the people of Pawmet: and in the bottome of the Bay, the people of Chawum. Towards the South and Southwest of this Cape, is found a long and dangerous shoale of sands and rocks. But so farre as I incircled it, I found thirtie fadom water aboard the shore, and a strong current: which makes mee thinke there is a Channell about this shoale; where is the best and greatest fish to be had, Winter and Summer, in all that Countrie. But, the Salvages say there is no Channell, but that the shoales beginne from the maine at Pawmet, to the Ile of Nausit; and so extends beyond their knowledge into the Sea. The next to this is Capawack, and those abounding Countries of copper, corne, people, and mineralls; which I went to discover this last yeare: but because

I miscarried by the way, I will leave them, till God please I have better acquaintance with them.

The Massachusets, they report, sometimes have warres with the Bashabes of Pennobskot; and are not alwaies friends with them of Chawun and their alliants: but now they are all friends, and have each trade with other, so farre as they have societie, on each others frontiers. For they make no such voiages as from Pennobskot to Cape Cod; seldom to Massachewset. In the North (as I have said) they begunne to plant corne, whereof the South part hath such plentie, as they have what they will from them of the North; and in the Winter much more plenty of fish and foule: but both Winter and Summer hath it in the one part or other all the yeare; being the meane and most indifferent temper, betwixt heat and colde, of all the regions betwixt the Lyne and the Pole: but the furs Northward are much better, and in much more plentie, then Southward.

A good Countrie.

The remarkeablest Iles and mountains for Land-markes are these; The highest Ile is Sorico, in the Bay of Pennobskot: but the three Iles and a rock of Matinnack are much furder in the Sea; Metinicus is also three plaine Iles and a rock, betwixt it and Monahigan: Monahigan is a rounde high Ile; and close by it Monanis, betwixt which is a small harbor where we ride. In Damerils Iles is such another: Sagadahock is knowne by Satquin, and foure or five Iles in the mouth. Smyths Iles are a heape together, none neere them, against Accominticus. The three Turks heads are three Iles seen far to Sea-ward in regard of the headland.

The land-markes.

The cheefe headlands are onely Cape Tragabigzanda and Cape Cod.

The cheefe mountaines, them of Pennobscot; the twinkling mountaine of Aucocisco; the greate mountaine of Sasanou; and the high mountaine of Massachusit: each of which you shall finde in the Mappe; their places, formes, and altitude. The waters are most pure, proceeding from the intrals of rockie mountaines; the hearbes and fruits are of many sorts and kindes: as alkermes, currans, or a fruit like currans, mulberries, vines, respices, goos-berries, plummes, walnuts, chesnuts, small nuts, etc. pumpions, gourds, strawberries, beans, pease, and mayze; a kinde or two

Hearbs.

of flax, wherewith they make nets, lines and ropes both small and great, verie strong for their quantities.

Woods.   Oke, is the chiefe wood; of which there is great difference in regard of the soyle where it groweth. firre, pyne, walnut, chesnut, birch, ash, elme, cypresse, ceder, mulberrie, plumtree, hazell, saxefrage, and many other sorts.

Birds.   Eagles, Gripes, diverse sorts of Haukes, Cranes, Geese, Brants, Cormorants, Ducks, Sheldrakes, Teale, Meawes, Guls, Turkies, Dive-doppers, and many other sorts, whose names I knowe not.

Fishes.   Whales, Grampus, Porkpisces, Turbut, Sturgion, Cod, Hake, Haddock, Cole, Cusk, or small Ling, Shark, Mackerell, Herring, Mullet, Base, Pinacks, Cunners, Pearch, Eels, Crabs, Lobsters, Muskles, Wilkes, Oysters, and diverse others etc.

Beasts.   Moos, a beast bigger then a Stagge; deere, red, and Fallow; Bevers, Wolves, Foxes, both blacke and other; Aroughconds, Wild-cats, Beares, Otters, Martins, Fitches, Musquassus, and diverse sorts of vermine, whose names I know not. All these and diverse other good things do heere, for want of use, still increase, and decrease with little diminution, whereby they growe to that abundance. You shall scarce finde any Baye, shallow shore, or Cove of sand, where you may not take many Clampes, or Lobsters, or both at your pleasure, and in many places lode your boat if you please; Nor Iles where you finde not fruits, birds, crabs, and muskles, or all of them, for taking, at a lowe water. And in the harbors we frequented, a little boye might take of Cunners, and Pinacks, and such delicate fish, at the ships sterne, more then sixe or tenne can eate in a daie; but with a casting-net, thousands when wee pleased: and scarce any place, but Cod, Cuske, Holybut, Mackerell, Scate, or such like, a man may take with a hooke or line what he will. And, in diverse sandy Baies, a man may draw with a net great store of Mullets, Bases, and diverse other sorts of such excellent fish, as many as his Net can drawe on shore: no River where there is not plentie of Sturgion, or Salmon, or both; all which are to be had in abundance observing but their seasons. But if a man will goe at Christmasse to gather Cherries in Kent, he may be deceived; though there be plentie in Summer: so, heere these plenties have each their seasons, as I have expressed. We for the most part had little but bread and vineger: and though the most part of July when the fishing decaied they wrought all day, laie abroade in the Iles all night, and lived on what they found, yet were not sicke: But I would wish none put himself long to such plunges; except necessitie constraine it: yet worthy is that person to starve that heere cannot live; if he have sense, strength and health: for, there is no such penury of these blessings in any place, but that a hundred men may, in one houre or two, make their provisions for a day: and hee that hath experience to mannage well these affaires, with fortie or thirtie honest industrious men, might well undertake (if they dwell in these parts) to subject the Salvages, and feed daily two or three hundred men, with as good corne, fish, and flesh, as the earth hath of those kindes, and yet make that labor but their pleasure: provided that they have engins, that be proper for their purposes.

A note for men that have great spirits, and smal meanes.   Who can desire more content, that hath small meanes; or but only his merit to advance his fortune, then to tread, and plant that ground hee hath purchased by the hazard of his life? If he have but the taste of virtue, and magnanimitie, what to such a minde can bee more pleasant, then planting and building a foundation for his Posteritie, gotte from the rude earth, by Gods blessing and his owne industrie, without prejudice to any? If hee have any graine of faith or zeale in Religion, what can hee doe lesse hurtfull to any; or more agreeable to God, then to seeke to convert those poore Salvages to know Christ, and humanitie, whose labors with discretion will triple requite thy charge and paines? What so truely sutes with honour and honestie, as the discovering things unknowne? erecting Townes, peopling Countries, informing the ignorant, reforming things unjust, teaching virtue; and gaine to our Native mother-countrie a kingdom to attend her; finde imployment for those that are idle, because they know not what to doe: so farre from wronging any, as to cause Posteritie to remember thee; and remembring thee, ever honour that remembrance with praise? Consider: What were the beginnings and endings of the Monarkies of the Chaldeans, the Syrians, the Grecians, and Romanes, but this one rule; What was it they would not doe, for the good of the commonwealth, or their Mother-citie? For example: Rome, What made her such a Monarchesse, but onely the adventures of her youth, not in riots at home; but in dangers abroade? and the justice and judgement out of their experience, when they grewe aged. What was their ruine and hurt, but this; The excesse of idlenesse, the fondnesse of Parents, the want of experience in Magistrates, the admiration of their undeserved honours, the contempt of true merit, their unjust jealosies, their politicke incredulities, their hypocriticall seeming goodnesse, and their deeds of secret lewdnesse? finally, in fine, growing onely formall temporists, all that their predecessors got in many years, they lost in few daies. Those by their pains and vertues became Lords of the world; they by their ease and vices became slaves to their servants. This is the difference betwixt the use of Armes in the field, and on the monuments of stones; the golden age and the leaden age, prosperity and miserie, justice and corruption, substance and shadowes, words and deeds, experience and imagination, making Commonwealths and marring Commonwealths, the fruits of vertue and the conclusions of vice.

Then, who would live at home idly (or thinke in himselfe any worth to live) onely to eate, drink, and sleepe, and so die? Or by consuming that carelesly, his friends got worthily? Or by using that miserably, that maintained vertue honestly? Or, for being descended nobly, pine with the vaine vaunt of great kindred, in penurie? Or (to maintaine a silly shewe of bravery) toyle out thy heart, soule, and time, basely, by shifts, tricks, cards, and dice? Or by relating newes of others actions, sharke here or there for a dinner, or supper; deceive thy friends, by faire promises, and dissimulation, in borrowing where thou never intendest to pay; offend the lawes, surfeit with excesse, burden thy Country, abuse thy selfe, despaire in want, and then couzen thy kindred, yea even thine owne brother, and wish thy parents death (I will not say damnation) to have their estates? though thou seest what honours, and rewards, the world yet hath for them will seeke them and worthily deserve them.

I would be sory to offend, or that any should mistake my honest meaning: for I wish good to all, hurt to none. But rich men for the most part are growne to that dotage, through their pride in their wealth, as though there were no accident could end it, or their life. And what hellish care do such take to

make it their owne miserie, and their Countries spoile, especially when there is most neede of their imployment? drawing
by all manner of inventions, from the Prince and his honest
subjects, even the vitall spirits of their powers and estates: as if
their Bagges, or Bragges, were so powerfull a defence, the malicious could not assault them; when they are the onely baite,
to cause us not to be onely assaulted; but betrayed and murdered in our owne security, ere we well perceive it.

An example   May not the miserable ruine of Constantinople,
of secure   their impregnable walles, riches, and pleasures last
covetousness.
       taken by the Turke (which are but a bit, in compari-
son of their now mightines) remember us, of the effects of private covetousness? at which time the good Emperour held
himselfe rich enough, to have such rich subjects, so formall in
all excesse of vanity, all kinde of delicacie, and prodigalitie. His
povertie when the Turke besieged, the citizens (whose mar-
chandizing thoughts were onely to get wealth, little conceiving the desperate resolution of a valiant expert enemy) left
the Emperour so long to his conclusions, having spent all he
had to pay his young, raw, discontented Souldiers; that so-
dainly he, they, and their citie were all a prey to the devouring
Turke. And what they would not spare for the maintenance of
them who adventured their lives to defend them, did serve
onely their enemies to torment them, their friends, and countrey, and all Christendome to this present day. Let this lamentable example remember you that are rich (seeing there are such
great theeves in the world to robbe you) not grudge to lend
some proportion, to breed them that have little, yet willing to
learne how to defend you: for, it is too late when the deede is
a-doing. The Romanes estate hath beene worse then this: for,
the meere covetousnesse and extortion of a few of them, so
mooved the rest, that not having any imployment, but contemplation; their great judgements grew to so great malice, as
themselves were sufficient to destroy themselves by faction:
Let this moove you to embrace imployment, for those whose
educations, spirits, and judgements, want but your purses; not
onely to prevent such accustomed dangers, but also to gaine
more thereby then you have. And you fathers that are either so
foolishly fond, or so miserably covetous, or so willfully ignorant, or so negligently carelesse, as that you will rather main-

taine your children in idle wantonness, till they growe your
masters; or become so basely unkinde, as they wish nothing
but your deaths; so that both sorts growe dissolute: and although you would wish them any where to escape the gallowes,
and ease your cares; though they spend you here one, two, or
three hundred pound a yeer; you would grudge to give halfe
so much in adventure with them, to obtaine an estate, which
in a small time but with a little assistance of your providence,
might bee better then your owne. But if an Angell should tell
you, that any place yet unknowne can afford such fortunes;
you would not beleeve him, no more then Columbus was
beleeved there was any such Land as is now the well knowne
abounding America; much lesse such large Regions as are yet
unknowne, as well in America, as in Affrica, and Asia, and
Terra incognita; where were courses for gentlemen (and them
that would be so reputed) more suiting their qualities, then
begging from their Princes generous disposition, the labours of
his subjects, and the very marrow of his maintenance.

I have not beene so ill bred, but I have tasted of
The Authors
conditions. Plenty and Pleasure, as well as Want and Miserie: nor
doth necessity yet, or occasion of discontent, force
me to these endeavors: nor am I ignorant what small thanke I
shall have for my paines; or that many would have the Worlde
imagine them to be of great judgement, that can but blemish
these my designes, by their witty objections and detractions:
yet (I hope) my reasons with my deeds, will so prevaile with
some, that I shall not want imployment in these affaires, to
make the most blinde see his owne senselesnesse, and incredulity; Hoping that gaine will make them affect that, which Religion, Charity, and the Common good cannot. It were but a
poore device in me, To deceive my selfe; much more the King,
and State, my Friends, and Countrey, with these inducements:
which, seeing his Majestie hath given permission, I wish all
sorts of worthie, honest, industrious spirits, would understand: and if they desire any further satisfaction, I will doe my
best to give it: Not to perswade them to goe onely; but goe
with them: Not leave them there; but live with them there. I
will not say, but by ill providing and undue managing, such
courses may be taken, may make us miserable enough: But if I
may have the execution of what I have projected; if they want

to eate, let them eate or never digest Me. If I performe what I say, I desire but that reward out of the gaines may sute my paines, quality, and condition. And if I abuse you with my tongue, take my head for satisfaction. If any dislike at the yeares end, defraying their charge, by my consent they should freely returne. I feare not want of companie sufficient, were it but knowne what I know of those Countries; and by the proofe of that wealth I hope yearely to returne, if God please to blesse me from such accidents, as are beyond my power in reason to prevent: For, I am not so simple, to thinke, that ever any other motive then wealth, will ever erect there a Commonweale; or draw companie from their ease and humours at home, to stay in New England to effect my purposes.

The planters pleasures, and profits.

And lest any should thinke the toile might be insupportable, though these things may be had by labour, and diligence: I assure my selfe there are who delight extreamly in vaine pleasure, that take much more paines in England, to enjoy it, then I should doe heere to gaine wealth sufficient: and yet I thinke they should not have halfe such sweet content: for, our pleasure here is still gaines; in England charges and losse. Heer nature and liberty affords us that freely, which in England we want, or it costeth us dearely. What pleasure can be more, then (being tired with any occasion a-shore) in planting Vines, Fruits, or Hearbs, in contriving their owne Grounds, to the pleasure of their owne mindes, their Fields, Gardens, Orchards, Buildings, Ships, and other works, etc. to recreate themselves before their owne doores, in their owne boates upon the Sea, where man woman and childe, with a small hooke and line, by angling, may take diverse sorts of excellent fish, at their pleasures? And is it not pretty sport, to pull up two pence, six pence, and twelve pence, as fast as you can hale and veare a line? He is a very bad fisher, cannot kill in one day with his hooke and line, one, two, or three hundred Cods: which dressed and dryed, if they be sould there for ten shillings the hundred, though in England they will give more then twentie; may not both the servant, the master, and marchant, be well content with this gaine? If a man worke but three dayes in seaven, he may get more then hee can spend, unlesse he will be excessive. Now that Carpenter, Mason, Gardiner, Taylor, Smith, Sailer, Forgers, or what other, may they not make this a pretty recreation though they fish but an houre in a day, to take more then they eate in a weeke: or if they will not eate it, because there is so much better choise; yet sell it, or change it, with the fisher men, or marchants, for any thing they want. And what sport doth yeeld a more pleasing content, and lesse hurt or charge then angling with a hooke, and crossing the sweete ayre from Ile to Ile, over the silent streames of a calme Sea? wherein the most curious may finde pleasure, profit, and content. Thus, though all men be not fishers: yet all men, whatsoever, may in other matters doe as well. For necessity doth in these cases so rule a Commonwealth, and each in their severall functions, as their labours in their qualities may be as profitable, because there is a necessary mutuall use of all.

Imployments for gentlemen. For Gentlemen, what exercise should more delight them, then ranging dayly those unknowne parts, using fowling and fishing, for hunting and hauking? and yet you shall see the wilde haukes give you some pleasure, in seeing them stoope (six or seaven after one another) an houre or two together, at the skuls of fish in the faire harbours, as those a-shore at a foule; and never trouble nor torment your selves, with watching, mewing, feeding, and attending them: nor kill horse and man with running and crying, See you not a hauk? For hunting also: the woods, lakes, and rivers, affoord not onely chase sufficient, for any that delights in that kinde of toyle, or pleasure; but such beasts to hunt, that besides the delicacy of their bodies for food, their skins are so rich, as may well recompence thy dayly labour, with a Captains pay.

Imployments for labourers. For labourers, if those that sowe hemp, rape, turnups, parsnips, carrats, cabidge, and such like; give 20, 30, 40, 50 shillings yearely for an acre of ground, and meat drinke and wages to use it, and yet grow rich: when better, or at least as good ground, may be had and cost nothing but labour; it seemes strange to me, any such should there grow poore.

My purpose is not to perswade children from their parents; men from their wives; nor servants from their masters: onely, such as with free consent may be spared: But that each parish, or village, in Citie, or Countrey, that will but apparell their fatherlesse children, of thirteene or fourteen years of age, or

young maried people, that have small wealth to live on; heere
by their labour may live exceeding well: provided alwaies that
first there bee a sufficient power to command them, houses to
receive them, meanes to defend them, and meet provisions for
them; for, any place may bee overlain: and it is most necessarie
to have a fortresse (ere this grow to practice) and sufficient
masters (as, Carpenters, Masons, Fishers, Fowlers, Gardiners,
Husbandmen, Sawyers, Smiths, Spinsters, Taylors, Weavers,
and such like) to take ten, twelve, or twentie, or as ther is occasion, for Apprentices. The Masters by this may quicklie growe
rich; these may learne their trades themselves, to doe the like;
to a generall and an incredible benefit, for King, and Countrey,
Master, and Servant.

It would bee an historie of a large volume, to re-
Examples of
the Spanyard. cite the adventures of the Spanyards, and Portugals,
their affronts, and defeats, their dangers and miseries; which with such incomparable honour and constant resolution, so farre beyond beleefe, they have attempted and
indured in their discoveries and plantations, as may well condemne us, of too much imbecillitie, sloth, and negligence: yet
the Authors of those new inventions, were held as ridiculous,
for a long time, as now are others, that doe but seek to imitate
their unparalleled vertues. And though we see daily their mountaines of wealth (sprong from the plants of their generous indevours) yet is our sensualitie and untowardnesse such, and so
great, that wee either ignorantly beleeve nothing; or so curiously contest, to prevent wee knowe not what future events;
that wee either so neglect, or oppresse and discourage the present, as wee spoile all in the making, crop all in the blooming;
and building upon faire sand, rather then rough rockes, judge
that wee knowe not, governe that wee have not, feare that
which is not; and for feare some should doe too well, force
such against their willes to be idle or as ill. And who is he hath
judgement, courage, and any industrie or qualitie with understanding, will leave his Countrie, his hopes at home, his certaine estate, his friends, pleasures) libertie, and the preferment
sweete England doth afford to all degrees, were it not to advance his fortunes by injoying his deserts? whose prosperitie
once appearing, will incourage others: but it must be cherished
as a childe, till it be able to goe, and understand it selfe; and

not corrected, nor oppressed above its strength, ere it knowe wherefore. A child can neither performe the office, nor deedes of a man of strength, nor indure that affliction He is able; nor can an Apprentice at the first performe the part of a Maister. And if twentie yeeres bee required to make a child a man, seven yeeres limited an apprentice for his trade: if scarce an age be sufficient to make a wise man a States man; and commonly, a man dies ere he hath learned to be discreet: If perfection be so hard to be obtained, as of necessitie there must bee practice, as well as theorick: Let no man much condemne this paradox opinion, to say, that halfe seaven yeeres is scarce sufficient, for a good capacitie, to learne in these affaires, how to carrie himselfe: and who ever shall trie in these remote places the erecting of a Colony, shall finde at the ende of seaven yeares occasion enough to use all his discretion: and, in the Interim all the content, rewards, gaines, and hopes will he necessarily required, to be given to the beginning, till it bee able to creepe, to stand, and goe, yet time enough to keepe it from running, for there is no feare it wil grow too fast, or ever to any thing; except libertie, profit, honor, and prosperitie there found, more binde the planters of those affaires, in devotion to effect it; then bondage, violence, tyranny, ingratitude, and such double dealing, as bindes free men to become slaves, and honest men turne knaves: which hath ever bin the ruine of the most popular common-weales; and is verie unlikelie ever well to begin in a new.

Who seeth not what is the greatest good of the

The blisse of Spaine. Spanyard, but these new conclusions, in searching those unknowne parts of this unknowne world? By which meanes hee dives even into the verie secrets of all his Neighbours, and the most part of the world: and when the Portugale and Spanyard had found the East and West Indies; how many did condemn themselves, that did not accept of that honest offer of Noble Columbus? who, upon our neglect, brought them to it, perswading our selves the world had no such places as they had found: and yet ever since wee finde, they still (from time to time) have found new Lands, new Nations, and trades, and still daily dooe finde both in Asia, Africa, Terra incognita, and America; so that there is neither Soldier nor Mechanick, from the Lord to the begger, but those parts afforde them all imploiment; and discharge their Native soile, of so many thousands of all sorts, that else, by their sloth, pride, and imperfections, would long ere this have troubled their neighbours, or have eaten the pride of Spaine it selfe.

Now he knowes little, that knowes not England may well spare many more people then Spaine, and is as well able to furnish them with all manner of necessaries. And seeing, for all they have, they cease not still to search for that they have not, and know not; It is strange we should be so dull, as not maintaine that which wee have, and pursue that wee knowe. Surely I am sure many would taste it ill, to bee abridged of the titles and honours of their predecessors: when if but truely they would judge themselves; looke how inferior they are to their noble vertues, so much they are unworthy of their honours and livings: which never were ordained for showes and shadowes, to maintaine idlenesse and vice; but to make them more able to abound in honor, by heroycall deeds of action, judgement, pietie, and vertue. What was it, They would not doe both in purse and person, for the good of the Commonwealth? which might move them presently to set out their spare kindred in these generous designes. Religion, above all things, should move us (especially the Clergie) if wee were religious, to shewe our faith by our workes; in converting those poore salvages, to the knowledge of God, seeing what paines the Spanyards take to bring them to their adulterated faith. Honor might move the Gentrie, the valiant, and industrious; and the hope and assurance of wealth, all; if wee were that we would seeme, and be accounted. Or be we so far inferior to other nations, or our spirits so far dejected, from our auncient predecessors, or our mindes so upon spoile, piracie, and such villany, as to serve the Portugall, Spanyard, Dutch, French, or Turke (as to the cost of Europe, too many dooe) rather then our God, our King, our Country, and our selves? excusing our idlenesse, and our base complaints, by want of imploiment; when heere is such choise of all sorts, and for all degrees, in the planting and discovering these North parts of America.

My second voyage to New England.   Now to make my words more apparent by my deeds; I was, the last yeare, 1615. to have staied in the

Countrie, to make a more ample triall of those conclusions with
sixteene men; whose names were

Thomas Dirmir.		Thomas Digbie.	
Edward Stalings.		Daniel Baker.	
Daniel Cage.	*Gentlemen.*	Adam Smith.	*Sailers.*
Francis Abbot.		Thomas Watson.	
John Gosling.		Walter Chissick.	
William Ingram.		John Hall.	
Robert Miter.			
David Cooper.	*Souldiers.*		
John Partridge,			
and two boies.			

I confesse, I could have wished them as many thousands, had
all other provisions bin in like proportion: nor would I have
had so fewe, could I have had meanes for more: yet (would
God have pleased wee had safely arrived) I never had the like
authoritie, freedom, and provision, to doe so well. The maine
assistance next God, I had to this small number, was my acquaintance among the Salvages; especially, with Dohannida,
one of their greatest Lords; who had lived long in England. By
the meanes of this proud Salvage, I did not doubt but quickly
to have gotte that credit with the rest of his friends, and alliants, to have had as many of them, as I desired in any designe
I intended, and that trade also they had, by such a kind of exchange of their Countrie commodities; which both with ease
and securitie in their seasons may be used. With him and diverse others, I had concluded to inhabit, and defend them
against the Terentynes; with a better power then the French
did them; whose tyranny did inforce them to imbrace my offer, with no small devotion. And though many may thinke me
more bolde then wise, in regard of their power, dexteritie,
treacherie, and inconstancie, having so desperately assaulted
and betraied many others: I say but this (because with so many,
I have many times done much more in Virginia, then I intended
heere, when I wanted that experience Virginia taught me) that
to mee it seemes no daunger more then ordinarie. And though
I know my selfe the meanest of many thousands, whose apprehensive inspection can pearce beyond the boundes of my ha-
bilities, into the hidden things of Nature, Art, and Reason: yet

I intreate such give me leave to excuse my selfe of so much im-becillitie, as to say, that in these eight yeares which I have been conversant with these affaires, I have not learned there is a great difference, betwixt the directions and judgement of experi-mentall knowledge, and the superficiall conjecture of variable relation: wherein rumor, humor, or misprision have such power, that oft times one is enough to beguile twentie, but twentie not sufficient to keep one from being deceived. There-fore I know no reason but to beleeve my own eies, before any mans imagination, that is but wrested from the conceits of my owne projects, and indeavours. But I honor, with all affection, the counsell and instructions of judiciall directions, or any other honest advertisement; so farre to observe, as they tie mee not to the crueltie of unknowne events.

These are the inducements that thus drew me to neglect all other imployments, and spend my time and best abilities in these adventures. Wherein, though I have had many discour-agements by the ingratitude of some, the malicious slanders of others, the falsenesse of friendes, the trechery of cowards, and slownesse of adventurers; but chiefly by one Hunt, who was Master of the ship, with whom oft arguing these projects, for a plantation, however hee seemed well in words to like it, yet he practiced to have robbed mee of my plots, and observations, and so to leave me alone in a desolate Ile, to the fury of famine, and all other extreamities (lest I should have acquainted Sir Thomas Smith, my Honourable good friend, and the Councell of Virginia) to the end, he and his associates, might secretly in-grosse it, ere it were knowne to the State: Yet that God that al-way hath kept me from the worst of such practices, delivered me from the worst of his dissimulations. Notwithstanding after my departure, hee abused the Salvages where hee came, and betrayed twenty seaven of these poore innocent soules, which he sould in Spaine for slaves, to moove their hate against our Nation, as well as to cause my proceedings to be so much the more difficult.

Now, returning in the Bark, in the fift of August, I arrived at Plimouth: where imparting those my purposes to my honourable friende Sir Ferdinando Gorge, and some others; I was so incouraged, and assured to have the managing their au-thoritie in those parts, during my life, that I ingaged my selfe to undertake it for them. Arriving at London, I found also many promise me such assistance, that I entertained Michaell Cooper the Master, who returned with mee, and others of the company. How hee dealt with others, or others with him I know not: But my publike proceeding gave such incouragement, that it became so well apprehended by some fewe of the Southren Company, as these projects were liked, and he furnished from London with foure ships at Sea, before they at Plimouth had made any provision at all, but onely a ship cheefely set out by sir Ferdinando Gorge; which upon Hunts late trecherie among the Salvages, returned as shee went, and did little or nothing, but lost her time. I must confesse I was beholden to the setters forth of the foure ships that went with Cooper; in that they offered mee that imploiment if I would accept it: and I finde, my refusall hath incurred some of their displeasures, whose favor and love I exceedingly desire, if I may honestly injoy it. And though they doe censure me as opposite to their proceedings; they shall yet still in all my words and deedes finde, it is their error, not my fault, that occasions their dislike: for having ingaged my selfe in this husinesse to the West Countrie; I had beene verie dishonest to have broke my promise; nor will I spend more time in discoverie, or fishing, till I may goe with a companie for plantation: for, I know my grounds. Yet every one that reades this booke can not put it in practice; though it may helpe any that have seene those parts. And though they endeavour to worke me even out of my owne designes, I will not much envy their fortunes: but, I would bee sory, their intruding ignorance should, by their defailements, bring those certainties to douhtfulnesse: So that the businesse prosper, I have my desire; be it by Londoner, Scot, Welch, or English, that are true subjects to our King and Countrey: the good of my Countrey is that I seeke; and there is more then enough for all, if they could bee content but to proceed.

The occasion of my returne.   At last it pleased Sir Ferdinando Gorge, and Master Doctor Sutliffe, Deane of Exceter, to conceive so well of these projects, and my former imploiments, as induced them to make a new adventure with me in those parts, whither they have so often sent to their continuall losse. By whose example, many inhabitants of the west Country, made promises of much more then was looked for, but their private emulations quickly qualified that heat in the greater number; so that the burden lay principally on them, and some few Gentlemen my friends, in London. In the end I was furnished with a Ship of 200. and another of 50. But ere I had sayled 120 leagues, shee broke all her masts; pumping each watch 5 or 6000 strokes: onely her spret saile remayned to spoon before the wind, till we had re-accommodated a Jury mast, and the rest, to returne for Plimouth. My Vice-admirall beeing lost, not knowing of this, proceeded her voyage: Now with the remainder of those provisions, I got out again in a small Barke of 60 tuns with 30 men (for this of 200 and provision for 70) which were the 16 before named, and 14 other saylors for the ship. With those I set saile againe the 24 of June: where what befell me (because my actions and writings are so publicke to the world, envy still seeking to scandalize my indeavours, and seeing no power but death, can stop the chat of ill tongues, nor imagination of mens mindes) lest my owne relations of those hard events, might by some constructors, be made doubtfull, I have thought it best to insert the examinations of those proceedings, taken by Sir Lewis Stukley a worthie Knight, and Viceadmirall of Devonshire; which were as followeth.

My reimbarkment, incounters with pyrats and imprisonment by the French.

Captaine Fry his ship 140 tuns, 36 cast peeces and murderers, 80 men; of which 40, or 50. were master gunners.

The examination of Daniel Baker, late Steward to Captaine John Smith in the returne of Plimouth; taken before Sir Lewis Stukley, Knight, the eight of December 1615.

Who saith, being chased two dayes by one Fry, an English Pirate, that could not board us, by reason of foule weather, Edmund Chambers, the Master, John Minter, his mate, Thomas Digby the Pilot, and others importuned his saide Captaine to yeeld; houlding it umpossible hee should defend himselfe: and that the saide Captaine should send them his boate, in that they had none: which at last he concluded upon these conditions, That Fry the Pyrate should vow not to take any thing from Captaine Smith, that might overthrowe his voyage, nor send more Pirats into his ship then hee liked off; otherwaies, he would make sure of them he had, and defend himselfe against the rest as hee could.

More: he confesseth that the quarter-masters and Chambers received golde of those Pirats; but how much, he knoweth not: Nor would his Captain come out of his Caben to entertaine them; although a great many of them had beene his saylers, and for his love would have wafted us to the Iles of Flowers.

At Fyall, wee were chased by two French Pyrats, who commanded us Amaine. Chambers, Minter, Digby, and others, importuned againe the Captaine to yeeld; alledging they were Turks, and would make them all slaves: or Frenchmen, and would throw them all over board if they shot but a peece; and that they were entertained to fish, and not to fight: untill the Captaine vowed to fire the powder and split the ship, if they would not stand to their defence; whereby at last wee went cleere of them, for all their shot.

The one of 200, the other 20.

The Admirall 140 tuns, 12 peeces, 12 murderers, 90 men, with long pistols, pocket pistols, musket, sword and poniard, the Vice-admirall 100 tuns, the Rere-admiral 60, the other 80: all had 250 men most armed as is said.

At Flowers, wee were chased by foure French men of warre; all with their close fights afore and after. And this examinants Captaine having provided for our defence, Chambers, Minter, Digby, and some others, againe importuned him to yeeld to the favour of those, against whom there was nothing but ruine by fighting: But if he would goe aboard them, in that hee could speake French, by curtesie hee might goe cleere; seeing they offered him such faire quarter, and vowed they were Protestants, and all of Rochell, and had the Kings commission onely to take Spaniards, Portugales, and Pyrats; which at last hee did: but they kept this examinates Captaine and some other of his company with him. The next day the French men of warre went aboard us, and tooke what they listed, and divided the company into their severall ships, and manned this examinates ship with the Frenchmen; and chased with her all the shippes they saw: untill about five or six dayes after upon better consideration, they surrendered the ship, and victualls, with the most part of our provision, but not our weapons.

More: he confesseth that his Captain exhorted them to performe their voyage, or goe for New found Land to returne fraughted with fish, where hee would finde meanes to proceed in his plantation: but Chambers and Minter grew upon tearms they would not; untill

The gentlemen and souldiers were ever willing to fight.

those that were Souldiers concluded with their Captaines resolution, they would; seeing they had clothes, victualls, salt, nets,
and lines sufficient, and expected their armes: and such other
things as they wanted, the French men promised to restore,
which the Captaine the next day went to seeke, and sent them
about loading of commodities, as powder, match, hookes, instruments, his sword and dagger, bedding, aqua vitæ, his commission, apparell, and many other things; the particulars he
remembreth not: But, as for the cloath, canvas, and the Captaines cloathes, Chambers, and his associats divided it amongst
themselves, and to whom they best liked; his Captaine not
having any thing, to his knowledge, but his wastecoat and
breeches. And in this manner going from ship to ship, to regaine our armes, and the rest; they seeing a sayle, gave chase
untill night. The next day being very foule weather, this examinate came so neere with the ship unto the French men of
warre, that they split the maine sayle on the others spret sayle
yard. Chambers willed the Captaine come aboard, or hee
would leave him: whereupon the Captaine commanded
Chambers to send his boate for him. Chambers replyed shee
was split (which was false) telling him hee might come if he
would in the Admiralls boat. The Captaines answer was, he
could not command her, nor come when hee would: so this
examinate fell on sterne; and that night left his said Captaine
alone amongst the French men, in this manner, by the command of Chambers, Minter, and others.

Daniel Cage, Edward Stalings, Gentlemen; Walter Chissell,
David Cooper, Robert Miller, and John Partridge,
beeing examined, doe acknowledge and confesse,
that Daniel Baker his examination above
writen is true.

Now the cause why the French detayned me
againe, was the suspicion this Chambers and Minter
gave them, that I would revenge my selfe, upon the
Bank, or in New found Land, of all the French I could there incounter; and how I would have fired the ship, had they not over-
perswaded mee: and many other such like tricks to catch but
opportunitie in this maner to leave me. And thus they returned
to Plimouth; and perforce with the French I thus proceeded.

A double
treachery.

Being a Fleet of eight or nine sayle, we watched for the West Indies fleet, till ill weather separated us from the other 8. Still

A fleet of nine French men of war, and fights with the Spaniards.

we spent our time about the Iles neere Fyall: where to keepe my perplexed thoughts from too much meditation of my miserable estate, I writ this discourse; thinking to have sent it you of his Majesties Councell, by some ship or other: for I saw their purpose was to take all they could. At last we were chased by one Captain Barra, an English Pyrat, in a small ship, with some twelve peeces of ordinance, about thirty men, and neer all starved. They sought by curtesie releefe of us; who gave them such faire promises, as at last wee betrayed Captaine Wolliston (his Lieftenant) and foure or five of their men aboard us, and then provided to take the rest perforce. Now my part was to be prisoner in the gunroum, and not to speake to any of them upon my life: yet had Barra knowledge what I was. Then Barra perceiving wel these French intents, made ready to fight, and Wolliston as resolutely regarded not their threats, which caused us demurre upon the matter longer, som sixteene houres; and then returned their prisoners, and some victualls also, upon a small composition. The next wee tooke was a small English man of Poole from New found Land. The great caben at this present, was my prison; from whence I could see them pillage those poore men of all that they had, and halfe their fish. When hee was gone, they sould his poore cloathes at the maine mast, by an outcry, which scarce gave each man seaven pence a peece. Not long after, wee tooke a Scot fraught from Saint Michaels to Bristow: hee had better fortune then the other. For, having but taken a boats loading of suger, marmelade, suckets, and such like, we discried foure sayle, after whom we stood; who forling their maine sayles attended us to fight. But our French spirits were content onely to perceive they were English red crosses. Within a very small time after, wee chased foure Spanish shippes came from the Indies: wee fought with them foure or five houres,

A prize worth 1600 crowns.

tore their sayles and sides; yet not daring to board them, lost them. A poore Carvell of Brasile, was the next we chased: and after a small fight, thirteene or

A prize worth 200000 crownes.

fourteene of her men being wounded, which was the better halfe, we tooke her, with 370 chests of sugar. The next was a West Indies man, of 160 tuns, with

1200 hides, 50 chests of cutchanell, 14 coffers of wedges of silver, 8000 ryalls of 8, and six coffers of the King of Spaines treasure, besides the pillage and rich coffers of many rich passengers. Two monethes they kept me in this manner to manage their fights against the Spaniards, and be a prisoner when they tooke any English. Now though the Captaine had oft broke his promise, which was to put me a-shore on the Iles, or the next ship he tooke; yet at last, he was intreated I should goe for France in the Carvell of sugar: himself resolved still to keepe the Seas. Within two dayes after, we were haled by two West Indy men: but when they saw us wave them for the King of France, they gave us their broad sides, shot through our mayne mast and so left us. Having lived thus, neer three moneths among those French men of warre; with much adoe, we arrived at the Gulion, not far from Rochel; where in stead of the great promises they alwaies fed me with, of double satisfaction, and full content, they kept me five or six daies prisoner in the Carvell, accusing me to bee him that burnt their Colony in New France; to force mee give them a discharge before the Judge of the Admiralty, and so stand to their curtesie for satisfaction, or lie in prison, or a worse mischiefe. To prevent this choise, in the end of such a storme that beat them all under

My escape from the French men.
Hatches, I watched my opportunity to get a-shore in their boat; where-into, in the darke night, I secretly got: and with a halfe pike that lay by me, put a drift for Rat Ile: but the Current was so strong and the Sea so great, I went a drift to Sea; till it pleased God the winde so turned with the tide, that although I was all this fearefull night of gusts and raine, in the Sea, the space of 12 houres, when many ships were driven a shore, and diverse split (and being with sculling and bayling the water tired, I expected each minute would sinke mee) at last I arrived in an oazie Ile by Charowne; where certaine fowlers found mee neere drowned, and halfe dead, with water, colde, and hunger. By those, I found meanes to gette to Rochell; where I understood the man of warre which we left at Sea, and the rich prize was split, the Captaine drowned and halfe his companie the same night, within seaven leagues of that place, from whence I escaped alone, in the little boate, by the mercy of God; far beyond all mens reason, or my expectation. Arriving at Rochell, upon my complaint to the

Judge of the Admiraltie, I founde many good words, and faire
promises; and ere long many of them that escaped drowning,
tolde mee the newes they heard of my owne death: these I arresting, their severall examinations did so confirme my complaint, it was held proofe sufficient. All which being performed
according to the order of justice, from under the judges hand;
I presented it to the English Ambassador then at Burdeaux,
where it was my chance to see the arrivall of the Kings great
mariage brought from Spaine. Of the wrack of the
rich prize some 36000 crownes worth of goods came
a shore and was saved with the Carvell, which I did
my best to arrest: the Judge did promise me I shold have justice; what will bee the conclusion as yet, I know not. But
under the colour to take Pirats and West-Indie men
(because the Spanyards will not suffer the French
trade in the West-Indies) any goods from thence,
thogh they take them upon the Coast of Spaine, are
lawfull prize; or from any of his territories out of the
limits of Europe.

Leaving thus my businesse in France, I returned
to Plimouth, to find them that had thus buried me
amongst the French: and not onely buried mee, but
with so much infamy, as such trecherous cowards
could suggest to excuse their villanies: But my clothes, bookes,
instruments, Armes, and what I had, they shared amongst
them, and what they liked; fayning, the French had all was
wanting; and had throwne them into the Sea, taken their ship,
and all, had they not runne away and left me as they did. The
cheeftaines of this mutinie that I could finde, I laied by the
heeles; the rest, like themselves, confessed the truth as you
have heard. Now how I have or could prevent these accidents,
I rest at your censures. But to the matter.

Newfound-land at the first, I have heard, was held as desperate a fishing, as this I project in New England. Placentia, and
the Banke, were also as doubtfull to the French: But,
for all the disasters happened mee, the businesse is
the same it was: and the five ships (whereof one was
reported more then three hundred tunnes) went forward; and found fish so much, that neither Izeland-
man, nor Newfound-land-man, I could heare of hath

Marginal notes:

Sir Thomas Edmunds

They betraied mee having the broad seale of England: and neere twentie sayle of English more, besides them concealed, in like maner were betrayed that year. My returne for England, 1615.

The successe of my vice Admirall and the foure ships of London, from New England.

beene there, will goe any more to either place, if they may goe thither. So, that upon the returne of my Viceadmirall that proceeded on her voyage when I spent my masts, from Plimouth this yeare are gone foure or five saile: and from London as many; onely to make voyages of profit: where the Englishmen have yet beene, all their returnes together (except Sir Francis Popphames) would scarce make one a saver of neere a douzen I could nominate; though there be fish sufficient, as I perswade my selfe, to fraught yearely foure or five hundred sayle, or as many as will goe. For, this fishing stretcheth along the Coast from Cape Cod to Newfound-land, which is seaven or eight hundered miles at the least; and hath his course in the deepes, and by the shore, all the yeare long; keeping their hants and feedings as the beasts of the field, and the birds of the aire. But, all men are not such as they should bee, that have undertaken those voiages: and a man that hath but heard of an instrument, can hardly use it so well, as hee that by use hath contrived to make it. All the Romanes were not Scipioes: nor all the Geneweses, Columbuses: nor all Spanyards, Corteses: had they dived no deeper in the secrets of their discoveries, then wee, or stopped at such doubts and poore accidentall chances; they had never beene remembred as they are: yet had they no such certainties to begin as wee. But, to conclude, Adam and Eve did first beginne this innocent worke, To plant the earth to remaine to posteritie; but not without labour, trouble and industrie. Noe, and his family, beganne againe the second plantation; and their seede as it still increased, hath still planted new Countries, and one countrie another: and so the world to that estate it is. But not without much hazard, travell, discontents, and many disasters. Had those worthie Fathers and their memorable off-spring not beene more diligent for us now in these Ages, then wee are to plant that yet unplanted, for the after livers: Had the seede of Abraham, our Saviour Christ, and his Apostles, exposed themselves to no more daungers to teach the Gospell, and the will of God then wee; Even wee our selves, had at this present been as Salvage, and as miserable as the most barbarous Salvage yet uncivilized. The Hebrewes, and Lacedæmonians, the Goths, the Grecians, the Romanes, and the rest, what was it they would not undertake to inlarge their Territories, enrich their subjects, resist their en-

emies? Those that were the founders of those great Monarchies and their vertues, were no silvered idle golden Pharises,
but industrious iron-steeled Publicans: They regarded more
provisions, and necessaries for their people, then jewels, riches,
ease, or delight for themselves. Riches were their servants, not
their Maisters. They ruled (as Fathers, not as Tyrantes) their
people as children, not as slaves: there was no disaster, could
discourage them; and let none thinke they incountered not
with all manner of incumbrances. And what have ever beene
the workes of the greatest Princes of the earth, but planting of
countries, and civilizing barbarous and inhumane Nations, to
civilitie and humanitie? whose eternall actions, fill our histories. Lastly, the Portugales, and Spanyards: whose everliving
actions, before our eyes will testifie with them our idlenesse,
and ingratitude to all posterities, and the neglect of our duties
in our pietie and religion we owe our God, our King, and
Countrie; and want of charity to those poore salvages, whose
Countrie wee challenge, use and possesse; except wee bee but
made to use, and marre what our Fore-fathers made, or but
onely tell what they did, or esteeme our selves too good to
take the like paines. Was it vertue in them, to provide that
doth maintaine us? and basenesse for us to doe the like for
others? Surely no. Then seeing we are not borne for our selves,
but each to helpe other, and our abilities are much alike at the
houre of our birth, and the minute of our death: Seeing our
good deedes, or our badde, by faith in Christs merits, is all we
have to carrie our soules to heaven, or hell: Seeing honour is
our lives ambition; and our ambition after death, to have an
honourable memorie of our life: and seeing by noe meanes
wee would bee abated of the dignities and glories of our Predecessors; let us imitate their vertues to bee worthily their
successors.

FINIS.

To his worthy Captaine,
the Author.

Oft thou hast led, when I brought up the Rere
In bloodie wars, where thousands have bin slaine.
   Then give mee leave, in this some part to beare;
And as thy servant, heere to read my name.
   Tis true, long time thou host my Captaine beene
In the fierce wars of Transilvania:
   Long ere that thou America *hadst seene,*
Or led wast captived in Virginia;
   Thou that to passe the worlds foure parts dost deeme
No more, then t'were to goe to bed, or drinke,
   And all thou yet hast done, thou dost esteeme
As nothing. This doth cause mee thinke
   That thou I'ave seene so oft approv'd in dangers
(And thrice captiv'd, thy valor still hath freed)
   Art yet preserved, to convert those strangers:
By God thy guide, I trust it is decreed.
   For mee: I not commend, but much admire
   Thy England yet unknowne to passers by-her.
   For it will praise it selfe in spight of me;
   Thou it, it thou, to all posteritie.

         Your true friend, and souldier,
                  Ed. Robinson.

172

To my honest Captaine,
the Author.

Malignant Times! What can be said or don,
But shall be censur'd and traduc't by some!
    This worthy Work, which thou hast bought so dear,
    Ne thou, nor it, Detractors neede to fear.
Thy words by deedes so long thou hast approv'd,
Of thousands knowe thee not thou art belov'd.
    And this great Plot will make thee ten times more
    Knowne and belov'd, than ere thou wert before.
I never knew a Warryer yet, but thee,
From wine, Tobacco, debts, dice, oaths, so free.
    I call thee Warrier: *and I make the bolder;*
    For, many a Captaine *now, was never Souldier*
Some such may swell at this: but (to their praise)
When they have don like thee, my Muse shall raise
    Their due deserts to Worthies yet to come,
    To live like thine (admir'd) till day of Doome.
        Your true friend, somtimes your soldier,
            Tho. Carlton.

NEW ENGLANDS TRIALS

Declaring the successe of 80 Ships
employed thither within these eight yeares;
and the benefit of that Countrey by
Sea and Land.

With the present estate of that happie
Plantation, begun but by 60 weake
men in the yeare 1620.

And how to build a Fleete of good Shippes
to make a little Navie Royall.

Written by Captaine John Smith, sometimes
Governour of Virginia, and
Admirall of New England.

The second Editon.

1622

TO THE MOST HIGH
And Excellent Prince Charles, Prince of Wales;
Duke of Cornewall, Yorke, and Albanie;
Marquis of Ormond, and Rothsey;
and Earle Palatine of Chester;
Heire of Great Britaine, France,
and Ireland, etc.

Sir,
  When scarce any would beleeve mee there was any such matter, your Highnesse did not disdaine to accept my description, and calld that New England, whose barbarous names you changed for such English, that none can denie but Prince Charles is the Godfather. Whereby I am bound in all reason and dutie to give you the best account I can how your child doth prosper: and although as yet it is not much unlike the Father in fortune, onely used as an instrument for other mens ends; yet the grace you bestowed on it by your Princely favour, hath drawn so many judgments now to behold it, that I hope shall find, it will give content to your Highnesse, satisfaction to them, and so increase the number of well-willers, New England will be able to reject her maligners, and attend Prince Charles with her dutifull obedience, with a trophie of honour, and a kingdome for a Prince. Therefore the great worke contained in this little booke, humbly desires your Princely patronage. No more but sacring all my best abilities to the exquisite judgement of your renowned vertues, I humbly kisse your gracious hands.
              Your Highnesse true and faithfull servant,
                          Jo. Smith.

TO THE RIGHT HONORABLE
And Right Worthy Adventurers,
to all Plantations and Discoveries,
their friends and well-willers,
especially of Virginia and New England.

Right Honorable,

I confesse it were more proper for me to be doing what I say, then writing what I know: but that it is not my fault, there is many a hundreth can testifie, if they please to remember what paines I have taken both particularly and generally to make this worke knowne, and procure meanes to put it in practise. What calumniations, doubts, or other mispritions hath opposed my endevours, I had rather forget then remember, but still to expresse my forwardnesse, to the consideration of your favourable constructions I present this short discourse of the proceedings and present estate of New England: if you please to peruse it, and make use of it, I am richly rewarded, though they be but the collections and observations of a plaine souldier, yet if you please to grace them with your countenance and good acceptance, I shall therein thinke my selfe happie, and hope that those labours may in time returne you such fruites as hereafter may perswade you to pardon this boldnesse, and accept them to be your honest servants.

Yours to command,
Jo. Smith.

NEW ENGLANDS TRIALS,
and Present Estate.

CONCERNING the description of this Countrey, six yeares ago I writ so largely, as in briefe I hope this may suffice you to remember, that New England is a part of America, betwixt the Degrees of 41. and 45. the very meane betwixt the North Pole and the Line. From 43. to 45. the coast is mountainous, rockie, barren and broken Iles that make many good harbours. The water is deepe, close to the shore; there are many rivers and fresh springs: few Salvages, but an incredible abundance of fish, fowle, wilde fruits, and good timber. From 43. to 41. and a half, an excellent mixed coast of stone, sand and clay, much corne, many people, some Iles, many good harbours, a temperate aire, and therein all things necessary for the building ships of any proportion, and good merchandize for their fraught, within a square of 12 leagues: 25 harbours I sounded; 30 severall Lordships I saw, and so neare as I could imagine, 3000 men. I was up one river fortie miles, crossed the mouths of many, whose heads are reported to be great lakes; where they kill their Bevers; inhabited with many people, who trade with those of New England, and them of Cannada.

The benefit of fishing, as Master Dee reporteth
in his Brittish Monarchie

He saith that it is more then 44 yeares ago, and it is more then 40 yeares since he writ it, that the Herring Busses out of the Low-countries, under the King of Spaine, were 500. besides 100 Frenchmen, and three or foure hundred saile of Flemmings.

The coasts of Wales and Lancashire was used by 300 saile of strangers.

Ireland at Baltemore fraughted yearely 300 saile of Spaniards, where King Edward the sixt intended to have made a strong Castle, because of the strait, to have tribute for fishing.

Blacke Rocke was yearely fished by three or foure hundred saile of Spaniards, Portugals and Biskiners.

Master Gentleman and many Fisher-men and
Fish-mongers with whom I have conferred, report,

The Hollanders raise yearely by Herring, Cod, and Ling,
3000000 pounds.

English and French by Salt-fish, poore John, Salmons and
Pilchards, 300000 pounds.

Hambrough and the Sound, for Sturgion, Lobsters and Eeles,
100000 pounds.

Cape Blanke for Tunny and Mullit, by the Biskiners and
Spaniards 30000 pounds.

But divers other learned experienced Observers
say, though it may seeme incredible,

That the Duke of Medina receiveth yearely tribute of the
fishers for Tunny, Mullit and Purgos, more then 10000 pounds.

Lubeck hath 700 ships: Hambrough 600: Embden lately a
fisher towne, 1400. whose customes by the profit of fishing
hath made them so powerfull as they be.

Holland and Zeland, not much greater then Yorkshire, hath
thirtie walled townes, 400 villages, and 20000 saile of shippes
and hoyes; 3600 are fishermen, whereof 100 are Doggers, 700
Pinckes and Welbotes, 700 Frand botes, Britters and Tode-
botes, with 1300 Busses, besides three hundred that yearely
fish about Yarmouth, where they sell their fish for gold; and fifteene yeares ago they had more then 116000 sea-faring men.

These fishing ships do take yearely 200000 Last of fish,
twelve barrels to a Last, which amounted to 3000000 pounds
by the Fishermens price, that 14 yeares ago did pay for their
tenths 300000 pound; which venting in Pumerland, Sprussia,
Denmarke, Lefland, Russia, Swethland, Germany, Netherlands,
England, or elsewhere, etc. make their returnes in a yeare about
7000000 pounds; and yet in Holland they have neither matter
to build ships, nor merchandize to set them foorth; yet by
their industrie they as much increase, as other Nations decay.
But leaving these uncertainties as they are, of this I am certaine, That the coast of England, Scotland, and Ireland, the
North Sea, with Ireland and the Sound, New-found land and
Cape Blanke, do serve all Europe, as well the land Townes as
Ports, and all the Christian shipping, with these sorts of Staple

fish which is transported, from whence it is taken, many a thousand mile, viz.

Herring.	Tunny.
Salt-fish.	Porgos.
poore John.	Caviare.
Sturgion.	Buttargo.
Mullit.	

Now seeing all these sorts of fish, or the most part of them, may be had in a land more fertile, temperate, and plentifull of all necessaries for the building of ships, boates and houses, and the nourishment of man; the seasons are so proper, and the fishings so neare the habitations we may there make, that New England hath much advantage of the most of those parts, to serve all Europe farre cheaper then they can, who at home have neither wood, salt, nor food, but at great rates; at Sea nothing but what they carry in their ships, an hundred or two hundred leagues from their habitation.

But New Englands fishings is neare land, where is helpe of wood, water, fruites, fowles, corne, or other refreshings need-full; and the Terceras, Mederas, Canaries, Spaine, Portugale, Provance, Savoy, Sicilia, and all Italy, as convenient markets for our dry Fish, greene Fish, Sturgion, Mullit, Caviare, and But-targo, as Norway, Swethland, Littuania or Germany, for their Herring, which is here also in abundance for taking; they re-turning but wood, pitch, tarre, soape-ashes, cordage, flaxe, waxe, and such like commodities: we, wines, oyles, sugars, silks, and such merchandize as the Straits affoord, whereby our profit may equalize theirs; besides the increase of shipping and Mariners. And for proofe hereof:

Proofe 1.
1614. With two ships sent out at the charge of Captain Marmaduke Roydon, Captain George Langam, Master John Buley and W. Skelton, I went from the Downes the third of March, and arived in New England the last of April, where I was to have stayed but with ten men to keep possession of those large territories, had the Whales proved, as curious information had assured me and my adven-turers, (but those things failed.) So having but fortie five men and boyes, we built seven boates, 37 did fish; my selfe with

eight others ranging the coast, I tooke a plot of what I could
see, got acquaintance of the inhabitants; 11000 Bever skins, 100
Martins, and as many Otters. 40000 of drie fish we sent for
Spaine; with the salt fish, traine oile and Furres, I returned for
England the 18 of July, and arived safe with my company the
latter end of August. Thus in six moneths I made my voyage
out and home; and by the labour of 45, got neare the value of
1500 pounds in those grosse commodities. This yeare also one
went from Plimmoth, set out by divers of the Isle of Wight
and the West country, by the directions and instructions of Sir
Ferdinando Gorge, spent their victuals, and returned with
nothing.

The Virginia Company upon this sent 4 good
ships; and because I would not undertake it for them,
having ingaged my selfe to them of the West, the
Londoners entertained the men that came home with me. They
set saile in January, and arived there in March; they found fish
enough untill halfe June, fraughted a ship of 300 Tuns, went
for Spaine, which was taken by the Turks; one went to Virginia
to relieve that Colonie, and two came for England with the
greene fish, traine oile and Furres within six moneths.

Proofe 2.
1615.

In January with 200 pounds in cash for adventure,
and six Gentlemen wel furnished, I went from London to the foure ships was promised, prepared for
me in the West country, but I found no such matter; notwithstanding at the last with a labyrinth of trouble I went from
Plimmoth with a ship of 200 Tuns, and one of fiftie: when the
fishing was done onely with 15 I was to stay in the country; but
ill weather breaking all my masts, I was forced to returne to
Plimmoth, where rather then lose all, reimbarking my selfe in a
Bark of 60 Tuns, how I escaped the English pyrates and the
French, and was betrayed by foure French men of warre, I referre you to the Description of New England: but my Vice-
Admirall, notwithstanding the latenesse of the yeare, setting
forth with me in March, the Londoners in January, she arived
in May, they in March, yet came home well fraught in August,
and all her men well, within 5 months, odde days.

Proofe 3.
1615.

The Londoners ere I returned from France, for all
their losse by the Turks, which was valued about
4000 pounds, sent two more in July; but such courses

Proofe 4.
1616.

they took by the Canaries to the West Indies, it was ten moneths ere they arived in New England, wasting in that time their seasons, victuall and healths, yet there they found meanes to refresh themselves, and the one returned, neare fraught with fish and traine, within 2 moneths after.

Proofe 5.
1616.

From Plimmoth went 4 ships, onely to fish and trade, some in Februarie, some in March, one of 200 Tuns got thither in a month, and went full fraught for Spain, the rest returned to Plimmoth well fraught, and their men well, within five moneths, odde dayes.

Proofe 6.
1616.

From London went two more, one of 200 Tuns, got thither in six weeks, and within six weeks after with 44 men and boyes was full fraught, and returned again into England within five moneths and a few daies; the other went to the Canaries with drie fish, which they sold at a great rate, for Rials of 8, and as I heard turned pirats.

Proofe 7.
1617.

I being at Plimmoth provided with 3 good ships, yet but fifteen men to stay with me in the country, was Wind-bound three moneths, as was many a hundred saile more, so that the season being past, the ships went for New-found-land, whereby my designe was frustrate, which was to me and my friends no small losse, in regard whereof here the Westerne Commissioners in the behalfe of themselves and the rest of the Companie, contracted with me by articles indented under our hands, to be Admirall of that Country during my life, and in the renewing of their Letters patents so to be nominated, halfe the fruits of our endevours theirs, the rest our owne; being thus ingaged, now the businesse doth prosper, some of them would willingly forget me; but I am not the first they have deceived.

Proofe 8.
1618.

There was foure good ships prepared at Plimmoth, but by reason of their disagreement, the season so wasted, as onely 2 went forward, the one being of 200 Tuns, returned well fraught for Plimmoth, and her men in health, within five moneths; the other of 80 Tuns, went for Bilbow with drie fish, and made a good returne. In this voyage Edward Rowcroft, alias Stallings, a valiant souldier, that had bin with me in Virginia, and seven yeares after went with me from Plimoth towards New England with Thomas Dirmer an understanding and an industrious Gentleman to inhabite it; all whose names with our proceedings you may reade at large in my description of New England, upon triall before the Judge of the Admiraltie, how when we had past the worst, for pure cowardize the Maister and sailers ran away with the ship and all I had, and left me alone among 8 or 9 French men of Warre in the yeare 1615. This Stallings went now againe in those ships, and having some wrong offered him in New England by a French man, he tooke him, and as he writ to me, he went with her to Virginia with fish, to trade with them for such commodities as they might spare; he knew both these countries well, yet he promised me the next Spring to meet me in New England; but the ship and he perished in Virginia.

This yeare againe, divers ships intending to go from Plimmoth, so disagreed, as there went but one of 200 Tuns, who stayed in the country about 6 weeks, with 38 men and boyes, had her fraught, which she sold at the first penie, for 2100 pounds, besides the Furres: so that every poore sailer that had but a single share, had his charges, and 16.l. 10.s. for his seven moneths worke. Master Thomas Dirmer having lived about a yeare in New-found-land, returning to Plimmoth, went for New England in this ship, and not only confirmes what I have writ, but so much more approved of it, that he stayed there with five or six men in a little boate; finding 2 or 3 Frenchmen among the savages, who had lost their ship, augmented his companie, with whom he ranged the coast to Virginia, where he was kindly welcomed and well refreshed; thence returned to New England again, where having bin a yeare, in his back-returne to Virginia, he was so wounded by the savages, he died upon it, them escaped were relieved at Virginia. Let not men attribute their great adventures and untimely deaths to unfortunatenesse, but rather wonder how God did so long preserve them, with so small meanes to do so much, leaving the fruits of their labours to be an encouragement to those our poore undertakings; and this for advantage as they writ unto me, that God had laid this Country open for us, and slaine the most part of the inhabitants by cruell warres and a mortall disease; for where I had seene 100 or 200 people, there is scarce ten to be found. From Pembrocks bays to Harrintons bay there is not 20; from thence to Cape An, some 30; from Taulbuts bay to the River Charles, about 40, and not any

Proofe 9.
1619.

of them touched with any sicknes, but one poore Frenchman that died.

Proofe 10.
1620.
For to make triall this yeare there is gone 6 or 7 saile from the West country, onely to fish, three of whom are returned, and as I was certainly informed, made so good a voyage, that every sailer for a single share had 20 pounds for his 7 moneths work, which is more then in 20 moneths he should have gotten had he gone for wages any where. Now though all the former ships have not made such good voyages as they expected, by sending opinionated unskilfull men, that had not experienced diligence to save that they tooke, nor take that there was; which now patience and practise hath brought to a reasonable kind of perfection: in despite of all detractors and calumniations, the Country yet hath satisfied all, the defect hath bin in their using or abusing it, not in it selfe nor me.

A plantation in New England.

Proofe 11.
1620.
Upon these inducements some few well disposed Gentlemen and Merchants of London and other places provided two ships, the one of 160 Tunnes, the other of 70; they left the coast of England the 23 of August, with about 120 persons, but the next day the lesser ship sprung a leake, that forced their returne to Plimmoth, where discharging her and 20 passengers, with the great ship and a hundred persons besides sailers, they set saile againe the sixt of September, and the ninth of November fell with Cape James; but being pestred nine weeks in this leaking unwholsome ship, lying wet in their cabbins, most of them grew very weake, and weary of the sea, then for want of experience ranging to and again, six weeks before they found a place they liked to dwell on, forced to lie on the bare ground without coverture in the extremitie of Winter, fortie of them died, and 60 were left in very weake estate at the ships coming away, about the fift of April following, and arived in England the sixt of May.

Proofe 12.
1620.
Immediatly after her arivall, from London they sent another of 55 Tunnes to supply them, with 37 persons, they set saile in the beginning of July, but being crossed by Westerly winds, it was the end of August ere they could passe Plimmoth, and arived at New Plimmoth in

New England the eleventh of November, where they found all the people they left in April, as is said, lustie and in good health, except six that died. Within a moneth they returned here for England, laded with clapboord, wainscot and walnut, with about three hogsheads of Bever skins, and some Saxefras, the 13 of December, and drawing neare our coast, was taken by a Frenchman, set out by the Marquis of Cera, Govenour of Ile Deu on the coast of Poytou, where they kept the ship, imprisoned the Master and companie, took from them to the value of about 500 pounds; and after 14 days sent them home with a poore supply of victuall, their owne being devoured by the Marquis and his hungry servants; they arived at London the 14 of Februarie, leaving all them they found and caried to New England well and in health, with victuall and corne sufficient till the next harvest.

The copie of Letter sent by this ship.

A Letter
from New
Plimmoth.   Loving cousin, at our arivall at New Plimmoth in New England, we found all our friends and planters in good health, though they were left sicke and weake with very small meanes, the Indians round about us peaceable and friendly, the country very pleasant and temperate, yeelding naturally of it self great store of fruites, as vines of divers sorts in great abundance; there is likewise walnuts, chesnuts, small nuts and plums, with much varietie of flowers, rootes, and herbs, no lesse pleasant then wholsome and profitable: no place hath more goose-berries and straw-berries, nor better, Timber of all sorts you have in England, doth cover the Land, that affoords beasts of divers sorts, and great flocks of Turkies, Quailes Pigeons and Partriges: many great lakes abounding with fish, fowle, Bevers and Otters. The sea affoords us as great plenty of all excellent sorts of sea-fish, as the rivers and Iles doth varietie of wilde fowle of most usefull sorts. Mines we find to our thinking, but neither the goodnesse nor qualide we know. Better grain cannot be then the Indian corne, if we will plant it upon as good ground as a man need desire. We are all freeholders, the rent day doth not trouble us, and all those good blessings we have, of which and what we list in their seasons for taking. Our companie are for most part very religious honest people; the word of God sincerely taught us every Sabbath:

so that I know not any thing a contented mind can here want. I desire your friendly care to send my wife and children to me, where I wish all the friends I have in England, and so I rest

Your loving kinsman
William Hilton.

Proofe 13.
1621.

From the West country went ten or twelve ships to fish, which were all well fraughted; those that came first at Bilbow made 17 pounds a single share, besides Bever, Otters and Martins skins; but some of the rest that came to the same ports that were already furnished, so glutted the market, their price was abated, yet all returned so well contented, they are a preparing to go againe.

For this
yeare 1622.

There is gone from the West of England onely to fish 35 ships, and about the last of April two more from London, the one of 100 Tuns, the other of 30, with some 60 passengers to supply the plantation with all necessary provisions. Now though the Turke and French hath bin somewhat too busie, would all the Christian Princes but be truly at unitie, as his royall Majestie our Soveraigne Lord and King desireth, 70 saile of good ships were sufficient to fire the most of his coasts in the Levant, and make such a guard in the straits of Hellespont, as would make the great Turke himselfe more afraid in Constantinople, then the smallest red crosse that crosses the seas would be, either of any French Piccaroun, or the pirats of Argere.

An abstract of Letters sent from the Collony
in New England, July 16. 1622.

Since the newes of the massacre in Virginia, though the Indians continue their wonted friendship, yet are we more wary of them then before; for their hands hath bin embrued in much English blood, onely by too much confidence, but not by force.

Here I must intreate a little your favours to digresse. They did not kill the English because they were Christians, but for their weapons and commodities, that were rare novelties; but now they feare we may beate them out of their dens, which Lions and Tygers would not admit but by force. But must this be an argument for an English man, or discourage any either in Virginia or New England? No: for I have tried them both. For Virginia, I kept that country with 38, and had not to eate but what we had from the savages. When I had ten men able to go abroad, our common wealth was very strong: with such a number I ranged that unknown country 14 weeks; I had but 18 to subdue them all, with which great army I stayed six weekes before their greatest Kings habitations, till they had gathered together all the power they could; and yet the Dutch-men sent at a needlesse excessive charge did helpe Powhatan how to betray me.

Of their numbers we were uncertaine; but them two honorable Gentlemen (Captaine George Percie and Captaine Francis West), two of the Phittiplaces, and some other such noble gentlemen and resolute spirits bore their shares with me, and now living in England, did see me take this murdering Opechankanough now their great King by the long locke on his head, with my pistole at his breast, I led him among his greatest forces, and before we parted made him fill our Bark of twenty Tuns with corne. When their owne wants was such, I have given them part againe in pittie, and others have bought it againe to plant their fields.

For wronging a souldier but the value of a peny, I have caused Powhatan send his owne men to James Towne to receive their punishment at my discretion. It is true in our greatest extremitie they shot me, slue three of my men, and by the folly of them that fled tooke me prisoner; yet God made Pocahontas the Kings daughter the meanes to deliver me: and thereby taught me to know their trecheries to preserve the rest. It was also my chance in single combat to take the King of Paspahegh prisoner, and by keeping him, forced his subjects to worke in chaines, till I made all the country pay contribution, having little else whereon to live.

Twise in this time I was their President, and none can say in all that time I had a man slaine: but for keeping them in that feare I was much blamed both there and here: yet I left 500 behind me that through their confidence in six months came most to confusion, as you may reade at large in the description of Virginia. When I went first to those desperate designes, it cost me many a forgotten pound to hire men to go; and procrastination caused more run away then went. But after the ice was broken, came many brave voluntaries: notwithstanding since I came from thence, the honorable Company have bin humble suiters to his Majestie to get vagabonds and condemned men to go thither; nay so much scorned was the name of Virginia, some did chuse to be hanged ere they would go thither, and were: yet for all the worst of spite, detraction and discouragement, and this lamentable massacre, there is more honest men now suters to go, then ever hath bin constrained knaves; and it is not unknown to most men of understanding, how happie many of those Collumners doe thinke themselves, that they might be admitted, and yet pay for their passage to go now to Virginia: and had I but meanes to transport as many as would go, I might have choise of 10000 that would gladly be in any of those new places, which were so basely contemned by ungratefull base minds.

To range this countrey of New England in like maner I had but eight, as is said, and amongst their bruite conditions I met many of their silly incounters, and without any hurt, God be thanked; when your West country men were many of them wounded and much tormented with the savages that assaulted their ship, as they did say themselves, in the first yeare I was there 1614. and though Master Hunt then Master with me did most basely in stealing some savages from that coast to sel, when he was directed to have gone for Spaine, yet that place was so remote from Capawuck, where Epenew should have fraughted them with gold ore, his fault could be no cause of their bad successe, however it is alledged for an excuse. I speake not this out of vainglory, as it may be some gleaners, or some was never there may censure me, but to let all men be assured by those examples, what those savages are that thus strangely doe murder and betray our country men. But to the purpose.

What is already writ of the healthfulnesse of the aire, the richnesse of the soile, the goodnes of the woods, the abundance of fruits, fish, and fowle in their season, they stil affirm that have bin there now neare 2 yeares, and at one draught they have taken 1000 basses, and in one night twelve hogsheads of herring. They are building a strong fort, they hope shortly to finish, in the interim they are wel provided: their number is about a hundred persons, all in health, and well neare 60 acres of ground well planted with corne, besides their gardens well replenished with useful fruits; and if their Adventurers would but furnish them with necessaries for fishing, their wants would quickly be supplied. To supply them this 16 of October is going the *Paragon* with 67 persons, and all this is done by privat mens purses. And to conclude in their owne words, should they write of all plenties they have found, they thinke they should not he beleeved.

For the 26 saile of ships, the most I can yet understand is, Master Ambrose Jennens of London, and Master Abraham Jennens of Plimmoth sent (their *Abraham*) a ship of 220 Tuns, and the *Nightingale* of Porchmouth of 100. whose fish at the first penie came to 3150 pounds: in all they were 35 saile: and where in Newfound land they shared six or seven pounds for a common man, in New England they shared 14 pounds; besides six Dutch and French ships made wonderfull returnes in furres.

Thus you may see plainely the yearely successe from New England (by Virginia) which hath bin so costly to this kingdome and so deare to me, which either to see perish or but bleed, pardon me though it passionate me beyond the bounds of modestie, to have bin sufficiently able to foresee it, and had neither power nor meanes how to prevent it. By that acquaintance I have with them, I may call them my children, for they have bin my wife, my hawks, my hounds, my cards, my dice, and in totall my best content, as indifferent to my heart as my left hand to my right; and notwithstanding all those miracles of disasters have crossed both them and me, yet were there not one English man remaining (as God he thanked there is some thousands) I would yet begin againe with as small meanes as I did at the first; not for that I have any secret encouragement from any I protest, more then lamentable experiences: for all their discoveries I can yet heare of, are but pigs of my owne sowe; nor more strange to me then to heare one tell me he hath gone from Billings gate and discovered Greenwich, Gravesend, Tilbery, Quinborow, Lee and Margit, which to those did never heare of them, though they dwell in England, might be made seem some rare secrets and great countries unknowne, except the relations of Master Dirmer.

In England some are held great travelers that have seene

1622.

Venice and Rome, Madrill and Algere, Prague or Ragousa, Constantinople or Jerusalem, and the Piramides of Egypt; that thinke it nothing to go to the Summer Iles or Virginia, which is as farre as any of them, and I hope in time will prove a more profitable and a more laudable journey. As for the danger, you see our Ladies and Gentlewomen account it nothing now to go thither; and therefore I hope all good men will better apprehend it, and not suffer them to languish in despaire, whom God so wonderfully and so oft hath preserved.

What here I have writ by relation, if it be not right, I humbly intreate your pardons, but I have not spared any diligence to learne the truth of them that have bin actors or sharers in those voyages: in some particulars they might deceive me, but in the substances they could not, for few could tell me any thing, except where they fished: but seeing all those have lived there, do confirme more then I have writ, I doubt not but all those testimonies with these new begun examples of plantation, will move both Citie and Country freely to adventure with me and my partners more then promises, seeing I have from his Majestie Letters Pattents, such honest, free and large conditions assured me from his Commissioners, as I hope wil satisfie any honest understanding.

But because some fortune tellers saith, I am unfortunate; had they spent their time as I have done, they would rather beleeve in God then their calculations, and peradventure have given as bad account of their actions; and therefore I intreat leave to answer those objectors, that think it strange if this be true, I have made no more use of it, and rest so long without emploiment, and hath no more reward nor preferment: to which I say:

I thinke it more strange they should taxe me before they have tried as much as I have both by land and sea, as well in Asia and Africa, as Europe and America, where my commanders were actors or spectators, they alwaies so freely rewarded me, I never needed to importunate, or could I ever learne to beg; what there I got, I have thus spent: these sixteen yeares I have spared neither paines nor money according to my abilitie, first to procure his Majesties Letters pattents, and a Company here to be the means to raise a company to go with me to Virginia, as is said: which beginning here and there cost me neare 5 yeares worke, and more then 500 pounds of my owne estate, besides all the dangers, miseries and incumbrances I endured gratis, where I stayed till I left 500 better provided then ever I was; from which blessed Virgin (ere I returned) sprung the fortunate habitation of Somer Iles.

This Virgins sister, now called New England, an. 1616. at my humble suit by our most gracious Prince Charles hath bin neare as chargeable to me and my friends: for all which although I never got shilling, but it cost me many a pound, yet I thinke my selfe happie to see their prosperities.

If it yet trouble a multitude to proceed upon these certainties, what think you I undertook when nothing was knowne, but that there was a vast land; I never had power and meanes to do any thing, though more hath bin spent in formall delayes then would have done the businesse; but in such a penurious and miserable manner as if I had gone a begging to build an universitie: where had men bin as forward to adventure their purses and performe the conditions they promised me, as to crop the fruites of my labours, thousands ere this had bin bettered by these designes. Thus betwixt the spur of Desire and the bridle of Reason I am neare ridden to death in a ring of despaire; the raines are in your hands, therefore I intreate you to ease me: and those that think I am either idle or unfortunate, may see the cause, and know: unlesse I did see better dealing, I have had warning enough, not to be so forward again at every motion upon their promises, unlesse I intended nothing but to cary newes. For now they dare adventure a ship, that when I went first, would not adventure a groate, so they may be at home again by Michaelmas: which makes me remember Master Hackluts; oh incredulitie! the wit of fooles, that slovenly do spit at all things faire; a sluggards cradle, a cowards castle, how easie it is to be an infidell: but to the purpose.

By this all men may perceive the ordinary performance of this voyage in five or six monethes, the plenty of fish is most certainly approved: and it is certain, from Cannada and New England within these six yeares hath come neare 20000 Bever skins. Now had each of those ships transported but some small quantitie of the most increasing beasts, fowles, fruit, plants and seeds, as I projected, by this time their increase might have bin sufficient for a thousand men. But the desire of present gain (in many) is so violent, and the endevors of many undertakers so negligent, every one so regarding their private gaine, that it is hard to effect any publick good, and impossible to bring them into a body, rule, or order, unlesse both authoritie and mony assist experiences. It is not a worke for every one to plant a Colonie; but when a house is built, it is no hard matter to dwell in it. This requireth all the best parts of art, judgement, courage, honestie, constancie, diligence and experience to do but neare well: your home bred ingrossing projectors shall finde there a great difference betwixt saying and doing. But to conclude, the fishing wil go forward if you plant it or no; whereby a Colonie may be transported with no great charge, that in a short time might provide such fraughts to buy of us there dwelling, as I would hope no ship should go or come empty from New England.

The charge of this is onely salt, nets, hookes, lines, knives, Irish rugs, course cloth, beades, glasse, and such trash, onely for fishing and trade with the savages, beside our owne neces-sary provisions, whose endevours wil quickly defray all this charge; and the savages have intreated me to inhabite where I will. Now all these ships, till this last yeare, have bin fished within a square of two or 3 leagues, and not one of them all would adventure any further, where questionlesse 500 saile may have their fraught better then in Island, Newfoundland, or elsewhere, and be in their markets before the other can have their fish in their ships, because New Englands fishing begins with February, the other not till mid May; the progression hereof tends much to the advancement of Virginia and the Bermudas, whose emptie ships may take in their fraught there, and would be a good friend in time of need to the inhabitants of New foundland.

The returnes made by the Westerne ships, are commonly de-vided into three parts, one for the owner of the ship, another for the Master and his companie, the third for the victuallers: which course being still permitted, wil be no hindrance to the plantation, go there never so many, but a meanes of trans-porting that yearly for little or nothing, which otherwise will cost many a hundred of pounds.

If a ship can gaine twentie, thirtie, fiftie in the 100, nay 300 for 100. in 7 moneths, as you see they have done, spending twise so much time in going and coming as in staying there: were I there planted, seeing the varietie of the fishings in their seasons serveth the most part of the yeare, and with a little labour we might make all the salt we need use. I can conceive no reason to distrust, but the doubling and trebling their gaines that are at all the former charge, and can fish but two moneths in a yeare: and if those do give 20. 30. or 40. shillings for an acre of land, or ship carpenters, forgers of iron, etc. that buy all things at a deare rate, grow rich; when they may have as good of all needful necessaries for taking (in my opinion) should not grow poore; and no commodity in Europe doth more decay then wood.

Master Dee recordeth in his Brittish Monarchie, that King Edgar had a navie of 4000 saile, with which he yearely made his progresse about this famous Monarchie of Great Brittaine, largely declaring the benefit thereof: whereupon it seemes he projected to our most memorable Queene Elizabeth, the erecting of a Fleete of 60 saile, he called a little Navie Royall; imitating the admired Pericles, Prince of Athens, that could never secure that tormented estate, untill he was Lord and Captain of the Sea.

At this none need wonder; for who knowes not, her Royall Majestie during her life, by the incredible adventures of her Royall Navy, and valiant souldiers and sea-men, notwithstanding all trecheries at home, the protecting and defending France and Holland, and reconquering Ireland, yet all the world by sea or land both feared, loved, and admired good Queen Elizabeth.

Both to maintaine and increase that incomparable honour (God be thanked) to her incomparable Successour, our most Royall Lord and Soveraigne King James, etc. this great Philosopher hath left this to his Majestie and his kingdomes consideration: That if the Tenths of the Earth be proper to God, it is also due by Sea: the Kings high wayes are common to passe, but not to dig for Mines or any thing; so Englands coasts are free to passe, but not to fish, but by his Majesties prerogative.

His Majesty of Spaine permits none to passe the Popes order for the East and West Indies, but by his permission, or at their perils. If all that world be so justly theirs, it is no injustice for England to make as much use of her own shores as strangers do, that pay to their own Lords the tenth, and not to the owner of those liberties any thing to speake of; whose subjects may neither take nor sell any in their territories: which small tribute would maintain this little Navie Royall, and not cost his Majestie a penny; and yet maintaine peace with all forreiners, and allow them more courtesie, then any nation in the world affoords to England.

It were a shame to alledge, that Holland is more worthy to enjoy our fishings as Lords thereof, because they have more skill to handle it then we, as they can our wooll and undressed cloth, notwithstanding all their wars and troublesome disorders.

To get mony to build this Navy, he saith, who would not spare the 100 peny of his Rents, and the 500 peny of his goods; each servant that taketh 40.s. wages, 4.d; and every forreiner of 7 yeares of age 4.d. for 7 yeares: not any of these but they will spend 3 times so much in pride, wantonnesse, or some superfluitie. And do any men love the securitie of their estates, that of themselves would not be humble suters to his Majestie to do this of free will as a voluntary benevolence, or but the one halfe of this, (or some such other course as I have propounded to divers of the Companies) free from any constraint, taxe, lottery or imposition, so it may be as honestly and truly employed as it is projected, the poorest mechanick in this kingdom would gaine by it. You might build ships of any proportion and numbers you please, five times cheaper then you can do here, and have good merchandize for their fraught in this unknowne land, to the advancement of Gods glorie, his Church and Gospel and the strengthening and reliefe of a great part of Christendome, without hurt to any, to the terror of pyrats, the amazement of enemies, the assistance of friends, the securing of Merchants, and so much increase of navigation to make Englands trade and shipping as much as any nation in the world, besides a hundred other benefits, to the generall good of all good subjects, and would cause thousands yet unborn blesse the time and all them that first put it in practise.

Now lest it should be obscured as it hath bin to private ends, or so weakly undertaken by our overweening incredulitie, that strangers may possesse it, whilest we contend for New Englands goods, but not Englands good; I present this to your Highnes and to all the Lords in England, hoping by your gracious good liking and approbation to move all the worthy Companies of

this noble Citie, and all the Cities and Countries in the whole
Land to consider of it, since I can finde them wood and halfe
victuall, with the aforesaid advantages, with what facilitie they
may build and maintaine this little Navie Royall, both with
honour, profit and content, and inhabite as good a country as
any in the world, within that parallel, which with my life and
what I have I wil endevour to effect, if God please, and you
permit. But no man will go from hence, to have lesse freedome
there then here; nor adventure all they have, to prepare the way
for them that know it not: and it is too well knowne there hath
bin so many undertakers of Patents and such sharing of them,
as hath bred no lesse discouragement then wonder, to heare
such great promises and so little performances. In the interim,
you see the Dutch and French already frequent it: and
God forbid them in Virginia or any of his Majesties
subjects should not have as free libertie as they. To
conclude, were it not for Master Pierce and a few
private Adventurers with him, what have we there
for all these inducements?

This yeare 3 ships went from London, set out by Maister John Farar and his Partners. The Bona nova 200 tunns. The Hopwell 70 The Darling 40.

As for them whom pride or covetousnes lulleth
asleep in a cradle of slothfull carelesnes, would they
but consider how all the great Monarchies of the earth have
bin brought to confusion; or but remember the late lamentable
experience of Constantinople; and how many Cities, Townes
and Provinces in the faire rich kingdoms of Hungaria, Transilvania, Wallachia and Moldavia; and how many thousands of
Princes, Earles, Barons, Knights, Merchants and others, have
in one day lost goods, lives and honors; or sold for slaves like
beasts in a market place; their wives, children and servants
slaine or wandring they knew not whither, dying or living in all
extremities of extreame miseries and calamities. Surely they
would not onely do this, but give all they have to enjoy peace
and libertie at home; or but adventure their persons abroad, to
prevent the conclusions of a conquering foe, who commonly
assaulteth and best prevaileth where he findeth wealth and
plentie (most armed) with ignorance and securitie.

Though the true condition of war is onely to suppresse the
proud, and defend the innocent and humble, as did that most
generous Prince Sigismundus Bather, Prince of those countries,
against them, whom under the colour of justice and pietie, to

maintaine their superfluitie of ambitious pride, thought all the world too little to maintaine their vice, and undoe them, or keepe them from abilitie to do any thing that would not admire and adore their honors, fortunes, covetousnes, falshood, bribery, crueltie, extortion, and ingratitude, which is worse then cowardize or ignorance, and all maner of vildnesse, cleane contrary to all honour, vertue and noblenesse.

Much more could I say, but lest I should be too tedious to your more serious affaires, I humbly crave your honorable and favourable constructions and pardons if any thing be amisse.

If any desire to be further satisfied, they may reade my Description of Virginia and New England, and peruse them with their severall Maps: what defect you finde in them, they shall find supplied in me or my authors, that thus freely hath throwne my selfe with my mite into the Treasury of my Countries good, not doubting but God will stir up some noble spirits to consider and examine if worthy Collumbus could give the Spaniards any such certainties for his designe, when Queene Isabel of Spaine set him foorth with fifteene saile. And though I can promise no Mines of gold, yet the warlike Hollanders let us imitate, but not hate, whose wealth and strength are good testimonies of their treasure gotten by fishing. Therefore (honorable and worthy Countrymen) let not the meannesse of the word Fish distaste you, for it will afford as good gold as the mines of Guiana or Tumbatu, with lesse hazard and charge, and more certaintie and facilitie; and so I humbly rest.

FINIS.

THE GENERALL HISTORIE

of

Virginia, New-England, and the Summer Isles
with the names of the Adventurers, Planters,
and Governours from their first beginning
An. 1584 to this present 1624.

With the Procedings of those Severall Colonies
and the Accidents that befell them in all their
Journeys and Discoveries.

Also the Maps and Descriptions of all those
Countryes, their Commodities, people,
Government, Customes, and Religion
yet knowne.

Divided into sixe Bookes.

By Captaine JOHN SMITH sometymes Governour
in those Countryes & Admirall
of New England.

1624

TO THE WORSHIPFULL
the Master Wardens and Societie
of the Cordwayners of the
Cittie of London.

Worthie Gentlemen

Not only in regard of your Courtisie and Love, Butt also of the Continuall use I have had of your Labours, and the hope you may make some use of mine, I salute yow with this Cronologicall discourse, whereof yow may understand with what infinite Difficulties and Dangers these Plantations first began, with ther yearlie proceedings, and the plaine description and Condition of those Countries; How many of your Companie have bin Adventurers, whose Names are omitted or not nominated in the Alphabett I know not, therefore I intreate yow better to informe me, that I may hereafter imprint yow amongst the Rest, Butt of this I am sure for want of Shooes among the Oyster Bankes wee tore our hatts and Clothes and those being worne, wee tied Barkes of trees about our Feete to keepe them from being Cutt by the shelles amongst which wee must goe or starve, yett how many thousand of Shooes hath bin transported to these plantations, how many soldiers Marriners and Saylers have bin and are likely to be encreased thereby, what vent your Commodities have had and still have, and how many Shipps and men of all Faculties have bin and are yearlie imployed I leave to your owne Judgments, and yett by reason of ill manadging, the Returnes have neither answered the generall Expectation, nor my desire; the Causes thereof yow may reade at Large in this Booke for your better Satisfaction, and I pray yow take it not in ill part that I present the same to yow in this manuscript Epistle soe late, for both it and I my self have bin soe overtired by attendances that this work of mine doth seeme to be Superannuated before it's Birth, notwithstanding Lett me intreat yow to give it Lodging in your Hall freelie to be perused for ever, in memorie of your Noblenesse towards mee, and my Love to God, my Countrie, your Societie, and those Plantations, Ever resting

Your's to use
John Smith

Constulta coronat.

The portraiture of the illustreous Princeße Frances Duchess of Richmon
and Lenox daugter of Thomas L: Howard of Bindon sonne of Thomas Duke of Norf
whose mother was Elisabeth daughter of Edward Duke of Buckingha
Anno 1625 insculptum a Guilh: Paßeo Londinum.

TO THE ILLUSTRIOUS
and Most Noble Princesse,
the Lady Francis, Duchesse
of Richmond and Lenox.

May it please your Grace,

This History, as for the raritie and varietie of the subject, so much more for the judicious Eyes it is like to undergoe, and most of all for that great Name, whereof it dareth implore Protection, might and ought to have beene clad in better robes then my rude military hand can cut out in Paper Ornaments. But because, of the most things therein, I am no Compiler by hearsay, but have beene a reall Actor; I take my selfe to have a propertie in them: and therefore have beene bold to challenge them to come under the reach of my owne rough Pen. That, which hath beene indured and passed through with hardship and danger, is thereby sweetned to the Actor, when he becometh the Relator. I have deeply hazarded my selfe in doing and suffering, and why should I sticke to hazard my reputation in Recording? He that acteth two parts is the more borne withall if he come short, or fayle in one of them. Where shall we looke to finde a Julius Cæsar, whose atchievments shine as cleare in his owne Commentaries, as they did in the field? I confesse, my hand, though able to weild a weapon among the Barbarous, yet well may tremble in handling a Pen among so many Judicious: especially when I am so bold as to call so piercing, and so glorious an Eye, as your Grace, to view these poore ragged lines.

Yet my comfort is, that heretofore honorable and vertuous Ladies, and comparable but amongst themselves, have offred me rescue and protection in my greatest dangers: even in forraine parts, I have felt reliefe from that sex. The beauteous Lady Tragabigzanda, when I was a slave to the Turkes, did all she could to secure me. When I overcame the Bashaw of Nalbrits in Tartaria, the charitable Lady Callamata supplyed my necessities. In the utmost of many extremities, that blessed Pokahontas, the great Kings daughter of Virginia, oft saved my life. When I escaped the crueltie of Pirats and most furious stormes, a long time alone in a small Boat at Sea, and driven

ashore in France, the good Lady Madam Chanoyes, bountifully assisted me.

And so verily these my adventures have tasted the same influence from your Gratious hand, which hath given birth to
the publication of this Narration. If therefore your Grace shall
daigne to cast your eye on this poore Booke, view I pray you
rather your owne Bountie (without which it had dyed in the
wombe) then my imperfections, which have no helpe but the
shrine of your glorious Name to be sheltered from censorious
condemnation. Vouchsafe some glimpse of your honorable aspect, to accept these my labours; to protect them under the
shadow of your excellent Name: which will inable them to be
presented to the Kings royall Majestie, the most admired Prince
Charles, and the Queene of Bohemia: your sweet Recommen-
dations will make it the worthier of their good countenances.
And as all my endevours are their due tribute: so this Page shall
recorde to posteritie, that my service shall be to pray to God,
that you may still continue the renowned of your sexe, the
most honored of men, and the highly blessed of God.

Your Graces faithfull and devoted servant,
John Smith.

A PREFACE
of foure Poynts.

I.
This plaine History humbly sheweth the truth; that our most royall King James hath place and opportunitie to inlarge his ancient Dominions without wronging any; (which is a condition most agreeable to his most just and pious resolutions:) and the Prince his Highness may see where to plant new Colonies. The gaining Provinces addeth to the Kings Crown: but the reducing Heathen people to civilitie and true Religion, bringeth honour to the King of Heaven. If his Princely wisedome and powerfull hand, renowned through the world for admirable government, please but to set these new Estates into order; their composure will be singular: the counsell of divers is confused; the generall Stocke is consumed; nothing but the touch of the Kings sacred hand can erect a Monarchy.

II.
Most noble Lords and worthy Gentlemen, it is your Honors that have imployed great paines and large expence in laying the foundation of this State, wherein much hath beene buried under ground, yet some thing hath sprung up, and given you a taste of your adventures. Let no difficulties alter your noble intentions. The action is an honour to your Country: and the issue may well reimburse you your summes expended. Our practices have hitherto beene but assayes, and are still to be amended. Let your bountie supply the necessities of weake beginnings, and your excellent judgements rectifie the proceedings; the returne cannot choose in the end but bring you good Commodities, and good contentments, by your shipping and fishing so usefull unto our Nation.

III.
Yee valiant and generous spirits, personall possessors of these new-found Territories, banish from among you Cowardise, covetousnes, jealousies, and idlenes, enemies to the raising your honours and fortunes; vertue, industry, and amitie, will make you good and great, and your merits live to ensuing Ages. You that in contempt of necessities, hazard your lives and estates, imploying your studies

and labours in these faire endevours, live and prosper as I desire my soule should prosper.

IIII.

For my selfe let emulation and envie cease, I ever intended my actions should be upright: now my care hath beene that my Relations should give every man they concerne, their due. But had I not discovered and lived in the most of those parts, I could not possibly have collected the substantiall truth from such a number of variable Relations, that would have made a Volume at least of a thousand sheets. Though the beginning may seeme harsh in regard of the Antiquities, brevitie, and names; a pleasanter Discourse ensues. The stile of a Souldier is not eloquent, but honest and justifiable; so I desire all my friends and well-wishers to excuse and accept it, and if any be so noble as to respect it, he that brought New England to light, though long since brought in obscuritie, he is againe to be found a true servant to all good designes.

So I ever rest yours to command,
John Smith

A GENTLEMAN
desirous to be unknowne,
yet a great Benefactor to Virginia,
his love to the Author,
the Company, and History.

Stay, reade, behold, skill, courage, knowledge, Arts;
Wonder of Nature: Mirror of our Clime.
Mars, Vulcan, Neptune *strive to have their parts,*
Rare Ornaments, rich honours of our time.

From far fetcht Indies, *and* Virginia's *soyle,*
Here Smith *is come to shew his Art and skill:*
He was the Smith *that hammered famins foyle,*
And on Powhatan's *Emperour had his will.*

Though first Columbus, Indies *true* Christofer;
Cabots, *brave* Florida, *much admirer;*
Meta Incognita, *rare* Martin Frobisher;
Gilberts *brave* Humphrey, Neptunes *devourer;*

Captaine Amadis, Raleighs *discoverer;*
Sir Richard Grenvill, Zealands *brave coaster:*
Drake, *doomes, drowne, death,* Spaines *scorner;*
Gosnolds *Relates,* Pring *prime observer.*

Though these be gone, and left behinde a name,
Yet Smith *is here to Anvile out a peece*
To after Ages, and eternall Fame,
That we may have the golden Jasons *fleece.*

He Vulcan *like did forge a true Plantation,*
And chain'd their Kings, to his immortall glory;
Restoring peace and plentie to the Nation,
Regaining honour to this worthy Story.

By him the Infidels *had due correction,*
He blew the bellowes still of peace and plentie:
He made the Indians *bow unto subjection,*
And Planters ne're return'd to Albion *empty.*

The Colonies pin'd, starv'd, staring, bones so feeble,
By his brave projects, proved strong againe:
The Souldiers' 'lowance he did seeke to treble,
And made the Salvage *in uncouth place remaine.*

He left the Countrey in prosperous happie state,
And plenty stood with peace at each mans doore:
Regarding not the Salvage *love nor hate:*
Themselves grew well, the Indians *wondrous poore.*

This there he did and now is home return'd,
To shew us all that never thither goe:
That in his heart, he deepely oft hath mourn'd,
Because the Action goeth on so slow.

> *Wise, Rich,*
>   *grave,*   *prize*
> *Brave,*   *Benefactors,*
> *Replant, want, continue still good Actors.*
>   *finde,*
>   *and*   *bring*
>   *kinde,*   *eyes*
> *Be*   *to blind;*
> *By Gods great might, give* Indians *light.*
>   *Bloud,*
>   *to*
>   *money,*
>   *doe*
> *Spend*   *that good,*
> *That may give* Indians *heav'nly food.*
>   *no lesse,*
>   *you*
>   *God*
>   *still*
> *And*   *shall blesse;*
> *Both you and yours the Lands possesse.*

S. M.

See here behold as in a Glasse,
All that is, or is and was.

T. T. 1624.

SAMUEL PURCHAS
of his friend Captaine John Smith,
and his Virginia.

Loe here SMITHS *Forge, where Forgery's Roague-branded,*
　　True Pegasus *is shoo'd, fetters are forged*
For Silke-sotts, Milk-sops, base Sloth, farre hence landed,
　　　　(Soile-chang'd, * *Soule-soil'd still)* Englands *dregs,*
　　　　discharged,
　　　　To plant (supplant!) Virginia, *home-disgorged:*
Where vertues praise frames good men Stories armour
　　'Gainst Time, Achilles-*like, with best Arts charged;*
　　Pallas, *all-arm'd, all-learn'd, can teach Sword-Grammar,*
　　Can Pens of Pikes; Armes t'Arts; to Scholar, Souldier hammer:

Can Pilgrim *make a* Maker; *all so well*
　　Hath taught, Smith *scoure my rustie out-worne* Muse,
And so conjur'd her in Virginian *Cell,*
　　　　That things unlearned long by want of use,
　　　　Shee fresh areeds me read, without abuse
By fabling. Arthurs *great Acts little made*
　　By greater lies she saith; seales Faith excuse
　　[a]*T*' Island, Groonland, Estotiland *to wade*
After lie-legends; Malgo, Brandon, *are Wares braide.*

The Fryer of Linne[b] *frights her with his block Art;*
　　Nor Brittish Bards *can tell where* Madoc[c] *planted.*
Cabots, Thorns, Elyots *truth have wonne her heart,*
　　　　Eldest discov'rers of New Worlds Cont'nent (granted
　　　　So had just Fates.) Colon *and* Vespuce *panted;*
This got the name[d], *last, least of Three; the Other*
　　New Worlds Isles found first: Cabot *is most chanted*
　　In Three-Mens-song; did more New World discover
Then both, then any; an hundred degrees coasted over.
Haile Sir Sebastian, Englands *Northern Pole,*
　　Virginia's *finder, Virgin* Eliza *nam'd it,*
Gave't Raleigh. (Rut, Prat, Hore, *I not enrole)*
　　　　Amadas *rites to* English *right first fram'd it.*
　　　　Lane *planted, return'd, nor had* English *tam'd it:*

Greenviles *and* Whites *men all slaine; New Plantation*
  JAMES *founds, Sloth confounds, feare, pride, faction sham'd*
    it:
Smiths *Forge mends all, makes chaines for* Savage *Nation,*
Frees, feeds the rest; the rest reade in his Bookes Relation.

*Cælum non animum mutant

[a]These are said a thousand yeares agoe to have beene in the North parts of America.

[b]He is said to discover the Pole 1360.

[c]Madoc ap Owen Planted some remote Western parts. 1170.

[d]America named of Americus Vesputius, which discovered les then Colon or Sir Sebastian Cabot, and the Continent later. Colon first found the Isles 1492. the Continent 1498. Above a yeare after Cabot had don it. He was set forth by Henry 7 and after by Henry 8. Knighted, and made grand Pilot of England by Edward 6 Under whom he procured the sending of Sir Hugh Willoughby, and discovery of Greenland and Russia: having by himself discovered on America from 67 North lat. to neere 40 South.

THOMAS MACARNESSE
to his worthy friend and Countryman,
Captaine John Smith.

Who loves *to* live *at home, yet* looke *abroad,*
    And know *both* passen *and* unpassen *road,*
The prime Plantation of an unknowne shore,
The men, *the* manners, fruitfulnesse, *and* store:
    Read but this little Booke, and then confesse,
    The lesse *thou* lik'st *and* lov'st, *thou* liv'st *the* lesse.

He writ it with great labour, for thy good,
Twice over, now in paper, *'fore in* blood;
It cost him deare, both paines, without an ayme
Of private *profit, for thy* publicke *gaine.*
    That thou mightst read *and* know *and safely* see,
    What he by practice, *thou by* Theoree.

Commend *him for his loyall loving heart,*
Or else come mend *him, and take thou his part.*

TO HIS FRIEND
Captaine John Smith,
and his Worke.

I know not how Desert more great can rise,
   Then out of Danger t' ane for good mens Good;
Nor who doth better winne th' Olympian *prize,*
   Than he whose Countryes Honor stirres his bloud;
     Private respects have private expectation,
     Publicke designes, should publish reputation.

This Gentleman whose Volumne heere is stoard
   With strange discoverie of G O D S strangest Creatures,
Gives us full view, how he hath Sayl'd, and Oar'd,
   And Marcht, full many myles, whose rough defeatures,
     Hath beene as bold, as puissant, up to binde
     Their barbarous strength's, to follow him dog-linde.

But wit, nor valour, now adayes payes scores
   For estimation; all goes now by wealth,
Or friends; tush! thrust the beggar out of dores
   That is not Purse-lyn'd; those which live by stealth
     Shall have their haunts; no matter what's the guest
     In many places; monies well come best.

But those who well discerne, esteeme not so:
   Nor I of thee brave Smith, *that hast beat out*
Thy Iron thus; though I but little know
   To what t'hast seene; yet I in this am stout:
     My thoughts, maps to my minde some accidents,
     That makes mee see thy greater presidents.
                              Jo: Done.

TO MY WORTHY
friend Captaine John Smith.

How great a part of knowledge had wee lost,
  Both of Virginia *and the* Summer Isles,
Had not thy carefull diligence and cost
  Inform'd us thus, with thy industrious stile!
Like Cæsar *now thou writ'st what thou hast done,*
These acts, this Booke will live while ther's a Sunne.
                                        Edw: Worseley.

TO HIS MUCH
respected Friend Captaine John Smith.

Envie avant. For Smith, *whose* Anvill *was* Experience,
  Could take his heart, *knew how and when to* Strike,
Wrought well this Peece; *till* After-negligence
  Mistaking temper, *Cold, or* Scorch'd; *or like*
Unskilfull workmen, that can never Fyle
  Nor Pollish *it, that takes in* Forge *such toyle:*
    Heere *Noble* Smith, *thou shewest the* Temper *true,*
    Which other Tampring-Tempres *never knew.*
                                        Ro: Norton.

TO HIS LOVING
friend Captaine John Smith.

Where actions speake the praises of a man,
  There, Pennes that use to flatter silent be,
Or if they speake, it is to scorne or scanne;
  For such with vertue seldome doe agree.

When I looke backe on all thy labours past,
  Thy travels, perils, losses oft sustaind

By Sea and Land; and (which is worst and last)
  Neglect *or* small reward, *so dearely gaind.*

I doe admire thy still undanted spirit;
  unwearied yet to worke thy Countries good.
This be thy praise then, due unto thy merit;
  For it th'hast venter'd life; and lost thy blood.

1.   2.   3.   1.   2.   3.
Truth, travayle, and Neglect, pure, painefull, most unkinde,
  1.   2.   3.   1.   2.   3.
Doth prove, consume, dismay, the soule, the corps, the minde.
                                            Edw: Ingham.

TO MY DEARE
friend by true Vertue ennobled
Captaine John Smith.

More then enough I cannot thee commend:
Whose both abilities and Love doe tend
So to advance the good of that Estate,
By English *charge, and Planters propagate*
Through heapes of painfull hazards; in the first
Of which, that Colony *thy Care hath nurst.*
And of ten that effected but with ten
That after thee, and now, three hundred men
Have faild in, 'mong the Salvages; *who shake*
At bruit of Thee, as Spaine *at Name of* Drake.
Which well appeares; considering the while
Thou governedst, nor force of theirs, ne guile
Lessend a man of thine; but since (I rue)
In Brittish *blood they deeply did imbrue*
Their Heathen hands. And (truth to say) we see,
Our selves wee lost, untimely leaving Thee.
Nor yet perceive I any got betweene
Thee and thy merit; which hath better beene
In prayse; or profit much; if counted just;

Free from the Weales abuse, or wronged trust.
Some few particulars perhaps have sped;
But wherin hath the publicke prospered?
Or is there more of those Vast Countries knowne,
Then by thy Labours and Relations showne
First, best? And shall wee love Thee now the lesse?
Farre be it! fit condignely to expresse
Thankes, by new Charge, or recompence; by whom,
Such past good hath, such future good may come.

David Wiffin.

NOBLE CAPTAINE
Smith, my worthy Friend

Not like the Age wherein thou liv'st, to lie
Buried in basenesse, sloth, or Ribaldrie
(For most doe thus) hast thou thy selfe applide;
But, in faire Actions, Merits height describe:
Which (like foure Theaters to set thee forth)
The worlds foure Quarters testifie thy worth.
The last whereof (America) best showes
Thy paines, and prayse; and what to thee shee owes,
(Although thy Sommer shone on th' Elder Three,
In as great Deeds as great varietie)
For opening to Her Selfe Her Selfe, in Two*
Of Her large Members; Now Ours, to our view.
Thereby endearing us to thy desart,
That doubly dost them to our hands impart;
There by thy Worke, Heere by thy Workes; By each
Maist thou Fames lasting Wreath (for guerdon) reach.
        And so become, in after Times t' ensue,
        A President for others, So to doe.

William Grent.

* *Virginia* now inhabited, and *New-England.*

TO HIS WORTHILY
affected Friend, Captaine John Smith.

Amongst so many that by learned skill,
Have given just prayse to thee, and to thy Booke,
Deare friend receive this pledge of my good will,
Whereon, if thou with acceptation looke,
And thinke it worthie, ranke amongst the rest:
Use thy discretion, I have done my best.

Ανώνυμος.

The Contents of the generall History, divided into six Books

The first Booke.

The second Booke.

Of Virginia now planted,
discovered by Captaine Smith.

1606 The Latitude, Temperature, and Capes; a description of Chisa-
      peack Bay, and seaven navigable Rivers that fall into it, with
      their severall Inhabitants, and diversitie of Language. pag. 265–
      273.

      Of things growing Naturally, as woods, fruits; gummes,
      berries, herbs, roots; also of beasts, birds, and fishes; how they
      divide the yeare, prepare their ground, plant their corne, and
      use it, and other victuall. pag. 273–280.

      What commodities may be had by industry. The description
      of the people, their numbers, constitutions, dispositions, attyre,
      buildings, lodgings and gardens, their usage of children, striking
      of fire, making their Bowes and Arrowes, knives, swords, tar-
      gets, and boats: how they spinne, make fish-hooks, and ginnes,
      and their order of hunting. Consultations and order in Warres.
      pag. 281–289.

      Their musicke, entertainment, trade, Physicke, Chirurgery
      and Charmes. Their Religion, God, burials ordinary and ex-
      traordinary, Temples, Priests, Ornaments, solemnities, Con-
      jurations, Altars, sacrifices, black boyes, and resurrection. pag.
      290–295.

      The manner of their government, their Emperor; his atten-
      dants, watch, treasury, wives, successors and authority: tenure
      of their lands, and manner of punishment, with some words of
      their Language Englished. pag. 296–303.

      And a Mappe of the Countrey of Virginia now planted.

The third Booke.

Of the Accidents and
Proceedings of the English.

The fourth Booke.

With their Proceedings after the alteration of the Government.

The fift Booke.

The sixt Booke.

A mappe of New England. How this country hath bin ac-
1614 counted but a miserable Desert. Captain Smiths first voyage;
what peace and warres he had with the Salvages, and within 6.
moneths returned with 1500 l. worth of commodities; got
Prince Charles to call it New-England. A Table of the old
names and the new. page. 588–592.

Captaine Hobsons voyage to Capawuk; the Londoners apprehend it. The situation: notes for ignorant undertakers. The
description of the Country. Staple Commodities; present proofe
of the healthfulnesse of the clime. Observations of the Hollanders chiefe trade. p. 593–600.

Examples of the altitude comparatively; the reasons why to
plant it. An example of the gaines every yeare; a description of
15. severall Countries in particular. Of their Kings, rivers, harbors, Isles, mountains, landmarks, fruits, woods, birds, fishes,
beasts, etc. and how as well Gentlemen as mecanicks, may be
imployed, and get much wealth, with the reasons and causes of
the defaylements. p. 601–620.

1615   Captaine Smiths second voyage; his ship neere foundered in
1616 the Sea; He reimbarketh himselfe; incountreth the English
Pyrats; fought with the French Pyrates; is betrayed by 4.
French men of warre; how he was released; his men ran from
him with ship and all; how he lived with the French men; what
fights they had, what prizes they tooke; the French mens ingratitude. 13 sayle cast away: how he escaped, proceeded in
France, returned for England, and punished them ran from
him. pag. 621–631.

1617   The yearely trialls of New-England; the benefit of fishing, as
1618 Master Dee, and divers report, and approved by the Hollan-
1619 ders Records; how it becomes so well apprehended, that more
then 150. have gone thither to fish, with an estimate of their
gaines, with many observations and Accidents. pag. 632–636.

1620   A Plantation in New-England; their first landing; divers
journeys and accidents; the description of the harbors, bayes,
lakes, and that place they inhabit, called New-Plimouth; conference with the Salvages; and kinde usage of the King of the
Massasoyts; a strange policie of Tusquantum. pag. 637–644.

1621   The Salvages make warres for their friendships; the English
1622 revenge their friends injuries. Notes and observations. They
lived two yeares without Supplyes; the death of Tusquantum;

Its not his part that is the best Translator,
To render word for word to every Author.

HOW ANCIENT AUTHORS REPORT, THE NEW-WORLD,

Now called America, was discovered: and part
thereof first Planted by the ENGLISH, called
VIRGINIA, with the Accidents and
Proceedings of the same.

The first Booke.

FOR the Stories of Arthur, Malgo, and Brandon, that say a
thousand yeares agoe they were in the North of America;
or the Fryer of Linn that by his blacke Art went to the North
pole in the yeare 1360. in that I know them not. Let this suffice.

The Chronicles of Wales report, that Madock,
1170.   sonne to Owen Guineth, Prince of Wales seeing his
two brethren at debate who should inherit, prepared
certaine Ships, with men and munition, and left his Country to
seeke adventures by Sea: leaving Ireland North he sayled west
till he came to a Land unknowne. Returning home and relating what pleasant and fruitfull Countries he had seene without Inhabitants, and for what barren ground his brethren and
kindred did murther one another, he provided a number of
Ships, and got with him such men and women as were desirous to live in quietnesse, that arrived with him in this new
Land in the yeare 1170: Left many of his people there and returned for more. But where this place was no History can show.

The Spanyards say Hanno a Prince of Carthage was
1492.   the first: and the next Christopher Cullumbus, a Ge-
noesian, whom they sent to discover those unknowne
parts, 1492.

But we finde by Records, Cullumbus offered his service in
the yeare 1488. to King Henry the seaventh; and by accident
undertooke it for the Spanyards. In the Interim King Henry
gave a Commission to John Cabot, and his three
1497.   sonnes, Sebastian, Lewis, and Santius. John and Sebastian well provided, setting sayle, ranged a great
part of this unknowne world, in the yeare 1497. For though

Cullumbus had found certaine Iles, it was 1498. ere he saw the Continent, which was a yeare after Cabot. Now Americus came a long time after, though the whole Continent to this day is called America after his name, yet Sebastian Cabot discovered much more then them all, for he sayled to about forty degrees Southward of the lyne, and to sixty-seaven towards the North: for which King Henry the eight Knighted him and made him grand Pilate of England. Being very aged King Edward the sixt gave him a Pention of 166^l.13^s.4^d. yearely. By his directions Sir Hugh Willowby was sent to finde out the Country of Russia, but the next yeare he was found frozen to death in his Ship, and all his Company.

Master Martin Frobisher was sent in the yeare 1576. by our most gracious Queene Elizabeth, to search for the Northwest passage, and Meta incognita: for which he was Knighted, honored, and well rewarded.

1576.

Sir Humphrey Gilbert a worthy Knight attempted a Plantation in some of those parts: and obtained Letters Pattents to his desire: but with this Proviso, He should maintaine possession in some of those vast Countries within the tearme of six yeares. Yet when he was provided with a Navy able to incounter a Kings power, even here at home they fell in divisions, and so into confusion, that they gave over the Designe ere it was begun, notwithstanding all this losse, his undanted spirit began againe, but his Fleet fell with New-found land, and he perished in his returne, as at large you may read in the third Volume of the English Voyages, written by Master Hackluit.

1583.

Upon all those Relations and inducements, Sir Walter Raleigh, a noble Gentleman, and then in great esteeme, undertooke to send to discover to the Southward. And though his occasions and other imployments were such he could not goe himselfe, yet he procured her Majesties Letters Pattents, and perswaded many worthy Knights and Gentlemen to adventure with him to finde a place fit for a Plantation. Their Proceedings followeth.

The most famous, renowned, and ever worthy of all memory, for her courage, learning, judgement, and vertue, Queene Elizabeth, granted her Letters Patents to Sir Walter Raleigh for the discovering and planting

1584.

new Lands and Countries, not actually possessed by any Christians. This Patenty got to be his assistants Sir Richard Grenvell the valiant, Master William Sanderson a great friend to all such noble and worthy actions, and divers other Gentlemen and Marchants, who with all speede provided two small Barkes well furnished with all necessaries, under the command of Captaine Philip Amidas and Captaine Barlow. The 27. of Aprill they set sayle from the Thames, the tenth of May passed the Canaries, and the tenth of June the West Indies: which unneedfull Southerly course, (but then no better was knowne) occasioned them in that season much sicknesse.

The second of July they fell with the coast of *Their arrivall.* Florida in shoule water, where they felt a most dilicate sweete smell, though they saw no land, which ere long they espied, thinking it the Continent: an hundred and twenty myles they sayled not finding any harbor. The first that appeared, with much difficulty they entred, and anchored, and after thankes to God they went to view the next Land adjoyning to take possession of it for the Queenes most excellent Majestie: which done, they found their first landing *Abundance of Grapes.* place very sandy and low, but so full of grapes that the very surge of the Sea sometimes over-flowed them: of which they found such plenty in all places, both on the sand, the greene soyle and hils, as in the plaines as well on every little shrub, as also climbing towardes the tops of high Cedars, that they did thinke in the world were not the like abundance.

We passed by the Sea-side towards the tops of the next hills being not high: from whence we might see the Sea *The Ile of Wokokon.* on both sides, and found it an Ile of twentie myles in length, and six in breadth, the vallyes replenished with goodly tall Cedars. Discharging our Muskets, such a flocke of Cranes, the most white, arose by us, with such a cry as if an Army of men had shouted altogether. This Ile hath many goodly Woods, and Deere, Conies, and Foule in incredible abundance, and using the Authors owne phrase, the Woods are not such as you finde in Bohemia, Moscovia, or Hercinia, barren and fruitlesse, but the highest and reddest Cedars of the world, bettering them of the Assores, Indies, or *In Lybanus are not many.* Libanus: Pynes, Cypres, Saxefras, the Lentisk that beareth Mastick, and many other of excellent smell and qualitie. Till the third day we saw not any of the people, then in a little Boat three of them appeared, one of them went on shore, to whom wee rowed, and he attended us without any signe of feare; after he had spoke much though we understood not a word, of his owne accord he came boldly aboord us, we gave him a shirt, a hat, wine and meate, which he liked well, and after he had well viewed the barkes and us, he went away in his owne Boat, and within a quarter of a myle of us in halfe an houre, had loaden his Boat with fish, with which he came againe to the poynt of land, and there devided it in two parts, poynting one part to the Ship, the other to the Pinnace, and so departed.

Conference with a Salvage.

The next day came divers Boats, and in one of them the Kings Brother, with forty or fifty men, proper people, and in their behaviour very civill; his name was Granganameo, the King is called Wingina, the Country Wingandacoa. Leaving his Boats a little from our Ships, he came with his trayne to the poynt: where spreading a Matte he sat downe. Though we came to him well armed, he made signes to us to sit downe without any shew of feare, stroking his head and brest, and also ours, to expresse his love. After he had made a long speech unto us, we presented him with divers toyes, which he kindly accepted. He was greatly regarded by his people, for none of them did sit, nor speake a word, but foure, on whom we bestowed presents also, but he tooke all from them, making signes all things did belong to him.

The Arrivall of the Kings brother.

The King himselfe in a conflict with a King his next neighbour and mortall enemy, was shot in two places through the body, and the thigh, yet recovered: whereby he lay at his chiefe towne six dayes journey from thence.

A day or two after shewing them what we had, Granganameo taking most liking to a Pewter dish, made a hole in it, hung it about his necke for a brest-plate: for which he gave us twenty Deere skins, worth twenty Crownes; and for a Copper Kettell, fiftie skins, worth fiftie Crownes. Much other trucke we had, and after two dayes he came aboord, and did eate and drinke with us very merrily. Not long after he brought his wife and children, they were but of meane stature, but well favoured and very bashfull; she had a long coat of Leather, and about her privities a peece of the

Trade with the Salvages.

same, about her forehead a band of white Corrall, and so had
her husband, in her eares were bracelets of pearle, hanging
downe to her middle, of the bignesse of great Pease; the rest of
the women had Pendants of Copper, and the Noblemen five
or sixe in an eare; his apparrell as his wives, onely the women
weare their haire long on both sides, and the men but on one;
they are of colour yellow, but their hayre is blacke, yet we saw
children that had very fayre Chesnut coloured hayre.

   After that these women had beene here with us, there came
downe from all parts great store of people, with Leather, Corrall, and divers kinde of dyes, but when Granganameo was present, none durst trade but himselfe, and them that wore red
Copper on their heads, as he did. When ever he came, he
would signifie by so many fires he came with so many boats,
that we might know his strength. Their Boats are but one
great tree, which is but burnt in the forme of a trough with
gins and fire, till it be as they would have it. For an armour he
would have ingaged us a bagge of pearle, but we refused, as
not regarding it, that wee might the better learn where it grew.
He was very just of his promise, for oft we trusted him, and he
would come within his day to keepe his word. He sent us commonly every day a brace of Bucks, Conies, Hares, and fish,
sometimes Mellons, Walnuts, Cucumbers, Pease, and
divers rootes. This Author sayth, their corne groweth
three times in five moneths; in May they sow, in July
reape; in June they sow, in August reape; in July sow, in August reape. We put some of our Pease in the ground, which in
ten dayes were 14. ynches high.

Note.

   The soyle is most plentifull, sweete, wholesome, and fruitfull of all other, there are about 14. severall sorts of sweete
smelling tymber trees: the most parts of the underwood, Bayes
and such like: such Okes as we, but far greater and better. After
this acquaintance, my selfe with seaven more went twenty myle
into the River Occam, that runneth toward the Cittie Ski-
coack, and the evening following we came to an Ile
called Roanoak, from the harbour where we entred
7. leagues; at the North end was 9. houses, builded
with Cedar, fortified round with sharpe trees, and the entrance
like a Turnpik. When we came towards it, the wife of Granganameo came running out to meete us, (her husband was

The Ile
Roanoak.

The great
courtesie of
a Woman.

absent) commanding her people to draw our Boat ashore for beating on the billowes, other she appoynted to carry us on their backes aland, others to bring our Ores into the house for stealing. When we came into the other roome, (for there was five in the house) she caused us to sit downe by a great fire; after tooke off our clothes and washed them, of some our stockings, and some our feete in warme water, and she her selfe tooke much paines to see all things well ordered, and to provide us victuall.

A banquet.

After we had thus dryed our selves, she brought us into an Inner roome, where she set on the bord standing a long the house somewhat like frumentie, sodden venison, and rosted fish; in like manner mellons raw, boyled rootes and fruites of divers kindes. There drinke is commonly water boyled with Ginger, sometimes with Saxefras, and wholsome herbes, but whilest the Grape lasteth they drinke wine. More love she could not expresse to entertaine us; they care but onely to defend themselves from the short winter, and feede on what they finde naturall in sommer. In this feasting house was their Idoll of whom they tould us uncredible things. When we were at meate two or three of her men came amongst us with their Bowes and Arrowes, which caused us to take our armes in hand. She perceiving our distrust, caused their Bowes and Arrowes to be broken, and they beaten out of the gate: but the evening approaching we returned to our boate, where at she much grieving brought our supper halfe boyled, pots and all, but when she saw us, but put our boat a little off from the shoar and lye at Anchor, perceiving our Jelousie, she sent divers men and 30. women to sit al night on the shoare side against us, and sent us five Mats to cover us from the raine, doing all she could to perswade us to her house. Though there was no cause of doubt, we would not adventure: for on our safety depended the voyage: but a more kinde loving people cannot be. Beyond this Ile is the maine land and the great river Occam, on which standeth a Towne called Pomeiock,

Skicoac a
great towne.

and six dayes higher, their City Skicoak: those people never saw it, but say there fathers affirme it to be above two houres journey about. Into this river falleth an other called Cipo, where is found many Mustells wherein are Pearles: likewise another River called Nomapona, on the one side whereof standeth a great towne called Chawanock, the Lord of the Country is not subject to Wingandacoa. Beyond him an other king they cal Menatonon. These 3. are in league each with other. Towards the south. 4. dayes journey is Sequotan, the southermost part of Wingandacoa.

Adjoyning to Secotan beginneth the country Po-
Pomouik. mouik, belonging to the King called Piamacum, in the Country Nusiok upon the great river Neus. These have mortall warres with Wingina, King of Winganda-coa. Betwixt Piemacum and the Lord of Secotan, a peace was concluded: notwithstanding there is a mortall malice in the Secotans, because this Piemacum invited divers men, and 30. women to a feast, and when they were altogether merry before their Idoll, which is but a meere illusion of the Devill, they su-dainly slew all the men of Secotan, and kept the women for their use. Beyond Roanoak are many Isles full of fruits and other Naturall increases, with many Townes a long the side of the Continent. Those Iles lye 200. myles in length, and be-tweene them and the mayne, a great long sea, in some places 20. 40. or 50. myles broad, in other more, somewhere lesse. And in this sea are 100. Iles of divers bignesses, but to get into it, you have but 3. passages and they very dangerous. Though this you see for most part be but the relations of Salvages, be-cause it is the first, I thought it not amisse to remember them as they are written by them that returned and arived in En-gland about the middest of September the same yeare. This discovery was so welcome into England that it pleased her
How the Majestie to call this Country of Wingandacoa, Vir-
Country was
called ginia, by which name now you are to understand
Virginia. how it was planted, disolved, renued, and enlarged,

The Performers of this voyage were these following.

Philip Amadas. Arthur Barlow.	*Captaines*
William Grenvill. John Wood. James Browewich. Henry Greene. Benjamen Wood. Simon Ferdinando.	*Of the* *Companie*

Nicholas Peryman.   *Of the*
John Hewes.   } *Companie*

Sir Richard Grenvills voyage to Virginia,
for Sir Walter Raleigh. 1585.

The 9. of Aprill he departed from Plimouth with 7. sayle: the chiefe men with him in command, were Master Ralph Layne, Master Thomas Candish Master John Arundel, Master Stukley, Master Bremige, Master Vincent, Master Heryot and Master John Clarke. The 14. day we fell with the Canaries, and the 7. of May with Dominico in the West Indies: we landed at Portorico, after with much a doe at Izabella on the north of Hispaniola, passing by many Iles. Upon the 20. we fell with the mayne of Florida, and were put in great danger upon Cape Fear. The 26. we Anchored at Wocokon, where the admiral had like to beene cast away, presently we sent to Wingina to Roanoak, and Master Arundell went to the mayne, with Manteo a salvage, and that day to Crooton. The 11. The Generall victualed for 8. dayes, with a selected company went to the maine, and discovered the Townes of Pomeiok, Aquascogoc, Secotan, and the great Lake called Paquipe. At Aquascogoc the Indians stole a silver Cup, wherefore we burnt the Towne and spoyled their corne, so returned to our fleete at Wocokon. Whence we wayed for Hatorask, where we rested, and Granganimeo, King Wingina's brother with Manteo came abord our Admirall, the Admirall went for Weapomeiok, and Master John Arundell for England. Our Generall in his way home tooke a rich loaden ship of 300. tunns, with which he arived at Plimouth the 18. of September. 1585.

(margin: Sir Richard Grenvils, voyage. 1585.)

These were left under the command of Master Ralph Layne to inhabite the Country, but they returned within a yeare.

Philip Amidas *Admirall.*   Master Rogers.
Master Thomas Heryot.   Master Harvy.
Master Acton.   Master Snelling.
Master Stafford.   Master Antony Russe.

Master Thomas Luddington.	Master Allen.
Master Marvyn.	Master Michaell Pollison.
Captaine Vaghan.	Master Thomas Bockner.
Master Kendall.	Master James Mason.
Master Gardiner.	Master David Salter.
Master Predeox.	Master James Skinner.

With divers others to the number of 108.

Touching the most remarkeable things of the Country and our proceeding from the 17. of August 1585. till the 18. of June 1586. we made Roanoack our habitation. The utmost of our discovery Southward was Secotan as we esteemed 80. leagues from Roanoacke. The passage from thence was thought a broad sound within the maine, being without kenning of land, yet full of flats and shoulds that our Pinnasse could not passe, and we had but one boat with 4. ores, that would carry but 15. men with their provisions for 7. dayes: so that because the winter approached we left those discoveries till a stronger supply. To the Northward; our farthest was to a Towne of the Chesapeacks, from Roanoack 130. myles. The passage is very shallow and dangerous by reason of the breadth of the sound and the little succour for a storme, but this teritory being 15. myle from the shoare, for pleasantnesse of seate, for temperature of climate, fertility of soyle and comoditie of the Sea, besides beares, good woods, Saxefras, Walnuts etc. is not to be excelled by any other whatsoever.

Their first Plantation.

There be sundry other Kings they call Weroances as the Mangoacks, Trypaniks and Opposians, which came to visit us.

To the northwest our farthest was Chawonock from Roanoack 130. myles our passage lyeth through a broad sound, but all fresh water, and the channell Navigable for a Ship, but out of it full of shoules.

Chawonoack.

The townes by the way by the water, are Passaquenock the womens towne, Chepanoc, Weapomeiok; from Muscamunge wee enter the river and jurisdiction of Chawonock, there it beginneth to straiten, and at Chawonock it is as Thames at Lambeth: betwixt them as we passed is goodly high land on the left hand, and there is a towne called Ohanock, where is a great corne field, it is subject to Chawonock, which is the greatest Province upon the river, and the Towne it selfe can put seven hundred men into the field, besides the forces of the rest. The King is lame, but hath more understanding then all the rest.

Chawonock 700. men.

The river of Moratoc is more famous then all the rest, and openeth into the sound of Weapomeiok, and where there is but a very small currant in Chawonock, it hath so strong a currant from the Southwest, as we doubted how to row against it. Strange things they report of the head of this river, and of Moratoc it selfe, a principall towne on it, and is thirtie or fortie dayes Journey to the head. This lame King is called Menatonon. When I had him prisoner two dayes, he told mee that 3. dayes Journey in a Canow up the river Chawonock, then landing and going foure dayes Journey Northeast, there is a King whose Country lyeth on the Sea, but his best place of strength is an Iland in a Bay invironed with deepe water, where he taketh that abundance of Pearle, that not onely his skins, and his nobles, but also his beds and houses are garnished therewith. This king was at Chawonock two yeares agoe to trade with blacke pearle, his worst sort whereof I had a rope, but they were naught; but that King he sayth hath store of white, and had trafficke with white men, for whom he reserved them; he promised me guides to him, but advised me to goe strong, for he was unwilling strangers should come in his Country, for his Country is populous and valiant men. If a supply had come in Aprill, I resolved to have sent a small Barke to the Northward to have found it, whilest I with small Boates and 200. men would have gone to the head of the river Chawonock, with sufficient guides by land, inskonsing my selfe every two dayes, where I would leave Garrisons for my retreat till I came to this Bay.

Menatonon his Relations of the Ile of Pearle, and a rich Mine, and the Sea by it.

Very neare unto it is the river of Moratoc, directly from the West, the head of it springeth out of a mayne Rocke, which standeth so neare the Sea, that in stormes the Sea beats over it into this fresh spring, that of it selfe at the surse is a violent streame. I intended with two Wherries and fortie persons to have Menatonons sonne for guide, to try this presently, till I could meete with some of the Moratocks, or Mangoaks, but hoping of getting more victuall from the Salvages, we as narrowly escaped starving in that Discovery as ever men did.

For Pemissapan who had changed his name of Wingina

Pemissapan
his trechery.

upon the death of his brother Granganameo, had given both the Chawonests, and Mangoaks word of my purpose: also he told me the Chawonocks had assembled two or three thousand to assault me at Roanok, urging me daily to goe against them, and them against us; a great assembly I found at my comming thether, which suddaine approach did so dismay them, that we had the better of them: and this confederacy against us was procured by Pemissapan him-

The discovery
of the river
Moratoc.

selfe our chiefe friend we trusted; he sent word also to the Moratoks and the Mangoaks, I came to invade them, that they all fled up into the high Country, so that where I assured my selfe both of succour and provision, I found all abandoned. But being thus farre on my journey 160. myles from home, and but victuals for two dayes, besides the casualties of crosse winds, stormes, and the Salvages trechery, though we intended no hurt to any: I gave my

A noble
resolution.

Company to understand we were onely drawne forth upon these vaine hopes by the Salvages to bring us to confusion: a Councell we held, to goe forward or returne, but they all were absolutely resolved but three, that whilst there was but one pynt of Corne for a man, they would not leave the search of that river; for they had two Mastive Dogs, which boyled with Saxefras leaves (if the worst fell out) upon them and the pottage they would live two dayes, which would bring them to the sound, where they should finde fish for two dayes more to passe it to Roanock, which two dayes they had rather fast then goe backe a foote, till they had seene the Mangoaks either as friends or foes.

Though I did forsee the danger and misery, yet the desire I had to see the Mangoaks was, for that there is a province called Chaunis Temoatan, frequented by them and well knowne to all those Countries, where is a mine of Copper they call *Wassador*; they say they take it out of a river that falleth swiftly from high rocks in shallow water, in great Bowles, covered with leather, leaving a part open to receive the mettall, which by the change

The strange
Mine of
Chaunis
Temoatan.

of the colour of the water where the spout falleth, they suddainly chop downe, and have the Bowle full, which they cast into the fire, it presently melteth, and doth yeeld in five parts at the first melting two parts mettall for three of Ore. The Mangoaks have such plenty of it,

they beautifie their, houses with great plates thereof: this the
Salvages report; and young Skiko the King of Chawonocks
sonne my prisoner, that had beene prisoner among the Mangoaks, but never at Chaunis Temoatan, for he sayd that was
twentie dayes journey overland from the Mangoaks.

Menatonon also confirmed all this, and promised me guids
to this mettall Country; by Land to the Mangoaks is but one
dayes journey, but seaven by water, which made me so willing
to have met them for some assay of this mettall: but when we
came there we found no creature, onely we might see where
had beene their fires. After our two dayes journey, and our victuals spent, in the evening, we heard some call as we thought
Manteo, who was with me in the boat; this made us glad, he
made them a friendly answer, which they answered with a song
we thought for welcome, but he told us they came to fight.
Presently they did let flie their Arrowes about the boat, but did
no hurt, the other boat scouring the shore we landed: but they
all were fled, and how to finde them wee knew not. So the next
morning we returned to the mouth of the river, that
cost us foure dayes rowing up, and here our dogs
pottage stood us in good stead, for we had nothing

The great
currant of
the river
Moratoc.

els: the next day we fasted being windbound, and could not
passe the sound, but the day following we came to Chip-
panum, where the people were fled, but their wires afforded us
fish: thus being neare spent, the next day God brought us to
Roanocke. I conclude a good Mine, or the South sea will make
this Country quickly inhabited, and so for pleasure and profit
comparable with any in the world: otherwise there will be
nothing worth the fetching. Provided there be found a better
harbour then yet there is, which must be Northward if there
be any. Master Vaughan, no lesse hoped of the goodnesse of
the Mine, then Master Heriot that the river Moratocks head,
either riseth by the Bay of Mexico, or very neare the South
Sea, or some part that openeth neare the same, which cannot
with that facilitie be done as from the Bay of Pearles, by insconsing foure dayes journey to the Chawonoks, Mangoaks,
and Moratocks, etc.

The conspiracy of Pemissapan; the Discovery of it; and our returne for England with Sir Francis Drake.

ENSENORE a Salvage, father to Pemissapan, the best friend we had after the death of Granganimeo, when I was in those Discoveries, could not prevaile any thing with the King from destroying us, that all this time God had preserved, by his good counsell to the King to be friendly unto us. Pemissapan thinking as the brute was in this last journey we were slaine and starved, began to blaspheme our God that would suffer it, and not defend us, so that old Ensenore had no more credit for us: for he began by all the devises he could to invade us. But in the beginning of this brute, when they saw us all returne, the report false, and had Manteo, and three Salvages more with us, how little we esteemed all the people we met, and feared neither hunger, killing, or any thing, and had brought their greatest Kings sonne prisoner with us to Roanock: it a little asswaged all his devises, and brought Ensenore in respect againe, that our God was good, and wee their friends, and our foes should perish, for we could doe them more hurt being dead, then living, and that being an hundred myles from them, shot, and strucke them sicke to death, and that when we die it is but for a time, then we returne againe. But that which wrought the most feare among them was the handy-worke of Almightie God. For certaine dayes after my returne, Menatonon sent messengers to me with Pearle, and Okisco King of Weopomeoke, to yeeld himselfe servant to the Queene of England. Okisco with twenty-foure of his principall men came to Pemissapan to acknowledge this dutie and subjection, and would performe it. All which so changed the heart of Pemissapan, that upon the advise of Ensenore, when we were ready to famish they came and made us wires, and planted their fields they intended to abandon (we not having one corne till the next harvest to sustaine us). This being done our old friend Ensenore dyed the twenty of Aprill, then all our enemies wrought with Pemissapan to put in practise his devises, which he easily imbraced, though they had planted corne by us, and at Dasamonpeack two leagues from us. Yet they got Okisco our tributary to get seven or eight hundred (and the Mandoages with the Chisapeans should doe the like) to meete (as their custome is) to solemnize the Funerall of Ensenore. Halfe of whom should lye hid, to cut off the straglers, seeking crabs and provision: the rest come out of the mayne upon the Signall by fire. Twenty of the principall of Pemissapans men had charge in the night to beset my house, put fire in the Reeds that covered it, which might cause me run out so naked and amazed, they might without danger knocke out my braines. The same order for Master Heriots, and the rest: for all should have beene fired at an instant. In the meane time they should sell us nothing, and in the night spoyle our wires, to make necessitie disperse us. For if we were but ten together, a hundred of them would not meddle with us. So our famine increased, I was forced to send Captaine Stafford to Croatan, with twentie to feed himselfe, and see if he could espie any sayle passe the coast; Master Predeox with ten to Hatarask upon the same occasion: and other small parties to the Mayne to live upon rootes and Oysters.

Pemissapan sequestring himselfe, I should not importune him for victuall, and to draw his troupes, found not the Chawonests so forward as he expected, being a people more faithfull and powerfull, and desired our friendships, and was offended with him for raising such tales, and all his projects were revealed to me by Skico my prisoner; who finding himselfe as well used by me, as Pemissapan tould me all. These troubles caused me send to Pemissapan, to put suspition in his head, I was to goe presently to Croatan to meete a Fleete came to me, though I knew no such matter: and that he would lend me men to fish and hunt. He sent me word he would come himselfe to Roanock; but delaying time eight dayes that all his men were there to be assembled, not liking so much company, I resolved the next day to goe visit him, but first to give them in the Ile a Canvisado, and at an instant to seaze on all their Canows about the Ile. But the towne tooke the Alarum before I ment it. For when I sent to take the Canows, he met one going from the shore, overthrew her and cut off two Salvages heads; whereupon the cry arose, being by their spyes perceived: for they kept as good watch over us, as we of them. Upon this they to their Bowes, and we

A slaughter of two Salvages.

to our Armes: three or foure of them at the first were slaine, the rest fled into the woods. The next morning I went to Dassamonpeack, and sent Pemissapan word I was going to Croatan, and tooke him in my way to complaine Osocon would have stole my prisoner Skico. Hereupon he did abide my comming, and being among eight of the principallest, I gave the watchword to my men, and immediately they had that they purposed for us. Himselfe being shot through with a Pistoll fell

Pemissapan slaine and 8. others.

downe as dead, but presently start up and ran away from them all, till an Irish Boy shot him over the buttocks, where they tooke him and cut off his head.

Seaven dayes after Captaine Stafford sent to me he descryed twentie-three Sayle. The next day came to me himselfe (of whom I must say this, from the first to the last, he neither spared labour, or perill by land or sea, fayre weather, or foule, to performe any serious service committed to him.) He brought me a letter from Sir Francis Drake, whose generous mind offered to supply all my defects, of shipping, boats, munition, victuall, clothes, and men to further this action: and upon good consultation and deliberation, he appointed me a ship of 70.

A most generous courtesie of Sir Francis Drake.

tuns, with an hundred men, and foure moneths victuals, two Pinnaces, foure small Boats, with two sufficient Masters, with sufficient Gangs. All this being made ready for me, suddenly arose such a storme for foure dayes, that had like to have driven the whole Fleete on shore: many of them were forced to the Sea, whereof my ship so lately given me was one, with all my provision and Company appoynted.

Notwithstanding, the storme ceasing, the Generall appointed me a ship of 170. tuns, with all provisions as before, to carry me into England the next August, or when I had performed such Discoveries as I thought fit. Yet they durst not undertake to bring her into the harbour, but she must ride in the road, leaving the care of the rest to my selfe, advising me to consider with my Company what was fittest, and with my best speed returne him answer.

Hereupon calling my Company together, who were all as privy of the Generals offer as my selfe; their whole request was, (in regard of all those former miseries, and no hope of the returne of Sir Richard Grenvill,) and with a generall consent, they desired me to urge him, we might all goe with him for England in his Fleete; for whose reliefe in that storme he had sustained more perill of wrack, then in all his honorable actions against his enemies. So with prayses to God we set sayle in June 1586. and arrived in Portsmouth the 27. of July the same yeare: Leaving this remembrance to posteritie.

Virginia abandoned.

> *To reason lend me thine attentive eares,*
> *Exempt thy selfe from mind-distracting cares:*
> *Least that's here thus projected for thy good;*
> *By thee rejected be, ere understood.*

> *Written by Master Ralph Layne, Governour.*

The Observations of Master Thomas Heriot in this Voyage.

For Marchandize and Victualls.

WHAT before is writ, is also confirmed by that learned Mathematician Master Thomas Heriot, with them in the Country, whose particular Relation of all the Beasts, Birds, Fishes, Foules, Fruites, and Rootes, and how they may be usefull; because I have writ it before for the most part in the Discourse of Captaine Amidas, and Captaine Layne, except Silk grasse, Worme silke, Flax like Hempe, Allum, Wapeih, or Terra sigillata, Tar, Rosen, and Turpentine, Civet-cats, Iron ore, Copper that held Silver, Coprose and Pearle: Let those briefes suffice, because I would not trouble you with one thing twice.

Commodities.

Dyes.

For Dyes, *Showmack*, the herbe *Wasebur*, little rootes called *Chapacor*, and the barke of a tree called by the Inhabitants *Tangomockonominge*, which are for divers sorts of Reds.

Dyes.

What more then is related is an herbe in Dutch called *Melden*, described like an Orange, growing foure foote high; the seede will make good broth, and

A strange salt.

the stalke burnt to ashes makes a kinde of Salt: other Salt they know not, and we used of it for Pot-herbs. Of their Tobacco we found plenty, which they esteeme their chiefe Physicke.

Ground nuts, *Tiswaw* we call China roots; they *Rootes.* grow in clusters, and bring forth a bryer stalke, but the leafe is far unlike, which will climbe up to the top of the highest tree: the use knowne is to cut it in small peeces, then stampe and straine it with water, and boyled makes a gelly good to eate. *Cassavia* growes in Marishes, which the Indians oft use for bread and broth. *Habascon* is like a Parsnip, naught of it selfe, except compounded: and their Leekes like those in England.

Sequenummener, a kinde of Berry like Capers, and *Fruits thats* three kinde of Berries like Acornes, called *Sagata-* *strange.* *menor, Osamenor*, and *Pummuckoner*.

Saquenuckot and *Maquowoc*, two kinde of beasts, greater then Conies, and very good meate; in some places *Beasts ex-* such plenty of gray Conies, like hayres, that all the *traordinary.* people make them mantels of their skins. I have the names of 28. severall sorts that are dispersed in the Country: of which 12. kindes we have discovered and good to eate; but the Salvages sometimes kill a Lyon and eate him.

There is plentie of Sturgeon in February, March, *Fish.* Aprill, and May; all Herings in abundance; some such as ours, but the most part of 18. 20. or 24. ynches long, and more. Trouts, Porpoises, Rayes, Mullets, Old-wives, Plaice, Tortoises both by Sea and Land: Crabs, Oysters, Mussels, Scalops, Periwinckles, Crevises, Secanauk: we have the Pictures of 12. sorts more, but their names we know not.

Turkyes, Stockdoves, Partridges, Cranes, Hernes, *Foules.* Swans, Geese, Parrots, Faulcons, Merlins. I have the names in their language of 86. severall sorts. Their woods are such as ours in England for the most part, except *Rakeock*, a great sweet tree, whereof they make their Canowes: and *Ascopo*, a kinde of tree like Lowrell, and Saxefras.

Their Natures and Manners.

Their Clothing, Townes, Houses, Warres, Arts, Tooles, handy crafts, and educations, are much like them in that part of Virginia we now inhabite: which at large you may read in the Description thereof. But the relation of their Religion is strange, as this Author reporteth.

Some Religion they have, which although it be farre from the truth, yet being as it is there is hope it may be the easier reformed. They beleeve there are many gods which they call *Mantoac*, but of different sorts and degrees. Also that there is one chiefe God that hath beene from all eternitie, who as they say when he purposed first to make the world, made first other gods of a principall order, to be as instruments to be used in the Creation and government to follow: And after the Sunne, Moone, and Starres, as pettie gods; and the instruments of the other order more principall. First (they say) were made waters, out of which by the gods were made all diversitie of creatures that are visible or invisible.

Their Religion.

How the world was made.

For mankinde they say a Woman was made first, which by the working of one of the gods conceived and brought forth children; and so they had their beginning, but how many yeares or ages since they know not; having no Records but onely Tradition from Father to sonne.

How man was made.

They thinke that all the gods are of humane shape, and therefore represent them by Images in the formes of men; which they call *Kewasowok*: one alone is called *Kewasa*; them they place in their Temples, where they worship, pray, sing, and make many offerings. The common sort thinke them also gods.

How they use their gods.

They beleeve the immortalitie of the Soule, when life departing from the body, according to the good or bad workes it hath done, it is carried up to the Tabernacles of the gods, to perpetuall happinesse, or to *Popogusso*, a great pit: which they thinke to be at the furthest parts of the world, where the Sunne sets, and there burne continually.

Whether they goe after death.

To confirme this they told me of two men that had beene lately dead, and revived againe; the one hapned but few yeares before our comming into the country; of a bad man, which being dead and buried, the next day the earth over him being seene to move, was taken up, who told them his soule was very neare entering into *Popogusso*, had not one of the gods saved him and gave him leave to returne againe, to teach his friends what they should doe to

Two men risen from death.

avoyd such torment. The other hapned the same yeare we were there, but sixtie myles from us, which they told me for news, that one being dead, buried, and taken up as the first, shewed, that although his body had layne dead in the grave, yet his soule lived, and had travailed far in a long broad way, on both sides whereof grew more sweet, fayre, and delicate trees and fruits, then ever he had seene before; at length he came to most brave and fayre houses, neare which he met his Father, that was dead long agoe, who gave him charge to goe backe, to shew his friends what good there was to doe, to injoy the pleasures of that place; which when hee had done hee should come againe.

The subtiltie of their Priests. What subtiltie so ever be in the Weroances, and Priests; this opinion worketh so much in the common sort, that they have great respect to their Governours: and as great care to avoyde torment after death, and to enjoy blisse. Yet they have divers sorts of punishments according to the offence, according to the greatnesse of the fact. And this is the sum of their Religion, which I learned by having speciall familiaritie with their Priests, wherein they were not so sure grounded, nor gave such credit, but through conversing with us, they were brought into great doubts of their owne, and no small admiration of ours: of which many desired to learne more then we had meanes for want of utterance in their Language to expresse.

Their simplicitie. Most things they saw with us as Mathematicall Instruments, Sea-Compasses; the vertue of the Loadstone, Perspective Glasses, burning Glasses: Clocks to goe of themselves; Bookes, writing, Guns, and such like; so far exceeded their capacities, that they thought they were rather the workes of gods then men; or at least the gods had taught us how to make them, which loved us so much better then them; and caused many of them give credit to what we spake concerning our God. In all places where I came, I did my best to make his immortall glory knowne. And I told them, although the Bible I shewed them, contained all; yet of it selfe, it was not of any such vertue as I thought they did conceive. Notwithstanding many would be glad to touch it, to kisse, and imbrace it, to hold it to their breasts, and heads, and stroke all their body over with it.

The King Wingina where we dwelt; would oft be
with us at Prayer. Twice he was exceeding sicke and
like to dye. And doubting of any helpe from his
Priests, thinking he was in such danger for offending us and
our God, sent for some of us to pray, and be a meanes to our
God, he might live with him after death. And so did many other
in the like case. One other strange Accident (leaving others)
will I mention before I end, which mooved the whole Country
that either knew or heard of us, to have us in wonderfull
admiration.

There was no Towne where they had practised any villany
against us (we leaving it unpunished, because we sought by all
possible meanes to winne them by gentlenes) but
within a few dayes after our departure, they began to
dye; in some Townes twenty, in some forty, in some
sixty, and in one an hundred an twenty, which was very many
in respect of their numbers. And this hapned in no place (we
could learn) but where we had bin, where they had used some
practise to betray us. And this disease was so strange, they
neither knew what it was, nor how to cure it; nor had they
knowne the like time out of minde; a thing specially observed
by us, as also by themselves, in so much that some of them
who were our friends, especially Wingina, had observed such
effects in foure or five Townes, that they were perswaded it
was the worke of God through our meanes: and that we by
him might kill and slay whom we would, without weapons,
and not come neare them. And thereupon, when they had any
understanding, that any of their enemies abused us in our
Journeyes, they would intreat us, we would be a meanes to our
God, that they, as the others that had dealt ill with us, might
dye in like sort: although we shewed them their requests were
ungodly; and that our GOD would not subject himselfe to any
such requests of men, but all things as he pleased came to
passe: and that we to shew our selves his true servants, ought
rather to pray for the contrary: yet because the effect fell out so
suddenly after, according to their desires, they thought it came
to pass by our meanes, and would come give us thankes in
their manner, that though we satisfied them not in words, yet
in deeds we had fulfilled their desires.

This marveilous Accident in all the Country wrought so

Their desire of salvation.

A wonderfull Accident.

strange opinions of us, that they could not tell whether to thinke us gods or men. And the rather that all the space of their sicknesse, there was no man of ours knowne to die, or much sicke. They noted also we had no women, nor cared for any of theirs: some therefore thought we were not borne of women, and therefore not mortall, but that we were men of an old generation many yeares past, and risen againe from immortalitie. Some would Prophesie there were more of our generation yet to come, to kill theirs and take their places. Those that were to come after us they imagined to be in the ayre, yet invisible and without bodies: and that they by our intreaties, for love of us, did make the people die as they did, by shooting invisible bullets into them.

Their strange opinions.

To confirme this, their Physicians to excuse their Ignorance in curing the disease, would make the simple people beleeve, that the strings of bloud they sucked out of the sicke bodies, were the strings wherein the invisible bullets were tyed, and cast. Some thought we shot them our selves from the place where we dwelt, and killed the people that had offended us, as we listed, how farre distant soever. And others said it was the speciall worke of God for our sakes, as we had cause in some sort to thinke no lesse, whatsoever some doe, or may imagine to the contrary; especially some Astrologers by the eclipse of the Sunne we saw that yeare before our Voyage, and by a Comet which began to appeare but a few dayes before the sicknesse began: but to exclude them from being the speciall causes of so speciall an Accident, there are farther reasons then I thinke fit to present or alledge.

These their opinions I have set downe, that you may see there is hope to imbrace the truth, and honor, obey, feare and love us, by good dealing and government: though some of our company towards the latter end, before we came away with Sir Francis Drake shewed themselves too furious, in slaying some of the people in some Townes, upon causes that on our part might have bin borne with more mildnesse; notwithstanding they justly had deserved it. The best neverthelesse in this, as in all actions besides, is to be indevoured and hoped; and of the worst that may happen, notice to be taken with consideration; and as much as may be eschewed; the better to allure them hereafter to Civilitie and Christianitie.

Thus you may see, *How*

Palling.

Nature her selfe delights her selfe in sundry Instruments,
That sundry things be done to decke the earth with Ornaments;
Nor suffers she her servants all should runne one race,
But wills the walke of every one frame in a divers pace;
That divers wayes and divers workes, the world might better
     grace.

          Written by Thomas Heriot, one of the Voyage.

How Sir Richard Grenvill went to relieve them.

IN the yeare of our Lord 1586. Sir Walter Raleigh and his Associates prepared a ship of a hundred tun, fraughted plentifully of all things necessary: but before they set sayle from England it was Easter. And arriving at Hatorask, they after some time spent in seeking the Collony up in the Country, and not finding them, returned with all the provision againe to England.

1586.

About 14. or 15. dayes after, Sir Richard Grenvill accompanied with three ships well appoynted, arrived there. Who not finding the aforesaid ship according to his expectation, nor hearing any newes of the Collony there seated, and left by him as is said 1585. travailing up and downe to seeke them, but when he could heare no newes of them, and found their habitation abandoned, unwilling to lose the possession of the Country, after good deliberation he landed fiftie men in the Ile of Roanoak, plentifully furnished with all manner of provision for two yeares: and so returned for England.

Sir Richard
Grenvill left
fiftie men.

Where many began strangely to discant of those crosse beginnings, and him; which caused me remember an old saying of Euripides.

Who broacheth ought thats new, to fooles untaught,
Himselfe shall judged be unwise, and good for naught.

Three Ships more sent to relieve them by Master White.

Master White his Voyages. 1587. WE went the old course by the west Indies, and Simon Ferdinando our continuall Pilot mistaking Virginia for Cape Fear, we fayled not much to have beene cast away, upon the conceit of our all-knowing Ferdinando, had it not beene prevented by the vigilancy of Captaine Stafford. We came to Hatorask the 22. of July, and with fortie of our best men, intending at Roanoack to find the 50 men left by Sir Richard Grenvill. But we found nothing but the bones of a man, and where the Plantation had beene, the houses unhurt, but overgrowne with weeds, and the Fort defaced, which much perplexed us.

By the History it seemes Simon Ferdinando did what he could to bring this voyage to confusion; but yet they all arrived at Hatorask. They repayred the old houses at Roanock, and One of the Councell slaine. Master George How, one of the Councell, stragling abroad, was slaine by the Salvages. Not long after Master Stafford with 20. men went to Croatan with Manteo, whose friends dwelled there: of whom we thought to have some newes of our 50 men. They at first made shew to fight, but when they heard Manteo, they threw away their Armes, and were friends, and desired there might be a token given to be knowne by, least we might hurt them by misprision, as the yeare before one had bin by Master Layne, that was ever their friend, and there present yet lame.

The next day we had conference with them concerning the people of Secotan, Aquascogoc, and Pomeiok, willing them of Croatan to see if they would accept our friendship, and renew our old acquaintance: which they willingly imbraced, and promised to bring their King and Governours to Roanoak, to confirme it. We also understood that Master Howe was slaine How the fiftie men were slaine. by the men of Wingina, of Dassamonpeack: and by them of Roanoack, that the fiftie men left by Sir Richard Grenvill, were suddainly set upon by three hundred of Secotan, Aquascogoc, and Dassamonpeack. First they intruded themselves among 11 of them by friendship, one they slew, the rest retyring to their houses, they set them on fire, that our men with what came next to hand were forced to make their passage among them; where one of them was shot in the mouth, and presently dyed, and a Salvage slaine by him. On both sides more were hurt; but our men retyring to the water side, got their boat, and ere they had rowed a quarter of a myle towards Hatorask, they tooke up foure of their fellowes, gathering Crabs and Oysters: at last they landed on a little Ile by Hatorask, where they remained a while, but after departed they knew not whether. So taking our leaves of the Croatans, we came to our Fleet at Hatorask.

The Governour having long expected the King and Governours of Pomeiok, Secotan, Aquascogoc, and Dassamonpeack, and the 7. dayes expired, and no newes of them, being also informed by those of Croatan, that they of Dassamonpeack slew Master How, and were at the driving our men from Roanoack he thought no longer to deferre the revenge. Wherefore about midnight, with Captaine Stafford, and twentiefoure men, whereof Manteo was one, for our guide, (that behaved himselfe towards us as a most faithfull English man) he set forward.

The next day by breake of day we landed, and got beyond their houses, where seeing them sit by the fire we assaulted them. The miserable soules amazed fled into the Reeds, where one was shot through, and we thought to have beene fully revenged, but we were deceived, for they were our friends come from Croatan to gather their corne, because they understood our enemies were fled after the death of Master How, and left all behinde them for the birds. But they had like to have payd too deare for it, had we not chanced upon a Weroances wife, with a childe at her backe, and a Salvage that knew Captaine Stafford, that ran to him calling him by his name. Being thus disappointed of our purpose, we gathered the fruit we found ripe, left the rest unspoyled, and tooke Menatonon his wife with her childe, and the rest with us to Roanoak. Though this mistake grieved Manteo, yet he imputed it to their own folly, because they had not kept promise to come to the governor at the day appointed. The 13. of August our Salvage Manteo was Christened, and called Lord of Dassamonpeack, in reward of his faithfulnesse. And the 18th, Ellinor the Governours daughter, and wife to Ananias Dare, was delivered of

An ill misprision.

A child borne in Virginia.

a daughter in Roanoak; which being the first Christian there borne, was called Virginia.

Our ships being ready to depart, such a storme arose, as the Admirall was forced to cut her Cables: and it was six dayes ere she could recover the shore, that made us doubt she had beene lost, because the most of her best men were on shore. At this time Controversies did grow betwixt our Governour and the Assistants, about choosing one of them 12. to goe as Factor for them all to England; for all refused save one, whom all men thought most insufficient: the Conclusion was by a generall consent, they would have the Governour goe himselfe, for that they thought none would so truly procure there supplyes as he. Which though he did what he could to excuse it, yet their importunitie would not cease till he undertooke it, and had it under all their hands how unwilling he was, but that necessity and reason did doubly constraine him. At their setting sayle for England, waighing Anchor, twelve of the men in the flyboat were throwne from the Capstern, by the breaking of a barre, and most of them so hurt, that some never recovered it. The second time they had the like fortune, being but 15. they cut the Cable and kept company with their Admirall to Flowres and Corvo; the Admirall stayed there looking for purchase: but the flyboats men grew so weake they were driven to Smerwick in the West of Ireland. The Governour went for England; and Simon Ferdinando with much adoe at last arrived at Portsmouth. 1587.

A controversie who to send for Factor to England.

The Names of those were landed in this Plantation were,

John White *Governour.*	John Samson.
Roger Bayley.	Thomas Smith.
Ananias Dare.	Dionis Harvie.
Simon Ferdinando.	Roger Prat.
Christopher Couper.	George How.
Thomas Stevens.	Antony Cage.

With divers others to the number of about 115.

The fift Voyage to Virginia; undertaken by Master John White. 1589.

1589. Master White his returne to Virginia. THE 20. of March three ships went from Plimouth, and passed betwixt Barbary and Mogador to Dominica in the West Indies. After we had done some exployts in those parts, the third of August wee fell with the low sandy Iles westward of Wokokon. But by reason of ill weather it was the 11, ere we could Anchor there; and on the 12. we came to Croatan, where is a great breach in 35. degrees and a halfe, in the Northeast poynt of the Ile. The 15. we came to Hatorask in 36. degrees and a terse, at 4. fadom, 3 leagues from shore: where we might perceive a smoake at the place where I left the Colony, 1587. The next morning Captaine Cooke, Captaine Spicer, and their companies, with two boats left our ships, and discharged some Ordnance to give them notice of our comming, but when we came there, we found no man, nor signe of any that had beene there lately: and so returned to our Boats. The next morning we prepared againe for Roanoack. Captaine Spicer had then sent his Boat ashore for water, so it was ten of the Clocke ere we put from the ships, which rode two myles from the shore. The Admirals boat, being a myle before the other, as she passed the bar, a sea broke into the boat and filled her halfe full of water: but by Gods good will, and the carefull stearage of Captaine Cook, though our provisions were much wet we safe escaped, the wind blew hard at Northeast, which caused so great a current and a breach upon the barre; Captaine Spicer passed halfe over, but by the indiscreet steering of Ralph Skinner, their boat was overset, the men that could catch hold hung about her, the next sea cast her on ground, where some let goe their hold to wade to shore, but the sea beat them downe The boat thus Captaine Spicer and seaven others drowned. tossed up and downe Captaine Spicer and Skinner hung there till they were drowne; but 4. that could swim a little, kept themselves in deeper water, were saved by the meanes of Captaine Cook, that presently upon the oversetting of their boat, shipped himselfe to save what he could. Thus of eleven, seven of the chiefest were drowned. This so discomfited all the Saylers, we had much to do to get them any more to seeke further for the Planters, but by their Captaines forwardnes at last they fitted themselves againe for Hatorask in 2 boats, with 19. persons. It was late ere we arrived, but seeing a fire through the woods, we sounded a Trumpet, but no answer could we heare. The next morning we went to it, but could see nothing but the grasse, and some rotten trees burning. We went up and downe the Ile, and at last found three faire Romane Letters carved CRO which presently we knew to signifie the place where I should find them, according to a secret note betweene them and me: which was to write the name of the place they would be in, upon some tree, dore, or post: and if they had beene in any distresse, to signifie it by making a crosse over it. For at my departure they intended to goe fiftie myles into the mayne. But we found no signe of distresse; then we went to a place where they were left in sundry houses, but we found them all taken downe, and the place strongly inclosed with a high Palizado, very Fortlike; and in one of the chiefe Posts carved in fayre capitall Letters CROATAN, without any signe of distresse, and many barres of Iron, two pigs of Lead, foure Fowlers, Iron shot, and such like heavie things throwne here and there, overgrowne with grasse and weeds. We went by the shore to seeke for their boats but could find none, nor any of the Ordnance I left them. At last some of the Sailers found divers Chists had beene hidden and digged up againe, and much of the goods spoyled, and scattered up and downe, which when I saw, I knew three of them to be my owne; but bookes, pictures, and all things els were spoyled. Though it much grieved me, yet it did much comfort me that I did know they were at Croatan; so we returned to our Ships, but had like to have bin cast away by a great storme that continued all that night.

They finde where they had buryed their provisions.

The next morning we weighed Anchor for Croatan: having the Anchor a-pike, the Cable broke, by the meanes whereof we lost another: letting fall the third, the ship yet went so fast a drift, we sayled not much there to have split. But God bringing us into deeper water; considering we had but one Anchor, and our provision neare spent, we resolved to goe forthwith to St. Johns Ile, Hispaniola, or Trinidado, to refresh our selves and seeke for purchase that Winter, and the next Spring come againe to seeke our Country-men. But our Vice Admirall would not, but went directly for England, and we our course for Trinidado. But within two dayes after, the wind changing, we were constrained for the Westerne Iles to refresh our selves, where we met with many of the Queenes ships our owne consort, and divers others, the 23. of September 1590. And thus we left seeking our Colony, that was never any of them found, nor scene to this day 1622. And this was the conclusion of this Plantation, after so much time, labour, and charge consumed. Whereby we see;

The end
of this
Plantation.

Not all at once, nor all alike, nor ever hath it beene,
That God doth offer and confer his blessings upon men.

Written by Master John White.

1602. *A briefe Relation of the Description of Elizabeths Ile, and some others towards the North part of Virginia; and what els they discovered in the yeare 1602. by Captaine Bartholomew Gosnoll, and Captaine Bartholomew Gilbert; and divers other Gentlemen their Associates.*

ALL hopes of Virginia thus abandoned, it lay dead and obscured from 1590. till this yeare 1602. that Captaine Gosnoll, with 32. and himselfe in a small Barke, set sayle from Dartmouth upon the 26. of March. Though the wind favoured us not at the first, but forced us as far Southward as the Asores, which was not much out of our way; we ran directly west from thence, whereby we made our journey shorter then heretofore by 500. leagues: the weaknesse of our ship, the badnes of our saylers, and our ignorance of the coast, caused us carry but a low sayle, that made our passage longer then we expected.

12. yeares it
lay dead.

On fryday the 11. of May we made land, it was somewhat low, where appeared certaine hummocks or hills in it: the shore white sand, but very rockie, yet overgrowne with fayre trees. Comming to an Anchor, 8 Indians in a Baske shallop,

with mast and sayle came boldly aboord us. It seemed by their
signes and such things as they had, some Biskiners had fished
there: being about the latitude of 43. But the harbour being
naught, and doubting the weather, we went not ashore, but
waighed, and stood to the Southward into the Sea. The next
morning we found our selves imbayed with a mightie head-
land: within a league of the shore we anchored, and
Captaine Gosnoll, my selfe, and three others went to
it in our boat, being a white sand and a bold coast.
Though the weather was hot, we marched to the highest hils
we could see, where we perceived this headland part of the
mayn, neare invironed with Ilands. As we were returning to
our ship, a good proper, lusty young man came to us, with
whom we had but small conference, and so we left him. Here
in 5. or 6. houres we tooke more Cod then we knew what to
doe with, which made us perswade our selves, there might be
found a good fishing in March, Aprill, and May.

Their first landing. (margin, at "Captaine Gosnoll")

At length we came among these fayre Iles, some a league, 2.
3. 5. or 6. from the Mayne, by one of them we anchored. We
found it foure myles in compasse, without house or inhabitant.
In it is a lake neare a myle in circuit; the rest overgrowne with trees, which so well as the bushes, were
so overgrowne with Vines, we could scarce passe
them. And by the blossomes we might perceive there would be
plenty of Strawberries, Respises, Gousberries, and divers other
fruits: besides, Deere and other Beasts we saw, and Cranes,
Hernes, with divers other sorts of fowle; which made us call it
Martha's Vineyard.

Martha's Vineyard (margin)

The rest of the Isles are replenished with such like; very
rocky, and much tinctured stone like Minerall.
Though we met many Indians, yet we could not see
their habitations: they gave us fish, Tobacco, and
such things as they had. But the next Isle we arrived at was but
two leagues from the Maine, and 16. myle about, invironed so
with creekes and coves, it seemed like many Isles linked together by small passages, like bridges. In it is many places of
plaine grasse, and such other fruits, and berries as before were
mentioned. In mid-May we did sow Wheat, Barley, Oates, and
Pease, which in 14. dayes sprung up 9. inches. The soyle is fat
and lusty: the crust therof gray, a foot or lesse in depth. It is

Elizabeths Island. (margin)

full of high timbred Okes, their leaves thrise so broad as ours:
Cedar straight and tall, Beech, Holly, Walnut, Hazell, Cherry
trees like ours, but the stalke beareth the blossom or fruit
thereof like a cluster of Grapes, forty or fiftie in a bunch. There
is a tree of Orange colour, whose barke in the feeling is as
smooth as Velvet. There is a lake of fresh water three myles in
compasse, in the midst an Isle containing an acre or thereabout, overgrowne with wood: here are many Tortoises, and
abundance of all sorts of foules, whose young ones we tooke and
eate at our pleasure. Grounds nuts as big as egges, as good as
Potatoes, and 40. on a string, not two ynches under ground.
All sorts of shell-fish, as Scalops, Mussels, Cockles, Crabs,
Lobsters, Welks, Oysters, exceeding good and very great; but
not to cloy you with particulars, what God and nature hath bestowed on those places, I refer you to the Authors owne writing at large. We called this Isle Elizabeths Isle, from whence
we went right over to the mayne, where we stood a while as
ravished at the beautie and delicacy of the sweetnesse, besides
divers cleare lakes, whereof we saw no end, and meadows very
large and full of greene grasse, etc.

Here we espyed 7. Salvages, at first they expressed some
feare, but by our courteous usage of them, they followed us to
the necke of Land, which we thought had beene severed from
the Mayne, but we found it otherwise. Here we imagined was
a river, but because the day was farre spent, we left to discover
it till better leasure. But of good Harbours, there is no doubt,
considering the Land is all rocky and broken lands. The next
day we determined to fortifie our selves in the Isle in the lake.
Three weekes we spent in building us there a house. But the
second day after our comming from the Mayne, 11. Canows
with neare 50. Salvages came towards us. Being unwilling they
should see our building, we went to, and exchanged with them
Knives, Hatchets, Beades, Bels, and such trifles, for some
Bevers, Luzernes, Martins, Foxes, wilde Catte skinnes, and such

A Copper
Mine.
like. We saw them have much red Copper, whereof
they make chaines, collars, and drinking cups, which
they so little esteemed they would give us for small
toyes, and signified unto us they had it out of the earth in the
Mayne: three dayes they stayed with us, but every night retyred two or three myle from us: after with many signes of love

and friendship they departed, seaven of them staying behind, that did helpe us to dig and carry Saxafras, and doe any thing they could, being of a comely proportion and the best condition of any Salvages we had yet incountred. They have no Beards but counterfeits, as they did thinke ours also was: for which they would have changed with some of our men that had great beards. Some of the baser sort would steale; but the better sort, we found very civill and just. We saw but three of their women, and they were but of meane stature, attyred in skins like the men, but fat and well favoured. The wholesomenesse and temperature of this climate, doth not onely argue the people to be answerable to this Description, but also of a perfect constitution of body, active, strong, healthfull, and very witty, as the sundry toyes by them so cunningly wrought may well testifie. For our selves, we found our selves rather increase in health and strength then otherwise; for all our toyle, bad dyet and lodging; yet not one of us was touched with any sicknesse. Twelve intended here a while to have stayed, but upon better consideration, how meanely we were provided, we left this Island (with as many true sorrowfull eyes as were before desirous to see it) the 18. of June, and arrived at Exmouth, the 23 of July.

Their return.

But yet mans minde doth such it selfe explay,
As Gods great Will doth frame it every way.

And,

Such thoughts men have, on earth that doe but live,
As men may crave, but God doth onely give.

Written by John Brierton one of the Voyage.

A Voyage of Captaine Martin Pring, with two Barks from Bristow, for the North part of Virginia. 1603.

1603.

BY the inducements and perswasions of Master Richard Hackluite, Master John Whitson being Major, with his brethren the Aldermen, and most of the Merchants of the Citie of

Bristow, raised a stocke of 1000l. to furnish out two Barkes, the one of 50. tuns, with 30. men and boyes, the other 26. tuns, with 13. men and boyes, having Martin Pring an understanding Gentleman, and a sufficient Mariner for Captaine, and Robert Salterne his Assistant, who had bin with Captaine Gosnoll there the yeare before for Pilot. Though they were much crossed by contrary windes upon the coast of England, and the death of that ever most memorable, miracle of the world, our most deare soveraigne Lady and Queene Elizabeth: yet at last they passed by the westerne Isles, and about the 7. of June, fell upon the north part of Virginia, about the degrees of fortie three. Where they found plentie of most sorts of fish, and saw a high country full of great woods of sundry sorts. As they ranged the coast at a place they named Whitson Bay, they were kindly used by the Natives, that came to them, in troupes, of tens, twenties, and thirties, and sometimes more. But because in this Voyage for most part they followed the course of Captaine Gosnoll, and have made no relation but to the same effect he writ before, we will thus conclude;

> *Lay hands unto this worke with all thy wit,*
> *But pray that God would speed and perfit it.*

Robert Salterne.

1605.

A relation of a Discovery towards the Northward of Virginia, by Captaine George Waymouth 1605. imployed thether by the right Honorable Thomas Arundell, Baron of Warder, in the Raigne of our most royall King James.

Upon tuesday the fift of March we set sayle from Ratcliffe, but by contrary winds we were forced into Dartmouth till the last of this moneth, then with 29. as good sea men, and all necessary provisions as could possibly be gotten, we put to sea; and the 24 of Aprill fell with Flowres and Corvo. We intended as we were directed towards the Southward of 39. But the winds so crossed us wee fell more Northwards about 41. and 20. minuits, we sounded at 100.

Dangerous shoules.

fathom, and by that we had run 6 leagues we had but 5. yet saw no land; from the mayne top we descryed a whitish sandy clift, West North-west some 6. leagues from us, but ere we had run two leagues further we found many shoules and breaches, sometimes in 4. fadom and the next throw 15. or 18. Being thus imbayed among those shoules, we were constrained to put back againe, which we did with no small danger, though both the winde and weather were as fayre as we could desire. Thus we parted from the Land, which we had not before so much desired, and at the first sight rejoyced, as now we all joyfully praysed God that he had delivered us from so eminent danger.

Here we found excellent Cod, and saw many Whales as we had done 2. or 3. daies before. Being thus con-strained to put to sea, the want of wood and water caused us take the best advantage of the winde, to fall with the shore wheresoever: but we found our Sea-cards most directly false. The 17. of May we made the Land againe, but it blew so hard, we durst not approach it. The next day it appeared to us a mayne high land, but we found it an Island of 6. myles in compasse: within a league of it we came to an anchor, and went on shore for wood and water, of which we found sufficient. The water gushing forth downe the rocky clifts in many places, which are all overgrown with Firre, Birch, Beech, and Oke, as the Verge is with Gous-berries, Strawberries, wild Pease, and Rose bushes, and much foule of divers sorts that breed among the rockes: here as in all places els where we came, we found Cod enough.

From hence we might discerne the mayne land and very high mountairies, the next day because we rode too open to the Sea, we waighed, and came to the Isles adjoyning to the mayn: among which we found an excellent rode, defended from all windes, for ships of any burthen, in 6. 7. 8. 9.or 10. fadom upon a clay oze. This was upon a Whitsonday, wherefore we called it Pentecost Harbour. Here I cannot omit for foolish feare of imputation of flattery, the painfull industry of our Captaine, who as at Sea he was alwayes most carefull and vigilant, so at land he refused no paines: but his labour was ever as much or rather more then any mans; which not onely incouraged others with better content, but also effected much with great expedition. We digged a Garden the

Side notes:

Cod and Whales.

Their first landing.

Pentecost harbour.

22. of May, where among our gardenseeds we sowed
Pease and Barley, which in 16, dayes grew up 8.
ynches, although this was but the crust of the ground,
and much inferiour to the mould we after found in the mayne.

After we had taken order for all our necessary businesses, we marched through two of these Isles. The biggest was 4. or 5. myles in compasse; we found here all sorts of ordinary trees, besides, Vines, Currants, Spruce, Yew, Angelica, and divers gummes: in so much many of our company wished themselves setled here. Upon the 30. our Captaine with 13. went to discover the mayne: we in the ship espyed 3. Canowes that came towards the ship. Which after they had well viewed, one of them came aboord with 3. men, and by our good usage of them not long after the rest, two dayes we had their companies, in all respects they are but like them at Elizabeths Isles, therefore this may suffice for their description. In this time our Captain had discovered a fayre river, trending into the mayne 40 myles, and returned backe to bring in the ship. The Salvages also kept their words and brought us 40. Bever, Otter, and sable skins, for the value of 5. shillings in knives, glasses, combes, and such toyes, and thus we used them so kindly as we could, because we intended to inhabit in their Country, they lying aboord with us and we ashore with them; but it was but as changing man for man as hostages, and in this manner many times we had their companies.

At last they desired our Captaine to goe with them to the mayne to trade with their *Bashabes*, which is their chiefe Lord, which we did, our boat well manned with 14. yet would they row faster with 3. Ores in their Canowes then we with 8. but when we saw our old acquaintance, would not stay aboord us as before for hostage, but did what they could to draw us into a narrow cirke, we exchanged one Owen Griffin with them for a yong fellow of theirs, that he might see if he could discover any trechery, as he did, for he found there assembled 283. Salvages with bowes and arrows, but not any thing at all to trade as they pretended. These things considered, we, conceited them to be but as all Salvages ever had beene, kinde till they found opportunitie to do mischiefe. Wherefore we determined to take some of them, before they should suspect we had discovered their plot, lest they should absent themselves from us, so the first that ever after came into the ship were three which we kept, and two we tooke on shore with much adoe, with two Canowes, their bowes and arrowes.

Five Salvages surprised.

Some time we spent in sounding all the Isles, channels, and inlets thereabouts, and we found 4. severall waies a ship might be brought into this Bay. In the interim there came 2. Canowes more boldly aboord us, signifying we should bring our ship to the place where he dwelt to trade. We excused our selves why we could not, but used them kindly, yet got them away with all the speed we could, that they should not be perceived by them in the houle, then we went up the river 26. myles, of which I had rather not write, then by my relation detract from it, it is in breadth a myle, neare 40. myles; and a channell of 6. 7. 8. 9. or 10. fadom, and on both sides every halfe myle gallant Coves, to containe in many of them 100 sayle, where they may lye on Oze without Cable or Anchor, onely mored with a Hauser, and it floweth 18. foot, that you may make, docke, or carine ships with much facilitie: besides the land is most rich, trending all along on both sides in an equall plaine, neither rocky nor mountainous, but verged with a greene border of grasse, doth make tender to the beholder her pleasant fertilitie, if by cleansing away the woods she were converted into meadow.

A description of the river.

The woods are great, and tall, such as are spoken of in the Islelands, and well watered with many fresh springs. Our men that had scene Oranoque so famous in the worlds eares, Reogrande, Loyer, and Seine, report, though they be great and goodly rivers, yet are not comparable to it. Leaving our ship we went higher, till we were 7. myles higher then the salt water flowed; we marched towards the mountains we had seene, but the weather was so hot, and our labour so great, as our Captaine was contented to returne: after we had erected a crosse we left this faire land and river, in which the higher we went the better we liked it, and returned to our ship. By the way we met a Canow that much desired one of our men to go up to their *Basshabes*, but we knew their intents, and so turned them off; and though we had both time and provision to have discovered much more, and might have found peradventure good trade, yet because our company was but small, we would

A Coniurer.

Their

C: S.

Their triumph about him

C: Smith bound to a tree to be shott to death 1607

How they tooke him prisoner in the Oaze 1607

C: Smith bindeth a salvage to his arme, fightah with the King of Pamaunkee and all his company, and slew 7 of them.

C: Smith takes the King of Paspahegh prisoner. A°. 1609.

35   Mountaynes forest
OULD   Waldens Oake
Masons bushe   L:D: Lenox rocks
VIR   GI   Mangoack Rich
Cawrnuock   Pananarec   Stuards
Nustoc   Secota   NI   Anadales
Setuoc
Cotan   Ceisls Harbor
Davers Ile   Piquimp
feare   Abigalls Iles
Salvage Ile   Box   DeHatton
Gordens Ila   P. Vaughan
Abbon   Ile Greeneuill
Accowdamus

35   Graven and extracted out of y generall

Idoll

A Preist

C. Smith taketh the King of Pamaunkees prisoner 1608

The Countrey wee now call Virginia beginneth at Cape Henry distant from Roanoack 60 miles, where was S.t Walter Raleigh's plantation. and because the people differ very little from them of Powhatan in any thing, I have inserted those figures in this place because of the conveniency.

A description of part of the adventures of Cap: Smith in Virginia.

steps
untaynes
fordss valley
ck flu:

Ramushonoq
A. Salvage Rocke
Beauchamps playne
Chavanok flu:

Ohanoack

Metocaum

Maraton

Mascoming

Chepanu

Heriots Ile

Pasquenock

P. Corbett

Ile

Arundells Ile

Ile

Alice
Smith

Capking

Segars grove
Chisapeack

Townsrows end

Mildmaids roade

Bacon.

Barkley

Adams Sound
C. Henry

ia, New England, and Somer Iles, by Robert Vaughan.

Vincere est Viuere

8 9 10

uges.

printed by James Reeue

King Powhatan comands C. Smith to be slayne, his daughter Pokahontas beggs his life, his thankfullness and how he subiected 39 of their kings, reade y history not hazzard so hopefull a businesse as this was, either for our private, or particular ends, being more regardfull of a publicke good, and promulgating Gods holy Church by planting Christianity, which was the intent of our adventurers so well as ours; returning by the Isles in the entry of the Sound we called them St. Georges Isles, and because on sunday we set out of England, on sunday also the 16. of June we departed hence. When we had run 30. leagues we had 40. fadom, then 70. then 100. After 2. or 3. watches more we were in 24. fadoms, where we tooke so much Cod as we did know what to doe with, and the 18. of July came to Dartmouth, and all our men as well God be thanked as when they went forth.

Thus may you see;

God hath not all his gifts bestowed on all or any one,
Words sweetest, and wits sharpest, courage, strength of bone;
All rarities of minde and parts doe all concurre in none.

Written by James Rosier one of the Voyage.

The second Booke.

THE SIXT VOYAGE.

1606.

To another part of Virginia, where now are
Planted our English Colonies, Whom God
increase and preserve: Discovered and
Described by Captaine JOHN SMITH,
sometimes Governour of the Countrey.

1606.

B Y these former relations you may see what incon-
veniences still crossed those good intents, and
how great a matter it was all this time to finde but a
Harbour, although there be so many. But this Virginia is a
Country in America betweene the degrees of 34. and
The latitude. 45. of the North latitude. The bounds thereof on the
East side are the great Ocean: on the South lyeth
Florida: on the North nova Francia: as for the West thereof,
the limits are unknowne. Of all this Country we purpose not
to speake, but onely of that part which was planted by the English men in the yeare of our Lord, 1606. And this is under the
degrees 37. 38. and 39. The temperature of this Country doth
agree well with English constitutions, being once seasoned to
the Country. Which appeared by this, that though by many
occasions our people fell sicke; yet did they recover by very
small meanes, and continued in health, though there were
other great causes, not onely to have made them sicke, but
even to end their dayes, etc.

The tem-
perature. The Sommer is hot as in Spaine; the Winter cold
as in France or England. The heat of sommer is in
June, July, and August, but commonly the coole
Breeses asswage the vehemency of the heat. The chiefe of winter is halfe December, January, February, and halfe March.
The colde is extreame sharpe, but here the Proverbe is true,
that no extreame long continueth.

In the yeare 1607. was an extraordinary frost in most of

Europe, and this frost was found as extreame in Virginia. But the next yeare for 8. or 10. dayes of ill weather, other 14. dayes would be as Sommer.

The windes here are variable, but the like thunder and lightning to purifie the ayre, I have seldome either seene or heard in Europe. From the Southwest came the greatest gusts with thunder and heat. The Northwest winde is commonly coole and bringeth faire weather with it. From the North is the greatest cold, and from the East and Southeast as from the Barmudas, fogs and raines.

The windes.

Some times there are great droughts, other times much raine, yet great necessitie of neither, by reason we see not but that all the raritie of needfull fruits in Europe, may be there in great plentie, by the industry of men, as appeareth by those we there Planted.

There is but one entrance by Sea into this Country, and that is at the mouth of a very goodly Bay, 18. or 20. myles broad. The cape on the South is called Cape Henry, in honour of our most noble Prince. The land white hilly sands like unto the Downes, and all along the shores great plentie of Pines and Firres.

The entrances.

Cape Henry.

The north Cape is called Cape Charles, in honour of the worthy Duke of Yorke. The Isles before it, Smith's Isles, by the name of the discoverer. Within is a country that may have the prerogative over the most pleasant places knowne, for large and pleasant navigable Rivers, heaven and earth never agreed better to frame a place for mans habitation; were it fully manured and inhabited by industrious people. Here are mountaines, hils, plaines, valleyes, rivers, and brookes, all running most pleasantly into a faire Bay, compassed but for the mouth, with fruitfull and delightsome land. In the Bay and rivers are many Isles both great and small, some woody, some plaine, most of them low and not inhabited. This Bay lyeth North and South, in which the water floweth neare 200. myles, and hath a channell for 140 myles, of depth betwixt 6 and 15 fadome, holding in breadth for the most part 10 or 14 myles. From the head of the Bay to the Northwest, the land is mountanous, and so in a manner from thence by a Southwest line; so that the more Southward, the farther off from the Bay are those mountaines.

Cape Charles.

The Country.

From which fall certaine brookes which after come to five principall navigable rivers. These run from the Northwest into the Southeast, and so into the West side of the Bay, where the fall of every River is within 20 or 15 myles one of another.

The mountaines. The mountaines are of divers natures: for at the head of the Bay the rockes are of a composition like Mill stones. Some of Marble, etc. And many peeces like Christall we found, as throwne downe by water from those mountaines. For in Winter they are covered with much snow, and when it dissolveth the waters fall with such violence, that it causeth great inundations in some narrow valleyes, which is scarce perceived being once in the rivers. These waters wash from the rocks such glistering tinctures, that the ground in some places seemeth as guilded, where both the rocks and the earth are so splendent to behold, that better judgements then ours might have beene perswaded, they contained more then probabilities.

The soyle. The vesture of the earth in most places doth manifestly prove the nature of the soyle to be lusty and very rich. The colour of the earth we found in diverse places, resembleth bole Armoniac, terra sigillata ad Lemnia, Fullers earth, Marle, and divers other such appearances. But generally for the most part it is a blacke sandy mould, in some places a fat slimy clay, in other places a very barren gravell. But the best ground is knowne by the vesture it beareth, as by the greatnesse of trees, or abundance of weeds, etc.

The valleyes. The Country is not mountanous, nor yet low, but such pleasant plaine hils, and fertile valleyes, one prettily crossing another, and watered so conveniently with fresh brookes and springs, no lesse com-

Plaines. modious, then delightsome. By the rivers are many plaine marishes, containing some 20 some 100. some 200 Acres, some more, some lesse. Other plaines there are few, but onely where the Salvages inhabit: but all overgrowne with trees and weeds, being a plaine wildernesse as God first made it.

On the west side of the Bay, we sayd were 5. faire and delightfull navigable rivers. The first of those, and the next to the mouth of the Bay hath his course from the West

The river Powhatan. Northwest. It is called Powhatan, according to the name of a principall country that lyeth upon it. The mouth of this river is neare three myles in breadth, yet doe

the shoules force the Channell so neare the land, that a Sacre
will overshoot it at point blanke. It is navigable 150 myles, the
shouldes and soundings are here needlesse to be expressed. It
falleth from Rockes farre west in a Country inhabited by a nation they call Monacans. But where it commeth into our discovery it is Powhatan. In the farthest place that was diligently
observed, are falles, rockes, shoules, etc. which makes it past
navigation any higher. Thence in the running downeward, the
river is enriched with many goodly brookes, which are maintained by an infinit number of small rundles and pleasant
springs, that disperse themselves for best service, as
The branches do the veines of a mans body. From the South there
fals into it: First, the pleasant river of Apamatuck.
Next more to the East are two small rivers of Quiyoughco-
hanocke. A little farther is a Bay wherein falleth 3 or 4 prettie
brookes and creekes that halfe intrench the Inhabitants of
Warraskoyac, then the river of Nandsamund, and lastly the
brooke of Chisapeack. From the North side is the river of
Chickahamania, the backe river of James Towne; another by
the Cedar Isle; where we lived ten weekes upon Oysters, then
a convenient harbour for Fisher boats at Kecoughtan, that so
turneth it selfe into Bayes and Creekes, it makes that place very
pleasant to inhabit; their cornefields being girded therein in a
manner as Peninsulaes. The most of these rivers are inhabited
by severall nations, or rather families, of the name of the rivers
They have also over those some Governour, as their King,
which they call Werowances. In a Peninsula on the North side
of this river are the English Planted in a place by
James Towne. them called James Towne, in honour of the Kings
most excellent Majestie.

The first and next the rivers mouth are the Ke-
The severall coughtans, who besides their women and children,
Inhabitants. have not past 20. fighting men. The Paspaheghes (on
whose land is seated James Towne, some 40 myles from the
Bay) have not past 40. The river called Chickahamania neare
250. The Weanocks 100. The Arrowhatocks 30. The place
called Powhatan, some 40. On the South side this river the Appamatucks have sixtie fighting men. The Quiyougcohanocks
25. The Nandsamunds 200. The Chesapeacks 100. Of this last
place the Bay beareth the name. In all these places is a severall

commander, which they call Werowance, except the Chickahamanians, who are governed by the Priests and their Assistants,
or their Elders called *Caw-cawwassoughes*. In sommer no place
affordeth more plentie of Sturgeon, nor in winter more abundance of foule, especially in the time of frost. I tooke once 52
Sturgeons at a draught, at another 68. From the later end of
May till the end of June are taken few, but yong Sturgeons of
two foot, or a yard long. From thence till the midst of September, them of two or three yards long and few others. And
in 4 or 5. houres with one Net were ordinarily taken 7 or 8:
often more, seldome lesse. In the small rivers all the yeare
there is good plentie of small fish, so that with hookes those
that would take paines had sufficient.

Foureteene myles Northward from the river Pow-
River Pamaunkee. hatan, is the river Pamaunkee, which is navigable 60
or 70 myles, but with Catches and small Barkes 30 or
40 myles farther. At the ordinary flowing of the salt water, it
The inhabi-tants. divideth it selfe into two gallant branches. On the
South side inhabit the people of Youghtanund, who
have about 60 men for warres. On the North branch
Mattapament, who have 30 men. Where this river is divided
the Country is called Pamaunkee, and nourisheth neare 300
able men. About 25. myles lower on the North side of this river
is Werawocomoco, where their great King inhabited when I
was delivered him prisoner; yet there are not past 40 able men.
Ten or twelve myles lower, on the South side of this river, is
Chiskiack, which hath some 40 or 50 men. These, as also Apamatuck, Irrohatock, and Powhatan, are their great Kings
chiefe alliance, and inhabitants. The rest his Conquests.

Before we come to the third river that falleth from
Payankatank. River. the mountaines, there is another river (some 30 myles
navigable) that commeth from the Inland, called
Payankatanke, the Inhabitants are about 50 or 60 serviceable
men.

The third navigable river is called Toppahanock.
Toppahanock River (This is navigable some 130 myles) At the top of it in-
habit the people called Mannahoacks amongst the
The inhabitants. mountaines, but they are above the place we describe.
Upon this river on the North side are the people Cut-
tatawomen, with 30 fighting men. Higher are the

Moraughtacunds, with 80. Beyond them Rapahanock with 100. Far above is another Cuttatawomen with 20. On the South is the pleasant seat of Nantaughtacund having 150 men. This river also as the two former, is replenished with fish and foule.

The fourth river is called Patawomeke, 6 or 7 myles in breadth. It is navigable 140 myles, and fed as the rest with many sweet rivers and springs, which fall from the bordering hils. These hils many of them are planted, and yeeld no lesse plentie and varietie of fruit, then the river exceedeth with abundance of fish. It is inhabited on both sides. First on the South side at the very entrance is Wighcocomoco and hath some 130 men, beyond them Sekacawone with 30. The Onawmanient with 100. And the Patawomekes more then 200. Here doth the river divide it selfe into 3 or 4 convenient branches. The greatest of the least is called Quiyough, trending Northwest, but the river it selfe turneth Northeast, and is still a navigable streame. On the Westerne side of this bought is Tauxenent with 40 men. On the North of this river is Secowocomoco with 40. Somewhat further Potapaco with 20. In the East part is Pamacaeack with 60. After Moyowance with 100. And lastly, Nacotchtanke with 80. The river above this place maketh his passage downe a low pleasant valley overshaddowed in many places with high rocky mountaines; from whence distill innumerable sweet and pleasant springs.

Patawomek, River.

The inhabitants.

The fift river is called Pawtuxunt, of a lesse proportion then the rest; but the channell is 16 fadome deepe in some places. Here are infinit skuls of divers kindes of fish more then elswhere. Upon this river dwell the people called Acquintanacksuak, Pawtuxunt, and Mattapanient. Two hundred men was the greatest strength that could be there perceived. But they inhabit together, and not so dispersed as the rest. These of all other we found most civill to give intertainement.

Pawtuxunt, River.

Thirtie leagues Northward is a river not inhabited, yet navigable; for the red clay resembling bole Armoniack we called it Bolus. At the end of the Bay where it is 6 or 7 myles in breadth, it divides it selfe into 4. branches, the best commeth Northwest from among

Bolus, River.

The head of the Bay.

the mountaines, but though Canows may goe a dayes journey
or two up it, we could not get two myles up it with
our boat for rockes. Upon it is seated the Sasquesahanocks, neare it North and by West runneth a
creeke a myle and a halfe: at the head whereof the Ebbe left us
on shore, where we found many trees cut with hatchets. The
next tyde keeping the shore to seeke for some Salvages; (for
within thirtie leagues sayling, we saw not any, being a barren
Country,) we went up another small river like a creeke 6 or 7
myle. From thence returning we met 7 Canowes of the Mas-
sowomeks, with whom we had conference by signes, for we
understood one another scarce a word: the next day we discovered the small river and people of Tockwhogh trending
Eastward.

Sasquesaha-nock.

Having lost our Grapnell among the rocks of Sasquesahanocks, we were then neare 200 myles from home, and our
Barge about two tuns, and had in it but 12 men to performe
this Discovery, wherein we lay above 12 weekes upon those
great waters in those unknowne Countries, having nothing
but a little meale, oatemeale and water to feed us, and scarce
halfe sufficient of that for halfe that time, but what provision
we got among the Salvages, and such rootes and fish as we
caught by accident, and Gods direction; nor had we a Mariner
nor any had skill to trim the sayles but two saylers and my selfe,
the rest being Gentlemen, or them were as ignorant in such
toyle and labour. Yet necessitie in a short time by good words
and examples made them doe that that caused them ever after
to feare no colours. What I did with this small meanes I leave
to the Reader to judge, and the Mappe I made of the Country,
which is but a small matter in regard of the magnitude thereof.
But to proceed, 60 of those Sasquesahanocks came to us with
skins, Bowes, Arrows, Targets, Beads, Swords, and Tobacco
pipes for presents. Such great and well proportioned men are
seldome seene, for they seemed like Giants to the English, yea
and to the neighbours, yet seemed of an honest and simple
disposition, with much adoe restrained from adoring us as
Gods. Those are the strangest people of all those Countries,
both in language and attire; for their language it
may well beseeme their proportions, sounding from
them, as a voyce in a vault. Their attire is the skinnes

*The
description
of a Sasque-
sahanough.*

of Beares, and Woolves, some have Cassacks made of Beares heads and skinnes, that a mans head goes through the skinnes neck, and the eares of the Beare fastned to his shoulders, the nose and teeth hanging downe his breast, another Beares face split behind him, and at the end of the nose hung a Pawe, the halfe sleeves comming to the elbowes were the neckes of Beares, and the armes through the mouth with pawes hanging at their noses. One had the head of a Woolfe hanging in a chaine for a Jewell, his Tobacco pipe three quarters of a yard long, prettily carved with a Bird, a Deere, or some such devise at the great end, sufficient to beat out ones braines: with Bowes, Arrowes, and clubs, sutable to their greatnesse. These are scarse knowne to Powhatan. They can make neare 600 able men, and are pallisadoed in their Townes to defend them from the Massawomekes their mortall enemies. Five of their chiefe Werowances came aboord us, and crossed the Bay in their Barge. The picture of the greatest of them is signified in the Mappe. The calfe of whose leg was three quarters of a yard about, and all the rest of his limbes so answerable to that pro-portion, that he seemed the goodliest man we ever beheld. His hayre, the one side was long, the other shore close with a ridge over his crowne like a cocks combe. His arrowes were five quarters long, headed with the splinters of a white christall-like stone, in forme of a heart, an inch broad, and an inch and a halfe or more long. These he wore in a Woolves skinne at his backe for his Quiver, his bow in the one hand and his clubbe in the other, as is described.

On the East side the Bay, is the river Tockwhogh, and upon it a people that can make 100 men, seated some seaven myles within the river: where they have a Fort very well pallisadoed and mantelled with barkes of trees. Next them is Ozinies with sixty men. More to the South of that East side of the Bay, the river Rapahanock, neere unto which is the river Kuskarawaock, Upon which is seated a people with 200 men. After that, is the river Tants Wighcocomoco, and on it a people with 100 men. The people of those rivers are of little stature, of another language from the rest, and very rude. But they on the river Acohanock with 40 men, and they of Accomack 80 men doth equalize any of

Tockwhogh, River.

Rapahanock, River.

Kuskara-waock River.

Wighco-comoco, River.

Accomack, River.

the Territories of Powhatan, and speake his language, who over all those doth rule as King.

Southward we went to some parts of Chawonock and the Mangoags to search for them left by Master White. Amongst those people are thus many severall Nations of sundry Languages, that environ Powhatans Territories. The Chawonockes, the Mangoags, the Monacans, the Mannahokes, the Masawomekes, the Powhatans, the Sasquesahanocks, the Atquanachukes, the Tockwoghes, and the Kuscarawaokes. All those not any one understandeth another but by Interpreters. Their severall habitations are more plainly described by this annexed Mappe, which will present to the eye, the way of the mountaines, and current of the rivers, with their severall turnings, bayes, shoules, Isles, Inlets, and creekes, the breadth of the waters, the distances of places, and such like. In which Mappe observe this, that as far as you see the little Crosses on rivers, mountaines, or other places have beene discovered; the rest was had by information of the Savages, and are set downe according to their instructions.

Chawoneck.

The severall languages.

> *Thus have I walkt a wayless way, with uncouth pace,*
> *Which yet no Christian man did ever trace:*
> *But yet I know this not affects the minde,*
> *Which eares doth heare, as that which eyes doe finde.*

Of such things which are naturally in Virginia, and how they use them.

VIRGINIA doth afford many excellent vegetables, and living Creatures, yet grasse there is little or none, but what groweth in low Marishes: for all the Countrey is overgrowne with trees, whose droppings continually turneth their grasse to weeds, by reason of the rancknes of the ground, which would soone be amended by good husbandry. The wood that is most common is Oke and Walnut, many of their Okes are so tall and

Why there is little grasse.

Woods with their fruits.

straight, that they will beare two foote and a halfe square of good timber for 20 yards long; Of this wood there is two or three severall kinds. The Acornes of one kinde, whose barke is more white then the other, and somewhat sweetish, which being boyled, at last affords a sweet oyle, that they keepe in gourds to annoint their heads and joynts. The fruit they eate made in bread or otherwise. There is also some Elme, some blacke Walnut tree, and some Ash: of Ash and Elme they make sope Ashes. If the trees be very great, the Ashes will be good, and melt to hard lumps, but if they be small, it will be but powder, and not so good as the other. Of walnuts there is 2 or 3 kindes; there is a kinde of wood we called Cypres, because both the wood, the fruit, and leafe did most resemble it, and of those trees there are some neare three fadome about at the root, very straight, and 50, 60, or 80 foot without a branch. By the dwelling of the Salvages are some great Mulbery trees, and in some parts of the Countrey, they are found growing naturally in prettie groves. There was an assay made to make silke, and surely the wormes prospered excellent well, till the master workeman fell sicke. During which time they were eaten with Rats.

    In some parts were found some Chesnuts, whose wild fruit equalize the best in France, Spaine, Germany, or Italy. Plums there are of three sorts. The red and white are like our hedge plums, but the other which they call *Putchamins*, grow as high as a Palmeta: the fruit is like a Medler; it is first greene, then yellow, and red when it is ripe; if it be not ripe, it will draw a mans mouth awry, with much torment, but when it is ripe, it is as delicious as an Apricot.

    They have Cherries, and those are much like a Damson, but for their tastes and colour we called them Cherries. We saw some few Crabs, but very small and bitter. Of vines great abundance in many parts that climbe the toppes of the highest trees in some places, but these beare but few grapes. Except by the rivers and savage habitations, where they are not overshadowed from the sunne, they are covered with fruit, though never pruined nor manured. Of those hedge grapes we made neere twentie gallons of wine, which was like our French Brittish wine, but cer-

Marginal notes: Elme.   Walnuts.   Supposed Cypres.   Mulberries.   Chesnuts.   Cherries.   Vines.

tainely they would prove good were they well manured. There is another sort of grape neere as great as a Cherry, this they call *Messamins*, they be fatte, and the juyce thicke. Neither doth the taste so well please when they are made in wine. They have a small fruit growing on little trees, husked like a Chesnut, but

Chechinqua-mins. the fruit most like a very small Acorne. This they call *Chechinquamins*, which they esteeme a great daintie. They have a berry much like our Gooseberry, in

Rawcomens. greatnesse, colour, and tast; those they call *Rawcomens*, and doe eat them raw or boyled. Of these naturall fruits they live a great part of the yeare, which they use in this manner; The Walnuts, Chesnuts, Acornes,

How they use their fruits. and *Chechinquamins* are dryed to keepe. When, they need walnuts they breake them betweene two stones, yet some part of the shels will cleave to the fruit. Then doe they dry them againe upon a Mat over a hurdle. After they put it into a morter of wood, and beat it very small: that done they mix it with water, that the shels may sinke to

Walnut milke. the bottome. This water will be coloured as milke, which they call *Pawcohiccora*, and keepe it for their use. The fruit like Medlers they call *Putchamins*, they cast upon hurdles on a Mat, and preserve them as Pruines. Of their Chesnuts and *Chechinquamins* boyled, they make both broath and bread for their chiefe men, or at their greatest feasts. Besides those fruit trees, there is a white Popular, and another tree like unto it, that yeeldeth a very cleare and an odoriferous

Gummes. Gumme like Turpentine, which some called Balsom.
Cedars.
Saxafras trees. There are also Cedars and Saxafras trees. They also yeeld gummes in a small proportion of themselves. Wee tryed conclusions to extract it out of the wood, but nature afforded more then our arts.

Berries. In the watry valleyes groweth a Berry which they call *Ocoughtanamnis* very much like unto Capers. These they dry in sommer. When they eat them they boile them neare halfe a day; for otherwise they dif-

Matoum. fer not much from poyson. *Mattoum* groweth as our Bents. The seed is not much unlike to Rie, though much smaller. This they use for a daintie bread buttered with deare suet.

Strawberries. During Sommer there are either Strawberries, which ripen in Aprill, or Mulberries which ripen in May and June. Raspises, hurts; or a fruit that the inhabitants call *Maracocks*, which is a pleasant wholsome fruit much like a Lemond. Many herbes in the spring are commonly dispersed throughout the woods, good for brothes and sallets, as Violets, Purslain, Sorrell, etc. Besides many we used whose names we know not.

Hearbes.

The chiefe root they have for food is called *Tockawhoughe*. It groweth like a flagge in Marishes. In one day a Salvage will gather sufficient for a weeke. These roots are much of the greatnesse and taste of Potatoes. They use to cover a great many of them with Oke leaves and Ferne, and then cover all with earth in the manner of a Cole-pit; over it, on each side, they continue a great fire 24 houres before they dare eat it. Raw it is no better then poyson, and being rosted, except it be tender and the heat abated, or sliced and dryed in the Sunne, mixed with sorrell and meale or such like, it will prickle and torment the throat extreamely, and yet in sommer they use this ordinarily for bread.

Rootes.

They have another roote which they call *Wighsacan*: as th'other feedeth the body, so this cureth their hurts and diseases. It is a small root which they bruise and apply to the wound. *Pocones* is a small root that groweth in the mountaines, which being dryed and beate in powder turneth red. And this they use for swellings, aches, annointing their joynts, painting their heads and garments. They account it very precious, and of much worth. *Musquaspen* is a roote of the bignesse of a finger, and as red as bloud. In drying, it will wither almost to nothing. This they use to paint their Mattes, Targets, and such like.

Wighsacan a roote.

Pocones a small roote.

Musquaspen a roote.

There is also Pellitory of Spaine, Sasafrage, and divers other simples, which the Apothecaries gathered, and commended to be good, and medicinable.

Pellitory. Sasafrage.

In the low Marishes grow plots of Onyons, containing an Acre of ground or more in many places; but they are small, not past the bignesse of the toppe of ones Thumbe.

Onyons.

Of beasts the chiefe are Deere, nothing differing from ours. In the deserts towards the heads of the

Their chiefe beasts are Deere.

rivers, there are many, but amongst the rivers few. There is a beast they call *Aroughcun*, much like a badger, but useth to live on trees as Squirrels doe. Their Squirrels some are neare as great as our smallest sort of wilde Rabbets, some blackish or blacke and white, but the most are gray.

Aroughcun. Squirrels.

A small beast they have they call *Assapanick*, but we call them flying Squirrels, because spreading their legs, and so stretching the largenesse of their skins, that they have beene seene to fly 30 or 40 yards. An Opassom hath a head like a Swine, and a taile like a Rat, and is of the bignesse of a Cat. Under her belly shee hath a bagge, wherein she lodgeth, carrieth, and suckleth her young. A *Mussascus* is a beast of the forme and nature of our water Rats, but many of them smell exceeding strongly of Muske. Their Hares no bigger then our Conies, and few of them to be found.

Assapanick, a Squirrel flying.

Opassom.

Mussascus.

Their Beares are very little in comparison of those of Muscovia and Tartaria. The Beaver is as big as an ordinary water dog, but his legs exceeding short. His forefeete like a dogs, his hinderfeet like a Swans. His taile somewhat like the forme of a Racket, bare without haire, which to eat the Salvages esteeme a great delicate. They, have many Otters, which as the Beavers they take with snares, and esteeme the skins great orna-ments, and of all those beasts they use to feed when they catch them. An *Utchunquoyes* is like a wilde Cat. Their Foxes are like our silver haired Conies, of a small proportion, and not smelling like those in England. Their Dogges of that Country are like their Woolves, and can-not barke but howle, and the Woolves not much bigger then our English Foxes. Martins, Powlecats, Weesels, and Minkes we know they have, because we have seene many of their skinnes, though very seldome any of them alive. But one thing is strange, that we could never per-ceive their Vermine destroy our Hennes, Egges, nor Chickens, nor doe any hurt, nor their flyes nor serpents any way perni-cious, where in the South parts of America they are alwayes dangerous, and often deadly.

Beares.

The Beaver.

Otters.

Utchunquoyes

Foxes.

Dogges.

Martins.

Polcats.

Weesels,

and Minkes.

Of Birds the Eagle is the greatest devourer. Hawkes

Birds.

there be of divers sorts, as our Falconers called them: Sparrow-hawkes, Lanarets, Goshawkes, Falcons and Osperayes, but they all prey most upon fish. Their Partridges are little bigger then our Quailes. Wilde Turkies are as bigge as our tame. There are Woosels or Blackbirds with red shoulders, Thrushes and divers sorts of small Birds, some red, some blew, scarce so bigge as a Wrenne, but few in Sommer. In Winter there are great plentie of Swans, Cranes, gray and white with blacke wings, Herons, Geese, Brants, Ducke, Wigeon, Dotterell, Oxeies, Parrats, and Pigeons. Of all those sorts great abundance, and some other strange kinds, to us unknowne by name. But in Sommer not any, or a very few to be seene.

Fish.

Of fish we were best acquainted with Sturgeon, Grampus, Porpus, Seales, Stingraies, whose tailes are very dangerous. Bretts, Mullets, white Salmonds, Trowts, Soles, Plaice, Herrings, Conyfish, Rockfish, Eeles, Lampreys, Catfish, Shades, Pearch of three sorts, Crabs, Shrimps, Crevises, Oysters, Cocles, and Muscles. But the most strange fish is a small one, so like the picture of St. George his Dragon, as possible can he, except his legs and wings, and the Toade-fish, which will swell till it be like to burst, when it commeth into the ayre.

The rockes.

Concerning the entrailes of the earth, little can be said for certaintie. There wanted good Refiners; for those that tooke upon them to have skill this way, tooke up the washings from the mountaines, and some moskered shining stones and spangles which the waters brought downe, flattering themselves in their owne vaine conceits to have beene supposed what they were not, by the meanes of that ore, if it proved as their arts and judgements expected. Onely this is certaine, that many regions lying in the same latitude, afford Mines very rich of divers natures. The crust also of these rockes would easily perswade a man to beleeve there are other Mines then yron and steele, if there were but meanes and men of experience that knew the Mine from Spar.

Of their Planted fruits in Virginia, and how they use them.

How they divide the yeare. THEY divide the yeare into five seasons. Their winter some call *Popanow*, the spring *Cattapeuk*, the sommer *Cohattayough*, the earing of their Corne *Nepinough*, the harvest and fall of leafe *Taquitock*. From September untill the midst of November are the chiefe feasts and sacrifice. Then have they plentie of fruits as well planted as naturall, as corne, greene and ripe, fish, fowle, and wilde beasts exceeding fat.

How they prepare the ground. The greatest labour they take, is in planting their corne, for the Country naturally is overgrowne with wood. To prepare the ground they bruise the barke of the trees neare the root, then doe they scortch the roots with fire that they grow no more. The next yeare with a crooked peece of wood they beat up the weeds by the rootes, and in that mould they plant their Corne. Their manner is this. They make a hole in the earth with a sticke, and into it they put foure graines of wheate and two of beanes. These holes they make foure foote one from another; Their women and children do continually keepe it with weeding, and when it is growne middle high, they hill it about like a hop-yard.

How they plant. In Aprill they begin to plant, but their chiefe plantation is in May, and so they continue till the midst of June. What they plant in Aprill they reape in August, for May in September, for June in October; Every stalke of their corne commonly beareth two eares, some three, seldome any foure, many but one, and some none. Every eare ordinarily hath betwixt 200 and 500 graines. The stalke being greene hath a sweet juice in it, somewhat like a sugar Cane, which is the cause that when they gather their corne greene, they sucke the stalkes: for as we gather greene pease, so doe they their corne being greene, which excelleth their old. They plant also pease they call *Assentamens*, which are the same they call in Italy, *Fagioli*. Their Beanes are the same the Turkes call *Garnanses*, but these they much esteeme for dainties.

How they use their Corne. Their corne they rost in the eare greene, and bruising it in a morter of wood with a Polt, lap it in rowles in the leaves of their corne, and so boyle it for a daintie. They also reserve that corne late planted that will not ripe, by roasting it in hot ashes, the heat thereof drying it. In winter they esteeme it being boyled with beanes for a rare dish, they call *Pausarowmena*. Their old wheat they first steepe a night in hot water, in the morning pounding it in a morter. They use a small basket for their Temmes, then pound againe the great, and so separating by dashing their hand in the basket, receive the flower in a platter made of wood, scraped to that forme with burning and shels. Tempering this flower with water, they make it either in cakes, covering them with ashes till they be baked, and then washing them in faire water, they drie presently with their owne heat: or else boyle them in water, eating the broth with the bread which they call *Ponap*. The groutes and peeces of the cornes remaining, by fanning in a Platter or in the wind, away, the branne they boyle 3 or 4 houres with water, which is an ordinary food they call *Ustatahamen*. But some more thriftie then cleanly, doe burne the core of the eare to powder, which they call *Pungnough*, mingling that in their meale, but it never tasted well in bread, nor broth. Their

How they fish and flesh they boyle either very tenderly, or
use their fish broyle it so long on hurdles over the fire, or else after
and flesh. the Spanish fashion, putting it on a spit, they turne first the one side, then the other, till it be as drie as their jerkin Beefe in the west Indies, that they may keepe it a moneth or more without putrifying. The broth of fish or flesh they eat as commonly as the meat.

In May also amongst their corne they plant
Planted fruits *Pumpeons*, and a fruit like unto a muske mellon, but lesse and worse, which they call *Macocks*. These increase exceedingly, and ripen in the beginning of July, and continue untill September. They plant also *Maracocks* a wild fruit like a Lemmon, which also increase infinitely. They begin to ripe in September, and continue till the end of October. When all their fruits be gathered, little els they plant, and this is done by their women and children; neither doth this long suffice them, for neare three parts of the yeare, they onely observe times and seasons, and live of what the Country naturally affordeth from hand to mouth, etc.

The Commodities in Virginia, or that
may be had by Industrie.

THE mildnesse of the ayre, the fertilitie of the soyle, and situation of the rivers are so propitious to the nature and use of man, as no place is more convenient for pleasure, profit, and mans sustenance, under that latitude or climat. Here will live any beasts, as horses, goats, sheepe, asses, hens, etc. as appeared by them that were carried thether. The waters, Isles, and shoales, are full of safe harbours for ships of warre or marchandize, for boats of all sorts, for transportation or fishing, etc. The Bay and rivers have much marchantable fish, and places fit for Salt coats, building of ships, making of Iron, etc.

A proofe cattell will live well.

Muscovia and Polonia doe yearely receive many thousands, for pitch, tarre, sope-ashes, Rosen, Flax, Cordage, Sturgeon, Masts, Yards, Wainscot, Firres, Glasse, and such like; also Swethland for Iron and Copper. France in like manner, for Wine, Canvas, and Salt. Spaine asmuch for Iron, Steele, Figges, Reasons, and Sackes. Italy with Silkes and Velvets consumes our chiefe Commodities. Holland maintaines it selfe by fishing and trading at our owne doores. All these temporize with other for necessities, but all as uncertaine as peace or warres. Besides the charge, travell, and danger in transporting them, by seas, lands, stormes, and Pyrats. Then how much hath Virginia the prerogative of all those flourishing Kingdomes, for the benefit of our Land, when as within one hundred myles all those are to be had, either ready provided by nature, or else to be prepared, were there but industrious men to labour. Onely of Copper we may doubt is wanting, but there is good probabilitie that both Copper and better Minerals are there to be had for their labour. Other Countries have it. So then here is a place, a nurse for souldiers, a practise for mariners, a trade for marchants, a reward for the good, and that which is most of all, a businesse (most acceptable to God) to bring such poore Infidels to the knowledge of God and his holy Gospell.

The Commodities.

Of the naturall Inhabitants of Virginia.

THE land is not populous, for the men be few; their far
greater number is of women and children. Within 60
The numbers   myles of James Towne, there are about some 5000
people, but of able men fit for their warres scarce
1500. To nourish so many together they have yet no meanes,
because they make so small a benefit of their land, be it never
Seaven   so fertile. Six or seaven hundred have beene the
hundred   most hath beene seene together, when they gathered
men were
the most   themselves to have surprised mee at Pamaunkee,
were seene   having but fifteene to withstand the worst of their
together
when they   fury. As small as the proportion of ground that hath
thought   yet beene discovered, is in comparison of that yet
to have
surprised   unknowne: the people differ very much in stature,
Captaine   especially in language, as before is expressed. Some
Smith.
being very great as the Sasquesahanocks; others very little, as
the Wighcocomocoes: but generally tall and straight,
A description of a comely proportion, and of a colour browne
of the people.
when they are of any age, but they are borne white.
Their hayre is generally blacke, but few have any beards. The
men weare halfe their heads shaven, the other halfe
The Barbers.   long; for Barbers they use their women, who with
two shels will grate away the hayre, of any fashion
The con-   they please. The women are cut in many fashions,
stitution.   agreeable to their yeares, but ever some part remaineth long. They are very strong, of an able body and full of
agilitie, able to endure to lie in the woods under a tree by the
fire, in the worst of winter, or in the weedes and grasse, in Ambuscado in the Sommer. They are inconstant in every
The   thing, but what feare constraineth them to keepe.
disposition.
Craftie, timerous, quicke of apprehension, and very
ingenuous. Some are of disposition fearefull, some bold, most
cautelous, all Savage. Generally covetous of Copper, Beads,
and such like trash. They are soone moved to anger, and so
malicious, that they seldome forget an injury: they seldome
steale one from another, least their conjurers should reveale it,
and so they be pursued and punished. That they are thus
feared is certaine, but that any can reveale their offences by
conjuration I am doubtfull. Their women are carefull not to be

suspected of dishonestie without the leave of their husbands.

The possessions. Each houshold knoweth their owne lands, and gardens, and most live of their owne labours. For their

Their attire. apparell, they are sometime covered with the skinnes of wilde beasts, which in Winter are dressed with the hayre, but in Sommer without. The better sort use large mantels of Deare skins, not much differing in fashion from the Irish mantels. Some imbrodered with white beads, some with Copper, other painted after their manner. But the common sort have scarce to cover their nakednesse, but with grasse, the leaves of trees, or such like. We have seene some use mantels made of Turky feathers, so prettily wrought and woven with threads that nothing could be discerned but the feathers. That was exceeding warme and very handsome. But the women are

Their ornaments. alwayes covered about their middles with a skin, and very shamefast to be seene bare. They adorne themselves most with copper beads and paintings. Their women, some have their legs, hands, breasts and face cunningly imbrodered with divers workes, as beasts, serpents, artificially wrought into their flesh with blacke spots. In each eare commonly they have 3 great holes, whereat they hang chaines, bracelets, or copper. Some of their men weare in those holes, a small greene and yellow coloured snake, neare halfe a yard in length, which crawling and lapping her selfe about his necke oftentimes familiarly would kisse his lips. Others weare a dead Rat tyed by the taile. Some on their heads weare the wing of a bird, or some large feather with a Rattell. Those Rattels are somewhat like the chape of a Rapier, but lesse, which they take from the taile of a snake. Many have the whole skinne of a Hawke or some strange foule, stuffed with the wings abroad. Others a broad peece of Copper, and some the hand of their enemy dryed. Their heads and shoulders are painted red with the roote *Pocone* brayed to powder, mixed with oyle, this they hold in sommer to preserve them from the heate, and in winter from the cold. Many other formes of paintings they use, but he is the most gallant that is the most monstrous to behold.

Their buildings. Their buildings and habitations are for the most part by the rivers, or not farre distant from some fresh spring. Their houses are built like our Arbors, of small young springs bowed and tyed, and so close covered with Mats, or the barkes of trees very handsomely, that not-withstanding either winde, raine, or weather, they are as warme as stooves, but very smoaky, yet at the toppe of the house there is a hole made for the smoake to goe into right over the fire.

Their
lodgings. Against the fire they lie on little hurdles of Reeds covered with a Mat, borne from the ground a foote and more by a hurdle of wood. On these round about the house they lie heads and points one by th'other against the fire, some covered with Mats, some with skins, and some starke naked lie on the ground, from 6 to 20 in a house.

Their gardens Their houses are in the midst of their fields or gar-dens, which are small plots of ground. Some 20 acres, some 40. some 100. some 200. some more, some lesse. In some places from 2 to 50 of those houses together, or but a little separated by groves of trees. Neare their habitations is little small wood or old trees on the ground by reason of their burning of them for fire. So that a man may gallop a horse amongst these woods any way, but where the creekes or Rivers shall hinder.

How they use their children. Men, women, and children have their severall names according to the severall humor of their Par-ents. Their women (they say) are easily delivered of childe, yet doe they love children very dearely. To make them hardie, in the coldest mornings they wash them in the rivers, and by painting and oyntments so tanne their skinnes, that after a yeare or two, no weather will hurt them.

The industrie of their women. The men bestow their times in fishing, hunting, warres, and such manlike exercises, scorning to be seene in any woman-like exercise, which is the cause that the women be very painefull, and the men often idle. The women and children doe the rest of the worke. They make mats, baskets, pots, morters, pound their corne, make their bread, prepare their victuals, plant their corne, gather their corne, beare all kind of burdens, and such like.

How they strike fire. Their fire they kindle presently by chafing a dry pointed sticke in a hole of a little square peece of wood, that firing it selfe, will so fire mosse, leaves, or any such like dry thing, that will quickly burne. In March and Aprill they live much upon their fishing wires; and feed on fish, Turkies, and Squirrels. In May and June they

The order of dyet.

plant their fields, and live most of Acornes, Walnuts, and fish. But to mend their dyet, some disperse themselves in small companies, and live upon fish, beasts, crabs, oysters, land Tortoises, strawberries, mulberries, and such like. In June, July, and August, they feed upon the rootes of *Tockwough* berries, fish, and greene wheat. It is strange to see how their bodies alter with their dyet, even as the deere and wilde beasts they seeme fat and leane, strong and weake. Powhatan their great King, and some others that are provident, rost their fish and flesh upon hurdles as before is expressed, and keepe it till scarce times.

How they make their bowes and arrowes.

For fishing, hunting, and warres they use much their bow and arrowes. They bring their bowes to the forme of ours by the scraping of a shell. Their arrowes are made some of straight young sprigs, which they head with bone, some 2 or 3 ynches long. These they use to shoot at Squirrels on trees. Another sort of arrowes they use made of Reeds. These are peeced with wood, headed with splinters of christall, or some sharpe stone, the spurres of a Turkey, or the bill of some bird. For his knife he hath the splinter of

Their knives.

a Reed to cut his feathers in forme. With this knife also, he will joynt a Deere, or any beast, shape his shooes, buskins, mantels, etc. To make the nock of his arrow he hath the tooth of a Beaver, set in a sticke, wherewith he grateth it by degrees. His arrow head he quickly maketh with a little bone, which he ever weareth at his bracer, of any splint of a stone, or glasse in the forme of a heart, and these they glew to the end of their arrowes. With the sinewes of Deere, and the tops of Deeres hornes boyled to a jelly, they make a glew that will not dissolve in cold water.

Their Targets and Swords.

For their warres also they use Targets that are round and made of the barkes of trees, and a sword of wood at their backes, but oftentimes they use for swords the horne of a Deere put through a peece of wood in forme of a Pickaxe. Some a long stone sharpned at both ends, used in the same manner. This they were wont to use also for hatchets, but now by trucking they have plentie of the same forme of yron. And those are their chiefe instruments and armes.

Their Boats.

Their fishing is much in Boats. These they make of

one tree by burning and scratching away the coales with stones and shels, till they have made it in forme of Trough. Some of them are an elne deepe, and fortie or fiftie foote in length, and some will beare 40 men, but the most ordinary are smaller, and will beare 10, 20, or 30. according to their bignesse. In stead of Oares, they use Paddles and stickes, with which they will row faster then our Barges. Betwixt their hands and thighes, their women use to spin, the barkes of trees, Deere sinewes, or a kind of grasse they call *Pemmenaw*, of these they make a thread very even and readily. This thread serveth for many uses. As about their housing, apparell, as also they make nets for fishing, for the quantitie as formally braded as ours. They make also with it lines for angles. Their hookes are either a bone grated as they nock their arrowes in the forme of a crooked pinne or fish-hooke, or of the splinter of a bone tyed to the clift of a little sticke, and with the end of the line, they tie on the bait. They use also long arrowes tyed in a line, wherewith they shoote at fish in the rivers. But they of Accawmack use staves like unto Javelins headed with bone. With these they dart fish swimming in the water. They have also many artificiall wires, in which they get abundance of fish.

How they spin.

Their fish-hookes.

In their hunting and fishing they take extreame paines; yet it being their ordinary exercise from their infancy, they esteeme it a pleasure and are very proud to be expert therein. And by their continuall ranging, and travell, they know all the advantages and places most frequented with Deere, Beasts, Fish, Foule, Roots, and Berries. At their huntings they leave their habitations, and reduce themselves into companies, as the Tartars doe, and goe to the most desert places with their families, where they spend their time in hunting and fowling up towards the mountaines, by the heads of their rivers, where there is plentie of game. For betwixt the rivers the grounds are so narrowe, that little commeth here which they devoure not. It is a marvell they can so directly passe these deserts, some 3 or 4 dayes journey without habitation. Their hunting houses are like unto Arbours covered with Mats. These their women beare after them, with Corne, Acornes, Morters, and all bag and baggage they use. When they come to the place of exercise, every man doth his best to shew

How they hunt.

his dexteritie, for by their excelling in those qualities, they get their wives. Fortie yards will they shoot levell, or very neare the marke, and 120 is their best at Random. At their huntings in the deserts they are commonly two or three hundred together. Having found the Deere, they environ them with many fires, and betwixt the fires they place themselves. And some take their stands in the midsts. The Deere being thus feared by the fires, and their voyces, they chase them so long within that circle, that many times they kill 6, 8, 10, or 15 at a hunting. They use also to drive them into some narrow poynt of land, when they find that advantage; and so force them into the river, where with their boats they have Ambuscadoes to kill them. When they have shot a Deere by land, they follow him like bloud-hounds by the bloud, and straine, and oftentimes so take them. Hares, Partridges, Turkies, or Egges, fat or leane, young or old, they devoure all they can catch in their power. In one of these huntings they found me in the discovery of the head of the river of Chickahamania, where they slew my men, and tooke me prisoner in a Bogmire, where I saw those exercises, and gathered these Observations.

One Salvage hunting alone. One Salvage hunting alone, useth the skinne of a Deere slit on the one side, and so put on his arme, through the neck, so that his hand comes to the head which is stuffed, and the hornes, head, eyes, eares, and every part as artificially counterfeited as they can devise. Thus shrowding his body in the skinne by stalking, he approacheth the Deere, creeping on the ground from one tree to another. If the Deere chance to find fault, or stand at gaze, he turneth the head with his hand to his best advantage to seeme like a Deere, also gazing and licking himselfe. So watching his best advantage to approach, having shot him, he chaseth him by his bloud and straine till he get him.

Their Consultations. When they intend any warres, the Werowances usually have the advice of their Priests and Conjurers, and their allies, and ancient friends, but chiefely the Priests determine their resolution. Every Werowance, or some lustie fellow, they appoint Captaine over every nation. They seldome make warre for lands or goods, but for women and Their enemies. children, and principally for revenge. They have many enemies, namely, all their westernly Countries beyond the mountaines, and the heads of the rivers. Upon the head of the Powhatans are the Monacans, whose chiefe habitation is at Rasauweak, unto whom the Mowhemenchughes, the Massinnacacks, the Monahassanughs, the Monasickapanoughs, and other nations pay tributes. Upon the head of the river of Toppahanock is a people called Mannahoacks. To these are contributers the Tauxanias, the Shackaconias, the Ontponeas, the Tegninateos, the Whonkenteaes, the Stegarakes, the Hassinnungaes, and divers others, all confederates with the Monacans, though many different in language, and be very barbarous, living for the most part of wild beasts and fruits. Beyond the mountaines from whence is the head of the river Patawomeke, the Salvages report inhabit their most mortall enemies, the Massawomekes, upon a great salt water, which by all likelihood is either some part of Cannada, some great lake, or some inlet of some sea that falleth into the South sea. These Massawomekes are a great nation and very populous. For the heads of all those rivers, especially the Pattawomekes, the Pautuxuntes, the Sasquesahanocks, the Tockwoughes are continually tormented by them: of whose crueltie, they generally complained, and very importunate they were with me, and my company to free them from these tormentors. To this purpose they offered food, conduct, assistance, and continuall subjection. Which I concluded to effect. But the councell then present emulating my successe, would not thinke it fit to spare me fortie men to be hazzarded in those unknowne regions, having passed (as before was spoken of) but with 12, and so was lost that opportunitie. Seaven boats full of these Massawomekes wee encountred at the head of the Bay; whose Targets, Baskets, Swords, Tobacco pipes, Platters, Bowes, and Arrowes, and every thing shewed, they much exceeded them of our parts, and their dexteritie in their small boats, made of the barkes of trees, sowed with barke and well luted with gumme, argueth that they are seated upon some great water.

Against all these enemies the Powhatans are constrained sometimes to fight. Their chiefe attempts are by Stratagems, trecheries, or surprisals. Yet the Werowances women and children they put not to death, but keepe them Captives. They

Massawomekes.

Their offer of subjection.

have a method in warre, and for our pleasures they shewed it us, and it was in this manner performed at Mattapanient.

Their manner of Battell. Having painted and disguised themselves in the fiercest manner they could devise. They divided themselves into two Companies, neare a hundred in a company. The one company called Monacans, the other Powhatans. Either army had their Captaine. These as enemies tooke their stands a musket shot one from another; ranked themselves 15 a breast, and each ranke from another 4 or 5 yards, not in fyle, but in the opening betwixt their fyles. So as the Reare could shoot as conveniently as the Front. Having thus pitched the fields: from either part went a messenger with these conditions, that whosoever were vanquished, such as escape upon their submission in two dayes after should live, but their wives and children should be prize for the Conquerours. The messengers were no sooner returned, but they approached in their orders; On each flanke a Serjeant, and in the Reare an Officer for Lieutenant, all duly keeping their orders, yet leaping and singing after their accustomed tune, which they use onely in Warres. Upon the first flight of arrowes they gave such horrible shouts and screeches, as so many infernall hell hounds could not have made them more terrible. When they had spent their arrowes, they joyned together prettily, charging and retyring, every ranke seconding other. As they got advantage they catched their enemies by the hayre of the head, and downe he came that was taken. His enemy with his wooden sword seemed to beat out his braines, and still they crept to the Reare, to maintaine the skirmish. The Monacans decreasing, the Powhatans charged them in the forme of a halfe Moone; they unwilling to be inclosed, fled all in a troope to their Ambuscadoes, on whom they led them very cunningly. The Monacans disperse themselves among the fresh men, whereupon the Powhatans retired, with all speed to their seconds; which the Monacans seeing, tooke that advantage to retire againe to their owne battell, and so each returned to their owne quarter. All their actions, voyces, and gestures, both in charging and retiring were so strained to the height of their qualitie and nature, that the strangenesse thereof made it seeme very delightfull.

For their Musicke they use a thicke Cane, on which
Their
Musicke. they pipe as on a Recorder. For their warres they have
a great deepe platter of wood. They cover the mouth
thereof with a skin, at each corner they tie a walnut, which
meeting on the backside neere the bottome, with a small rope
they twitch them together till it be so tought and stiffe, that
they may beat upon it as upon a drumme. But their chiefe instruments are Rattles made of small gourds, or Pumpeons shels.
Of these they have Base, Tenor, Countertenor, Meane, and
Treble. These mingled with their voyces sometimes twenty or
thirtie together, make such a terrible noise as would rather
Their enter-
tainment. affright, then delight any man. If any great commander arrive at the habitation of a Werowance,
they spread a Mat as the Turkes doe a Carpet for him
to sit upon. Upon another right opposite they sit themselves.
Then doe all with a tunable voice of shouting bid him welcome. After this doe two or more of their chiefest men make
an Oration, testifying their love. Which they doe with such vehemency, and so great passions, that they sweat till they drop,
and are so out of breath they can scarce speake. So that a man
would take them to be exceeding angry, or stark mad. Such
victuall as they have, they spend freely, and at night where his
lodging is appointed, they set a woman fresh painted red with
Pocones and oyle, to be his bed-fellow.

Their manner of trading is for copper, beads, and
Their trade. such like, for which they give such commodities as
they have, as skins, foule, fish, flesh, and their Country Corne. But their victualls are their chiefest riches.

Every spring they make themselves sicke with
Their
Phisicke. drinking the juyce of a roote they call *Wighsacan*,
and water; whereof they powre so great a quantitie,
that it purgeth them in a very violent manner; so that in three
or foure dayes after, they scarce recover their former
Their
Chirurgery. health. Sometimes they are troubled with dropsies,
swellings, aches, and such like diseases; for cure
whereof they build a Stove in the forme of a Dove-house with
mats, so close that a few coales therein covered with a pot, will
make the patient sweat extreamely. For swellings also they use
small peeces of touchwood, in the forme of cloves, which
pricking on the griefe they burne close to the flesh, and from

thence draw the corruption with their mouth. With this roote *Wighsacan* they ordinarily heale greene wounds. But to scarrifie a swelling, or make incision, their best instruments are some splinted stone. Old ulcers, or putrified hurts are seldome seene cured amongst them. They have many professed Phisicians, who with their charmes and Rattles, with an infernall rout of words and actions, will seeme to sucke their inward griefe from their navels, or their grieved places; but of our Chirurgians they were so conceited, that they beleeved any Plaister would heale any hurt.

Their charms to cure.

> *But 'tis not alwayes in Phisicians skill,*
> *To heale the Patient that is sicke and ill:*
> *For sometimes sicknesse on the Patients part,*
> *Proves stronger farre then all Phisicians art.*

Of their Religion.

THERE is yet in Virginia no place discovered to be so Savage, in which they have not a Religion, Deere, and Bow, and Arrowes. All things that are able to doe them hurt beyond their prevention, they adore with their kinde of divine worship; as the fire, water, lightning, thunder, our Ordnance, peeces, horses, etc. But their chiefe God they worship is the Devill. Him they call *Okee*, and serve him more of feare then love. They say they have conference with him, and fashion themselves as neare to his shape as they can imagine. In their Temples they have his image evill favouredly carved, and then painted and adorned with chaines of copper, and beads, and covered with a skin, in such manner as the deformitie may well suit with such a God. By him is commonly the sepulcher of their Kings. Their bodies are first bowelled, then dried upon hurdles till they be very dry, and so about the most of their joynts and necke they hang bracelets, or chaines of copper, pearle, and such like, as they use to weare, their inwards they stuffe with copper beads, hatchets, and such trash. Then lappe they them very carefully in white skins, and so rowle them in mats for their

Their God.

How they bury their Kings

winding sheets. And in the Tombe which is an arch made of mats, they lay them orderly. What remaineth of this kinde of wealth their Kings have, they set at their feet in baskets. These Temples and bodies are kept by their Priests.

Their ordinary burials.

For their ordinary burials, they dig a deepe hole in the earth with sharpe stakes, and the corpse being lapped in skins and mats with their jewels, they lay them upon stickes in the ground, and so cover them with earth. The buriall ended, the women being painted all their faces with blacke cole and oyle, doe sit twenty foure houres in the houses mourning and lamenting by turnes, with such yelling and howling, as may expresse their great passions.

Their Temples.

In every Territory of a Werowance is a Temple and a Priest, two or three or more. Their principall Temple or place of superstition is at Uttamussack at Pamaunkee, neare unto which is a house, Temple, or place of Powhatans.

Upon the top of certaine red sandy hils in the woods, there are three great houses filled with images of their Kings, and Devils, and Tombes of their Predecessors. Those houses are neare sixtie foot in length built arbour-wise, after their building. This place they count so holy as that but the Priests and Kings dare come into them; nor the Salvages dare not goe up the river in boats by it, but they solemnly cast some peece of copper, white beads, or *Pocones* into the river, for feare their *Okee* should be offended and revenged of them.

Thus,

> *Feare was the first their Gods begot:*
> *Till feare began, their Gods were not.*

Their ornaments for their Priests.

In this place commonly are resident seaven Priests. The chiefe differed from the rest in his ornaments, but inferior Priests could hardly be knowne from the common people, but that they had not so many holes in their eares to hang their jewels at. The ornaments of the chiefe Priest were certaine attires for his head made thus. They tooke a dosen, or 16, or more snakes skins and stuffed them with mosse, and of Weesels and other Vermines skins a good many. All these they tie by their tailes, so as all their tailes meete in the toppe of their head like a great Tassell. Round about this Tassell is as it were a crowne of feathers, the skins hang round about his head, necke, and shoulders, and in a manner cover his face. The faces of all their Priests are painted as ugly as they can devise, in their hands they had every one his Rattle, some base, some smaller. Their devotion was most in songs, which the chiefe Priest beginneth and the rest followed him, sometimes he maketh invocations with broken sentences by starts and strange passions, and at every pause, the rest give a short groane.

> *Thus seeke they in deepe foolishnesse,*
> *To climbe the height of happinesse.*

It could not be perceived that they keepe any day as more holy then other; But onely in some great distresse of want, feare of enemies, times of triumph and gathering together their fruits, the whole Country of men, women, and children come together to solemnities. The manner of their devotion is, sometimes to make a great fire, in the house or fields, and all to sing and dance about it with Rattles and shouts together, foure or five houres. Sometimes they set a man in the midst, and about him they dance and sing, he all the while clapping his hands, as if he would keepe time, and after their songs and dauncings ended they goe to their Feasts.

The times of solemnities.

> *Through God begetting feare,*
> *Mans blinded minde did reare*
> *A hell-god to the ghosts;*
> *A heaven-god to the hoasts;*
> *Yea God unto the Seas:*
> *Feare did create all these.*

They have also divers conjurations, one they made when I was their prisoner; of which hereafter you shall reade at large.

Their conjurations.

They have also certaine Altar stones they call *Paw-corances*, but these stand from their Temples, some by their houses, others in the woods and wildernesses, where they have had any extraordinary accident, or incounter. And as you travell, at those stones they will tell you the cause why they were there

Their Altars.

Sacrifices to the water.

erected, which from age to age they instruct their children, as their best records of antiquities. Upon these they offer bloud, Deere suet, and Tobacco. This they doe when they returne from the Warres, from hunting, and upon many other occasions. They have also another superstition that they use in stormes, when the waters are rough in the Rivers and Sea coasts. Their Conjurers runne to the water sides, or passing in their boats, after many hellish outcryes and invocations, they cast Tobacco, Copper, *Pocones*, or such trash into the water, to pacifie that God whom they thinke to be very angry in those stormes. Before their dinners and suppers the better sort will take the first bit, and cast it in the fire, which is all the grace they are knowne to use.

In some part of the Country they have yearely a sacrifice of children. Such a one was at Quiyoughcohanock some ten myles from James Towne, and thus performed. Fifteene of the properest young boyes, betweene ten and fifteene yeares of age they painted white. Having brought them forth, the people spent the forenoone in dancing and singing about them with Rattles. In the afternoone they put those children to the roote of a tree. By them all the men stood in a guard, every one having a Bastinado in his hand, made of reeds bound together. This made a lane betweene them all along, through which there were appointed five young men to fetch these children: so every one of the five went through the guard to fetch a childe each after other by turnes, the guard fiercely beating them with their Bastinadoes, and they patiently enduring and receiving all defending the children with their naked bodies from the unmercifull blowes, that pay them soundly, though the children escape. All this while the women weepe and cry out very passionately, providing mats, skins, mosse, and dry wood, as things fitting their childrens funerals. After the children were thus passed the guard, the guard tore down the trees, branches and boughs, with such violence that they rent the body, and made wreaths for their heads, or bedecked their hayre with the leaves. What els was done with the children, was not seene, but they were all cast on a heape, in a valley as dead, where they made a great feast for all the company. The Werowance being de-

Their solemn Sacrifices of children, which they call Blackboyes.

Those Blackboyes are made so mad with a kind of drinke, that they will doe any mischiefe, at the command of their Keepers.

manded the meaning of this sacrifice, answered that the children were not all dead, but that the *Okee* or Divell did sucke the bloud from their left breast, who chanced to be his by lot, till they were dead, but the rest were kept in the wildernesse by the young men till nine moneths were expired, during which time they must not converse with any, and of these were made their Priests and Conjurers. This sacrifice they held to be so necessary, that if they should omit it, their *Okee* or Devill, and all their other *Quiyoughcosughes*, which are their other Gods, would let them have no Deere, Turkies, Corne, nor fish, and yet besides, he would make a great slaughter amongst them.

They thinke that their Werowances and Priests which they also esteeme *Quiyoughcosughes*, when they are dead, doe goe beyond the mountaines towards the setting of the sunne, and ever remaine there in forme of their *Okee*, with their heads painted with oyle and *Pocones*, finely trimmed with feathers, and shall have beads, hatchets, copper, and Tobacco, doing nothing but dance and sing, with all their Predecessors. But the common people they suppose shall not live after death, but rot in their graves like dead dogs.

Their resurrection.

To divert them from this blind Idolatry, we did our best endevours, chiefly with the Werowance of Quiyoughcohanock, whose devotion, apprehension, and good disposition, much exceeded any in those Countries, who although we could not as yet prevaile, to forsake his false Gods, yet this he did beleeve that our God as much exceeded theirs, as our Gunnes did their Bowes and Arrowes, and many times did send to me to James Towne, intreating me to pray to my God for raine, for their Gods would not send them any. And in this lamentable ignorance doe these poore soules sacrifice themselves to the Devill, not knowing their Creator; and we had not language sufficient, so plainly to expresse it as make them understand it; which God grant they may.

For,

> *Religion 'tis that doth distinguish us,*
> *From their bruit humor, well we may it know;*
> *That can with understanding argue thus,*
> *Our God is truth, but they cannot doe so.*

Of the manner of the Virginians Government

ALTHOUGH the Country people be very barbarous, yet have they amongst them such government, as that their Magistrates for good commanding, and their people for due subjection, and obeying, excell many places that would be counted very civill. The forme of their Common-wealth is a Monarchicall government, one as Emperour ruleth over many Kings or Governours. Their chiefe ruler is called Powhatan, and taketh his name of his principall place of dwelling called Powhatan. But his proper name is Wahunsonacock. Some Countries he hath which have beene his ancestors, and came unto him by inheritance, as the Country called Powhatan, Arrohateck, Appamatuck, Pamaunkee, Youghtanund, and Mattapanient. All the rest of his Territories expressed in the Mappe, they report have beene his severall Conquests. In all his ancient inheritances, he hath houses built after their manner like arbours, some 30. some 40. yards long, and at every house provision for his entertainement according to the time. At Werowcomoco on the Northside of the river Pamaunkee, was his residence, when I was delivered him prisoner, some 14 myles from James Towne, where for the most part, he was resident, but at last he tooke so little pleasure in our neare neighbourhood, that he retired himselfe to Orapakes, in the desert betwixt Chickahamania and Youghtanund. He is of personage a tall well proportioned man, with a sower looke, his head somwhat gray, his beard so thinne, that it seemeth none at all, his age neare sixtie; of a very able and hardy body to endure any labour. About his person ordinarily attendeth a guard of 40 or 50 of the tallest men his Country doth afford. Every night upon the foure quarters of his house are foure Sentinels, each from other a flight shoot, and at every halfe houre one from the Corps du guard doth hollow, shaking his lips with his finger betweene them; unto whom every Sentinell doth answer round from his stand: if any faile, they presently send forth an officer that beateth him extreamely.

A myle from Orapakes in a thicket of wood, he hath a house in which he keepeth his kinde of Treasure, as skinnes, copper, pearle, and beads, which he storeth up against the time of his death and buriall. Here also

A description of Powhatan.

His attendance and watch.

His treasury.

is his store of red paint for oyntment, bowes and arrowes, Targets and clubs. This house is fiftie or sixtie yards in length, frequented onely by Priests. At the foure corners of this house stand foure Images as Sentinels, one of a Dragon, another a Beare, the third like a Leopard, and the fourth like a giantlike man, all made evill favouredly, according to their best workemanship.

He hath as many women as he will, whereof when

His wives.

he lieth on his bed, one sitteth at his head, and another at his feet, but when he sitteth, one sitteth on his right hand and another on his left. As he is weary of his women, he bestoweth them on those that best deserve them at his hands. When he dineth or suppeth, one of his women before and after meat, bringeth him water in a wooden platter to wash his hands. Another waiteth with a bunch of feathers to wipe them in stead of a Towell, and the feathers when he hath wiped are dryed againe. His kingdomes descend not

His successors

to his sonnes nor children, but first to his brethren, whereof he hath 3. namely, Opitchapan, Opechancanough, and Catataugh, and after their decease to his sisters. First to the eldest sister, then to the rest, and after them to the heires male or female of the eldest sister, but never to the heires of the males.

He nor any of his people understand any letters, whereby to write or reade, onely the lawes whereby he ruleth is

Their authoritie.

custome. Yet when he listeth his will is a law and must be obeyed: not onely as a King, but as halfe a God they esteeme him. His inferiour Kings whom they call Werowances, are tyed to rule by customes, and have power of life and death at their command in that nature. But this word Werowance, which we call and construe for a King, is a common word, whereby they call all commanders: for they have but few words in their language, and but few occasions to use

The tenor of their lands.

any officers more then one commander, which commonly they call Werowance, or *Caucorouse* which is Captaine. They all know their severall lands, and habitations, and limits, to fish, foule, or hunt in, but they hold all of their great Werowance Powhatan, unto whom they pay tribute of skinnes, beads, copper, pearle, deere, turkies, wild beasts, and corne. What he commandeth they dare not disobey in the least thing. It is strange to see with what great feare and adoration, all these people doe obey this Powhatan. For at his feet they present whatsoever he commandeth, and at the least frowne of his brow, their greatest spirits will tremble with feare: and no marvell, for he is very terrible and tyrannous in punishing such as offend him. For example, he caused certaine malefactors to be bound hand and foot, then having of many fires gathered great store of burning coales, they rake these coales round in the forme of a cockpit, and in the midst they cast the offenders to broyle to death. Sometimes he causeth the heads of them that offend him, to be laid upon the altar or sacrificing stone, and one with clubbes beats out their braines. When he would punish any notorious enemy or malefactor, he causeth him to be tyed to a tree, and with Mussell shels or reeds, the executioner cutteth off his joynts one after another, ever casting what they cut of into the fire; then doth he proceed with shels and reeds to case the skinne from his head and face; then doe they rip his belly and so burne him with the tree and all. Thus themselves reported they executed George Cassen. Their ordinary correction is to beate them with cudgels. We have seene a man kneeling on his knees, and at Powhatans command, two men have beate him on the bare skin, till he hath fallen senselesse in a sound, and yet never cry nor complained. And he made a woman for playing the whore, sit upon a great stone, on her bare breech twenty-foure houres, onely with corne and water, every three dayes, till nine dayes were past, yet he loved her exceedingly: notwithstanding there are common whores by profession.

His manner of punishments. (margin note)

In the yeare 1608, he surprised the people of Payankatank his neare neighbours and subjects. The occasion was to us un-knowne, but the manner was thus. First he sent divers of his men as to lodge amongst them that night, then the Ambusca-does environed all their houses, and at the houre appointed, they all fell to the spoyle, twenty-foure men they slew, the long haire of the one side of their heads, with the skinne cased off with shels or reeds, they brought away. They surprised also the women, and the children, and the Werowance. All these they presented to Powhatan. The Werowance, women and children became his prisoners, and doe him service. The lockes of haire with their skinnes he hanged on a line betwixt two trees. And thus he made ostentation of his triumph at Werowocomoco, where he intended to have done as much to mee and my company.

And this is as much as my memory can call to minde worthy of note; which I have purposely collected, to satisfie my friends of the true worth and qualitie of Virginia. Yet some bad natures will not sticke to slander the Countrey, that will slovenly spit at all things, especially in company where they can finde none to contradict them. Who though they were scarce ever ten myles from James Towne, or at the most but at the falles; yet holding it a great disgrace that amongst so much action, their actions were nothing, exclaime of all things, though they never adventured to know any thing; nor ever did any thing but devoure the fruits of other mens labours. Being for most part of such tender educations, and small experience in Martiall accidents, because they found not English Cities, nor such faire houses, nor at their owne wishes any of their accustomed dainties, with feather beds and downe pillowes, Tavernes and Alehouses in every breathing place, neither such plentie of gold and silver and dissolute libertie, as they expected, had little or no care of any thing, but to pamper their bellies, to fly away with our Pinnaces, or procure their meanes to returne for England. For the Country was to them a misery, a ruine, a death, a hell, and their reports here, and their actions there according.

Some other there were that had yearely stipends to passe to and againe for transportation: who to keepe the mysterie of the businesse in themselves, though they had neither time nor meanes to know much of themselves; yet all mens actions or relations they so formally tuned to the temporizing times simplicitie, as they could make their ignorances seeme much more, then all the true actors could by their experience. And those with their great words deluded the world with such strange promises, as abused the businesse much worse then the rest. For the businesse being builded upon the foundation of their fained experience, the planters, the money and meanes have still miscarried: yet they ever returning, and the planters so farre absent, who could contradict their excuses? which, still to maintaine their vaine glory and estimation, from time to time have used such diligence as made them passe for truths, though nothing more false. And that the adventurers might be thus abused, let no man wonder; for the wisest living is soonest abused by him that hath a faire tongue and a dissembling heart.

There were many in Virginia meerely projecting, verball, and idle contemplators, and those so devoted to pure idlenesse, that though they had lived two or three yeares in Virginia, lordly, necessitie it selfe could not compell them to passe the Peninsula, or Pallisadoes of James Towne, and those witty spirits, what would they not affirme in the behalfe of our transporters, to get victuall from their ships, or obtaine their good words in England, to get their passes. Thus from the clamors, and the ignorance of false informers, are sprung those disasters that sprung in Virginia: and our ingenious verbalists were no lesse plague to us in Virginia, then the Locusts to the Egyptians. For the labour of twentie or thirtie of the best onely preserved in Christianitie by their industry, the idle livers of neare two hundred of the rest: who living neere ten moneths of such naturall meanes, as the Country naturally of it selfe afforded, notwithstanding all this, and the worst fury of the Salvages, the extremitie of sicknesse, mutinies, faction, ignorances, and want of victuall; in all that time I lost but seaven or eight men, yet subjected the salvages to our desired obedience, and received contribution from thirtie five of their Kings, to protect and assist them against any that should assault them, in which order they continued true and faithfull, and as subjects to his Majestie, so long after as I did governe there, untill I left the Countrey: since, how they have revolted, the Countrie lost, and againe replanted, and the businesses hath succeded from time to time, I referre you to the relations of them returned from Virginia, that have beene more diligent in such Observations.

John Smith writ this with his owne hand.

———

Because many doe desire to know the manner of their Language, I have inserted these few words.

Ka ka torawincs yowo. What call you this.
Nemarough, a man.
Crenepo, a woman.
Marowanchesso, a boy.
Yehawkans, Houses.

Matchcores, Skins, or garments.
Mockasins, Shooes.
Tussan, Beds.
Pokatawer, Fire.
Attawp, A bow.
Attonce, Arrowes.
Monacookes, Swords.
Aumouhhowgh, A Target.
Pawcussacks, Gunnes.
Tomahacks, Axes.
Tockahacks, Pickaxes.
Pamesacks, Knives.
Accowprets, Sheares.
Pawpecones, Pipes.
Mattassin, Copper.
Ussawassin, Iron, Brasse, Silver, or any white mettall.
Musses, Woods.
Attasskuss, Leaves, weeds, or grasse.
Chepsin, Land.
Shacquohocan. A stone.
Wepenter, A cookold.
Suckahanna, Water.
Noughmass, Fish.
Copotone, Sturgeon.
Weghshaughes, Flesh.
Sawwehone, Bloud.
Netoppew, Friends.
Marrapough, Enemies.
Maskapow, the worst of enemies.
Mawchick chammay, The best of friends.
Casacunnakack, peya quagh acquintan uttasantasough, In how many daies will there come hither any more English Ships.

Their Numbers.

Necut, 1.
Ningh, 2.
Nuss, 3.
Yowgh, 4.
Paranske, 5.

Comotinch, 6.
Toppawoss, 7.
Nusswash, 8.
Kekatawgh, 9.
Kaskeke, 10.

They count no more but by tennes as followeth.

Case, how many.
Ninghsapooeksku, 20.
Nussapooeksku, 30.
Yowghapooeksku, 40.
Parankestassapooeksku, 50.
Comatinchtassapooeksku, 60.
Nussswashtassapooeksku, 80.
Kekataughtassapooeksku, 90.
Necuttoughtysinough, 100.
Necuttweunquaough, 1000.
Rawcosowghs, Dayes.
Keshowghes, Sunnes.
Toppquough, Nights.
Nepawweshowghs, Moones.
Pawpaxsoughes, Yeares.
Pummahumps, Starres.
Osies, Heavens.
Okees, Gods.
Quiyoughcosoughs, Pettie Gods, and their affinities.
Righcomoughes, Deaths.
Kekughes, Lives.
Mowchick woyawgh tawgh noeragh kaquere mecher, I am very
     hungry? what shall I eate?
Tawnor nehiegh Powhatan, Where dwels Powhatan.
Mache, nehiegh yourowgh, Orapaks. Now he dwels a great way
     hence at Orapaks.
Uttapitchewayne anpechitchs nehawper Werowacomoco, You lie,
     he staid ever at Werowacomoco.
Kator nehiegh mattagh neer uttapitchewayne, Truely he is there
     I doe not lie.
*Spaughtynere keragh werowance mawmarinough kekaten
     wawgh peyaquaugh.* Run you then to the King Mawmary-
     nough and bid him come hither.

Utteke, e peya weyack wighwhip, Get you gone, and come againe quickly.

Kekaten Pokahontas patiaquagh niugh tanks manotyens neer mowchick rawrenock audowgh, Bid Pokahontas bring hither two little Baskets, and I will give her white Beads to make her a Chaine.

FINIS.

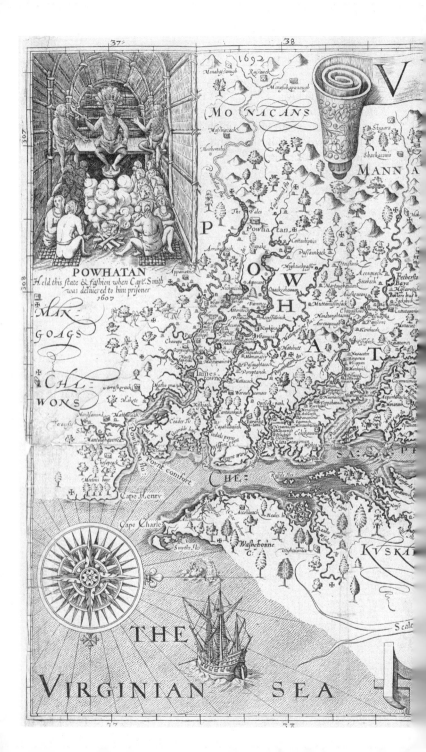

37

38

1692

Menahosinugh   Rassawek

Monasukapanaugh

MO NACANS

Massinacack

Mahoc

S[t]egara

Shackaconia

MANNA

T   The Fales

Powha tan   Rattachopco

Arrohateck   Orapaks   Passaunkack

Mrghtuckpassu   Utmstank

POWHATAN   Apecant   Quackcohowaon   Accoquock   Secobeck   Fetherston

Held this state & fashion when Capt. Smith   Nechanicok   Pamuno   Menaskunt   Baye

was deliuered to him prisoner   Attamuskin   Martuoughquaunk

1607   Pomuno   Chesapeack

Accossiwinck   Anskewaeeus   Fioughs

MA[R]   Cinquoateck   Muttamussinsak   Poruptanck   Fioughs

GOAGS   Chewapo   Wecuttanow   Nandtaughtacuud   Cuttatawamen

Aeawck   Weanock   Matahunt   Mataxent

CHI=   Apanaock   Mathpament   Wiahuck   Pamancock

WONS   Nantapoyac   Mamanahunt   Wiahuck   Mataxent

Nakefte   Mamanaliock   Pemancock

Nandsamund   Matahoock   Iames   Ozanies   Wiahuck

Mattachick   towne   Werowocomaco

Shapanack   Ceader Ile   Opileeuank

Mantughquemke   Capahoiack   Incale peyne   Matalaeack

Chesapeack   Poynt comfort   Kifkeack   ffina peyne   Gome Wamb   SA   P

Mortons baye   CHE: Raesyfles

Cape Henry

Cape Charles   Accohanock   Keales Is

Smyths Ilo   Accomack   KVSKA

Washeborne   Wighcocomoca

C.

THE   Scale

VIRGINIAN   SEA

Massaw- *Massawomeck* Omecks

RGINIA

Signification of these markes,
To the crosses hath bin discouered,
what beyond is by relation
Kings houses 2 ⊞
Ordinary houses 2 ○

Demo=
crites
tree

Burtons *Mount*

Pemaacack

N

Tananyent

Namaßingakent

Assaomeck

Namoraughquena

Natachtanto

Matchotanke

Cattamens

Nacotchtante

Quadasuaus

Guernestars reaake

Blands
C:

Cep[...]

The Sasquef= ahanougs
are a Gyant like peo= ple &
Vthowe thus a tyred

S A S Q V E

Attaock

Tesinigh

S A H A N

Quadroque

O V G H

BAY

Dawses Ily

* ß: nes Iles*

Browe= kees Forest

Ozinies

Berue word

Porte Peraut

Sasquesahanough

Tockwogh flu:

Smyths falles

Sasquesahanough flu:

Gunters Harbour

Peregrins mount

TOCK
WOGHS

and halfe

Legnies

Chickahokin

A T O V

Aquanachuke

A N A C

H V K E S

Macock

Described by Captayn John Smith
by William Hole
1606

Page 41
Smith

The third Booke.

THE PROCEEDINGS
AND ACCIDENTS OF
The English Colony in Virginia,
Extracted from the Authors
following, by WILLIAM SIMONS,
Doctour of Divinitie.

Chapter I.

1606. Sir Thomas Smith Treasurer.

IT might well be thought, a Countrie so faire (as Virginia is) and a people so tractable, would long ere this have beene quietly possessed, to the satisfaction of the adventurers, and the eternizing of the memory of those that effected it. But because all the world doe see a defailement; this following Treatise shall give satisfaction to all indifferent Readers, how the businesse hath bin carried: where no doubt they will easily understand and answer to their question, how it came to passe there was no better speed and successe in those proceedings.

The first mover of the action.

Captaine Bartholomew Gosnoll, one of the first movers of this plantation, having many yeares solicited many of his friends, but found small assistants; at last prevailed with some Gentlemen, as Captaine John Smith, Master Edward-Maria Wingfield, Master Robert Hunt, and divers others, who depended a yeare upon his projects, but nothing could be effected, till by their great charge and industrie, it came to be apprehended by certaine of the Nobilitie, Gentry, and Marchants, so that his Majestic by his letters patents, gave commission for establishing Councels, to direct here; and to governe, and to execute there. To effect this, was spent another yeare, and by that, three ships were provided, one of 100 Tuns, another of 40. and a Pinnace of 20. The transportation of the company was committed to Captaine Christopher Newport, a Marriner well practised for the Westerne parts of America. But their orders for government were put in a box, not to be opened, nor the governours knowne untill they arrived in Virginia.

Orders for government.

On the 19 of December, 1606. we set sayle from Blackwall, but by unprosperous winds, were kept six weekes in the sight of England; all which time, Master Hunt our Preacher, was so weake and sicke, that few expected his recovery. Yet although he were but twentie myles from his habitation (the time we were in the Downes) and notwithstanding the stormy weather, nor the scandalous imputations (of some few, little better then Atheists, of the greatest ranke amongst us) suggested against him, all this could never force from him so much as a seeming desire to leave the busines, but preferred the service of God, in so good a voyage, before any affection to contest with his godlesse foes, whose disasterous designes (could they have prevailed) had even then overthrowne the businesse, so many discontents did then arise, had he not with the water of patience, and his godly exhortations (but chiefly by his true devoted examples) quenched those flames of envie, and dissention.

We watered at the Canaries, we traded with the Salvages at Dominica; three weekes we spent in refreshing our selves amongst these west-India Isles; in Gwardalupa we found a bath so hot, as in it we boyled Porck as well as over the fire. And at a little Isle called Monica, we tooke from the bushes with our hands, neare two hogs-heads full of Birds in three or foure houres. In Mevis, Mona, and the Virgin Isles, we spent some time, where, with a lothsome beast like a Crocodil, called a Gwayn, Tortoises, Pellicans, Parrots, and fishes, we daily feasted. Gone from thence in search of Virginia, the company was not a little discomforted, seeing the Marriners had 3 dayes passed their reckoning and found no land, so that Captaine Ratliffe (Captaine of the Pinnace) rather desired to beare up the helme to returne for England, then make further search. But God the guider of all good actions, forcing them by an extreame storme to hull all night, did drive them by his providence to their desired Port, beyond all their expectations, for never any of them had seene that coast. The first land they made they called Cape Henry; where thirtie of them recreating themselves on shore, were assaulted by five Salvages, who hurt

Monica an unfrequented Isle full of Birds.

Their first landing.

two of the English very dangerously. That night was the box opened, and the orders read, in which Bartholomew Gosnoll, John Smith, Edward Wingfield, Christopher Newport, John Ratliffe, John Martin, and George Kendall, were named to be the Councell, and to choose a President amongst them for a yeare, who with the Councell should governe. Matters of moment were to be examined by a Jury, but determined by the major part of the Councell, in which the President had two voyces. Untill the 13 of May they sought a place to plant in, then the Councell was sworne, Master Wingfield was chosen President, and an Oration made, why Captaine Smith was not admitted of the Councell as the rest.

Matters of government.

Now falleth every man to worke, the Councell contrive the Fort, the rest cut downe trees to make place to pitch their Tents; some provide clapbord to relade the ships, some make gardens, some nets, etc. The Salvages often visited us kindly. The Presidents overweening jealousie would admit no exercise at armes, or fortification, but the boughs of trees cast together in the forme of a halfe moone by the extraordinary paines and diligence of Captaine Kendall. Newport, Smith, and twentie others, were sent to discover the head of the river: by divers small habitations they passed, in six dayes they arrived at a Towne called Powhatan, consisting of some twelve houses, pleasantly seated on a hill; before it three fertile Isles, about it many of their cornefields, the place is very pleasant, and strong by nature, of this place the Prince is called Powhatan, and his people Powhatans, to this place the river is navigable: but higher within a myle, by reason of the Rockes and Isles, there is not passage for a small Boat, this they call the Falles, the people in all parts kindly intreated them, till being returned within twentie myles of James towne, they gave just cause of jealousie, but had God not blessed the discoverers otherwise then those at the Fort, there had then beene an end of that plantation; for at the Fort, where they arrived the next day, they found 17 men hurt, and a boy slaine by the Salvages, and had it not chanced a crosse barre shot from the Ships strooke downe a bough from a tree amongst them, that caused them to retire, our men had all

The discovery of the Falles and Powhatan.

The Fort assaulted by the Salvages.

beene slaine, being securely all at worke, and their armes in dry
fats.

Hereupon the President was contented the Fort should be
pallisadoed, the Ordnance mounted, his men armed and exercised, for many were the assaults, and ambuscadoes of the Salvages, and our men by their disorderly stragling were often
hurt, when the Salvages by the nimblenesse of their heeles well
escaped. What toyle we had, with so small a power to guard
our workemen adayes, watch all night, resist our enemies, and
effect our businesse, to relade the ships, cut downe trees, and
prepare the ground to plant our Corne, etc., I referre to the
Readers consideration. Six weekes being spent in this manner,
Captaine Newport (who was hired onely for our transportation) was to returne with the ships. Now Captaine Smith, who
all this time from their departure from the Canaries was restrained as a prisoner upon the scandalous suggestions of some
of the chiefe (envying his repute) who fained he intended to
usurpe the government, murther the Councell, and make himselfe King, that his confederats were dispersed in all the three
ships, and that divers of his confederats that revealed it, would
affirme it, for this he was committed as a prisoner: thirteene
weekes he remained thus suspected, and by that time the ships
should returne they pretended out of their commisserations,
to referre him to the Councell in England to receive a check,
rather then by particulating his designes make him so odious
to the world, as to touch his life, or utterly overthrow his reputation. But he so much scorned their charitie, and publikely
defied the uttermost of their crueltie, he wisely prevented their
policies, though he could not suppresse their envies, yet so well
he demeaned himselfe in this businesse, as all the company did
see his innocency, and his adversaries malice, and those suborned to accuse him, accused his accusers of subornation; many
untruthes were alledged against him; but being so apparently
disproved, begat a generall hatred in the hearts of the company against such unjust Commanders, that the President was
adjudged to give him 200^l. so that all he had was seized upon,
in part of satisfaction, which Smith presently returned to the
Store for the generall use of the Colony. Many were the mischiefes that daily sprung from their ignorant (yet ambitious)

spirits; but the good Doctrine and exhortation of our Preacher Master Hunt reconciled them, and caused Captaine Smith to be admitted of the Councell; the next day all received the Communion, the day following the Salvages voluntarily desired peace, and Captaine Newport returned for England with newes; leaving in Virginia 100. the 15 of June 1607.

Captain Newports returne for England.

By this observe;

> *Good men did ne'r their Countries ruine bring.*
> *But when evill men shall injuries beginne;*
> *Not caring to corrupt and violate*
> *The judgements-seats for their owne Lucr's sake:*
> *Then looke that Country cannot long have peace,*
> *Though for the present it have rest and ease.*

The names of them that were the first Planters, were these following.

1607. Sir Thomas Smith Treasurer.

Master Edward Maria Wingfield.
Captaine Bartholomew Gosnoll.
Captaine John Smith.
Captaine John Ratliffe.
Captaine John Martin.
Captaine George Kendall.
} *Councel.*

Master Robert Hunt *Preacher.*
Master George Percie.
Anthony Gosnoll.
George Flower.
Captaine Gabriell Archer.
Robert Fenton.
Robert Ford.
William Bruster.
Edward Harrington.
Dru Pickhouse.
Thomas Jacob.
John Brookes.
Ellis Kingston.
Thomas Sands.
Benjamin Beast.
} *Gentlemen.*

Jehu Robinson.
Thomas Mouton.
Eustace Clovill.
Stephen Halthrop.
Kellam Throgmorton.
Edward Morish.
Nathaniell Powell.
Edward Browne.
Robert Behethland.
John Penington.
Jeremy Alicock.
George Walker.
Thomas Studley.
Richard Crofts.
Nicholas Houlgrave.
Thomas Webbe.
John Waller.   } *Gentlemen.*
John Short.
William Tankard.
William Smethes.
Francis Snarsbrough.
Richard Simons.
Edward Brookes.
Richard Dixon.
John Martin.
Roger Cooke.
Anthony Gosnold.
Thomas Wotton, *Chirurgian.*
John Stevenson.
Thomas Gore.
Henry Adling.
Francis Midwinter.
Richard Frith.
William Laxon.
Edward Pising.   } *Carpenters.*
Thomas Emry.
Robert Small.
John Laydon.
William Cassen.   } *Labourers.*
George Cassen.

Thomas Cassen. \
William Rodes. \
William White. \
Old Edward. \
Henry Tavin. \
George Goulding. \
John Dods. \
William Johnson. \
William Unger.

Labourers.

James Read, *Blacksmith.* \
Jonas Profit, *Sailer.* \
Thomas Cowper, *Barber.* \
William Garret, *Bricklayer.* \
Edward Brinto, *Mason.* \
William Love, *Taylor.* \
Nicholas Scot, *Drummer.* \
William Wilkinson, *Chirurgian.* \
Samuell Collier, *boy.* \
Nathaniell Pecock, *boy.* \
James Brumfield, *boy.* \
Richard Mutton, *boy.* \
With divers others to the number of 100.

Chapter II.
What happened till the first supply.

BEING thus left to our fortunes, it fortuned that within ten dayes scarce ten amongst us could either goe, or well stand, such extreame weaknes and sicknes oppressed us. And thereat none need marvaile, if they consider the cause and reason, which was this; whilest the ships stayed, our allowance was somewhat bettered, by a daily proportion of Bisket, which the sailers would pilfer to sell, give, or exchange with us, for money, Saxefras, furres, or love. But when they departed, there remained neither taverne, beere-house, nor place of reliefe, but the common Kettell. Had we beene as free from all sinnes as

The occasion of sicknesse.

The Sailers abuses.

gluttony, and drunkennesse, we might have beene canonized
for Saints; But our President would never have beene admitted, for ingrossing to his private, Oatmeale, Sacke, Oyle,
Aquavitæ, Beefe, Egges, or what not, but the Kettell; that indeed he allowed equally to be distributed, and that was halfe a
pint of wheat, and as much barley boyled with water for a man
a day, and this having fryed some 26. weekes in the ships hold,
contained as many wormes as graines; so that we might truely
call it rather so much bran then corne, our drinke was water,
our lodgings Castles in the ayre: with this lodging and dyet,
our extreame toile in bearing and planting Pallisadoes, so
strained and bruised us, and our continuall labour in the extremitie of the heat had so weakened us, as were cause sufficient to have made us as miserable in our native Countrey, or
any other place in the world. From May, to September, those
that escaped, lived upon Sturgeon, and Sea-crabs, fiftie in this
time we buried, the rest seeing the Presidents projects to escape these miseries in our Pinnace by flight
(who all this time had neither felt want nor sicknes)
so moved our dead spirits, as we deposed him; and established
Ratcliffe in his place, (Gosnoll being dead) Kendall deposed,
Smith newly recovered, Martin and Ratcliffe was by his care
preserved and relieved, and the most of the souldiers recovered, with the skilfull diligence of Master Thomas Wotton our
Chirurgian generall. But now was all our provision spent, the
Sturgeon gone, all helps abandoned, each houre expecting
the fury of the Salvages; when God the patron of all good indevours, in that desperate extremitie so changed the
hearts of the Salvages, that they brought such plenty
of their fruits, and provision, as no man wanted.

A bad President.

Plentie unexpected.

And now where some affirmed it was ill done of the Councell to send forth men so badly provided, this incontradictable
reason will shew them plainely they are too ill advised to nourish such ill conceits; first, the fault of our going was our owne,
what could be thought fitting or necessary we had, but what
we should find, or want, or where we should be, we were all
ignorant, and supposing to make our passage in two moneths,
with victuall to live, and the advantage of the spring to worke;
we were at Sea five moneths, where we both spent our victuall
and lost the opportunitie of the time, and season to plant, by

the unskilfull presumption of our ignorant transporters, that understood not at all, what they undertooke.

Such actions have ever since the worlds beginning beene subject to such accidents, and every thing of worth is found full of difficulties, but nothing so difficult as to establish a Common-wealth so farre remote from men and meanes, and where mens mindes are so untoward as neither doe well themselves, nor suffer others. But to proceed.

The new President and Martin, being little beloved, of weake judgement in dangers, and lesse industrie in peace, committed the managing of all things abroad to Captaine Smith: who by his owne example, good words, and faire promises, set some to mow, others to binde thatch, some to build houses, others to thatch them, himselfe alwayes bearing the greatest taske for his owne share, so that in short time, he provided most of them lodgings, neglecting any for himselfe. This done, seeing the Salvages superfluitie beginne to decrease (with some of his workemen) shipped himselfe in the Shallop to search the Country for trade. The want of the language, knowledge to mannage his boat without sailes, the want of a sufficient power, (knowing the multitude of the Salvages) apparell for his men, and other necessaries, were infinite impediments, yet no discouragement. Being but six or seaven in company he went downe the river to Kecoughtan, where at first they scorned him, as a famished man, and would in derision offer him a handfull of Corne, a peece of bread, for their swords and muskets, and such like proportions also for their apparell. But seeing by trade and courtesie there was nothing to be had, he made bold to try such conclusions as necessitie inforced, though contrary to his Commission: Let fly his muskets, ran his boat on shore, whereat they all fled into the woods. So marching towards their houses, they might see great heapes of corne: much adoe he had to restraine his hungry souldiers from present taking of it, expecting as it hapned that the Salvages would assault them, as not long after they did with a most hydeous noyse. Sixtie or seaventie of them, some blacke, some red, some white, some party-coloured, came in a square order, singing and dauncing out of the woods, with their *Okee* (which was an Idoll made of skinnes, stuffed with mosse, all painted and hung with chaines and copper)

The building of James Towne.

The beginning of Trade abroad.

borne before them: and in this manner being well armed, with Clubs, Targets, Bowes and Arrowes, they charged the English, that so kindly received them with their muskets loaden with Pistoll shot, that downe fell their God, and divers lay sprauling on the ground; the rest fled againe to the woods, and ere long sent one of their *Quiyoughkasoucks* to offer peace, and redeeme their *Okee*. Smith told them, if onely six of them would come unarmed and loade his boat, he would not only be their friend, but restore them their *Okee*, and give them Beads, Copper, and Hatchets besides: which on both sides was to their contents performed: and then they brought him Venison, Turkies, wild foule, bread, and what they had, singing and dauncing in signe of friendship till they departed. In his returne he discovered the Towne and Country of Warraskoyack.

> *Thus God unboundlesse by his power,*
> *Made them thus kind, would us devour.*

Amoris, a Salvage his best friend slaine for loving us.

Smith perceiving (notwithstanding their late miserie) not any regarded but from hand to mouth (the company being well recovered) caused the Pinnace to be provided with things fitting to get provision for the yeare following; but in the interim he made 3. or 4.

The Discovery of Chickahamina.

journies and discovered the people of Chickahamania: yet what he carefully provided the rest carelesly spent. Wingfield and Kendall living in disgrace, seeing all things at randome in the absence of Smith, the companies dislike of their Presidents weaknes, and their small love to Martins never mending sicknes, strengthened themselves with the sailers, and other confederates to regaine their former credit and authority, or at least such meanes abord the Pinnace, (being fitted to saile as Smith had appointed for trade) to alter her course and to goe for England. Smith unexpectedly returning had the plot discovered to him, much trouble he had to prevent it, till with store of sakre and musket shot he forced them stay or sinke in the river, which action cost the life of captaine Kendall. These brawles are so disgustfull, as some will say they were better forgotten, yet all men of good judgement will conclude, it were better their basenes should be manifest to the world, then the busines beare the scorne and shame of their excused disorders. The President and captaine Archer not

long after intended also to have abandoned the country, which
project also was curbed, and suppressed by Smith. The Spaniard
Another never more greedily desired gold then he victuall,
project to
abandon the nor his souldiers more to abandon the Country, then
country. he to keepe it. But finding plentie of Corne in the
river of Chickahamania where hundreds of Salvages in divers
places stood with baskets expecting his comming. And now the
winter approaching, the rivers became so covered with swans,
geese, duckes, and cranes, that we daily feasted with good
bread, Virginia pease, pumpions, and putchamins, fish, fowle,
and diverse sorts of wild beasts as fat as we could eate them: so
that none of our Tuftaffaty humorists desired to goe for England. But our Comædies never endured long without a
Tragedie; some idle exceptions being muttered against Captaine Smith, for not discovering the head of Chickahamania
river, and taxed by the Councell, to be too slow in so worthy
an attempt. The next voyage hee proceeded so farre that with
much labour by cutting of trees in sunder he made his passage,
but when his Barge could passe no farther, he left her in a
broad bay out of danger of shot, commanding none should
goe a shore till his returne: himselfe with two English and two
Salvages went up higher in a Canowe, but hee was not long
absent, but his men went a shore, whose want of government,
gave both occasion and opportunity to the Salvages to surprise
one George Cassen, whom they slew, and much failed not to
have cut of the boat and all the rest. Smith little dreaming of
*Jehu that accident, being got to the marshes at the rivers
Robinson
and Thomas head, twentie myles in the desert, had his* two men
Emry slaine. slaine (as is supposed) sleeping by the Canowe, whilst
himselfe by fowling sought them victuall, who finding he was
beset with 200. Salvages, two of them hee slew, still defending
himselfe with the ayd of a Salvage his guid, whom he bound to
his arme with his garters, and used him as a buckler, yet he was
shot in his thigh a little, and had many arrowes that stucke in
his cloathes but no great hurt, till at last they tooke him prisoner. When this newes came to James towne, much was their
sorrow for his losse, fewe expecting what ensued. Six or seven
weekes those Barbarians kept him prisoner, many strange triumphes and conjurations they made of him, yet hee so demeaned himselfe amongst them, as he not onely diverted them

from surprising the Fort, but procured his owne libertie, and got himselfe and his company such estimation amongst them, that those Salvages admired him more then their owne *Qui-youckosucks.* The manner how they used and delivered him, is as followeth.

Captaine Smith taken prisoner. The Salvages having drawne from George Cassen whether Captaine Smith was gone, prosecuting that oportunity they followed him with 300. bow-men, conducted by the King of Pamaunkee, who in divisions searching the turnings of the river, found Robinson and Emry by the fire side, those they shot full of arrowes and slew. Then finding the Captaine, as is said, that used the Salvage that was his guide as his sheld (three of them being slaine and divers other so gauld) all the rest would not come neere him. Thinking thus to have returned to his boat, regarding them, as he marched, more then his way, slipped up to the middle in an oasie creeke and his Salvage with him, yet durst they not come to him till being neere dead with cold, he threw away his armes. Then according to their composition they drew him forth and led him to the fire, where his men were slaine. Diligently they chafed his benummed limbs. He demanding for their Captaine, they shewed him Opechankanough, King of Pamaunkee, to whom he gave a round Ivory double compass Dyall. Much they marvailed at the playing of the Fly and Needle, which they could see so plainely, and yet not touch it, because of the glasse that covered them. But when he demonstrated by that Globe-like Jewell, the roundnesse of the earth, and skies, the spheare of the Sunne, Moone, and Starres, and how the Sunne did chase the night round about the world continually; the greatnesse of the Land and Sea, the diversitie of Nations, varietie of complexions, and how we were to them Antipodes, and many other such like matters, they all stood as amazed with admiration. Notwithstanding, within an houre after they tyed him to a tree, and as many as could stand about him prepared to shoot him, but the King holding up the Compass in his hand, they all laid downe their Bowes and Arrowes, and in a triumphant manner led him to Orapaks, where he was after their manner kindly feasted, and well used.

The order they observed in their triumph. Their order in conducting him was thus; Drawing themselves all in fyle, the King in the middest had all their Peeces and Swords borne before him. Captaine Smith was led after him by three great Salvages, holding him fast by each arme: and on each side six went in fyle with their Arrowes nocked. But arriving at the Towne (which was but onely thirtie or fortie hunting houses made of Mats, which they remove as they please, as we our tents) all the women and children staring to behold him, the souldiers first all in fyle performed the forme of a Bissone so well as could be; and on each flanke, officers as Serjeants to see them keepe their order. A good time they continued this exercise, and then cast themselves in a ring, dauncing in such severall Postures, and singing and yelling out such hellish notes and screeches; being strangely painted, every one his quiver of Arrowes, and at his backe a club; on his arme a Fox or an Otters skinne, or some such matter for his vambrace; their heads and shoulders painted red, with Oyle and *Pocones* mingled together, which Scarlet-like colour made an exceeding handsome shew; his Bow in his hand, and the skinne of a Bird with her wings abroad dryed, tyed on his head, a peece of copper, a white shell, a long feather, with a small rattle growing at the tayles of their snakes tyed to it, or some such like toy. All this while Smith and the King stood in the middest guarded, as before is said, and after three dances they all departed. Smith they conducted to a long house, where thirtie or fortie tall fellowes did guard him, and ere long more bread and venison was brought him then would have served twentie men, I thinke his stomacke at that time was not very good; what he left they put in baskets and tyed over his head. About midnight they set the meate againe before him, all this time not one of them would eate a bit with him, till the next morning they brought him as much more, and then did they eate all the old, and reserved the new as they had done the other, which made him thinke they would fat him to eat him. Yet in this desperate estate to defend him from the cold, one Maocassater brought him his gowne, in requitall of some beads and toyes Smith had given him at his first arrivall in Virginia.

How he should have beene slaine at Orapacks.   Two dayes after a man would have slaine him (but that the guard prevented it) for the death of his sonne, to whom they conducted him to recover the poore man then breathing his last. Smith told them that at

James towne he had a water would doe it, if they would let him fetch it, but they would not permit that; but made all the preparations they could to assault James towne, craving his advice, and for recompence he should have life, libertie, land, and women. In part of a Table booke he writ his minde to them at the Fort, what was intended, how they should follow that direction to affright the messengers, and without fayle send him such things as he writ for. And an Inventory with them. The difficultie and danger, he told the Salvages, of the Mines, great gunnes, and other Engins exceedingly affrighted them, yet according to his request they went to James towne, in as bitter weather as could be of frost and snow, and within three dayes returned with an answer.

How he saved James towne from being surprised.

But when they came to James towne, seeing men sally out as he had told them they would, they fled; yet in the night they came againe to the same place where he had told them they should receive an answer, and such things as he had promised them, which they found accordingly, and with which they returned with no small expedition, to the wonder of them all that heard it, that he could either divine, or the paper could speake: then they led him to the Youghtanunds, the Mattapanients, the Payankatanks, the Nantaughtacunds, and Onawmanients upon the rivers of Rapahanock, and Patawomek, over all those rivers, and backe againe by divers other severall Nations, to the Kings habitation at Pamaunkee, where they entertained him with most strange and fearefull Conjurations;

How they did Conjure him at Pamaunkee.

> *As if neare led to hell,*
> *Amongst the Devils to dwell.*

Not long after, early in a morning a great fire was made in a long house, and a mat spread on the one side, as on the other, on the one they caused him to sit, and all the guard went out of the house, and presently came skipping in a great grim fellow, all painted over with coale, mingled with oyle; and many Snakes and Wesels skins stuffed with mosse, and all their tayles tyed together, so as they met on the crowne of his head in a tassell; and round about the tassell was as a Coronet of feathers, the skins hanging round about his head, backe, and shoulders, and in a manner covered his face; with a hellish voyce and a rattle in his hand. With most strange gestures and passions he began his invocation, and environed the fire with a circle of meale; which done, three more such like devils came rushing in with the like antique tricks, painted halfe blacke, halfe red: but all their eyes were painted white, and some red stroakes like Mutchato's, along their cheekes: round about him those fiends daunced a pretty while, and then came in three more as ugly as the rest; with red eyes, and white stroakes over their blacke faces, at last they all sat downe right against him; three of them on the one hand of the chiefe Priest, and three on the other. Then all with their rattles began a song, which ended, the chiefe Priest layd downe five wheat cornes: then strayning his armes and hands with such violence that he sweat, and his veynes swelled, he began a short Oration: at the conclusion they all gave a short groane; and then layd down three graines more. After that, began their song againe, and then another Oration, ever laying downe so many cornes as before, till they had twice incirculed the fire; that done, they tooke a bunch of little stickes prepared for that purpose, continuing still their devotion, and at the end of every song and Oration, they layd downe a sticke betwixt the divisions of Corne. Till night, neither he nor they did either eate or drinke, and then they feasted merrily, with the best provisions they could make. Three dayes they used this Ceremony; the meaning whereof they told him, was to know if he intended them well or no. The circle of meale signified their Country, the circles of corne the bounds of the Sea, and the stickes his Country. They imagined the world to be flat and round, like a trencher, and they in the middest. After this they brought him a bagge of gunpowder, which they carefully preserved till the next spring, to plant as they did their corne; because they would be acquainted with the nature of that seede. Opitchapam the Kings brother invited him to his house, where, with as many platters of bread, foule, and wild beasts, as did environ him, he bid him wellcome; but not any of them would eate a bit with him, but put up all the remainder in Baskets. At his returne to Opechancanoughs, all the Kings women, and their children, flocked about him for their parts, as a due by Custome, to be merry with such fragments.

But his waking mind in hydeous dreames did oft see wondrous
*   shapes,*
Of bodies strange, and huge in growth, and of stupendious makes.

At last they brought him to Meronocomoco, where was
Powhatan their Emperor. Here more then two hundred of
those grim Courtiers stood wondering at him, as he
had beene a monster; till Powhatan and his trayne
had put themselves in their greatest braveries. Before

How
Powhatan
entertained
him.

a fire upon a seat like a bedsted, he sat covered with a great
robe, made of Rarowcun skinnes, and all the tayles hanging by.
On either hand did sit a young wench of 16 or 18 yeares, and
along on each side the house, two rowes of men, and behind
them as many women, with all their heads and shoulders
painted red; many of their heads bedecked with the white
downe of Birds; but every one with something: and a great
chayne of white beads about their necks. At his entrance
before the King, all the people gave a great shout. The Queene
of Appamatuck was appointed to bring him water to wash his
hands, and another brought him a bunch of feathers, in stead
of a Towell to dry them: having feasted him after their best
barbarous manner they could, a long consultation was held,
but the conclusion was, two great stones were brought before
Powhatan: then as many as could layd hands on him, dragged
him to them, and thereon laid his head, and being ready with
their clubs, to beate out his braines, Pocahontas the Kings

How
Pocahontas
saved his life.

dearest daughter, when no intreaty could prevaile,
got his head in her armes, and laid her owne upon
his to save him from death: whereat the Emperour
was contented he should live to make him hatchets, and her
bells, beads, and copper; for they thought him as well of all occupations as themselves. For the King himselfe will make his
owne robes, shooes, bowes, arrowes, pots; plant, hunt, or doe
any thing so well as the rest.

> *They say he bore a pleasant shew,*
> *But sure his heart was sad.*
> *For who can pleasant be, and rest,*
> *That lives in feare and dread:*
> *And having life suspected, doth*
> *It still suspected lead.*

Two dayes after, Powhatan having disguised himselfe in the most fearefullest manner he could, caused Captaine Smith to be brought forth to a great house in the woods, and there upon a mat by the fire to be left alone. Not long after from behinde a mat that divided the house, was made the most dolefullest noyse he ever heard; then Powhatan more like a devill then a man with some two hundred more as blacke as himselfe, came unto him and told him now they were friends, and presently he should goe to James towne, to send him two great gunnes, and a gryndstone, for which he would give him the Country of Capahowosick, and for ever esteeme him as his sonne Nantaquoud. So to James towne with 12 guides Powhatan sent him. That night they quarterd in the woods, he still expecting (as he had done all this long time of his imprisonment) every houre to be put to one death or other: for all their feasting. But almightie God (by his divine providence) had mollified the hearts of those sterne Barbarians with compassion. The next morning betimes they came to the Fort, where Smith having used the Salvages with what kindnesse he could, he shewed Rawhunt, Powhatans trusty servant two demi-Culverings and a millstone to carry Powhatan: they found them somewhat too heavie; but when they did see him discharge them, being loaded with stones, among the boughs of a great tree loaded with Isickles, the yce and branches came so tumbling downe, that the poore Salvages ran away halfe dead with feare. But at last we regained some conference with them, and gave them such toyes, and sent to Powhatan, his women, and children such presents, as gave them in generall full content. Now in James Towne they were all in combustion, the strongest preparing once more to run away with the Pinnace; which with the hazzard of his life, with Sakre falcon and musket shot, Smith forced now the third time to stay or sinke. Some no better then they should be, had plotted with the President, the next day to have put him to death by the Leviticall law, for the lives of Robinson and Emry, pretending the fault was his that had led them to their ends: but he quickly tooke such order with such Lawyers, that he layd them by the heeles till he sent some of them prisoners for England. Now ever once in foure or five dayes, Pocahontas with her attendants, brought him so much provision,

Marginal notes:

How Powhatan sent him to James Towne.

The third project to abandon the Countrey.

that saved many of their lives, that els for all this had starved with hunger.

> *Thus from numbe death our good God sent reliefe,*
> *The sweete asswager of all other griefe.*

His relation of the plenty he had seene, especially at Wera-wocomoco, and of the state and bountie of Powhatan, (which till that time was unknowne) so revived their dead spirits (especially the love of Pocahontas) as all mens feare was abandoned. Thus you may see what difficulties still crossed any good indevour: and the good successe of the businesse being thus oft brought to the very period of destruction; yet you see by what strange means God hath still delivered it. As for the insufficiency of them admitted in Commission, that error could not be prevented by the Electors; there being no other choise, and all strangers to each others education, qualities, or disposition. And if any deeme it a shame to our Nation to have any mention made of those inormities, let them peruse the Histories of the Spanyards Discoveries and Plantations, where they may see how many mutinies, disorders, and dissentions have accompanied them, and crossed their attempts: which being knowne to be particular mens offences; doth take away the generall scorne and contempt, which malice, presumption, covetousnesse, or ignorance might produce; to the scandall and reproach of those, whose actions and valiant resolutions deserve a more worthy respect.

A true proofe of Gods love to the action.

Now whether it had beene better for Captaine Smith, to have concluded with any of those severall projects, to have abandoned the Countrey, with some ten or twelve of them, who were called the better sort, and have left Master Hunt our Preacher, Master Anthony Gosnoll, a most honest, worthy, and industrious Gentleman, Master Thomas Wotton, and some 27 others of his Countrymen to the fury of the Salvages, famine, and all manner of mischiefes, and inconveniences, (for they were but fortie in all to keepe possession of this large Country;) or starve himselfe with them for company, for want of lodging: or but adventuring abroad to make them provision, or by his opposition to preserve the action, and save all their lives; I leave to the censure of all honest men to consider. But

Of two evils the lesse was chosen.

We men imagine in our Jolitie,
That 'tis all one, or good or bad to be.
But then anone wee alter this againe,
If happily wee feele the sence of paine;
For then we're turn'd into a mourning vaine.

Written by Thomas Studley, the first Cape Merchant in Virginia,
Robert Fenton, Edward Harrington, and J. S.

Chapter III.
The Arrivall of the first supply, with their Proceedings, and the Ships returne.

ALL this time our care was not so much to abandon the Countrey; but the Treasurer and Councell in England, were as diligent and carefull to supply us. Two good ships they sent us, with neare a hundred men, well furnished with all things could be imagined necessary, both for them and us; The one commanded by Captaine Newport: the other by Captaine Francis Nelson, an honest man, and an expert Marriner. But such was the lewardnesse of his Ship (that though he was within the sight of Cape Henry) by stormy contrary winds was he forced so farre to Sea, that the West Indies was the next land, for the repaire of his Masts, and reliefe of wood and water. But Newport got in and arrived at James Towne, not long after the redemption of Captaine Smith. To whom the Salvages, as is sayd, every other day repaired, with such provisions that sufficiently did serve them from hand to mouth: part alwayes they brought him as Presents from their Kings, or Pocahontas; the rest he as their Market Clarke set the price himselfe, how they should sell: so he had inchanted these poore soules being their prisoner; and now Newport, whom he called his Father arriving, neare as directly as he foretold, they esteemed him as an Oracle, and had them at that submission he might command them what he listed. That God that created all things they knew he adored

The Phœnix from Cape Henry forced to the West Indies.

for his God: they would also in their discourses tearme the
God of Captaine Smith.

Their opinion
of our God.
Thus the Almightie was the bringer on,
The guide, path, terme, all which was God alone.

But the President and Councell so much envied his estimation among the Salvages, (though we all in generall equally
participated with him of the good thereof,) that they wrought
it into the Salvages understandings (by their great bounty in
giving foure times more for their commodities then Smith appointed) that their greatnesse and authoritie as much exceeded
his, as their bountie and liberalitie. Now the arrivall of this first
supply so overjoyed us, that wee could not devise too much to
please the Marriners. We gave them libertie to trucke or trade
at their pleasures. But in a short time it followed, that could
not be had for a pound of Copper, which before was sould us
for an ounce: thus ambition and sufferance cut the throat of
our trade, but confirmed their opinion of the greatnesse of
Captaine Newport, (wherewith Smith had possessed Powhatan) especially by the great presents Newport often sent him,
before he could prepare the Pinnace to goe and visit him: so
that this great Savage desired also to see him. A great coyle
there was to set him forward. When he went he was accompanied with Captaine Smith, and Master Scrivener, a very wise
understanding Gentleman, newly arrived and admitted of the
Councell, with thirtie or fortie chosen men for their
guard. Arriving at Werowocomoco, Newports conceit of this great Savage bred many doubts and suspitions of trecheries, which Smith to make appeare was needlesse,
with twentie men well appointed, undertooke to encounter
the worst that could happen: Knowing

Smiths
revisiting
Powhatan.

All is but one, and selfe-same hand, that thus
Both one while scourgeth, and that helpeth us.

Nathaniell Powell			John Taverner		
Robert Behethland			William Dyer		
Michell Phittiplace	}	*Gentlemen.*	Thomas Coe	}	*Gentlemen.*
William Phittiplace			Thomas Hope		
Anthony Gosnoll			Anas Todkill		
Richard Wyffin					

These, with nine others (whose names I have forgotten) comming a-shore, landed amongst a many of creekes, over which they were to passe such poore bridges, onely made of a few cratches, thrust in the ose, and three or foure poles laid on them, and at the end of them the like, tyed together onely with barkes of trees, that it made them much suspect those bridges were but traps. Which caused Smith to make diverse Salvages goe over first, keeping some of the chiefe as hostage till halfe his men was passed, to make a guard for himselfe and the rest. But finding all things well, by two or three hundred Salvages they were kindly conducted to their towne. Where Powhatan strained himselfe to the utmost of his greatnesse to entertaine them, with great shouts of joy, Orations of protestations; and with the most plenty of victualls he could provide to feast them. Sitting upon his bed of mats, his pillow of leather imbrodered (after their rude manner with pearle and white Beads) his attyre a faire robe of skinnes as large as an Irish mantell: at his head and feete a handsome young woman: on each side his house sat twentie of his Concubines, their heads and shoulders painted red, with a great chaine of white beads about each of their neckes. Before those sat his chiefest men in like order in his arbour-like house, and more then fortie platters of fine bread stood as a guard in two fyles on each side the doore. Foure or five hundred people made a guard behinde them for our passage; and Proclamation was made, none upon paine of death to presume to doe us any wrong or discourtesie. With many pretty Discourses to renew their old acquaintance, this great King and our Captaine spent the time, till the ebbe left our Barge aground. Then renewing their feasts with feates, dauncing and singing, and such like mirth, we quartered that night with Powhatan. The next day Newport came a shore and received as much content as those people could give him: a boy named Thomas Salvage was then given unto Powhatan, whom Newport called his sonne; for whom Powhatan gave him Namontack his trustie servant, and one of a shrewd, subtill capacitie. Three or foure dayes more we spent in feasting, dauncing, and trading, wherein Powhatan carried himselfe so proudly, yet discreetly (in his salvage manner) as made us all admire his

Powhatan his entertainement.

The exchange of a Christian for a Salvage.

naturall gifts, considering his education. As scorning to trade as his subjects did; he bespake Newport in this manner.

Captaine Newport it is not agreeable to my greatnesse, in this pedling manner to trade for trifles; and I esteeme you also a great Werowance. Therefore lay me downe all your commodities together; what I like I will take, and in recompence give you what I thinke fitting their value.

Powhatans speech.

Captaine Smith being our interpreter, regarding Newport as his father, knowing best the disposition of Powhatan, tould us his intent was but onely to cheate us; yet Captaine Newport thinking to out brave this Salvage in ostentation of greatnesse, and so to bewitch him with his bountie, as to have what he listed, it so hapned, that Powhatan having his desire, valued his corne at such a rate, that I thinke it better cheape in Spaine: for we had not foure bushells for that we expected to have twentie hogsheads. This bred some unkindnesse betweene our two Captaines; Newport seeking to please the unsatiable desire of the Salvage, Smith to cause the Salvage to please him; but smothering his distast to avoyd the Salvages suspition, glanced in the eyes of Powhatan many trifles, who fixed his humor upon a few blew beades. A long time he importunately desired them, but Smith seemed so much the more to affect them, as being composed of a most rare substance of the coulour of the skyes, and not to be worne but by the greatest kings in the world. This made him halfe madde to be the owner of such strange Jewells: so that ere we departed, for a pound or two of blew beades, he brought over my king for 2. or 300. Bushells of corne; yet parted good friends. The like entertainment we found of Opechankanough king of Pamaunkee, whom also he in like manner fitted (at the like rates) with blew beads, which grew by this meanes, of that estimation, that none durst weare any of them but their great kings, their wives and children. And so we returned all well to James towne, where this new supply being lodged with the rest, accidentally fired their quarters and so the towne, which being but thatched with reeds, the fire was so fierce as it burnt their Pallisado's, (though eight or ten yards distant) with their Armes, bedding, apparell,

Differences of opinions.

James towne burnt.

and much private provision. Good Master Hunt our Preacher lost all his Library and all he had but the cloathes on his backe: yet none never heard him repine at his losse. This happned in the winter in that extreame frost, 1607. Now though we had victuall sufficient I meane onely of Oatmeale, meale and corne, yet the Ship staying 14. weekes when shee might as wel have beene gone in 14. dayes, spent a great part of that, and neare all the rest that was sent to be landed. When they departed what there discretion could spare us, to make a little poore meale or two, we called feastes, to relish our mouthes: of each somwhat they left us, yet I must confesse, those that had either money, spare clothes credit to give billes of paiment, gold rings, furrs, or any such commodities, were ever welcome to this removing taverne, such was our patience to obay such vile Commanders, and buy our owne provisions at 15. times the value, suffering them feast (we bearing the charge) yet must not repine, but fast, least we should incurre the censure of factious and seditious persons: and then leakage, ship-rats, and other casualities occasioned them losse, but the vessels and remnants (for totals) we were glad to receave with all our hearts to make up the account, highly commending their providence for preserving that, least they should discourage any more to come to us. Now for all this plenty our ordynary was but meale and water, so that this great charge little releeved our wants, whereby with the extremitie of the bitter cold frost and those defects, more then halfe of us dyed; I cannot deny but both Smith and Skrivener did their best to amend what was amisse, but with the President went the major part, that there homes were to short. But the worst was our guilded refiners with their golden promises made all men their slaves in hope of recompences; there was no talke, no hope, no worke, but dig gold, wash gold, refine gold, loade gold, such a bruit of gold, that one mad fellow desired to be buried in the sands least they should by there art make gold of his bones: little neede there was and lesse reason, the ship should stay, there wages run on, our victualls consume 14. weekes, that the Mariners might say, they did helpe to build such a golden Church that we can say the raine washed neere to nothing in 14. dayes. Were it that captaine Smith would not applaude all those

A ship Idely loytering 14. weekes.

The effect of meere Verbalists.

A needlesse charge.

golden inventions, because they admitted him not to the sight of their trialls nor golden consultations, I know not; but I have heard him oft question with Captaine Martin and tell him, except he could shew him a more substantiall triall, he was not inamoured with their durty skill, breathing out these and many other passions, never any thing did more torment him, then to see all necessary busines neglected, to fraught such a drunken ship with so much guilded durt. Till then we never accounted, Captaine Newport a refiner, who being ready to set saile for England, and we not having any use of Parliaments, Plaies, Petitions, Admiralls, Recorders, Interpreters, Chronologers, Courts of Plea, nor Justices of peace, sent Master Wingfield and Captaine Archer home with him, that had ingrossed all those titles, to seeke some better place of imployment.

A returne to England.

> *Oh cursed gold those, hunger-starved movers,*
> *To what misfortunes lead'st thou all those lovers!*
> *For all the* China *wealth, nor* Indies *can*
> *Suffice the minde of an av'ritious man.*

Chapter IIII.
The Arrivall of the Phœnix; *her returne;*
and other Accidents.

The rebuilding James Towne.

THE authoritie now consisting in Captaine Martin, and the still sickly President, the sale of the Stores commodities maintained his estate, as an inheritable revenew. The spring approaching, and the Ship departing, Master Scrivener and Captaine Smith devided betwixt them the rebuilding James towne; the repairing our Pallizadoes; the cutting downe trees; preparing our fields; planting our corne, and to rebuild our Church, and recover our Store house. All men thus busie at their severall labours, Master Nelson arrived with his lost *Phœnix*; lost (I say) for that we all deemed him lost. Landing safely all his men, (so well he had mannaged his ill hap,) causing the Indian Isles to feede his company, that his victuall to that we had gotten, as is said before, was neare after

our allowance sufficient for halfe a yeare. He had not any thing
but he freely imparted it, which honest dealing (being a Marriner) caused us admire him: we would not have wished more
then he did for us. Now to relade this ship with some good
tydings, the President (not holding it stood with the dignitie

Sixtie
appointed to
discover the
Monacans. of his place to leave the Fort) gave order to Captaine
Smith to discover and search the commodities of the
Monacans Countrey beyond the Falls. Sixtie able
men was allotted them, the which within six dayes, Smith had
so well trained to their armes and orders, that they little feared
with whom they should incounter: yet so unseasonable was the
time, and so opposit was Captaine Martin to any thing, but
onely to fraught this ship also with his phantasticall gold, as
Captaine Smith rather desired to relade her with Cedar, (which
was a present dispatch) then either with durt, or the hopes and
reports of an uncertaine discovery, which he would performe
when they had lesse charge and more leisure.

But,

> *The God of Heav'n, He eas'ly can*
> *Immortalize a mortall man,*
> *With glory and with fame.*
> *The same God, ev'n as eas'ly may*
> *Afflict a mortall man, I say,*
> *With sorrow and with shame.*

Whilst the conclusion was a resolving, this hapned.

Powhatan (to expresse his love to Newport) when he de-

An ill
example to
sell swords
to Salvages. parted, presented him with twentie Turkies, conditionally to returne him twentie swords, which
immediately was sent him; now after his departure
he presented Captaine Smith with the like luggage, but not
finding his humor obeyed in not sending such weapons as he
desired, he caused his people with twentie devices to obtaine
them. At last by ambuscadoes at our very Ports they would take
them perforce, surprise us at worke, or any way; which was so
long permitted, they became so insolent there was no rule; the

The
Presidents
weaknesse. command from England was so strait not to offend
them, as our authoritie-bearers (keeping their houses)
would rather be any thing then peace-breakers. This
charitable humor prevailed, till well it chanced they medled

with Captaine Smith, who without farther deliberation gave them such an incounter, as some he so hunted up and downe the Isle, some he so terrified with whipping, beating, and imprisonment, as for revenge they surprised two of our forraging disorderly souldiers, and having assembled their forces, boldly threatned at our Ports to force Smith to redeliver seven Salvages, which for their villanies he detained prisoners, or we were all but dead men. But to try their furies he sallied out amongst them, and in lesse then an houre, he so hampred their insolencies, they brought them his two men, desiring peace without any further composition for their prisoners. Those he examined, and caused them all beleeve, by severall vollies of shot one of their companions was shot to death, because they would not confesse their intents and plotters of those villanies. And thus they all agreed in one point, they were directed onely by Powhatan to obtaine him our weapons, to cut our owne throats, with the manner where, how, and when, which we plainly found most true and apparant: yet he sent his messengers, and his dearest daughter Pocahontas with presents to excuse him of the injuries done by some rash untoward Captaines his subjects, desiring their liberties for this time, with the assurance of his love for ever. After Smith had given the prisoners what correction he thought fit, used them well a day or two after, and then delivered them Pocahontas, for whose sake onely he fayned to have saved their lives, and gave them libertie. The patient Councell that nothing would move to warre with the Salvages, would gladly have wrangled with Captaine Smith for his crueltie, yet none was slaine to any mans knowledge, but it brought them in such feare and obedience, as his very name would sufficiently affright them; where before, wee had sometime peace and warre twice in a day, and very seldome a weeke, but we had some trecherous villany or other.

Smiths attempt to suppresse the Salvages insolencies.

Powhatans excuse.

The fraught of this Ship being concluded to be Cedar, by the diligence of the Master, and Captaine Smith, she was quickly reladed: Master Scrivener was neither idle nor slow to follow all things at the Fort; the Ship being ready to set sayle, Captaine Martin being alwayes very sickly, and unserviceable, and desirous to injoy the credit of his

A ship fraught with Cedar.

supposed Art of finding the golden Mine, was most willingly admitted to returne for England. For

> *He hath not fill'd his lapp,*
> *That still doth hold it oap.*

From the writings of Thomas Studley, and Anas Todkill.

Their Names that were landed in this Supply.

Mathew Scrivener *appointed to be one of the Councell.*
Michaell Phittiplace.
William Phittiplace.
Ralph Morton.
Richard Wyffing.
John Taverner.
William Cantrell.
Robert Barnes.
Richard Fetherstone.
George Hill.
George Pretty.
Nathaniell Causy.
Peter Pory.
Robert Cutler.
Michaell Sicklemore.
William Bentley.
Thomas Coe.
Doctor Russell.
Jeffrey Abbot.
Edward Gurgana.
Richard Worley.
Timothy Leeds.
Richard Killingbeck.
William Spence.
Richard Prodger.
Richard Pots.
Richard Mullinax.
William Bayley.
Francis Perkins.
John Harper.
George Forest.

} *Gentlemen.*

John Nichols. } *Gentlemen.*
William Grivell. }

Raymond Goodison.
William Simons.
John Spearman.
Richard Bristow.
William Perce.
James Watkins.
John Bouth.
Christopher Rods.
Richard Burket.
James Burre.
Nicholas Ven. } *Labourers.*
Francis Perkins.
Richard Gradon.
Rawland Nelstrop.
Richard Savage.
Thomas Savage.
Richard Milmer.
William May.
Vere.
Michaell.
Bishop Wiles.

Thomas Hope.
William Ward.
John Powell. } *Taylers.*
William Yong.
William Beckwith.
Larence Towtales.

Thomas Field. } *Apothecaries.*
John Harford. }

Daniel Stallings, *Jeweller.*
William Dawson, *a refiner.*
Abram Ransack, *a refiner.*
William Johnson, *a Goldsmith.*
Peter Keffer, *a gunsmith.*
Robert Alberton, *a perfumer.*
Richard Belfield, *a Goldsmith.*
Post Ginnat, *a Chirurgion.*
John Lewes, *a Copper.*

Robert Cotton, *a Tobacco-pipe-maker.*
Richard Dole, *a Blacksmith.*
And divers others to the number of 120.

Chapter V.
The Accidents that hapned in the Discovery of the Bay of Chisapeack.

THE prodigalitie of the Presidents state went so deepe into our small store, that Smith and Scrivener tyed him and his Parasites to the rules of proportion. But now Smith being to depart, the Presidents authoritie so overswayed the discretion of Master Scrivener, that our store, our time, our strength and labours were idely consumed to fulfill his phantasies. The second of June 1608. Smith left the Fort to performe his Discovery with this Company,

Walter Russell, *Doctor of Physicke.*	
Ralfe Murton.	
Thomas Momford.	
William Cantrill.	
Richard Fetherston.	*Gentlemen.*
James Burne.	
Michell Sicklemore.	
Jonas Profit.	
Anas Todkill.	
Robert Small.	
James Watkins.	*Souldiers.*
John Powell.	
James Read.	
Richard Keale.	

These being in an open Barge neare three tuns burthen, leaving the *Phœnix* at Cape Henry, they crossed the Bay to the Easterne shore, and fell with the Isles called Smiths Isles, after our Captaines name. The first people we saw were two grim and stout Salvages upon Cape Charles, with long poles like Javelings, headed with bone, they boldly demanded what we were, and what we would; but after many circumstances they seemed very kinde, and directed us to Accomack, the habitation of their Werowance, where we were kindly intreated. This King was the comliest, proper, civill Salvage we incountred. His Country is a pleasant fertile clay soyle, some small creekes; good Harbours for small Barks, but not for Ships. He told us of a strange accident lately happened him, and it was, two children being dead; some extreame passions, or dreaming visions, phantasies, or affection moved their parents againe to revisit their dead carkases, whose benummed bodies reflected to the eyes of the beholders such delightfull countenances, as though they had regained their vitall spirits. This as a miracle drew many to behold them, all which being a great part of his people, not long after dyed, and but few escaped. They spake the language of Powhatan, wherein they made such descriptions of the Bay, Isles, and rivers, that often did us exceeding pleasure. Passing along the coast, searching every inlet, and Bay, fit for harbours and habitations. Seeing many Isles in the midst of the Bay we bore up for them, but ere we could obtaine them, such an extreame gust of wind, rayne, thunder, and lightening happened, that with great danger we escaped the unmercifull raging of that Ocean-like water. The highest land on the mayne, yet it was but low, we called Keales hill, and these uninhabited Isles, Russels Isles. The next day searching them for fresh water, we could find none, the defect whereof forced us to follow the next Easterne Channell, which brought us to the river of Wighcocomoco. The people at first with great fury seemed to assault us, yet at last with songs and daunces and much mirth became very tractable, but searching their habitations for water, we could fill but three barricoes, and that such puddle, that never till then we ever knew the want of good water. We digged and searched in many places, but before two daies were expired, we would have refused two barricoes of gold for one of that puddle water of Wighcocomoco. Being past these Isles which are many in number, but all naught for habitation, falling with a high land upon the mayne, we found a great Pond of fresh water, but so exceeding hot wee supposed it some bath; that place we called poynt Ployer, in honor of that most

A strange mortalitie of Salvages.

Russels Isles.

Wighcocomoco.

An extreame want of fresh water.

honourable House of Mousay in Britaine, that in an extreame extremitie once relieved our Captaine. From Wighcocomoco to this place, all the coast is low broken Isles of Morap, growne a myle or two in breadth, and ten or twelve in length, good to cut for hay in Summer, and to catch fish and foule in Winter: but the Land beyond them is all covered over with wood, as is the rest of the Country.

Being thus refreshed in crossing over from the maine to other Isles, we discovered the winde and waters so much increased with thunder, lightning, and raine, that our mast and sayle blew overbord and such mighty waves overracked us in that small barge that with great labour we kept her from sinking by freeing out the water. Two dayes we were inforced to inhabite these uninhabited Isles which for the extremitie of gusts, thunder, raine, stormes, and ill wether we called Limbo. Repairing our saile with our shirts, we set sayle for the maine and fell with a pretty convenient river on the East called Cuskarawaok, the people ran as amazed in troups from place to place, and divers got into the tops of trees, they were not sparing of their arrowes, nor the greatest passion they could expresse of their anger. Long they shot, we still ryding at an Anchor without there reatch making all the signes of friendship we could. The next day they came unarmed, with every one a basket, dancing in a ring, to draw us on shore: but seeing there was nothing in them but villany, we discharged a volly of muskets charged with pistoll shot, whereat they all lay tumbling on the grownd, creeping some one way, some another into a great cluster of reedes hard by; where there companies lay in Ambuscado. Towards the evening we wayed, and approaching the shoare, discharging five or six shot among the reedes, we landed where there lay a many of baskets and much bloud, but saw not a Salvage. A smoake appearing on the other side the river, we rowed thither, where we found two or three little houses, in each a fire, there we left some peeces of copper, beads, bells, and looking glasses, and then went into the bay, but when it was darke we came backe againe. Early in the morning foure Salvages came to us in their Canow, whom we used with such courtesie, not knowing what we were, nor had done, having beene in the bay a fishing, bade us stay and ere long they would

Their Barge neare sunke in a gust.

Cuskarawaock.

returne, which they did and some twentie more with them; with whom after a little conference, two or three thousand men women and children came clustring about us, every one presenting us with something, which a little bead would so well requite, that we became such friends they would contend who should fetch us water, stay with us for hostage, conduct our men any whither, and give us the best content. Here doth inhabite the people of Sarapinagh, Nause, Arseek, and Nantaquak the best Marchants of all other Salvages. They much extolled a great nation called Massawomekes, in search of whom we returned by Limbo: this river but onely at the entrance is very narrow, and the people of small stature as them of Wighcocomoco, the Land but low, yet it may prove very commodious, because it is but a ridge of land betwixt the Bay and the maine Ocean. Finding this Easterne shore, shallow broken Isles, and for most part without fresh water, we passed by the straites of Limbo for the Westerne shore: so broad is the bay here, we could scarce perceive the great high clifts on the other side: by them we Anchored that night and called them Riccards Cliftes. 30. leagues we sayled more Northwards not finding any inhabitants, leaving all the Easterne shore, lowe Islandes, but overgrowne with wood, as all the Coast beyond them so farre as wee could see: the Westerne shore by which we sayled we found all along well watered, but very mountanous and barren, the vallies very fertill, but extreame thicke of small wood so well as trees, and much frequented with Wolves, Beares, Deere and other wild beasts. We passed many shallow creekes, but the first we found Navigable for a ship, we called Bolus, for that the clay in many places under the clifts by the high water marke, did grow up in red and white knots as gum out of trees; and in some places so participated together as though they were all of one nature, excepting the coulour, the rest of the earth on both sides being hard sandy gravell, which made us thinke it Bole-Armoniack and Terra sigillata. When we first set sayle some of our Gallants doubted nothing but that our Captaine would make too much hast home, but having lien in this small barge not above 12. or 14. dayes, oft tyred at the Oares, our bread spoyled with wet so much that it was rotten (yet so good were their stomacks that they could disgest it)

The first notice of the Massawomeks.

Bolus River.

they did with continuall complaints so importune him now to returne, as caused him bespeake them in this manner.

Gentlemen if you would remember the memorable history of Sir Ralph Layne, how his company importuned him to proceed in the discovery of Moratico, alleadging they had yet a dog, that being boyled with Saxafras leaves, would richly feede them in their returnes; then what a shame would it be for you (that have bin so suspitious of my tendernesse) to force me returne, with so much provision as we have, and scarce able to say where we have beene, nor yet heard of that we were sent to seeke? You cannot say but I have shared with you in the worst which is past; and for what is to come, of lodging, dyet, or whatsoever, I am contented you allot the worst part to my selfe. As for your feares that I will lose my selfe in these unknowne large waters, or be swallowed up in some stormie gust; abandon these childish feares, for worse then is past is not likely to happen: and there is as much danger to returne as to proceede. Regaine therefore your old spirits for returne I will not (if God please) till I have scene the Massawomeks, found Patawomek, or the head of this water you conceit to be endlesse.

The discovery of Patawomek.

Two or 3. dayes we expected winde and wether, whose adverse extremities added such discouragement, that three or foure fell sicke, whose pittifull complaints caused us to returne, leaving the bay some nine miles broad, at nine and ten fadome water.

Ambuscadoes of Salvages.

The 16. of June we fell with the river Patowomek: feare being gone, and our men recovered, we were all content to take some paines, to know the name of that seven mile broad river: for thirtie myles sayle, we could see no inhabitants: then we were conducted by two Savages up a little bayed creeke, towards Onawmanient, where all the woods were layd with ambuscado's to the number of three or foure thousand Salvages, so strangely paynted, grimed and disguised, shouting, yelling and crying as so many spirits from hell could not have shewed more terrible. Many bravado's they made, but to appease their fury, our Captaine prepared with as seeming a willingnesse (as they) to incounter them. But the grazing of our bullets upon the water (many being shot on purpose they might see them) with the Ecco of the woods so amazed them, as downe went their bowes and arrowes; (and exchanging hostage) James Watkins was sent six myles up the woods to their

Kings habitation. We were kindly used of those Salvages, of whom we understood, they were commanded to betray us, by the direction of Powhatan, and he so directed from the discontents at James towne, because our Captaine did cause them stay in their country against their wills.

The like incounters we found at Patowomek, Cecocawonee and divers other places: but at Moyaones, Nacotchtant and Toags the people did their best to content us. Having gone so high as we could with the bote, we met divers Salvages in Canowes, well loaden with the flesh of Beares, Deere, and other beasts, whereof we had part, here we found mighty Rocks, growing in some places above the grownd as high as the shrubby trees, and divers other solid quarries of divers tinctures: and divers places where the waters had falne from the high mountaines they had left a tinctured spangled skurfe, that made many bare places seeme as guilded. Digging the growne above in the highest clifts of rocks, we saw it was a claie sand so mingled with yellow spangles as if it had beene halfe pin-dust. In our returne inquiring still for this Matchqueon, the king of Patawomeke gave us guides to conduct us up a little river called Quiyough, up which we rowed so high as we could. Leaving the bote, with six shot, and divers Salvages, he marched seven or eight myle before they came to the mine: leading his hostages in a small chaine they were to have for their paines, being proud so richly to be adorned. The mine is a great Rocky mountaine like Antimony; wherein they digged a great hole with shells and hatchets: and hard by it, runneth a fayre brooke of Christall-like water, where they wash a way the drosse and keepe the remainder, which they put in little baggs and sell it all over the country to paint there bodyes, faces, or Idols; which makes them looke like Blackmores dusted over with silver. With so much as we could carry we returned to our bote, kindly requiting this kinde king and all his kinde people. The cause of this discovery was to search this mine, of which Newport did assure us that those small baggs (we had given him) in England he had tryed to hold halfe silver; but all we got proved of no value: also to search what furrs, the best whereof is at Cuscarawaoke, where is made so much *Rawranoke* or white beads that occasion as much dissention among the Salvages, as

A trecherous project.

A myne like Antimony.

gold and silver amongst Christians; and what other mineralls, rivers, rocks, nations, woods, fishings, fruites, victuall, and what other commodities the land afforded: and whether the bay were endlesse or how farre it extended: of mines we were all ignorant, but a few Bevers, Otters, Beares, Martins and minkes we found, and in divers places that aboundance of fish, lying so thicke with their heads above the water, as for want of nets (our barge driving amongst them) we attempted to catch them

An aboundant plenty of fish. with a frying pan: but we found it a bad instrument to catch fish with: neither better fish, more plenty, nor more variety for smal fish, had any of us ever scene in any place so swimming in the water, but they are not to be caught with frying pans: some small codd also we did see swim close by the shore by Smiths Iles, and some as high as Riccards Clifts. And some we have found dead upon the shore.

How to deale with the Salvages. To express all our quarrels, trecheries and incounters amongst those Salvages I should be too tedious: but in breefe, at all times we so incountred them, and curbed their insolencies, that they concluded with presents to purchase peace; yet we lost not a man: at our first meeting our Captaine ever observed this order to demand their bowes and arrowes, swordes, mantells and furrs, with some childe or two for hostage, whereby we could quickly perceive, when they intended any villany. Having finished this discovery (though our victuall was neere spent) he intended to see his imprisonment-acquaintances upon the river of Rapahanock, by many called Toppahanock, but our bote by reason of the ebbe, chansing to grownd upon a many shoules lying in the entrances, we spyed many fishes lurking in the reedes: our Captaine sporting himselfe by nayling them to the grownd with his sword, set us all a fishing in that manner: thus we tooke more in owne houre then we could eate in a day. But it chansed our Captaine taking

Captaine Smith neare killed with a Stingray. a fish from his sword (not knowing her condition) being much of the fashion of a Thornback, but a long tayle like a ryding rodde, whereon the middest is a most poysoned sting, of two or three inches long, bearded like a saw on each side, which she strucke into the wrest of his arme neere an inch and a halfe: no bloud nor wound was seene, but a little blew spot, but the torment was instantly so extreame, that in foure houres had so swolen his hand, arme and shoulder, we all with much sorrow concluded his funerall, and prepared his grave in an Island by, as himselfe directed: yet it pleased God by a precious oyle Docter Russell at the first applyed to it when he sounded it with probe (ere night) his tormenting paine was so well asswaged that he eate of the fish to his supper, which gave no lesse joy and content to us then ease to himselfe, for which we called the Island Stingray Isle after the name of the fish.

The Salvages affrighted with their owne suspition. Having neither Chirurgian, nor Chirurgery, but that preservative oyle we presently set sayles for James towne, passing the mouthes of the rivers of Payankatank, and Pamaunkee, the next day we safely arrived at Kecougtan. The simple Salvages seeing our Captaine hurt, and an other bloudy by breaking his shinne, our numbers of bowes, arrowes, swords, mantles, and furrs, would needes imagine we had beene at warres (the truth of these accidents would not satisfie them) but impatiently importuned us to know with whom. Finding their aptnesse to beleeve we fayled not (as a great secret) to tell them any thing that might affright them, what spoyle we had got and made of the Massawomeks. This rumor went faster up the river then our Barge, that arrived at Waraskoyack the 20 of July; where trimming her with painted streamers, and such devises as we could, we made them at James towne jealous of a Spanish Frigot, where we all God be thanked safely arrived the 21 of July. There we found the last Supply were all sicke, the rest some lame, some bruised, all unable to doe any thing but complaine of the pride Needlesse misery at James towne. and unreasonable needlesse crueltie of the silly President, that had riotously consumed the store: and to fulfill his follies about building him an unnecessary building for his pleasure in the woods, had brought them all to that misery; that had we not arrived, they had as strangely tormented him with revenge: but the good newes of our Discovery, and the good hope we had by the Salvages relation, that our Bay had stretched into the South Sea, or somewhat neare it, appeased their fury; but conditionally that Ratliffe should be deposed, and that Captaine Smith would take upon him the government, as by course it did belong. Their request being effected, he substituted Master Scrivener his deare friend in the Presidency, equally distributing those private provisions the other had ingrossed, appointing more honest officers to assist master Scrivener (who then lay exceeding sicke of a Callenture) and in regard of the weaknesse of the company, and heate of the yeare, they being unable to worke, he left them to live at ease, to recover their healths, but imbarked himselfe to finish his Discovery.

Written by Walter Russell, Anas Todkill,
and Thomas Momford.

Chapter VI.
The Government surrendred to Master Scrivener.
What happened the second Voyage in discovering the Bay.

THE 24 of July, Captaine Smith set forward to finish the discovery with twelve men: their names were

Nathaniell Powell.	
Thomas Momford.	
Richard Fetherston.	
Michell Sicklemore.	*Gentlemen.*
James Bourne.	
Anthony Bagnall, *Chirurgian.*	
Jonas Profit.	
Anas Todkill.	
Edward Pising.	
Richard Keale.	*Souldiers.*
James Watkins.	
William Ward.	

The wind being contrary caused our stay two or three dayes at Kecoughtan: the King feasted us with much mirth, his people were perswaded we went purposely to be revenged of the Massawomeks. In the evening we fired a few rackets, which flying in the ayre so terrified the poore Salvages, they supposed nothing unpossible we attempted; and desired to assist us. The first night we anchored at Stingray Isle. The next day crossed Patawomeks river, and hasted to the river Bolus. We went not much further before we

The Salvages admire fireworkes.

might see the Bay to divide in two heads, and arriving there we found it divided in foure, all which we searched so farre as we could sayle them. Two of them we found inhabited, but in crossing the Bay, we incountred 7 or 8 Canowes full of Massawomeks. We seeing them prepare to assault us, left our Oares and made way with our sayle to incounter them, yet were we but five with our Captaine that could stand, for within 2 dayes after we left Kecoughtan, the rest (being all of the last supply) were sicke almost to death, untill they were seasoned to the Country. Having shut them under our Tarpawling, we put their hats upon stickes by the Barges side, and betwixt two hats a man with two peeces, to make us seeme many, and so we thinke the Indians supposed those hats to be men, for they fled with all possible speed to the shore, and there stayed, staring at the sayling of our barge till we anchored right against them. Long it was ere we could draw them to come unto us. At last they sent two of their company unarmed in a Canow, the rest all followed to second them if neede required. These two being but each presented with a bell, brought aboord all their fellowes, presenting our Captaine with venison, beares flesh, fish, bowes, arrowes, clubs, targets, and beares-skinnes. We understood them nothing at all, but by signes, whereby they signified unto us they had beene at warres with the Tockwoghes, the which they confirmed by shewing us their greene wounds, but the night parting us, we imagined they appointed the next morning to meete, but after that we never saw them.

An Incounter with the Massawomeks at the head of the Bay.

Entring the river of Tockwogh, the Salvages all armed, in a fleete of boats, after their barbarous manner, round invironed us; so it chanced one of them could speake the language of Powhatan, who perswaded the rest to a friendly parley. But when they saw us furnished with the Massawomeks weapons, and we faining the invention of Kecoughtan, to have taken them perforce; they conducted us to their pallizadoed towne, mantelled with the barkes of trees, with scaffolds like mounts, brested about with brests very formally. Their men, women, and children with daunces, songs, fruits, furres, and what they had, kindly welcommed us, spreading mats for us to sit on, stretching their best abilities to expresse their loves.

An Incounter with the Tockwhoghs.

Hatchets
from the
Sasquesa-
hanocks. Many hatchets, knives, peeces of iron, and brasse, we saw amongst them, which they reported to have from the Sasquesahanocks, a mightie people and mortall enemies with the Massawomeks. The Sasquesahanocks inhabit upon the chiefe Spring of these foure branches of the Bayes head, two dayes journey higher then our barge could passe for rocks, yet we prevailed with the Interpreter to take with him another Interpreter, to perswade the Sasquesahanocks to come visit us, for their language are different. Three or foure dayes we expected their returne, then sixtie of those gyant-like people came downe, with presents of Venison, Tobacco-pipes three foot in length, Baskets, Targets, Bowes and Arrowes. Five of their chiefe Werowances came boldly aboord us to crosse the Bay for Tockwhogh, leaving their men and Canowes; the wind being so high they durst not passe.

Our order was daily to have Prayer, with a Psalme, at which solemnitie the poore Salvages much wondred, our Prayers being done, a while they were busied with a consultation till they had contrived their businesse. Then they began in a most passionate manner to hold up their hands to the Sunne, with a
The Sasque-
sahanocks
offer to the
English. most fearefull song, then imbracing our Captaine, they began to adore him in like manner: though he rebuked them, yet they proceeded till their song was finished: which done with a most strange furious action, and a hellish voyce, began an Oration of their loves; that ended, with a great painted Beares skin they covered him: then one ready with a great chayne of white Beads, weighing at least six or seaven pound, hung it about his necke, the others had 18 mantels, made of divers sorts of skinnes sowed together; all these with many other toyes they layd at his feete, stroking their ceremonious hands about his necke for his Creation to be their Governour and Protector, promising their aydes, victualls, or what they had to be his, if he would stay with them, to defend and revenge them of the Massawomeks. But we left them at Tockwhogh, sorrowing for our departure, yet we promised the next yeare againe to visit them. Many descriptions and discourses they made us, of Atquanachuck, Massawomek, and other people, signifying they inhabit upon a great water beyond the mountaines, which we understood to be some great lake, or the river of Canada: and from the French to have their

hatchets and Commodities by trade. These know no more of the territories of Powhatan, then his name, and he as little of them, but the Atquanachuks are on the Ocean Sea.

The highest mountaine we saw Northward wee called Perigrines mount, and a rocky river, where the Massawomeks went up, Willowbyes river, in honor of the towne our Captaine was borne in, and that honorable house the Lord Willowby, his most honored good friend. The Sasquesahanocks river we called Smiths falles; the next poynt to Tockwhogh, Pisings poynt; the next it poynt Bourne. Powells Isles and Smals poynt is by the river Bolus; and the little Bay at the head Profits poole; Watkins, Reads, and Momfords poynts are on each side Limbo; Ward, Cantrell, and Sicklemore, betwixt Patawomek and Pamaunkee, after the names of the discoverers. In all those places and the furthest we came up the rivers, we cut in trees so many crosses as we would, and in many places made holes in trees, wherein we writ notes, and in some places crosses of brasse, to signifie to any, Englishmen had beene there.

Thus having sought all the inlets and rivers worth noting, we returned to discover the river of Pawtuxunt; these people we found very tractable, and more civill then any. We promised them, as also the Patawomeks to revenge them of the Massawomeks, but our purposes were crossed.

Pawtuxunt, River.

In the discovery of this river some call Rapahanock, we were kindly entertained by the people of Moraughtacund; here we incountered our old friend Mosco, a lusty Salvage of Wighcocomoco upon the river of Patawomek. We supposed him some French mans sonne, because he had a thicke blacke bush beard, and the Salvages seldome have any at all, of which he was not a little proud, to see so many of his Countrymen. Wood and water he would fetch us, guide us any whether, nay, cause divers of his Countrymen helpe us towe against winde or tyde from place to place till we came to Patawomek: there he rested till we returned from the head of the river, and occasioned our conduct to the mine we supposed Antimony. And in the place he fayled not to doe us all the good he could, perswading us in any case not to goe to the Rapahanocks, for they would kill us for being friends with the Moraughtacunds that but lately had

Rapahanock, River.

The exceeding love of the Salvage Mosco.

stolne three of the Kings women. This we did thinke was but
that his friends might onely have our trade: so we
crossed the river to the Rapahanocks. There some 12
or 16 standing on the shore, directed us a little Creeke
where was good landing, and Commodities for us in three or
foure Canowes we saw lie there: but according to our custome, we demanded to exchange a man in signe of love, which
after they had a little consulted, foure or five came up to the
middles, to fetch our man, and leave us one of them, shewing
we need not feare them, for they had neither clubs, bowes, nor
arrowes. Notwithstanding, Anas Todkill, being sent on shore
to see if he could discover any Ambuscadoes, or what they
had, desired to goe over the playne to fetch some wood, but
they were unwilling, except we would come into the Creeke,
where the boat might come close ashore. Todkill by degrees
having got some two stones throwes up the playne, perceived
two or three hundred men (as he thought) behind the trees, so
that offering to returne to the Boat, the Salvages assayed to
carry him away perforce, that he called to us we were betrayed,
and by that he had spoke the word, our hostage was over-
boord, but Watkins his keeper slew him in the water. Immediately we let fly amongst them, so that they fled, and Todkill
escaped, yet they shot so fast that he fell flat on the ground ere
he could recover the boat. Here the Massawomek Targets
stood us in good stead, for upon Mosco's words, we had set
them about the forepart of our Boat like a forecastle, from
whence we securely beat the Salvages from off the plaine without any hurt: yet they shot more then a thousand Arrowes,
and then fled into the woods. Arming our selves with these
light Targets (which are made of little small sticks woven betwixt strings of their hempe and silke grasse, as is our Cloth,
but so firmely that no arrow can possibly pierce them:) we
rescued Todkill, who was all bloudy by some of them who
were shot by us that held him, but as God pleased he had no
hurt; and following them up to the woods, we found some
slaine, and in divers places much bloud. It seems all their arrowes were spent, for we heard no more of them. Their
Canows we tooke; the arrowes we found we broke, save them
we kept for Mosco, to whom we gave the Canowes for his
kindnesse, that entertained us in the best triumphing manner,

Our fight with the Rapahanocks.

and warlike order in armes of conquest he could procure of the Moraughtacunds.

The Salvages disguised like bushes fight. The rest of the day we spent in accomodating our Boat, in stead of thoules wee made stickes like Bedstaves, to which we fastened so many of our Massawomek Targets, that invironed her as wast clothes. The next morning we went up the river, and our friend Mosco followed us along the shore, and at last desired to goe with us in our Boat. But as we passed by Pisacack, Matchopeak, and Mecuppom, three Townes situated upon high white clay clifts; the other side all a low playne marish, and the river there but narrow. Thirtie or fortie of the Rapahanocks, had so accommodated themselves with branches, as we tooke them for little bushes growing among the sedge, still seeing their arrowes strike the Targets, and dropped in the river: whereat Mosco fell flat in the Boat on his face, crying the Rapahanocks, which presently we espied to be the bushes, which at our first volley fell downe in the sedge: when wee were neare halfe a myle from them, they shewed themselves dauncing and singing very merrily.

The Kings of Pissassack, Nandtaughtacund, and Cuttatawomen, used us kindly, and all their people neglected not any thing to Mosco to bring us to them. Betwixt Secobeck and Massawteck is a small Isle or two, which causeth the river to be broader then ordinary; there it pleased God to take one of our Company called Master Fetherstone, that all the time he had beene in this Country, had behaved himselfe, honestly, valiantly, and industriously, where in a little Bay we called Fetherstones Bay wee buryed him with a volley of shot: the rest notwithstanding their ill dyet, and bad lodging, crowded in so small a Barge, in so many dangers never resting, but alwayes tossed to and againe, had all well recovered their healths. The next day wee sayled so high as our Boat would float, there setting up crosses, and graving our names in the trees. Our Sentinell saw an arrow fall by him, though we had ranged up and downe more then an houre in digging in the earth, looking of stones, herbs, and springs, not seeing where a Salvage could well hide himselfe.

Our fight with the Manahaacks. Upon the alarum by that we had recovered our armes, there was about an hundred nimble Indians skipping from tree to tree, letting fly their arrows so fast as they could: the trees here served us for Baricadoes as well as they. But Mosco did us more service then we expected, for having shot away his quiver of Arrowes, he ran to the Boat for more. The Arrowes of Mosco at the first made them pause upon the matter, thinking by his bruit and skipping, there were many Salvages. About halfe an houre this continued, then they all vanished as suddainly as they approached. Mosco followed them so farre as he could see us, till they were out of sight. As we returned there lay a Salvage as dead, shot in the knee, but taking him up we found he had life, which Mosco seeing, never was Dog more furious against a Beare, then Mosco was to have beat out his braines, so we had him to our Boat, where our Chirurgian who went with us to cure our Captaines hurt of the Stingray, so dressed this Salvage that within an houre after he looked somewhat cheare-fully, and did eate and speake. In the meane time we contented Mosco in helping him to gather up their arrowes, which were an armefull, whereof he gloried not a little. Then we desired Mosco to know what he was, and what Countries were beyond the mountaines; the poore Salvage mildly answered, he and all with him were of Hasinninga, where there are three Kings more, like unto them, namely the King of Stegora, the King of Tauxuntania, and the King of Shakahonea, that were come to Mohaskahod, which is onely a hunting Towne, and the bounds betwixt the Kingdome of the Mannahocks, and the Nand-taughtacunds, but hard by where we were. We demanded why they came in that manner to betray us, that came to them in peace, and to seeke their loves; he answered, they heard we were a people come from under the world, to take their world from them. We asked him how many worlds he did know, he replyed, he knew no more but that which was under the skie that covered him, which were the Powhatans, with the Mona-cans, and the Massawomeks, that were higher up in the moun-taines. Then we asked him what was beyond the mountaines, he answered the Sunne: but of any thing els he knew nothing; *because the woods were not burnt. These and many such questions wee de-manded, concerning the Massawomeks, the Mona-cans, their owne Country, and where were the Kings

A Salvage shot and taken prisoner.

His relation of their countries.

*They cannot travell but where the woods are burnt.

of Stegora, Tauxsintania, and the rest. The Monacans he sayd were their neighbours and friends, and did dwell as they in the hilly Countries by small rivers, living upon rootes and fruits, but chiefly by hunting. The Massawomeks did dwell upon a great water, and had many boats, and so many men that they made warre with all the world. For their Kings, they were gone every one a severall way with their men on hunting: But those with him came thither a fishing till they saw us, notwithstanding they would be altogether at night at Mahaskahod. For his relation we gave him many toyes, with perswasions to goe with us, and he as earnestly desired us to stay the comming of those Kings that for his good usage should be friends with us, for he was brother to Hasinninga. But Mosco advised us presently to be gone, for they were all naught, yet we told him we would not till it was night. All things we made ready to entertain what came, and Mosco was as diligent in trimming his arrowes. The night being come we all imbarked, for the river was so narrow, had it beene light the land on the one side was so high, they might have done us exceeding much mischiefe. All this while the King of Hasinninga was seeking the rest, and had consultation a good time what to doe. But by their espies seeing we were gone, it was not long before we heard their arrowes dropping on every side the Boat; we caused our Salvages to call unto them, but such a yelling and hallowing they made that they heard nothing, but now and then a peece, ayming so neare as we could where we heard the most voyces. More then 12 myles they followed us in this manner; then the day appearing, we found our selves in a broad Bay, out of danger of their shot, where wee came to an anchor, and fell to breakfast. Not so much as speaking to them till the Sunne was risen; being well refreshed, we untyed our Targets that covered us as a Deck, and all shewed our selves with those shields on our armes, and swords in our hands, and also our prisoner Amoroleck; a long discourse there was betwixt his Countrimen and him, how good wee were, how well wee used him, how wee had a Patawomek with us, loved us as his life, that would have slaine him had we not preserved him, and that he should have his libertie would they be but friends; and to doe us any hurt it was impossible. Upon this they all hung their Bowes and Quivers

How we concluded peace with the foure kings of Monahoke.

upon the trees, and one came swimming aboord us with a Bow tyed on his head, and another with a Quiver of Arrowes, which they delivered our Captaine as a present, the Captaine having used them so kindly as he could, told them the other three Kings should doe the like, and then the great King of our world should be their friend, whose men we were. It was no sooner demanded but performed, so upon a low Moorish poynt of Land we went to the shore, where those foure Kings came and received Amoroleck: nothing they had but Bowes, Arrowes, Tobacco-bags, and Pipes: what we desired, none refused to give us, wondering at every thing we had, and heard we had done: our Pistols they tooke for pipes, which they much desired, but we did content them with other Commodities, and so we left foure or five hundred of our merry Mannahocks, singing, dauncing, and making merry, and set sayle for Moraughtacund.

How we became friends with the Rapahanocks.

In our returnes we visited all our friends, that rejoyced much at our Victory against the Mannahocks, who many times had Warres also with them, but now they were friends, and desired we would be friends with the Rapahanocks, as we were with the Mannahocks. Our Captaine told them, they had twise assaulted him that came onely in love to doe them good, and therefore he would now burne all their houses, destroy their corne, and for ever hold them his enemies, till they made him satisfaction; they desired to know what that should be: he told them they should present him the Kings Bow and Arrowes, and not offer to come armed where he was; that they should be friends with the Moraughtacunds his friends, and give him their Kings sonne in pledge to performe it, and then all King James his men should be their friends. Upon this they presently sent to the Rapahanocks to meete him at the place where they first fought, where would be the Kings of Nantautacund and Pissassac: which according to their promise were there so soone as we; where Rapahanock presented his Bow and Arrowes, and confirmed all we desired, except his sonne, having no more but him he could not live without him, but in stead of his sonne he would give him the three women Moraughtacund had stolne. This was accepted: and so in three or foure Canowes, so many as could went with us to Moraughtacund, where Mosco made them such relations, and gave to his friends so many Bowes and Arrowes, that they no lesse loved him then admired us. The 3 women were brought our Captaine, to each he gave a chayne of Beads: and then causing Moraughtacund, Mosco, and Rapahanock stand before him, bid Rapahanock take her he loved best, and Moraughtacund chuse next, and to Mosco he gave the third. Upon this away went their Canowes over the water, to fetch their venison, and all the provision they could, and they that wanted Boats swam over the river: the darke commanded us then to rest. The next day there was of men, women, and children, as we conjectured, six or seaven hundred, dauncing, and singing, and not a Bow nor Arrow seene amongst them. Mosco changed his name Uttasanta-sough, which we interpret Stranger, for so they call us. All promising ever to be our friends, and to plant Corne purposely for us; and we to provide hatchets, beads, and copper for them, we departed, giving them a Volley of shot, and they us as loud shouts and cryes as their strengths could utter. That night we anchored in the river of Payankatank, and discovered it so high as it was navigable, but the people were most a hunting, save a few old men, women, and children, that were tending their corne, of which they promised us part when we would fetch it, as had done all the Nations where ever we had yet beene.

The dis-
covery of
Payankatank.

In a fayre calme, rowing towards poynt Comfort, we anchored in Gosnolls Bay, but such a suddaine gust surprised us in the night with thunder and rayne, that we never thought more to have seene James Towne. Yet running before the wind, we sometimes saw the Land by the flashes of fire from heaven, by which light onely we kept from the splitting shore, untill it pleased God in that blacke darknesse to preserve us by that light to finde poynt Comfort: there refreshing our selves, because we had onely but heard of the Chisapeacks and Nandsamunds, we thought it as fit to know all our neighbours neare home, as so many Nations abroad.

A notable
trechery of
the Nand-
samunds.

So setting sayle for the Southerne shore, we sayled up a narrow river up the country of Chisapeack; it hath a good channell, but many shoules about the entrance. By that we had sayled six or seaven myles, we saw two or three little garden plots with their houses, the shores

overgrowne with the greatest Pyne and Firre trees wee ever
saw in the Country. But not seeing nor hearing any people,
and the river very narrow, we returned to the great river, to see
if we could finde any of them. Coasting the shore towards
Nandsamund, which is most Oyster-bankes; at the mouth of
that river, we espied six or seaven Salvages making their wires,
who presently fled: ashore we went, and where they wrought
we threw divers toyes, and so departed. Farre we were not
gone ere they came againe, and began to sing, and daunce,
and recall us: and thus we began our first acquaintance. At last
one of them desired us to goe to his house up that river, into
our Boat voluntarily he came, the rest ran after us by the shore
with all shew of love that could be. Seaven or eight myles we
sayled up this narrow river: at last on the Westerne shore we
saw large Cornefields, in the midst a little Isle, and in it was
abundance of Corne; the people he told us were all a hunting,
but in the Isle was his house, to which he invited us with much
kindnesse: to him, his wife, and children, we gave such things
as they seemed much contented them. The others being come,
desired us also to goe but a little higher to see their houses:
here our host left us, the rest rowed by us in a Canow, till we
were so far past the Isle the river became very narrow. Here we
desired some of them to come abord us, wherat pausing a
little, they told us they would but fetch their bows and arrowes
and goe all with us, but being a-shore and thus armed, they
perswaded us to goe forward, but we could neither perswade
them into their Canow, nor into our Boat. This gave us cause
to provide for the worst. Farre we went not ere seaven or eight
Canowes full of men armed appeared following us, staying to
see the conclusion. Presently from each side the river came arrowes so fast as two or three hundred could shoot
them, whereat we returned to get the open. They in
the Canowes let fly also as fast, but amongst them
we bestowed so many shot, the most of them leaped
overboord and swam ashore, but two or three escaped by
rowing. Being against their playnes: our Muskets they found
shot further then their Bowes, for wee made not twentie shot
ere they all retyred behind the next trees. Being thus got out of
their trap, we seised on all their Canowes, and moored them in

The fight
with the
Chisapeacks
and Nand-
samunds.

the midst of the open. More then an hundred arrowes stucke in our Targets, and about the boat, yet none hurt, onely Anthony Bagnall was shot in his Hat, and another in his sleeve. But seeing their multitudes, and suspecting as it was, that both the Nandsamunds, and the Chisapeacks were together, we thought it best to ryde by their Canowes a while, to bethinke if it were better to burne all in the Isle, or draw them to composition, till we were provided to take all they had, which was sufficient to feed all our Colony: but to burne the Isle at night it was concluded. In the interim we began to cut in peeces their Canowes, and they presently to lay downe their bowes, making signes of peace: peace we told them we would accept, would they bring us their Kings bowes and arrowes, with a chayne of pearle; and when we came againe give us foure hundred baskets full of Corne, otherwise we would breake all their boats, and burne their houses, and corne, and all they had. To performe all this they alledged onely the want of a Canow; so we put one a drift and bad them swim to fetch her: and till they performed their promise, wee would but onely breake their Canowes. They cryed to us to doe no more, all should be as we would: which presently they performed, away went their bowes and arrowes, and tagge and ragge came with their baskets: so much as we could carry we tooke, and so departing good friends, we returned to James Towne, where we safely arrived the 7. of September, 1608. There we found Master Scrivener, and divers others well recovered: many dead; some sicke: the late President prisoner for mutiny: by the honest diligence of Master Scrivener, the harvest gathered, but the provision in the store much spoyled with rayne. Thus was that summer (when little wanted) consumed and spent, and nothing done (such was the government of Captaine Ratliffe) but onely this discovery; wherein to expresse all the dangers, accidents, and incounters this small number passed in that small Barge, by the scale of proportion, about three thousand myles, with such watery dyet in those great waters and barbarous Countries (till then to any Christian utterly unknowne) I rather referre their merit to the censure of the courteous and experienced Reader, then I would be tedious or partiall being a partie.

How they became friends.

The proceeding at James Towne.

But to this place to come who will adventure,
with judgements guide and reason how to enter:
Finds in this worlds broad sea, with winde and tyde,
Ther's safer sayle then any where beside.
But 'cause to wanton novices it is
A Province full of fearefulnesse I wiss;
Into the great vast deepe to venter out:
Those shallow rivers let them coast about.
And by a small Boat learne there first, and marke,
How they may come to make a greater Barke.

Written by Anthony Bagnall, Nathanaell Powell,
and Anas Todkill.

Chapter VII.
The Presidency surrendred to Captaine Smith:
the Arrivall and returne of the second Supply.
And what happened.

T HE tenth of September, by the Election of the Councell, and request of the Company, Captaine Smith received the Letters Patents: which till then by no meanes he would accept, though he was often importuned thereunto.

Now the building of Ratliffes Pallace stayed as a thing need-lesse; the Church was repaired; the Store-house recovered; buildings prepared for the Supplyes, we expected; the Fort re-duced to a five-square forme; the order of the Watch renewed; the squadrons (each setting of the Watch) trained; the whole Company every Saturday exercised, in the plaine by the west Bulwarke, prepared for that purpose, we called Smithfield: where sometimes more then an hundred Salvages would stand in an amazement to behold, how a fyle would batter a tree, where he would make them a marke to shoot at; the boats trimmed for trade, which being sent out with Lieutenant Percy, in their journey incountred the second Supply, that brought them backe to discover the Country of Monacan. How or why Captaine Newport obtained such a private Commission, as not to returne without a lumpe of gold, a certaintie of the South sea, or one of the lost company sent out by Sir Walter Raleigh, I know not; nor why he brought such a five peeced Barge, not to beare us to that South sea, till we had borne her over the mountaines, which how farre they extend is yet un-knowne. As for the Coronation of Powhatan, and his presents of Bason and Ewer, Bed, Bedstead, Clothes, and such costly novelties, they had beene much better well spared then so ill spent, for wee had his favour much better onely for a playne peece of Copper, till this stately kinde of soliciting, made him so much overvalue him-selfe, that he respected us as much as nothing at all. As for the hyring of the Poles and Dutch-men, to make Pitch, Tar, Glasse, Milles, and Sope ashes when the Country is replenished with people, and necessaries, would have done well, but to send them and seaventie more without victualls to worke, was not so well advised nor considered of, as it should have beene. Yet this could not have hurt us had they beene 200. though then we were 130 that wanted for our selves. For we had the Salvages in that decorum (their harvest being newly gathered) that we feared not to get victuals for 500. Now was there no way to make us miserable, but to neglect that time to make provision whilst it was to be had, the which was done by the direction from England to per-forme this strange discovery, but a more strange Coronation to loose that time, spend that victualls we had, tyre and starve our men, having no meanes to carry victuals, munition, the hurt or sicke, but on their owne backes. How or by whom they were invented I know not: but Captaine Newport we onely accounted the Author, who to effect these projects, had so guilded mens hopes with great promises, that both Com-pany and Councell concluded his resolution for the most part: God doth know they little knew what they did, nor under-stood their owne estates to conclude his conclusions, against all the inconveniences the foreseeing President alledged. Of this Supply there was added to the Councell, one Captaine Richard Waldo, and Captaine Wynne, two auncient Souldiers, and valiant Gentlemen, but yet ignorant of the busines, (being but newly arrived.) Ratliffe was also permitted to have his voyce, and Master

Marginal notes:

Powhatans scorne when his courtesie was most deserved.

No better way to overthrow the busines then by our instructors.

A consulta-tion, where all the Councell was against the President.

Scrivener, desirous to see strange Countries: so that although Smith was President, yet the Major part of the Councell had the authoritie and ruled it as they listed. As for clearing Smiths objections, how Pitch and Tarre, Wainscot, Clapbord, Glasse, and Sope ashes, could be provided, to relade the ship, or provision got to live withall, when none was in the Country, and that we had, spent, before the ship departed to effect these projects. The answer was, Captaine Newport undertooke to fraught the Pinnace of twentie tunnes with Corne in going and returning in his Discovery, and to refraught her againe from Werowocomoco of Powhatan. Also promising a great proportion of victualls from the Ship; inferring that Smiths propositions were onely devices to hinder his journey, to effect it himselfe; and that the crueltie he had used to the Salvages, might well be the occasion to hinder these Designes, and seeke revenge on him. For which taxation all workes were left, and 120 chosen men were appointed for Newports guard in this Discovery. But Captaine Smith to make cleare all those seeming suspitions, that the Salvages were not so desperate as was pretended by Captaine Newport, and how willing (since by their authoritie they would have it so) he was to assist them what he could, because the Coronation would consume much time, he undertooke himselfe their message to Powhatan, to intreat him to come to James Towne to receive his presents. And where Newport durst not goe with lesse then 120. he

Captaine
Smith goeth
with 4. to
Powhatan,
when
Newport
feared with
120.

onely tooke with him Captaine Waldo, Master Andrew Buckler, Edward Brinton, and Samuel Collier: with these foure he went over land to Werowocomoco, some 12 myles; there he passed the river of Pamaunkee in a Salvage Canow. Powhatan being 30 myles of, was presently sent for: in the meane time, Pocahontas and her women entertained Captaine Smith in this manner.

In a fayre plaine field they made a fire, before which, he sitting upon a mat, suddainly amongst the woods was heard such a hydeous noise and shreeking, that the English betooke themselves to their armes, and seized on two or three old

A Virginia
Maske.

men by them, supposing Powhatan with all his power was come to surprise them. But presently Pocahontas came, willing him to kill her if any hurt were intended, and the beholders, which were men, women, and children, satisfied the Captaine there was no such matter. Then presently they were presented with this anticke; thirtie young women came naked out of the woods, onely covered behind and before with a few greene leaves, their bodies all painted, some of one colour, some of another, but all differing, their leader had a fayre payre of Bucks hornes on her head, and an Otters skinne at her girdle, and another at her arme, a quiver of arrowes at her backe, a bow and arrowes in her hand; the next had in her hand a sword, another a club, another a pot-sticke; all horned alike: the rest every one with their severall devises. These fiends with most hellish shouts and cryes, rushing from among the trees, cast themselves in a ring about the fire, singing and dauncing with most excellent ill varietie, oft falling into their infernall passions, and solemnly againe to sing and daunce; having spent neare an houre in this Mascarado, as they entred in like manner they departed.

The Womens
entertaine-
ment. Having reaccommodated themselves, they solemnly invited him to their lodgings, where he was no sooner within the house, but all these Nymphes more tormented him then ever, with crowding, pressing, and hanging about him, most tediously crying, Love you not me? love you not me? This salutation ended, the feast was set, consisting of all the Salvage dainties they could devise: some attending, others singing and dauncing about them; which mirth being ended, with fire-brands in stead of Torches they conducted him to his lodging.

Thus did they shew their feats of armes, and others art in dauncing:
Some other us'd there oaten pipe, and others voyces chanting.

Captaine
Smiths
message. The next day came Powhatan. Smith delivered his message of the presents sent him, and redelivered him Namontack he had sent for England, desiring him to come to his Father Newport, to accept those presents, and conclude their revenge against the Monacans. Whereunto this subtile Savage thus replyed.

Powhatans
answer. If your King have sent me Presents, I also am a King, and this is my land: eight dayes I will stay to receive them. Your Father is to come to me, not I to him, nor yet to your Fort, neither will I bite at such a bait: as for the Monacans I can revenge my owne injuries, and as for Atquanachuk, where you say your brother was slaine, it is a contrary way from those parts you suppose it; but for any salt water beyond the mountaines, the Relations you have had from my people are false.

Whereupon he began to draw plots upon the ground (according to his discourse) of all those Regions. Many other discourses they had (yet both content to give each other content in complementall Courtesies) and so Captaine Smith returned with this Answer.

Upon this the Presents were sent by water which is neare an hundred myles, and the Captains went by land with fiftie good shot. All being met at Werowocomoco, the next day was appointed for his Coronation, then the presents were brought him, his Bason and Ewer, Bed and furniture set up, his scarlet Cloke and apparell with much adoe put on him, being perswaded by Namontack they would not hurt him: but a foule trouble there was to make him kneele to receive his Crowne, he neither knowing the majesty nor meaning of a Crowne, nor bending of the knee, endured so many perswasions, examples, and instructions, as tyred them all; at last by leaning hard on his shoulders, he a little stooped, and three having the crowne in their hands put it on his head, when by the warning of a Pistoll the Boats were prepared with such a volley of shot, that the King start up in a horrible feare, till he saw all was well. Then remembring himselfe, to congratulate their kindnesse, he gave his old shooes and his mantell to Captaine Newport: but perceiving his purpose was to discover the Monacans, he laboured to divert his resolution, refusing to lend him either men or guides more then Namontack; and so after some small complementall kindnesse on both sides, in requitall of his presents he presented Newport with a heape of wheat eares that might containe some 7 or 8 Bushels, and as much more we bought in the Towne, wherewith we returned to the Fort.

Powhatans Coronation.

The Ship having disburdened her selfe of 70 persons, with the first Gentlewoman and woman-servant that arrived in our Colony. Captaine Newport with 120 chosen men, led by Captaine Waldo, Lieutenant Percie, Captaine Winne, Master West, and Master Scrivener, set forward for the discovery of Monacan, leaving the President at the

The discovery of Monacan.

Fort with about 80. or 90. (such as they were) to relade the Ship. Arriving at the Falles we marched by land some fortie myles in two dayes and a halfe, and so returned downe the same path we went. Two townes we discovered of the Monacans, called Massinacak and Mowhemenchouch, the people neither used us well nor ill, yet for our securitie we tooke one of their petty Kings, and led him bound to conduct us the way. And in our returnes searched many places we supposed Mines, about which we spent some time in refyning, having one William Callicut, a refyner fitted for that purpose. From that crust of earth we digged, he perswaded us to beleeve he extracted some small quantitie of silver; and (not unlikely) better stuffe might be had for the digging. With this poore tryall, being contented to leave this fayre, fertile, well watered Country; and comming to the Falles, the Salvages fayned there were

How the Salvages deluded Captaine Newport.

divers ships come into the Bay, to kill them at James Towne. Trade they would not, and finde their Corne we could not; for they had hid it in the woods: and being thus deluded, we arrived at James Towne, halfe sicke, all complaining, and tyred with toyle, famine, and discontent, to have onely but discovered our guilded hopes, and such fruitlesse certainties, as Captaine Smith fortold us.

> *But those that hunger seeke to slake,*
> *Which thus abounding wealth would rake:*
> *Not all the gemmes of* Ister *shore,*
> *Nor all the gold of* Lydia's *store,*
> *Can fill their greedie appetite;*
> *It is a thing so infinite.*

No sooner were we landed, but the President dispersed so many as were able, some for Glasse, others for Tarre, Pitch, and Sope ashes, leaving them with the Fort to the Councels oversight, but 30 of us he conducted downe the river some 5 myles from James towne, to learne to make Clapbord, cut downe trees, and lye in woods. Amongst the rest he had chosen Gabriel Beadle, and John Russell, the onely two gallants of this last Supply, and both proper Gentlemen. Strange were these pleasures to their conditions; yet lodging, eating, and drinking, working or playing, they but doing as the President did himselfe. All these things were carried so pleasantly as

within a weeke they became Masters: making it their delight to
heare the trees thunder as they fell; but the Axes so oft blistered their tender fingers, that many times every third blow
had a loud othe to drowne the eccho; for remedie of which
sinne, the President devised how to have every mans othes
numbred, and at night for every othe to have a Cann
of water powred downe his sleeve, with which every
offender was so washed (himselfe and all) that a man
should scarce heare an othe in a weeke.

A punishment for swearing.

For he who scornes and makes but jests of cursings, and his othe,
He doth contemne, not man but God, nor God, nor man, but both.

By this, let no man thinke that the President and these Gentlemen spent their times as common Wood haggers at felling
of trees, or such other like labours, or that they were pressed to
it as hirelings, or common slaves; for what they did, after they
were but once a little inured, it seemed and some conceited it,
onely as a pleasure and recreation, yet 30 or 40 of
such voluntary Gentlemen would doe more in a day
then 100 of the rest that must be prest to it by compulsion, but twentie good workemen had beene better then
them all.

3. Men better then 1000.

Master Scrivener, Captaine Waldo, and Captaine Winne at
the Fort, every one in like manner carefully regarded their
charge. The President returning from amongst the woods,
seeing the time consumed and no provision gotten, (and the
Ship lay idle at a great charge and did nothing) presently imbarked himselfe in the discovery barge, giving order to the
Councell to send Lieutenant Percie after him with the next
barge that arrived at the Fort; two Barges he had
himselfe and 18 men, but arriving at Chickahamania,
that dogged Nation was too well acquainted with our
wants, refusing to trade, with as much scorne and insolency as
they could expresse. The President perceiving it was Powhatans policy to starve us, told them he came not so much for
their Corne, as to revenge his imprisonment, and the death of
his men murthered by them, and so landing his men and
readie to charge them, they immediately fled: and presently
after sent their Ambassadors with corne, fish, foule, and what
they had to make their peace, (their Corne being that yeare

The Chicka-hamania's forced to contribution.

but bad) they complained extreamely of their owne wants, yet fraughted our Boats with an hundred Bushels of Corne, and in like manner Lieutenant Percies, that not long after arrived, and having done the best they could to content us, we parted good friends, and returned to James towne.

A bad reward for well-doing.

Though this much contented the Company, (that feared nothing more then starving) yet some so envied his good successe, that they rather desired to hazzard a starving, then his paines should prove so much more effectuall then theirs. Some projects there were invented by Newport and Ratliffe, not onely to have deposed him, but to have kept him out of the Fort; for that being President, he would leave his place and the Fort without their consents, but their homes were so much too short to effect it, as they themselves more narrowly escaped a greater mischiefe.

A good Taverne in Virginia.

All this time our old Taverne made as much of all them that had either money or ware as could be desired: by this time they were become so perfect on all sides (I meane the souldiers, saylers, and Salvages) as there was tenne times more care to maintaine their damnable and private trade, then to provide for the Colony things that were necessary.

A bad trade of the masters and saylers.

Neither was it a small policy in Newport and the Marriners to report in England we had such plentie, and bring us so many men without victuals, when they had so many private Factors in the Fort, that within six or seaven weeks, of two or three hundred Axes, Chissels, Hows, and Pick-axes, scarce twentie could be found: and for Pike-heads, shot, Powder, or any thing they could steale from their fellowes, was vendible; they knew as well (and as secretly) how to convey them to trade with the Salvages for Furres, Baskets, *Mussaneeks*, young Beasts, or such like Commodities, as exchange them with the Saylers for Butter, Cheese, Beefe, Porke, Aqua vitæ, Beere, Bisket, Oatmeale, and Oyle: and then fayne all was sent them from their friends. And though Virginia affoorded no Furres for the Store, yet one Master in one voyage hath got so many by this indirect meanes, as he confessed to have sold in England for 30^l.

Those are the Saint-seeming Worthies of Virginia, that have notwithstanding all this meate, drinke, and wages; but now they begin to grow weary, their trade being both perceived and prevented; none hath beene in Virginia that hath observed any thing, which knowes not this to be true, and yet the losse, the scorne, the misery, and shame, was the poore Officers, Gentlemen, and carelesse Governours, who were all thus bought and sold; the adventurers cousened, and the action overthrowne by their false excuses, informations, and directions. By this let all men judge, how this businesse could prosper, being thus abused by such pilfring occasions. And had not Captaine Newport cryed *Peccavi*, the President would have discharged the ship, and caused him to have stayed one yeare in Virginia, to learne to speake of his owne experience.

Master Scrivener was sent with the Barges and Pinnace to Werowocomoco, where he found the Salvages more readie to fight then trade; but his vigilancy was such as prevented their projects, and by the meanes of Namontack got three or foure hogsheads of Corne, and as much *Pocones*, which is a red roote, which then was esteemed an excellent Dye.

Master Scriveners voyage to Werowocomoco.

Captaine Newport being dispatched, with the tryals of Pitch, Tarre, Glasse, Frankincense, Sope ashes; with that Clapboord and Waynscot that could be provided: met with Master Scrivener at poynt Comfort, and so returned for England. We remaining were about two hundred.

The Copy of a Letter sent to the Treasurer
and Councell of Virginia from Captaine Smith,
then President in Virginia.

Right Honorable, etc.

I Received your Letter, wherein you write, that our minds are so set upon faction, and idle conceits in dividing the Country without your consents, and that we feed You but with ifs and ands, hopes, and some few proofes; as if we would keepe the mystery of the businesse to our selves: and that we must expresly follow your instructions sent by Captain Newport: the charge of whose voyage amounts to neare two thousand pounds, the which if we cannot defray by the Ships returne, we are like to remain as banished men. To these particulars I humbly intreat your Pardons if I offend you with my rude Answer.

For our factions, unlesse you would have me run away and leave the Country, I cannot prevent them: because I do make many stay that would els fly any whether. For the idle Letter sent to my Lord of Salisbury, by the President and his confederats, for dividing the

Country etc. What it was I know not, for you saw no hand of mine to it; nor ever dream't I of any such matter. That we feed you with hopes, etc. Though I be no scholer, I am past a schoole-boy; and I desire but to know, what either you, and these here doe know, but that I have learned to tell you by the continuall hazard of my life. I have not concealed from you any thing I know; but I feare some cause you to beleeve much more then is true.

Expresly to follow your directions by Captaine Newport, though they be performed, I was directly against it; but according to our Commission, I was content to be overruled by the major part of the Councell, I feare to the hazard of us all; which now is generally confessed when it is too late. Onely Captaine Winne and Captaine Waldo I have sworne of the Councell, and Crowned Powhatan according to your instructions.

For the charge of this Voyage of two or three thousand pounds, we have not received the value of an hundred pounds. And for the quartred Boat to be borne by the Souldiers over the Falles, Newport had 120 of the best men he could chuse. If he had burnt her to ashes, one might have carried her in a bag; but as she is, five hundred cannot, to a navigable place above the Falles. And for him at that time to find in the South Sea, a Mine of gold; or any of them sent by Sir Walter Raleigh: at our Consultation I told them was as likely as the rest. But during this great discovery of thirtie myles, (which might as well have beene done by one man, and much more, for the value of a pound of Copper at a seasonable tyme) they had the Pinnace and all the Boats with them, but one that remained with me to serve the Fort. In their absence I followed the new begun workes of Pitch and Tarre, Glasse, Sope-ashes, and Clapboord, whereof some small quantities we have sent you. But if you rightly consider, what an infinite toyle it is in Russia and Swethland, where the woods are proper for naught els, and though there be the helpe both of man and beast in those ancient Common-wealths, which many an hundred yeares have used it, yet thousands of those poore people can scarce get necessaries to live, but from hand to mouth. And though your Factors there can buy as much in a week as will fraught you a ship, or as much as you please; you must not expect from us any such matter, which are but a many of ignorant miserable soules, that are scarce able to get wherewith to live, and defend our selves against the inconstant Salvages: finding but here and there a tree fit for the purpose, and want all things els the Russians have. For the Coronation of Powhatan, by whose advice you sent him such presents, I know not; but this give me leave to tell you, I feare they will be the confusion of us all ere we heare from you againe. At your Ships arrivall, the Salvages harvest was newly gathered, and we going to buy it, our owne not being halfe sufficient for so great a number. As for the two ships loading of Corne Newport promised to provide us from Powhatan, he brought us but foureteene Bushels; and from the Monacans nothing, but the most of the men sicke and neare famished. From your Ship we had not provision in victuals worth twenty pound, and we are more then two hundred to live upon this: the one halfe sicke, the other little better. For the Saylers (I confesse) they daily make good cheare, but our dyet is a little meale and water, and not sufficient of that. Though there be fish in the Sea, foules in the ayre, and Beasts in the woods, their bounds are so large, they so wilde, and we so weake and ignorant, we cannot much trouble them. Captaine Newport we much suspect to be the Authour of those inventions. Now that you should know, I have made you as great a discovery as he, for lesse charge then he spendeth you every meale; I have sent you this Mappe of the Bay and Rivers, with an annexed Relation of the Countries and Nations that inhabit them, as you may see at large. Also two barrels of stones, and such as I take to be good Iron ore at the least; so devided, as by their notes you may see in what places I found them. The Souldiers say many of your officers maintaine their families out of that you send us: and that Newport hath an hundred pounds a yeare for carrying newes. For every master you have yet sent can find the way as well as he, so that an hundred pounds might be spared, which is more then we have all, that helpe to pay him wages. Captaine Ratliffe is now called Sicklemore, a poore counterfeited Imposture. I have sent you him home, least the company should cut his throat. What he is, now every one can tell you: if he and Archer returne againe, they are sufficient to keepe us alwayes in factions. When you send againe I intreat you rather send but thirty Carpenters, husbandmen, gardiners, fisher men, blacksmiths, masons, and diggers up of trees, roots, well provided; then a thousand of such as we have: for except wee be able both to lodge them, and feed them, the most will consume with want of necessaries before they can be made good for any thing. Thus if you please to consider this account, and of the unnecessary wages to Captaine Newport, or his ships so long lingering and staying here (for notwithstanding his boasting to leave us victuals for 12 moneths, though we had 89 by this discovery lame and sicke, and but a pinte of Corne a day for a man, we were constrained to give him three hogsheads of that to victuall him homeward) or yet to send into Germany or Poleland for glasse-men and the rest, till we be able to sustaine our selves, and relieve them when they come. It were better to give five hundred pound a tun for those grosse Commodities in Denmarke, then send for them hither, till more necessary things be provided. For in over-toyling our weake and unskilfull bodies, to satisfie this desire of present profit, we can scarce ever recover our selves from one Supply to another. And I humbly intreat you hereafter, let us know what we should receive, and not stand to the Saylers courtesie to leave us what they please, els you may charge us with what you will, but we not you with any thing. These are the causes that have kept us in Virginia, from laying such a foundation, that ere this might have given much better content and satisfaction; but as yet you must not looke for any profitable returnes: so I humbly rest.

———

The Names of those in this Supply, were these: with their Proceedings and Accidents.

Captaine Peter Winne, } *were appoynted to be of the Councell.*
Captaine Richard Waldo, }

Master Francis West, *brother to the Lord La Warre.*

Thomas Graves.		Hugh Wolleston.	
Raleigh Chroshaw.		John Hoult.	
Gabriel Beadle.		Thomas Norton.	
John Beadle.		George Yarington.	
John Russell.		George Burton.	
William Russell.		Thomas Abbay.	*Gentlemen.*
John Cuderington.	*Gentlemen.*	William Dowman.	
William Sambage.		Thomas Maxes.	
Henry Leigh.		Michael Lowick.	
Henry Philpot.		Master Hunt.	
Harmon Harrison.		Thomas Forrest.	
Daniel Tucker.		John Dauxe.	
Henry Collins.			
Thomas Phelps.		Thomas Dawse.	
John Prat.		Thomas Mallard.	
John Clarke.		William Tayler.	
Jeffrey Shortridge.		Thomas Fox.	
Dionis Oconor.		Nicholas Hancock.	
Hugh Winne.		Walker.	*Labourers.*
David ap Hugh.	*Tradesmen.*	Williams.	
Thomas Bradley.		Floud.	
John Burras.		Morley.	
Thomas Lavander.		Rose.	
Henry Bell.		Scot.	
Master Powell.		Hardwyn.	
David Ellis.			
Thomas Gibson.		Milman.	*Boyes.*
		Hilliard.	

Mistresse Forrest, and Anne Burras her maide; eight Dutch men and Poles, with some others, to the number of seaventie persons. etc.

These poore conclusions so affrighted us all with famine, that the President provided for Nandsamund, and tooke with him Captaine Winne, and Master Scrivener, then returning from Captaine Newport. These people also long denied him not onely the 400 Baskets of Corne they promised, but any trade at all; (excusing themselves they had spent most they had, and were commanded by Powhatan to keepe that they had, and not to let us come into their river) till we were constrained to begin with them perforce. Upon the discharging of our Muskets they all fled and shot not an Arrow; the first house we came to we set on fire, which when they perceived, they desired we would make no more spoyle, and they would give us halfe they had: how they collected it I know not, but before night they loaded our three Boats; and so we returned to our quarter some foure myles downe the River, which was onely the open woods under the lay of a hill, where all the ground was covered with snow, and hard frozen; the snow we digged away and made a great fire in the place; when the ground was well dryed, we turned away the fire; and covering the place with a mat, there we lay very warme. To keepe us from the winde we made a shade of another Mat; as the winde turned we turned our shade, and when the ground grew cold we removed the fire. And thus many a cold winter night have wee laine in this miserable manner, yet those that most commonly went upon all those occasions, were alwayes in health, lusty, and fat. For sparing them this yeare, the next yeare they promised to plant purposely for us; and so we returned to James towne. About this time there was a marriage betwixt John Laydon and Anne Burras; which was the first marriage we had in Virginia.

Nandsamund forced to contribution.

The first marriage in Virginia.

Long he stayed not, but fitting himselfe and Captaine Waldo with two Barges. From Chawopo, Weanock, and all parts thereabouts, all the people were fled, as being jealous of our intents; till we discovered the river and people of Apamatuck; where we found not much, that they had we equally divided, but gave them copper, and such things as contented them in consideration. Master Scrivener and Lieutenant Percie went also abroad, but could find nothing.

Apamatuck discovered.

The President seeing the procrastinating of time, was no course to live, resolved with Captaine Waldo (whom he knew to be sure in time of need) to surprise Powhatan, and all his provision, but the unwillingnesse of Captaine Winne, and Master Scrivener, for some private respect, plotted in England to ruine Captaine Smith, did their best to hinder their project; but the President whom no perswasions could perswade to starve, being invited by Powhatan to come unto him: and if he would send him but men to build him a house, give him a gryndstone, fiftie swords, some peeces, a cock and a hen, with much copper and beads, he would load his Ship with Corne. The President not ignorant of his devises and subtiltie, yet unwilling to neglect any opportunitie, presently sent three Dutchmen and two English, having so small allowance, few were able to doe any thing to purpose: knowing there needed no better a Castle to effect this project, tooke order with Captaine Waldo to second him, if need required; Scrivener he left his substitute, and set forth with the Pinnace, two Barges, and fortie-six men, which onely were such as voluntarily offered themselves for his Journey, the which by reason of Master Scriveners ill successe, was censured very desperate, they all knowing Smith would not returne emptie, if it were to be had; howsoever, it caused many of those that he had appointed, to find excuses to stay behinde.

Chapter VIII.
Captaine Smiths Journey to Pamaunkee.

THE twentie-nine of December he set forward for Werowoco-moco: his Company were these;

In the Discovery Barge himselfe.

Robert Behethland.		Raleigh Chrashow.	
Nathanael Graves.	*Gentlemen.*	Michael Sicklemore.	*Gentlemen.*
John Russell.		Richard Worley.	
Anas Todkill.		Jeffrey Shortridge.	
William Love.	*Souldiers.*	Edward Pising.	*Souldiers.*
William Bentley.		William Ward.	

In the Pinnace.

Lieutenant Percie, *brother to the Earle of Northumberland.*
Master Francis West, *brother to the Lord La Warre.*
William Phittiplace, *Captaine of the Pinnace.*

Michael Phittiplace.		
Jeffrey Abbot, *Serjeant*	*Gentlemen.*	Jonas Profit, *Master.*
William Tankard.		Robert Ford, *Clarke of the Councell.*
George Yarington.		
James Browne.		
Edward Brinton.	*Souldiers.*	John Dods, *Souldier.*
George Burton.		Henry Powell, *Souldier.*
Thomas Coe.		

Thomas Gipson, David Ellis, Nathanael Peacock, *Saylers.* John Prat, George Acrig, James Read, Nicholas Hancock, James Watkins, Thomas Lambert, foure Dutch-men, and Richard Salvage were sent by land before to build the house for Powhatan against our Arrivall.

This company being victualled but for three or foure dayes, lodged the first night at Warraskoyack, where the President tooke sufficient provision. This kind King did his best to divert him from seeing Powhatan, but perceiving he could not prevaile, he advised in this manner. Captaine Smith, you shall find Powhatan to use you kindly, but trust him not, and be sure he have no oportunitie to seize on your Armes; for he hath sent for you onely to cut your throats. The Captaine thanking him for his good counsell: yet the better to try his love, desired guides to Chawwonock; for he would send a present to that King, to bind him his friend. To performe this journey was sent Master Sicklemore, a very valiant, honest, and a painefull Souldier: with him two guides, and directions how to seeke for the lost company of Sir Walter Raleighs, and silke Grasse. Then we departed thence, the President assuring the King perpetuall love; and left with him Samuel Collier his Page to learne the Language.

The good counsell of Warraskoyack.

> *So this Kings deeds by sacred Oath adjur'd.*
> *More wary proves, and circumspect by ods:*
> *Fearing at least his double forfeiture;*
> *To offend his friends, and sin against his Gods.*

The next night being lodged at Kecoughtan; six or seaven dayes the extreame winde, rayne, frost and snow caused us to keepe Christmas among the Salvages, where we were never more merry, nor fed on more plentie of good Oysters, Fish, Flesh, Wild-foule, and good bread; nor never had better fires in England, then in the dry smoaky houses of Kecoughtan: but departing thence, when we found no houses we were not curious in any weather to lye three or foure nights together under the trees by a fire, as formerly is sayd. An hundred fortie eight foules the President, Anthony Bagnall, and Serjeant Pising did kill at three shoots. At Kiskiack the frost and contrary winds forced us three or foure dayes also (to suppresse the insolency of those proud Salvages) to quarter in their houses, yet guard our Barge, and cause them give us what we wanted; though we were but twelve and himselfe, yet we never wanted shelter where we found any houses. The 12 of January we arrived at Werowocomoco, where the river was frozen neare halfe a myle from the shore; but to neglect no time, the President with his Barge so far had approached by breaking the ice, as the ebbe left him amongst those oasie shoules, yet rather then to lye there frozen to death, by his owne example he taught them to march neere middle deepe, a flight shot through this muddy frozen oase. When the Barge floated, he appoynted two or three to returne her aboord the Pinnace. Where for want of water in melting the ice, they made fresh water, for the river there was salt. But in this march Master Russell, (whom none could perswade to stay behinde) being somewhat ill, and exceeding heavie, so overtoyled himselfe as the rest had much adoe (ere he got ashore) to regaine life into his dead benummed spirits. Quartering in the next houses we found, we sent to Powhatan for provision, who sent us plentie of bread, Turkies, and Venison; the next day having feasted us after his ordinary manner, he began to aske us when we would be gone: fayning he sent not for us, neither had he any corne; and his people much lesse: yet for fortie swords he would procure us fortie Baskets. The President shewing him the men there present that brought him the message and conditions, asked Powhatan how it chanced he became so forgetfull;

Marginal notes:

Plentie of victualls.

148 Foules killed at three shootes.

thereat the King concluded the matter with a merry laughter, asking for our Commodities, but none he liked without gunnes and swords, valuing a Basket of Corne more precious then a Basket of Copper; saying he could eate his Corne, but not the Copper.

Captaine Smith seeing the intent of this subtill Salvage began to deale with him after this manner.

Powhatan, though I had many courses to have made my provision, yet beleeving your promises to supply my wants, I neglected all to satisfie your desire: and to testifie my love, I send you my men for your building, neglecting mine owne. What your people had you have engrossed, forbidding them our trade: and now you thinke by consuming the time, we shall consume for want, not having to fulfill your strange demands. As for swords and gunnes, I told you long agoe I had none to spare; and you must know those I have can keepe me from want: yet steale or wrong you I will not, nor dissolve that friendship we have mutually promised, except you constraine me by our bad usage.

Captaine Smiths discourse to Powhatan.

The King having attentively listned to this Discourse, promised that both he and his Country would spare him what he could, the which within two dayes they should receive. Yet Captaine Smith, sayth the King,

some doubt I have of your comming hither, that makes me not so kindly seeke to relieve you as I would: for many doe informe me, your comming hither is not for trade, but to invade my people, and possesse my Country; who dare not come to bring you corne, seeing you thus armed with your men. To free us of this feare, leave aboord your weapons, for here they are needlesse, we being all friends, and for ever Powhatans.

Powhatans reply and flattery.

With many such discourses they spent the day, quartering that night in the Kings houses. The next day he renewed his building, which hee little intended should proceede. For the Dutch-men finding his plentie, and knowing our want, and perceiving his preparations to surprise us, little thinking we could escape both him and famine; (to obtaine his favour) revealed to him so much as they knew of our estates and projects, and how to prevent them. One of them being of so great a spirit, judgement, and resolution, and a hireling that was certaine of his wages for his labour, and ever well used both he and his Countrymen; that the President knew not whom better to trust; and not knowing any fitter for that imployment, had sent him as a spy to discover Powhatans intent, then little doubting his honestie, nor could ever be certaine of his villany till neare halfe a yeare after.

Whilst we expected the comming in of the Country, we wrangled out of the King ten quarters of Corne for a copper Kettell, the which the President perceiving him much to affect, valued it at a much greater rate; but in regard of his scarcity he would accept it, provided we should have as much more the next yeare, or els the Country of Monacan. Wherewith each seemed well contented, and Powhatan began to expostulate the difference of Peace and Warre after this manner.

Captaine Smith, you may understand that I having seene the death of all my people thrice, and not any one living of those three generations but my selfe; I know the difference of Peace and Warre better then any in my Country. But now I am old and ere long must die, my brethren, namely Opitchapam, Opechancanough, and Kekataugh, my two sisters, and their two daughters, are distinctly each others successors. I wish their experience no lesse then mine, and your love to them no lesse then mine to you. But this bruit from Nandsamund, that you are come to destroy my Country, so much affrighteth all my people as they dare not visit you. What will it availe you to take that by force you may quickly have by love, or to destroy them that provide you food. What can you get by warre, when we can hide our provisions and fly to the woods? whereby you must famish by wronging us your friends. And why are you thus jealous of our loves seeing us unarmed, and both doe, and are willing still to feede you, with that you cannot get but by our labours? Thinke you I am so simple, not to know it is better to eate good meate, lye well, and sleepe quietly with my women and children, laugh and be merry with you, have copper, hatchets, or what I want being your friend: then be forced to flie from all, to lie cold in the woods, feede upon Acornes, rootes, and such trash, and be so hunted by you, that I can neither rest, eate, nor sleepe; but my tyred men must watch, and if a twig but breake, every one cryeth there commeth Captaine Smith: then must I fly I know not whether: and thus with miserable feare, end my miserable life, leaving my pleasures to such youths as you, which through your rash unadvisednesse may quickly as miserably end, for want of that, you never know where to

Powhatans discourse of peace and warre.

finde. Let this therefore assure you of our loves, and every yeare our friendly trade shall furnish you with Corne; and now also, if you would come in friendly manner to see us, and not thus with your guns and swords as to invade your foes.

To this subtill discourse, the President thus replyed.

Captaine Smiths Reply. Seeing you will not rightly conceive of our words, we strive to make you know our thoughts by our deeds; the vow I made you of my love, both my selfe and my men have kept. As for your promise I find it every day violated by some of your subjects: yet we finding your love and kindnesse, our custome is so far from being ungratefull, that for your sake onely, we have curbed our thirsting desire of revenge; els had they knowne as well the crueltie we use to our enemies, as our true love and courtesie to our friends. And I thinke your judgement sufficient to conceive, as well by the adventures we have undertaken, as by the advantage we have (by our Armes) of yours: that had we intended you any hurt, long ere this we could have effected it. Your people comming to James Towne are entertained with their Bowes and Arrowes without any exceptions; we esteeming it with you as it is with us, to weare our armes as our apparell. As for the danger of our enemies, in such warres consist our chiefest pleasure: for your riches we have no use: as for the hiding your provision, or by your flying to the woods, we shall not so unadvisedly starve as you conclude, your friendly care in that behalfe is needlesse, for we have a rule to finde beyond your knowledge.

Many other discourses they had, till at last they began to trade. But the King seeing his will would not be admitted as a law, our guard dispersed, nor our men disarmed, he (sighing) breathed his minde once more in this manner.

Powhatans importunity to have us unarmed to betray us. Captaine Smith, I never use any Werowance so kindely as your selfe, yet from you I receive the least kindnesse of any. Captaine Newport gave me swords, copper, cloathes, a bed, tooles, or what I desired; ever taking what I offered him, and would send away his gunnes when I intreated him: none doth deny to lye at my feet, or refuse to doe what I desire, but onely you; of whom I can have nothing but what you regard not, and yet you will have whatsoever you demand. Captaine Newport you call father, and so you call me; but I see for all us both you will doe what you list, and we must both seeke to content you. But if you intend so friendly as you say, send hence your armes, that I may beleeve you; for you see the love I beare you, doth cause me thus nakedly to forget my selfe.

THE PORTRAICTUER OF CAPTAYNE IOHN SMITH / ADMIRALL OF NEW ENGLAND.

Æ.ta 37
A° 1616

These are the Lines that shew thy Face; but those
That shew thy Grace and Glory, brighter bee:
Thy Faire-Discoueries and Fowle-Overthrowes
Of Salvages, much Civill'zd by thee
Best shew thy Spirit; and to it Glory Wyn;
So, thou art Brasse without, but Golde within.

1. Simon van de Passe, *The Portraictuer of Captayne John Smith* (1617)

2. John Payne, *His Combat with Grualgo* (1630)

Within the illustration:

Capt SMITH led Captiue to the BASHAW of NALBRITS in TARTARIA. Chap·12·

Smith

Drub·man

Bashaw

3. John Payne, *Capt. Smith Led Captive to the Bashaw of Nalbrits in Tartaria* (1630)

4. Theodor de Bry, *The arrival of the Englishemen in Virginia* (1590)

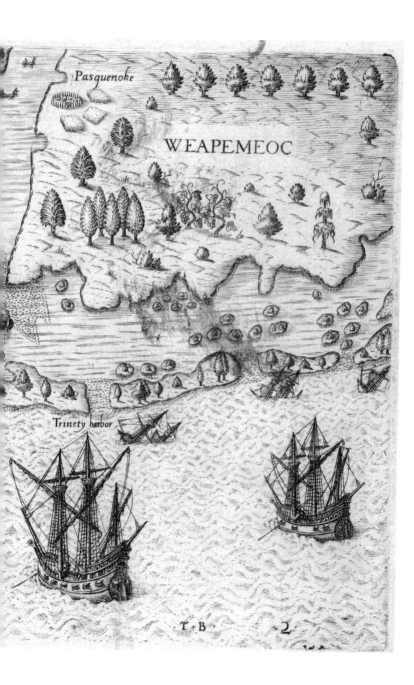

Pasquenoke

WEAPEMEOC

Trinety harbor

T. B. 2

5. Theodor de Bry, *Americæ pars, Nunc Virginia dicta* (1590)

CHAWA

R
NO
G
I
A

I

Americæ
pars, Nunc Virginia
dicta, primum ab Anglis
inuenta, sumtibus Dn Walteri
Raleigh, Equestris ordinis Viri
Anno Dñi M·D·LXXXV regni Vero
Sereniss. nostræ Reginæ Elisabethæ
XXVII
Huius Vero Historia peculiari
Libro descripta est, additis
etiam Indigenarum
Iconibus

Ramushonnok

Ohaunook

nuc
Metocuuem

Catokinge

Waratan

Mascoming

Skicoak

W E A P E

Chesepiooc sinus

Comokee

Chepanuu M E O C

Chesepiooc

Apasus

Pasquenoke

Trinety harbor

OCCIDENS

MERIDIES

SEPTENTRIO

ORIENS

6. Theodor de Bry, *Their Idol Kiwasa* (1590)

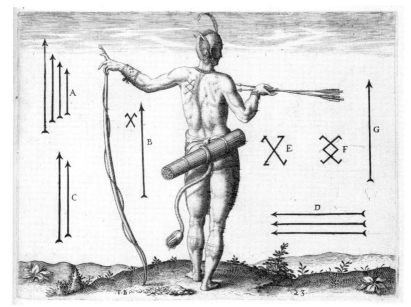

7. Theodor de Bry, *The Marckes of sundrye of the Cheif mene of Virginia* (1590)

C: S:
How they tooke him prisoner in the Oaze 1607
C.S.
C. Smith bindeth a saluage to his arme, fighteth with the King of Pamaunkee and all his company, and slew 3 of them.
8. Robert Vaughan, *How they tooke him prisoner in the Oaze* (1624)

Their

C: S

triumph about him

C: Smith bound to a tree to be shott to death
1607

9. Robert Vaughan, *Their triumph about him* (1624)

C S
King Powhatan comands C: Smith to be slayne, his
daughter Pokahontas beggs his life his thankfullness
and how he subiected 39 of their kings. reade ÿ history.
printed by James Reeve

10. Robert Vaughan, *King Powhatan commands C. Smith to be slayne* (1624)

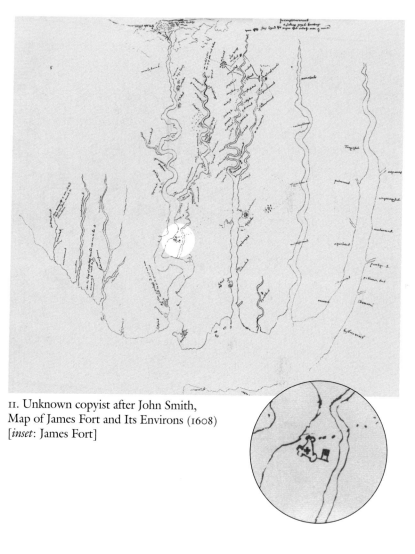

11. Unknown copyist after John Smith,
Map of James Fort and Its Environs (1608)
[*inset*: James Fort]

12. Robert Vaughan, *C: Smith taketh the King of Pamaunkee prisoner* (1624)

C: Smith takes the King of Paspahegh prisoner. Aº 1609.

13. Robert Vaughan, *C: Smith takes the King of Paspahegh prisoner* (1624)

Text around oval portrait:

MATOAKA ALS REBECCA FILIA POTENTISS : PRINC : POWHATANI IMP : VIRGINIÆ.

Ætatis suæ 21. A.
1616.

Matoaks als Rebecka daughter to the mighty Prince
Powhatan Emperour of Attanoughskomouck als virginia
converted and baptized in the Christian faith, and
wife to the wor.ᵗ Mr. Joh Rolff.

Si: Paß: sculp: Compton Holland excud:

14. Simon van de Passe, *Matoaka als Rebecca* (1616–17)

Smith seeing this Salvage but trifle the time to cut his throat, procured the Salvages to breake the ice, that his Boate might come to fetch his corne and him: and gave order for more men to come on shore, to surprise the King, with whom also he but trifled the time till his men were landed: and to keepe him from suspicion, entertained the time with this reply.

Captaine Smiths discourse to delay time, till he found oportunity to surprise the King.

  Powhatan you must know, as I have but one God, I honour but one King; and I live not here as your subject, but as your friend to pleasure you with what I can. By the gifts you bestow on me, you gaine more then by trade: yet would you visit mee as I doe you, you should know it is not our custome, to sell our curtesies as a vendible commodity. Bring all your countrey with you for your guard, I will not dislike it as being over jealous. But to content you, tomorrow I will leave my Armes, and trust to your promise. I call you father indeed, and as a father you shall see I will love you: but the small care you have of such a childe caused my men perswade me to looke to my selfe.

Powhatans plot to have murdered Smith.

  By this time Powhatan having knowledge his men were ready whilest the ice was a breaking, with his luggage women and children, fled. Yet to avoyd suspicion, left two or three of the women talking with the Captaine, whilest hee secretly ran away, and his men that secretly beset the house. Which being presently discovered to Captaine Smith, with his pistoll, sword, and target hee made such a passage among these naked Divels; that at his first shoot, they next him tumbled one over another, and the rest quickly fled some one way some another: so that without any hurt, onely accompanied with John Russell, hee obtained the *corps du guard.* When they perceived him so well escaped, and with his eighteene men (for he had no more with him a shore) to the uttermost of their skill they sought excuses to dissemble the matter: and Powhatan to excuse his flight and the sudden comming of this multitude, sent our Captaine a great bracelet and a chaine *A chaine of pearle sent the Captaine for a present.* of pearle, by an ancient Oratour that bespoke us to this purpose, perceiving even then from our Pinnace, a Barge and men departing and comming unto us.

Captaine Smith, our Werowance is fled, fearing your gunnes, and knowing when the ice was broken there would come more men, sent these numbers but to guard his corne from stealing, that might happen without your knowledge: now though some bee hurt by your misprision, yet Powhatan is your friend and so will for ever continue. Now since the ice is open, he would have you send away your corne, and if you would have his company, send away also your gunnes, which so affright his people, that they dare not come to you as hee promised they should.

Pretending to kill our men loaded with baskets, we caused them do it themselves.

Then having provided baskets for our men to carry our corne to the boats, they kindly offered their service to guard our Armes, that none should steale them. A great many they were of goodly well proportioned fellowes, as grim as Divels; yet the very sight of cocking our matches, and being to let fly, a few wordes caused them to leave their bowes and arrowes to our guard, and beare downe our corne on their backes; wee needed not importune them to make dispatch. But our Barges being left on the oase by the ebbe, caused us stay till the next high-water, so that wee returned againe to our old quarter. Powhatan and his Dutch-men brusting with desire to have the head of Captaine Smith, for if they could but kill him, they thought all was theirs, neglected not any oportunity to effect his purpose. The Indians with all the merry sports they could devise, spent the time till night: then they all returned to Powhatan, who all this time was making ready his forces to surprise the house and him at supper. Notwithstanding the eternall all-seeing God did

Pocahontas bewrayes her fathers deceit to kill us.

prevent him, and by a strange meanes. For Pocahontas his dearest jewell and daughter, in that darke night came through the irksome woods, and told our Captaine great cheare should be sent us by and by: but Powhatan and all the power he could make, would after come kill us all, if they that brought it could not kill us with our owne weapons when we were at supper. Therefore if we would live shee wished us presently to bee gone. Such things as shee delighted in, he would have given her: but with the teares running downe her cheekes, shee said shee durst not be seene to have any: for if Powhatan should know it, she were but dead, and so shee ranne away by her selfe as she came. Within lesse then an houre came eight or ten lusty fellowes, with great platters of venison and other victuall, very importunate to have us put out our matches (whose smoake made them sicke) and sit down to

our victuall. But the Captaine made them taste every dish,
which done hee sent some of them backe to Powhatan, to bid
him make haste for hee was prepared for his comming. As for
them hee knew they came to betray him at his supper: but hee
would prevent them and all their other intended villanies: so
that they might be gone. Not long after came more messengers, to see what newes; not long after them others. Thus wee
spent the night as vigilantly as they, till it was high-water, yet
seemed to the salvages as friendly as they to us: and that wee
were so desirous to give Powhatan content, as hee requested,
wee did leave him Edward Brynton to kill him foule, and the
Dutch-men to finish his house; thinking at our returne from
Pamaunkee the frost would be gone, and then we might finde
a better oportunity if necessity did occasion it, little dreaming
yet of the Dutch-mens treachery, whose humor well suted this
verse:

Is any free, that may not live as freely as he list?
Let us live so, then w'are as free, and bruitish as the best.

Chapter IX.
How wee escaped surprising at Pamaunkee.

The Dutch
men deceive
Captaine
Winne.

WE had no sooner set sayle but Powhatan returned,
and sent Adam and Francis (two stout Dutch-men)
to James towne: who faining to Captaine Winne that
all things were well, and that Captaine Smith had use of their
armes, wherefore they requested new (the which were given
them) they told him their comming was for some extraordinary tooles, and shift of apparell; by which colourable excuse
they obtained six or seaven more to their confederacie, such
expert theeves, that presently furnished them with a great
many swords, pike-heads, peeces, shot, powder and such like:
Salvages they had at hand to carry it away, and the next day
they returned unsuspected, leaving their confederates to follow, and in the interim to convay them such things as they
could: for which service they should live with Powhatan as his

chiefe affected, free from those miseries that would happen the Colony. Samuel their other consort Powhatan kept for their pledge, whose diligence had provided them three hundred of The Dutch men furnish the Salvages with Armes. their kinde of hatchets; the rest fifty swords, eight peeces, and eight pikes. Brynton and Richard Salvage seeing the Dutch-men so diligent to accommodate the Salvages with weapons, attempted to have gotten to James towne, but they were apprehended, and expected ever when to be put to death.

Within two or three dayes we arrived at Pamaunkee, the King as many dayes entertained us with feasting and much mirth. And the day appointed to beginne our trade, the President, Lieutenant Percie, Master West, Master Russell, Master Behethland, Master Crashaw, Master Powell, Master Ford, and some others to the number of fifteene, went up to Opechancanoughs house a quarter of a mile from the river, where wee found nothing but a lame fellow and a boy: and all the houses round about of all things abandoned. Not long wee stayed ere the King arrived, and after him came diverse of his people loaden with bowes and arrowes: but such pinching commodities, and those esteemed at such a value, as our Captaine began with the King after this manner.

Smiths Speech to Opechan-canough. Opechancanough, the great love you professe with your tongue, seemes meere deceit by your actions. Last yeere you kindly fraughted our ship: but now you have invited mee to starve with hunger: you know my want, and I your plenty; of which by some meanes I must have part: remember it is fit for Kings to keepe their promise. Here are my commodities, whereof take your choice, the rest I will proportion fit bargains for your people.

The King seemed kindly to accept his offer, and the better to colour his project, sold us what they had to our owne content, promising the next day more company, better provided. The Barges and Pinnace being committed to the charge of Master Phetiplace; the President with his old fifteene marched up to 700. Salvages beset the En-glish being but 16. the Kings house, where wee found foure or five men newly arrived, each with a great basket. Not long after came the King, who with a strained cheerfulnesse held us with discourse what paines he had taken to keep his promise; till Master Russell brought us in newes that we were all betrayed: for at least seven hundred Salvages well armed, had invironed the house, and beset the fields. The King conjecturing what Russell related, wee could well perceive how the extremity of his feare bewrayed his intent: whereat some of our company seeming dismaied with the thought of such a multitude; the Captaine encouraged us to this effect.

Smiths speech to his Company.

Worthy Countrey-men, were the mischiefes of my seeming friends no more then the danger of these enemies, I little cared were they as many more: if you dare doe, but as I. But this is my torment, that if I escape them, our malicious Councell with their open mouthed Minions, will make me such a peace breaker (in their opinions in England) as will breake my necke. I could wish those here, that make these seeme Saints, and me an oppressor. But this is the worst of all, wherein I pray you aid mee with your opinions. Should wee beginne with them and surprise the King, we cannot keepe him and defend well our selves. If wee should each kill our man, and so proceed with all in the house; the rest will all fly: then shall wee get no more then the bodies that are slaine, and so starve for victuall. As for their fury it is the least danger; for well you know, being alone assaulted with two or three hundred of them, I made them by the helpe of God compound to save my life. And wee are sixteene, and they but seaven hundred at the most; and assure your selves, God will so assist us, that if you dare stand but to discharge your pieces, the very smoake will bee sufficient to affright them. Yet howsoever, let us fight like men, and not die like sheepe: for by that meanes you know God hath oft delivered mee, and so I trust will now. But first, I will deale with them, to bring it to passe wee may fight for something, and draw them to it by conditions. If you like this motion, promise me you will be valiant.

The time not permitting any argument, all vowed to execute whatsoever hee attempted, or die: whereupon the Captaine in plaine tearmes told the King this.

Smiths offer to Opechan-canough.

I see Opechancanough your plot to murder me, but I feare it not. As yet your men and mine have done no harme, but by our direction. Take therefore your Armes, you see mine, my body shall bee as naked as yours: the Isle in your river is a fit place, if you be contented: and the conquerour (of us two) shall be Lord and Master over all our men. If you have not enough, take time to fetch more, and bring what number you will; so every one bring a basket of corne, against all which I will stake the value in copper, you see I have but fifteene, and our game shall be, the Conquerour take all.

Opechanca-
noughs
device to
betray Smith. The King being guarded with forty or fifty of his chiefe men, seemed kindly to appease Smiths suspicion of unkindnesse, by a great present at the doore, they intreated him to receive. This was to draw him out of the doore, where the bait was guarded with at least two hundred men, and thirty lying under a great tree (that lay thwart as a barricado) each his arrow nocked ready to shoot. The President commanded one to go see what kind of deceit this was, and to receive the present; but hee refused to doe it: yet the Gentlemen and all the rest were importunate to goe, but he would not permit them, being vexed at that Coward: and commanded Lieutenant Percie, Master West, and the rest to make good the house; Master Powell and Master Behethland he commanded to guard the doore, and in such a rage Smith taketh
the King
prisoner. snatched the King by his long locke in the middest of his men, with his Pistoll readie bent against his brest. Thus he led the trembling King, neare dead with feare amongst all his people: who delivering the Captaine his Vambrace, Bow, and Arrowes, all his men were easily intreated to cast downe their Armes, little dreaming any durst in that manner have used their King: who then to escape himselfe bestowed his presents in good sadnesse, and causing a great many of them come before him unarmed, holding the King by the hayre (as is sayd) he spake to them to this effect.

Smiths
discourse
to the
Pamaunkees. I see (you Pamaunkees) the great desire you have to kill me, and my long suffering your injuries hath imboldened you to this presumption. The cause I have forborne your insolencies, is the promise I made you (before the God I serve) to be your friend, till you give me just cause to be your enemy. If I keepe this vow, my God will keepe me, you cannot hurt me, if I breake it, he will destroy me. But if you shoot but one Arrow to shed one drop of bloud of any of my men, or steale the least of these Beads, or Copper, I spurne here before you with my foot; you shall see I will not cease revenge (if once I begin) so long as I can heare where to finde one of your Nation that will not deny the name of Pamaunk. I am not now at Rassaweak halfe drowned with myre, where you tooke me prisoner; yet then for keeping your promise and your

good usage and saving my life, I so affect you, that your denyals of your trechery, doe halfe perswade me to mistake my selfe. But if I be the marke you ayme at, here I stand, shoot he that dare. You promised to fraught my Ship ere I departed, and so you shall, or I meane to load her with your dead carcasses, yet if as friends you will come and trade, I once more promise not to trouble you, except you give me the first occasion, and your King shall be free and be my friend, for I am not come to hurt him or any of you.

The Salvages dissemble their intent. Upon this away went their Bowes and Arrowes, and men, women, and children brought in their Commodities: two or three houres they so thronged about the President and so overwearied him, as he retyred himselfe to rest, leaving Master Behethland and Master Powell to receive their presents, but some Salvages perceiving him fast asleepe, and the guard somewhat carelesly dispersed, fortie or fiftie of their choise men each with a club, or an English sword in his hand began to enter the house with two or three hundred others, that pressed to second them. The noyse and hast they made in, did so shake the house they awoke him from his sleepe, and being halfe amazed with this suddaine sight, betooke him strait to his sword and Target; Master Chrashaw and some others charged in like manner; whereat they quickly thronged faster backe then before forward. The house thus cleansed, the King and some of his auncients we kept yet with him, who with a long Oration, excused this intrusion. The rest of the day was spent with much kindnesse, the companie againe Their excuse and reconcilement. renewing their presents with their best provisions, and whatsoever he gave them they seemed therewith well contented.

Now in the meane while since our departure, this hapned at our Fort. Master Scrivener having received Letters from England to make himselfe either Cæsar or nothing, he began to decline in his affection to Captaine Smith, that ever regarded him as himselfe, and was willing to crosse the surprising of Powhatan. Some certaine daies after the Presidents departure, he would needs goe visit the Isle of Hogs, and tooke with him Captaine Waldo (though the President had appointed him to be ready to second his occasions) with Master Anthony Gosnoll and eight others; but so violent was the wind (that extreame frozen time) that the Boat sunke, but where or how none doth know. The Skiff was much over-loaden, and would scarce have lived in that extreame tempest had she beene empty: but by no perswasion he could be diverted, though both Waldo and an hundred others doubted as it hapned. The Salvages were the first that found their bodies, which so much the more encouraged them to effect their projects. To advertise the President of this heavie newes, none could be found would undertake it, but the Jorney was often refused of all in the Fort, untill Master Richard Wyffin undertooke alone the performance thereof.

The losse of Master Scrivener and others with a Skiff.

In this Journey he was incountred with many dangers and difficulties in all parts as he passed. As for that night he lodged with Powhatan, perceiving such preparation for warre, not finding the President there: he did assure himselfe some mischiefe was intended. Pocahontas hid him for a time, and sent them who pursued him the cleane contrary way to seeke him; but by her meanes and extraordinary bribes and much trouble in three dayes travell, at length he found us in the middest of these turmoyles. This unhappy newes the President swore him to conceale from the company, and so dissembling his sorrow with the best countenances he could, when the night approched went safely aboord with all his Souldiers; leaving Opechancanough at libertie, according to his promise, the better to have Powhatan in his returne.

Master Wyffins desperate journey.

Now so extreamely Powhatan had threatned the death of his men, if they did not by some meanes kill Captaine Smith: that the next day they appointed all the countrey should come to trade unarmed: yet unwilling to be trecherous, but that they were constrained, hating fighting with him almost as ill as hanging, such feare they had of bad successe. The next morning the Sunne had not long appeared, but the fields appeared covered with people and Baskets, to tempt us on shore; but nothing was to be had without his presence, nor they would not indure the sight of a gun. When the President saw them begin to depart, being unwilling to loose such a bootie, he so well contrived the Pinnace, and his Barges with Ambuscadoes, as onely with Lieutenant Percie, Master West, and Master Russell, with their Armes went on shore; others he appointed unarmed to receive what was brought. The Salvages flocked before him in heapes,

Powhatan constraineth his men to be trecherous.

The third attempt to betray us.

and the banke serving as a trench for a retreat, he drew them fayre open to his Ambuscado's. For he not being to be perswaded to goe visit their King, the King knowing the most of them unarmed, came to visit him with two or three hundred men, in the forme of two halfe Moones; and with some twentie men, and many women loaden with painted Baskets. But when they approached somewhat neare us, their women and children fled. For when they had environed and beset the fields in this manner, they thought their purpose sure, yet so trembled with feare as they were scarse able to nock their Arrowes: Smith standing with his three men ready bent, beholding them till they were within danger of our Ambuscado's, who upon the word discovered themselves, and he retyred to the Barge. Which the Salvages no sooner perceived, then away they fled, esteeming their heeles for their best advantage.

That night we sent Master Chrashaw, and Master Ford to James towne to Captaine Winne. In the way betweene Werowocomoco and the Fort they met foure or five of the Dutchmens Confederates going to Powhatan: the which to excuse those Gentlemens suspition of their running to the Salvages, returned to the Fort and there continued.

The Salvages hearing our Barge goe downe the river in the night, were so terribly affrayde, that we sent for more men (we having so much threatned their ruine, and the rasing of their houses, boats, and wires) that the next day the King sent our Captaine a chayne of Pearle, to alter his purpose and stay his men: promising though they wanted themselves, to fraught our ship and bring it aboord to avoyd suspicion. So that five or six dayes after, from all parts of the Country within ten or twelve myles in the extreame frost and snow, they brought us provision on their naked backes.

A chayne of pearle sent to obtaine peace.

Yet notwithstanding this kindnesse and trade, had their art and poyson beene sufficient, the President, with Master West, and some others had beene poysoned; it made them sicke, but expelled it selfe. Wecuttanow, a stout young fellow, knowing he was suspected for bringing this present of poyson, with fortie or fiftie of his chiefe companions (seeing the President but with a few men at Potauncak) so proudly braved it, as though he expected to incounter a revenge. Which the President perceiving in the

The President poysoned: the offender punished.

midst of his company, did not onely beate, but spurned him like a dogge, as scorning to doe him any worse mischiefe. Whereupon all of them fled into the woods, thinking they had done a great matter to have so well escaped: and the townsmen remaining presently fraughted our Barge to be rid of our companies, framing many excuses to excuse Wecuttanow, (being sonne to their chiefe King, but Powhatan) and told us if we would shew them him that brought the poyson, they would deliver him to us to punish as we pleased. Men may thinke it strange there should be such a stirre for a little corne, but had it beene gold with more ease wee might have got it; and had it wanted, the whole Colony had starved. Wee may be thought very patient to endure all those injuries, yet onely with fearing them wee got what they had. Whereas if we had taken revenge, then by their losse, we should have lost our selves. We searched also the Countries of Youghtanund and Mattapanient, where the people imparted that little they had with such complaints and teares from the eyes of women and children, as he had beene too cruell to have beene a Christian, that would not have beene satisfied and moved with compassion. But had this hapned in October, November, and December, when that unhappie discovery of Monacan was made, and when we might have fraughted a ship of fortie tuns, and twise as much might have beene had from the Rivers of Rapahanock, Patawomek, and Pawtuxunt.

The Salvages want and povertie.

The maine occasion of our thus temporizing with them was, to part friends as we did, to give the lesse cause of suspition to Powhatan to fly, by whom we now returned with a purpose to have surprised him and his provision. For effecting whereof (when we came against the Towne) the President sent Master Wyffin and Master Coe ashore to discover and make way for his intended project. But they found that those damned Dutch-men had caused Powhatan to abandon his new house and Werowocomoco, and to carry away all his corne and provision: and the people they found so ill affected, that they were in great doubt how to escape with their lives. So the President finding his intent frustrated, and that there was nothing now to be had, and therefore an unfit time to revenge their abuses, sent Master Michael Phittiplace by Land to James towne, whether we sayled with all the speed we

The Dutchmen did much hurt.

could; wee having in this Journey (for 25ˡ. of Copper, and 50ˡ. of Iron and Beads) enough to keepe 46 men six weekes, and every man for his reward a moneths provision extraordinary (no Trade being allowed but for the store) we got neare 200ˡ waight of deere suet, and delivered to the Cape Merchant 479 Bushels of Corne.

Those temporizing proceedings to some may seeme too charitable, to such a daily daring trecherous people: to others not pleasing, that we washed not the ground with their blouds, nor shewed such strange inventions in mangling, murdering, ransacking, and destroying (as did the Spanyards) the simple bodies of such ignorant soules; nor delightfull, because not stuffed with Relations of heapes and mynes of gold and silver, nor such rare commodities, as the Portugals and Spanyards found in the East and West Indies. The want whereof hath begot us (that were the first undertakers) no lesse scorne and contempt, then the noble conquests and valiant adventures beautified with it, prayse and honour. Too much I confesse the world cannot attribute to their ever memorable merit: and to cleare us from the blind worlds ignorant censure, these few words may suffice any reasonable understanding.

It was the Spanyards good hap to happen in those

An Apology
for the first
Planters.

parts where were infinite numbers of people, who had manured the ground with that providence, it affoorded victualls at all times. And time had brought them to that perfection, they had the use of gold and silver, and the most of such commodities as those Countries affoorded: so that, what the Spanyard got was chiefely the spoyle and pillage of those Countrey people, and not the labours of their owne hands. But had those fruitfull Countries beene as salvage, as barbarous, as ill peopled, as little planted, laboured, and manured, as Virginia: their proper labours it is likely would have produced as small profit as ours. But had Virginia beene peopled, planted, manured, and adorned with such store of precious Jewels, and rich commodities as was the Indies: then had we not gotten and done as much as by their examples might be expected from us, the world might then have traduced us and our merits, and have made shame and infamy our recompence and reward.

But we chanced in a Land even as God made it, where we

found onely an idle, improvident, scattered people, ignorant of the knowledge of gold or silver, or any commodities, and carelesse of any thing but from hand to mouth, except bables of no worth; nothing to incourage us, but what accidentally we found Nature afforded. Which ere we could bring to recompence our paines, defray our charges, and satisfie our Adventurers; we were to discover the Countrey, subdue the people, bring them to be tractable, civill, and industrious, and teach them trades, that the fruits of their labours might make us some recompence, or plant such Colonies of our owne, that must first make provision how to live of themselves, ere they can bring to perfection the commodities of the Country: which doubtlesse will be as commodious for England as the west Indies for Spaine, if it be rightly mannaged: notwithstanding all our home-bred opinions, that will argue the contrary, as formerly some have done against the Spanyards and Portugalls. But to conclude, against all rumor of opinion, I onely say this, for those that the three first yeares began this Plantation; notwithstanding all their factions, mutinies, and miseries, so gently corrected, and well prevented: peruse the Spanish Decades; the Relations of Master Hackluit, and tell me how many ever with such small meanes as a Barge of 2 tuns, sometimes with seaven, eight, or nine, or but at most, twelve or sixteene men, did ever discover so many fayre and navigable Rivers, subject so many severall Kings, people, and Nations, to obedience, and contribution, with so little bloudshed.

And if in the search of those Countries we had hapned where wealth had beene, we had as surely had it as obedience and contribution, but if we have overskipped it, we will not envie them that shall find it: yet can we not but lament, it was our fortunes to end when we had but onely learned how to begin, and found the right course how to proceed.

By Richard Wyffin, William Phittiplace,
Jeffrey Abbot, and Anas Todkill.

Chapter X.
How the Salvages became subject to the English.

When the Ships departed, all the provision of the Store (but that the President had gotten) was so rotten with the last Summers rayne, and eaten with Rats and Wormes, as the Hogges would scarcely eate it. Yet it was the Souldiers dyet till our returnes, so that we found nothing done, but our victuals spent, and the most part of our tooles, and a good part of our Armes conveyed to the Salvages. But now casting up the Store, and finding sufficient till the next harvest, the feare of starving was abandoned, and the company divided into tens, fifteens, or as the businesse required; six houres each day was spent in worke, the rest in Pastime and merry exercises, but the untowardnesse of the greatest number caused the President advise as followeth.

The Presidents advice to the Company. Countrymen, the long experience of our late miseries, I hope is sufficient to perswade every one to a present correction of himselfe, and thinke not that either my pains, nor the Adventurers purses, will ever maintaine you in idlenesse and sloath. I speake not this to you all, for divers of you I know deserve both honour and reward, better then is yet here to be had: but the greater part must be more industrious, or starve, how ever you have beene heretofore tollerated by the authoritie of the Councell, from that I have often commanded you. You see now that power resteth wholly in my selfe: you must obey this now for a Law, that he that will not worke shall not eate (except by sicknesse he be disabled) for the labours of thirtie or fortie honest and industrious men shall not be consumed to maintaine an hundred and fiftie idle loyterers. And though you presume the authoritie here is but a shadow, and that I dare not touch the lives of any but my owne must answer it: the Letters patents shall each weeke be read to you, whose Contents will tell you the contrary. I would wish you therefore without contempt seeke to observe these orders set downe, for there are now no more Counsellers to protect you, nor curbe my endevours. Therefore he that offendeth, let him assuredly expect his due punishment.

He made also a Table, as a publicke memoriall of every mans deserts, to incourage the good, and with shame to spurre on the rest to amendment. By this many became very industrious, yet more by punishment performed their businesse, for all were so tasked, that there was no excuse could prevaile to deceive him: yet the Dutch-mens consorts so closely convayed them powder, shot, swords, and tooles, that though we could find the defect, we could not finde by whom, till it was too late.

The Dutch-mens plot to murther Captaine Smith. All this time the Dutch men remaining with Powhatan, (who kindly entertained them to instruct the Salvages the use of our Armes) and their consorts not following them as they expected; to know the cause, they sent Francis their companion, a stout young fellow, disguised like a Salvage, to the Glasse-house, a place in the woods neare a myle from James Towne; where was their Rendezvous for all their unsuspected villany. Fortie men they procured to lie in Ambuscado for Captaine Smith, who no sooner heard of this Dutch-man, but he sent to apprehend him (but he was gone) yet to crosse his returne to Powhatan, the Captaine presently dispatched 20. shot after him, himselfe returning from the Glasse-house alone. By the way he incountred the King of Paspahegh, a most strong stout Salvage, whose perswasions not being able to perswade him to his Ambush, seeing Smith taketh the King of Paspahegh prisoner. him onely armed but with a faucheon, attempted to have shot him, but the President prevented his shoot by grapling with him, and the Salvage as well prevented him for drawing his faucheon, and perforce bore him into the River to have drowned him. Long they strugled in the water, till the President got such hold on his throat, he had neare strangled the King; but having drawne his faucheon to cut off his head, seeing how pittifully he begged his life, he led him prisoner to James Towne, and put him in chaynes.

The Dutch-man ere long was also brought in, whose villany though all this time it was suspected, yet he fayned such a formall excuse, that for want of language Captaine Winne understood him not rightly, and for their dealings with Powhatan, that to save their lives they were constrained to accommodate his armes, of whom he extreamely complained to have detained them perforce, and that he made this escape with the hazard of his life, and meant not to have returned, but was onely walking in the woods to gather Walnuts. Yet for all this faire tale, there was so small appearance of truth, and the plaine confession of Paspahegh of his trechery, he went by the heeles: Smith purposing to regaine the Dutch-men, by the saving his life. The poore Salvage did his best by his daily messengers to

Powhatan, but all returned that the Dutch-men would not returne, neither did Powhatan stay them; and to bring them fiftie myles on his mens backes they were not able. Daily this Kings wives, children, and people came to visit him with presents, which he liberally bestowed to make his peace. Much trust they had in the Presidents promise: but the King finding his guard negligent, though fettered yet escaped. Captaine Winne thinking to pursue him found such troupes of Salvages to hinder his passage, as they exchanged many vollies of shot for flights of Arrowes. Captaine Smith hearing of this in returning to the Fort, tooke two Salvages prisoners, called Kemps and Tussore, the two most exact villaines in all the Country. With these he sent Captaine Winne and fiftie choise men, and Lieutenant Percie, to have regained the King, and revenged this injury, and so had done, if they had followed his directions, or beene advised with those two villaines, that would have betrayed both King and kindred for a peece of Copper, but he trifling away the night, the Salvages the next morning by the rising of the Sunne, braved him to come ashore to fight: a good time both sides let fly at other, but we heard of no hurt, onely they tooke two Canowes, burnt the Kings house, and so returned to James towne.

Captaine Smith taketh two Salvages prisoners.

The President fearing those Bravado's would but incourage the Salvages, began againe himselfe to try his conclusions; whereby six or seaven were slaine, as many made prisoners. He burnt their houses, tooke their Boats, with all their fishing wires, and planted some of them at James towne for his owne use, and now resolved not to cease till he had revenged himselfe of all them had injured him. But in his journey passing by Paspahegh towards Chickahamania, the Salvages did their best to draw him to their Ambuscadoes; but seeing him regardlesly passe their Country, all shewed themselves in their bravest manner. To try their valours he could not but let fly, and ere he could land, they no sooner knew him, but they threw downe their armes and desired peace. Their Orator was a lustie young fellow called Okaning, whose worthy discourse deserveth to be remembred. And thus it was:

The Salvages desire Peace.

Okaning his Oration.

Captaine Smith, my Master is here present in the company, thinking it Captaine Winne, and not you, (of him he intended to have beene revenged) having never offended him. If he hath offended you in escaping your imprisonment, the fishes swim, the foules fly, and the very beasts strive to escape the snare and live. Then blame not him being a man. He would intreat you remember, you being a prisoner, what paines he tooke to save your life. If since he hath injured you he was compelled to it: but howsoever, you have revenged it with our too great losse. We perceive and well know you intend to destroy us, that are here to intreat and desire your friendship, and to enjoy our houses and plant our fields, of whose fruit you shall participate: otherwise you will have the worse by our absence; for we can plant any where, though with more labour, and we know you cannot live if you want our harvest, and that reliefe we bring you. If you promise us peace, we will beleeve you; if you proceed in revenge we will abandon the Country.

Upon these tearmes the President promised them peace, till they did us injury, upon condition they should bring in provision. Thus all departed good friends, and so continued till Smith left the Countrey.

A Salvage smoothered at James towne, and recovered.

Arriving at James Towne, complaint was made to the President, that the Chickahamanians, who all this while continued trade and seemed our friends, by colour thereof were the onely theeves. And amongst other things a Pistoll being stolne and the theefe fled, there was apprehended two proper young fellowes, that were brothers, knowne to be his confederates. Now to regaine this Pistoll, the one was imprisoned, the other was sent to returne the Pistoll againe within twelve houres, or his brother to be hanged. Yet the President pittying the poore naked Salvage in the dungeon, sent him victuall and some Char-coale for a fire: ere midnight his brother returned with the Pistoll, but the poore Salvage in the dungeon was so smoothered with the smoake he had made, and so pittiously burnt, that wee found him dead. The other most lamentably bewayled his death, and broke forth into such bitter agonies, that the President to quiet him, told him that if hereafter they would not steale, he would make him alive againe: but he little thought he could be recovered. Yet we doing our best with Aqua vitæ and Vineger, it pleased God to restore him againe to life, but so drunke and affrighted, that he seemed Lunaticke, the which as much tormented and grieved the other, as before to see him dead. Of which maladie upon promise of their good behaviour, the President promised to recover him: and so caused him to be layd by a fire to sleepe, who in the morning having well slept, had recovered his perfect senses, and then being dressed of his burning, and each a peece of Copper given them, they went away so well contented, that this was spread among all the Salvages for a miracle, that Captaine Smith could make a man alive that was dead.

Two or three Salvages slaine in drying Powder.

Another ingenuous Salvage of Powhatans, having gotten a great bag of Powder, and the backe of an Armour, at Werowocomoco amongst a many of his companions, to shew his extraordinary skill, he did dry it on the backe as he had scene the Souldiers at James Towne. But he dryed it so long, they peeping over it to see his skill, it tooke fire, and blew him to death, and one or two more, and the rest so scorched, they had little pleasure to meddle any more with powder.

These and many other such pretty Accidents, so amazed and affrighted both Powhatan, and all his people, that from all parts with presents they desired peace; returning many stolne things which we never demanded nor thought of; and after that, those that were taken stealing, both Powhatan and his people have sent them backe to James towne, to receive their punishment; and all the Country became absolute as free for us, as for themselves.

Chapter XI.
What was done in three moneths having Victualls. The Store devoured by Rats, how we lived three moneths of such naturall fruits as the Country affoorded.

Now we so quietly followed our businesse, that in three moneths wee made three or foure Last of Tarre, Pitch, and Sope ashes; produced a tryall of Glasse; made a Well in the Fort of excellent sweet water, which till then was wanting; built some twentie houses; recovered our Church; provided Nets and Wires for fishing; and to stop the disorders of our disorderly

theeves, and the Salvages, built a Blockhouse in the neck of
our Isle, kept by a Garrison to entertaine the Salvages trade,
and none to passe nor repasse Salvage nor Christian without
the presidents order. Thirtie or forty Acres of ground we
digged and planted. Of three sowes in eighteene moneths, increased 60, and od Piggs. And neere 500. chickings brought up
themselves without having any meat given them: but the Hogs
were transported to Hog Isle: where also we built a block-
house with a garison to give us notice of any shipping, and for
their exercise they made Clapbord and waynscot, and cut
downe trees. We built also a fort for a retreat neere a convenient River upon a high commanding hill, very hard to be assalted and easie to be defended, but ere it was finished this
defect caused a stay.

Great
extremitie
by Rats.
          In searching our casked corne, we found it halfe
rotten, and the rest so consumed with so many thousands of Rats that increased so fast, but there originall was from the ships, as we knew not how to keepe that little
we had. This did drive us all to our wits end, for there was
nothing in the country but what nature afforded. Untill this
time Kemps and Tassore were fettered prisoners, and did
double taske and taught us how to order and plant our fields:
whom now for want of victuall we set at liberty, but so well
they liked our companies they did not desire to goe from us.
And to expresse their loves for 16. dayes continuance, the Countrie people brought us (when least) 100. a day, of Squirrils,
Turkyes, Deere and other wilde beasts: But this want of corne
occasioned the end of all our works, it being worke sufficient
to provide victuall. 60. or 80. with Ensigne Laxon was sent
downe the river to live upon Oysters, and 20. with liutenant
Percy to try for fishing at Poynt Comfort: but in six weekes
they would not agree once to cast out the net, he being sicke
and burnt sore with Gunpouder. Master West with as many
went up to the falls, but nothing could be found but a few
Acornes; of that in store every man had their equall proportion.
Till this present, by the hazard and indevours of some thirtie or
fortie, this whole Colony had ever beene fed. We had more

Bread made
of dried
Sturgeon.
Sturgeon, then could he devoured by Dog and Man,
of which the industrious by drying and pounding,
mingled with Caviare, Sorell and other wholesome

hearbes would make bread and good meate: others would gather as much *Tockwhogh* roots, in a day as would make them bread a weeke, so that of those wilde fruites, and what we caught, we lived very well in regard of such a diet. But such was the strange condition of some 150, that had they not beene forced *nolens, volens,* perforce to gather and prepare their victuall they would all have starved or have eaten one another. Of those wild fruits the Salvages often brought us, and for that, the President would not fullfill the unreasonable desire, of those distracted Gluttonous Loyterers, to sell not only our kettles, hows, tooles, and Iron, nay swords, pieces, and the very Ordnance and howses, might they have prevayled to have beene but Idle: for those Salvage fruites, they would have had imparted all to the Salvages, especially for one basket of Corne they heard of to be at Powhatans, fifty myles from our Fort. Though he bought neere halfe of it to satisfie their humors, yet to have had the other halfe, they would have sould their soules, though not sufficient to have kept them a weeke. Thousands were their exclamations, suggestions and devises, to force him to those base inventions to have made it an occasion to abandon the Country. Want perforce constrained him to indure their exclaiming follies, till he found out the author, one Dyer a most crafty fellow and his ancient Maligner, whom he worthily punished, and with the rest he argued the case in this maner.

Their desire to destroy themselves.

Fellow souldiers, I did little thinke any so false to report, or so many to be so simple to be perswaded, that I either intend to starve you, or that Powhatan at this present hath corne for himselfe, much lesse for you; or that I would not have it, if I knew where it were to be had. Neither did I thinke any so malitious as now I see a great many; yet it shal not so passionate me, but I will doe my best for my worst maligner. But dreame no longer of this vaine hope from Powhatan, nor that I will longer forbeare to force you, from your Idlenesse, and punish you if you rayle. But if I finde any more runners for Newfoundland with the Pinnace, let him assuredly looke to arive at the Gallows. You cannot deny but that by the hazard of my life many a time I have saved yours, when (might your owne wills have prevailed) you would have starved; and will doe still whether I will or noe; But I protest by that God that made me, since necessitie hath not power to force you to gather for your selves those

The Presidents order for the drones

fruites the earth doth yeeld, you shall not onely gather for your selves, but those that are sicke. As yet I never had more from the store then the worst of you: and all my English extraordinary provision that I have, you shall see me divide it amongst the sick. And this Salvage trash you so scornfully repine at; being put in your mouthes your stomackes can disgest, if you would have better you should have brought it; and therefore I will take a course you shall provide what is to be had. The sick shall not starve, but equally share of all our labours; and he that gathereth not every day as much as I doe, the next day shall be set beyond the river, and be banished from the Fort as a drone, till he amend his conditions or starve.

But some would say with Seneca.

> *I know those things thou sayst are true good Nurse,*
> *But fury forceth me to follow worse.*
> *My minde is hurried headlong up and downe:*
> *Desiring better counsell, yet finds none.*

But seven of 200 dyed in nine moneths.   This order many murmured was very cruell, but it caused the most part so well bestirre themselves, that of 200. (except they were drowned) there died not past seven: as for Captaine Winne and Master Leigh they were dead ere this want hapned, and the rest dyed not for want of such as preserved the rest. Many were billetted amongst the Salvages, whereby we knew all their passages, fields and habitations, how to gather and use there fruits as well as themselves; for they did know wee had such a commanding power at James towne they durst not wrong us of a pin.

The Salvages returne our fugitives.   So well those poore Salvages used us that were thus billetted, that divers of the Souldiers ran away to search Kemps and Tassore our old prisoners. Glad were these Salvages to have such an oportunity to testifie their love unto us, for in stead of entertaining them, and such things as they had stollen, with all their great Offers, and promises they made them how to revenge their injuryes upon Captaine Smith; Kemps first made himselfe sport, in shewing his countrie men (by them) how he was used, feeding them with this law, who would not work must not eat, till they were neere starved indeede, continually threatning to beate them to death: neither could they get from him, till hee and his consorts brought them perforce to our Captaine, that so well contented him and punished them, as many others that intended also to follow them, were rather contented to labour at home, then adventure to live idlely amongst the Salvages; (of whom there was more hope to make better Christians and good subjects, then the one halfe of those that counterfeited themselves both.) For so affraide was al those kings and the better sort of the people to displease us, that some of the baser sort that we have extreamly hurt and punished for there villanies would hire us, we should not tell it to their kings, or countrymen, who would also repunish them, and yet returne them to James towne to content the President for a testimony of their loves.

Master Sicklemores Journey to Chawwonoke

Master Sicklemore well returned from Chaw-wonoke; but found little hope and lesse certaintie of them were left by Sir Walter Raleigh. The river, he saw was not great, the people few, the countrey most over growne with pynes, where there did grow here and there straglingly *Pemminaw*, we call silke grasse. But by the river the ground was good, and exceeding furtill;

Master Powels jorney to the Mangoags.

Master Nathanael Powell and Anas Todkill were also by the Quiyoughquohanocks conducted to the Mangoags to search them there: but nothing could they learne but they were all dead. This honest proper good promise-keeping king, of all the rest did ever best affect us, and though to his false Gods he was very zealous, yet he would confesse our God as much exceeded his as our Gunns did his Bow and Arrowes, often sending our President many presents, to pray to his God for raine or his corne would perish, for his Gods were angry. Three dayes jorney they conducted them through the woods, into a high country towards the South-west: where they saw here and there a little corne field, by some little spring or smal brooke, but no river they could see: the people in all respects like the rest, except there language: they live most upon rootes, fruites and wilde beasts; and trade with them towards the sea and the fatter countrys for dryed fish and corne, for skins.

The Dutch mens projects.

All this time to recover the Dutch-men and one Bentley another fugitive, we imployed one William Volday, a Zwitzar by birth, with Pardons and prom-ises to regaine them. Little we then suspected this double vil-lane, of any villany; who plainly taught us, in the most trust was the greatest treason; for this wicked hypocrite, by the seeming

hate he bore to the lewd conditions of his cursed country men,
(having this oportunity by his imployment to regaine them)
convayed them every thing they desired to effect their projects, to distroy the Colony. With much devotion they expected
the Spaniard, to whom they intended good service, or any
other, that would but carry them from us. But to begin with
the first oportunity; they seeing necessitie thus inforced us to
disperse our selves, importuned Powhatan to lend them but
his forces, and they would not onely distroy our Hoggs, fire
our towne, and betray our Pinnace; but bring to his service and
subjection the most of our company. With this plot they had
acquainted many Discontents, and many were agreed to there
Devilish practise. But one Thomas Douse, and Thomas Mallard (whose christian hearts relented at such an unchristian act)
voluntarily revealed it to Captaine Smith, who caused them to
conceale it, perswading Douse and Mallard to proceed in their
confedracie: onely to bring the irreclamable Dutch men and
the inconstant Salvages in such a maner amongst such Ambuscado's as he had prepared, that not many of them should returne from our Peninsula. But this brute comming to the eares
of the impatient multitude they so importuned the President
to cut off those Dutch men, as amongst many that offered to
cut their throats before the face of Powhatan, the first was
Lieutenant Percy, and Master John Cuderington, two Gentlemen of as bold resolute spirits as could possibly be found. But
the President had occasion of other imploiment for them, and
gave way to Master Wyffin and Sarjeant Jeffrey
Abbot, to goe and stab them or shoot them. But the
Dutch men made such excuses, accusing Volday
whom they supposed had revealed their project, as Abbot
would not, yet Wyffing would, perceiving it but deceit. The
King understanding of this their imployment, sent presently his
messengers to Captaine Smith to signifie it was not his fault to
detaine them, nor hinder his men from executing his command:
nor did he nor would he mantaine them, or any to occasion his
displeasure.

Two Gentlemen sent to the Germans.

But whilst this businesse was in hand, Arrived one
Captaine Argall, and Master Thomas Sedan, sent by
Master Cornelius to truck with the Collony, and fish
for Sturgeon, with a ship well furnished, with wine and much

The first arrivall of Captaine Argall.

other good provision. Though it was not sent us, our necessities was such as inforced us to take it. He brought us newes of a great supply and preparation for the Lord La Warre, with letters that much taxed our President for his heard dealing with the Salvages, and not returning the shippes fraughted. Notwithstanding we kept this ship tell the fleete arrived. True it is Argall lost his voyage, but we revictualled him, and sent him for England, with a true relation of the causes of our defailments, and how imposible it was to returne that wealth they expected, or observe there instructions to indure the Salvages insolencies, or doe any thing to any purpose, except they would send us men and meanes that could produce that they so much desired: otherwise all they did was lost, and could not but come to confusion. The villany of Volday we still dissembled. Adam upon his pardon came home but Samuell still stayed with Powhatan to heare further of there estates by this supply. Now all their plots Smith so well understood, they were his best advantages to secure us from any trechery, could be done by them or the Salvages: which with facility he could revenge when he would, because all those countryes more feared him then Powhatan, and hee had such parties with all his bordering neighbours: and many of the rest for love or feare would have done any thing he would have them, upon any commotion, though these fugitives had done all they could to perswade Powhatan, King James would kill Smith, for using him and his people so unkindly.

By this you may see for all those crosses, trecheries, and dissentions, how hee wrestled and overcame (without bloudshed) all that happened: also what good was done; how few dyed; what food the Countrey naturally affoordeth; what small cause there is men should starve, or be murthered by the Salvages, that have discretion to mannage them with courage and industrie. The two first yeares, though by his adventures, he had oft brought the Salvages to a tractable trade, yet you see how the envious authoritie ever crossed him, and frustrated his best endevours. But it wrought in him that experience and estimation amongst the Salvages, as otherwise it had bin impossible, he had ever effected that he did. Notwithstanding the many miserable, yet generous and worthy adventures, he had oft and long endured in the wide world, yet in this case he was againe to learne his Lecture by experience. Which with thus much adoe having obtained, it was his ill chance to end, when he had but onely learned how to begin. And though he left those unknowne difficulties (made easie and familiar) to his unlawfull successors, (who onely by living in James Towne, presumed to know more then all the world could direct them:) Now though they had all his Souldiers, with a tripple power, and twice tripple better meanes; by what they have done in his absence, the world may see what they would have done in his presence, had he not prevented their indiscretions: it doth justly prove, what cause he had to send them for England; and that he was neither factious, mutinous, nor dishonest. But they have made it more plaine since his returne for England; having his absolute authoritie freely in their power, with all the advantages and opportunitie that his labours had effected. As I am sorry their actions have made it so manifest, so I am unwilling to say what reason doth compell me, but onely to make apparant the truth, least I should seeme partiall, reasonlesse, and malicious.

Chapter XII.
The Arrivall of the third Supply.

The alteration of the government.

To redresse those jarres and ill proceedings, the Treasurer, Councell, and Company of Virginia, not finding that returne, and profit they expected; and them ingaged there, not having meanes to subsist of themselves, made meanes to his Majestie, to call in their Commission, and take a new in their owne names, as in their owne publication, 1610. you may reade at large. Having thus annihilated the old by vertue of a Commission made to the right Honourable, Sir Thomas West, Lord de la Warre, to be Generall of Virginia; Sir Thomas Gates, his Lieutenant; Sir George Somers, Admirall; Sir Thomas Dale, high Marshall; Sir Fardinando Wainman, Generall of the Horse; and so all other offices to many other worthy Gentlemen, for their lives: (though not any of them had ever beene in Virginia, except Captaine Newport, who was also by Patent made vice Admirall:) those noble Gentlemen drew in such great summes of money, that they sent Sir Thomas Gates, Sir George Somers, and Captaine Newport with nine shippes, and five hundred people, who had each of them a Commission, who first arrived to call in the old, without the knowledge or consent of them, that had endured all those former dangers to beat the path, not any regard had at all of them. All things being ready, because those three Captaines could not agree for place, it was concluded they should goe all in one ship, so all their three Commissions were in that Ship with them called the *Sea-Venture*. They set sayle from England in May 1609. A small Catch perished at Sea in a Hericano: the Admirall with an hundred and fiftie men, with the two Knights, and their new Commission, their Bils of Loading, with all manner of directions, and the most part of their provision arrived not. With the other seaven Ships as Captaines arrived Ratliffe, whose right name (as is sayd) was Sicklemore, Martin, and Archer, with Captaine Wood, Captaine Webbe, Captaine Moone, Captaine King, Captaine Davis, and divers Gentlemen of good meanes, and great parentage. But the first as they had beene troublesome at Sea, began againe to marre all ashore: for though (as is said) they were formerly sent for England, yet now returning againe, graced by the titles of Captaines of the passengers, seeing the Admirall wanting, and great probabilitie of her losse, strengthened themselves with those new companies, so exclaiming against Captaine Smith, that they mortally hated him ere ever they saw him. Who understanding by his Scouts the arrivall of such a Fleet, little dreaming of any such supply, supposed them Spanyards. But he quickly so determined and ordered our affaires, as we little feared their Arrivall, nor the successe of our incounter; nor were the Salvages any way negligent for the most part, to ayd and assist us with their best power. Had it so beene we had beene happy; for we would not have trusted them but as our foes, where receiving them as our Countreymen and friends, they did what they could to murther our President, to surprise the Store, the Fort, and our lodgings, to usurpe the government, and make us all their servants and slaves, till they could consume us and our remembrance; and

1609.
Sir Thomas Smith Treasurer.

The losse of Virginia.

The Salvages offer to fight under our colours.

rather indeed to supplant us then supply us, as master William
Box an honest Gentleman in this voyage thus relateth.

In the tayle of a Hericano wee were separated from the Admirall,
which although it was but the remainder of that Storme, there is seldome any such in England, or those Northerne parts of Europe.
Some lost their Masts, some their Sayles blowne from their Yards; the
Seas so over-raking our Ships, much of our provision was spoyled, our
Fleet separated, and our men sicke, and many dyed, and in this miserable estate we arrived in Virginia.

But in this Storme,

> When ratling Thunder ran along the Clouds;
> Did not the Saylers poore, and Masters proud
> A terror feele as strucke with feare of God?
> Did not their trembling joynts then dread his rod?
> Least for foule deeds and black mouth'd blasphemies,
> The rufull time be come that vengeance cryes.

To a thousand mischiefes those lewd Captaines led
this lewd company, wherein were many unruly
Gallants, packed thither by their friends to escape ill
destinies, and those would dispose and determine of the
government, sometimes to one, the next day to another; to day
the old Commission must rule, to morrow the new, the next
day neither, in fine they would rule all, or ruine all: yet in charitie we must endure them thus to destroy us, or by correcting
their follies, have brought the worlds censure upon us to be
guiltie of their blouds. Happie had we beene had they never
arrived, and we for ever abandoned, and as we were left to our
fortunes: for on earth for the number was never more confusion, or misery, then their factions occasioned.

The President seeing the desire those Braves had to rule;
seeing how his authoritie was so unexpectedly changed, would
willingly have left all, and have returned for England. But
seeing there was small hope this new Commission would arrive,
longer he would not suffer those factious spirits to proceede. It
would be too tedious, too strange, and almost incredible;
should I particularly relate the infinite dangers, plots, and practices, he daily escaped amongst this factious crew; the chiefe
whereof he quickly layd by the heeles, till his leasure better

Mutinies.

served to doe them justice: and to take away all occasions of
further mischiefe, Master Percie had his request granted to
returne for England, being very sicke; and Master West with
an hundred and twentie of the best he could chuse, he sent to
the Falles; Martin with neare as many to Nand-
*The planting
Nandsamund.* samund, with their due proportions of all provisions
according to their numbers.

Now the Presidents yeare being neare expired, he made Captaine Martin President to follow the order for the election of a
President every yeare: but he knowing his owne insufficiency,
and the companies untowardnesse and little regard of him,
within three houres after resigned it againe to Captaine Smith,
and at Nandsamund thus proceeded. The people being contributers used him kindly; yet such was his jealous feare, in the
The breach midst of their mirth, he did surprise this poore naked
of peace with King, with his Monuments, houses, and the Isle he
the Salvages. inhabited, and there fortified himselfe; but so apparantly distracted with feare, as imboldened the Salvages to assault him, kill his men, release their King, gather and carry away
a thousand bushels of Corne, he not once offering to intercept
them; but sent to the President then at the Falles for thirtie
good shot; which from James Towne immediately was sent him.
But he so well imployed them they did just nothing, but returned complaining of his tendernesse: yet he came away with
them to James Towne, leaving his company to their fortunes.

Here I cannot omit the courage of George Forrest, that had
seaventeene Arrowes sticking in him, and one shot through
him, yet lived sixe or seaven dayes, as if he had small hurt, then
for want of Chirurgery dyed.

Master West having seated his men by the Falles, presently
returned to revisit James Towne: the President followed him to
see that company seated; met him by the way, wondering at his
so quicke returne; and found his company planted so inconsiderately, in a place not onely subject to the rivers inundation,
but round invironed with many intollerable inconveniences.

Powhatan For remedie whereof he presently sent to Pow-
bought for hatan to sell him the place called Powhatan, pro-
Copper. mising to defend him against the Monacans. And
these should be his Conditions (with his people) to resigne him
the Fort and houses, and all that Countrey for a proportion of

Copper; that all stealing offenders should be sent him, there to receive their punishment; that every house as a Custome should pay him a Bushell of Corne for an inch square of Copper, and a proportion of *Pocones*, as a yearely tribute to King James for their protection, as a dutie; what else they could spare to barter at their best discretions.

But both this excellent place and those good Con-
ditions did those furies refuse, contemning both him, his kinde care and authoritie. So much they depended on the Lord Generals new Commission, as they regarded none: the worst they could doe to shew their spights they did; supposing all the Monacans Country, gold; and none should come there but whom they pleased. I doe more then wonder to thinke how onely with five men, he either durst or would adventure as he did, (knowing how greedie they were of his bloud) to land amongst them, and commit to imprisonment
all the Chieftaines of those mutinies, till by their multitudes being an hundred and twentie they forced him to retyre: yet in that interim he surprised one of their Boates, wherewith he returned to their ship; where in deed was their provision, which also he tooke, and well it chanced he found the Marriners so tractable and constant, or there had beene small possibilitie he had ever escaped. There were divers other of better reason and experience, that from their first landing, hearing the generall good report of his old Souldiers, and seeing with their eyes his actions so well mannaged with discretion, as Captaine Wood, Captaine Webbe, Captaine Moone, Captaine FitzJames, Master William Powell, Master Partridge, Master White, and divers others, when they perceived the malice of Ratliffe and Archer, and their faction, left their companies, and ever rested his faithfull friends. But the worst was that the poore Salvages, that daily brought in their contribution to the President, that disorderly company so tormented those poore soules, by stealing their
corne, robbing their gardens, beating them, breaking their houses and keeping some prisoners; that they daily complained to Captaine Smith, he had brought them for Protectors, worse enemies then the Monacans themselves: which though till then, for his love they had endured, they desired pardon if hereafter they defended themselves;

since he would not correct them, as they had long expected he would. So much they importuned him to punish their misdemeanors, as they offered (if he would leade them) to fight for him against them. But having spent nine dayes in seeking to reclaime them; shewing them how much they did abuse themselves with these great guilded hopes of the South Sea Mines, commodities, or victories, they so madly conceived; then seeing nothing would prevaile, he set sayle for James Towne.

Thus oft we see from small greene wounds, and from a little griefe,
A greater sore and sicknesse growes, then will admit reliefe:
For thus themselves they did beguile, and with the rest play'd theefe.

Now no sooner was the Ship under sayle, but the Salvages assaulted those hundred and twentie in their Fort, finding some stragling abroad in the woods: they slew many, and so affrighted the rest, as their prisoners escaped, and they safely retyred, with the swords and cloakes of those they had slaine. But ere wee had sayled halfe a league, our ship grounding, gave us once more libertie to summon them to a parley; where we found them all so strangely amazed with this poore silly assault of twelve Salvages, that they submitted themselves upon any tearmes to the Presidents mercy; who presently put by the heeles six or seaven of the chiefe offenders: the rest he seated gallantly at Powhatan, in that Salvage Fort, readie built, and prettily fortified with poles and barkes of trees, sufficient to have defended them from all the Salvages in Virginia, dry houses for lodgings and neere two hundred acres of ground ready to be planted, and no place we knew so strong, so pleasant and delightfull in Virginia for which we called it Non-such. The Salvages also hee presently appeased, redelivering to either party their former losses. Thus all were friends.

An assalt by the Salvages

The planting of Non-such.

New officers appointed to command, and the President againe ready to depart, at that instant arrived Captaine West, whose gentle nature (by the perswasions and compassion of those mutinous prisoners, alledging they had onely done this for his honor) was so much abused, that to regaine their old hopes, new turboyles did arise. For they a-shore being possessed of all there victuall, munition, and every thing, grew to that height in their former

The Salvages appeased.

factions, as the President left them to their fortunes: they returned againe to the open ayre at Wests Fort, abandoning Non-such, and he to James towne with his best expedition, but this hapned him in that Journey.

Sleeping in his Boate, (for the ship was returned two daies before) accidentallie, one fired his powder-bag, which tore the flesh from his body and thighes, nine or ten inches square in a most pittifull manner; but to quench the tormenting fire, frying him in his cloaths he leaped over-boord into the deepe river, where ere they could recover him he was neere drowned. In this estate without either Chirurgian, or Chirurgery he was to goe neere an hundred myles. Arriving at James towne, causing all things to be prepared for peace or warres to obtaine provision, whilest those things were providing, Ratliffe, Archer, and the rest of their Confederates, being to come to their trials; their guiltie consciences, fearing a just reward for their deserts, seeing the President, unable to stand, and neere bereft of his senses by reason of his torment, they had plotted to have murdered him in his bed. But his heart did faile him that should have given fire to that mercilesse Pistoll. So not finding that course to be the best, they joyned together to usurpe the government, thereby to escape their punishment. The President, had notice of their projects, the which to withstand, though his old souldiers importuned him but permit them to take their heads that would resist his command, yet he would not suffer them, but sent for the Masters of the ships, and tooke order with them for his returne for England. Seeing there was neither Chirurgian, nor Chirurgery in the Fort to cure his hurt, and the ships to depart the next day, his Commission to be suppressed he knew not why, himselfe and souldiers to be rewarded he knew not how, and a new commission granted they knew not to whom (the which disabled that authority he had, as made them presume so oft to those mutinies as they did:) besides so grievous were his wounds, and so cruell his torments (few expecting he could live) nor was hee able to follow his busines to regaine what they had lost, suppresse those factions, and range the countries for provision as he intended; and well he knew in those affaires his owne actions and presence was as requisit as his directions, which now could not be, he went presently abroad, resolving there to appoint them governours, and to take order for the mutiners, but he could fade none hee thought fit for it would accept it. In the meanetime, seeing him gone, they perswaded Master Percy to stay, who was then to goe for England, and be their President.

The causes why Smith left the Countrey and his Commission. Within lesse then an houre was this mutation begun and concluded. For when the Company understood Smith would leave them, and saw the rest in Armes called Presidents and Councellors, divers began to fawne on those new commanders, that now bent all their wits to get him resigne them his Commission: who after much adoe and many bitter repulses; that their confusion (which he tould them was at their elbowes) should not be attributed to him, for leaving the Colony without a Commission, he was not unwilling they should steale it, but never would he give it to such as they.

And thus,

> Strange violent forces drew us on unwilling:
> Reason perswading 'gainst our loves rebelling.
> We saw and knew the better, ah curse accurst!
> That notwithstanding we imbrace the worst.

But had that unhappie blast not hapned, he would quickly have qualified the heate of those humors, and factions, had the ships but once left them and us to our fortunes; and have made that provision from among the Salvages, as we neither feared Spanyard, Salvage, nor famine; nor would have left Virginia, nor our lawfull authoritie, but at as deare a price as we had bought it, and payd for it. What shall I say but thus, we left him, that in all his proceedings, made Justice his first guide, and experience his second, even hating basenesse, sloath, pride, and indignitie, more then any dangers; that never allowed more for himselfe, then his souldiers with him; that upon no danger would send them where he would not lead them himselfe; that would never see us want, what he either had, or could by any meanes get us; that would rather want then borrow, or starve then not pay; that loved action more then words, and hated falshood and covetousnesse worse then death; whose adventures were our lives, and whose losse our deaths.

Leaving us thus with three ships, seaven boats, commodities

readie to trade, the harvest newly gathered, ten weeks provision in the store, foure hundred nintie and od persons, twentie-foure Peeces of Ordnance, three hundred Muskets, Snaphances, and Firelockes, Shot, Powder, and Match sufficient, Curats, Pikes, Swords, and Morrions, more then men; the Salvages, their language, and habitations well knowne to an hundred well trayned and expert Souldiers; Nets for fishing; Tooles of all sorts to worke; apparell to supply our wants; six Mares and a Horse; five or sixe hundred Swine; as many Hennes and Chickens; some Goats; some sheepe; what was brought or bred there remained. But they regarding nothing but from hand to mouth, did consume that wee had, tooke care for nothing, but to perfect some colourable complaints against Captaine Smith. For effecting whereof three weekes longer they stayed the Ships, till they could produce them. That time and charge might much better have beene spent, but it suted well with the rest of their discretions.

Besides James towne that was strongly Pallizadoed, containing some fiftie or sixtie houses, he left five or sixe other severall Forts and Plantations: though they were not so sumptuous as our successors expected, they were better then they provided any for us. All this time we had but one Carpenter in the Countrey, and three others that could doe little, but desired to be learners: two Blacksmiths; two saylers, and those we write labourers were for most part footmen, and such as they that were Adventurers brought to attend them, or such as they could perswade to goe with them, that never did know what a dayes worke was, except the Dutch-men and Poles, and some dozen other. For all the rest were poore Gentlemen, Tradsmen, Serving-men, libertines, and such like, ten times more fit to spoyle a Common-wealth, then either begin one, or but helpe to maintaine one. For when neither the feare of God, nor the law, nor shame, nor displeasure of their friends could rule them here, there is small hope ever to bring one in twentie of them ever to be good there. Notwithstanding, I confesse divers amongst them, had better mindes and grew much more industrious then was expected: yet ten good workemen would have done more substantiall worke in a day, then ten of them in a weeke. Therefore men may rather wonder how we could doe so much, then use us so badly, because we did no more, but leave those examples to make others beware, and the fruits of all, we know not for whom.

The ends of the Dutch-men. But to see the justice of God upon these Dutch-men; Valdo before spoke of, made a shift to get for England, where perswading the Merchants what rich Mines he had found, and great service he would doe them, was very well rewarded, and returned with the Lord La Warre: but being found a meere Imposter, he dyed most miserably. Adam and Francis his two consorts were fled againe to Pow-hatan, to whom they promised at the arrivall of my Lord, what wonders they would doe, would he suffer them but to goe to him. But the King seeing they would be gone, replyed; You that have betrayed Captaine Smith to mee, will certainely be-tray me to this great Lord for your peace: so caused his men to beat out their braines.

To conclude, the greatest honour that ever belonged to the greatest Monarkes, was the inlarging their Dominions, and erecting Common-weales. Yet howsoever any of them have at-tributed to themselves, the Conquerors of the world: there is more of the world never heard of them, then ever any of them all had in subjection: for the Medes, Persians, and Assyrians, never Conquered all Asia, nor the Grecians but part of Europe and Asia. The Romans indeed had a great part of both, as well as Affrica: but as for all the Northerne parts of Europe and Asia, the interior Southern and Westerne parts of Affrica, all America and Terra incognita, they were all ignorant: nor is our knowl-edge yet but superficiall. That their beginnings, ending, and limitations were proportioned by the Almightie is most evi-dent: but to consider of what small meanes many of them have begun is wonderfull. For some write that even Rome her selfe, during the Raigne of Romulus, exceeded not the number of a thousand houses. And Carthage grew so great a Potentate, that at first was but incirculed in the thongs of a Bulls skinne, as to fight with Rome for the Empire of the world. Yea Venice at this time the admiration of the earth, was at first but a Marish, inhabited by poore Fishermen. And likewise Ninivie, Thebes, Babylon, Delus, Troy, Athens, Mycena and Sparta, grew from small beginnings to be most famous States, though now they retaine little more then a naked name. Now this our yong Common-wealth in Virginia, as you have read once consisted but of 38 persons, and in two yeares increased but to 200. yet by this small meanes so highly was approved the Plantation in Virginia, as how many Lords, with worthy Knights, and brave Gentlemen pretended to see it, and some did, and now after the expence of fifteene yeares more, and such massie summes of men and money, grow they disanimated? If we truely consider our Proceedings with the Spanyards, and the rest, we have no reason to despayre, for with so small charge, they never had either greater Discoveries, with such certaine tryals of more severall Commodities, then in this short time hath beene returned from Virginia, and by much lesse meanes. New England was brought out of obscuritie, and affoorded fraught for neare 200 sayle of ships, where there is now erected a brave Plantation. For the happines of Summer Isles, they are no lesse then either, and yet those have had a far lesse, and a more difficult beginning, then either Rome, Carthage, or Venice.

Written by Richard Pots, Clarke of the Councell,
William Tankard, and G.P.

Now seeing there is thus much Paper here to spare, that you should not be altogether cloyed with Prose; such Verses as my worthy Friends bestowed upon New England, I here present you, because with honestie I can neither reject, nor omit their courtesies.

In the deserved Honour of the Author,
Captaine John Smith, and his Worke.

Damn'd Envie *is a sp'rite, that ever haunts*
Beasts, mis-nam'd Men; Cowards, or Ignorants.
But, onely such shee followes, whose deare WORTH
(Maugre her malice) sets their glory forth.
If this faire Overture, then, take not; It
Is Envie's *spight (deare friend) in men of wit;*
Or Feare, *lest morsels, which our mouthes possesse,*
Might fall from thence; or else, tis Sottishnesse.
If either; (I hope neither) thee they raise;

Thy *Letters are as Letters in thy praise;
Who, by their vice, improve *(when they* reproove)
Thy vertue; so, in hate, procure thee Love.
Then, On firme Worth: this Monument I frame;
Scorning for any Smith to forge *such* fame.

       John Davies, Herefordshire

*Hinderers.

To his worthy Captaine the Author,

That which wee call the subject of all Storie,
Is Truth: which in this Worke of thine gives glorie
To all that thou hast done. Then, scorne the spight
Of Envie; *which doth no mans Merits right.*
My sword may helpe the rest: my Pen no more
Can doe, but this; I'ave said enough before.

  Your sometime Souldier, J. Codrinton, now Templer.

To my Worthy Friend and Cosen, Captaine John Smith.

It over-joyes my heart, when as thy Words
Of these designes, with deeds I doe compare.
Here is a Booke, such worthy truth affords,
None should the due desert thereof impare:
Sith thou, the man, deserving of these Ages,
Much paine hast ta'en for this our Kingdomes good,
In Climes unknowne, 'Mongst Turks and Salvages,
T'inlarge our bounds; though with thy losse of blood.
Hence damn'd Detraction: stand not in our way.
Envie, it selfe, will not the Truth gainesay.

       N. Smith.

In the deserved Honour of my honest and worthy Captaine, John Smith, and his Worke.

Captaine and friend; when I peruse thy Booke
(With Judgements eyes) into my heart I looke:
And there I finde (what sometimes Albion knew)
A Souldier, to his Countries-honour, true.
Some fight for wealth; and some for emptie praise;
But thou alone thy Countries Fame to raise.
With due discretion, and undanted heart,
I (oft) so well have seene thee act thy Part
In deepest plunge of hard extreamitie,
As forc't the troups of proudest foes to flie.
Though men of greater Ranke and lesse desert
Would Pish-away thy Praise, it can not start
From the true Owner: for, all good mens tongues
Shall keepe the same. To them that Part belongs.
If, then, Wit, Courage, and Successe should get
Thee Fame; the Muse for that is in thy debt:
A part whereof (least able though I be)
Thus here I doe disburse, to honor Thee.

Raleigh Crashaw.

Michael Phettiplace, William Phettiplace, and Richard Wiffing, Gentlemen, and Souldiers under Captaine Smiths command: In his deserved honour for his Worke, and Worth.

Why may not wee in this Worke have our Mite,
That had our share in each black day and night,
When thou Virginia foild'st, yet kept'st unstaind;
And held'st the King of Paspeheh enchaind.
Thou all alone this Salvage sterne didst take.
     Pamaunkees King wee saw thee captive make
Among seaven hundred of his stoutest men,
To murther thee and us resolved; when
Fast by the hayre thou ledst this Salvage grim,
Thy Pistoll at his breast to governe him:

Which did infuse such awe in all the rest
(Sith their drad Soveraigne thou had'st so distrest)
That thou and wee (poore sixteene) safe retir'd
Unto our helplesse Ships. *Thou (thus admir'd)*
Didst make proud Powhatan, *his subjects send*
To James *his Towne, thy censure to attend:*
And all Virginia's *Lords, and pettie Kings,*
Aw'd by thy venue, crouch, and Presents brings
To gaine thy grace; so dreaded thou hast beene:
And yet a heart more milde is seldome seene;
So, making Valour Vertue, really;
Who hast nought in thee counterfeit, or slie;
If in the sleight be not the truest Art,
That makes men famoused for faire desert.

Who saith of thee, this savors of vaine glorie,
Mistakes both thee and us, and this true Storie.
If it be ill in Thee, so well to doe;
Then, is ill in Us, to praise thee too.
But, if the first be well done; it is well,
To say it doth (if so it doth) excell.
Praise is the guerdon of each deare desert
Making the praised act the praised part
With more alacritie : Honours *Spurre is* Praise;
Without which, it (regardlesse) soone decaies.

And for this paines of thine wee praise thee rather,
That future Times may know who was the father
Of that rare Worke (New England) *which may bring,*
Praise to thy God, *and profit to thy* King.

The Fourth Booke.

TO MAKE PLAINE THE
TRUE PROCEEDINGS

of the Historie for 1609. we must follow the
examinations of Doctor Simons, and two
learned Orations published by the Companie;
with the relation of the Right Honourable
the Lord De la Ware.

*What happened in the first government after the
alteration in the time of Captaine George Piercie
their Governour.*

The planting
Point
Comfort. THE day before Captaine Smith returned for England with the ships, Captaine Davis arrived in
a small Pinace, with some sixteene proper men more:
To these were added a company from James towne, under the
command of Captaine John Sickelmore alias Ratliffe, to inhabit Point Comfort. Captaine Martin and Captaine
West, having lost their boats and neere halfe their
men among the Salvages, were returned to James
towne; for the Salvages no sooner understood Smith was gone,
but they all revolted, and did spoile and murther all they incountered. Now wee were all constrained to live onely on that
Smith had onely for his owne Companie, for the rest had consumed their proportions, and now they had twentie Presidents
with all their appurtenances: Master Piercie our new President,
was so sicke hee could neither goe nor stand. But ere all was
consumed, Captaine West and Captaine Sickelmore, each with
a small ship and thirtie or fortie men well appointed, sought
abroad to trade. Sickelmore upon the confidence of Powhatan,
with about thirtie others as carelesse as himselfe, were all
slaine, onely Jeffrey Shortridge escaped, and Pokahontas the
Kings daughter saved a boy called Henry Spilman, that lived
many yeeres after, by her meanes, amongst the Patawomekes.

1609 (margin note)

Powhatan still as he found meanes, cut off their Boats, denied them trade, so that Captaine West set saile for England. Now we all found the losse of Captaine Smith, yea his greatest maligners could now curse his losse: as for corne, provision and contribution from the Salvages, we had nothing but mortall wounds, with clubs and arrowes; as for our Hogs, Hens, Goats, Sheepe, Horse, or what lived, our commanders, officers and Salvages daily consumed them, some small proportions sometimes we tasted, till all was devoured; then swords, armes, pieces, or any thing, wee traded with the Salvages, whose cruell fingers were so oft imbrewed in our blouds, that what by their crueltie, our Governours indiscretion, and the losse of our ships, of five hundred within six moneths after Captaine Smiths departure, there remained not past sixtie men, women and children, most miserable and poore creatures; and those were preserved for the most part, by roots, herbes, acornes, walnuts, berries, now and then a little fish: they that had startch in these extremities, made no small use of it; yea, even the very skinnes of our horses. Nay, so great was our famine, that a Salvage we slew, and buried, the poorer sort tooke him up againe and eat him, and so did divers one another boyled and stewed with roots and herbs: And one amongst the rest did kill his wife, powdered her, and had eaten part of her before it was knowne, for which hee was executed, as hee well deserved; now whether shee was better roasted, boyled or carbonado'd, I know not, but of such a dish as powdered wife I never heard of. This was that time, which still to this day we called the starving time; it were too vile to say, and scarce to be beleeved, what we endured: but the occasion was our owne, for want of providence, industrie and government, and not the barrennesse and defect of the Countrie, as is generally supposed; for till then in three yeeres, for the numbers were landed us, we had never from England provision sufficient for six moneths, though it seemed by the bils of loading sufficient was sent us, such a glutton is the Sea, and such good fellowes the Mariners; we as little tasted of the great proportion sent us, as they of our want and miseries, yet notwithstanding they ever overswayed and ruled the businesse, though we endured all that is said, and chiefly lived on what this good Countrie naturally afforded; yet had wee beene even in Paradice it selfe with these

Governours, it would not have beene much better with us; yet there was amongst us, who had they had the government as Captaine Smith appointed, but that they could not maintaine it, would surely have kept us from those extremities of miseries. This in ten daies more, would have supplanted us all with death.

The arrivall of Sir Thomas Gates. But God that would not this Countrie should be unplanted, sent Sir Thomas Gates, and Sir George Sommers with one hundred and fiftie people most happily preserved by the Bermudas to preserve us: strange it is to say how miraculously they were preserved in a leaking ship, as at large you may reade in the insuing Historie of those Ilands.

The Government resigned to Sir Thomas Gates, 1610.

1610. WHEN these two Noble Knights did see our miseries, being but strangers in that Countrie, and could understand no more of the cause, but by conjecture of our clamours and complaints, of accusing and excusing one another: They embarked us with themselves, with *James towne abandoned.* the best meanes they could, and abandoning James towne, set saile for England, whereby you may see the event of the government of the former Commanders left to themselves; although they had lived there many yeeres as formerly hath beene spoken (who hindred now their proceedings, Captaine Smith being gone.)

At noone they fell to the Ile of Hogs, and the next morning to Mulbery point, at what time they descried the Long-boat of the Lord la Ware, for God would not have it so abandoned. For this honourable Lord, then Governour of the Countrie, met them with three ships exceedingly well furnished with all necessaries fitting, who againe returned them to the abandoned James towne.

Out of the observations of
William Simmons Doctor of Divinitie.

The government devolved to the Lord la Ware.

His Lordship arrived the ninth of June 1610. accompanied with Sir Ferdinando Waynman, Captaine Houlcroft, Captaine Lawson, and divers other Gentlemen of sort; the tenth he came up with his fleet, went on shore, heard a Sermon, read his Commission, and entred into consultation for the good of the Colonie, in which secret counsell we will a little leave them, that we may duly observe the revealed counsell of God. Hee that shall but turne up his eie, and behold the spangled canopie of heaven, or shall but cast downe his eie, and consider the embroydered carpet of the earth, and withall shall marke how the heavens heare the earth, and the earth the Corne and Oile, and they relieve the necessities of man, that man will acknowledge Gods infinite providence: But hee that shall further observe, how God inclineth all casuall events to worke the necessary helpe of his Saints, must needs adore the Lords infinite goodnesse; never had any people more just cause, to cast themselves at the very footstoole of God, and to reverence his mercie, than this distressed Colonie; for if God had not sent Sir Thomas Gates from the Bermudas, within foure daies they had almost beene famished; if God had not directed the heart of that noble Knight to save the Fort from fiering at their shipping, for many were very importunate to have burnt it, they had beene destitute of a present harbour and succour: if they had abandoned the Fort any longer time, and had not so soone returned, questionlesse the Indians would have destroied the Fort, which had beene the meanes of our safeties amongst them and a terror. If they had set saile sooner, and had lanched into the vast Ocean, who would have promised they should have incountered the Fleet of the Lord la Ware, especially when they made for New found land, as they intended, a course contrarie to our Navie approaching. If the Lord la Ware had not brought with him a yeeres provision, what comfort would those poore soules have received, to have beene relanded to a second distruction? This was the arme of the Lord of Hosts, who would have his people passe the red Sea and Wildernesse, and then to possesse the land of Canaan: It was divinely spoken of Heathen

Socrates, If God for man be carefull, why should man bee over-distrustfull? for he hath so tempered the contrary qualities of the Elements,

That neither cold things want heat, nor moist things dry,
Nor sad things spirits, to quicken them thereby,
Yet make they musicall content of contrarietie,
Which conquer'd, knits them in such links together,
They doe produce even all this whatsoever.

The Lord Governour, after mature deliberation, delivered some few words to the Companie, laying just blame upon them, for their haughtie vanities and sluggish idlenesse, earnestly intreating them to amend those desperate follies, lest hee should be compelled to draw the sword of Justice, and to cut off such delinquents, which he had rather draw, to the shedding of his vitall bloud, to protect them from injuries; heartning them with relation of that store hee had brought with him, constituting officers of all conditions, to rule over them, allotting every man his particular place, to watch vigilantly, and worke painfully: This Oration and direction being received with a generall applause, you might shortly behold the idle and restie diseases of a divided multitude, by the unitie and authoritie of this government to be substantially cured. Those that knew not the way to goodnesse before, but cherished singularitie and faction, can now chalke out the path of all respective dutie and service: every man endevoureth to outstrip other in diligence: the French preparing to plant the Vines, the English labouring in the Woods and grounds; every man knoweth his charge, and dischargeth the same with alacritie. Neither let any man be discouraged, by the relation of their daily labour (as though the sap of their bodies should bee spent for other mens profit) the setled times of working, to effect all themselves, or as the Adventurers need desire, required no more paines than from six of the clocke in the morning, untill ten, and from two in the afternoone, till foure, at both which times they are provided of spirituall and corporall reliefe. First, they enter into the Church, and make their praiers unto God, next they returne to their houses and receive their proportion of food. Nor should it bee conceived that this businesse excludeth Gentlemen whose breeding never knew what a daies labour meant, for though they cannot digge, use the Spade, nor practice the Axe, yet may the staied spirits of any condition, finde how to imploy the force of knowledge, the exercise of counsell, the operation and power of their best breeding and qualities. The houses which are built, are as warme and defensive against wind and weather, as if they were tiled and slated, being covered above with strong boards, and some matted round with Indian mats. Our forces are now such as are able to tame the furie and trecherie of the Salvages: Our Forts assure the Inhabitants, and frustrate all assaylants. And to leave no discouragement in the heart of any, who personally shall enter into this great action, I will communicate a double comfort; first, Sir George Sommers, that worthy Admirall hath undertaken a dangerous adventure for the good of the Colonie.

Sir George Sommers returne to the Bermudas.

Upon the 15. of June, accompanied with Captaine Samuel Argall, hee returned in two Pinaces unto the Bermudas, promising (if by any meanes God will open a way to that Iland of Rocks) that he would soone returne with six moneths provision of flesh; with much crosse weather at last hee there safely arrived, but Captaine Argall was forced backe againe to James towne, whom the Lord De la Ware not long after sent to the River of Patawomeke, to trade for Corne; where finding an English boy, one Henry Spilman, a young Gentleman well descended, by those people preserved from the furie of Powhatan, by his acquaintance had such good usage of those kinde Salvages, that they fraughted his ship with Corne, wherewith he returned to James towne.

The other comfort is, that the Lord la Ware hath built two new Forts, the one called Fort Henry, the other Fort Charles, in honour of our most noble Prince, and his hopefull brother, upon a pleasant plaine, and neare a little Rivilet they call Southampton River; they stand in a wholsome aire, having plentie of Springs of sweet water, they command a great circuit of ground, containing Wood, Pasture and Marsh, with apt places for Vines, Corne and Gardens; in which Forts it is resolved, that all those that come out of England, shall be at their first landing quartered, that the wearisomnesse of the Sea, may bee refreshed in this pleasing part of the Countrie, and Sir Thomas Gates hee sent for England. But to correct some injuries of the Paspahegs, he sent Captaine

The building Fort Henry and Fort Charles.

Pearcie, Master Stacy, and fiftie or threescore shot, where the Salvages flying, they burnt their houses, tooke the Queene and her children prisoners, whom not long after they slew.

The fertilitie of the soile, the temperature of the climate, the forme of government, the condition of our people, their daily invocating of the Name of God being thus expressed; why should the successe, by the rules of mortall judgement, bee disparaged? why should not the rich harvest of our hopes be seasonably expected? I dare say, that the resolution of Cæsar in France, the designes of Alexander, the discoveries of Hernando Cortes in the West, and of Emanuel, King of Portugal, in the East, were not encouraged upon so firme grounds of state and possibilitie.

But his Lordship being at the fales, the Salvages assaulted his troopes and slew three or foure of his men. Not long after, his Honour growing very sicke, he returned for England the 28. of March; in the ship were about five and fiftie men, but ere we arrived at Fyall, fortie of us were neare sicke to death, of the Scurvie, Callenture, and other diseases: the Governour being an English-man, kindly used us, but small reliefe we could get, but Oranges, of which we had plenty, whereby within eight daies wee recovered, and all were well and strong by that they came into England.

Written by William Box.

The Counsell of Virginia finding the smalnesse of that returne which they hoped should have defrayed the charge of a new supply, entred into a deep consultation, whether it were fit to enter into a new Contribution, or in time to send for them home, and give over the action, and therefore they adjured Sir Thomas Gates to deale plainly with them, who with a solemne and a sacred oath replyed, That all things before reported were true, and that all men know that wee stand at the devotion of politicke Princes and States, who for their proper utilitie, devise all courses to grind our Merchants, and by all pretences to confiscate their goods, and to draw from us all manner of gaine by their inquisitive inventions, when in Virginia, a few yeeres labour by planting and husbandry, will furnish all our defects with honour and securitie.

Out of a Declaration published by the Counsell, 1610.

*The government left againe to Captaine George Piercie,
and the returne of the Lord la Ware,
with his Relation to the Councell.*

1611.
Sir Thomas
Smith
Treasurer.

My Lords, now by accident returned from my charge at Virginia, contrary either to my owne desire, or other mens expectations, who spare not to censure me, in point of dutie, and to discourse and question the reason, though they apprehend not the true cause of my returne, I am forced out of a willingnesse to satisfie every man,

The Relation
of the Lord la
Ware.

to deliver unto your Lordships and the rest of this assemblie, in what state I have lived ever since my arrivall to the Colonie, what hath beene the just cause of my sudden departure, and on what tearmes I have left the same, the rather because I perceive, that since my comming into England, such a coldnesse and irresolution is bred in many of the Adventurers, that some of them seeke to withdraw their payments, by which the action must be supported, making this my returne colour of their needlesse backwardnesse and unjust protraction: which that you may the better understand, I was welcomed to James towne by a violent ague; being cured of it, within three weekes after I began to be distempered with other grievous sicknesses which successively and severally assailed me, for besides a relapse into the former disease, which with much more violence held me more than a moneth, and brought me to greater weaknesse; the flux surprised mee, and kept me many daies, then the crampe assaulted my weake body with strong paines, and after, the gout; all those drew me to that weaknesse, being unable to stirre, brought upon me the scurvie, which though in others it be a sicknesse of slothfulnesse, yet was it in me an effect of weaknesse, which never left me, till I was ready to leave the world.

In these extremities I resolved to consult with my friends, who finding nature spent in me, and my body almost consumed, my paines likewise daily increasing, gave me advice to preferre a hopefull recoverie, before an assured ruine, which must necessarily have ensued, had I lived but twentie daies longer in Virginia, wanting at that instant both food and Physicke, fit to remedie such extraordinary diseases; wherefore I shipped my

selfe with Doctor Bohun and Captaine Argall, for Mevis in the
West Indies, but being crossed with Southerly winds, I was
forced to shape my course for the Westerne Iles, where I found
helpe for my health, and my sicknesse asswaged, by the meanes
of fresh dyet, especially Oranges and Limons, an undoubted
remedie for that disease: then I intended to have returned
backe againe to Virginia, but I was advised not to hazard my
selfe, before I had perfectly recovered my strength: so I came
for England; in which accident, I doubt not but men of judgement will imagine, there would more prejudice have happened
by my death there, than I hope can doe by my returne.

For the Colony I left it to the charge of Captaine George
Piercie, a Gentleman of honour and resolution, until the comming of Sir Thomas Dale, whose Commission was likewise
to bee determined upon the arrivall of Sir Thomas Gates, according to the order your Lordships appointed: the number I
left were about two hundred, the most in health, and provided
of at least ten moneths victuall, and the Countrie people tractable and friendly. What other defects they had, I found by Sir
Thomas Gates at the Cowes; his Fleet was sufficiently furnished with supplies, but when it shall please God that Sir
Thomas Dale, and Sir Thomas Gates shall arrive in Virginia
100. Kine and with the extraordinarie supply of 100. Kine, and 200.
200. Swine
sent to Swine, besides store of other provision, for the main-
Virginia. tenance of the Colonie, there will appeare that successe in the action, as shall give no man cause of distrust, that
hath already adventured, but incourage every good minde to
further so good a worke, as will redound both to the glory of
God, to the credit of our nation, and the comfort of all those
that have beene instruments in the furthering of it.

Out of the Lord la Wares discourse,
published by Authoritie, 1611.

The government surrendred to Sir Thomas Dale,
who arrived in Virginia the tenth of May, 1611.
out of Master Hamors Booke.

BEFORE the Lord la Ware arrived in England, the Councell
and Companie had dispatched away Sir Thomas Dale with
three ships, men and cattell, and all other provisions
necessarie for a yeere; all which arrived well the tenth
of May 1611. where he found them growing againe
to their former estate of penurie, being so improvident as not to put Corne in the ground for their
bread, but trusted to the store, then furnished but with three
moneths provision; his first care therefore was to imploy all
hands about setting of Corne, at the two Forts at Kecoughtan,
Henry and Charles, whereby, the season then not fully past,
though about the end of May, wee had an indifferent crop of
good Corne.

1611.
Sir Thomas
Smith Trea-
surer.
The arrivall
of Sir
Thomas Dale.

This businesse taken order for, and the care and trust of it
committed to his under-Officers, to James towne he hastened,
where most of the companie were at their daily and
usuall works, bowling in the streets; these hee imployed about necessarie workes, as felling Timber,
repayring their houses ready to fall on their heads, and providing pales, posts and railes, to impale his purposed new towne,
which by reason of his ignorance, being but newly arrived, hee
had not resolved where to seat; therefore to better his knowledge, with one hundred men he spent some time in viewing
the River of Nansamund, in despight of the Indians then our
enemies; then our owne River to the Fales, where upon a high
land, invironed with the maine River, some twelve miles from
the Fales, by Arsahattock, he resolved to plant his new towne.

His
preparation
to build a
new towne.

It was no small trouble to reduce his people so timely to
good order, being of so ill a condition, as may well witnesse his
severitie and strict imprinted booke of Articles, then needfull
with all extremitie to be executed; now much mitigated; so as
if his Lawes had not beene so strictly executed, I see not how
the utter subversion of the Colonie should have beene prevented, witnesse Webbes and Prices designe the first yeere, since
that of Abbots, and others, more dangerous than the former.

Here I entreat your patience for an Apologie, though not a pardon. This Jeffrey Abbots, how ever this Author censures him, and the Governour executes him, I know he had long served both in Ireland and Netherlands, here hee was a Sargeant of my Companie, and I never saw in Virginia a more sufficient Souldier, lesse turbulent, a better wit, more hardy or industrious, nor any more forward to cut off them that sought to abandon the Countrie, or wrong the Colonie; how ingratefully those deserts might bee rewarded, envied or neglected, or his farre inferiors preferred to over-top him, I know not, but such occasions might move a Saint, much more a man, to an unadvised passionate impatience, but how ever, it seemes he hath beene punished for his offences, that was never rewarded

Divers mutinie suppressed.

for his deserts. And even this Summer Cole and Kitchins plot with three more, bending their course to Ocanahowan, five daies journey from us, where they report are Spaniards inhabiting. These were cut off by the Salvages, hired by us to hunt them home to receive their deserts: So as Sir Thomas Dale hath not beene so tyrannous nor severe by the halfe, as there was occasion, and just cause for it, and though the manner was not usuall, wee were rather to have regard to those, whom we would have terrified and made fearefull to commit the like offences, than to the offenders justly condemned, for amongst them so hardned in evill, the feare of a cruell, painfull and unusuall death more restraines them, than death it selfe. Thus much I have proceeded of his endevours, untill the comming of Sir Thomas Gates, in preparing himselfe to proceed as he intended.

Now in England againe to second this noble Knight, the Counsell and Companie with all possible expedition prepared for Sir Thomas Gates six tall ships, with three hundred men, and one hundred Kine and other Cattell, with munition and all other manner of provision that could be thought needfull; and about the first or second of August 1611. arrived safely at James towne.

The government returned againe to Sir Thomas Gates, 1611.

The second arrivall of Sir Thomas Gates.

THESE worthy Knights being met, after their welcoming salutations, Sir Thomas Dale acquainted him what he had done, and what he intended, which designe Sir Thomas Gates well approving, furnished him with three hundred and fiftie men, such as himselfe made choice of. In the beginning of September, 1611. hee set saile, and arrived where hee intended to build his new towne: within ten or twelve daies he had invironed it with a pale, and in honour of our noble Prince Henry, called it Henrico. The next worke he did, was building at each corner of the Towne, a high commanding Watch-house, a Church, and Store-houses; which finished, hee began to thinke upon convenient houses for himselfe and men, which with all possible speed hee could he effected, to the great content of his companie, and all the Colonie.

The building of Henrico.

This towne is situated upon a necke of a plaine rising land, three parts invironed with the maine River, the necke of land well impaled, makes it like an Ile; it hath three streets of well framed houses, a handsome Church, and the foundation of a better laid, to bee built of Bricke, besides Store-houses, Watch-houses, and such like: Upon the verge of the River there are five houses, wherein live the honester sort of people, as Farmers in England, and they keepe continuall centinell for the townes securitie. About two miles from the towne, into the Maine, is another pale, neere two miles in length from River to River, guarded with severall Commanders, with a good quantitie of Corne-ground impailed, sufficiently secured to maintaine more than I suppose will come this three yeeres.

On the other side of the River, for the securitie of the towne, is intended to be impaled for the securitie of our Hogs, about two miles and a halfe, by the name of Hope in Faith, and Coxendale, secured by five of our manner of Forts, which are but Palisadoes, called Charitie Fort, Mount Malado, a guest house for sicke people, a high seat and wholesome aire, Elisabeth Fort, and Fort Patience: And here hath Master Whitaker chosen his Parsonage, impaled a faire framed Parsonage, and one hundred acres called Rocke hall, but these are not halfe finished.

About Christmas following, in this same yeere 1611. in regard of the injurie done us by them of Apamatuck, Sir Thomas Dale, without the losse of any, except some few Salvages, tooke it and their Corne, being but five miles by land from Henrico, and considering how commodious it might be for us, resolved to possesse and plant it, and at the instant called it the new Bermudas, whereunto hee hath laid out and annexed to the belonging freedome and corporation for ever, many miles of Champian and Woodland ground in severall hundreds, as the upper and nether hundreds, Rochdale hundred, West Sherly hundred, and Digs his hundred. In the nether hundred he first began to plant, for there is the most Corne-ground, and with a pale of two miles, cut over from River to River, whereby we have secured eight English miles in compasse; upon which circuit, within halfe a mile of each other, are many faire houses already built, besides particular mens houses neere to the number of fiftie. Rochdale, by a crosse pale welnigh foure miles long, is also planted with houses along the pale, in which hundred our Hogs and Cattell have twentie miles circuit to graze in securely. The building of the Citie is referred till our harvest be in, which he intends to make a retreat against any forraigne enemie.

The building the Bermudas.

About fiftie miles from these is James towne, upon a fertill peninsula, which although formerly scandaled for an unhealthfull aire, wee finde it as healthfull as any other part of the Countrie; it hath two rowes of houses of framed timber, and some of them two stories, and a garret higher, three large Storehouses joined together in length, and hee hath newly strongly impaled the towne. This Ile, and much ground about it, is much inhabited: To Kecoughtan we accounted it fortie miles, where they live well with halfe that allowance the rest have from the store, because of the extraordinarie quantitie of Fish, Fowle and Deere; as you may reade at large in the Discoveries of Captaine Smith. And thus I have truly related unto you the present estate of that small part of Virginia wee frequent and possesse.

Since there was a ship fraughted with provision, and fortie

1612.
Sir Thomas
Smith
Treasurer.
Captaine
Argals
arrivall. men; and another since then with the like number
and provision, to stay twelve moneths in the Countrie, with Captaine Argall, which was sent not long
after. After hee had recreated and refreshed his Companie, hee was sent to the River Patawomeake, to
trade for Corne, the Salvages about us having small quarter,
but friends and foes as they found advantage and opportunitie:
But to conclude our peace, thus it happened. Captaine Argall,
having entred into a great acquaintance with Iapazaws, an old
friend of Captaine Smiths, and so to all our Nation, ever since
hee discovered the Countrie: hard by him there was Pocahontas, whom Captaine Smiths Relations intituleth the Numparell
of Virginia, and though she had beene many times a preserver
of him and the whole Colonie, yet till this accident shee was
never seene at James towne since his departure, being at Patawomeke, as it seemes, thinking her selfe unknowne, was easily
by her friend Iapazaws perswaded to goe abroad with him and
his wife to see the ship, for Captaine Argall had promised him

How
Pocahontas
was taken
prisoner. a Copper Kettle to bring her but to him, promising
no way to hurt her, but keepe her till they could
conclude a peace with her father; the Salvage for this
Copper Kettle would have done any thing, it seemed by the
Relation; for though she had seene and beene in many ships,
yet hee caused his wife to faine how desirous she was to see
one, and that hee offered to beat her for her importunitie, till
she wept. But at last he told her, if Pocahontas would goe with
her, hee was content: and thus they betraied the poore innocent Pocahontas aboord, where they were all kindly feasted in
the Cabbin. Iapazaws treading oft on the Captaines foot, to
remember he had done his part, the Captaine when he saw his
time, perswaded Pocahontas to the Gun-roome, faining to have
some conference with Iapazaws, which was onely that she
should not perceive hee was any way guiltie of her captivitie:
so sending for her againe, hee told her before her friends, she
must goe with him, and compound peace betwixt her Countrie and us, before she ever should see Powhatan, whereat the
old Jew and his wife began to howle and crie as fast as Pocahontas, that upon the Captaines faire perswasions, by degrees
pacifying her selfe, and Iapazaws and his wife, with the Kettle
and other toies, went merrily on shore, and shee to James

towne. A messenger forthwith was sent to her father, that his daughter Pocahontas he loved so dearely, he must ransome with our men, swords, peeces, tooles, etc. hee trecherously had stolne.

This unwelcome newes much troubled Powhatan, because hee loved both his daughter and our commodities well, yet it was three moneths after ere hee returned us any answer: then by the perswasion of the Councell, he returned seven of our men, with each of them an unserviceable Musket, and sent us word, that when wee would deliver his daughter, hee would make us satisfaction for all injuries done us, and give us five hundred bushels of Corne, and for ever be friends with us. That he sent, we received in part of payment, and returned him this answer: That his daughter should be well used, but we could not beleeve the rest of our armes were either lost or stolne from him, and therefore till hee sent them, we would keepe his daughter.

Seven English returned from Powhatan prisoners.

This answer, it seemed, much displeased him, for we heard no more from him a long time after, when with Captaine Argals ship, and some other vessels belonging to the Colonie, Sir Thomas Dale, with a hundred and fiftie men well appointed, went up into his owne River, to his chiefe habitation, with his daughter; with many scornfull bravado's they affronted us, proudly demanding why wee came thither; our reply was, Wee had brought his daughter, and to receive the ransome for her that was promised, or to have it perforce. They nothing dismayed thereat, told us, We were welcome if wee came to fight, for they were provided for us, but advised us, if wee loved our lives to retire; else they would use us as they had done Captaine Ratcliffe: We told them, wee would presently have a better answer; but we were no sooner within shot of the shore than they let flie their Arrowes among us in the ship.

Sir Thomas Dale his voyage to Pamaunke.

Being thus justly provoked, wee presently manned our Boats, went on shore, burned all their houses, and spoiled all they had we could finde; and so the next day proceeded higher up the River, where they demanded why wee burnt their houses, and wee, why they shot at us: They replyed, it was some stragling Salvage, with many other excuses, they intended no hurt, but were our friends: We told

A man shot in the forehead.

them, wee came not to hurt them, but visit them as friends also. Upon this we concluded a peace, and forthwith they dispatched messengers to Powhatan, whose answer, they told us, wee must expect foure and twentie houres ere the messengers could returne: Then they told us, our men were runne away for feare we would hang them, yet Powhatans men were runne after them; as for our Swords and Peeces, they should be brought us the next day, which was only but to delay time; for the next day they came not. Then we went higher, to a house of Powhatans, called Matchot, where we saw about foure hundred men well appointed; here they dared us to come on shore, which wee did; no shew of feare they made at all, nor offered to resist our landing, but walking boldly up and downe amongst us, demanded to conferre with our Captaine, of his comming in that manner, and to have truce till they could but once more send to their King to know his pleasure, which if it were not agreeable to their expectation, then they would fight with us, and defend their owne as they could, which was but onely to deferre the time, to carrie away their provision; yet wee promised them truce till the next day at noone, and then if they would fight with us, they should know when we would begin by our Drums and Trumpets.

Two of Powhatans sonnes come to see Pocahontas. Upon this promise, two of Powhatans sonnes came unto us to see their sister, at whose sight, seeing her well, though they heard to the contrarie, they much rejoiced, promising they would perswade her father to redeeme her, and for ever be friends with us. And upon this, the two brethren went aboord with us, and we sent Master John Rolfe and Master Sparkes to Powhatan, to acquaint him with the businesse; kindly they were entertained, but not admitted the presence of Powhatan, but they spoke with Opechancanough, his brother and successor; hee promised to doe the best he could to Powhatan, all might be well. So it being Aprill, and time to prepare our ground and set our Corne, we returned to James Towne, promising the forbearance of their performing their promise, till the next harvest.

The mariage of Pocahontas to Master John Rolfe. Long before this, Master John Rolfe, an honest Gentleman, and of good behaviour, had beene in love with Pocahontas, and she with him, which thing at that instant I made knowne to Sir Thomas Dale by a letter

1613.
Sir Thomas
Smith
Treasurer. from him, wherein hee intreated his advice, and she acquainted her brother with it, which resolution Sir Thomas Dale well approved: the brute of this mariage came soone to the knowledge of Powhatan, a thing acceptable to him, as appeared by his sudden consent, for within ten daies he sent Opachisco, an old Uncle of hers, and two of his sons, to see the manner of the mariage, and to doe in that behalfe what they were requested, for the confirmation thereof, as his deputie; which was accordingly done about the first of Aprill: And ever since wee have had friendly trade and commerce, as well with Powhatan himselfe, as all his subjects.

Besides this, by the meanes of Powhatan, we became in league with our next neighbours, the Chicahama-nias, a lustie and a daring people, free of themselves. These people, so soone as they heard of our peace with Powhatan, sent two messengers with presents to Sir Thomas Dale, and offered them his service, excusing all former injuries, hereafter they would ever be King James his subjects, and relinquish the name of Chickahamania, to be called Tassantessus, as they call us, and Sir Thomas Dale there Governour, as the Kings Deputie; onely they desired to be governed by their owne Lawes, which is eight of their Elders as his substitutes. This offer he kindly accepted, and appointed the day hee would come to visit them.

The Chica-hamanias desire friendship.

When the appointed day came, Sir Thomas Dale and Captaine Argall with fiftie men well appointed, went to Chickahamania, where wee found the people expecting our comming, they used us kindly, and the next morning sate in counsell, to conclude their peace upon these conditions:

Articles of Peace. First, they should for ever bee called Englishmen, and bee true subjects to King James and his Deputies.

Secondly, neither to kill nor detaine any of our men, nor cattell, but bring them home.

Thirdly, to bee alwaies ready to furnish us with three hundred men, against the Spaniards or any.

Fourthly, they shall not enter our townes, but send word they are new Englishmen.

Fiftly, that every fighting man, at the beginning of harvest, shall bring to our store two bushels of Corne, for tribute, for which they shall receive so many Hatchets.

Lastly, the eight chiefe men should see all this performed, or receive the punishment themselves: for their diligence they should have a red coat, a copper chaine, and King James his picture, and be accounted his Noblemen.

All this they concluded with a generall assent, and a great shout to confirme it: then one of the old men began an Oration, bending his speech first to the old men, then to the young, and then to the women and children, to make them understand how strictly they were to observe these conditions, and we would defend them from the furie of Powhatan, or any enemie whatsoever, and furnish them with Copper, Beads, and Hatchets; but all this was rather for feare Powhatan and we, being so linked together, would bring them againe to his subjection; the which to prevent, they did rather chuse to be protected by us, than tormented by him, whom they held a Tyrant. And thus wee returned againe to James towne.

The benefit of libertie in the planters.

When our people were fed out of the common store, and laboured jointly together, glad was he could slip from his labour, or slumber over his taske he cared not how, nay, the most honest among them would hardly take so much true paines in a weeke, as now for themselves they will doe in a day, neither cared they for the increase, presuming that howsoever the harvest prospered, the generall store must maintaine them, so that wee reaped not so much Corne from the labours of thirtie, as now three or foure doe provide for themselves. To prevent which, Sir Thomas Dale hath allotted every man three Acres of cleare ground, in the nature of Farmes, except the Bermudas, who are exempted, but for one moneths service in the yeere, which must neither bee in seed-time, nor harvest; for which doing, no other dutie they pay yeerely to the store, but two barrels and a halfe of

Ensigne Spence the first Farmer in Virginia.

Corne (from all those Farmers, whereof the first was William Spence, an honest, valiant, and an industrious man, and hath continued from 1607. to this present) from those is expected such a contribution to the store, as wee shall neither want for our selves, nor to entertaine our supplies; for the rest, they are to worke eleven moneths for the store, and hath one moneth onely allowed them to get provision to keepe them for twelve, except two bushels of

Corne they have out of the store; if those can live so, why should any feare starving, and it were much better to denie them passage, that would not ere they come, bee content to ingage themselves to those conditions: for onely from the slothfull and idle drones, and none else, hath sprung the manifold imputations, Virginia innocently hath undergone; and therefore I would deter such from comming here, that cannot well brooke labour, except they will undergoe much punishment and penurie, if they escape the skurvie: but for the industrious, there is reward sufficient, and if any thinke there is nothing but bread, I referre you to his relations that discovered the Countrie first.

The government left to Sir Thomas Dale upon Sir Thomas Gates returne for England.

Captaine Argals voyage to Port Royall.

SIR Thomas Dale understanding there was a plantation of Frenchmen in the north part of Virginia, about the degrees of 45. sent Captaine Argall to Port Royall and Sancta Crux, where finding the Frenchmen abroad dispersed in the Woods, surprized their Ship and Pinnace, which was but newly come from France, wherein was much good apparel, and other provision, which he brought to James towne, but the men escaped, and lived among the Salvages of those Countries.

1614. Sir Thomas Smith Treasurer.

It pleased Sir Thomas Dale, before my returne to England, because I would be able to speake somewhat of my owne knowledge, to give mee leave to visit Powhatan and his Court: being provided, I had Thomas Salvage with mee, for my Interpreter, with him and two Salvages for guides, I went from the Bermuda in the morning, and came to Matchot the next night, where the King lay upon the River of Pamaunke; his entertainment was strange to me, the boy he knew well, and told him; My child, I gave you leave, being my boy, to goe see your friends, and these foure yeeres I have not seene you, nor heard of my owne man Namontack I sent to England, though many ships since have beene returned thence: Having done with him, hee began with mee, and demanded for the chaine of pearle he sent his brother Sir Thomas Dale at his first arrivall, which was a token betwixt them, when ever hee should send a messenger from himselfe to him, he should weare that chaine about his necke, since the peace was concluded, otherwaies he was to binde him and send him home.

Master Hamars journey to Powhatan. It is true Sir Thomas Dale had sent him such word, and gave his Page order to give it me, but he forgot it, and till this present I never heard of it, yet I replyed I did know there was such an order, but that was when upon a sudden he should have occasion to send an Englishman without an Indian Guide; but if his owne people should conduct his messenger, as two of his did me who knew my message, it was sufficient; with which answer he was contented, and so conducted us to his house, where was a guard of two hundred Bow-men, that alwaies attend his person. The first thing he did, he offered me a pipe of Tobacco, then asked mee how his brother Sir Thomas Dale did, and his daughter, and unknowne sonne, and how they lived, loved and liked; I told him his brother was well, and his daughter so contented, she would not live againe with him; whereat he laughed, and demanded the cause of my comming: I told him my message was private, and I was to deliver it onely to himselfe and Papaschicher, one of my guides that was acquainted with it; instantly he commanded all out of the house, but onely his two Queenes, that alwaies sit by him, and bade me speake on.

His message to Powhatan. I told him, by my Interpreter, Sir Thomas Dale hath sent you two pieces of Copper, five strings of white and blue Beads, five woodden Combes, ten Fish-hookes, a paire of Knives, and that when you would send for it, hee would give you a Grind-stone; all this pleased him: but then I told him his brother Dale, hearing of the fame of his youngest daughter, desiring in any case he would send her by me unto him, in testimonie of his love, as well for that he intended to marry her, as the desire her sister had to see her, because being now one people, and hee desirous for ever to dwell in his Countrie, he conceived there could not be a truer assurance of peace and friendship, than in such a naturall band of an united union.

I needed not entreat his answer by his oft interrupting mee in my speech, and presently with much gravitie he thus replyed.

Powhatans answer.

I gladly accept your salute of love and peace, which while I live, I shall exactly keepe, his pledges thereof I receive with no lesse thanks, although they are not so ample as formerly he had received; but for my daughter, I have sold her within this few daies to a great Werowance, for two bushels of *Rawrenoke*, three daies journie from me. I replyed, I knew his greatnesse in restoring the *Rawrenoke*, might call her againe to gratifie his brother, and the rather, because she was but twelve yeeres old, assuring him, besides the band of peace, hee should have for her, three times the worth of the *Rawrenoke*, in Beads, Copper, Hatchets, etc. His answer was, he loved his daughter as his life, and though hee had many children, hee delighted in none so much as shee, whom if he should not often behold, he could not possibly live, which she living with us he could not do, having resolved upon no termes to put himselfe into our hands, or come amongst us; therefore desired me to urge him no further, but returne his brother this answer: That I desire no former assurance of his friendship, than the promise hee hath made, from me he hath a pledge, one of my daughters, which so long as she lives shall be sufficient, when she dies, he shall have another: I hold it not a brotherly part to desire to bereave me of my two children at once. Farther, tell him though he had no pledge at all, hee need not distrust any injurie from me or my people; there have beene too many of his men and mine slaine, and by my occasion there shall never be more, (I which have power to performe it, have said it) although I should have just cause, for I am now old, and would gladly end my daies in peace; if you offer me injurie, my countrie is large enough to goe from you: Thus much I hope will satisfie my brother. Now because you are wearie, and I sleepie, wee will thus end. So commanding us victuall and lodging, we rested that night, and the next morning he came to visit us, and kindly conducted us to the best cheere hee had.

William Parker recovered.

While I here remained, by chance came an Englishman, whom there had beene surprized three yeeres agoe at Fort Henry, growne so like, both in complexion and habit like a Salvage, I knew him not, but by his tongue: hee desired mee to procure his libertie, which I intended, and so farre urged Powhatan, that he grew discontented, and told mee, You have one of my daughters, and I am content, but you cannot see one of your men with mee, but you must have him away, or breake friendship; if you must needs have him, you shall goe home without guides, and if any evill befall you, thanke your selves: I told him I would, but if I returned not well, hee must expect a revenge, and his brother might have just cause to suspect him. So in passion he left me till supper, and then gave me such as hee had with a cheerefull countenance: About midnight hee awaked us, and promised in the morning my returne with Parker; but I must remember his brother to send him ten great pieces of Copper, a Shaving-knife, a Frowe, a Grind-stone, a Net, Fish-hookes, and such toies; which lest I should forget, he caused me write in a table-booke he had; how ever he got it, it was a faire one, I desired hee would give it me; he told me, no, it did him much good in shewing to strangers, yet in the morning when we departed, having furnished us well with provision, he gave each of us a Bucks skin as well dressed as could be, and sent two more to his sonne and daughter: And so we returned to James towne.

Written by Master Ralph Hamor and John Rolph.

From a letter of Sir Thomas Dale and Master Whitakers.

I have read the substance of this relation, in a Letter written by Sir Thomas Dale, another by Master Whitaker, and a third by Master John Rolfe; how carefull they were to instruct her in Christianity, and how capable and desirous shee was thereof, after she had beene some time thus tutored, shee never had desire to goe to her father, nor could well endure the society of her owne nation: the true affection she constantly bare her husband was much, and the strange apparitions and violent passions he endured for her love, as he deeply protested, was wonderful, and she openly renounced her countries idolatry, confessed the faith of Christ, and was baptized, but either the coldnesse of the adventurers, or the bad usage of that was collected, or both, caused this worthy Knight to write thus. Oh why should so many Princes and Noblemen ingage themselves, and thereby intermedling herein, have caused a number of soules transport themselves, and be transported hither? Why should they, I say, relinquish this so glorious an action: for if their ends be to build God a Church, they ought to persevere; if otherwise, yet their honour ingageth them to be constant; howsoever they stand affected, here is enough to content them. These are the things have animated me to stay a little season from them, I am bound in conscience to returne unto; leaving all contenting pleasures and mundall delights, to reside here with much turmoile, which I will rather doe than see Gods glory diminished, my King and Country dishonoured, and these poore soules I have in charge revived, which would quickly happen if I should leave them; so few I have with me fit to command or manage the businesse: Master Whitaker their Preacher complaineth, and much museth, that so few of our English Ministers, that were so hot against the surplice and subscription come hether, where neither is spoken of. Doe they not wilfully hide their talents, or keepe themselves at home, for feare of losing a few pleasures; be there not any among them of Moses his minde, and of the Apostles, that forsooke all to follow Christ, but I refer them to the Judge of all hearts, and to the King that shall reward every one according to his talent.

From Virginia, June 18. 1614.

The businesse being brought to this perfection, Captaine Argall returned for England, in the latter end of June, 1614. ariving in England, and bringing this good tidings to the Councell and company by the assistances of Sir Thomas Gates, that also had returned from Virginia but the March before; it was presently concluded, that to supply this good successe with all expedition, the standing Lottery should be drawne with all diligent conveniency, and that posterity may remember upon occasion to use the like according to the declaration, I thinke it not amisse to remember thus much.

The Contents of the declaration of the
Lottery published by the Counsell.

1615.
Sir Thomas
Smith
Treasurer. IT is apparent to the world, by how many former Proclamations, we manifested our intents, to have drawn out the great standing Lottery long before this, which not falling out as we desired, and others expected, whose monies are adventured therein, we thought good therefore for the avoiding all unjust and sinister constructions, to resolve the doubts of all indifferent minded, in three speciall points for their better satisfaction.

But ere I goe any farther, let us remember there was a running Lottery, used a long time in Saint Pauls Church-yard, where this stood, that brought into the Treasury good summes of mony dayly, though the Lot was but small.

Now for the points, the first is, for as much as the Adventurers came in so slackly for the yeere past, without prejudice to the generality, in losing the blankes and prises, we were forced to petition to the honourable Lords, who out of their noble care to further this Plantation, have recommended their Letters to the Countries, Cities, and good townes in England, which we hope by sending in their voluntary Adventurers, will sufficiently supply us.

The second for satisfaction to all honest well affected minds, is, that though this expectation answer not our hopes, yet wee have not failed in our Christian care, the good of that Colony, to whom we have lately sent two sundry supplies, and were they but now supplied with more hands, wee should soone resolve the division of the Country by Lot, and so lessen the generall charge.

The third is our constant resolution, that seeing our credits are so farre ingaged to the honourable Lords and the whole State, for the drawing this great Lottery, which we intend shall be without delay, the 26. of June next, desiring all such as have undertaken with bookes to solicit their friends, that they will not with-hold their monies till the last moneth be expired, lest we be unwillingly forced to proportion a lesse value and number of our Blankes and Prises which hereafter followeth.

Welcomes.

Crownes.

To him that first shall be drawne out with a blanke, 100
To the second,   50
To the third,   25
To him that every day during the drawing of this
    Lottery, shall bee first drawne out with a blanke, 10

Prizes.

Crownes.

1	Great Prize of	4500
2	Great Prizes, each of	2000
4	Great Prizes, each of	1000
6	Great Prizes, each of	500
10	Prizes, each of	300
20	Prizes, each of	200
100	Prizes, each of	100
200	Prizes, each of	50
400	Prizes, each of	20
1000	Prizes, each of	10
1000	Prizes, each of	8
1000	Prizes, each of	6
4000	Prizes, each of	4
1000	Prizes, each of	3
1000	Prizes, each of	2

Rewards.

Crownes

To him that shall be last drawne out with a blanke,   25
To him that putteth in the greatest Lot, under one
    name,   400
To him that putteth in the second greatest number,   300
To him that putteth in the third greatest number,   200
To him that putteth in the fourth greatest number,   100
If divers be of equall number, their rewards are
    to be divided proportionally.

Addition of new Rewards.

Crownes.

The blanke that shall bee drawne out next before
    the great Prize shall have   25

The blanke that shall be drawne out next after the
   said great Prize   25
The blancks that shall be drawne out immediatly
   before the two next great Prizes, shall have each
   of them   20
The severall blankes next after them, each shall have   20
The severall blankes next before the foure great
   Prizes, each shall have   15
The severall blankes next after them, each shall have   15
The severall blankes next before the six great Prizes,
   each shall have   10
The severall blankes next after them, each shall have   10

The prizes, welcomes, and rewards, shall be payed in ready
Mony, Plate, or other goods reasonably rated; if any dislike of
the plate or goods, he shall have mony, abating only the tenth
part, except in small prizes of ten Crownes or under.

The mony for the Adventurers is to be paied to Sir Thomas
Smith, Knight, and Treasurer for Virginia, or such Officers as
he shall apoint in City or Country, under the common seale of
the company for the receit thereof.

All prizes, welcomes and rewards drawne where ever they
dwell, shall of the Treasurer have present pay, and whosoever
under one name or poesie payeth three pound in ready money,
shall receive six shillings and eight pence, or a silver spoone of
that value at his choice.

About this time it chanced a Spanish ship, beat too
and againe before point Comfort, and at last sent a
shore their boat, as desirous of a Pilot. Captaine James
Davis the governor, immediatly gave them one, but he was no
sooner in the boat, but a way they went with him, leaving
three of their companions behind them; this sudden accident
occasioned some distrust, and a strict examination of those
three thus left, yet with as good usage as our estate could
afford them. They only confessed having lost their Admirall,
accident had forced them into those parts, and two of them
were Captaines, and in chiefe authority in the fleet, thus they
lived till one of them was found to be an Englishman, and had
been the Spaniards Pilot for England in 88. and having here induced some male-contents, to beleeve his projects, to run

A Spanish Ship in Virginia.

away with a small barke, which was apprehended, some executed, and he expecting but the Hangmans curtesie, directly
confessed that two or three Spanish ships was at Sea, purposely
to discover the estate of the Colony, but their Commission was
not to be opened till they arrived in the Bay, so that of any
thing more he was utterly ignorant. One of the Spaniards at
last dyed, the other was sent for England, but this reprieved, till
Sir Thomas Dale hanged him at Sea in his voyage homeward;
the English Pilot they carried for Spaine, whom after a long
time imprisonment, with much sute was returned for England.

1616.
Sir Thomas
Smith
Treasurer.

Whilst those things were effecting, Sir Thomas
Dale, having setled to his thinking all things in good
order, made choice of one Master George Yearly, to
be Deputy Governour in his absence, and so returned for England, accompanied with Pocahontas the Kings Daughter, and
Master Rolfe her husband, and arrived at Plimmoth the 12. of
June. 1616.

The government left to Captaine Yearly.

A digression.

Now a little to commentary upon all these proceedings, let me leave but this as a caveat by the way;
if the alteration of government hath subverted great
Empires, how dangerous is it then in the infancy of a common-
weale? The multiplicity of Governors is a great damage to any
State, but uncertaine daily changes are burdensome, because
their entertainments are chargeable, and many will make hay
whilst the sunne doth shine, how ever it shall faire with the
generality.

This deare bought Land with so much bloud and cost, hath
onely made some few rich, and all the rest losers. But it was intended at the first, the first undertakers should be first preferred and rewarded, and the first adventurers satisfied, and
they of all the rest are the most neglected; and those that never
adventured a groat, never see the Country, nor ever did any
service for it, imploied in their places, adorned with their
deserts, and inriched with their ruines; and when they are fed

fat, then in commeth others so leane as they were, who through their omnipotency doth as much. Thus what one Officer doth, another undoth, only ayming at their owne ends, thinking all the world derides his dignity, cannot fill his Coffers being in authority with any thing. Every man hath his minde free, but he can never be a true member to that estate, that to enrich himselfe beggers all the Countrie. Which bad course, there are many yet in this noble plantation, whose true honour and worth as much scornes it, as the others loves it; for the Nobilitie and Gentrie, there is scarce any of them expects any thing but the prosperitie of the action: and there are some Merchants and others, I am confidently perswaded, doe take more care and paines, nay, and at their continuall great charge, than they could be hired to for the love of money, so honestly regarding the generall good of this great worke, they would hold it worse than sacrilege, to wrong it but a shilling, or extort upon the common souldier a penny. But to the purpose, and to follow the Historie.

The government of Captaine Yearley. Master George Yearly now invested Deputie Governour by Sir Thomas Dale, applied himselfe for the most part in planting Tobacco, as the most present commoditie they could devise for a present gaine, so that every man betooke himselfe to the best place he could for the purpose: now though Sir Thomas Dale had caused such an abundance of corne to be planted, that every man had sufficient, yet the supplies were sent us, came so unfurnished, as quickly eased us of our superfluitie. To relieve their necessities, he sent to the Chickahamanias for the tribute Corne Sir Thomas Dale and Captaine Argall had conditioned for with them: But such a bad answer they returned him, that hee drew together one hundred of his best shot, with whom he went to Chickahamania; the people in some places used him indifferently, but in most places with much scorne and contempt, telling him he was but Sir Thomas Dales man, and they had payed his Master according to condition, but to give any to him they had no such order, neither would they obey him as they had done his Master; after he had told them his authoritie, and that he had the same power to enforce them that Dale had, they dared him to come on shore to fight, presuming more of his not daring, than their owne valours. Yearly seeing their insolencies, made

no great difficultie to goe on shore at Ozinies, and they as
little to incounter him: but marching from thence towards
Mamanahunt, they put themselves in the same order they
see us, lead by their Captaine Kissanacomen, Governour of
Ozinies, and so marched close along by us, each as threatning
other who should first begin. But that night we quartered
against Mamanahunt, and they passed the River. The next day
we followed them; there are few places in Virginia had then
more plaine ground together, nor more plentie of Corne,
which although it was but newly gathered, yet they had hid it
in the woods where we could not finde it: a good time we spent
thus in arguing the cause, the Salvages without feare standing
in troupes amongst us, seeming as if their countenances had
beene sufficient to dant us: what other practises they had I
know not; but to prevent the worst, our Captaine caused us all
to make ready, and upon the word, to let flie among them,
where he appointed: others also he commanded to seize on
them they could for prisoners; all which being done
according to our direction, the Captaine gave the
word, and wee presently discharged, where twelve lay,
some dead, the rest for life sprawling on the ground,
twelve more we tooke prisoners, two whereof were
brothers, two of their eight Elders, the one tooke by Sergeant
Boothe, the other by Robert a Polonian; Neere one hundred
bushels of Corne we had for their ransomes, which was promised the Souldiers for a reward, but it was not performed: now
Opechankanough had agreed with our Captaine for the sub-
jecting of those people, that neither hee nor Powhatan could
ever bring to their obedience, and that he should make no
peace with them without his advice: in our returne by Ozinies
with our prisoners wee met Opechankanough, who with much
adoe, fained with what paines hee had procured their peace,
the which to requite, they called him the King of Ozinies, and
brought him from all parts many presents of Beads, Copper,
and such trash as they had; here as at many other times wee
were beholding to Captaine Henry Spilman our Interpreter, a
Gentleman had lived long time in this Countrie, and sometimes a prisoner among the Salvages, and done much good
service, though but badly rewarded. From hence we marcht
towards James towne, we had three Boats loaded with Corne

*Twelve
Salvages
slaine, twelve
prisoners
taken, and
peace
concluded.*

and other luggage, the one of them being more willing to be at James towne with the newes than the other, was overset, and eleven men cast away with the Boat, Corne and all their provision; notwithstanding this put all the rest of the Salvages in that feare, especially in regard of the great league we had with Opechankanough, that we followed our labours quietly, and in such securitie, that divers salvages of other Nations, daily frequented us with what provisions they could get, and would guide our men on hunting, and oft hunt for us themselves. Captaine Yearly had a Salvage or two so well trained up to their peeces, they were as expert as any of the English, and one hee kept purposely to kill him fowle. There were divers others had Salvages in like manner for their men. Thus we lived together, as if wee had beene one people, all the time Captaine Yearley staied with us, but such grudges and discontents daily increased among our selves, that upon the arrivall of Captaine Argall, sent by the Councell and Companie to bee our Governour, Captaine Yearley returned for England in the yeere 1617.

Eleven men cast away.

A bad president.

From the writings of Captaine Nathaniel Powell, William Cantrill, Sergeant Boothe, Edward Gurganey.

During this time, the Lady Rebecca, alias Pocahontas, daughter to Powhatan, by the diligent care of Master John Rolfe her husband and his friends, was taught to speake such English as might well bee understood, well instructed in Christianitie, and was become very formall and civill after our English manner; shee had also by him a childe which she loved most dearely, and the Treasurer and Company tooke order both for the maintenance of her and it, besides there were divers persons of great ranke and qualitie had beene very kinde to her; and before she arrived at London, Captaine Smith to deserve her former courtesies, made her qualities knowne to the Queenes most excellent Majestie and her Court, and writ a little booke to this effect to the Queene: An abstract whereof followeth.

Pocahontas instructions.

To the most high and vertuous Princesse Queene Anne
of Great Brittanie.

Most admired Queene,

The love I beare my God, my King and Countrie, hath so
oft emboldened mee in the worst of extreme dangers, that now
honestie doth constraine mee presume thus farre beyond my
selfe, to present your Majestie this short discourse: if ingratitude be a deadly poyson to all honest vertues, I must bee guiltie
of that crime if I should omit any meanes to bee thankfull. So
it is,

A relation to   That some ten yeeres agoe being in Virginia, and
Queene   taken prisoner by the power of Powhatan their chiefe
Anne, of
Pocahontas.   King, I received from this great Salvage exceeding
great courtesie, especially from his sonne Nantaquaus, the most
manliest, comeliest, boldest spirit, I ever saw in a Salvage, and
his sister Pocahontas, the Kings most deare and wel-beloved
daughter, being but a childe of twelve or thirteene yeeres of
age, whose compassionate pitifull heart, of my desperate estate, gave me much cause to respect her: I being the first
Christian this proud King and his grim attendants ever saw:
and thus inthralled in their barbarous power, I cannot say I felt
the least occasion of want that was in the power of those my
mortall foes to prevent, notwithstanding al their threats. After
some six weeks fatting amongst those Salvage Courtiers, at the
minute of my execution, she hazarded the beating out of her
owne braines to save mine, and not onely that, but so prevailed
with her father, that I was safely conducted to James towne,
where I found about eight and thirtie miserable poore and
sicke creatures, to keepe possession of all those large territories
of Virginia, such was the weaknesse of this poore Common-
wealth, as had the Salvages not fed us, we directly had starved.

And this reliefe, most gracious Queene, was commonly
brought us by this Lady Pocahontas, notwithstanding all these
passages when inconstant Fortune turned our peace to warre,
this tender Virgin would still not spare to dare to visit us, and
by her our jarres have beene oft appeased, and our wants still
supplyed; were it the policie of her father thus to imploy her, or
the ordinance of God thus to make her his instrument, or her
extraordinarie affection to our Nation, I know not: but of
this I am sure; when her father with the utmost of his policie

and power, sought to surprize mee, having but eighteene with mee, the darke night could not affright her from comming through the irkesome woods, and with watered eies gave me intelligence, with her best advice to escape his furie; which had hee knowne, hee had surely slaine her. James towne with her wild traine she as freely frequented, as her fathers habitation; and during the time of two or three yeeres, she next under God, was still the instrument to preserve this Colonie from death, famine and utter confusion, which if in those times had once beene dissolved, Virginia might have line as it was at our first arrivall to this day. Since then, this businesse having beene turned and varied by many accidents from that I left it at: it is most certaine, after a long and troublesome warre after my departure, betwixt her father and our Colonie, all which time shee was not heard of, about two yeeres after shee her selfe was taken prisoner, being so detained neere two yeeres longer, the Colonie by that meanes was relieved, peace concluded, and at last rejecting her barbarous condition, was maried to an English Gentleman, with whom at this present she is in England; the first Christian ever of that Nation, the first Virginian ever spake English, or had a childe in mariage by an Englishman, a matter surely, if my meaning bee truly considered and well understood, worthy a Princes understanding.

Thus most gracious Lady, I have related to your Majestie, what at your best leasure our approved Histories will account you at large, and done in the time of your Majesties life, and however this might bee presented you from a more worthy pen, it cannot from a more honest heart, as yet I never begged any thing of the state, or any, and it is my want of abilitie and her exceeding desert, your birth, meanes and authoritie, hir birth, vertue, want and simplicitie, doth make mee thus bold, humbly to beseech your Majestie to take this knowledge of her, though it be from one so unworthy to be the reporter, as my selfe, her husbands estate not being able to make her fit to attend your Majestie: the most and least I can doe, is to tell you this, because none so oft hath tried it as my selfe, and the rather being of so great a spirit, how ever her stature: if she should not be well received, seeing this Kingdome may rightly have a Kingdome by her meanes; her present love to us and Christianitie, might turne to such scorne and furie, as to divert all this good to the worst of evill, where finding so great a Queene should doe her some honour more than she can imagine, for being so kinde to your servants and subjects, would so ravish her with content, as endeare her dearest bloud to effect that, your Majestie and all the Kings honest subjects most earnestly desire: And so I humbly kisse your gracious hands.

Being about this time preparing to set saile for New-England, I could not stay to doe her that service I desired, and she well deserved; but hearing shee was at Branford with divers of my friends, I went to see her:

Pocahontas meeting in England with Captaine Smith.

After a modest salutation, without any word, she turned about, obscured her face, as not seeming well contented; and in that humour her husband, with divers others, we all left her two or three houres, repenting my selfe to have writ she could speake English. But not long after, she began to talke, and remembred mee well what courtesies shee had done: saying, You did promise Powhatan what was yours should bee his, and he the like to you; you called him father being in his land a stranger, and by the same reason so must I doe you: which though I would have excused, I durst not allow of that title, because she was a Kings daughter; with a well set countenance she said, Were you not afraid to come into my fathers Countrie, and caused feare in him and all his people (but mee) and feare you here I should call you father; I tell you then I will, and you shall call mee childe, and so I will bee for ever and ever your Countrieman. They did tell us alwaies you were dead, and I knew no other till I came to Plimoth; yet Powhatan did command Uttamatomakkin to seeke you, and know the truth, because your Countriemen will lie much.

Uttamaco-mack, ob-servations of his usage.

This Salvage, one of Powhatans Councell, being amongst them held an understanding fellow; the King purposely sent him, as they say, to number the people here, and informe him well what wee were and our state. Arriving at Plimoth, according to his directions, he got a long sticke, whereon by notches hee did thinke to have kept the number of all the men hee could see, but he was quickly wearie of that taske: Comming to London, where by chance I met him, having renewed our acquaintance, where many were desirous to heare and see his behaviour, hee told me Powhatan did bid him to finde me out, to shew him our God, the King,

Queene, and Prince, I so much had told them of: Concerning God, I told him the best I could, the King I heard he had seene, and the rest hee should see when he would; he denied ever to have seene the King, till by circumstances he was satisfied he had: Then he replyed very sadly, You gave Powhatan a white Dog, which Powhatan fed as himselfe, but your King

Pocahontas her enter-tainment with the Queene. gave me nothing, and I am better than your white Dog.

The small time I staid in London, divers Courtiers and others, my acquaintances, hath gone with mee to see her, that generally concluded, they did thinke God had a great hand in her conversion, and they have seene many English Ladies worse favoured, proportioned and behavioured, and as since I have heard, it pleased both the King and Queenes Majestie honourably to esteeme her, accompanied with that honourable Lady the Lady De la Ware, and that honourable Lord her husband, and divers other persons of good qualities, both publikely at the maskes and otherwise, to her great satisfaction and content, which doubtlesse she would have deserved, had she lived to arrive in Virginia.

The government devolved to Captaine Samuel Argall, 1617.

1617. Sir Thomas Smith Treasurer. THE Treasurer, Councell and Companie, having well furnished Captaine Samuel Argall, the Lady Pocahontas alias Rebecca, with her husband and others, in the good ship called the *George*, it pleased God at Gravesend to take this young Lady to his mercie, where shee made not more sorrow for her unexpected death, than joy to the beholders, to heare and see her make so religious and godly an end. Her little childe Thomas Rolfe therefore was left

The death of Pocahontas. at Plimoth with Sir Lewis Stukly, that desired the keeping of it. Captaine Hamar his vice-Admirall was gone before, but hee found him at Plimoth. In March they set saile 1617. and in May he arrived at James towne, where hee was kindly entertained by Captaine Yearley and his Companie in a martiall order, whose right hand file was led by an Indian. In James towne he found but five or six houses, the

Church downe, the Palizado's broken, the Bridge in pieces, the Well of fresh water spoiled; the Store-house they used for the Church, the market-place, and streets, and all other spare places planted with Tobacco, the Salvages as frequent in their houses as themselves, whereby they were become expert in our armes, and had a great many in their custodie and possession, the Colonie dispersed all about, planting Tobacco. Captaine Argall not liking those proceedings, altered them agreeable to his owne minde, taking the best order he could for repairing those defects which did exceedingly trouble us; we were constrained every yeere to build and repaire our old Cottages, which were alwaies a decaying in all places of the Countrie, yea, the very Courts of Guard built by Sir Thomas Dale, was ready to fall, and the Palizado's not sufficient to keepe out Hogs. Their number of people were about 400. but not past 200. fit for husbandry and tillage: we found there in all one hundred twentie eight cattell, and fourescore and eight Goats, besides innumerable numbers of Swine, and good plentie of Corne in some places, yet the next yeere the Captaine sent out a Frigat and a Pinnace, that brought us neere six hundred bushels more, which did greatly relieve the whole Colonie: For from the tenants wee seldome had above foure hundred bushels of rent Corne to the store, and there was not remaining of the Companies companie, past foure and fiftie men, women and Children.

1000. bushels of Corne from the Salvages.

1618. Sir Thomas Smith Treasurer.   This yeere having planted our fields, came a great drought, and such a cruell storme of haile, which did such spoile both to the Corne and Tobacco, that wee reaped but small profit, the Magazine that came in the *George*, being five moneths in her passage, proved very badly conditioned, but ere she arrived, we had gathered and made up our Tobacco, the best at three shillings the pound, the rest at eighteene pence.

To supply us, the Councell and Company with all possible care and diligence, furnished a good ship of some two hundred and fiftie tunne, with two hundred people and the Lord la Ware. They set saile in Aprill, and tooke their course by the westerne Iles, where the Governour of the Ile of Saint Michael received the Lord la Ware, and honourably feasted him, with all the content hee could give him. Going from thence, they

were long troubled with contrary winds, in which time many
of them fell very sicke, thirtie died, one of which number was
that most honourable Lord Governour the Lord la
Ware, whose most noble and generous disposition,
is well knowne to his great cost, had beene most forward in this businesse for his Countries good : Yet this tender
state of Virginia was not growne to that maturitie, to maintaine such state and pleasure as was fit for such a personage,
with so brave and great attendance: for some small number of
adventrous Gentlemen to make discoveries, and lie in Garrison, ready upon any occasion to keepe in feare the inconstant
Salvages, nothing were more requisite; but to have more to wait
and play than worke, or more commanders and officers than
industrious labourers was not so necessarie: for in Virginia, a
plaine Souldier that can use a Pick-axe and spade, is better than
five Knights, although they were Knights that could breake a
Lance; for men of great place, not inured to those incounters;
when they finde things not sutable, grow many times so discontented, they forget themselves, and oft become so carelesse, that a discontented melancholy brings them to much
sorrow, and to others much miserie. At last they stood in for
the coast of New-England, where they met a small Frenchman,
rich of Bevers and other Furres. Though wee had here but
small knowledge of the coast nor countrie, yet they tooke such
an abundance of Fish and Fowle, and so well refreshed themselves there with wood and water, as by
the helpe of God thereby, having beene at Sea sixteene weekes, got to Virginia, who without this reliefe had
beene in great danger to perish. The French-men made them
such a feast, with such an abundance of varietie of Fish, Fowle
and Fruits, as they all admired, and little expected that wild
wildernesse could affoord such wonderfull abundance of plentie. In this ship came about two hundred men, but very little
provision, and the ship called the *Treasurer* came in againe not
long after with fortie passengers; the Lord la Wares ship lying
in Virginia three moneths, wee victualled her with threescore
bushels of Corne, and eight Hogsheads of flesh, besides other
victuall she spent whilest they tarried there: this ship brought
us advice that great multitudes were a preparing in England to
bee sent, and relied much upon that victuall they should finde

The death of
the Lord la
Ware.

They are
relieved in
New-En-
gland.

here: whereupon our Captaine called a Councell, and writ to the Councell here in England the estate of the Colonie, and what a great miserie would insue, if they sent not provision as well as people; and what they did suffer for want of skilfull husbandmen, and meanes to set their Ploughs on worke, having as good ground as any man can desire, and about fortie Bulls and Oxen, but they wanted men to bring them to labour, and Irons for the Ploughs, and harnesse for the Cattell. Some thirtie or fortie acres wee had sowne with one Plough, but it stood so long on the ground before it was reaped, it was most shaken, and the rest spoiled with the Cattell and Rats in the Barne, but no better Corne could bee for the quantitie.

Richard Killingbeck being with the Captaine at Kekoughtan, desired leave to returne to his wife at Charles hundred, hee went to James towne by water, there he got foure more to goe with him by land, but it proved that he intended to goe trade with the Indians of Chickahamania, where making shew of the great quantitie of trucke they had, which the Salvages perceiving, partly for their trucke, partly for revenge of some friends they pretended should have beene slaine by Captaine Yearley, one of them with an English peece shot Killingbeck dead, the other Salvages assaulted the rest and slew them, stripped them, and tooke what they had: But fearing this murther would come to light, and might cause them to suffer for it, would now proceed to the perfection of villanie; for presently they robbed their *Machaco-mocko* house of the towne, stole all the Indian treasure thereout, and fled into the woods, as other Indians related. On Sunday following, one Farfax that dwelt a mile from the towne, going to Church, left his wife and three small children safe at home, as he thought, and a young youth: she supposing praier to be done, left the children, and went to meet her husband; presently after came three or foure of those fugitive Salvages, entred the house, and slew a boy and three children, and also another youth that stole out of the Church in praier time, meeting them, was likewise murdered. Of this disaster the Captaine sent to Opechankanough for satisfaction, but he excused the matter, as altogether ignorant of it, at the same time the Salvages that were robbed were complaining to

Richard Killingbeck and foure other murdered by the Salvages.

Their Church and Storehouse.

Farfax, three children and two boyes also murdered.

Opechankanough, and much feared the English would bee revenged on them, so that Opechankanough sent to Captaine
Argall, to assure him the peace should never be broken by him,
desiring that he would not revenge the injurie of those fugitives upon the innocent people of that towne, which towne he
should have, and sent him a basket of earth, as possession given
of it, and promised, so soone as possibly they could catch these
robbers, to send him their heads for satisfaction, but he never
performed it.

Samuel Argall, John Rolfe.

A relation from Master John Rolfe, June 15. 1618.

CONCERNING the state of our new Common-wealth, it is
somewhat bettered, for we have sufficient to content our selves,
though not in such abundance as is vainly reported
in England. Powhatan died this last Aprill, yet the
Indians continue in peace. Itopatin his second
brother succeeds him, and both hee and Opechankanough have
confirmed our former league. On the eleventh of May, about
ten of the clocke in the night, happened a most fearefull tempest, but it continued not past halfe an houre, which powred
downe hailestones eight or nine inches about, that
none durst goe out of their doores, and though it
tore the barke and leaves of the trees, yet wee finde
not they hurt either man or beast; it fell onely about James
towne, for but a mile to the East, and twentie to the West
there was no haile at all. Thus in peace every man followed his
building and planting without any accidents worthy of note.
Some private differences happened betwixt Captaine Bruster
and Captaine Argall, and Captaine Argall and the Companie
here in England; but of them I am not fully informed, neither
are they here for any use, and therefore unfit to be remembred.
In December one Captaine Stallings, an old planter in those
parts, being imployed by them of the West countrie for a
fishing voyage, in New-England, fell, foule of a Frenchman
whom hee tooke, leaving his owne ship to returne for England,

Marginal notes: Powhatans death. | Haile-stones eight inches about.

himselfe with a small companie remained in the French barke, some small time after upon the coast, and thence returned to winter in Virginia.

The government surrendred to Sir George Yearley.

1619.
Sir Edwin
Sands
Treasurer.
Master John
Farer
Deputie.

For to begin with the yeere of our Lord, 1619. there arrived a little Pinnace privatly from England about Easter for Captaine Argall, who taking order for his affaires, within foure or five daies returned in her, and left for his Deputy, Captaine Nathaniel Powell. On the eighteenth of Aprill, which was but ten or twelve daies after, arrived Sir George Yearley, by whom we understood Sir Edwin Sands was chosen Treasurer, and Master John Farrar his Deputy, and what great supplies was a preparing to be sent us, which did ravish us so much with joy and content, we thought our selves now fully satisfied, for our long toile and labours, and as happy men as any in the world. Notwithstanding, such an accident hapned Captaine Stallings, the next day his ship was cast away, and he not long after slaine in a private quarrell. Sir George Yearly to beginne his government, added to be of his councell, Captaine Francis West, Captaine Nathaniel Powell, Master John Pory, Master John Rolfe, and Master William Wickam, and Master Samuel Macocke, and propounded to have a generall assembly with all expedition. Upon the twelfth of this Moneth, came in a Pinnace of Captaine Bargraves, and on the seventeenth Captaine Lownes, and one Master Euans,

Waraskoyack
planted.

who intended to plant themselves at Waraskoyack, but now Ophechankanough will not come at us, that causes us suspect his former promises.

In May came in the *Margaret* of Bristoll, with foure and thirty men, all well and in health, and also many devout gifts, and we were much troubled in examining some scandalous letters sent into England, to disgrace this Country with barrennesse, to discourage the adventurers, and so bring it and us to ruine and confusion; notwithstanding, we finde by them of best experience, an industrious man not other waies imploied, may well tend foure akers of Corne, and 1000. plants of Tobacco, and where they say an aker will yeeld but three or foure barrels, we have ordinarily foure or five, but of new ground six, seven, and eight, and a barrell of Pease and Beanes, which we esteeme as good as two of Corne, which is after thirty or forty bushels an aker, so that one man may provide Corne for five, and apparell for two by the profit of his Tobacco; they say also English Wheat will yeeld but sixteene bushels an aker, and we have reaped thirty: besides to manure the Land, no place hath more white and blew Marble than here, had we but Carpenters to build and make Carts and Ploughs, and skilfull men that know how to use them, and traine up our cattell to draw them, which though we indevour to effect, yet our want of experience brings but little to perfection but planting Tobaco, and yet of that many are so covetous to have much, they make little good; besides there are so many sofisticating Tobaco-mungers in England, were it never so bad, they would sell it for Verinas, and the trash that remaineth should be Virginia, such devilish bad mindes we know some of our owne Country-men doe beare, not onely to the businesse, but also to our mother England her selfe; could they or durst they as freely defame her.

A barrell they account foure bushels.

The 25. of June came in the *Triall* with Corne and Cattell all in safety, which tooke from us cleerely all feare of famine; then our governour and councell caused Burgesses to be chosen in all places, and met at a generall Assembly, where all matters were debated thought expedient for the good of the Colony, and Captaine Ward was sent to Monahigan in new England, to fish in May, and returned the latter end of May, but to small purpose, for they wanted Salt: the *George* also was sent to New-found-land with the Cape Merchant, there she bought fish, that defraied her charges, and made a good voyage in seven weekes. About the last of August came in a dutch man of warre that sold us twenty Negars, and Iapazous King of Patawomeck, came to James towne, to desire two ships to come trade in his River, for a more plentifull yeere of Corne had not beene in a long time, yet very contagious, and by the trechery of one Poule, in a manner turned heathen, wee were very jealous the Salvages would surprize us. The Governours have bounded foure Corporations; which is the Companies, the University, the

Their time of Parlament.

Foure corporations named.

Governours and Gleabe land: Ensigne William Spencer, and Thomas Barret a Sergeant, with some others of the ancient Planters being set free, weare the first farmers that went forth, and have chosen places to their content, so that now knowing their owne land, they strive who should exceed in building and planting. The fourth of November the *Bona nova* came in with all her people lusty and well; not long after one Master Dirmer sent out by some of Plimoth for New-England, arrived in a Barke of five tunnes, and returned the next Spring; notwithstanding the ill rumours of the unwholsomnesse of James towne, the new commers that were planted at old Paspaheghe,

Captaine Wards exploit. little more then a mile from it, had their healths better then any in the Country. In December Captaine Ward returned from Patawomeck, the people there dealt falsly with him, so that hee tooke 800. bushels of Corne from them perforce. Captaine Woodliffe of Bristol came in not long after, with all his people lusty and in health, and we had two particular Governors sent us, under the titles of Deputies to the Company, the one to have charge of the Colledge Lands, the other of the Companies: Now you are to understand, that because there have beene many complaints against the Governors, Captaines, and Officers in Virginia, for buying and selling men and boies, or to bee set over from one to another for a yeerely rent, was held in England a thing most intolerable, or that the tenants or lawfull servants should be put from their places, or abridged their Covenants, was so odious, that the very report thereof brought a great scandall to the generall action. The Councell in England did send many good and worthy instructions for the amending those abuses, and appointed a hundred men should at the Companies charge be allotted and provided to serve and attend the Governour during the time of his government, which number he was to make good at his departure, and leave to his Successor in like manner, fifty to the Deputy-Governour of the College land, and fifty to the Deputy of the Companies land, fifty to the Treasurer, to the Secretary five and twenty, and more to the Marshall and Cape merchant; which they are also to leave to their successors, and likewise to every particular Officer such a competency, as he might live well in his Office, without oppressing any under their charge, which good law I pray God it be well observed, and then we may truly say in Virginia, we are the most happy people in the world.

By me John Rolfe.

The number of Ships and men.
There went this yeere by the Companies records, 11. ships, and 1216. persons to be thus disposed on: Tenants for the Governors land fourescore, besides fifty sent the former spring; for the Companies land a hundred and thirty, for the College a hundred, for the Glebe land fifty, young women to make wives ninety, servants for publike service fifty, and fifty more whose labours were to bring up thirty of the infidels children, the rest were sent to private Plantations.

Gifts given.
Two persons unknowne have given faire Plate and Ornaments for two Communion Tables, the one at the College, the other at the Church of Mistris Mary Robinson, who towards the foundation gave two hundred pound. And another unknowne person sent to the Treasurer five hundred and fifty pounds, for the bringing up of the salvage children in Christianity. Master Nicholas Farrar deceased, hath by his Will given three hundred pounds to the College, to be paid when there shall be ten young Salvages placed in it, in the meane time foure and twenty pound yeerely to bee distributed unto three discreet and godly young men in the Colony, to bring up three wilde young infidels in some good course of life, also there were granted eleven Pattents, upon condition to transport people and cattle to increase the Plantations.

But few performe them.

A desperat Sea-fight betwixt two Spanish men of warre, and a small English ship, at the Ile of Dominica going to Virginia, by Captaine Anthony Chester.

1620.
The Earle of Southampton Treasurer, and Master John Ferrar Deputy.
HAVING taken our journey towards Virginia in the beginning of February, a ship called the *Margaret and John*, of one hundred and sixty tuns, eight Iron Peeces and a Falcon, with eightie Passengers besides Sailers; After many tempests and foule weather, about

the foureteenth of March we were in thirteene degrees and an
halfe of Northerly latitude, where we descried a ship at hull; it
being but a faire gale of wind, we edged towards her to see
what she was, but she presently set saile, and ran us quickly out
of sight: This made us keepe our course for Mettalina, and the
next day passing Dominica, we came to an anchor at Guardalupo, to take in fresh water. Six. French-men there
cast away sixteene moneths agoe came aboord us;
they told us a Spanish man of Warre but seven daies
before was seeking his consort, and this was she we descried at
hull. At Mevis we intended to refresh our selves, having beene
eleven weeks pestered in this unwholsome ship; but there we
found two tall ships with the Hollanders colours, but necessitie
forcing us on shore, we anchored faire by them, and in friendly
manner sent to hale them: but seeing they were
Spaniards, retiring to our ship, they sent such a volley
of shot after us, that shot the Boat, split the Oares,
and some thorow the clothes, yet not a man hurt; and then
followed with their great Ordnance, that many times overracked our ship, which being so cumbred with the Passengers
provisions, our Ordnance was not well fitted, nor any thing as
it should have beene. But perceiving what they were, we fitted
our selves the best we could to prevent a mischiefe, seeing
them warp themselves to windward, we thought it not good to
be boorded on both sides at an anchor, we intended to set saile,
but that the Vice-Admirall battered so hard our star-boord
side, that we fell to our businesse, and answered their
unkindnesse with such faire shot from a Demiculvering, that shot her betweene wind and water,
whereby she was glad to leave us and her Admirall
together. Comming faire by our quarter, he tooke in his Holland flag, and put forth his Spanish colours, and so haled us.

We quietly and quickly answered him, both what wee were,
and whither bound, relating the effect of our Commission, and
the cause of our comming thither for water, and not to annoy
any of the King of Spaines Subjects, nor any. She commanded
us amaine for the King of Spaine, we replied with inlarging the
particulars what friends both the Kings our Masters were, and
as we would doe no wrong, we would take none. They commanded us aboord to shew our Commission, which we re-

A French-
man cast
away at
Guardalupo.

The
Spaniards
begin.

The Vice-
Admirall shot
betweene
wind and
water.

fused, but if they would send their Boat to us willingly they should see it. But for answer they made two great shot at us, with a volley of small shot, which caused us to leave the decks; then with many ill words they laid us aboord, which caused us to raise our maine saile, and give the word to our small shot which lay close and ready, that paid them in such sort, they quickly retired. The fight continued halfe an houre, as if we had beene invironed with fire and smoke, untill they discovered the waste of our ship naked, where they bravely boorded us loofe for loofe, hasting with pikes and swords to enter, but it pleased God so to direct our Captaine, and encourage our men with valour, that our pikes being formerly placed under our halfe deck, and certaine shot lying close for that purpose under the Port holes, encountred them so rudely, that their fury was not onely rebated, but their hastinesse intercepted, and their whole company beaten backe, many of our men were hurt, but I am sure they had two for one.

The manner of their fight.

In the end they were violently repulsed, untill they were re-inforced to charge againe by their commands, who standing upon their honors, thought it a great indignity to be so af-fronted, which caused a second charge, and that answered with a second beating backe: whereat the Captaine grew in-raged, and constrained them to come on againe afresh, which they did so effectually, that questionlesse it had wrought an al-teration, if the God that tosseth Monarchies, and teareth Mountaines, had not taught us to tosse our Pikes with pros-perous events, and powred out a volley of small shot amongst them, whereby that valiant Commander was slaine, and many of his Souldiers dropped downe likewise on the top of the hatches. This we saw with our eies, and rejoyced with it at our hearts, so that we might perceive good suc-cesse comming on, our Captaine presently tooke ad-vantage of their discomfiture, though with much comiseration of that resolute Captaine, and not onely plied them againe with our Ordnance, but had more shot under the Pikes, which was bestowed to good purpose, and amazed our enemies with the suddennesse.

The Captaine slaine.

Amongst the rest, one Lucas, our Carpenters Mate, must not be forgotten, who perceiving a way how to annoy them; As they were thus puzled and in a

A worthy exploit of Lucas.

confusion, drew out a Minion under the halfe decke, and there bent it upon them in such a manner, that when it was fired, the cases of stones and peeces of Iron fell upon them so thick, as cleared the decke, and slew many, and in short time we saw few assailants, but such as crept from place to place covertly from the fury of our shot, which now was thicker than theirs: for although as far as we may commend our enemies, they had done something worthy of commendations; yet either wanting men, or being overtaken with the unlooked for valour of our men, they now began to shrinke, and give us leave to be wanton with our advantage. Yet we could onely use but foure peece of Ordnances, but they served the turne as well as all the rest: for she was shot so oft betweene wind and water, we saw they were willing to leave us, but by reason she was fast in the latch of our cable, which in haste of weighing our anchor hung aloofe, she could not cleare her selfe as she wrought to doe, till one cut the Cable with an axe, and was slaine by freeing us. Having beene aboord us two hours and an halfe, seeing her selfe cleere, all the shot wee had plaied on both sides, which lasted till we were out of shot, then we discovered the Vice-Admirall comming to her assistance, who began afarre off to ply us with their Ordnances, and put us in minde we had another worke in hand. Whereupon we separated the dead and hurt bodies, and manned the ship with the rest, and were so well incouraged wee waifed them amaine. The Admirall stood aloofe off, and the other would not come within Falcon shot, where she lay battering us till shee received another paiment from a Demiculvering, which made her beare with the shore for smooth water to mend her leakes. The next morning they both came up againe with us, as if they had determined to devour us at once, but it seemed it was but a bravado, though they forsooke not our quarter for a time within Musket shot; yet all the night onely they kept us company, but made not a shot. During which time we had leasure to provide us better than before: but God bethanked they made onely but a shew of another assault, ere suddenly the Vice-Admirall fell a starne, and the other lay shaking in the wind, and so they both left us. The fight continued six houres, and was the more unwelcome, because we were so ill provided, and had no intent to fight, nor give occasion to dis-

The event of the fight.

turbe them. As for the losse of men, if Religion had not taught us what by the providence of God is brought to passe, yet daily experience might informe us, of the dangers of wars, and perils at sea, by stormes tempests, shipwracks, encounters with Pirats, meeting with enemies, crosse winds, long voiages, unknowne shores, barbarous Nations, and an hundred inconveniences, of which humane pollicies are not capable, nor mens conjectures apprehensive. We lost Doctor Bohun, a worthy valiant Gentleman, (a long time brought up amongst the most learned Surgeons, and Physitions in Netherlands, and this his second journey to Virginia:) and seven slaine out right, two died shortly of their wounds; sixteene was shot, whose limbs God be thanked was recovered without maime, and now setled in Virginia: how many they lost we know not, but we saw a great many lie on the decks, and their skuppers runne with bloud, they were about three hundred tunnes apeece, each sixteene or twentie Brasse-peeces. Captaine Chester, who in this fight had behaved himselfe like a most vigilant, resolute, and a couragious souldier, as also our honest and valiant master, did still so comfort and incourage us by all the meanes they could, at last to all our great contents we arrived in Virginia, and from thence returned safely to England.

The Names of the Adventurers for Virginia, Alphabetically set downe, according to a printed Booke, set out by the Treasurer and Councell in this present yeere, 1620.

A

Sir William Aliffe.
Sir Roger Aston.
Sir Anthony Ashley.
Sir John Akland.
Sir Anthonie Aucher.
Sir Robert Askwith.
Doctor Francis Anthony.
Charles Anthony.
Edward Allen.
Edmund Allen Esquire.
John Allen.
Thomas Allen.
William Atkinson, Esquire.
Richard Ashcroft.
Nicholas Andrews.
John Andrews the elder.

John Andrews the younger.
James Ascough.
Giles Allington.
Morris Abbot.
Ambrose Asten.
James Askew.
Anthony Abdey.
John Arundell, Esquire.

B

Edward, Earle of Bedford
James, Lord Bishop of Bathe
    and Wells.
Sir Francis Barrington.
Sir Morice Barkley.
Sir John Benet.
Sir Thomas Beamont.
Sir Amias Bamfield.
Sir John Bourcher.
Sir Edmund Bowyer.
Sir Thomas Bludder.
Sir George Bolles.
Sir John Bingley.
Sir Thomas Button.
Sir Henry Beddingfield.
Companie of Barbers-
    Surgeons.
Companie of Bakers.
Richard Banister.
John Bancks.
Miles Bancks.
Thomas Barber.
William Bonham.
James Bryerley.
William Barners.
Anthony Barners, Esquire.
William Brewster.
Richard Brooke.
Hugh Brooker, Esquire.

Ambrose Brewsey.
John Brooke.
Matthew Bromridge.
Christopher Brooke, Esquire.
Martin Bond.
Gabriel Beadle.
John Beadle.
David Borne.
Edward Barnes.
John Badger.
Edmund Branduell.
Robert Bowyer, Esquire.
Robert Bateman.
Thomas Britton.
Nicholas Benson.
Edward Bishop.
Peter Burgoney.
Thomas Burgoney.
Robert Burgoney.
Christopher Baron.
Peter Benson.
John Baker.
John Bustoridge.
Francis Burley.
William Browne.
Robert Barker.
Samuel Burnham.
Edward Barkley.
William Bennet.
Captaine Edward Brewster.
Thomas Brocket.
John Bullock.
George Bache.
Thomas Bayly.
William Barkley.
George Butler.
Timothie Bathurst.
George Burton.
Thomas Bret.
Captaine John Brough.

Thomas Baker.

John Blunt.

Thomas Bayly.

Richard and Edward Blunt.

Mineon Burrell.

Richard Blackmore.

William Beck.

Benjamin Brand.

John Busbridge.

William Burrell.

William Barret.

Francis Baldwin.

Edward Barber.

Humphrey Basse.

Robert Bell.

Matthew Bromrick.

John Beaumont.

George Barkley.

Peter Bartle.

Thomas Bretton.

John Blount.

Arthur Bromfeld Esquire.

William Berbloke.

Charles Beck.

C

George, Lord Archbishop of Canterburie.

William Lord Cranborne, now Earle of Salisburie.

William Lord Compton, now Earle of North-hampton.

William Lord Cavendish, now Earle of Devonshire.

Richard, Earle of Clanricard.

Sir William Cavendish now Lord Cavendish.

Gray, Lord Chandos.

Sir Henry Cary.

Sir George Calvert.

Sir Lionell Cranfield.

Sir Edward Cecill.

Sir Robert Cotten.

Sir Oliver Cromwell.

Sir Anthony Cope.

Sir Walter Cope.

Sir Edward Carr.

Sir Thomas Conisbie.

Sir George Cary.

Sir Edward Conwey.

Sir Walter Chute.

Sir Edward Culpeper.

Sir Henry Cary, Captaine.

Sir William Craven.

Sir Walter Covert.

Sir George Coppin.

Sir George Chute.

Sir Thomas Coventry.

Sir John Cutts.

Lady Cary.

Company of Cloth-workers.

Citie of Chichester.

Robert Chamberlaine.

Richard Chamberlaine.

Francis Covill.

William Coyse, Esquire.

Abraham Chamberlaine.

Thomas Carpenter.

Anthony Crew.

Richard Cox.

William Crosley.

James Chatfeild.

Richard Caswell.

John Cornelis.

Randall Carter.

Executors of Randall Carter.

William Canning.

Edward Carue, Esquire.

Thomas Cannon, Esquire.

Richard Champion.
Rawley Crashaw.
Henry Collins.
Henry Cromwell.
John Cooper.
Richard Cooper.
John Casson.
Thomas Colthurst.
Allen Cotten.
Edward Cage.
Abraham Carthwright.
Robert Coppin.
Thomas Conock.
John Clapham.
Thomas Church.
William Carpenter.
Laurence Campe.
James Cambell.
Christopher Cletheroe.
Matthew Cooper.
George Chamber.
Captaine John Cooke.
Captaine Thomas Conwey,
    Esquire.
Edward Culpeper, Esquire.
Master William Crashaw.
Abraham Colmer.
John Culpeper.
Edmund Colbey.
Richard Cooper.
Robert Creswell.
John Cage, Esquire.
Matthew Cavell.
William Crowe.
Abraham Carpenter.
John Crowe.
Thomas Cordell.
Richard Connock, Esquire.
William Compton.
William Chester.

Thomas Covel.
Richard Carmarden, Esquire.
William and Paul Canning.
Henry Cromwell, Esquire.
Simon Codrington.
Clement Chichley.
James Cullemore.
William Cantrell.

D

Richard, Earle of Dorset.
Edward Lord Denny.
Sir John Digbie, now
    Lord Digbie.
Sir John Doderidge.
Sir Drew Drewry the elder.
Sir Thomas Dennis.
Sir Robert Drewry.
Sir John Davers.
Sir Dudley Digs.
Sir Marmaduke Dorrel.
Sir Thomas Dale.
Sir Thomas Denton.
Companie of Drapers.
Thomas Bond, Esquire.
David Bent, Esquire.
Companie of Dyers.
Towne of Dover.
Master Richard Deane,
    Alderman.
Henry Dawkes.
Edward Dichfleld.
William Dunne.
John Davis.
Matthew Dequester.
Philip Durdent.
Abraham Dawes.
John Dike.
Thomas Draper.

Lancelot Davis.
Rowley Dawsey.
William Dobson, Esquire.
Anthony Dyot, Esquire.
Avery Dranfield.
Roger Dye.
John Downes.
John Drake.
John Delbridge.
Benjamin Decroe.
Thomas Dyke.
Jeffery Duppa.
Daniel Darnelly.
Sara Draper.
Clement and
    Henry Dawkney.

E

Thomas, Earle of Exeter.
Sir Thomas Everfield.
Sir Francis Egiock.
Sir Robert Edolph.
John Eldred, Esquire.
William Evans.
Richard Evans.
Hugh Evans.
Raph Ewens, Esquire.
John Elkin.
John Elkin.
Robert Evelin.
Nicholas Exton.
John Exton.
George Etheridge.

F

Sir Moyle Finch.
Sir Henry Fanshaw.
Sir Thomas Freake.
Sir Peter Fretchvile.

Sir William Fleetwood.
Sir Henry Fane.
Company of Fishmongers.
John Fletcher.
John Farmer.
Martin Freeman, Esquire.
Ralph Freeman.
William and Ralph Freeman.
Michael Fetiplace.
William Fettiplace.
Thomas Forrest.
Edward Fleetwood, Esquire.
William Felgate.
William Field.
Nicholas Ferrar.
John Farrar.
Giles Francis.
Edward Fawcet.
Richard Farrington.
John Francklin.
Richard Frith.
John Ferne.
George Farmer.
Thomas Francis.
John Fenner.
Nicholas Fuller, Esquire.
Thomas Foxall.
William Fleet.
Peter Franck, Esquire.
Richard Fishborne.
William Faldoe.
John Fletcher, and Company.
William Ferrars.

G

Lady Elizabeth Gray.
Sir John Gray.
Sir William Godolfine.
Sir Thomas Gates.

Sir William Gee.
Sir Richard Grobham.
Sir William Garaway.
Sir Francis Goodwin.
Sir George Goring.
Sir Thomas Grantham.
Company of Grocers.
Company of Goldsmiths.
Company of Girdlers.
John Geering.
John Gardiner.
Richard Gardiner.
John Gilbert.
Thomas Grave.
John Gray.
Nicholas Grice.
Richard Goddard.
Thomas Gipps.
Peter Gates.
Thomas Gibbs, Esquire.
Laurence Greene.
William Greenwell.
Robert Garset.
Robert Gore.
Thomas Gouge.
Francis Glanvile, Esquire.

H

Henry, Earle of Huntington.
Lord Theophilus Haward,
    Lord Walden.
Sir John Harrington, Lord
    Harington.
Sir John Hollis, now Lord
    Hautein.
Sir Thomas Holecroft.
Sir William Harris.
Sir Thomas Harefleet.

Sir George Haiward.
Sir Warwicke Heale.
Sir Baptist Hicks.
Sir John Hanham.
Sir Thomas Horwell.
Sir Thomas Hewit.
Sir William Herrick.
Sir Eustace Hart.
Sir Pory Huntley.
Sir Arthur Harris.
Sir Edward Heron.
Sir Persevall Hart.
Sir Ferdinando Heiborne.
Sir Lawrence Hide.
Master Hugh Hamersley,
    Alderman.
Master Richard Heron,
    Alderman.
Richard Humble, Esquire.
Master Richard Hackleuit.
Edward Harrison.
George Holeman.
Robert Hill.
Griffin Hinton.
John Hawkins.
William Hancocke.
John Harper.
George Hanger.
John Holt.
John Huntley.
Jeremy Heiden.
Ralph Hamer.
Ralph Hamer, Junior.
John Hodgeson.
John Hanford.
Thomas Harris.
Richard Howell.
Thomas Henshaw.
Leonard Harwood

Tristram Hill.
Francis Haselridge.
Tobias Hinson.
Peter Heightley.
George Hawkenson.
Thomas Hackshaw.
Charles Hawkens.
John Hodgis.
William Holland.
Robert Hartley.
Gregory Herst.
Thomas Hodgis.
William Hodgis.
Roger Harris.
John Harris.
Master John Haiward.
James Haiward.
Nicholas Hide, Esquire.
John Hare, Esquire.
William Hackwell, Esquire.
Gressam Hoogan.
Humfrey Hanford.
William Haselden.
Nicholas Hooker.
Doctor Anthony Hunton.
John Hodsale.
George Hooker.
Anthony Hinton.
John Hogsell.
Thomas Hampton.
William Hicks.
William Holiland.
Ralph Harison.
Harman Harison.

J

Sir Thomas Jermyn.
Sir Robert Johnson.

Sir Arthur Ingram.
Sir Francis Jones.
Company of Ironmongers.
Company of Inholders.
Company of Imbroyderers.
Bailiffes of Ipswich.
Henry Jackson.
Richard Ironside.
Master Robert Johnson
  Alderman.
Thomas Jones.
William Jobson.
Thomas Johnson.
Thomas Jadwine.
John Josua.
George Isam.
Philip Jacobson.
Peter Jacobson.
Thomas Jaxson Senior.
James Jewell.
Gabriel Jaques.
Walter Jobson.
Edward James.
Zachary Jones, Esquire.
Anthony Irbye, Esquire.
William I-anson.
Humfrey Jobson.

K

Sir Valentine Knightley.
Sir Robert Killegrew.
Sir Charles Kelke.
Sir John Kaile.
Richard Kirrill.
John Kirrill.
Raph King.
Henry Kent.
Towne of Kingslynne.

John Kettleby, Esquire.
Walter Kirkham, Esquire.

L

Henry, Earle of Lincolne.
Robert, Lord Lisle, now
   Earle of Leicester.
Thomas, Lord Laware.
Sir Francis Leigh.
Sir Richard Lovelace.
Sir William Litton.
Sir John Lewson.
Sir William Lower.
Sir Samuel Leonard.
Sir Samson Leonard.
Company of Lethersellers.
Thomas Laughton.
William Lewson.
Peter Latham.
Peter Van Lore.
Henry Leigh.
Thomas Levar.
Christofer Landman.
Morris Lewellin.
Edward Lewis.
Edward Lewkin.
Peter Lodge.
Thomas Layer
Thomas Lawson.
Francis Lodge.
John Langley.
David Loide.
John Levitt.
Thomas Fox and Luke
   Lodge.
Captaine Richard Linley.
Arnold Lulls.
William Lawrence.
John Landman.

Nicholas Lichfield.
Nicholas Leate.
Gedeon de Laune.

M

Philip Earle of Montgomerie.
Doctor George Mountaine,
   now Lord Bishop of
   Lincolne.
William Lord Mounteagle,
   now Lord Morley.
Sir Thomas Mansell.
Sir Thomas Mildmay.
Sir William Maynard.
Sir Humfrey May.
Sir Peter Manhood.
Sir John Merrick.
Sir George More.
Sir Robert Mansell.
Sir Arthur Mannering.
Sir David Murrey.
Sir Edward Michelborn.
Sir Thomas Middleton.
Sir Robert Miller.
Sir Cavaliero Maicott.
Doctor James Meddus.
Richard Martin, Esquire.
Company of Mercers.
Company of Merchant
   Taylors.
Otho Mowdite.
Captaine John Martin.
Arthur Mouse.
Adrian More.
Thomas Mountford.
Thomas Morris.
Ralph Moorton.
Francis Mapes.
Richard Maplesden.

James Monger.
Peter Monsell.
Robert Middleton.
Thomas Maile.
John Martin.
Josias Maude.
Richard Morton.
George Mason.
Thomas Maddock.
Richard Moore.
Nicholas Moone.
Alfonsus van Medkerk.
Captaine Henry Meoles.
Philip Mutes.
Thomas Mayall.
Humfrey Marret.
Jarvis Mundz.
Robert Mildmay.
William Millet.
Richard Morer.
John Miller.
Thomas Martin.
John Middleton.
Francis Middleton.

N

Dudly, Lord North.
Francis, Lord Norris.
Sir Henry Nevill of
    Barkshire.
Thomas Nicols.
Christopher Nicols.
William Nicols.
George Newce.
Joseph Newberow.
Christopher Newgate.
Thomas Norincott.
Jonathan Nuttall.
Thomas Norton.

O

William Oxenbridge,
    Esquire.
Robert Offley.
Francis Oliver.

P

William, Earle of Pembroke.
William, Lord Paget.
John, Lord Petre.
George Percy, Esquire.
Sir Christofer Parkins.
Sir Amias Preston.
Sir Nicholas Parker.
Sir William Poole.
Sir Stephen Powell.
Sir Henry Peyton.
Sir James Perrot.
Sir John Pettus.
Sir Robert Payne.
William Payne.
John Payne.
Edward Parkins.
Edward Parkins his widow.
Aden Perkins.
Thomas Perkin.
Richard Partridge.
William Palmer.
Miles Palmer.
Robert Parkhurst.
Richard Percivall, Esquire.
Richard Poyntell.
George Pretty.
George Pit.
Allen Percy.
Abraham Peirce.
Edmund Peirce.
Phenice Pet.
Thomas Philips.

Henry Philpot.
Master George Procter.
Robert Penington.
Peter Peate.
John Prat.
William Powell.
Edmund Peashall.
Captaine William Proude.
Henry Price.
Nicholas Pewriffe.
Thomas Pelham.
Richard Piggot.
John Pawlet, Esquire.
Robert Pory.
Richard Paulson.

Q

William Quicke.

R

Sir Robert Rich, now Earle
　of Warwicke.
Sir Thomas Row.
Sir Henry Rainsford.
Sir William Romney.
Sir John Ratcliffe.
Sir Steven Ridlesdon.
Sir William Russell.
Master Edward Rotheram,
　Alderman.
Robert Rich.
Tedder Roberts.
Henry Robinson.
John Russell.
Richard Rogers.
Arthur Robinson.
Robert Robinson.
Millicent Ramsden.
John Robinson.

George Robins.
Nichalas Rainton.
Henry Rolffe.
John Reignolds.
Elias Roberts.
Henry Reignolds, Esquire.
William Roscarrocke,
　Esquire.
Humfrey Raymell.
Richard Robins.

S

Henry, Earle of
　Southampton.
Thomas, Earle of Suffolke.
Edward Semer, Earle of
　Hartford.
Robert, Earle of Salisbury.
Mary, Countesse of
　Shrewsbury.
Edmund, Lord Sheffeld.
Robert, Lord Spencer.
John, Lord Stanhope.
Sir John Saint-John.
Sir Thomas Smith.
Sir John Samms.
Sir John Smith.
Sir Edwin Sandys.
Sir Samuel Sandys.
Sir Steven Some.
Sir Raph Shelton.
Sir Thomas Stewkley.
Sir William Saint-John.
Sir William Smith.
Sir Richard Smith.
Sir Martin Stutevill.
Sir Nicolas Salter.
Doctor Matthew Sutcliffe, of
　Exeter.

Captaine John Smith.
Thomas Sandys, Esquire.
Henry Sandys, Esquire.
George Sandys, Esquire.
Company of Skinners.
Company of Salters.
Company of Stationers.
John Stokley.
Richard Staper.
Robert Shingleton.
Thomas Shipton.
Cleophas Smith.
Richard Strongtharm.
Hildebrand Spruson.
Matthew Scrivener.
Othowell Smith.
George Scot.
Hewet Stapers.
James Swift.
Richard Stratford.
Edmund Smith.
Robert Smith.
Matthias Springham.
Richard Smith.
Edward Smith.
Jonathan Smith.
Humfrey Smith.
John Smith.
George Swinhow.
Joseph Some.
William Sheckley.
John Southick.
Henry Shelley.
Walter Shelley.
Richard Snarsborow.
George Stone.
Hugh Shepley.
William Strachey.
Urion Spencer.
John Scarpe.

Thomas Scott.
William Sharpe.
Steven Sparrow.
Thomas Stokes.
Richard Shepard.
Henry Spranger.
William Stonnard.
Steven Sad.
John Stockley.
Thomas Stevens.
Matthew Shepard.
Thomas Sherwell.
William Seabright, Esquire.
Nicholas Sherwell.
Augustine Steward.
Thomas Stile.
Abraham Speckhard.
Edmund Scot.
Francis Smalman.
Gregory Sprint, Esquire.
Thomas Stacey.
William Sandbatch.
Augustine Stuard, Esquire.

T

Sir William Twisden.
Sir William Throckmorton.
Sir Nicholas Tufton.
Sir John Trever.
Sir Thomas Tracy.
George Thorpe, Esquire.
Doctor William Turner.
The Trinity house.
Richard Turner.
John Taverner.
Daniel Tucker.
Charles Towler.
William Tayler.
Leonard Townson.

Richard Tomlins.
Francis Tate, Esquire.
Andrew Troughton.
George Tucker.
Henry Timberlake.
William Tucker.
Lewis Tite.
Robert Thornton.

V

Sir Horatio Vere.
Sir Walter Vaughan.
Henry Vincent.
Richard Venne.
Christopher Vertue.
John Vassell.
Arthur Venne.

W

Henry Bishop of Worcester.
Francis West, Esquire.
Sir Ralph Winwood.
Sir John Wentworth.
Sir William Waad.
Sir Robert Wroth.
Sir Percival Willoby.
Sir Charles Wilmott.
Sir John Wats.
Sir Hugh Worrell.
Sir Edward Waterhouse.
Sir Thomas Wilsford.
Sir Richard Williamson.
Sir John Wolstenholm.
Sir Thomas Walsingham.
Sir Thomas Watson.
Sir Thomas Wilson.
Sir John Weld.
Mistris Katherine West, now
    Lady Conway.

John Wroth, Esquire.
Captaine Maria Winckfield,
    Esquire.
Thomas Webb.
Rice Webb.
Edward Webb.
Sands Webb.
Felix Wilson.
Thomas White.
Richard Wiffen.
William Williamson.
Humfrey Westwood.
Hugh Willeston.
Thomas Wheatley.
William Wattey.
William Webster.
James White.
Edmund Winne.
John West.
John Wright.
Edward Wooller.
Thomas Walker.
John Wooller.
John Westrow.
Edward Welch.
Nathaniel Waad.
Richard Widowes.
David Waterhouse,
    Esquire
Captaine Owen Winne.
Randall Wetwood.
George Wilmer, Esquire.
Edward Wilkes.
Leonard White.
Andrew Willmer.
Clement Willmer.
George Walker.
William Welbie.
Francis Whistler.
Thomas Wells.

Captaine Thomas Winne.
John Whittingham.
Thomas Wheeler.
William Willet.
Devereux Woogam.
John Walker.
Thomas Wood.
John Willet.
Nicholas Wheeler.
Thomas Wale.
William Wilston.
John Waller.
William Ward.
William Willeston.
John Water.

Thomas Warr, Esquire.
David Wiffen.
Garret Weston.

Y

Sir George Yeardley, now
   Governour of Virginia.
William Yong.
Simon Yeomans.

Z

Edward, Lord Zouch.
John Zouch, Esquire.

That most generous and most honourable Lord, the Earle of South-hampton, being pleased to take upon him the title of Treasurer, and Master John Farrar his Deputy, with such instructions as were necessary, and admonitions to all Officers to take heede of extortion, ingrosing commodities, forestalling of markets, especially to have a vigilant care, the familiarity of the Salvages living amongst them made them not way to betray or surprize them, for the building of Guest-houses to relieve the weake in, and that they did wonder in all this time they had made no discoveries, nor knew no more then the very place whereon they did inhabit, nor yet could ever see any returne for all this continuall charge and trouble, therefore they sent to be added to the Councell seven Gentlemen, namely Master Thorp, Captaine Nuce, Master Tracy, Captaine Middleton, Captaine Blount, Master John Pountas, and Master Harwood, with men, munition, and all things thought fitting, but they write from Virginia, many of the Ships were so pestred with diseased people, and thronged together in their passage, there was much sicknesse and a great mortality, wherfore they desired rather a few able sufficient men well provided, then great multitudes, and because there were few accidents of note, but private advertisements by letters, we will conclude this yeere, and proceed to the next.

Collected out of the Councels letters for Virginia.

The instructions and advertisements for this yeere were both from England and Virginia, much like the last: only whereas before they had ever a suspicion of Opechankanough, and all the rest of the Salvages, they had an eye over him more then any, but now they all write so confidently of their assured peace with the Salvages, there is now no more feare nor danger either of their power or trechery, so that every man planteth himselfe where he pleaseth, and followeth his businesse securely. But the time of Sir George Yearley being neere expired, the Councel here made choise of a worthy young Gentleman Sir Francis Wyat to succeed him, whom they forthwith furnished and provided, as they had done his Predecessors, with all the necessary instructions all these times had acquainted them for the conversion of the Salvages, the suppressing of planting Tobacco, and planting of Corne, not depending continually to be supplied by the Salvages, but in case of necessity to trade with them, whom long ere this, it hath beene promised and expected should have beene fed and relieved by the English, not the English by them; and carefully to redresse all the complaints of the needlesse mortality of their people, and by all diligence seeke to send something home to satisfie the Adventurers, that all this time had only lived upon hopes, grew so weary and discouraged, that it must now be substance that must maintaine their proceedings, and not letters, excuses and promises; seeing they could get so much and such great estates for themselves, as to spend after the rate of 100. pounds, 2, 3, 4, 5, 6, 7, 8, 9, 10. nay some 2000. or 3000. pounds yearely, that were not worth so many pence when they went to Virginia, can scarce containe themselves either in diet, apparell, gaming, and all manner of such superfluity, within a lesse compasse than our curious, costly, and consuming Gallants here in England, which cannot possibly be there supported, but either by oppressing the Comminalty there, or deceiving the generality here (or both.)

Extracted out of the Councels Letters for Virginia.

From Virginia, by the relations of the Chieftains there, and many I have conferred with, that came from thence hither, I have much admired to heare of the incredible pleasure, profit and plenty this Plantation doth abound in, and yet could never heare of any returne but Tobacco, but it hath oft amazed me to understand how strangely the Salvages hath beene taught the use of our armes, and imploied in hunting and fowling with our fowling peeces, and our men rooting in the ground about Tobacco like Swine; besides that, the Salvages that doe little but continually exercise their bow and arrowes, should dwell and lie so familiarly amongst our men that practised little but the Spade, being so farre asunder, and in such small parties dispersed, and neither Fort, exercise of armes used, Ordnances mounted, Courts of guard, nor any preparation nor provision to prevent a forraine enemy, much more the Salvages howsoever; for the Salvages uncertaine conformity I doe not wonder, but for their constancy and conversion, I am and ever have beene of the opinion of Master Jonas Stockam a Minister in Virginia, who even at this time, when all things were so prosperous, and the Salvages at the point of conversion, against all their Governours and Councels opinions, writ to the Councell and Company in England to this effect.

May 28.

We that have left our native country to sojourne in a strange land, some idle spectators, who either cowardly dare not, or covetously will not adventure either their purses or persons in so commendable a worke; others supporting Atlas of this almost unsupportable burdens as your selves, without whose assistance this Virginia Firmament (in which some) and I hope in short time will shine many more glorious Starres, though there be many Italiannated and Spaniolized Englishmen envies our prosperities, and by all their ignominious scandals they can devise seekes to dishearten what they can, those that are willing to further this glorious enterprize, to such I wish according to the decree of Darius, that whosoever is an enemy to our peace, and seeketh either by getting monipolicall patents, or by forging unjust tales to hinder our welfare, that his house were pulled downe, and a paire of gallowes made of the wood, and he hanged on them in the place.

Master Stockams relation.

As for those lasie servants, who had rather stand all day idle, than worke, though but an houre in this Vineyard, and spend their substance riotously, than cast the superfluity of their wealth into your Treasury, I leave them as they are to the eternall Judge of the world.

But you right worthy, that hath adventured so freely, I will not examine, if it were for the glory of God, or your desire of gaine, which it
may be you expect should flow unto you with a full tide, for the conversion of the Salvages: I wonder you use not the meanes, I confesse
you say well to have them converted by faire meanes, but they scorne
to acknowledge it, as for the gifts bestowed on them they devoure
them, and so they would the givers if they could, and though many
have endevoured by all the meanes they could by kindnesse to convert them, they finde nothing from them but derision and ridiculous
answers. We have sent boies amongst them to learne their Language,
but they returne worse than they went; but I am no States-man, nor
love I to meddle with any thing but my Bookes, but I can finde no
probability by this course to draw them to goodnesse; and I am perswaded if Mars and Minerva goe hand in hand, they will effect more
good in an houre, then those verball Mercurians in their lives, and till
their Priests and Ancients have their throats cut, there is no hope to
bring them to conversion.

The government of Sir Francis Wyat.

ABOUT October arrived Sir Francis Wyat, with
Master George Sands, appointed Treasurer, Master
Davison Secretary, Doctor Pot the Physician, and
Master Cloyburne the Surgian, but much provision
was very badly conditioned, nay the Hogs would not eat that
Corne they brought, which was a great cause of their sicknesse
and mortality, and whatsoever is said against the Virginia Corne,
they finde it doth better nourish than any provision is sent
thither; the Sailers still they complaine are much to blame for
imbesling the provisions sent to private men, killing of Swine,
and disorderly trucking; for which some order would be taken.

In them nine Ships that went with Sir Francis Wyat not one
Passenger died, at his arrivall he sent Master Thorpe to
Opechancanough, whom hee found much satisfied with his
comming, to confirme their leagues as he had done his Predecessors, and so contented his people should coinhabit amongst
them, and hee found more motions of Religion in him than
could be imagined: every man betaking himselfe to his quarter, it was ordered, that for every head they should plant but

The arrivall of Sir Francis Wyat.

1000. Plants of Tobacco, and upon each plant nine leaves, which will be about 100. weight, the Corne being appointed but at two shillings and six pence the bushell, required such labour, it caused most men neglect it, and depend upon trade; where were it rated at ten shillings the bushell, every man would indevour to have plenty to sell to the new commers, or any that wanted, and seldome any is transported from England, but it standeth in as much, besides the hazard and other necessaries, the Ships might transport of that burden. The 22. of November arrived Master Gookin out of Ireland, with fifty men of his owne, and thirty Passengers, exceedingly well furnished with all sorts of provision and cattle, and planted himselfe at Nuports-newes: the Cotten trees in a yeere grew so thicke as ones arme, and so high as a man: here any thing that is planted doth prosper so well as in no place better. For the mortality of the people accuse not the place, for of the old Planters and the families scarce one of twenty miscarries, onely the want of necessaries are the occasions of those diseases. And so wee will conclude this yeere with the shipping and numbers sent.

Out of the Councels Letters from Virginia.

This yeere was sent one and twenty saile of Ships that imployed more than 400. sailers and 1300. men, women and children of divers faculties, with fourescore cattle; the *Tiger* fell in the Turkes hands, yet safely escaped, and by the returne of their letters from thence, the company is assured there can bee no fitter place of Mines, Wood and Water for Iron than there; and the French men affirme no Country is more proper for Vines, Olives, Silke, Rice and Salt, etc. of which the next yeere they promise a good quantity.

Gifts

THE Gentlemen and Mariners that came in the *Royall James* from the East-Indies, gave towards the building of a free Schoole 70. pound, eight shillings, and six

(side notes) Master Gookins Plantation. The number of Ships and men The number of Ships and men Gifts given.

pence; and an unknowne person to further it, sent thirtie pounds; and another in like manner five and twentie pounds; another refusing to be made knowne, gave fortie shillings yeerely for a Sermon before the Virginia companie: also another that would not be knowne, sent for the College at Henrico, many excellent good religious bookes, worth ten pound, and a most curious Map of al that coast of America. Master Thomas Bargrave their Preacher there deceased, gave a Librarie valued at one hundred Markes: and the Inhabitants hath made a contribution of one thousand and five hundred pounds, to build a house for the entertaining of strangers. This yeere also

Patents granted.
there was much suing for Patents for Plantations, who promised to transport such great multitudes of people: there was much disputing concerning those divisions, as though the whole land had beene too little for them: six and twentie obtained their desires, but as yet not past six hath sent thither a man; notwithstanding many of them would have more, and are not well contented; whom I would intreat, and all other wranglers, to peruse this saying of honest Claudius.

> *See'st not the world of Natures worke, the fairest well, I*
> *wot,*
> *How it, it selfe together ties, as in a true-loves knot.*
> *Nor seest how th' Elements ayre combin'd, maintaine one*
> *constant plea,*
> *How midst of heaven contents the Sunne, and shore*
> *containes the sea;*
> *And how the aire both compasseth, and carrieth still*
> *earths frame,*
> *Yet neither pressing burdens it, nor parting leaves the same.*

The observations of Master John Pory Secretarie of Virginia, in his travels.

HAVING but ten men meanly provided to plant the Secretaries land on the Easterne shore neere Acomack, Captaine

My journey to the Easterne shore.

Wilcocks plantation, the better to secure and assist each other. Sir George Yearley intending to visit Smiths Iles, fell so sicke that he could not, so that he sent me with Estinien Moll a French-man, to finde a convenient place to make salt in. Not long after Namenacus the King of Pawtuxunt, came to us to seeke for Thomas Salvage our Interpreter. Thus insinuating himselfe, he led us into a thicket, where all sitting downe, he shewed us his naked brest; asking if we saw any deformitie upon it, we told him, No; No more, said hee, is the inside, but as sincere and pure; therefore come freely to my Countrie and welcome: which wee promised wee would within six weekes after. Having taken a muster of the companies tenants, I went to Smiths Iles, where was our Salt-house: not farre off wee found a more convenient place, and so returned to James towne.

A good place to make salt in

Being furnished the second time, wee arrived at Aquohanock, and conferred with Kiptopeke their King. Passing Russels Ile and Onancoke, we arrived at Pawtuxunt: the discription of those places, you may reade in Captaine Smiths discoveries, therefore needlesse to bee writ againe. But here arriving at Attoughcomoco the habitation of Namenacus and Wamanato, his brother, long wee staied not ere they came aboord us with a brasse Kettle, as bright without as within, ful of boyled Oisters. Strict order was given none should offend us, so that the next day I went with the two Kings a hunting, to discover what I could in their confines. Wamanato brought mee first to his house, where hee shewed mee his wife and children, and many Corne-fields; and being two miles within the woods a hunting, as the younger conducted me forth, so the elder brought me home, and used me as kindly as he could, after their manner. The next day he presented me twelve Bever skinnes and a Canow, which I requited with such things to his content, that he promised to keepe them whilst hee lived, and burie them with him being dead. Hee much wondered at our Bible, but much more to heare it was the Law of our God, and the first Chapter of Genesis expounded of Adam and Eve, and simple mariage; to which he replyed, hee was like Adam in one thing, for he never had but one wife at once: but he, as all the rest, seemed more willing of other discourses they better understood. The next day the two

The King of Pawtuxunts entertainment.

Kings with their people, came aboord us, but brought nothing
according to promise; so that Ensigne Salvage challenged Namenacus the breach of three promises, viz. not in giving him a
Boy, nor Corne, though they had plentie, nor Moutapass a
fugitive, called Robert Marcum, that had lived 5. yeeres
amongst those northerly nations, which hee cunningly answered by excuses. Womanato it seemes, was guiltlesse of this
falshood, because hee staied alone when the rest were gone. I
asked him if he desired to bee great and rich; he answered,
They were things all men aspired unto: which I told him he
should be, if he would follow my counsell, so he gave me two
tokens, which being returned by a messenger, should suffice to
make him confident the messenger could not abuse us.

Some things being stolne from us, he tooke such order that
they were presently restored, then we interchanged presents:
in all things hee much admired our discretions, and gave us
a guide that hee called brother, to conduct us up the River:
by the way we met with divers that stil tould us of Marcum:
and though it was in October, we found the Countrie very hot,
and their Corne gathered before ours at James towne.
The next day we went to Paccamaganant, and they
directed us to Assacomoco, where their King Cas-
satowap had an old quarrell with Ensigne Salvage, but now
seeming reconciled, went with us, with another Werowance
towards Mattapanient, where they perswaded us ashore upon
the point of a thicket; but supposing it some trecherie, we returned to our boat: farre we had not gone from the shore, but
a multitude of Salvages sallied out of the wood, with all the ill
words and signes of hostilitie they could. When wee saw plainly
their bad intent, wee set the two Werowances at libertie, that
all this while had line in the Cabbin, as not taking any notice of
their villanie, because we would convert them by courtesie.
Leaving them as we found them, very civil and subtill, wee returned the same way wee came, to the laughing Kings on the
Easterne shore, who told us plainly, Namanicus would also
have allured him into his Countrie, under colour of trade to
cut his throat. Hee told us also Opechancanough had imployed Onianimo to kill Salvage, because he brought the trade
from him to the Easterne shore, and some disgrace hee had
done his sonne, and some thirteene of his people before one

The trecherie
of Nama-
nicus.

hundred of those Easterlings in rescuing Thomas Graves whom they would have slaine, where hee and three more did challenge the thirteene Pamaunkes to fight, but they durst not, so that all those Easterlings so derided them, that they came there no more.

Thomas Salvages good service.   This Thomas Salvage, it is sixteene yeeres since he went to Virginia, being a boy, hee was left with Powhatan, for Namontacke, to learne the language, and as this Author affirmeth, with much honestie and good successe hath served the publike without any publike recompence, yet had an arrow shot through his body in their service. This laughing King at Accomack, tels us the land is not two daies journy over in the broadest place, but in some places a man may goe in halfe a day, betwixt the Bay and the maine Ocean, where inhabit many people, so that by the narrownesse of the Land there is not many Deere, but most abundance of Fish and Fowle. Kiptope his brother rules as his Lieutenant, who seeing his younger brother more affected by the people than himselfe, freely resigned him the moitie of his Countrie, applying himselfe onely to husbandry and hunting, yet nothing neglected in his degree, nor is hee carelesse of any thing concernes the state, but as a vigilant and faithfull Counceller, as hee is an affectionated Brother, bearing the greater burden in government, though the lesser honour, where cleane contrary they on the Westerne shore, the younger beares the charge, and the elder the dignitie. Those are the best husbands of any Salvages we know: for they provide Corne to serve them all the yeare, yet spare; and the other not for halfe the yeare, yet want. They are the most civill and tractable people we have met with, and by little sticks will keepe as just an account of their promises, as by a tally. In their mariages they observe a large distance, as well in affinitie as consanguinitie; nor doe they use that devillish custome in making black Boyes. There may be on this shore about two thousand people: they on the West would invade them, but that they want Boats to crosse the Bay, and so would divers other Nations, were they not protected by us. A few of the Westerly Runnagados had conspired against the laughing King, but fearing their treason was discovered, fled to Smiths Iles, where they made a massacre of Deere and Hogges; and thence to Rickahake, betwixt

Chissapeack and Nansamund, where they now are seated under the command of Itoyatin, and so I returned to James Towne, where I found the government rendred to Sir Francis Wyat. In February also he travelled to the South River Chawonock, some sixtie miles over land, which he found to be a very fruitfull and pleasant Country, yeelding two harvests in a yeare, and found much of the Silke grasse formerly spoken of, was kindly used by the people, and so returned.

Captaine Each sent to build a Fort to secure the Countrey.

1622.
The Earle of
Southampton
Iᴛ was no small content to all the Adventurers to heare of the safe arrivall of all those ships and companies, which was thought sufficient to have made a Plantation of themselves: and againe to second them, was sent
Treasurer,
and Nicolas
Farrar
Deputy.
Captaine Each in the *Abigale*, a ship of three or foure hundred tunnes, who hath undertaken to make a Block-house amongst the Oyster banks, that shall secure the River. The furnishing him with Instruments, cost three hundred pounds; but the whole charge and the ships re-
Five and
twentie sent
only to build
Barks and
Boats.
turne, will be neere two thousand pounds. In her went Captaine Barwicke with five and twentie men for the building ships and Boats, and not other waies to be imploied: and also a selected number to build the East Indie Schoole, but as yet from Virginia little returnes but private mens Tobacco, and faire promises of plentie of Iron, Silke, Wine, and many other good and rich commodities, besides the speedy conversion of the Salvages, that at first were much discouraged from living amongst them, when they were debarred the use of their peeces; therefore it was disputed as a matter of State, whether such as would live amongst them should use them or not, as a bait to allure them; or at least such as should bee called to the knowledge of Christ. But because it was a great trouble for all causes to be brought to James Towne for a triall, Courts were appointed in convenient places to releeve them: but as they can make no Lawes in Virginia till they be ratified here; so they thinke it but reason,

none should bee inacted here without their consents, because they onely feele them, and must live under them. Still they complaine for want of Corne, but what must be had by Trade, and how unwilling any Officer when he leaveth his place, is to make good his number of men to his Successor, but many of them during their times to help themselves, undoes the Company: for the servants you allow them, or such as they hire, they plant on their private Lands, not upon that belongeth to their office, which crop alwaies exceeds yours, besides those which are your tenants to halfes, are forced to row them up and downe, whereby both you and they lose more then halfe. Nor are those officers the ablest or best deserving, but make their experience upon the companies cost, and your land lies unmanured to any purpose, and will yeeld as little profit to your next new officers.

The massacre upon the two and twentieth of March.

The death of Nemattanow, writ by Master Wimp.

THE Prologue to this Tragedy, is supposed was occasioned by Nemattanow, otherwise called Jack of the Feather, because hee commonly was most strangely adorned with them; and for his courage and policy, was accounted amongst the Salvages their chiefe Captaine, and immortall from any hurt could bee done him by the English. This Captaine comming to one Morgans house, knowing he had many commodities that hee desired, perswaded Morgan to goe with him to Pamaunke to trucke, but the Salvage murdered him by the way; and after two or three daies returned againe to Morgans house, where he found two youths his Servants, who asked for their Master: Jack replied directly he was dead; the Boyes suspecting as it was, by seeing him weare his Cap, would have had him to Master Thorp: But Jack so moved their patience, they shot him, so he fell to the ground, put him in a Boat to have him before the Governor, then seven or eight miles from them. But by the way Jack finding the pangs of death upon him, desired of the Boyes two things; the one was, that they would not make it knowne hee was slaine with a bullet; the other, to bury him amongst the English. At the losse of this Salvage Opechankanough much grieved and repined, with great threats of revenge; but the English returned him such terrible answers, that he cunningly dissembled his intent, with the greatest signes he could of love and peace, yet within foureteene daies after he acted what followeth.

Sir Francis Wyat at his arrivall was advertised, he found the Countrey setled in such a firme peace, as most men there thought sure and unviolable, not onely in regard of their promises, but of a necessitie. The poore weake Salvages being every way bettered by us, and safely sheltred and defended, whereby wee might freely follow our businesse: and such was the conceit of this conceited peace, as that there was seldome or never a sword, and seldomer a peece, except for a Deere or Fowle, by which assurances the most plantations were placed straglingly and scatteringly, as a choice veine of rich ground invited them, and further from neighbours the better. Their houses generally open to the Salvages, who were alwaies friendly fed at their tables, and lodged in their bed-chambers, which made the way plaine to effect their intents, and the conversion of the Salvages as they supposed.

Security a bad guard.

Having occasion to send to Opechankanough about the middle of March, hee used the Messenger well, and told him he held the peace so firme, the sky should fall or he dissolved it; yet such was the treachery of those people, when they had contrived our destruction, even but two daies before the massacre, they guided our men with much kindnesse thorow the woods, and one Browne that lived among them to learne the language, they sent home to his Master; yea, they borrowed our Boats to transport themselves over the River, to consult on the devillish murder that insued, and of our utter extirpation, which God of his mercy (by the meanes of one of themselves converted to Christianitie) prevented, and as well on the Friday morning that fatall day, being the two and twentieth of March, as also in the evening before, as at other times they came unarmed into our houses, with Deere, Turkies, Fish, Fruits, and other provisions to sell us, yea in some places sat downe at breakfast with our people, whom immediatly with their owne tooles they slew most barbarously,

The manner of the massacre.

house, and then came to tell them in the dwelling house of it to quench it; all the men ran towards it, but Master Hamer not suspecting any thing, whom the Salvages pursued, shot them full of arrowes, then beat out their braines. Hamer having finished a letter hee was a writing, followed after to see what was the matter, but quickly they shot an arrow in his back, which caused him returne and barricado up the doores, whereupon the Salvages set fire on the house. Harisons Boy finding his Masters peece loaded, discharged it at randome, at which bare report the Salvages all fled, Baldwin still discharging his peece, and Master Hamer with two and twentie persons thereby got to his house, leaving their owne burning. In like manner, they had fired Lieutenant Basse his house, with all the rest there about, slaine the people, and so left that Plantation.

Captaine Ralfe Hamer with forty escapeth. Captaine Hamer all this while not knowing any thing, comming to his Brother that had sent for him to go hunt with the King, meeting the Salvages chasing some, yet escaped, retired to his new house then a building, from whence he came; there onely with spades, axes, and brickbats, he defended himselfe and his Company till the Salvages departed. Not long after, the Master from the ship had sent six Musketiers, with which he recovered their Merchants store-house, where he armed ten more, and so with thirtie more unarmed workmen, found his Brother and the rest at Baldwins: Now seeing all they had was burnt and consumed, they repaired to James Towne with their best expedition; yet not far from Martins hundred, where seventy three were slaine, was a little house and a small family, that heard not of any of this till two daies after.

All those, and many others whom they have as maliciously murdered, sought the good of those poore brutes, that thus despising Gods mercies, must needs now as miscreants be corrected by Justice: to which leaving them, I will knit together the thred of this discourse. At the time of the massacre, there were three or foure ships in James River, and one in the next, and daily more to come in, as there did within fourteene daies The Salvages attempt to surprise a ship. after, one of which they indevoured to have surprised: yet were the hearts of the English ever stupid, and averted from beleeving any thing might weaken their hopes, to win them by kinde usage to Christianitie. But divers write from thence, that Almighty God hath his great worke in this Tragedy, and will thereout draw honor and glory to his name, and a more flourishing estate and safetie to themselves, and with more speed to convert the Salvage children to himselfe, since he so miraculously hath preserved the English; there being yet, God be praised, eleven parts of twelve remaining, whose carelesse neglect of their owne safeties, seemes to have beene the greatest cause of their destructions: yet you see, God by a converted Salvage that disclosed the plot, saved the rest, and the Pinnace then in Pamaunkes River, whereof (say they) though our sinnes made us unworthy of so glorious a conversion, yet his infinite wisdome can neverthelesse bring it to passe, and in good time, by such meanes as we thinke most unlikely: for in the delivery of them that survive, no mans particular carefulnesse saved one person, but the meere goodnesse of God himselfe, freely and miraculously preserving whom he pleased.

The Letters of Master George Sands, a worthy Gentleman, and many others besides them returned, brought us this unwelcome newes, that hath beene heard at large in publike Court, that the Indians and they lived as one Nation, yet by a generall combination in one day plotted to subvert the whole Colony, and at one instant, though our severall Plantations were one hundred and fortie miles up on River on both sides.

But for the better understanding of all things, you must remember these wilde naked natives live not in great numbers together, but dispersed, commonly in thirtie, fortie, fiftie, or sixtie in a company. Some places have two hundred, few places more, but many lesse; yet they had all warning given them one from another in all their habitations, though farre asunder, to meet at the day and houre appointed for our destruction at al our several Plantations; some directed to one place, some to another, all to be done at the time appointed, which they did accordingly: Some entring their houses under colour of trading, so tooke their advantage; others drawing us abroad under faire pretences, and the rest suddenly falling upon those that were at their labours.

Six of the Councell slaine.   Six of the counsell suffered under this treason, and the slaughter had beene universall, if God had not put it into the heart of an Indian, who lying in the house of one Pace, was urged by another Indian his Brother, that lay with him the night before to kill Pace, as he should doe Perry which was his friend, being so commanded from their King; telling him also how the next day the execution should be finished: Perrys Indian presently arose and reveales it to Pace, that used him as his sonne; and thus them that escaped was saved by this one converted Infidell. And though three hundred fortie seven were slaine, yet thousands of ours were by the meanes of this alone thus preserved, for which Gods name he praised for ever and ever.

How it was revealed. Pace upon this, securing his house, before day rowed to James Towne, and told the Governor of it, whereby they were prevented, and at such other Plantations as possibly intelligence could be given: and where they saw us upon our guard, at the sight of a peece they ranne away; but the rest were most slaine, their houses burnt, such Armes and Munition as they found they tooke away, and some cattell also they destroied. Since wee finde Opechankanough the last yeare had practised with a King on the Easterne shore, to furnish him with a kind of poison, which onely growes in his Country to poison us. But of this bloudy acte never griefe and shame possessed any people more then themselves, to be thus butchered by so naked and cowardly a people, who dare not stand the presenting of a staffe in manner of a peece, nor an uncharged peece in the hands of a woman. (But I must tell those Authors, though some might be thus cowardly, there were many of them had better spirits.)

Memoran-dums. Thus have you heard the particulars of this mas-sacre, which in those respects some say will be good for the Plantation, because now we have just cause to destroy them by all meanes possible: but I thinke it had beene much better it had never happened, for they have given us an hundred times as just occasions long agoe to subject them, (and I wonder I can heare of none but Master Stockam and Master Whitaker of my opinion.) Moreover, where before we were troubled in cleering the ground of great Timber, which was to them of small use: now we may take their owne plaine fields and Habitations, which are the pleasantest places in the Countrey. Besides, the Deere, Turkies, and other Beasts and Fowles will exceedingly increase if we beat the Salvages out of the Countrey, for at all times of the yeare they never spare Male nor Female, old nor young, egges nor birds, fat nor leane, in season or out of season with them, all is one. The like they did in our Swine and Goats, for they have used to kill eight in tenne more then we, or else the wood would most plentifully abound with victuall; besides it is more easie to civilize them by conquest then faire meanes; for the one may be made at once, but their civilizing will require a long time and much industry. The manner how to suppresse them is so often related and approved, I omit it here: And you have twenty examples of the Spaniards how they got the West-Indies, and forced the treacherous and rebellious Infidels to doe all manner of drudgery worke and slavery for them, themselves living like

Captaine Smith.

Souldiers upon the fruits of their labours. This will make us more circumspect, and be an example to posteritie: (But I say, this might as well have beene put in practise sixteene yeares agoe as now.)

His Majesties gift.

Thus upon this Anvill shall wee now beat our selves an Armour of proofe hereafter to defend us against such incursions, and ever hereafter make us more circumspect: but to helpe to repaire this losse, besides his Majesties bounty in Armes, he gave the Company out of the Tower, and divers other Honorable persons have renewed

London sets out 100 persons.

their adventures, we must not omit the Honorable Citie of London, to whose endlesse praise wee may speake it, are now setting forward one hundred persons, and divers others at their owne costs are a repairing, and all good men doe thinke never the worse of the businesse for all these disasters.

What growing state was there ever in the world which had not the like? Rome grew by oppression, and rose upon the backe of her enemies: and the Spaniards have had many of those counterbuffes, more than we. Columbus, upon his returne from the West-Indies into Spaine, having left his people with the Indies, in peace and promise of good usage amongst them, at his returne backe found not one of them living, but all treacherously slaine by the Salvages. After this againe, when the Spanish Colonies were increased to great numbers, the Indians from whom the Spaniards for trucking stuffe used to have all their corne, generally conspired together to plant no more at all, intending thereby to famish them; themselves living in the meane time upon Cassava, a root to make bread, onely then knowne to themselves. This plot of theirs by the Spaniards oversight, that foolishly depended upon strangers for their bread, tooke such effect, and brought them to such misery by the rage of famine, that they spared no uncleane nor loathsome beast, no not the poisonous and hideous Serpents, but eat them up also, devouring one death to save them from another; and by this meanes their whole Colony well-neere surfeted, sickned and died miserably, and when they had againe recovered this losse, by their incontinency an infinite number of them died on the Indian disease, we call the French Pox, which at first being a strange and an unknowne malady, was deadly upon whomsoever it lighted: then had they a little flea called Nigua, which got betweene the skinne and the flesh before they were aware, and there bred and multiplied, making swellings and putrifactions, to the decay and losse of many of their bodily members.

A lamentable example, too oft approved.

Againe, divers times they were neere undone by their ambition, faction, and malice of the Commanders. Columbus, to whom they were also much beholden, was sent with his Brother in chaines into Spaine; and some other great Commanders killed and murdered one another. Pizzaro was killed by Almagros sonne, and him Vasco beheaded, which Vasco was taken by Blasco, and Blasco was likewise taken by Pizzaros Brother: And thus by their covetous and spightfull quarrels, they were ever shaking the maine pillars of their Commonweale. These and many more mischiefes and calamities hapned them, more then ever did to us, and at one time being even at the last gaspe, had two ships not arrived with supplies as they did, they were so disheartned, they were a leaving the Countrey: yet we see for all those miseries they have attained to their ends at last, as is manifest to all the world, both with honour, power, and wealth: and whereas before few could be hired to goe to inhabit there, now with great sute they must obtaine it; but where there was no honesty, nor equity, nor sanctitie, nor veritie, nor pietie, nor good civilitie in such a Countrey, certainly there can bee no stabilitie.

Note this conclusion.

Therefore let us not be discouraged, but rather animated by those conclusions, seeing we are so well assured of the

goodnesse and commodities may bee had in Virginia, nor is it
to be much doubted there is any want of Mines of most sorts,
no not of the richest, as is well knowne to some yet living that
can make it manifest when time shall serve: and yet to thinke
that gold and silver Mines are in a country otherwise most rich
and fruitfull, or the greatest wealth in a Plantation, is but a
popular error, as is that opinion likewise, that the gold and sil-

How the
Spaniards
raise their
wealth in the
West Indies.
ver is now the greatest wealth of the West Indies at
this present. True it is indeed, that in the first conquest the Spaniards got great and mighty store of
treasure from the Natives, which they in long space
had heaped together, and in those times the Indians shewed
them entire and rich Mines, which now by the relations of
them that have beene there, are exceedingly wasted, so that
now the charge of getting those Metals is growne excessive,
besides the consuming the lives of many by their pestilent
smoke and vapours in digging and refining them, so that all
things considered, the cleere gaines of those metals, the Kings
part defraied, to the Adventurers is but small, and nothing
neere so much as vulgarly is imagined; and were it not for
other rich Commodities there that inrich them, those of the
Contraction house were never able to subsist by the Mines
onely; for the greatest part of their Commodities are partly
naturall, and partly transported from other parts of the world,
and planted in the West-Indies, as in their mighty wealth of
Sugarcanes, being first transported from the Canaries; and in
Ginger and other things brought out of the East-Indies, in
their Cochanele, Indicos, Cotton, and their infinite store of
Hides, Quick-silver, Allum, Woad, Brasill woods, Dies, Paints,
Tobacco, Gums, Balmes, Oiles, Medicinals and Perfumes, Sas-
saparilla, and many other physicall drugs: These are the meanes
whereby they raise that mighty charge of drawing out their
gold and silver to the great and cleare revenue of their King.
Now seeing the most of those commodities, or as usefull, may
be had in Virginia by the same meanes, as I have formerly said;
let us with all speed take the priority of time, where also may
be had the priority of place, in chusing the best seats of the
Country, which now by vanquishing the salvages, is like to
offer a more faire and ample choice of fruitfull habitations,

then hitherto our gentlenesse and faire comportments could attaine unto.

The numbers that were slaine in those severall Plantations.

At Captaine Berkleys Plantation, himselfe and 21. others, seated at the Falling-Crick, 66. miles from James City.   22

2 Master Thomas Sheffelds Plantation, some three miles from the Falling-Crick, himselfe and 12. others.   13

3 At Henrico Iland, about two miles from Sheffelds Plantation.   6

4 Slaine of the College people, two miles from Henrico.   17

5 At Charles City, and of Captaine Smiths men.   5

6 At the next adjoyning Plantation.   8

7 At William Farrars house.   10

8 At Berkley hundred, five miles from Charles City, Master Thorp and   10

9 At Westover, a mile from Berkley.   2

10 At Master John Wests Plantation.   2

11 At Captaine Nathaniel Wests Plantation.   2

12 At Lieutenant Gibs his Plantation.   12

13 At Richard Owens house, himselfe and   6

14 At Master Owen Macars house, himselfe and   3

15 At Martins hundred, seven miles from James City.   73

16 At another place.   7

17 At Edward Bennets Plantation.   50

18 At Master Waters his house, himselfe and   4

19 At Apamatucks River, at Master Peirce his Plantation, five miles from the College.   4

20 At Master Macocks Divident, Captaine Samuel Macock, and   4

21 At Flowerdieu hundred, Sir George Yearleys Plantation.   6

22 On the other side opposite to it.   7

23 At Master Swinhows house, himselfe and   7

24 At Master William Bickars house, himselfe and   4

25	At Weanock, of Sir George Yearleys people.	21
26	At Powel Brooke, Captaine Nathaniel Powel, and	12
27	At Southampton hundred.	5
28	At Martin Brandons hundred.	7
29	At Captaine Henry Spilmans house.	2
30	At Ensigne Spences house.	5
31	At Master Thomas Peirce his house by Mulbery Ile, himseife and	4

The whole number 347.

Men in this taking bittered with affliction,
Better attend, and mind, and marke Religion,
For then true voices issue from their hearts,
Then speake they what they thinke in inmost parts,
The truth remaines, they cast off fained Arts.

How they were reduced to five or six places.

This lamentable and so unexpected a disaster caused them all beleeve the opinion of Master Stockam, and drave them all to their wits end: it was twenty or thirty daies ere they could resolve what to doe, but at last it was concluded, all the petty Plantations should be abandoned, and drawne onely to make good five or six places, where all their labours now for the most part must redound to the Lords of those Lands where they were resident. Now for want of Boats, it was impossible upon such a sudden to bring also their cattle, and many other things, which with much time, charge and labour they had then in possession with them; all which for the most part at their departure was burnt, ruined

Gookins and Jordens resolutions.

and destroyed by the Salvages. Only Master Gookins at Nuports-newes would not obey the Commanders command in that, though hee had scarce five and thirty of all sorts with him, yet he thought himselfe sufficient against what could happen, and so did to his great credit and the content of his Adventurers. Master Samuel Jorden gathered together but a few of the straglers about him at Beggers-bush, where he fortified and lived in despight of the enemy. Nay, Mistrisse Proctor, a proper, civill, modest Gentlewoman did the like, till perforce the English Officers forced her and all them with her to goe with them, or they would fire her house themselves, as the Salvages did when they were gone, in whose despight they had kept it, and what they had a moneth or three weekes after the Massacre; which was to their hearts a griefe beyond comparison, to lose all they had in that manner, onely to secure others pleasures. Now here in England it was thought, all those remainders might presently have beene reduced into fifties or hundreds in places most convenient with what they had, having such strong houses as they reported they had, which with small labour might have beene made invincible Castles against all the Salvages in the Land, and then presently raised a company, as a running Armie to torment the Barbarous and secure the rest, and so have had all that Country betwixt the Rivers of Powhatan and Pamaunke to range and sustaine them; especially all the territories of Kecoughtan, Chiskact and Paspahege, from Ozenies to that branch of Pamaunke, comming from Youghtanund, which strait of land is not past 4. or 5. miles, to have made a peninsula much bigger then the Summer Iles, invironed with the broadest parts of those two maine Rivers, which for plenty of such things as Virginia affords is not to be exceeded, and were it well manured, more then sufficient for ten thousand men. This, were it well understood, cannot but be thought better then to bring five or six hundred to lodge and live on that, which before would not well receive and maintaine a hundred, planting little or nothing, but spend that they have upon hopes out of England, one evill begetting another, till the disease is past cure: Therefore it is impossible but such courses must produce most fearefull miseries and extreme extremities; if it prove otherwise, I should be exceeding glad. I confesse I am somewhat too bold to censure other mens actions being not present, but they have done as much of me; yea many here in England that were never there, and also many there that knowes little more then their Plantations, but as they are informed; and this doth touch the glory of God, the honour of my Country, and the publike good so much, for which there hath beene so many, faire pretences, that I hope none will be angry for speaking my opinion, seeing the old Proverbe doth allow losers leave to speake; and Du Bartas saith,

The opinion of Captaine Smith.

Even as the wind the angry Ocean moves,
Wave hunteth Wave, and Billow Billow shoves,

So doe all Nations justell each the other,
And so one people doe pursue another,
And scarce a second hath the first unhoused,
Before a third him thence againe have roused.

The
providence
of Captaine
Nuse.
Amongst the multitude of these severall Relations, it appeares Captaine Nuse seeing many of the difficulties to ensue, caused as much Corne to be planted as he could at Elizabeths city, and though some destroyed that they had set, fearing it would serve the Salvages for Ambuscadoes, trusting to releefe by trade, or from England, which hath ever beene one cause of our miseries, for from England wee have not had much, and for trading, every one hath not Ships, Shalops, Interpreters, men and provisions to performe it, and those that have, use them onely for their owne private gaine, not the publike good, so that our beginning this yeere doth cause many to distrust the event of the next. Here wee will leave Captaine Nuse for a while, lamenting the death of Captaine Norton, a valiant industrious Gentleman, adorned with many good qualities, besides Physicke and Chirurgery, which for the publike good he freely imparted to all gratis, but most bountifully to the poore; and let us speake a little of Captaine Croshaw amongst the midst of those broiles in the River of Patawomeke.

Captaine
Croshaw his
voyage to
Patawomek.
Being in a small Barke called the *Elizabeth*, under the command of Captaine Spilman, at Cekacawone, a Salvage stole aboord them, and told them of the Massacre, and that Opechancanough had plotted with his King and Country to betray them also, which they refused, but them of Wighcocomoco at the mouth of the river had undertaken it; upon this Spilman went thither, but the Salvages seeing his men so vigilant and well armed, they suspected themselves discovered, and to colour their guilt, the better to delude him, so contented his desire in trade, his Pinnace was neere fraught; but seeing no more to be had, Croshaw went to Patawomek, where he intended to stay and trade for himselfe, by reason of the long acquaintance he had with this King that so earnestly entreated him now to be his friend, his countenancer, his Captaine and director against the Pazaticans, the Nacotchtanks, and Moyaons his mortall enemies. Of this oportunity Croshaw

was glad, as well to satisfie his owne desire in some other purpose he had, as to keepe the King as an opposite to Opechancanough, and adhere him unto us, or at least make him an
instrument against our enemies; so onely Elis Hill stayed with
him, and the Pinnace returned to Elizabeths City; here shall
they rest also a little, till we see how this newes was entertained
in England.

The arrivall of
this newes in
England.

It was no small griefe to the Councell and Company, to understand of such a supposed impossible
losse, as that so many should fall by the hands of men
so contemptible; and yet having such warnings, especially by
the death of Nemattanow, whom the Salvages did thinke was
shot-free, as he had perswaded them, having so long escaped
so many dangers without any hurt. But now to leape out of
this labyrinth of melancholy, all this did not so discourage the
noble adventurers, nor divers others still to undertake new severall Plantations, but that divers ships were dispatched away,
for their supplies and assistance thought sufficient. Yet Captaine Smith did intreat and move them to put in practise his
old offer, seeing now it was time to use both it and him, how
slenderly heretofore both had beene regarded, and because it
is not impertinent to the businesse, it is not much amisse to
remember what it was.

The project and offer of Captaine John Smith, to the Right Honourable, and Right Worshipfull Company of Virginia.

Captaine
Smiths offer
to the
Company.

IF you please I may be transported with a hundred
Souldiers and thirty Sailers by the next Michaelmas,
with victuall, munition, and such necessary provision, by Gods assistance, we would endevour to inforce the
Salvages to leave their Country, or bring them in that feare and
subjection that every man should follow their businesse securely, whereas now halfe their times and labours are spent in
watching and warding, onely to defend, but altogether unable
to suppresse the Salvages, because every man now being for

himselfe will be unwilling to be drawne from their particular labours, to be made as pack-horses for all the rest, without any certainty of some better reward and preferment then I can understand any there can or will yet give them.

These I would imploy onely in ranging the Countries, and tormenting the Salvages, and that they should be as a running Army till this were effected, and then settle themselves in some such convenient place, that should ever remaine a garison of that strength, ready upon any occasion against the Salvages, or any other for the defence of the Countrey, and to see all the English well armed, and instruct them their use. But I would have a Barke of one hundred tunnes, and meanes to build sixe or seven Shalops, to transport them where there should bee occasion.

Towards the charge, because it is for the generall good, and what by the massacre and other accidents, Virginia is disparaged, and many men and their purses much discouraged, how ever a great many doe hasten to goe, thinking to bee next heires to all the former losses, I feare they will not finde all things as they doe imagine; therefore leaving those gilded conceits, and dive into the true estate of the Colony; I thinke if his Majestie were truly informed of their necessitie, and the benefit of this project, he would be pleased to give the custome of Virginia, and the Planters also according to their abilities would adde thereto such a contribution, as would be fit to maintaine this garison till they be able to subsist, or cause some such other collections to be made, as may put it with all expedition in practice; otherwise it is much to be doubted, there will neither come custome, nor any thing from thence to England within these few yeares.

Now if this should be thought an imploiment more fit for ancient Souldiers there bred, then such new commers as may goe with me; you may please to leave that to my discretion, to accept or refuse such voluntaries, that will hazard their fortunes in the trialls of these events, and discharge such of my company that had rather labour the ground then subdue their enemies: what releefe I should have from your Colony I would satisfie and spare them (when I could) the like courtesie. Notwithstanding these doubts, I hope to feede them as well as defend them, and yet discover you more land unknowne then they all yet know, if you will grant me such priviledges as of necessity must be used.

For against any enemy we must be ready to execute the best can be devised by your state there, but not that they shall either take away my men, or any thing else to imploy as they please by vertue of their authority, and in that I have done somewhat for New-England as well as Virginia, so I would desire liberty and authority to make the best use I can of my best experiences, within the limits of those two Patents, and to bring them both in one Map, and the Countries betwixt them, giving alwaies that respect to the Governors and government, as an Englishman doth in Scotland, or a Scotchman in England, or as the regiments in the Low-countries doe to the Governors of the Townes and Cities where they are billited, or in Garrison, where though they live with them, and are as their servants to defend them, yet not to be disposed on at their pleasure, but as the Prince and State doth command them, and for my owne paines in particular I aske not any thing but what I can produce from the proper labour of the Salvages.

Their Answer.

I CANNOT say, it was generally from the Company, for being published in their Court, the most that heard it liked exceeding well of the motion, and some would have been very large Adventurers in it, especially Sir John Brookes and Master David Wyffin, but there were such divisions amongst them, I could obtaine no answer but this, the charge would be too great; their stocke was decayed, and they did thinke the Planters should doe that of themselves if I could finde meanes to effect it; they did thinke I might have leave of the Company, provided they might have halfe the pillage, but I thinke there are not many will much strive for that imploiment, for except it be a little Corne at some time of the yeere is to be had, I would not give twenty pound for all the pillage is to be got amongst the Salvages in twenty yeeres: but because they supposed I spake only for my owne ends, it were

Their answer.

good those understand providents for the Companies good they so much talke of, were sent thither to make triall of their profound wisdomes and long experiences.

About this time also was propounded a proposition concerning a Sallery of five and twenty hundred pounds to be raised out of Tobacco, as a yeerely pension to bee paid to certaine Officers for the erecting a new office, concerning the sole importation of Tobacco, besides his Majesties custome, fraught, and all other charges. To nominate the undertakers, favourers and opposers, with their arguments *pro* and *con* would bee too tedious and needlesse being so publikely knowne; the which to establish, spent a good part of that yeere, and the beginning of the next. This made many thinke wonders of Virginia, to pay such pensions extraordinary to a few here that were never there, and also in what state and pompe some Chieftaines and divers of their associates live in Virginia, and yet no money to maintaine a Garrison, pay poore men their wages, nor yet five and twenty pence to all the Adventurers here, and very little to the most part of the Planters there, bred such differences in opinion it was dissolved.

The manner of the Sallary.

Now let us returne to Captaine Croshaw at Patawomek, where he had not beene long ere Opechancanough sent two baskets of beads to this King, to kill him and his man, assuring him of the Massacre he had made, and that before the end of two Moones there should not be an Englishman in all their Countries: this fearefull message the King told this Captaine, who replied, he had seene both the cowardise and trechery of Opechancanough sufficiently tried by Captaine Smith, therefore his threats he feared not, nor for his favour cared, but would nakedly fight with him or any of his with their owne swords; if he were slaine, he would leave a letter for his Country men to know, the fault was his owne, not the Kings; two daies the King deliberated upon an answer, at last told him the English were his friends, and the Salvage Emperour Opitchapam now called Toyatan, was his brother, therefore there should be no bloud shed betwixt them, so hee returned the Presents, willing the Pamaunkes to come no more in his Country, lest the English, though against his will, should doe them any mischiefe.

Captaine Croshaw staies at Patawomek, and his adventures.

Not long after, a Boat going abroad to seeke out some

The escape of
Waters and
his Wife.
releefe amongst the Plantations, by Nuports-newes met such ill weather, though the men were saved they lost their boat, which the storme and waves cast upon the shore of Nandsamund, where Edward Waters one of the three that first stayed in Summer Iles, and found the great peece of Amber-greece, dwelling in Virginia at this Massacre, hee and his wife these Nandsamunds kept Prisoners till it chanced they found this Boat, at which purchase they so rejoyced, according to their custome of triumph, with songs, dances and invocations, they were so busied, that Waters and his wife found opportunity to get secretly into their Canow, and so crossed the River to Kecoughtan, which is nine or ten miles, whereat the English no lesse wondred and rejoyced, then the Salvages were madded with discontent. Thus you may see how many desperate dangers some men escape, when others die that have all things at their pleasure.

The arrivall of
Captaine
Hamar at
Patawomek.
All men thinking Captaine Croshaw dead, Captaine Hamer arriving with a Ship and a Pinnace at Patawomeke, was kindly entertained both by him and the King; that Don Hamar told the King he came for Corne: the King replied hee had none, but the Nacotchtanks and their confederats had, which were enemies both to him and them; if they would fetch it, he would give them 40. or 50 choise Bow-men to conduct and assist them. Those Salvages with some of the English they sent, who so well played their parts, they slew 18. of the Nacotchtanks, some write but 4. and some they had a long skirmish with them; where the Patawomeks were so eager of revenge, they drive them not onely out of their towne, but all out of sight through the woods, thus taking what they liked, and spoiling the rest, they retired to

Croshaws
Fort and plot
for trade.
Patawomek, where they left Captaine Croshaw, with foure men more, the rest set saile for James towne.

Captaine Croshaw now with five men and himselfe found night and day so many Alarums, he retired into such a convenient place, that with the helpe of the Salvages, hee had quickly fortified himselfe against all those wilde enemies. Captaine Nuse his Pinnace meeting Hamar by the way understanding all this, came to see Captaine Croshaw: after their best enterchanges of courtesies, Croshaw writ to Nuse the estate of the place where he was, but understanding by them the poore estate of the Colony, offered if they would send him but a bold Shallop, with men, armes and provision for trade, the next Harvest he would provide them Corne sufficient, but as yet it being the latter end of June, there was little or none in all the Country.

Captaine Madyson sent to Patawomek.

This being made knowne to the Governour and the rest, they sent Captaine Madyson with a ship and pinnace, and some six and thirtie men: those Croshaw a good time taught the use of their armes, but receiving a letter from Boyse his Wife, a prisoner with nineteene more at Pamaunke, to use meanes to the Governour for their libertie; So hee dealt with this King, hee got first two of his great men to goe with him to James towne, and eight daies after to send foure of his counsell to Pamaunke, there to stay till he sent one of his two to them, to perswade Opachankanough to send two of his with two of the Patawomekes, to treat about those prisoners, and the rest should remaine their hostage at Pamaunke; but the Commanders, at James towne, it seemes, liked not of it, and so sent the Patawomekes backe againe to their owne Countrie, and Captaine Croshaw to his owne habitation.

The industry of Captaine Nuse.

All this time we have forgot Captaine Nuse, where we left him but newly acquainted with the Massacre, calling all his next adjoyning dispersed neighbours together, he regarded not the pestring his owne house, nor any thing to releeve them, and with all speed entrenched himselfe, mounted three peece of Ordnance, so that within 14. daies, he was strong enough to defend himselfe from all the Salvages, yet when victuall grew scant, some that would forrage without order, which he punished, neere occasioned a mutiny. Notwithstanding, he behaved himselfe so fatherly and kindly to them all, they built two houses for them he daily expected from England, a faire Well of fresh water mantled with bricke, because the River and Cricks are there brackish or salt; in all which things he plaied the Sawyer, Carpenter, Dauber, Laborer, or any thing; wherein though his courage and heart were steeled, he found his body was not made of Iron, for hee had many sicknesses, and at last a Dropsie, no lesse griefe to himselfe, then sorrow to his Wife and all under his government. These crosses and losses were no small increasers of his malady, nor the thus abandoning our Plantations, the losse of our Harvest, and also Tobacco which was as our money; the Vineyard our Vineyetours had brought to a good forwardnesse, bruised and destroyed with Deere, and all things ere they came to perfection, with weeds, disorderly persons or wild beasts; so that as we are I cannot perceive but the next yeere will be worse, being still tormented with pride and flattery, idlenesse and covetousnesse as though they had vowed heere to keepe their Court with all the pestilent vices in the world for their attendants, inchanted with a conceited statelinesse, even in the very bottome of miserable senselesnesse.

Captaine Powel kils 3. Salvages. Shortly after, Sir George Yearly and Captaine William Powel, tooke each of them a company of well disposed Gentlemen and others to seeke their enemies. Yearley ranging the shore of Weanock, could see nothing but their old houses which he burnt, and so went home: Powel searching another part, found them all fled but three he met by chance, whose heads hee cut off, burnt their houses, and so returned; for the Salvages are so light and swift, though wee see them (being so loaded with armour) they have much advantage of us though they be cowards.

The opinion of Captaine Smith. I confesse this is true, and it may cause some suppose they are grown invincible: but will any goe to catch a Hare with a Taber and a Pipe? for who knowes not though there be monsters both of men and beasts, fish and fowle, yet the greatest, the strongest, the wildest, cruellest, fiercest and cunningest, by reason, art and vigilancy, courage and industry hath beene slaine, subjected or made tame, and those are still but Salvages as they were, onely growne more bold by our owne simplicities, and still will be worse and worse till they be tormented with a continuall pursuit, and not with lying inclosed within Palizados, or affrighting them out of your sights, thinking they have done well, can but defend themselves: and to doe this to any purpose, will require both charge, patience and experience. But to their proceedings.

Sir George Yearleys journy to Accomack. About the latter end of June, Sir George Yearley accompanied with the Councell, and a number of the greatest Gallants in the Land, stayed three or foure daies with Captaine Nuse, he making his moane to a chiefe man amongst them for want of provision for his Company, the great Commander replied hee should turne them to

his greene Corne, which would make them plumpe and fat:
these fields being so neere the Fort, were better regarded and
preserved then the rest, but the great mans command, as we
call them, was quickly obeied, for though it was scarce halfe
growne either to the greatnesse or goodnesse, they devoured
it greene though it did them small good. Sir George with his
company went to Accomack to his new Plantation, where he
staied neere six weekes; some Corne he brought home, but as
he adventured for himselfe, he accordingly enjoyed the benefit; some pety Magazines came this Summer, but either the re-
straint by Proclamation, or want of Boats, or both, caused few
but the Chieftaines to be little better by them. So long as Captaine Nuse had any thing we had part; but now all being spent,

Captaine
Nuse his
misery.

and the people forced to live upon Oisters and Crabs,
they became so faint no worke could be done; and
where the Law was, no worke, no meat, now the
case is altered, to no meat, no worke; some small quantity of
Milke and Rice the Captaine had of his owne, and that he
would distribute gratis as he saw occasion; I say gratis, for I
know no place else, but it was sold for ready paiment: those
eares of Corne that had escaped till August, though not ripe
by reason of the late planting, the very Dogs did repaire to the
Corne fields to seeke them as the men till they were hanged;
and this I protest before God is true that I have related, not to
flatter Nuse, nor condemne any, but all the time I have lived in
Virginia, I have not seene nor heard that any Commander hath
taken such continuall paines for the publike, or done so little
good for himselfe, and his vertuous wife was no lesse charitable and compassionate according to her power. For my owne
part, although I found neither Mulberies planted, houses built,
men nor victuall provided, as the honourable Adventurers did
promise mee in England; yet at my owne charge, having made
these preparations, and the silke-Wormes ready to be covered,
all was lost, but my poore life and children, by the Massacre,

An Alarum,
foure slaine.

the which as God in his mercy did preserve, I continually pray we may spend to his glory. The 9. of
September, we had an alarum, and two men at their
labours slaine; the Captaine, though extreme sicke, sallied
forth, but the Salvages lay hid in the Corne fields all night,
where they destroyed all they could, and killed two men more,

much mischiefe they did to Master Edward Hills cattle, yet he alone defended his house though his men were sicke and could doe nothing, and this was our first assault since the Massacre.

The kindnesse of the King of Patawomek. About this time Captaine Madyson passed by us, having taken Prisoners, the King of Patawomek, his sonne, and two more, and thus it happened; Madyson not liking so well to live amongst the Salvages as Croshaw did, built him a strong house within the Fort, so that they were not so sociable as before, nor did they much like Poole the Interpreter; many Alarums they had, but saw no enemies: Madyson before his building went to Moyaones, where hee got provision for a moneth, and was promised much more, so he returned to Patawomek and built this house, and was well used by the Salvages. Now by the foure great men the King sent to Pamaunke for the redemption of the Prisoners, Madyson sent them a letter, but they could neither deliver it nor see them: so long they stayed that the King grew doubtfull of their bad usage, that hee swore by the Skyes, if they returned not well, he would have warres with Opechankanough so long as he had any thing: at this time two of Madysons men ranne from him, to finde them he sent Master John Upton and three more with an Indian guide to Nazatica, where they heard they were. At this place was a King beat out of his Country by the Necosts, enemies to the Patawomeks; this expulsed King though he professed much love to the Patawomeks, yet hee loved not the King because he would not helpe him to revenge his injuries, but to our Interpreter Poole hee protested great love, promising if any treason were, he would reveale it; our guide conducted this Bandyto with them up to Patawomek, and there kept him; our Fugitives we found the Patawomeks had taken and brought home, and the foure great men returned from Pamaunke; not long after, this expulsed King desired private conference with Poole, urging him to sweare by his God never to reveale what hee would tell him, Poole promised he would not; then quoth this King, those great men that went to Pamaunke, went not as you suppose they pretended, but to contract with Opechankanough how to kill you all here, and these are their plots.

A Salvages policy. First, they will procure halfe of you to goe a fishing to their furthest towne, and there set upon them, and cut off the rest; if that faile, they will faine a place where are many strangers would trade their Furres, where they will perswade halfe of you to goe trade, and there murder you and kill them at home; and if this faile also, then they will make Alarums two nights together, to tire you out with watching, and then set upon you, yet of all this, said he, there is none acquainted but the King and the great Conjurer.

Madison takes the King and kils 30. or 40.

This being made known to the Captain, we all stood more punctually upon our guard, at which the Salvages wondering, desired to know the cause; we told them we expected some assault from the Pamaunkes, whereat they seemed contented, and the next day the King went on hunting with two of our men, and the other a fishing and abroad as before, till our Shallop returned from James towne with the two Salvages, sent home with Captaine Croshaw: by those the Governour sent to Madyson, that this King should send him twelve of his great men; word of this was sent to the King at another towne where he was, who not comming presently with the Messenger, Madyson conceited hee regarded not the message, and intended as he supposed the same treason. The next morning the King comming home, being sent for, he came to the Captaine and brought him a dish of their daintiest fruit; then the Captaine fained his returne to James towne, the King told him he might if he would, but desired not to leave him destitute of aid, having so many enemies about him; the Captaine told him he would leave a guard, but intreated his answer concerning the twelve great men for the Governour; the King replied, his enemies lay so about him he could not spare them, then the Captaine desired his sonne and one other; my sonne, said the King, is gone abroad about businesse, but the other you desire you shall have, and that other sits by him, but that man refused to goe, whereupon Madyson went forth and locked the doore, leaving the King, his sonne, and foure Salvages, and five English men in the strong house, and setting upon the towne with the rest of his men, slew thirty or forty men, women and children; the King demanding the cause, Poole told him the treason, crying out to intreat the Captaine cease from such cruelty: but having slaine and made flye all in the towne, hee returned, taxing the poore King of treason, who denied to the death not to know of any such matter, but said, This is some plot of them that told it, onely to kill mee for being your friend. Then Madyson willed him, to command none of his men should shoot at him as he went aboord, which he presently did, and it was performed: so Madyson departed, leading the King, his sonne, and two more to his ship, promising when all his men were shipped, he should re-

The King set at liberty. turne at libertie; notwithstanding he brought them to James towne, where they lay some daies, and after were sent home by Captaine Hamer, that tooke Corne for their ransome, and after set saile for New found Land.

> *But, alas the cause of this was onely this*
> *They understood, nor knew what was amisse.*

A digression. Ever since the beginning of these Plantations, it hath beene supposed the King of Spaine would invade them, or our English Papists indevour to dissolve them. But neither all the Counsels of Spaine, nor Papists in the world could have devised a better course to bring them all to ruine, then thus to abuse their friends, nor could there ever have beene a better plot, to have overthrowne Opechankanough then Captaine Chroshaws, had it beene fully managed with expedition. But it seemes God is angry to see Virginia made a stage where nothing but murder and indiscretion contends for victory.

Their proceedings of the other plantations. Amongst the rest of the Plantations all this Summer little was done, but securing themselves and planting Tobacco, which passes there as current Silver, and by the oft turning and winding it, some grow rich, but many poore, notwithstanding ten or twelve ships or more hath arrived there since the massacre, although it was Christmas ere any returned, and that returne greatly revived all mens longing expectation here in England: for they brought newes, that notwithstanding their extreme sicknesse many were recovered, and finding the Salvages did not much trouble them, except it were sometimes some disorderly straglers they cut off. To lull

300 surpriseth Nandsamund. them the better in securitie, they sought no revenge till their Corne was ripe, then they drew together three hundred of the best Souldiers they could, that would leave their private businesse, and adventure themselves

amongst the Salvages to surprize their Corne, under the conduct of Sir George Yearley, being imbarked in convenient shipping, and all things necessary for the enterprise, they went first
to Nandsamund, where the people set fire on their owne
houses, and spoiled what they could, and then fled with what
they could carry; so that the English did make no slaughter
amongst them for revenge. Their Corne fields being newly
gathered, they surprized all they found, burnt the houses remained unburnt, and so departed. Quartering about Kecoughtan, after the Watch was set, Samuell Collyer one of
the most ancientest Planters, and very well acquainted with their language and habitation, humors
and conditions, and Governor of a Towne, when the Watch
was set going the round, unfortunately by a Centinell that discharged his peece, was slaine.

Samuell Collyer slaine.

Thence they sailed to Pamaunke, the chiefe seat of
Opechankanough, the contriver of the massacre: the
Salvages seemed exceeding fearefull, promising to
bring them Sara, and the rest of the English yet living, with all
the Armes, and what they had to restore, much desiring peace,
and to give them any satisfaction they could. Many such devices they fained to procrastinate the time ten or twelve daies,
till they had got away their Corne from all the other places up
the River, but that where the English kept their quarter: at last,
when they saw all those promises were but delusions, they
seised on all the Corne there was, set fire on their houses: and
in following the Salvages that fled before them, some few of
those naked Devils had that spirit, they lay in ambuscado, and
as our men marched discharged some shot out of English
peeces, and hurt some of them flying at their pleasures where
they listed, burning their empty houses before them as they
went to make themselves sport: so they escaped, and Sir George
returned with Corne, where for our paines we had three
bushels apeece, but we were enjoyned before we had it, to pay
ten shillings the bushell for fraught and other charges. Thus by
this meanes the Salvages are like as they report, to endure no
small misery this Winter, and that some of our men are returned to their former Plantations.

They surprise Pamaunke.

What other passages or impediments hapned in
their proceedings, that they were not fully revenged

The opinion of Captaine Smith.

of the Salvages before they returned, I know not; nor could ever heare more, but that they supposed they slew two, and how it was impossible for any men to doe more then they did: yet worthy Ferdinando Courtus had scarce three hundred Spaniards to conquer the great Citie of Mexico, where thousands of Salvages dwelled in strong houses: but because they were a civilized people, had wealth, and those meere Barbarians as wilde as beasts have nothing; I intreat your patience to tell you my opinion, which if it be Gods pleasure I shall not live to put in practice, yet it may be hereafter usefull for some, but howsoever I hope not hurtfull to any, and this it is.

How to subject all the Salvages in Virginia. Had these three hundred men beene at my disposing, I would have sent first one hundred to Captaine Rawley Chroshaw to Patawomek, with some small Ordnance for the Fort, the which but with daily exercising them, would have struck that love and admiration into the Patowomeks, and terror and amazement into his enemies, which are not farre off, and most seated upon the other side the River, they would willingly have beene friends, or have given any composition they could, before they would be tormented with such a visible feare.

Now though they be generally perfidious, yet necessity constraines those to a kinde of constancy because of their enemies, and neither my selfe that first found them, Captaine Argall, Chroshow, nor Hamar, never found themselves in fifteene yeares trials: nor is it likely now they would have so hostaged their men, suffer the building of a Fort, and their women and children amongst them, had they intended any villany; but suppose they had, who would have desired a better advantage then such an advertisement, to have prepared the Fort for such an assault, and surely it must be a poore Fort they could hurt, much more take, if there were but five men in it durst discharge a peece: Therefore a man not well knowing their conditions, may be as wel too jealous as too carelesse; Such another Lope Skonce would I have had at Onawmanient, and one hundred men more to have made such another at Atquacke upon the River of Toppahanock, which is not past thirteene miles distant from Onawmanient: each of which twelve men would keepe, as well as twelve thousand, and spare all the rest to bee imploied as there should be occasion. And all this with

these numbers might easily have beene done, if not by courtesie, yet by compulsion, especially at that time of September
when all their fruits were ripe, their beasts fat, and infinite
numbers of wilde Fowle began to repaire to every creeke, that
men if they would doe any thing, could not want victuall. This
done, there remained yet one hundred who should have done
the like at Ozinieke, upon the River of Chickahamania, not
past six miles from the chiefe habitations of Opechankanough.
These small Forts had beene cause sufficient to cause all the
Inhabitants of each of those Rivers to looke to themselves.
Then having so many Ships, Barks, and Boats in Virginia as
there was at that present, with what facility might you have
landed two hundred and twentie men, if you had but onely
five or six Boats in one night; forty to range the branch of
Mattapanyent, fortie more that of Youghtanund, and fortie
more to keepe their randivous at Pamaunke it selfe. All which
places lie so neere, they might heare from each other within
foure or five houres, and not any of those small parties, if there
were any valour, discretion, or industry in them, but as sufficient as foure thousand, to force them all to contribution, or
take or spoile all they had. For having thus so many convenient
randevous to releeve each other, though all the whole Countries had beene our enemies, where could they rest, but in the
depth of Winter we might burne all the houses upon all those
Rivers in two or three daies? Then without fires they could not
live, which they could not so hide but wee should finde, and
quickly so tire them with watching and warding, they would
be so weary of their lives, as either fly all their Countries, or
give all they had to be released of such an hourely misery. Now
if but a small number of the Salvages would assist us, as there
is no question but divers of them would; And to suppose they
could not be drawne to such faction, were to beleeve they are
more vertuous then many Christians, and the best governed
people in the world. All the Pamaunkes might have beene dispatched as well in a moneth as a yeare, and then to have dealt
with any other enemies at our pleasure, and yet made all this
toile and danger but a recreation.

If you think this strange or impossible, 12 men with my selfe
I found sufficient, to goe where I would adaies, and surprise a
house with the people, if not a whole towne in a night, or in-

counter all the power they could make, as a whole Army, as formerly at large hath beene related: And it seemes by these small parties last amongst them, by Captaine Crashow, Hamar, and Madyson, they are not growne to that excellency in policy and courage but they might bee encountred, and their wives and children apprehended. I know I shall bee taxed for writing so much of my selfe, but I care not much, because the judiciall know there are few such Souldiers as are my examples, have writ their owne actions, nor know I who will or can tell my intents better then my selfe.

Some againe finde as much fault with the Company for medling with so many Plantations together, because they that have many Irons in the fire some must burne; but I thinke no if they have men enow know how to worke them, but howsoever, it were better some burne then have none at all. The King of Spaine regards but how many powerfull Kingdomes he keepes under his obedience, and for the Salvage Countries he hath subjected, they are more then enow for a good Cosmographer to nominate, and is three Mole-hills so much to us; and so many Empires so little for him? For my owne part, I cannot chuse but grieve, that the actions of an Englishman should be inferior to any, and that the command of England should not be as great as any Monarchy that ever was since the world began, I meane not as a Tyrant to torment all Christendome, but to suppresse her disturbers, and conquer her enemies.

> For the great Romans got into their hand
> The whole worlds compasse, both by Sea and Land,
> Or any seas, or heaven, or earth extended,
> And yet that Nation could not be contented.

The arrivall of Captaine Butler, and his accidents.   Much about this time arrived a small Barke of Barnestable, which had beene at the Summer Iles, and in her Captaine Nathaniel Butler, who having beene Governor there three yeares, and his Commission expired, he tooke the opportunity of this ship to see Virginia: at James Towne he was kindly entertained by Sir Francis Wyat the Governor. After he had rested there foureteene daies, he fell up with his ship to the River of Chickahamania, where meeting Captaine William Powell, joyning together such forces as they had to the number of eighty, they set upon the

Chickahamanians, that fearefully fled, suffering the English to spoile all they had, not daring to resist them. Thus he returned to James towne, where hee staied a moneth, at Kecoughtan as much more, and so returned for England.

But riding at Kecoughtan, Master John Argent, sonne to Doctor Argent, a young Gentleman that went with Captaine Butler from England to this place, Michael Fuller, William Gany, Cornelius May, and one other going ashore with some goods late in a faire evening, such a sudden gust did arise, that drive them thwart the River, in that place at least three or foure miles in bredth, where the shore was so shallow at a low water, and the Boat beating upon the Sands, they left her, wading neere halfe a mile, and oft up to the chin: So well it hapned, Master Argent had put his Bandileir of powder in his hat, which next God was all their preservations: for it being February, and the ground so cold, their bodies became so benumbed, they were not able to strike fire with a steele and a stone hee had in his pocket; the stone they lost twice, and thus those poore soules groping in the darke, it was Master Argents chance to finde it, and with a few withered leaves, reeds, and brush, make a small fire, being upon the Chisapeaks shore, their mortall enemies, great was their feare to be discovered. The joyfull morning appearing, they found their Boat and goods drive ashore, not farre from them, but so split shee was unserviceable: but so much was the frost, their clothes did freeze upon their backs, for they durst not make any great fire to dry them, lest thereby the bloudy Salvages might discry them, so that one of them died the next day, and the next night digging a grave in the Sands with their hands, buried him. In this bodily feare they lived and fasted two daies and nights, then two of them went into the Land to seeke fresh water; the others to the Boat to get some meale and oyle, Argent and his Comrado found a Canow, in which they resolved to adventure to their ship, but shee was a drift in the River before they returned: thus frustrate of all hopes, Captaine Butler the third night ranging the shore in his Boat to seeke them, discharged his Muskets, but they supposing it some Salvages had got some English peeces, they grew more perplexed then ever, so he returned and lost his labour. The fourth day they unloaded their Boat, and stopping her leakes

A strange deliverance of Master Argent and others.

with their handkerchiefes, and other rags, two rowing, and two bailing out the water; but farre they went not ere the water grew upon them so fast, and they so tired, they thought themselves happy to be on shore againe, though they perceived the Indians were not farre off by their fires. Thus at the very period of despaire, Fuller undertooke to sit a stride upon a little peece of an old Canow; so well it pleased God the wind and tide served, by padling with his hands and feet in the water, beyond all expectation God so guided him three or foure houres upon this boord, he arrived at their ship, where they no lesse amazed then he tired, they tooke him in. Presently as he had concluded with his Companions, he caused them discharge a peece of Ordnance if he escaped, which gave no lesse comfort to Master Argent and the rest, then terror to those Plantations that heard it, (being late) at such an unexpected alarum: but after, with warme clothes and a little strong water, they had a little recovered him, such was his courage and care of his distressed friends, he returned that night againe with Master Felgate to conduct him to them, and so giving thanks to God for so hopelesse a deliverance, it pleased his Divine power, both they and their provision came safely aboord, but Fuller they doubt will never recover his benumbed legs and thighes.

Now before Butlers arrivall in England, many hard speeches were rumored against him for so leaving his charge, before he received order from the Company: Divers againe of his Souldiers as highly commended him, for his good government, art, judgement and industry. But to make the misery of Virginia appeare that it might be reformed in time, how all those Cities, Townes, Corporations, Forts, Vineyards, Nurseries of Mulberies, Glasse-houses, Iron forges, Guest-houses, Silke-wormes, Colleges, the Companies great estate, and that plenty some doe speake of here, are rather things in words and paper then in effect, with divers reasons of the causes of those defects; if it were false, his blame nor shame could not be too much: but if there bee such defects in the government, and distresse in the Colony, it is thought by many it hath beene too long concealed, and requireth rather reformation then disputation: but however, it were not amisse to provide for the worst, for the best will help it selfe. Notwithstanding, it was apprehended so hardly, and examined with that passion, that the brute thereof was spread abroad with that expedition, it did more hurt then the massacre; and the fault of all now by the vulgar rumour, must be attributed to the unwholesomnesse of the ayre, and barrennesse of the Countrey, as though all England were naught, because the Fens and Marshes are unhealthy; or barren, because some will lie under windowes and starve in Cheap-side, rot in Goales, die in the street, highwaies, or any where, and use a thousand devices to maintaine themselves in those miseries, rather then take any paines, to live as they may by honest labour, and a great part of such like are the Planters of Virginia, and partly the occasion of those defailements.

1623.
How
Captaine
Spilman was
left in the
River of
Patawomek.
The Earle of
Southampton
Treasurer.

In the latter end of this last yeare, or the beginning of this, Captaine Henrie Spilman a Gentleman, that hath lived in those Countries thirteene or foureteene yeares, one of the best Interpreters in the Land, being furnished with a Barke and six and twentie men, hee was sent to trucke in the River of Patawomek, where he had lived a long time amongst the Salvages, whether hee presumed too much upon his acquaintance amongst them, or they sought to be revenged of any for the slaughter made amongst them by the English so lately, or hee sought to betray them, or they him, are all severall relations, but it seemes but imaginary: for then returned report they left him ashore about Patawomek, but the name of the place they knew not, with one and twentie men, being but five in the Barke, the Salvages ere they suspected any thing, boorded them with their Canowes, and entred so fast, the English were amazed, till a Sailer gave fire to a peece of Ordnance onely at randome; at the report whereof, the Salvages leapt over-boord, so distracted with feare, they left their Canowes and swum a shore; and presently after they heard a great brute amongst the Salvages a shore, and saw a mans head throwne downe the banke, whereupon they weighed Anchor and returned home, but how he was surprised or slaine, is uncertaine.

Thus things proceed and vary not a jot.
Whether we know them, or we know them not.

A particular of such necessaries as either private families, or single persons, shall have cause to provide to goe to Virginia, whereby greater numbers may in part conceive the better how to provide for themselves.

Apparell.

A Monmoth Cap.	1s.	10d.
3 falling bands.	1s.	3d.
3 shirts.	7s.	6d.
1 Waste-coat.	2s.	2d.
1 suit of Canvase.	7s.	6d.
1 suit of Frize.	10s.	
1 suit of Cloth.	15s.	
3 paire of Irish stockings.	4s.	
4 paire of shooes.	8s.	8d.
1 paire of garters.		10d.
1 dozen of points.		3d.
1 paire of Canvas sheets.	8s.	
7 ells of Canvas to make a bed and boulster, to be filled in Virginia, serving for two men.	8s.	
5 ells of course Canvas to make a bed at Sea for two men.	5s.	
1 course rug at sea for two men.	6s.	
	4l.	

Victuall for a whole yeare for a man, and so after the rate for more.

8 bushels of meale.	2l.	
2 bushels of pease.	6s.	
2 bushels of Otemeale.	9s.	
1 gallon of Aquavitæ.	2s.	6d.
1 gallon of oyle.	3s.	6d.
2 gallons of Vineger.	2s.	
	3l.	3s.

Armes for a man, but if halfe your men be armed it is well, so all have swords and peeces.

1 Armor compleat, light.	17s.	
1 long peece five foot and a halfe, neere Musket bore.	1l.	2s.
1 Sword.	5s.	
1 Belt.	1s.	

1 Bandilier.		1s.	6d.
20 pound of powder.		18s.	
60 pound of shot or Lead,			
Pistoll and Goose shot.		5s.	
	3l.	9s.	6d.

Tooles for a family of six persons,
and so after the rate for more.

5 broad howes at 2s. a peece.		10s.	
5 narrow howes at 16d. a peece.		6s.	8d.
2 broad axes at 3s. 8d. a pecce.		7s.	4d.
5 felling axes at 18d. a peece.		7s.	6d.
2 steele handsawes at 16d. a			
peece.		2s.	8d
2 two handsawes at 5s. a peece.		10s.	
1 whipsaw, set and filed, with			
box, file and wrest.		10s.	
2 hammers 12d. a peece.		2s.	
3 shovels 18d. a peece.		4s.	6d.
2 spades at 18d. a peece.		3s.	
2 Augers at 6d. a peece.		1s.	
6 Chissels at 6d. a peece.		3s.	
2 Percers stocked 4d. a peece.			8d.
3 Gimblets at 2d. a peece.			6d.
2 Hatchets at 21d. a peece.		3s.	6d.
2 frowes to cleave pale 18d. each	3s.		
2 hand Bills 20d. a peece.		3s.	4d.
1 Grindstone.		4s.	
Nailes of all sorts to the value of	2l.		
2 Pickaxes.		3s.	
	6l.	2s.	8d.

Houshold implements for a family of six
persons; and so for more or lesse after the rate.

1 Iron pot.		7s.	
1 Kettell.		6s.	
1 large Frying pan.		2s.	6d.
1 Gridiron.		1s.	6d.
2 Skellets.		5s.	
1 Spit.		2s.	
Platters, dishes, spoones of			
wood		4s.	
	1l.	8s.	

For Sugar, Spice, and Fruit, and at Sea for six men.	12s.	6d.
So the full charge after this rate for each person, will amount about the summe of	12l.	10s.
The passage of each man is	6l.	
The fraught of these provisions for a man, will be about halfe a tun, which is	1l.	10s.
So the whole charge will amount to about	20l.	

Now if the number be great, Nets, Hooks and Lines, but Cheese, Bacon, Kine and Goats must be added. And this is the usuall proportion the Virginia Company doe bestow upon their Tenents they send.

A briefe relation written by Captaine Smith to his Majesties Commissioners for the reformation of Virginia, concerning some aspersions against it.

HONOURABLE Gentlemen, for so many faire and Navigable Rivers so neere adjoyning, and piercing thorow so faire a naturall Land, free from any inundations, or large Fenny unwholsome Marshes, I have not seene, read, nor heard of: And for the building of Cities, Townes, and Wharfage, if they will use the meanes, where there is no more ebbe nor floud, Nature in few places affoords any so convenient. For salt Marshes or Quagmires, in this tract of James Towne River I know very few; some small Marshes and Swamps there are, but more profitable then hurtfull: and I thinke there is more low Marsh ground betwixt Eriffe and Chelsey, then Kecoughton and the Falls, which is about one hundred and eighty miles by the course of the River.

The causes of our first miseries. Being enjoyned by our Commission not to unplant nor wrong the Salvages, because the channell was so neere the shore, where now is James Towne, then a thicke grove of trees; wee cut them downe, where the Salvages pretending as much kindnesse as could bee, they hurt

and slew one and twenty of us in two houres: At this time our
diet was for most part water and bran, and three ounces of
little better stuffe in bread for five men a meale, and thus we
lived neere three moneths: our lodgings under boughes of
trees, the Salvages being our enemies, whom we neither knew
nor understood; occasions I thinke sufficient to make men
sicke and die.

But 38 En-
glish in all
Virginia.

Necessity thus did inforce me with eight or nine,
to try conclusions amongst the Salvages, that we got
provision which recovered the rest being most sicke.
Six weeks I was led captive by those Barbarians, though some
of my men were slaine, and the rest fled, yet it pleased God to
make their great Kings daughter the means to returne me safe
to James towne, and releeve our wants, and then our Common-
wealth was in all eight and thirty, the remainder of one hundred and five.

Proofes of the
healthfulnesse
of the
Countrey.

Being supplied with one hundred and twenty, with
twelve men in a boat of three tuns, I spent foureteene weeks in those large waters; the contents of
the way of my boat protracted by the skale of proportion, was
about three thousand miles, besides the River we dwell upon,
where no Christian knowne ever was, and our diet for the
most part what we could finde, yet but one died.

How the
Salvages
became
subjected.

The Salvages being acquainted, that by command
from England we durst not hurt them, were much
imboldned; that famine and their insolencies did
force me to breake our Commission and instructions, cause
Powhatan fly his Countrey, and take the King of Pamaunke
Prisoner; and also to keepe the King of Paspahegh in shackels,
and put his men to double taskes in chaines, till nine and thirty
of their Kings paied us contribution, and the offending Salvages sent to James towne to punish at our owne discretions: in
the two last yeares I staied there, I had not a man slaine.

All those conclusions being not able to prevent the bad
events of pride and idlenesse, having received another supply

How we lived
of the natural
fruits of the
Countrey.

of seventie, we were about two hundred in all, but
not twentie work-men: In following the strict directions from England to doe that was impossible at
that time; So it hapned, that neither wee nor they had any
thing to eat, but what the Countrey afforded naturally; yet of

eightie who lived upon Oysters in June and July, with a pint of corne a week for a man lying under trees, and 120 for the most part living upon Sturgion, which was dried til we pounded it to powder for meale, yet in ten weeks but seven died.

Proofe of the Commodities we returned. It is true, we had of Tooles, Armes, and Munition sufficient, some Aquavitæ, Vineger, Meale, Pease, and Otemeale, but in two yeares and a halfe not sufficient for six moneths, though by the bils of loading the proportions sent us, would well have contented us, notwithstanding we sent home ample proofes of Pitch, Tar, Sope Ashes, Wainskot, Clapboord, Silke grasse, Iron Ore, some Sturgion and Glasse, Saxefras, Cedar, Cypris, and blacke Walnut, crowned Powhaton, sought the Monacans Countrey, according to the instructions sent us, but they caused us neglect more necessary workes: they had better have given for Pitch and Sope ashes one hundred pound a tun in Denmarke: Wee also maintained five or six severall Plantations.

What we built. James towne being burnt, wee rebuilt it and three Forts more, besides the Church and Store-house, we had about fortie or fiftie severall houses to keepe us warme and dry, invironed with a palizado of fourteene or fifteene foot, and each as much as three or foure men could carrie. We digged a faire Well of fresh water in the Fort, where wee had three Bulwarks, foure and twentie peece of Ordnance, of Culvering, Demiculvering, Sacar and Falcon, and most well mounted upon convenient plat-formes, planted one hundred acres of Corne. We had but six ships to transport and supply us, and but two hundred seventy seven men, boies, and women, by whose labours Virginia being brought to this kinde of perfection, the most difficulties past, and the foundation thus laid by this small meanes; yet because we had done no more, they called in our Commission, tooke a new in their owne names, and appointed us neere as many offices and Officers as I had Souldiers, that neither knew us nor wee them, without our consents or knowledge; since there have gone more then one hundred ships of other proportions, and eight or ten thousand people. Now if you please to compare what hath beene spent, sent, discovered and done this fifteene yeares, by that we did in the three first yeares, and every Governor that hath beene there since, give you but such an account as this, you may easily finde what hath beene the cause of those disasters in Virginia.

Then came in Captaine Argall, and Master Sedan, in a ship of Master Cornelius, to fish for Sturgion, who had such good provision, we contracted with them for it, whereby we were better furnished then ever.

Not long after came in seven ships, with about three hundred people; but rather to supplant us then supply us, their Admirall with their authoritie being cast away in the Bermudas, very angry they were we had made no better provision for them. Seven or eight weekes we withstood the inundations of these disorderly humors, till I was neere blowne to death with Gun-powder, which occasioned me to returne for England.

In the yeare 1609 about Michaelmas, I left the Countrey, as is formerly related, with three ships, *How I left the Country.* seven Boats, Commodities to trade, harvest newly gathered, eight weeks provision of Corne and Meale, about five hundred persons, three hundred Muskets, shot, powder, and match, with armes for more men then we had. The Salvages their language and habitation, well knowne to two hundred expert Souldiers; Nets for fishing, tooles of all sorts, apparell to supply their wants: six Mares and a Horse, five or six hundred Swine, many more Powltry, what was brought or bred, but victuall there remained.

Having spent some five yeares, and more then five *My charge.* hundred pounds in procuring the Letters Patents and setting forward, and neere as much more about New England, etc. Thus these nineteene yeares I have here and there not spared any thing according to my abilitie, nor the best advice I could, to perswade how those strange miracles of misery might have beene prevented, which lamentable experience plainly taught me of necessity must insue, but few would beleeve me till now too deerely they have paid for it.

Wherefore hitherto I have rather left all then under-*My reward.* take impossibilities, or any more such costly taskes at such chargeable rates: for in neither of those two Countries have I one foot of Land, nor the very house I builded, nor the ground I digged with my owne hands, nor ever any content or satisfaction at all, and though I see ordinarily those two Countries shared before me by them that neither have them nor knowes them, but by my descriptions: Yet that doth not so much trouble me, as to heare and see those contentions and divisions which will hazard if not ruine the prosperitie of Virginia, if present remedy bee not found, as they have hindred many hundreds, who would have beene there ere now, and makes them yet that are willing to stand in a demurre.

For the Books and Maps I have made, I will thanke him that will shew me so much for so little recompence, and beare with their errors till I have done better. For the materials in them I cannot deny, but am ready to affirme them both there and here, upon such grounds as I have propounded, which is to have but one hundred fifty men to subdue againe the Salvages, fortifie the Countrey, discover that yet unknowne, and both defend and feed their Colony, which I most humbly refer to his Majesties most judiciall judgement, and the most honourable Lords of his Privy Councell, you his trusty and well-beloved Commissioners, and the Honourable company of Planters and well-willers to Virginia, New-England and Sommer-Ilands.

Out of these Observations it pleased his Majesties Commissioners for the reformation of Virginia, to desire my answer to these seven Questions.

Question 1. What conceive you is the cause the Plantation hath prospered no better since you left it in so good a for-wardnesse?

Answer. Idlenesse and carelesnesse brought all I did in three yeeres in six moneths to nothing, and of five hundred I left, scarce threescore remained, and had Sir Thomas Gates not got from the Bermudas, I thinke they had beene all dead before they could be supplied.

Question 2. What conceive you should be the cause, though the Country be good, there comes nothing but Tobacco?

Answer. The oft altering of Governours it seemes causes every man make use of his time, and because Corne was stinted at two shillings six pence the bushell, and Tobacco at three shillings the pound, and they value a mans labour a yeere worth fifty or threescore pound, but in Corne not worth ten pound, presuming Tobacco will furnish them with all things; now make a mans labour in Corne worth threescore pound, and in Tobacco but ten pound a man, then shall they have Corne sufficient to entertaine all commers, and keepe their people in health to doe any thing, but till then, there will be little or nothing to any purpose.

Question 3. What conceive you to have beene the cause of the Massacre, and had the Salvages had the use of any peeces in your time, or when, or by whom they were taught?

Answer. The cause of the Massacre was the want of marshall discipline, and because they would have all the English had by destroying those they found so carelesly secure, that they were not provided to defend themselves against any enemy, being so dispersed as they were. In my time, though Captaine Nuport furnished them with swords by truck, and many fugitives did the like, and some Peeces they got accidentally, yet I got the most of them againe, and it was death to him that should shew a Salvage the use of a Peece. Since I understand they became so good shot, they were imployed for Fowlers and Huntsmen by the English.

Question 4. What charge thinke you would have setled the government both for defence and planting when you left it?

Answer. Twenty thousand pound would have hyred good labourers and mechanicall men, and have furnished them with cattle and all necessaries, and 100. of them would have done more then a thousand of those that went, though the Lord Laware, Sir Ferdinando Waynman, Sir Thomas Gates and Sir Thomas Dale were perswaded to the contrary, but when they had tried, they confessed their error.

Question 5. What conceive you would be the remedy and the charge?

Answer. The remedy is to send Souldiers and all sorts of labourers and necessaries for them, that they may be there by next Michaelmas, the which to doe well will stand you in five thousand pound, but if his Majesty would please to lend two of his Ships to transport them, lesse would serve, besides the benefit of his grace to the action would encourage all men.

Question 6. What thinke you are the defects of the government both here and there?

Answer. The multiplicity of opinions here, and Officers there, makes such delaies by questions and formalitie, that as much time is spent in complement as in action; besides, some are so desirous to imploy their ships, having six pounds for every Passenger, and three pounds for every tun of goods, at which rate a thousand ships may now better be procured then one at the first, when the common stocke defrayed all fraughts, wages, provisions and Magazines, whereby the Ships are so pestred, as occasions much sicknesse, diseases and mortality, for though all the Passengers die they are sure of their fraught; and then all must be satisfied with Orations, disputations, excuses and hopes. As for the letters of advice from hence, and their answers thence, they are so well written, men would beleeve there were no great doubt of the performance, and that all things were wel, to which error here they have beene ever much subject; and there not to beleeve, or not to releeve the true and poore estate of that Colony, whose fruits were commonly spent before they were ripe, and this losse is nothing to them here, whose great estates are not sensible of the losse of their adventures, and so they thinke, or will not take notice; but it is so with all men: but howsoever they thinke or dispose of all things at their pleasure, I am sure not my selfe onely, but a thousand others have not onely spent the most of their estates, but the most part have lost their lives and all, onely but to make way for the triall of more new conclusions, and he that now will adventure but twelve pounds ten shillings, shall have better respect and as much favour then he that sixteene yeere agoe adventured as much, except he have money as the other hath, but though he have adventured five hundred pound, and spent there never so much time, if hee have no more and not able to begin a family of himselfe, all is lost by order of Court.

But in the beginning it was not so, all went then out of one purse, till those new devices have consumed both mony and purse; for at first there were but six Patentees, now more then a thousand, then but thirteene Counsailors, now not lesse then an hundred; I speake not of all, for there are some both honourable and honest, but of those Officers, which did they manage their owne estates no better then the affaires of Virginia, they would quickly fall to decay so well as it; but this is most evident, few Officers in England it hath caused to turne Banquerupts, nor for all their complaints would leave their places, neither yet any of their Officers there, nor few of the rest but they would be at home, but fewer Adventurers here will adventure any more till they see the businesse better established, although there be some so wilfully improvident they care for nothing but to get thither, and then if their friends be dead, or want themselves, they die or live but poorely for want of necessaries, and to thinke the old Planters can releeve them were too much simplicity; for who here in England is so charitable to feed two or three strangers, have they never so much; much lesse in Virginia where they want for themselves. Now the generall complaint saith, that pride, covetousnesse, extortion and oppression in a few that ingrosses all, then sell all againe to the comminalty at what rate they please, yea even men, women and children for who will give most, occasions no small mischiefe amongst the Planters.

As for the Company, or those that doe transport them, provided of necessaries, God forbid but they should receive their charges againe with advantage, or that masters there should not have the same privilege over their servants as here, but to sell him or her for forty, fifty, or threescore pounds, whom the Company hath sent over for eight or ten pounds at the most, without regard how they shall be maintained with apparell, meat, drinke and lodging, is odious, and their fruits sutable, therefore such merchants it were better they were made such merchandize themselves, then suffered any longer to use that trade, and those are defects sufficient to bring a well setled Common-wealth to misery, much more Virginia.

Question 7. How thinke you it may be rectified?

Answer. If his Majestie would please to intitle it to his Crowne, and yearely that both the Governours here and there may give their accounts to you, or some that are not ingaged in the businesse, that the common stocke bee not spent in maintaining one hundred men for the Governour, one hundred for two Deputies, fifty for the Treasurer, five and twenty for the Secretary, and more for the Marshall and other Officers who were never there nor adventured any thing, but onely preferred by favour to be Lords over them that broke the ice and beat the path, and must teach them what to doe. If any thing happen well, it is their glory; if ill, the fault of the old directors, that in all dangers must endure the worst, yet not five hundred of them have so much as one of the others; also that there bee some present course taken to maintaine a Garrison to suppresse the Salvages, till they be able to subsist, and that his Majesty would please to remit his custome, or it is to be feared they will lose custome and all, for this cannot be done by promises, hopes, counsels and countenances, but with sufficient workmen and meanes to maintaine them, not such delinquents as here cannot be ruled by all the lawes in England. Yet when the foundation is laid, as I have said, and a common-wealth established, then such there may better be constrained to labour then here: but to rectifie a common-wealth with debaushed people is impossible, and no wise man would throw himselfe into such a society, that intends honestly, and knowes what he undertakes, for there is no Country to pillage as the Romans found: all you expect from thence must be by labour.

For the government I thinke there is as much adoe about it as the Kingdomes of Scotland and Ireland, men here conceiting Virginia as they are, erecting as many stately Offices as Officers with their attendants, as there are labourers in the Countrey, where a Constable were as good as twenty of their Captaines, and three hundred good Souldiers and labourers better then all the rest that goe onely to get the fruits of other mens labours by the title of an office. Thus they spend Michaelmas rent in Mid-summer Moone, and would gather their Harvest before they have planted their Corne.

As for the maintenance of the Officers, the first that went never demanded any, but adventured good summes, and it seemes strange to me, the fruits of all their labours, besides the expence of an hundred and fifty thousand pounds, and such multitudes of people, those collaterall Officers could not maintaine themselves so well as the old did, and having now such liberty to doe to the Salvages what they will, the others had not. I more then wonder they have not five hundred Salvages to worke for them towards their generall maintenance, and as many more to returne some content and satisfaction to the Adventurers, that for all their care, charge and diligence, can heare nor see nothing but miserable complaints; therefore under your correction to rectifie all, is with all expedition to passe the authority to them who will releeve them, lest all bee consumed ere the differences be determined. And except his Majestie undertake it, or by Act of Parlament some small tax may be granted throughout his Dominions, as a Penny upon every Poll, called a headpenny; two pence upon every Chimney, or some such collection might be raised, and that would be sufficient to give a good stocke, and many servants to sufficient men of any facultie, and transport them freely for paying onely homage to the Crowne of England, and such duties to the publike good as their estates increased reason should require. Were this put in practice, how many people of what quality you please, for all those disasters would yet gladly goe to spend their lives there, and by this meanes more good might be done in one yeere, then all those pety particular undertakings will effect in twenty.

For the Patent the King may, if he please, rather take it from them that have it, then from us who had it first, pretending to his Majesty what great matters they would doe, and how little we did, and for any thing I can conceive, had we remained still as at first, it is not likely we could have done much worse; but those oft altering of governments are not without much charge, hazard and losse. If I be too plaine, I humbly crave your pardon; but you requested me, therefore I doe but my duty. For the Nobility, who knowes not how freely both in their Purses and assistances many of them have beene to advance it, committing the managing of the businesse to inferiour persons, amongst whom questionlesse also many have done their utmost best, sincerely and truly according to their conceit, opinion and understanding; yet grosse errors have beene committed, but no man lives without his fault; for my owne part, I have so much adoe to amend my owne, I have no leisure to looke into any mans particular, but those in generall I conceive to be true. And so I humbly rest

Yours to command, J.S.

The King hath pleased to take it into his consideration. Thus those discords, not being to be compounded among themselves, nor yet by the extraordinary diligences, care and paines of the noble and right worthy Commissioners, Sir William Jones, Sir Nicholas Fortescue, Sir Francis Gofton, Sir Richard Sutton, Sir Henry Bourgchier and Sir William Pit; a *Quo warranto* was granted against Master Deputy Farrar, and 20. or 30. others of that party to plead their causes before the Judges in Westminster hall: now notwithstanding all the Relations, Examinations, and intercepting of all Letters whatsoever came from thence, yet it seemes they were so farre unsatisfied and desired to know the truth, as well for the preservation of the Colony, as to give content and doe all men right, they sent two Commissioners strictly to examine the true estate of the Colony. Upon whose returne after mature deliberation, it pleased his royall Majesty to suppresse the course of the Court at Deputy Farrars, and that for the present ordering the affaires of Virginia, untill he should make a more full settlement thereof, the Lord Viscount

Mandevile, Lord President of his Majesties Privie Councell, and also other Privy Councellors, with many understanding Knights and Gentlemen, should every Thursday in the afternoone meet at Sir Thomas Smiths in Philpot lane, where all men whom it should concerne may repaire, to receive such directions and warrant for their better security, as more at large you may see in the Proclamation to that effect, under the great Seale of England, dated the 15. of July, 1624. But as for the relations last returned, what numbers they are, how many Cities, Corporations, townes, and houses, cattle and horse they have, what fortifications or discoveries they have made, or revenge upon the Salvages; who are their friends or foes, or what commodities they have more then Tobacco, and their present estate or what is presently to be put in execution, in that the Commissioners are not yet fully satisfied in the one, nor resolved in the other, at this present time when this went to the Presse, I must intreat you pardon me till I be better assured.

Thus far I have travelled in this Wildernesse of Virginia, not being ignorant for all my paines this discourse will be wrested, tossed and turned as many waies as there is leaves; that I have writ too much of some, too little of others, and many such like objections. To such I must answer, in the Companies name I was requested to doe it, if any have concealed their approved experiences from my knowledge, they must excuse me: as for every fatherles or stolne relation, or whole volumes of sofisticated rehearsals, I leave them to the charge of them that desire them. I thanke God I never undertooke any thing yet any could tax me of carelesnesse or dishonesty, and what is hee to whom I am indebted or troublesome? Ah! were these my accusers but to change cases and places with me but 2. yeeres, or till they had done but so much as I, it may be they would judge more charitably of my imperfections. But here I must leave all to the triall of time, both my selfe, Virginia's preparations, proceedings and good events, praying to that great God the protector of all goodnesse to send them as good successe as the goodnesse of the action and Country deserveth, and my heart desireth.

FINIS.

THE GENERALL HISTORIE OF THE BERMUDAS,

now called the Summer Iles, from their
beginning in the yeere of our Lord 1593.
to this present 1624. with their proceedings,
accidents and present estate.

B EFORE we present you the matters of fact, it is fit to offer
to your view the Stage whereon they were acted, for as
Geography without History seemeth a carkasse without motion, so History without Geography, wandreth as a
Vagrant without a certaine habitation. Those Ilands
lie in the huge maine Ocean, and two hundred
leagues from any continent, situated in 32. degrees and 25.
minutes, of Northerly latitude, and distant from England West
South-West, about 3300. miles, some twenty miles in length,
and not past two miles and a halfe in breadth, environed with
Rocks, which to the North-ward, West-ward, and South-East,
extend further then they have bin yet well discovered: by reason of those Rocks the Country is naturally very strong, for
there is but two places, and scarce two, unlesse to them who
know them well, where shipping may safely come in, and those
now are exceeding well fortified, but within is roome to entertaine a royall Fleet: the Rocks in most places appeare at a low
water, neither are they much covered at a high, for it ebbs and
flowes not past five foot; the shore for most part is a Rocke, so
hardened with the sunne, wind and sea, that it is not apt to be
worne away with the waves, whose violence is also broke by
the Rocks before they can come to the shore: it is very uneven,
distributed into hills and dales; the mold is of divers colours,
neither clay nor sand, but a meane betweene; the red which resembleth clay is the worst, the whitest resembling sand and the
blackest is good, but the browne betwixt them both which
they call white, because there is mingled with it a white meale
is the best: under the mould two or three foot deep, and

*The
description of
the Iles.*

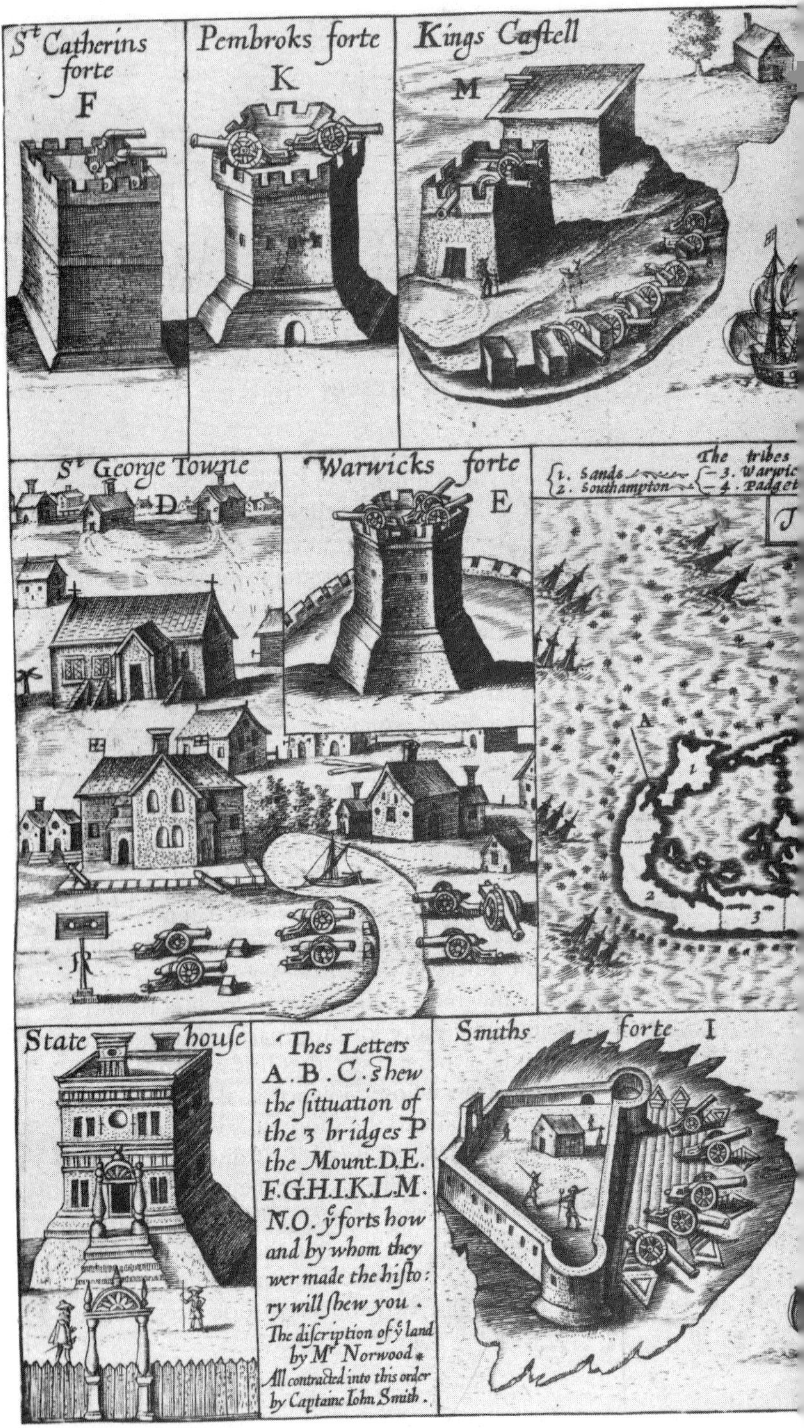

St Catherins forte F

Pembroks forte K

Kings Castell M

St George Towne D

Warwicks forte E

The tribes
1. Sands — 3. Warwic
2. Southampton — 4. Padget

State house

Thes Letters A.B.C. shew the sittuation of the 3 bridges P the Mount.D.E. F.G.H.I.K.L.M. N.O. y̆ forts how and by whom they wer made the histo: ry will shew you. The discription of y̆ land by Mr Norwood. All contracted into this order by Captaine Iohn Smith.

Smiths forte I

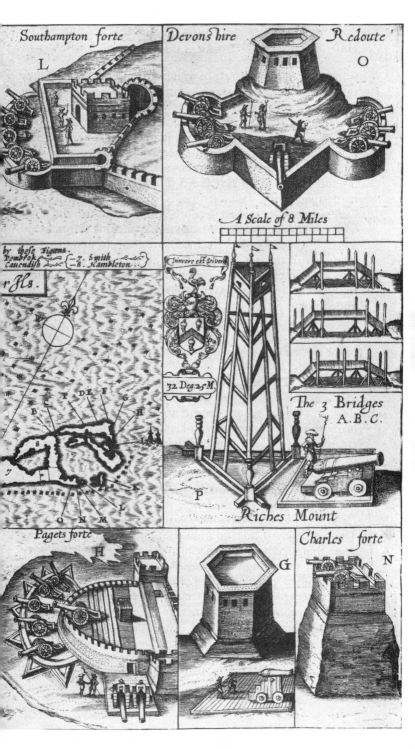

Southampton forte L

Devonshire Redoute O

A Scale of 8 Miles

by these Figures.
Pembrok
Cauendish } 7. Smith
8. Hambleton

r Hs.

Vincere est Vivere

32 Deg:25 M.

The 3 Bridges
A.B.C.

Riches Mount P

Pagets forte H

G

Charles forte N

sometimes lesse, is a kinde of white hard substance which they call the Rocke: the trees usually fasten their roots in it; neither is it indeed rocke or stone, or so hard, though for most part more harder then Chalke; nor so white, but pumish-like and spungy, easily receiving and containing much water. In some places Clay is found under it, it seemes to be ingendred with raine water, draining through the earth, and drawing with it of his substance unto a certaine depth where it congeales; the hardest kinde of it lies under the red ground like quarries, as it were thicke slates one upon another, through which the water hath his passage, so that in such places there is scarce found any fresh water, for all or the most part of the fresh water commeth out of the Sea draining through the sand, or that substance called the Rocke, leaving the salt behinde, it becomes fresh: sometimes we digged wells of fresh water which we finde in most places, and but three or foure paces from the Sea side, some further, the most part of them would ebbe and flow as the Sea did, and be levell or little higher then the superficies of the sea, and in some places very strange, darke and cumbersome Caves.

The clime, temper and fertility. The aire is most commonly cleere, very temperate, moist, with a moderate heat, very healthfull and apt for the generation and nourishing of all things, so as many things transported from hence yeeld a farre greater increase, and if it be any living thing it becomes fatter and better; by this meanes the country is so replenished with Hens and Turkies, within the space of three or foure yeeres, that many of them being neglected, forsake the houses and become wilde, and so live in great abundance; the like increase there is in Hogs, tame Conies, and other Cattle according to their kindes. There seemes to be a continuall Spring, which is the cause some things come not to that maturity and perfection as were requisite; and though the trees shed their leaves, yet they are alwaies full of greene; the Corne is the same they have in Virginia, and the West-Indies: of this and many other things without plowing or much labour, they have two Harvests every yeere, for they set about March, which they gather in July; and againe in August, which they reape in December; and little slips of Fig-trees and Vines doe usually beare fruit within the yeere, and sometimes in lesse; but we finde not the Grapes as yet come to any perfection; the like fertility it hath in Oranges and Limons, Pomgranates, and other things. Concerning the serenity and beauty of the skie, it may as truly be said of those Ilands as ever it was said of the Rhodes, that there is no one day throughout the 12. moneths, but that in some houre thereof, the sun lookes singularly and cleere upon them: for the temperature it is beyond all others most admirable; no cold there is beyond an English Aprill, nor heat much greater then an ordinary July in France, so that frost and snow is never seene here, not stinking and infectious mists very seldome, by reason of the maine Ocean, there is some wind stirring that cooles the aire: the winter they have observes the time with ours, but the longest daies and nights are shorter then ours almost by two houres.

Trees and Fruits.

We found it at first all overgrowne with weeds, and plants of severall kinds, as many tall and goodly Cedars, infinite store of Palmetoes, numbers of Mulberies, wild Olive-trees store, with divers others unknowne both by name and nature, so that as yet they become lost to many usefull imployments, which time and industry no doubt will one day discover, and even already certaine of the most notorious of them have gotten them appellations from their apparent effects, as the Prickell-peare which growes like a shrub by the ground, with broad thick leaves, all over-armed with long and sharpe dangerous thornes, the fruit being in forme not much unlike a small greene Peare, and on the outside of the same colour, but within bloud red, and exceeding full of juice; with graines not much unlike the Pomgranat, and colouring after its nature.

The Prickell Peare.

The poison weed.

The poysoned weed is much in shape like our English Ivy, but being but touched, causeth rednesse, itching, and lastly blisters, the which howsoever after a while passe away of themselves without further harme, yet because for the time they are somewhat painfull, it hath got it selfe an ill name, although questionlesse of no ill nature.

The red weed.

Here is also frequently growing a certaine tall Plant, whose stalke being all over covered with a red rinde, is thereupon termed the red weed, the root whereof being soked in any liquor, but a small quantity of the Juice drunke alone, procures a very forcible vomit, and yet is generally used by the people, and found very effectuall against the paines and distempers of the stomacke.

A kinde of Wood-bind there is likewise by the Sea very commonly to bee found, which runnes upon trees twining it selfe like a Vine: the fruit somewhat resembles a Beane, but somewhat flatter, the which any way eaten worketh excellently in the nature of a purge, and though very vehemently, yet without all perill. Contrary to this, another small tree there is, which causeth costivenesse; there is also a certaine Plant like a bramble bush, which beares a long yellow fruit, having the shell very hard, and within it a hard berry, that beaten and taken inwardly purgeth gently. There is another fruit much like our Barberies, which being beaten or brused betweene the teeth, sets all the mouth on an extreme heat very terrible for the time, to avoid which they are swallowed downe whole, and found of the same or better operation then the red Pepper, and thence borroweth the name. In the bottome of the Sea there is growing upon the Rocks a large kinde of Plant in the forme of a Vine leafe, but far more spread with veines in colour of a pale red, very strangely interlaced and woven one into another, which we call the Feather, but the vertue thereof is altogether unknowne, but only regarded for the rarity. Now besides these naturall productions, providences and paines since the Plantation have offered divers others seeds and plants, which the soile hath greedily imbraced and cherished, so that at this present 1623. there are great abundance of white, red and yellow coloured Potatoes, Tobacco, Sugar-canes, Indicos, Parsnips, exceeding large Radishes, the American bread, the Cassado root, the Indian Pumpian, the Water-millon, Musk-millon, and the most delicate Pine-apples, Plantans, and Papawes, also the English Artichoke, Pease, etc. briefly whatsoever else may be expected for the satisfaction either of curiosity, necessity or delight.

Neither hath the aire for her part been wanting with due supplies of many sorts of Fowles, as the gray and white Hearne, the gray and greene Plover, some wilde Ducks and Malards, Coots and Red-shankes, Sea-wigions, Gray-bitterns, Cormorants, numbers of small Birds

The purging Beane.

The costive tree.

Red Pepper.

The Sea feather.

Fruits transported.

Birds.

like Sparrowes and Robins, which have lately beene destroyed by the wilde Cats, Wood-pickars, very many Crowes, which since this Plantation are kild, the rest fled or seldome seene except in the most uninhabited places, from whence they are observed to take their flight about sun set, directing their course towards the North-west, which makes many conjecture there are some more Ilands not far off that way. Sometimes are also seene Falcons and Jar-falcons, Ospraies, a Bird like a Hobby, but because they come seldome, they are held but as passengers; but above all these, most deserving observation and respect are those two sorts of Birds, the one for the tune of his voice, the other for the effect, called the Cahow, and

Egge-Birds.

Egge-bird, which on the first of May, a day constantly observed, fall a laying infinite store of Eggs neere as big as Hens, upon certaine small sandie baies especially in Coupers Ile; and although men sit downe amongst them when hundreds have bin gathered in a morning, yet there is hath stayed amongst them till they have gathered as many more: they continue this course till Midsummer, and so tame and feareles, you must thrust them off from their Eggs with your hand; then they grow so faint with laying, they suffer them to breed and take infinite numbers of their yong to eat, which are very excellent meat.

Cahowes.

The Cahow is a Bird of the night, for all the day she lies hid in holes in the Rocks, where they and their young are also taken with as much ease as may be, but in the night if you but whoop and hollow, they will light upon you, that with your hands you may chuse the fat and leave the leane; those they have only in winter: their Eggs are as big as hens, but they are speckled, the other white. Master Norwood hath taken twenty dozen of them in three or foure houres, and since there hath beene such havocke made

The Tropicke Bird and the Pemblicos presagements.

of them, they were neere all destroyed, till there was a strict inhibition for their preservation. The Tropicke bird is white, as large as a Pullet, with one onely long Feather in her taile, and is seldome seene far distant from other of the Tropicks: another small Bird there is, because she cries Pemblyco they call her so, she is seldome seene in the day but when she sings, as too oft she doth very clamorously; too true a Prophet she proves of huge winds and boysterous weather: there were a kinde of small Owles in great abundance, but they are now all slaine or fled: some tame Ducks, Geese and Pigeons there are, but the two latter prosper not.

Concerning vermine and noisome creatures, there **Of Vermine.** are not many, but onely Rats and Cats, there increased since the Plantation, but how they agree together you shall heare hereafter. The Musketas and Flies are also too busie, with a certaine India Bug, called by the Spaniards a Cacarootch, the which creeping into Chests they eat and defile with their ill-sented dung: also the little Ants in summer time are so troublesome, they are forced to dry their figs upon high frames, and anoint their feet with tar, wherein they sticke, else they would spoile them all ere they could be dryed: Wormes in the earth also there are, but too many, so that to keepe them from destroying their Corne and Tobacco, they are forced to worme them every morning, which is a great labour, else all would be destroyed. Lizards there were many and very large, but now none, and it is said they were **Note.** destoyed by the Cat. Certaine Spiders also of very large size are found hanging upon trees, but instead of being any way dangerous as in other places, they are here of a most pleasing aspect, all over drest, as it were with Silver, Gold, and Pearle, and their Webs in the Summer woven from tree to tree, are generally a perfect raw silke, and that as well in regard of substance as colour, and so strong withall, that divers Birds bigger than Black-birds, being like Snipes, are often taken and snared in them as a Net: then what would the Silke-worme doe were shee there to feede upon the continuall greene Mulbery?

But above all the rest of the Elements, the Sea is **Fishes.** found most abundantly liberall: hence have they as much excellent Fish, and as much variety as need be desired. The most of which being unknowne to our Northerne parts, got there new names, either for their shapes or conditions; as the large Rocke-fish from his like hew, and haunting amongst the Rocks, the fat Hog-fish from his swine-like shape and snout: for this is not the old knowne Hog-fish with brussels on his backe; the delicate Amber-fish from his taste and smell, Angell-fish, Cony-fish, the small yellow taile from that naturall painting; the great Growper from his odde and strange grunting, some of them yet knowne to the Americans, as the Purgoose, the Cavallo, the Gar-fish, Flying-fish and Morerayes: the rest are common to other Continents; as the Whale in great numbers, the Sharke, the Pilot-fish, the Sea-Breame, the Oyster and Lobster, with divers others; twenty Tortoises have beene taken in a day, and some of them will affoord halfe a bushell of Egges, and suffice to feed forty men at a meale. And thus have you briefely epitomized Mother Natures benefits to this little, yet dainty spot of earth. Neither were it ingenuity to conceale wherein shee inclineth to the Stepdame, especially since the particulars are so few, as rather requisite Antidotes against idlenesse to rouse up industry, then any great cause of much distaste, much lesse despaire: and of those to speake troth, there are onely two: viz. the Winds, and the Wormes, especially in the Spring and Autumne; and thus conditioned as yet we will let rest these small Ilands, in the midst of this mightie and maine Ocean, so invironed on every side, by infinite numbers of uncertaine scattered Rocks, lying shallowly hid under the surface of the water, a league, two, three, foure, or five, to Sea, to the which advantagers added by art, as hereafter you shall heare at large, and finde described in the Map. It may well be concluded to be the most impregnable place in the world, and although the Amber Greece, Pearles, nor Tobacco, are of that quantity and certainty to be relied upon to gaine wealth; yet by practise and experience they finde, by Silke, Saffron, Indico, Madar, Sugarcanes, Wine, Oile, and such like great profit may be expected: yet were those hopelesse in regard of their conveniency to nourish and maintaine themselves, and releeve them shall visit them with wood, water, and other necessaries, besides what an eye-sore they are already becommed to them that have them not, and how deare and pretious to them that have them, I thinke none will deny but they are well worth the keeping: and so we will proceed to the accidents that befell the first finders; also the proceedings of the first Planters and their successors, Master Norrod, Thomas Sparkes, and divers others.

The most hurtfull things in those Iles.

A briefe relation of the shipwracke of Henry May.

1593. How it
is supposed
they were
called the
Bermudas. How these Iles came by the name of Bermudas, or the infinite number of blacke Hogs, or so fearefull to the world, that many called them the Ile of Devils, that all men did shun as Hell and perdition; I will not expostulate, nor trouble your patiences with those uncertaine antiquities further then thus; our men found divers crosses, peeces of Spanish monies here and there. Two or three wracks also they found, by certaine inscriptions to bee some Spanish, some Dutch, some French; but the greatest rumour is, that a Spanish ship called *Bermudas* was there cast away, carrying Hogges to the West-Indies that swam a shore, and there increased: how the Spaniards escaped is uncertaine: but they say, from that ship those Iles were first called Bermudas, which till then for six thousand yeares had beene namelesse.

But the first English-man that was ever in them, was one Henry May, a worthy Mariner that went with Captaine Lancaster to the East-Indies 1591. and in their returne by the West-Indies, being in some distresse, sent this Henry May for England by one Mounsier de la Barbotier, to acquaint the Merchants with their estate. The last of November, saith May, we departed from Laguna in Hispaniola, and the seventeenth of December following, we were cast away upon the North-west of the Bermudas; the Pilots about noone made themselves Southwards of the Iles twelve leagues, and demanded of the Captaine their Wine of hight as out of all danger, which they had: but it seemes they were either drunke, or carelesse of their charge; for through their negligences a number of good men were cast away. I being but a stranger amongst fiftie and odde French-men, it pleased God to appoint me to be one of them should be saved. In this extremity we made a raft, which we towed with our Boat, there were but six and twentie of us saved; and I seeing scarce roome for the one halfe, durst not passe in amongst them till the Captaine called me along with him, leaving the better halfe to the seas mercy: that day we rowed till within two houres of night ere we could land, being neere dead with thirst, every man tooke his way to seeke fresh water, at length, by searching amongst many weeds, we found some raine water, but in the maine are many faire Baies, where we had enough for digging.

The building
and calking
their Barke. Now it pleased God before our ship split we saved our Carpenters tooles, some Nailes, Sailes, and Tacklings, wherewith we went roundly to worke, and built a Barke of eighty tunnes: In stead of Pitch, we made Lime, mixed with Tortoise oyle, and as the Carpenters calked her, I and another paied the seames with this plaster, which being in Aprill, became quickly dry, and as hard as a stone.

His returne
for England. In Aprill it was so hot, we feared our water would faile, two great Chests wee made, which we calked as our ship; those we stowed on each side our maine Mast, filled them with water and thirtie live Tortoises: wee found many Hogges, but so leane wee could not eat them; the tops of the Palmeta berries was our bread, and the juyce we got out of the trees we cut downe our drinke, and of the leaves, which are more then an Ell long, we covered our Cabens, and made our beds, and found many of those provisions as is related, but little foule weather. The eleventh of May it pleased God to set us cleere of the Ile, after wee had lived there five moneths: and the twentieth wee fell with Cape Britton, neere New found Land, where refreshing our selves with wood and water, and such things as we could get of the Salvages, it seemed a good Countrey, but we staied not past foure houres before we set saile for the banke of New found land, where wee met many ships, but not any would take in a man of us, untill it pleased God we met a Barke of Fawmothe, which received us for a little time, and with her we tooke a French ship, wherein I left Captaine de la Barbotier, my deare friend, and all his Company: and in August arrived at Falmouth in this honest English Barke, 1594.

Written by me Henry May.

The first English ship knowne to have beene cast away upon the Bermudas 1609. From the relation of Master Jordan, Master John Euens, Master Henry Shelly, and divers others.

You have heard, that when Captaine Smith was Governor of Virginia, there were nine ships sent with Sir Thomas Gates, and Sir George Somers, and Captaine Nuport with five hundred people, to take in the old Commission, and rectifie a new government: they set saile in May, and in the height of thirty degrees of Northerly latitude, they were taken with an extreme storm, or rather a part of Hericano, upon the five and twentieth of July, which as they write, did not onely separate them from the Fleet, but with the violent working of the Seas, their ship became so shaken, torne, and leake, she received so much water as covered two tire of Hogsheads above the ballace, that they stood up to the middles, with Buckets, Baricos, and Kettles, to baile out the water. Thus bailing and pumping three daies and three nights without intermission, and yet the water seemed rather to increase then diminish, in so much that being all utterly spent with labour, were even resolved without any hope to shut up the hatches, and commit themselves to the mercy of the Sea, which is said to be mercilesse, or rather to the mercy of Almighty God, whose mercy farre exceeds all his workes; seeing no sense or hope in mans apprehension, but presently to sinke: some having some good and comfortable waters, fetched them and dranke one to another, as taking their last leaves untill a more happy, and a more joyfull meeting in a more blessed world, when it pleased God out of his most gracious and mercifull providence, so to direct and guide their ship for her most advantage;

A most desperate estate by a storm.

That Sir George Somers all this time sitting upon the poupe, scarce taking leisure to eat nor sleepe, coning the ship to keepe her as upright as he could, otherwaies she must long ere that needs have foundered, most wishedly and happily descried land; whereupon he most comfortably incouraged them to follow their worke, many of them being fast asleepe: this unlooked for welcome newes, as if it

The care and judgement of Sir George Somers.

had bin a voice from heaven, hurrieth them all above hatches, to looke for that they durst scarce beleeve, so that improvidently forsaking that taske which imported no lesse then their lives, they gave so dangerous advantage to their greedy enemy the salt water, which still entred at the large breaches of their poore wooden castle, as that in gaping after life, they had wellnigh swallowed their death. Surely it is impossible any should not be urged to doe his best, and although they knew it that place all men did so shun, yet they spread all the saile they could to attaine them: for not long it was before they strucke upon a rocke, till a surge of the sea cast her from thence, and so from one to another, till most luckily at last so upright betwixt two, as if she had beene in the stocks, till this they expected but every blow a death: But now behold, suddenly the wind gives place to a calme, and the billowes, which each by overtaking her, would in an instant have shivered her in peeces, become peaceable and still, so that with all conveniency and ease, they unshipped all their goods, victuall, and persons into their Boats, and with extreme joy, even almost to amazednesse, arrived in safetie, though more then a league from the shore, without the losse of a man; yet were they in all one hundred and fiftie: yet their deliverance was not more strange in falling so happily upon the land, as their feeding and preservation was beyond their hopes; for you have heard, it hath beene to the Spaniards more fearefull then an Utopian Purgatory, and to all Sea-men no lesse terrible then an inchanted den of Furies and Devils, the most dangerous, unfortunate, and forlorne place in the world, and they found it the richest, healthfullest and pleasantest they ever saw, as is formerly said.

An evident token of Gods mercy.

Sir George Somers his first ranging the land.

Being thus safe on shore, they disposed themselves to search the Iles for food and water; others to get a shore what they could from the ship; not long Sir George wandred but found such a fishing, that in halfe an houre with a hooke and line, he tooke so many as sufficed the whole company, in some places they were so thicke in the Coves, and so great, they durst not goe in lest they should bite them, and these rocke fish are so great two will load a man, and fatter nor better fish cannot be. Master Shelly found a Bay neere a quarter of a mile over, so full of Mullets, as none of them before had ever seene or heard of the like: the next day seeking to kill them with fis-gigs, they strucke so many the water in many places was red with bloud, yet caught not one, but with a net they caught so many as they could draw a shore, with infinite number of Pilchards and divers other sorts; great craw-fishes in a night by making a fire they have taken in great quantity. Sir George had twice his hooke and line broke out of his hand, but the third time he made it so strong he caught the same fish, which had pulled him into the Sea had not his men got hold of him, whereby he had his three hookes againe that were found in her belly. At their first hunting for hogs they found such abundance, they killed 32 and this hunting and fishing was appointed to Captaine Robert Walsingham, and Master Henry Shelly for the company in general: they report they killed at least 500. besides Pigs, and many that were killed by divers others; for the birds in their seasons, the facility to make their cabens of Palmeta leaves, caused many of them utterly forget or desire ever to returne from thence, they lived in such plenty, peace and ease.

What meanes they made to send to Virginia. But let us remember how the Knights began to resolve in those desperat affaires: many projects they had, but at last it was concluded, to decke their long boat with their ship hatches; which done, with all expedition they sent Master Raven, a very sufficient Mariner, with eight more in her to Virginia, to have shipping from thence to fetch them away; three weekes or a moneth they expected her returne, but to this day she was never more heard of; all this time was spent in searching the Iles: now although God still fed them with this abundance of plenty, yet such was the malice of envy or ambition, for all this good service done by Sommers, such a great difference fell amongst their Commanders, that they lived asunder in this distresse, rather as meere strangers then distressed friends: but necessity so commanded, patience had the victory.

A mariage, and two children borne. Two ships at this time by those severall parties were a building; in the meane time two children were borne, the Boy was called Bermudas, the Girle Bermuda, and amongst all those sorrowes they had a merry English mariage; the forme of those Iles you may see at large in the Map of Master Norwood, where you may plainly see no place knowne hath better walls, nor a broader ditch. But having finished and rigged their two new Cedar ships with such provisions they saved from the *Sea-adventurer* they left amongst the Rocks, they called the one the *Patience*, the other the *Deliverance*; they used Lime and Oile, as May did, for Pitch and Tar. Sir George Summers had in his Barke no Iron at all but one bolt in her Keele; now having made their provisions of victuall and all things ready, they set saile the tenth of May 1610. onely leaving two men behinde them, called Christopher Carter and Edward Waters, that for their offences, or the suspition they had of their judgements, fled into the woods, and there rather desired to end their daies then stand to their trials and the event of justice; for one of their consorts was shot to death, and Waters being tied to a tree also to be executed, had by chance a Knife about him, and so secretly cut the Rope, he ran into the woods where they could not finde him. There were two Salvages also sent from Virginia by Captain Smith, the one called Namuntack, the other Matchumps, but some such differences fell betweene them, that Matchumps slew Namuntack, and having made a hole to bury him, because it was too short, he cut of his legs and laid them by him, which murder he concealed till he was in Virginia.

Their arrivall
in Virginia. The foure and twentieth of the same moneth they arrived in Virginia at James towne, where they found but threescore persons, as you may reade at large in the History of Virginia, of the five hundred left by Captaine Smith, also of the arrivall of the Lord Laware, that met them thus bound for England, returned them backe, and understanding what plenty there was of hogs and other good things in the Bermudas, was desirous to send thither to supply his necessary occasions; whereupon Sir George Summers, the best acquainted with the place, whose noble minde ever regarded a generall good more then his owne ends, though above threescore yeeres of age, and had meanes in England sutable to his ranke, offered himselfe by Gods helpe to performe this dangerous voyage againe for the Bermudas, which was kindly accepted, so upon the 19. of June, he imbarked in his Cedar ship, about the burthen of thirty tunnes, and so set saile.

Sir George
Summers his
returne to the
Bermudas. Much foule and crosse weather he had, and was forced to the North parts of Virginia, where refreshing himselfe upon this unknowne coast, he could not bee diverted from the search of the Bermudas, where at last with his company he safely arrived: but such was his diligence with his extraordinary care, paines and industry to dispatch his businesse, and the strength of his body not answering the ever memorable courage of his minde, having lived so long in such honourable services, the most part of his well beloved and vertuous life, God and nature here determined, should ever remaine a perpetuall memory of his much bewailed sorrow for his death: finding his time but short, after he had taken the best course he could to settle his estate, like a valiant Captaine he exhorted them with all diligence to be constant to those Plantations, and with all expedition to returne to Virginia. In that very place which we now call Saint Georges towne, this noble Knight died, whereof the place taketh the name. But his men, as men amazed, seeing the death of him who was even as the life of them all, embalmed his body and set saile for England, being the first that ever went to seeke those Ilands, which have beene ever since called Summers Iles, in honour of his worthy memory, leaving three men behind them, that voluntarily stayed, whose names were Christopher Carter, Edward Waters, there formerly left as is said, and Edward Chard. This Cedar ship at last with his dead body arrived at Whit-Church in Dorsetshire, where by his friends he was honourably buried, with many vollies of shot, and the rites of a Souldier, and upon his tombe was bestowed this Epitaph.

His Epitaph.

Hei mihi Virginia quod tam cito præterit Æstas,
Autumnus sequitur, sæviet inde et hiems;
At ver perpetuum nascetur, et Anglia læta,
Decerpit flores florida terra tuas.

In English thus:

Alas Virginia's Summer so soone past,
Autumne succeeds and stormy Winters blast,
Yet Englands joyfull Spring with joyfull showers,
O Florida, shall bring thy sweetest flowers.

The honour of this resolution belongs principally to Carter, for through his importunity, not to leave such a place abandoned, Chard and Waters were moved to stay with him, and the rest promised with all the

The proceedings of the three men.

speed they could againe to revisit them. But the ship once out of sight, those three Lords, the sole inhabitants of all those Ilands, began to erect their little common wealth for a while with brotherly regency, repairing the ground, planting Corne, and such seeds and fruits as they had, building a house, etc. Then making privy search amongst the crevises and corners of those craggy Rocks, what this maine Ocean since the worlds creation had throwne amongst them, at last they chanced upon the greatest peece of Amber-greece was ever seene or heard of in one lumpe, being in weight fourescore pound, besides divers other small peeces.

A peece of Amber-greece of 80. pound weight.

But now being rich, they grew so proud and ambitious, contempt tooke such place, they fell out for superiority, though but three forlorne men, more then three thousand miles from their native Country, and but small hope ever to see it againe. Notwithstanding, they sometimes fell from words to blowes about meere trifles: in one of which fights, one of them was bitten with his owne dog, as if the dumbe beast would reprove them of their folly; at last Chard and Waters, the two greater spirits, must try it out in the field, but Carter wisely stole away their weapons, affecting rather to live amongst his enemies, then by being rid of them live alone; and thus those miserable men lived full two yeeres, so that all their clothes were neere worne cleane from their backs, and their hopes of any forraine releefe as naked as their bodies. At last they began to recover their wits, yet in a fashion perhaps would have cost them dearer then when they were mad; for concluding a tripartite peace of their Matachin warre, they resolved to frame as good a Boat as they could, and therein to make a desperate attempt for Virginia, or New found Land; but no sooner were they entred into that resolution, but they descried a saile standing in for the shore, though they neither knew what she was, nor what she would, they were so over-joyed, with all possible speed they went to meet her, and according to their hearts desire she proved an English-man, whom they safely conducted into their harbour.

How they were supplied. 1611.

Now you are to understand, that Captaine Matthew Somers, Nephew and heire to Sir George, that returned with his dead body, though both he and his Company did their utmost in relating all those passages to their Countrey-men and adventurers, their relations were beleeved but as travellers tales, till it came to be apprehended by some of the Virginia Company, how beneficiall it might be, and helpfull to the Plantation in Virginia, so that some one hundred and twentie of them bought the pretended right of all the Company, and had sent this ship to make a triall; but first they had obtained Letters Patents of the Kings most excellent Majestie. Sir Thomas Smith was elected Treasurer and Governor heere, and Master Richard More to be Governor of the Iles and Colony there.

The first beginning of a Colonie in the Somer Iles, under the command of Master Richard More, extracted out of a plot of Master Richard Norwood Surveior, and the relations of divers others.

The arrivall of Master More. 1612. Sir Thomas Smith Treasurer. MASTER MORE thus finding those three men not onely well and lusty, but well stored with divers sorts of provisions, as an Acre of Corne ready to be gathered, numbers of Pumpions and Indian Beanes, many Tortoises ready taken, good store of hogs flesh salted, and made in flitches of Bacon, were very good, and so presently landed his goods and sixty persons towards the beginning of July 1612. upon the South side of Smiths Ile.

Their differences about the Amber-greece. Not long after his arrivall, More having some private intelligence of this Amber-greece, tooke first Chard in examination, he being one of the three the most masterfull spirit, what Amber-greece, Pearle, Treasure, or other Commodities they had found. Chard no lesse witty then resolute, directly answered; Not any thing at all but the fruits of the Ile, what his fellowes had done he knew not, but if they had, he doubted not but to finde it out, and then hee should know it certainly. This he spake onely to win time to sweare his Consorts to secrecy, and he would finde the meanes how they should all returne in that ship with it all for England, otherwise they should be deceived of all. Till this was effected they thought every houre an age; now for the better conveiance of it aboord, they acquainted it to Captaine Davis, master of the ship, and one Master Edwin Kendall, that for their secrecy and transportation should participate with them: Without further ceremony the match was accepted, and absolutely concluded, the plot laid, time and place set downe to have it aboord. But Carter, were it for feare the Governor at last should know of it, to whom so oft they had denied it; or that the rest should deceive him, is uncertaine; but most certaine it is, he revealed all the plot to Master More: To get so much wealth he knew would please them in England, though it did displease all his Company, and to lose such a prize he would not for hazarding a mutiny. So first hee revealed himselfe to Kendall in faire tearmes, reproving his dishonesty, but not being answered according to his expectation, he committed both Chard and him to prison. The next Sabbath day Davis comming on shore, More also taxed with very hard language and many threats, to lay him fast also if he mended not his manners; Davis for the present replied little, but went with him to the place of praier: but in the midst of divine service he goeth away, commanding all his Sea-men to follow him presently aboord, where he encourageth them to stand to him like men, and hee would free the Prisoners, have all the Ambergreece for themselves, and so be gone.

The Governor hearing of this resolution, prepares with his company to repulse force with force, so that a generall expectance of a civill uncivill warre possessed every man; but this threatning gust passed over more calmlier then was expected; for Davis having better advised with himselfe, repented his rashnesse, and desired a reconcilement with the Governor. Peace thus concluded, Kendall was set at libertie, but Chard was condemned, and upon the ladder to be hanged for his obstinacy; yet upon better consideration More reprived him, but kept him a prisoner all the time he staied in the Country, which was generally thought a very bad reward for his great desert, and that there was more of this Amber-greece imbeziled, then would have contented all the finders, that never had any consideration at all. The greatest part though More thus recovered, yet Davis and Kendall had so much, either by the ignorance or connivency of the Governors, that arriving in England, they prepared themselves for a

Chard in danger of hanging.

new voiage; at last they two falling out, the Company having notice thereof, so tormented them both, they gave over their voiage, and durst not be seene a long time after.

Master Mores industry in fortifying and planting.   The Governor thus rid of the ship and those discontents, removed his seat from Smiths Ile to Saint Georges, after he had fitted up some small Cabbens of Palmeta leaves for his wife and family, in that valley where now stands their prime towne called St. Georges, hee began to apply himselfe to fortifie the Countrey, and training his men in the exercise of armes. For although he was but a Carpenter, he was an excellent Artist, a good Gunner, very witty and industrious: he built and laid the foundation of eight or nine Forts, called the Kings Castle, Charles Fort, Pembrookes Fort, Smiths Fort, Pagits Fort, Gates Fort, Warwicks Castle, Saint Katharines Fort, etc. mounting in them all the Ordnance he had, preparing the ground to build Houses, plant Corne, and such Fruits as they had.

Being thus busied, and as the necessitie of the time required, keeping his men somewhat hard at worke, Master Keath his Minister, were it by the secret provocation of some drones, that grew weary of their taskes, or his affection to popularity is not certaine: But he begins to tax the Governor in the Pulpit, hee did grinde the faces of the poore, oppressing his Christian brethren with Pharaohs taxes. More finding this in short time, might breed ill bloud, called the Company together and also the Minister, urging them plainly, to tell him wherein he had deserved those hard accusations: whereupon, with an universall cry they affirmed the contrary, so that Keath downe on his knees to aske him forgivenesse. But Master More kindly tooke him up, willing him to kneele to God, and hereafter be more modest and charitable in his speeches; notwithstanding two other discontents so upbraided More with that doctrine, and stood to maintaine it, he impaneled a Jury, with a great deale of seeming much adoe he would hang them being condemned, one of them with the very feare, fell into a dead Palsie; so that the other was set at libertie, and proved after a very good labourer.

A contention of the Minister against the Governor.

Two peeces weighed out of the Sea Adventure.   Many conclusions he tried about the *Sea-venture* the wracke of Sir George Somers, but he got onely for his paines but two peece of Ordnance. Having framed a Church of timber, it was blowne downe by a tempest, so that he built another in a more closer place with Palmeta leaves.

The first supply.
Before this yeere was expired, the adventerers sent them an adviso with thirtie Passengers and good provisions, to prepare with all expedition for their defence against the Spaniard, whom they understood ere long would visit them: This occasioned him to keepe all his men together in that Ile so hard at worke, that wanting libertie to goe abroad for food, living onely on that they had, and expected daily to receive from England, they were so over-toiled, many fell sicke, but none died. Very earnest this ship was to have all the Amber-greece, which Master More perceiving, was the chiefest cause of their comming, and that it was the onely loadstone to draw from England still more supplies; for all the expresse command sent from the Company, he returned this ship but with the one third part; so from thence she went to Virginia, and not long after arrived safely in England.

1613.
The second supply. Sir Thomas Smith Treasurer.
But before her returne the Company sent the *Martha* with sixtie Passengers more; they arrived in June with one Master Bartlet to survey the Iland, and the estate of the Colonie, with expresse command for all the Amber-greece: but More perceiving him not as he would have him, and that the Company began to mistrust him, would send no more but another third part, wherewith they returned, leaving a French-man to make triall of the Mulberies for Silke, but he did not bring any thing to perfection; excusing himselfe, they were not the right Mulberies he expected. About this time they were in hope of a small crop of Tobacco, but it was most spoiled for want of knowledge to use it. Now in England Master More became amongst the Merchants marvelous distastfull, for the detaining so long the Amber-greece; which delaies they so much abhorred, they forthwith dispatched the *Elizabeth* the second time and forty Passengers, much rebuking More for so long detaining the Amber-greece: for the which, having now no more colourable excuses, he delivered it, wherewith the ship went to Virginia, and thence home. In this ship was brought the first Potato roots, which flourished exceedingly for a time, till by negligence they were almost lost (all but

A strange increase of Potatoes.

two cast-away roots) that so wonderfully have increased, they are a maine releefe to all the Inhabitants. This ship was not long gone but there came two Spanish ships, sounding with their Boat, which attempted to come in: but from the Kings Castle Master More made but two shot, which caused them presently depart. Marke here the handy-worke of the divine providence, for they had but three quarters of a barrell of powder, and but one shot more, and the powder by carelesnesse was tumbled downe under the mussels of the two peeces, were discharged, yet not touched with fire when they were discharged.

The attempt of two Spanish ships.

This feare thus past, appeares another much worse, which was the extremity of famine; in this extremity God sent Captaine Daniel Elfrid with a carvell of meale which a little relieved them, but brought withall so many Rats, that within two yeeres after neere ruined all; now though Elfrid had deceived his friend Fisher of this Carvell in the West-Indies, they revenged Fishers injury, for Elfrid had his passage for England, and they made use of all he had. Some two moneths after, came in the *Blessing* with an hundred Passengers; and two daies after the *Starre* with a hundred and fourescore more, amongst which were many Gentlemen, as Master Lower for Marshall, Master Barret, Master Felgate, and divers others; but very unproper for what they undertooke. Within fourteene daies after came in the *Margaret* and two Frygats, and in them one hundred and threescore Passengers; also Master Bartlet came now expresly to divide the Country into Tribes, and the Tribes into shares. But Master More finding no mention made of any part for himselfe nor all of them with him, as he was promised in England, by no meanes would admit of any division, nor suffer his men from finishing their fortifications, which was so necessary, it was his maine ambition to see that accomplished; but such unkindnesse grew betwixt this Master Bartlet and the Governour, that the rude multitude with all the disdaine they could devise caused Bartlet returne for England as he came. About this time William Millington was drawne into the Sea by a fish, but never after ever seene.

The neglect of this division was very hardly conceited in England, so that Master More grew more and more in dislike with the company; notwithstanding he followed the building

1614.
A great
famine and
mortalitie. Sir
Thomas
Smith
Treasurer.
of these Forts so earnestly, neglecting planting of Corne, till their store was neere all consumed, whereby they became so feeble and weake, some would not, others could not goe abroad to seeke releefe, but starved in their houses, and many that went abroad, through weaknesse were subject to be suddenly surprized with a disease called the Feauges, which was neither paine nor sicknesse, but as it were the highest degree of weaknesse, depriving them of power and ability from the execution of any bodily exercises, whether it were working, walking, or what else: being thus taken, if any presently gave them food, many times they straight recovered, yet some after a little rest would bee able to walke, but if they found not present succour, died.

A strange
being of
Ravens.
About this time or immediatly before, came in a company of Ravens, which continued amongst them all the time of this mortality and then departed, which for any thing knowne, neither before nor since were ever seene or heard of: this with divers other reasons caused Master More to goe out to Sea, to see if he could discover any other Ilands, but he went not farre ere ill weather forced him backe; and it were a noble adventure of him would undertake to make more perfect all the dangers are about the Summer Iles.

All workes
abandoned to
get onely
victuals.
Thus famine and misery caused Governour More leave all his workes, and send them abroad to get what they could; one hundred and fifty of the most weake and sicke he sent to Coupers Ile, where were such infinite numbers of the Birds called Cahowes, which were so fearelesse they might take so many as they would, and that admired abundance of fish, that the extremity of their hunger, and their gluttony was such, those heavenly blessings they so consumed and wasted by carelesnesse and surfetting, many of them died upon those silly Birds that offered themselves to the slaughter, which the Governour understanding, caused them for change of aire to be removed to Port-royall, and a Company of Fishers with a Boat to releeve them with fish, but the Gange grew so lazie the poore weaklings still died; they that remained killed the Cattle they found in the Ile, faining the heat caused them to runne into the Sea and so were drowned; so that the Governour sent againe for them home, but some

obtained leave still to live abroad; one amongst the rest hid himselfe in the Woods, and lived onely on Wilkes and land Crabs, fat and lusty many moneths, but most of them being at Saint Georges, ordinarily was taken one hundred and fifty or two hundred great fishes daily for their food; for want of hookes and lines, the Smith made hookes of old swords, and lines of old ropes, but finding all those poore Engines also decay, they sent one of the two Frigats last left with them for England, to tell them of this misery. All which was now attributed to Master Mores perversnesse, who at first when he got the Amber-Greece had not such a generall applause, but now all the worst could possibly be suggested was too good for him; yet not knowing for the present how to send a better, they let him continue still, though his time was neere expired, and with all speed sent the *Welcome* fraught with provision, where shee well arrived, and proved her selfe as welcome in deed as in name; for all those extremities, Master Lewes Hues writeth, not one of all those threescore that first beganne this Plantation was dead, which shewes it was not impossible, but industry might have prevented a great part of the others sluggish carelesnesse.

A supply, and Master Mores returne.   This ship much refreshed this miserable Colony, but Master More seeing they sent not for him, his time being now expired, understanding how badly they reputed him in England, and that his imploiment now was more for their owne ends then any good for himselfe, resolved directly to returne with this ship. Having setled all things in the best order he could, left the government to the charge of the counsell of six to succeed each other monethly, till they had further directions from England; whose names were Captaine Miles Kendall, Captaine John Mansfield, Thomas Knight, Charles Caldycot, Edward Waters, and Christopher Carter, with twelve others for their assistances. More thus taking leave of those Ilands, arrived in England, much wrangling they had, but at last they confirmed him according to promise eight shares of Land, and so he was dismissed of his charge, with shew of favour and much friendship.

The rule of the six Governors.

1615.
Sir Thomas
Smith
Treasurer.

THE first thing they did was casting of lots, who should rule first, which lot lighted upon Master Caldicot. This last supply somewhat abated the extremitie of their miseries, and the better in that their fortifications being finished, they had the more leasure to goe abroad with that meanes was brought to that purpose to fish. Chard as you have heard, whom all this while More had kept Prisoner, they set at libertie: now by reason of their former miseries, little or nothing could be done; yet this Governor having thus concluded his moneth, and prepared a Frigot and two and thirtie men, hee imbarked himselfe with two other of his fellow counsellers; namely, Knight and Waters for the West-Indies, to get Fruits and Plants, Goats, young Cattle, and such like. But this poore vessell, whether through ill weather, or want of Mariners, or both, in stead of the Indies fell with the Canaries, where taking a poore Portugall, the which they manned with ten of their owne people, as soone after separated from her in a storme, and the next day was taken by a French Pickaroune, so that the Frigot out of hope of her prize, makes a second time for the West-Indies, where she no sooner arrived, but foundred in the sea; but the men in their Boat recovered a desolate Ile, where after some few moneths stay, an English Pyrat tooke them in, and some of them at last got for England, and some few yeares after returned to the Somer Iles.

Captaine John Mansfield his moneth.

The Frigot thus gone, Captaine Mansfield succeeded. Then was contrived a petition, as from the generalitie, unto the triumvirat Governors; wherein they supplicated, that by no meanes they should resigne the government to any should come from England, upon what tearmes soever, untill six moneths after the returne of their ship sent to the West-Indies: about this unwarrantable action, Master Lewes Hues their Preacher was so violent in suppressing it, that such discontents grew betwixt the Governors and him, and divisions among the Company, he was arraigned, condemned, and imprisoned, but not long detained before released. Then the matter fell so hotly againe to be disputed betwixt him and one Master Keath

a Scotch-man, that professed schollership, that made all the
people in a great combustion: much adoe there was, till at last
as they sate in the Church and ready to proceed to a judiciary
course against Master Hues, suddenly such an extreme gust of
wind and weather so ruffled in the trees and Church; some
cried out, A miracle; others, it was but an accident common in
those Iles, but the noise was so terrible it dissolved the assembly: notwithstanding, Master Hues was againe imprisoned,
and as suddenly discharged; but those factions were so confused, and their relations so variable, that such unnecessary circumstances were better omitted then any more disputed.

Master
Carter.
Captaine
Kendall
Captaine
Mansfield.

This mans moneth thus ended, begins Master
Carter, which was altogether spent in quietnesse,
and then Captaine Miles Kendall had the rule, whose
moneth was also as quietly spent as his Predecessors.
Then Captaine Mansfield begins his second moneth, when the
ship called the *Edwin* arrived with good supplies. About this
time divers Boats going to sea were lost, and some men
drowned; and many of the Company repaired to Master Hues,
that there might bee a Councell according to Master Mores
order of six Governours, and twelve Assistants, whereupon
grew as many more such silly brawles as before, which at last
concluded with as simple a reconciliation. In the interim happened to a certaine number of private persons as miserable and
lamentable an accident, as ever was read or heard of, and thus
it was:

In the month of March, a time most subject of all
A wonderfull
accident.
others to such tempests; on a Friday there went
seven men in a boat of two or three tunnes to fish.
The morning being faire, so eager they were of their journey,
some went fasting: neither carried they either meat or drinke
with them, but a few Palmeta berries, but being at their fishing
place some foure leagues from the shoare, such a tempest
arose, they were quickly driven from the sight of land in an
overgrowne Sea, despairing of all hope, onely committing
themselves to Gods mercy, let the boat drive which way shee
would. On Sunday the storme being somewhat abated, they
hoysed saile as they thought towards the Island. In the evening
it grew starke calme; so that being too weake to use their
oares, they lay a drift that night. The next morning Andrew

Hilliard, for now all his companions were past strength either to helpe him or themselves: before a small gale of wind spred his saile againe. On Tuesday one died, whom they threw over board. On Wednesday three. And on Thursday at night the sixt. All these but the last were buried by Hilliard in the Sea, for so weake hee was growne hee could not turne him over as the rest, whereupon hee stripped him, ripping his belly with his knife, throwing his bowels into the water, hee spread his body abroad tilted open with a sticke, and so lets it lie as a cisterne to receive some lucky raine-water, and this God sent him presently after, so that in one small shoure hee recovered about foure spoonefuls of raine water to his unspeakeable refreshment; he also preserved neere halfe a pint of blood in a shooe, which he did sparingly drinke of to moist his mouth: two severall daies he fed on his flesh, to the quantity of a pound, on the eleventh day from his losing the sight of land, two flying fishes fals in his boat, whose warme jucie blood hee sucked to his great comfort. But within an houre after to his greater comfort you will not doubt, he once againe descried the land, and within foure houres after was cast upon a rocke neere to Port royall, where his boat was presently split in pieces, but himselfe, though extreamly weake, made shift to clamber up so steepe and high a rocke, as would have troubled the ablest man in the Ile to have done that by day hee did by night.

Being thus astride on a rocke, the tumbling Sea had gotten such possession in his braines, that a good while it was before his giddy head would suffer him to venture upon the forsaking it: towards the morning he craules a shore, and then to his accomplished joy descernes where hee is, and travels halfe a day without any refreshment then water, whereof wisely and temperately he stinted himselfe, otherwise certainely hee had drunke his last. In which case hee attaines a friends house: where at the first they tooke him for a ghost, but at last acknowledged and received him with joy, his story after some houres of recovery of strength to tell it, heard out with admiration: he was not long after conveyed to the towne, where he received his former health, and was living in the yeere 1622.

Treasure found in the Summer Iles. The next newes that happened in this time of ease, was, that a merry fellow having found some few Dollars against the Flemish wracke, the bruit went currant the treasure was found, and they all made men. Much adoe there was to prevent the purloining of it, before they had it: where after they had tyred themselves with searching, that they found, amounted not to above twenty pounds starling, which is not unlike but to be the remainder of some greater store, washed from some wracke not farre from the shore.

A new Governor chosen.

The company by the *Edwin* receiving newes of the revels were kept in Sommer Iles, resolved to make choice of a new Governour, called Master Daniel Tuckar, that a long time had bin a planter in Virginia in the government of Captaine Smith. All things being furnished for his voyage; hee set saile in the *George,* consorted with the *Edwin,* with many passengers, which being discovered by them in those Iles, they supposed them the Frigot sent to the West Indies; but when they understood what they were, much preparation they made to resist the new Governour. Many great ostentations appeared on both sides, but when the quondam Governour did see his men for most part forsake him; all was very well and quietly compounded, and with much kindnesse received and welcomed a shore, where his Commission was no sooner read, then they accepted and acknowledged him for their Governour.

The Government of Captaine Daniel Tuckar.

1616. Sir Thomas Smith Treasurer.

ABOUT the midst of May arrived this Governor, where finding the Inhabitants both abhorring all exacted labour, as also in a manner disdaining and grudging much to be commanded by him; it could not but passionate any man living. But at last according to the Virginia order, hee set every one was with him at Saint Georges, to his taske, to cleere grounds, fell trees, set corne, square timber, plant vines and other fruits brought out of England. These by their taske Masters by breake a day repaired to the wharfe, from thence to be imployed to the place of their imployment, till nine of the clocke, and then in the after-noone from three till Sunne-set. Beside meat, drinke and cloaths, they had for a time a certaine kinde of brasse money with a hogge on the one side, in memory of the abundance of hogges was found at their first landing.

Captaine Tuckars proceedings. This course thus squared, imitating divers orders used in Virginia, by Sir Thomas Dale: he began by them to looke into his instructions given by the Company. Whereupon by one Master Richard Norwood a Survayor, sent over for that purpose, in the time of Master Moore, hee began to lay out the eight tribes in the maine, which were to consist of fifty shares to a tribe; and twenty five acers to every share. He also began to plant some Colony men, on some of the especiall shares. He swore also certaine of the chiefe men of every tribe to bee Bailiffes thereof; and appointed as many men as hee was able for all supplied shares. The goods landed in the store houses hee sent from thence, and dispersed it to his workemen in generall: some Boats also began to be builded; but the pinace called the *Thomas* suspected might make an escape, was laid up in a docke, where shee yet remaineth.

A Barke sent to the West Indies. In the beginning of the second moneth of his government, he directed warrants to all the Bailiffes, for the holding of a generall Assise at Saint Georges, and appointed Master Stokes Lieutenant of the Kings Castle at the Gurnets head. The *Edwin* came with him he sent to the West Indies by directions from England, to trade with the natives, for cattell, corne, plants, and other commodities. A course of great importance, which had it been pursued, would certainly have produced more hopefull effects for the good of the Colony, then all the supplies and Magazines from England hath or will in a long time.

Presently after her departure began the Assises, The Assises. executed by his Deputy. The chiefe matter handled was the hanging one John Wood a French man, for speaking many distastefull and mutinous speeches against the Governour, to shew the rest by that example, the power of his authority, which after with his owne hands he so oft executed with a bastinado amongst the poorer sort; many tearmed it a cruelty, not much lesse then tyranny: but the sequell is more The strange adventure of five men in a boat. then strange.

So it was that five of them, seeing by no meanes they could get passage for England, resolved to undergoe all hazards but they would make an escape from such servitude. The chiefe mariner and plotter of this businesse, was Richard Sanders and his confederates, William Goodwin a ship Carpenter, Thomas Harison a Joyner, James Barker a Gentleman, and Henry Puet. These repairing to the Governour, and with pleasing insinuations told him, if hee would allow them but things necessary, they would build him a boat of two or three tunnes, with a close decke, should goe a fishing all weathers. The Governour halfe proud that hee had brought his men to so good a passe, as he conceived, to offer themselves to so necessary a worke; instantly with all willingnesse furnished them with all things they could desire, and many faire promises to incourage them to performe it with all expedition. Having made choise of a place most fit from molestation, they went forward with that expedition, that in a short time shee was brought to perfection. By this time, the ship that brought the Governour, being ready to depart, hee sends a lusty gange to goe fetch his new boat to carry him aboard, but arriving at the place where she was built, they could heare no more of her, but she was gone the last evening to Sea, to try how shee would saile. Much search and dispute was where this boat should be: but at last they found divers letters in the cabbins, to this effect, directed to the Governour, and other their friends: that their hard and bad usage was so intolerable, and their hope so small ever againe to see their Countrey, or be delivered from such servitude, they did rather chuse to put themselves to that desperate hazard to goe for England, in which if they miscaried, as it was much to be mistrusted, their lives and bloods should be required at their hands was the cause. A compasse Diall Barker had borrowed of Master Hues, to whom he writ that as hee had oft perswaded them to patience, and that God would pay them though none did: hee must now bee contented with the losse of his Diall, with his owne doctrine. Such leasure they found to bee merry when in the eye of reason they were marching into a most certaine ruine. The Governour being thus satisfied of their escape, extreamly threatned them no lesse then a hanging, but the stormes of the Ocean they now more feared then him; good provision by bartering they had got from the ship, where Goodwin in a bravado told the Mariners, though he could not be permitted to goe with them, yet peradventure hee might be in England before them, whereat the Master and his Mate laughed merrily. But having beene now under saile three weekes, the winds so favoured them, they felt nothing of what they had cause to feare: then a blustering gale blowing in their teeth, put them to much extremity for divers dayes, then becomming more gentle away they past prosperously some eight or ten dayes more, till meeting a French Piccaroune of whom they desired succour, hee like himselfe tooke from them what hee liked, leaving them not so much as a crosse-staffe to observe withall, and so cast them off: their course still they continued till their victuall began to fall to the lowest ebbe; and the very knees of their small vessell were halfe hewed away for fire wood. At last to their infinit joy they arrived in Ireland, where the Earle of Tomund honorably entertained them, and caused the boat to be hung up for a Monument, and well she might, for shee had sailed more then 3300. miles by a right line thorow the maine Sea, without any sight of land, and I thinke, since God made the world, the like navigation was never done, nor heard of. This fortunate Sanders going to the East Indies, in the rifling some ships there tooke, it was his chance to buy an old chest, for three or foure shillings, but because it wanted a key hee repented his bargaine, and would gladly have sold it againe for lesse. A certaine time it lay tossed to and fro as a thing hee little regarded, but at last having little to doe, hee broke it open, where he found a thousand pounds starling, or so much gold as bought him in England a good estate, which leaving with his wife he returned againe to the East Indies.

The *George* setting saile three dayes after this escape, the Governour seazed and confiscated all that those fugitives left behinde them. Within a weeke after returned the *Edwin* from the West Indies, furnished with figges, pynes, sugar-canes, plantaines, papawes and divers other plants, which were presently replanted, and since increased into greater numbers, also an Indian and a Negar, and so much *ligna vitæ* as defrayed all the charge. The Governor thus busied amongst his plants, making hedges of Figtrees, and Pomgranets, and severall divisions by Palizadoes for the defence of their guarding and keeping their cattell, for in such husbandry qualities he well deserved great commendations. The

Plants from the West Indies.

Adventurers to supply him sent with all speed they could the *Hopewell,* a small Barke, but an excellent sailer, and in her one Captaine Powell an excellent Mariner, and well ac-

The exploits of Captain Powell.

quainted in the Indies where he was to goe trade, after he had landed his passengers in the Summer Iles: but in his journey at the Westerne Iles meeting a Brasile man, hee liked the suger and passengers so well, hee mand the Carvill with his owne men, and continued his course, but bethinking himself how this would be entertained at the Summer Iles, hee found such doubts, hee went directly for the West Indies to take time to resolve what to doe: arriving there hee met a French rover, one every way as cunning as himselfe, but much more trecherous. A great league of kindnesse is soone made betweene them, upon confidence whereof, Powell and some of the chiefe with him being invited aboord him, is easily entised, and in the midst of their cups both hee and his company treacherously made prisoners; and thus was forced to give him their prise, or hang at the yards arme with all his company. Having set them a shore, away goes the French man; Powels ship being but hard by, presently fetcht them all a boord, but finding his victuall neere spent, and no hope at all to recover his prize, set his Portugales on shore, and set saile for the Summer Iles; where safely arriving, hee declared the whole passage to the Governour, lest some other in telling might make it worse, of which the Governour seemed well enough to approve.

This Governour still spent his time in good hus-

The second Assise.

bandry, although some of the snarling sort here in England, whom nothing will please, writ to him hee was fitter to be a Gardiner then a Governour: some time he spent in digging of a great pond, but that worke proved altogether unprofitable: about that time was held the second Assise. The greatest matter passed, was a Proclamation against the spoile of Cahowes, but it came too late, for they were most destroyed before: a platforme hee caused to be erected by Pagits Fort, where a good Fort were very necessary. Captaine Powell not having performed his service in the West Indies, he conditioned with the Company, is sent thither againe by this Governour, and thirteene or fourteene of his best men, furnished with all things necessary. In the meane time the Company understanding, that in January, February and March, there are many Whales, for which fishing they sent the *Neptune*, a tall ship well provided with every thing fitting for that purpose. But before she arrived, Captaine Tuckar, who had brought also with him most provisions for that imploiment, sent three good Shalops to try what could be done, but whether it was the swiftnes of the Whale in swimming, or the condition of the place, certaine it is for all their labour and hazard, they could kill none, though they strucke many.

1617.
The third
Assise. Sir
Thomas
Smith
Treasurer. To begin his second yeere, he called the third Assise, where divers were punished as their faults deserved: three were condemned to die; two were reprived, but the third was hanged: the next day there was also a levy for the repairing two Forts; but that labour tooke not such effect as was intended, for want of good directions.

The countrey
neere
devoured
with rats. But the great God of heaven being angry at somewhat happened in those proceedings, caused such an increase of silly rats, in the space of two yeeres so to abound, before they regarded them, that they filled not onely those places where they were first landed, but swimming from place to place, spread themselves into all parts of the Countrey, insomuch that there was no Iland but it was pestered with them; and some fishes have beene taken with rats in their bellies, which they caught in swimming from Ile to Ile: their nests they had almost in every tree, and in most places their burrowes in the ground like conies: they spared not the fruits of the plants, or trees, nor the very plants themselves, but ate them up. When they had set their corne, the rats would come by troupes in the night and scratch it out of the ground. If by diligent watch any escaped till it came to earing, it should then very hardly escape them: and they became noysome even to the very persons of men. They used all the diligence they could for the destroying of them, nourishing cats both wilde and tame, for that purpose; they used ratsbane, and many times set fire on the woods, that oft ran halfe a mile before it was extinct; every man was enjoyned to set twelve traps, and some of their owne accord have set neere an hundred, which they ever visited twice or thrice in a night; they also trained up their dogges to hunt them, wherein they became so expert, that a good dog in two or three houres would kil forty or fifty. Many

other devices they used to destroy them, but could not prevaile, finding them still increasing against them: nay they so
devoured the fruits of the earth, that they were destitute of
bread for a yeere or two; so that when they had it afterwards,
they were so wained from it, they easily neglected to eat it with
their meat. Besides they endevoured so much for the planting
Tobacco for present gaine, that they neglected many things
might more have prevailed for their good, which caused
amongst them much weaknesse and mortality, since the beginning of this vermine.

At last it pleased God, but by what meanes it is

A strange
confusion of
rats.

not well knowne, to take them away; in so much that
the wilde cats and many dogs which lived on them,
were famished, and many of them leaving the woods, came
downe to their houses, and to such places where they use to
garbish their fish, and became tame. Some have attributed the
destruction of them to the encrease of wild cats, but that is not
likely they should be so suddenly encreased rather at that time,
then foure yeeres before; and the chiefe occasion of this sup-
position was, because they saw some companies of them leave
the woods, and slew themselves for want of food. Others by the
coldnesse of winter, which notwithstanding is never so great
there, as with us in March, except it be in the wind: besides the
rats wanted not the fethers of young birds and chickins, which
they daily killed, and Palmeta mosse to build themselves
warme nests out of the wind, as usually they did; neither doth
it appeare that the cold was so mortall to them, seeing they
would ordinarily swimme from place to place, and bee very fat
even in the midst of winter. It remaineth then, that as God
doth sometimes effect his will without subordinate and secondary causes, so wee need not doubt, but that in the speedy encrease of this vermine; as also by the preservation of so many
of them by such weake meanes as they then enjoyed, and especially in the so sudden removall of this great annoyance, there
was joyned with and besides the ordinary and manifest
meanes, a more mediate and secret worke of God.

About this time Henry Long, with seven others in an extreame storme were cast away, but three of them escaped. One
of them being asked what hee thought in the worst of that extremity, answered, he thought nothing but gallowes claime thy

right, and it seemes God well heard his prayer, and rewarded his ingratitude; for he was hanged within halfe a yeere after. In that March also five men went to Sea, but as yet was never heard of, and three more drowned in a boat. By Hilliards house grew a very faire Cedar, which by a thunder clap was rent almost to small shivers, and a man stood by him, and Samuel Tanton, most fearfully blasted, yet neither they, the house, nor a little childe, yet a paire of racks in the house was all torne to fitters. The *Neptune* not long after arriving to fish for whale, her fortune proved no better then the Governours, yet some are of opinion, profit might be made by them.

The returne of Master Powel from the Indies. In May they discried foure saile, so that manning all their Forts, they stood two daies in Armes, expecting what they were; at last they found it Master Powell returned from the West-Indies in the *Hopewell*, where missing such trade as he expected, these three Frigots comming in his way, he could not chuse but take them; Meale, Hides and Munition was their lading. Faire weather the Governor made with Powell, till he had got all the goods into his owne possession, and then called Powell to a strict account for doing such an unwarrantable act; much a doe then was betwixt the taker and receiver; but Powell was glad to be excused to answer it in England, leaving all hee had taken behinde him in the Iles: The *Neptune* also returned with him, but noble Powell lost all his pay and pillage for this yeeres worke. For which the Company sent for to Tuckar, so that he also lost his part as well as Powell: Notwithstanding, the Governour by this meanes being strong in shipping, fitted the Carvill with twelve men, under the command of Edward Waters formerly spoken of, and sent them to Virginia about such businesse as hee had conceived. Arriving there, they obtained some goates, and hogs, and what they could spare, and so returned for the Summer Iles; but whether they could not finde the Iles for want of skill, or beaten off by ill weather, or the ill will they bare the Governor, it matters not much: but they bare up again for Virginia, where they all remained, and would returne no more to Summer Iles.

A supposed mutiny by Master Pollard, and Master Rich. The Governour thinking to make some use of the hides, set some that professed themselves Tanners, to make tryall of their skill; but they lost their labours and spoiled the hides. Also he called another Assise concerning a poore fellow called Gabriel, for concealing some speeches Master Pollard and Master Rich should use, tending to the disreputation of the Governour, and his injustice and cruelties; which being brought within the compasse of sedition and mutiny, though a yeere agoe; many were called in question about it, although every one ordinarily had spoke as much. Yet Gabriel for example sake was condemned to bee hanged, and was upon the ladder, but reprieved. The other two Master Pollard, and Master Rich were imprisoned, but upon better consideration, the fact appeared so small and ridiculous, upon their submission they were pardoned, and restored to their places.

The division of the Summer Iles into Tribes, by Master Richard Norwood, Surveyor.

1618.
The division of the Iles into Tribes.
Sir Thomas Smith Treasurer.

ACCORDING to the directions of the Councell and Company, as they had determined by lot, Master Norwood tooke a plot of the Ile, and divided it with as much faithfulnes as he could, assigning to every Adventurer his share or proportion, as namely, to lay out a large proportion, to bee called the generall land, and imployed for publike uses, as for the maintenance of the Governour, Ministers, Commanders of Forts, souldiers, and such like: and to this end was assigned St. Georges Iland, St. Davids Iland, Longbridge Iland, Smiths Iland, Coopers Iland, Cony Iland, Nonesuch Iland, part of the maine, and sundry other small Iles. The rest was to be divided into eight parts, each part to be called a tribe, and to have his denomination of some principall person that was Adventurer therein: and accordingly the first Tribe to bee Eastward, was then called Bedfords Tribe, now Hamiltons: the second, Smiths Tribe: the third, Cavendish, now Devonshires: the fourth, Pembrooks: the fift, Pagits: the sixt, Mansils, now Warwicks: the seventh, Southhampton: the eighth, Sands: in the honours of the Right honorable the Marquis Hamilton, Sir Thomas Smith, the Earle of

Devonshire, the Earle of Pembrooke, the Lord Pagit, the Earle of Warwicke, the Earle of Southhampton, and Sir Edwin Sands. Againe each of those Tribes were to bee divided into fifty parts, called shares; and every Adventurer to have his shares in these tribes as was determined, by casting lots in England, the manner of it appeares by the Map, and more largely by his Booke of the Survay of the Countrey, which is in the Records of the Colony. And then began this which was before as you have heard, but as an unsetled and confused Chaos, to receive a disposition, forme, and order, and become indeed a Plantation.

The names of the Adventurers, and their shares in every Tribe, according to the survey, and the best information yet ascertained, of any of their alterations.

Hamiltons Tribe.	Shares.
James, Lord Marquis Hamilton	6
Sir Edward Harwood.	4
Master John Delbridge.	3
Master John Dike.	3
Master Ellis Roberts.	2
Master Robert Phips.	1
Master Ralph King.	1
Master Quicks assignes.	2
Master William Canning.	4
Master William Canning.	1
Master William Web.	1
Master John Bernards assignes.	2
Master Elias Roberts Junior.	1
Master John Gearing.	2
Master Cleophas Smith.	2
Robert Earle of Warwick.	4
Master Thomas Covell.	3
Master Greenwels assignes.	1
Master Cley.	1
Master Powlson.	2
Master John Dike.	1 ½

	Shares.
Common land for conveniency.	25
Master John Dike.	1 ½
Master George Thorps assignes.	1

2. Smiths Tribe.

Sir Dudley Digs assignes.	2
Master Richard Edwards.	2
Master William Pane.	4
Master Robert Smith.	2
Master George Barkley assignes.	5
Sir Samuel Sands.	1
Master Anthony Pennistone.	4
Sir Edwin Sands.	5
Sir Thomas Smith.	5
Master Richard More.	4
Master Adam Brumfield	2
Master Robert Johnson Alderman.	5
Master John Wroth.	3
Master George Smith.	4

3. Devonshire Tribe.

Master Anthony Penistone.	2
Master John Dike.	1
Master John Dike.	1
Master John Bernards heires.	2
Robert Earle of Warwick.	2
Master Francis West.	2
William Lord Cavendish.	5
William Earle of Devonshire.	5
Master Edward Luckin.	5
Master Edward Ditchfield.	1
Master Edward Ditchfield.	4
Master William Nicols.	2
Master Edward Ditchfield.	1
Master John Fletcher.	2
Master Gedion Delawne.	2
Master Anthony Pennistone.	3
Master Best.	2
Master Edward Luckin.	2
Master Richard Rogers.	2
Master William Palmer.	4

4. Pembrookes Tribe.

	Shares.
Master George Smith.	
Gleab land.	4
Master Nicholas Hide.	2
Sir Lawrence Hide.	1
Master Thomas Judwyn.	1
William Earle of Pembrooke.	2
Master Richard Edwards.	10
Master Harding.	1
Master Richard Edwards.	1
Master Elias Roberts.	1
Master Richard Edwards.	1
Master Jacobsons assignes.	1
Master John Farrar.	1
Master Nicholas Farrar.	1
Master Nicholas Farrar.	1
Master William Canning.	2
Master Richard Martin.	2
Master Moris Abbot.	2
Master Richard Caswell.	1
Master Richard Caswell.	2
Master William Caswell.	1
Master Richard Edwards.	2
Master Richard Caswell.	1
Master Richard Edwards.	1
Master George Sands assignes.	2
Master William Paine.	2

5. Pagits Tribe.

	Shares.
Master John Chamberlaine.	
Master Thomas Ayres, and	5
Master Richard Wiseman.	4
Master Richard Wiseman	1
William Lord Pagit.	10
Master William Palmer.	4
Master Bagnell.	5
Master John Bale.	1
Master Wheatley.	4
Master Christopher Barron.	4
Master John Wodall.	1
Master John Wodall.	1
Master Lewis.	2
Master Owen Arthors assignes.	2

Shares.

Master George Etheridge.	4
	2
Sir William Wade.	1
Master John Bernards heires.	1

6. Warwicks Tribe.

Master Wheatley.	2
Captaine Daniel Tuckar.	2
Master William Felgate.	1
Robert Earle of Warwicke.	5
Master George Smith.	5
Master Samuel Tickner.	2
Master Francis Mevell.	1
Master Stephen Sparrow.	1
Master Joseph Man.	5
Captaine Daniel Tuckar.	2
Master Elias More.	1
Doctor. Anthony Hunton	2
Master Francis Moverill.	1
Master Richard Poulson	1
Master Mathew Shephard.	1
Master George Tuckar.	10
Master Charles Clitheroe.	1
Master George Swinow.	2
Master Richard Tomlings.	1
Master Francis Meverill.	1
Master John Waters.	2
Master Martin Bond.	2

7. Southamptons Tribe.

Captaine Daniel Tuckar.	4
Master John Britton.	1
Master Richard Chamberland.	3
Master Leonard Harwods assignes.	1
Master John Banks.	1
Sir Nathanael Rich.	12
Robert Earle of Warwicke.	3
Master Richard More.	6
Master George Scot. ⎫	
Master Edward Scot. ⎬	6
Master Anthony Abdy. ⎭	
Henry Earle of Southampton.	4
Master Andrew Broumfield.	2
Master Henry Timbed.	2

	Shares.
Sir Thomas Hewet.	2
Master Perce.	1
Sir Ralph Winwood.	2

8. Sandys Tribe.

	Shares.
Master George Barcklies heires.	5
Sir Edwin Sands.	5
Master Jerom Hidon.	10
Master Thomas Millin and Master John Cuffe.	2
Master Robert Chamberlaine.	2
Master Abraham Chamberlaine.	1
Master George Smith.	2
Master Robert Gore.	3
Sir Edward Sackvile.	1
Sir John Dauers.	1
Master Robert Gore.	2
Master John Delbridge.	1
Master John Wroth.	1
Master John Wests heires.	4
Master Richard Chamberlaine.	10

Touching the common ground in each Tribe, as also the over-plus, you may finde that at large in the Booke of Surveyes amongst their Records.

Now though the Countrey was small, yet they could not conveniently have beene disposed and well setled, without a true description and a survey of it; and againe, every man being setled where he might constantly abide, they knew their businesse, and fitted their houshold accordingly: then they built no more Cabbens, but substantiall houses, they cleered their grounds, and planted not onely such things as would yeeld them their fruits in a few moneths, but also such as would affoord them profit within a few yeares, so that in a short time the Countrey began to aspire, and neerely approach unto that happinesse and prosperitie, wherein now it flourisheth, etc.

The first
Magazin.
1618.

But to follow the History; upon the best plot of ground could be found, the Governor prevailed so much with the generalitie, they built a faire house of Cedar, which being done, he appropriated it to himselfe, which occasioned exceeding much distaste. About this time arrived the *Diana* with a good supply of men and provision, and the first Magazin ever seene in those Iles; which course is not so much commended here, as cursed and abhorred by reason of enhansements of all the Inhabitants there; six or seven weeks this ship staied, then having towards her fraught thirtie thousand weight of Tobacco; which proving good, and comming to a lucky Market, gave great encouragement to the Adventurers to goe lustily forward in their Plantation, and without such successe, there is nothing but grudging and repining. But about the appropriation of this new built house, many bad discontents grew betwixt the oppressed Colony and the Governor, especially betwixt him and the Minister, and Lewes, who would neither be feared with threats nor imprisonment, that their malice continued till they met in England, of which the Minister made the cause so plaine, hee very well and honestly it seemes, discharged himselfe.

Now in those times of these endlesse uncivill broiles, two desperate men and a proper Gentlewoman got into a Boat, and thinking to make an escape to Virginia, as appeared by some Letters they left behinde them were never more heard on. The very next moneth after the like was attempted by six others, so desirous they were to be rid of their servitude; but their plot being discovered by one of their societie, they were apprehended, arraigned, and condemned to be hanged: the next day being led with halters about their neckes to the place of execution, one was hanged, and the rest reprived.

Two exploits of desperate Fugitives.

The *Diana* arriving well in England, for all the infinite numbers of complaints, the Tobacco did helpe to sweeten all manner of grievances, yet it bred a distaste in the opinions of so many, they began to thinke of another Governor; but for that time it was so qualified by divers of his friends, they dispatched away the *Blessing*, which arrived in the Somer Iles. Though their generall Letter was faire and courteous to the Governor, yet by the report of the Passengers and divers particular letters from his friends, it was assured him his cruelty and covetousnesse, for all his paines and industry was much disliked, nor was he like to enjoy his house, and that

The arrivall of the Blessing.

land he had planted for himselfe, by the extreme oppression of the Comminalty. This caused so many jelousies to arise in his conceit, that at last he fully resolved to returne by this ship, that no sooner set saile from England, then they proceeded to the nomination of a new Governor. Many were presented according to the affections of those that were to give in their voices, but it chiefely rested betwixt one Captaine Southwell, and one Master Nathaniel Butler, where wee will leave them a while to the consideration of the Court and Company. Now Captaine Tuckar having instituted Captaine Kendall one of the six Governors before spoken of for his substitute, returned with this ship directly for England, as well to excuse himselfe of those objections he suspected, as to get assured him the house and land he had alotted for himselfe, lest it might otherwise be disposed of in his absence.

Collected out of their Records by N. B. and the relations of
Master Pollard, and divers others.

The Government of Captaine Miles Kendall, Deputy for Captaine Tuckar.

THE unexpected returne of Captaine Tuckar, caused a demurre in the election of the new Governor; some perswading these oft changes were so troublesome, dangerous, and chargeable, it were best to continue Captaine Kendall; others againe stood for Captaine Tuckar, but during the time of these opinions, the *Gilliflower* was dispatched with a supply. Now I should have remembred, Tuckar was no sooner out of the harbour, but he met Master Elfred in a ship called the *Treasurer,* sent from Virginia to trade: by her he writ to his Deputy Master Kendall, to have a care of all things, and beware of too much acquaintance with this ship, which hee suspected was bound for the West-Indies. Notwithstanding, Elfred received what kindnesse the Ile could afford; he promised to revisit them at his returne; this done, because they would not be governlesse when his Deputiship was expired,

The arrivall of two ships.

there was a generall assembly, and by that Election Kendall was confirmed to succeed still Governor. Now they began to apply themselves to the finishing some plat-forme about Smiths Fort, and laying the foundation of a Church to be built of Cedar, till the *Gillyflower* arrived with some private letters to Kendall, how he was elected Governor of those Iles for three yeeres. During her stay they held their Assises, where for some few suspected facts three were condemned, and the better to terrifie the rest, led to the place of execution, but reprieved; divers of the rest had their faults pardoned, and the *Gilliflower* set saile for New found land.

The love and kindnesse, honesty and industry of this Captaine Kendall, hath beene very much com-mended; by others, somewhat disliked: but an Angell in those imploiments cannot please all men, yet this considera-tion bred much ill bloud as well here as there, so that the Com-pany directly concluded, Captaine Butler should with what expedition they could, goe to be their Governor: In the Interim they tooke the opportunitie of a ship, called the *Sea-flower*, bound for Virginia, and by her sent a Preacher and his Family, with divers Passengers, and newes of a new Governor. This bred a great distaste amongst many, that still they should have new officers and strangers for their Governors they never heard of, and themselves still kept there whether they would or no, without any preferment, no nor scarce any of them their inhabiting, to have any land at all of their owne, but live all as tenants, or as other mens poore servants.

Captaine Butler chosen Governor.

About this time came in Captaine Kerby with a small Barke from the West-Indies, who having refreshed himselfe, was very kindly used by the Governor and so departed. Not long after a Dutch Frigot was cast away upon the Westerne shore, yet by the helpe of the English they saved the men, though the ship perished amongst the Rocks. A little after one Ensigne Wood being about the loading of a peece, by thrusting a pike into the concavitie, grating upon the shot, or somewhat about the powder, strucke fire within her and so discharged, but wounded him cruelly and blew him into the Sea, though hee was got out by some that stood by him, yet hee died of those wounds. Within two or three daies after, Captaine Elfred now comes in a second time: but of that we shall say more in the government of Captaine Butler, who presently after arrived with a good supply, and was kindly entertained by Captaine Kendall and all the Colony.

From a relation of Thomas Sparks, and divers others.

The Government of Captaine Nathaniel Butler.

A plat-forme burnt, and much hurt by a Hericano. 1619.

CAPTAINE BUTLER being arrived the twentieth of October, 1619. some mutterings there was how to maintaine their election of Captaine Kendall, but better remembring themselves, that conceit quickly dissolved. The next day, Kendall, the Ministers, and the Counsell went aboord to salute the new Governor, where after they had dined with the best entertainment he could give them; they saw the Redout belonging to the Kings Castle by a mischance on fire, whither he repaired with all the meanes he could to quench it; but all the platforme and cariages were consumed before their faces, and they could not helpe it. Two daies after he went up to the Towne, had his Commission publikely read, made a short speech to the Company, and so tooke upon him the government. Then presently he began to repaire the most necessary defects: The next moneth came in the *Garland,* sent from England six or seven weekes before him; so that being seventeene weeks in her voyage, it was so tedious and grievous to divers of the Fresh-water Passengers, that such a sicknesse bred amongst them, many died as well Sailers as Passengers. Having taken the best order he could for their releefe, passed through all the Tribes, and held his first Assise in Captaine Tuckars house at the over-plus. Towards the last of this moneth of November there arose a most terrible storme or Hericano, that blew up many great trees by the roots: the *Warwick* that brought the Governor was cast away, but the *Garland* rid by her, saved her selfe by cutting downe her Masts; and not long after a second storme, no lesse violent then the first, wherein the Mount which was a frame of wood built by Master More for a Watch-tower to looke out to Sea, was blowne up by the roots, and all that Winter crop of corne blasted: And thus was the new Governor welcomed.

With the beginning of the new yeere he began his first peece of fortification, upon a Rocke which flankers the Kings Castle, and finding the ship called the *Treasurer* starke rotten and unserviceable, hee tooke nine peeces of Ordinance from her to serve other uses. The *Garland* for want of meanes, could not make her voiage to Virginia as she was appointed; wherefore he entertained her to returne to England, with all the Tabacco they had in the Ile. It was January before she departed, in which time shee failed not much to have beene twice cast away. But those strange and unavoidable mischances, rather seemed to quicken the Governors industry then to dull it. Having finished the Church begun by Captaine Kendall, with an infinite toile and labour he got three peeces out of the wracke *Warwicke*. Having an excellent Dutch Carpinter he entertained of them that were cast away in the Dutch Frigot; he imploied him in building of Boats, whereof they were in exceeding great want. In February they discovered a tall ship beating too and againe, as it seemed by her working, being ignorant of the Coast; some thought her a Spaniard to view their Forts, which stand most to that part she so neerely approached; some, English; but the most, some Dutch man of Warre: The wind blew so high, they durst not send out a Boat, though they much doubted she would be foule of their Rocks, but at last she bore up rommy for the Sea, and we heard of her no more. That evening, a lucky fellow it should seeme he was, that found a peece of Ambergreece of eight ounces, as he had twice before, which bringing to the Governor, he had ready money for the one halfe, after three pound an ounce, according to their order of Court, to encourage others to looke out for more, and prevent the mischiefe insueth by concealing of it.

Within a few daies after, they descried two Frigots that came close to the shore, and sent a Letter to the Governor, writ in Italian, that they were Hollanders had beene in the West-Indies, and desired but to arrive, refresh themselves with wood and water, and so be gone. The Governor forthwith sent them to understand, that being there under his Majestie of England to command those Iles, he was to carrie himselfe a friend to his friends, and an enemy to his enemies; if therefore he could shew a lawfull Commission for

The refortifying the Kings Castle.

Amber-greece found.

The arrivall of two Dutch Frigots.

his being honestly and nobly emploied, he and his should be kindly welcome, otherwise they were to adventure at their perills. But his Commission was so good, he staied there two moneths, and was so well fitted with Oile and Bacon, they were all glad and happy of this Dutch Captaine Scoutans arrivall, with many thanks to their old friend Captaine Powell that had conducted him thither: the Colony being exceedingly in great want and distresse, bought the most part of it at reasonable rates, so Captaine Scoutan returned to the West-Indies, and Captaine Powell for his part in the Low-Countries. Whilest these things were in action, the Adventurers in England made many a long looke for their ships; at last the *Garland* brought them all the newes, but the Tobacco was so spoiled either in the leaking ship, or the making up, it caused a great suspicion there could none was good come from those Iles; where (were they but perfit in the cure) questionlesse it would be much better then a great quantitie of that they sell for Verinas, and many a thousand of it in London hath beene bought and sold by that title.

The Governor being cleere of those distractions, falls upon the restoring of the burnt Redoubt, where he cuts out a large new plat-forme, and mounts seven great peece of Ordnance upon new cariages of Cedar. Now amongst all those troubles, it was not the least to bring the two Ministers to subscribe to the Booke of Common Praier, which all the Bishops in England could not doe. Finding it high time to attempt some conformitie, bethought himselfe of the Liturgie of Garnsey and Jarse, wherein all those particulars they so much stumbled at, were omitted. No sooner was this propounded, but it was gladly imbraced by them both, whereupon the Governor translated it verbatim out of French into English, and caused the eldest Minister upon Easter day to begin the use thereof at St. Georges towne, where himselfe, most of the Councell, Officers and Auditorie received the Sacrament: the which forme they continued during the time of his government.

The differences betwixt the Ministers.

Much about this time, in such a faire morning, that had invited many Boats farre out to the Sea to fish, did rise such a Hericano that much indangered them all, so that one of them with two Boies were driven to

The rebuilding the Mount.

Sea and never more heard of. The Ministers thus agreed, a Proclamation was published for keeping of the Sabbath, and all the defective cariages he endevoured to have renewed, builded a small Boat of Cedar onely to goe with Ores, to be ready upon any occasion to discover any shipping, and tooke order every Fort should have the like: Also caused numbers of Cedars to be brought from divers places in flotes, to rebuild the Mount, which with an unspeakable toile, was raised seven foot higher then before, and a Falcon mounted at the foot, to be alwaies discharged for a warning to all the Forts upon the discovery of any shipping, and this he called Rich Mount. This exceeding toile and labour, having no Cattle but onely mens strengths, caused many petitions to the Governour, that all those generall works might cease till they had reaped their harvests, in that they were in great distresse for victuall; which hee so well answered, their owne shames did cause them desist from that importunity, and voluntarily performe as much as hee required.

The Tombe of Sir George Summers   Finding accidentally a little crosse erected in a by place, amongst a many of bushes, understanding there was buried the heart and intrailes of Sir George Summers, hee resolved to have a better memory for so worthy a Souldier, then that. So finding also a great Marble stone brought out of England, hee caused it by Masons to bee wrought handsomely and laid over the place, which hee invironed with a square wall of hewen stone, Tombe like; wherein hee caused to bee graven this Epitaph he had composed, and fixed it upon the Marble stone; and thus it was,

> *In the yeere 1611,*
> *Noble Sir* George Summers *went hence to heaven;*
> *Whose well tri'd worth that held him still imploid,*
> *Gave him the knowledge of the world so wide.*
> *Hence 't was by heavens decree, that to this place*
> *He brought new guests, and name to mutuall grace.*
> *At last his soule and body being to part,*
> *He here bequeath'd his entrails and his heart.*

Their manner of lawes reformed.   Upon the sixt of June began the second Assise, that reduced them to the direct forme used in England. For besides the Governour and Councell, they have the Bailiffes of the Tribes, in nature of the Deputy Lieutenants of the shires in England, for to them are all precepts and warrants directed, and accordingly answered and respected; they performe also the duties of Justices of Peace, within their limits. The subordinate Officers to these in every tribe, are the Constables, Head-borowes, and Church-wardens; these are the triers of the Tobacco, which if they allow not to be marchantable, is burnt: and these are the executioners of their civill and politicke causes.

Martiall
Officers.

For points of warre and martiall affaires, they have the Governour for Lieutenant generall, the Sergeant major, Master of Ordinance, Captaines of Companies, Captaines of Forts, with their severall officers, to traine and exercise those numbers under their charge, in martiall discipline.

Civill Officers
and Courts.

Concerning their Courts for decision of right and justice, the first, though last in constitution, is their generall assembly; allowed by the state in England, in the nature of a Parliament, consisting of about forty persons; viz. the Governour, the Counsell, the Bailiffes of the tribes, and two Burgesses of each tribe chosen by voyces in the tribe, besides such of the Clergie as the Governour thinkes most fit, to be held once a yeere, as you shal heare more thereof hereafter. The next Court is the Assise or Jayles of deliverie, held twice every yeere, in Christmas, and Whitson weeke, for all criminall offenders, and civill causes betwixt party and party; as actions of debt, trespasse, battery, slander, and the like: and these are determined by a Jury of twelve men, and above them is also a grand Jury to examine matters of greater consequence. The last day of the Assise might also well be held a Court, for hearing the trangressions in matters of contempt, mis-behaviour towards any Magistrate, riots, seditious speakers, contemners of warrants, and such like: there are also as occasion shall require, many matters heard by the Governor, or his Officers, and oft justice done in severall places, but those are but as daies of hearing, and as preparatives against their Courts, etc.

The second
Assise.

At this last Assize eighteene were arrained for criminall causes, a number very extraordinary considering the place; but now occasioned by reason of the hard yeere, and the store of ill chosen new commers; of these, some were censured to the whipping post, some burned in the hand, but two were condemned to die, yet the one was reprieved, the other hanged; this done, every man returned to his home: many trials they made againe about the *Warwicke*, but to small purpose, her Ordnance being lashed so fast they could not be unloosed, till the ropes and decks were rotten, yet some few buttes of beare being flote they got, which though it had lien six moneths under water was very good, notwithstanding the next yeere they recovered five peeces of Ordnance.

A generall assemblie in manner a Parliament.

Upon the first of August, according to the Companies instructions from England, began the generall assembly at the towne of Saint George, which was the first these Iles ever had; consisting as is said, of the Governour, Councell, Bailiffes, and Burgesses, and a Secretarie to whom all bils were presented, and by him openly read in the house, also a Clerke to record the Acts, being thirty two in all; fifteene of which being sent into England, were by a generall consent received and enacted, the titles whereof are these following: as for all the reasons for them, they would be too tedious to recite.

Their Acts.

The first was against the unjust sale and letting of apprentises and other servants, and this was especially for the righting the undertakers in England. The second, concerning the disposing of aged, diseased, and impotent persons, for it being considered how carelesse many are in preferring their friends, or sending sometimes any they can procure to goe, such unserviceable people should be returned back at their charge that sent them, rather then be burdensome to the poore Inhabitants in the Iles. The third, the necessary manning the Kings Castle, being the key of the Ile, that a garison of twelve able men should bee there alwaies resident: and 3000. eares of corne, and 1000. pounds of Tobacco payed them by the generality yeerely, as a pension. The fourth, against the making unmarchantable Tobacco, and Officers sworne to make true trials, and burne that was naught. The fift, injoyned the erection of certaine publike bridges, and the maintenance of them. The sixt, for a continuall supply of victuall for all the Forts, to bee preserved, till some great occasion to use it. The seventh was, for two fixed dayes every yeere for the Assises. The eight, commands the making of high-waies, and prohibiting the passage over mens grounds and planted fields, as well to prevent the spoyling of gardens, as conveniencie to answer any alarum. The ninth, for the preserving young tortoises and birds, that were carelesly destroyed. The tenth, provided against vagabonds, and prohibited the entertainement of other mens servants. The eleventh, compelled the setting of a due quantity of corne for every family. The twelfth, the care corne being set, enjoyned the keeping up of their poultry till it was past their reaches. The thirteenth, for the preservation of sufficient fences, and against the felling of marked trees appointed for bounds. The fourteenth, granted to a levy for a thousand pound weight of Tobacco, towards the payment of publike workes, as the bridges and the mount. The fifteenth, for the enjoyning an acknowledgement and acception of all resident Governours, and the warranting him to continue, though his time be expired, till the arrivall of a legitimate successor from England, to prevent all unmeet and presumptuous elections, besides it was desired by petition in England, the new Governour should live two months as a private man after his arrivall, if his predecessor did stay so long, the better to learne and observe his course. And these are the contents of those fifteene Acts, applied as you may perceive: which the lawes of England could not take notice of, because every climate hath somewhat to it selfe in that kinde in particular; for otherwise as it is conceived, it had beene a high impudency and presumption to have medled with them, or indeed with any such as these lawes, that had with such great judgement and justice alwaies provided for.

The arrivall of the Magazin ship. No sooner was this businesse over, but the Magazin ship is discovered, and that night came into the Harbour, but in a very weake and sickly case, having cast over board twenty or thirty of her people, and so violent was the infection, that the most part of the sailers, as well as passengers, were so sicke, or dismaid, or both, that the Master confessed, had they stayed at the Sea but a weeke longer, they had all perished. There arrived with this ship divers Gentlemen of good fashion, with their wives and families; but many of them crasie by the tediousnesse of the voyage: howsoever most of them, by the excellent salubrity of the aire, then which the world hath not a better, soone after recovered; yet some there were that died presently after they got ashore, it being certainly the quality of the place, either to kill, or cure quickly, as the bodies are more or lesse corrupted. By this ship the Company sent a supply of ten persons for the generality, but of such bad condition that it seemed they had picked the Males out of Newgate, the Females from Bridewell: As the Governour found it his best course, to grant out the women to such as were so greedy of wives, and would needs have them for better for worse; and the men hee placed in the Kings Castle for souldiers. But this bad, weake, sickly supply being dispersed for their best reliefe, by the much imployment of his boats in remooving them, many of his owne men became infected, so that for some weekes, they were not able to doe him any service at all. Strict instructions also they brought for the planting of Sugar canes, for which the Iland being rockie and dry, is so unproper, that few as yet have beene seene to prosper: yet there are others hold the contrary opinion, that there is raine so ordinarily, the Iles are so moist, as produceth all their plants in such infinit abundance: there is no great reason to suspect this, were it rightly used, more then the rest. Seventy thousand weight of Tobacco being prepared towards her fraught, she returned for England. No sooner was shee gone then came in another, sent by the Company and generality, well conditioned, but shee failed not much to have beene cast away amongst those dangerous and terrible rocks; by her came also expresse command, they should entertaine no other ships, then were directly sent from the Company: this caused much grudging, and indeed a generall distraction and exclamation among the Inhabitants, to be thus constrained to buy what they wanted, and sell what they had at what price the Magazin pleased, and to debarre true men from comming to them for trade or reliefe, that were daily received in all the harbours in England. So long this ship stayed going for fraught and wages, the Master not caring how long he lay at that rate in a good harbour, the Governour was ready to send her away by Proclamation. Thus ended the first yeere of the government of Captaine Butler.

With the first of the second yeere were held the Assises, where all the Bailiffes were fined for not giving a beginning to

1620.
The building
of three
bridges and
other works.
the building of the bridges; there was also an order to restraine the excessive wages all handicrafts men would have: and that the Church-wardens should meet twice a yeere, to have all their presentments made perfect against the Assises. The Assises done, all the ablest men were trained in their armes, and then departed to their owne homes. The towne thus cleered, he made certaine new carriages for some demy Culverings, and a large new store-house of Cedar for the yeerely Magazines goods; finished Warwicks Fort begun by Master More, and made a new platforme at Pagits Fort, also a faire house of lime and stone for the Townes-house. The three bridges appointed by the generall assembly, was followed with such diligence, though they were more then an hundred, or an hundred and twenty foot in length, having the foundation and arches in the Sea, were raised and accomplished, so that man or beast with facility might passe them.

The generall
Assises,
and the
proceedings.
At Whitsonday was held the fourth generall Assise at Saint Georges, where were tryed twenty severall causes; foure or five were whipped or burnt in the hand, for breaking of houses: also an order was made, that the party cast in the triall of any cause, should pay to every of the Jurours foure pence: moreover, that not past ten leaves at the most should grow upon a plant of Tobacco, and that also in the making it up, a distinction should diligently be observed of two kinds, a better and a worse: then they built a strong stone house for the Captaine of the Kings Castle and *corps du guard*; and repaired what defects they could finde in the platformes and carriages.

Captaine Powell so oft mentioned, having beene in the West Indies for the States of Holland, came to an anchor within shot of their Ordnance, desiring admittance for wood and water, of which hee had great need, but the Governor would not permit him, so he weighed and departed, whereat the company were so madded, it was not possible to constraine them to cease their exclamations against the Companies inhibition, till they were weary with exclaming: But still for their better defence, not thinking themselves sufficiently secure, having finished two new plat-formes more, arrived the Magazin ship, but her Master was dead, and many of the Passengers, the rest for

most part very sicke; and withall, a strange and wonderfull report of much complaint made against the Governor to the
Company in England, by some of them returned in the last
yeeres shipping: but it was eight daies before she could get in
by reason of ill weather, being forced againe to Sea; so that
time, they kept every night continually great fires, she might
see the Ile as well by night as day; but at last she arrived, and
he plainly understood, he had more cause a great deale to
looke for misconstruction of all his service then an acknowl-
edgment, much lesse a recompence any better then his predecessors; but it is no new thing to requite the best desert with
the most vildest of ingratitude.

A strange   The very next daies night after the arrivall of the
deliverance of Magazins ship, newes was brought the Governor by
a Spanish
wracke.   a dismaied Messenger from Sands his Tribe, that one
hundred Spaniards were landed in that part, and divers ships
discovered at Sea, whereupon he presently manned the Forts,
and instantly made thitherward in person with twentie men,
determining as he found cause to draw together more strength
by the way. Being got thither by the breake of the next day, in
stead of an enemy which he expected, he met onely with a
company of poore distressed Portugals and Spaniards, who in
their passage from Carthagena in the West-Indies, in consort
with the Spanish fleet of Plait; by the same storme that had indangered the Magazin ship, lost theirs upon those terrible
Rocks, being to the number of seventy persons, were strangely
preserved; and the manner was thus.

About Sunne-set their ship beating amongst the Rocks,
some twenty of the Sailers got into the Boat with what treasure
they could, leaving the Captaine, the Master, and all the rest to
the mercy of the Sea. But a Boy not past foureteene yeares of
age that leaped after to have got into the Boat, missing that
hope, it pleased God he got upon a Chest a drift by him,
whereon they report he continued two daies, and was driven
neere to the cleane contrary part of the Ile, where he was
taken up neere dead, yet well recovered. All this night the ship
sticking fast, the poore distressed in her the next day spying
land, made a raft, and were those gave the alarum first a shore
about three of the clocke in the after noone. The morning after,
about seven of the clocke came in the Boat to a place called

Mangrove Bay; and the same day their Carpenter was driven a shore upon a Planke neere Hog Bay. There was a Gentlewoman that had stood wet up to the middle upon the raft from the ship to the shore, being big with childe; and although this was upon the thirteenth of September, she tooke no hurt, and was safely delivered of a Boy within three daies after. The best comfort could be given them in those extremities they had, although some of the baser sort had beene rifling some of them before the Governors arrivall: Also the Spanish Captaine and the chiefe with him, much complained of the treachery of his men to leave him in that manner, yet had conveyed with them the most of the money they could come by, which he easily missed; whereupon hee suddenly caused all them he accused, to be searched, and recovered to the value of one hundred and fortie pounds starling, which he delivered into the Captaines hands, to be imploied in a generall purse towards their generall charge: during their stay in the Iles, some of the better sort, nine or ten weeks dieted at his owne table, the rest were billited amongst the Inhabitants at foure shillings the weeke, till they found shipping for their passage, for which they paied no more then the English paied themselves; and for the passage of divers of them, the Governor was glad to stand bound to the Master; some others that were not able to procure such friendship, were so constrained to stay in the Iles, till by their labours they had got so much as would transport them; and thus they were preserved, releeved, and delivered.

How they solemnized the powder treason, and the arrivall of two ships. In the moneth insuing arrived the second ship, and she also had lost her Master, and divers of her Passengers; in her came two Virginian Women to be married to some would have them, that after they were converted and had children, they might be sent to their Countrey and kindred to civilize them. Towards the end of this moneth came in the third ship with a small Magazin, having sold what she could, caried the rest to Virginia, and never did any of those Passengers complaine either of their good diet, or too good usage at sea; but the cleane contrary still occasioned many of those extremities. The fift of November the damnable plot of the powder treason was solemnized, with Praiers, Sermons, and a great Feast, whereto the Governor invited the chiefe of the Spaniards, where drinking the

Kings health, it was honored with a quicke volly of small shot,
which was answered from the Forts with the great Ordnance,
and then againe concluded with a second volley of small shot;
neither was the afternoone without musicke and dancing, and
at night many huge bone-fires of sweet wood.

The Spaniards to expresse their thankfulnesse at
their departure, made a deed of gift to the Governor
of whatsoever he could recover of the wracked ship;
but the ships as they went out came so dangerously
upon a Rock, that the poore Spaniards were so dismaied,
swearing this place was ominous unto them, especially the
women, that desired rather to goe a shore and die howsoever,
than adventure any further in such a labyrinth of dangers, but
at last she got cleere without danger, and well to England; the
other went to Virginia, wherein the Governor sent two great
Chests filled with all such kinds and sorts of Fruits and Plants
as their Ilands had; as Figs, Pomgranats, Oranges, Lemons,
Sugar-canes, Plantanes, Potatoes, Papawes, Cassado roots, red
Pepper, the Prickell Peare, and the like. The ships thus dispatched, hee goeth into the maine, and so out to sea to the
Spanish wracke. He had beene there before presently after her
ruine, for never had ship a more sudden death, being now split
in peeces all under water. He found small hope to recover any
thing, save a Cable and an Anchor, and two good Sacars; but
the wind was so high hee was forced to returne, being ten miles
from the shore, onely with three Murderers, which
were knowne to be the same Captaine Kendall had
sold to Captaine Kerby, whose ship was taken by two
men of warre of Carthagena, the most of his men
slaine or hanged, and he being wounded, died in the woods.
Now their Pilot being at this service, got thus those three
Murderers to their ship, and their ship thus to the Bermudas,
as the Spaniards remaining related to the Governor and others.

Having raised three small Bulwarkes at South-
hamptons Fort, with two Curtaines, and two Rav-
ilings, which indeed is onely the true absolute peece
of fortification in the Iles; Christmas being come, and the prefixed day of the Assise; divers were whipped and burnt in the
hand, onely three young boyes for stealing were condemned,
and at the very point of hanging reprived. The Governour

The
Spaniards
returne, and
in danger
againe. 1621.

Three
English
Murderers
found in the
Spanish
wracke.

Their Assises,
and other
passages.

then sent his Lieutenant all over the maine to distribute Armes to those were found most fit to use them, and to give order for their randezvous, which were hanged up in the Church. About this time it chanced a pretty secret to be discovered to preserve their corne from the fly, or weavell, which did in a manner as much hurt as the rats. For the yeere before having made a Proclamation that all Corne should be gathered by a certaine day, because many lazy persons ranne so after the ships to get Beere and Aquavitæ, for which they will give any thing they have, much had beene lost for want of gathering. This yeare having a very faire crop, some of the Inhabitants, none of the best husbands, hastily gathered it for feare of the penaltie, threw it in great heaps into their houses unhusked, and so let it lie foure or five moneths, which was thought would have spoiled it: where the good husbands husked it, and with much labour hung it up, where the Flies did so blow on it, they increased to so many Weavels, they generally complained of great losse; but those good fellowes that never cared but from hand to mouth, made their boasts, that not a graine of theirs had beene touched nor hurt, there being no better way to preserve it then by letting it lie in its huske, and spare an infinite labour formerly had beene used. There were also very luckily about this time found out divers places of fresh water, of which many of the Forts were very destitute, and the Church-wardens and Side-men were very busie in correcting the prophaners of the Sabbath, Drunkards, Gamesters, and such like. There came also from Virginia a small Barke with many thanks for the presents sent them; much Aquavitæ, Oile, Sacke and Bricks they brought in exchange of more Fruits and Plants, Ducks, Turkies and Lime-stone, of which she had plenty, and so returned. During the aboad of the stay of this ship, the mariage of one of the Virginia maides was consummated with a husband fit for her, attended with more then one hundred guests, and all the dainties for their dinner could be provided; they made also another triall to fish for Whales, but it tooke no more effect then the former: this was done by the Master of the Virginia ship that professed much skill that way, but having fraughted his ship with Limestone, with 20000. weight of Potatoes, and such things as he desired, returned for Virginia.

Aprill and May were spent in building a strong
new Prison, and perfecting some of the Fortifications, and by the labour of twenty men in fourteene
daies was got from the Spanish wracke foure excellent good
Sacres, and mounted them at the Forts. Then began the generall Assize, where not fewer then fifty civill, or rather uncivill
actions were handled, and twenty criminall prisoners brought
to the bar; such a multitude of such vild people were sent to
this Plantation, that he thought himselfe happy his time was so
neere expired: three of the foulest acts were these: the first for
the rape of a married woman, which was acquitted by a senselesse Jury; the second for buggering a Sow, and the third for
Sodomy with a boy, for which they were hanged; during the
time of the imprisonment of this Buggerer of the Sow, a Dung-
hill Cocke belonging to the same man did continually haunt a
Pigge of his also, and to the wonder of all them that saw it who
were many, did so frequently tread the Pigge as if it had beene
one of his Hens, that the Pigge languished and died within a
while after, and then the Cocke resorted to the very same Sow
(that this fellow was accused for) in the very same manner; and
as an addition to all this, about the same time two Chickens
were hatched, the one whereof had two heads, the other
crowed very loud and lustily within twelve houres after it was
out of the shell. A desperate fellow being to bee arraigned for
stealing a Turky, rather then he would endure his triall, secretly
conveighed himselfe to Sea in a little Boat, and never since was
ever heard of, nor is he ever like to be, without an exceeding
wonder, little lesse then a miracle. In June they made another
triall about the Spanish wracke, and recovered another Sacre
and a Murderer, also he caused to be hewed out of the maine
Rocke a paire of large staires for the convenient landing of
goods and passengers, a worke much to the beauty and benefit
of the towne. With twenty chosen men, and two excellent
Divers, the Governour went himselfe to the wracke *Warwick,*
but they could recover but one Murderer, from
thence he went to the *Sea-adventure,* the wracke of
Sir George Summers, the hull though two or three
fathomes in the water, they found unperished and with much a
doe weighed a Sacre, her sheat Anchor, divers barres of Iron
and pigs of Lead, which stood the Plantation in very great

A strange Sodomy.

More trialls about the wracks.

stead. Towards the end of July he went to seeke for a wracke they reported lay under water with her hatches spiked up, but they could not finde her, but from the Spanish wracke lay there by they weighed three faire Sacres more, and so returned through the Tribes to Saint Georges: some were also imployed to seeke out beds of Oisters for Pearle, some they found, some seed Pearle they got, but out of one little shell above all the rest they got about 120. small Pearle, but somewhat defective in their colour.

The time of Captain Butlers government drawing neere an end, the Colony presented unto him divers grievances, to intreat him to remember to the Lords and Company in England at his returne: also they appointed two to be joyned with him, with letters of credence to solicit in their behalfe those grievances following: First, they were defrauded of the food of their soules: for being not fewer then one thousand and five hundred people, dispersed in length twenty miles, they had at that present but one Minister, nor never had but two, and they so shortned of their promises, that but onely for meere pity they would have forsaken them. Secondly, neglected in the safety of their lives by wants of all sorts of munition. Thirdly, they had beene censured contrary to his Majesties Lawes, and not allowed them the benefit of their booke as they are in England, but by Captaine Butler. Fourthly, they were frustrated of many of their covenants, and most extremely pinched and undone by the extortion of the Magazine, for although their Tobacco was stinted but at two shillings sixpence the pound, yet they pitched their commodities at what rate they pleased. Fifthly, their fatherlesse children are left in little better condition then slaves, for if their Parents die in debt, their children are made as bondmen till the debt be discharged: these things being perfected, there grew a great question of one Heriot for plotting of factions and abusing the Governour, for which he was condemned to lose his eares, yet he was used so favourably he lost but the part of one in all.

The Planters complaints.

The returne of Captaine Butler.

By this time it being growne past the wonted season of the comming in of ships from England, after a generall longing and expectation, especially of the Governour, whose Commission being neere upon expiration, gave him cause to wish for a meane of deliverance from so troublesome and thanklesse an imploiment as he had hitherto found it; a saile is discovered, and long it was not before shee arrived in the Kings Castle-Harbour: this Barke was set out by two or three private men of the Company, and having landed her supplies, was to goe for Virginia; by her the Governour received certaine advertisements of the carriage and behaviour of the Spaniards, which he had relieved as you have heard the yeere before; that quite contrary both to his merit, their vow, and his owne expectation, they made clamours against him, the which being seconded by the Spanish Ambassadour, caused the State to fall in examination about it; whereupon having fully cleared their ingratefulnesse and impudency, and being assured of the choice of a successor that was to be expected within five or six weekes; hee was desirous to take the opportunity of this Barke, and to visit the Colony in Virginia in his returne for England: leaving the government to Captaine Felgat, Captaine Stokes, Master Lewis Hewes, Master Nedom and Master Ginner. But now his time being fully expired, and the fortifications finished, viz. The Kings Castle wherein were mounted upon sufficient Platformes sixteene peece of Ordnances: In Charles Fort two; In Southampton Fort five, betwixt which and the Castle passeth the Chanell into the Harbour, secured by three and twenty peeces of good artillery to play upon it. In Cowpers Ile is Pembrocks Fort, where is two Peeces. The Chanell of Saint George is guarded by Smiths Fort, and Pagits Fort, in which is eleven peece of Ordnance. Saint George towne is halfe a league within the Harbour, commanded by Warwicks Fort, where are three great Peeces, and on the Wharfe before the Governours house eight more, besides the warning Peece by the mount, and three in Saint Katharines; so that in all there are ten Fortresses and two and fifty peeces of Ordnance sufficient and serviceable: their formes and situations you may see more plainlier described in the Map; and to defend those, he left one thousand five hundred persons with neere a hundred boats, and the Ile well replenished with store of such fruits, provisions and Poultry, as is formerly related; yet for so departing and other occasions, much difference hath beene betwixt him and some of the Company, as any of his Predecessors, which I rather wish were reconciled, then to be a reporter of such unprofitable dissentions.

For

Till trechery and faction, and avarice be gone,
Till envy and ambition, and backbiting be none,
Till perjury and idlenesse, and injury be out,
And truly till that villany the worst of all that rout;
Unlesse those vises banisht be, what ever Forts you have,
A hundred walls together put will not have power to save.

Master John Barnard sent to be Governour.

1622.
The Lord
Cavendish
Treasurer.
Master
Nicholas
Farrar
Deputy.

To supply this place was sent by the noble adventurers John Bernard, a Gentleman both of good meanes and quality, who arrived within eight daies after Butlers departure with two ships, and about one hundred and forty passengers with armes and all sorts of munition and other provisions sufficient. During the time of his life which was but six weekes in reforming all things he found defective, he shewed himselfe so judiciall and industrious as gave great satisfaction, and did generally promise vice was in great danger to be suppressed, and vertue and the Plantation much advanced; but so it hapned that both he and his wife died in such short time they were both buried in one day and one grave, and Master John Harrison chosen Governour till further order came from England.

What hapned in the government of Master John Harrison.

1623.
Sir Edward
Sackvil
Treasurer.
Master
Gabriel
Barber
Deputy.

They are still much troubled with a great short worme that devours their Plants in the night, but all the day they lie hid in the ground, and though early in the morning they kill so many, they would thinke there were no more, yet the next morning you shall finde as many. The Caterpillers to their fruits are also as pernicious, and the land Crabs in some places are as thicke in their

Borowes as Conies in a Warren, and doe much hurt; besides all this, there hapned this yeere a very heavy disaster, for a ship wherein there had beene much swearing and blaspheming used all the voyage, and landed what she had to leave in those Iles, jovially froliking in their Cups and Tobacco, by accident fired the Powder, that at the very instant blew up the great Cabin, and some one way and some another, it is a wonder to thinke how they could bee so blowne out of the gun-roome into the Sea, where some were taken up living, so pitifully burned, their lives were worse then so many deaths, some died, some lived, but eighteene were lost at this fatall blast, the ship also immediatly sunke with threescore barrels of meale sent for Virginia, and all the other provision in her was thus lost.

Now to consider how the Spaniards, French, and Dutch, have beene lost and preserved in those invincible Iles, yet never regarded them but as monuments of miseries, though at this present they all desire them; How Sir Thomas Gates, and Sir George Summers being ready to sinke in the sea were saved, what an incredible abundance of victuall they found, how it was first planted by the English, the strange increase of Rats, and their sudden departure, the five men came for England in a boat, the escape of Hilliard, and the rest of those accidents there hapned, a man would thinke it a tabernacle of miracles, and the worlds wonder, that from such a Paradise of admiration who would thinke should spring such wonders of afflictions as are onely fit to be sacrificed upon the highest altars of sorrow, thus to be set upon the highest Pinacles of content, and presently throwne downe to the lowest degree of extremity, as you see have beene the yeerely succeedings of those Plantations; the which to overcome, as it is an incomparable honour, so it can be no dishonour if a man doe miscarry by unfortunate accidents in such honourable actions, the which renowne and vertue to attaine hath caused so many attempts by divers Nations besides ours, even to passe through the very amazement of adventures. Upon the relation of this newes the Company hath sent one Captaine Woodhouse, a Gentleman of good repute and great experience in the warres, and no lesse provident then industrious and valiant: then returned report, all goeth well there. It is too true, in the absence of the noble Treasurer, Sir Edward Sackvill, now Earle

Note.

of Dorset, there have beene such complaints betwixt the Planters and the Company, that by command the Lords appointed Sir Thomas Smith againe Treasurer, that since then according to their order of Court he is also elected, where now we must leave them all to their good fortune and successe, till we heare further of their fortunate proceedings.

FINIS.

To his friend Captaine Smith, upon his description of New-England.

Sir; your Relations I have read: which shew,
Ther's reason I should honour, them and you:
And if their meaning I have understood,
I dare to censure thus: Your Project's good;
And may (if follow'd) doubtlesse quit the paine,
With honour, pleasure and a trebble game;
Beside the benefit that shall arise
To make more happy our Posterities.
   For would we daigne to spare, though 'twere no more
Then what ore-fils, and surfets us in store,
To order Nature's fruitfulnesse a while
In that rude Garden, you New-England stile;
With present good, ther's hope in after-daies
Thence to repaire what Time and Pride decaies
In this rich Kingdome. And the spacious West
Being still more with English bloud possest,
The proud Iberians shall not rule those Seas,
To checke our ships from sailing where they please;
Nor future times make any forraine power
Become so great to force a bound to Our.
   Much good my minde foretels would follow hence
With little labour, and with lesse expence.
Thrive therefore thy Designe, who ere envy:
England may joy in England's Colony,

1624.
Sir Thomas
Smith
Treasurer,
and Master
Edwards
Deputy.

Virginia *seeke her Virgin sisters good,*
Be blessed in such happy neighbourhood:
  Or, whatsoere Fate pleaseth to permit,
  Be thou still honour'd for first moving it.
                George Wither, *e societate* Lincolniense

To that worthy and generous Gentleman, my very good friend, Captaine Smith.

May Fate thy Project prosper, that thy name
May be eternized with living fame:
  Though foule Detraction Honour would pervert,
  And Envie ever waits upon desert:
In spight of Pelias, *when his hate lies cold,*
Returne as Jason *with a fleece of gold.*
  Then after-ages shall record thy praise,
  That a New-England *to this Ile didst raise:*
And when thou di'st (as all that live must die)
Thy fame live here; thou, with Eternity.
                        R. Gunnell.

To his worthy Captaine, the Author.

Oft thou hast led, when I brought up the Rere
In bloudy wars, where thousands have beene slaine.
  Then give me leave in this some part to beare;
  And as thy servant, here to reade my name.
  Tis true, long time thou hast my Captaine beene
In the fierce warres of Transilvania:
  Long ere that thou America *hadst seene,*
Or led wast captiv'd in Virginia;
  Thou that to passe the worlds foure parts dost deeme
No more, then t'were to goe to bed, or drinke,
  And all thou yet host done, thou dost esteeme

As nothing. This doth cause me thinke
  That thou I'ave seene so oft approv'd in dangers,
(And thrice captiv'd, thy valour still hath freed)
  Art yet preserved, to convert those strangers:
By God thy guide I trust it is decreed.
  For me: I not commend but much admire
  Thy England yet unknowne to passers by-her.
For it will praise it selfe in spight of me;
Thou it, it thou, to all posterity.

                    Your true friend and souldier, Ed. Robinson.

To my honest Captaine, the Author.

Malignant Times! What can be said or done,
But shall be censur'd and traduc't by some!
  This worthy Worke, which thou hast bought so deare,
  Ne thou, nor it, Detractors need to feare.
Thy words by deeds so long thou hast approv'd,
Of thousands know thee not thou art belov'd.
  And this great Plot will make thee ten times more
  Knowne and belov'd, than ere thou wert before.
I never knew a Warrier yet, but thee,
From wine, Tobacco, debts, dice, oaths, so free.
  I call thee Warrier: *and I make the bolder;*
  For, many a Captaine *now, was never Souldier.*
Some such may swell at this: but (to their praise)
When they have done like thee, my Muse shall raise
  Their due deserts to Worthies yet to come,
  To live like thine (admir'd) till day of Doome.
    Your true friend, sometimes your souldier, Tho. Carlton.

The Sixth Booke.

THE GENERALL HISTORIE
OF NEW-ENGLAND.

ONCERNING this History you are to understand the Letters-Patents granted by his Majesty in 1606. for the limitation of Virginia, did extend from 34. to 44. which was divided in two parts; namely, the first Colony and the second: the first was to the honourable City of London, and such as would adventure with them to discover and take their choice where they would, betwixt the degrees of 34. and 41. The second was appropriated to the Cities of Bristol, Exeter and Plimoth, etc. and the West parts of England, and all those that would adventure and joine with them, and they might make their choise any where betwixt the degrees of 38. and 44. provided there should bee at least 100. miles distance betwixt these 2. Colonies, each of which had lawes, privileges and authoritie, for the government and advancing their severall Plantations alike. Now this part of America hath formerly beene called Norumbega, Virginia, Nuskoncus, Penaquida, Cannada, and such other names as those that ranged the Coast pleased. But because it was so mountainous, rocky and full of Iles, few have adventured much to trouble it, but as is formerly related. Notwithstanding, that honourable Patron of vertue, Sir John Popham, Lord chiefe Justice of England, in the yeere 1606. procured meanes and men to possesse it, and sent Captaine George Popham for President, Captaine Rawley Gilbert for Admirall, Captaine Edward Harlow master of the Ordnance, Captaine Robert Davis, Sargeant-Major, Captaine Elis Best, Marshall, Master Seaman, Secretary, Captaine James Davis to be Captaine of the Fort, Master Gome Carew, chiefe Searcher: all those were of the Councell, who with some hundred more were to stay in the Country: they set saile from Plimoth the last of May, and fell with Monahigan the eleventh of August. At Sagadahock 9. or 10. leagues southward, they planted themselves at the mouth

Sir Francis
Popham
Treasurer.

of a faire navigable River, but the coast all thereabouts most extreme stony and rocky: that extreme frozen Winter was so cold they could not range nor search the Country, and their provision so small, they were glad to send all but 45. of their company backe againe: their noble President Captaine Popham died, and not long after arrived two ships well provided of all necessaries to supply them, and some small time after another, by whom understanding of the death of the Lord chiefe Justice, and also of Sir John Gilbert, whose lands there the President Rawley Gilbert was to possesse according to the adventurers directions, finding nothing but extreme extremities, they all returned for England in the yeere 1608. and thus this Plantation was begunne and ended in one yeere, and the Country esteemed as a cold, barren, mountainous, rocky Desart.

Notwithstanding, the right Honourable Henry Earle of South-hampton and those of the Ile of Wight, imploied Captaine Edward Harlow to discover an Ile supposed about Cape Cod, but they found their plots had much abused them, for falling with Monahigan, they found onely Cape Cod no Ile but the maine. There they detained three Salvages aboord them, called Pechmo, Monopet and Pekenimne, but Pechmo leapt over board, and got away; and not long after with his consorts cut their Boat from their sterne, got her on shore, and so filled her with sand, and guarded her with Bowes and Arrowes the English lost her: not farre from thence they had three men sorely wounded with Arrowes. Anchoring at the Ile of Nohono, the Salvages in their Canowes assaulted the Ship till the English Guns made them retire, yet here they tooke Sakaweston, that after he had lived many yeeres in England went a Souldier to the warres of Bohemia. At Capawe they tooke Coneconam and Epenow, but the people at Agawom used them kindly, so with five Salvages they returned for England, yet Sir Francis Popham sent divers times one Captaine Williams to Monahigan onely to trade and make core fish, but for any Plantations there was no more speeches. For all this, as I liked Virginia well, though not their proceedings, so I desired also to see this country, and spend some time in trying what I could finde for all those ill rumors and disasters.

From the relations of Captaine Edward Harlow
and divers others.

My first
voyage to
New-
England.
1614.

In the month of Aprill 1614. at the charge of Captaine Marmaduke Roydon, Captaine George Lang-
man, Master John Buley and Master William Skelton,
with two ships from London, I chanced to arrive at
Monahigan an Ile of America, in 43½ of Northerly latitude:
our plot was there to take Whales, for which we had one
Samuel Cramton and divers others expert in that faculty, and
also to make trialls of a Mine of gold and copper; if those
failed, Fish and Furs were then our refuge to make our selves
savers howsoever: we found this Whale-fishing a costly conclusion, we saw many and spent much time in chasing them, but
could not kill any. They being a kinde of Jubartes, and not the
Whale that yeelds Fins and Oile as we expected; for our gold it
was rather the Masters device to get a voyage that projected it,
then any knowledge he had at all of any such matter; Fish and
Furs were now our guard, and by our late arrivall and long lingring about the Whale, the prime of both those seasons were
past ere wee perceived it, wee thinking that their seasons
served at all times, but we found it otherwise, for by the middest of June the fishing failed, yet in July and August some
were taken, but not sufficient to defray so great a charge as our

The
commodities
I got
amounted to
1500. pounds.

stay required: of dry fish we made about forty thousand, of Cor-fish about seven thousand. Whilest the
Sailers fished, my selfe with eight others of them
might best bee spared, ranging the Coast in a small Boat, we
got for trifles neere eleven thousand Bever skinnes, one hundred Martins, as many Otters, and the most of them within the
distance of twenty leagues: we ranged the Coast both East and
West much further, but Eastward our commodities were not
esteemed, they were so neere the French who afforded them
better, with whom the Salvages had such commerce that only
by trade they made exceeding great voyages, though they were
without the limits of our precincts; during the time we tried
those conclusions, not knowing the coast, nor Salvages habitations: with these Furres, the traine Oile and Cor-fish, I returned for England in the Barke, where within six moneths
after our departure from the Downes, wee safely arrived backe;
the best of this fish was sold for 5. li. the hundred, the rest by
ill usage betwixt three pounds and 50. shillings. The other ship
stayed to fit her selfe for Spaine with the dry fish which was

The trechery of Master Hunt.

sold at Maligo at forty Rialls the Quintall, each hundred weighing two quintals and a halfe. But one Thomas Hunt the Master of this ship (when I was gone) thinking to prevent that intent I had to make there a Plantation, thereby to keepe this abounding Countrey still in obscuritie, that onely he and some few Merchants more might enjoy wholly the benefit of the Trade, and profit of this Countrey, betraied foure and twenty of those poore Salvages aboord his ship, and most dishonestly and inhumanely for their kinde usage of me and all our men, caried them with him to Maligo, and there for a little private gaine sold those silly Salvages for Rials of eight; but this vilde act kept him ever after from any more imploiment to those parts. Now because at this time I had taken a draught of the Coast, and called it New England, yet so long he and his Consorts drowned that name with the Eccho of Cannaday, and some other ships from other parts also, that upon this good returne the next yeere went thither, that at last I presented this Discourse with the Map, to our most gracious Prince Charles, humbly intreating his Highnesse hee would please to change their barbarous names for such English, as posteritie might say Prince Charles was their God-father, which for your better understanding both of this Discourse and the Map, peruse this Schedule, which will plainly shew you the correspondency of the old names to the new, as his Highnesse named them.

v Prince rles called most arkable es in New land.

The old names.	The new names.
Cape Cod.	Cape James.
The Harbor at Cape Cod.	Milforth haven.
Chawum.	Barwick.
Accomack.	Plimoth.
Sagoquas.	Oxford.
Massachusets Mount.	Chevit hills.
Massachusits River.	Charles River.
Totan.	Famouth.
A great Bay by Cape Anne.	Bristow.

The old names.	The new names.
Cape Tragabigsanda.	Cape Anne.
Naemkeck.	Bastable.
Aggawom.	Southampton.
Smiths Iles.	Smiths Iles.

Passataquack.	Hull.
Accominticus.	Boston.
Sassanows Mount.	Snowdon hill.
Sowocatuck.	Ipswich.
Bahanna.	Dartmouth.
A good Harbor within that Bay.	Sandwich.
Aucociscos Mount.	Shuters hill.
Aucocisco.	The Base.
Aumoughcawgen.	Cambridge.
Kenebecka.	Edenborow.
Sagadahock.	Leth.
Pemmayquid.	Saint Johns towne.
Segocket.	Norwich.
Mecadacut.	Dunbarton.
Pennobscot.	Aberden.
Nusket.	Low mounds.

Those being omitted I named my selfe.

Monahigan.	Barties Iles.
Matinack.	Willowbies Iles.
Metinacus.	Haughtons Iles.

The rest of the names in the Map, are places that had no names we did know.

Aspersions against New England.

But to continue the History succeedingly as neere with the day and yeere as may bee. Returning in the Barke as is said; it was my ill chance to put in at Plimoth, where imparting those my purposes to divers I thought my friends, whom as I supposed were interested in the dead Patent of this unregarded Countrey, I was so encouraged and assured to have the managing their authoritie in those parts during my life, and such large promises, that I ingaged my selfe to undertake it for them. Arriving at London, though some malicious persons suggested there was no such matter to be had in that so bad abandoned Countrey, for if there had, other could have found it so well as I; therefore it was to be suspected I had robbed the French men in New France or Cannada, and the Merchants set me forth seemed not to regard it, yet I found so many promised me such assistance, that I entertained Michael Cooper the Master of the Barke, that returned with me and others of the Company: how he dealt with others, or others with him, I know not; but my publike proceeding gave such encouragement, that it became so well apprehended by some few of the Virginia Company, as those projects for fishing onely was so well liked, they furnished Couper with foure good ships to Sea, before they at Plimoth had made any provision at all for me; but onely a small Barke set out by them of the Ile of Wight. Some of Plimoth, and divers Gentlemen of the West Countrey, a little

Captaine Hobson his voiage to Capawuk. before I returned from New England, in search for a Mine of Gold about an Ile called Capawuck, Southwards from the Shoules of Cape James, as they were informed by a Salvage called Epenew; that having deluded them as it seems thus to get home, seeing they kept him as a prisoner in his owne Countrey, and before his friends, being a man of so great a stature, he was shewed up and downe London for money as a wonder, and it seemes of no lesse courage and authoritie, then of wit, strength, and proportion: for so well he had contrived his businesse, as many reported he intended to have surprised the ship; but seeing it could not be effected to his liking, before them all he leaped over-boord. Many shot they made at him, thinking they had slaine him, but so resolute they were to recover his body, the master of the ship was wounded, and many of his company; And thus they lost him, and not knowing more what to do, returned againe to England with nothing, which so had discouraged all your West Countrey men, they neither regarded much their promises, and as little either me or the Countrey, till they saw the London ships gone and me in Plimoth according to my promise, as hereafter shall be related.

I must confesse I was beholden to the setters forth of the foure ships that went with Couper, in that they offered me that

The Londoners send foure good ships to New England. imploiment if I would accept it; and I finde still my refusall incurred some of their displeasures, whose love and favour I exceedingly desired; and though they doe censure me opposite to their proceedings, they shall yet still in all my words and deeds finde, it is their error, not my fault that occasions their dislike: for having ingaged my selfe in this businesse to the West Countrey, I had beene very dishonest to have broke my promise, nor will I spend more time in discovery or fishing, till I may goe with a Company for a Plantation; for I know my grounds, yet every one to whom I tell them, or that reads this Booke, cannot put it in practise, though it may helpe any that hath seene or not seene to know much of those parts: And though they endevour to worke me out of my owne designes, I will not much envy their fortunes: but I would be sorry their intruding ignorance should by their defailments bring those certainties to doubtfulnesse. So that the businesse prosper I have my desire, be it by whomsoever that are true subjects to our King and Countrey: the good of my Countrey is that I seeke, and there is more then enough for all, if they could be contented.

The situation of New England.

New England is that part of America in the Ocean Sea, opposite to Nova Albion in the South Sea, discovered by the most memorable Sir Francis Drake in his Voyage about the world, in regard whereof this is stiled New England, being in the same latitude. New France of it is Northwards, Southwards is Virginia, and all the adjoyning continent with new Granado, new Spaine, new Andolosia, and the West-Indies. Now because I have beene so oft asked such strange questions of the goodnesse and greatnesse of those spatious Tracts of Land, how they can be thus long unknowne, or not possessed by the Spaniards, and many such like demands; I intreat your pardons if I chance to be too plaine or tedious in relating my knowledge for plaine mens satisfaction.

Notes of Florida.

Florida is the next adjoyning to the Indies, which unprosperously was attempted to be planted by the French, a Countrey farre bigger then England, Scotland, France and Ireland, yet little knowne to any Christian, but by the wonderfull endevours of Ferdinando de Soto, a valiant Spaniard, whose writings in this age is the best guide knowne to search those parts.

Notes of Virginia.

Virginia is no Ile as many doe imagine, but part of the Continent adjoyning to Florida, whose bounds may be stretched to the magnitude thereof, without offence to any Christian Inhabitant, for from the degrees of thirtie to forty eight, his Majesty hath now enlarged his Letters Patents. The Coast extending Southwest and North-east about sixteene or seventeene hundred miles, but to follow it aboord the shore may well be three thousand miles at the least: of which twentie miles is the most gives entrance into the Bay of Chisapeacke, where is the London Plantation, within which is a Countrey, as you may perceive by the Map, of that little I discovered, may well suffice three hundred thousand people to inhabit: but of it, and the discoveries of Sir Ralph Laine and Master Heriot, Captaine Gosnold, and Captaine Waymouth, they have writ so largely, that posteritie may be bettered by the fruits of their labours. But for divers others that have ranged those parts since, especially this Countrey now called New England, within a kenning sometimes of the shore; some touching in one place, some in another; I must intreat them pardon me for omitting them, or if I offend in saying, that their true descriptions were concealed, or never were well observed, or died with the Authors, so that the Coast is yet still but even as a Coast unknowne and undiscovered. I have had six or seven severall plots of those Northerne parts, so unlike each to other, or resemblance of the Country, as they did me no more good then so much waste paper, though they cost me more, it may bee it was not my chance to see the best; but lest others may be deceived as I was, or through dangerous ignorance hazard themselves as I did, I have drawne a Map from point to point, Ile to Ile, and Harbour to Harbour, with the Soundings, Sands, Rocks, and Land-markes, as I passed close aboord the shore in a little Boat; although there bee many things to bee observed, which the haste of other affaires did cause me to omit: for being sent more to get present Commodities, then knowledge of any discoveries for any future good, I had not power to search as I would; yet it will serve to direct any shall goe that waies to safe Harbours and the Salvages habitations: what Merchandize and Commodities for their labours they may finde, this following discourse shall plainly demonstrate.

Observations for presumptuous ignorant directors. Thus you may see of these three thousand miles, more then halfe is yet unknowne to any purpose, no not so much as the borders of the Sea are yet certainly discovered: as for the goodnesse and true substance of the Land, we are for most part yet altogether ignorant of them, unlesse it be those parts about the Bay of Chisapeack and Sagadahock, but onely here and there where we have touched or seene a little, the edges of those large Dominions which doe stretch themselves into the maine, God doth know how many thousand miles, whereof we can yet no more judge, then a stranger that saileth betwixt England and France, can describe the harbours and dangers by landing here or there in some River or Bay, tell thereby the goodnesse and substance of Spaine, Italy, Germany, Bohemia, Hungaria, and the rest; nay, there are many have lived fortie yeeres in London, and yet have scarce beene ten miles out of the Citie: so are there many have beene in Virginia many yeeres, and in New England many times, that doe know little more then the place they doe inhabit, or the Port where they fished, and when they come home, they will undertake they know all Virginia and New England, as if they were but two Parishes or little Ilands. By this you may perceive how much they erre, that thinke every one that hath beene in Virginia or New England, understandeth or knoweth what either of them are; Or that the Spaniards know one halfe quarter of those large Territories they possesse, no not so much as the true circumference of Terra incognita, whose large Dominions may equalize the goodnesse and greatnesse of America for any thing yet knowne. It is strange with what small power he doth range in the East-Indies, and few will understand the truth of his strength in America: where having so much to keepe with such a pampered force, they need not greatly feare his fury in Sommer Iles, Virginia, or New England, beyond whose bounds America doth stretch many thousand miles. Into the frozen parts whereof, one Master Hutson an English Mariner, did make the greatest discoverie of any Christian I know, where hee unfortunately was left by his cowardly Company, for his exceeding deserts, to end and die a most miserable death.

For Affrica, had not the industrious Portugals ranged her unknowne parts, who would have sought for wealth amongst those fried Regions of blacke brutish Negars, where notwithstanding all their wealth and admirable adventures and endevours more then one hundred and fortie yeeres, they know not one third part of those blacke habitations. But it is not a worke for every one to manage such an affaire, as make a discovery and plant a Colony, it requires all the best parts of art, judgement, courage, honesty, constancy, diligence, and industry, to doe but neere well; some are more proper for one thing then another, and therein best to be imploied: and nothing breeds more confusion then misplacing and misimploying men in their undertakings. Columbus, Courtes, Pitzara, Zoto, Magilanus, and the rest served more then a Prentiship, to learne how to begin their most memorable attempts in the West-Indies, which to the wonder of all ages successefully they effected, when many hundreds of others farre above them in the worlds opinion, being instructed but by relation, came to shame and confusion in actions of small moment, who doubtlesse in other matters were both wise, discreet, generous and couragious. I say not this to detract any thing from their incomparable merits, but to answer those questionlesse questions, that keepe us backe from imitating the worthinesse of their brave spirits, that advanced themselves from poore Souldiers to great Captaines, their posterity to great Lords, their King to be one of the greatest Potentates on earth, and the fruits of their labours his greatest power, glory, and renowne.

The Description of New England.

THAT part we call New England, is betwixt the degrees of fortie one and fortie five, the very meane betwixt the North pole and the line; but that part this Discourse speaketh of, stretcheth but from Penobscot to Cape Cod, some seventie five leagues by a right line distant each from other; within which bounds I have seene at least fortie severall habitations upon the Sea Coast, and sounded about five and twentie excellent good Harbours, in many whereof there is anchorage for five hundred saile of ships of any burden; in some of them for one thousand, and more then two hundred Iles overgrowne with good Timber of divers sorts of wood, which doe make so many Harbours, as required a longer time then I had to be well observed.

The principall habitation Northward we were at, was Pennobscot: Southward along the Coast and up the Rivers, we found Mecadacut, Segocket, Pemaquid, Nusconcus, Sagadahock, Aumoughcowgen, and Kenebeke; and to those Countries belong the people of Segotago, Paghhuntanuck, Pocopassum, Taughtanakagnet, Warbigganus, Nassaque, Masherosqueck, Wawrigweck, Moshoquen, Wakcogo, Pasharanack, etc. To these are alied in confederacy, the

The principall Countries or governments.

Countries of Aucocisco, Accomynticus, Passataquack, Aggawom, and Naemkeck: All these for any thing I could perceive,
differ little in language, fashion, or government, though most
of them be Lords of themselves, yet they hold the Bashabes of
Penobscot, the chiefe and greatest amongst them.

The next I can remember by name, are Mattahunts, two
pleasant Iles of Groves, Gardens, and Corne fields a league in
the Sea from the maine: Then Totant, Massachuset, Topent,
Secassaw, Totheet, Nasnocomacack, Accomack, Chawum,
Patuxet, Massasoyts, Pakanokick: then Cape Cod, by which is
Pawmet and the Ile Nawset, of the language and aliance of
them of Chawum; the others are called Massachusets, and
differ somewhat in language, custome, and condition: for their
Trade and Merchandize, to each of their principall families or
habitations, they have divers Townes and people belonging,
and by their relations and descriptions, more then twentie severall habitations and rivers that stretch themselves farre into
the Countrey, even to the Borders of divers great Lakes, where
they kill and take most of their Otters. From Pennobscot to
Sagadahoc, this Coast is mountainous, and Iles of huge Rockes,
but over-growne for most part, with most sorts of excellent
good woods, for building Houses, Boats, Barks or Ships, with
an incredible abundance of most sorts of Fish, much Fowle,
and sundry sorts of good Fruits for mans use.

Betwixt Sagadahock, and Sowocatuck, there is but two or
three Sandy Bayes, but betwixt that and Cape James very many:
especially the Coast of the Massachusets is so indifferently
mixed with high Clay or Sandy clifts in one place, and the tracts
of large long ledges of divers sorts, and Quaries of stones in
other places, so strangely divided with tinctured veines of
divers colours: as Free-stone for building, Slate for tyling,
smooth stone to make Furnasses and Forges for Glasse and
Iron, and Iron Ore sufficient conveniently to melt in them;
but the most part so resembleth the Coast of Devonshire, I
thinke most of the clifts would make such Lime-stone: if they
bee not of these qualities, they are so like they may deceive a
better judgement then mine: all which are so neere adjoyning
to those other advantages I observed in these parts, that if the
Ore prove as good Iron and Steele in those parts as I know it
is within the bounds of the Countrey, I dare ingage my head

(having but men skilfull to worke the Simples there growing) to have all things belonging to the building and rigging of ships of any proportion and good Merchandise for their fraught, within a square of ten or foureteene leagues, and it were no hard matter to prove it within a lesse limitation.

A proofe of an excellent clime. And surely by reason of those sandy clifts, and clifts of rocks, both which we saw so planted with Gardens and Corne fields, and so well inhabited with a goodly, strong, and well proportioned people, besides the greatnesse of the Timber growing on them, the greatnesse of the Fish, and the moderate temper of the aire (for of five and forty not a man was sicke, but two that were many yeares diseased before they went, notwithstanding our bad lodging and accidentall diet) who can but approve this a most excellent place, both for health and fertilitie: and of all the foure parts of the world I have yet seene not inhabited, could I have but means to transport a Colony, I would rather live here then any where, and if it did not maintaine it selfe, were we but once indifferently well fitted, let us starve.

Staple Commodities present. The maine staple from hence to bee extracted for the present, to produce the rest, is Fish, which howbeit may seeme a meane and a base Commoditie; yet who will but truly take the paines and consider the sequell, I thinke will allow it well worth the labour. It is strange to see, what great adventures the hopes of setting forth men of warre to rob the industrious innocent would procure, or such massie promises in grosse, though more are choaked then well fed Observations of the Hollanders. with such hastie hopes. But who doth not know that the poore Hollanders chiefely by fishing at a great charge and labour in all weathers in the open Sea, are made a people so hardy and industrious, and by the venting this poore Commoditie to the Easterlings for as meane, which is Wood, Flax, Pitch, Tarre, Rozen, Cordage, and such like; which they exchange againe to the French, Spaniards, Portugals, and English, etc. for what they want, are made so mighty, strong, and rich, as no state but Venice of twice their magnitude is so well furnished, with so many faire Cities, goodly Townes, strong Fortresses, and that abundance of shipping, and all sorts of Merchandize, as well of Gold, Silver, Pearles, Diamonds, pretious Stones, Silkes, Velvets, and Cloth of Gold; as Fish,

Pitch, Wood, or such grosse Commodities? What voiages and discoveries, East and West, North and South, yea about the world, make they? What an Army by Sea and Land have they long maintained, in despight of one of the greatest Princes of the world, and never could the Spaniard with all his Mines of Gold and Silver, pay his debts, his friends, and Army, halfe so truly as the Hollanders still have done by this contemptible Trade of Fish. Divers (I know) may alleage many other assistances; but this is the chiefest Mine, and the Sea the source of those silver streames of all their vertue, which hath made them now the very miracle of industry, the onely paterne of perfection for these affaires: and the benefit of fishing is that Primum Mobile that turnes all their spheares to this height, of plentie, strength, honor, and exceeding great admiration.

Herring, Cod, and Ling, is that triplicitie, that makes their wealth and shippings multiplicitie such as it is: and from which (few would thinke it) they should draw so many millions yeerely as they doe, as more in particular in the trials of New England you may see; and such an incredible number of ships, that breeds them so many Sailers, Mariners, Souldiers, and Merchants, never to be wrought out of that Trade, and fit for any other. I will not deny but others may gaine as well as they that will use it, though not so certainly, nor so much in quantitie, for want of experience: and this Herring they take upon the Coast of England and Scotland, their Cod and Ling upon the Coast of Izeland, and in the North seas,

Note.

If wee consider what gaines the Hamburgans, the Biskinners, and French make by fishing; nay, but how many thousands this fiftie or sixty yeeres have beene maintained by New found land, where they take nothing but small Cod, where of the greatest they make Cor-fish, and the rest is hard dried, which we call Poore-John, would amaze a man with wonder. If then from all those parts such paines is taken for this poore gaines of Fish, especially by the Hollanders, that hath but little of their owne, for building of ships and setting them to sea; but at the second, third, fourth, or fift hand, drawne from so many parts of the world ere they come together to be used in those voiages: If these (I say) can gaine, why should we more doubt then they; but doe much better, that may have most of all those things at our doores for taking and making, and here are no hard Landlords to racke us with high rents, or extorting fines, nor tedious pleas in Law to consume us with their many yeeres disputation for Justice; no multitudes to occasion such impediments to good orders as in popular States: so freely hath God and his Majestie bestowed those blessings on them will attempt to obtaine them, as here every man may be master of his owne labour and land, or the greatest part (if his

Note.

Majesties royall meaning be not abused) and if he have nothing but his hands, he may set up his Trade; and by industry quickly grow rich, spending but halfe that time well, which in England we abuse in idlenesse, worse, or as ill. Here is ground as good as any lieth in the height of forty one, forty two, forty three, etc. which is as temperate, and as fruitfull as any other parallel in the world.

Examples of the Altitude comparatively.

As for example, on this side the line, West of it in the South Sea, is Nova Albion, discovered as is said by Sir Francis Drake: East from it is the most temperate part of Portugall, the ancient Kingdomes of Galizia, Bisky, Navarre, Aragon, Cattilonia, Castillia the old, and the

In Spaine.

most moderatest of Castillia the new, and Valentia, which is the greatest part of Spaine; which if the Histories be true, in the Romans time abounded no lesse with gold and silver Mines, then now the West-Indies, the Romans then using the Spaniards to worke in those Mines, as now the Spaniards doe the Indians. In France the Provinces of Gascony, Langadocke, Avignon, Province, Dolphine, Pyamont, and Turyne, are in the same parallel, which are the best

In France.

and richest parts of France. In Italy the Provinces of Genua, Lumbardy, and Verona, with a great part of the most famous state of Venice, the Dukedomes of Bononia, Mantua, Ferrara, Ravenna, Bolognia, Florence, Pisa, Sienna, Urbine, Ancona, and the ancient Citie and Countrey of Rome, with a great part of the Kingdome of Naples. In

In Greece.

Slavonia, Istria, and Dalmatia, with the Kingdomes of Albania. In Grecia those famous Kingdomes of Macedonia, Bulgaria, Thessalia, Thracia, or Romania, where is seated the most pleasant and plentifull Citie in Europe, Constantinople.

In Asia.

In Asia in the same latitude, are the temperatest

Beyond the line. parts of Natolia, Armenia, Persia, and China; besides divers other large Countries and Kingdomes in those most milde and temperate Regions of Asia. Southward in the same height is the richest of Gold Mines, Chily, and Baldivia, and the mouth of the great River of Plate, etc. for all the rest of the world in that height is yet unknowne. Besides these reasons, mine owne eies that have seene a great part of those Cities and their Kingdomes (as well as it) can finde no advantage they have in Nature but this, they are beautified by the long labour and diligence of industrious people and art; This is onely as God made it when hee created the world: Therefore I conclude, if the heart and intrailes of those Regions were sought, if their Land were cultured, planted, and manured by men of industry, judgement, and experience; what hope is there, or what need they doubt, having the advantages of the Sea, but it might equalize any of these famous Kingdomes in all commodities, pleasures, and conditions, seeing even the very edges doe naturally affoord us such plentie, as no ship need returne away emptie: and onely use but the season of the Sea, Fish will returne an honest gaine, besides all other advantages, her treasures having yet never beene opened, nor her originals wasted, consumed, nor abused.

The particular staple commodities that may be had by industry. And whereas it is said the Hollanders serve the Easterlings themselves, and other parts that want with Herring, Ling, and wet Cod: The Easterlings, a great part of Europe, with Sturgion and Caviare, as the Blacke Sea doth Grecia, Podolia, Sagovia, Natolia, and the Hellespont. Cape Blanke, Spaine, Portugall, and the Levant, with Mulit and Puttargo. New found land, the most part of the chiefe Southerne Ports in Europe, with a thin Poore-John, which hath beene so long, so much over-laied with Fishers, as the fishing decaieth, so that many oft times are constrained to returne with a small fraught. Norway and Poland affoords Pitch and Tarre, Masts and Yards. Sweathland and Russia, Iron and Ropes. France and Spaine, Canvase, Wine, Steele, Iron, and Oile. Italy and Greece, Silkes and Fruits. I dare boldly say, because I have seene naturally growing or breeding in those parts, the same materials that all these are made of, they may as well bee had here, or the most part of them within the distance of seventie leagues for some few ages, as from all those parts, using but the same meanes to have them that they doe; but surely in Virginia, their most tender and daintiest fruits or commodities, would be as perfit as theirs, by reason of the heat, if not in New England, and with all those advantages.

The nature of the ground approved. First, the ground is so fertill, that questionlesse it is capable of producing any Graine, Fruits, or Seeds, you will sow or plant, growing in the Regions afore-named: But it may be not to that perfection of delicacy, be-cause the Summer is not so hot, and the Winter is more cold in those parts we have yet tried neere the Sea side, then wee finde in the same height in Europe or Asia: yet I made a Garden upon the top of a Rocky Ile in three and forty degrees and an halfe, foure leagues from the maine in May, that grew so well, as it served us for Sallets in June and July. All sorts of Cattle may here be bred and fed in the Iles or Peninsulaes securely for nothing. In the Interim, till they increase (if need be) ob-serving the seasons, I durst undertake to have Corne enough from the Salvages for three hundred men, for a few trifles; and if they should be untowards, as it is most certaine they will, thirtie or fortie good men will be sufficient to bring them all in subjection, and make this provision, if they understand what to doe; two hundred whereof may eight or nine moneths in the yeere be imploied in helping the Fisher-men, till the rest provide other necessaries, fit to furnish us with other Com-modities.

The seasons for fishing approved. In March, Aprill, May, and halfe June, heere is Cod in abundance; in May, June, July, and August, Mullit and Sturgion, whose Roes doe make Caviare and Puttargo; Herring, if any desire them: I have taken many out of the bellies of Cods, some in nets; but the Salvages compare the store in the Sea with the haires of their heads: and surely there are an incredible abundance upon this Coast. In the end of August, September, October, and November, you may have Cod againe to make Core-fish or Poore-John: Hake you may have when the Cod failes in Summer, if you will fish in the night, which is better then Cod. Now each hundred you take here, is as good as two or three hundred in New found Land; so that halfe the labour in hooking, splitting and turning, is saved: And you may have your fish at what market you will, before they have any in New found land, where their fishing is chiefely but in June and July, where it is here in March, Aprill, May, September, October and November, as is said; so that by reason of this Plantation, the Merchants may have their fraught both out and home, which yeelds an advantage worth consideration. Your Core-fish you may in like manner transport as you see cause, to serve the Ports in Portugall, as Lisbone, Avera, Port Aport, and divers others, (or what market you please) before your Ilanders returne. They being tied to the season in the open Sea, and you having a double season, and fishing before your doores, may every night sleep quietly ashore with good cheere, and what fires you will, or when you please with your wives and family: they onely and their ships in the maine Ocean, that must carie and containe all they use, besides their fraught. The Mullits here are in that abundance, you may take them with nets sometimes by hundreds, where at Cape Blanke they hooke them; yet those are but a foot and a halfe in length; these two, three, or foure, as oft I have measured, which makes me suspect they are some other kinde of fish, though they seeme the same, both in fashion and goodnesse. Much Salmon some have found up the Rivers as they have passed, and here the aire is so temperate, as all these at

Imploiment for poore people and fatherlesse children.

any time may be preserved. Now, young Boies and Girles Salvages, or any other bee they never such idlers, may turne, carie or returne a fish, without either shame or any great paine: He is very idle that is past twelve yeeres of age and cannot doe so much, and she is very old that cannot spin a threed to make Engins to catch a fish.

The facilitie of the Plantation.

For their transportation, the ships that goe there to fish may transport the first: who for their passage will spare the charge of double manning their ships, which they must do in New found land to get their fraught; but one third part of that company are onely proper to serve a stage, carie a Barrow, and turne Poore-John; notwithstanding, they must have meat, drinke, clothes, and passage so well as the rest. Now all I desire is but this, That those that voluntarily will send shipping, should make here the best choice they can, or accept such as shall bee presented them to serve them at that rate: and their ships returning leave such with me, with the value of that they should receive comming home, in such provisions and necessarie tooles, armes, bedding, apparell, salt, nets, hookes, lines, and such like, as they spare of the remainings; who till the next returne may keepe their Boats, and doe them many other profitable offices. Provided, I have men of abilitie to teach them their functions, and a company fit for Souldiers to be ready upon any occasion, because of the abuses that have beene offered the poore Salvages, and the libertie that both French and English, or any that will, have to deale with them as they please; whose disorders will be hard to reforme, and the longer the worse: Now such order with facilitie might be taken, with every Port, Towne, or Citie, with free power to convert the benefit of their fraughts to what advantage they please, and increase their numbers as they see occasion, who ever as they are able to subsist of themselves, may begin the new Townes in New England, in memory of their old: which freedome being confined but to the necessitie of the generall good, the event (with Gods helpe) might produce an honest, a noble, and a profitable emulation.

Salt upon Salt may assuredly be made, if not at the *Present Commodities.* first in ponds, yet till they be provided this may be used: then the ships may transport Kine, Horse, Goats, course Cloth, and such Commodities as we want; by whose arrivall may be made that provision of fish to fraught the ships that they stay not; and then if the Sailers goe for wages it matters not, it is hard if this returne defray not the charge: but care must be had they arrive in the Spring, or else that provision be made for them against winter. Of *Kermes.* certaine red berries called Kermes, which is worth ten shillings the pound, but of these have beene sold *Musquasses.* for thirty or forty shillings the pound, may yeerely be gathered a good quantity. Of the Muskrat may be well raised gaines worth their labour, that will endevour *Bevers.* to make triall of their goodnesse. Of Bevers, Otters and Martins, blacke Foxes, and Furres of price, may yeerely be had six or seven thousand, and if the trade of the French were prevented, many more: 25000. this yeere were brought from those northerne parts into France, of which trade we may have as good part as the French *Mines.* if we take good courses. Of Mines of Gold and Silver,

Copper, and probabilities of Lead, Crystall and Allum, I could say much if relations were good assurances; it is true indeed, I made many trialls according to the instructions I had, which doth perswade me I need not despaire but that there are metals in the Country: but I am no Alcumist, nor will promise more then I know: which is, who will undertake the rectifying of an iron Forge, if those that buy meat and drinke, coles, ore, and all necessaries at a deare rate, gaine, where all these things are to be had for taking up, in my opinion cannot lose.

Woods.

Of woods, seeing there is such plenty of all sorts, if those that build ships and boats, buy wood at so great a price, as it is in England, Spaine, France and Holland, and all other provisions for the nourishment of mans life, live well by their trade; when labour is all required to take these necessaries without any other tax, what hazard will be here but to doe much better, and what commodity in Europe doth more decay then wood? for the goodnesse of the ground, let us take it fertill or barren, or as it is, seeing it is certaine it beares fruits to nourish and feed man and beast as well as England, and the Sea those severall sorts of fishes I have related: thus seeing all good things for mans sustenance may with this facility be had by a little extraordinary labour, till that transported be increased, and all necessaries for shipping onely for labour, to which may added the assistance of the Salvages which may easily be had, if they be discreetly handled in their kinds, towards fishing, planting, and destroying woods. What gaines might be raised if this were followed (when there is but once men to fill your store houses dwelling there, you may serve all Europe better and farre cheaper then can the Iland Fishers, or the Hollanders, Cape-blanke, or Newfound land, who must be at much more charge then you) may easily be conjectured by this example.

An example of the gaines upon every yeere or six moneths returne.

Two thousand will fit out a ship of 200. tunnes, and one of 100. tuns, if of the dry fish they both make fraught, that of 200. and goe for Spaine, sell it but at ten shillings a quintall, but commonly it gives fifteene or twenty, especially when it commeth first, which amounts to 3. or 4000. pound, but say but ten, which is the lowest, allowing the rest for waste, it amounts at that rate to 2000. which is the whole charge of your two ships and the equipage, then the returne of the mony and the fraught of the ship for the vintage or any other voyage is cleere gaine, with your ship of one hundred tunnes of traine Oile and Cor-fish, besides the Bevers and other commodities, and that you may have at home within six moneths if God please to send but an ordinary passage; then saving halfe this charge by the not staying of your ships, your victuall, overplus of men and wages, with her fraught thither with necessaries for the Planters, the Salt being there made, as also may the nets and lines within a short time; if nothing may be expected but this, it might in time equalize your Hollanders gaines, if not exceede them, having their fraughts alwaies ready against the arrivall of the ships, this would so increase our shipping and sailers, and so incourage and imploy a great part of our Idlers and others that want imployment fitting their qualities at home, where they shame to doe that they would doe abroad, that could they but once taste the sweet fruits of their owne labours, doubtlesse many thousands would be advised by good discipline to take more pleasure in honest industry, then in their humors of dissolute idlenesse.

A description of the Countrey in particular, and their situations.
But to returne a little more to the particulars of this Countrey, which I intermingle thus with my projects and reasons, not being so sufficiently yet acquainted in those parts, to write fully the estate of the Sea, the Aire, the Land, the Fruits, the Rocks, the People, the Government, Religion, Territories, Limitations, Friends and Foes: But as I gathered from their niggardly relations in a broken language, during the time I ranged those Countries, etc. the most Northerne part I was at, was the Bay of Pennobscot, which is East and West, North and South, more then ten leagues: but such were my occasions, I was constrained to be satisfied of them I found in the Bay, that the River ranne farre up into the Land, and was well inhabited with many people, but they were from their habitations, either fishing amongst the Iles, or hunting the Lakes and Woods for Deere and Bevers: the Bay is full of great Iles of one, two, six or eight miles in length, which divides it into many faire and excellent good Harbours. On the East of it are the Tarrentines, their mortall enemies, where inhabit the French, as they report, that live with those people as one Nation or Family: And Northwest

of Pennobscot is Mecaddacut, at the foot of a high Mountaine, a kinde of fortresse against the Tarrentines, adjoyning to the high Mountaines of Pennobscot, against whose feet doth beat the Sea; but over all the Land, Iles, or other impediments, you may well see them fourteene or eighteene leagues from their situation. Segocket is the next, then Nuskoncus, Pemmaquid, and Sagadahock: up this River, where was the Westerne Plantation, are Aumoughcawgen, Kinnebeke, and divers others, where are planted some Corne fields. Along this River thirtie or fortie miles, I saw nothing but great high clifts of barren Rocks overgrowne with Wood, but where the Salvages dwell there the ground is excellent fat, and fertill. Westward of this River is the Country of Aucocisco, in the bottome of a large deepe Bay, full of many great Iles, which divides it into many good Harbours. Sawocotuck is the next, in the edge of a large Sandy Bay, which hath many Rockes and Iles, but few good Harbours, but for Barkes I yet know; but all this Coast to Pennobscot, and as farre as I could see Eastward of it is nothing, but such high craggy clifty Rockes and stony Iles, that I wonder such great Trees could grow upon so hard foundations. It is a Countrey rather to affright then delight one, and how to describe a more plaine spectacle of desolation, or more barren, I know not, yet are those rocky Iles so furnished with good Woods, Springs, Fruits, Fish and Fowle, and the Sea the strangest Fish-pond I ever saw, that it makes me thinke, though the coast be rocky and thus affrightable, the Vallies and Plaines and interior parts may well notwithstanding be very fertill. But there is no Country so fertill hath not some part barren, and New-England is great enough to make many Kingdomes and Countries, were it all inhabited. As you passe the coast still westward, Accominticus and Passataquack are two convenient Harbours for small Barkes; and a good Country within their craggy clifts. Augoan is the next: this place might content a right curious judgement, but there are many sands at the entrance of the Harbour, and the worst is, it is imbayed too farre from the deepe Sea; here are many rising hils, and on their tops and descents are many corne fields and delightfull groves: On the East is an Ile of two or three leagues in length, the one halfe plaine marish ground, fit for pasture or salt Ponds, with many faire high groves of Mulbery trees and

Gardens; there is also Okes, Pines, Walnuts, and other wood to make this place an excellent habitation, being a good and safe Harbour.

Naiemkeck, though it be more rocky ground, for Augoan is sandy, not much inferiour neither for the harbour, nor any thing I could perceive but the multitude of people: from hence doth stretch into the Sea the faire headland Tragabigzanda, now called Cape An, fronted with the three Iles wee called the three Turkes heads; to the north of this doth enter a great Bay, where we found some habitations and Corne fields, they report a faire River and at least 30. habitations doth possesse this Country. But because the French had got their trade, I had no leisure to discover it: the Iles of Mattahunts are on the west side of this Bay, where are many Iles and some Rocks that appeare a great height above the water like the Pyramides in Ægypt, and amongst them many good Harbours, and then the country of the Massachusits, which is the Paradice of all those parts, for here are many Iles planted with Corne, Groves, Mulberies, salvage Gardens and good Harbours, the Coast is for the most part high clayie sandy clifts, the sea Coast as you passe shewes you all along large Corne fields, and great troupes of well proportioned people: but the French having remained here neere six weekes, left nothing for us to take occasion to examine the Inhabitants relations, viz. if there be three thousand people upon those Iles, and that the River doth pierce many daies journey the entrailes of that Country: we found the people in those parts very kinde, but in their fury no lesse valiant, for upon a quarrell we fought with forty or fifty of them, till they had spent all their Arrowes, and then we tooke six or seven of their Canowes, which towards the evening they ransomed for Bever skinnes, and at Quonahasit falling out there but with one of them, he with three others crossed the Harbour in a Canow to certaine rockes whereby wee must passe, and there let flie their Arrowes for our shot, till we were out of danger, yet one of them was slaine, and another shot through his thigh.

An Indian slaine, another shot.

Then come you to Accomacke an excellent good Harbour, good land, and no want of any thing but industrious people: after much kindnesse, wee fought also with them, though some were hurt, some slaine, yet within an houre after they became friends. Cape Cod is the next presents it selfe, which is onely a headland of high hils, over-growne with shrubby Pines, hurts and such trash, but an excellent harbour for all weathers. This Cape is made by the maine Sea on the one side, and a great Bay on the other in forme of a Sickell, on it doth inhabit the people of Pawmet, and in the bottome of the Bay them of Chawum: towards the South and South-west of this Cape, is found a long and dangerous shoule of rocks and sand, but so farre as I incercled it, I found thirty fathome water and a strong currant, which makes mee thinke there is a chanell about this Shoule, where is the best and greatest fish to be had winter and summer in all the Country; but the Salvages say there is no Chanell, but that the Shoales beginne from the maine at Pawmet to the Ile of Nawset, and so extends beyond their knowledge into the Sea. The next to this is Capawucke, and those abounding Countries of Copper, Corne, People and Mineralls, which I went to discover this last yeere, but because I miscarried by the way I will leave them till God please I have better acquaintance with them.

The Massachusets they report sometimes have warres with the Bashabes of Pennobscot, and are not alwaies friends with them of Chawum and their alliance; but now they are all friends, and have each trade with other so farre as they have society on each others frontiers, for they make no such voyages as from Pennobscot to Cape Cod, seldome to Massachuset. In the North as I have said they have begun to plant Corne, whereof the south part hath such plenty as they have what they will from them of the North, and in the Winter much more plenty of fish and fowle, but both Winter and Summer hath it in one part or other all the yeere, being the meane and most indifferent temper betwixt heat and cold, of all the Regions betwixt the Line and the Pole, but the Furs Northward are much better, and in much more plenty then Southward.

The remarkablest Iles and Mountaines for land Markes are these: the highest Ile is Sorico in the Bay of Pennob- scot, but the three Iles, and the Iles of Matinack are much further in the Sea: Metynacus is also three plaine Iles, but many great Rocks: Monahigan is a round high Ile, and close by it Monanis, betwixt which is a small Harbour where we rid; in Damerils Iles is such another, Sagadahocke is

The land Markes.

knowne by Satquin, and foure or five Iles in their mouth.
Smiths Iles are a heape together, none neere them against Ac-
comintycus: the three Turkes heads, are three Iles, seene farre
to Sea-ward in regard of the Head-land. The chiefe Headlands, are onely Cape Tragabigzanda, and Cape Cod, now
called Cape James, and Cape Anne.

The chiefe Mountaines, them of Pennobscot, the twinkling
Mountaine of Acocisco, the great Mountaine of Sassanow, and
the high Mountaine of Massachuset. Each of which you shall
finde in the Map, their places, forme, and altitudes. The waters
are most pure, proceeding from the intrailes of rocky Mountaines: the Herbs and Fruits are of many sorts and
kinds, as Alkermes, Currans, Mulberies, Vines,
Respises, Gooseberies, Plums, Wall-nuts, Chesse-
nuts, Small-nuts, Pumpions, Gourds, Strawberies, Beanes,
Pease, and Maize; a kinde or two of Flax, wherewith they make
Nets, Lines, and Ropes, both small and great, very strong for
their quantities.

Herbs and Fruits

Oake is the chiefe wood, of which there is great
difference, in regard of the soyle where it groweth,
Firre, Pine, Wall-nut, Chesse-nut, Birtch, Ash, Elme,
Cipris, Cedar, Mulbery, Plum tree, Hazell, Saxefras, and many
other sorts.

Woods.

Eagles, Grips, divers sorts of Hawkes, Craines,
Geese, Brants, Cormorants, Ducks, Cranes, Swannes,
Sheldrakes, Teale, Meawes, Gulls, Turkies, Dive-
doppers, and many other sorts whose names I know not.

Birds.

Whales, Grompus, Porkpisces, Turbut, Sturgion,
Cod, Hake, Haddocke, Cole, Cuske or small Ling,
Sharke, Mackarell, Herring, Mullit, Base, Pinnacks,
Cunners, Pearch, Eeles, Crabs, Lobsters, Mustels, Wilks, Ois-
ters, Clamps, Periwinkels, and divers others, etc.

Fishes.

Moos, a beast bigger than a Stag, Deare red and
fallow, Bevers, Wolves, Foxes both blacke and other,
Aroughcunds, wilde Cats, Beares, Otters, Martins,
Fitches, Musquassus, and divers other sorts of Vermin whose
names I know not: all these and divers other good things doe
here for want of use still increase and decrease with little
diminution, whereby they grow to that abundance, you shall
scarce finde any bay, shallow shore or Cove of sand, where you

Beasts.

may not take many clamps or Lobsters, or both at your pleasure, and in many places load your Boat if you please, nor Iles
where you finde not Fruits, Birds, Crabs, and Mustels, or all of
them; for taking at a low water. Cod, Cuske, Hollibut, Scate,
Turbut, Mackarell, or such like are taken plentifully in divers
sandy Bayes, store of Mullit, Bases, and divers other sorts of
such excellent fish as many as their Net can hold: no River
where there is not plenty of Sturgion, or Salmon, or both, all
which are to be had in abundance observing but their seasons:
but if a man will goe at Christmas to gather Cherries in Kent,
though there be plenty in Summer, he may be deceived; so
here these plenties have each their seasons, as I have expressed;
we for the most part had little but bread and Vinegar, and
though the most part of July when the fishing decayed, they
wrought all day, lay abroad in the Iles all night, and lived on
what they found, yet were not sicke: But I would wish none
long put himselfe to such plunges, except necessity constraine
it: yet worthy is that person to starve that here cannot live if he
have sense, strength and health, for there is no such penury of
these blessings in any place but that one hundred men may in
two or three houres make their provisions for a day, and he that
hath experience to manage these affaires, with forty or thirty
honest industrious men, might well undertake (if they dwell in
these parts) to subject the Salvages, and feed daily two or three
hundred men, with as good Corne, Fish, and Flesh as the

A note for
men that
have great
spirits and
small meanes.

earth hath of those kinds, and yet make that labour
but their pleasure: provided that they have Engines
that be proper for their purposes. Who can desire
more content that hath small meanes, or but onely
his merit to advance his fortunes, then to tread and plant that
ground he hath purchased by the hazard of his life; if hee have
but the taste of vertue and magnanimity, what to such a minde
can bee more pleasant then planting and building a foundation
for his posterity, got from the rude earth by Gods blessing and
his owne industry without prejudice to any, if hee have any
graine of faith or zeale in Religion, what can he doe lesse hurtfull to any, or more agreeable to God, then to seeke to convert
those poore Salvages to know Christ and humanity, whose
labours with discretion will triple requite thy charge and paine;
what so truly sutes with honour and honesty, as the discovering

things unknowne, erecting Townes, peopling Countries, informing the ignorant, reforming things unjust, teaching vertue and gaine to our native mother Country; a Kingdome to attend her, finde imploiment for those that are idle, because they know not what to doe: so farre from wronging any, as to cause posterity to remember thee, and remembring thee, ever honour that remembrance with praise. Consider what were the beginnings and endings of the Monarchies of the Chaldeans, the Syrians, the Grecians and Romans, but this one rule; what was it they would not doe for the good of their common weale, or their mother City? For example: Rome, what made her such a Monarchesse, but onely the adventures of her youth, not in riots at home, but in dangers abroad, and the justice and judgement out of their experiences when they grew aged; what was their ruine and hurt but this, the excesse of idlenesse, the fondnesse of parents, the want of experience in Majestrates, the admiration of their undeserved honours, the contempt of true merit, their unjust jealousies, their politike incredulities, their hypocriticall seeming goodnesse and their deeds of secret lewdnesse; finally in fine, growing onely formall temporists, all that their Predecessors got in many yeeres they lost in a few daies: those by their paines and vertues became Lords of the world, they by their ease and vices became slaves to their servants; this is the difference betwixt the use of armes in the field, and on the monuments of stones, the golden age and the leaden age, prosperity and misery, justice and corruption, substance and shadowes, words and deeds, experience and imagination, making common weales, and marring common weales, the fruits of vertue, and the conclusions of vice.

Then who would live at home idly, or thinke in himselfe any worth to live, onely to eat, drinke and sleepe, and so die; or by consuming that carelesly, his friends got worthily, or by using that miserably that maintained vertue honestly, or for being descended nobly, and pine with the vaine vaunt of great kindred in penury, or to maintaine a silly shew of bravery, toile out thy heart, soule and time basely; by shifts, tricks, Cards and Dice, or by relating newes of other mens actions, sharke here and there for a dinner or supper, deceive thy friends by faire promises and dissimulation, in borrowing where thou never meanest to pay, offend the Lawes, surfet with excesse, burthen thy Countrie, abuse thy selfe, despaire in want, and then cousen thy Kindred, yea even thy owne brother, and wish thy Parents death (I will not say damnation) to have their estates, though thou seest what honours and rewards the world yet hath for them, that will seeke them and worthily deserve them.

I would bee sorry to offend, or that any should mistake my honest meaning; for I wish good to all, hurt to none: but rich men for the most part are growne to that dotage through their pride in their wealth, as though there were no accident could end it or their life.

And what hellish care doe such take to make it their owne misery and their Countries spoile, especially when there is most need of their imploiment, drawing by all manner of inventions from the Prince and his honest Subjects, even the vitall spirits of their powers and estates: as if their baggs or brags were so powerfull a defence, the malicious could not assault them, when they are the onely bait to cause us not onely to bee assaulted, but betrayed and murthered in our owne security ere wee will perceive it.

An example of secure covetousnesse. May not the miserable ruine of Constantinople, their impregnable walls, riches and pleasures last taken by the Turke, which were then but a bit in comparison of their mightinesse now, remember us of the effects of private covetousnesse, at which time the good Emperour held himselfe rich enough, to have such rich subjects, so formall in all excesse of vanity, all kinde of delicacy and prodigality: his poverty when the Turke besieged the Citizens (whose merchandizing thoughts were onely to get wealth) little conceiving the desperat resolution of a valiant expert enemy, left the Emperour so long to his conclusions, having spent all he had to pay his young raw discontented Souldiers, that suddenly he, they, and their City were all a prey to the devouring Turke, and what they would not spare for the maintenance of them who adventured their lives to defend them, did serve onely their enemies to torment them, their friends and Country, and all Christendome to this present day. Let this lamentable example remember you that are rich (seeing there are such great theeves in the world to rob you) not grudge to lend some proportion to breed them that have little, yet willing to learne how to defend you, for it is too late when the deed is doing.

The Romans estate hath beene worse then this, for the meere covetousnesse and extortion of a few of them so moved the rest, that not having any imploiment but contemplation, their great judgements grew to so great malice, as themselves were sufficient to destroy themselves by faction; let this move you to imbrace imployment, for those whose educations, spirits and judgements want but your purses, not only to prevent such accustomed dangers, but also to gaine more thereby then you have; and you fathers that are either so foolishly fond, or so miserably covetous, or so wilfully ignorant, or so negligently carelesse, as that you will rather maintaine your children in idle wantonnesse till they grow your masters, or become so basely unkinde that they wish nothing but your deaths, so that both sorts grow dissolute, and although you would wish them any where to escape the Gallowes and ease your cares, though they spend you here one, two or three hundred pound a yeere, you would grudge to give halfe so much in adventure with them to obtaine an estate, which in a small time, but with a little assistance of your providence, might bee better then your owne; but if an Angell should tell you any place yet unknowne can affoord such fortunes, you would not beleeve it, no more then Columbus was beleeved there was any such land, as is now the well knowne abounding America, much lesse such large Regions as are yet unknowne, as well in America, as in Africa and Asia, and Terra incognita.

I have not beene so ill bred but I have tasted of plenty and pleasure, as well as want and misery; nor doth necessity yet, or occasion of discontent force me to these endevours, nor am I ignorant what small thankes I shall have for my paines, or that many would have the world imagine them to bee of great judgement, that can but blemish these my designes, by their witty objections and detractions, yet (I hope) my reasons with my deeds will so prevaile with some, that I shall not want imploiment in these affaires, to make the most blinde see his owne senselesnesse and incredulity, hoping that gaine will make them affect that which Religion, Charity and the common good cannot. It were but a poore

The Authors conditions.

device in mee to deceive my selfe, much more the King and
State, my Friends and Country with these inducements, which
seeing his Majesty hath given permission, I wish all sorts of
worthy honest industrious spirits would understand, and if
they desire any further satisfaction, I will doe my best to give
it, not to perswade them to goe onely, but goe with them; not
leave them there, but live with them there: I will not say but by
ill providing and undue managing, such courses may bee taken
may make us miserable enough: but if I may have the execution of what I have projected, if they want to eat, let them eat
or never digest mee; If I performe what I say, I desire but that
reward out of the gaines may sute my paines, quality and condition, and if I abuse you with my tongue, take my head for
satisfaction. If any dislike at the yeeres end, defraying their
charge, by my consent they should freely returne; I feare not
want of company sufficient, were it but knowne what I know
of these Countries, and by the proofe of that wealth I hope
yeerely to returne, if God please to blesse me from such accidents as are beyond my power in reason to prevent; for I am
not so simple to thinke that ever any other motive then wealth
will ever erect there a common wealth, or draw company from
their ease and humors at home, to stay in New-England to
effect my purposes.

The Planters
pleasures and
profit.

And lest any should thinke the toile might be insupportable, though these things may bee had by
labour and diligence; I assure my selfe there are who
delight extremely in vaine pleasure, that take much more paines
in England to enjoy it, then I should doe here to gaine wealth
sufficient, and yet I thinke they should not have halfe such
sweet content: for our pleasure here is still gaines, in England
charges and losse; here nature and liberty affoords us that
freely which in England we want, or it costeth us deerely. What
pleasure can bee more then being tired with any occasion a
shore, in planting Vines, Fruits, or Herbes, in contriving their
owne grounds to the pleasure of their owne minds, their
Fields, Gardens, Orchards, Buildings, Ships, and other workes,
etc. to recreate themselves before their owne doores in their
owne Boats upon the Sea, where man, woman and childe, with
a small hooke and line, by angling may take divers sorts of excellent Fish at their pleasures; and is it not pretty sport to pull

up two pence, six pence, and twelve pence, as fast as you can hale and vere a line; hee is a very bad Fisher cannot kill in one day with his hooke and line one, two, or three hundred Cods, which dressed and dryed, if they bee sold there for ten shillings a hundred, though in England they will give more then twenty, may not both servant, master and Merchant be well content with this gaine? if a man worke but three daies in seven, hee may get more then hee can spend unlesse hee will bee exceedingly excessive. Now that Carpenter, Mason, Gardiner, Tailer, Smith, Sailer, Forger, or what other, may they not make this a pretty recreation, though they fish but an houre in a day, to take more then they can eat in a weeke, or if they will not eat it, because there is so much better choise, yet sell it or change it with the Fisher-men or Merchants for any thing you want, and what sport doth yeeld a more pleasing content, and lesse hurt and charge then angling with a hooke, and crossing the sweet aire from Ile to Ile, over the silent streames of a calme Sea, wherein the most curious may finde profit, pleasure and content.

Thus though all men be not fishers, yet all men whatsoever may in other matters doe as well, for necessity doth in these cases so rule a common wealth, and each in their severall functions, as their labours in their qualities may be as profitable because there is a necessary mutuall use of all.

Imploiments for Gentlemen. For Gentlemen, what exercise should more delight them then ranging daily these unknowne parts, using fowling and fishing for hunting and hawking, and yet you shall see the wilde Hawkes give you some pleasure in seeing them stoupe six or seven times after one another an houre or two together, at the skulls of Fish in the faire Harbours, as those a shore at a fowle, and never trouble nor torment your selves with watching, mewing, feeding, and attending them, nor kill horse and man with running and crying, See you not a Hawke? For hunting also, the Woods, Lakes and Rivers affoord not onely chase sufficient for any that delights in that kinde of toile or pleasure, but such beasts to hunt, that besides the delicacie of their bodies for food, their skinnes are so rich, as they will recompence thy daily labour with a Captaines pay.

For Labourers, if those that sow Hempe, Rape, Turnups,

Parsnips, Carrats, Cabidge, and such like; give twentie, thirtie, fortie, fiftie shillings yeerely for an Acre
of Land, and meat, drinke, and wages to use it, and
yet grow rich: when better, or at least as good ground may bee
had and cost nothing but labour; it seemes strange to me any
such should grow poore.

My purpose is not to perswade children from their parents
men from their wives, nor servants from their masters; onely
such as with free consent may bee spared: but that each Parish,
or Village, in Citie, or Countrey, that will but apparell their
fatherlesse children of thirteene or foureteene yeeres of age, or
young maried people that have small wealth to live on, here by
their labour may live exceeding well. Provided alwaies, that
first there be a sufficient power to command them, houses to
receive them, meanes to defend them, and meet provisions for
them, for any place may be over-laine: and it is most necessary
to have a fortresse (ere this grow to practise) and sufficient
masters, of all necessarie, mecanicall qualities, to take ten or
twelve of them for Apprentises; the Master by this may quickly
grow rich, these may learne their trades themselves to doe the
like, to a generall and an incredible benefit for King and Countrey, Master and Servant.

It would be a History of a large volume, to recite
the adventures of the Spaniards and Portugals, their
affronts and defeats, their dangers and miseries;
which with such incomparable honor, and constant resolution,
so farre beyond beleefe, they have attempted and indured in
their discoveries and plantations, as may well condemne us of
too much imbecillitie, sloth, and negligence; yet the Authors
of these new inventions were held as ridiculous for a long time,
as now are others that doe but seeke to imitate their unparal-
leld vertues, and though we see daily their mountaines of
wealth (sprung from the Plants of their generous indevours)
yet is our sensualitie and untowardnesse such, and so
great, that we either ignorantly beleeve nothing, or
so curiously contest, to prevent we know not what
future events; that we either so neglect, or oppresse and discourage the present, as wee spoile all in the making, crop all in
the blooming; and building upon faire Sand rather then upon
rough Rocks, judge that we know not, governe that wee have

Imploiments for Labourers.

Examples of the Spaniards.

The causes of our defailments.

not, feare that which is not; and for feare some should doe too well, force such against their wils to be idle, or as ill. And who is hee hath judgement, courage, and any industry or quality with understanding, will leave his Country, his hopes at home, his certaine estate, his friends, pleasures, libertie, and the preferment sweet England doth affoord to all degrees, were it not to advance his fortunes by enjoying his deserts, whose prosperitie once appearing, will encourage others: but it must be cherished as a childe, till it be able to goe and understand it selfe, and not corrected nor oppressed above its strength, ere it know wherefore. A childe can neither performe the office nor deeds of a man of strength, nor endure that affliction he is able: nor can an Apprentise at the first performe the part of a Master, and if twentie yeeres be required to make a childe a man, seven yeeres limited an Apprentise for his trade: if scarce an age be sufficient to make a wise man a States-man, and commonly a man dies ere he hath learned to be discreet; if perfection be so hard to be obtained, as of necessitie there must be Practice as well as Theoricke: Let no man then condemne this paradox opinion, to say that halfe seven yeres is scarce sufficient for a good capacitie to learne in these affaires how to carrie himselfe. And who ever shall try in these remote places the erecting of a Colony, shall finde at the end of seven yeeres occasion enough to use all his discretion: and in the Interim, all the content, rewards, gaines, and hopes, will be necessarily required, to be given to the beginning, till it be able to creepe, to stand, and goe, and to encourage desert by all possible meanes; yet time enough to keepe it from running, for there is no feare it will grow too fast, or ever to any thing, except libertie, profit, honor, and prosperitie there found, more binde the Planters of those affaires in devotion to effect it; then bondage, violence, tyrannie, ingratitude, and such double dealing, as bindes free men to become slaves, and honest men turne knaves; which hath ever beene the ruine of the most popular Common-weales, and is very unlikely ever well to begin anew.

The blisse of Spaine. Who seeth not what is the greatest good of the Spaniard, but these new conclusions in searching those unknowne parts of this unknowne world; by which meanes he dives even into the very secrets of all his neighbours, and the most part of the world; and when the Portugals and Spaniards had found the East and West-Indies, how many did condemne themselves, that did not accept of that honest offer of Noble Columbus, who upon our neglect brought them to it, perswading our selves the world had no such places as they had found: and yet ever since we finde, they still (from time to time) have found new Lands, new Nations, and Trades, and still daily doe finde, both in Asia, Affrica, Terra incognita, and America, so that there is neither Souldier nor Mechanicke, from the Lord to the Begger, but those parts affoords them all imploiment, and discharges their native soile of so many thousands of all sorts, that else by their sloth, pride, and imperfections, would long ere this have troubled their neighbours, or have eaten the pride of Spaine it selfe.

Now hee knowes little that knowes not England may well spare many more people then Spaine, and is as well able to furnish them with all manner of necessaries; and seeing for all they have, they cease not still to search for that they have not, and know not; it is strange we should be so dull, as not maintaine that which we have, and pursue that we know: Surely, I am sure many would take it ill, to be abridged of the titles and honors of their predecessors; when if but truly they would judge themselves, looke how inferior they are to their Noble Vertues, so much they are unworthy of their honors and livings, which never were ordained for shewes and shadowes, to maintaine idlenesse and vice, but to make them more able to abound in honor, by Heroicall deeds of action, judgement, pietie, and vertue. What was it both in their purse and person they would not doe, for the good of their Common-wealth, which might move them presently to set out their spare children in these generous designes; Religion above all things should move us, especially the Clergie, if we are religious, to shew our faith by our works, in converting those poore Salvages to the knowledge of God, seeing what paines the Spaniards takes to bring them to their adultered faith. Honor might move the Gentry, the valiant, and industrious, and the hope and assurance of wealth, all, if we were that we would seeme, and be accounted; or be we so farre inferior to other Nations, or our spirits so farre dejected from our ancient predecessors, or our mindes so upon spoile, piracy, and such villany, as to serve the Portugall,

Spaniard, Dutch, French, or Turke, (as to the cost of Europe too many doe) rather then our God, our King, our Country, and our selves; excusing our idlenesse and our base complaints by want of imploiment, when here is such choice of all sorts, and for all degrees, in the planting and discovering these North parts of America.

My second voyage to New England.

My second Voiage to New England. 1615.

In the yeere of our Lord 1615. I was imploied by many my friends of London, and Sir Ferdinando Gorges, a noble Knight, and a great favourer of those actions, who perswaded the reverend Deane of Exeter Doctor Sutliffe, and divers Merchants of the West, to entertaine this Plantation. Much labour I had taken to bring the Londoners and them to joyne together, because the Londoners have most Money, and the Westerne men are most proper for fishing; and it is neere as much trouble, but much more danger, to saile from London to Plimoth, then from Plimoth to New England, so that halfe the voiage would thus be saved, yet by no meanes I could prevaile, so desirous they were both to be Lords of this fishing. Now to make my words more apparant by my deeds, to begin a Plantation for a more ample triall of those conclusions, I was to have staied there but with sixteene men, whose names were;

Thomas Dirmer. Edward Stallings. Daniel Cage. Francis Abbot.	*Gentlemen.*
John Gosling. William Ingram. David Cooper. John Partridge.	*Souldiers.*
Thomas Digby. Daniel Baker. Adam Smith. Thomas Watson. Walter Chisell.	*were to learne to be Sailers.*

Robert Miller.
And two Boyes $\Big\}$ *were to learne to be Sailers.*

I confesse I could have wished them as many thousands, had all other provisions beene in like proportion; nor would I have had so few, could I have had means for more: yet would God have pleased we had safely arrived, I doubted not but to have performed more then I promised, and that many thousands

The ground and plot for our plantation.

ere this would have bin there ere now. The maine assistance next God I had to this small number, was my acquaintance amongst the Salvages, especially with Dohoday, one of their greatest Lords, who had lived long in England, and another called Tantum, I caried with mee from England, and set on shore at Cape Cod; by the meanes of this proud Salvage, I did not doubt but quickly to have got that credit amongst the rest of the Salvages and their alliance, to have had as many of them as I desired in any designe I intended, and that trade also they had by such a kinde of exchange of their Countrey Commodities, which both with ease and securitie might then have beene used with him and divers others: I had concluded to inhabit and defend them against the Tarentines, with a better power then the French did them; whose tyrannie did inforce them to embrace my offer with no small devotion: and though many may think me more bold then wise, in regard of their power, dexteritie, treachery, and inconstancy, having so desperately assaulted, and betraied many others; I say but this (because with so many, I have many times done much more in Virginia then I intended here, when I wanted that experience Virginia taught mee) that to me it seemes no more danger then ordinary: and though I know my selfe the meanest of many thousands, whose apprehensive inspection can pierce beyond the bounds of my abilities, into the hidden things of Nature, Art, and Reason: yet I intreat such, give mee leave to excuse my selfe of so much imbecillitie, as to say, that in these eighteene yeeres which I have beene conversant with these affaires, I have not learned, there is a great difference betwixt the directions and judgement of experimentall knowledge, and the superficiall conjecture of variable relation: wherein rumour, humour, or misprision have such power, that oft times one is enough to beguile twentie, but twentie not sufficient to keepe one from being deceived. Therefore I know no reason but to beleeve my owne eies before any mans imagination, that is but wrested from the conceits of my owne projects and endevours, but I honor with all affection, the counsell and instructions of judiciall directions, or any other honest advertisement, so farre to observe, as they tie me not to the crueltie of unknowne events. These are the inducements that thus drew

The meanes used to prevent it and me.

me to neglect all other imploiments, and spend my time and best abilities in these adventures, wherein though I have had many discouragements, by the ingratitude of some, the malicious slanders of others, the falsenesse of friends, the treachery of cowards, and slownesse of Adventurers.

How I set saile and returned.

Now you are to remember, as I returned first from New England at Plimoth, I was promised foure good ships ready prepared to my hand the next Christmas, and what conditions and content I would desire, to put this businesse in practise, and arriving at London, foure more were offered me with the like courtesie. But to joyne the Londoners and them in one, was most impossible; so that in January with two hundred pound in Cash for adventure, and six Gentlemen well furnished, I went from London to the foure ships were promised me at Plimoth, but I found no such matter: and the most of those that had made such great promises, by the bad returne of the ship went for Gold, and their private emulations, were extinct and qualified. Notwithstanding at last, with a labyrinth of trouble, though the greatest of the burden lay on me, and a few of my particular friends, I was furnished with a ship of two hundred tunnes, and another of fiftie: But ere I had sailed one hundred and twentie leagues, she brake all her Masts, pumping each watch five or six thousand strokes; onely her spret-saile remained to spoone before the winde, till we had re-accommodated a Jury-mast to returne for Plimoth, or founder in the Seas.

My reimbarkement, encounter with Pirats, and imprisonment by the French.

My Vice-Admirall being lost, not knowing of this, proceeded her voyage; now with the remainder of those provisions, I got out againe in a small Barke of sixtie tuns with thirty men (for this of two hundred, and provision for seventie), which were the sixteene before named, and foureteene other Sailers for the ship; with those I set saile againe the foure and twentieth of June, where what befell me (because my actions and writings are so publike to the world) envy still seeking to scandalize my endevours, and seeing no power but death can stop the chat of ill tongues, nor imagination of mens minds, lest my owne relations of those hard events might by some constructors bee made doubt-full, I have thought it best to insert the examinations of those proceedings, taken by Sir Lewis Stukeley, a worthy Knight, and Vice-Admirall of Devonshire, which was as followeth.

The Examination of Daniel Baker, late Steward to
Captaine John Smith, in the returne of Plimoth,
taken before Sir Lewis Stukeley Knight,
the eighth of December, 1615.

The effect in briefe was this: being chased by one Fry an English Pirat, Edward Chambers the Master, John Minter his Mate, Thomas Digby the Pylot, and divers others importuned him to yeeld; much swaggering wee had with them, more then the Pirats, who agreed upon such faire conditions as we desired, which if they broke, he vowed to sinke rather then be abused. Strange they thought it, that a Barke of threescore tuns with foure guns should stand upon such termes, they being eightie expert Sea-men, in an excellent ship of one hundred and fortie tuns, and thirty six cast Peeces and Murderers: But when they knew our Captaine, so many of them had beene his Souldiers, and they but lately runne from Tunis, where they had stolne this ship, wanted victuall, and in combustion amongst themselves, would have yeelded all to his protection, or wafted us any whither: but those mutinies occasioned us to reject their offer, which afterward we all repented. For at Fiall we met two French Pirats, the one of two hundred tuns, the other thirty: no disgrace would cause our mutiners fight, till the Captaine offered to blow up the ship rather then yeeld, till hee had spent all his powder: so that together by the eares we went, and at last got cleere of them for all their shot. At Flowers we were againe chased with foure French men of warre, the Admirall one hundred and fortie tuns, and ninety men well armed; the rest good ships, and as well provided: much parly we had, but vowing they were Rochilers, and had a Commission from the King onely to secure true men, and take Portu-

gals, Spaniards, and Pirats, and as they requested, our Captaine
went to shew his Commission, which was under the broad
Seale, but neither it nor their vowes they so much respected, but
they kept him, rifled our ship, manned her with French men,
and dispersed us amongst their Fleet: within five or six daies
they were increased to eight or nine saile. At last they surrendred us our ship, and most of our provisions, the defects they
promised the next day to supply, and did. Notwithstanding,
there was no way but our mutiners would for England, though
we were as neere New England, till the major part resolved
with our Captaine to proceed. But the Admirall sending his
Boat for our Captaine, they espying a Saile, presently gave
chase, whereby our mutiners finding an opportunitie in the
night ran away, and thus left our Captaine in his Cap, Bretches,
and Wast-coat, alone among the French men: his clothes,
armes, and what he had, our mutiners shared among them,
and with a false excuse, faining for feare lest he should turne
man of warre, they returned for Plimoth: fifteene of us being
Land-men, not knowing what they did.

Daniel Gage, Edward Stalings, Walter Chisell, David Cooper,
Robert Miller, and John Partridge, upon oath affirmes this
for truth before the Vice-Admirall.

Now the cause why the French detained mee
againe, was the suspition this Chambers and Minter
gave them, that I would revenge my selfe upon the
Banke, or in New found land, of all the French I could there
encounter, and how I would have fired the ship, had they not
over-perswaded me: and that if I had but againe my Armes, I
would rather sinke by them, then they should have from me but
the value of a Bisket; and many other such like tales
to catch but opportunitie in this manner to leave me,
and thus they returned to Plimoth, and perforce
with the French men I thus proceeded. Being a fleet
of eight or nine saile, we watched for the West-Indies fleet, till
ill weather separated us from the other eight: still wee spent
our time about the Iles of the Assores, where to keepe my perplexed thoughts from too much meditation of my miserable
estate, I writ this Discourse, thinking to have sent it to you of
his Majesties Councell by some ship or other, for I saw their

A double treachery.

A fleet of nine French men of war, and fights with the Spaniard.

purpose was to take all they could. At last we were chased by one Captaine Barra, an English Pirat in a small ship, with some twelve Peece of Ordnance, about thirty men, and neere all starved. They sought by courtesie releefe of us, who gave them such faire promises, as at last they betraied Captaine Wollistone his Lieutenant, and foure or five of his men aboord us, and then provided to take the rest perforce. Now my part was to be prisoner in the Gun-roome, and not to speake to any of them upon my life, yet had Barra knowledge what I was. Then Barra perceiving well those French intents, made ready to fight, and Wollistone as resolutely regarded not their threats, which caused us demurre upon the matter longer some six-teene houres, and then returned them againe Captaine Wollistone and all their Prisoners, and some victuall also upon a small composition: But whilest we were bartering thus with them; a Carvill before our faces got under the Castle of Gratiosa, from whence they beat us with their Ordnance.

A prise of Fish.

The next wee tooke was a small English man of Poole from New found land: the great Cabben at this present was my prison, from whence I could see them pillage these poore men of all that they had, and halfe their fish: when hee was gone, they sold his poore clothes at the maine Mast by an out-cry, which scarce gave each man seven pence a peece.

A Scotch prise.

Not long after we tooke a Scot fraught from Saint Michaels to Bristow, he had better fortune then the other; for having but taken a Boats loading of Sugar, Marmelade, Suckets, and such like, we descried foure saile, after whom we stood, who forling their maine Sailes attended us to fight, but our French spirits were content onely to perceive they were English red Crosses. Within a very small time after wee chased 4. Spanish ships that came from the Indies, we fought with them foure or five houres, tore their sailes and sides with many a shot betwixt wind and weather, yet not daring to boord them, lost them, for which all the Sailers ever after hated the Captaine as a professed coward.

A prise worth 36000 crownes.

A poore Carvill of Brasile was the next wee chased; and after a small fight, thirteene or foureteene of her men being wounded, which was the better halfe, we tooke her with three hundred and seventy chests of Sugar, one hundred hides, and thirty thousand Rialls of eight.

The next was a ship of Holland, which had lost her Consorts in the Streights of Magilans, going for the South sea. She was put roomy. She also these French men with faire promises, cunningly betraied to come aboord them to shew their Commission, and so made prise of all: the most of the Dutch-men we tooke aboord the Admirall, and manned her with Frenchmen, that within two or three nights after ran away with her for France, the wounded Spaniards we set on shore on the Ile of Tercera, the rest we kept to saile the Carvill.

Within a day or two after, we met a West-Indies man of warre, of one hundred and sixtie tuns, a forenoone wee fought with her, and then tooke her with one thousand one hundred Hides, fiftie Chests of Cutchanele, foureteene Coffers of wedges of Silver, eight thousand Rialls of eight and six Coffers of the King of Spaines Treasure, besides the good pillage and rich Coffers of many rich Passengers.

A prise worth 200000 crownes.

Two moneths they kept me in this manner to manage their fights against the Spaniards, and bee a Prisoner when they tooke any English. Now though the Captaine had oft broke his promise, which was to put me on shore the Iles, or the next ship he tooke; yet at the last he was contented I should goe in the Carvill of Sugar for France, himselfe seeming as resolved to keepe the Seas, but the next morning we all set saile for France, and that night we were separated from the Admirall and the rich prise by a storme. Within two daies after wee were hailed by two West-Indies men: but when they saw us waife them for the King of France, they gave us their broad sides, shot thorow our maine Mast, and so left us. Having lived now this Summer amongst those French men of warre, with much adoe we arrived at the Gulion, not farre from Rotchell: where in stead of the great promises they alwaies fed me with, of double satisfaction and full content, and tenne thousand Crownes was generally concluded I should have; they kept me five or six daies Prisoner in the Carvill, accusing me to be he that burnt their Colony in New France, to force me to give them a discharge before the Judge of the Admiraltie, and stand to their courtesies for satisfaction, or lie in prison, or a worse mischiefe:

Indeed this was in the time of combustion, that the Prince of Cundy was with his Army in the field, and every poore Lord, or men in authoritie, as little Kings of themselves: For this injury was done me by them that set out this voyage (not by the Sailers) for they were cheated of all as well as I, by a few Officers aboord, and the owners on shore.

But to prevent this choise, in the end of such a storme that beat them all under hatches, I watched my opportunitie to get a shore in their Boat, whereinto in the darke night I secretly got, and with a halfe Pike that lay by me, put a drift for Rat Ile: but the currant was so strong, and the Sea so great, I went a drift to Sea, till it pleased God the wind so turned with the tide, that although I was all this fearefull night of gusts and raine in the Sea the space of twelve houres, when many ships were driven ashore, and divers split: (and being with skulling and bayling the water tired, I expected each minute would sinke me) at last I arrived in an Oazy Ile by Charowne, where certaine Fowlers found me neere drowned, and halfe dead, with water, cold, and hunger. My Boat I pawned to finde meanes to get to Rotchell; where I understood our man of war and the rich prize, wherein was the Captaine called Mounsieur Poyrune, and the thirtie thousand Rialls of eight we tooke in the Carvill, was split, the Captaine drowned and halfe his Company the same night, within six or seven leagues of that place; from whence I escaped in the little Boat by the mercy of God, far beyond all mens reason or my expectation. Arriving at Rotchell, upon my complaint to the Judge of the Admiraltie, I found many good words and faire promises, and ere long many of them that escaped drowning, told me the newes they heard of my owne death: These I arresting, their severall examinations did so confirme my complaint, it was held proofe sufficient. All which being performed according to their order of justice, from under the Judges hand, I presented it to Sir Thomas Edmonds, then Ambassadour at Burdeaux, where it was my chance to see the arrivall of the Kings great mariage brought from Spaine.

My escape from the French men.

What law I had.

Here it was my good fortune to meet my old friend Master Crampton, that no lesse grieved at my losse, then willingly to his power did supply my wants, and I must confesse, I was more beholden to the French men that escaped drowning in the man of warre, Madam Chanoyes at Rotchell, and the Lawyers of Burdeaux, then all the rest of my Country-men I met in France. Of the wracke of the rich prise, some three thousand six hundred crownes worth of goods came ashore, and was saved with the Carvill, which I did my best to arrest: the Judge promised I should have Justice, what will be the conclusion as yet I know not. But under the couler to take Pirats and the West-Indie men (because the Spaniards will not suffer the French to trade in the West-Indies) any goods from thence, though they take them upon the Coast of Spaine are lawfull prize, or from any of his Teritories out of the limits of Europe: and as they betraied me, though I had the broad-seale, so did they rob and pillage twentie saile of English men more, besides them I knew not of the same yeere.

My returne for England.   Leaving thus my businesse in France I returned to Plimoth, to finde them had thus buried me amongst the French; and not onely buried me, but with so much infamy as such treacherous cowards could suggest to excuse their villanies. The Chiefetaines of this mutiny that I could finde, I laid by the heeles, the rest like themselves confessed the truth, as you have heard. Now how I have or could prevent these accidents, having no more meanes, I rest at your censures; but to proceed to the matter; yet must I sigh and say, How oft hath Fortune in the world (thinke I) brought slavery, freedome, and turned all diversly. Newfoundland I have heard at the first, was held as desperate a fishing as this I project for New England; Placentia, and the Banke were also as doubtfull to the French: But for all the disasters hapned me, the businesse is the same it was, and the five ships went from London, whereof one was reported more then three hundred tunnes, found fish so much, that neither Izeland man, nor Newfoundland man I could heare of hath bin there, will go any more to either place, if they may go thither. So that upon the good returne of my Vice-Admirall, this yeere are gone 4 or 5 saile from

The successe of my Vice-Admirall.   Plimoth, and from London as many, only to make voyages of profit: whereas if all the English had bin there till my returne, put all their returnes together, they would scarce make one a favour of neere a dozen I could nominate, except one sent by Sir Francis Popham; though there be fish sufficient, as I am perswaded, to fraught yeerely foure or five hundred Saile, or as many as will goe. For this fishing stretcheth along the Sea Coast from Cape James to New-foundland, which is seven or eight hundred miles at the least, and hath his course in the deepes, and by the shore, all the yere long, keeping their hants and feedings, as the beasts of the field, and the birds of the aire. But all men are not such as they should be, that have undertaken those voyages: All the Romans were not Scipioes, nor Carthagenians Hanibals, nor all the Genoeses Columbusses, nor all the Spaniards Courteses: had they dived no deeper in the secrets of their discoveries then we, or stopped at such doubts and poore accidentall chances, they had never beene remembred as they are, yet had they no such certainties to begin as we.

But to conclude, Adam and Eve did first begin this innocent worke to plant the earth to remaine to posterity, but not without labour, trouble, and industry. Noe and his family began againe the second Plantation; and their seed as it still increased, hath still planted new Countries, and one Countrey another, and so the world to that estate it is: but not without much hazard, travell, mortalities, discontents, and many disasters. Had those worthy Fathers, and their memorable offspring, not beene more diligent for us now in these ages, then we are to plant that yet is unplanted for the after livers. Had the seed of Abraham, our Saviour Christ, and his Apostles, exposed themselves to no more dangers to teach the Gospell then we, even wee our selves had at this present beene as salvage, and as miserable as the most barbarous Salvage, yet uncivilized. The Hebrewes and Lacedemonians, the Gothes, the Grecians, the Romanes, and the rest, what was it they would not undertake to inlarge their Teritories, enrich their subjects, resist their enemies. Those that were the founders of those great Monarchies and their vertues, were no silvered idle golden Pharises, but industrious Iron steeled Publicans: They regarded more provisions and necessaries for their people, then jewels, riches, ease, or delight for themselves; Riches were their Servants, not their Masters. They ruled (as Fathers, not as Tirants) their people as Children, not as Slaves; there was no disaster could discourage them; and let none thinke they incountred not with all manner of incumbrances. And what hath ever beene the worke of the greatest Princes of the Earth, but planting of Countries, and civilizing barbarous and inhumane Nations to civilitie and humanitie, whose eternall actions fills our Histories.

Lastly, the Portugals and Spaniards, whose ever-living actions before our eies will testifie with them our idlenesse, and ingratitude to all posterities, and the neglect of our duties, in our pietie and religion we owe our God, our King and Countrey; and want of Charitie to those poore Salvages, whose Countrey wee challenge, use and possesse; except wee be but made to use, and marre what our fore-fathers made, or but onely tell what they did, or esteeme our selves too good to take the like paines. Was it vertue in them to provide that doth maintaine us, and basenesse in us to doe the like for others? Surely no. Then seeing we are not borne for our selves, but each to help other, and our abilities are much alike at the houre of our birth, and the minute of our death: seeing our good deeds or our bad by faith in Christs merits, is all we have, to carie our soules to heaven or hell. Seeing honor is our lives ambition, and our ambition after death to have an honorable memory of our life: and seeing by no meanes we would be abated of the dignities and glories of our predecessors, let us imitate their vertues to be worthily their successors: to conclude with Lucretius,

> *Its want of reason, or its reasons want*
> *Which doubts the minde and judgement, so doth dant,*
> *That those beginnings makes men not to grant.*

> *John Smith writ this with his owne hand.*

Here followeth a briefe Discourse of the trials of New England, with certaine Observations of the Hollanders use and gaine by fishing, and the present estate of that happy Plantation, begun but by sixtie weake men, in the yeere of our Lord 1620. and how to build a fleet of good ships to make a little Navy Royall, by the former Author.

Master Dee
his report.

HE saith, that it is more then foure and fortie yeeres agoe, and it is more then fortie yeeres agoe since he writ it; that the Herring Busses out of the Low Countries under the King of Spaine, were five hundred, besides one hundred French men, and three or foure hundred saile of Flemings. The Coast of Wales and Lancashire was used by 300 Saile of Strangers. Ireland at Baltimore, fraughted yeerely three hundred saile of Spaniards, where King Edward the sixt intended to have made a strong Castle, because of the straight to have tribute for fishing. Black Rocke was yerely fished by three or foure hundred saile of Spaniards, Portugals, and Biskiners.

The benefit
of fishing, as
Master
Gentleman
and others
report.

The Hollanders raise yeerely by Herring, Cod, and Ling, thirty thousand pounds: English and French, by Salt-fish, Poore-John, Salmons, and Pilchards, three hundred thousand pounds: Hambrough and the Sound, for Sturgion, Lobsters and Eeles, one hundred thousand pounds: Cape Blanke for Tunny and Mullit, by the Biskiners and Spaniards, thirty thousand pounds.

That the Duke of Medina receiveth yeerely tribute of the Fishers, for Tunny, Mullit, and Porgos, more then ten thousand pounds. Lubecke hath seven hundred ships; Hambrough

The Records
of Holland
and other
learned
observers

six hundred; Emden lately a Fisher towne, one thousand foure hundred, whose customes by fishing hath made them so powerfull as they be. Holland and Zeland not much greater then Yorkeshire, hath thirty walled Townes, foure hundred Villages, and twenty thousand saile of Ships and Hoies; three thousand six hundred are Fisher-men, whereof one hundred are Doggers, seven hundred Pinkes and Well-Boats, seven hundred Strand-boats, Britters, and Tode-boats, with thirteene hundred Busses, besides three hundred that yeerely fish about Yarmouth, where they sell their fish for

Gold: and fifteene yeeres agoe they had more then an hundred and sixteene thousand Sea-faring men.

These fishing ships doe take yeerely two hundred thousand last of fish, twelve barrels to a last, which amounts to 3000000. pounds by the fisher mens price, that 14. yeeres agoe did pay for their tenths three hundred thousand pound, which venting in Pumerland, Sprussia, Denmarke, Lefeland, Russia, Swethland, Germany, Netherlands, England, or else where, etc. makes their returnes in a yeere about threescore and ten hundred thousand pounds, which is seven millions; and yet in Holland there is neither matter to build ships nor merchandize to set them forth, yet by their industry they as much increase as other nations decay; but leaving these uncertainties as they are, of this I am certaine.

That the coast of England, Scotland and Ireland, the North Sea with Island and the Sound, Newfound-land and Cape Blanke, doe serve all Europe, as well the land townes as ports, and all the Christian shipping, with these sorts of staple fish, which is transported from whence it is taken many a thousand mile, viz. Herring, salt Fish, Poore-John, Sturgion, Mullit, Tunny, Porgos, Caviare, Buttargo.

Now seeing all these sorts of fish, or the most part of them may be had in a land more fertill, temperate and plentifull of all necessaries, for the building of ships, boats and houses, and the nourishment of man, the seasons are so proper, and the fishings so neere the habitations we may there make, that New-England hath much advantage of the most of those parts, to serve all Europe farre cheaper then they can, who at home have neither wood, salt, nor food, but at great rates, at Sea nothing but what they carry in their ships, an hundred or two hundred leagues from their habitation. But New-Englands fishings is neere land, where is helpe of Wood, Water, Fruits, Fowles, Corne or other refreshings needfull, and the Terceras, Mederas, Canaries, Spaine, Portugall, Provance, Savoy, Sicillia, and all Italy, as convenient markets for our dry fish, greene fish, Sturgion, Mullit, Caviare and Buttargo, as Norway, Swethland, Littuania or Germany for their Herring, which is heare also in abundance for taking; they returning but Wood, Pitch, Tar, Sope-ashes, Cordage, Flax, Wax, and such like commodities; wee Wines, Oiles, Sugars, Silkes, and such merchandize as the Straits affoord, whereby our profit may equalize theirs, besides the increase of shipping and Marriners: and for proofe hereof,

1614. In the yeere of our Lord 1614. you have read how I went from London: also the next yeere 1615. how
1615. foure good ships went from London, and I with two more from Plimoth, with all our accidents, successes
1616. and returnes: in the yeere 1616. ere I returned from France, the Londoners for all their losse by the Turkes, sent foure ships more; foure more also went from
1617. Plimoth; after I returned from France, I was perswaded againe to goe to Plimoth with divers of my friends with one hundred pound for our adventures besides our charges, but wee found all things as untoward as before, and all their great promises nothing but aire: yet to prepare the voyage against the next yeere, having acquainted a great part of the Nobility with it, and ashamed to see the Prince his Highnesse till I had done some what worthy his Princely view;

My sute to the Country. I spent that Summer in visiting the Cities and Townes of Bristoll, Exeter, Bastable, Bodnam, Perin, Foy, Milborow, Saltash, Dartmouth, Absom, Tattnesse, and the most of the Gentry in Cornewall and Devonshire, giving them Bookes and Maps, shewing how in six moneths the most of those ships had made their voyages, and some in lesse, and with what good successe; by which incitation they seemed so well contented, as they promised twenty saile of ships should goe with mee next yeere, and in regard of my paines, charge, and former losses, the westerne Commissioners in behalfe of themselves and the rest of the Company, and them hereafter that should be joyned to them, contracted with me by articles indented under our hands, to be Admirall of that Country during my life, and in the renewing of their Letters-Patents so to be nominated. Halfe the fruits of our endevours to be theirs, the rest our owne; being thus ingaged, now the businesse is made plaine and likely to prosper, some of them would not onely forget me and their promises, but also obscure me, as if I had never beene acquainted in the businesse, but I am not the first they have deceived.

1618. There was foure good ships prepared at Plimoth, but by reason of their disagreement, the season so wasted, as onely two went forward, the one being of two hundred tunnes, returned well fraught to Plimoth, and her men in health, within five moneths; the other of fourescore tunnes went for Bilbow with drie fish and made a good returne. In this voyage Edward Rowcroft, alias Stallings, a valiant Souldier, that had beene with me in Virginia, and was with me also when I was betrayed by the French, was sent againe in those ships, and having some wrong offered him there by a French man, he tooke him, and as he writ to me, went with him to Virginia with fish, to trade with them for such commodities as they might spare: he had not past ten or twelve men, and knew both those countries well, yet he promised me the next spring to meet me in New-England, but the ship and he both perished in Virginia.

This yeere againe, divers ships intending to goe from Plimoth, so disagreed, there went but one of two hundred tunnes, who stayed in the Country about six weeks, which with eight and thirty men and boies had her fraught, which she sold at the first penny for 2100. pounds, besides the Furres: so that every poore Sailer that had but a single share had his charges and sixteene pound ten shillings for his seven moneths worke. Master Thomas Dirmire an understanding and industrious Gentleman, that was also with me amongst the French men, having lived about a yeere in Newfoundland, returning to Plimoth, went for New-England in this ship, so much approved of this Country, that he staied there with five or six men in a little Boat, finding two or three French men amongst the Salvages who had lost their ship, augmented his company, with whom he ranged the Coast to Virginia, where he was kindly welcommed and well refreshed, thence returned to New-England againe, where having beene a yeere, in his backe returne to Virginia he was so wounded by the Salvages, he died upon it; let not men attribute these their great adventures, and untimely deaths to unfortunatenesse, but rather wonder how God did so long preserve them with so small meanes to doe so much, leaving the fruits of their labours to be an incouragement to those our poore undertakings, and as warnings for us not to undertake such great workes with such small meanes, and this for advantage as they writ unto me, that God had laid this Country open for us, and

1619.

slaine the most part of the inhabitants by civill warres and a mortall disease, for where I had seene one hundred or two hundred Salvages, there is scarce ten to be found, and yet not any one of them touched with any sicknesse but one poore French man that died;

> *They say this plague upon them thus sore fell,*
> *It was because they pleas'd not* Tantum *well.*

From the West Country to make triall this yeere

1620.

onely to fish, is gone six or seven saile, three of which I am certainly informed made so good a voyage, that every Sailer that had a single share had twenty pound for his seven moneths work, which is more then in twenty moneths he should have gotten, had he gone for wages any where. Now although these former ships have not made such good voiages as they expected, by sending opinionated unskilfull men, that had not experienced diligence to save that they tooke, nor take that there was, which now patience and practice hath brought to a reasonable kinde of perfection; in despight of all detractors and calumniations the Country yet hath satisfied all, the defect hath beene in their using or abusing it, not in it selfe nor me: But,

> *A due desert, for fortune makes provision*
> *For Knaves and Fooles, and men of base condition.*

Now all these proofes and this relation I now called

My sute to the Citie.

New-Englands triall. I caused two or three thousand of them to be printed, one thousand with a great many Maps both of Virginia and New-England, I presented to thirty of the chiefe Companies in London at their Halls, desiring either generally or particularly (them that would) to imbrace it, and by the use of a stocke of five thousand pound, to ease them of the superfluity of the most of their companies that had but strength and health to labour; neere a yeere I spent to understand their resolutions, which was to me a greater toile and torment, then to have beene in New-England about my businesse but with bread and water, and what I could get there by my labour; but in conclusion, seeing nothing would be effected, I was contented as well with this losse of time and charge as all the rest.

A Plantation in New-England.

Upon these inducements some few well disposed
Gentlemen, and Merchants of London and other
places, provided two ships, the one of a hundred and
threescore tunnes, the other of threescore and ten, they left
the Coast of England the two and thirtieth of August, with
about a hundred and twenty persons, but the next day the
lesser ship sprung a leake, that forced their returne to Plimoth,
where discharging her and twenty passengers; with the greater
ship and one hundred passengers besides Sailers, they set saile
againe the sixt of September, and the ninth of November fell
with Cape James, but being pestred nine weekes in this leaking
unwholsome ship, lying wet in their Cabins, most of them
grew very weake and weary of the Sea; then for want of experience, ranging two and againe six weekes before they found a
place they liked to dwell on, forced to lie on the bare ground
without coverture, forty of them died, and threescore were left
in very weake estate at the ships comming away, about the fifth
of Aprill following, and arrived in England the sixth of May.
Though the Harbour be good, the shore is so shallow, they
were forced to wade a great way up to the knees in water, and
used that that did them much hurt; and little fish they found
but Whailes, and a great kinde of Mustell so fat, that few did eat
of them that were not sicke: these miseries occasioned some
discord, and gave some appearance of faction, but all was so
reconciled, that they united themselves by common consent
under their hands, to a kinde of combination of a body politike, by vertue whereof to inact and constitute lawes and ordinances, and Officers from time to time, as should bee thought
most convenient for their generall good.

Sixteene or seventeene daies they could doe little
for want of their Shallop which was amending, yet
Captaine Miles Standish, unto whom was joyned in
Councell, William Bradford, Stephen Hopkins and Edward
Tilly, went well armed a shore, and by that time they had gone
a mile, met five or six Indians that fled into the Woods: we
traced them by the footing eight or ten miles, then the night
approaching we made a fire, by which we lay that night, and
the next morning followed the Salvages by their tract, thinking

1620. (margin)

Their first journy by land. (margin)

to finde their habitations, but by the way we found a Deere
amongst many faire springs of water, where we refreshed our
selves; then we went a shore and made a fire, that they at the
ship might perceive where we were, and so marched to a place
where we supposed was a River; by the way we saw many
Vines, Saxefras, haunts of Deere and Fowle, and some fifty
Acres of plaine ground had beene planted by the Indians,
where were some of their graves; from thence we followed a
path that brought us through three or foure fields that had bin
planted that yeere; in one grave we digged, we found a basket
or two of Indian Corne, so much as we could carry we tooke
with us, the rest we buried as we found it, and so proceeded to
the place we intended, but we found it not such a Harbour as
we expected; and so we returned, till the night caused us take
up our lodging under a tree, where it rained six or seven houres:
the next morning as we wandred, we passed by a tree, where a
young sprig was bowed downe over a bough, and some
Acornes strewed under it, which was one of their Gins to a
catch a Deere, and as we were looking at it, Bradford was suddenly caught by the leg in a noosed Rope, made as artificially
as ours; as we passed we see a lease of Bucks, sprung some Partriges, and great flocks of wilde Geese and Ducks, and so we
returned well wearied to our ship.

Their first
journy by
Shallop.

Master Jones our Master with foure and thirty
men, also went up and downe in the frost and snow,
two or three daies in the extremity of the cold, but
could finde no harbour; only among the old graves we got
some ten bushels of Corne, some Beanes, and a bottle of Oile;
and had we not thus haply found it, we had had no Corne for
seede, so that place we ever called Corne-hill; the next day Master Jones with the Corne and our weakest men returned to the
Ship, but eighteene of us quartered there that night, and in
the morning following the paths, wee found in the Snow in a
field a greater hill or grave then the rest, diging it wee found
first a Mat, under that a boord three quarters long, painted and
carved with three Tyns at the top like a Cronet, betweene the
Mats also were Bowles, Traies and Dishes and such trash, at
length we found a faire new Mat, and under that two bundles,
the one biggar the other lesse; in the greater wee found a great
quantity of fine red powder like a kinde of imbalmement, and

yeelded a strong but no offensive smell, with the bones and skull of a man that had fine yellow haire still on it, and some of the flesh unconsumed, a Knife, a Pack-needle, and two or three old Iron things was bound up in a Sailers canvase Cassocke, also a paire of cloth Breeches; in the lesse bundle we found likewise of the same powder, and the bones and head of a little childe; about the legs and other parts of it was bound strings and braslets of white beades, there was also a little Bow, and some other odde knacks, the prettiest we tooke, and covered againe the corps as they were: not farre from thence were two of their houses, where were a great deale of their miserable houshold stuffe, which we left as wee found, and so returned to our Boat, and lay aboord that night.

Many arguments we had to make here our Planta-

Accidents.

tion or not; in the Interim, Mistris White was brought to bed of a young sonne, which was called Perigrine: and a Sailer shooting at a Whale, his peece flew in peeces stocke and all, yet he had no hurt. A foolish boy discharging his fathers peece hard by halfe a barrell of Powder, and many people by it, it pleased God it escaped firing, so that no hurt was done.

Their second journey by water to finde a place to plant in.

But to make a more certaine discovery where to seat our selves, Captaine Standish, Master Carver, William Bradford, Edward Winslow, John Tilly, Edward Tilly, with divers others to the number of seventeene, upon the sixt of December set saile, and having sailed six or seven leagues, we espied eight or ten Salvages about a dead Grampus: still following the shore we found two or three more cast up by the ill weather, many we see in the water, therefore we called it Grampus Bay: Ships may ride well in it, but all the shore is very shallow flats of sand; at last seven or eight of us went a shore, many fields we saw where the Salvages had inhabited, and a buriall place incompassed with a Palizado, so we returned to our Shallop, in the night we heard a hideous cry and howling of Wolves and Foxes; in the morning as we were ready to goe into our Shallop, one of our men being in the woods, came running crying, Indians, Indians, and with all their Arrowes flying amongst us, some of our men being in the boat, and their Armes a shore, so well it chanced, Captaine Standish with two or three more discharged their

peeces till the rest were ready, one Salvage more
stout then the rest kept under a tree, till he had shot
three or foure Arrowes, and endured three or foure
Musket shot, but at last they all fled, this was about breake of
day in the morning when they saw us, and we not them.

Having the wind faire, we sailed along the coast 8.
or 10. leagues, thinking to have got to a Harbour
where one of our company had beene, within 8.
leagues of Cape Cod, for neither cricke nor Harbour in this
bay we could finde; and the wind so increased, our Rudder
broke, and our Mast flew over-boord, that we were in danger
to be cast away, but at last it pleased God we were in a harbor
we knew not, thinking it one we were acquainted with, this we
found to be an Ile where we rid that night, and having well
viewed the land about it, and sounded the Bay to be a good
Harbour for our ship, compassed with good land, and in it two
faire Iles, where there is in their seasons innumerable store of
all sorts of fish and fowle, good water, much plaine land, which
hath beene planted; with this newes we returned to our ship,
and with the next faire wind brought her thither, being but
within the sight of Cape Cod; in the meane time
Goodwife Alderton was delivered of a sonne, but
dead borne. Upon the 28. of December, so many as
could went to worke upon the hill, where we purposed to build our Platforme for our ordnance, which doth
command all the Plaine and the Bay, and from whence wee
may see far into the Sea, and be easily impailed, so in the afternoone we went to measure out the grounds, and divided our
company into 19. families, alotting to every person halfe a
poule in bredth and three in length, and so we cast lots where
every man should lie, which we staked out, thinking this proportion enough at the first to impale for lodgings and gardens.

Francis Billington from the top of a tree seeing a
great water some three miles from us in the land,
went with the Masters Mate, and found it two great
Lakes of fresh water, the bigger five or six miles in circuit, and
an Ile in it of a Cables length square; the other three miles in
compasse, full of fish and fowle, and two brooks issuing from
it, which will be an excellent helpe in time for us, where they
saw seven or eight Indian houses, but no people. Foure being

Their first fight with the Salvages.

The description of their place to plant in.

Another Boy borne in New-England.
Their first Plantation.

Two faire Lakes.

sent a mile or two from our plantation, two of them stragling
into the woods was lost, for comming to a Lake of
water they found a great Deere, having a mastive

Two men lost
themselves in
the woods.

Bitch and a Spanell with them, they followed so farre
they could not finde the way backe, that afternoone it rained,
and did freeze and snow at night; their apparell was very thin,
and had no weapons but two sickles, nor any victuals, nor
could they finde any of the Salvages habitations; when the
night came they were much perplexed that they had no other
bed then the earth, nor coverture then the skies, but that they
heard, as they thought, two Lions roaring a long time together
very nigh them, so not knowing what to doe, they resolved to
climbe up into a tree, though that would be an intollerable
cold lodging. Expecting their comming they stood at the trees
root, and the bitch they held fast by the necke, for shee would
have beene gone to the Lions or what they were, that as it
chanced came not nigh them, so they watched the tree that extreme cold night, and in the morning travelling againe, passing
by many lakes, brooks and woods, and in one place where the
Salvages had burnt 4. or 5. miles in length, which is a fine
champion Country, in the afternoone they discovered the two
Iles in their Bay, and so that night neere famished they got to
their Plantation, from whence they had sent out men every
way to seeke them; that night the house they had built and
thatched, where lay their armes, bedding, powder, etc. tooke
fire and was burnt. The Coast is so shoule, the ship rides more
then a mile from the Fort, but God be thanked no man was
hurt though much was burnt.

Their first
conference
with a
Salvage.

All this time we could not have conference with a
Salvage, though we had many times seene them and
had many alarums, so that we drew a Councell, and
appointed Captaine Standish to have the command of all martiall actions, but even in the time of consultation the Salvages
gave an alarum: the next day also as wee were agreeing upon
his orders, came a tall Salvage boldly amongst us, not fearing
any thing, and kindly bad us welcome in English; he was a Sag-
amo, towards the North, where the ships use to fish, and did
know the names of most of the Masters that used thither: such
victuall as we had we gave him, being the first Salvage we yet
could speake with, he told us this place where we were was

called Patuxet, and that all the people three or foure yeeres agoe there died on the plague: in a day or two we could not be rid of him, then he returned to the Massasoyts from whence he came, where is some sixty people, but the Nawsits are 100.

strong, which were they encountred our people at the first. Two daies after this Samoset, for so was his name, came againe, and brought five or six of the Massasoyts with him, with certaine skinnes, and certaine tooles they had got that we had left in the woods at their alarums: much friendship they promised, and so departed, but Samoset would not leave us, but fained himselfe sicke, yet at last he went to entreat the Salvages come againe to confirme a peace: now the third time, as we were consulting of our Marshall orders, two Salvages appeared, but when we went to them they vanished: not long after came Samoset, and Squanto, a native of Patuxet where we dwell, and one of them carried into Spaine by Hunt, thence brought into England, where a good time he lived; and now here signified unto us, their great Sachem of Massasoyt, with Quadaquina his brother, and all their men, was there by to see us: not willing to send our Governour, we sent Edward Winslow with presents to them both, to know their minds, making him to understand by his Interpreters how King James did salute him and was his friend; after a little conference with twenty of his men, he came over the brooke to our Plantation, where we set him upon a rug, and then brought our Governour to him with Drums and Trumpets; where after some circumstances, for they use few complements, we treated of peace with them to this effect.

That neither he nor any of his should injury or doe hurt to any of us; if they did, he should send us the offender, that we might punish him, and wee would doe the like to him: if any did unjustly warre against him, we would aid him, as he should us against our enemies, and to send to his neighbour confederats to certifie them of this, that they might likewise be comprised in these conditions, that when any of them came to us, they should leave their Bow and Arrowes behinde them, as we would our peeces when we came to them, all which the King seemed to like well of, and was applauded of his followers. In his person hee is a very lusty man, in his best yeeres, an able body, grave of countenance, and spare of speech: in his attire little differing from the rest; after all was done, the Governour conducted him to the brooke, but kept our hostage till our messengers returned: in like manner we used Quaddaquina, so all departed good friends.

Two of his people would have staied with us, but wee would not permit them, onely Samoset and Squanto wee entertained kindly; as yet wee have found they intend to keepe promise, for they have not hurt our men they have found stragling in the Woods, and are afraid of their powerfull Adversaries the Narrohiggansets, against whom hee hopes to make use of our helpe. The next day Squanto went a fishing for Eeles, and in an houre he did tread as many out of the Ose with his feet as he could lift with his hand, not having any other instrument.

A journey to Pakanoki. But that we might know their habitations so well as they ours, Stephen Hopkins and Edward Winslow had Squantum for their guide and Interpreter; to Packanoki, the habitation of the King of Massasoyt, with a red horsemans coat for a present, to entreat him by reason we had not victuall to entertaine them as we would, he would defend his people so much from visiting us; and if hee did send, he should alwaies send with the Messenger a copper Chaine they gave him, that they might know he came from him, and also give them some of his Corne for seede: that night they lodged at Namascet, some fifteene miles off: by the way we found ten or twelve women and children that still would pester us till we were weary of them, perceiving it is the manner of them, where victuall is to bee gotten with most ease, there they will live; but on that River of Namaschet have beene many habitations of the Salvages that are dead, and the land lies waste, and the River abounding with great plenty of fish, and hath beene much frequented by the French.

A great courage of two old Salvages. The next day travelling with six or seven Indians, where we were to wade over the River, did dwell onely two old men of that Nation then living, that thinking us enemies, sought the best advantage they could to fight with us, with a wonderfull shew of courage, but when they knew us their friends they kindly welcommed us; after we came How the King used them. to a towne of the Massasoits, but at Pakanoki the King was not: towards night he arrived and was very proud, both of our message and presents, making a great oration to all his people, Was not he Massasoit, Commander of the country about him, was not such a towne his, and the people of it, and 20. townes more he named was his? and should they not bring their skins to us? to which they answered, they were his and they would; victual they had none, nor any lodging, but a poore planke or two, a foot high from the ground, wheron his wife and he lay at the one end, we at the other, but a thin Mat upon them, two more of his chiefe men pressed by and upon us, so that we were worse weary of our lodging then of our journey. Although there is such plenty of fish and fowle and wild beasts, yet are they so lasie they will not take paines to catch it till meere hunger constraine them, for in two or three daies we had scarce a meales meat, whereby we were so faint, we were glad to be at home: besides what for the fleas, and their howling and singing in the night in their houses, and the Musketas without doores, our heads were as light for want of sleepe, as our bellies empty for want of meat. The next voiage we made was in a Shallop with ten men to Nawsit, sixteene miles from us, to fetch a Boy was lost in the Woods we heard was there, whom Aspinet their King had bedecked like a salvage, but very kindly he brought him to us, and so returned well to Patuxet.

A voyage to
Nawsit.

Immediatly after the arrivall of the last ship, they sent another of five and fifty tuns to supply them; with seven and thirty persons they set saile in the beginning of July, but being crossed by westernly winds, it was the end of August ere they could passe Plimoth, and arrived in New-England at New-Plimoth, now so called the 11. of November, where they found all the people they left so ill, lusty and well for all their poverties, except six that died: a moneth they stayed ere they returned to England, loaded with Clapboord, Wainscot and Wallnut, with about three hogsheads of Bever skinnes the 13. of December: and drawing neere our coast was set on by a French man set out by the Marquesse of Cera, Governour of Ile Deu, where they kept the ship, imprisoned the Master and company, tooke from them to the value of 500. pound, and after 14. daies sent them home with a poore supply of victuall, their owne being devoured by the Marquesse and his hungry servants.

1621.

Now you are to understand this 37. brought nothing, but

relied wholly on us to make us more miserable then before, which the Sachem Couanacus no sooner understood, but sent to Tusquantum our Interpreter, a bundle of new arrowes in a Snakes skinne; Tusquantum being absent, the Messenger departed, but when we understood it was a direct challenge, we returned the skin full of powder and shot, with an absolute defiance, which caused us finish our fortification with all expedition. Now betwixt our two Salvages, Tusquantum and Hobbamock, grew such great emulation, we had much adoe to know which best to trust. In a journey we undertooke, in our way we met a Salvage of Tusquantums, that had cut his face fresh bleeding, to assure us Massasoyt our supposed friend, had drawne his forces to Packanokick to assault us. Hobomak as confidently assured us it was false, and sent his wife as an espy to see; but when she perceived all was well, shee told the King Massasoyt how Tusquantum had abused him, divers Salvages also hee had caused to beleeve we would destroy them, but he would doe his best to appease us; this he did onely to make his Country-men beleeve what great power hee had with us to get bribes on both sides, to make peace or warre when he would, and the more to possesse them with feare, he perswaded many we had buried the plague in our store house, which wee could send when we listed whither wee would, but at last all his knavery being discovered, Massasowat sent his knife with Messengers for his head or him, being his subject; with much adoe we appeased the angry King and the rest of the Salvages, and freely forgave Tusquantum, because he speaking our language we could not well be without him.

A journey to the Towne of Namaschet, in defence of the King of Massasoyt, against the Narrohigganses, and the supposed death of Squantum.

A GREAT difference there was betwixt the Narrohigganses and the Massasoytes, that had alwaies a jealousie; Coubatant one of their petty Sachems was too conversant with the Narrohigganses, this Coubatant lived much at Namaschet, and much stormed at our peace with his King and others; also at Squantum, and Tokamahamon, and Hobomak our friends, and chiefe occasioners of our peace, for which he sought to murther Hobomak; yet Tokamahamon went to him upon a rumour he had taken Masasoyt prisoner, or forced him from his Country, but the other two would not, but in privat to see if they could heare what was become of their King; lodging at Namaschet they were discovered to Coubatant, who surprized the house and tooke Squantum, saying, if hee were dead the English had lost their tongue; Hobomak seeing that, and Coubatant held a knife at his brest, being a strong lusty fellow, brake from them and came to New-Plimoth, full of sorrow for Squantum, whom he thought was slaine.

The next day we sent ten men with him armed to be revenged of Coubatant, who conducted us neere Namaschet, where we rested and refreshed our selves til midnight, and then we beset the house as we had resolved; those that entred the house demanded for Coubatant, but the Salvages were halfe dead with feare, we charged them not to stirre, for we came to hurt none but Coubatant for killing Squantum, some of them seeking to escape was wounded, but at last perceiving our ends, they told us Coubatant was gone and all his men, and Squantum was yet living, and in the towne; in this hurly burly we discharged two peeces at randome, which much terrified all the inhabitants except Squantum and Tokamahamon, who though they knew not the end of our comming, yet assured themselves of our honesties, that we would not hurt them; the women and children hung about Hobomak, calling him friend, and when they saw we would hurt no women, the young youths cryed we are women; to be short, we kept them all, and whilest we were searching the house for Coubatant, Hobomak had got to the top, and called Squantum and Tokamahamon, which came unto us accompanied with others, some armed, others naked, those that had bowes we tooke them from them, promising them againe when it was day: the house wee tooke for our quarter that night and discharged the prisoners, and the next morning went to breakfast to Squantums house; thither came all them that loved us to welcome us, but all Coubatants faction was fled, then we made them plainly know the cause of our com-

They surprise the Salvages.

ming, and if their King Massasoyt were not well, we would be revenged upon the Narrohiggansets, or any that should doe injury to Hobomak, Squantum, or any of their friends; as for those were wounded we were sorry for it, and offered our Surgion should heale them, of this offer a man and a woman accepted, that went home with us, accompanied with Squantum, and many other knowne friends, that offered us all the kindnesse they could.

From the West of England there is gone ten or twelve ships to fish, which were all well fraughted: those that came first at Bilbow, made seventeene pound a single share, besides Bevers, Otters, and Martins skinnes; but some of the rest that came to the same ports, that were all ready furnished, so glutted the market, that the price was abated, yet all returned so well contented, that they are a preparing to goe againe.

There is gone from the West Countrey onely to fish, five and thirtie ships, and about the last of Aprill two more from London; the one of one hundred tunnes, the other of thirtie, with some sixtie Passengers to supply the Plantation. Now though the Turke and French hath beene somewhat too busie in taking our ships, would all the Christian Princes be truly at unitie, as his Royall Majestie our Soveraigne King James desireth, seventie Saile of good ships were sufficient to fire the most of his Coasts in the Levant, and make such a guard in the Straights of Hellespont, as would make the great Turke himselfe more affraid in Constantinople, then the smallest Red-Crosse that crosses the Seas would be, either of any French Pickaroun, or the Pirats of Agere.

An abstract of divers Relations sent from the Colony in New England, July 16. 1622.

SINCE the massacre in Virginia, though the Indians continue their wonted friendship, yet wee are more wary of them then before; for their hands hath beene imbrued in much English bloud, onely by too much confidence, but not by force, and we have had small supplies of

1622.

Notes and observations.

any thing but men. Here I must intreat a little your favours to digresse, they did not kill the English in Virginia, because they were Christians: but for their weapons and Copper, which were rare novelties; but now they feare we may beat them out of their dens, which Lions and Tigers will not admit but by force. But must this be an argument for an English man, and discourage any in Virginia or New England: No, for I have tried them both, as you may reade at large in the Historie of Virginia; notwithstanding since I came from thence, the Honourable Company hath beene humble suiters to his Majestie, to get vagabonds and condemned men to goe thither; nay, so the businesse hath beene so abused, that so much scorned was the name of Virginia, some did chuse to be hanged ere they would goe thither, and were: Yet for all the worst of spight, detraction, and discouragement, and this lamentable massacre, there is more honest men now suiters to goe, then ever hath beene constrained knaves. And it is not unknowne to most men of understanding, how happy many of those Callumners hath thought themselves that they might be admitted; and yet pay for their passage to goe now to Virginia, and I feare mee there goeth too many of those, that hath shifted heere till they could no longer; and they will use that qualitie there till they hazard all.

To range this Countrey of New England in like manner, I had but eight, as is said, and amongst their bruit conditions, I met many of their silly encounters, and I give God thankes, without any hurt at all to me, or any with mee. When your West-Countrey men were so wounded and tormented with the Salvages, though they had all the Politicke directions that had beene gathered from all the secret informations could be heard of, yet they found little, and returned with nothing. I speak not this out of vaine-glory, as it may be some gleaners, or some who were never there may censure me; but to let all men be assured by those examples, what those Salvages are, that thus strangely doe murder and betray our Countrymen: but to the purpose;

They lived two yeeres without supply.   The *Paragon* with thirtie seven men sent to releeve them, miscaried twice upon our English Coast, whereby they failed of their supplies. It is true, there hath beene taken one thousand Bases at a draught; and in one night twelve Hogsheads of Herrings: but when they wanted all necessaries both for fishing and sustinance, but what they could get with their naked industry, they indured most extreme wants, having beene now neere two yeeres without any supply to any purpose, it is a wonder how they should subsist, much lesse so to resist the Salvages, fortifie themselves, plant sixtie acres of Corne, besides their Gardens that were well replenished with many usuall fruits. But in the beginning of July

Westons Plantation.

came in two ships of Master Westons, though we much wanted our selves, yet we releeved them what we could: and to requite us, they destroied our Corne and Fruits then planted, and did what they could to have done the like to us. At last they were transported to Wichaguscusset at the Massachusets, where they abused the Salvages worse then us. We having neither Trade, nor scarce any thing remaining, God sent in one Master Jones, and a ship of Westons had beene at Monahigan amongst the Fisher-men, that for Bever skinnes and such Merchandize as wee had, very well refreshed us, though at deere rates. Weston left also his men a small Barke, and much good provision, and so set saile for England. Then wee joyned with them to trade to the Southward of Cape Cod, twice or thrice wee were forced to returne; first by the death of their Governor; then the sicknesse of Captaine Standish. At last our Governor Master Bradford undertooke it himselfe to have found the passage betwixt the Shoules and

The death of Tusquantum.

the Maine, then Tusquantum our Pilot died, so that we returned to the Massachusets, where we found the trade spoiled, and nothing but complaints betwixt the Salvages and the English. At Nawset we were kindly used and had good trade, though we lost our Barge, the Salvages carefully kept both her wracke, and some ten Hogsheads of Corne three moneths, and so we returned some by land, some in the ship.

Tusquantum at his death desired the English to pray he might go dwell with the English mens God, for theirs was a good God.

Captaine Standish being recovered, went to fetch them both, and traded at Namasket and Monomete, where the people had the plague, a place much frequented with Dutch and French. Here the Sachem put a man to death for killing his fellow at play, wherein they are so violent, they will play their coats from their backs, and also their wives, though many miles from them. But our provision decaying, Standish is sent to Mattachist, where they pretended their wonted love; yet it plainly appeared they intended to kill him. Escaping thence, wee went to Monomete, where we found nothing but bad countenances. Heare one Wittuwamat a notable villaine, would boast how many French and English hee had slaine: This Champion presenting a Dagger to the Sachem Canacum he had got from the English, occasioned us to understand how they had contrived to murder all the English in the Land, but having such a faire opportunitie, they would begin heere with us. Their scornfull usage made the Captaine so passionate to appease his anger and choler, their intent made many faire excuses for satisfaction: Scar a lusty Salvage, alwaies seeming the most to effect us, bestowed on us the best presents he had without any recompence, saying; Hee was rich enough to bestow such favours on his friends, yet had undertaken to kill the Captaine himselfe, but our vigilencies so prevented the advantage they expected, we safely returned, little suspecting in him any such treachery.

They contrive to murder all the English.

During this time a Dutch ship was driven a shore at Massasowat, whose King lay very sicke, now because it is a generall custome then for all their friends to visit them: Master Winslow, and Master Hamden, with Habamok for their guide, were sent with such Cordialls as they had to salute him; by the way they so oft heard the King was dead, Habamok would breake forth in those words, My loving Sachem, my loving Sachem, many have I knowne, but never any like thee, nor shall ever see the like amongst the Salvages; for he was no lier, nor bloudy and cruell like other Indians, in anger soone reclaimed, he would be ruled by reason, not scorning the advice of meane men, and governed his men better with a few strokes, then others with many: truly loving where he loved, yea he feared wee had not a faithfull friend left amongst all his Countrey-men, shewing how oft he had restrained their malice, much more with much passion he spoke to this purpose, till at last we arrived where we found the Dutchmen but newly gone, and the house so full we could hardly get in. By their charmes they distempered us that were well, much more him that was sicke, women rubbing him to keepe heat in him; but their charmes ended, understanding of

The sicknesse of King Massasowat.

us, though he had lost his sight, his understanding failed not; but taking Winslow by the hand, said, Art thou Winslow, Oh Winslow, I shall never see thee againe!

His cure by the English.

Hobamock telling him what restauratives they had brought, he desired to taste them, with much adoe they got a little Confexion of many comfortable Conserves into his mouth, as it desolved he swallowed it, then desolving more of it in water, they scraped his tongue, which was al furred and swolne, and washed his mouth, and then gave him more of it to eat, and in his drinke, that wrought such an alteration in him in two or three houres, his eies opened to our great contents; with this and such brothes as they there provided for him, it pleased God he recovered: and thus the manner of his sicknesse and cure caused no small admiration amongst them.

During the time of their stay to see his recovery, they had sent to New Plimoth for divers good things for him, which he tooke so kindly, that he fully revealed all the former conspiracies against us, to which he had oft beene moved; and how that all the people of Powmet, Nawset, Succonet, Mattachist, Manamet, Augawam, and Capawac were joyned to murder us; therefore as we respected our lives, kill them of Massachuset that were the authors; for take away the principals and the plot wil cease, thus taking our leaves, and arriving at our fort, we found our brave liberall friend of Pamet drawing Standish to their Ambuscados, which being thus discovered, we sent him away, as though he knew nor suspected any thing. Them at the Massachusets, some were so vilde they served the Salvages for victuall, the rest sent us word the Salvages were so insolent, they would assault them though against their Commission, so fearefull they were to breake their Commission, so much time was spent in consultations, they all were famished, till Wassapinewat againe came and told them the day of their execution was at hand.

The Kings thankfulnesse.

A bad example.

Captaine Standish sent to suppresse the Salvages.

Then they appointed Standish with eight chosen men, under colour of Trade to catch them in their owne trap at Massachuset, and acquaint it with the English in the Towne, where arriving he found none in the Barke, and most of the rest without Armes, or scarce clothes, wandering abroad, all so sencelesly secure, he more then wondered they were not all slaine, with much adoe he got the most of them to their Towne. The Salvages suspecting their plots discovered, Pecksuot a great man, and of as great a spirit, came to Habamak, who was then amongst them, saying; Tell Standish we know he is come to kill us, but let him begin when he dare. Not long after many would come to the Fort and whet their Knives before him, with many braving speeches. One amongst the rest was by Wittawamat bragging he had a Knife, that on the handle had the picture of a womans face, but at home I have one hath killed both French and English, and that hath a mans face on it, and by and by these two must marrie: but this here, by and by shall see, and by and by eat, but not speake; Also Pecksuot being of a greater stature then the Captaine, told him, though he were a great Captaine he was but a little man, and I though no Sachem, yet I am of great strength and courage. These things Standish bare patiently for the present; but the next day seeing he could not get many of them together, but these two Roarers, and two more being in a convenient roome, and his company about him, Standish

Two desperate Salvages slaine.

seased on Pecksuots Knife then hanging about his necke, wherewith he slew him, and the rest slew Wittuwamat and the other Salvage, but the youth they tooke, who being Brother to Wittuwamat, and as villanous as himselfe, was hanged. It is incredible how many wounds they indured, catching at their weapons without any feare or bruit, till the last gasp. Habamack stood by all this time very silent, but all ended, he said, Yesterday Pecksuot bragged of his strength and stature, but I see you are big enough to lay him on the ground.

The Salvages overcommed.

The Towne he left to the guard of Westons people: three Salvages more were slaine; upon which rumour they all fled from their houses. The next day they met with a file of Salvages that let fly their Arrowes, shot for shot till Hobamack shewed himselfe, and then they fled. For all this, a Salvage Boy to shew his innocency, came boldly unto us and told us: Had the English Fugitives but finished the three Canowes they were a making, to have taken the ship, they would have done as much to all the English, which was onely the cause they had forborne so long. But now consulting and considering their estates, those that went in the Pinnace to

Barty Iles to get passage for England, the rest to New Plimoth, where they were kindly entertained. The Sachem Obtakeest, and Powas, and divers other were guilty, the three fugitives in their fury there slew; but not long after so distracted were those poore scattered people, they left their habitations, living in swamps, where with cold and infinite diseases they endured much mortalitie, suing for peace, and crying the God of England is angry with them. Thus you see where God pleases, as some flourish, others perish.

Now on all hands they prepare their ground, and about the middest of Aprill, in a faire season they begin to plant till the latter end of May; but so God pleased, that in six weekes after the latter setting there scarce fell any raine; so that the stalke was first set, began to eare ere it came to halfe growth, and the last not like to yeeld any thing at all. Our Beanes also seemed so withered, we judged all utterly dead, that now all our hopes were overthrowne, and our joy turned into mourning. And more to our sorrow, we heard of the twice returne of the *Paragon*, that now the third time was sent us three moneths agoe, but no newes of her: onely the signes of a wracke we saw on the Coast which wee judged her. This caused not every of us to enter into a private consideration betwixt God and our consciences, but most solemnly to humble our selves before the Lord by fasting and praying, to releeve our dejected spirits by the comforts of his mercy. In the morning when wee assembled all together, the skies were as cleere, and the drought as like to continue as ever; yet our exercise continued eight or nine houres. Before our departure, the skies were all over-cast, and on the next morning distilled such soft, sweet, moderate showers, continuing foureteene daies, mixed with such seasonable weather, as it was hard to say, whether our withered Corne, or drooping affections were most quickned and revived; such was the bounty and mercy of God. Of this the Indians by the meanes of Hobamock tooke notice, who seeing us use this exercise in the midst of the weeke, said; It was but three daies since Sunday, and desired to know the reason; which when hee understood, he and all of them admired the goodnesse of God towards us, shewing the difference betwixt their conjurations and our praiers, and what

1623.

An extreme drought.

A wonderfull blessing and signe of Gods love.

stormes and dangers they oft receive thereby. To expresse our thankfulnesse, wee assembled together another day, as before, and either the next morning, or not long after, came in two ships to supply us, and all their Passengers well except one, and he presently recovered. For us, notwithstanding all these wants, there was not a sicke person amongst us. The greater ship we returned fraught; the other wee sent to the Southward, to trade under the command of Captaine Altom. So that God be thanked, we desire nothing, but what we will returne Commodities to the value.

> Thus all men finde our great God he,
> That never wanted nature,
> To teach his truth, that onely he
> Of every thing is Author.

Forty saile sent to fish.

For this yeere from England is gone about fortie saile of ships, only to fish, and as I am informed, have made a farre better voyage then ever.

Now some new great observers will have this an Iland, because I have writ it is the Continent: others report, that the people are so bruit, they have no religion, wherein surely they are deceived; for my part, I never heard of any Nation in the world which had not a Religion, deare, bowes and arrowes. They beleeve as doe the Virginians, of many divine powers, yet of one above all the rest, as the Southerne Virginians call their chiefe God Kewassa, and that wee now inhabit Oke, but both their Kings Werowance. The Masachusets call their great God Kiehtan, and their Kings there abouts Sachems: The Penobscotes their greatest power Tantum, and their Kings Sagomos. Those where is this Plantation, say Kiehtan made all the other Gods: also one man and one woman, and of them all mankinde, but how they became so dispersed they know not. They say, at first there was no King but Kiehtan that dwelleth farre westerly above the heavens, whither all good men goe when they die, and have plentie of all things. The bad men goe thither also and knocke at the doore, but he bids them goe wander in endlesse want and miserie, for they shall not stay there. They never saw Kiehtan, but they hold it a great charge and dutie, that one age teach another; and to him they make feasts, and cry and sing for plentie

Their Religion.

and victorie, or any thing is good. They have another Power they call *Hobamock,* which wee conceive the Devill, and upon him they call to cure their wounds and diseases: when they are curable he perswades them he sent them, because they have displeased him; but if they be mortall, then he saith, *Kiehtan* sent them, which makes them never call on him in their sicknesse. They say this *Hobamock* appeares to them somtimes like a Man, a Deere, or an Eagle, but most commonly like a Snake; not to all, but only to their *Powahs* to cure diseases, and *Undeses,* which is one of the chiefe next the King, and so bold in the warres, that they thinke no weapon can kill them: and those are such as conjure in Virginia, and cause the people to doe what they list.

For their Government: every Sachem is not a King, **Their Government.** but their great Sachems have divers Sachems under their protection, paying them tribute, and dare make no warres without his knowledge; but every Sachem taketh care for the Widowes, Orphans, the aged and maimed, nor will they take any to first wife, but them in birth equall to themselves, although they have many inferior Wives and Concubins that attend on the principall; from whom he never parteth, but any of the rest when they list. They inherit by succession, and every one knowes their owne bounds. To his men, hee giveth them land, also bounded, and what Deere they kill in that circuit, he hath the fore-part; but if in the water, onely the skin: But they account none a man, till hee hath done some notable exploit: the men are most imploied in hunting, the women in slavery; the younger obey the elders: their names are variable; they have harlots and honest women: the harlots never marrie, or else are widowes. They use divorcement, and the King commonly punisheth all offenders himselfe: when a maid is maried, she cutteth her haire, and keepes her head covered till it be growne againe. Their arts, games, musicke, attire, burials, and such like, differ very little from the Virginians, onely for their Chronicles they make holes in the ground, as the others set up great stones.

Out of the Relations of Master Edward Winslow.

An answer to Objections.   Now I know the common question is, For all those miseries, where is the wealth they have got, or the Gold or Silver Mines? To such greedy unworthy minds I say once againe: The sea is better then the richest Mine knowne, and of all the fishing ships that went well provided, there is no complaint of losse nor misery, but rather an admiration of wealth, profit, and health. As for the land were it never so good, in two yeeres so few of such small experience living without supplies so well, and in health, it was an extraordinary blessing from God. But that with such small meanes they should subsist, and doe so much, to any understanding judgement is a wonder. Notwithstanding, the vaine expectation of present game in some, ambition in others, that to be great would have all else slaves, and the carelesnesse in providing supplies, hath caused those defailements in all those Plantations, and how ever some bad conditions will extoll the actions of any Nation but their owne: yet if we may give credit to the Spaniards, Portugals, and French writings, they indured as many miseries, and yet not in twenty yeeres effected so much, nay scarce in fortie.

The ordinary voyage to goe to Virginia or New-England.

Thus you may see plainly the yeerely successe from New England by Virginia, which hath beene so costly to this Kingdome, and so deare to me, which either to see perish, or but bleed; Pardon me though it passionate me beyond the bounds of modesty, to have beene sufficiently able to fore-see their miseries, and had neither power nor meanes to prevent it. By that acquaintance I have with them, I call them my children, for they have beene my Wife, my Hawks, Hounds, my Cards, my Dice, and in totall, my best content, as indifferent to my heart, as my left hand to my right. And not-withstanding, all those miracles of disasters have crossed both them and me, yet were there not an Englishman remaining, as God be thanked notwithstanding the massacre there are some thousands; I would yet begin againe with as small meanes as I did at first, not that I have any secret encouragement (I protest) more then lamentable experience; for all their discoveries I have yet heard of, are but Pigs of my owne Sow, nor more strange to me, then to heare one tell me hee hath gone from Billingsgate and discovered Gravesend, Tilbury, Quinborow, Lee, and Margit, which to those did never heare of them, though they dwell in England, might bee made some rare secrets and great Countries unknowne, except some few Relations of Master Dirmer. In England, some are held great travellers that have seene Venice, and Rome, Madrill, Toledo, Sivill, Algere, Prague, or Ragousa, Constantinople, or Jerusalem, and the Piramides of Egypt; that thinke it nothing to goe to Summer Iles, or Virginia, which is as far as any of them; and I hope in time will prove a more profitable and a more laudable journey: as for the danger, you see our Ladies and Gentlewomen account it nothing now to goe thither; and therefore I hope all good men will better apprehend it, and not suffer them to languish in despaire, whom God so wonderfully and oft hath preserved.

What here I have writ by Relation, if it be not right I humbly intreat your pardons, but I have not spared any diligence to learne the truth of them that have beene actors, or sharers in those voyages; In some particulars they might deceive mee, but in the substance they could not: for few could tell me any thing, except where they fished. But seeing all those have lived there, doe confirme more then I have writ, I doubt not but all those testimonies with these new begun examples of Plantation, will move both Citie and Country, freely to adventure with me more then promises.

The objections against me.　But because some Fortune-tellers say, I am unfortunate; had they spent their time as I have done, they would rather beleeve in God then their calculations, and peradventure have given as bad an account of their actions, and therefore I intreat leave to answer those objecters, that thinke it strange, if this be true, I have made no more use of it, rest so long without imploiment, nor have no more reward nor preferment: To which I say;

My answer.　I thinke it more strange they should tax me, before they have tried as much as I have, both by land and sea, as well in Asia and Affrica, as Europe and America, where my Commanders were actors or spectators, they alwaies so freely rewarded me, I never needed bee importunate, or could I ever learne to beg: What there I got, I have spent; yet in Virginia I staied, till I left five hundred behinde me better provided then ever I was, from which blessed Virgin (ere I returned) sprung the fortunate habitation of Summer Iles.

This Virgins Sister, now called New England, at my humble sute, by our most gracious Prince Charles, hath beene neere as chargeable to me and my friends: for all which, although I never got shilling but it cost mee a pound, yet I would thinke my selfe happy could I see their prosperities.

But if it yet trouble a multitude to proceed upon *Considera-* these certainties, what thinke you I undertooke when *tions.* nothing was knowne but that there was a vast land? I never had power and meanes to doe any thing, though more hath beene spent in formall delaies then would have done the businesse, but in such a penurious and miserable manner, as if I had gone a begging to build an Universitie: where had men beene as forward to adventure their purses, and performe the conditions they promised mee, as to crop the fruits of my labours, thousands ere this had beene bettered by these designes. Thus betwixt the spur of desire and the bridle of reason, I am neere ridden to death in a ring of despaire; the reines are in your hands, therefore I intreat you ease me, and those that thinke I am either idle or unfortunate, may see the cause and know: unlesse I did see better dealing, I have had warning enough not to be so forward againe at every motion upon their promises, unlesse I intended nothing but to carie newes; for now they dare adventure a ship, that when I went first would not adventure a groat, so they may be at home againe by Michaelmas, which makes me remember and say with Master Hackluit; Oh incredulitie the wit of fooles, that slovingly doe spit at all things faire, a sluggards Cradle, a Cowards Castle, how easie it is to be an Infidell. But to the matter: By this all men may perceive, the ordinary performance of this voyage in five or six moneths, the plentie of fish is most certainly approved; and it is certaine, from Cannada and New England, within these six yeeres hath come neere twenty thousand Bever skinnes: Now had each of these ships transported but some small quantitie of the most increasing Beasts, Fowles, Fruits, Plants, and Seeds, as I projected; by this time their increase might have beene sufficient for more then one thousand men: But the desire of present game (in many) is so violent, and the endevours of many undertakers so negligent, every one so regarding their private game, that it is hard to effect any publike good, and impossible to bring them into a body, rule, or order, unlesse both honesty, as well as authoritie and money, assist experience. But your home-bred ingrossing Projecters will at last finde, there is a great difference betwixt saying and doing, or those that thinks their directions can be as soone and easily performed, as they can conceit them; or that their conceits are the fittest things to bee put in practise, or their countenances maintaine Plantations. But to conclude, the fishing will goe forward whether you plant it or no; whereby a Colony may be then transported with no great charge, that in short time might provide such fraughts, to buy on us there dwelling, as I would hope no ship should goe or come emptie from New England.

The charge of this is onely Salt, Nets, Hookes, Lines, Knives, Irish-rugges, course cloth, Beads, Glasse, and such trash, onely for fishing and trade with the Salvages, besides our owne necessarie provisions, whose endevours would quickly defray all this charge, and the Salvages did intreat me to inhabit where I would. Now all those ships till these last two yeeres, have beene fishing within a square of two or three leagues, and scarce any one yet will goe any further in the Port they fish in, where questionlesse five hundred may have their fraught as well as elsewhere, and be in the market ere others can have the fish in their ships, because New Englands fishing begins in February, in Newfoundland not till the midst of May; the progression hereof tends much to the advancement of Virginia and Summer Iles, whose empty ships may take in their fraughts there, and would be also in time of need a good friend to the Inhabitants of Newfoundland.

The returnes made by the Westerne men, are commonly divided in three parts; one for the owner of the ship; another for the Master and his Company; the third for the victualers, which course being still permitted, will be no hinderance to the Plantation as yet goe there never so many, but a meanes of transporting that yeerely for little or nothing, which otherwise wil cost many hundreds of pounds. If a ship can gaine twenty, thirty, fifty in the hundred; nay three hundred for one hundred in seven or ten moneths, as you see they have done, spending twice so much time in comming and going as in staying there: were I there planted, seeing the variety of the fishings serve the most part of the yeere, and with a little labour we might make all the Salt we need use, as is formerly said, and

The charge.

The order of the westerne men.

The gaines.

can conceive no reason to distrust of good successe by Gods assistance; besides for the building of ships, no place hath more convenient Harbours, ebbe, nor floud, nor better timber; and no Commoditie in Europe doth more decay then wood.

Master Dee his opinion for the building of ships.

MASTER Dee recordeth in his Brittish Monarchy, that King Edgar had a Navy of foure thousand saile, with which he yeerely made his progresse, about this famous Monarchy of Great Britaine, largely declaring the benefit thereof; whereupon hee projected to our most memorable Queene Elizabeth, the erecting of a Fleet of sixty Saile, he called a little Navy Royall: imitating that admired Pericles Prince of Athens, that could never secure that tormented estate, untill he was Lord and Captaine of the Sea. At this none need wonder, for who knowes not her Royall Majestie during her life, by the incredible adventures of her Royall Navy, and valiant Souldiers and Sea-men, notwithstanding all treacheries at home, the protecting and defending France and Holland, and reconquering Ireland; yet all the world by Sea and Land both feared or loved, and admired good Queene Elizabeth. Both to maintaine and increase that incomparable honour (God be thanked) to her incomparable Successor, our most Royall Lord and Soveraigne King James, this great Philosopher hath left this to his Majestie and his Kingdomes consideration: that if the tenths of the earth be proper to God, it is also due by Sea. The Kings high waies are common to passe, but not to dig for Mines or any thing: So Englands Coasts are free to passe but not to fish, but by his Majesties Prerogative.

His Majesty of Spaine permits none to passe the Popes order, for the East and West Indies but by his permission, or at their perils; if all that world be so justly theirs, it is no injustice for England to make as much use of her owne shores as strangers doe, that pay to their owne Lords the tenth, and not to the owner of those liberties any thing to speake of, whose subjects may neither take nor sell any in their Teritories: which small tribute would maintaine this little Navy Royall, and not cost his Majesty a peny, and yet maintaine peace with all Forrainers, and allow them more courtesie then any Nation in the world affords to England. It were a shame to alleage, that Holland is more worthy to enjoy our fishing as Lords thereof, because they have more skill to handle it then we, as they can our wooll and undressed Cloth, notwithstanding all their warres and troublesome disorders.

How to get money to build this little Navy. To get money to build this Navy, he saith, who would not spare the one hundreth penny of his rents, and the five hundreth penny of his goods; each servant that taketh forty shillings wages, foure pence; and every forrainer of seven yeeres of age foure pence, for seven yeeres; not any of these but they will spend three times so much in pride, wantonnesse, or some superfluitie: And doe any men love the securitie of their estates, that of themselves would not bee humble suters to his Majesty to doe this of free will as a voluntary benevolence, or but the one halfe of this (or some such other course as I have propounded to divers of the Companies) free from any constraint, tax, lottery, or imposition; so it may be as honestly and truly imploied, as it is projected, the poorest Mechanicke in this Kingdom would gaine by it. Then you might build ships of any proportion and numbers you please, five times cheaper then you can doe here, and have good merchandize for their fraught in this unknowne Land, to the advancement of Gods glory, his Church and Gospel, and the strengthning and releefe of a great part of Christendome without hurt to any, to the terror of Pirats, the amazement of enemies, the assistance of friends, the securing Merchants, and so much increase of Navigation, to make Englands trade and shipping as much as any Nations in the world, besides a hundred other benefits, to the generall good of all true subjects, and would cause thousands yet unborne to blesse the time, and all them that first put it in practise.

Contention for New-Englands goods, not her good. Now lest it should be obscured as it hath beene to privat ends, or so weakely undertaken by our overweening incredulity, that strangers may possesse it whilest we contend for New-Englands goods, but not Englands good; I have presented it as I have said, to the Prince and Nobility, the Gentry and Commonalty, hoping at last it will move the whole land to know it and consider of it; since I can finde them wood and halfe victuall, with the foresaid advantages: were this Country planted, with what facility they may build and maintaine this little Navy Royall, both with honour, profit and content, and inhabit as good a Country as any in the world within that paralell, which with my life and what I have, I will endevour to effect, if God please and you permit. But no man will goe from hence to have lesse freedome there then here, nor adventure all they have to prepare the way for them will scarce thanke them for it; and it is too well knowne there have beene so many undertakers of Patents, and such sharing of them, as hath bred no lesse discouragement then wonder, to heare such great promises and so little performance; in the Interim, you see the French and Dutch already frequent it, and God forbid they in Virginia, or any of his Majesties subjects, should not have as free liberty as they. To conclude, were it not for Master Cherley and a few private adventurers with them, what have we there for all these inducements? As for them whom pride or covetousnesse lulleth asleepe in a Cradle of slothfull carelesnesse, would they but consider how all the great Monarchies of the earth have beene brought to confusion, or but remember the late lamentable experiences of Constantinople, and how many Cities, Townes and Provinces, in the faire rich Kingdoms of Hungaria, Transilvania, Wallachia and Moldavia, and how many thousands of Princes, Earles, Barons, Knights, Merchants, and others, have in one day lost goods, lives and honours, or sold for slaves like beasts in a market place, their wives, children and servants slaine, or wandring they knew not whither, dying or living in all extremities of extreme miseries and calamities, surely they would not onely doe this, but give all they have to enjoy peace and liberty at home, or but adventure their persons abroad; to prevent the conclusions of a conquering Foe, who commonly assaulteth and best prevaileth where he findeth wealth and plenty, most armed with ignorance and security.

The necessity of martiall power.

Though the true condition of warre is onely to suppresse the proud and defend the innocent, as did that most generous Prince Sigismundus, Prince of those Countries, against them whom under the colour of justice and piety, to maintaine their superfluity of ambitious pride, thought all the world too little to maintaine their vice, and undoe them, or keepe them from ability to doe any thing, that would not admire and adore their honours, fortunes, covetousnesse, falshood, bribery, cruelty, extortion, and ingratitude, which is worse then cowardize or ignorance, and all manner of vildnesse, cleane contrary to all honour, vertue, and noblenesse.

John Smith writ this with his owne hand.

Here follow certaine notes and observations of Captaine Charles Whitbourne concerning New-found land, which although every master trained up in fishing, can make their proportions of necessaries according to their custome, yet it is not much amisse here to insert them, that every one which desires the good of those actions know them also. Besides in his Booke intituled, *A discovery of New-found land, and the commodities thereof,* you shall finde many excellent good advertisements for a Plantation; and how that most yeeres this Coast hath beene frequented with 250. saile of his Majesties subjects, which supposing but 60. tunnes a peece, one with another, they amount to 15000. tunnes, and allowing 25. men and boies to every Barke, they will make 5000. persons, whose labours returne yeerely to about 135000. pound sterling, besides the great numbers of Brewers, Bakers, Coupers, Ship-Carpenters, Net-makers, Rope-makers, Hooke-makers, and the most of all other mecanicall trades in England.

The charge of setting forth a ship of 100. tuns
with 40. persons, both to make a fishing voyage,
and increase the Plantation.

	l.	s.	d.
Inprimis, 11000. weight of Bisket at 15s. a 100. weight.	82.	10.	
26 Tun of Beere and Sider at 53.s. 4.d. a Tun.	69.	7.	
2 Hogsheads of English Beefe.	10.		
2 Hogsheads of Irish Beefe.	5.		
10 Fat Hogs salted with Salt and Caske.	10.	10.	
30 Bushels of Pease.	6.		

	l.	s.	d.
2 Ferkins of Butter.	3.		
200 Waight of Cheese.	2.	10.	
1 Bushell of Mustard-seed.		6.	
1 Hogshead of Vinegar.	1.	5.	
Wood to dresse meat withall.	1.		
1 Great Copper Kettle.	2.		
2 Small Kettles.	2.		
2 Frying-Pans.		3.	4.
Platters, Ladles and Cans.	1.		
a paire of Bellowes for the Cooke.		2.	6.
Taps, Boriers and Funnels.		2.	
Locks for the Bread roomes.		2.	6.
100 weight of Candles.	2.	10.	
130 quarters of Salt at 2.s. the Bushell.	104.		
Mats and dinnage to lie under it.	2.	10.	
Salt Shovels.		10.	
Particulars for the 40. persons to keepe 8. fishing boats at Sea, with 3. men in every boat, imploies 24.; and 500. foot of Elme boords of an inch thicke, 8.s. each one.	2.		
2000 Nailes for the 8. Boats, at 13.s. 4.d. a 1000	1.	6.	8.
4000 Nailes at 6.s. 8.d. a 1000.	1.	6.	8.
2000 Nailes at 5.d. a 100.		8.	
500 weight of pitch at 8.s. a 100.	2.		
2000 of good orlop nailes.	2.	5.	
More for other small necessaries.	3.		
A barrell of Tar.		10.	
200 weight of black Ocome.	1.		
Thrums for pitch Maps.		1.	6.
Bolls, Buckets and Pumps.	1.		
2 brazen Crocks.	2.		
Canvas to make Boat sailes and small ropes, at 25.s. for each saile.	12.	10.	
10 rode Ropes which contain 600. weight, at 30.s. the 100.	10.		
12 dozen of fishing lines.	6.		
24 dozen of fishing hookes.	2.		
for Squid line.		3.	
For Pots and liver maunds.		18.	
Iron works for the boats ruthers.	2.		

	l.	s.	d.
10 Kipnet Irons.		10.	
Twine to make kipnets and gagging hooks.		6.	
10 good Nets at 26.s. a net.	13.		
2 Saynes, a great and a lesse.	12.		
200 weight of Sow-lead.	1.		
2 couple of ropes for the Saynes.	1.		
Dry-fats to keepe them in.		6.	
Twine for store.		5.	
Flaskets and bread Baskets.		15.	
For haire cloth.	10.		
3. Tuns of vinegar caske, for water	1.	6.	8.
1 douzen of Deale Bourds.		10.	
2 Barrels of Oatmeale.	1.	6.	
100 weight of Spikes.	2.	5.	
2 good Axes, 4. hand Hatchets, 4. Drawers, 2. drawing Irons.		16.	
3 yards of wollen cloth for cuffs.		10.	
8 yards of good Canvasse.		10.	
A Grind-stone or two.		6.	
2000 of poore John to spend in going.	6.	10.	
1 Hogshead of Aquavitæ	4.		
4 arme Sawes, 4. Handsawes, 4. thwart Sawes, 3. Augers, 2. Crowes of Iron, 3. Sledges, 4. shod Shovels, 2. Picaxes, 4. Matocks, and 4. Hammers.	5.		
The totall summe is	420.	1.	4.

All these provisions the Master or Purser is to be account-able what is spent and what is left, with those which shall con-tinue there to plant, and of the 40. thus provided for the voyage, ten may well be spared to leave behind them, with 500. weight of Bisket, 5. hogsheads of Sider or beere, halfe a hogshead of Beefe, 4. sides of dry Bakon, 4. bushell of Pease, halfe a ferkin of Butter, halfe 100. weight of Cheese, a pecke of Mustard-seed, a barrell of Vinegar, 12. pound of Candles, 2. pecks of Oatmeale, halfe a hogshead of Aquavitæ, 2. copper Kettles, 1. brasse Crock, 1. Frying-pan, a Grindstone, and all the Hatchets, Woodhooks, Sawes, Augers, etc. and all other iron tooles, with the 8. Boats and their implements, and spare salt, and what else they use not in a readinesse from yeere to yeere, and in the meane time served them to helpe to build their houses, cleanse land, and further their fishing whilst the ships are wanting.

By his estimation and calculation these 8. Boats with 22. men in a Summer doe usually kill 25000. fish for every Boat, which may amount to 200000. allowing 120. fishes to the 100. sometimes they have taken above 35000. for a Boat, so that they load not onely their owne ship, but provide great quantities for sacks, or other spare ships which come thither onely to buy the overplus: if such ships come not, they give over taking any more, when sometimes there hath beene great abundance, because there is no fit houses to lay them in till another yeere, now most of those sacks goeth empty thither, which might as well transport mens provision and cattle at an easie rate as nothing, either to New-England or New-found land, but either to transport them for nothing or pay any great matter for their liberty to fish, will hardly effect so much as freedome as yet; nor can this be put in practice as before I said, till there be a power there well planted and setled to entertaine and defend them, assist and releeve them as occasion shall require, otherwaies those small divisions will effect little, but such miserable conclusions as both the French and we too long have tried to our costs. Now commonly 200000. fish will load a ship of 100. tunnes in New-found land, but halfe so many will neere doe it in New-England, which carried to Toloune or Merselus, where the custome is small, and the Kintall lesse then 90. English pounds weight, and the prise when least, 12. shillings the Kintall, which at that rate amounts to 1320.l. starling; and the ship may either there be discharged or imployed as hath beene said to refraught for England, so that the next yeere she may be ready to goe her fishing voyage againe, at a farre cheaper rate then before.

To this adde but 12. tuns of traine oile, which delivered in New-found land is 10.l. the tun, makes 120.l. then it is hard if there be not 10000. of Cor-fish, which also sold there at 5.l. the 1000. makes 50.l. which brought to England, in some places yeelds neere halfe so much more; but if at Merselus it be sold for 16.s. the Kentall, as commonly it is, and much dearer, it amounts to 1760.l. and if the Boats follow the fishing till the

15. of October, they may take 80000. more, which with their traine in New-found land at 4.l. the 1000. will amount to 320.l. which added to 1320.l. with 120.l. for Oile, and 10000. of Cor-fish 50.l. and the overplus at Merselus, which will be 440.l. make the totall 2250.l. which divided in three parts according to their custome, the Victualer hath for the former particulars, amounting to 420.l. 751.l. so all the charge defraied, hee gaines 331.l. 11.ŝ. then for the fraught of the ship there is 751.l. and so much for the Master and his company, which comparing with the voiages hath beene made to New-England, you may easily finde which is the better though both bee good. But now experience hath taught them at New-Plimoth, that in Aprill there is a fish much like a Herring that comes up into the small Brookes to spawne, and where the water is not knee deepe, they will presse up through your hands, yea though you beat at them with Cudgels, and in such abundance as is incredible, which they take with that facility they manure their land with them when they have occasion; after those the Cod also presseth in such plenty, even into the very Harbours, they have caught some in their armes, and hooke them so fast, three men oft loadeth a Boat of two tuns in two houres, where before they used most to fish in deepe water.

The facility of the fishing lately observed.

The present estate of New-Plimoth.

The present estate of the plantation at New-Plimoth. 1624.

AT New-Plimoth there is about 180 persons, some cattell and goats, but many swine and poultry, 32 dwelling houses, whereof 7 were burnt the last winter, and the value of five hundred pounds in other goods; the Towne is impaled about halfe a mile compasse. In the towne upon a high Mount they have a Fort well built with wood, lome, and stone, where is planted their Ordnance: Also a faire Watch-tower, partly framed for the Sentinell, the place it seemes is healthfull, for in these last three yeeres, notwithstanding their great want of most necessaries, there hath not one died of the first planters, they have made a saltworke, and

with that salt preserve the fish they take, and this yeare hath
fraughted a ship of 180. tunnes. The Governour is one Master
William Bradford, their Captaine Miles Standish, a bred
Souldier in Holland; the chiefe men for their assistance is Master Isaak Alderton, and divers others as occasion
serveth; their Preachers are Master William Bruster
and Master John Layford.

Their order
of govern-
ment.

    The most of them live together as one family or houshold,
yet every man followeth his trade and profession both by sea
and land, and all for a generall stocke, out of which they have
all their maintenance, untill there be a divident betwixt the
Planters and the Adventurers. Those Planters are not servants
to the Adventurers here, but have onely councells of directions
from them, but no injunctions or command, and all the masters
of families are partners in land or whatsoever, setting their
labours against the stocke, till certaine yeeres be expired for
the division: they have young men and boies for their Apprentises and servants, and some of them speciall families, as Ship-
carpenters, Salt-makers, Fish-masters, yet as servants upon
great wages. The Adventurers which raised the stocke to begin
and supply this Plantation were about 70. some Gentlemen,
some Merchants, some handy-crafts men, some adventuring
great summes, some small, as their estates and affection
served. The generall stocke already imploied is about 7000.l.
by reason of which charge and many crosses, many of them
would adventure no more, but others that knowes, so great a
designe cannot bee effected without both charge, losse and
crosses, are resolved to goe forward with it to their powers;
which deserve no small commendations and encouragement.
These dwell most about London, they are not a corporation,
but knit together by a voluntary combination in a society without constraint or penalty, aiming to doe good and to plant Religion; they have a President and Treasurer, every yeere newly
chosen by the most voices, who ordereth the affaires of their
Courts and meetings, and with the assent of the most of them,
undertaketh all ordinary businesses, but in more weighty affaires, the assent of the whole Company is required. There hath
beene a fishing this yeere upon the Coast about 50. English
ships: and by Cape Anne, there is a Plantation a beginning by

the Dorchester men, which they hold of those of New-Plimoth, who also by them have set up a fishing worke; some talke there is some other pretended Plantations, all whose good proceedings the eternal God protect and preserve. And these have beene the true proceedings and accidents in those Plantations.

Now to make a particular relation of all the acts and orders in the Courts belonging unto them, of the anihilating old Patents and procuring new; with the charge, paines and arguments, the reasons of such changes, all the treaties, consultations, orations, and dissentions about the sharing and dividing those large territories, confirming of Counsailers, electing all sorts of Officers, directions, Letters of advice, and their answers, disputations about the Magazines and Impositions, suters for Patents, positions for Freedomes, and confirmations with complaints of injuries here, and also the mutinies, examinations, arraignements, executions, and the cause of the so oft revolt of the Salvages at large, as many would have had, and it may be some doe expect it would make more quarrels then any of them would willingly answer, and such a volume as would tire any wise man but to read the contents; for my owne part I rather feare the unpartiall Reader wil thinke this rather more tedious then necessary: but he that would be a practitioner in those affaires, I hope will allow them not only needfull but expedient: but how ever, if you please to beare with those errors I have committed, if God please I live, my care and paines shall endevour to be thankfull: if I die, accept my good will: If any desire to be further satisfied, what defect is found in this, they shall finde supplied in me, that thus freely have throwne my selfe with my mite into the Treasury of my Countries good, not doubting but God will stirre up some noble spirits to consider and examine if worthy Columbus could give the Spaniards any such certainties for his designe, when Queene Isabel of Spaine set him forth with 15. saile, and though I promise no Mines of gold, yet the warlike Hollanders let us imitate but not hate, whose wealth and strength are good testimonies of their treasury gotten by fishing; and New-England hath yeelded already by generall computation one hundred thousand pounds at the least. Therefore honourable and worthy Country men, let not the meannesse of the word fish distaste you, for it will afford as good gold as the Mines of Guiana or Potassie, with lesse hazard and charge, and more certainty and facility.

J.S.

FINIS.

THE TRUE TRAVELS, ADVENTURES, AND OBSEVATIONS

of

Captaine JOHN SMITH,

In Europe, Asia, Affrica, and America, from *Anno Domini* 1593. to 1629.

His Accidents and Sea-fights in the Straights; his Service
and Stratagems of warre in Hungaria, Transilvania, Wallachia, and
Moldavia, against the Turks, and Tartars; his three single combats
betwixt the Christian Armie and the Turkes.

After how he was taken prisoner by the Turks, sold for a Slave, sent into
Tartaria; his description of the Tartars, their strange manners and customes
of Religions, Diets, Buildings, Warres, Feasts, Ceremonies, and
Living; how hee slew the Bashaw of Nalbrits in Cambia,
and escaped from the Turkes and Tartars.

Together with a continuation of his generall History of Virginia,
Summer-Iles, New England, and their proceedings, since 1624 to this
present 1629; as also of the new Plantations of the great
River of the Amazons, the Iles of St. Christopher, Mevis,
and Barbados in the West Indies.

All written by actuall Authours, whose names
you shall finde along the History.

1630

Vincere est Viuere

Accordamus

Fecill scu

TO THE RIGHT HONOURABLE,
William *Earle of Pembroke*,
Lord Steward of his Majesties
most Honourable Houshold.
Robert *Earle of Lindsey*,
Great Chamberlaine of England.
Henrie *Lord Hunsdon*, *Vicount Rochford*,
Earle of Dover.
And all your Honourable Friends
and Well-willers.

My Lords:

Sir Robert Cotton, that most learned Treasurer of Antiquitie, having by perusall of my Generall Historie, and
others, found that I had likewise undergone divers other as
hard hazards in the other parts of the world, requested me to
fix the whole course of my passages in a booke by it selfe,
whose noble desire I could not but in part satisfie; the rather,
because they have acted my fatall Tragedies upon the Stage,
and racked my Relations at their pleasure. To prevent therefore all future misprisions, I have compiled this true discourse.
Envie hath taxed me to have writ too much, and done too
little; but that such should know, how little I esteeme them, I
have writ this, more for the satisfaction of my friends, and all
generous and well disposed Readers: To speake only of my
selfe were intolerable ingratitude; because, having had so many
co-partners with me; I cannot make a Monument for my selfe,
and leave them unburied in the fields, whose lives begot me
the title of a Souldier; for as they were companions with me in
my dangers, so shall they be partakers with me in this Tombe.

For my Sea Grammar (caused to bee printed by my worthy
friend, Sir Samuel Saltonstall) hath found such good entertainment abroad, that I have beene importuned by many noble
persons, to let this also passe the Presse. Many of the most eminent Warriers, and others, what their swords did, their penns
writ: Though I bee never so much their inferiour, yet I hold it
no great errour, to follow good examples; nor repine at them,
will doe the like.

673

And now my most Honourable good Lords, I know not to whom I may better present it, than to your Lordships, whose friendships, as I conceive, are as much to each others, as my duty is to you all; and because you are acquainted both with my endevours, and writings, I doubt not, but your honours will as well accept of this, as of the rest, and Patronize it under the shadow of your most noble vertues, which I am ever bound in all duty to reverence, and under which I hope to have shelter, against all stormes that dare threaten.

Your Honours to be commanded,
John Smith.

The Contents of the severall Chapters.

TO MY WORTHY FRIEND,
Captaine John Smith.

Two greatest Shires of England *did thee beare,*
Renowned Yorkshire, *Gaunt-stild* Lancashire;
But what's all this? even Earth, Sea, Heaven above,
Tragabigzanda, Callamata's *love,*
Deare Pocahontas, *Madam* Shanoi's *too,*
Who did what love with modesty could doe:
Record thy worth, thy birth, which as I live,
Even in thy reading such choice solace give,
As I could wish (such wishes would doe well)
Many such Smiths *in this our* Israel.

R. Brathwait.

TO MY NOBLE
brother and friend,
Captaine John Smith.

Thou hast a course so full of honour runne,
Envy may snarle, as dogges against the Sunne
May barke, not bite: for what deservedly
With thy lifes danger, valour, pollicy,
Quaint warlike stratagems, abillity
And judgement, thou hast got, fame sets so high
Detraction cannot reach: thy worth shall stand
A patterne to succeeding ages, and
Cloth'd in thy owne lines, ever shall adde grace,
Unto thy native Country and thy race;
And when dissolv'd, laid in thy mothers wombe,
These, Cæsar-*like,* Smiths *Epitaph and tombe.*

Anthony Fereby.

TO HIS VALIANT
and deserving friend,
Captaine John Smith.

Mongst Frenchmen, Spanyards, Hungars, Tartars, Turks,
And wilde Virginians *too, this tells thy works:*
Now some will aske, what benefit? what gaine?
Is added to thy store for all this paine?
Th' art then content to say, content is all,
Th'ast got content for perils, paine and thrall;
Tis lost to looke for more: for few men now
Regard Wit, Learning, Valour; but allow
The quintessence of praise to him that can
Number his owne got gold, and riches, than
Th' art Valiant, Learned, Wise; Pauls *counsell will,*
Admire thy merits, magnifie thy skill.
The last of thine to which I set my hand
Was a Sea Grammar; *this by Sea and Land,*
Serves us for imitation: I know none,
That like thy selfe hast come, and runne, and gone,
To such praise-worthy actions: bee't approv'd,
Th'ast well deserv'd of best men to be lov'd:
If France, *or* Spaine, *or any forren soile*
Could claime thee theirs, for these thy paines and toile,
Th' adst got reward and honour: now adayes,
What our owne natives doe, we seldome praise.

Good men will yeeld thee praise; then sleight the rest;
Tis best praise-worthy to have pleas'd the best.

Tuissimus Ed. Jorden.

TO MY WORTHY FRIEND,
Captaine John Smith.

Deare noble Captaine, who by Sea and Land,
To act the earnest of thy name hast hand
And heart; who canst with skill designe the Fort,
The Leaguer, Harbour, City, Shore, and Port:
Whose sword and pen in bold, ruffe, Martiall wise,
Put forth to try and beare away the prize,
From Cæsar *and* Blaize Monluc: *Can it be,*
That Men alone in Gonnels *fortune see*
Thy worth advanc'd? no wonder since our age,
Is now at large a Bedlem or a Stage.

Rich. James.

TO HIS WORTHY FRIEND,
Captaine John Smith.

Thou that hast had a spirit to flie like thunder,
Without thy Countries charge through those strange dangers,
Doth make my muse amaz'd, and more to wonder,
That thy deserts should shared be by strangers,
And thou neglected; (ah miracle!) most lamented,
At thy great patience thus to rest contented.

For none can truly say thou didst deceive,
Thy Souldiers, Sailers, Merchants, nor thy friends,
But all from thee a true account receive,
Yet nought to thee all these thy vertues brings;
Is none so noble to advance thy merit,
If any be, let him thy praise inherit.

Ma. Hawkins.

TO MY WORTHY FRIEND,
Captaine John Smith.

To combate with three Turks in single du'le,
  Before two Armies, who the like hath done?
Slaine thy great Jailor; found a common weale
  In faire America *where; thou hast wonne*
No lesse renowne amongst their Savage Kings,
  Than Turkish warres, that thus thy honour sings.

Could not those tyrants daunt thy matchlesse spirit,
  Nor all the cruelty of envies spight:
Will not thy Country yet reward thy merit,
  Nor in thy acts and writings take delight?
Which here in so few sheets doth more expresse
  Than volumes great, this is thy happinesse.

Richard Meade.

TO MY WELL DESERVING
friend, Captaine John Smith.

Thou hast no need to covet new applause,
  Nor doe I thinke vaine-glory moves thee to it;
But since it is thy will (though without cause)
  To move a needlesse thing, yet will I doe it:
Doe it in briefe I will, or else I doe the wrong,
  And say, read or'e Captaine Smiths *former song;*
His first then will invite thee to his latter:
  Reader 'tis true; *I am not brib'd to flatter.*

Edw. Ingham.

TO HIS APPROVED
friend, the Authour;
Captaine John Smith.

The old Greeke Bard, *counts him the onely man,*
  Who knowes strange Countries, like his Ithacan,
  And wise, as valiant, by his observation,
  Can tell the severall customes of each Nation:
All these are met in thee, who will not then
Repute thee in the ranke of worthiest men?

  To th' Westerne world to former times unknowne,
  Thy active spirit hath thy valour showne:
  The Turks *and* Tartars *both can testifie,*
  Thee t' have deserv'd a Captaines dignity;
But verse thou need'st not to expresse thy worth,
Thy acts, this booke doe plainly set it forth.

M. Cartner.

TO THE VALOUROUS
and truly-vertuous souldier,
Captaine John Smith.

No* Faith in Campe? *tis false: see pious* Smith
Hath brought stragling Astræa *backe, and with*
An all-outdaring spirit made Valour *stand*
Upheld by Vertue *in bold* Mars *his land:*
If Valourous, *be praise; how great's his* Name?
Whose Valour *joynd with* Vertue *laud's his* Fame.
T'was Homers *boast of wise* Laertes *sonne,*
†*Well-read in men and Cities: than thou none*
(*Great* Smith) *of these can more true tales rehearse;*
What want thy praises then, but Homers *verse?*

*Nulla fides pietasque viris, qui castra sequuntur.
†πολλῶν δ' ἀιθρώπων ἴδεν ἀϛεα, χj νόον ἔγνω. Hom. Odyss. *a.*

Jn Smithum Distichon.

Quisque suæ sortis* Faber: an Faber exstitit unquam
  Te (Smithe) fortunæ verior usque suæ?

*Appius.

I. C.
C. P.

TO HIS NOBLE FRIEND,
Captaine John Smith.

To see bright honour sparkled all in gore,
Would steele a spirit that ne're fought before:
And that's the height of Fame, when our best bloud,
Is nobly spilt in actions great and good:
So thou hast taught the world to purchase Fame,
Rearing thy story on a glorious frame,
And such foundation doth thy merits make it,
As all detractions rage shall never shake it;
Thy actions crowne themselves, and thy owne pen,
Gives them the best and truest Epiphonem.

Brian O Rourke.

TO HIS TRULY
deserving friend,
Captaine John Smith.

Can one please all? there's none from Censure *free,*
To looke for't then it were absurd in thee;
It's easie worke to censure sweetest Layes,
Where Ignorance *is* Judge *thou'd have no praise:*
Wisdome *I know will mildly judge of all,*
Envious hearts, tongues, pennes, are dippt in Gall.
Proud malignant times will you now bring forth
Monsters *at least to snarle at others worth;*

O doe not so, but wisely looke on him
That wrought such Honours *for his* Countries King:
Of Turks *and* Tartars *thou hast wonne the field,*
The great Bashaw *his* Courage *thou host quel'd;*
In the Hungarian warre *thou'st shewd thy* Arts,
Prov'd thy Selfe *a* Souldier *true in all parts:*
Thy Armes *are deckt with that thy* Sword *hath wonne,*
Which mallice can't out-weare till day be done:
For three proud Turks *in single fight thou'st slue,*
Their Heads adorne *thy* Armes, *for witnesse true;*
Let Mars *and* Neptune *both with* Pregnant *wit,*
Extoll thy due deserts, Ile pray for it.

Salo. Tanner.

Capt SMITH throwne into the Sea gott safe to Shore, and was releeued Chap. 2.

The Coast of Tunis BARBARIE

Bugia

S.t Mayies Ile

The Coast of SAVOY

NICE

Tollonnt

Part of the Trauels of C. TARTARS, and others. ex.

How hee releeued OLVMPA

His three single Combats before REGALL in TRANSILVANIA His Encounter with TVRBASHAW Chap. 7.

His Combat with GRVALG C.

Capt SMITH led Captiue to the BASHAW of NALBRITS in TARTARIA. Chap. 12.

Smith   Drub. man   Basham

Three TVRKS heads in

P.Sigismundus

P.Moyses

MRien Dr. sculptor

How he was presented to

SMITH a mongst TVRKES
t of the HISTORY by IOHN PAYN

stagem of Lights Chap. 4

The Siege of REGALL in Transiluania Chap 7

threehundred horsmen.

How he slew BONNY:MVLGRO. Chap · 7

him for Armes. Chap · 8

Capt SMITH Killeth the BASHAW
of Nalbrits and on his horse
escapeth Chap · 17

VNDVS. Chap · 8

London Printed
by Iames Reeue

THE TRUE TRAVELS,
ADVENTURES, AND
OBSERVATIONS

Of Captaine John Smith,
in *Europe*, *Asia*, *Africke*, and *America*:
beginning about the yeere 1593, and
continued to this present 1629.

Chapter I.
His Birth; Apprentiship; Going into France;
His beginning with ten shillings and three pence;
His Service in Netherlands; His bad passage
into Scotland; His returne to Willoughby; And how
he lived in the Woods.

H E was borne in Willoughby in Lincolne-shire, and a
Scholler in the two Free-schooles of Alford and Louth.
His father anciently descended from the ancient Smiths of
Crudley in Lancashire; his mother from the Rickards at great
Heck in York-shire.

His parents dying when he was about thirteene yeeres of age,
left him a competent meanes, which hee not being capable to
manage, little regarded; his minde being even then set upon
brave adventures, sould his Satchell, bookes, and all he had, intending secretly to get to Sea, but that his fathers death stayed
him. But now the Guardians of his estate more regarding it
than him, he had libertie enough, though no meanes, to get
beyond the Sea. About the age of fifteene yeeres hee was
bound an Apprentice to Master Thomas Sendall of Linne, the
greatest Merchant of all those parts; but because hee would
not presently send him to Sea, he never saw his master in eight
yeeres after.

At last he found meanes to attend Master Perigrine Barty
into France, second sonne to the Right Honourable Perigrine,
that generous Lord Willoughby, and famous Souldier; where
comming to his brother Robert, then at Orleans, now Earle of

Linsey, and Lord great Chamberlaine of England; being then but little youths under Tutorage: his service being needlesse, within a moneth or six weekes they sent him backe againe to his friends; who when he came from London they liberally gave him (but out of his owne estate) ten shillings to be rid of him; such oft is the share of fatherlesse children: but those two Honourable Brethren gave him sufficient to returne for England. But it was the least thought of his determination, for now being freely at libertie in Paris, growing acquainted with one Master David Hume, who making some use of his purse, gave him Letters to his friends in Scotland to preferre him to King James. Arriving at Roane, he better bethinkes himselfe, seeing his money neere spent, downe the River he went to Haver de grace, where he first began to learne the life of a souldier: Peace being concluded in France, he went with Captaine Joseph Duxbury into the Low-countries, under whose Colours having served three or foure yeeres, he tooke his journey for Scotland, to deliver his Letters.

At Ancusan he imbarked himselfe for Lethe, but as much danger, as shipwracke and sicknesse could endure, hee had at the holy Ile in Northumberland neere Barwicke: (being recovered) into Scotland he went to deliver his Letters.

After much kinde usage amongst those honest Scots at Ripweth and Broxmoth, but neither money nor meanes to make him a Courtier, he returned to Willoughby in Lincolne-shire; where within a short time being glutted with too much company, wherein he took small delight, he retired himselfe into a little wooddie pasture, a good way from any towne, invironed with many hundred Acres of other woods: Here by a faire brook he built a Pavillion of boughes, where only in his cloaths he lay. His studie was Machiavills Art of warre, and Marcus Aurelius; his exercise a good horse, with his lance and Ring; his food was thought to be more of venison than any thing else; what he wanted his man brought him. The countrey wondering at such an Hermite; His friends perswaded one Seignior Theadora Polaloga, Rider to Henry Earle of Lincolne, an excellent Horse-man, and a noble Italian Gentleman, to insinuate into his wooddish acquaintances, whose Languages and good discourse, and exercise of riding drew him to stay with him at Tattersall. Long these pleasures could not content him, but hee returned againe to the Low-Countreyes.

Chapter II.
The notable villany of foure French Gallants; and his revenge; Smith throwne over-board; Captaine La Roche of Saint Malo releeves him.

THUS when France and Netherlands had taught him to ride a Horse and use his Armes, with such rudiments of warre, as his tender yeeres in those martiall Schooles could attaine unto; he was desirous to see more of the world, and trie his fortune against the Turkes, both lamenting and repenting to have seene so many Christians slaughter one another. Opportunitie casting him into the company of foure French Gallants well attended, faining to him the one to be a great Lord, the rest his Gentlemen, and that they were all devoted that way; over-perswaded him to goe with them into France, to the Dutchesse of Mercury, from whom they should not only have meanes, but also Letters of favour to her noble Duke, then Generall for the Emperour Rodolphus in Hungary; which he did, with such ill weather as winter affordeth, in the darke night they arrived in the broad shallow In-let of Saint Valleries sur Some in Picardie; his French Lord knowing he had good apparell, and better furnished with money than themselves, so plotted with the Master of the ship to set his and their owne trunckes a shore leaving Smith aboard till the boat could returne, which was the next day after towards evening; the reason hee alleaged was the sea went so high hee could come no sooner, and that his Lord was gone to Amiens where they would stay his comming; which treacherous villany, when divers other souldiers, and passengers understood, they had like to have slaine the Master, and had they knowne how, would have runne away with the ship.

Comming on shore hee had but one Carralue, was forced to sell his cloake to pay for his passage. One of the souldiers, called Curzianvere, compassionating

A notable villan of foure French Gallants.

A Carralue is value a penny.

his injury, assured him this great Lord Depreau was only the sonne of a Lawyer of Mortaigne in base Britany, and his Attendants Cursell, La Nelie, and Monferrat, three young citizens, as arrant cheats as himselfe; but if he would accompany him, he would bring him to their friends, but in the interim supplied his wants: thus travelling by Deepe, Codebeck, Humphla, Pount-demer in Normandie, they came to Cane in base Normandie; where both this noble Curzianvere, and the great Prior of the great Abbey of Saint Steven (where is the ruinous Tombe of William the Conquerour,) and many other of his friends kindly welcomed him, and brought him to Mortaigne, where hee found Depreau and the rest, but to small purpose; for Master Curzianvere was a banished man, and durst not be seene, but to his friends: yet the bruit of their cosenage occasioned the Lady Collumber, the Baron Larshan, the Lord Shasghe, and divers other honourable persons, to supply his wants, and with them to recreate himselfe so long as hee would: but such pleasant pleasures suited little with his poore estate, and his restlesse spirit, that could never finde content, to receive such noble favours, as he could neither deserve nor requite: but wandring from Port to Port to finde some man of war, spent that he had, and in a Forest, neere dead with griefe and cold, a rich Farmer found him by a faire Fountaine under a tree: This kinde Pesant releeved him againe to his content, to follow his intent. Not long after, as he passed thorow a great grove of trees, betweene Pounterson and Dina in Britaine, it was his chance to meet Cursell, more miserable than himselfe: His piercing injuries had so small patience, as without any word they both drew, and in a short time Cursell fell to the ground, where from an old ruinated Tower the inhabitants seeing them, were satisfied, when they heard Cursell confesse what had formerly passed; and that how in the dividing that they had stolne from him, they fell by the ears amongst themselves, that were actors in it; but for his part, he excused himselfe to be innocent as well of the one, as of the other. In regard of his hurt, Smith was glad to be so rid of him, directing his course to an honourable Lord, the Earle of Ployer, who during the warre in France, with his two brethren, Viscount Poomory, and Baron d' Mercy, who had beene brought up in England;

Here he incountred one of the theeves.

The noblenesse of the Earle of Ployer.

by him he was better refurnished than ever. When they had shewed him Saint Malo, Mount Saint Michael, Lambal, Simbreack, Lanion, and their owne faire Castle of Tuncadeck, Gingan, and divers other places in Britanny, (and their Brittish Cornwaile) taking his leave, he tooke his way to Raynes, the Britaines chiefe Citie, and so to Nantes, Poyters, Rochell, and Burdeaux. The rumour of the strength of Bayon in Biskay, caused him to see it; and from thence tooke his way from Leskar in Biearne, and Paw in the kingdom of Navar to Tolouza in Gascoigne, Bezers and Carcassone, Narbone, Montpellier, Nimes in Languedock, and thorow the Country of Avignion, by Arles to Marcellos in Province, there imbarking himselfe for Italy, the ship was enforced to Tolonne, and putting againe to sea, ill weather so grew upon them, they anchored close aboard the shore, under the little Isle of S. Mary, against Neice in Savoy. Here the inhumane Provincialls, with a rabble of Pilgrimes of divers Nations going to Rome, hourely cursing him, not only for a Hugonoit, but his Nation they swore were all Pyrats, and so vildly railed on his dread Soveraigne Queene Elizabeth, and that they never should have faire weather so long as hee was aboard them; their disputations grew to that passion, that they threw him over-board, yet God brought him to that little Isle, where was no inhabitants, but a few kine and goats. The next morning he espied two ships more riding by them, put in by the storme, that fetched him aboard, well refreshed him, and so kindly used him, that he was well contented to trie the rest of his fortune with them. After he had related unto them his former discourse, what for pitie, and the love of the Honourable Earle of Ployer, this noble Britaine his neighbour, Captaine la Roche of Saint Malo, regarded and entertained him for his well respected friend. With the next faire wind they sailed along by the Coast of Corsica and Sardinia, and crossing the gulfe of Tunis, passed by Cape Bona to the Isle of Lampadosa, leaving the coast of Barbary till they came at Cape Rosata, and so along the African shore, for Alexandria in Ægypt. There delivering their fraught, they went to Scandaroone; rather to view what ships was in the Roade, than any thing else: keeping their course by Cypres and the coast of Asia, sayling by Rhodes, the Archipellagans, Candia, and the coast of Grecia,

An inhumane act of the Provincialls in casting him over-board.

Captain La Roche releeves him.

and the Isle of Zaffalonia. They lay to and againe a few dayes betwixt the Isle of Corfue and the Cape of Otranto in the Kingdome of Naples, in the Entrance of the Adriatike sea.

Chapter III.
A desperate Sea-fight in the Straights;
His passage to Rome, Naples, and the view of Italy.

Betwixt the two Capes they meet with an Argosie of Venice, it seemed the Captaine desired to speake with them, whose untoward answer was such, as slew them a man; whereupon the Britaine presently gave them the broad-side, then his Sterne, and his other broad-side also, and continued the chase, with his chase peeces, till he gave them so many broad-sides one after another, that the Argosies sayles and tackling was so torne, she stood to her defence, and made shot for shot; twice in one houre and a halfe the Britaine boarded her, yet they cleared themselves, but clapping her aboard againe, the Argosie fired him, which with much danger to them both was presently quenched. This rather augmented the Britaines rage, than abated his courage; for having reaccommodated himselfe againe, shot her so oft betweene wind and water, shee was readie to sinke, then they yeelded; the Britaine lost fifteene men, she twentie, besides divers were hurt, the rest went to worke on all hands; some to stop the leakes, others to guard the prisoners that were chained, the rest to rifle her. The Silkes, Velvets, Cloth of gold, and Tissue, Pyasters, Chicqueenes and Sultanies, which is gold and silver, they unloaded in foure and twentie houres, was wonderfull, whereof having sufficient, and tired with toile, they cast her off with her company, with as much good merchandize as would have fraughted such another Britaine, that was but two hundred Tunnes, she foure or five hundred.

To repaire his defects, hee stood for the coast of Calabria, but hearing there was six or seven Galleyes at Mesina hee departed thence for Malta, but the wind comming faire, he kept his course along the coast of the Kingdome of Sicilia by Sardinia and Corsica, till he came to the Road of Antibo in Pea-

A desperate sea-fight.

mon, where he set Smith on shore with five hundred chicqueenes, and a little box God sent him worth neere as much
more. Here he left this noble Britaine, and embarked himselfe
for Lygorne, being glad to have such opportunitie and meanes
to better his experience by the view of Italy; and having passed
Tuskany, and the Countrey of Sieana, where hee found his
deare friends, the two Honourable Brethren, the
Lord Willoughby and his Brother cruelly wounded,
in a desperate fray, yet to their exceeding great honour. Then to Viterbo and many other Cities he came
to Rome, where it was his chance to see Pope
Clement the eight, with many Cardinalls, creepe up
the holy Stayres, which they say are those our Saviour Christ
went up to Pontius Pilate, where bloud falling from his head,
being pricked with his crowne of thornes, the drops are marked
with nailes of steele, upon them none dare goe but in that
manner, saying so many *Ave-Maries* and *Pater-nosters*, as is
their devotion, and to kisse the nailes of steele: But on each
side is a paire of such like staires, up which you may goe, stand,
or kneele, but divided from the holy Staires by two walls: right
against them is a Chappell, where hangs a great silver Lampe,
which burneth continually, yet they say the oyle neither increaseth nor diminisheth. A little distant is the ancient Church
of Saint John de Laterane, where he saw him say Masse, which
commonly he doth upon some Friday once a moneth. Having
saluted Father Parsons, that famous English Jesuite, and satisfied himselfe with the rarities of Rome, he went downe the
River of Tiber to Civita Vechia, where he embarked himselfe
to satisfie his eye with the faire Citie of Naples, and her Kingdomes nobilitie; returning by Capua, Rome and Seana, he passed
by that admired Citie of Florence, the Cities and Countries of
Bolonia, Ferrara, Mantua, Padua and Venice, whose Gulfe he
passed from Malamoco and the Adriatike Sea for Ragouza,
spending some time to see that barren broken coast of Albania
and Dalmatia, to Capo de Istria, travelling the maine of poore
Slavonia by Lubbiano, till he came to Grates in Steria, the Seat
of Ferdinando Arch-duke of Austria, now Emperour of Alma-
nia: where he met an English man, and an Irish Jesuite, who
acquainted him with many brave Gentlemen of good qualitie,
especially with the Lord Ebersbaught, with whom trying such

Marginal note: The Popes holy Staires brought from Jerusalem, whereon (they say) Christ went up to Pontius Pilate.

conclusions, as he projected to undertake, preferred him to Baron Kisell, Generall of the Artillery, and he to a worthy Collonell, the Earle of Meldritch, with whom going to Vienne in Austria, under whose Regiment, in what service, and how he spent his time, this ensuing Discourse will declare.

Chapter IV.
The Siege of Olumpagh; An excellent Stratagem by Smith; Another not much worse.

The siege of Olumpagh. AFTER the losse of Caniza, the Turkes with twentie thousand besieged the strong Towne of Olumpagh so straightly, as they were cut off from all intelligence and hope of succour; till John Smith, this English Gentleman, acquainted Baron Kisell, Generall of the Arch-dukes Artillery, he had taught the Governour, his worthy friend, such a Rule, that he would undertake to make him know any thing he intended, and have his answer, would they bring him but to some place where he might make the flame of a Torch seene to the Towne; Kisell inflamed with this strange invention; Smith made it so plaine, that forthwith hee gave him guides, who in the darke night brought him to a mountaine, where he shewed three Torches equidistant from other, which plainly appearing to the Towne, the Governour presently apprehended, and answered againe with three other fires in like manner; each knowing the others being and intent; Smith, though distant seven miles, signified to him these words: On Thursday at night I will charge on the East, at the Alarum, salley you; Ebersbaught answered he would, and thus it was done: First he writ his message as briefe, you see, as could be, then divided the Alphabet in two parts thus;

A. b. c. d. e. f. g. h. i. k. l.
1. 1. 1. 1. 1. 1. 1. 1. 1. 1. 1.
m. n. o. p. q. r. s. t. v. w. x. y. z.
2. 2. 2. 2. 2. 2. 2. 2. 2. 2. 2. 2.

The first part from A. to L. is signified by shewing and hiding one linke, so oft as there is letters from A. to *An excellent Stratagem.* that letter you meane; the other part from M. to Z. is mentioned by two lights in like manner. The end of a word is signified by shewing of three lights, ever staying your light at that letter you meane, till the other may write it in a paper, and answer by his signall, which is one light, it is done, beginning to count the letters by the lights, every time from A. to M. by this meanes also the other returned his answer, whereby each did understand other. The Guides all this time having well viewed the Campe, returned to Kisell, who, doubting of his power being but ten thousand, was animated by the Guides, how the Turkes were so divided by the River in two parts, they could not easily second each other. To which *Another Stratagem.* Smith added this conclusion; that two or three thousand pieces of match fastened to divers small lines of an hundred fathome in length being armed with powder, might all be fired and stretched at an instant before the Alarum, upon the Plaine of Hysnaburg, supported by two staves, at each lines end, in that manner would seeme like so many Musketteers; which was put in practice; and being discovered by the Turkes, they prepared to encounter these false fires, thinking there had beene some great Armie: whilest Kisell with his ten thousand being entred the Turks quarter, who ranne up and downe as men amazed. It was not long ere Ebersbaught was pell-mell with them in their Trenches; in which distracted confusion, a third part of the Turkes, that besieged that side towards Knousbruck, were slaine; many of the rest drowned, but all fled. The other part of the Armie was so busied to resist the false fires, that Kisell before the morning put two thousand good souldiers in the Towne, and with small losse was retired; the Garrison was well releeved with that they found in the Turkes quarter, which caused the Turkes to raise their siege and returne to Caniza: and Kisell with much honour was received at Kerment, and occasioned the Author a good reward and preferment, to be Captaine of two hundred and fiftie Horse-men, under the Conduct of Colonell Voldo, Earle of Meldritch.

Chapter V.
The siege of Stowlle-wesenburg; The effects of Smiths Fire-workes; A worthy exploit of Earle Rosworme; Earle Meldritch takes the Bashaw prisoner.

A GENERALL rumour of a generall peace, now spred it selfe over all the face of those tormented Countries: but the Turke intended no such matter, but levied souldiers from all parts he could. The Emperour also, by the assistance of the Christian Princes, provided three Armies, the one led by the Arch-duke Mathias, the Emperours brother, and his Lieutenant Duke Mercury to defend Low Hungary, the second, by Ferdinando the Arch-duke of Steria, and the Duke of Mantua his Lieutenant to regaine Caniza; the third by Gonzago, Governour of High Hungary, to joyne with Georgio Busca, to make an absolute conquest of Transilvania.

Duke Mercury with an Armie of thirtie thousand, whereof neere ten thousand were French, besieged Stowlle-wesenburg, otherwise called Alba Regalis, a place so strong by Art and Nature, that it was thought impregnable. At his first comming, the Turkes sallied upon the Germane quarter, slew neere five hundred, and returned before they were thought on. The next night in like manner they did neere as much to the Bemers, and Hungarians; of which fortune still presuming, thinking to have found the French quarter as carelesse, eight or nine hundred of them were cut in pieces and taken prisoners. In this encounter Monsieur Grandvile, a brave French Colonell, received seven or eight cruell wounds, yet followed the Enemie to the Ports; he came off alive, but within three or foure dayes died.

The siege of Alba Regalis.

Earle Meldritch, by the information of three or foure Christians, (escaped out of the Towne) upon every Alarum, where there was greatest assemblies and throng of people, caused Captaine Smith to put in practice his fiery Dragons, hee had demonstrated unto him, and the Earle Von Sulch at Comora, which hee thus performed: Having prepared fortie or fiftie round-bellied earthen pots, and filled them with hand Gunpowder, then covered them with Pitch, mingled

The effect of good fire-works.

with Brimstone and Turpentine; and quartering as many Musket-bullets, that hung together but only at the Center of the division, stucke them round in the mixture about the pots, and covered them againe with the same mixture, over that a strong Searcloth, then over all a good thicknesse of Towze-match well tempered with oyle of Lin-seed, Campheer, and powder of Brimstone, these he fitly placed in Slings, graduated so neere as they could to the places of these Assemblies. At mid-night upon the Alarum, it was a fearfull sight to see the short flaming course of their flight in the aire, but presently after their fall, the lamentable noise of the miserable slaughtered Turkes was most wonderfull to heare: Besides, they had fired that Suburbe at the Port of Buda in two or three places, which so troubled the Turkes to quench, that had there beene any meanes to have assaulted them, they could hardly have resisted the fire, and their enemies. The Earle Rosworme, contrary to the opinion of all men, would needs undertake to finde meanes to surprize the Segeth and Suburbe of the Citie, strongly de-fended by a muddie Lake, which was thought impassable.

A worthy exploit of Earle Rosworme. The Duke having planted his Ordnance, battered the other side, whilest Rosworme, in the darke night, with every man a bundle of sedge and bavins still throwne before them, so laded up the Lake, as they surprized that unregarded Suburbe before they were discovered: upon which unexpected Alarum, the Turkes fled into the Citie, and the other Suburbe not knowing the matter, got into the Citie also, leaving their Suburbe for the Duke, who, with no great resistance, tooke it, with many peeces of Ordnance; the Citie, being of no such strength as the Suburbs, with their owne Ordnance was so battered, that it was taken perforce, with such a mercilesse execution, as was most pitifull to behold. The Bashaw notwithstanding drew together a partie of five hun-dred before his owne Pallace, where he intended to die; but seeing most of his men slaine before him, by the valiant Cap-

Earle Meldritch takes the Bashaw prisoner. taine Earle Meldritch, who tooke him prisoner with his owne hands; and with the hazard of himselfe saved him from the fury of other troopes, that did pull downe his Pallace, and would have rent him in peeces, had he not beene thus preserved. The Duke thought his victory much honoured with such a Prisoner; tooke order hee should bee used like a Prince, and with all expedition gave charge presently to repaire the breaches, and the ruines of this famous Citie, that had beene in the possession of the Turkes neere threescore yeares.

Chapter VI.
A brave encounter of the Turkes Armie with the Christians; Duke Mercury overthroweth Assan Bashaw; Hee divides the Christian Armie; His noblenesse and death.

MAHOMET, the great Turke, during the siege, had raised an Armie of sixtie thousand men to have releeved it; but hearing it was lost, he sent Assan Bashaw, Generall of his Armie, the Bashaw of Buda, Bashaw Amaroz, to see if it were possible to regaine it; The Duke understanding there could be no great experience in such a new levied Armie as Assan had; having put a strong Garrison into it: and with the brave Colonell Rosworme, Culnits, Meldritch, the Rhine-Grave, Vahan and many others; with twenty thousand good souldiers, set forward to meet the Turke in the Plaines of Girke. Those two Armies encountred as they marched, where began a hot and bloudy Skirmish betwixt them, Regiment against Regiment, as they came in order, till the night parted them: Here Earle Meldritch was so invironed amongst those halfe circuler Regiments of Turkes, they supposed him their Prisoner, and his Regiment lost; but his two most couragious friends, Vahan and Culnits, made such a passage amongst them, that it was a terror to see how horse and man lay sprawling and tumbling, some one way, some another on the ground. The Earle there at that time made his valour shine more bright than his armour, which seemed then painted with Turkish bloud, he slew the brave Zanzack Bugola, and made his passage to his friends, but neere halfe his Regiment was slaine. Captain Smith had his horse slaine under him, and himselfe sore wounded; but he was not long unmounted, for there was choice enough of horses, that wanted masters. The Turke thinking the victory sure against the Duke, whose Armie, by the Siege and the Garrison, he had left behind him, was much weakned, would not be content with one, but he would have all; and lest the Duke should returne to Alba Regalis, he sent that night twenty thousand to besiege the Citie, assuring them he would keepe the Duke or any other from releeving them. Two or three dayes they lay each by other, entrenching themselves; the Turkes daring the Duke daily to a sett battell, who at length drew out his Army, led by the Rhine-Grave, Culnits and Meldritch, who upon their first encounter, charged with that resolute and valiant courage, as disordered not only the formost squadrons of the Turkes, but enforced all the whole Armie to retire to the Campe, with the losse of five or six thousand, with the Bashaw of Buda, and foure or five Zanzacks, with divers other great Commanders, two hundred Prisoners, and nine peeces of Ordnance. At that instant appeared, as it were, another Armie comming out of a valley over a plaine hill, that caused the Duke at that time to be contented, and to retire to his Trenches; which gave time to Assan to reorder his disordered squadrons: Here they lay nine or ten dayes, and more supplies repaired to them, expecting to try the event in a sett battell; but the souldiers on both parties, by reason of their great wants and approach of winter, grew so discontented, that they were ready of themselves to breake up the Leager; the Bashaw retiring himselfe to Buda, had some of the Reare Troopes cut off. Amaroz Bashaw hearing of this, found such bad welcome at Alba Regalis, and the Towne so strongly repaired, with so brave a Garrison, raised his siege, and retired to Zigetum.

Duke Mercury overthroweth Assan Bassa.

The Duke understanding that the Arch-duke Ferdinando had so resolutely besieged Caniza, as what by the losse of Alba Regalis, and the Turks retreat to Buda, being void of hope of any reliefe, doubted not but it would become againe the Christians. To the furtherance whereof, the Duke divided his Armie into three parts. The Earle of Rosworme went with seven thousand to Caniza; the Earle of Meldritch with six thousand he sent to assist Georgio Busca against the Transilvanians, the rest went with himselfe to the Garrisons of Strigonium and Komara; having thus worthily behaved himselfe, he arrived at Vienne; where the Arch-dukes

Duke Mercury divideth his Armie

and the Nobilitie with as much honour received him, as if he had conquered all Hungaria; his very Picture they esteemed would make them fortunate, which thousands kept as curiously as a precious relique. To requite this honour, preparing himselfe to returne into France, to raise new Forces against the next yeare, with the two Arch-dukes, Mathias and Maximilian, and divers others of the Nobilitie, was with great magnificence conducted to Nurenburg, there by them royally feasted; (how it chanced is not knowne;) but the next morning he was found dead, and his brother in law died two dayes after; whose hearts, after this great triumph, with much sorrow were carried into France.

Duke Mercury and his brother in law die suddenly.

Chapter VII.

The unhappie Siege of Caniza; Earle Meldritch serveth Prince Sigismundus; Prince Moyses besiegeth Regall; Smiths three single combats; His Patent from Sigismundus, and reward.

THE worthy Lord Rosworme had not a worse journey to the miserable Seige of Caniza, (where by the extremitie of an extraordinary continuing tempest of haile, wind, frost and snow, in so much that the Christians were forced to leave their Tents and Artillery, and what they had; it being so cold that three or foure hundred of them were frozen to death in a night, and two or three thousand lost in that miserable flight in the snowie tempest, though they did know no enemie at all to follow them:) than the noble Earle of Meldritch had to Transilvania, where hearing of the death of Michael and the brave Duke Mercury, and knowing the policie of Busca, and the Prince his Roialtie, being now beyond all beleefe of men, in possession of the best part of Transilvania, perswaded his troopes, in so honest a cause, to assist the Prince against the Turke, rather than Busca against the Prince.

The unhappie siege of Caniza.

The souldiers being worne out with those hard payes and travells, upon hope to have free libertie to make bootie upon what they could get possession of from the Turkes, was easily

Earle
Meldritch
serveth
Prince
Sigismundus.
perswaded to follow him whithersoever. Now this noble Earle was a Transilvanian borne, and his fathers Countrey yet inhabited by the Turkes; for Transilvania was yet in three divisions, though the Prince had the hearts both of Country and people; yet the Frontiers had a Garrison amongst the unpassable mountaines, some for the Emperour, some for the Prince, and some for the Turke: to regaine which small estate, hee desired leave of the Prince to trie his fortunes, and to make use of that experience, the time of twentie yeares had taught him in the Emperours service, promising to spend the rest of his dayes for his countries defence in his Excellencies service. The Prince glad of so brave a Commander, and so many expert and ancient souldiers, made him Campe-master of his Armie, gave him all necessary releefe for his troopes and what freedome they desired to plunder the Turkes.

Earle
Meldritch
maketh
incursions to
discover
Regall.
The Earle having made many incursions into the Land of Zarkam among those rockie mountaines, where were some Turks, some Tartars, but most Bandittoes, Rennegadoes, and such like, which sometimes hee forced into the Plaines of Regall, where is a Citie not only of men and fortifications, strong of it selfe, but so environed with mountaines, that made the passages so difficult, that in all these warres no attempt had beene made upon it to any purpose: Having satisfied himselfe with the Situation, and the most convenient passages to bring his Armie unto it: The earth no sooner put on her greene habit, than the Earle overspread her with his armed troopes. To possesse himselfe first of the most convenient passage, which was a narrow valley betwixt two high mountaines; he sent Colonell Veltus with his Regiment, dispersed in companies to lye in Ambuscado, as he had directed them, and in the morning to drive all the cattell they could finde before a Fort in that passage, whom he supposed would sally, seeing but some small partie, to recover their prey; which tooke such good successe, that the Garrison was cut off by the Ambuscado, and Veltus seized on the Skonces, which was abandoned. Meldritch glad of so fortunate a beginning, it was six dayes ere he could with six thousand Pioners make passage for his Ordnance: The Turkes having such warning, strengthned the Towne so with men and provision,

that they made a scorne of so small a number as Meldritch brought with him before the Citie, which was but eight thousand. Before they had pitched their Tents, the Turkes sallied in such abundance, as for an houre they had rather a bloudy battell than a skirmish, but with the losse of neere fifteene hundred on both sides. The Turkes were chased till the Cities Ordnance caused the Earle to retire. The next day Zachel Moyses, Generall of the Armie, pitched also his tents with nine thousand foot and horse, and six and twenty peeces of Ordnance; but in regard of the situation of this strong Fortresse, they did neither feare them nor hurt them, being upon the point of a faire promontory, environed on the one side within halfe a mile with an un-usefull mountaine, and on the other side with a faire Plaine, where the Christians encamped, but so commanded by their Ordnance, they spent neere a month in entrenching themselves, and raising their mounts to plant their batteries; which slow proceedings the Turkes oft derided, that their Ordnance were at pawne, and how they grew fat for want of exercise, and fearing lest they should depart ere they could assault their Citie, sent this Challenge to any Captaine in the Armie.

Moyses besiegeth Regall.

That to delight the Ladies, who did long to see some courtlike pastime, the Lord Turbashaw did defie any Captaine, that had the command of a Company, who durst combate with him for his head: The matter being discussed, it was accepted, but so many questions grew for the undertaking, it was decided by lots, which fell upon Captaine Smith, before spoken of.

Truce being made for that time, the Rampiers all beset with faire Dames, and men in Armes, the Christians in Battalio; Turbashaw with a noise of Howboyes entred the field well mounted and armed; on his shoulders were fixed a paire of great wings, compacted of Eagles feathers within a ridge of silver, richly garnished with gold and precious stones, a Janizary before him, bearing his Lance, on each side another leading his horse; where long hee stayed not, ere Smith with a noise of Trumpets, only a Page bearing his Lance, passing by him with a courteous salute, tooke his ground with such good successe, that at the sound of the charge, he passed the Turke thorow the sight of his Beaver, face, head and all, that he fell dead to the ground, where

Three single Combates.
1

alighting and unbracing his Helmet, cut off his head, and the
Turkes tooke his body; and so returned without any hurt at all.
The head hee presented to the Lord Moses, the Generall, who
kindly accepted it, and with joy to the whole armie he was generally welcomed.

2

The death of this Captaine so swelled in the heart
of one Grualgo, his vowed friend, as rather inraged
with madnesse than choller, he directed a particular
challenge to the Conquerour, to regaine his friends head, or
lose his owne, with his horse and Armour for advantage, which
according to his desire, was the next day undertaken: as before
upon the sound of the Trumpets, their Lances flew in peeces
upon a cleare passage, but the Turke was neere unhorsed. Their
Pistolls was the next, which marked Smith upon the placard;
but the next shot the Turke was so wounded in the left arme,
that being not able to rule his horse, and defend himselfe, he
was throwne to the ground, and so bruised with the fall, that
he lost his head, as his friend before him; with his horse and
Armour; but his body and his rich apparell was sent backe to
the Towne.

Every day the Turkes made some sallies, but few skirmishes
would they endure to any purpose. Our workes and approaches
being not yet advanced to that height and effect which was of
necessitie to be performed; to delude time, Smith with so
many incontradictable perswading reasons, obtained leave that
the Ladies might know he was not so much enamoured of
their servants heads, but if any Turke of their ranke would
come to the place of combate to redeeme them, should have
his also upon the like conditions, if he could winne it.

3

The challenge presently was accepted by Bonny
Mulgro. The next day both the Champions entring
the field as before, each discharging their Pistoll,
having no Lances, but such martiall weapons as the defendant
appointed, no hurt was done; their Battle-axes was the next,
whose piercing bils made sometime the one, sometime the
other to have scarce sense to keepe their saddles, specially the
Christian received such a blow that he lost his Battle-axe, and
failed not much to have fallen after it, wherat the supposing
conquering Turk, had a great shout from the Rampiers. The
Turk prosecuted his advantage to the uttermost of his power;

yet the other, what by the readinesse of his horse, and his judgement and dexterity in such a businesse, beyond all mens expectation, by Gods assistance, not onely avoided the Turkes violence, but having drawne his Faulchion, pierced the Turke so under the Culets thorow backe and body, that although he alighted from his horse, he stood not long ere hee lost his head, as the rest had done.

Chapter VIII.

Georgio Busca an Albane his ingratitude to Prince Sigismundus; Prince Moyses his Lieutenant, is overthrowne by Busca, Generall for the Emperour Rodolphus; Sigismundus yeeldeth his Countrey to Rodolphus; Busca assisteth Prince Rodoll in Wallachia.

THIS good successe gave such great encouragement to the whole Armie, that with a guard of six thousand, three spare horses, before each a Turkes head upon a Lance, he was conducted to the Generalls Pavillion with his Presents. Moyses received both him and them with as much respect as the occasion deserved, embracing him in his armes; gave him a faire Horse richly furnished, a Semitere and belt worth three hundred ducats; and Meldritch made him Sergeant major of his Regiment. But now to the siege, having mounted six and twenty peeces of Ordnance fifty or sixty foot above the Plaine, made them so plainly tell his meaning, that within fifteene dayes two breaches were made, which the Turkes as valiantly defended as men could; that day was made a darksome night, but by the light that proceeded from the murdering Muskets, and peace-making Canon, whilest their slothfull Governour lay in a Castle on the top of a high mountaine, and like a valiant Prince asketh what's the matter, when horrour and death stood amazed each at other, to see who should prevaile to make him victorious: Moyses commanding a generall assault upon the sloping front of the high Promontory, where the Barons of Budendorfe and Oberwin lost neere halfe their

Regall assaulted and taken. Regiments, by logs, bags of powder, and such like, tumbling downe the hill, they were to mount ere they could come to the breach; notwithstanding with an incredible courage they advanced to the push of the Pike with the defendants, that with the like courage repulsed, till the Earle Meldritch, Becklefield and Zarvana, with their fresh Regiments seconded them with that fury, that the Turks retired and fled into the Castle, from whence by a flag of truce they desired composition. The Earle remembring his fathers death, battered it with all the Ordnance in the Towne, and the next day tooke it; all he found could beare Armes he put to the sword, and set their heads upon stakes round about the walles, in the same manner they had used the Christians, when they tooke it. Moyses having repaired the Rampiers, and throwne downe the worke in his Campe, he put in it a strong Garrison, though the pillage he had gotten in the Towne was much, having beene for a long time an impregnable den of theeves; yet the losse of the Armie so intermingled the sowre with the sweet, as forced Moyses to seek a further revenge, that he sacked Veratio, Solmos, and Kupronka, and with two thousand prisoners, most women and children, came to Esenberg, not farre from the Princes Palace, where he there Encamped.

Sigismundus comming to view his Armie, was presented with the Prisoners, and six and thirtie Ensignes; where celebrating thanke to Almightie God in triumph of those victories, hee was made acquainted with the service Smith had done at Olumpagh, Stowle-Wesenburg and Regall, for which with great honour hee gave him three Turkes heads in a Shield for his Armes, by Patent, under his hand and Seale, with an Oath ever to weare them in his Colours, his Picture in Gould, and three hundred Ducats, yearely for a Pension.

The Patent. SIGISMUNDUS BATHORI, *Dei gratia Dux.* Transilvaniæ, Wallachiæ *et* Vandalorum; *Comes* Anchard, Salford, Growenda; *Cunctis his literis significamus qui eas lecturi aut audituri sunt, concessam licentiam aut facultatem* Iohanni Smith, *natione* Anglo Geñeroso, 250. *militum Capitaneo sub Illustrisimi et Gravissimi* Henrici Volda, *Comitis*

de Meldri, Salmariæ, et Peldoiæ *primario, ex* 1000. *equitibus et* 1500. *peditibus bello* Ungarico *conductione in Provincias suprascriptas sub Authoritate nostra: cui servituti omni laude perpetuaque, memoria dignum præbuit sese erga nos, ut virum strenuum pugnantem pro aris et focis decet. Quare è favore nostro militario ipsum ordine condonavimus, et in Sigillum illius tria* Turcica *Capita designare et deprimer concessimus, quæ ipse gladio suo ad Urbem* Regalem *in singulari prælio vicit, mactavit, atque; decollavit in* Transilvaniæ *Provincia: Sed fortuna cum variabilis ancepsque; sit idem forte fortuito in* Wallachia *Provincia Anno Domini* 1602. *die Mensis Novembris* 18. *cum multis aliis etiam Nobilibus et aliis quibusdam militibus captus est à Domino* Bascha *electo ex* Cambia *regionis* Tartariæ, *cujus severitate adductus salutem quantam potuit quæsivit, tantumque effecit, Deo omnipotente adjuvante, ut deliberavit se, et ad suos Commilitones revertit; ex quibus ipsum liberavimus, et hæcnobis testimonia habuit ut majori licentia frueretur qua dignus esset, jam tendet in patriam suam dulcissiman: Rogamus ergo omnes nostros charissimos, confinitimos, Duces, Principes, Comites, Barones, Gubernatores Urbium et Navium in eadem Regione el cæterarum Provinciarum in quibus ille residere conatus fuerit ut idem permittatur Capitaneus libere sine obstaculo omni versari. Hæc facientes pergraium nobis feceritis. Signatum* Lesprizia *in* Misnia *die Mensis Decembris* 9. *Anno Domini* 1603. *Gum Privilegio propriæ Majestatis.*   SIGISMUNDUS BATHORI.

UNIVERSIS, *et singulis, cujuscunque loci, status, gradus, ordinis, ac conditionis ad quos hoc præsens scriptum pervenerit,* Guilielmus Segar *Eques auratus aliàs dictus Garterus Principalis Rex Armorum* Anglicorum, *Salutem.* Sciatis, *quod Ego prædictus Garterus, notum, testatumque facio, quod Patentem suprascriptum, cum manu propria prædicti Ducis* Transilvaniæ *subsignatum, et Sigillo suo affixum, Vidi: et Copiam veram ejusdem (in perpetuam rei memoriam) transcripsi, et recordavi in Archivis, et Registris Officii Armorum. Datum* Londini 19. *die Augusti, Anno Domini* 1625. *Annoque Regni Domini nostri* CAROLI *Dei gratia Magnæ* Britanniæ, Franciæ, *et* Hiberniæ *Regis, Fidei Defensoris, etc. Primo.*

GUILIELMUS SEGAR, Garterus.

The same in English.

Sigismundus Bathor, by the Grace of God, Duke of Transilvania, Wallachia, and Moldavia, Earle of Anchard, Salford and Growenda; to whom this Writing may come or appeare. Know that We have given leave and licence to John Smith an English Gentleman, Captaine of 250. Souldiers, under the most Generous and Honourable Henry Volda, Earle of Meldritch, Salmaria, and Peldoia, Colonell of a thousand horse, and fifteene hundred foot, in the warres of Hungary, and in the Provinces aforesaid under our authority;

whose service doth deserve all praise and perpetuall memory towards us, as a man that did for God and his Country overcome his enemies: Wherefore out of Our love and favour, according to the law of Armes, We have ordained and given him in his shield of Armes, the figure and description of three Turks heads, which with his sword before the towne of Regall, in single combat he did overcome, kill, and cut off, in the Province of Transilvania. But fortune, as she is very variable, so it chanced and happened to him in the Province of Wallachia, in the yeare of our Lord, 1602. the 18. day of November, with many others, as well Noble men, as also divers other Souldiers, were taken prisoners by the Lord Bashaw of Cambia, a Country of Tartaria; whose cruelty brought him such good fortune, by the helpe and power of Almighty God, that hee delivered himselfe, and returned againe to his company and fellow souldiers, of whom We doe discharge him, and this hee hath in witnesse thereof, being much more worthy of a better reward; and now intends to returne to his owne sweet Country. We desire therefore all our loving and kinde kinsmen, Dukes, Princes, Earles, Barons, Governours of Townes, Cities, or Ships, in this Kingdome, or any other Provinces he shall come in, that you freely let passe this the aforesaid Captaine, without any hinderance or molestation, and this doing, with all kindnesse we are alwayes ready to doe the like for you. Sealed at Lipswick in Misenland, the ninth of December, in the yeare of our Lord, 1603.

With the proper privilege   SIGISMUNDUS BATHOR.
of his Majestie.

To all and singular, in what place, state, degree, order, or condition whatsoever, to whom this present writing shall come: I, William Segar, Knight, otherwise Garter, and principall King of Armes of England, wish health. Know that I the aforesaid Garter, do witnesse and approve, that this aforesaid Patent, I have seene, signed, and sealed, under the proper hand and Seale Manual of the said Duke of Transilvania, and a true coppy of the same, as a thing for perpetuall memory, I have subscribed and recorded in the Register and office of the Heralds of Armes. Dated at London the nineteenth day of August, in the yeare of our Lord, 1625. and in the first yeare of our

Soveraigne Lord Charles by the grace of God, King of great
Britaine, France, and Ireland; Defender of the faith, etc.

WILLIAM SEGAR.

Chapter IX.
Sigismundus sends Ambassadours unto the Emperour; the conditions re-assured; He yeeldeth up all to Busca, and returneth to Prague.

Busca having all this time beene raising new forces, was commanded from the Emperour againe to invade Transilvania,
which being one of the fruitfullest and strongest Countries in
those parts, was now rather a desart, or the very spectacle of
desolation; their fruits and fields overgrowne with weeds, their
Churches and battered Palaces and best buildings, as for feare,
hid with Mosse and Ivy; being the very Bulwarke and Rampire
of a great part of Europe, most fit by all Christians to have
beene supplyed and maintained, was thus brought to ruine by
them it most concerned to support it. But alas, what is it, when
the power of Majestie pampered in all delights of pleasant vanity, neither knowing nor considering the labour of the Plough-
man, the hazard of the Merchant, the oppression of Statesmen;
nor feeling the piercing torments of broken limbes, and invet-
erated wounds, the toilsome marches, the bad lodging, the
hungry diet, and the extreme misery that Souldiers endure to
secure all those estates, and yet by the spight of malicious detraction, starves for want of their reward and recompences;
whilest the politique Courtier, that commonly aimes more at
his owne honors and ends, than his Countries good, or his
Princes glory, honour, or security, as this worthy Prince too
well could testifie. But the Emperor being certified how weak
and desperate his estate was, sent Busca againe with a great
Army, to trie his fortune once more in Transilvania. The Prince
considering how his Country and subjects were consumed, the
small means he had any longer to defend his estate, both against
the cruelty of the Turke, and the power of the Emperor, and

the small care the Polanders had in supplying him, as they had promised, sent to Busca to have truce, till messengers might be sent to the Emperour for some better agreement, where-with Busca was contented. The Ambassadours so prevailed, that the Emperour re-assured unto them the conditions he had promised the Prince at their confederacie for the lands in Silesia, with 60000. ducats presently in hand, and 50000. ducats yearely as a pension. When this conclusion was knowne to Moyses, his Lieftenant then in the field with the Army, that would doe any thing rather than come in subjection to the Germans, he encouraged his Souldiers, and without any more adoe marched to encounter Busca, whom he found much better provided than he expected; so that be-twixt them in six or seven houres, more than five or six thousand on both sides lay dead in the field. Moyses thus overthrowne, fled to the Turks at Temesware, and his scattered troopes some one way, some another.

Busca in Transilvania overthroweth Moyses.

The Prince understanding of this so sudden and unexpected accident, onely accompanied with an hundred of his Gentry and Nobility, went into the campe to Busca, to let him know, how ignorant he was of his Lieftenants errour, that had done it without his direction or knowledge, freely offering to per-forme what was concluded by his Ambassadours with the Em-perour; and so causing all his Garrisons to come out of their strong holds, he delivered all to Busca for the Emperour, and so went to Prague, where he was honourably received, and established in his possessions, as his Emperiall Majestie had promised. Busca assembling all the Nobility, tooke their oaths of allegeance and fidelity, and thus their Prince being gone, Transilvania became againe subject to the Emperour.

Sigismundus yeeldeth his country to Busca.

Now after the death of Michael, Vavoyd of Wal-lachia, the Turke sent one Jeremie to be their Vavoyd or Prince; whose insulting tyranny caused the people to take Armes against him, so that he was forced to flie into the confines of Moldavia; and Busca in the behalfe of the Emper-our, proclaimed the Lord Rodoll in his stead. But Jeremy having assembled an Army of forty thousand Turks, Tartars, and Moldavians, returned into Wallachia. Rodoll not yet able to raise such a power, fled into Transilvania to Busca, his an-

Busca assisteth Rodoll in Wallachia.

cient friend; who considering well of the matter, and how good it would be for his owne security to have Wallachia subject to the Emperour, or at least such an employment for the remainders of the old Regiments of Sigismundus, (of whose greatnesse and true affection hee was very suspitious,) sent them with Rodoll to recover Wallachia, conducted by the valiant Captaines, the Earle Meldritch, Earle Veltus, Earle Nederspolt, Earle Zarvana, the Lord Bechleleld, the Lord Budendorfe, with their Regiments, and divers others of great ranke and quality, the greatest friends and alliances the Prince had; who with thirty thousand, marched along by the river Altus, to the streights of Rebrinke, where they entred Wallachia, encamping at Raza; Jeremie lying at Argish, drew his Army into his old campe, in the plaines of Peteske, and with his best diligence fortified it, intending to defend himselfe till more power came to him from the Crym-Tartar. Many small parties that came to his campe, Rodoll cut off; and in the nights would cause their heads to be throwne up and downe before the trenches. Seven of their Porters were taken, whom Jeremie commanded to be flayed quicke, and after hung their skinnes upon poles, and their carkasses and heads on stakes by them.

Chapter X.
The battell of Rotenton; a pretty stratagem of fire-workes by Smith.

Rodoll not knowing how to draw the enemie to battell, raised his Armie, burning and spoyling all where he came, and returned againe towards Rebrinke in the night, as if he had fled upon the generall rumour of the Crym-Tartars comming, which so inflamed the Turkes of a happy victory, they urged Jeremy against his will to follow them. Rodoll seeing his plot fell out as he desired, so ordered the matter, that having re-gained the streights, he put his Army in order, that had beene neere two dayes pursued, with continuall skirmishes in his Reare, which now making head against the enemie, that followed with their whole Armie in the best manner they could, was furiously charged with six

A battell betwixt Rodoll and Jeremie

thousand Hydukes, Wallachians, and Moldavians, led by three
Colonells, Oversall, Dubras, and Calab, to entertaine the time
till the rest came up; Veltus and Nederspolt with their Regiments, entertained them with the like courage, till the Zanzacke Hamesbeg, with six thousand more, came with a fresh
charge, which Meldritch and Budendorfe, rather like enraged
lions, than men, so bravely encountred, as if in them only had
consisted the victory; Meldritchs horse being slaine under him,
the Turks pressed what they could to have taken him prisoner,
but being remounted, it was thought with his owne hand he
slew the valiant Zanzacke, whereupon his troopes retyring, the
two proud Bashawes, Aladin, and Zizimmus, brought up the
front of the body of their battell. Veltus and Nederspolt having
breathed, and joyning their troopes with Becklefield and
Zarvana, with such an incredible courage charged the left
flancke of Zizimmus, as put them all in disorder, where Zizimmus the Bashaw was taken prisoner, but died presently upon
his wounds. Jeremie seeing now the maine battell of Rodoll
advance, being thus constrained, like a valiant Prince in his
front of the Vantgard, by his example so bravely encouraged
his souldiers, that Rodoll found no great assurance of the victorie. Thus being joyned in this bloudy massacre, that there
was scarce ground to stand upon, but upon the dead carkasses,
which in lesse than an hower were so mingled, as if each Regiment had singled out other. The admired Aladin that day did
leave behinde him a glorious name for his valour, whose death
many of his enemies did lament after the victory, which at that
instant fell to Rodoll. It was reported Jeremie was also slaine,
but it was not so, but fled with the remainder of his Armie to
Moldavia, leaving five and twenty thousand dead in
the field, of both Armies. And thus Rodoll was seated
againe in his Soveraignty, and Wallachia became subject to the Emperour.

Wallachia subjected to the Emperour.

But long he rested not to settle his new estate, but there
came newes, that certaine Regiments of stragling Tartars, were
forraging those parts towards Moldavia. Meldritch with thirteene thousand men was sent against them, but when they
heard it was the Crym-Tartar and his two sonnes, with an Armie
of thirty thousand; and Jeremie, that had escaped with fourteene or fifteene thousand, lay in ambush for them about

Langanaw, he retired towards Rottenton, a strong garrison for Rodoll; but they were so invironed with these hellish numbers, they could make no great haste for skirmishing with their scouts, forragers, and small parties that still encountred them. But one night amongst the rest, having made a passage through a wood, with an incredible expedition, cutting trees thwart each other to hinder their passage, in a thicke fogge early in the morning, unexpectedly they met two thousand loaded with pillage, and two or three hundred horse and cattell; the most of them were slaine and taken prisoners, who told them where Jeremie lay in the passage, expecting the Crym-Tartar that was not farre from him. Meldritch intending to make his passage perforce, was advised of a pretty stratagem by the English Smith, which presently he thus accomplished; for having accommodated two or three hundred truncks with wilde fire, upon the heads of lances, and charging the enemie in the night, gave fire to the truncks, which blazed forth such flames and sparkles, that it so amazed not onely their horses, but their foot also; that by the meanes of this flaming encounter, their owne horses turned tailes with such fury, as by their violence overthrew Jeremy and his Army, without any losse at all to speake of to Meldritch. But of this victory long they triumphed not; for being within three leagues of Rottenton, the Tartar with neere forty thousand so beset them, that they must either fight, or be cut in peeces flying. Here Busca and the Emperour had their desire; for the Sunne no sooner displayed his beames, than the Tartar his colours; where at midday he stayed a while, to see the passage of a tyrannicall and treacherous imposture, till the earth did blush with the bloud of honesty, that the Sunne for shame did hide himselfe, from so monstrous sight of a cowardly calamity. It was a most brave sight to see the banners and ensignes streaming in the aire, the glittering of Armour, the variety of colours, the motion of plumes, the forrests of lances, and the thicknesse of shorter weapons, till the silent expedition of the bloudy blast from the murdering Ordnance, whose roaring voice is not so soone heard, as felt by the aymed at object, which made among them a most lamentable slaughter.

Chapter XI.
The names of the English that were slaine in the battell of Rottenton; and how Captaine Smith is taken prisoner; and sold for a slave.

IN the valley of Veristhorne, betwixt the river of Altus, and the mountaine of Rottenton, was this bloudy encounter, where the most of the dearest friends of the noble Prince Sigismundus perished. Meldritch having ordered his eleven thousand in the best manner he could, at the foot of the mountaine upon his flancks, and before his front, he had pitched sharpe stakes, their heads hardned in the fire, and bent against the ene- mie, as three battalion of Pikes, amongst the which also there was digged many small holes. Amongst those stakes was ranged his footmen, that upon the charge was to retire, as there was occasion. The Tartar having ordered his 40000. for his best advantage, appointed Mustapha Bashaw to beginne the battell, with a generall shout, all their Ensignes displaying, Drummes beating, Trumpets and Howboyes sounding. Nederspolt and Mavazo with their Regiments of horse most valiantly encountred, and forced them to retire; the Tartar Begolgi with his Squadrons, darkening the skies with their flights of numberles arrowes, who was as bravely encoun- tred by Veltus and Oberwin, which bloudie slaughter contin- ued more than an houre, till the matchlesse multitude of the Tartars so increased, that they retired within their Squadrons of stakes, as was directed. The bloudy Tartar, as scorning he should stay so long for the victorie, with his massie troopes prosecuted the charge: but it was a wonder to see how horse and man came to the ground among the stakes, whose disor- dered troopes were there so mangled, that the Christians with a loud shout cryed Victoria; and with five or six field peeces, planted upon the rising of the mountaine, did much hurt to the enemy that still continued the battell with that furie, that Meldritch seeing there was no possibilitie long to prevaile, joyned his small troopes in one body, resolved directly to make his passage or die in the conclusion; and thus in grosse gave a generall charge, and for more than halfe an houre made his way plaine before him, till the maine battel of the Crym-Tartar

The battell of Rottenton.

with two Regiments of Turkes and Janizaries so overmatched them, that they were overthrowen. The night approaching, the Earle with some thirteene or fourteene hundred horse, swamme the River, some were drowned, all the rest slaine or taken prisoners: And thus in this bloudy field, neere 30000. lay, some headlesse, armelesse and leglesse, all cut and mangled; where breathing their last, they gave this knowledge to the world, that for the lives of so few, the Crym-Tartar never paid dearer. But now the Countreyes of Transilvania and Wallachia, (subjected to the Emperour) and Sigismundus that brave Prince his Subject and Pensioner, the most of his Nobilitie, brave Captaines and Souldiers, became a prey to the cruell devouring Turke: where had the Emperor been as ready to have assisted him, and those three Armies led by three such worthy Captaines, as Michael, Busca, and Himselfe, and had those three Armies joyned together against the Turke, let all men judge, how happie it might have beene for all Christendome: and have either regained Bulgaria, or at least have beat him out of Hungaria, where hee hath taken much more from the Emperour, than hath the Emperour from Transilvania.

Extracted out of a Booke intituled, The warres of Hungaria, Wallachia, and Moldavia, written by Francisco Ferneza, a learned Italian, the Princes Secretarie, and translated by Master Purchas.

In this dismal battell, where Nederspolt, Veltus, Zarvana, Mavazo, Bavell, and many other Earles, Barons, Colonels, Captaines, brave Gentlemen, and Souldiers were slaine. Give mee leave to remember the names of our owne Country-men with him in those exploits, that as resolutely as the best in the defence of Christ and his Gospell, ended their dayes, as Baskerfield, Hardwicke, Thomas Milemer, Robert Mullineux, Thomas Bishop, Francis Compton, George Davison, Nicholas Williams, and one John a Scot, did what men could doe, and when they could doe no more, left there their bodies in testimonie of their mindes; only Ensigne Carleton and Sergeant Robinson escaped: but Smith among the slaughtered dead bodies, and many a gasping soule, with toile and wounds lay groaning among the rest, till being found by the Pillagers hee was able to live, and perceiving by his armor and habit, his ransome might be better to them, than his death, they led him prisoner with many others; well they used him till his wounds were cured, and at Axopolis they

The English men in this Battell.

were all sold for slaves, like beasts in a market-place, where
everie Merchant, viewing their limbs and wounds, caused other
slaves to struggle with them, to trie their strength, hee fell to
the share of Bashaw Bogall, who sent him forthwith to Adri-
nopolis, so for Constantinople to his faire Mistresse for a slave.
By twentie and twentie chained by the neckes, they marched in
file to this great Citie, where they were delivered to their severall Masters, and he to the young Charatza Tragabigzanda.

Chapter XII.
How Captaine Smith was sent prisoner thorow the
Blacke and Dissabacca Sea in Tartaria;
the description of those Seas, and his usage.

THIS Noble Gentlewoman tooke sometime occasion to shew
him to some friends, or rather to speake with him, because
shee could speake Italian, would feigne her selfe sick when she
should goe to the Banians, or weepe over the graves, to know
how Bogall tooke him prisoner; and if he were as the Bashaw
writ to her, a Bohemian Lord conquered by his hand, as hee
had many others, which ere long hee would present her, whose
ransomes should adorne her with the glorie of his conquests.

But when she heard him protest he knew no such matter,
nor ever saw Bogall till he bought him at Axopolis, and that
hee was an English-man, onely by his adventures made a Captaine in those Countreyes. To trie the truth, shee found meanes
to finde out many could speake English, French, Dutch, and
Italian, to whom relating most part of these former passages
he thought necessarie, which they so honestly reported to her,
she tooke (as it seemed) much compassion on him; but having
no use for him, lest her mother should sell him, she sent him
to her brother, the Tymor Bashaw of Nalbrits, in the Countrey
of Cambia, a Province in Tartaria.

Here now let us remember his passing in this
speculative course from Constantinople by Sander,
Screwe, Panassa, Musa, Lastilla, to Varna, an ancient
Citie upon the Blacke Sea. In all which journey, having little

How he was
sent into
Tartaria.

more libertie, than his eyes judgement since his captivitie, he might see the Townes with their short Towers, and a most plaine, fertile, and delicate Countrey, especially that most admired place of Greece, now called Romania, but from Varna, nothing but the Blacke Sea water, till he came to the two Capes of Taur and Pergilos, where hee passed the Straight of Niger, which (as he conjectured) is some ten leagues long, and three broad, betwixt two low lands, the Channell is deepe, but

The description of the Dissabacca Sea.

at the entrance of the Sea Dissabacca, their are many great Osie-shoulds, and many great blacke rockes, which the Turkes said were trees, weeds, and mud, throwen from the in-land Countryes, by the inundations and violence of the Current, and cast there by the Eddy. They sayled by many low Iles, and saw many more of those muddy rockes, and nothing else, but salt water, till they came betwixt Susax and Curuske, only two white townes at the entrance of the river Bruapo appeared: In six or seven dayes saile, he saw foure or five seeming strong castles of stone, with flat tops and battlements about them, but arriving at Cambia, he was (according to their custome) well used. The river was there more than halfe a mile broad. The Castle was of a large circumference, fourteene or fifteene foot thicke, in the foundation some six foot from the wall, is a Pallizado, and then a Ditch of about fortie foot broad full of water. On the west side of it, is a Towne all of low flat houses, which as he conceived could bee of no great strength, yet it keepes all them barbarous Countreyes about it in admiration and subjection. After he had stayed there three dayes; it was two dayes more before his guides brought him to Nalbrits, where the *Tymor* then was resident, in a great vast stonie Castle with many great Courts about it, invironed with high stone wals, where was quartered their Armes, when they first subjected those Countreyes, which only live to labour for those tyrannicall Turkes.

Smith his usage in Tartaria.

To her unkinde brother, this kinde Ladie writ so much for his good usage, that hee halfe suspected, as much as she intended; for shee told him, he should there but sojourne to learne the language, and what it was to be a Turke, till time made her Master of her selfe. But the *Tymor* her brother, diverted all this to the worst of crueltie, for within an houre after his arrivall, he caused his *Drubman* to strip him

naked, and shave his head and beard so bare as his hand, a
great ring of iron, with a long stalke bowed like a sickle, rivet-
ted about his necke, and a coat made of Ulgries haire, guarded
about with a peece of an undrest skinne. There were many
more Christian slaves, and neere an hundred *Forsades* of
Turkes and Moores, and he being the last, was slave of slaves
to them all. Among these slavish fortunes there was no great
choice; for the best was so bad, a dog could hardly have lived
to endure, and yet for all their paines and labours no more regarded than a beast.

Chapter XIII.
The Turkes diet; the Slaves diet; the attire of the Tartars; and manner of Warres and Religions, etc.

The *Tymors*
diet of
Cambia is as
the Turkes. THE *Tymor* and his friends fed upon *Pillaw*, which
is boiled Rice and Garnances, with little bits of mut-
ton or *Buckones*, which is rosted peeces of Horse,
Bull, Ulgrie, or any beasts. *Samboyses* and *Muselbits* are great
dainties, and yet but round pies, full of all sorts of flesh they
can get chopped with varietie of herbs. Their best drinke is
Coffa, of a graine they call *Coava*, boiled with water; and *Sher-
becke*, which is only honey and water; Mares milke, or the milke
of any beast, they hold restorative: but all the Comminaltie
drinke pure water. Their bread is made of this *Coava*,
The Slaves
diet. which is a kinde of blacke wheat, and *Cuskus* a small
white seed like *Millya* in Biskay: but our common
victuall, the entrailes of Horse and Ulgries; of this cut in small
peeces, they will fill a great Cauldron, and being boiled with
Cuskus, and put in great bowles in the forme of chaffing-dishes,
they sit round about it on the ground, after they have raked it
thorow so oft as they please with their foule fists, the remainder was for the Christian slaves. Some of this broth they would
temper with *Cuskus* pounded, and putting the fire off from the
hearth, powre there a bowle full, then cover it with coales till it
be baked, which stewed with the remainder of the broth, and
some small peeces of flesh, was an extraordinarie daintie.

The better sort are attired like Turkes, but the plaine Tartar hath a blacke sheepe skinne over his backe, and two of the legs tied about his necke; the other two about his middle, with another over his belly, and the legs tied in the like manner behinde him: then two more made like a paire of bases, serveth him for breeches; with a little close cap to his skull of blacke felt, and they use exceeding much of this felt, for carpets, for bedding, for Coats, and Idols. Their houses are much worse than your Irish, but the In-land Countreyes have none but Carts and Tents, which they ever remove from Countrey to Countrey, as they see occasion, driving with them infinite troopes of blacke sheepe, Cattell and Ulgries, eating all up before them, as they goe.

The Attire of those Tartars.

For the Tartars of Nagi, they have neither Towne, nor house, corne, nor drinke; but flesh and milke. The milke they keepe in great skinnes like *Burracho's*, which though it be never so sower, it agreeth well with their strong stomackes. They live all in *Hordias*, as doth the Crim-Tartars, three or foure hundred in a company, in great Carts fifteene or sixteene foot broad, which is covered with small rods, wattled together in the forme of a birds nest turned up-wards, and with the ashes of bones tempered with oile, Camels haire, and a clay they have: they lome them so well, that no weather will pierce them, and yet verie light. Each *Hordia* hath a *Murse*, which they obey as their King. Their Gods are infi-nite. One or two thousand of those glittering white Carts drawen with Camels, Deere, Buls, and Ulgries, they bring round in a ring, where they pitch their Campe; and the *Murse,* with his chiefe alliances, are placed in the midst. They doe much hurt when they can get any *Stroggs*, which are great boats used upon the river Volga, (which they call *Edle*) to them that dwell in the Countrey of Perolog, and would doe much more, were it not for the Muscovites Garrisons that there inhabit.

The Tartars of Nagi and their manners.

Chapter XIIII.
The description of the Crym-Tartars; their houses and carts; their Idolatry in their lodgings.

The description tion of the Crym-Tartars Court.

Now you are to understand, Tartary and Scythia are all one, but so large and spacious, few or none could ever perfectly describe it, nor all the severall kinds of those most barbarous people that inhabit it. Those we call the Crym-Tartars, border upon Moldavia, Podolia, Lituania, and Russia, are much more regular than the interior parts of Scythia. This great Tartarian Prince, that hath so troubled all his neighbours, they alwayes call Chan, which signifieth Emperour; but we, the Crym-Tartar. He liveth for most part in the best champion plaines of many Provinces; and his removing Court is like a great Citie of houses and tents, drawne on Carts, all so orderly placed East and West, on the right and left hand of the Prince his house, which is alwayes in the midst towards the South, before which none may pitch their houses, every one knowing their order and quarter, as in an Armie.

His houses and carts.

The Princes houses are very artificially wrought, both the foundation, sides, and roofe of wickers, ascending round to the top like a Dove-coat; this they cover with white felt, or white earth tempered with the powder of bones, that it may shine the whiter; sometimes with blacke felt, curiously painted with vines, trees, birds, and beasts; the breadth of the Carts are eighteene or twenty foot, but the house stretcheth foure or five foot over each side, and is drawne with ten or twelve, or for more state, twenty Camels

Baskets.

and Oxen. They have also great baskets, made of smaller wickers like great chests, with a covering of the same, all covered over with blacke felt, rubbed over with tallow and sheeps milke, to keepe out the raine; prettily bedecked with painting or feathers; in those they put their houshold stuffe and treasure, drawne upon other carts for that purpose. When they take downe their houses, they set the doore alwayes towards the South, and their carts thirtie or fortie foot distant on each side, East and West, as if they were two walls: the women also have most curious carts; every one of his wives hath a great one for herselfe, and so many other for her attendants, that they seeme as many Courts, as he hath wives. One great Tartar or Nobleman, will have for his particular, more than an hundred of those houses and carts, for his severall offices and uses, but set so farre from each other, they will seeme like a great village. Having taken their houses from the

Their idolatrie in their lodgings.

carts, they place the Master alwayes towards the North; over whose head is alwayes an Image like a Puppet, made of felt, which they call his brother; the women on his left hand, and over the chiefe Mistris her head, such another brother, and betweene them a little one, which is the keeper of the house; at the good wives beds-feet is a kids skinne, stuffed with wooll, and neere it a Puppet looking towards the Maids; next the doore another, with a dried cowes udder, for the women that milke the kine, because only the men milke mares; every morning those Images in their orders

Cossmos is Mares milke.

they besprinkle with that they drinke, bee it *Cossmos*, or whatsoever, but all the white mares milke is reserved for the Prince. Then without the doore, thrice to the South, every one bowing his knee in honour of the fire; then the like to the East, in honour of the aire; then to the West, in honour of the water; and lastly to the North, in behalfe of the dead. After the servant hath done this duty to the foure quarters of the world, he returnes into the house, where his fellowes stand waiting, ready with two cups and two basons to give their master, and his wife that lay with him that night, to wash and drinke, who must keepe him company all the day following; and all his other wives come thither to drinke, where hee keepes his house that day; and all the gifts presented him till night, are laid up in her chests; and at the doore a bench full of cups, and drinke for any of them to make merry.

Chapter XV.

Their feasts; common diet; Princes estate; buildings; tributes; lawes; slaves; entertainment of Ambassadours.

Their feasts.

FOR their feasts they have all sorts of beasts, birds, fish, fruits, and hearbs they can get, but the more variety of wilde ones is the best; to which they have excellent drinke made of rice, millit, and honey, like wine; they have also wine, but in Summer they drinke most *Cossmos*, that standeth ready alwayes at the entrance of the doore, and by it a fidler; when the master of the house beginneth to drinke, they all cry, ha, ha, and the fidler playes, then they all clap their hands and dance, the men before their Masters, the women before their Mistresses; and ever when he drinks, they cry as before; then the fidler stayeth till they drinke all round; sometimes they will drinke for the victory; and to provoke one to drinke, they will pull him by the ears, and lugge and draw him, to stretch and heat him, clapping their hands, stamping with their feet, and dancing before the champions, offering them cups, then draw them backe againe to increase their appetite; and thus continue till they be drunke, or their drinke done, which they hold an honour, and no infirmity.

Though the ground be fertile, they sow little corne, yet the Gentlemen have bread and hony-wine; grapes they have plenty, and wine privately, and good flesh and fish; but the common sort stamped millit, mingled with milke and water. They call *Cassa* for meat, and drinke any thing; also any beast unprofitable for service they kill, when they are like to die, or however they die, they will eat them, guts liver and all; but the most fleshy parts they cut in thinne slices, and hang it up in the Sunne and wind without salting, where it will drie so hard, it will not putrifie in a long time. A Ramme they esteeme a great feast among forty or fiftie, which they cut in peeces boiled or roast, put it in a great bowle with salt and water, for other sauce they have none; the master of the feast giveth every one a peece, which he eateth by himselfe, or carrieth away with him. Thus their hard fare makes them so infinite in Cattell, and their great number of captived women to breed upon, makes them so populous. But neere the Christian frontiers, the baser sort make little cottages of wood, called *Ulusi*, daubed over with durt, and beasts dung covered with sedge; yet in Summer they leave them, beginning their progresse in Aprill, with their wives, children, and slaves, in their carted houses, scarce convenient for foure or five persons; driving their flocks towards Perecopya, and sometimes into Taurica, or Osow, a towne upon

Their common diet.

How they become populous.

the river Tanais, which is great and swift, where the Turke hath a garrison; and in October returne againe to their Cottages. Their Clothes are the skinnes of dogges, goats, and sheepe, lined with cotton cloath, made of their finest wooll, for of their worst they make their felt, which they use in aboundance, as well for shooes and caps, as houses, beds, and Idolls; also of the coarse wooll mingled with horse haire, they make all their cordage. Notwithstanding this wandring life, their Princes sit in great state upon beds, or carpits, and with great reverence are attended both by men and women, and richly served in plate, and great silver cups, delivered upon the knee, attired in rich furres, lined with plush, or taffity, or robes of tissue. These Tartars possesse many large and goodly plaines, wherein feed innumerable herds of horse and cattell, as well wilde as tame; which are Elkes, Bisones, Horses, Deere, Sheepe, Goates, Swine, Beares, and divers others.

Their Princes state.

In those countries are the ruines of many faire Monasteries, Castles, and Cities, as Bacasaray, Salutium, Almassary, Perecopya, Cremum, Sedacom, Capha, and divers others by the Sea, but all kept with strong garrisons for the great Turke, who yearely by trade or trafficke, receiveth the chiefe commodities those fertile countries afford, as Bezer, Rice, Furres, Hides, Butter, Salt, Cattell, and Slaves, yet by the spoiles they get from the secure and idle Christians, they maintaine themselves in this Pompe. Also their wives, of whom they have as many as they will, very costly, yet in a constant custome with decency.

Ancient buildings.

Commodities for tribute to the Turke.

They are Mahometans, as are the Turks, from whom also they have their Lawes, but no Lawyers, nor Attournies, onely Judges, and Justices in every Village, or *Hordia*; but capitall criminalls, or matters of moment, before the Chan himselfe, or Privie Counsells, of whom they are alwayes heard, and speedily discharged; for any may have accesse at any time to them, before whom they appeare with great reverence, adoring their Princes as Gods, and their spirituall Judges as Saints; for Justice is with such integrity and expedition executed, without covetousnesse, bribery, partiality, and brawling, that in six moneths they have sometimes scarce six causes to heare. About the Princes court none but his

Good lawes, yet no lawyers.

guard weares any weapon, but abroad they goe very strong, because there are many bandytos, and Theeves.

   They use the Hungarians, Russians, Wallachians, and Moldavian slaves (whereof they have plenty) as beasts to every worke; and those Tartars that serve the Chan, or noblemen, have only victuall and apparell, the rest are generally nasty, and idle, naturally miserable, and in their warres better theeves than souldiers.

Their slaves.

 This Chan hath yeerely a Donative from the King of Poland, the Dukes of Lituania, Moldavia, and Nagagon Tartars; their Messengers commonly he useth bountifully, and verie nobly, but sometimes most cruelly; when any of them doth bring their Presents, by his houshold Officers they are entertained in a plaine field, with a moderate proportion of flesh, bread and wine, for once; but when they come before him, the Sultaines, Tuians, Ulans, Marhies, his chiefe Officers and Councellors attend, one man only bringeth the Ambassadour to the Court gate, but to the Chan he is led betweene two Councellors; where saluting him upon their bended knees, declaring their message, are admitted to eat with him, and presented with a great silver cup full of Mead from his owne hand, but they drinke it upon their knees: when they are dispatched, he invites them againe, the feast ended, they go backe a little from the Palace doore, and rewarded with silke Vestures wrought with gold downe to their anckles, with an horse or two, and sometimes a slave of their owne Nation; in them robes presently they come to him againe, to give him thankes, take their leave, and so depart.

His entertainment of Ambassadours.

Chapter XVI.
How he levieth an Armie; their Armes and Provision; how he divideth the spoile; and his service to the Great Turke.

WHEN he intends any warres, he must first have leave of the Great Turke, whom hee is bound to assist when hee commandeth, receiving daily for himselfe and chiefe of his Nobilitie, pensions from the Turke, that holds

How he levieth an Armie.

all Kings but slaves, that pay tribute or are subject to any: signifying his intent to all his subjects, within a moneth commonly he raiseth his Armie, and everie man is to furnish
himselfe for three monethes victuals, which is parched Millit, or
grownd to meale, which they ordinarily mingle with water (as
is said) hard cheese or cruds dried, and beaten to powder, a
little will make much water like milke, and dried flesh, this they
put also up in sackes: The Chan and his Nobles have some
bread and Aquavitæ, and quicke cattell to kill when they please,
wherewith verie sparingly they are contented. Being provided
with expert Guides, and got into the Countrey he intends to
invade, he sends forth his Scouts to bring in what prisoners
they can, from whom he will wrest the utmost of their knowledge fit for his purpose: having advised with his Councell,
what is most fit to be done, the Nobilitie, according to their
antiquitie, doth march; then moves he with his whole Armie: if
hee finde there is no enemie to oppose him, he adviseth how
farre they shall invade, commanding everie man (upon paine
of his life) to kill all the obvious Rusticks; but not to hurt any
women, or children.

  Ten, or fifteene thousand, he commonly placeth,
The manner
of his warres. where hee findeth most convenient for his standing
Campe; the rest of his Armie hee divides in severall
troops, bearing ten or twelve miles square before them, and
ever within three or foure dayes returne to their Campe, putting
all to fire and sword, but that they carrie with them backe to
their Campe; and in this scattering manner he will invade a
Countrey, and be gone with his prey, with an incredible expedition. But if he understand of an enemie, he will either fight in
Ambuscado, or flie; for he will never fight any battell if he can
chuse, but upon treble advantage; yet by his innumerable
flights of arrowes, I have seene flie from his flying troopes, we
could not well judge, whether his fighting or flying was most
dangerous, so good is his horse, and so expert his bowmen; but
if they be so intangled they must fight, there is none can bee
more hardy, or resolute in their defences.

  Regaining his owne borders, he takes the tenth of
How he
divides the
spoile. the principall captives, man, woman, childe, or beast
(but his captaines that take them, will accept of some
particular person they best like for themselves) the rest are

divided amongst the whole Armie, according to every mans desert, and quality; that they keepe them, or sell them to who will give most; but they will not forget to use all the meanes they can, to know their estates, friends, and quality, and the better they finde you, the worse they will use you, till you doe agree to pay such a ransome, as they will impose upon you; therefore many great persons have endured much misery to conceale themselves, because their ransomes are so intolerable: their best hope is of some Christian Agent, that many times commeth to redeeme slaves, either with mony, or man for man; those Agents knowing so well the extreme covetousnesse of the Tartars, doe use to bribe some Jew or Merchant, that feigning they will sell them againe to some other nation, are oft redeemed for a very small ransome.

How the Chan doth serve the great Turke.

But to this Tartarian Armie, when the Turke commands, he goeth with some small artillery; and the Nagagians, Perecopens, Crimes, Osovens, and Cersessians, are his tributaries; but the Petigorves, Oczaconians, Byalogordens, and Dobrucen Tartars, the Turke by covenant commands to follow him, so that from all those Tartars he hath had an Army of an hundred and twenty thousand excellent, swift, stomackfull Tartarian horse, for foot they have none. Now the Chan, his Sultaines and nobility, use Turkish, Caramanian, Arabian, Parthian, and other strange Tartarian horses; the swiftest they esteeme the best; seldome they feede any more at home, than they have present use for; but upon their plaines is a short wodde like heath, in some countries like gaile, full of berries, farre much better than any grasse.

Their Armes.

Their Armes are such as they have surprised or got from the Christians or Persians, both brest-plates, swords, semiteres, and helmets; bowes and arrowes they make most themselves, also their bridles and saddles are indifferent, but the nobility are very handsome, and well armed like the Turkes, in whom consisteth their greatest glory; the ordinary sort have little armor, some a plaine young pole unshaven, headed with a peece of iron for a lance; some an old Christian pike, or a Turks cavarine; yet those tattertimallions will have two or three horses, some foure or five, as well for service, as for to eat; which makes their Armies seem thrice so many as there are souldiers. The Chan himselfe hath about his person ten thousand chosen Tartars and Janizaries, some small Ordnance, and a white mares taile, with a peece of greene taffity on a great Pike, is carried before him for a standard; because they hold no beast so precious as a white mare, whose milke is onely for the King and nobility, and to sacrifice to their Idolls; but the rest have ensignes of divers colours.

For all this miserable knowledge, furniture, and equipage, the mischiefe they doe in Christendome is wonderfull, by reason of their hardnesse of life and constitution, obedience, agilitie, and their Emperours bountie, honours, grace, and dignities he ever bestoweth upon those, that have done him any memorable service in the face of his enemies.

The Caspian Sea, most men agree that have passed it, to be in length about 200. leagues, and in breadth an hundred and fifty, environed to the East, with the great desarts of the Tartars of Turkamane; to the West, by the Circasses, and the mountaine Caucasus; to the North, by the river Volga, and the land of Nagay; and to the South, by Media, and Persia: this sea is fresh water in many places, in others as salt as the great Ocean; it hath many great rivers which fall into it, as the mighty river of Volga, which is like a sea, running neere two thousand miles, through many great and large Countries, that send into it many other great rivers; also out of Saberya, Yaick, and Yem, out of the great mountaine Caucasus, the river Sirus, Arash, and divers others, yet no Sea neerer it than the blacke Sea, which is at least an hundred leagues distant: in which Country live the Georgians, now part Armenians, part Nestorians; it is neither found to increase or diminish, or empty it selfe any way, except it be under ground, and in some places they can finde no ground at two hundred fadome.

A description of the Caspian Sea.

Many other most strange and wonderfull things are in the land of Cathay towards the North-east, and Chyna towards the South-east, where are many of the most famous Kingdomes in the world; where most arts, plenty, and curiosities are in such abundance, as might seeme incredible, which hereafter I will relate, as I have briefly gathered from such authors as have lived there.

Chapter XVII.

How captaine Smith escaped his captivity; slew the Bashaw of Nalbrits in Cambia; his passage to Russia, Transilvania, and the middest of Europe to Affrica.

ALL the hope he had ever to be delivered from this thraldome, was only the love of Tragabigzanda, who surely was ignorant of his bad usage; for although he had often debated the matter with some Christians, that had beene there a long time slaves, they could not finde how to make an escape, by any reason or possibility; but God beyond mans expectation or imagination helpeth his servants, when they least thinke of helpe, as it hapned to him. So long he lived in this miserable estate, as he became a thresher at a grange in a great field, more than a league from the *Tymors* house; the Bashaw as he oft used to visit his granges, visited him, and tooke occasion so to beat, spurne, and revile him, that forgetting all reason, he beat out the *Tymors* braines with his threshing bat, for they have no flailes; and seeing his estate could be no worse than it was, clothed himselfe in his clothes, hid his body under the straw, filled his knapsacke with corne, shut the doores, mounted his horse, and ranne into the desart at all adventure; two or three dayes thus fearfully wandring he knew not whither, and well it was he met not any to aske the way; being even as taking leave of this miserable world, God did direct him to the great way or Castragan, as they call it, which doth crosse these large territories, and generally knowne among them by these markes.

In every crossing of this great way is planted a post, and in it so many bobs with broad ends, as there be wayes, and every bob the figure painted on it, that demonstrateth to what part that way leadeth; as that which pointeth towards the Cryms Country, is marked with a halfe Moone, if towards the Georgians and Persia, a blacke man, full of white spots, if towards China, the picture of the Sunne, if towards Muscovia, the signe of a Crosse, if towards the habitation of any other Prince, the figure whereby his standard is knowne. To his dying spirits thus God added some comfort in this melancholy journey, wherein if he had met any of that vilde generation, they had made him their slave, or knowing the figure engraven in the iron about his necke, (as all slaves have) he had beene sent backe againe to his master; sixteene dayes he travelled in this feare and torment, after the Crosse, till he arrived at Æcopolis, upon the river Don, a garrison of the Muscovites. The governour after due examination of those his hard events, tooke off his irons, and so kindly used him, he thought himselfe new risen from death, and the good Lady Callamata, largely supplied all his wants.

This is as much as he could learne of those wilde Countries, that the Country of Cambia is two dayes journy from the head of the great river Bruapo, which springeth from many places of the mountaines of Innagachi, that joyne themselves together in the Poole Kerkas; which they account for the head, and falleth into the Sea Dissabacca, called by some the lake Meotis, which receiveth also the river Tanais, and all the rivers that fall from the great Countries of the Circassi, the Cartaches, and many from the Tauricaes, Precopes, Cummani, Cossunka, and the Cryme; through which Sea he sailed, and up the river Bruapo to Nalbrits, and thence through the desarts of Circassi to Æcopolis, as is related; where he stayed with the Governour, till the Convoy went to Coragnaw; then with his certificate how hee found him, and had examined with his friendly letters sent him by Zumalacke to Caragnaw, whose Governour in like manner so kindly use him, that by this meanes he went with a safe conduct to Letch, and Donka, in Cologoske, and thence to Berniske, and Newgrod in Seberia, by Rezechica, upon the river Niper, in the confines of Littuania; from whence with as much kindnesse he was convoyed in like manner by Coroski, Duberesko, Duzihell, Drohobus, and Ostroge in Volonia; Saslaw and Lasco in Podolia; Halico and Collonia in Polonia; and so to Hermonstat in Transilvania. In all his life he seldome met with more respect, mirth, content, and entertainment; and not any Governour where he came, but gave him somewhat as a present, besides his charges; seeing themselves as subject to the like calamity. Through those poore continually forraged Countries there is no passage, but with the Carravans or Convoyes; for they are Countries rather to be pitied, than envied;

The description of Cambia, and his passage to Russia.

His observations in his journey to Transilvania, through the midst of Europe.

and it is a wonder any should make warres for them. The Villages are onely here and there a few houses of straight Firre trees, laid heads and points above one another, made fast by notches at the ends more than a mans height, and with broad split boards, pinned together with woodden pinnes, as thatched for coverture. In ten Villages you shall scarce finde ten iron nailes, except it be in some extraordinary mans house. For their Townes, Æcopolis, Letch, and Donko, have rampiers made of that woodden walled fashion, double, and betwixt them earth and stones, but so latched with crosse timber, they are very strong against any thing but fire; and about them a deepe ditch, and a Palizado of young Firre trees: but most of the rest have only a great ditch cast about them, and the ditches earth is all their rampier; but round well environed with Palizadoes. Some have some few small peeces of small Ordnance, and slings, calievers, and muskets, but their generallest weapons are the Russe bowes and arrowes; you shall find pavements over bogges, onely of young Firre trees laid crosse one over another, for two or three houres journey, or as the passage requires, and yet in two dayes travell you shall scarce see six habitations. Notwithstanding to see how their Lords, Governours, and Captaines are civilized, well attired and acoutred with Jewells, Sables, and Horses, and after their manner with curious furniture, it is wonderfull; but they are all Lords or slaves, which makes them so subject to every invasion.

In Transilvania he found so many good friends, that but to see, and rejoyce himselfe (after all those encounters) in his native Country, he would ever hardly have left them, though the mirrour of vertue their Prince was absent. Being thus glutted with content, and neere drowned with joy, he passed high Hungaria by Fileck, Tocka, Cassovia, and Underoroway, by Ulmicht in Moravia, to Prague in Bohemia; at last he found the most gracious Prince Sigismundus, with his Colonell at Lipswick in Misenland, who gave him his Passe, intimating the service he had done, and the honours he had received, with fifteene hundred ducats of gold to repaire his losses: with this he spent some time to visit the faire Cities and Countries of Drasdon in Saxonie, Magdaburgh and Brunswicke; Cassell in Hessen; Wittenberg, Ullum, and Minikin in Bavaria; Aughsbrough, and her Universities; Hama, Franckford, Mentz, the

Palatinate; Wormes, Speyre, and Strausborough; passing Nancie in Loraine, and France by Paris to Orleans, hee went downe the river of Loyer, to Angiers, and imbarked himselfe at Nantz in Britanny, for Bilbao in Biskay, to see Burgos, Valiadolid, the admired monasterie of the Escuriall, Madrill, Toledo, Cordua, Cuedyriall, Civill, Cheryes, Cales, and Saint Lucas in Spaine.

Chapter XVIII.
The observations of Captaine Smith; Master Henrie Archer and others in Barbarie.

BEING thus satisfied with Europe and Asia, understanding of the warres in Barbarie, hee went from Gibralter to Guta and Tanger, thence to Saffee, where growing into acquaintance with a French man of warre, the Captaine and some twelve more went to Morocco, to see the ancient monuments of that large renowned Citie: it was once the principall Citie in Barbarie, situated in a goodly plaine Countrey, 14. miles from the great Mount Atlas, and sixtie miles from the Atlanticke Sea; but now little remaining, but the Kings Palace, which is like a Citie of it selfe, and the Christian Church, on whose flat square steeple is a great brouch of iron, whereon is placed the three golden Bals of Affrica: the first is neere three Ells in circumference, the next above it somewhat lesse, the uppermost the least over them, as it were an halfe Ball, and over all a prettie guilded Pyramides. Against those golden Bals hath been shot many a shot, their weight is recorded 700. weight of pure gold, hollow within, yet no shot did ever hit them, nor could ever any Conspirator attaine that honor as to get them downe. They report the Prince of Morocco betrothed himselfe to the Kings Daughter of Æthiopia, he dying before their marriage, she caused those three golden Balls to be set up for his Monument, and vowed virginitie all her life. The Alfantica is also a place of note, because it is invironed with a great wall, wherein lye the goods of all the Merchants securely guarded. The Juderea

The three golden Bals of Affrica.

The description of Morocco.

is also (as it were) a Citie of it selfe, where dwell the Jewes: the rest for the most part is defaced: but by the many pinnacles and towers, with Balls on their tops, hath much appearance of much sumptuousnesse and curiositie. There have been many famous Universities, which are now but stables for Fowles and Beasts, and the houses in most parts lye tumbled one above another; the walls of Earth are with the great fresh flouds washed to the ground; nor is there any village in it, but tents for Strangers, Larbes and Moores. Strange tales they will tell of a great Garden, wherein were all sorts of Birds, Fishes, Beasts, Fruits and Fountaines, which for beautie, Art and pleasure, exceeded any place knowne in the world, though now nothing but dung-hils, Pigeon-houses, shrubs and bushes. There are yet many excellent fountaines adorned with marble, and many arches, pillers, towers, ports and Temples; but most only reliques of lamentable ruines and sad desolation.

When Mully Hamet reigned in Barbarie, hee had three sonnes, Mully Shecke, Mully Sidan, and Mully Befferres, he a most good and noble King, that governed well with peace and plentie, till his Empresse, more cruell than any beast in Affrica, poysoned him, her owne daughter, Mully Shecke his eldest sonne borne of a Portugall Ladie, and his daughter, to bring Mully Sidan to the Crowne now reigning, which was the cause of all those brawles and warres that followed betwixt those Brothers, their children, and a Saint that start up, but he played the Devill.

A bloudie Empresse.

King Mully Hamet was not blacke, as many suppose, but Molata, or tawnie, as are the most of his subjects; everie way noble, kinde and friendly, verie rich and pompous in State and Majestie, though hee sitteth not upon a Throne nor Chaire of Estate, but crosse legged upon a rich Carpet, as doth the Turke, whose Religion of Mahomet, with an incredible miserable curiositie they observe. His Ordinarie Guard is at least 5000 but in progresse he goeth not with lesse than 20000. horsemen, himselfe as rich in all his Equipage, as any Prince in Christendome, and yet a Contributor to the Turke. In all his Kingdome were so few good Artificers, that hee entertained from England, Gold-smiths, Plummers, Carvers, and Polishers of stone, and Watch-makers, so much hee delighted in

King Mully Hamet, or the Great Zeriff of Barbarie.

His great love to English-men.

the reformation of workmanship, hee allowed each of them ten shillings a day standing fee, linnen, woollen, silkes, and what they would for diet and apparell, and custome-free to transport, or import what they would; for there were scarce any of those qualities in his Kingdomes, but those, of which there are divers of them living at this present in London. Amongst the rest, one Master Henry Archer, a Watch-maker, walking in Morocco, from the Alfantica to the Juderea, the way being verie foule, met a great Priest, or a Sante (as they call all great Clergy-men) who would have thrust him into the durt for the way; but Archer, not knowing what he was, gave him a box on the eare, presently he was apprehended, and condemned to have his tongue cut out, and his hand cut off: but no sooner it was knowen at the Kings Court, but 300. of his Guard came, and broke open the Prison, and delivered him, although the fact was next degree to Treason.

The strange love of a Lyon.

Concerning this Archer, there is one thing more worth noting: Not farre from Mount Atlas, a great Lionesse in the heat of the day, did use to bathe her selfe, and teach her young Puppies to swimme in the river Cauzeff, of a good bredth; yet she would carrie them one after another over the river; which some Moores perceiving watched their opportunitie, and when the river was betweene her and them, stole foure of her whelps, which she perceiving, with all the speed shee could passed the river, and comming neere them they let fall a whelpe (and fled with the rest) which she tooke in her mouth, and so returned to the rest: a Male and a Female of those they gave Master Archer, who kept them in the Kings Garden, till the Male killed the Female, then he brought it up as a Puppy-dog lying upon his bed, till it grew so great as a Mastiffe, and no dog more tame or gentle to them hee knew: but being to returne for England, at Saffee he gave him to a Merchant of Marsellis, that presented him to the French King, who sent him to King James, where it was kept in the Tower seven yeeres: After one Master John Bull, then servant to Master Archer, with divers of his friends, went to see the Lyons, not knowing any thing at all of him; yet this rare beast smelled him before hee saw him, whining, groaning, and tumbling, with such an expression of acquaintance, that being informed by the Keepers how hee came thither; Master Bull so prevailed, the Keeper opened the grate, and Bull went in: But no Dogge could fawne more on his Master, than the Lyon on him, licking his feet, hands, and face, skipping and tumbling to and fro, to the wonder of all the beholders; being satisfied with his acquaintance, he made shift to get out of the grate. But when the Lyon saw his friend gone, no beast by bellowing, roaring, scratching, and howling, could expresse more rage and sorrow, nor in foure dayes after would he either eat or drinke.

Another kinde Lyon in Morocco.   In Morocco, the Kings Lyons are all together in a Court, invironed with a great high wall; to those they put a young Puppy-dogge: the greatest Lyon had a sore upon his necke, which this Dogge so licked that he was healed: the Lyon defended him from the furie of all the rest, nor durst they eat till the Dogge and he had fed; this Dog grew great, and lived amongst them many yeeres after.

The descrip- tion of Fez.   Fez also is a most large and plentifull Countrey, the chiefe Citie is called Fez, divided into two parts; old Fez, containing about 80. thousand housholds, the other 4000. pleasantly situated upon a River in the heart of Barbarie, part upon hils, part upon plaines, full of people, and all sorts of Merchandise. The great Temple is called Caru-cen, in bredth seventeene Arches, in length 120. borne up with 2500. white marble pillars: under the chiefe Arch, where the Tribunall is kept, hangeth a most huge lampe, compassed with 110. lesser, under the other also hang great lamps, and about some are burning fifteene hundred lights. They say they were all made of the bels the Arabians brought from Spaine. It hath three gates of notable height, Priests and Officers so many, that the circuit of the Church, the Yard, and other houses, is little lesse than a mile and an halfe in compasse; there are in this Citie 200. Schooles, 200. Innes, 400. water-mils, 600. water-Conduits, 700. Temples and Oratories; but fiftie of them most stately and richly furnished. Their Alcazer or Burse is walled about, it hath twelve gates, and fifteen walks covered with tents, to keepe the Sun from the Merchants, and them that come there. The Kings Palace, both for strength and beautie is excellent, and the Citizens have many great privileges. Those two Countreyes of Fez and Morocco, are the best part of all Barbarie, abounding with people, cattell, and all good neces-

A briefe
description
of the most
unknowen
parts of
Affrica. saries for mans use. For the rest, as the Larbes, or Mountainers, the Kingdomes of Cocow, Algier, Tripoly, Tunis, and Ægypt; there are many large histories of them in divers languages, especially that writ by that most excellent Statesman, John de Leo, who afterward turned Christian. The unknowen Countries of Ginny and Binne, this six and twentie yeeres have beene frequented with a few English ships only to trade, especially the river of Senaga, by Captaine Brimstead, Captaine Brockit, Master Crump, and divers others. Also the great river of Gambra, by Captaine Jobson, who is returned in thither againe in the yeere 1626. with Master William Grent, and thirteene or fourteene others, to stay in the Countrey, to discover some way to those rich mines of Gago or Tumbatu, from whence is supposed the Moores of Barbarie have their gold, and the certaintie of those supposed descriptions and relations of those interiour parts, which daily the more they are sought into, the more they are corrected. For surely, those interiour parts of Affrica are little knowen to either English, French, or Dutch, though they use much the Coast; therefore wee will make a little bold with the observations of the Portugalls.

Chapter XIX.
The strange discoveries and observations of the Portugalls in Affrica.

How the
Portugalls
coasted to the
East Indies. THE Portugalls on those parts have the glorie, who first coasting along this Westerne shore of Affrica, to finde passage to the East Indies, within this hundred and fiftie yeeres, even from the Streights of Gibralter, about the Cape of Bone Esperance to the Persian Gulfe, and thence all along the Asian Coast to the Moluccas, have subjected many great Kingdomes, erected many Common-wealths, built many great and strong Cities; and where is it they have not beene by trade or force? no not so much as Cape de Verd, and Serraleone; but most Bayes or Rivers, where there is any trade to bee had, especially gold, or conveniencie for refreshment,

but they are scattered; living so amongst those Blacks, by time and cunning they seeme to bee naturalized amongst them. As for the Isles of the Canaries, they have faire Townes, many Villages, and many thousands of people rich in commodities.

Odoardo Lopez, a noble Portugall, Anno Dom.

Or Edward. 1578. imbarquing himselfe for Congo to trade, where he found such entertainment, finding the King much oppressed with enemies, hee found meanes to bring in the Portugalls to assist him, whereby he planted there Christian Religion, and spent most of his life to bring those Countreyes to the Crowne of Portugall, which he describeth in this manner.

The Kingdome of Congo is about 600. miles diameter any way, the chiefe Citie called St. Salvadore, seated upon an exceeding high mountaine, 150. miles from the Sea, verie fertile, and inhabited with more than 100000. persons; where is an excellent prospect over all the plaine Countreyes about it, well watered, lying (as it were) in the Center of this Kingdome, over all which the Portugalls now command, though but an handfull in comparison of Negroes. They have flesh and fruits verie plentifull of divers sorts.

The Kingdome of Congo.

This Kingdom is divided into five Provinces, viz. Bamba, Sundi, Pango, Batta and Pembo; but Bamba is the principall, and can affoord 400000. men of warre. Elephants are bred over all those Provinces, and of wonderfull greatnesse; though some report they cannot kneele, nor lye downe, they can doe both, and have their joynts as other creatures for use: with their fore-feet they will leape upon trees to pull downe the boughes, and are of that strength, they will shake a great Cocar tree for the nuts, and pull downe a good tree with their tuskes, to get the leaves to eat, as well as sedge and long grasse, Cocar nuts and berries, etc. which with their trunke they put in their mouth, and chew it with their smaller teeth; in most of those Provinces, are many rich mines, but the Negars opposed the Portugalls for working in them.

Wilde Elephants.

The Kingdome of Angola is wonderfull populous, and rich in mines of silver, copper, and most other mettalls; fruitfull in all manner of food, and sundry sorts of cattell, but dogges flesh they love better than any other meat; they use few clothes, and no Armour; bowes, arrowes,

The Kingdome of Angola.

and clubs, are their weapons. But the Portugalls are well armed against those engines, and doe buy yearely of those Blacks more than five thousand slaves, and many are people exceeding well proportioned.

The Kingdome of Anchicos. The Anchicos are a most valiant nation, but most strange to all about them. Their Armes are Bowes, short and small, wrapped about with serpents skinnes, of divers colours, but so smooth you would thinke them all one with the wood, and it makes them very strong; their strings little twigs, but exceeding tough and flexible; their arrowes short, which they shoot with an incredible quicknesse. They have short axes of brasse and copper for swords; wonderfull loyall and faithfull, and exceeding simple, yet so active,

A strange mony. they skip amongst the rockes like goats. They trade with them of Nubea, and Congo, for *Lamache*, which is a small kinde of shell fish, of an excellent azure colour, male and female, but the female they hold most pure; they value them at divers prices, because they are of divers sorts, and those they use for coine, to buy and sell, as we doe gold and silver; nor will they have any other money in all those Countries, for which they give Elephants teeth; and slaves for salt, silke, linnen cloth, glasse-beads, and such like Portugall commodities.

A shambles of mans flesh. They circumcise themselves, and marke their faces with sundry slashes from their infancie. They keepe a shambles of mans flesh, as if it were beefe, or other victuall; for when they cannot have a good market for their slaves; or their enemies they take, they kill, and sell them in this manner; some are so resolute, in shewing how much they scorne death, they will offer themselves and slaves, to this butchery to their Prince and friends; and though there be many nations will eat their enemies, in America and Asia, yet none but those are knowne to be so mad, as to eat their slaves and friends also.

Their Religions and Idols. Religions and idolls they have as many, as nations and humours; but the devill hath the greatest part of their devotions, whom all those Blacks doe say is white; for there are no Saints but Blacks.

But besides those great Kingdomes of Congo, Angola, and Azichi, in those unfrequented parts are the kingdomes of

Divers nations yet unknowne, and the wonders of Affrica. Lango, Matania, Buttua, Sofola, Mozambeche, Quivola, the Isle of Saint Lawrence, Mombaza, Metruda, the Empires of Monomatopa, Monemugi, and Presbiter John, with whom they have a kinde of trade, and their rites, customes, climates, temperatures, and commodities by relation. Also of great Lakes, that deserve the names of Seas, and huge mountaines of divers sorts, as some scorched with heat, some covered with snow; the mountaines of the Sunne, also of the Moone, some of crystall, some of iron, some of silver, and mountaines of gold, with the originall of Nilus; likewise sundry sorts of cattell, fishes, Fowles, strange beasts, and monstrous serpents; for Affrica was alwayes noted to be a fruitfull mother of such terrible creatures; who meeting at their watering places, which are but Ponds in desart places, in regard of the heat of the Country, and their extremities of nature, make strange copulations, and so ingender those extraordinary monsters. Of all these you may reade in the history of this Edward Lopez, translated into English by Abraham Hartwell, and dedicated to John, Lord Archbishop of Canterbury, 1597. But because the particulars are most concerning the conversion of those Pagans, by a good poore Priest, that first converted a Noble man, to convert the King, and the rest of the Nobility; sent for so many Priests and ornaments into Portugall, to solemnize their baptismes with such magnificence, which was performed with such strange curiosities, that those poore Negros adored them as Gods, till the Priests grew to that wealth, a Bishop was sent to rule over them, which they would not endure, which endangered to spoile all before they could bee reconciled. But not to trouble you too long with those rarities of uncertainties; let us returne againe to Barbary, where the warres being ended, and Befferres possessed of Morocco, and his fathers treasure, a new bruit arose amongst them, that Muly Sidan, was raising an Armie against him, who after tooke his brother Befferres prisoner; but by reason of the uncertainty, and the perfidious, treacherous, bloudy murthers rather than warre, amongst those perfidious, barbarous Moores, Smith returned with Merham, and the rest to Saffe, and so aboard his Ship, to try some other conclusions at Sea.

Chapter XX.
A brave Sea fight betwixt two Spanish men of warre, and Captaine Merham, with Smith.

MERHAM a captaine of a man of war then in the Road, invited captaine Smith, and two or three more of them aboord with him, where he spared not any thing he had to expresse his kindnesse, to bid them welcome, till it was too late to goe on shore, so that necessitie constrained them to stay aboord; a fairer Evening could not bee, yet ere midnight such a storme did arise, they were forced to let slip Cable, and Anchor, and put to Sea; spooning before the wind, till they were driven to the Canaries; in the calmes they accommodated themselves, hoping this strange accident might yet produce some good event; not long it was before they tooke a small Barke comming from Teneryf, loaded with Wine; three or foure more they chased, two they tooke, but found little in them, save a few passengers, that told them of five Dutch men of warre, about the Isles, so that they stood for Boyadora, upon the Affrican shore, betwixt which and Cape Noa, they descried two saile. Merham intending to know what they were, hailed them; very civilly they dansed their topsailes, and desired the man of warre to come aboord them, and take what he would, for they were but two poore distressed Biskiners. But Merham the old fox, seeing himselfe in the lions pawes, sprung his loufe, the other tacked after him, and came close up to his nether quarter, gave his broad side, and so loufed up to wind-ward; the Vice-Admirall did the like, and at the next bout, the Admirall with a noise of Trumpets, and all his Ordnance, mur-therers, and muskets, boorded him on his broad side; the other in like manner on his ley quarter, that it was so darke, there was little light, but fire and smoake; long he stayed not, before he fell off, leaving 4. or 5. of his men sprawling over the grating; after they had battered Merham about an houre, they boorded him againe as before; and threw foure kedgers or grapnalls in iron chaines, then shearing off they thought so to have torne downe the grating; but the Admiralls yard was so intangled in their shrouds, Merham had time to discharge two crosse barre shot amongst them, and divers bolts of iron made for that purpose, against his bow, that made such a breach, he feared they both should have sunke for company; so that the Spaniard was as yare in slipping his chained Grapnalls, as Merham was in cutting the tackling, kept fast their yards in his shrouds; the Vice-admirall presently cleared himselfe, but spared neither his Ordnance nor Muskets to keepe Merham from getting away, till the Admirall had repaired his leake; from twelve at noone, till six at night, they thus interchanged one volly for another; then the Vice-admirall fell on starne, staying for the Admirall that came up againe to him, and all that night stood after Merham, that shaped his course for Mamora, but such small way they made, the next morning they were not three leagues off from Cape Noa. The two Spanish men of warre, for so they were, and well appointed, taking it in scorne as it seemed, with their chase, broad side, and starne, the one after the other, within Musket shot, plying their ordnance; and after an houres worke commanded Merham a maine for the King of Spaine upon faire quarter; Merham dranke to them, and so discharged his quarter peeces: which pride the Spaniard to revenge, boorded him againe, and many of them were got to the top to unsling the maine saile, which the Master and some others from the round house, caused to their cost to come tumbling downe; about the round house the Spaniards so pestered, that they were forced to the great Cabben and blew it up; the smoake and fire was so vehement, as they thought the Ship on fire; they in the fore castle were no lesse assaulted, that blew up a peece of the grating, with a great many of Spaniards more; then they cleared themselves with all speed, and Merham with as much expedition to quench the fire with wet clothes and water, which beganne to grow too fast. The Spaniard still playing upon him with all the shot they could; the open places presently they covered with old sailes, and prepared themselves to fight to the last man. The angry Spaniard seeing the fire quenched, hung out a flagge of truce to have but a parley; but that desperate Merham knew there was but one way with him, and would have none, but the report of his Ordnance, which hee did know well how to use for his best advantage. Thus they spent the next after-noone, and halfe that night, when the Spanyards either lost them, or left them. Seven and twentie

men Merham had slaine, and sixteene wounded, and could
finde they had received 140. great shot. A wounded Spanyard
they kept alive confessed, they had lost 100. men in the Admirall, which they did feare would sinke, ere she could recover a
Port. Thus reaccommodating their sailes, they sailed for Sancta
Cruse, Cape Goa, and Magadore, till they came againe to Saffee, and then he returned into England.

Chapter XXI.
The continuation of the generall Historie of Virginia; the Summer Iles; and New England; with their present estate from 1624. to this present 1629.

CONCERNING these Countreyes, I would be sorrie to trouble
you with repeating one thing twice, as with their Maps, Commodities, People, Government and Religion yet knowen, the
beginning of those plantations, their numbers and names, with
the names of the Adventurers, the yeerely proceedings of everie
Governour both here and there. As for the misprisions, neglect, grievances, and the causes of all those rumours, losses and
crosses that have happened; I referre you to the Generall Historie, where you shall finde all this at large; especially to those
pages, where you may read my letter of advice to the Councell
and Company, what of necessitie must be done, or lose all and
leave the Countrey, pag. 70. what commodities I sent home,
pag. 163. my opinion and offer to the Company, to feed and
defend the Colonies, pag. 150. my account to them here of my
actions there, pag. 163. my seven answers to his Majesties
Commissioners: seven questions what hath hindered Virginia,
and the remedie, pag. 165. How those noble Gentlemen spent
neere two yeares in perusing all letters came from thence; and
the differences betwixt many factions, both here and there,
with their complaints; especially about the Sallerie, which
should have beene a new office in London, for the well ordering the sale of Tobacco, that 2500. pounds should yearely
have beene raised out of it, to pay foure or five hundred
pounds yearly to the Governor of that Companie; two or three

hundred to his Deputie; the rest into stipends of thirtie or fiftie pounds yearely for their Clerks and under Officers which were never there, pag. 153. but not one hundred pounds for all them in Virginia, nor any thing for the most part of the Adventurers in England, except the undertakers for the Lotteries, Setters out of ships, Adventurers of commodities, also their Factors and many other Officers, there imployed only by friendship to raise their fortunes out of the labours of the true industrious planters by the title of their office, who under the colour of sinceritie, did pillage and deceive all the rest most cunningly: For more than 150000. pounds have beene spent out of the common stocke, besides many thousands have beene there consumed, and neere 7000. people that there died, only for want of good order and government, otherwise long ere this there would have beene more than 20000. people, where after twentie yeeres spent onely in complement, and trying new conclusions, was remaining scarce 1500. with some few cattell.

Then the Company dissolved, but no account of any thing; so that his Majestie appointed Commissioners to oversee, and give order for their proceedings. Being thus in a manner left to themselves, since then within these foure yeeres, you shall see how wonderfully they have increased beyond expectation; but so exactly as I desired, I cannot relate unto you: For although I have tired my selfe in seeking and discoursing with those returned thence, more than would a voyage to Virginia; few can tell me any thing, but of that place or places they have inhabited, and he is a great traveller that hath gone up and downe the river of James Towne, been at Pamaunke, Smiths Iles, or Accomack; wherein for the most part they keepe one tune of their now particular abundance, and their former wants, having beene there, some sixteene yeeres, some twelve, some six, some neere twentie, etc. But of their generall estate, or any thing of worth, the most of them doth know verie little to any purpose.

Now the most I could understand in generall, was from the relation of Master Nathaniel Cawsey, that lived there with mee, and returned Anno Dom. 1627. and some others affirme; Sir George Yerley was Governour, Captaine Francis West, Doctor John Poot, Captain Roger Smith, Captaine Matthewes, Captaine Tucker, Master Cla-

Their estate 1627.

bourne, and Master Farrer of the Councell: their habitations many. The Governour, with two or three of the Councell, are for most part at James Towne, the rest repaire thither as there is occasion; but everie three moneths they have a generall meeting, to consider of their publike affaires.

Their numbers then were about 1500. some say rather 2000. divided into seventeene or eighteene severall Plantations; the greatest part thereof towards the falls, are so inclosed with Pallizadoes they regard not the Salvages; and amongst those Plantations above James Towne, they have now found meanes to take plentie of fish, as well with lines, as nets, and where the waters are the largest, having meanes, they need not want.

Their numbers.

Upon this River they seldome see any Salvages, but in the woods, many times their fires: yet some few there are, that upon their opportunitie have slaine some few stragglers, which have beene revenged with the death of so many of themselves; but no other attempt hath beene made upon them this two or three yeares.

Their condition with the Salvages.

Their Cattle, namely Oxen, Kine, Buls, they imagine to be about 2000. Goats great store and great increase; the wilde Hogs, which were infinite, are destroyed and eaten by the Salvages: but no family is so poore, that hath not tame Swine sufficient; and for Poultrie, he is a verie bad husband breedeth not an hundred in a yeere, and the richer sort doth daily feed on them.

Their increase of Cattle and Poultrie.

For bread they have plentie, and so good, that those that make it well, better cannot be: divers have much English corne, especially Master Abraham Perce, which prepared this yeere to sow two hundred acres of English wheat, and as much with barley, feeding daily about the number of sixtie persons at his owne charges.

Plenty of Corne.

For drinke, some malt the Indian corne, others barley, of which they make good Ale, both strong and small, and such plentie thereof, few of the upper Planters drinke any water: but the better sort are well furnished with Sacke, Aquavitæ, and good English Beere.

Their drinke.

Their servants commonly feed upon Milke Homini, which is bruized Indian corne pounded, and boiled thicke, and milke for the sauce; but boiled

Their servants diet.

with milke, the best of all will oft feed on it, and leave their
flesh; with milke, butter and cheese; with fish, Bulls flesh, for
they seldome kill any other, etc. And everie one is so applyed
to his labour about Tobacco and Corne, which doth yeeld
them such profit, they never regard any food from the Salvages, nor have they any trade or conference with them, but
upon meere accidents and defiances: and now the Merchants
have left it, there have gone so many voluntarie ships within
this two yeeres, as have furnished them with Apparell, Sacke,
Aquavitæ, and all necessaries, much better than ever before.

Their Armes
and exercise.

For Armes, there is scarce any man but he is furnished with a Peece, a Jacke, a Coat of Maile, a Sword,
or Rapier; and everie Holy-day, everie Plantation
doth exercise their men in Armes, by which meanes, hunting
and fowling, the most part of them are most excellent markmen.

Their health
and dis-
coveries.

For Discoveries they have made none, nor any
other commoditie than Tobacco doe they apply
themselves unto, though never any was planted at
first. And whereas the Countrey was heretofore held most intemperate and contagious by many, now they have houses,
lodgings and victuall, and the Sunne hath power to exhale up
the moyst vapours of the earth, where they have cut downe
the wood, which before it could not, being covered with
spreading tops of high trees; they finde it much more healthfull than before; nor for their numbers, few Countreyes are
lesse troubled with death, sicknesse, or any other disease, nor
where overgrowne women become more fruitfull.

The present
estate of
Virginia 1629.

Since this, Sir George Yerley died 1628. Captaine
West succeeded him; but about a yeere after returned for England: Now Doctor Poot is Governour, and the rest of the Councell as before: James Towne is
yet their chiefe seat, most of the wood destroyed, little corne
there planted, but all converted into pasture and gardens,
wherein doth grow all manner of herbs and roots we have in
England in abundance, and as good grasse as can be. Here
most of their Cattle doe feed, their Owners being most some
one way, some another, about their plantations, and returne
againe when they please, or any shipping comes in to trade.
Here in winter they have hay for their Cattell, but in other
places they browze upon wood, and the great huskes of their

Master Hutchins.

Five thousand people. Five thousand cattell. Goats, Hogs, and Poultry, infinite.

corne, with some corne in them, doth keepe them well. Master Hutchins saith, they have 2000. Cattle, and about 5000. people; but Master Floud, John Davis, William Emerson, and divers others, say, about five thousand people, and five thousand kine, calves, oxen, and bulls; for goats, hogs, and poultry; corne, fish, deere, and many sorts of other wilde beasts; and fowle in their season, they have so much more than they spend, they are able to feed three or foure hundred men more than they have; and doe oft much releeve many ships, both there, and for their returne; and this last yeare was there at least two or three and twenty saile. They have oft much salt fish from New England, but fresh fish enough, when they will take it; Peaches in abundance at Kecoughtan; Apples, Peares, Apricocks, Vines, figges, and other fruits some have planted, that prospered exceedingly, but their diligence about Tobacco, left them to be spoiled by the cattell, yet now they beginne to revive; Mistresse Pearce, an honest industrious woman, hath beene there neere twentie yeares, and now returned, saith,

Good Hospitality.

shee hath a Garden at James towne, containing three or foure acres, where in one yeare shee hath gathered neere an hundred bushels of excellent figges; and that of her owne provision she can keepe a better house in Virginia, than here in London for 3. or 400. pounds a yeare, yet went thither with little or nothing. They have some tame geese, ducks, and turkies. The masters now do so traine up their servants and youth in shooting deere, and fowle, that the youths will kill them as well as their Masters. They have two brew-houses, but they finde the Indian corne so much better than ours, they beginne to leave sowing it. Their Cities and Townes are onely scattered houses, they call plantations, as are our Country Villages, but no Ordnance mounted. The Forts Captaine Smith left a building, so ruined, there is scarce mention where they were; no discoveries of any thing more, than the curing of Tobacco, by which hitherto, being so present a commodity of gaine, it hath brought them to this abundance; but that they are so disjoynted, and every one commander of himselfe, to plant what he will: they are now so well provided, that they are able to subsist; and if they would joyne together now to worke upon Sope-ashes, Iron, Rape-oile, Mader, Pitch and Tarre, Flax and Hempe; as for their Tobacco, there comes from many places such abundance, and the charge so great, it is not worth the bringing home.

There is gone, and now a going, divers Ships; as Captaine Perse, Captaine Prine, with Sir John Harvy to be their governour, with two or three hundred people; there is also some from Bristow, and other parts of the West Country a preparing, which I heartily pray to God to blesse, and send them a happy and prosperous voyage.

Nathaniel Causie, Master Hutchins, Master Floud,
John Davis, William Emerson, Master Willam,
Barnet, Master Cooper, and others.

Chapter XXII.
The proceedings and present estate of the Summer Iles, from An. Dom. 1624 to this present 1629.

FROM the Summer Iles, Master Ireland, and divers others report, their Forts, Ordnance, and proceedings, are much as they were in the yeare 1622. as you may read in the generall History, page 199. Captaine Woodhouse governour. There are few sorts of any fruits in the West Indies, but they grow there in abundance; yet the fertility of the soile in many places decayeth, being planted every yeare; for their Plantaines, which is a most delicate fruit, they have lately found a way, by pickling or drying them, to bring them over into England, there being no such fruit in Europe, and wonderfull for increase. For fish, flesh, figs, wine, and all sorts of most excellent hearbs, fruits, and rootes they have in abundance. In this Governours time, a kinde of Whale, or rather a Jubarta, was driven on shore in Southampton tribe from the west, over an infinite number of rocks, so bruised, that the water in the Bay where she lay, was all oily, and the rocks about it all bedasht with Parmacitty, congealed like ice, a good quantity we gathered, with which we commonly cured any byle, hurt, or bruise; some burnt it in their lamps, which blowing out, the very snuffe will burne, so long as there is any of the oile remaining, for two or three dayes together.

The next Governour, was Captaine Philip Bell, whose time being expired, Captaine Roger Wood possessed his place, a worthy Gentleman of good desert, and hath lived a long time in the Country; their numbers are about two or three thousand, men, women, and children, who increase there exceedingly; their greatest complaint, is want of apparell, and too much custome, and too many officers; the pity is, there are more men than women, yet no great mischiefe, because there is so much lesse pride: the cattell they have increase exceedingly; their forts are well maintained by the Merchants here, and Planters there; to be briefe, this Ile is an excellent bit, to rule a great horse.

All the Cohow birds and Egbirds are gone; seldome any wilde cats seene; no Rats to speake of; but the wormes are yet very troublesome; the people very healthfull; and the Ravens gone; fish enough, but not so neere the shore as it used, by the much beating it; it is an Ile that hath such a rampire and a ditch, and for the quantity so manned, victualled, and fortified, as few in the world doe exceed it, or is like it.

The 22. of March, two ships came from thence; the *Peter Bonaventure*, neere two hundred tunnes, and sixteene peeces of Ordnance; the Captaine, Thomas Sherwin; The Master, Master Edward Some, like him in condition, a goodly, lusty, proper, valiant man: the *Lydia*, wherein was Master Anthony Thorne, a smaller ship; were chased by eleven ships of Dunkerk; being thus overmatched, Captaine Sherwin was taken by them in Turbay, only his valiant Master was slaine; the ship with about seventy English men, they carried betwixt Dover and Callis, to Dunkerk; but the *Lydia* safely recovered Dartmouth.

These noble adventurers for all those losses, patiently doe beare them; but they hope the King and state will understand it is worth keeping, though it afford nothing but Tobacco, and that now worth little or nothing, custome and fraught payed, yet it is worth keeping, and not supplanting; though great men feele not those losses, yet Gardiners, Carpenters, and Smiths doe pay for it.

From the relation of Robert Chesteven, and others.

Chapter XXIII.
The proceedings and present estate of NewEngland,
since 1624. to this present 1629.

W HEN I went first to the North part of Virginia, where the Westerly Colony had beene planted, it had dissolved it selfe within a yeare, and there was not one Christian in all the land. I was set forth at the sole charge of foure Merchants of London; the Country being then reputed by your westerlings, a most rockie, barren, desolate desart; but the good returne I brought from thence, with the maps and relations I made of the Country, which I made so manifest, some of them did beleeve me, and they were well embraced, both by the Londoners, and Westerlings, for whom I had promised to undertake it, thinking to have joyned them all together, but that might well have beene a worke for Hercules. Betwixt them long there was much contention; the Londoners indeed went bravely forward; but in three or foure yeares, I and my friends consumed many hundred pounds amongst the Plimothians, who only fed me but with delayes, promises, and excuses, but no performance of any thing to any purpose. In the interim, many particular ships went thither, and finding my relations true, and that I had not taken that I brought home from the French men, as had beene reported; yet further for my paines to discredit me, and my calling it New England, they obscured it, and shadowed it, with the title of Cannada, till at my humble suit, it pleased our most Royall King Charles, whom God long keepe, blesse, and preserve, then Prince of Wales, to confirme it with my map and booke, by the title of New England; the gaine thence returning did make the fame thereof so increase, that thirty, forty, or fifty saile, went yearly only to trade and fish; but nothing would bee done for a plantation, till about some hundred, of your Brownists of England, Amsterdam, and Leyden, went to New Plimouth, whose humorous ignorances, caused them for more than a yeare, to endure a wonderfull deale of misery, with an infinite patience; saying my books and maps were much better cheape to teach them, than my selfe; many other have used the like good husbandry, that have payed soundly in trying their

The effect of niggardlinesse. selfe-willed conclusions; but those in time doing well, divers others have in small handfulls undertaken to goe there, to be severall Lords and Kings of themselves, but most vanished to nothing; notwithstanding the fishing ships, made such good returnes, at last it was ingrossed by twenty Pattenties, that divided my map into twenty parts, and cast lots for their shares; but mony not comming in as they expected, procured a Proclamation, none should goe thither without their licences to fish; but for every thirty tunnes of shipping, to pay them five pounds; besides, upon great penalties, neither to trade with the natives, cut downe wood for their stages, without giving satisfaction, though all the Country is nothing but wood, and none to make use of it, with many such other pretences, for to make this Country plant it selfe, by its owne wealth: hereupon most men grew so discontented, that few or none would goe; so that the Pattenties, who never one of them had beene there, seeing those projects would not prevaile, have since not hindred any to goe that would, that within these few last yeares, more have gone thither than ever.

A new plantation 1629. Now this yeare 1629. a great company of people of good ranke, zeale, meanes, and quality, have made a great stocke, and with six good ships in the moneths of Aprill and May, they set saile from Thames, for the Bay of the Massachusetts, otherwise called Charles River; viz. the *George Bonaventure*, of twenty peeces of Ordnance, the *Talbot* nineteene, the *Lions-whelpe* eight, the *May-flower* fourteene, the *Foure Sisters*, foureteene, the *Pilgrim* foure, with three hundred and fifty men, women, and children; also an hundred and fifteene head of Cattell, as horse, mares, and neat beast; one and forty goats, some Conies, with all provision for houshold, and apparell; six peeces of great Ordnance for a Fort, with Muskets, Pikes, Corselets, Drums, Colours, with all provisions necessary for a plantation, for the good of man; other particulars I understand of no more, than is writ in the generall historie of those Countries.

But you are to understand, that the noble Lord chiefe Justice Popham, Judge Doderege; the Right Honourable Earles of Pembroke, Southampton, Salesbury, and the rest, as I take it, they did all thinke, as I and them went with me, did; That had those two Countries beene planted, as it was intended, that no other nation should come plant betwixt us. If ever the King of Spaine and we should fall foule, those Countries being so capable of all materialls for shipping, by this might have beene owners of a good Fleet of ships, and to have releeved a whole Navy from England upon occasion; yea, and to have furnished England with the most Easterly commodities; and now since, seeing how conveniently the Summer Iles fell to our shares, so neere the West Indies, wee might with much more facility than the Dutchmen have invaded the West Indies, that doth now put in practice, what so long hath beene advised on, by many an honest English States-man.

Those Countries Captaine Smith oft times used to call his children that never had mother; and well he might, for few fathers ever payed dearer for so little content; and for those that would truly understand, how many strange accidents hath befallen them and him; how oft up, how oft downe, sometimes neere desperate, and ere long flourishing, cannot but conceive Gods infinite mercies and favours towards them. Had his designes beene to have perswaded men to a mine of gold, though few doth conceive either the charge or paines in refining it, nor the power nor care to defend it; or some new Invention to passe to the South Sea; or some strange plot to invade some strange Monastery: or some portable Countrie; or some chargeable Fleet to take some rich Caracks in the East Indies; or Letters of Mark to rob some poore Merchants; what multitudes of both people and mony, would contend to be first imployed: but in those noble endevours (now) how few of quality, unlesse it be to beg some Monopolie; and those seldome seeke the common good, but the commons goods; as you may reade at large in his generall history, page 217, 218, 219. his generall observations and reasons for this plantation; for yet those Countries are not so forward but they may become as miserable as ever, if better courses be not taken than is; as this Smith will plainly demonstrate to his Majesty; or any other noble person of ability, liable generously to undertake it; how within a short time to make Virginia able to resist any enemy, that as yet lieth open to all; and yeeld the King more custome within these few yeares, in certaine staple commodities, than ever it did in Tobacco; which now not being

Notes of inconveniencie.

worth bringing home, the custome will bee as uncertaine to the King, as dangerous to the plantations.

Chapter XXIIII.

A briefe discourse of divers voyages made unto the goodly Countrey of Guiana, and the great River of the Amazons; relating also the present Plantation there.

It is not unknowen how that most industrious and honourable Knight Sir Walter Rauleigh, in the yeare of our Lord 1595. taking the Ile of Trinidado, fell with the Coast of Guiana Northward of the Line ten degrees, and coasted the Coast; and searched up the River Oranoca: where understanding that twentie severall voyages had beene made by the Spanyards, in discovering this Coast and River; to finde a passage to the great Citie of Mano, called by them the Eldorado, or the Golden Citie: he did his utmost to have found some better satisfaction than relations: But meanes failing him, hee left his trustie ser- Sparrow left to seeke the great Citie of Mano. vant Francis Sparrow to seeke it, who wandring up and downe those Countreyes, some fourteene or fifteene yeares, unexpectedly returned: I have heard him say, he was led blinded into this Citie by Indians; but little discourse of any purpose touching the largenesse of the report of it; his body seeming as a man of an uncurable consumption, shortly dyed here after in England. There are above thirtie faire rivers that fall into the Sea, betweene the River of Amazons and Oranoca, which are some nine degrees asunder.

Captaine Charles Ley. In the yeare 1605. Captaine Ley, brother to that noble Knight Sir Oliver Ley, with divers others, planted himselfe in the River Weapoco, wherein I should have beene a partie; but hee dyed, and there lyes buried, and the supply miscarrying, the rest escaped as they could.

Sir Thomas Roe. Sir Thomas Roe, well knowen to be a most noble Gentleman, before he went Lord Ambassadour to the Great Mogoll, or the Great Turke, spent a yeare or two upon this Coast, and about the River of the Amazones, wherein he most imployed Captaine Matthew Mor-

Captain Morton. ton, an expert Sea-man in the discoverie of this famous River, a Gentleman that was the first shot and
mortally supposed wounded to death, with me in Virginia, yet
since hath beene twice with command in the East Indies; Also

Captaine William White, and divers others worthy

Captaine White. and industrious Gentlemen, both before and since,
hath spent much time and charge to discover it more
perfitly, but nothing more effected for a Plantation, till it was
undertaken by Captaine Robert Harcote, 1609.

This worthy Gentleman, after he had by Commis-

Captain Harcote. sion made a discoverie to his minde, left his brother
Michael Harcote, with some fiftie or sixtie men in
the River Weapoco, and so presently returned to England,
where he obtained by the favour of Prince Henrie, a large
Patent for all that Coast called Guiana, together with the famous River of Amazones, to him and his heires: but so many
troubles here surprized him, though he did his best to supply
them, he was not able, only some few hee sent over as passengers with certaine Dutch-men, but to small purpose. Thus this
businesse lay dead for divers yeeres, till Sir Walter Rauleigh, accompanied with many valiant Souldiers and brave Gentlemen,
went his last voyage to Guiana, amongst the which was Captaine Roger North, brother to the Right Honourable the Lord
Dudley North, who upon this voyage having stayed and seene
divers Rivers upon this Coast, tooke such a liking to those
Countreyes, having had before this voyage more perfect and
particular information of the excellencie of the great River of
the Amazones, above any of the rest, by certaine Englishmen
returned so rich from thence in good commodities, they
would not goe with Sir Walter Rauleigh in search of gold; that
after his returne for England, he endevoured by his best abilities to interest his Countrey and state in those faire Regions,
which by the way of Letters Patents unto divers Noblemen and
Gentlemen of qualitie, erected into a company and perpetuitie
for trade and plantation, not knowing of the Interest of Captaine Harcote.

Whereupon accompanied with 120. Gentlemen and

Captaine Roger North. others, with a ship, a pinnace and two shallops, to
remaine in the Countrey, hee set saile from Plimouth

the last of April 1620, and within seven weekes after hee arrived
well in the Amazones, only with the losse, of one old man:
some hundred leagues they ran up the River to settle his men,
where the sight of the Countrey and people so contented
them, that never men thought themselves more happie: Some
English and Irish that had lived there some eight yeeres, only
supplyed by the Dutch, hee reduced to his company and to
leave the Dutch: having made a good voyage, to the value of
more than the charge, he returned to England with divers
good commodities besides Tobacco: So that it may well be
conceived, that if this action had not beene thus crossed, the
Generalitie of England had by this time beene wonne and encouraged therein. But the time was not yet come, that God
would have this great businesse effected, by reason of the great
power the Lord Gundamore, Ambassadour for the King of
Spaine, had in England, to crosse and ruine those proceedings,
and so unfortunate Captaine North was in this businesse, hee
was twice committed prisoner to the Tower, and the goods detained, till they were spoiled, who beyond all others was by
much the greatest Adventurer and Loser.

   Notwithstanding all this, those that he had left in
Nota bene. the Amazons would not abandon the Countrey.
   Captaine Thomas Painton, a worthy Gentleman, his
Lieutenant dead. Captaine Charles Parker, brother to the
Right Honourable the Lord Morley, lived there six yeeres after;
Master John Christmas, five yeeres, so well, they would not returne, although they might, with divers other Gentle-men of
qualitie and others: all thus destitute of any supplyes from England. But all authoritie being dissolved, want of government
did more wrong their proceedings, than all other crosses whatsoever. Some releefe they had sometime from the Dutch, who
knowing their estates, gave what they pleased and tooke what
they list. Two brothers Gentlemen, Thomas and William
Hixon, who stayed three yeeres there, are now gone to stay in
the Amazons, in the ships lately sent thither.

  The businesse thus remaining in this sort, three private men
left of that Company, named Master Thomas Warriner, John
Rhodes, and Robert Bims, having lived there about two yeeres,
came for England, and to be free from the disorders that did
grow in the Amazons for want of Government amongst their

Countrey-men, and to be quiet amongst themselves, made meanes to set themselves out for St. Christophers; their whole number being but fifteene persons, that payed for their passage in a ship going for Virginia, where they remained a yeare before they were supplyed, and then that was but foure or five men. Thus this Ile, by this small beginning, having no interruption by their owne Countrey, hath now got the start of the Continent and maine Land of Guiana, which hath beene layd apart and let alone untill that Captaine North, ever watching his best opportunitie and advantage of time in the state, hath now againe pursued and set on foot his former designe. Captaine Harcote being now willing to surrender his grant, and to joyne with Captaine North, in passing a new Patent, and to erect a company for trade and plantation in the Amazons, and all the Coast and Countrey of Guiana for ever. Whereupon, they have sent this present yeare in Januarie, and since 1628. foure ships with neere two hundred persons; the first ship with 112. men, not one miscarried; the rest went since, not yet heard of, and are preparing another with their best expedition: and since Januarie is gone from Holland, 100. English and Irish, conducted by the old Planters.

This great River lieth under the Line, the two chiefe head lands North and South, are about three degrees asunder, the mouth of it is so full of many great and small Iles, it is an easie matter for an unexperienced Pilot to lose his way. It is held one of the greatest rivers in America, and as most men thinke, in the world: and commeth downe with such a fresh, it maketh the Sea fresh more than thirtie miles from the shore. Captaine North having seated his men about an hundred leagues in the Maine, sent Captaine William White, with thirtie Gentlemen and others, in a pinnace of thirtie tun, to discover further, which they did some two hundred leagues, where they found the River to divide it selfe in two parts, till then all full of Ilands, and a Countrey most healthfull, pleasant and fruitfull; for they found food enough, and all returned safe and in good health: In this discoverie they saw many Townes well inhabited, some with three hundred people, some with five, six, or seven hundred; and of some they understood to be of so many thousands, most differing verie much, especially in their languages:

whereof they suppose by those Indians, they understand are many hundreds more, unfrequented till then by any Christian, most of them starke naked, both men, women and children, but they saw not any such giant-like women as the Rivers name importeth. But for those where Captaine North hath seated his company, it is not knowen where Indians were ever so kinde to any Nation, not sparing any paines, danger or labour, to feed and maintaine them. The English following their buildings, fortifications and sugar-workes; for which they have sent most expert men, and with them all things necessarie for that purpose; to effect which, they want not the helpe of those kinde Indians to produce; and many other good commodities, which (God willing) will ere long make plaine and apparent to this Kingdome, and all the Adventurers and Well-willers to this Plantation, to bee well worthy the cherishing and following with all alacritie.

Chapter XXV.
The beginning and proceedings of the new plantation of St. Christopher by Captaine Warner.

MASTER Ralfe Merifield and others, having furnished this worthy industrious Gentleman, hee arrived at St. Christophers, as is said, with fifteene men, the 28. of Januarie, 1623. viz. William Tested, John Rhodes, Robert Bims, Master Benifield, Sergeant Jones, Master Ware, William Royle, Rowland Grascocke, Master Bond, Master Langley, Master Weaver, Edward Warner their Captaines sonne, and now Deputy-Governour till his fathers returne, Sergeant Aplon, one Sailor and a Cooke: At their arrivall they found three French-men, who sought to oppose Captaine Warner, and to set the Indians upon us; but at last we all became friends, and lived with the Indians a moneth, then we built a Fort, and a house, and planting fruits, by September we made a crop of Tobacco; but upon the nineteenth of September came a Hericano and blew it away, all this

1623.

A Hericano.

while wee lived upon Cassada bread, Potatoes, Plantines, Pines, Turtels, Guanes, and fish plentie; for drinke wee had *Nicnobbie*.

The 18. of March 1624. arrived Captaine Jefferson with three men passengers in the *Hope-well* of London, with some trade for the Indians, and then we had another crop of Tobacco, in the meane time the French had planted themselves in the other end of the Ile; with this crop Captaine Warner returned for England in September, 1625.

In his absence came in a French pinnace, under the command of Monsieur de Nombe, that told us, the Indians had slaine some French-men in other of the Charybes Iles, and that there were six Peryagoes, which are huge great trees formed as your Canowes, but so laid out on the sides with boords, they will seeme like a little Gally: six of those, with about foure or five hundred strange Indians came unto us, we bade them be gone, but they would not; whereupon we and the French joyned together, and upon the fifth of November set upon them, and put them to flight: upon New-yeares Even they came againe, found three English going about the Ile, whom they slue.

Untill the fourth of August, we stood upon our guard, living upon the spoile and did nothing. But now Captaine Warner arriving againe with neere an hundred people, then we fell to worke and planting as before; but upon the fourth of September, came such a Hericano, as blew downe all our houses, Tobacco, and two Drums into the aire we know not whither, drove two ships on shore that were both split; all our provision thus lost, we were very miserable, living onely on what we could get in the wilde woods, we made a small party of French and English to goe aboord for provision, but in their returning home, eight French men were slaine in the harbour.

Thus wee continued till neere June that the Tortels came in, 1627. but the French being like to starve, sought to surprize us, and all the Cassado, Potatos, and Tobacco we had planted, but we did prevent them. The 26. of October, came in Captaine William Smith, in the *Hope-well*, with some Ordnance, shot and powder, from the Earle of

1624.

1625.

Their fight with the Indians.

1626.

A Hericano.

Eight French slaine.

1627.

Carlile; with Captaine Pelham and thirty men, about that time also came the *Plow*; also a small ship of Bristow, with Captaine Warners wife, and six or seven women more.

Upon the 25. of November, the Indians set upon the French, for some injury about their women, and slew six and twentie French men, five English, and three Indians. Their weapons are bowes and arrowes; their bowes are never bent, but the string lies flat to the bow; their arrowes a small reed, foure or five foot long, headed some with the poysoned sting of the taile of a Stingray, some with iron, some with wood, but all so poysoned, that if they draw but bloud, the hurt is incurable.

Three Indians slaine.

The next day came in Captaine Charles Saltonstall, a young Gentleman, son of Sir Samuell Saltonstall, who brought with him good store of all commodities to releeve the plantation; but by reason some Hollanders, and others, had bin there lately before him, who carried away with them all the Tobacco, he was forced to put away all his commodities upon trust till the next crop; in the meane time hee resolved there to stay, and imploy himselfe and his company in planting Tobacco, hoping thereby to make a voyage, but before he could be ready to returne for England, a Hericano hapning, his ship was split, to his great losse, being sole Merchant and owner himselfe, notwithstanding forced to pay to the Governour, the fift part of his Tobacco, and for fraught to England, three pence a pound, and nine pence a pound custome, which amounts together to more than threescore pound in the hundred pound, to the great discouragement of him and many others, that intended well to those plantations. Neverthelesse he is gone againe this present yeare 1629. with a ship of about three hundred tunnes, and very neere two hundred people, with Sir William Tuffton, Governour for the Barbados, and divers gentlemen, and all manner of commodities fit for a plantation.

The arrivall of many English ships.

Captaine Prinne, Captaine Stone, and divers others, came in about Christmas; so that this last yeare there hath beene about thirtie saile of English, French, and Dutch ships, and all the Indians forced out of the Ile, for they had done much mischiefe amongst the French, in cutting their throats, burning their houses, and spoyling their Tobacco; amongst the rest

Tegramund, a little childe the Kings sonne, his parents being slaine, or fled, was by great chance saved, and carefully brought to England by Master Merifield, who brought him from thence, and bringeth him up as his owne children.

The description of the Ile.

It lyeth seventeene degrees Northward of the line, about an hundred and twenty leagues from the Cape de tres Puntas, the neerest maine land in America, it is about eight leagues in length, and foure in bredth; an Iland amongst 100. Iles in the West Indies, called the Caribes, where ordinarily all them that frequent the West Indies, refresh themselves; those most of them are rocky, little, and mountainous, yet frequented with the Canibals; many of them inhabited, as Saint Domingo, Saint Mattalin, Saint Lucia, Saint Vincent, Granada, and Margarita, to the Southward; Northward, none but Saint Christophers, and it but lately, yet they will be ranging Marigalanta, Guardalupo, Deceado, Monserat, Antigua, Mevis, Bernardo, Saint Martin, and Saint Bartholomew, but the worst of the foure Iles possessed by the Spanyard, as Portorico or Jamica, is better than them all; as for Hispaniola, and Cuba, they are worthy the title of two rich Kingdomes, the rest not respected by the Spanyards, for want of harbors, and their better choice of good land, and profit in the maine. But Captaine Warner, having beene very familiar with Captaine Painton, in the Amazon, hearing his information of this St. Christophers; and having made a yeares tryall, as it is said, returned for England, joyning with Master Merifield, and his friends, got Letters Pattents, from King James, to plant and possesse it. Since then, the Right Honourable the Earle of Carlile, hath got Letters Pattents also, not only of that, but all the Caribes Iles about it, who is now chiefe Lord of them, and the English his tenants, that doe possesse them; over whom he appointeth such Governours and Officers, as their affaires require; and although there be a great custome imposed upon them, considering their other charges, both to feed and maintaine themselves; yet there is there, and now a going, neere upon the number of three thousand people; where by reason of the rockinesse and thicknesse of the woods

The springs, temper, and seasons.

in the Ile, it is difficult to passe, and such a snuffe of the Sea goeth on the shore, ten may better defend, than fifty assault. In this Ile are many springs, but yet water is scarce againe in many places; the valleyes and sides of the hills very fertile, but the mountaines harsh, and of a sulphurous composition; all overgrowne with Palmetas, Cotten trees, Lignum vitæ, and divers other sorts, but none like any in Christendome, except those carried thither; the aire very pleasant and healthfull, but exceeding hot, yet so tempered with coole breaths, it seemes very temperate to them, that are a little used to it; the trees being always greene, the daies and nights alwayes very neere equal in length, alwayes Summer; only they have in their seasons great gusts and raines, and somtimes a Hericano, which is an overgrowne, and a most violent storme.

A strange hatching of egges for beasts.   In some of those Iles, are cattell, goats, and hogges, but here none but what they must carry; Gwanes they have, which is a little harmelesse beast, like a Crokadell, or Aligator, very fat and good meat, she layes egges in the sand, as doth the land Crabs, which live here in abundance, like Conies in Boroughs, unlesse about May, when they come downe to the Sea side, to lay in the sand, as the other; and all their egges are hatched by the heat of the Sunne.

Fish.   From May to September they have good store of Tortasses, that come out of the Sea to lay their egges in the sand, and are hatched as the other; they will lay halfe a pecke at a time, and neere a bushell ere they have done; and are round like Tenis-balls: this fish is like veale in taste, the fat of a brownish colour, very good and wholsome. We seeke them in the nights, where we finde them on shore, we turne them upon their backs, till the next day we fetch them home, for they can never returne themselves, being so hard a cart may goe over them; and so bigge, one will suffice forty or fifty men to dinner. Divers sorts of other fish they have in abundance, and Prawnes most great and excellent, but none will keepe sweet scarce twelve houres.

Birds.   The best and greatest is a Passer Flaminga, which walking at her length is as tall as a man; Pigeons, and Turtle Doves in abundance; some Parrots, wilde Hawkes, but divers other sorts of good Sea fowle, whose names we know not.

Roots.   Cassado is a root planted in the ground, of a wonderfull increase, and will make very good white bread, but the Juyce ranke poyson, yet boyled, better than wine; Potatos, Cabbages and Radish plenty.

Fruits. Mayes, like the Virginia wheat; we have Pine-apples, neere so bigge as an Hartichocke, but the most daintiest taste of any fruit; Plantains, an excellent, and a most increasing fruit; Apples, Prickell Peares, and Pease, but differing all from ours. There is Pepper that groweth in a little red huske, as bigge as a Walnut, about foure inches in length, but the long cods are small, and much stronger, and better for use, than that from the East Indies. There is two sorts of Cotten, the silke Cotten as in the East Indies, groweth upon a small stalke, as good for beds as downe; the other upon a shrub, and beareth a cod bigger than a Walnut, full of Cotten wooll: *Anotto* also groweth upon a shrub, with a cod like the other, and nine or ten on a bunch, full of Anotto, very good for Dyers, though wilde; Sugar Canes, not tame, 4. or 5. foot high; also Masticke, and Locus trees; great and hard timber, Gourds, Muske Melons, Water Melons, Lettice, Parsly; all places naturally beare purslaine of it selfe; Sope-berries like a Musket bullet, that washeth as white as Sope; in the middle of the root is a thing like a sedge, a very good fruit, we call Pen-gromes; a Pappaw is as great as an apple, coloured like an Orange, and good to eat; a small hard nut, like a hazell nut, growes close to the ground, and like this growes on the Palmetas, which we call a Mucca nut; Mustard-seed will grow to a great tree, but beares no seed, yet the leaves will make good mustard; the Mancinell tree the fruit is poyson; good figs in abundance; but the Palmeta serveth to build Forts and houses, the leaves to cover them, and many other uses; the juyce we draw from them, till we sucke them to death, (is held restorative) and the top for meat doth serve us as Cabbage; but oft we want poudered Beefe, and Bacon, and many other needfull necessaries.

by Thomas Simons, Rowland Grascocke,
Nicholas Burgh, and others.

Chapter XXVI.
The first planting of the Barbados.

THE Barbados lies South-west and by South, an hundred leagues from Saint Christophers, threescore leagues West and South from Trinidado, and some fourescore leagues from Cape de Salinos, the next part of the maine. The first planters brought thither by Captaine Henry Powel, were forty English, with seven or eight Negros; then he went to Disacuba in the maine, where he got thirty Indians, men, women, and children, of the Arawacos, enemies both to the Caribes, and the Spaniards. The Ile is most like a triangle, each side forty or fifty miles square, some exceeding great rocks, but the most part exceeding good ground; abounding with an infinite number of Swine, some Turtles, and many sorts of excellent fish; many great ponds wherein is Ducke and Mallard; excellent clay for pots, wood and stone for building, and a spring neere the middest of the Ile of Bitume, which is a liquid mixture like Tarre, that by the great raines falls from the tops of the mountaines, it floats upon the water in such abundance, that drying up, it remaines like great rocks of pitch, and as good as pitch for any use.

A description of the Ile.

The Mancinell apple, is of a most pleasant sweet smell, of the bignesse of a Crab, but ranke poyson, yet the Swine and Birds have wit to shun it; great store of exceeding great Locus trees, two or three fadome about, of a great height, that beareth a cod full of meale, will make bread in time of necessity. A tree like a Pine, beareth a fruit so great as a Muske Melon, which hath alwayes ripe fruit, flowers, or greene fruit, which will refresh two or three men, and very comfortable; Plumb trees many, the fruit great and yellow, which but strained into water in foure and twenty houres will be very good drinke; wilde figge trees there are many; all those fruits doe fat the hogges, yet at some times of the yeare they are so leane, as carrion; Gwane trees beare a fruit so bigge as a Peare, good and wholsome; Palmetaes of three severall sorts; Papawes, Prickle Peares good to eat or make drinke; Cedar trees very tall and great; Fusticke trees are very great and the wood yellow, good for dying; sope berries, the

Fruits and trees.

kernell so bigge as a sloe, and good to eat; Pumpeons in abundance; Goards so great as will make good great bottles, and cut
in two peeces good dishes and platters; many small brooks of
very good water; Ginni wheat, Cassado, Pines and Plantaines;
all things we there plant doe grow exceedingly, so well as Tobacco; the corne, pease, and beanes, cut but away the stalke,
young sprigs will grow, and so beare fruit for many yeares together, without any more planting; the Ile is overgrowne with
wod or great reeds, those wods which are soft are exceeding
light and full of pitch, and those that are hard, are so hard and
great, they are as hard to cut as stone.

Master John Powell came thither the fourth of
Their numbers. August 1627. with forty five men, where we stayed
three weeks, and then returning, left behind us about
an hundred people, and his sonne John Powell for his Deputy,
as Governour; but there have beene so many factions amongst
them, I cannot from so many variable relations give you any
certainty for their orderly Government: for all those plenties,
much misery they have endured, in regard of their weaknesse
at their landing, and long stay without supplies; therefore
those that goe thither, it were good they carry good provision
with them; but the Ile is most healthfull, and all things planted
doe increase abundantly: and by this time there is, and now a
going, about the number of fifteene or sixteene hundred
people.

Sir William Curtine, and Captaine John Powell, were the
first and chiefe adventurers to the planting this fortunate Ile;
which had beene oft frequented by men of Warre to refresh
themselves, and set up their shallops; being so farre remote
from the rest of the Iles, they never were troubled with any of
the Indies. Harbours they have none, but exceeding good
Rodes, which with a small charge might bee very well fortified;
it doth ebbe and flow foure or five foot, and they cannot perceive there hath ever beene any Hericano in that Ile.

From the relations of Captaine John White,
and Captaine Wolverstone.

Chapter XXVII.
The first plantation of the Ile of Mevis.

The description of the Ile. BECAUSE I have ranged and lived amongst those Ilands, what my authours cannot tell me, I thinke it no great errour in helping them to tell it my selfe. In this little Ile of Mevis, more than twenty yeares agoe, I have remained a good time together, to wod, and water and refresh my men; it is all woddy, but by the Sea side South-ward there are sands like downes, where a thousand men may quarter themselves conveniently; but in most places the wod groweth close to the water side, at a high water marke, and in some places so thicke of a soft spungy wood like a wilde figge tree, you cannot get through it, but by making your way with hatchets, or fauchions: whether it was the dew of those trees, or of some others, I am not certaine, but many of our men became so tormented with a burning swelling all over their bodies, they seemed like scalded men, and neere mad with paine; here we found a great Poole, wherein bathing themselves, *The Bath.* they found much ease; and finding it fed with a pleasant small streame that came out of the woods, we found the head halfe a mile within the land, distilling from a many of rocks, by which they were well cured in two or three dayes. Such factions here we had, as commonly attend such voyages, that a paire of gallowes was made, but Captaine Smith, for whom they were intended, could not be perswaded to use them; but not any one of the inventers, but their lives by justice fell into his power, to determine of at his pleasure, whom with much mercy he favoured, that most basely and unjustly would have betrayed him.

A great misprision. The last yeare, 1628. Master Littleton, with some others got a Pattent of the Earle of Carlile, to plant the Ile called the Barbados, thirty leagues North-ward of Saint Christophers; which by report of their informers, and undertakers, for the excellencie and pleasantnesse thereof, they called Dulcina, but when they came there, they found it such a barren rocke, they left it; although they were told as much before, they would not beleeve it, perswading themselves, those contradicters would get it for themselves, was thus by their cunning opinion, the deceiver of themselves; for seeing it lie conveniently for their purpose in a map, they had not patience to know the goodnesse or badnesse, the inconvenience nor probabilities of the quality, nor quantity; which errour doth predominate in most of our homebred adventurers, that will have all things as they conceit and would have it; and the more they are contradicted, the more hot they are; but you may see by many examples in the generall history, how difficult a matter it is, to gather the truth from amongst so many forren and severall relations, except you have exceeding good experience both of the Countries, people, and their conditions; and those ignorant undertakings, have beene the greatest hinderance of all those plantations.

At last because they would be absolute, they came
Their
numbers. to Mevis, a little Ile by Saint Christophers; where they seated themselves, well furnished with all necessaries, being about the number of an hundred, and since increased to an hundred and fifty persons, whereof many were old planters of Saint Christophers, especially Master Anthony Hinton, and Master Edward Tompson. But because all those Iles for most part are so capable to produce, and in nature like each other, let this discourse serve for the description of them all. Thus much concerning those plantations, which now after all this time, losse, and charge, should they be abandoned, suppressed, and dissolved, were most lamentable; and surely seeing they all strive so much about this Tobacco, and that the fraught thereof, and other charges are so great, and so open to any enemie, by that commodity they cannot long subsist.

And it is a wonder to me to see such miracles of mischiefes in men; how greedily they pursue to dispossesse the planters of the Name of Christ Jesus, yet say they are Christians, when so much of the world is unpossessed; yea, and better land than they so much strive for, murthering so many Christians, burning and spoiling so many cities, villages, and Countries, and subverting so many kingdomes, when so much lieth vast, or only possessed by a few poore Savages, that more serve the Devill for feare, than God for love; whose ignorance we pretend to reforme, but covetousnesse, humours, ambition, faction, and pride, hath so many instruments, we performe very little to any purpose; nor is there either honour or profit to be got by any that are so vile, to undertake the subversion, or hinderance of any honest intended christian plantation.

Certaine exploits of Captaine Smith.

Now to conclude the travels and adventures of Captaine Smith; how first he planted Virginia, and was set ashore with about an hundred men in the wilde woods; how he was taken prisoner by the Savages, by the King of Pamaunke tied to a tree to be shot to death, led up and downe their Country to be shewed for a wonder; fatted as he thought, for a sacrifice for their Idoll, before whom they conjured him three dayes, with strange dances and invocations, then brought him before their Emperor Powhatan, that commanded him to be slaine; how his daughter Pocahontas saved his life, returned him to James towne, releeved him and his famished company, which was but eight and thirty to possesse those large dominions; how he discovered all the severall nations, upon the rivers falling into the Bay of Chisapeacke; stung neere to death with a most poysoned taile of a fish called Stingray: how Powhatan out of his Country tooke the kings of Pamaunke and Paspahegh prisoners, forced thirty nine of those kings to pay him contribution, subjected all the Savages: how Smith was blowne up with gunpowder, and returned for England to be cured.

Also how hee brought our new England to the subjection of the kingdome of great Britaine; his fights with the Pirats, left alone amongst a many French men of Warre, and his ship ran from him; his Sea-fights for the French against the Spaniards; their bad usage of him; how in France in a little boat he escaped them; was adrift all such a stormy night at Sea by himselfe, when thirteene French Ships were split, or driven on shore by the Ile of Ree, the generall and most of his men drowned, when God to whom be all honour and praise, brought him safe on shore to all their admirations that escaped; you may read at large in his generall history of Virginia, the Summer Iles, and New England.

Chapter XXVIII.
The bad life, qualities and conditions of Pyrats; and how they taught the Turks and Moores to become men of warre.

As in all lands where there are many people, there are some theeves, so in all Seas much frequented, there are some pyrats; the most ancient within the memory of threescore yeares was one Callis, who most refreshed himselfe upon the Coast of Wales; Clinton and Pursser his companions, who grew famous, till Queene Elizabeth of blessed memory, hanged them at Wapping; Flemming was as expert and as much sought for as they, yet such a friend to his Country, that discovering the Spanish Armado, he voluntarily came to Plimouth, yeelded himselfe freely to my Lord Admirall, and gave him notice of the Spaniards comming; which good warning came so happily and unexpectedly, that he had his pardon, and a good reward; some few Pirats there then remained; notwithstanding it is incredible how many great and rich prizes the little barques of the West Country daily brought home, in regard of their small charge; for there are so many difficulties in a great Navy, by wind and weather, victuall, sicknesse, losing and finding one another, they seldome defray halfe the charge: but for the grace, state, and defence of the Coast and narrow Seas, a great Navy is most necessary, but not to attempt any farre voyage, except there be such a competent stocke, they want not wherewith to furnish and supply all things with expedition; but to the purpose.

The difficulties of a great Navie.

After the death of our most gracious Queene Elizabeth, of blessed memory, our Royall King James, who from his infancy had reigned in peace with all Nations; had no imployment for those men of warre, so that those that were rich rested with that they had; those that were poore and had nothing but from hand to mouth, turned Pirats; some, because they became sleighted of those for whom they had got much wealth; some, for that they could not get their due; some, that had lived bravely, would not abase themselves to poverty; some vainly, only to get a name; others for revenge, covetousnesse, or as ill; and as they found themselves

What occasioneth Pirats.

more and more oppressed, their passions increasing with discontent, made them turne Pirats.

Now because they grew hatefull to all Christian Princes, they retired to Barbary, where although there be not many good Harbours, but Tunis, Argier, Sally, Mamora, and Tituane, there are many convenient Rodes, or the open Sea, which is their chiefe Lordship: For their best harbours Massalqueber, the townes of Oran, Mellila, Tanger, and Cuta, within the Streights, are possessed by the Spaniards; without the Streights they have also Arzella, and Mazagan; Mamora likewise they have lately taken, and fortified. Ward a poore English sailer, and Dansker a Dutchman, made first here their Marts, when the Moores knew scarce how to saile a ship; Bishop was Ancient, and did little hurt; but Easton got so much, as made himselfe a Marquesse in Savoy; and Ward lived like a Bashaw in Barbary; those were the first that taught the Moores to be men of warre. Gennings, Harris, Tompson, and divers others, were taken in Ireland, a Coast they much frequented, and died at Wapping. Hewes, Bough, Smith, Walsingam, Ellis, Collins, Sawkwell, Wollistone, Barrow, Wilson, Sayres, and divers others, all these were Captaines amongst the Pirats, whom King James mercifully pardoned; and was it not strange, a few of these should command the Seas. Notwithstanding the Malteses, the Pope, Florentines, Genoeses, French, Dutch, and English, Gallies, and Men of Warre, they would rob before their faces, and even at their owne Ports, yet seldome more than three, foure, five or six in a Fleet: many times they had very good ships, and well manned, but

commonly in such factions amongst themselves, and so riotous, quarrellous, treacherous, blasphemous, and villanous, it is more than a wonder they could so long continue, to doe so much mischiefe; and all they got, they basely consumed it amongst Jewes, Turks, Moores, and whores.

The best was, they would seldome goe to Sea, so long as they could possibly live on shore, being compiled of English, French, Dutch, and Moores, (but very few Spanyards, or Italians) commonly running one from another, till they became so disjoynted, disordered, debawched, and miserable, that the Turks and Moores beganne to command them as slaves, and force them to instruct them in their best skill, which many an accursed runnagado, or Christian turned Turke did,

Runnagados. till they have made those Sally men, or Moores of Barbary so powerfull as they be, to the terror of all the Straights, and many times they take purchase in the maine Ocean, yea sometimes even in the narrow Seas in England, and those are the most cruell villaines in Turkie, or Barbarie; whose natives are very noble, and of good natures, in comparison of them.

To conclude, the misery of a Pirate (although

Advertise-
ments for
wilde heads. many are as sufficient Sea-men as any) yet in regard of his superfluity, you shall finde it such, that any wise man would rather live amongst wilde beasts, than them; therefore let all unadvised persons take heed, how they entertaine that quality; and I could wish Merchants, Gentlemen, and all setters forth of ships, not to bee sparing of a competent pay, nor true payment; for neither Souldiers nor Sea-men can live without meanes, but necessity will force them to steale; and when they are once entered into that trade, they are hardly reclaimed. Those titles of Sea-men and Souldiers, have beene most worthily honoured and esteemed, but now regarded for most part, but as the scumme of the world; regaine therefore your wonted reputations, and endevour rather to adventure to those faire plantations of our English Nation; which however in the beginning were scorned and contemned, yet now you see how many rich and gallant people come from thence, who went thither as poore as any Souldier or Sailer, and gets more in one yeare, than you by Piracie in seven. I intreat you therefore to consider, how many thousands yearely goe thither; also how many Ships and Sailers are imployed to transport them, and what custome they yearely pay to our most Royall King Charles, whose prosperity and his Kingdomes good, I humbly beseech the immortall God ever to preserve and increase.

FINIS.

ADVERTISEMENTS

For the unexperienced Planters of
New-England, or any where.

OR,

The Path-way to experience to erect a Plantation.

With the yearely proceedings of this Country in Fishing
and Planting, since the yeare 1614. to the yeare 1630.
and their present estate.

Also how to prevent the greatest inconveniences, by their
proceedings in Virginia, and other Plantations,
by approved examples.

With the Countries Armes, a description of the Coast,
Harbours, Habitations, Land-markes, Latitude and
Longitude: with the Map allowed by our Royall
King Charles.

By Captaine John Smith, sometimes Governour of
Virginia, and Admirall of New-England.

1631

GENS · IN COGNI TA·MIHI SERVIET

TO THE MOST
Reverend Father in God,
GEORGE Lord Arch-Bishop of Canterburie
his Grace, Primate and Metropolitan
of all England:
and
The Right Reverend
Father in God, SAMUEL
Lord Arch-Bishop of Yorke
his Grace, Primate and Metropolitan
of England.

My most Gracious Good Lords, I desire to leave testimony to the world, how highly I honour as well the Miter as the Lance: therefore where my last Booke presented three most honourable Earles with a subject of Warre, and received from them favourable acceptance: the worke I now prosecute, concerning the Plantation of New-England, for the increase of Gods Church, converting Salvages, and enlarging the Kings Dominions, prostrates it selfe humbly to your Graces; who as you are in the name of Prelacy to this Kingdome, so you are to mee in goodnesse both Fathers and Protectors unexpectedly. God long preserve your Gracious lives, and continue favour

Unto both your Graces most devoted servant,
John Smith.

TO THE READER.

Honest Reader,

Apelles by the proportion of a foot, could make the whole proportion of a man: were hee now living, he might goe to schoole, for now are thousands can by opinion proportion Kingdomes, Cities, and Lordships, that never durst adventure to see them. Malignancy, I expect from those, have lived 10. or 12. yeares in those actions, and returne as wise as they went, claiming time and experience for their tutor, that can neither shift Sun nor Moone, nor say their Compasse, yet will tell you of more than all the world, betwixt the Exchange, Pauls and Westminster: so it be newes, it matters not what, that will passe currant when truth must be stayed with an army of conceits that can make or marre any thing, and tell as well what all England is by seeing but Milford haven, as what Apelles was by the picture of his great toe. Now because examples give a quicker impression than arguments, I have writ this discourse to satisfie understanding, wisdome, and honesty, and not such as can doe nothing but finde fault with that they neither know nor can amend. So I rest

Your friend
John Smith.

THE SEA MARKE.

Aloofe, aloofe, and come no neare,
    the dangers doe appeare;
Which if my ruine had not beene
    you had not seene:
I onely lie upon this shelfe
    to be a marke to all
    which on the same might fall,
That none may perish but my selfe.

If in or outward you be bound,
    doe not forget to sound;
Neglect of that was cause of this
    to steare amisse.
The Seas were calme, the wind was faire,
    that made me so secure,
    that now I must indure
All weathers be they foule or faire.

The Winters cold, the Summers heat,
    alternatively beat
Upon my bruised sides, that rue
    because too true
That no releefe can ever come.
    But why should I despaire
    being promised so faire
That there shall be a day of Dome.

The Contents.

Chapter 13.

Their great supplies, present estate and accidents, advantage.

Chapter 14.

Ecclesiasticall government in Virginia, authority from the Arch Bishop, their beginning at Bastable now called Salem.

Chapter 15.

The true modell of a plantation, tenure, increase of trade, true examples, necessity of expert Souldiers, the names of all the first discoverers for plantations and their actions, what is requisite to be in the Governour of a plantation, the expedition of Queene Elizabeths Sea Captaines.

ADVERTISEMENTS:
Or, The Path-way to Experience
to erect a Plantation.

Chapter 1.
What people they are that beginne this plantation: the bane of Virginia: strange misprisions of wise men.

THE Warres in Europe, Asia, and Affrica, taught me how to subdue the wilde Salvages in Virginia and New-England, in America; which now after many a stormy blast of ignorant contradictors, projectors, and undertakers, both they and I have beene so tossed and tortured into so many extremities, as despaire was the next wee both expected, till it pleased God now at last to stirre up some good mindes, that I hope will produce glory to God, honour to his Majesty, and profit to his Kingdomes, although all our Plantations have beene so foyled and abused, their best good willers have beene for the most part discouraged, and their good intents disgraced, as the generall History of them will at large truly relate you.

Pardon me if I offend in loving that I have cherished truly, by the losse of my prime fortunes, meanes, and youth: If it over-glad me to see Industry her selfe

No Brownist nor Separatist admitted.

adventure now to make use of my aged endevours, not by such (I hope) as rumour doth report, a many of discontented Brownists, Anabaptists, Papists, Puritans, Separatists, and such factious Humorists, for no such they will suffer among them, if knowne, as many of the chiefe of them have assured mee, and the much conferences I have had with many of them, doth confidently perswade me to write thus much in their behalfe.

I meane not the Brownists of Leyden and Amsterdam at New-Plimoth, who although by accident, ignorance, and wilfulnesse, have indured with a wonderfull patience, many losses and extremities; yet they subsist and prosper so well, not any of them will abandon the Country, but to the utmost of their powers increase their numbers: But of those which are gone *What they are that beginne this Plantation.* within this eighteene moneths for Cape Anne, and the Bay of the Massachusets: those which are their chiefe Undertakers are Gentlemen of good estate, some of 500, some a thousand pound land a yeere, all which they say they will sell for the advancing this harmlesse and pious worke; men of good credit and well-beloved in their Country, not such as flye for debt, or any scandall at home, and are good Catholike Protestants according to the reformed Church of England, if not, it is well they are gone: the rest of them men of good meanes, or Arts, Occupations, and Qualities, much more fit for such a businesse, and better furnished of all necessaries if they arrive well, than was ever any Plantation went out of England: I will not say but some of them may be more precise than needs, nor that they all be so good as they should be, for Christ had but twelve Apostles, and one was a traitor; and if there be no dissemblers among them, it is more than a wonder: therefore doe not condemne all for some; but however they have as good authority from his Majesty as they could desire, if they doe ill, the losse is but their owne; if well, a great glory and exceeding good to this Kingdome, to make good at last what all our former con-*The bane of Virginia.* clusions have disgraced. Now they take not that course the Virginia company did for the Planters there, their purses and lives were subject to some few here in London who were never there, that consumed all in Arguments, Projects, and their owne conceits, every yeere trying new conclusions, altering every thing yearely as they altered opinions, till they had consumed more than two hundred thousand pounds, and neere eight thousand mens lives.

It is true, in the yeere of our Lord 1622. they were about seven or eight thousand English indifferently well furnished with most necessaries, and many of them grew to that height of bravery, living in that plenty and excesse, that went thither not worth any thing, made the Company here thinke all the world was Oatmeale there, and all this proceeded by surviving those that died, nor were they ignorant to use as curious tricks there as here, and out of the juice of Tabacco, which at first they sold at such good rates, they regarded nothing but Tabacco; a commodity then so vendable, it provided them all things: and the loving Salvages their kinde friends, they trained so well up to shoot in a Peece, to hunt and kill them fowle, they became more expert than our owne Country-men, whose labours were more profitable to their Masters in planting Tabacco, and other businesse.

The differences betwixt my beginning in Virginia and the proceedings of my successors. This superfluity caused my poore beginnings scorned, or to be spoken of but with much derision, that never sent Ship from thence fraught, but onely some small quantities of Wainscot, Clap-board, Pitch, Tar, Rosin, Sope-ashes, Glasse, Cedar, Cypresse, Blacke Walnut, Knees for Ships, Ash for Pikes, Iron Ore none better, some Silver Ore, but so poore it was not regarded; better there may be, for I was no Mineralist, some Sturgion, but it was too tart of the Vinegar, which was of my owne store, for little came from them which was good; and Wine of the Countries wilde Grapes, but it was too sowre, yet better than they sent us any: in two or three yeeres but one Hogshead of Claret. Onely spending my time to revenge my imprisonment upon the harmlesse innocent Salvages, who by my cruelty I forced to feed me with their contribution, and to send any offended my idle humour to James towne to punish at mine owne discretion; or keepe their Kings and subjects in chaines, and make them worke. Things cleane contrary to my Commission; whilest I and my company tooke our needlesse pleasures in discovering the Countries about us, building of Forts, and such unnecessary fooleries, where an Egge-shell (as they writ) had beene sufficient against such enemies; neglecting to answer the Merchants expectations with profit, feeding the Company onely with Letters and tastes of such commodities as we writ the Country would afford in time by industry, as Silke, Wines, Oyles of Olives, Rape, and Linsed, Rasons, Prunes, Flax, Hempe, and Iron, as for Tabacco, wee never then dreamt of it.

Now because I sent not their ships full fraught home with those commodities, they kindly writ to me, if we failed the next returne, they would leave us there as banished men, as if houses and all those commodities did grow naturally, only for us to take at our pleasure, with such tedious Letters, directions, and instructions, and most contrary to that was fitting, we did admire how it was possible such wise men could so torment themselves and us with such strange absurdities and impossibilities, making Religion their colour, when all their aime was nothing but present profit, as most plainly appeared, by sending us so many Refiners, Gold-smiths, Jewellers, Lapidaries, Stone-cutters, Tabacco-pipe-makers, Imbroderers, Perfumers, Silke-men, with all their appurtenances, but materialls, and all those had great summes out of the common stocke: and so many spies and super-intendents over us, as if they supposed we would turne Rebels, all striving to suppresse and advance they knew not what: at last got a Commission in their owne names, promising the King custome within seven yeares, where we were free for one and twenty, appointing the Lord De-la-ware for Governour, with as many great and stately officers, and offices under him, as doth belong to a great Kingdome, with good summes for their extraordinary expences; also privileges for Cities, Charters for Corporations, Universities, Free-schooles, and Glebe-land, putting all those in practice before there were either people, students, or schollers to build or use them, or provision and victuall to feed them were then there: and to amend this, most of the Tradesmen in London that would adventure but twelve pounds ten shillings, had the furnishing the Company of all such things as belonged to his trade, such jugling there was betwixt them, and such intruding Committies their associats, that all the trash they could get in London was sent us to Virginia, they being well payed for that was good. Much they blamed us for not converting the Salvages, when those they sent us were little

A strange mistake in wise men.

better, if not worse, nor did they all convert any of those we sent them to England for that purpose. So doating of Mines of gold, and the South Sea, that all the world could not have devised better courses to bring us to ruine than they did themselves, with many more such like strange conceits; by this you may avoid the like inconveniences, and take heed by those examples, you have not too many irons in the fire at once, neither such change of Governours, nor such a multitude of Officers, neither more Masters, Gentlemen, Gentlewomen, and children, than you have men to worke, which idle charge you will finde very troublesome, and the effects dangerous, and one hundred good labourers better than a thousand such Gallants as were sent me, that could doe nothing but complaine, curse, and despaire, when they saw our miseries, and all things so cleane contrary to the report in England, yet must I provide as well for them as for my selfe.

Chapter 2.

Needlesse custome, effect of flattery, cause of misery, factions, carelesse government, the dissolving the Company and Patent.

The effect of flattery, the cause of misery.

THIS the Mariners and Saylers did ever all they could to conceale, who had alwayes both good fare, and good pay for the most part, and part out of our owne purses, never caring how long they stayed upon their voyage, daily feasting before our faces, when wee lived upon a little corne and water, and not halfe enough of that, the most of which we had from amongst the Salvages. Now although there be Deere in the woods, Fish in the rivers, and Fowles in abundance in their seasons; yet the woods are so wide, the rivers so broad, and the beasts so wild, and wee so unskilfull to catch them, wee little troubled them nor they us: for all this our letters that still signified unto them the plaine truth, would not be beleeved, because they required such things as was most necessary: but their opinion was otherwayes, for they desired but to packe over so many as they could, saying necessity would make them get victuals for themselves, as for good labourers they were more usefull here in England: but they found it otherwayes; the charge was all one to send a workman as a roarer, whose clamors to appease, we had much adoe to get fish and corne to maintaine them from one supply till another came with more loyterers without victuals still to make us worse and worse, for the most of them would rather starve than worke; yet had it not beene for some few that were Gentlemen, both by birth, industry, and discretion, we could not possibly have subsisted.

Many did urge I might have forced them to it, having authority that extended so farre as death: but I say, having neither meat, drinke, lodging, pay, nor hope of any thing, or preferment: and seeing the Merchants onely did what they listed with all they wrought for, I know not what punishment could be greater than that they indured; which miseries caused us alwaies to be in factions, the most part striving by any meanes to abandon the Country, and I with my party to prevent them and cause them stay. But indeed the cause of our factions was bred here in England, and grew to that maturity among themselves that spoyled all, as all the Kingdome and other Nations can too well testifie: Yet in the yeare 1622. there were about seven or eight thousand English, as hath beene said, so well trained, secure, and well furnished, as they reported and conceited. These simple Salvages their bosome friends, I so much oppressed, had laid their plot how to cut all their throats in a morning, and upon the 22. of March, so innocently attempted it, they slew three hundred forty seven, set their houses on fire, slew their cattell, and brought them to that distraction and confusion within lesse than a yeare, there were not many more than two thousand remaining: the which losse to repaire the company did what they could, till they had consumed all their stocke as is said; then they broke, not making any account, nor giving satisfaction to the Lords, Planters, Adventurers, nor any, whose noble intents had referred the managing of this intricate businesse to a few that lost not by it; so that his Majesty recalled their Commission, and by more just cause: then they perswaded King James

Take heed of factions bred in England.

The Massacre in Virginia.

How the company dissolved.

to call in ours, which were the first beginners without our knowledge or consent, disposing of us and all our indevours at their pleasures.

Chapter 3.
A great comfort to new England, it is no Iland: a strange plague.

The abundance of victuals now in Virginia. NOTWITHSTANDING since they have beene left in a manner, as it were, to themselves, they have increased their numbers to foure or five thousand, and neere as many cattell, with plenty of Goats, abundance of Swine, Poultry and Corne, that as they report, they have sufficient and to spare, to entertaine three or four hundred people, which is much better than to have many people more than provision. Now having glutted the world with their too much overabounding Tabacco: Reason, or necessity, or both, will cause them, I hope, learne in time better to fortifie themselves, and make better use of the trials of their grosse commodities that I have propounded, and at the first sent over: and were it not a lamentable dishonour so goodly a Countrey after so much cost, losse, and trouble, should now in this estate not bee regarded and supplied. And to those of New-England may it not be a great comfort to have so neare a neighbour of their owne Nation, that may furnish them with their spare cattell, swine, poultry, and other roots and fruits, much better than A great comfort for New England by Virginia. from England. But I feare the seed of envy, and the rust of covetousnesse doth grow too fast, for some would have all men advance Virginia to the ruine of New-England; and others the losse of Virginia to sustaine New-England, which God of his mercy forbid: for at first it was intended by that most memorable Judge Sir John Popham, then Lord chiefe Justice of England, and the Lords of his Majesties Privy Councel, with divers others, that two Colonies should be planted, as now they be, for the better strengthening each other against all occurrences; the which to performe, shal ever be in my hearty prayers to Almighty God, to increase and continue that mutuall love betwixt them for ever.

By this you may perceive somewhat, what unexpected inconveniences are incident to a plantation,
especially in such a multitude of voluntary contributers, superfluity of officers, and unexperienced
Commissioners. But it is not so, as yet, with those
for New-England; for they will neither beleeve nor use such
officers, in that they are overseers of their owne estates, and so
well bred in labour and good husbandry as any in England,
where as few as I say was sent me to Virginia, but these were
naught here and worse there.

The differences betwixt the beginning of Virginia, and them of Salem.

Now when these shall have laid the foundations,
and provided meanes beforehand, they may entertain all the poore artificers and laborers in England,
and their families which are burthensome to their Parishes and
Countries where they live upon almes and benevolence for
want of worke, which if they would but pay for their transportation, they should never be troubled with them more; for
there is vast land enough for all the people in England, Scotland, and Ireland: and it seemes God hath provided
this Country for our Nation, destroying the natives
by the plague, it not touching one Englishman,
though many traded and were conversant amongst them; for
they had three plagues in three yeares successively neere two
hundred miles along the Sea coast, that in some places there
scarce remained five of a hundred, and as they report thus it
began:

A necessary consideration.

New-England is no Iland but the maine continent.

A fishing ship being cast away upon the coast, two of the men
escaped on shore; one of them died, the other lived among the
natives till he had learned their language: then he perswaded
them to become Christians, shewing them a Testament, some
parts thereof expounding so well as he could, but they so much
derided him, that he told them hee feared his God would destroy them: whereat the King assembled all his people about a
hill, himselfe with the Christian standing on the top,
demanded if his God had so many people and able
to kill all those? He answered yes, and surely would,
and bring in strangers to possesse their land: but so long they
mocked him and his God, that not long after such a sicknesse
came, that of five or six hundred about the Massachusets there
remained but thirty, on whom their neighbours fell and slew

A strange plague among the Salvages.

twenty eight: the two remaining fled the Country till the English came, then they returned and surrendred their Countrey and title to the English: if this be not true in every particular, excuse me, I pray you, for I am not the Author: but it is most certaine there was an exceeding great plague amongst them; for where I have seene two or three hundred, within three yeares after remained scarce thirty, but what disease it was the Salvages knew not till the English told them, never having seene, nor heard of the like before.

Chapter 4.
Our right to those Countries,
true reasons for plantations, rare examples.

By what right wee may possesse those Countries lawfully.

MANY good religious devout men have made it a great question, as a matter in conscience, by what warrant they might goe to possesse those Countries, which are none of theirs, but the poore Salvages. Which poore curiosity will answer it selfe; for God did make the world to be inhabited with mankind, and to have his name knowne to all Nations, and from generation to generation: as the people increased they dispersed themselves into such Countries as they found most convenient. And here in Florida, Virginia, New-England, and Cannada, is more land than all the people in Christendome can manure, and yet more to spare than all the natives of those Countries can use and culturate. And shall we here keepe such a coyle for land, and at such great rents and rates, when there is so much of the world uninhabited, and as much more in other places, and as good, or rather better than any wee possesse, were it manured and used accordingly. If this be not a reason sufficient to such tender consciences; for a copper kettle and a few toyes, as beads and hatchets, they will sell you a whole Countrey; and for a small matter, their houses and the ground they dwell upon; but those of the Massachusets have resigned theirs freely.

True reasons for those plantations.

Now the reasons for plantations are many; Adam and Eve did first begin this innocent worke to plant the earth to remaine to posterity, but not without labour, trouble, and industry: Noah and his family began againe the second plantation, and their seed as it still increased, hath still planted new Countries, and one Country another, and so the world to that estate it is; but not without much hazard, travell, mortalities, discontents, and many disasters: had those worthy Fathers and their memorable off-spring not beene more diligent for us now in those ages, than wee are to plant that yet unplanted for after-livers. Had the seed of Abraham, our Saviour Christ Jesus and his Apostles, exposed themselves to no more dangers to plant the Gospell wee so much professe, than we, even we our selves had at this present beene as Salvages, and as miserable as the most barbarous Salvage, yet uncivilized. The Hebrewes, Lacedemonians, the Goths, Grecians, Romans, and the rest, what was it they would not undertake to inlarge their Territories, inrich their subjects, and resist their enemies. Those that were the founders of those great Monarchies and their vertues, were no silvered idle golden Pharisies, but industrious honest hearted Publicans, they regarded more provisions and necessaries for their people, than jewels, ease and delight for themselves; riches was their servants, not their masters; they ruled as fathers, not as tyrants; their people as children, not as slaves; there was no disaster could discourage them; and let none thinke they incountered not with all manner of incumbrances, and what hath ever beene the worke of the best great Princes of the world, but planting of Countries, and civilizing barbarous and inhumane Nations to civility and humanity, whose eternall actions fils our histories with more honour than those that have wasted and consumed them by warres.

Rare examples of the Spaniards, Portugals, and the Ancients. Lastly, the Portugals and Spaniards that first began plantations in this unknowne world of America till within this 140. yeares, whose everlasting actions before our eyes, will testifie our idlenesse and ingratitude to all posterity, and neglect of our duty and religion wee owe our God, our King, and Countrey, and want of charity to those poore Salvages, whose Countries we challenge, use, and possesse, except wee be but made to marre what our forefathers made, or but only tell what they did, or esteeme our selves too good to take the like paines where there is so much reason, liberty, and action offers it selfe, having as much power and meanes as others: why should English men despaire and not doe so much as any? Was it vertue in those Heros to provide that doth maintaine us, and basenesse in us to doe the like for others to come? Surely no; then seeing wee are not borne for our selves but each to helpe other, and our abilities are much alike at the howre of our birth and minute of our death: seeing our good deeds or bad, by faith in Christs merits, is all wee have to carry our soules to heaven or hell: Seeing honour is our lives ambition, and our ambition after death, to have an honourable memory of our life: and seeing by no meanes wee would be abated of the dignitie and glorie of our predecessors, let us imitate their vertues to be worthily their successors, or at least not hinder, if not further them that would and doe their utmost and best endevour.

Chapter 5.
My first voyage to new England, my returne and profit.

<small>My first voyage to Norumbega now called New-England. 1614.</small>

To begin with the originals of the voyages to those coasts, I referre you to my generall history; for New-England by the most of them was esteemed a most barren rocky desart: Notwithstanding at the sole charge of foure Merchants of London and my selfe, 1614. within eight weekes sayling I arrived at Monahigan an Ile in America in 43. degrees 39. minutes of Northerly latitude. Had the fishing for Whale proved as we expected, I had stayed in the Country; but we found the plots wee had, so false, and the seasons for fishing and trade by the unskilfulnesse of our Pylot so much mistaken, I was contented, having taken by hookes and lines with fifteene or eighteene men at most, more than 60000. Cod in lesse than a moneth: whilest my selfe with eight others of them might best be spared, by an houre glasse of three moneths, ranging the coast in a small boat,

<small>We got 1500. pound in six moneths.</small>

got for trifles eleven hundred Bever skins beside Otters and Martins; all amounting to the value of fifteene hundred pound, and arrived in England with all my men in health in six or seven moneths: But Northward the French returned this yeare to France five and twenty thousand bevers and good furres, whilest we were contending about Patents and Commissions, with such fearefull incredulity that more dazeled our eyes than opened them. In this voyage I tooke the description of the coast as well by map as writing, and called it New-England; but malicious mindes amongst Sailers and others, drowned that name with the eccho of Nusconcus, Canaday, and Penaquid; till at my humble sute, our most gracious King Charles, then Prince of Wales, was pleased to confirme it by that title, and did change the barbarous names of their principall Harbours and habitations for such English, that posterity may say, King Charles was their Godfather; and in my opinion it should seeme an unmannerly presumption in any that doth alter them without his leave.

25000. Bevers sent to France.

My second voyage was to beginne a Plantation, and to doe what else I could, but by extreme tempests that bore neare all my Masts by the boord, being more than two hundred leagues at Sea, was forced to returne to Plimoth with a Jury-Mast. The third was intercepted by English and French Pyrats, by my trecherous company that betrayed me to them, who ran away with my Ship and all that I had, such enemies the Sailers were to a Plantation, and the greatest losse being mine, did easily excuse themselves to the Merchants in England, that still provided to follow the fishing: much difference there was betwixt the Londoners and the Westerlings to ingrosse it, who now would adventure thousands, that when I went first would not adventure a groat; yet there went foure or five good Ships, but what by their dissention, and the Turkes men of warre that tooke the best of them in the Straits, they scarce saved themselves this yeare. At my returne from France I did my best to have united them, but that had beene more than a worke for Hercules, so violent is the folly of greedy covetousnesse.

My second and third voyage. 1615. 1616.

Chapter 6.

A description of the Coast, Harbours, Habitations, Land-marks, Latitude, Longitude, with the map.

A description of the Country.

THIS Country wee now speake of, lyeth betwixt 41. and 44½ the very meane for heat and cold betwixt the Equinoctiall and the North Pole, in which I have sounded about five and twenty very good Harbors; in many whereof is Ancorage for five hundred good ships of any burthen, in some of them for a thousand, and more than three hundred Iles overgrowne with good timber, or divers sorts of other woods; in most of them (in their seasons) plenty of wilde fruits, Fish, and Fowle, and pure springs of most excellent water pleasantly distilling from their rockie foundations. The principall habitations I was at North-ward, was Pennobscot, who are in warres with the Terentines, their next Northerly neighbours. Southerly up the Rivers, and along the Coast, wee found Mecadacut, Segocket, Pemmaquid, Nusconcus, Sagadahock, Satquin, Aumughcawgen, and Kenabeca: to those belong the Countries and people of Segotago, Pauhuntanuck, Pocopassum, Taughtanakagnet, Wabigganus, Nassaque, Masherosqueck, Wawrigwick, Moshoquen, Waccogo, Pasharanack, etc. To those are alied in confederacy, the Countries of Aucocisco, Accominticus, Passataquak, Augawoam and Naemkeck, all these for any thing I could perceive differ little in language or any thing, though most of them be Sagamos, and Lords of themselves, yet they hold the Bashabes of Pennobscot the chiefe and greatest amongst them. The next is Mattahunt, Totant, Massachuset, Paconekick, then Cape Cod, by which is Pawmet, the Iles Nawset and Capawuck, neere which are the shoules of Rocks and sands that stretch themselves into the maine Sea twenty leagues, and very dangerous betwixt the degrees of 40. and 41.

Now beyond Cape Cod, the land extendeth it selfe Southward to Virginia, Florida, the West-Indies, the Amazons, and Brasele, to the straits of Magelanus, two and fifty degrees Southward beyond the Line; all those great Countries, differing as they are in distance North or South from the Equinoctiall, in temper, heat, cold,

Under the Equinoctiall, twelve houres day, and twelve night.

Woods, Fruits, Fishes, Beasts, Birds, the increase and decrease
of the night and day, to six moneths day and six moneths
night. Some say, many of those Nations are so brute they have
no Religion, wherein surely they may be deceived, for my part
I never saw nor heard of any Nation in the world which had
not Religion, Deare, Bowes, and Arrowes. Those in New-
England, I take it, beleeve much alike as those in Virginia, of
many divine Powers, yet of one above all the rest; as
Their Religion. the Southerly Virginians call their chiefe God *Kewassa*, and that we now inhabit, *Okee*, but all their
Kings *Werowances.* The Massachusets call their great God *Kich-
tan*, and their Kings *Sachemes;* and that we suppose their
Devill, they call *Habamouk.* The Pennobscots, their God, *Tantum*, their Kings, *Sagamos.* About those Countries are abundance of severall Nations and languages, but much alike in
their simple curiosities, living and workemanship, except the
wilde estate of their chiefe Kings, etc.

Of whose particular miserable magnificence, yet most happy
in this, that they never trouble themselves with such variety of
Apparell, Drinkes, Viands, Sawses, Perfumes, Preservatives, and
nicities as we; yet live as long, and much more healthfull and
hardy: also the deities of their chiefest Gods, Priests, Conjurers,
Religion, Temples, Triumphs, Physicke, and Chirurgerie, their
births, educations, duty of their women, exercise for their men;
how they make all their Instruments and Engines to cut downe
Trees, make their Cloaths, Boats, Lines, Nets, Fish-hooks,
Weres, and Traps, Mats, Houses, Pots, Platters, Morters, Bowes,
Arrowes, Targets, Swords, Clubs, Jewels, and Hatchets. Their
severall sorts of Woods, Serpents, Beasts, Fish, Fowle, Roots,
Berries, Fruits, Stones, and Clay. Their best trade, what is most
fit to trade with them. With the particulars of the charge of a
fishing voyage, and all the necessaries belonging to it, their
best countries to vent it for their best returnes; also the particulars for every private man or family that goeth to plant, and
the best seasons to goe or returne thence, with the particular
description of the Salvages, Habitations, Harbours, and Land
markes, their Latitude, Longitude, or severall distance, with
their old names and the new by the Map augmented. Lastly,
the power of their Kings, obedience of their subjects, Lawes,
executions, planting their Fields, Huntings, Fishings, the

manner of their warres and treacheries yet knowne; and in generall, their lives and conversation, and how to bridle their brute, barbarous, and salvage dispositions: of all these particulars you may reade at large in the generall History of Virginia, New-England, and the Summer Iles, with many more such strange actions and accidents, that to an ordinary capacity might rather seeme miracles than wonders possibly to bee effected, which though they are but wound up as bottoms of fine silke, which with a good needle might be flourished into a far larger worke, yet the Images of great things are best discerned, contracted into smaller glasses.

Chapter 7.
New Englands yearely trials, the planting new Plimoth, supprisals prevented, their wonderfull industry and fishing.

1617.
Eight ships
to fish.

For all those differences there went eight tall ships before I arrived in England, from France, so that I spent that yeare in the West Country, to perswade the Cities, Townes, and Gentrie for a Plantation, which the Merchants very little liked, because they would have the coast free only for themselves, and the Gentlemen were doubtfull of their true accounts; oft and much it was so disputed, that at last they promised me the next yeere twenty saile well furnished, made me Admirall of the Country for my life under their hands, and the Colonels Seale for New-England; and in renewing their Letters Patents, to be a Patentee for my paines, yet nothing but a voluntary fishing was effected for all this aire.

1618.
1619.
1620.
Eight and
thirty men
in six weeks
tooke two
thousand
one hundred
pounds worth
of fish.

In those yeares many Ships made exceeding good voyages, some in six moneths, others in five, but one of two hundred tunne in six weekes, with eight and thirty men and boyes had her fraught, which shee sold at the first penny for one and twenty hundred pounds, besides her Furres. Six or seven more went out of the West, and some Sailers that had but a single share, had twenty pounds, and at home againe in seven moneths, which was more than such a one should have got in twenty moneths, had he gone for wages any where: yet for all this, in all this time, though I had divulged to my great labour, cost, and losse, more than seven thousand Bookes and Maps, and moved the particular Companies in London, as also Noblemen, Gentlemen, and Merchants for a Plantation, all availed no more than to hew Rocks with Oister-shels, so fresh were the living abuses of Virginia and the Summer Iles in their memories.

At last, upon those inducements, some well disposed Brownists, as they are tearmed, with some Gentlemen and Merchants of Layden and Amsterdam, to save charges, would try their owne conclusions, though with great losse and much miserie, till time had taught them to see their owne error; for such humorists will never beleeve well, till they bee beaten with their owne rod.

1621.

They were supplied with a small Ship with seven and thirty passengers, who found all them were left after they were seated, well, all but six that died, for all their poverties: in this ship they returned the value of five hundred pounds, which was taken by a French-man upon the coast of England.

1622.
Seven and thirty saile to fish.

There is gone from the West to fish five and thirty saile, two from London with sixty passengers for them at New-Plimoth, and all made good voyages. Now you are to understand, the seven and thirty passengers miscarrying twice upon the coast of England, came so ill provided, they onely relyed upon that poore company they found, that had lived two yeares by their naked industry, and what the Country naturally afforded; it is true, at first there hath beene taken a thousand Bayses at a draught, and more than twelve hogsheads of Herrings in a night, of other fish when and what they would, when they had meanes; but wanting most necessaries for fishing and fowling, it is a wonder how they could subsist, fortifie themselves, resist their enemies, and plant their plants.

In July, a many of stragling forlorne Englishmen, whose wants they releeved, though wanted themselves; the which to requite, destroyed their Corne and Fruits, and would have done the like to them, and have surprised what they had; the salvages also intended the like, but wisely they slew the salvage

Captaines, and revenged those injuries upon the fugitive English, that would have done the like to them.

Chapter 8.
Extremity next despaire, Gods great mercy, their estate, they make good salt, an unknowne rich myne.

A<small>T</small> New-Plimoth, having planted there Fields and Gardens, such an extraordinary drought insued, all things withered, that they expected no harvest; and having long expected a supply, they heard no newes, but a wracke split upon their Coast, they supposed their Ship: thus in the very labyrinth of despaire, they solemnly assembled themselves together nine houres in prayer. At their departure, the parching faire skies all overcast with blacke clouds, and the next morning, such a pleasant moderate raine continued fourteene daies, that it was hard to say, whether their withered fruits or drooping affections were most revived; not long after came two Ships to supply them, with all their Passengers well, except one, and he presently recovered; for themselves, for all their wants, there was not one sicke person amongst them: the greater Ship they returned fraught with commodities. This yeare went from England, onely to fish, five and forty saile, and have all made a better voyage than ever.

1623.

In this Plantation there is about an hundred and fourescore persons, some Cattell, but many Swine and Poultry: their Towne containes two and thirty houses, whereof seven were burnt, with the value of five or six hundred pounds in other goods, impailed about halfe a mile, within which within a high Mount, a Fort, with a Watch-tower, well built of stone, lome, and wood, their Ordnance well mounted, and so healthfull, that of the first Planters not one hath died this three yeares: yet at the first landing at Cape Cod, being an hundred passengers, besides twenty they had left behind at Plimoth for want of good take heed, thinking to finde all things better than I advised them, spent six or seven weekes in wandring up and downe in frost and snow, wind and raine, among

Five and forty saile to fish.
1624.

the woods, cricks, and swamps, forty of them died, and three-score were left in most miserable estate at New-Plimoth, where their Ship left them, and but nine leagues by Sea from where they landed, whose misery and variable opinions, for want of experience, occasioned much faction, till necessity agreed them. These disasters, losses, and uncertainties, made such disagreement among the Adventurers in England, who beganne to repent, and rather lose all, than longer continue the charge, being out of purse six or seven thousand pounds, accounting my bookes and their relations as old Almanacks. But the Planters, rather than leave the Country, concluded absolutely to supply themselves, and to all their adventurers pay them for nine yeares two hundred pounds yearely without any other account; where more than six hundred Adventurers for Virginia, for more than two hundred thousand pounds, had not six pence. Since they have made a salt worke, wherewith they preserve all the fish they take, and have fraughted this yeare a ship of an hundred and fourescore tun, living so well they desire nothing but more company, and what ever they take, returne commodities to the value.

They make store of good salt.

Thus you may plainly see, although many envying I should bring so much from thence, where many others had beene, and some the same yeare returned with nothing, reported the Fish and Bevers I brought home, I had taken from the French men of Canada, to discourage any from beleeving me, and excuse their owne misprisions, some onely to have concealed this good Country (as is said) to their private use; others taxed me as much of indiscretion, to make my discoveries and designes so publike for nothing, which might have beene so well managed by some concealers, to have beene all rich ere any had knowne of it. Those, and many such like wise rewards, have beene my recompences, for which I am contented, so the Country prosper, and Gods name bee there praised by my Country-men, I have my desire; and the benefit of this salt and fish, for breeding Mariners and building ships, will make so many fit men to raise a Common-wealth, if but managed, as my generall history will shew you; it might well by this have beene as profitable as the best Mine the King of Spaine hath in his West Indies.

An incredible rich mine.

Chapter 9.
Notes worth observation: miserablenesse no good husbandry.

Now if you but truly consider how many strange accidents have befallen those plantations and my selfe,
how oft up, how oft downe, sometimes neere despaire, and ere long flourishing; how many scandals and
Spanolized English have sought to disgrace them, bring them
to ruine, or at least hinder them all they could; how many have
shaven and couzened both them and me, and their most honourable supporters and well-willers, cannot but conceive Gods
infinite mercy both to them and me. Having beene a slave to
the Turks, prisoner amongst the most barbarous Salvages, after
my deliverance commonly discovering and ranging those large
rivers and unknowne Nations with such a handfull of ignorant
companions, that the wiser sort often gave mee for lost,
alwayes in mutinies, wants and miseries, blowne up with gunpowder; A long time prisoner among the French Pyrats, from
whom escaping in a little boat by my selfe, and adrift, all such
a stormy winter night when their ships were split, more than
an hundred thousand pound lost, wee had taken at sea, and
most of them drownd upon the Ile of Ree, not farre from
whence I was driven on shore in my little boat, etc. And many
a score of the worst of winter moneths lived in the fields, yet to
have lived neere 37. yeares in the midst of wars, pestilence and
famine; by which, many an hundred thousand have died about
mee, and scarce five living of them went first with me to Virginia, and see the fruits of my labours thus well begin to prosper: Though I have but my labour for my paines, have I not
much reason both privately and publikely to acknowledge it
and give God thankes, whose omnipotent power onely delivered me to doe the utmost of my best to make his name
knowne in those remote parts of the world, and his loving
mercy to such a miserable sinner.

Notes worthy observation.

Had my designes beene to have perswaded men to
a mine of gold, as I know many have done that knew
no such matter; though few doe conceive either the
charge or paines in refining it, nor the power nor care to defend

Goods ill gotten ill spent.

it; or some new invention to passe to the South sea, or some strange plot to invade some strange Monastery; or some chargeable Fleet to take some rich Charaques, or letters of mart, to rob some poore Merchant or honest fisher men; what multitudes of both people and money would contend to be first imployed. But in those noble indevours now how few, unlesse it bee to begge them as Monopolies, and those seldome seeke the common good, but the commons goods, as the 217. the 218. and the 219. pages in the generall history will shew. But only those noble Gentlemen and their associates, for whose better incouragements I have recollected those experienced memorandums, as an Apologie against all calumniating detracters, as well for my selfe as them.

Miserablenesse no good husbandry. Now since them called Brownists went, some few before them also having my bookes and maps, presumed they knew as much as they desired, many other directers they had as wise as themselves, but that was best that liked their owne conceits; for indeed they would not be knowne to have any knowledge of any but themselves, pretending onely Religion their governour, and frugality their counsell, when indeed it was onely their pride, and singularity, and contempt of authority; because they could not be equals, they would have no superiours: in this fooles Paradise, they so long used that good husbandry, they have payed soundly in trying their owne follies, who undertaking in small handfuls to make many plantations, and to bee severall Lords and Kings of themselves, most vanished to nothing, to the great disparagement of the generall businesse, therefore let them take heed that doe follow their example.

Chapter 10.
The mistaking of Patents, strange effects, incouragements for servants.

1625.
1626.
1627.
1628. Who would not thinke that all those certainties should not have made both me and this Country have prospered well by this? but it fell out otherwayes, for

by the instigation of some, whose policy had long watched their oportunity by the assurance of those profitable returnes, procured new Letters Patents from King James, drawing in many Noblemen and others to the number of twenty, for Patentees, dividing my map and that tract of land from the North Sea to the South Sea, East and West, which is supposed by most Cosmographers at least more than two thousand miles; and from 41. degrees to 48. of Northerly latitude about 560. miles; the bounds Virginia to the South, the South Sea to the West, Canada to the North, and the maine Ocean to the East; all this they divided in twenty parts, for which they cast lots, but no lot for me but Smiths Iles, which are a many of barren rocks, the most overgrowne with such shrubs and sharpe whins you can hardly passe them; without either grasse or wood, but three or foure short shrubby old Cedars. Those Patentees procured a Proclamation, that no ship should goe thither to fish but pay them for the publike, as it was pretended, five pound upon every thirty tuns of shipping, neither trade with the natives, cut downe wood, throw their balast over-boord, nor plant without commission, leave and content to the Lord of that division or Mannor; some of which for some of them I beleeve will be tenantlesse this thousand yeare. Thus whereas this Country, as the contrivers of those projects, should have planted it selfe of it selfe, especially all the chiefe parts along the coast the first yeare, as they have oft told me, and chiefly by the fishing ships and some small helpe of their owne, thinking men would be glad upon any termes to be admitted under their protections: but it proved so contrary, none would goe at all. So for feare to make a contempt against the Proclamation it hath ever since beene little frequented to any purpose, nor would they doe any thing but left it to it selfe.

The effect of the last great Patent.

A Proclamation for New-England.

Thus it lay againe in a manner vast, till those noble Gentlemen thus voluntarily undertooke it, whom I intreat to take this as a memorandum of my love, to make your plantations so neere and great as you can; for many hands make light worke, whereas yet your small parties can doe nothing available; nor stand too much upon the letting, setting, or selling those wild Countries, nor impose too much upon the commonalty either by your maggazines, which

Memoran-dums for masters.

commonly eat out all poore mens labours, nor any other too hard imposition for present gaine; but let every man so it bee by order allotted him, plant freely without limitation so much as hee can, bee it by the halfes or otherwayes: And at the end of five or six yeares, or when you make a division, for every acre he hath planted, let him have twenty, thirty, forty, or an hundred; or as you finde hee hath extraordinarily deserved, by it selfe to him and his heires for ever; all his charges being defrayed to his lord or master, and publike good: In so doing, a

Incourage-
ments for
servants. servant that will labour, within foure or five yeares may live as well there as his master did here: for where there is so much land lie waste, it were a madnesse in a man at the first to buy, or hire, or pay any thing more than an acknowledgement to whom it shall be due; and hee is double mad that will leave his friends, meanes, and freedome in England, to be worse there than here. Therefore let all men have as much freedome in reason as may be, and true dealing, for it is the greatest comfort you can give them, where the very name of servitude will breed much ill bloud, and become odious to God and man; but mildly temper correction with mercy, for I know well you will have occasion enough to use both; and in thus doing, doubtlesse God will blesse you, and quickly triple and multiply your numbers, the which to my utmost I will doe my best indevour.

Chapter II.
The planting Bastable or Salem and Charlton, a description of the Massachusets.

1629.
The planting
Salem. In all those plantations, yea, of those that have done least, yet the most will say, we were the first; and so every next supply, still the next beginner: But seeing history is the memory of time, the life of the dead, and the happinesse of the living; because I have more plainly discovered, and described, and discoursed of those Countries than any as yet I know, I am the bolder to continue the story, and doe all men right so neere as I can in those new beginnings, which hereafter perhaps may bee in better request than a forest of nine dayes pamphlets.

Their provisions for Salem.   In the yeare 1629. about March, six good ships are gone with 350. men, women, and children, people professing themselves of good ranke, zeale, meanes and quality: also 150. head of cattell, as horse, mares, and neat beasts; 41. goats, some conies, with all provision for houshold and apparell; six peeces of great Ordnance for a Fort, with Muskets, Pikes, Corslets, Drums and Colours, with all provisions necessary for the good of man. They are seated about 42. degrees and 38. minutes, at a place called by the natives Naemkecke, by our Royall King Charles, Bastable; but now by the planters, Salem; where they arrived for most part exceeding well, their cattell and all things else prospering exceedingly, farre beyond their expectation.

The planting Salem and Charlton.   At this place they found some reasonable good provision and houses built by some few of Dorchester, with whom they are joyned in society with two hundred men, an hundred and fifty more they have sent to the Massachusets, which they call Charlton, or Charles Towne: I tooke the fairest reach in this Bay for a river, whereupon I called it Charles river, after the name of our Royall King Charles; but they find that faire Channell to divide it selfe into so many faire branches as make forty or fifty pleasant Ilands within that excellent Bay, where the land is of divers and *A description of the Massachusets Bay.* sundry sorts, in some places very blacke and fat, in others good clay, sand and gravell, the superficies neither too flat in plaines, nor too high in hils. In the Iles you may keepe your hogs, horse, cattell, conies or poultry, and secure for little or nothing, and to command when you list, onely having a care of provision for some extraordinary cold winter. In those Iles, as in the maine, you may make your nurseries for fruits and plants where you put no cattell; in the maine you may shape your Orchards, Vineyards, Pastures, Gardens, Walkes, Parkes, and Corne fields out of the whole peece as you please into such plots, one adjoyning to another, leaving every of them invironed with two, three, foure, or six, or so many rowes of well growne trees as you will, ready growne to your hands, to defend them from ill weather, which in a champion you could not in many ages; and this at first you may doe with as much facility, as carelesly or ignorantly cut downe all before you, and then after better consideration make ditches, pales, plant young trees with an excessive charge and labour, seeing you may have so many great and small growing trees for your maineposts, to fix hedges, palisados, houses, rales, or what you will; which order in Virginia hath not beene so well observed as it might: where all the woods for many an hundred mile for the most part grow streight, like unto the high grove or tuft of trees, upon the high hill by the house of that worthy Knight Sir Humphrey Mildmay, so remarkable in Essex in the Parish of Danbery, where I writ this discourse, but much taller and greater, neither grow they so thicke together by the halfe, and much good ground betweene them without shrubs, and the best is ever knowne by the greatnesse of the trees and the vesture it beareth. Now in New-England the trees are commonly lower, but much thicker and firmer wood, and more proper for shipping, of which I will speake a little, being the chiefe engine wee are to use in this worke, and the rather for that within a square of twenty leagues, you may have all, or most of the chiefe materials belonging to them, were they wrought to their perfection as in other places.

Of all fabricks a ship is the most excellent, requiring more art in building, rigging, sayling, trimming, defending, and moaring, with such a number of severall termes and names in continuall motion, not understood of any landman, as none would thinke of, but some few that know them; for whose better instruction I writ my Sea-Grammar, a booke most necessary for those plantations, because there is scarce any thing belonging to a ship, but the Sea-termes, charge and duty of every officer is plainly expressed, and also any indifferent capacity may conceive how to direct an unskilfull Carpenter or Sailer to build Boats and Barkes sufficient to saile those coasts and rivers, and put a good workman in minde of many things in this businesse hee may easily mistake or forget. But to be excellent in this faculty is the master-peece of all the most necessary workmen in the world. The first rule or modell thereof being directed by God himselfe to Noah for his Arke, which he never did to any other building but his Temple, which is tossed and turned up and downe the world with the like dangers, miseries, and extremities as a ship,

The master-peece of workmanship.

sometimes tasting the fury of the foure Elements, as well as shee, by unlimited tyrants in their cruelty for tortures, that it is hard to conceive whether those inhumanes exceed the beasts of the Forrest, the birds of the Aire, the fishes of the Sea, either in numbers, greatnesse, swiftnesse, fiercenesse or cruelty; whose actions and varieties, with such memorable observations as I have collected, you shall finde with admiration in my history of the Sea, if God be pleased I live to finish it.

Chapter 12.
Extraordinary meanes for building, many caveats, increase of corne, how to spoyle the woods, for any thing, their healths.

Extraordinary
meanes for
buildings. For the building houses, townes, and fortresses, where shall a man finde the like conveniency, as stones of most sorts, as well lime stone, if I be not much deceived, as Iron stone, smooth stone, blew slate for covering houses, and great rockes we supposed Marble, so that one place is called the marble harbour: There is grasse plenty, though very long and thicke stalked, which being neither mowne nor eaten, is very ranke, yet all their cattell like and prosper well therewith, but indeed it is weeds, herbs, and grasse growing together, which although they be good and sweet in the Summer, they will deceive your cattell in winter; Caveats for
cattell. therefore be carefull in the Spring to mow the swamps, and the low Ilands of Auguan, where you may have harsh sheare-grasse enough to make hay of, till you can cleare ground to make pasture, which will beare as good grasse as can grow any where, as now it doth in Virginia; and unlesse you make this provision, if there come an extraordinary winter, you will lose many of them and hazard the rest, especially if you bring them in the latter end of Summer, or before the grasse bee growne in the Spring, comming weake from Sea. All things they plant prosper exceedingly: but one man of 13. gallons of Indian corne, reaped that yeare 364. bushels London measure, as they confidently report, at which

I much wonder, having planted many bushels, but no such increase.

How to spoyle the woods for pasture and corne.

The best way wee found in Virginia to spoile the woods, was first to cut a notch in the barke a hand broad round about the tree, which pill off and the tree will sprout no more, and all the small boughs in a yeare or two will decay, the greatest branches in the root they spoyle with fire, but you with more ease may cut them from the body and they will quickly rot: betwixt those trees they plant their corne, whose great bodies doe much defend it from extreme gusts, and heat of the Sunne, where that in the plaines, where the trees by time they have consumed, is subject to both; and this is the most easie way to have pasture and corne fields, which is much more fertile than the other: in Virginia they never manure their overworne fields, which is very few, the ground for most part is so fertile: but in New-England they doe, sticking at every plant of corne, a herring or two, which commeth in that season in such abundance, they may take more than they know what to doe with.

A silly complaint of cold, the reason and remedy.

Some infirmed bodies, or tender educats, complaine of the piercing cold, especially in January and February, yet the French in Canada, the Russians, Swethlanders, Polanders, Germans, and our neighbour Hollanders, are much colder and farre more Northward, for all that, rich Countreyes and live well. Now they have wood enough if they will but cut it, at their doores to make fires, and traine oyle with the splinters of the roots of firre trees for candles, where in Holland they have little or none to build ships, houses, or any thing but what they fetch from forren Countries, yet they dwell but in the latitude of Yorkshire, and New-England is in the heighth of the North cape of Spaine, which is 10. degrees, 200. leagues, or 600. miles nearer the Sunne than wee, where upon the mountaines of Bisky I have felt as much cold, frost, and snow as in England, and of this I am sure, a good part of the best Countries and kingdomes of the world, both Northward and Southward of the line, lie in the same paralels of Virginia and New-England, as at large you may finde in the 201. page of the generall history.

Thus you may see how prosperously thus farre they have proceeded, in which course by Gods grace they may continue;

Provisoes for passengers and saylers at sea.

but great care would be had they pester not their ships too much with cattell nor passengers, and to make good conditions for your peoples diet, for therein is used much legerdemaine, therefore in that you cannot be too carefull to keepe your men well, and in health at Sea: in this case some masters are very provident, but the most part so they can get fraught enough, care not much whether the passengers live or die, for a common sailer regards not a landman, especially a poore passenger, as I have seene too oft approved by lamentable experience, although we have victualled them all at our owne charges.

Chapter 13.
Their great supplies, present estate and accidents, advantage.

1630. Their present estate.

WHO would not thinke but that all those trials had beene sufficient to lay a foundation for a plantation, but we see many men many mindes, and still new Lords, new lawes: for those 350. men with all their cattell that so well arived and promised so much, not being of one body, but severall mens servants, few could command and fewer obey, lived merrily of that they had, neither planting or building any thing to any purpose, but one faire house for the Governour, till all was spent and the winter approached; then they grew into many diseases, and as many inconveniences, depending only of a supply from England, which expected Houses, Gardens, and Corne fields ready planted by them for their entertainment.

It is true, that Master John Wynthrop, their now Governour, a worthy Gentleman both in estate and esteeme, went so well provided (for six or seven hundred people went with him) as could be devised, but at Sea, such an extraordinarie storme encountred his Fleet, continuing ten daies, that of two hundred Cattell which were so tossed and brused, threescore and ten died, many of their people fell sicke, and in this perplexed estate, after ten weekes, they arrived in New-England at severall times, where they found threescore of their people dead, the rest sicke, nothing done, but all complaining, and all things so contrary to their expectation, that now every monstrous humor began to shew it selfe. And to second this, neare as many more came after them, but so ill provided, with such multitudes of women and children, as redoubled their necessities.

This small triall of their patience, caused among them no small confusion, and put the Governour and his Councell to their utmost wits; some could not endure the name of a Bishop, others not the sight of a Crosse nor Surplesse, others by no meanes the booke of common Prayer. This absolute crue, only of the Elect, holding all (but such as themselves) reprobates and cast-awaies, now make more haste to returne to Babel, as they tearmed England, than stay to enjoy the land they called Canaan; somewhat they must say to excuse themselves.

The fruits of counterfeits.

Those he found Brownists, hee let goe for New-Plimoth, who are now betwixt foure or five hundred, and live well without want, some two hundred of the rest he was content to returne for England, whose clamors are as variable as their humours and Auditors; some say they could see no timber of two foot diameter, some the Country is all Woods, others they drunke all the Springs and Ponds dry, yet like to famish for want of fresh water; some of the danger of the rattell Snake; and that others sold their provisions at what rates they pleased to them that wanted, and so returned to England great gainers out of others miseries; yet all that returned are not of those humors.

Notwithstanding all this, the noble Governour was no way disanimated, neither repents him of his enterprise for all those mistakes, but did order all things with that temperance and discretion, and so releeved those that wanted with his owne provision, that there is six or seven hundred remained with him, and more than 1600. English in all the Country, with three or foure hundred head of Cattell, as for Corne they are very ignorant: If upon the coast of America, they doe not before the end of this October (for toies) furnish themselves with two or three thousand bushels of Indian Corne, which is better than ours, and in a short time cause the Salvages to doe them as good service as their owne men, as I did in Virginia, and yet neither use cruelty nor tyranny amongst them; a consequence well worth putting in practice: and till it be effected, they will hardly doe well. I know ignorance will say it is impossible, but this impossible taske, ever since the massacre in Virginia, I have beene a suter to have undertaken, but with 150. men, to have got Corne, fortified the Country, and discovered them more land than they all yet know or have demonstrated: but the Merchants common answer was, necessity in time would force the Planters doe it themselves, and rather thus husbandly to lose ten sheepe, than be at the charge of a halfe penny worth of Tarre.

Who is it that knowes not what a small handfull of *Note well.* Spaniards in the West Indies, subdued millions of the inhabitants, so depopulating those Countries they conquered, that they are glad to buy Negroes in Affrica at a great rate, in Countries farre remote from them, which although they bee as idle and as devilish people as any in the world, yet they cause them quickly to bee their best servants; notwithstanding, there is for every foure or five naturall Spaniards, two or three hundred Indians and Negros, and in Virginia and New-England more English than Salvages, that can assemble themselves to assault or hurt them, and it is much better to helpe to plant a country than unplant it and then replant it: but there Indians were in such multitudes, the Spaniards had no other remedy; and ours such a few, and so dispersed, it were nothing in a short time to bring them to labour and obedience.

It is strange to me, that English men should not doe as much as any, but upon every sleight affront, in stead to amend it, we make it worse; notwithstanding the worst of all those rumours, the better sort there are constant in their resolutions, and so are the most of their best friends here; and making provision to supply them, many conceit they make a dearth here, which is nothing so; for they would spend more here than they transport thither. One Ship this Summer with twenty cattell, and forty or fifty passengers, arived all well, and the Ship at home againe in nine weekes: another for all this exclamation of want, is returned with 10000. Corfish, and fourescore Kegs of Sturgion, which they did take and save when the season was neare past, and in the very heat of Summer, yet as good as can be. Since another ship is gone from Bristow, and many more a providing to follow them with all speed.

Thus you may plainly see for all these rumours, they are in no such distresse as is supposed: as for their mischances, misprisions, or what accidents may befall them, I hope none is so malicious, as attribute the fault to the Country nor mee; yet if some blame us not both, it were more than a wonder; for I am not ignorant that ignorance and too curious spectators, make it a great part of their profession to censure (however) any mans actions, who having lost the path to vertue, will make most excellent shifts to mount up any way; such incomparable connivency is in the Devils most punctuall cheaters, they will hazard a joint, but where God hath his Church they wil have a Chapel; a mischiefe so hard to be prevented, that I have thus plainly adventured to shew my affection, through the weaknesse of my abilitie, you may easily know them by their absolutenesse in opinions, holding experience but the mother of fooles, which indeed is the very ground of reason, and he that contemnes her in those actions, may finde occasion enough to use all the wit and wisdome hee hath to correct his owne folly, that thinkes to finde amongst those salvages such Churches, Palaces, Monuments, and Buildings as are in England.

Chapter 14.
Ecclesiasticall government in Virginia, authority from the Arch Bishop, their beginning at Bastable now called Salem.

Ecclesiasticall government in Virginia.

Now because I have spoke so much for the body, give me leave to say somewhat of the soule; and the rather because I have beene demanded by so many, how we beganne to preach the Gospell in Virginia, and by what authority, what Churches we had, our order of service, and maintenance for our Ministers, therefore I thinke it not amisse to satisfie their demands, it being the mother of all our

Plantations, intreating pride to spare laughter, to understand her simple beginning and proceedings.

When I went first to Virginia, I well remember, wee did hang an awning (which is an old saile) to three or foure trees to shadow us from the Sunne, our walls were rales of wood, our seats unhewed trees, till we cut plankes, our Pulpit a bar of wood nailed to two neighbouring trees, in foule weather we shifted into an old rotten tent, for we had few better, and this came by the way of adventure for new; this was our Church, till wee built a homely thing like a barne, set upon Cratchets, covered with rafts, sedge, and earth, so was also the walls: the best of our houses of the like curiosity, but the most part farre much worse workmanship, that could neither well defend wind nor raine, yet wee had daily Common Prayer morning and evening, every Sunday two Sermons, and every three moneths the holy Communion, till our Minister died, but our Prayers daily, with an Homily on Sundaies; we continued two or three yeares after till more Preachers came, and surely God did most mercifully heare us, till the continuall inundations of mistaking directions, factions, and numbers of unprovided Libertines neere consumed us all, as the Israelites in the wildernesse.

Their estates at this day. Notwithstanding, out of the relicks of our miseries, time and experience had brought that Country to a great happinesse, had they not so much doated on their Tabacco, on whose fumish foundation there is small stability: there being so many good commodities besides, yet by it they have builded many pretty Villages, faire houses, and Chapels, which are growne good Benefices of 120. pounds a yeare, besides their owne mundall industry, but James towne was 500. pounds a yeare, as they say, appointed by the Councell here, allowed by the Councell there, and confirmed by the Archbishop of Canterbury his Grace, Primate and Metropolitan of all England, Anno 1605. to master Richard Hacluit, Prebend of Westminster, who by his authority sent master Robert Hunt, an honest, religious, and couragious Divine; during whose life our factions were oft qualified, our wants and greatest extremities so comforted, that they seemed easie in comparison of what we endured after his memorable death.

Now in New-England they have all our examples

to teach them how to beware, and choice men, wee
most ignorant in all things, or little better, therfore
presage not the event of all such actions by our defailements:
For they write, they doubt not ere long to be able to defend
themselves against any indifferent enemy; in the interim, they
have Preachers erected among themselves, and Gods true Religion (they say) taught amongst them, the Sabbath day observed, the common Prayer (as I understand) and Sermons
performed, and diligent catechizing, with strict and carefull
exercise, and commendable good orders to bring those people
with whom they have to deale withall into a Christian conversation, to live well, to feare God, serve the King, and love the
Country; which done, in time from both those Plantations
may grow a good addition to the Church of England; but
Rome was not built in one day, whose beginnings was once as
unhopefull as theirs, and to make them as eminent shall be my
humble and hearty prayers.

But as yet it is not well understood of any authority they have
sought for the government and tranquillity of the Church,
which doth cause those suspicions of factions in Religion,

wherein although I be no Divine, yet I hope without
offence I may speake my opinion as well in this as I
have done in the rest. He that will but truly consider
the greatnesse of the Turks Empire and power here
in Christendome, shall finde the naturall Turkes are generally
of one religion, and the Christians in so many divisions and
opinions, that they are among themselves worse enemies than
the Turkes, whose dis-joyntednesse hath given him that opportunity to command so many hundred thousand of Christians as he doth, where had they beene constant to one God,
one Christ, and one Church, Christians might have beene
more able to have commanded as many Turkes, as now the
Turkes doe poore miserable Christians. Let this example remember you to beware of faction in that nature; for my owne
part, I have seene many of you here in London goe to Church
as orderly as any.

Therefore I doubt not but you will seeke to the
prime authority of the Church of England, for such
an orderly authority as in most mens opinions is fit

for you both to intreat for and to have, which I thinke will not be denied; and you have good reason, seeing you have such liberty to transport so many of his Majesties subjects, with all sorts of cattell, armes, and provision as you please, and can provide meanes to accomplish, nor can you have any certaine releefe, nor long subsist without more supplies from England. Besides, this might prevent many inconveniences may insue, and would clearely take away all those idle and malicious rumours, and occasion you many good and great friends and assistance you yet dreame not of; for you know better than I can tell, that the maintainers of good Orders and Lawes is the best preservation next God of a Kingdome: but when they are stuffed with hypocrisie and corruption, that state is not doubtfull but lamentable in a well setled Common-wealth, much more in such as yours, which is but a beginning, for as the Lawes corrupt, the state consumes.

Chapter 15.
The true modell of a plantation, tenure, increase of trade, true examples, necessity of expert Souldiers, the names of all the first discoverers for plantations and their actions, what is requisite to be in the Governour of a plantation, the expedition of Queene Elizabeths Sea Captaines.

The effect of a Citadell, or the true modell of a Plantation. IN regard of all that is past, it is better of those slow proceedings than lose all, and better to amend late than never; I know how hatefull it is to envy, pride, flattery, and greatnesse to be advised, but I hope my true meaning wise men will excuse, for making my opinion plaine; I have beene so often and by so many honest men intreated for the rest, the more they mislike it, the better I like it my selfe.

Concerning this point of a Cittadell, it is not the least, though the last remembred: therefore seeing you have such good meanes and power of your owne I never had, with the best convenient speed may be erect a Fort, a Castle or Cittadell, which in a manner is all one; towards the building, provision, and maintenance thereof, every man for every acre he doth culturate to pay foure pence yearely, and some small matter out of every hundred of fish taken or used within five or ten miles, or as you please about it, it being the Center as a Fortresse for ever belonging to the State, and when the charge shall be defrayed to the chiefe undertaker, in reason, let him be Governour for his life: the overplus to goe forward to the erecting another in like manner in a most convenient place, and so one after another, as your abilities can accomplish, by benevolences, forfeitures, fines, and impositions, as reason and the necessitie of the common good requireth; all men holding their lands on those manners as they doe of Churches, Universities, and Hospitals, but all depending upon one principall, and this would avoid all faction among the Superiours, extremities from the comminalty, and none would repine at such payments, when they shall see it justly imployed for their owne defence and security; as for corruption in so small a Government, you may quickly perceive, and punish it accordingly.

The condition of trade and freedome. Now as his Majesty hath made you custome-free for seven yeares, have a care that all your Country men shall come to trade with you, be not troubled with Pilatage, Boyage, Ancorage, Wharfage, Custome, or any such tricks as hath beene lately used in most of new Plantations, where they would be Kings before their folly; to the discouragement of many, and a scorne to them of understanding, for Dutch, French, Biskin, or any will as yet use freely the Coast without controule, and why not English as well as they: Therefore use all commers with that respect, courtesie, and liberty is fitting, which in a short time will much increase your trade and shipping to fetch it from you, for as yet it were not good to adventure any more abroad with factors till you bee better provided; now there is nothing more inricheth a Common-wealth than much trade, nor no meanes better to increase than small custome, as Holland, Genua, Ligorne, and divers other places can well tell you, and doth most beggar those places where they take most custome, as Turkie, the Archipelagan Iles, Cicilia, the Spanish ports, but that their officers will connive to inrich themselves, though undoe the State.

In this your infancy, imagine you have many eyes attending your actions, some for one end, and some onely to finde fault; neglect therefore no opportunity, to informe his Majesty truly your orderly proceedings, which if it be to his liking, and contrary to the common rumour here in England, doubtlesse his Majesty will continue you custome free, till you have recovered your selves, and are able to subsist; for till such time, to take any custome from a Plantation, is not the way to make them prosper, nor is it likely those Patentees shall accomplish any thing; that will neither maintaine them nor defend them, but with Countenances, Councells, and advice, which any reasonable man there may better advise himselfe, than one thousand of them here who were never there; nor will any man, that hath any wit, throw himselfe into such a kinde of subjection, especially at his owne cost and charges; but it is too oft seene that sometimes one is enough to deceive one hundred, but two hundred not sufficient to keepe one from being deceived.

I speake not this to discourage any with vaine feares, but
The Spaniards glory. could wish every English man to carry alwaies this Motto in his heart; Why should the brave Spanish Souldiers brag. The Sunne never sets in the Spanish dominions, but ever shineth on one part or other we have conquered for our King; who within these few hundred of yeares, was one of the least of most of his neighbours; but to animate us to doe the like for ours, who is no way his inferior; and truly there is no pleasure comparable to a generous spirit; as good imploiment in noble actions, especially amongst Turks, Heathens, and Infidels, to see daily new Countries, people, fashions, governments, stratagems, releeve the oppressed, comfort his friends, passe miseries, subdue enemies, adventure upon any feazable danger for God and his Country: it is true, it is a happy thing to be borne to strength, wealth, and honour, but that which is got by prowesse and magnanimity is the truest lustre; and those can the best distinguish content, that have escaped most honourable dangers, as if out of every extremity he found himselfe now borne to a new life to learne how to amend and maintaine his age.

Provisoes for exercise of armes. Those harsh conclusions have so oft plundered me in those perplexed actions, that if I could not freely expresse my selfe to them doth second them, I should thinke my selfe guilty of a most damnable crime worse than ingratitude; however some overweining capricious conceits, may attribute it to vaine-glory, ambition, or what other idle Epithete such pleased to bestow on me: But such trash I so much scorne, that I presume further to advise those, lesse advised than my selfe, that as your fish and trade increaseth, so let your forts and exercise of armes, drilling your men at your most convenient times, to ranke, file, march, skirmish, and retire, in file, manaples, battalia, or ambuskados, which service there is most proper; also how to assault and defend your forts, and be not sparing of a little extraordinary shot and powder to make them mark-men, especially your Gentlemen, and those you finde most capable, for shot must be your best weapon, yet all this will not doe unlesse you have at least 100. or as many as you can, of expert, blouded, approved good Souldiers, who dare boldly lead them, not to shoot a ducke, a goose, or a dead marke, but at men, from whom you must expect such as you send. The want of this, and the presumptuous assurance of literall Captaines, was the losse of the French and Spaniards in Florida, each surprising other, and lately neare the ruine of Mevis and Saint Christophers in the Indies: also the French at Port Riall, and those at Canada, now your next English neighbours: Lastly, Cape Britton not far from you, called New-Scotland. Questionlesse there were some good Souldiers among them, yet somewhat was the cause they were undone by those that watched the advantage of opportunity: for as rich preyes make true men theeves; so you must not expect, if you be once worth taking and unprovided, but by some to bee attempted in the like manner: to the prevention whereof, I have not beene more willing at the request of my friends to print this discourse, than I am ready to live and dye among you, upon conditions suting my calling and profession to make good, and Virginia and New-England, my heires, executors, administrators and assignes.

A reference to the actions of all our prime discoverers and planters.   Now because I cannot expresse halfe that which is necessary for your full satisfaction and instruction belonging to this businesse in this small pamphlet, I referre you to the generall history of Virginia, the Summer Iles, and New-England; wherein you may plainly see

all the discoveries, plantations, accidents, the misprisions and
causes of defailments of all those noble and worthy Captaines;
Captaine Philip Amadas, and Barlow; that most renowned
Knight Sir Richard Greenvile, worthy Sir Ralph Layne, and
learned Master Hariot, Captaine John White, Captaine Bartholomew Gosnold, Captaine Martin Pring, and George Waymouth, with mine owne observations by sea, rivers and land,
and all the governours that yearely succeeded mee in Virginia.
Also those most industrious Captaines, Sir George Summers,
and Sir Thomas Gates, with all the governours that succeeded
them in the Summer Iles. Likewise the plantation of Sagadahock, by those noble Captaines, George Popham, Rawley
Gilbert, Edward Harlow, Robert Davis, James Davis, John
Davis, and divers others, with the maps of those Countries:
with it also you may finde the plantations of Saint Christophers, Mevis, the Berbados, and the great river of the Amazons, whose greatest defects, and the best meanes to amend
them are there yearely recorded, to be warnings and examples
to them that are not too wise to learne to understand.

This great worke, though small in conceit, is not a worke for
every one to mannage such an affaire, as make a discovery, and plant a Colony, it requires all the best
parts of art, judgement, courage, honesty, constancy,
diligence, and industry, to doe but neere well; some
are more proper for one thing than another, and therein best
to be imployed, and nothing breeds more confusion than misplacing and misimploying men in their undertakings. Columbus, Curtes, Pitzara, Zotto, Magellanus, and the rest, served
more than an apprentiship to learne how to begin their most
memorable attempts in the West Indies, which to the wonder
of all ages, succesfully they effected, when many hundreds
farre above them in the worlds opinion, being instructed but
by relation, scorning to follow their blunt examples, but in
great state, with new inventions came to shame and confusion
in actions of small moment, who doubtlesse in other matters,
were both wise, discreet, generous and couragious. I say not
this to detract any thing from their noblenesse, state, nor greatnesse, but to answer those questionlesse questions that keepe
us from imitating the others brave spirits, that advanced themselves from poore Souldiers to great Captaines, their posterity

*What is
requisite to
be in a
Governour of
a plantation.*

to great Lords, and their King to be one of the greatest potentates on earth, and the fruits of their labours his greatest glory,
power, and renowne.

The expeditions of Queene Elizabeths Sea-Captaines.

Till his greatnesse and security made his so rich remote and dispersed plantations such great booties
and honours, to the incomparable Sir Francis Drake,
the renowned Captaine Candish, Sir Richard
Luson, Sir John Hawkins, Captaine Carlile, and Sir Martin Fur-
bisher, etc. and the most memorable and right honourable
Earles, Cumberland, Essex, Southampton, and Nottingham
that good Lord Admirall, with many hundreds of brave English
Souldiers, Captaines and Gentlemen, that have taught the
Hollanders to doe the like: Those would never stand upon a
demurre who should give the first blow, when they see peace
was onely but an empty name, and no sure league, but impuis-
sance to doe hurt, found it better to buy peace by warre, than
take it up at interest of those could better guide penknives
than use swords; and there is no misery worse than be conducted by a foole, or commanded by a coward; for who can indure to be assaulted by any, see his men and selfe imbrued in
their owne bloud, for feare of a checke, when it is so contrary
to nature and necessity, and yet as obedient to government
and their Soveraigne, as duty required. Now your best plea is
to stand upon your guard, and provide to defend as they did
offend, especially at landing: if you be forced to retire, you
have the advantage five for one in your retreat, wherein there
is more discipline, than in a brave charge; and though it seeme
lesse in fortune, it is as much in valour to defend as to get, but
it is more easie to defend than assault, especially in woods
where an enemy is ignorant. Lastly, remember as faction, pride,
and security, produces nothing but confusion, miserie and dis-
solution; so the contraries well practised will in short time
make you happy, and the most admired people of all our plantations for your time in the world.

John Smith writ this with his owne hand.

FINIS.

OTHER NARRATIVES OF ROANOKE, JAMESTOWN, AND THE FIRST ENGLISH SETTLEMENT OF AMERICA

ARTHUR BARLOWE

Discourse of the First Voyage

THE first voyage made to the coastes of America, with two barkes, wherein were Captaines Master Philip Amadas, and Master Arthur Barlowe, who discovered part of the Countrey, now called Virginia, Anno 1584: Written by one of the said Captaines, and sent to sir Walter Raleigh, knight, at whose charge, and direction, the said voyage was set foorth.

The 27. day of Aprill, in the yeere of our redemption, 1584. we departed the west of England, with two barkes, well furnished with men and victuals, having receyved our last, and perfect directions by your letters, confirming the former instructions, and commandements delivered by your selfe at our leaving the river of Thames. And I thinke it a matter both unnecessarie, for the manifest discoverie of the Countrey, as also for tediousnes sake, to remember unto you the diurnall of our course, sailing thither, and returning: onely I have presumed to present unto you this briefe discourse, by which you may judge how profitable this land is likely to succeede, as well to your selfe, (by whose direction and charge, and by whose servants this our discoverie hath beene performed) as also to her Highnes, and the Common wealth, in which we hope your wisedome will be satisfied, considering, that as much by us hath bene brought to light, as by those small meanes, and number of men we had, could any way have bene expected, or hoped for.

The tenth of May, we arrived at the Canaries, and the tenth of June in this present yeere, we were fallen with the Islands of the West Indies, keeping a more southeasterly course then was needefull, because we doubted that the current of the Baye of Mexico, disbogging betweene the Cape of Florida, and the Havana, had bene of greater force then afterwards we found it to be; At which Islands we found the aire very unwholesome, and our men grewe for the most part ill disposed: so that

having refreshed our selves with sweete water, and fresh victual, we departed the twelfth daye after our arrivall there. These
Islands, with the rest adjoyning, are so well knowen to your
selfe, and to many others, as I will not trouble you, with the
remembrance of them.

The second of July, we found shole water, which smelt so
sweetely, and was so strong a smell, as if we had bene in the
midst of some delicate garden, abounding with all kind of odoriferous flowers, by which we were assured, that the land could
not be farre distant: and keeping good watch, and bearing but
slacke saile, the fourth of the same moneth, we arrived upon the
coast, which we supposed to be a continent, and firme lande,
and wee sailed along the same, a hundred and twentie English
miles, before we could finde any entrance, or river issuing into
the Sea. The first that appeared unto us, we entred, though
not without some difficultie, and caste anker about three harquebushot within the havens mouth, on the left hande of the
same: and after thankes given to God for our safe arrivall
thither, we manned our boates, and went to viewe
the lande next adjoyning, and to take possession of
the same, in the right of the Queenes most excellent
Majestie, as rightfull Queene, and Princesse of the same: and
after delivered the same over to your use, according to her
Majesties grant, and letters patents, under her Highnes great
Seale. Which being performed, according to the ceremonies
used in such enterprises, wee viewed the lande about us, being
whereas we first landed, very sandie, and lowe towards the
water side, but so full of grapes, as the very beating, and surge
of the Sea overflowed them, of which we founde such plentie,
as well there, as in all places else, both on the sande, and on the
greene soile on the hils, as in the plaines, as well on every little
shrubbe, as also climing towardes the toppes of the high
Cedars, that I thinke in all the world the like aboundance is
not to be founde: and my selfe having seene those partes of
Europe that most abound, finde such difference, as were incredible to be written.

We passed from the Sea side, towardes the toppes of those
hils next adjoyning, being but of meane heigth, and from
thence wee behelde the Sea on both sides to the North, and to
the South, finding no ende any of both waies. This lande laye

July 13.
possessions
taken.

stretching it selfe to the West, which after wee founde to be but an Island of twentie leagues long, and not above sixe miles broade. Under the banke or hill, whereon we stoode, we be-helde the vallies replenished with goodly Cedar trees, and having discharged our harquebushot, such a flocke of Cranes (the most part white) arose under us, with such a crye redou-bled by many Ecchoes, as if an armie of men had showted all together.

This Island had many goodly woods, full of Deere, Conies, Hares, and Fowle, even in the middest of Summer, in incredi-ble aboundance. The woodes are not such as you finde on Bohemia, Moscovia, or Hyrcania, barren and fruitlesse, but the highest, and reddest Cedars of the world, farre bettering the Cedars of the Açores, of the Indias, or of Lybanus, Pynes, Cypres, Sassaphras, the Lentisk, or the tree that beareth the Masticke, the tree that beareth the rinde of black Sinamon, of which Master Winter brought from the Streights of Magel-lane, and many other of excellent smell, and qualitie. We re-mained by the side of this Island two whole daies, before we sawe any people of the Countrey: the third daye we espied one small boate rowing towards us, having in it three persons: this boate came to the landes side, foure harquebushot from our shippes, and there two of the people remaining, the thirde came along the shoare side towards us, and we being then all within boord, he walked up and downe uppon the point of the lande next unto us: then the Master, and the Pilot of the Ad-mirall, Simon Ferdinando, and the Captaine Philip Amadas, my selfe, and others, rowed to the lande, whose comming this fellowe attended, never making any shewe of feare, or doubt. And after he had spoken of many things not understoode by us, we brought him with his owne good liking, aboord the shippes, and gave him a shirt, a hatte, and some other things, and made him taste of our wine, and our meate, which he liked very well: and after having viewed both barkes, he departed, and went to his owne boate againe, which hee had left in a little Cove, or Creeke adjoyning: assoone as hee was two bowe shoote into the water, hee fell to fishing, and in lesse then halfe an howre, he had laden his boate as deepe, as it could swimme, with which he came againe to the pointe of the lande, and there he de-vided his fishe into two partes, pointing one part to the shippe, and the other to the Pinnesse: which after he had (as much as he might,) requited the former benefits receaved, he departed out of our sight.

The next day there came unto us divers boates, and in one of them the Kings brother, accompanied with fortie or fiftie men, very handsome, and goodly people, and in their behaviour as mannerly, and civill, as any of Europe. His name was Granganimeo, and the King is called Wingina, the countrey Wingandacoa, (and nowe by her Majestie, Virginia,) the manner of his comming was in this sorte: hee left his boates altogether, as the first man did a little from the shippes by the shoare, and came along to the place over against the shippes, followed with fortie men. When hee came to the place, his servants spread a long matte uppon the grounde, on which he sate downe, and at the other ende of the matte, foure others of his companie did the like: the rest of his men stoode round about him, somewhat a farre off: when wee came to the shoare to him with our weapons, he never mistrusted any harme to be offered from us, but sitting still, he beckoned us to come and sitte by him, which we perfourmed: and beeing sette, hee makes all signes of joy, and welcome, striking on his head, and his breast, and afterwardes on ours, to shewe we were all one, smiling, and making shewe the best hee could, of all love, and familiaritie. After hee had made a long speech unto us, wee presented him with divers thinges, which hee receaved very joyfully, and thankefully. None of his companye durst to speake one worde all the tyme: onely the foure which were at the other ende, spake one in the others eare very softly.

The King is greatly obeyed, and his brothers, and children reverenced: the King himselfe in person was at our beeing there sore wounded, in a fight which he had with the King of the next Countrey, called Wingina, and was shotte in two places through the bodye, and once cleane thorough the thigh, but yet he recovered: by reason whereof, and for that hee laye at the chiefe Towne of the Countrey, beeing six days journeye off, wee sawe him not at all.

After wee had presented this his brother, with such things as we thought he liked, we likewise gave somewhat to the other that sate with him on the matte: but presently he arose, and tooke all from them, and put it into his owne basket, making signes and tokens, that all things ought to be delivered unto him, and the rest were but his servants, and followers. A daye or two after this, we fell to trading with them, exchanging some thinges that we had for Chammoys, Buffe, and Deere skinnes: when we shewed him all our packet of merchandize, of all things that he saw, a bright tinne dishe most pleased him, which he presently tooke up, & clapt it before his breast, & after made a hole in the brimme thereof, & hung it about his necke, making signes, that it would defende him against enemies arrowes: for those people maintaine a deadlie and terrible warre, with the people and King adjoyning. We exchanged our tinne dishe for twentie skinnes, woorth twentie Crownes, or twentie Nobles: and a copper kettle for fiftie skinnes woorth fiftie Crownes. They offered us very good exchange for our hatchets, and axes, and for knives, and would have given any thing for the swordes: but we would not depart with any. After two or three daies, the Kings brother came aboord the shippes, and dranke wine, and ate of our meate, and of our bread, and liked exceedingly thereof: and after a few daies overpassed, he brought his wife with him to the shippes, his daughter, and two or three little children: his wife was very well favored, of meane stature, and very bashfull: she had on her backe a long cloke of leather, with the furre side next to her bodie, and before her a peece of the same: about her forehead, she had a broad bande of white Corrall, and so had her husband many times: in her eares she had bracelets of pearles, hanging downe to her middle, (whereof wee delivered your Worship a litle bracelet) and those were of the bignes of good pease. The rest of her women of the better sorte had pendants of copper, hanging in every eare, and some of the children of the Kings brother, and other Noble men, have five or sixe in every eare: he himselfe had upon his head a broad plate of golde, or copper, for being unpolished we knew not what metall it should be, neither would he by any meanes suffer us to take it off his head, but feeling it, it would bowe very easily: His apparell was as his wives, onely the women weare their haire long on both sides, and the men but on one: They are of colour yellowish, and their haire blacke for the most, and yet we sawe children that had very fine aburne, and chestnut colour haire.

After that these women had bene there, there came downe

from all parts great store of people, bringing with them leather, corrall, divers kindes of dies very excellent, and exchanged with us: but when Granganimeo, the kings brother was present, none durst to trade but himselfe, except such as weare redde peeces of copper on their heades, like himselfe: for that is the difference between the Noble men, and Governours of Countries, and the meaner sort. And we both noted there, and you have understood since by these men, which we brought home, that no people in the worlde carry more respect to their King, Nobililtie, and Governours, then these doe. The Kings brothers wife, when she came to us, as she did many times, shee was followed with fortie or fiftie women alwaies: and when she came into the shippe, she left them all on lande, saving her two daughters, her nurce, and one or two more. The Kings brother alwaies kept this order, as many boates as he would come withall to the shippes, so many fires would he make on the shoare a farre off, to the ende wee might understand with what strength, and companie he approched. Their boates are made of one tree, either of Pine, or of Pitch trees: a wood not commonly knowen to our people, nor found growing in England. They have no edge tooles to make them withall: if they have any, they are very fewe, and those it seemes they had twentie yeeres since, which as those two men declared, was out of a wracke which happened upon their coast of some Christian shippe, being beaten that way by some storme, and outragious weather, whereof none of the people were saved, but onely the shippe, or some part of her, being cast upon the sande, out of whose sides they drewe the nailes, and spikes, and with those they made their best instruments. Their manner of making their boates, is this: they burne downe some great tree, or take such as are winde fallen, and putting myrrhe, and rosen upon one side thereof, they sette fire into it, and when it hath burnt it hollowe, they cutte out the coale with their shels, and ever where they would burne it deeper or wider, they laye on their gummes, which burneth away the timber, and by this meanes they fashion very fine boates, and such as will transport twentie men. Their oares are like scoopes, and many times they sette with long pooles, as the depth serveth.

The Kings brother had great liking of our armour, a sworde, and divers other things, which we had: and offered to laye a great boxe of pearle in gage for them: but wee refused it for this time, because we would not make them knowe, that wee esteemed thereof, untill we had understoode in what places of the Countrey the pearle grewe: which nowe your Worshippe doth very well understand.

He was very just of his promise: for many times wee delivered him merchandize uppon his worde, but ever he came within the daye, and performed his promise. Hee sent us every daye a brase or two of fatte Buckes, Conies, Hares, Fishe, the best of the worlde. Hee sent us divers kindes of fruites, Melons, Walnuts, Cucumbers, Gourdes, Pease, and divers rootes, and fruites very excellent good, and of their Countrey corne, which is very white, faire, and well tasted, and groweth three times in five moneths: in Maye they sowe, in July they reape, in June they sowe, in August they reape: in July they sow, in September they reape: onely they cast the corne into the ground, breaking a little of the soft turfe with a woodden mattocke, or pickeaxe: our selves prooved the soile, and put some of our Pease into the ground, and in tenne daies they were of fourteene ynches high: they have also Beanes very faire, of divers colours, and wonderfull plentie: some growing naturally, and some in their gardens, and so have they both wheat and oates.

The soile is the most plentifull, sweete, fruitfull, and wholesome of all the world: there are above foureteene severall sweete smelling timber trees, and the most part of the underwoods are Bayes, and such like: they have those Okes that we have, but farre greater and better. After they had bene divers times aboord our shippes, my selfe, with seven more, went twentie mile into the River, that runneth toward the Citie of Skicoake, which River they call Occam: and the evening following, we came to an Island, which they call Roanoak, distant from the harbour by which we entred, seven leagues: and at the North ende thereof, was a village of nine houses, built of Cedar, and fortified round about with sharpe trees, to keep out their enemies, and the entrance into it made it like a turne pike very artificially: when we came towards it, standing neere unto the waters side, the wife of Grangyno, the Kings brother, came running out to meete us very cheerefully, and friendly, her husband was not then in the village: some of her people she commanded to drawe our boate on the shoare, for the beating

of the billoe: others shee appointed to carry us on their backes
to the dry ground, and others to bring our oares into the house,
for feare of stealing. When we were come into the utter roome,
having five roomes in her house, she caused us to sitte downe
by a great fire, and after tooke off our clothes, and washed
them, and dried them againe: some of the women pulled off
our stockings, and washed them, some washed our feete in
warme water, and shee her selfe tooke great paines to see all
thinges ordered in the best manner shee coulde, making great
haste to dresse some meate for us to eate.

After we had thus dried our selves, shee brought us into the
inner roome, where shee set on the boord standing along
the house, some wheate like furmentie, sodden Venison, and
roasted, fishe sodden, boyled, and roasted, Melons rawe, and
sodden, rootes of divers kindes, and divers fruites: their drinke
is commonly water, but while the grape lasteth, they drinke
wine, and for want of caskes to keepe it all the yeere after, they
drinke water, but it is sodden with Ginger in it, and blacke
Sinamon, and sometimes Sassaphras, and divers other wholesome, and medicinable hearbes and trees. We were entertained
with all love, and kindnes, and with as much bountie, after
their manner, as they could possibly devise. Wee found the
people most gentle, loving, and faithfull, void of all guile, and
treason, and such as lived after the manner of the golden age.
The earth bringeth foorth all things in aboundance, as in the
first creation, without toile or labour. The people onely care to
defend them selves from the cold, in their short winter, and to
feede themselves with such meate as the soile affoordeth: their
meate is very well sodden, and they make broth very sweete,
and savorie: their vessels are earthen pots, very large, white, and
sweete: their dishes are woodden platters of sweete timber:
within the place where they feede, was their lodging, and within
that their Idoll, which they worship, of which they speake uncredible things. While we were at meate, there came in at the
gates, two or three men with their bowes, and arrowes, from
hunting, whome when we espied, we beganne to looke one to
wardes another, and offered to reach our weapons: but assoone as she espied our mistrust, she was very much mooved,
and caused some of her men to runne out, and take away their
bowes, and arrowes, and breake them, and withall beate the

poore fellowes out of the gate againe. When we departed in the evening, and would not tarry all night, she was very sorie, and gave us into our boate our supper halfe dressed, pots, and all, and brought us to our boates side, in which wee laye all night, remooving the same a pretie distance from the shoare: shee perceiving our jealousie, was much grieved, and sent divers men, and thirtie women, to sitte all night on the bankes by us, and sent us into our boates fine mattes to cover us from the rayne, using very many wordes to intreate us to rest in their houses: but because wee were fewe men, and if wee had miscarried, the voyage had beene in very great daunger, wee durst not adventure any thing, although there was no cause of doubt: for a more kinde and loving people, there can not be found in the world, as farre as we have hitherto had triall.

Beyonde this Islande, there is the maine lande, and over against this Islande falleth into this spatious water, the great river called Occam, by the Inhabitants on which standeth a Towne called Pemeoke, and six daies journey further upon the same is situate their greatest citie, called Schycoake, which this people affirme to be very great: but the Savages were never at it, onely they speak of it, by the report of their Fathers, and other men, whome they have heard affirme it, to be above one daies journey about.

Into this river falleth another great river, called Cipo, in which there is found great store of the Muscels, in which there are pearles: likewise there descendeth into this Occam, another river, called Nomopana, on the one side whereof standeth a great Towne, called Chowanoake, and the Lord of that Towne and Countrey, is called Pooneno: this Pooneno is not subject to the King of Wingandacoa, but is a free Lorde. Beyonde this Countrey, is there another King, whome they call Menatoan, and these three Kinges are in league with eache other. Towards the Sunne set, foure daies journey, is situate a Towne called Sequotan, which is the Westermost Town of Wingandacoa, neere unto which, sixe and twentie yeeres past, there was a shippe cast away, whereof some of the people were saved, and those were white people, whom the Countrey people preserved.

And after ten daies, remaining in an out Island uninhabited, called Wococan, they with the helpe of some of the dwellers of Sequotan, fastened two boates of the Countrey together, and made mastes unto them, and sailes of their shirtes, and having taken into them such victuals as the Countrey yeelded, they departed after they had remained in this out Island three weekes: but shortly after, it seemed they were cast away, for the boates were found uppon the coast, cast aland in another Island adjoyning: other then these, there was never any people apparelled, or white of colour, either seene, or heard of amongst these people, and these aforesaide were seene onely of the Inhabitants of Sequotan: which appeared to be very true, for they wondred mervelously when we were amongest them, at the whitenes of our skinnes, ever coveting to touch our breastes, and to view the same: besides they had our shippes in marvelous admiration, and all things els was so strange unto them, as it appeared that none of them had ever seene the like. When we discharged any peece, were it but a harquebush, they would tremble thereat for very feare, and for the strangenes of the same: for the weapons which themselves use, are bowes and arrowes: the arrowes are but of small canes, headed with a sharpe shell, or tooth of a fishe sufficient enough to kill a naked man. Their swordes are of wood hardened: likewise they use woodden breastplates for their defense. They have besides a kinde of clubbe, in the ende whereof they fasten the sharpe hornes of a stagge, or other beast. When they goe to warres, they carry with them their Idoll, of whome they aske counsell, as the Romanes were woont of the Oracle of Apollo. They sing songs as they march to wardes the battell, in steede of drummes, and trumpets: their warres are very cruell, and bloodie, by reason whereof, and of their civill dissentions, which have happened of late yeeres amongest them, the people are marvelously wasted, and in some places, the Countrey left desolate.

Adjoyning unto this Towne aforesaide called Sequotan, beginneth a Countrey called Ponouike, belonging to another King, whom they call Piemacum, and this King is in league with the next King, adjoyning towardes the setting of the Sunne, and the Countrey Neiosioke, situate uppon the side of a goodly River, called Neus: these Kings have mortall warre with Wingina, King of Wingandacoa, but about two yeeres past, there was a peace made betweene the King Piemacum, and the Lorde of Sequotan, as these men which we have brought with us into England, have made us understande: but there remaineth a mortall malice in the Sequotanes, for many injuries and slaughters done uppon them by this Peimacum. They invited divers men, and thirtie women, of the best of his Countrey, to their Towne to a feast: and when they were altogether merrie, and praying before their Idoll, which is nothing else, but a meere illusion of the Devill: the Captaine or Lorde of the Towne came suddenly upon them, and slewe them every one, reserving the women, and children: and these two have oftentimes since perswaded us to surprise Piemacum his Towne, having promised, and assured us, that there will be founde in it great store of commodities. But whether their perswasion be to the ende they may be revenged of their enemies, or for the love they beare to us, we leave that to the triall hereafter.

Beyond this Island, called Croonoake, are many Islands, very plentifull of fruites and other naturall increases, together with many Townes, and villages, along the side of the continent, some bounding upon the Islands, and some stretching up further into the land.

When we first had sight of this Countrey, some thought the first lande we sawe, to be the continent: but after wee entred into the Haven, wee sawe before us another mightie long Sea: for there lieth along the coast a tracte of Islands, two hundreth miles in length, adjoyning to the Ocean sea, and betweene the Islands, two or three entrances: when you are entred betweene them (these Islands being very narrowe, for the most part, as in most places sixe miles broad, in some places lesse, in fewe more,) then there appeareth another great Sea, containing in bredth in some places, fortie, and in some fiftie, in some twentie miles over, before you come unto the continent: and in this inclosed Sea, there are about a hundreth Islands of divers bignesses, whereof one is sixteene miles long, at which we were, finding it to be a most pleasant, and fertile ground, replenished with goodly Cedars, and divers other sweete woods, full of Currans, of flaxe, and many other notable commodities, which we at that time had no leasure to view. Besides this Island, there are many, as I have saide, some of two, of three, of foure, of five miles, some more, some lesse, most beautifull, and pleasant to behold, replenished with Deere, Conies, Hares, and divers beastes, and about them the goodliest and best fishe in the world, and in greatest aboundance.

Thus Sir, we have acquainted you with the particulars of our discoverie, made this present voyage, as farre foorth, as the shortnes of the time we there continued, would affoord us to take viewe of: and so contenting our selves with this service at this time, which we hope hereafter to inlarge, as occasion and assistance shall be given, we resolved to leave the Countrey, and to apply our selves to returne for England, which we did accordingly, and arrived safely in the West of England, about the middest of September.

And whereas we have above certified you of the Countrey, taken in possession by us, to her Majesties use, and so to yours, by her Majesties grant, wee thought good for the better assurance thereof to recorde some of the particular Gentlemen, and men of accompt, who then were present, as witnesses of the same, that thereby all occasion of cavill to the title of the Countrey, in her Majesties behalfe, may be prevented, which other wise, such as like not the action may use, and pretend, whose names are:

Master Philip Amadas,
Master Arthur Barlowe, } Captaines.

William Greeneville,
John Wood,
James Browewich,
Henrie Greene,
Benjamin Wood,
Simon Ferdinando,
Nicholas Petman,
John Hewes, } Of the companie.

The Journal of the Tiger

THE voyage made by Sir Richard Greenvile, for Sir Walter Ralegh, to Virginia, in the yeere, 1585.

The 19. day of Maye, in the yeere above saide, wee departed from Plymmouth, our fleete consisting of the number of seven sailes, to wit, the Tyger, of the burden of seven score tunnes: a Flie boate called the Roe Bucke, of the like burden: the Lyon of a hundred tunnes, or thereabouts: the Elizabeth, of fiftie tunnes, and the Dorothie, a small barke, whereunto were also adjoyned for speedie services, 2. small Pinnesses. The principall Gentlemen of our companie, were, Master Ralfe Lane, Master Thomas Candishe, Master John Arundell, Master Raimund, Master Stukely, Master Bremige, Master Vincent, and Master John Clarke, and divers others, whereof some were Captaines, and other some Assistants for counsell, and good directions in the voyage.

The 14. day of Aprill, we fell with Lançacota, and Forte Ventura, Isles of the Canaries, and from thence we continued our course for Dominica, one of the Antiles of the West India, wherewith we fell the 7. day of Maye, and the 10. day following, we came to an anker at Cotesa, a little Island situate neere to the Island of S. John, where wee landed, and refreshed our selves all that day.

The 15. day of Maye, we came to an anker, in the Baye of Muskito, in the Island of S. John, within a Fawlcon shot of the shoare: where our Generall Sir Richard Greenvill, and the most part of our companie landed, and began to fortifie, very neere to the sea side: the river ranne by the one side of our forte, and the other two sides were environed with woods.

The 13. day we began to builde a new pinnesse within the Fort, with the timber that we then felled in the countrey, some part whereof we fet three myle up in the land, and brought it to our Fort upon trucks, the Spaniards not daring to make or offer resistance.

The 16. day, there appeared unto us out of the woods 8. horsemen of the Spaniards, about a quarter of a myle from our Fort, staying about halfe an hower in viewing our forces: but as soone as they saw x. of our shot marching towards them, they presently retyred into the woodes.

The 19. day, Master Candish, who had bene seperated from our fleete in a storme in the Bay of Portingal arrived at Cotesa, within the sight of the Tiger: we thinking him a farre off to have ben either a Spaniard or French man of warre thought it good to waigh ankers, and to goe roome with him, which the Tyger did, and discerned him at last to be one of our Consorts, for joy of whose comming our ships discharged their ordinance, and saluted him, according to the manner of the Seas.

The 22. day, 20. other Spanishe horsemen shewed them selves to us upon the other side of the river: who being seene, our General dispatched 20. footemen towards them, and two horsemen of ours, mounted upon Spanish horses, which wee before had taken in the time of our being on the Iland: they shewed to our men a flagge of truce, and made signes to have a parle with us: whereupon two of our men went halfe of the way upon the sands, and two of theirs came and met them: the two Spaniards offred very great salutations to our men, but began according to their Spanish proud humors, to expostulate with them, about their arrival, and fortifying in their countrie, who notwithstanding by our mens discrete answers were so cooled, that wheras they were told, that our principal intention was onely to furnish our selves with water, and victuals, and other necessaries wherof we stood in neede, which we craved might be yelded us with faire, and friendly means, otherwise our resolution was to practise force, and to releeve our selves by the sworde: the Spaniards in conclusion, seeing our men so resolute, yelded to our requestes with large promises of all curtesie, and great favor, and so our men and theirs departed.

The 23. day our pinnesse was finished, and lanched, which being done, our Generall with his Captaines, and Gentlemen, marched up into the Country about the space of 4. myles, where in a plaine marsh, they stayed expecting the comming of the Spanyards according to their promise, to furnish us with victuals: who keeping their old custome for perjurie and breache of promise came not, whereupon our General fired the woods thereabout, and so retired to our Fort, which the same day was fired also, and each man came aboord to be ready to set saile the next morning.

The 29. day we set saile from Saint Johns, being many of us stoong before upon shoare with the Muskitoes: but the same night wee tooke a Spanish Frigat, which was forsaken by the Spanyards upon the sight of us, and the next day in the morning very early, wee tooke another Frigat, with good and rich fraight, and divers Spaniards of accompt in her, which afterwards we ransomed for good round summes, and landed them in Saint Johns.

The 26. day our Lieutenant Master Ralfe Lane, went in one of the Frigats which we had taken, to Roxo bay upon the Southwest side of Saint Johns, to fetch salt, being thither conducted by a Spanish Pilot: as soone as he arrived there, he landed with his men, to the number of 20. and intrenched him selfe upon the sandes immediatly, compassing one of their salt hils within the trench: who being seene of the Spanyards, there came downe towards him two or three troopes of horsemen, and footemen, who gave him the looking, and gazing on, but durst not come neere him to offer any resistance, so that Master Lane mauger their troopes, caried their salt aboord and laded his Frigat, and so returned againe to our fleete the 29. day, which road at Saint Germans Bay. The same day we all departed, and the next day arrived in the Iland of Hispaniola.

June.

The 1. day of June we ankered at Isabella, in the North side of Hispaniola.

The 3. day of June, the Governor of Isabella, and Captaine of the Port de Plata, beeing certifyed by the reports of sundry Spanyards, who had bene wel intertained aboord our shippes by our General, that in our fleete were many brave, and gallant Gentlemen, who greatly desired to see the Governor aforesaid, he thereupon sent gentle commendations to our Generall, promising within a few daies to come to him in person, which he performed accordingly.

The 5. day the foresaid governor, accompanied with a lusty Frier, & 20. other Spaniards, with their servants, & Negroes, came downe to the sea side, where our ships road at anker, who being seene, our General manned immediatly the most part of his boats with the chiefe men of our fleete, every man appointed, and furnished in the best sort: at the landing of our Generall, the Spanishe Governor received him very curteously, and the Spanish Gentlemen saluted our English Gentlemen, and their inferiour sort did also salute our Souldiers and Sea men, liking our men, and likewise their qualities, although at the first, they seemed to stand in feare of us, and of so many of our boats, whereof they desired that all might not land their men, yet in the end, the curtesies that passed on both sides were so great, that all feare and mistrust on the Spanyardes part was abandoned.

In the meane time while our English Generall and the Spanish Governor discoursed betwixt them of divers matters, as of the state of the Country, the multitude of the Townes and people, and the commodities of the Iland, our men provided two banquetting houses covered with greene boughs, the one for the gentlemen, the other for the servants, and a sumptuous banquet was brought in served by us all in Plate, with the sound of trumpets, and consort of musick, wherewith the Spanyards were more than delighted. Which banquet being ended, the Spanyardes in recompense of our curtesie, caused a great heard of white buls, and kyne, to be brought together from the Mounteines, and appointed for every Gentlemen and Captaine that woulde ride, a horse ready sadled, and then singled out three of the best of them to be hunted by horsemen after their manner, so that the pastime grew very plesant for the space of three houres, wherein all three of the beasts were killed, whereof one tooke the sea, and there was slaine with a musket. After this sport, many rare presents and gifts were given and bestowed on both partes, and the next day wee plaied the Marchants in bargaining with them by way of trucke and exchange for divers of their commodities, as horses, mares, kyne, buls, goates, swine, sheepe, bul hydes, sugar, ginger, pearle, tabacco, and such like commodities of the Iland.

The 7. day we departed with great good will from the Spanyardes from the Island of Hispaniola: but the wiser sort do impute this greate shew of friendship, and curtesie used towardes us by the Spanyards rather to the force that we were of, and the vigilancie, and watchfulnes that was amongst us, then to any harty good will, or sure freindly intertainment: for doubtlesse if they had bene stronger than wee, we might have looked for no better curtesie at their handes, then Master John Hawkins received at saint John de Ullua, or John Oxnam neere the streights of Dariene, and divers others of our Countrymen in other places.

The 8. day we ankred at a small Iland to take Seales which in that place wee understood to have bene in great quantitie, where the Generall and certaine others with him in the pinnesse, were in very great danger to have bene all cast away, but by the helpe of God they escaped the hazard, and returned aboord the Admirall in safetie.

The 9. day we arrived and landed in the Isle of Caycos, in which Islande we searched for salt pondes, upon the advertisement, and information of a Portingall: who in deede abused our General and us, deserving a halter for his hire, if it had so pleased us.

The 12. we ankered at Guanema, and landed.

The 15. and 16. we ankered and landed at Sygateo.

The 20. we fell with the mayne of Florida.

The 23. wee were in great danger of a Wracke on a breache called the Cape of Feare.

The 24. we came to anker in a harbor where we caught in one tyde so much fishe as woulde have yelded us xx. pounds in London: this was our first landing in Florida.

The 26. we came to anker at Wocokon.

The 29. wee waighed anker to bring the Tyger into the harbour, where through the unskilfulnesse of the Master whose name was Fernando, the Admirall strooke on grounde, and sunke.

July.

The 3. we sent word of our arriving at Wococon, to Wingino at Roanocke.

The 6. Master John Arundell was sent to the mayne, and Manteio with him: and Captayne Aubry, and Captaine Boniten the same day were sent to Croatoan, where they found two of our men left there, with 30. other by Captaine Reymond, some 20. daies before.

The 8. Captaine Aubry, and Captaine Boniten returned with two of our men found by them to us at Wocokon.

The 11. day the Generall accompanied in his Tilt boate with Master John Arundell, Master Stukelye, and divers other Gentelmen, Master Lane, Master Candish, Master Harriot, and 20. others in the new pinnesse, Captaine Amadas, Captaine Clarke, with tenne others in a ship boate, Francis Brooke, and John White in another ship boate, passed over the water from Ococon to the mayne land victualled for eight dayes, in which voyage we first discovered the townes of Pomioke, Aquascogoc and Secota, and also the great lake called by the Savages Paquype, with divers other places, and so returned with that discovery to our Fleete.

The 12. we came to the Towne of Pomeioke.

The 13. we passed by water to Aquascococke.

The 15. we came to Secotan and were well intertayned there of the Savages.

The 16. we returned thence, and one of our boates with the Admirall was sent to Aquascococke to demaund a silver cup which one of the Savages had stolen from us, and not receiving it according to his promise, we burnt, and spoyled their corne, and Towne, all the people beeing fledde.

The 18. we returned from the discovery of Secotan, and the same day came aboord our fleete ryding at Wocokon.

The 21. our fleete ankering at Wokocon, we wayed anker for Hatoraske.

The 27. our fleete ankered at Hatoraske, and there we rested.

The 29. Grangino, brother to King Wingino, came aboord the Admirall, and Manteo with him.

August.

The 2. The Admirall was sent to Weapemeoke.

The 5. Master John Arundell was sent for England.

The 25. our Generall wayed anker, and set saile for England.

About the 31. he tooke a Spanish ship of 300. tunne richly loaden, boording her with a boate made with boards of chests, which fell a sunder, and sunke at the shippes side, assoone as ever hee and his men were out of it.

September.

The 10. of September, by foule weather the Generall then shipped in the prise lost sight of the Tyger.

October.

The sixt the Tyger fell with the landes ende, and the same day came to an anker at Falmouth.

The 18. the Generall came with the prise to Plymmouth, and was courteously received by diverse of his worshipfull friends.

RALPH LANE

Discourse on the First Colony

An account of the particularities of the imployments of the English men left in Virginia by Sir Richard Greenevill under the charge of Master Ralfe Lane Generall of the same, from the 17. of August, 1585. untill the 18. of June 1586. at which time they departed the Countrie: sent and directed to Sir Walter Ralegh.

That I may proceed with order in this discourse, I thinke it requisite to devide it into two partes. The first shall declare the particularities of such partes of the Country within the mayne, as our weake number, and supply of things necessary did inable us to enter into the discovery thereof.

The second part, shall set downe the reasons generally moving us to resolve on our departure at the instant with the General Sir Frauncis Drake, and our common request for passage with him, when the barkes, pinnesses, and boates with the Masters and Mariners ment by him to bee left in the Countrie for the supply of such, as for a further time ment to have stayed there, were caried away with tempest, and foule weather: In the beginning whereof shalbe declared the conspiracie of Pemisapan, with the Savages of the mayne to have cutt us off, &c.

2 parts of this discourse.

*The first part declaring the particularities
of the Countrey of Virginia.*

First therefore touching the particularities of the Countrey, you shal understand our discovery of the same hath bene extended from the Iland of Roanoak, (the same having bene the place of our settlement or inhabitation) into the South, into the North, into the Northwest, and into the West.

The uttermost place to the Southward of any discoverie was Secotan, being by estimation foure score miles distant from

Roanoak. The passage from thence was thorowe a broad sound within the mayne, the same being without kenning of land, and yet full of flats and shoales: we had but one boate with foure oares to passe through the same, which boat could not carry above fifteene men with their furniture, baggage, and victuall for seven dayes at the most: and as for our Pinnesse, besides that she drewe too deepe water for that shalow sound, she would not stirre for an oare: for these and other reasons (winter also being at hand) we thought good wholly to leave the discovery of those partes untill our stronger supplie.

To the Northwarde our furthest discoverie was to the Chesepians, distant from Roanoak about 130. miles, the passage to it was very shalow and most dangerous, by reason of the breadth of the sound, and the little succour that upon any flawe was there to be had.

The ex-cellency of the seate of Chesepiok. But the Territorie and soyle of the Chesepians (being distant fifteene miles from the shoare) was for pleasantnes of seate, for temperature of Climate, for fertilitie of soyle, and for the commoditie of the Sea, besides multitude of beares (being an excellent good victual, with great woods of Sassafras, and Wall nut trees) is not to be excelled by any other whatsoever.

There be sundry Kings, whom they call Weroances, and Countries of great fertilitie adjoyning to the same, as the Man-doages, Tripanicks, and Opossians, which all came to visit the Colonie of the English, which I had for a time appointed to be resident there.

To the Northwest the farthest place of our discoverie was to Choanoke distant from Roanoak about 130. miles. Our passage thither lyeth through a broad sound, but all fresh water, and the chanell of a great depth, navigable for good shipping, but out of the chanell full of shoales.

The Townes about the waters side situated by the way, are these following: Pysshokonnok, The womans Towne, Chipa-num, Weopomiok, Muscamunge, and Mattaquen: all these being under the jurisdiction of the king of Weopomiok, called Okisco: from Muscamunge we enter into the River, and juris-diction of Choanoke: There the River beginneth to straighten untill it come to Choanoke, and then groweth to be as nar-rowe as the Thames betweene Westminster, and Lambeth.

Betweene Muscamunge and Choanoke upon the left hand
as we passe thither, is a goodly high land, and there is a Towne
which we called the blinde Towne, but the Savages called it
Ooanoke, and hath a very goodly corne field belonging unto
it: it is subject to Choanoke.

The Towne
of Choanoke
able to make
700. men of
warre.

Choanoke it selfe is the greatest Province and
Seigniorie lying upon that River, and the very Towne
it selfe is able to put 700. fighting men into the
fielde, besides the forces of the Province it selfe.

The King of the sayd Province is called Menatonon, a man
impotent in his lims, but otherwise for a Savage, a very grave
and wise man, and of very singular good discourse in matters
concerning the state, not onely of his owne Countrey, and the
disposition of his owne men, but also of his neighbours round
about him as wel farre as neere, and of the commodities that
eche Countrey yeeldeth. When I had him prisoner with me,
for two dayes that we were together, he gave mee more understanding and light of the Countrey then I had received by all
the searches and salvages that before I or any of my companie
had had conference with: it was in March last past 1586.
Amongst other things he tolde me, that going three dayes
journey in a canoa up his River of Choanoke, and then de-
scending to the land, you are within foure dayes journey to
passe over land Northeast to a certaine Kings countrey, whose

An Iland
in a Bay.

Province lyeth upon the Sea, but his place of greatest
strength is an Iland situate as he described unto me
in a Bay, the water round about the Iland very deepe.

Pearles in
exceeding
quantitie.

Out of this Bay hee signified unto mee, that this
King had so great quantitie of Pearle, and doeth so
ordinarily take the same, as that not onely his owne
skins that he weareth, and the better sort of his gentlemen and
followers, are full set with the sayd Pearle, but also his beds,
and houses are garnished with them, and that hee hath such
quantitie of them, that it is a wonder to see.

He shewed me that the sayd King was with him at Choanoak two yeeres before, and brought him certaine Pearle, but
the same of the worst sort, yet was he faine to buy them of him
for copper at a deere rate, as he thought: He gave me a rope of
the same Pearle, but they were blacke, and naught, yet many
of them were very great, and a fewe amongst a number very

orient and round, all which I lost with other things of mine, comming aborde Sir Francis Drake his Fleete: yet he tolde me that the sayd King had great store of Pearle that were white, great, and round, and that his blacke Pearle his men did take out of shalowe water, but the white Pearle his men fished for in very deepe water.

It seemed to mee by his speech, that the sayde king had traffike with white men that had clothes as we have, for these white Pearle, and that was the reason that he would not depart with other then with blacke Pearles, to those of the same Countrey.

The king of Choanoak promised to give me guides to goe over land into that kings Countrey whensoever I would: but he advised me to take good store of men with mee, and good store of victuall, for he sayd, that king would be loth to suffer any strangers to enter into his Countrey, and especially to meddle with the fishing for any Pearle there, and that hee was able to make a great many of men into the fielde, which he sayd would fight very well.

Hereupon I resolved with my selfe, that if your supplie had come before the end of April, and that you had sent any store of boats or men, to have had them made in any reasonable time, with a sufficient number of men, and victuals to have found us untill the new corne were come in, I woulde have sent a small Barke with two Pinnesses about by Sea to the Northwarde to have found out the Bay he spake of, and to have sounded the barre if there were any, which shoulde have ridden there in the sayd Bay about that Iland, while I with all the small boats I could make, and with two hundreth men would have gone up to the head of the River of Choanoak, with the guides that Menatonon would have given, which I would have bene assured should have bene of his best men, (for I had his best beloved sonne prisoner with me) who also should have kept me companie in an handlocke with the rest foote by foote all the voyage over land.

My meaning was further at the head of the River in the place of my descent where I would have left my boates to have raysed a sconse with a small trench, and a pallisado upon the top of it, in the which, and in the garde of my boates I would have left five and twentie, or thirtie men, with the rest would I have marched with as much victuall as every man could have carried, with their furniture, mattocks, spades and axes, two dayes journey. In the ende of my marche upon some convenient plot would I have raised another sconse according to the former, where I would have left 15. or 20. And if it would have fallen out conveniently, in the way I woulde have raised my sayd sconse upon some corne fielde, that my companie might have lived upon it.

Whether Master Ralph Lane meant to remoove. And so I would have holden this course of insconsing every two dayes march, untill I had bene arrived at the Bay or Porte he spake of: which finding to be worth the possession, I would there have raised a mayne forte, both for the defence of the harboroughs, and our shipping also, and would have reduced our whole habitation from Roanoak and from the harborough and port there (which by proofe is very naught) unto this other before mentioned, from whence, in the foure dayes march before specified, could I at all times returne with my companie backe unto my boats ryding under my sconse, very neere whereunto directly from the West runneth a most notable River, and in all those partes most famous, called the River of Morotico. This River openeth into the broad sound of Weopomiok: And whereas the River of Choanoak, and all the other sounds, and Bayes, salt and fresh, shewe no currrant in the world in calme weather, but are mooved altogether in the winde: This River of Morotico hath so violent a currant from the West and Southwest, that it made me almost of opinion that with oares it would scarse be navigable: it passeth with many creeks and turnings, and for space of thirtie miles rowing, and more, it is as broad as the Thames betwixt Greenwich, and the Ile of dogges, in some place more, and in some lesse: the currant runneth as strong being entred so high into the River, as London bridge upon a vale water.

And for that not onely Menatonon, but also the Savages of Morotico themselves doe report strange things of the head of that River, and that from Morotico it selfe, which is a principall Towne upon that River, it is thirtie dayes as some of them say, and some say fourtie dayes voyage to the head thereof, which head they say springeth out of a maine rocke in that abundance, that forthwith it maketh a most violent streame: and further, that this huge rocke standeth nere unto a Sea, that many times in stormes (the winde comming outwardly from the Sea) the waves thereof are beaten into the said fresh streame, so that the fresh water for a certaine space, groweth salt and brackish:

I tooke a resolution with my selfe, having dismissed Menatonon upon a ransome agreed for, and sent his sonne into the Pinnesse to Roanoak, to enter presently so farre into that River with two double whirries, and fourtie persons one or other, as I could have victuall to carrie us, untill we could meete with more either of the Moratiks, or of the Mangoaks, which is another kinde of Savages, dwelling more to the Westwarde of the sayd River: but the hope of recovering more victuall from the Savages made me and my company as narowly to escape starving in that discoverie before our returne, as ever men did that missed the same.

For Pemisapan, who had changed his name of Wingina upon the death of his brother Granganimo, had given both the Choanists & Mangoaks word of my purpose touching them, I having bin inforced to make him privie to the same, to be served by him of a guide to the Mangoaks, and yet he did never rest to solicite continually my going upon them, certifying me of a generall assembly even at that time made by Menatonon at Choanoak of all his Weroances, & allyes to the number of 3000. bowes preparing to come upon us at Roanoak, and that the Mangoaks also were joyned in the same confederacie, who were able of themselves to bring as many more to the enterprise: And true it was, that at that time the assembly was holden at Choanoak about us, as I found at my comming thither, which being unlooked for did so dismay them, as it made us have the better hand at them. But this confederacie against us of the Choanists and Mangoaks was altogether and wholly procured by Pemisapan himselfe, as Menatonon confessed unto me, who sent them continuall worde that our purpose was fully bent to destroy them: on the other side he tolde me that they had the like meaning towards us.

Wingina changeth his name

Hee in like sort having sent worde to the Mangoaks of mine intention to passe up into their River, and to kill them (as he sayd) both they and the Moratiks, with whome before we were entred into a league, and they had ever dealt kindely with us, abandoned their Townes along the River, and retyred themselves with their *Crenepoes, and

Their women

their corne within the mayne: insomuch as having passed three dayes voyage up the River, we could not meete a man, nor finde a graine of corne in any their Townes: whereupon considering with my selfe, that wee had but two dayes victuall left, and that wee were then 160. miles from home, besides casualtie of contrarie windes or stormes, and suspecting treason of our owne Savages in the discoverie of our voyage intended, though we had no intention to be hurtfull to any of them, otherwise then for our copper to have had corne of them: I at night upon the corps of garde, before the putting foorth of centinels, advertised the whole companie of the case wee stoode in for victuall, and of mine opinion that we were betrayed by our owne Savages, and of purpose drawen foorth by them, upon vaine hope to be in the ende starved, seeing all the Countrey fledde before us, and therefore while we had those two dayes victuall left, I thought it good for us to make our return homewarde, and that it were necessarie for us to get the other side of the sound of Weopomiok in time, where we might be relieved upon the weares of Chypanum, and the womans Towne, although the people were fled.

Thus much I signified unto them, as the safest way: neverthelesse, I did referre it to the greatest number of voyces, whether we should adventure the spending of our whole victuall in some further viewe of that most goodly River in hope to meete with some better hap, or otherwise to retyre our selves backe againe.: And for that they might be the better advised, I willed them to deliberate all night upon the matter, and in the morning at our going aborde to set our course according to the desires of the greatest part. Their resolution fully and wholly was (and not three found to be of the contrary opinion) that whiles there was left one halfe pinte of corne for a man, that we should not leave the search of that River, and that there were in the companie two mastives, upon the pottage of which sassafras leaves (if the worst fell out) the companie would make shift to live two dayes, which time would bring them downe the currant to the mouth of the River, and to the entrie of the sound, and in two dayes more at the farthest they hoped to crosse the sounde and to bee relieved by the weares, which two dayes they would fast rather then be drawen backe a foote till they had seene the Mangoaks, either as friends or foes. This resolution of theirs did not a little please mee, since it came of themselves, although for mistrust of that which afterwards did happen, I pretended to have bene rather of the contrary opinion.

And that which made me most desirous to have some doings with the Mangoaks either in friendship or otherwise to have had one or two of them prisoners, was, for that it is a thing most notorious to all the countrey, that there is a Province to the which the sayd Mangoaks have recourse and traffike up that River of Moratico, which hath a marveilous and most strange Minerall. This Mine is so notorious amongst them, as not onely to the Savages dwelling up the sayde river, and also to the Savages of Choanoke, and all them to the westward, but also to all them of the mayne: the countries name is of fame, and is called Chaunis Temoatan.

A marvellous Mineral in the countrey of Chaunis Temoatan.

The mineral they say is Wassador, which is copper, but they call by the name of Wassador every mettall whatsoever: they say it is of the couler of our copper, but our copper is better then theirs: and the reason is for that it is redder and harder, whereas that of Chaunis Temoatan is very soft, and pale: they say that they take the sayd mettall out of a river that falleth very swift from hie rocks, and hyls, and they take it in shallowe water: the manner is this. They take a great bowle by their discription as great as one of our targets, and wrap a skinne over the hollowe part thereof, leaving one part open to receive in the minerall: that done, they watch the comming downe of the currant, and the change of the couler of the water, and then suddenly chop downe the said bowle with the skin, and receive into the same as much oare as will come in, which is ever as much as their bowle wil hold, which presently they cast into a fire, and forthwith it melteth, and doeth yeelde in 5. partes, at the first melting, two parts of metall for three partes of oare. Of this metall the Mangoaks have so great store, by report of all the savages adjoyning, that they beautifie their houses with great plates of the same: and this to be true, I received by report of all the country, and particularly by yong Skiko, the King of Choanokes sonne my prisoner, who also himselfe had bene prisoner with the Mangoaks, and set downe all the particularities to mee before mentioned: but hee had not bene at Chawnis Temoatan himselfe: for he sayd, it was twentie dayes journey overlande from the Mangoaks, to the saide minerall country, and that they passed through certaine other territories betweene them and the Mangoaks, before they came to the said country.

Upon reporte of the premisses, which I was inquisitive in all places where I came to take very particular information of, by all the savages that dwelt towards those parts, and especially of Menatonon himselfe, who in every thing did very particularly informe mee, and promised mee guides of his owne men, who shoulde passe over with mee, even to the sayde country of Chaunis Temoatan, (for over lande from Choanok to the Mangoaks is but one dayes journey from sunne rysing to sunne setting, whereas by water it is 7. daies with the soonest:) These things I say, made me verie desirous by all meanes possible to recover the Mangoaks, to get some of that their copper for an assay, and therefore I willingly yeelded to their resolution: But it fell out very contrarie to all expectation, and likelyhood: for after two dayes travell, and our whole victual spent, lying on shoare all night, wee could never see man, onely fires wee might perceive made alongst the shoare where we were to passe, and up into the countrie untill the very last day. In the evening whereof, about three of the clocke we heard certaine savages call as we thought, Manteo, who was also at that time with mee in boate, whereof we all being verie glad, hoping of some friendly conference with them, and making him to answere them, they presently began a song, as we thought in token of our welcome to them: but Manteo presently betooke him to his peece, and tolde mee that they ment to fight with us: which

A conflict begun by the Savages.

word was not so soone spoken by him, and the light horseman ready to put to shoare, but there lighted a vollie of their arrowes amongst them in the boate, but did no hurt God be thanked to any man. Immediatly, the other boate lying ready with their shot to skoure the place for our hand weapons to land upon, which was presently done, although the lande was very high and steepe, the Savages forthwith quitted the shoare, and betooke themselves to flight: we landed, and having fayre and easily followed for a smal time after them, who had wooded themselves we know not where: the sunne drawing then towards the setting, and being then assured that the next day, if wee would pursue them, though wee might happen to meete with them, yet we should bee assured to meete with none of their victuall, which we then had good cause to thinke of, therefore choosing for the companie a convenient grounde in safetie to lodge in for the night, making a strong corps of garde, and putting out good centinels, I determined the next morning before the rising of the sunne to be going backe againe, if possibly wee might recover the mouth of the river into the broade sownde, which at my first motion I found my whole companie ready to assent unto: for they were nowe come to their dogs porredge, that they had bespoken for themselves, if that befell them which did, and I before did mistrust we should hardly escape. The ende was, we came the next

The great current of the River of Morottico.   day by night to the rivers mouth within 4. or 5. miles of the same, having rowed in one day downe the currant, as much as in 4. dayes we had done against the

same: we lodged upon an Islande, where wee had nothing in the worlde to eate but pottage of sassafras leaves, the like whereof for a meate was never used before as I thinke. The broad sownde wee had to passe, the next day all fresh and fasting: that day the winde blewe so strongly, and the billow so great, that there was no possibilitie of passage without sinking of our boates. This was upon Easter eve, which was fasted very trulie. Upon Easter day in the morning the wind comming very calme, wee entred the sownde, and by 4. of the clocke we were at Chipanum, wher all the Savages that wee had left there were fled, but their wears did yeelde us some fish, as God was pleased not utterly to suffer us to be lost: for some of our companie of the light horsemen were far spent. The next morning we arrived at our home Roanoke.

I have set downe this voyage somewhat particularly, to the ende it may appeare unto you (as true it is) that there wanted no great good will from the most to the least amongst us, to have perfited this discoverie of the mine: for that the discovery of a good mine, by the goodnesse of God, or a passage to the Southsea, or someway to it, and nothing els can bring this country in request to be inhabited by our nation. And with the discovery of any of the two above shewed, it willbe the most sweete, and healthfullest climate, and therewithall the most fertile soyle, being manured in the world: and then will Sassafras, and many other rootes & gummes there found make good

Marchandise and lading for shipping, which otherwise of themselves will not bee worth the fetching.

Provided also, that there be found out a better harborough then yet there is, which must bee to the Northward, if any there be, which was mine intention to have spent this summer in the search of, and of the mine of Chawnis Temoatan: the one I would have done, if the barks that I should have had of Sir Francis Drake, by his honorable curtesie, had not bene driven away by storme: the other if your supply of more men, and some other necessaries had come to us in any convenient sufficiencie. For this river of Moratico promiseth great things, and by the opinion of Master Harriots the heade of it by the description of the country, either riseth from the bay of Mexico, or els from very neere unto the same, that openeth out into the South sea.

And touching the Minerall, thus doth Master Yougham affirme, that though it be but copper, seeing the Savages are able to melt it, it is one of the richest Minerals in the worlde.

Wherefore a good harborough founde to the Northward, as before is sayd, and from thence foure dayes overland, to the river of Choanoak sconses being raysed, from whence againe overlande through the province of Choanoak one dayes voyage to the first towne of the Mangoaks up the river of Moratico by the way, as also upon the sayd river for the defence of our boats like sconses being set, in this course of proceeding you shall cleare your selfe from all those dangers and broad shallowe sownds before mentioned, and gayne within foure dayes travell into the heart of the mayne 200. myles at the least, and so passe your discoverie into that most notable, and to the likeliest partes of the mayne, with farre greater felicitie then otherwise can bee performed.

Thus sir, I have though simply, yet truely set downe unto you, what my labour with the rest of the gentlemen, and poore men of our company, (not without both payne, and perill which the lorde in his mercy many wayes delivered us from) could yeelde unto you, which might have bene performed in some more perfection, if the lorde had bene pleased that onely that which you had provided for us had at the first bene left with us, or that he had not in his eternall providence now at the last set some other course in these things, then the wisedome of man could looke into, which truely the carying away, by a most strange, & unlooked for storme all our provision, with barks, master, Marryners, and sundrie also of mine owne company, all having bene so curteously supplyed by the Generall Sir Francis Drake, the same having bene most sufficient to have performed the greatest part of the premisses, must ever make me to thinke, the hand of God only, (for some his good purpose to my selfe yet unknowne), to have bene in the matter.

The second part touching the conspiracy of Pemisapan, the discoverie of the same, and at the last, of our request to depart with Sir Francis Drake for England.

Ensenore a savage father to Pemisapan being the only frend to our nation that we had amongst them, and about the king, dyed the 20. of April, 1586. hee alone, had before opposed himselfe in their consultations against al matters proposed against us, which both the king, and all the rest of them after Grangemoes death, were very willing to have preferred. And he was not onely by the meere providence of God during his life, a meane to save us from hurt, as poysonings and such like, but also to doe us very great good, and singulerly in this.

The king was advised and of himselfe disposed, as a ready meane to have assuredly brought us to ruine in the moneth of March, 1586, himselfe also with all his Savages to have runne away from us, and to have left his ground in the Island unsowed, which if he had done, there had bene no possibilitie in common reason, (but by the immediate hande of God) that we could have bene preserved from starving out of hand. For at that time wee had no weares for fishe, neither could our men skill of the making of them, neither had wee one grayne of corne for seede to put into the ground.

In mine absence on my voyage that I had made against the Chaonists, and Mangoaks, they had raised a bruite among themselves, that I and my company were part slayne, and part starved by the Chaonists, and Mangoaks. One part of this tale was too true, that I and mine were likely to be starved, but the other false.

Neverthelesse untill my returne, it tooke such effect in Pemisapans breast, and in those against us, that they grew not onely into contempt of us, but also (contrary to their former

reverend opinion in shew, of the almightie God of heaven, and
Jesus Christ, whome wee serve and worship, whome before
they woulde acknowledge and confesse the onely God:) nowe
they began to blaspheme, and flatly to say, that our Lord God
was not God, since hee suffered us to sustaine much hunger,
and also to be killed of the Renapoaks, for so they call by that
generall name, all the inhabitants of the whole mayne, of what
province soever. Insomuch as olde Ensenore, neither any of his
fellowes, coulde for his sake have no more credite for us: and it
came so farre that the King was resolved to have presently
gone away as is aforesaid.

But even in the beginning of this bruite I returned, which
when hee sawe contrarie to his expectation, and the advertisement that he had received: that not only my selfe, and my
company were al safe, but also by report of his owne 3. savages,
which had bene with mee besides Manteo in that voyage, that
is to say, Tetepano, his sisters husband Eracano, and Cossine,
and that the Chaonists, and Mangoaks, (whose name, and multitude besides their valour is terrible to al the rest of the provinces) durst not for the most part of them abide us, and that
those that did abide us were killed, and that we had taken
Menatonon prisoner, and brought his sonne that he best loved
to Roanoak with me, it did not a little asswage all devises against
us: on the other side, it made Ensenors opinions to be received
againe with greater respects. For hee had often before tolde
them, and then renewed those his former speeches, both
to the king and the rest, that wee were the servants of God,
and that wee were not subject to be destroyed by them: but
contrariwise, that they were amongst them that sought our destruction, should finde their owne, and not be able to worke
ours, and that we being dead men were able to doe them more
hurt, then now we coulde do being alive: an opinion very confidently at this day holden by the wisest amongst them, and of
their olde men, as also, that they have bene in the night, beeing
100. myles from any of us in the ayre shot at, and stroken by
some men of ours, that by sicknesse had dyed among them:
and many of them holde opinion, that wee be dead men returned into the worlde againe, and that we doe not remayne
dead but for a certaine time, and that then we returne againe.

All these speeches then againe grew in ful credite with them, the King and all touching us, when hee saw the small troupe returned againe, and in that sort from those whose very names were terrible unto them: but that which made up the matter on our side for that time, was an accident, yea rather, (as all the rest was) the good providence of the Almightie for the saving of us, which was this.

Within certaine dayes after my returne from the said journey, Menatonon sent a messengere to visite his sonne the prisoner with me, and sent me certaine pearle for a present, or rather as Pemisapan told me, for the ransome of his sonne, and therefore I refused them: but the greatest cause of his sending then, was to signifie unto me, that hee had commaunded Okisko king of Weopomiok, to yelde himselfe servant, and homager, to the great Weroanza of England, and after her to Sir Walter Ralegh: to perfourme which commandement received from Menatonon, the sayd Okisko joyntly with this Menatonons messenger, sent foure and twentie of his principallest men to Roanoak to Pemisapan, to signifie that they were readie to perfourme the same, and so had sent those his men to let me knowe, that from that time forwarde hee, and his successours were to acknowledge her Majestie their onely Soveraigne, and next unto her, as is aforesayde.

All which being done, and acknowledged by them all, in the presence of Pemisapan his father, and all his Savages in counsel then with him, it did for the time, thorowly (as it seemed) change him in disposition toward us: Insomuch as forthwith Ensenore wan this resolution of him, that out of hand he should goe about, & withall, to cause his men to set up weares forthwith for us: both which he, at that present went in hand withal & did so labour the expedition of it, that in the end of April, he had sowed a good quantitie of ground, so much as had bene sufficient, to have fed our whole company (God blessing the grouth) and that by the belly for a whole yere: besides that he gave us a certaine plot of grounde for our selves to sowe. All which put us in marveilous comfort, if we could passe from The be-
ginning of
their harvest
in Julie. Aprill, untill the beginning of July, (which was to have bene the beginning of their harvest,) that then a newe supplie out of Englande or els our owne store would well inough maintayne us: All our feare was of the two moneths betwixt, in which meane space, if the Savages should not helpe us, with Cassada, and Chyna, and that our weares should fayle us, (as often they did) wee might very well starve, notwithstanding the growing corne, like the starving horse in the stable, with the growing grasse, as the proverbe is, which we very hardlye had escaped but onely by the hand of God, as it pleased him to try us. For within few dayes after, as before is sayde Ensenore our friende dyed, who was no sooner dead, but certaine of our great enemies about Pemisapan, as Osocan a Weroance, Tanaquiny and Wanchese most principally, were in hand again to put their old practises in ure against us, which were readily imbraced, & al their former devises against us renewed, & new brought in question.

But that of starving us, by their forbearing to sowe, was broken by Ensenore in his life, by having made the king all at one instant to sowe his grounde not onely in the Islande but also at Addesmocopeia in the mayne, within two leagues over against us. Neverthelesse there wanted no store of mischevous practises among them, and of all they resolved principally of this following.

The conspiracie of Pemisapan. First that Okisko, king of Weopomiok, with the Mandoages, should bee moved, and with great quantitie of copper intertayned to the number of seven, or 800. bowes to the enterprise the matter thus to be ordred. They of Weopomiok should be invited to a certaine kind of moneths minde which they do use to solemnise in their Savage maner for any great personage dead, and should have bene for Ensenore. At this instant also should the Mandoaks, who were a great people with the Chesepians, and their friends to the number of 700. of them be armed at a day appoynted to the mayne of Addesmocopeio, and there lying close at the signe of fyers, which should interchangeably be made on both sides, when Pemisapan with his troup above named should have executed me, and some of our Weroances (as they called all our principall officers,) the mayne forces of the rest should have come over into the Iland where they ment to have dispatched the rest of the company, whome they did imagine to finde both dismayed and dispersed abroade in the Islande seeking of crabs, and fish to live withall. The manner of their enterprise was this.

Tarraquine and Andacon two principall men about Pemisapan, and very lustie fellowes with twentie more appointed to them had the charge of my person to see an order taken for the same, which they ment should in this sort have bene executed. In the dead time of the night they would have beset my house, and put fire in the reedes, that the same was covered with: meaning (as it was likelye) that my selfe woulde have come running out of a sudden amazed in my shirt without armes, upon the instant whereof they woulde have knocked out my braynes.

The same order was given to certaine of his fellowes, for Master Herriots: so for all the rest of our better sort, all our houses at one instant being set on fire as afore is sayde, and that as well for them of the forte, as for us at the towne. Now to the end that we might be the fewer in number together, and so be the more easilie dealt withall (for in deede ten of us with our armes prepared, were a terrour to a hundred of the best sort of them,) they agreed and did immediatly put it in practise, that they should not for any copper, sell us any victuals whatsoever: besides that in the night they should send to have our weares robbed, and also to cause them to be broken and once being broken never to be repayred againe by them. By this meanes the King stood assured, that I must bee enforced for lacke of sustenance, there to disband my company into sundry places to live upon shell fishe, for so the Savages themselves doe, going to Ottorasko, Croatoan, and other places fishing and hunting, while their grownds be in sowing, and their corne growing, which fayled not his expectation. For the famine grewe so extreeme among us, our weares fayling us of fish, that I was enforced to send captaine Stafford with 20. with him to Croatoan my lord Admirals Island to serve two turnes in one, that is to say to feede himselfe, and his company, and also to keepe watch, if any shipping came upon the coast to warne us of the same. I sent master Pridiox with the Pynnesse to Otterasco, and ten with him, with the Provost Marshal to live there, and also to wayte for shipping: also I sent every weeke 16. or 20. of the rest of the companie to the mayne over against us, to live of Casada, and oysters.

The sufficiencye of our men to deale against the Savages, 10. to 100.

The savages live by fishing, and hunting, till harvest.

In the meane while Pemisapan went of purpose to Addesmocopeio for 3. causes, the one, to see his grounds there broken up, and sowed for a second croppe: the other to withdrawe himselfe from my dayly sending to him for supply of victuall for my company, for hee was afrayde to denye me any thing, neither durst he in my presence but by colour, and with excuses, which I was content to accept for the time, meaning in the ende as I had reason, to give him the jumpe once for all: but in the meane whiles, as I had ever done before, I and mine bare all wrongs, and accepted of all excuses.

My purpose was to have relyed my selfe with Menatonon, and the Chaonists, who in truth as they are more valiant people and in greater number then the rest, so are they more faithfull in their promises, and since my late being there, had given many tokens of earnest desire they had to joyne in perfect league with us, and therefore were greatly offended with Pemisapan and Weopomiok for making him beleeve such tales of us.

The third cause of his going to Addesmacopeio was to dispatch his messengers to Weopomiok, and to the Mandoages, as aforesaid, al which he did with great impresse of copper in hand, making large promises to them of greater spoyle.

The answere within fewe dayes after, came from Weopomiok, which was devided into two parts. First for the King Okisko, who denyed to be of the partie for himselfe, or any of his especial followers, and therefore did immediatly retyre himselfe with his force into the mayne: the other was concerning the rest of the sayd province who accepted of it: and in like sort the Mandoags received the imprest.

The day of their assembly aforesayd at Roanoak, was appointed the 10. of July: all which the premises were discovered by Skyco, the king Menatonon his sonne my prisoner, who having once attempted to run away, I laid him in the bylboes, threatning to cut off his head, whome I remitted at Pemisapans request: whereupon he being perswaded that he was our enemie to the death, he did not only feede him with himselfe, but also made him acquainted with all his practises. On the other side, the yong man finding himself as well used at my hand, as I had meanes to shew, and that all my companie made much of him, he flatly discovered all unto me, which also afterwards was revealed unto me by one of Pemisapans owne men, the night before he was slaine.

These mischiefes being al instantly upon mee, and my companie to be put in execution, stood mee in hand to study how to prevent them, and also to save all others, which were at that time as aforesaid so farre from me: whereupon I sent to Pemisapan to put suspition out of his heade, that I ment presently to goe to Croatoan, for that I had heard of the arival of our fleete, (thought I in trueth had neither heard nor hoped for so good adventure,) and that I meant to come by him, to borrow of his men to fish for my company, and to hunt for me at Croatoan, as also to buy some foure dayes provision to serve for my voyage.

He sent mee word that he would himselfe come over to Roanoak, but from day to day hee deferred, only to bring the Weopomioks with him, and the Mandoags, whose time appoynted was within 8. dayes after. It was the last day of May, 1586. when all his owne savages began to make their assembly at Roanoak, at his commandement sent abroad unto them, and I resolved not to stay longer upon his comming over, since he ment to come with so good company, but thought good to go, and visite him with such as I had, which I resolved to do the next day: but that night I ment by the way to give them in the Island a Canuisado, and at the instant to sease upon all the Canoas about the Island to keepe him from advertisements.

But the towne tooke the allarum, before I ment it to them: the occasion was this. I had sent the Master of the light horsemen with a few with him, to gather up all the Canoas in the setting of the sunne, & to take as many as were going from us to Adesmocopeio, but to suffer any that came from thence to land: he met with a Canoa, going from the shoare, and overthrew the Canoa, and cut off 2. savages heads: this was not done so secretly but hee was discovered from the shoare, wherupon the cry arose: for in trueth they, privie to their owne villanous purposes against us, held as good espial upon us, both day and night, as we did upon them.

The slaughter, and surprise of the Savages.

The allarum given, they tooke themselves to their bowes, and we to our armes: some three or foure of them at the first were slayne with our shot, the rest fled into the woods: The next morning with the light horseman, & one Canoa, taking 25. with the Colonel of the Chesepians, and the Serjeant major, I went to Adesmocopeio, and being landed sent Pemisapan word by one of his owne savages that met me at the shore, that I was going to Croatoan, and ment to take him in the way to complaine unto him of Osocon, who the night past was conveying away my prisoner, whom I had there present tied in an handlocke: hereupon the king did abide my comming to him, and finding my selfe amidst 7. or 8. of his principal Weroances, & followers, (not regarding any of the common sort) I gave the watchword agreed upon, (which was Christ our victory,) and immediatly those his chiefe men, and himselfe, had by the mercie of God for our deliverance, that which they had purposed for us. The king himselfe being shot thorow by the Colonell with a pistoll lying on the ground for dead, & I looking as watchfully for the saving of Manteos friends, as others were busie that none of the rest should escape, suddenly he started up, and ran away as though he had not bene touched, insomuch as he overran all the companie, being by the way shot thwart the buttocks by mine Irish boy with my Petronell. In the end an Irish man serving me, one Nugent and the deputie provost undertooke him, and following him in the woods overtooke him, and I in some doubt least we had lost both the king, and my man by our owne negligence to have bene intercepted by the Savages, we met him returning out of the woods with Pemisapans head in his hand.

Pemisapan slaine.

This fell out the first of June, 1586. and the 8. of the same came advertisement to me from captaine Stafford, lying at my lord Admirals Island, that he had discovered a great Fleete of 23. sailes: but whether they were friends or foes, he could not yet discerne, he advised me to stand upon as good gard as I could.

The 9. of the said moneth, he himselfe came unto me, having that night before, and that same day travelled by land 20. miles, and I must truly report of him from the first to the last, he was the gentleman that never spared labour or perill either by land or water, faire weather or fowle, to performe any service committed unto him.

A letter from sir Francis Drake.

He brought me a letter from the Generall sir Francis Drake, with a most bountifull and honourable offer for the supplie of our necessities to the performance of the action, we were entered into, and that not onely of victuals, munition and clothing, but also of barkes, pinnaces and boates, they also by him to be victualled, manned, and furnished to my contentation.

The 10. day he arrived in the road of our bad harborough, and comming there to an anker, the 11. day I came to him, whom I found in deeds most honourably to performe that which in writing and message he had most curteously offered, he having aforehand propounded the matter to all the captains of his Fleete, and got their liking and consent thereto.

With such thanks unto him and his captaines for his care both of us and of our action, not as the matter deserved, but as I could both for my companie and my selfe, I (being afore-hand) prepared what I would desire, craved at his
1   hands that it would please him to take with him into England a number of weake, and unfit men for my good action, which I would deliver to him, and in place of them to supply me of his company, with oare men, artificers, and others.

That he would leave us so much shipping and
2   victuall, as about August then next followyng, would cary me and all my companie into England, when we had discovered somwhat that for lacke of needfull provision in time left with us as yet remained undone.

That it would please him withall to leave some
3   sufficient masters not onely to cary us into England, when time should be, but also to search the coast for some better harborow if there were any, and especially to helpe us to some small boats and oare men.

4   Also for a supplie of calievers, handweapons, match and lead, tooles, apparell, and such like.

He having received these my requests according to his usu-all commendable maner of governement (as it was told me) calling his captaines to counsell, the resolution was that I should send such of my officers of my companie, as I used in such matters, with their notes to goe aboord with him, which were the master of the victuals, the keeper of the store, and the Vicetreasurer, to whom he appointed foorthwith for me the Francis, being a very proper barke of 70. tunnes, and tooke present order for bringing of victuall aboord her for 100. men for foure moneths withall my other demaunds whatsoever, to the uttermost.

And further appointed for me two fine pinnaces, and 4. small boats, and that which was to performe all his former liberalitie towards us, was that he had gotten the full assents of two of as sufficient experimented masters as were any in his fleete, by judgement of them that knewe them, with very sufficient gings to tarie with mee, and to employ themselves most earnestly in the action, as I should appoynt them, untill the terme which I promised of our returne into England agayne. The names of one of those masters was Abraham Kendall, the other Griffith Herne.

While these things were in hand, the provision aforesayd being brought, and in bringing a boord, my sayd masters being also gone aboord, my sayd barkes having accepted of their charge, and mine owne officers with others in like sort of my company with them, all which was dispatched by the said Generall the 12. of the said moneth: the 13. of the same there arose such an unwonted storme, and continued foure dayes that had like to have driven all on shore, if the Lord had not held his holy hand over them, and the generall very providently foreseene the worst himselfe, then about my dispatch putting himselfe aboord: but in the ende having driven sundry of the Fleete to put to sea the Francis also with all my provisions, my two masters, and my company aboord, shee was seene to be free from the same, and to put cleare to sea.

This storme having continued from the 13. to the 16. of the moneth, and thus my barke put away as aforesayd, the Generall comming a shore, made a new proffer to me, which was a shippe of 170. tunnes, called the Barke Bonner, with a sufficient master and guide to tarie with mee the time appointed, and victualled sufficiently to carie mee and my companie into England with all provisions as before: but hee tolde mee that he would not for any thing undertake to have her brought into our harbour, and therefore hee was to leave her in the roade, and to leave the care of the rest unto my selfe, and advised me to consider with my companie of our case, and to deliver presently unto him in writing, what I would require him to doe for us: which being within his power, hee did assure me as well for his Captaines, as for himselfe should be most willingly performed.

Hereupon calling such Captaines and Gentlemen of my companie as then were at hand, who were all as privie as my selfe to the Generals offer, their whole request was to mee, that considering the case that we stood in, the weaknesse of our companie, the small number of the same, the carying away of our first appointed barke, with those two especiall masters, with our principall provisions in the same, by the very hand of God as it seemed, stretched out to take us from thence: considering also, that his second offer, though most honourable of his part, yet of ours not to be taken, insomuch as there was no possibility for her with any safetie to be brought into the harbour: Seeing furthermore, our hope for supplie with sir Richard Greenvill, so undoubtedly promised us before Easter, not yet come, neither then likely to come this yeere considering the doings in England for Flaunders, and also for America, that therefore I would resolve my selfe, with my companie to goe into England in that Fleete, and accordingly to make request to the Generall in all our names, that he would bee pleased to give us present passage with him. Which request of ours by my selfe delivered unto him, hee most readily assented unto, and so hee sending immediately his pinnaces unto our Island for the fetching away of fewe that there were left with our baggage, the weather was so boysterous, and the pinnaces so often on ground, that the most of all wee had, with all our Cardes, Bookes and writings, were by the Saylers cast over boord, the greater number of the Fleete being much agrieved with their long and daungerous abode in that miserable road.

From whence the Generall in the name of the Almightie, waying his ankers (having bestowed us among his Fleete) for the reliefe of whom hee had in that storme sustained more perill of wracke then in all his former most honourable actions against the Spaniards, with praises unto God for all, set saile the 19. of June, 1586. and arrived in Portesmouth, the 27. of Julie the same yeere.

JOHN WHITE

Narrative of His Voyage

THE fourth voyage made to Virginia, with three shippes, in the yeere, 1587. Wherein was transported the second Colonie.

In the yeere of our Lorde, 1587. Sir Walter Ralegh intending to persevere in the planting of his Countrey of Virginia, prepared a newe Colonie of one hundred and fiftie men to be sent thither, under the charge of John White, whom he appointed Governour, and also appointed unto him twelve Assistants, unto whome he gave a Charter, and incorporated them by the name of Governour, and Assistants of the Citie of Ralegh in Virginia.

Aprill.

Our Fleete being in number three saile, viz. the Admirall, a shippe of one hundred and twentie tunnes: a Flie boate, and a Pinnesse, departed the sixe and twentieth of Aprill from Portesmouth, and the same day came to an anker at the Cowes, in the Isle of Wight, where wee staied eight daies.

Maye.

The 5. of Maye, at nine of the clocke at night, we came to Plymmouth, where we remained the space of two daies.

The 8. we waied anker at Plymmouth, and departed thence for Virginia.

The 16. Simon Ferdinando Master of our Admirall, lewdly forsooke our Flie boate, leaving her distressed in the Baye of Portingall.

June.

*One of the Isles of the Indias, inhabited with Savages.

The 19. we fell with *Dominica, and the same evening we sailed betweene it, and Guadalupe: the 21. the Flie boat also fell with Dominica.

The 22. we came to an anker at an Isle, called Santa Cruz, where all the planters were set on land, staying there till the 25. of the same moneth. At our first landing on this Island, some of our women, and men, by eating a small fruite, like greene apples, were fearefully troubled with a sudden burning in their mouthes, and swelling of their tongues so bigge, that some of them could not speake. Also a child by sucking one of those womens breastes, had at that instant his mouth set on such a burning, that it was strange to see how the infant was tormented for the time: but after 24. howres, it ware away of it selfe.

Also the first night of our being on this Island, we took five great Torteses, some of them of such bignes, that sixteene of our strongest men were tired with carrying of one of them but from the Sea side, to our cabbins. In this Island we found no watring place, but a standing ponde, the water whereof was so evill, that many of our companie fell sicke with drinking thereof: and as many as did but wash their faces with that water, in the morning before the Sunne had drawen away the corruption, their faces did so burne, and swell, that their eies were shut up, and could not see in five or sixe diaes or longer.

The second day of our abode there, we sent foorth some of our men to search the Island for fresh water, three one way, and two another way. The Governour also, with sixe others, went up to the toppe of an high hill, to view the Island, but could perceive no signe of any men, or beastes, nor any goodnes, but Parots, and trees of Guiacum. Returning backe to our Cabbins another way, he found in the discent of a hill, certaine potsheards of savage making, made of the earth of that Island: whereupon it was judged, that this Island was inhabited with Savages, though Fernando had tolde us for certaine, the contrarie. The same day at night, the rest of our companie very late returned to the Governour. The one companie affirmed, that they had seene in a valley, eleven Savages, and divers houses halfe a mile distant from the steepe, or toppe of the hill where they staied. The other companie had found running out of a high rock, a very faire spring of water, whereof they brought three bottles to the companie: for before that time, wee drank the stinking water of the pond.

The same second day at night, Captaine Stafford, with the

pinnesse, departed from our fleete, riding at Santa Cruz, to an
Island, called Beake, lying neere S. Johns, being so directed by
Ferdinando, who assured him he should there finde great plen-
tie of sheepe. The next day at night, our planters left Santa
Cruz, and came all aboord, and the next morning after, being
the 25. or June, we waied anker, and departed from Santa Cruz.

The seven and twentieth we came to anker at Cottea, where
we found the pinnesse riding, at our comming.

The 28. we waied anker at Cottea, and presently came to
anker at S. Johns in Musketas Bay, where we spent three daies
unprofitably in taking in freshe water, spending in the meane
time more beere, then the quantitie of the water we came
unto.

Julie.

*Musketas
Baye, is a
harbour upon
the South
side of S.
Johns Island,
where we
take in fresh
water.

The first we waied anker at *Muskitoes Baye,
where were left behind two Irish men of our companie, Darbie Glauen, and Denice Carrell, bearing
along the coast of S. Johns, till evening, at which time
we fell with Rosse Baye. At this place Fernando had
promised wee should take in salt, and had caused us
before, to make and provide as many sackes for that purpose,
as we could. The Governour also, for that he understoode
there was a Towne in the bottome of the Baye, not farre from
the salt hils, appointed thirtie shotte, ten pikes, and ten targets,
to man the pinnesse, and to goe a land for salt. Fernando perceaving them in a readines, sent to the Governour, using great
perswasions with him, not to take in salt there, saying that he
knewe not well, whether the same were the place or not: also,
that if the pinnesse went into the Bay, she could not without
great danger come backe, till the next day at night, and that if
in the meane time any storme should rise, the Admirall were
in danger to be cast away. Whilest he was thus perswading, he
caused the lead to be cast, and having craftily brought the
shippe in three fathome, and a halfe water, he suddenly began to sweare, and teare God in peeces, dissembling great
danger, crying to him at the helme, beare up hard, beare up
hard: so we went off, and were disappointed of our salt, by his
meanes.

The next day, sailing along the West ende of S. Johns, the

*A pleasant and fruitfull Countrey, lying on the west ende of S. Johns Island where groweth plentie of Oringes, Lemmons, Plantyns, and Pynes.

Governour determined to goe a land in S. Germans *Baye, to gather yong plants of Oringes, Pines, Mameas, and Platonos, to set at Virginia, which we knewe might easily be had, for that they growe neere the shoare, and the places where they grewe, well knowen to the Governour, and some of the planters: but our Simon denied it, saying: he would come to anker at Hispaniola, and there lande the Governour, and some other of the Assistants, with the pinnesse, to see if he could speake with his friend Alanson, of whome he hoped to be furnished both of cattell, and all such thinges as wee woulde have taken in at S. Johns: but hee meant nothing lesse, as it plainely did appeare to us afterwards.

The next day after, being the third of Julie, wee sawe Hispaniola, and bare with the coast all that day, looking still when the pinnesse should be prepared to goe for the place where Fernando his friend Alanson was: but that day passed, and we sawe no preparation for landing in Hispaniola.

The 4. of Julie, sailing along the coast of Hispaniola, untill the next day at noone, and no preparation yet seene for the staying there, we having knowledge that we were past the place where Alanson dwelt, and were come with Isabella: hereupon Fernando was asked by the Governour, whether he meant to speake with Alanson, for the taking in of cattell, and other things, according to his promise, or not: but he answered, that he was now past the place, and that Sir Walter Ralegh tolde him, the French Ambassador certified him, that the king of Spaine had sent for Alanson into Spaine: wherefore he thought him dead, and that it was to no purpose to touch there in any place, at this voyage.

The next day, we left sight of Hispaniola, and haled off for Virginia, about 4. of the clocke in the afternoone.

The sixt of Julie, wee came to the Islande Caycos, wherein Fernando saide were two salt pondes, assuring us if they were drie, wee might finde salt to shift with, untill the next supplie, but it prooved as true as the finding of sheepe at Beake. In this Island, whilest Ferdinando solaced himself a shoare, with one of the company, in part of the Island, others spent the latter part of that day in other parts of the Island, some to seeke the salt ponds, some fowling, some hunting Swannes, whereof we caught many. The next daye, earely in the morning we waied anker, leaving Caycos, with good hope, the first lande that wee sawe next, should be Virginia.

About the 16. of July, we fell with the maine of Virginia, which Simon Fernando tooke to be the Island of Croatoan, where we came to an anker, and rode there two or three daies: but finding himselfe deceaved, he waied, and bare along the coast, where in the night, had not Captaine Stafforde bene more carefull in looking out, then our Simon Fernando, wee had beene all caste away upon the breache, called the Cape of Feare, for wee were come within two cables length upon it: such was the carelesnes, and ignorance of our Master.

The two and twentieth of Julie, we arrived safe at Hatoraske, where our shippe and pinnesse ankered: the Governour went aboord the pinnesse, accompanied with fortie of his best men, intending to passe up to Roanoake foorthwith, hoping there to finde those fifteene Englishmen, which Sir Richard Greenvill had left there the yeere before, with whome he meant to have conference, concerning the state of the Countrey, and Savages, meaning after he had so done, to returne againe to the fleete, and passe along the coast, to the Baye of Chesepiok, where we intended to make our seate and forte, according to the charge given us among other directions in writing, under the hande of Sir Walter Ralegh: but assoone as we were put with our pinnesse from the shippe, a Gentleman by the meanes of Fernando, who was appointed to returne for England, called to the sailers in the pinnesse, charging them not to bring any of the planters backe againe, but leave them in the Island, except the Governour, and two or three such as he approoved, saying that the Summer was farre spent, wherefore hee would land all the planters in no other place. Unto this were all the sailers, both in the pinnesse, and shippe, perswaded by the Master, wherefore it booted not the Governour to contend with them, but passed to Roanoake, and the same night, at Sunne set, went aland on the Island, in the place where our fifteene men were left, but we found none of them, nor any signe, that they had bene there, saving onely we found the bones of one of those fifteene, which the Savages had slaine long before.

The 23. of July, the Governour, with divers of his companie, walked to the North ende of the Island, where Master Ralfe

Lane had his forte, with sundry necessarie and decent dwelling houses, made by his men about it the yeere before, where wee hoped to finde some signes, or certaine knowledge of our fifteene men. When we came thither, wee found the forte rased downe, but all the houses standing unhurt, saving the neather roomes of them, and also of the forte, were overgrowen with Melons of divers sortes, and Deere within them, feeding on those Mellons: so we returned to our companie, without hope of ever seeing any of the fifteene men living.

The same day order was given, that every man should be imploied for the repairing of those houses, which we found standing, and also to make other newe Cottages, for such as shoulde neede.

The 25. our Flie boat, and the rest of our planters, arrived, all safe at Hatoraske, to the great joye, and comfort of the whole companie: but the Master of our Admirall, Fernando grieved greatly at their safe comming: for he purposely left them in the Baye of Portingall, and stole away from them in the night, hoping that the Master thereof, whose name was Edward Spicer, for that he never had beene in Virginia, would hardly finde the place, or els being left in so dangerous a place as that was, by meanes of so many men of warre, as at that time were aboord, they should surely be taken, or slaine: but God disappointed his wicked pretenses.

The eight and twentieth, George Howe, one of our twelve Assistants was slaine by divers Savages, which were come over to Roanoake, either of purpose to espie our companie, and what number we were, or els to hunt Deere, whereof were many in the Island. These Savages beeing secretly hidden among high reedes, where oftentimes they finde the Deere asleepe, and so kill them, espied our man wading in the water alone, almost naked, without any weapon, save onely a smal forked sticke, catching Crabs therewithall, and also being strayed two miles from his companie, shotte at him in the water, where they gave him sixeteene wounds with their arrowes: and after they had slain him with their woodden swordes, beat his head in peeces, and fled over the water to the maine.

On the thirtieth of Julie, Master Stafford, and twentie of our men, passed by water to the Island of Croatoan, with Manteo, who had his mother, and many of his kinred, dwelling in that

Island, of whome we hoped to understande some newes of our fifteene men, but especially to learne the disposition of the people of the Countrey towards us, and to renew our olde friendshippe with them. At our first landing, they seemed as though they would fight with us: but perceaving us begin to marche with our shot towards them, they turned their backes, and fled. Then Manteo their countreyman, called to them in their owne language, whom, assoone as they heard, they returned, and threwe away their bowes, and arrowes, and some of them came unto us, embracing and entertaining us friendly, desiring us not to gather or spill any of their corne, for that they had but little. We answered them, that neither their corne, nor any other thing of theirs, should be diminished by any of us, and that our comming was onely to renew the olde love, that was betweene us, and them, at the first, and to live with them as brethren, and friendes: which answere seemed to please them well, wherefore they requested us to walke up to their Towne, who there feasted us after their manner, and desired us earnestly, that there might be some token or badge given them of us, whereby we might know them to be our friendes, when we met them any where out of the Towne or Island. They told us further, that for want of some such badge, divers of them were hurt the yeere before, beeing founde out of the Island by Master Lane his companie, whereof they shewed us one, which at that very instant laye lame, and had lien of that hurt ever since: but they said, they knew our men mistooke them, and hurt them in steade of Winginoes men, wherefore they held us excused.

August.

The next day, we had conference further with them, concerning the people of Secota, Aquascogoc, & Pomioek, willing them of Croatoan, to certifie the people of those townes, that if they would accept our friendship, we would willingly receave them againe, and that all unfriendly dealings past on both partes, should be utterly forgiven, and forgotten. To this the chiefe men of Croatoan answered, that they would gladly doe the best they could, and within seven daies, bring the Weroances and chiefe Governours of those townes with them, to our Governour at Roanoak, or their answere. We also understoode of the men of Croatoan, that our man Master Howe, was slaine by the remnant of Winginoes men, dwelling then at Dasamongueponke, with whom Winchese kept companie: and also we understood by them of Croatoan, how that the 15. Englishmen left at Roanoak the yeere before, by Sir Richard Greenvill, were suddenly set upon, by 30. of the men of Secota, Aquascogoc, and Dasamongueponke, in manner following. They conveied themselves secretly behind the trees, neere the houses, where our men carelesly lived: and having perceaved that of those 15. they could see but 11. onely, two of those Savages appeared to the 11. Englishmen, calling to them by friendly signes, that but two of their chiefest men should come unarmed to speake with those two Savages, who seemed also to be unarmed. Wherefore the two of the chiefest of our Englishmen, went gladly to them: but whilest one of those Savages traitorously embraced one of our men, the other with his sword of wood, which he had secretly hidden under his mantell, stroke him on the head, and slewe him, and presently the other eight and twentie Savages shewed themselves: the other Englishmen perceaving this, fled to his companie, whome the Savages pursued with their bowes, and arrowes, so fast, that the Englishmen were forced to take the house, wherein all their victuall, and weapons were: but the Savages foorthwith set the same on fire, by means whereof, our men were forced to take up such weapons as came first to hand, and without order to runne foorth among the Savages, with whom they skirmished above an howre. In this skirmish, another of our men was shotte into the mouth with an arrowe, whereof he died: and also one of the Savages was shot into the side by one of our men, with a wild fire arrowe, whereof he died presently. The place where they fought, was of great advantage to the Savages, by means of the thicke trees, behinde which the Savages through their nimblenes, defended themselves, and so offended our men with their arrowes, that our men being some of them hurt, retired fighting to the water side, where their boate lay, with which they fled towards Hatorask. By that time they had rowed but a quarter of a mile, they espied their foure fellowes comming from a creeke thereby, where they had bene to fetch Oysters: these foure they receaved into their boate, leaving Roanoake, and landed on a little Island on the right hand of our entrance into the harbour of Hatorask, where they remained a while, but afterward departed, whither, as yet we knowe not.

Having nowe sufficiently dispatched our busines at Croatoan, the same day wee departed friendly, taking our leave, and came aboord the fleete at Hatoraske.

The eight of August, the Governour having long expected the comming of the Weroanses of Pomioake, Aquascoquos, Secota, and Dasamongueponke, seeing that the seven daies were past, within which they promised to come in, or to send their answers by the men of Croatoan, and no tidings of them heard, being certainly also informed by those men of Croatoan, that the remnant of Wingino his men, which were left alive, who dwelt at Dasamongueponke, were they which had slaine George Howe, and were also at the driving of our eleven Englishmen from Roanoake, he thought to differre the revenging thereof no longer. Wherefore the same night, about midnight, he passed over the water, accompanied with Captaine Stafford, and 24. men, whereof Manteo was one, whome wee tooke with us to be our guide to the place where those Savages dwelt, where he behaved himselfe toward us as a most faithfull English man.

The next day, being the ninth of August, in the morning so earely, that it was yet darke, wee landed neere the dwelling place of our enemies, and very secretly conveyed our selves through the woods, to that side, where we had their houses betweene us and the water: and having espied their fire, and some sitting about it, we presently sette on them: the miserable soules herewith amased, fledde into a place of thicke reedes, growing fast by, where our men perceaving them, shotte one of them through the bodie with a bullet, and therewith wee entred the reedes, among which wee hoped to acquite their evill doing towards us, but wee were deceaved, for those Savages were our friendes, and were come from Croatoan, to gather the corne, and fruite of that place, because they understoode our enemies were fledde immediately after they had slaine George Howe, and for haste had left all their corne, Tabacco, and Pompions standing in such sorte, that all had beene devoured of the birdes, and Deere, if it had not been gathered in time: but they had like to have paide deerely for it:

for it was so darke, that they beeing naked, and their men and women apparelled all so like others, we knewe not but that they were all men: and if that one of them, which was a Weroans wife, had not had her childe at her backe, she had beene slaine in steede of a man, and as happe was, another Savage knewe Master Stafford, and ranne to him, calling him by his name, whereby he was saved. Finding our selves thus disappointed of our purpose, wee gathered all the corne, Pease, Pumpions, and Tabacco, that we found ripe, leaving the rest unspoiled, and tooke Menatoan his wife, with the yong childe, and the other Savages with us over the water to Roanoak. Although the mistaking of these Savages somewhat grieved Manteo, yet he imputed their harme to their owne follie, saying to them, that if their Weroans had kept their promise in comming to the Governour, at the day appointed, they had not knowen that mischance.

The 13. of August, our Savage Manteo, by the commandment of Sir Walter Ralegh, was christened in Roanoak, and called Lord thereof, and of Dasamongueponke, in reward of his faithfull service.

The 18. Elenora, daughter to the Governour, and wife to Ananias Dare, one of the Assistants, was delivered of a daughter in Roanoak, and the same was christened there the Sunday following, and because this childe was the first Christian borne in Virginia, she was named Virginia. By this time our shippes had unlanded the goods and victuals of the planters, and began to take in wood, and fresh water, and to newe calke and trimme them for England: the planters also prepared their letters, and tokens, to send backe into England.

Our two shippes, the Lyon, and the Flieboate, almost ready to depart, the 21. of August, there arose such a tempest at northeast, that our Admirall then riding out of the harbour, was forced to cut his cables, and put to Sea, where he laye beating off and on, six dayes before hee coulde come to us againe, so that wee feared hee had beene cast away, and the rather, for that at the tyme that the storme tooke them, the moste, and best of their Saylers, were left aland.

At this time some controversies rose betweene the Governour and Assistants, about choosing two out of the twelve Assistants, which should goe backe as factors for the companie into England: for every one of them refused, save onely one, which all the other thought not sufficient: but at length, by much perswading of the Governour, Christopher Cooper onely agreed to goe for England: but the next day, through the perswasion of divers of his familiar friendes, he changed his minde, so that now the matter stoode as at the first.

The next day, the 22. of August, the whole companie, both of the Assistants, and planters, came to the Governour, and with one voice requested him to returne himselfe into England, for the better and sooner obtaining of supplies, and other necessaries for them: but he refused it, and alleaged many sufficient causes, why he would not: the one was, that he could not so suddenly returne backe againe, without his great discredite, leaving the action, and so many, whome he partly had procured through his perswasions, to leave their native Countrey, and undertake that voyage, and that some enemies to him, and the action at his returne into England, would not spare to slander falsely both him, and the action, by saying he went to Virginia, but politikely, and to no other ende, but to leade so many into a Countrey, in which he never meant to stay himselfe, and there to leave them behind him. Also he alleaged, that seing they intended to remove 50. miles further up into the maine presently, he being then absent, his stuffe and goods, might be both spoiled, and most of it pilfered away in the carriage, so that at his returne, hee should be either forced to provide himselfe of all such things againe, or els at his comming againe to Virginia, finde himselfe utterly unfurnished, whereof already he had found some proofe, beeing but once from them but three daies. Wherefore he concluded, that he would not goe himselfe.

The next day, not onely the Assistants, but divers others, as well women, as men, beganne to renewe their requests to the Governour againe, to take uppon him to returne into England for the supplie, and dispatch of all such thinges, as there were to be done, promising to make him their bonde under all their handes, and seales, for the safe preserving of all his goods for him at his returne to Virginia, so that if any part thereof were spoiled, or lost, they would see it restored to him, or his Assignes, whensoever the same should be missed, and demanded: which bonde, with a testimonie under their handes, and seales, they foorthwith made, and delivered into his hands. The copie of the testimonie, I thought good to set downe.

May it please you, her Majesties Subjects of England, wee your friendes and Countrey men, the planters in Virginia, doe by these presents let you, and every of you to understande, that for the present and speedie supplie of certaine our knowen, and apparent lackes, and needes, most requisite and necessarie for the good and happie planting of us, or any other in this lande of Virginia, wee all of one minde, and consent, have most earnestly intreated, and uncessantly requested John White, Governour of the planters in Virginia, to passe into England, for the better and more assured helpe, and setting forward of the foresayde supplies: and knowing assuredly that he both can best, and will labour, and take paines in that behalfe for us all, and hee not once, but often refusing it, for our sakes, and for the honour, and maintenance of the action, hath at last, though much against his will, through our importunacie, yeelded to leave his government, and all his goods among us, and himselfe in all our behalfes to passe into Englande, of whose knowledge, and fidelitie in handling this matter, as all others, wee doe assure our selves by these presents, and will you to give all credite thereunto. the five and twentieth of August.

The Governour beeing at the last, through their extreame intreating, constrayned to returne to England, having then but halfe a daies respit to prepare him selfe for the same, departed from Roanoake, the seven and twentieth of August in the morning: and the same daye about midnight, came aboord the Flie boate, who already had waied anker, and rode without the barre, the Admirall riding by them, who but the same morning was newly come thither againe. The same day, both the shippes waied anker, and sette saile for England: at this waying their ankers, twelve of the men which were in the Flieboat, were throwen from the Capestone, which by meanes of a barre that brake, came so fast about upon them, that the other two barres thereof stroke and hurt most of them so sore, that some of them never recovered it: neverthelesse they assaied presently againe to waigh their anker, but being so weakened with the first fling, they were not able to weigh it, but were throwen downe, and hurt the seconde time. Wherefore having in all but fifteene men aboord, and most of them by this infortunate beginning so bruised, and hurt, they were forced to cut their Cable, and lesse their anker. Neverthelesse, they kept companie with the Admirall, untill the seventeenth of September, at which time wee fell with Corvo, and sawe Flores.

September.

The eighteenth, perceaving of all our fifteene men in the Flie boat, there remained but five, which by meanes of the former mischance, were able to stande to their labour: wherefore understanding that the Admirall meant not to make any haste for England, but linger about the Islande of Tercera for purchase, the Flie boate departed for Englande with letters, where we hoped by the helpe of God to arrive shortly: but by that time wee had continued our course homeward, about twentie dayes, having had sometimes scarse, and variable windes, our fresh water also by leaking almost consumed, there arose a storme at Northeast, which for 6. dayes ceased not to blowe so exceeding, that we were driven further in those 6. then wee could recover in thirteene daies: in which time others of our saylers began to fall very sicke, and two of them dyed, the weather also continued so close, that our Master sometimes in foure daies together could see neither Sunne nor starre, and all the beverage we could make, with stinking water, dregges of beere, and lees of wine which remained, was but 3. gallons, and therefore now we expected nothing but by famyne to perish at Sea.

October.

The 16. of October we made land, but we knew not what land it was, bearing in with the same land at that day: about Sunne set we put into a harbour, where we found a Hulke of Dublin, and a pynesse of Hampton ryding, but we knew not as yet what place this was, neither had we any boate to goe a shoare, untill the pinnesse sent off their boate to us with 6. or 8. men, of whom we understood we were in Smewicke in the west parts of Ireland: they also releeved us presently with fresh water, wyne, and other fresh meate.

The 18. the Governour, and the Master ryd to Dingen Cushe, 5. myles distant, to take order of the new victualling of our Flye boate for England, and for reliefe of our sicke and hurt men, but within 4. dayes after the boatswane, the steward, and the boatswanes mate dyed aboord the flyeboate, and the 28. the Masters mate and two of our chiefe Saylers were brought sicke to Dingen.

November.

The first the Governour shipped him selfe in a ship called the Monkie, which at that time was readie to put to sea from Dingen for England, leaving the Flyeboat and all his company in Ireland, the same day we set sayle, and on the third day we fel with the Northside of the lands end, and were shut up the Severne, but the next day we duobled the same, for Monts Bay.

The 5. the Governour landed in England at Martasew, neere Saint Michaels mount in Cornewall.

The 8. we arrived at Hampton, where we understood that our consort the Admirall was come to Portsmouth, and had bene there three weekes before: and also that Fernando the Master with all his company were not onely come home without any purchase, but also in such weaknesse by sicknes, and death of their cheefest men, that they were scarse able to bring their ship into the harbour, but were forced to let fall anker without, which they could not way againe, but might all have perished there, if a small barke by great hap had not come to them to helpe them. The names of the chiefe men that dyed are these, Roger Large, John Mathew, Thomas Smith, and some other saylers, whose names I know not at the writing hereof. Anno Domini 1587.

THOMAS HARIOT

A Briefe and True Report

A BRIEFE and true report of the new found land of Virginia: of the commodities there found and to be raysed, as well marchantable, as others for victuall, building and other necessarie uses for those that are and shalbe the planters there; and of the nature and manners of the naturall inhabitants: Discovered by the English Colony there seated by Sir Richard Greinvile Knight in the yeere 1585. which remained under the government of Rafe Lane Esquier, one of her Majesties Equieres, during the space of twelve monethes: at the speciall charge and direction of the Honourable Sir Walter Raleigh Knight, Lord Warden of the stanneries; who therein hath beene favoured and authorised by her Majestie and her letters patents:

Directed to the Adventurers, Favourers, and Welwillers of the action, for the inhabiting and planting there:

By Thomas Hariot; servant to the abovenamed Sir Walter, a member of the Colony, and there imployed in discovering.

Imprinted at London 1588.

———

Rafe Lane one of her Majesties Equieres, and Governour of the Colony of Virginia above mentioned for the time there resident.

To the gentle Reader wisheth all happines in the Lord.

Albeit (Gentle Reader) the credite of the reports in this treatise contained, can little be furthered by the testimonie of one as my selfe, through affection judged partiall, though without desert: Neverthelesse, for somuch as I have bene requested by some my particular friends, who conceive more rightly of me, to deliver freely my knowledge of the same; not onely for the satisfying of them, but also for the true enformation of anie other whosoever, that comes not with a prejudicate minde to the reading thereof: Thus much upon my credit I am to affirme: that things universally are so truely set downe in this treatise

by the authour thereof, an Actor in the Colony, or a man no
lesse for his honesty then learning commendable: as that I dare
boldly avouch it may very well passe with the credit of trueth
even amongst the most true relations of this age. Which as for
mine owne part I am readie any way with my word to acknowledge, so also (of the certaintie thereof assured by mine
owne experience) with this my publique assertion, I doe affirme
the same. Farewell in the Lorde.

———

To the Adventurers, Favourers, and Welwillers of the enterprise for the inhabiting and planting of Virginia.

Since the first undertaking by Sir Walter Raleigh to deale in
the action of discovering of that Countrey which is now called
and known by the name of Virginia, many voyages having bin
thither made at sundrie times to his great charge; as first in
the yere 1584, and afterwardes in the yeeres 1585, 1586, and now
of late this last yeere of 1587: There have bin divers and variable
reportes, with some slaunderous and shamefull speeches
bruited abroade by many that returned from thence. Especially of that discovery which was made by the Colony transported by Sir Richard Greinvile in the yeare 1585, being of all
the others the most principal, and as yet of most effect, the time
of their abode in the countrey beeing a whole yeare, when as in
the other voyage before they staied but sixe weekes, and the
others after were onelie for supply and transportation, nothing
more being discovered then had been before. Which reports
have done not a litle wrong to many that otherwise would have
also favoured & adventured in the action, to the honour and
benefite of our nation, besides the particular profite and credite which would redound to them selves the dealers therein, as
I hope by the sequele of events to the shame of those that have
avouched the contrary, shalbe manifest: if you the adventurers,
favourers and welwillers do but either encrease in number, or
in opinion continue, or having bin doubtfull renewe your good
liking and furtherance to deale therein according to the worthinesse thereof alreadye found and as you shall understand
hereafter to be requisite. Touching which woorthines through
cause of the diversitie of relations and reportes, manye of your
opinions coulde not bee firme, nor the mindes of some that
are well disposed, bee setled in any certainte.

I have therefore thought it good, beeing one that have beene in the discoverie, and in dealing with the naturall inhabitantes specially imploied; and having therefore seene and knowne more then the ordinarie: to impart so much unto you of the fruites of our labours, as that you may knowe how injuriously the enterprise is slaundered. And that in publik manner at this present, chiefelie for two respectes.

First, that some of you which are yet ignorant or doubtfull of the state thereof, may see that there is sufficient cause why the chiefe enterpriser with the favour of her Majestie, notwithstanding suche reportes; hath not onelie since continued the action by sending into the countrey againe, and replanting this last yeere a new Colony; but is also readie according as the times and meanes will affoorde, to follow and prosecute the same.

Secondly, that you seeing and knowing the continuance of the action by the view hereof you may generally know & learne what the countrey is; & thereupon consider how your dealing therein, if it proceede, may returne you profit and gaine; bee it either by inhabiting & planting or otherwise in furthering thereof.

And least that the substance of my relation should be doubtful unto you, as of others by reason of their diversitie; I will first open the cause in a few wordes, wherefore they are so different, referring my selfe to your favourable constructions, and to be adjudged of as by good consideration you shall finde cause.

Of our companie that returned some for their misdemeanour and ill dealing in the countrey have beene there worthily punished, who by reason of their badde natures, have maliciously not onelie spoken ill of their Governours, but for their sakes slaundered the countrie it selfe. The like also have those done which were of their consort.

Some being ignorant of the state thereof, notwithstanding since their returne amongst their friendes and acquaintance and also others, especially if they were in companie where they might not be gainesaide; woulde seeme to knowe so much as no men more, and make no men so great travailers as themselves. They stood so much as it maie seeme upon their credite and reputation that having been a twelve moenth in the countrey, it woulde have beene a great disgrace unto them as they thought, if they coulde not have saide much whether it were true or false. Of which some have spoken of more then ever they saw or otherwise knew to bee there; othersome have not bin ashamed to make absolute deniall of that which although not by them, yet by others is most certainely and there plentifully knowne. And othersome make difficulties of those things they have no skill of.

The cause of their ignorance was, in that they were of that many that were never out of the Iland where wee were seated, or not farre, or at the leastwise in few places els, during the time of our aboade in the countrey: or of that many that after gold and silver was not so soone found, as it was by them looked for, had little or no care of any other thing but to pamper their bellies; or of that many which had litle understanding, lesse discretion, and more tongue then was needfull or requisite.

Some also were of a nice bringing up, only in cities or townes, or such as never (as I may say) had seene the world before. Because there were not to bee found any English cities, nor such faire houses, nor at their owne wish any of their olde accustomed daintie food, nor any soft beds of downe or feathers, the countrey was to them miserable, & their reports thereof according.

Because my purpose was but in briefe to open the cause of the varietie of such speeches; the particularities of them, and of many envious, malicious, and slaunderous reports and devices els, by our owne countreymen besides; as trifles that are not worthy of wise men to bee thought upon, I meane not to trouble you withall: but will passe to the commodities, the substance of that which I have to make relation of unto you.

The treatise whereof, for your more readie view & easier understanding, I will divide into three speciall parts. In the first I will make the declaration of such commodities there alreadie found or to be raised, which will not onely serve the ordinary turnes of you which are and shall bee the planters and inhabitants, but such an overplus sufficiently to bee yelded, or by men of skill to bee provided, as by way of trafficke and exchaunge with our owne nation of England, will enrich your selves the providers: those that shal deal with you; the enterprisers in general, and greatly profit our owne countrey men, to supply them with most things which heretofore they have bene faine to provide, either of strangers or of our enemies: which commodities for distinction sake I call Merchantable.

In the second, I will set downe all the commodities which wee know the countrey by our experience doeth yeld of it selfe for victuall, and sustenance of mans life; such as is usually fed upon by the inhabitants of the countrey, as also by us during the time we were there.

In the last part I will make mention generally of such other commodities besides, as I am able to remember, and as I shall thinke behoofull for those that shall inhabite, and plant there to knowe of, which specially concerne building, as also some other necessary uses: with a briefe description of the nature and maners of the people of the countrey.

The first part of Merchantable commodities.

Silke of grasse, or grasse Silke. There is a kind of grasse in the countrey uppon the blades whereof there groweth very good silke in forme of a thin glittering skin to bee stript of. It groweth two foot and a halfe high or better: the blades are about two foot in length, and half inch broad. The like groweth in Persia, which is in the selfe same climate as Virginia, of which very many of the silke works that come from thence into Europe are made. Hereof if it be planted and ordered as in Persia, it cannot in reason be otherwise, but that there will rise in shorte time great profite to the dealers therein, seeing there is so great use and vent thereof as well in our countrey as els where. And by the meanes of sowing & planting it in good ground, it will be farre greater, better, and more plentifull then it is. Although notwithstanding there is great store thereof in many places of the countrey growing naturally and wilde, Which also by proof here in England, in making a piece of silke Grogran, we found to be excellent good.

Worme Silke. In many of our journeys we found silke wormes fayre and great; as bigge as our ordinary walnuts. Although it hath not beene our happe to have found such plentie, as elswhere to be in the countrey we have heard of, yet seeing that the countrey doth naturally breede and nourish them, there is no doubt but if art be added in planting of mulberry trees, and others fitte for them in commodious places, for their feeding and nourishing, and some of them carefully gathered and hus-

banded in that sort as by men of skill is knowne to be necessarie: there will rise as great profite in time to the Virginians,
as thereof doth now to the Persians, Turkes, Italians and
Spaniards.

Flaxe and Hempe. The trueth is that of Hempe and Flaxe
there is no great store in any one place together, by reason it is
not planted but as the soile doth yeeld it of it selfe: and howsoever the leafe, and stemme or stalke doe differ from ours; the
stuffe by the judgement of men of skill is altogether as good as
ours. And if not, as further proofe should finde otherwise, we
have that experience of the soile, as that there cannot bee
shewed anie reason to the contrary, but that it will grow there
excellent well, and by planting will be yeelded plentifully: seeing there is so much ground whereof some may well be applyed to such purposes. What benefite heereof may growe in
cordage and linnens who can not easily understand?

Allum. There is a veine of earth along the sea coast for the
space of fourtie or fiftie miles, whereof by the judgement of
some that have made triall heere in England, is made good
Allum, of that kind which is called Roche allum. The richnesse
of such a commoditie is so well knowne that I need not to saye
any thing thereof. The same earth doth also yeeld White
Copresse, Nitrum, and Alumen plumeum, but nothing so
plentifully as the common Allum, which be also of price, and
profitable.

Wapeih, a kinde of earth so called by the naturall inhabitants,
very like to terra Sigillata: and having beene refined, it hath
beene found by some of our Phisitions and Chirurgeons to bee
of the same kinde of vertue and more effectuall. The inhabitants
use it very much for the cure of sores and woundes: there is in
divers places great plentie, and in some places of a blewe sort.

Pitch, Tarre, Rozen and Turpentine. There are those kindes
of trees which yeelde them abundantly and great store. In the
very same Iland where we were seated, being fifteene miles of
length, and five or six miles in breadth, there are few trees els
but of the same kind, the whole Iland being full.

Sassafras, called by the inhabitants Winauk, a kinde of wood
of most pleasant and sweete smel; and of most rare vertues in
phisick for the cure of many diseases. It is found by experience
to bee far better and of more uses then the wood which is

called Guaiacum, or Lignum vitae. For the description, the maner of using, and the manifold vertues thereof, I refer you to the booke of Monardes, translated and entituled in English, The joyfull newes from the West Indies.

Cedar, a very sweet wood & fine timber; whereof if nests of chests be there made, or timber thereof fitted for sweet & fine bedsteads, tables, deskes, lutes, virginalles & many things else, (of which there hath beene proofe made already), to make up fraite with other principal commodities will yeeld profite.

Wine: There are two kinds of grapes that the soile doth yeeld naturally: the one is small and sowre of the ordinarie bignesse as ours in England: the other farre greater & of himselfe lushious sweet. When they are planted and husbanded as they ought, a principall commoditie of wines by them may be raised.

Oyle: There are two sortes of Walnuttes, both holding oyle, but the one farre more plentifull then the other. When there are milles & other devices for the purpose, a commodity of them may be raised because there are infinite store. There are also three severall kindes of Berries in the forme of Oke akornes, which also by the experience and use of the inhabitantes, wee find to yeelde very good and sweete oyle. Furthermore, the Beares of the countrey are commonly very fatte, and in some places there are many: their fatnesse because it is so liquid, may well be termed oyle, and hath many speciall uses.

Furres: All along the Sea coast there are great store of Otters, which beyng taken by weares and other engines made for the purpose, wil yeelde good profite. Wee hope also of Marterne furres, and make no doubt by the relation of the people but that in some places of the countrey there are store, although there were but two skinnes that came to our handes. Luzarnes also we have understanding of, although for the time we saw none.

Deare Skinnes dressed after the maner of Chamoes or undressed are to be had of the naturall inhabitants thousands yeerely by way of trafficke for trifles: and no more wast or spoyle of Deare then is and hath beene ordinarily in time before.

Civet cattes: In our travailes, there was founde one to have beene killed by a savage or inhabitant: and in another place the smell where one or more had lately beene before: whereby we gather besides then by the relation of the people that there are some in the countrey: good profite will rise by them.

Iron: In two places of the countrey specially, one about fourescore and the other six score miles from the Fort or place where we dwelt: we found neere the water side the ground to be rockie, which by the triall of a minerall man, was found to holde yron richly. It is founde in many places of the country else. I knowe nothing to the contrarie, but that it maie bee allowed for a good merchantable commoditie, considering there the small charge for the labour and feeding of men: the infinite store of wood: the want of wood and deerenesse thereof in England: & the necessity of ballasting of shippes.

Copper: A hundred and fiftie miles into the maine in two townes we founde with the inhabitaunts divers small plates of copper, that had beene made as we understood, by the inhabitantes that dwell farther into the countrey, where as they say are mountains and Rivers that yeelde also whyte graynes of Mettall, which is to be deemed Silver. For confirmation whereof at the time of our first arrivall in the Countrey, I sawe with some others with mee, two small peeces of silver grosly beaten about the weight of a Testrone, hangyng in the ears of a *Wiroans* or chiefe Lord that dwelt about fourescore myles from us; of whom thorowe inquiry, by the number of dayes and the way, I learned that it had come to his handes from the same place or neere, where I after understood the copper was made and the white graines of mettall founde. The aforesaide copper wee also founde by triall to holde silver.

Pearle: Sometimes in feeding on muscles wee found some pearle; but it was our hap to meet with ragges, or of a pide colour; not having yet discovered those places where wee heard of better and more plentie. One of our companie; a man of skill in such matters, had gathered together from among the savage people aboute five thousande: of which number he chose so many as made a fayre chaine, which for their likenesse and uniformitie in roundnesse, orientnesse, and pidenesse of many excellent colours, with equalitie in greatnesse, were very fayre and rare; and had therefore beene presented to her Majestie, had wee not by casualtie, and through extremity of a storme, lost them with many things els in comming away from the countrey.

Sweet Gummes of divers kinds, and many other Apothecary drugges, of which we will make speciall mention, when we shall receive it from such men of skill in that kynd, that in taking reasonable paines shall discover them more particularly then wee have done; and than now I can make relation of, for want of the examples I had provided and gathered, and are nowe lost, with other things by casualtie before mentioned.

Dyes of divers kindes: There is Shoemake well knowen, and used in England for blacke; the seede of an hearbe called *Wasewówr*, little small rootes called *Cháppacor*, and the barke of the tree called by the inhabitaunts *Tangómockomindge*: which Dies are for divers sortes of red: their goodnesse for our English clothes remayne yet to be proved. The inhabitants use them onely for the dying of hayre, the colouring of their faces, and Mantles made of Deare skinnes; and also for the dying of Rushes to make artificiall workes withall in their Mattes and Baskettes; having no other thing besides that they account of, apt to use them for. If they will not prove merchantable there is no doubt but the Planters there shall finde apt uses for them, as also for other colours which wee knowe to be there.

Oade; a thing of so great vent and use amongst English Diers, which can not be yeelded sufficiently in our owne countrey for spare of ground, may be planted in Virginia, there being ground enough. The grouth thereof need not to be doubted, when as in the Ilands of the Asores it groweth plentifully, which is in the same climate. So likewise of Madder.

We caryed thither Suger canes to plant, which beeing not so well preserved as was requisit, & besides the time of the yere being past for their setting when we arrived, wee could not make that proofe of them as wee desired. Notwithstanding, seeing that they grow in the same climate, in the South part of Spaine and in Barbary, our hope in reason may yet continue. So likewise for Orenges and Lemmons. There may be planted also Quinses. Whereby may grow in reasonable time if the action be diligently prosecuted, no small commodities in Sugers, Suckets, and Marmalades.

Many other commodities by planting may there also bee raised, which I leave to your discret and gentle considerations: and many also bee there, which yet we have not discovered. Two more commodities of great value, one of certaintie, and the other in hope, not to be planted, but there to be raised & in short time to be provided and prepared, I might have specified. So likewise of those commodities already set downe I might have said more; as of the particular places where they are founde and best to be planted and prepared: by what meanes and in what reasonable space of time they might be raised to profit and in what proportion; but because others then welwillers might be therewithall acquainted, not to the good of the action, I have wittingly omitted them: knowing that to those that are well disposed I have uttered, according to my promise and purpose, for this part sufficient.

The second part of suche commodities as Virginia is knowne to yeelde for victuall and sustenance of mans life, usually fed upon by the naturall inhabitants: as also by us, during the time of our aboade. And first of such as are sowed and husbanded.

Pagatowr, a kinde of graine so called by the inhabitants; the same in the West Indies is called Mayze: English men call it Guinny wheate or Turkie wheate, according to the names of the countreys from whence the like hath beene brought. The graine is about the bignesse of our ordinary English peaze and not much different in forme and shape: but of divers colours: some white, some red, some yellow, and some blew. All of them yeelde a very white and sweet flowre: being used according to his kinde it maketh a very good bread. Wee made of the same in the countrey some mault, whereof was bruwed as good Ale as was to bee desired. So likewise by the helpe of hops therof may bee made as good Beere. It is a graine of marveillous great increase; of a thousand, fifteene hundred and some two thousand fold. There are three sortes, of which two are ripe in eleven and twelve weeks at the most: sometimes in ten, after the time they are set, and are then of height in stalke about sixe or seven foote. The other sort is ripe in fourteene, and is about ten foote high, of the stalkes some beare foure heads, some three, some one, and some two: every head conteining five, sixe, or seven hundred graines within a few more or lesse. Of these graines besides bread, the inhabitants make victuall, eyther by parching them, or seething them whole untill they be broken; or boyling the floure with water into a pappe.

Okindgíer, called by us Beanes, because in greatnesse &

partly in shape they are like to the Beanes in England; saving
that they are flatter, of more divers colours, and some pide.
The leafe also of the stemme is much different. In taste they are
altogether as good as our English peaze.

Wickonzówr, called by us Peaze, in respect of the beanes, for
distinction sake, because they are much lesse; although in
forme they litle differ: but in goodnesse of taste much, & are
far better then our English peaze. Both the beanes and peaze
are ripe in tenne weekes after they are set. They make them
vicutall either by boyling them all to pieces in a broth, or boil-
ing them whole untill they bee soft and beginne to breake as is
used in England, eyther by themselves, or mixtly together:
Sometimes they mingle of the wheate with them. Sometime
also beeing whole sodden, they bruse or pound them in a
morter, & thereof make loaves of lumps of dowishe bread,
which they use to eat for varietie.

Macócqwer, according to their severall formes, called by us
Pompions, Mellions, and Gourdes, because they are of the like
formes as those kinds in England. In Virginia such of severall
formes are of one taste and very good, and do also spring from
one seed. There are two sorts; one is ripe in the space of a
moneth, and the other in two moneths.

There is an hearbe which in Dutch is called *Melden*. Some of
those that I describe it unto take it to be a kinde or Orage; it
groweth about foure or five foote high: of the seede thereof
they make a thicke broth, and pottage of a very good taste: of
the stalke by burning into ashes they make a kind of salt earth,
wherewithall many use sometimes to season their broths; other
salte they knowe not. Wee our selves used the leaves also for
pot-hearbes.

There is also another great hearbe, in forme of a Marigolde,
about six foot in height, the head with the floure is a spanne
in breadth. Some take it to be Planta Solis: of the seeds heereof
they make both a kinde of bread and broth.

All the aforesayd commodities for victuall are set or sowed,
sometimes in groundes apart and severally by themselves, but
for the most part together in one ground mixtly: the manner
thereof, with the dressing and preparing of the ground, because
I will note unto you the fertilitie of the soile; I thinke good
briefly to describe.

The ground they never fatten with mucke, dounge, or any other thing, neither plow nor digge it as we in England, but onely prepare it in sort as followeth. A few daies defore they sowe or set, the men with wooden instruments, made almost in forme of mattockes or hoes with long handles; the women with short peckers or parers, because they use them sitting, of a foote long and about five inches in breadth: doe only break the upper part of the ground to rayse up the weedes, grasse, & olde stubbes of corne stalks with their rootes. The which after a day or twoes drying in the Sunne, being scrapte up into many small heapes, to save them labour for carrying them away; they burne into ashes. (And whereas some may thinke that they use the ashes for to better the ground, I say that then they would either disperse the ashes abroade, which wee observed they do not, except the heapes bee too great: or else would take speciall care to set their corne where the ashes lie, which also wee finde they are carelesse of.) And this is all the husbanding of their ground that they use.

Then their setting or sowing is after this maner. First for their corne, beginning in one corner of the plot, with a pecker they make a hole, wherein they put foure graines, with that care they touch not one another (about an inch asunder) and cover them with the moulde againe: and so through out the whole plot, making such holes and using them after such maner: but with this regard, that they bee made in rankes, every ranke differing from other halfe a fadome or a yarde, and the holes also in every ranke, as much. By this means there is a yard spare ground betwene every hole: where according to discretion here and there, they set as many Beans and Peaze; in divers places also among the seedes of *Macócqwer*, *Melden* and Planta solis.

The ground being thus set according to the rate by us experimented, an English Acre conteining fourtie pearches in length, and foure in breadth, doeth there yeeld in croppe or ofcome of corne, beanes, and peaze, at the least two hundred London bushelles, besides the *Macócqwer*, *Melden*, and Planta solis: When as in England fourtie bushelles of our wheate yeelded out of such an acre is thought to be much.

I thought also good to note this unto you, that you which shall inhabite and plant there, maie know how specially that countrey corne is there to be preferred before ours: Besides the manifold waies in applying it to victuall, the increase is so much that small labour and paines is needful in respect that must be used for ours. For this I can assure you that according to the rate we have made proofe of, one man may prepare and husband so much grounde (having once borne corne before) with lesse then foure and twentie hours labour, as shall yeeld him victuall in a large proportion for the twelvemoneth, if hee have nothing else, but that which the same ground will yeelde, and of that kinde onelie which I have before spoken of: the saide ground being also but of five and twentie yards square. And if neede require, but that there is ground enough, there might be raised out of one and the selfsame ground two harvestes or ofcomes; for they sowe or set and may at anie time when they thinke good from the middest of March untill the end of June: so that they also set when they have eaten of their first croppe. In some places of the countrey notwithstanding they have two harvests, as we have heard, out of one and the same ground.

For English corne neverthelesse whether to use or not to use it, you that inhabite maie doe as you shall have farther cause to thinke best. Of the grouth you need not to doubt: for barlie, oates and peaze, we have seene proof of, not beeing purposely sowen but fallen casually in the worst sort of ground, and yet to be as faire as any we have ever seene here in England. But of wheat, because it was musty and had taken salt water we could make no triall: and of rye we had none. Thus much have I digressed and I hope not unnecessarily: nowe will I returne againe to my course and intreate of that which yet remaineth apperteining to this Chapter.

There is an herbe which is sowed apart by it selfe & is called by the inhabitants *uppówoc*: In the West Indies it hath divers names, according to the severall places & countreys where it groweth and is used: The Spaniardes generally call it Tobacco. The leaves thereof being dried and brought into pouder, they use to take the fume or smoke thereof by sucking it through pipes made of claie, into their stomacke and heade; from whence it purgeth superfluous fleame & other grosse humors, openeth all the pores & passages of the body: by which meanes the use thereof, not only preserveth the body from obstructions; but also if any be, so that they have not beene of too long continuance, in short time breaketh them: wherby their bodies are notably preserved in health, & know not many greevous diseases wherewithall wee in England are oftentimes afflicted.

This *Uppówoc* is of so precious estimation amongest them, that they thinke their gods are marvelously delighted therwith: Wherupon sometime they make hallowed fires & cast some of the pouder therein for a sacrifice: being in a storme uppon the waters, to pacifie their gods, they cast some up into the aire and into the water: so a weare for fish being newly set up, they cast some therein and into the aire: also after an escape of danger, they cast some into the aire likewise: but all done with strange gestures, stamping, sometime dauncing, clapping of hands, holding up of hands, & staring up into the heavens, uttering therewithal and chattering strange words & noises.

We our selves during the time we were there used to suck it after their manner, as also since our returne, & have found manie rare and wonderfull experiments of the vertues thereof; of which the relation woulde require a volume by it selfe: the use of it by so manie of late men & women of great calling as else and some learned Phisitions also, is sufficient witnes.

And these are all the commodities for sustenance of life that I know and can remember they use to husband: all else that followe, are founde growing naturally or wilde.

Of Rootes.

Openauk are a kind of roots of round forme, some of the bignes of walnuts, some far greater, which are found in moist & marish grounds growing many together one by another in ropes, as though they were fastnened with a string. Being boiled or sodden they are very good meate.

Okeepenauk are also of round shape, found in dry grounds: some are the bignes of a mans head. They are to be eaten as they are taken out of the ground, for by reason of their drinesse they will neither roste nor seeth. Their tast is not so good as of the former roots, notwithstanding for want of bread & sometimes for a varietie the inhabitants use to eate them with fish or flesh, and in my judgement they doe as well as the household bread made of rie heare in England.

Kaishucpenauk a white kind of roots about the bignes of

hen egs & neere of that forme: their tast was not so good to our seeming as the other, and therefore their place and manner of growing not so much cared for by us: the inhabitants notwithstanding used to boile & eate many.

Tsinaw a kind of roote much like unto that which in England is called the China root brought from the East Indies. And we know not anie thing to the contrary but that it maie be of the same kinde. These roots grow manie together in great clusters and do bring foorth a brier stalke, but the leafe in shape farre unlike: which beeing supported by the trees it groweth neerest unto, will reach or climbe to the top of the highest. From these roots while they be new or fresh beeing chopt into small pieces & stampt, is strained with water a juice that maketh bread, & also being boiled, a very good spoonemeate in maner of a gelly, and is much better in tast, if it bee tempered with oyle. This *Tsinaw* is not of that sort which by some was caused to be brought into England for the China roote, for it was discovered since, and is in use as is afore said: but that which was brought hither is not yet knowne, neither by us nor by the inhabitants to serve for any use or purpose, although the rootes in shape are very like.

Coscúshaw, some of our company tooke to bee that kinde of root which the Spaniards in the West Indies call *Cassavy*, whereupon also many called it by that name: it groweth in very muddie pooles and moist groundes. Being dressed according to the countrey maner, it maketh a good bread, and also a good sponemeate, and is used very much by the inhabitants. The juice of this root is poison, and therefore heede must be taken before any thing be made therewithall: Either the rootes must bee first sliced and dried in the Sunne, or by the fire, and then being pounded into floure wil make good bread: or els while they are greene they are to bee pared, cut into pieces, and stampt; loves of the same to be laid neere or over the fire untill it be soure, and then being well pounded againe, bread, or spone meate very good in taste, and holesome may be made thereof.

Habascon is a root of hoat taste almost of the forme and bignesse of a Parseneepe, of it selfe it is no victuall, but onely a helpe beeing boiled together with other meates.

There are also Leekes, differing little from ours in England that grow in many places of the countrey, of which, when we came in places where they were, wee gathered and eate many, but the naturall inhabitants never.

Of Fruites.

Chestnuts, there are in divers places great store: some they use to eate rawe, some they stampe and boile to make spoone-meate, and with some being sodden they make such a manner of dowe bread as they use of their beanes before mentioned.

Walnuts: There are two kindes of Walnuts, and of them in-finit store: In many places where are very great woods for many miles together the third part of trees are walnut-trees. The one kind is of the same taste and forme or litle differing from ours of England, but that they are harder and thicker shelled: the other is greater, and hath a verye ragged and harde shell: but the kernell great, verie oylie and sweete. Besides their eating of them after our ordinarie maner, they breake them with stones and pound them in morters with water to make a milk which they use to put into some sorts of their spoon-meate; also among their sodde wheat, peaze, beanes and pom-pions which maketh them have a farre more pleasant taste.

Medlars a kinde of verie good fruit, so called by us chieflie for these respectes: first in that they are not good until they be rotten: then in that they are open at the head as our medlars, and are about the same bignesse: otherwise in taste and colour they are farre different: for they are as red as cheries and very sweet: but whereas the cherie is sharpe sweet, they are lushious sweet.

Metaquesúnnauk, a kinde of pleasaunt fruite almost of the shape & bignesse of English peares, but that they are of a per-fect red colour as well within as without. They grow on a plant whose leaves are verie thicke and full of prickles as sharpe as needles. Some that have bin in the Indies, where they have seen that kind of red die of great price, which is called Cochinile, to grow, doe describe his plant right like unto this of *Metaque-súnnauk* but whether it be the true cochinile or a bastard or a wilde kinde, it cannot yet be certified, seeing that also as I heard, Cochinile is not of the fruite but found on the leaves of the plant; which leaves for such matter we have not so specially observed.

Grapes there are of two sorts which I mentioned in the marchantable commodities.

Straberies there are as good & as great as those which we have in our English gardens.

Mulberies, Applecrabs, Hurts or Hurtleberies, such as wee have in England.

Sacquenúmmener a kinde of berries almost like unto capres but somewhat greater which grow together in clusters upon a plant or herbe that is found in shalow waters: being boiled eight or nine houres according to their kind, are very good meat and holesome, otherwise if they be eaten they will make a man for the time franticke or extremely sicke.

There is a kinde of reed which beareth a seed almost like unto our rie or wheat, & being boiled is good meate.

In our travailes in some places wee found wilde peaze like unto ours in England but that they were lesse, which are also good meate.

Of a kinde of fruite or berrie in forme of Acornes.

There is a kind of berrie or acorne, of which there are five sorts that grow on several kinds of trees; the one is called *Sagatémener*, the second *Osámener*, the third *Pummuckóner*. These kinds of acorns they use to drie upon hurdles made of reeds with fire underneath almost after the maner as we dry malt in England. When they are to be used they first water them until they be soft & then being sod they make a good victual, either to eate so simply, or els being also pounded, to make loaves or lumpes of bread. These be also the three kinds of which, I said before, the inhabitants used to make sweet oyle.

Another sort is called *Sapúmmener*, which being boiled or parched doth eate and taste like unto chestnuts. They sometime also make bread of this sort.

The fifth sort is called *Mangúmmenauk*, and is the acorne of their kinde of oake, the which beeing dried after the maner of the first sortes, and afterward watered they boile them, & their servants or sometime the chiefe themselves, either for variety or for want of bread, doe eate them with their fish or flesh.

Of Beastes.

Deare, in some places, there are great store: neere unto the

Sea coast they are of the ordinarie bignes as ours in England, & some lesse: but further up into the countrey where there is better feed they are greater: they differ from ours onely in this, their tailes are longer and the snags of their hornes looke backward.

Conies, Those that we have seen & al that we can heare of are of a grey colour like unto hares: in some places there are such plentie that all the people of some townes make them mantles of the furre or flue of the skinnes of those they usually take.

Saquénuckot & *Maquówoc*; two kinds of small beastes greater then conies which are very good meat. We never tooke any of them our selves but sometime eate of such as the inhabitants had taken & brought unto us.

Squirels, which are of a grey colour, we have taken and eaten. Beares which are all of blacke colour. The beares of this countrey are good meat; the inhabitants in time of winter do use to take & eate manie, so also sometime did wee. They are taken commonlie in this sort. In some Ilands or places where they are, being hunted for, as soone as they have spiall of a man they presently run awaie, & then being chased they clime and get up the next tree they can, from whence with arrowes they are shot downe starke dead, or with those wounds that they may after easily be killed; we sometime shotte them downe with our callevers.

I have the names of eight & twenty severall sortes of beasts which I have heard of to be here and there dispersed in the countrie, especially in the maine: of which there are only twelve kinds that we have yet discovered, & of those that be good meat we know only them before mentioned. The inhabitants sometime kill the Lyon, and eat him: and we somtime as they came to our hands of their Wolves or wolvish Dogges, which I have not set downe for good meat, least that some would understand my judgement therein to be more simple then needeth, although I could alleage the difference in taste of those kindes from ours, which by some of our company have beene experimented in both.

Of Foule.

Turkie cockes and Turkie hennes: Stockdoves: Partridges: Cranes: Hernes: & in Winter great store of Swannes & Geese.

Of al sorts of fowle I have the names in the countrie language of fourescore and sixe of which number besides those that be named, we have taken, eaten, & have the pictures as they were there drawne with the names of the inhabitaunts of severall strange sorts of water foule eight, and seventeene kinds more of land foul, although wee have seene and eaten of many more, which for want of leasure there for the purpose could not bee pictured: and after wee are better furnished and stored upon further discovery, with their strange beastes, fishe, trees, plants, and hearbes, they shalbe also published.

There are also Parats, Faulcons, & Marlin haukes, which although with us they bee not used for meate, yet for other causes I thought good to mention.

Of Fishe.

For foure monethes of the yeere, February, March, Aprill and May, there are plentie of Sturgeons. And also in the same moneths of Herrings, some of the ordinary bignesse as ours in England, but the most part farre greater, of eighteene, twentie inches, and some two foote in length and better; both these kindes of fishe in those monethes are most plentifull, and in best season, which wee found to bee most delicate and pleasaunt meate.

There are also Troutes: Porpoises: Rayes: Oldwives: Mullets: Plaice: and very many other sortes of excellent good fish, which we have taken & eaten, whose names I know not but in the countrey language; we have of twelve sorts more the pictures as they were drawn in the countrey with their names.

The inhabitants use to take them two maner of wayes, the one is by a kinde of wear made of reedes which in that countrey are very strong. The other way, which is more strange, is with poles made sharpe at one ende, by shooting them into the fish after the maner as Irishmen cast dartes; either as they are rowing in their boats or els as they are wading in the shallowes for this purpose.

There are also in many places plentie of these kindes which follow.

Sea crabbes, such as we have in England.

Oysters, some very great, and some small; some rounde and some of a long shape: They are founde both in salt water and brackish, and those that we had out of salt water are far better than the other, as in our owne countrey.

Also Muscles: Scalopes: Periwinkles: and Crevises.

Seékanauk, a kinde of crustie shel fishe which is good meate about a foote in breadth, having a crustie tayle, many legges like a crab; and her eyes in her backe. They are found in shallowes of salt waters, and sometimes on the shoare.

There are many Tortoyses both of lande and sea kinde, their backes & bellies are shelled very thicke; their head, feete, and taile, which are in appearance, seeme ougly as though they were members of a serpent or venemous: but notwithstanding they are very good meate, as also their egges. Some have bene founde of a yard in bredth and better.

And thus have I made relation of all sortes of victuall that we fed upon for the time we were in Virginia, as also the inhabitants themselves, as farre foorth as I knowe and can remember or that are specially worthy to bee remembered.

The third and last part of such other thinges as is behoofull for those which shall plant and inhabit to know of; with a description of the nature and manners of the people of the countrey.

Of commodities for building and other necessary uses.

Those other things which I am more to make rehearsall of, are such as concerne building, and other mechanicall necessarie uses, as divers sortes of trees for house & shiptimber, and other uses els: Also lime, stone, and brick, least that being not mentioned some might have bene doubted of, or by some that are malicious reported the contrary.

Okes, there are as faire, straight, tall, and as good timber as any can be, and also great store, and in some places very great.

Walnut trees, as I have saide before very many, some have bene seen excellent faire timber of foure & five fadome, & above fourescore foote streight without bough.

Firre trees fit for masts of ships, some very tall & great.

Rakiock, a kinde of trees so called that are sweet wood of which the inhabitants that were neere unto us doe commonly make their boats or Canoes of the forme of trowes; onely with the helpe of fire, hatchets of stones, and shels; we have knowen some so great being made in that sort of one tree that they have carried well xx. men at once, besides much baggage: the timber being great, tal, streight, soft, light, & yet tough enough I thinke (besides other uses) to be fit also for masts of ships.

Cedar, a sweete wood good for seelings, Chests, Boxes, Bedsteeds, Lutes, Virginals, and many things els, as I have also said before. Some of our company which have wandered in some places where I have not bene, have made certaine affirmation of Cyprus which for such and other excellent uses is also a wood of price and no small estimation.

Maple, and also Wich-hazle, whereof the inhabitants use to make their bowes.

Holly a necessary thing for the making of birdlime.

Willowes good for the making of weares and weeles to take fish after the English manner, although the inhabitants use onely reedes, which because they are so strong as also flexible, doe serve for that turne very well and sufficiently.

Beech and Ashe, good for caske, hoopes: and if neede require, plowe work, as also for many things els.

Elme.

Sassafras trees.

Ascopo a kinde of tree very like unto Lawrell, the barke is hoat in taste and spicie, it is very like to that tree which Monardus describeth to be Cassia Lignea of the West Indies.

There are many other strange trees whose names I know not but in the Virginian language, of which I am not nowe able, neither is it so convenient for the present to trouble you with particular relation: seeing that for timber and other necessary uses, I have named sufficient. And of many of the rest but that they may be applied to good use, I know no cause to doubt.

Now for Stone, Bricke and Lime, thus it is. Neere unto the Sea coast where wee dwelt, there are no kinde of stones to bee found (except a fewe small pebbles about foure miles off) but such as have bene brought from farther out of the maine. In some of our voiages wee have seene divers hard raggie stones, great pebbles, and a kinde of gray stone like unto marble, of which the inhabitants make their hatchets to cleeve wood. Upon inquirie wee heard that a little further up into the Countrey were of all sortes verie many, although of Quarries they are ignorant, neither have they use of any store whereupon they should have occasion to seeke any. For if everie housholde have one or two to cracke Nuttes, grinde shelles, whet copper, and sometimes other stones for hatchets, they have enough: neither use they any digging, but onely for graves about three foote deepe: and therefore no marvalle that they know neither Quarries, nor lime stones, which both may bee in places neerer then they wot of.

In the meane time untill there be discovery of sufficient store in some place or other convenient, the want of you which are and shalbe the planters therein may be as well supplied by Bricke: for the making whereof in divers places of the countrey there is clay both excellent good, and plentie; and also by lime made of Oister shels, and of others burnt, after the maner as they use in the Iles of Tenet and Shepy, and also in divers other places of England: Which kinde of lime is well knowne to bee as good as any other. And of Oister shels there is plentie enough: for besides divers other particular places where are abundance, there is one shallowe sounde along the coast, where for the space of many miles together in length, and two or three miles in breadth, the grounde is nothing els beeing but halfe a foote or a foote under water for the most part.

Thus much can I say furthermore of stones, that about 120. miles from our fort neere the water in the side of a hill was found by a Gentleman of our company, a great veine of hard ragge stones, which I thought good to remember unto you.

Of the nature and manners of the people.

It resteth I speake a word or two of the naturall inhabitants, their natures and maners, leaving large discourse thereof until time more convenient hereafter: nowe onely so farre foorth, as that you may know, how that they in respect of troubling our inhabiting and planting, are not to be feared, but that they shall have cause both to feare and love us, that shall inhabite with them.

They are a people clothed with loose mantles made of Deere skins, & aprons of the same rounde about their middles; all els naked; of such a difference of statures onely as wee in England, having no edge tooles or weapons of yron or steele to offend us withall, neither knowe they how to make any: those weapons y^t they have, are onlie bowes made of Witch hazle, &

arrowes of reeds, flat edged truncheons also of wood about a yard long, neither have they any thing to defend themselves but targets made of barks, and some armours made of stickes wickered together with thread.

Their townes are but small, & neere the sea coast but fewe, some containing but 10. or 12. houses: some 20. the greatest that we have seene have bene but of 30. houses: if they be walled it is only done with barks of trees made fast to stakes, or els with poles onely fixed upright and close one by another.

Their houses are made of small poles made fast at the tops in rounde forme after the maner as is used in many arbories in our gardens of England, in most townes covered with barkes, and in some with artificiall mattes made of long rushes, from the tops of the houses downe to the ground. The length of them is commonly double to the breadth, in some places they are but 12. and 16. yardes long, and in other some we have seene of foure and twentie.

In some places of the countrey one onely towne belongeth to the government of a *Wiróans* or chiefe Lorde; in other some two or three, in some sixe, eight, & more; the greatest *Wiróans* that yet we had dealing with had but eighteene townes in his government, and able to make not above seven or eight hundred fighting men at the most. The language of every government is different from any other, and the further they are distant the greater is the difference.

Their maner of warres amongst themselves is either by sudden surprising one an other most commonly about the dawning of the day, or moone light, or els by ambushes, or some suttle devises. Set battles are very rare, except it fall out where there are many trees, where eyther part may have some hope of defence, after the deliverie of every arrow, in leaping behind some or other.

If there fall out any warres betweene us & them, what their fight is likely to bee, we having advantages against them so many maner of waies, as by our discipline, our strange weapons and devises else, especially by ordinance great and small, it may be easily imagined; by the experience we have had in some places, the turning up of their heeles against us in running away was their best defence. In respect of us they are a people poore, and for want of skill and judgement in the knowledge and use of our things, doe esteeme our trifles before thinges of greater value: Notwithstanding in their proper manner considering the want of such meanes as we have, they seeme very ingenious; For although they have no such tooles, nor any such craftes, sciences and artes as wee; yet in those things they doe, they shewe excellencie of wit. And by howe much they upon due consideration shall finde our manner of knowledges and craftes to exceede theirs in perfection, and speed for doing or execution, by so much the more is it probable that they shoulde desire our friendships & love, and have the greater respect for pleasing and obeying us. Whereby may bee hoped if meanes of good government bee used, that they may in short time be brought to civilitie, and the imbracing of true religion.

Some religion they have alreadie, which although it be farre from the truth, yet beyng as it is, there is hope it may bee the easier and sooner reformed.

They beleeve that there are many Gods which they call *Montóac*, but of different sortes and degrees; one onely chiefe and great God, which hath bene from all eternitie. Who as they affirme when hee purposed to make the worlde, made first other goddes of a principall order to bee as meanes and instruments to be used in the creation and government to follow; and after the Sunne, Moone, and Starres as pettie gods, and the instruments of the other order more principall. First they say were made waters, out of which by the gods was made all diversitie of creatures that are visible or invisible.

For mankinde they say a woman was made first, which by the working of one of the goddes, conceived and brought foorth children: And in such sort they say they had their beginning. But how many yeeres or ages have passed since, they say they can make no relation, having no letters nor other such meanes as we to keepe recordes of the particularities of times past, but onely tradition from father to sonne.

They thinke that all the gods are of humane shape, & therefore they represent them by images in the formes of men, which they call *Kewasówak* one alone is called *Kewás*; them they place in houses appropriate or temples, which they call *Machicómuck*; Where they worship, praie, sing, and make manie times offerings unto them. In some *Machicómuck*; we have seene but one *Kewás*, in some two, and in other some three; The common sort thinke them to be also gods.

They beleeve also the immortalitie of the soule, that after this life as soone as the soule is departed from the bodie, according to the workes it hath done, it is eyther carried to heaven the habitacle of gods, there to enjoy perpetuall blisse and happinesse, or els to a great pitte or hole, which they thinke to bee in the furthest partes of their part of the worlde toward the sunne set, there to burne continually: the place they call *Popogusso*.

For the confirmation of this opinion, they tolde mee two stories of two men that had been lately dead and revived againe, the one happened but few yeres before our comming into the countrey of a wicked man which having beene dead and buried, the next day the earth of the grave being seene to move, was taken up againe; Who made declaration where his soule had beene, that is to saie, very neere entring into *Popogusso*, had not one of the gods saved him and gave him leave to returne againe, and teach his friends what they should doe to avoid that terrible place or torment.

The other happened in the same yeere wee were there, but in a towne that was three score miles from us, and it was tolde mee for straunge newes that one beeing dead, buried and taken up againe as the first, shewed that although his bodie had lien dead in the grave, yet his soule was alive, & had travailed farre in a long broade waie, on both sides whereof grewe most delicate and pleasaunt trees, bearing more rare and excellent fruites, then ever hee had seene before or was able to expresse, and at length came to most brave and faire houses, neere which hee met his father, that had beene dead before, who gave him great charge to goe backe againe and shew his friendes what good they were to doe to enjoy the pleasures of that place, which when he had done he should after come againe.

What subtilty soever be in the *Wiroances* and Priestes, this opinion worketh so much in manie of the common and simple sort of people that it maketh them have great respect to their Governours, and also great care what they do, to avoid torment after death, and to enjoy blisse; although notwithstanding there is punishment ordained for malefactours, as stealers, whoremoongers, and other sortes of wicked doers; some punished with death, some with forfeitures, some with beating, according to the greatnes of the factes.

And this is the summe of their religion, which I learned by having special familiarity with some of their priestes. Wherein they were not so sure grounded, nor gave such credite to their traditions and stories, but through conversing with us they were brought into great doubts of their owne, and no small admiration of ours, with earnest desire in many, to learne more then we had means for want of perfect utterance in their language to expresse.

Most things they sawe with us, as Mathematicall instruments, sea compasses, the vertue of the loadstone in drawing yron, a perspective glasse whereby was shewed manie strange sightes, burning glasses, wildefire woorkes, gunnes, bookes, writing and reading, spring clocks that seeme to goe of themselves, and manie other thinges that wee had, were so straunge unto them, and so farre exceeded their capacities to comprehend the reason and meanes how they should be made and done, that they thought they were rather the works of gods then of men, or at the leastwise they had bin given and taught us of the gods. Which made manie of them to have such opinion of us, as that if they knew not the trueth of god and religion already, it was rather to be had from us, whom God so specially loved then from a people that were so simple, as they found themselves to be in comparison of us. Whereupon greater credite was given unto that we spake of concerning such matters.

Manie times and in every towne where I came, according as I was able, I made declaration of the contentes of the Bible; that therein was set foorth the true and onelie GOD, and his mightie woorkes, that therein was contayned the true doctrine of salvation through Christ, with manie particularities of Miracles and chiefe poyntes of religion, as I was able then to utter, and thought fitte for the time. And although I told them the booke materially & of it self was not of anie such vertue, as I thought they did conceive, but onely the doctrine therein contained; yet would many be glad to touch it, to embrace it, to kisse it, to hold it to their brests and heades, and stroke over all their bodie with it; to shew their hungrie desire of that knowledge which was spoken of.

The *Wiroans* with whom we dwelt called Wingina, and many

of his people would be glad many times to be with us at our praiers, and many times call upon us both in his owne towne, as also in others whither he sometimes accompanied us, to pray and sing Psalmes; hoping thereby to bee partaker of the same effectes which wee by that meanes also expected.

Twise this *Wiroans* was so grievously sicke that he was like to die, and as hee lay languishing, doubting of anie helpe by his owne priestes, and thinking he was in such daunger for offending us and thereby our god, sent for some of us to praie and bee a meanes to our God that it would please him either that he might live, or after death dwell with him in blisse, so likewise were the requestes of manie others in the like case.

On a time also when their corne began to wither by reason of a drougth which happened extraordinarily, fearing that it had come to passe by reason that in some thing they had displeased us, many would come to us & desire us to pray to our God of England, that he would preserve their corne, promising that when it was ripe we also should be partakers of the fruite.

There could at no time happen any strange sicknesse, losses, hurtes, or any other crosse unto them, but that they would impute to us the cause or meanes therof for offending or not pleasing us.

One other rare and strange accident, leaving others, will I mention before I ende, which moved the whole countrey that either knew or hearde of us, to have us in wonderfull admiration.

There was no towne where wee had any subtile devise practised against us, we leaving it unpunished or not revenged (because we sought by all meanes possible to win them by gentlenesse) but that within a few dayes after our departure from everie such towne, the people began to die very fast, and many in short space; in some townes about twentie, in some fourtie, in some sixtie, & in one six score, which in trueth was very manie in respect to their numbers. This happened in no place that wee coulde learne but where we had bene where they used some practise against us, and after such time; The disease also was so strange, that they neither knew what it was, nor how to cure it; the like by report of the oldest men in the countrey never happened before, time out of minde. A thing specially observed by us, as also by the naturall inhabitants themselves.

Insomuch that when some of the inhabitantes which were our friends & especially the *Wiroans* Wingina had observed such effects in foure or five towns to follow their wicked practises, they were perswaded that it was the worke of our God through our meanes, and that wee by him might kil and slaie whom wee would without weapons and not come neere them.

And thereupon when it had happened that they had understanding that any of their enemies had abused us in our journeyes, hearing that wee had wrought no revenge with our weapons, & fearing upon some cause the matter should so rest: did come and intreate us that we woulde bee a meanes to our God that they as others that had dealt ill with us might in like sort die; alleaging how much it would be for our credite and profite, as also theirs; and hoping furthermore that we would do so much at their requests in respect of the friendship we professe them.

Whose entreaties although wee shewed that they were ungodlie, affirming that our God would not subject himself to any such praiers and requests of men: that in deede all thinges have beene and were to be done according to his good pleasure as he had ordained: and that we to shew our selves his true servants ought rather to make petition for the contrarie, that they with them might live together with us, bee made partakers of his trueth & serve him in righteousnes; but notwithstanding in such sort, that wee referre that as all other things, to bee done according to his divine will & pleasure, and as by his wisedome he had ordained to be best.

Yet because the effect fell out so suddenly and shortly after according to their desires, they thought neverthelesse it came to passe by our meanes, and that we in using such speeches unto them did but dissemble the matter, and therefore came unto us to give us thankes in their manner that although wee satisfied them not in promise, yet in deedes and effect we had fulfilled their desires.

This marvelous accident in all the countrie wrought so strange opinions of us, that some people could not tel whether to thinke us gods or men, and the rather because that all the space of their sicknesse, there was no man of ours knowne to die, or that was specially sicke: they noted also that we had no women amongst us, neither that we did care for any of theirs.

Some therefore were of opinion that wee were not borne of women, and therefore not mortall, but that wee were men of an old generation many yeeres past then risen againe to immortalitie.

Some woulde likewise seeme to prophesie that there were more of our generation yet to come, to kill theirs and take their places, as some thought the purpose was by that which was already done.

Those that were immediately to come after us they imagined to be in the aire, yet invisible & without bodies, & that they by our intreaty & for the love of us did make the people to die in that sort as they did by shooting invisible bullets into them.

To confirme this opinion, their phisitions to excuse their ignorance in curing the disease, would not be ashamed to say, but earnestly make the simple people beleeve, that the strings of blood that they sucked out of the sicke bodies, were the strings wherewithall the invisible bullets were tied and cast.

Some also thought that we shot them our selves out of our pieces from the place where we dwelt, and killed the people in any such towne that had offended us as we listed, howe farre distant from us soever it were.

And other some saide that it was the speciall woorke of God for our sakes, as wee our selves have cause in some sorte to thinke no lesse, whatsoever some doe or may imagine to the contrarie, specially some Astrologers knowing of the Eclipse of the Sunne which wee saw the same yeere before in our voyage thytherward, which unto them appeared very terrible. And also of a Comet which beganne to appeare but a fewe daies before the beginning of the said sicknesse. But to conclude them from being the speciall causes of so speciall an accident, there are farther reasons then I thinke fit at this present to be alleadged.

These their opinions I have set downe the more at large, that it may appeare unto you that there is good hope they may be brought through discreet dealing and governement to the imbracing of the trueth, and consequently to honour, obey, feare and love us.

And although some of our companie towardes the ende of the yeare, shewed themselves too fierce, in slaying some of the people, in some towns, upon causes that on our part, might easily enough have bene borne withall: yet notwithstanding because it was on their part justly deserved, the alteration of their opinions generally & for the most part concerning us is the lesse to bee doubted. And whatsoever els they may be, by carefulnesse of our selves neede nothing at all to be feared.

The best neverthelesse in this in all actions besides is to be endeavoured and hoped, & of the worst that may happen notice to bee taken with consideration, and as much as may be eschewed.

The conclusion.

Now I have as I hope made relation not of so fewe and smal things but that the countrey of men that are indifferent & wel disposed maie be sufficiently liked: If there were no more knowen then I have mentioned, which doubtlesse and in great reason is nothing to that which remaineth to bee discovered, neither the soile, nor commodities. As we have reason so to gather by the difference we found in our travails; for although all which I have before spoken of, have bene discovered & experimented not far from the sea coast where was our abode & most of our travailing: yet sometimes as we made our journeies farther into the maine and countrey; we found the soyle to bee fatter; the trees greater and to growe thinner; the grounde more firme and deeper mould; more and larger champions; finer grasse and as good as ever we saw any in England; in some places rockie and farre more high and hillie ground; more plentie of their fruites; more abundance of beastes; the more inhabited with people, and of greater pollicie & larger dominions, with greater townes and houses.

Why may wee not then looke for in good hope from the inner parts of more and greater plentie, as well of other things, as of those which wee have already discovered? Unto the Spaniardes happened the like in discovering the maine of the West Indies. The maine also of this countrey of Virginia, extending some wayes so many hundreds of leagues, as otherwise then by the relation of the inhabitants wee have most certaine knowledge of, where yet no Christian Prince hath any possession or dealing, cannot but yeeld many kinds of excellent commodities, which we in our discoverie have not yet seene.

What hope there is els to be gathered of the nature of the climate, being answerable to the Iland of Japan, the land of China, Persia, Jury, the Ilandes of Cyprus and Candy, the South parts of Greece, Italy, and Spaine, and of many other notable and famous countreis, because I meane not to be tedious, I leave to your owne consideration.

Whereby also the excellent temperature of the ayre there at all seasons, much warmer then in England, and never so violently hot, as sometimes is under & between the Tropikes, or nere them; cannot bee unknowne unto you without further relation.

For the holsomnesse thereof I neede to say but this much: that for all the want of provision, as first of English victuall, excepting for twentie daies, wee lived onely by drinking water and by the victuall of the countrey, of which some sorts were very straunge unto us, and might have bene thought to have altered our temperatures in such sort, as to have brought us into some greevous and dangerous diseases: Secondly the want of English meanes for the taking of beastes, fishe, and foule, which by the helpe only of the inhabitants and their meanes, could not bee so suddenly and easily provided for us, nor in so great number & quantities, nor of that choise as otherwise might have bene to our better satisfaction and contentment. Some want also wee had of clothes. Furthermore, in all our travailes, which were most speciall and often in the time of winter, our lodging was in the open aire upon the grounde. And yet I say for all this, there were but foure of our whole company (being one hundreth and eight) that died all the yeere and that but at the latter ende thereof and upon none of the aforesaide causes. For all foure especially three were feeble, weake, and sickly persons before ever they came thither, and those that knew them much marveyled that they lived so long beeing in that case, or had adventured to travaile.

Seeing therefore the ayre there is so temperate and holsome, the soyle so fertile, and yeelding such commodities as I have before mentioned, the voyage also thither to and fro being sufficiently experimented, to bee perfourmed thrice a yeere with ease and at any season thereof: And the dealing of Sir Water

Raleigh so liberall in large giving and graunting lande there, as is alreadie knowen, with many helpes and furtherances els: (The least that hee hath graunted hath beene five hundred acres to a man onely for the adventure of his person) I hope there remaine no cause whereby the action should be misliked.

If that those which shall thither travaile to inhabite and plant bee but reasonably provided for the first yere, as those are which were transported the last, and beeing there doe use but that diligence and care as is requisit, and as they may with ease: There is no doubt but for the time following they may have victuals that is excellent good and plentie enough; some more Englishe sortes of cattaile also hereafter, as some have bene before, and are there yet remayning, may and shall bee God willing thither transported: So likewise our kinde of fruites, rootes, and hearbes, may bee there planted and sowed, as some have bene alreadie, and prove wel: And in short time also they may raise of these sortes of commodities which I have spoken of as shall both enrich them selves, as also others that shall deale with them.

And this is all the fruites of our labours, that I have thought necessary to advertise you of at this present: what els concerneth the nature and manners of the inhabitants of Virginia: The number with the particularities of the voyages thither made; and of the actions of such as have bene by Sir Water Raleigh therein and there imployed, many worthy to bee remembred; as of the first discoverers of the Countrey: of our Generall for the time Sir Richard Greinvile; and after his departure, of our Governour there Master Rafe Lane; with divers other directed and imployed under theyr governement: Of the Captaynes and Masters of the voyages made since for transportation; of the Governour and assistants of those alreadie transported, as of many persons, accidents, and thinges els, I have ready in a discourse by it self in maner of a Chronicle according to the course of times and when time shall bee thought convenient shall be also published.

Thus referring my relation to your favourable constructions, expecting good successe of the action, from him which is to be acknowledged the authur and governour not onely of this but of all things els, I take my leave of you, this moneth of February. 1588.

JOHN WHITE

Narrative of the 1590 Voyage

THE fift voyage of Master John White into the West Indies and parts of America called Virginia, in the yeere 1590.

The 20 of March the three shippes the Hopewell, the John Evangelist, and the Little John, put to Sea from Plymmouth with two small Shallops.

The 25 at midnight both our Shallops were sunke being towed at the ships stearnes by the Boatswaines negligence.

On the 30 we saw a head us that part of the coast of Barbary, lying East of Cape Cantyn, and the Bay of Asaphi.

The next day we came to the Ile of Mogador, where rode, at our passing by, a Pinnesse of London called the Mooneshine.

Aprill.

On the first of Aprill we ankored in Santa Cruz rode, where we found two great shippes of London lading in Sugar, of whom we had 2 shipboats to supply the losse of our Shallops.

On the 2 we set sayle from the rode of Santa Cruz, for the Canaries.

On Saturday the 4 we saw Alegranza, the East Ile of the Canaries.

On Sunday the 5 of Aprill we gave chase to a double flyboat, the which, we also the same day fought with, and tooke her, with losse of three of their men slaine, and one hurt.

On Munday the 6 we saw Grand Canarie, and the next day we landed and tooke in fresh water on the Southside thereof.

On the 9 we departed from Grand Canary, and framed our course for Dominica.

The last of Aprill we saw Dominica, and the same night we came to an anker on the Southside thereof.

May.

The first of May in the morning many of the Salvages came

aboord our ships in their Canowes, and did traffique with us; we also the same day landed and entered their Towne from whence we returned the same day aboord without any resistance of the Salvages; or any offence done to them.

The 2 of May our Admirall and our Pinnesse departed from Dominica leaving the John our Vice admirall playing off and on about Dominica, hoping to take some Spaniard outwardes bound to the Indies; the same night we had sight of three smal Ilands called Los Santos, leaving Guadalupe and them on our starboord.

The 3 we had sight of S. Christophers Iland, bearing Northeast and by East off us.

On the 4 we sayled by the Virgines, which are many broken Ilands, lying at the East ende of S. Johns Iland; and the same day towards evening we landed upon one of them called Blanca, where we killed an incredible number of foules: here we stayed but three houres, & from thence stood into the shore Northwest, and having brought this Iland Southeast off us, we put towards night thorow an opening or swatch, called The passage, lying betwene the Virgines, and the East end of S. John: here the Pinnesse left us and sayled on the South side of S. John.

The 5 and 6 the Admirall sayled along the Northside of S. John, so neere the shore that the Spaniards discerned us to be men of warre; and therefore made fires along the coast as we sailed by, for so their custome is, when they see any men of warre on their coasts.

The 7 we landed on the Northwest end of S. John, where we watered in a good river called Yaguana, and the same night following we tooke a Frigate of tenne Tunne comming from Gwathanelo laden with hides and ginger. In this place Pedro a Mollato, who knewe all our state, ranne from us to the Spaniards.

On the 9 we departed from Yaguana.

The 13 we landed on an Iland called Mona, whereon were 10 or 12 houses inhabited of the Spaniards; these we burned & tooke from them a Pinnesse, which they had drawen a ground and sunke, and carried all her sayles, mastes, and rudders into the woods, because we should not take him away; we also chased the Spaniards over all the Iland; but they hid them in caves, hollow rockes, and bushes, so that we could not find them.

On the 14 we departed from Mona, and the next day after wee came to an Iland called Saona, about 5 leagues distant from Mona, lying on the Southside of Hispaniola neere the East end: betweene these two Ilands we lay off and on 4 or 5 dayes, hoping to take some of the Domingo fleete doubling this Iland, as a neerer way to Spaine then by Cape Tyburon, or by Cape S. Anthony.

On Thursday being the 19 our Viceadmirall, from whom we departed at Dominica, came to us at Saona, with whom we left a Spanish Frigate, and appointed him to lie off and on other five daies betweene Saona and Mona to the ende aforesaid; then we departed from them at Saona for Cape Tyburon. Here I was enformed that our men of the Viceadmirall, at their departure from Dominica brought away two young Salvages, which were the chiefe Casiques sonnes of that Countrey and part of Dominica, but they shortly after ran away from them at Santa Cruz Iland, where the Viceadmirall landed to take in ballast.

On the 21 the Admirall came to the Cape Tyburon, where we found the John Evangelist our Pinnesse staying for us: here we tooke in two Spaniards almost starved on the shore, who made a fire to our ships as we passed by. Those places for an 100 miles in length are nothing els but a desolate and meere wildernesse, without any habitation of people, and full of wilde Bulles and Bores, and great Serpents.

The 22 our Pinnesse came also to an anker in Aligato Bay at cape Tyburon. Here we understood of Master Lane, Captaine of the Pinnesse; how he was set upon with one of the kings Gallies belonging to Santo Domingo, which was manned with 400 men, who after he had fought with him 3 or 4 houres, gave over the fight & forsooke him, without any great hurt done in eyther part.

Master William Lane.

The 26 the John our Vizadmirall came to us to cape Tyburon, and the Frigat which we left with him at Saona. This was the appointed place where we should attend for the meeting with the Santo Domingo Fleete.

On Whitsunday Even at Cape Tyburon one of our boyes ranne away from us, and at ten dayes end returned to our ships almost starved for want of food. In sundry places about this part of Cape Tyburon we found the bones and carkases of divers men, who had persished (as wee thought) by famine in those woods, being either stragled from their company, or landed there by some men of warre.

June.

On the 14 of June we tooke a smal Spanish frigat which fell amongst us so suddenly, as he doubled the point at the Bay of Cape Tyburon, where we road, so that he could not escape us. This Frigat came from Santo Domingo, and had but 3 men in her, the one was an expert Pilot, the other a Mountainer, and the third a Vintener, who escaped all out of prison at Santo Domingo, purposing to fly to Yaguana which is a towne in the West parts of Hispaniola where many fugitive Spaniards are gathered together.

Spanish fugitives.

The 17 being Wednesday Captaine Lane was sent to Yaguana with his Pinnesse and a Frigat to take a shippe, which was there taking in fraight, as we understood by the old Pylot, whom we had taken three dayes before.

The 24 the Frigat returned from Captaine Lane at Yaguana, and brought us word to cape Tyburon, that Captaine Lane had taken the shippe, with many passengers and Negroes in the same; which proved not so rich a prize as we hoped for, for that a Frenchman of warre had taken and spoyled her before we came. Neverthelesse her loading was thought worth 1000 or 1300 pounds, being hides, ginger, Cannafistula, Copper-pannes, and Cassavi.

July.

Edward Spicer.

The second of July Edward Spicer whom we left in England came to us at Cape Tyburon, accompanied with a small Pinnesse, whereof one Master Harps was Captaine. And the same day we had sight of a fleete of 14 saile all of Santo Domingo, to whom we presently gave chase, but they upon the first sight of us fled, and separating themselves scattered here and there: Wherefore we were forced to divide our selves and so made after them untill 12 of the clocke at night. But then by reason of the darkenesse we lost sight of ech other, yet in the end the Admirall and the Moonelight happened to be together the same night at the fetching up of the Vizadmirall of the Spanish fleete, against whom the next morning we fought and tooke him, with losse of one of our men and two hurt, and of theirs 4 slaine and 6 hurt. But what was become of our Viceadmirall, our Pinnesse, and Prize, and two Frigates, in all this time, we were ignorant.

The 3 of July we spent about rifling, romaging and fitting the Prize to be sailed with us.

The 6 of July we saw Jamayca the which we left on our larboord, keeping Cuba in sight on our starboord.

Upon the 8 of July we saw the Iland of Pinos, which lieth on the Southside of Cuba nigh unto the West end or Cape called Cape S. Anthony. And the same day we gave chase to a Frigat, but at night we lost sight of her, partly by the slow sayling of our Admirall, & lacke of the Moonelight our Pinnesse, whom Captaine Cooke had sent to the Cape the day before.

On the 11 we came to Cape S. Anthony, where we found our consort the Moonelight and her Pinnesse abiding for our comming, of whom we understood that the day before there passed by them 22 saile, some of them of the burden of 300 and some 400 tunnes loaden with the Kings treasure from the maine, bound for Havana; from this 11 of July untill 22 we were much becalmed: and the winde being scarse, and the weather exceeding hoat, we were much pestered with the Spaniards we had taken: wherefore we were driven to land all the Spaniards saving three, but the place where we landed them was of their owne choise on the Southside of Cuba neere unto the Organes and Rio de Puercos.

The 23 we had sight of the Cape of Florida, and the broken Ilands therof called the Martires.

The 25 being S. James day in the morning, we fell with the Matanças, a head-land 8 leagues towards the East of Havana, where we purposed to take fresh water in, and make our abode two or three dayes.

On Sunday the 26 of July plying too and fro betweene the Matanças and Havana, we were espied of three small Pinnasses of S. John de Ullua bound for Havana, which were exceeding richly loaden. These 3 Pinnasses came very boldly up unto us, and so continued untill they came within musket shot of us. And we supposed them to be Captaine Harps pinnesse, and two small Frigats taken by Captaine Harpe: wherefore we shewed our flag. But they presently upon the sight of it turned about & made all the saile they could from us toward the shore, & kept themselves in so shallow water, that we were not able to follow them, and therefore gave them over with expence of shot & pouder to no purpose. But if we had not so rashly set out our flagge, wee might have taken them all three, for they would not have knowen us before they had bene in our hands. This chase brought us so far to leeward as Havana: wherefore not finding any of our consorts at the Matanças, we put over again to the cape of Florida, & from thence thorow the chanel of Bahama.

On the 28 the Cape of Florida bare West off us.

The 30 we lost sight of the coast of Florida, and stood to Sea for to gaine the helpe of the current which runneth much swifter a farre off then in sight of the coast. For from the Cape to Virginia all along the shore are none but eddie currents, setting to the South and Southwest.

The state of the currents from the cape of Florida to Virginia.

The 31 our three ships were clearely disbocked, the great prize, the Admirall, and the Mooneshine, but our prize being thus disbocked departed from us without taking leave of our Admirall or consort, and sayled directly for England.

August.

On the first of August the winde scanted, and from thence forward we had very fowle weather with much raine, thundering, and great spouts, which fell round about us nigh unto our ships.

The 3 we stoode againe in for the shore, and at midday we tooke the height of the same. The height of that place we found to be 34 degrees of latitude. Towards night we were within three leagues of the Low sandie Ilands West of Wokokon. But the weather continued so exceeding foule, that we could not come to an anker nye the coast: wherefore we stood off againe to Sea untill Monday the 9 of August.

Sandie Ilands West of Wokokon.

On munday the storme ceased, and we had very great likelihood of faire weather: therefore we stood in againe for the shore: & came to an anker at 11 fadome in 35 degrees of latitude, within a mile of the shore, where we went on land on the narrow sandy Iland, being one

They land in 35 degrees.

of the Ilandes West of Wokokon: in this Iland we tooke in some fresh water and caught great store of fish in the shallow water. Betweene the maine (as we supposed) and that Iland it was but a mile over and three or foure foote deepe in most places.

On the 12 in the morning we departed from thence and toward night we came to an anker at the Northeast end of the Iland of Croatoan, by reason of a breach which we perceived to lie out two or three leagues into the Sea: here we road all that night.

A breach 2 or 3 leagues into Sea.

The 13 in the morning before we wayed our ankers, our boates were sent to sound over this breach; our ships riding on the side thereof at 5 fadome; and a ships length from us we found but 4 and a quarter, and then deeping and shallowing for the space of two miles, so that sometimes we found 5 fadome, and by & by 7, and within two casts with the lead 9, & then 8, next cast 5, & then 6, & then 4, & then 9 againe, and deeper; but 3 fadome was the least, 2 leagues off from the shore. This breach is in 35 degr. & a halfe, & lyeth at the very Northeast point of Croatoan, wheras goeth a fret out of the maine Sea into the inner waters, which part the Ilandes and the maine land.

Great diversity of soundings.

The 15 of August towards Evening we came to an anker at Hatorask, in 36 degr. and one third, in five fadom water, three leagues from the shore. At our first comming to anker on this shore we saw a great smoke rise in the Ile Raonoak neere the place where I left our Colony in the yeere 1587, which smoake put us in good hope that some of the Colony were there expecting my returne out of England.

Hatorask in 36 degr. & a terce.

The 16 and next morning our 2 boates went a shore, & Captaine Cooke, & Captain Spicer, & their company with me, with intent to passe to the place at Roanoak where our countreymen were left. At our putting from the ship we commanded our Master gunner to make readie 2 Minions and a Falkon well loden, and to shoot them off with reasonable space betweene every shot, to the ende that their reportes might bee heard to the place where wee hoped to finde some of our people. This was accordingly performed, & our twoe boats put off unto the shore, in the Admirals boat we sounded all the way and found from our shippe untill we came within a mile of the shore nine, eight, and seven fadome: but before we were halfe way betweene our ships and the shore we saw another great smoke to the Southwest of Kindrikers mountes: we therefore thought good to goe to that second smoke first: but it was much further from the harbour where we landed, then we supposed it to be, so that we were very sore tired before wee came to the smoke. But that which grieved us more was that when we came to the smoke, we found no man or signe that any had bene there lately, nor yet any fresh water in all this way to drinke. Being thus wearied with this journey we returned to the harbour where we left our boates, who in our absence had brought their caske a shore for fresh water, so we deferred our going to Roanoak untill the next morning, and caused some of those saylers to digge in those sandie hilles for fresh water whereof we found very sufficient. That night wee returned aboord with our boates and our whole company in safety.

They land.

Fresh water found in sandy hilles.

The next morning being the 17 of August, our boates and company were prepared againe to goe up to Roanoak, but Captaine Spicer had then sent his boat ashore for fresh water, by meanes whereof it was ten of the clocke aforenoone before we put from our ships which were then come to an anker within two miles of the shore. The Admirals boat was halfe way toward the shore, when Captaine Spicer put off from his ship. The Admirals boat first passed the breach, but not without danger of sinking, for we had a sea brake into our boat which filled us halfe full of water, but by the will of God and carefull styrage of Captaine Cooke we came safe ashore, saving onely that our furniture, victuals match and powder were much wet and spoyled. For at this time the winde blue at Northeast and direct into the harbour so great a gale, that the Sea brake extremely on the barre, and the tide went very forcibly at the entrance. By that time our Admirals boate was halled ashore, and most of our things taken out to dry, Captaine Spicer came to the entrance of the breach with his mast standing up, and was halfe passed over, but by the rash and undiscreet styrage of Ralph Skinner his Masters mate, a very dangerous Sea brake into their boate and overset them quite, the men kept the boat some in it, and some hanging on it, but the next sea set the boat on ground, where it beat so, that some of them were forced to let goe their hold, hoping to wade ashore, but the Sea

still beat them downe, so that they could neither stand nor
swimme, and the boat twise or thrise was turned the
keele upward; whereon Captaine Spicer and Skinner
hung untill they sunke, & seene no more. But foure
that could swimme a litle kept themselves in deeper water and
were saved by Captain Cookes meanes, who so soone as he saw
their oversetting, stripped himselfe, and foure other that could
swimme very well, & with all haste possible rowed unto them,
& saved foure. They were a 11 in all, & 7 of the chiefest were
drowned, whose names were Edward Spicer, Ralph Skinner,
Edward Kelley, Thomas Bevis, Hance the Surgion, Edward
Kelborne, Robert Coleman. This mischance did so much dis-
comfort the saylers, that they were all of one mind not to goe
any further to seeke the planters. But in the end by the commandement & perswasion of me and Captaine Cooke, they
prepared the boates: and seeing the Captaine and me so resolute, they seemed much more willing. Our boates and all
things fitted againe, we put off from Hatorask, being the number of 19 persons in both boates: but before we could get to the
place, where our planters were left, it was so exceeding darke,
that we overshot the place a quarter of a mile: there we espied
towards the North end of the Iland the light of a great fire
thorow the woods, to the which we presently rowed: when wee
came right over against it, we let fall our Grapnel neere the
shore, & sounded with a trumpet a Call, & afterwardes many
familiar English tunes of Songs, and called to them friendly;
but we had no answere, we therefore landed at day-breake, and
comming to the fire, we found the grasse & sundry rotten trees
burning about the place. From hence we went thorow the
woods to that part of the Iland directly over against Dasamongwepeuk, & from thence we returned by the water side,
round about the Northpoint of the Iland, untill we came to the
place where I left our Colony in the yeere 1586. In all this way
we saw in the sand the print of the Salvages feet of 2 or 3 sorts
troaden that night, and as we entred up the sandy banke upon a
tree, in the very browe thereof were curiously carved these faire
Romane letters CRO: which letters presently we knew to signifie the place, where I should find the planters seated, according
to a secret token agreed upon betweene them & me at my last
departure from them, which was, that in any wayes they should

Captaine
Spicer
drowned.

not faile to write or carve on the trees or posts of the dores the name of the place where they should be seated; for at my comming away they were prepared to remove from Roanoak 50 miles into the maine. Therefore at my departure from them in Anno 1587 I willed them, that if they should happen to be distressed in any of those places, that then they should carve over the letters or name, a Crosse ✠ in this forme, but we found no such signe of distresse. And having well considered of this, we passed toward the place where they were left in sundry houses, but we found the houses taken downe, and the place very strongly enclosed with a high palisado of great trees, with cortynes and flankers very Fort-like, and one of the chiefe trees or postes at the right side of the entrance had the barke taken off, and 5. foote from the ground in fayre Capitall letters was graven CROATOAN without any crosse or signe of distresse; this done, we entred into the palisado, where we found many barres of Iron, two pigges of Lead, foure yron fowlers, Iron sacker-shotte, and such like heavie things, throwen here and there, almost overgrowen with grasse and weedes. From thence wee went along by the water side, towards the poynt of the Creeke to see if we could find any of their botes or Pinnisse, but we could perceive no signe of them, nor any of the last Falkons and small Ordinance which were left with them, at my departure from them. At our returne from the Creeke, some of our Saylers meeting us, tolde us that they had found where divers chests had bene hidden, and long sithence digged up againe and broken up, and much of the goods in them spoyled and scattered about, but nothing left, of such things as the Savages knew any use of, undefaced. Presently Captaine Cooke and I went to the place, which was in the ende of an olde trench, made two yeeres past by Captaine Amadas: wheere wee found five Chests, that had been carefully hidden of the Planters, and of the same chests three were my owne, and about the place many of my things spoyled and broken, and my bookes torne from the covers, the frames of some of my pictures and Mappes rotten and spoyled with rayne, and my armour almost eaten through with rust; this could bee no other but the deede of the Savages our enemies at Dasamongwepeuk, who had watched the departure of our men to Croatoan; and assoone as they were departed, digged up every place where they suspected any thing to be buried: but although it much grieved me to see such spoyle of my goods, yet on the other side I greatly joyed that I had safely found a certaine token of their safe being at Croatoan, which is the place where Manteo was borne, and the Savages of the Iland our friends.

When we had seene in this place so much as we could, we returned to our Boates, and departed from the shoare towards our Shippes, with as much speede as we could: For the weather beganne to overcast, and very likely that a foule and stormie night would ensue. Therefore the same Evening with much danger and labour, we got our selves aboard, by which time the winde and seas were so greatly risen, that wee doubted our Cables and Anchors would scarcely holde untill Morning; wherefore the Captaine caused the Boate to be manned with five lusty men, who could swimme all well, and sent them to the little Iland on the right hand of the Harbour, to bring aboard sixe of our men, who had filled our caske with fresh water: the Boate the same night returned aboard with our men, but all our Caske ready filled they left behinde, unpossible to bee had aboard without danger of casting away both men and Boates; for this night prooved very stormie and foule.

The next Morning it was agreed by the Captaine and my selfe, with the Master and others, to wey anchor, and goe for the place at Croatoan, where our planters were: for that then the winde was good for that place, and also to leave that Caske with fresh water on shoare in the Iland untill our returne. So then they brought the cable to the Capston, but when the anchor was almost apecke, the Cable broke, by meanes whereof we lost another Anchor, wherewith we drove so fast into the shoare, that wee were forced to let fall a third Anchor; which came so fast home that the Shippe was almost aground by Kenricks mounts: so that wee were forced to let slippe the Cable ende for ende. And if it had not chanced that wee had fallen into a chanell of deeper water, closer by the shoare then wee accompted of, wee could never have gone cleare of the poynt that lyeth to the Southwardes of Kenricks mounts. Being thus cleare of some dangers, and gotten into deeper waters, but not without some losse; for wee had but one Cable and Anchor left us of foure, and the weather grew to be fouler and fouler; our victuals scarse, and our caske and fresh water lost: it

Theire sitting at meate .

23. *Theire sitting at meate*

One of their Religious men

24. *One of their Religious men*

The manner of their fishing

25. *The manner of their fishing*

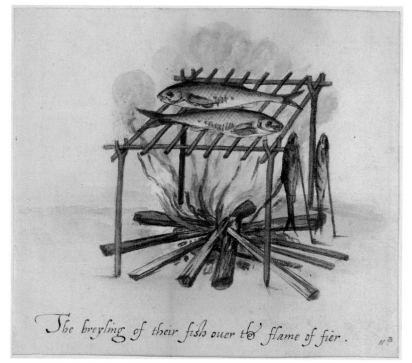

The broyling of their fish ouer the flame of fier.

nᵒ 3

26. *The broyling of their fish over the flame of fier*

A chiefe Herowan

27. *A chiefe Herowan*

The manner of their attire and
painting them selues when
they goe to their generall
huntings, or at theire
Solemne feasts.

28. *The manner of their attire and painting them selves*

The flyer

29. *The flyer*

was therefore determined that we should goe for Saint John or some other Iland to the Southward for fresh water. And it was further purposed, that if wee could any wayes supply our wants of victuals and other necessaries, either at Hispaniola, Sant John, or Trynidad, that then wee should continue in the Indies all the Winter following, with hope to make 2. rich voyages of one, and at our returne to visit our countrymen at Virginia. The captaine and the whole company in the Admirall (with my earnest petitions) thereunto agreed, so that it rested onely to knowe what the Master of the Moonelight our consort would doe herein. But when we demanded them if they would accompany us in that new determination, they alleged that their weake and leake Shippe was not able to continue it; wherefore the same night we parted, leaving the Moone-light to goe directly for England, and the Admirall set his course for Trynidad, which course we kept two dayes.

They leave the coast of Virginia.

On the 28. the winde changed, and it was sette on foule weather every way: but this storme brought the winde West and Northwest, and blewe so forcibly, that wee were able to beare no sayle, but our fore-course halfe mast high, wherewith wee ranne upon the winde perforce, the due course for England, for that wee were dryven to change our first determination for Trynidad, and stoode for the Ilands of Açores, where wee purposed to take in fresh water, and also there hoped to meete with some English men of warre about those Ilands, at whose hands wee might obtaine some supply of our wants. And thus continuing our course for the Açores, sometimes with calmes, and sometimes with very scarce windes, on the fifteenth of September the winde came South Southeast, and blew so exceedingly, that wee were forced to lye atry all that day. At this time by account we judged our selves to be about twentie leagues to the West of Cuervo and Flores, but about night the storme ceased, and fayre weather ensued.

On Thursday the seventeenth wee saw Cuervo and Flores, but we could not come to anker the night, by reason the winde shifted. The next Morning being the eighteenth, standing in againe with Cuervo, we escryed a sayle ahead us, to whom we gave chase: but when wee came neere him, we knew him to be a Spanyard, and hoped to make sure purchase of him; but we understood at our speaking with him, that he was a prize, and of the Domingo fleete already taken by the John our consort, in the Indies. We learned also of this prize, that our Viceadmirall and Pinnisse had fought with the rest of the Domingo fleete, and had forced them with their Admirall to flee unto Jamaica under the Fort for succour, and some of them ran themselves aground, whereof one of them they brought away, and tooke out of some others so much as the time would permit. And further wee understood of them, that in their returne from Jamaica about the Organes neere Cape Saint Anthony, our Viceadmirall mette with two Shippes of the mayne land, come from Mexico, bound for Havana, with whom he fought: in which fight our Viceadmirals Lieutenant was slaine, and the Captaines right arme strooken off, with foure other of his men slaine, and sixteene hurt, But in the ende he entred, and tooke one of the Spanish shippes, which was so sore shot by us under water, that before they could take out her treasure, she sunke; so that we lost thirteen Pipes of silver which sunke with her, besides much other rich marchandize. And in the meane time the other Spanish shippe being pearced with nine shotte under water, got away; whom our Viceadmirall intended to pursue: but some of their men in the toppe made certaine rockes, which they saw above water neere the shoare, to be Gallies of Havana and Cartagena, comming from Havana to rescue the two Ships; Wherefore they gave over their chase, and went for England. After this intelligence was given us by this our prize, he departed from us, and went for England.

On Saturday the 19. of September we came to an Ancre neere a small village on the North side of Flores, where we found ryding 5. English men of warre, of whom wee understood that our Viceadmirall and Prize were gone thence for England. One of these five was the Moonelight our consort, who upon the first sight of our comming into Flores, set sayle and went for England, not taking any leave of us.

On Sunday the 20. the Mary Rose, Admirall of the Queenes fleete, wherein was Generall Sir John Hawkins, stood in with Flores, and divers other of the Queenes ships, namely the Hope, the Nonpareilia, The Rainebow, the Swift-sure, the Foresight, with many other good merchants ships of warre, as the Edward Bonaventure, the Marchant Royal, the Amitie, the

Eagle, the Dainty of sir John Hawkins, and many other good ships and pinnesses, all attending to meete with the king of Spaines fleete, comming from Terra firma of the West Indies.

The 22. of September we went aboard the Raynebow, and towards night we spake with the Swift-sure, and gave him 3. pieces. The captaines desired our company; wherefore we willingly attended on them: who at this time with 10. other ships stood for Fajal. But the Generall with the rest of the Fleete were separated from us, making two fleetes, for the surer meeting with the Spanish fleete.

On Wednesday the 23. we saw Gratiosa, where the Admiral and the rest of the Queens fleete were come together. The Admirall put forth a flag of counsel, in which was determined that the whole fleete should go for the mayne, and spred themselves on the coasts of Spaine and Portugal, so farre as conveniently they might, for the surer meeting of the Spanish fleete in those parts.

The 26. we came to Fajal, where the Admiral with some other of the fleete ankred, othersome plyed up and downe betweene that and the Pico untill midnight, at which time the Antony shot off a piece and weyed, shewing his light: after whom the whole fleete stood to the East, the winde at Northeast by East.

On Sunday the 27. towards Evening wee tooke our leave of the Admirall and the whole fleete, who stood to the East. But our shippe accompanied with a Flyboate stoode in againe with S. George, where we purposed to take in more fresh water, and some other fresh victuals.

On Wednesday the 30. of September, seeing the winde hang so Northerly, that wee could not atteine the Iland of S. George, we gave over our purpose to water there, and the next day framed our due course for England.

October.

The 2. of October in the Morning we saw S. Michaels Iland on our Starre board quarter.

The 23. at 10. of the clocke afore noone, we saw Ushant in Britaigne.

On Saturday the 24. we came in safetie, God be thanked, to an anker at Plymmouth.

GEORGE PERCY

Discourse

OBSERVATIONS gathered out of a Discourse of the Plantation of the Southerne Colonie in Virginia by the English, 1606. Written by that Honorable Gentleman Master George Percy.

On Saturday, the twentieth of December in the yeere 1606 the fleet fell from London, and the fift of January we anchored in the Downes: but the winds continued contrarie so long, that we were forced to stay there some time, where wee suffered great stormes, but by the skilfulnesse of the Captaine wee suffered no great losse or danger.

The twelfth day of February at night we saw a blazing Starre, and presently a storme. The three and twentieth day we fell with the Iland of Mattanenio in the West Indies. The foure and twentieth day we anchored at Dominico, within fourteene degrees of the Line, a very faire Iland, the Trees full of sweet and good smels inhabited by many Savage Indians, they were at first very scrupulous to come aboord us. Wee learned of them afterwards that the Spaniards had given them a great overthrow on this Ile, but when they knew what we were, there came many to our ships with their Canoas, bringing us many kinds of sundry fruites, as Pines, Potatoes, Plantons, Tobacco, and other fruits, and Roane Cloth abundance, which they had gotten out of certaine Spanish ships that were cast away upon that Iland. We gave them Knives, Hatchets for exchange which they esteeme much, wee also gave them Beades, Copper Jewels which they hang through their nosthrils, eares, and lips, very strange to behold, their bodies are all painted red to keepe away the biting of Muscetos, they goe all naked without covering: the haire of their head is a yard long, all of a length pleated in three plats hanging downe to their wastes, they suffer no haire to grow on their faces, they cut

The next day Cap. Smith was suspected for a supposed Mutinie, though never no such matter. Trade at Dominica

their skinnes in divers workes, they are continually in warres, and will eate their enemies when they kill them, or any stranger if they take them. They will lap up mans spittle, whilst one spits in their mouthes in a barbarous fashion like Dogges. These people and the rest of the Ilands in the West Indies, and Brasill, are called by the names of Canibals, that will eate mans flesh, these people doe poyson their Arrow heads, which are made of fishes bone: they worship the Devill for their God, and have no other beliefe. Whilest we remayned at this Iland we saw a Whale chased by a Thresher and a Sword-fish: they fought for the space of two houres, we might see the Thresher with his flayle layon the monstrous blowes which was strange to behold: in the end these two fishes brought the Whale to her end.

Brutish-nesse of the Dominicans

Fight betwixt a Whale, the Thresher and Sword-fish

The sixe and twentieth day, we had sight of Marigalanta, and the next day wee sailed with a slacke saile alongst the Ile of Guadalupa, where we went ashore, and found a Bath which was so hot, that no man was able to stand long by it, our Admirall Captaine Newport caused a piece of Porke to be put in it: which boyled it so in the space of halfe an houre as no fire could mend it. Then we went aboord and sailed by many Ilands, as Mounserot and an Iland called Saint Christopher, both unhabited about; about two a clocke in the afternoone wee anchored at the Ile of Mevis. There the Captaine landed all his men being well fitted with Muskets and other convenient Armes, marched a mile into the Woods; being commanded to stand upon their guard, fearing the treacherie of the Indians, which is an ordinary use amongst them and all other Savages on this Ile, we came to a Bath standing in a Valley betwixt two Hils; where wee bathed our selves and found it to be of the nature of the Bathes in England, some places hot and some colder: and men may refresh themselves as they please, finding this place to be so convenient for our men to avoid diseases, which will breed in so long a Voyage, wee incamped our selves on this Ile sixe dayes, and spent none of our ships victuall, by reason our men some went a hunting, some a fouling, and some a fishing, where we got great store of Conies, sundry kinds of fowles, and great plentie of fish. We kept Centinels and

Margalanta

Guadalupa
Bath very hot

Mevis

Bath at Mevis

Commodities there

Courts de gard at every Captaines quarter, fearing wee should be assaulted by the Indians, that were on the other side of the Iland: wee saw none nor were molested by any: but some few we saw as we were a hunting on the Iland. They would not come to us by any meanes, but ranne swiftly through the Woods to the Mountaine tops; so we lost the sight of them: whereupon we made all the haste wee could to our quarter, thinking there had beene a great ambush of Indians there abouts. We past into the thickest of the Woods where we had almost lost our selves, we had not gone aboue halfe a mile amongst the thicke, but we came into a most pleasant Garden, being a hundred paces square on every side, having many Cotton-trees growing in it with abundance of Cotton-wooll, and many Guiacum trees: wee saw the goodliest tall trees growing so thick about the Garden, as though they had beene set by Art which made us marvell very much to see it.

The third day, wee set saile from Mevis: the fourth

Aprill day we sailed along by Castutia and by Saba: This day we anchored at the Ile of Virgines, in an excellent Bay able to harbour a hundred Ships: if this Bay stood in England, it would be a great profit and commoditie to the Land.

On this Iland wee caught great store of Fresh-fish,

Tortoises and abundance of Sea Tortoises, which served all our Fleet three daies, which were in number eight score persons. We also killed great store of wilde Fowle, wee cut the Barkes of certaine Trees which tasted much like Cinnamon, and very hot in the mouth. This Iland in some places hath very good ground, straight and tall Timber. But the greatest discom-

Mevis water
unwholsome moditie that wee have seene on this Iland is that it hath no Fresh-water, which makes the place void of any Inhabitants.

Upon the sixt day, we set saile and passed by Becam, and by Saint John deportorico. The seventh day, we arrived at Mona: where wee watered, which we stood in great need of, seeing that our water did smell so vildly that none of our men was able to indure it. Whilst some of the Saylers were a filling the Caskes with water, the Captaine, and the rest of the Gentlemen, and the other Soldiers marched up in the Ile six myles, thinking to find some other provision to maintaine our victualling; as wee marched we killed two wild Bores, and saw a huge wild Bull, his hornes was an ell betweene the two tops. Wee also killed Guanas, in fashion of a Serpent, and speckled like a Toade under the belly. These wayes that wee went, being so troublesome and vilde going upon the sharpe Rockes, that many of our men fainted in the march, but by good fortune wee lost none but one Edward Brookes Gentleman, whose fat melted within him by the great heate and drought of the Countrey: we were not able to relieve him nor our selves, so he died in that great extreamitie.

<small>Ed. Brookes faint with thirst</small>

The ninth day in the afternoone, we went off with our Boat to the Ile of Moneta, some three leagues from Mona, where we had a terrible landing, and a troublesome getting up to the top of the Mountaine or Ile, being a high firme Rocke step, with many terrible sharpe stones: After wee got to the top of the Ile, we found it to bee a fertill and a plaine ground, full of goodly grasse, and abundance of Fowles of all kindes, they flew over our heads as thicke as drops of Hale; besides they made such a noise, that wee were not able to heare one another speake. Furthermore, wee were not able to set our feet on the ground, but either on Fowles or Egges which lay so thicke in the grasse: Wee laded two Boats full in the space of three houres, to our great refreshing.

<small>Moneta</small>

<small>Store of fowles</small>

The tenth day we set saile, and disimboged out of the West Indies, and bare our course Northerly. The fourteenth day we passed the Tropicke of Cancer. The one and twentieth day, about five a clocke at night there began a vehement tempest, which lasted all the night, with winds, raine, and thunders in a terrible manner. Wee were forced to lie at Hull that night, because we thought wee had beene nearer land then wee were. The next morning, being the two and twentieth day wee sounded; and the three and twentieth and foure and twenteth day, but we could find no ground. The five and twentieth day we sounded, and had no ground at an hundred fathom.

<small>We were driven to try that night, and by the storme were forced neere the shoare, not knowing where we were</small>

The six and twentieth day of Aprill, about foure a clocke in the morning, wee descried the Land of Virginia: the same day wee entred into the Bay of Chesupioc directly, without any let or hindrance; there wee landed and discovered a little way, but wee could find nothing worth the speaking of, but faire

They land in
Virginia
meddowes and goodly tall Trees, with such Fresh-
waters running through the woods, as I was almost
ravished at the first sight thereof.

At night, when wee were going aboard, there came the Savages creeping upon all foure, from the Hills like Beares, with
their Bowes in their mouthes, charged us very desperately in
the faces, hurt Captaine Gabrill Archer in both his hands, and
a sayler in two places of the body very dangerous. After they
had spent their Arrowes, and felt the sharpnesse of our shot,
they retired into the Woods with a great noise, and so left us.

The seven and twentieth day we began to build up our Shallop: the Gentlemen and Souldiers marched eight miles up into
the Land, we could not see a Savage in all that march, we came
to a place where they had made a great fire, and had beene
newly a rosting Oysters: when they perceived our comming,
they fled away to the Mountaines, and left many of the Oysters
in the fire: we eat some of the Oysters, which were very large
and delicate in taste.

The eighteenth day we lanched our Shallop, the Captaine
and some Gentlemen went in her, and discovered up the Bay,
we found a River on the Southside running into the Maine; we
entered it and found a very shoald water, not for any Boats to
swim: Wee went further into the Bay, and saw a plaine plot of
ground where we went on Land, and found the place five mile
in compasse, without either Bush or Tree, we saw nothing
there but a Cannow, which was made out of the whole tree,
which was five and fortie foot long by the Rule. Upon this plot
of ground we got good store of Mussels and Oysters, which
lay on the ground as thicke as stones: wee opened some, and
found in many of them Pearles. Wee marched some three or
foure miles further into the Woods, where we saw great
smoakes of fire. Wee marched to those smoakes and found that
the Savages had beene there burning downe the grasse, as wee
thought either to make their plantation there, or else to give
signes to bring their forces together, and so to give us battell.
We past through excellent ground full of Flowers of divers kinds
and colours, and as goodly trees as I have seene, as Cedar,

Strawberries
Cipresse, and other kindes: going a little further we
came into a little plat of ground full of fine and beautifull Strawberries, foure times bigger and better

than ours in England. All this march we could neither see Savage nor Towne. When it grew to be towards night we stood backe to our Ships, we sounded and found it shallow water for a great way, which put us out of all hopes for getting any higher with our Ships, which road at the mouth of the River. Wee rowed over to a point of Land, where wee found a channell, and sounded six, eight, ten, or twelve fathom:
Point Comfort
which put us in good comfort. Therefore wee named that point of Land, Cape Comfort.

The nine and twentieth day we set up a Crosse at Chesupioc Bay, and named that place Cape Henry. Thirtieth day, we came with our ships to Cape Comfort; where we saw five Savages running on the shoare; presently the Captaine caused the shallop to be manned, so rowing to the shoare, the Captaine called to them in signe of friendship, but they were at first very timersome, until they saw the Captain lay his hand on his heart: upon that they laid down their Bowes and Arrowes, and came very boldly to us, making signes to come a shoare to their
Kecoughtan
Towne, which is called by the Savages Kecoughtan. Wee coasted to their Towne, rowing over a River running into the Maine, where these Savages swam over with their Bowes and Arrowes in their mouthes.

When we came over to the other side, there was a many of other Savages which directed us to their Towne, where we were entertained by them very kindly. When we came first a Land they made a dolefull noise, laying their faces to the ground, scratching the earth with their nailes. We did thinke that they had beene at their Idolatry. When they had ended their Ceremonies, they went into their houses and brought out mats and laid upon the ground, the chiefest of them sate all in a rank: the meanest sort brought us such dainties as they had, & of their bread which they make of their Maiz or Gennea wheat, they would not suffer us to eat unlesse we sate down, which
Tobacco
we did on a Mat right against them. After we were well satisfied they gave us their Tabacco, which they tooke in a pipe made artificially of earthe as ours are, but far bigger, with the bowle fashioned together with a piece
Singing and Dancing
of fine copper. After they had feasted us, they shewed us, in welcome, their manner of dancing, which was in this fashion: one of the Savages standing in the

midst singing, beating one hand against another, all the rest
dancing about him, shouting, howling, and stamping against
the ground, with many Anticke tricks and faces, making noise
like so many Wolves or Devils. One thing of them I observed;
when they were in their dance they kept stroke with their feet
just one with another, but with their hands, heads, faces, and
bodies, every one of them had a severall gesture: so they continued for the space of halfe an houre. When they had ended their
dance, the Captaine gave them Beades and other trifling Jewells. They hang through their eares Fowles legs: they shave the
right side of their heads with a shell, the left side they weare of
an ell long tied up with an artificiall knot, with a many of
Foules feathers sticking in it. They goe altogether naked, but
their privities are covered with Beasts skinnes beset commonly
with little bones, or beasts teeth: some paint their bodies blacke,
some red, with artificiall knots of sundry lively colours, very
beautifull and pleasing to the eye, in a braver fashion then they
in the West Indies.

    The fourth day of May, we came to the King or Werowance
of Paspihe: where they entertained us with much wel-
A long
oration   come; an old Savage made a long Oration, making a
foule noise uttering his speech with a vehement ac-
tion, but we knew little what they meant. Whilst we were in
company with the Paspihes, the Werowance of Rapahanna
came from the other side of the River in his Cannoa: he seemed
to take displeasure of our being with the Paspihes: he would
faine have had us come to his Towne, the Captaine was unwilling; seeing that the day was so far spent he returned backe
to his ships for that night.

    The next day, being the fift of May, the Werowance of Rapa-
hanna sent a Messenger to have us come to him. We entertained the said Messenger, and gave him trifles which pleased
him: Wee manned our shallop with Muskets and Targatiers sufficiently: this said Messenger guided us where our determination was to goe. When wee landed, the Werowance of
Rapahanna came downe to the water side with all his traine, as
goodly men as any I have seene of Savages or Chris-
A Flute made
of a Reed   tians: the Werowance comming before them playing
on a Flute made of a Reed, with a Crown of Deares
haire colloured red, in fashion of a Rose fastened about his

knot of haire, and a great Plate of Copper on the other side of his head, with two long Feathers in fashion of a paire of Hornes placed in the midst of his Crowne. His body was painted all with Crimson, with a Chaine of Beads about his necke, his face painted blew, besprinkled with silver Ore as wee thought, his eares all behung with Braslets of Pearle, and in either eare a Birds Claw through it beset with fine Copper or gold, he entertained us in so modest a proud fashion, as though he had beene a Prince of civil government, holding his countenance without laughter or any such ill behaviour; he caused his Mat to be spred on the ground, where hee sate downe with a great Majestie, taking a pipe of Tabacco: the rest of his company standing about him. After he had rested a while he rose, and made signes to us to come to his Towne: Hee went formost, and all the rest of his people and our selves followed him up a steepe Hill where his Palace was settled. Wee passed through the Woods in fine paths, having most pleasant Springs which issued from the Mountaines: Wee also went through the goodliest Corne fieldes that ever was seene in any Countrey. When wee came to Rapahannos Towne, hee entertained us in good humanitie.

The eight day of May we discovered up the River. We landed in the Countrey of Apamatica, at our landing, there came many stout and able Savages to resist us with their Bowes and Arrowes, in a most warlike manner, with the swords at their backes beset with sharpe stones, and pieces of yron able to cleave a man in sunder. Amongst the rest one of the chiefest standing before them crosse-legged, with his Arrow readie in his Bow in one hand, and taking a Pipe of Tobacco in the other, with a bold uttering of his speech, demanded of us our being there, willing us to bee gone. Wee made signes of peace, which they perceived in the end, and let us land in quietnesse.

The twelfth day we went backe to our ships, and Archers Hope discovered a point of Land, called Archers Hope, which was sufficient with a little labour to defend our selves against any Enemy. The soile was good and fruitfull, with excellent good Timber. There are also great store of Vines in bignesse of a mans thigh, running up to the tops of the Trees in great abundance. We also did see many Squirels, Conies, Black Birds with crimson wings, and divers other

Fowles and Birds of divers and sundrie collours of crimson, Watchet, Yellow, Greene, Murray, and of divers other hewes naturally without any art using.

We found store of Turkie nests and many Egges, if it had not beene disliked, because the ship could not ride neere the shoare, we had setled there to all the Collonies contentment.

The thirteenth day, we came to our seating place in Paspihas Countrey, some eight miles from the point of Land, which I made mention before: where our shippes doe lie so neere the shoare that they are moored to the Trees in six fathom water.

The fourteenth day we landed all our men which were set to worke about the fortification, and others some to watch and ward as it was convenient. The first night of our landing, about midnight, there came some Savages sayling close to our quarter: presently there was an alarum given; upon that the savages ran away, and we not troubled any more by them that night. Not long after there came two Savages that seemed to be Commanders, bravely drest, with Crownes of coloured haire upon their heads, which came as Messengers from the Werowance of Paspihæ; telling us that their Werowance was comming and would be merry with us with a fat Deare.

The eighteenth day, the Werowance of Paspihæ came himselfe to our quarter, with one hundred Savages armed, which garded him in a very warlike manner with Bowes and Arrowes, thinking at that time to execute their villany. Paspihæ made great signes to us to lay our Armes away. But we would not trust him so far: he seeing he could not have convenient time to worke his will, at length made signes that he would give us as much land as we would desire to take. As the Savages were in a throng in the Fort, one of them stole a Hatchet from one of our company, which spied him doing the deed: whereupon he tooke it from him by force, and also strooke him over the arme: presently another Savage seeing that, came fiercely at our man with a wooden sword, thinking to beat out his braines. The Werowance of Paspiha saw us take to our Armes, went suddenly away with all his company in great anger.

The nineteenth day, my selfe and three or foure more walking

*Their Planta-
tion at
James Towne*

Land given

*These
Savages are
naturally
great theeves*

into the Woods by chance wee espied a path-way like to an Irish pace: wee were desirous to knowe whither it would bring us; we traced along some foure miles, all the way as wee went, having the pleasantest Suckles, the ground all flowing over with faire flowers of sundry colours and kindes, as though it had beene in any Garden or Orchard in England. There be many Strawberries, and other fruits unknowne: wee saw the Woodes full of Cedar and Cypresse trees, with other trees, which issues out sweet Gummes like to Balsam: wee kept on our way in this Paradise, at length wee came to a Savage Towne, where wee found but few people, they told us the rest were gone a hunting with the Werowance of Paspiha: we stayed there a while, and had of them Strawberries, and other things; in the meane time one of the Savages came running out of his house with a Bowe and Arrowes and ranne mainly through the Woods: then I beganne to mistrust some villanie, that he went to call some companie, and so betray us, wee made all the haste away wee could: one of the Savages brought us on the way to the Wood side, where there was a Garden of Tobacco, and other fruits and herbes, he gathered Tobacco, and distributed to every one of us, so wee departed.

The twentieth day the Werowance of Paspiha sent fortie of his men with a Deere, to our quarter: but they came more in villanie than any love they bare us: they faine would have layne in our Fort all night, but wee would not suffer them for feare of their treachery. One of our Gentlemen having a Target which hee trusted in, thinking it would beare out a flight shot, hee set it up against a tree, willing one of the Savages to shoot; who tooke from his backe an Arrow of an elle long, drew it strongly in his Bowe, shoots the Target a foote thorow, or better: which was strange, being that a Pistoll could not pierce it. Wee seeing the force of his Bowe, afterwards set him up a steele Target; he shot again, and burst his arrow all to pieces, he presently pulled out another Arrow, and bit it in his teeth, and seemed to bee in a great rage, so hee went away in great anger. Their Bowes are made of tough Hasell, their strings of Leather, their Arrowes of Canes or Hasell, headed with very sharpe stones, and are made artifically like a broad Arrow: other some of their Arrowes are headed with

Their arrowes

the ends of Deeres hornes, and are feathered very artificially. Paspha was as good as his word; for he sent Venison, but the Sawse came within few dayes after.

At Port Cotage in our Voyage up the River, we saw a Savage Boy about the age of ten yeeres, which had a head of hair of a perfect yellow and a reasonable white skinne, which is a Miracle amongst all Savages.

Yellow haired Virginian

This River which wee have discovered is one of the famousest Rivers that ever was found by any Christian, it ebbes and flowes a hundred and threescore miles where ships of great burthen may harbour in safetie. Wheresoever we landed upon this River, wee saw the goodliest Woods as Beech, Oke, Cedar, Cypresse, Wal-nuts, Sassafras and Vines in great abundance, which hang in great clusters on many Trees, and other Trees unknowne, and all the grounds bespred with many sweet and delicate flowres of divers colours and kindes. There are also many fruites as Strawberries, Mulberries, Rasberries and Fruits unknowne, there are many branches of this River, which runne flowing through the Woods with great plentie of fish of all kindes, as for Sturgeon all the World cannot be compared to it. In this Countrey I have seene many great and large Medowes* having excellent good pasture for any Cattle. There is also great store of Deere both Red and Fallow. There are Beares, Foxes, Otters, Bevers, Muskats, and wild beasts unknowne.

River of Pohatan

*Low Marshes

The foure and twentieth day wee set up a Crosse at the head of this River, naming it Kings River, where we proclaimed James King of England to have the most right unto it. When wee had finished and set up our Crosse, we shipt our men and made for James Fort. By the way wee came to Pohatans Towre where the Captaine went on shore suffering none to goe with him, hee presented the Commander of this place with a Hatchet which hee tooke joyfully, and was well pleased.

Wee came downe the River

But yet the Savages murmured at our planting in the Countrie, whereupon this Werowance made answere againe very wisely of a Savage, Why should you bee offended with them as long as they hurt you not, nor take any thing away by force, they take but a little waste ground, which doth you nor any of us any good.

I saw Bread made by their women which doe all their drugerie. The men takes their pleasure in hunting and their warres, which they are in continually one Kingdome against another. The manner of baking of bread is thus, after they pound their wheat into flowre with hote water, they make it into paste, and worke it into round balls and Cakes, then they put it into a pot of seething water, when it is sod throughly, they lay it on a smooth stone, there they harden it as well as in an Oven.

Bread how made

There is notice to be taken to know married women from Maids, the Maids you shall alwayes see the fore part of their head and sides shaven close, the hinder part very long, which they tie in a plate hanging downe to their hips. The married women weares their haire all of a length, and is tied of that fashion that the Maids are. The women kinde in this Countrey doth pounce and race their bodies, legges, thighes, armes and faces with a sharpe Iron, which makes a stampe in curious knots, and drawes the proportion of Fowles, Fish, or Beasts, then with paintings of sundry lively colours, they rub it into the stampe which will never be taken away, because it is dried into the flesh where it is sered.

Distinct habit of Maids and Wives

The Savages beare their yeeres well, for when wee were at Pamonkies, wee saw a Savage by their report was above eight score yeeres of age. His eyes were sunke into his head, having never a tooth in his mouth, his haire all gray with a reasonable bigge beard, which was as white as any snow. It is a Miracle to see a Savage have any haire on their faces, I never saw, read, nor heard, any have the like before. This Savage was as lustie and went as fast as any of us, which was strange to behold.

Savage 160. yeeres old. Bearded.

The fifteenth day of June, we had built and finished our Fort which was triangle wise, having three Bulwarkes at every corner like a halfe Moone, and foure or five pieces of Artillerie mounted in them, we had made our selves sufficiently strong for these Savages, we had also sowne most of our Corne on two Mountaines, it sprang a mans height from the ground, this Countrey is a fruitfull soile, bearing many goodly and fruitfull Trees, as Mulberries, Cherries, Walnuts, Ceders, Cypresse, Sassafras, and Vines in great abundance.

Cap.
Newports
departure   Munday the two and twentieth of June, in the morning Captaine Newport in the Admirall departed from James Port for England.

Captaine Newport being gone for England, leaving us (one hundred and foure persons) verie bare and scantie of victualls, furthermore in warres and in danger of the Savages. We hoped after a supply which Captaine Newport promised within twentie weekes. But if the beginners of this action doe carefully further us, the Country being so fruitfull, it would be as great a profit to the Realme of England, as the Indies to the King of Spaine, if this River which wee have found had beene discovered in the time of warre with Spaine, it would have been a commoditie to our Realme, and a great annoyance to our enemies. The seven and twentieth of July the King of Rapahanna, demanded a Canoa which was restored, lifted up his hand to the Sunne, which they worship as their God, besides he laid his hand on his heart, that he would be our speciall friend. It is a generall rule of these people when they swere by their God The Savages
use to
sacrifice to
the Sunne which is the Sunne, no Christian will keepe their Oath better upon this promise. These people have a great reverence to the Sunne above all other things at the rising and setting of the same, they sit downe lifting up their hands and eyes to the Sunne making a round Circle on the ground with dried Tobacco, then they began to pray making many Devillish gestures with a Hellish noise foaming at the mouth, staring with their eyes, wagging their heads and hands in such a fashion and deformitie as it was monstrous to behold.

The sixt of August there died John Asbie of the bloudie Flixe. The ninth day died George Flowre of the swelling. The tenth day died William Bruster Gentleman, of a wound given by the Savages, and was buried the eleventh day.

The fourteenth day, Jerome Alikock Ancient, died of a wound, the same day Francis Midwinter, Edward Moris Corporall died suddenly.

The fifteenth day, their died Edward Browne and Stephen Galthrope. The sixteenth day, their died Thomas Gower Gentleman. The seventeenth day, their died Thomas Mounslic. The eighteenth day, there died Robert Pennington, and John Martine Gentleman, The nineteenth day, died Drue Piggase Gentleman. The two and twentieth day of August, there died

Captaine Bartholomew Gosnold one of our Councell, he was honourably buried, having all the Ordnance in the Fort shot off with many vollies of small
shot.

After Captaine Gosnols death, the Councell could hardly
agree by the dissention of Captaine Kendall, which afterward
was committed about hainous matters which was proved
against him.

The foure and twentieth day, died Edward Harington and
George Walker, and were buried the same day. The sixe
and twentieth day, died Kenelme Throgmortine. The seven
and twentieth day died William Roods. The eight and twentieth day died Thomas Stoodie, Cape Merchant.

The fourth day of September died Thomas Jacob Sergeant.
The fift day, there died Benjamin Beast. Our men were destroyed with cruell diseases as Swellings, Flixes, Burning Fevers,
and by warres, and some departed suddenly, but for the most
part they died of meere famine. There were never
Englishmen left in a forreigne Countrey in such miserie as wee were in this new discovered Virginia. Wee
watched every three nights lying on the bare cold ground what
weather soever came warded all the next day, which brought
our men to bee most feeble wretches, our food was but a small
Can of Barlie sod in water to five men a day, our drinke cold
water taken out of the River, which was at a floud verie salt, at
a low tide full of slime and filth, which was the destruction of
many of our men. Thus we lived for the space of five moneths
in this miserable distresse, not having five able men to man our
Bulwarkes upon any occasion. If it had not pleased God to
have put a terrour in the Savages hearts, we had all perished
by those vild and cruell Pagans, being in that weake estate as
we were; our men night and day groaning in every corner of
the Fort most pittifull to heare, if there were any conscience
in men, it would make their harts to bleed to heare the pittiful
murmurings & out-cries of our sick men without reliefe every
night and day for the space of sixe weekes, some departing out
of the World, many times three or foure in a night, in the
morning their bodies trailed out of their Cabines like
Dogges to be buried: in this sort I did see the mortalitie of divers of our people.

It pleased God, after a while, to send those people which were our mortall enemies to releeve us with victuals, as Bread, Corne, Fish, and Flesh in great plentie, which was the setting up of our feeble men, otherwise wee had all perished. Also we were frequented by divers Kings in the Countrie, bringing us store of provision to our great comfort.

The eleventh day, there was certaine Articles laid against Master Wingfield which was then President, thereupon he was not only displaced out of his President ship, but also from being of the Councell. Afterwards Captaine John Ratcliffe was chosen President.

The eighteenth day, died one Ellis Kinistone which was starved to death with cold. The same day at night, died one Richard Simmons. The nineteenth day, there died one Thomas Mouton.

William White (having lived with the Natives) re-
He was a made man
ported to us of their customes in the morning by breake of day, before they eate or drinke both men, women and children, that be above tenne yeeres of age runnes into the water, there washes themselves a good while till the Sunne riseth, then offer Sacrifice to it, strewing Tobacco on
*The rest is omitted, being more fully set downe in Cap. Smiths Relations
the water or Land, honouring the Sunne as their God, likewise they doe at the setting of the *Sunne

GABRIEL ARCHER

A Relatyon of the Discovery of Our River

A RELATYON of the Discovery of our River, from James Forte into the Maine: made by Captain Christofer Newport: and sincerely written and observed by a gent. of ye Colony.

Thursday the xxith of May, Captain Newport (having fitted our shallup with provision and all necessaryes belonging to a discovery) tooke 5 . gentlemen . 4 . Maryners . and . 14 . Saylours, with whome he proceeded with a perfect resolutyon not to returne, but either to finde the head of this Ryver, the Laake mentyoned by others heretofore, the Sea againe, the Mountaynes Apalatsi, or some issue.

May 21.

The names of the Dys- coverers are thes	} Captain Christofer Newport
George Percye esq. Captain Gabriell Archer Captain Jhon Smyth Master Jhon Brookes Master Thomas Wotton Francys Nellson John Collson Robert Tyndall Mathew Fytch	} Maryners

   1 Jonas Poole
   2 Robert Markham
   3 John Crookdeck
   4 Olyver Browne
   5 Benjamyn White
   6 Rychard Genoway
   7 Thomas Turnbrydg
   8 Thomas Godword

9 Robert Jackson
10 Charles Clarke
11 Stephen
12 Thomas Skynner
13 Jeremy Deale
14 Danyell

Thus from James Fort we tooke our leave about noone, and by night we were up the Ryver . 18 . myle at a lowe meadow point, which I call Wynauk. Here came the people, and entertayned us with Daunces and much rejoycing. This kyngdome Wynauk is full of pearle muskles. the kyng of Paspeiouh and this king is at oddes, as the Paspeians tould me, and Demonstrated by their hurtes: heere we anckored all night.

May 22   Fryday, omitting no tyme, we passed up some . 16 . myle further, where we founde an Ilet, on which were many Turkeys, and greate store of yonge byrdes like Black birdes, whereof wee tooke Dyvers, which wee brake our fast withall. Now spying . 8 . salvages in a Canoa, we haled them by our worde of kyndnes; Wingapoh, and they came to us. In conference by signes with them, one seemed to understand our intentyon, and offred with his foote to describe the river to us: So I gave him a pen and paper (shewing first the use) and he layd out the whole River from the Chesseian bay to the end of it so farr as passadg was for boates: he tolde us of two Ilettes in the Ryver we should passe by, meaning that one whereon we were, and then come to an overfall of water, beyond that of two kyngdomes which the Ryver Runes by then a greate Distance of, the mountaines Quirank as he named them: beyond which by his relation is that which we expected. This fellow parting from us promised to procure us wheate if we would stay a little before, and for that intent went back againe to provide it: but we coming by the place where he was, with many more very Desirous of our Company, stayd not, as being eagre of our good tydinges. He notwithstanding with two wemen and another fellow of his owne consort, followed us some six mile with basketes full of Dryed oysters, and mett us at a point, where calling to us, we went ashore and bartred with them for most of their victualls. Here the shoare began to be full of greate Cobble stones, and higher land. The

Ryver skantes of his breadth . 2 . mile before we come to the
Ilet mentyoned which I call Turkey Ile: yet keepes it a quarter
of a mile broade most comonly, and depe water for shipping.
This fellow with the rest overtooke us agayne upon the doubling of another point: Now they had gotten mulberyes, little
sweete nuttes like Acorns (a verye good fruite) wheate, beanes
and mulberyes sodd together and gave us. Some of them desired to be sett over the Ryver, which we dyd, and they parted.
Now we passed a Reach of . 3 . mile ½ . in length, highe stony
grownd on Popham syde . 5 . or 6 . fadome . 8 . oares length
from the shoare. This daye we went about . 38 . mile and came
to an Ankre at a place I call poore Cottage; where we went
ashore, and were used kyndly by the people, wee sodd our kettle by the water syde within nighte, and rested aboorde.

Satterday we passed a few short reaches; and . 5 .
May 23   mile of poore Cottage we went a shore. Heer we
found our kinde Comrades againe, who had gyven
notice all along as they came of us: by which we were entertayned with much Courtesye in every place. We found here a
Wiroans (for so they call their kynges) who satt upon a matt of
Reedes, with his people about him: He caused one to be layd
for Captain Newport, gave us a Deare roasted; which according
to their Custome they seethed againe: His people gave us mullberyes, sodd wheate and beanes, and he caused his weomen to
make Cakes for us. He gave our Captaine his Crowne which
was of Deares hayre dyed redl. Certifying him of our intentyon
up the Ryver, he was willing to send guydes with us. This we
found to be a kyng subject to Pawatah (the Cheife of all the
kyngdomes) his name is Arahatec: the Country Arahatecoh.
Now as we satt merye banquetting with them, seeing their
Daunces, and taking Tobacco, Newes came that the greate
kyng Powatah was come: at whose presence they all rose of
their mattes (save the kyng Arahatec); separated themselves
aparte in fashion of a Guard, and with a long shout they
saluted him. Him wee saluted with silence sitting still on our
mattes, our Captaine in the myddest; but presented (as before
we dyd to kyng Arahatec) gyftes of dyvers sortes, as penny
knyves, sheeres, belles, beades, glasse toyes &c. more amply
then before. Now this king appointed . 5 . men to guyde us up
the River, and sent Postes before to provyde us victuall. I

caused now our kynde Consort that described the River to us,
to draw it againe before kyng Arahatec, who in every thing
consented to this draught, and it agreed with his first relatyon.
This we found a faythfull fellow, he was one that was appointed guyde for us. Thus parting from Arahatecs joye, we
found the people on either syde the Ryver stand in Clusters all
along, still proferring us victualls, which of some were accepted; as our guydes (that were with us in the boate) pleased,
and gave them requitall. So after we had passed some 10. myle,
which (by the pleasure and joye we tooke of our kinde in-
terteynment, and for the Comfort of our happy & hopefull
Discovery) we accompted scarce . 5 . we came to the second
Ilet Described in the Ryver; over against which on Popham
syde is the habitatyon of the greate kyng Pawatah: which I call
Pawatahs Towre; it is scituat upon a highe Hill by the water
syde, a playne betweene it and the water . 12 . score over,
wheron he sowes his wheate, beane, peaze, tobacco, pompions, gowrdes, Hempe, flaxe &c. And were any Art used to the
naturall state of this place, it would be a goodly habitatyon:
Heere we were conducted up the Hill to the kyng, with
whome we found our kinde king Arahatec: Thes . 2 . satt by
themselves aparte from all the rest (save one who satt by
Powatah, and what he was I could not gesse but they told me
he was no Wiroans): Many of his company satt on either syde:
and the mattes for us were layde right over against the kynges.
He caused his weomen to bring us vittailes, mulberyes, strawberryes &c. but our best entertaynment was frendly wellcome.
In discoursing with him, we founde that all the kyngdomes
from the Chessipians were frendes with him, and (to use his
owne worde) Cheisc. which is all one with him or under him.
Also wee perceived the Chessipian to be an Enemye generally
to all thes kyngdomes: upon which I tooke occasion to signifye
our displeasure with them also: making it knowne that we refused to plant in their Country; that we had warres with them
also, shewing hurtes scarce whole received by them, for which
we vowed revenge, after their maner, pointing to the Sunne:
Further we certifyed him that we were frendes with all his
people & kyngdomes, neither had any of them offred us ill, or
used us unkyndly. Hereupon he (very well understanding by
the wordes and signes we made; the significatyon of our mean-

ing) moved of his owne accord a leauge of fryndship with us; which our Captain kyndly imbraced; and for concluding therof, gave him his gowne, put it on his back himselfe, and laying his hand on his breast saying Wingapoh Chemuze (the most kynde wordes of salutatyon that may be) he satt downe. Now the Day Drawing on, we made signe to be gone, wherwith he was contented; and sent . 6 . men with us: we also left a man with him, and departed. But now rowing some 3 . myle in shold water we came to an overfall, impassible for boates any further. Here the water falles Downe through great mayne Rockes, from ledges of Rockes above . 2 . fadome highe: in which fall it maketh Divers little Ilettes, on which might be placed 100 . water milnes for any uses. Our mayne Ryver ebbs and flowes . 4 . foote even to the skert of this Downfall. Shippes of . 200 . or . 300 . toonne may come to within . 5 . myle hereof, and the rest Deepe inoughe for Barges, or small vessells that drawe not above . 6 . foote water. Having viewed this place, betweene Content and greefe we left it for the night, determyning the next Day to fitt our selfe for a march by Land. So we road all night betweene Pawatahs Tower and that Ilet I call   whereon is 6 . or . 7 . families. One of our Guydes which we had from Arahatacs Joy whose name was Navirans, and now we found to be brother in Lawe to king Arahatec, desired to sleepe in the boate with us: we permitted him, and used him with all the kyndnes we coulde: He proved a very trustye frend, as after is Declared. Now we sent for our man to Pawatah, who coming tolde us of his entertaynment, how they had prepared mattes for him to lye on, gave him store of victualls, and made asmuch on him as coulde be.

Sonday, Whitsonday, our Captayne caused two
May 24 peeces of porke to be sodd a shore with pease; to which he invyted King Pawatah: for Arahatec perswading himselfe we would come Downe the Ryver that night, went home before Dynner, for preparatyon against our Coming. But in presence of them both it fell out that we missing two bullet-bagges which had shot and Dyvers trucking toyes in them: we Complayned to theis kynges, who instantly caused them all to be restored, not wanting any thing. Howbeit they had Devyded the shott and toyes to (at least) a dozen severall persons; and those also in the Ilet over the water: One also

having stollen a knyfe, brought it againe upon this Comaunde
before we supposed it lost, or had made any signe for it: So
Captaine Newport gave thanckes to the Kinges and rewarded
the theeves with the same toyes they had stollen, but kept the
bulletes: yet he made knowne unto them the Custome of
England to be Death for such offences.

Now Arahatec departed, and it being Dynner tyme, King
Pawatah with some of his people satt with us, brought of his
Dyet, & we fedd familiarly, without sitting in his state as before;
he eat very freshly of our meate, Dranck of our beere, Aquavite, and Sack. Dynner Done we entred into Discourse of the
Ryver how far it might be to the head therof, where they gat
their Copper, and their Iron, and how many Dayes Jornye it
was to Monanacah, Rahowacah and the Mountaines Quirank:
requesting him to have guydes with us also in our intended
march; for our Captaine Determyned to have travelled two or
. 3 . dayes Jornye a foote up the Ryver: but without gyving any
answer to our Demaundes, he shewde he would meete us himselfe at the overfall and so we parted. This Navirans accompanyed us still in the boate. According to his promyse he mett us;
where the fellow whome I have called our kynde Consort, he
that followed us from Turkey Ile, at the Coming of Pawatah
made signe to us we must make a shoute, which we Dyd. Now
sitting upon the banck by the overfall beholding the same, he
began to tell us of the tedyous travell we should have if wee
proceeded any further, that it was a Daye and a halfe Jorney to
Monanacah, and if we Went to Quirank, we should get no vittailes and be tyred, and sought by all meanes to disswade our
Captayne from going any further: Also he tolde us that the Monanacah was his Enimye, and that he came Downe at the fall of
the leafe and invaded his Countrye. Now What I conjecture of
this I have left to a further experience. But our Captayne out
of his Discretyon (though we would faine have seene further,
yea and himselfe as Desirous also) Checkt his intentyon and
retorned to his boate; as holding it much better to please the
kyng (with whome and all of his Comaund he had made so
faire Way) then to prosecute his owne fancye or satisfye our requestes: So upon one of the little Ilettes at the mouth of the
falls he sett up a Crosse with this inscriptyon Jacobus Rex.
1607. and his owne name belowe: At the erecting hereof we

prayed for our kyng and our owne prosperous succes in this his Actyon, and proclaymed him kyng, with a greate showte. The kyng Pawatah was now gone (and as we noted somewhat Distasted with our importunity of proceeding up further) and all the Salvages likewise save Navirans, who seeing us set up a Crosse with such a shoute, began to admire; but our Captayne told him that the two Armes of the Crosse signifyed kyng Powatah and himselfe, the fastening of it in the myddest was their united Leaug, and the shoute the reverence he dyd to Pawatah. which cheered Navirans not a litle. Also (which I have omytted) our Captayne before Pawatah Departed shewed him that if he would, he would gyve the Wiroans of Monanacah into his handes, and make him king of that Country, making signes to bring to his ayde . 500 . men, which pleased the kyng muche, and upon this (I noted) he told us the tyme of the yere when his enemyes assaile him.

So farr as we could Discerne the River above the overall, it was full of huge Rockes: About a myle of, it makes a pretty bigg Iland; It runnes up betweene highe Hilles which increase in height one above another so farr as wee sawe. Now our kynde Consortes relatyon sayth (which I dare Well beleeve, in that I found not any one report false of the River so farr as we tryed, or that he tolde us untruth in any thing ells whatsoever) that after a Dayes jorney or more, this River devydes it selfe into two branches, which both come from the mountaynes Quirank. Here he whispered with me that their caquassan was gott in the bites of Rockes and betweene Cliffes in certayne vaynes.

Having ended thus of force our Discovery, our Captayne intended to call of kyng Pawatah, and sending Navirans up to him he came downe to the water syde, where he went a shore single unto him, presented him with a hatchet, and staying but till Naviraus had tolde (as we trewly perceived) the meaning of our setting up the Crosse, which we found Dyd exceedingly rejoyce him, he came a boorde, with the kyndest farewell that possible might be. Now at our putting off the boate, Navirans willed us to make a shout, which we Dyd two severall times, at which the King and his Company weaved their skinnes about their heades answering our shout with gladnes in a frendly fashion.

This night (though late) we came to Arahatec Joy, where we

found the king ready to entertayne us, and had provided some victualls for us, but he tolde us he was very sick, & not able to sitt up long with us, so we repaired aborde.

Monday he came to the Water syde, and we went
May 25   a shore to him agayne. He tolde us that our hott
Drynckes he thought caused his greefe, but that he was well agayne, and we were very wellcome. He sent for another Deere which was roasted and after sodd for us (as before) Our Captayne caused his Dynner to be Dressed a shore also. Thus we satt banquetting all the forenoone. some of his people led us to their houses, shewed us the growing of their Corne & the maner of setting it, gave us Tobacco, wallnutes, mulberyes, strawberryes, and Respises. One shewed us the herbe called in their tongue wisacan, which they say heales poysoned woundes, it is like lyverwort or bloudwort. One gave me a Roote wherewith they poison their Arrowes. they would shew us any thing we Demaunded, and laboured very much by signes to make us understand their Languadg.

Naviraus our guyde and this Kings brother made a complaint to Arahatec, that one of his people prest into our boate to vyolently upon a man of ours; which Captaine Newport (understanding the pronenes of his owne men to such injuryes) misconstruing the matter, sent for his owne man, bound him to a tree before King Arahatec, and with a Cudgell soundly beate him. the king perceiving the error, stept up and stayde our Captaynes hand And sytting still a while, he spyed his owne man that Dyd the injurye: upon which he silently rose, and made towardes the fellow, he seeing him come, runn away, after ran the king, so swiftly as I assure my selfe he might gyve any of our Company . 6 . score in . 12 . with the king ran also Dyvers others, who all returning brought Cudgells and wandes in their handes all to be tewed, as if they had beaten him extreamly. At Dynner our Captayne gave the kyng a glasse and some Aquavitæ therin, shewing him the benefytt of the Water, for which he thanckt him kindly: and taking our Leave of him, he promised to meete us at a point not farr of: where he hath another house, which he performed, withall, sending men into the woodes to kill a Dere for us if they could. This place I call mulbery shade. He caused heere to be prepared for us pegatewk-Apoan which is bread of their wheat made in Rolles and Cakes; this the weomen make, & are very clenly about it; We had parched meale, excellent good, sodd beanes, which eate as sweete as filbert kernells in a maner, strawberryes & mulberyes new shaken of the tree dropping on our heades as we satt: He made ready a land turtle which we eate, & shewed that we was hartely rejoyced in our Company. He was Desirous to have a Musket shott of, shewing first the maner of their owne skirmishes, which we perceive is violent Cruell and full of Celerity; they use a tree to Defend them in fight, and having shott an Enemy that he fall, they maull him with a short wodden sworde. Our Captayne caused a gentle-man Discharge his peece Souldyer like before him, at which noyse he started, stopt his eares, and exprest much feare, so likewise all about him; some of his people being in our boate leapt over boorde at the wonder hereof: but our course of kyndnes after, & letting him to witt that wee never use this thunder but against our enemyes, yea and that we would assist him with thes to Terrify & kill his Adversaryes, he rejoyced the more, and we found it bred a better affectyon in him towardes us; so that by his signes we understood he would or long be with us at our Fort. Captayne Newport bestowed on him a redd wastcote, which highly pleased him, and so Departed, gyving him also . 2 . shoutes as the boate went of. This night we Went some   mile, and ankored at a place I Call kynd womans care which is   mile from Mulbery shade. Here we came within night, yet was there ready for us of bread new made, sodden wheate and beanes, mullberyes, and some fishe undressed more then all we could eate. Moreover thes people seemed not to crave any thing in requitall, Howbeit our Cap-tain voluntarily distributed guiftes.

Tuesday We parted from kynd womans care, and

May 26   by Directyon of Navirans (who still accompanyed in the boate with us) went a shore at a place I call Queene Apumatecs bowre. He caryed us along through a plaine Lowe grownd prepared for seede, part wherof had ben lately Cropt: and assending a pretty Hill, we sawe the Queene of this Country comminge in selfe same fashion of state as Pawatah or Arahatec; yea rather with more majesty: she had an usher before her who brought her to the matt prepared under a faire mulbery tree, where she satt her Downe by her selfe

with a stayed Countenance, she would permitt none to stand
or sitt neere her: she is a fatt lustie manly woman: she had much
Copper about her neck, a Crownet of Copper upon her hed:
she had long black haire, which hanged loose downe her back
to her myddle, which only part was Covered with a Deares
skyn, & ells all naked. She had her woemen attending on her
adorned much like her selfe (save they Wanted the Copper).
Here we had our accustomed Cates, Tobacco and wellcome.
Our Captayne presented her with guyftes liberally, wherupon
shee cheered somwhat her Countenance; and requested him
to shoote of a peece whereat (we noted) she shewed not neere
the like feare as Arahatec though he be a goodly man. She had
much Corne in the grownd: she is subject to Pawatah as the
rest are; yet within herselfe of as greate authority as any of her
neighbour Wyoances. Captain Newport stayd here some . 2 .
houres & Departed.

Now Leaving her, Naviraus Dyrected us to one of kyng Pamaunches howses some . 5 . myle from the Queenes Bower.
Here We were entertayned with greate joye and gladnes, the
people falling to Daunce, the weomen to preparing vitailes,
some boyes were sent to Dive for muskles, they gave us Tobacco, and very kyndly saluted us.

This kyng (sitting in maner of the rest) so set his Countenance stryving to be stately, as to our seeming he became foole.
Wee gave him many presentes, and certifyed him of our Jorney
to the falles our League with the greate kyng Pawatah, a most
certayne frendship with Arahatec and kynde entertaynment of
the Queene: that we were professed Enemyes to the Chessepi-
ans, and would assist King Pawatah against the Monanacans;
with this he seemed to be much rejoyced; and he would have
had our Captayne staye with him all night, which he refused
not, but single with the king walked above two flight shott,
shewing therby his trew meaning without Distrust or feare.
Howbeit, we followed a Loofe of, and coming up to a gallant
mulbery tree, we founde Divers preparing vittailes for us: but
the kyng seing our intentyon Was to accompany our Captaine,
he alltered his purpose and weaved us in kyndnes to our boate.
This Wyroans Pamaunche I holde to inhabite a Rych land of
Copper and pearle. His Country lyes into the land to another
Ryver, which by relatyon and Descriptyon of the Salvages

comes also from the Mountaynes Quirank, but a shorter Jorney. The Copper he had, as also many of his people, was very flexible, I bowed a peece of the thickness of a shilling rounde about my finger, as if it had ben lead: I found them nice in parting with any; They weare it in their eares, about their neckes in Long lynckes, and in broade plates on their heades: So we made no greate enquyry of it, neither seemed Desirous to have it. The kyng had a Chaine of pearle about his neck thrice Double, the third parte of them as bygg as pease, which I could not valew lesse worth then . 3 . or . 400 .[li] had the pearle ben taken from the muskle as it ought to be. His kyngdome is full of Deare (so also is moste of all the kyngdomes:) he hath (as the rest likewise) many ryche furres. This place I call Pamaunches pallace, howbeit by Nauviraus his wordes the kyng of Winauk is possessor hereof. The platt of grownd is bare without wood some . 100 . acres, where are set beanes, wheate, peaze, Tobacco, Gourdes, pompions, and other thinges unknowne to us in our tongue.

Now having left this kyng in kyndnes and frendship: We crossed over the Water to a sharpe point which is parte of Winauk on Salisbury syde (this I call careles point) Here some of our men went a shore with Naviraus, mett . 10 . or . 12 . Salvages, who offering them neither victualls nor Tobacco, they requitted their Courtesy with the like, and left them. This night we came to point Winauk right against which we rested all night. There was an olde man with King Pamaunche (which I omitted in place to specify) who wee understood to be . 110 . yere olde; for Navirans with being with us in our boate had learned me so much of the Languadg, & was so excellently ingenious in signing out his meaning, that I could make him understand me, and perceive him also wellny in any thing. But this knowledg our Captaine gatt by taking a bough and singling of the leaves, let one drop after another, saying caische which is . 10 . so first Navirans tooke . 11 . beanes and tolde them to us, pointing to this olde fellow, then 110. beanes; by which he awnswered to our demaund for . 10 . yeres a beane, and also every yere by it selfe. This was a lustye olde man, of a sterne Countenance, tall & straight, had a thinne white beard, his armes overgrowne with white haires, and he went as strongly as any of the rest.

Wensday we went a shore at point Winauk, where
May 27   Navirans caused them to goe a fisshing for us, and
they brought us in a shorte space good store: Thes
seemed our good frindes but (the cause I knowe not) heere
Navirans tooke some Conceyt, and though he shewed no discontent, yet would he by no meanes goe any further with us;
saying he would but goe upto kyng Arahatek, and then within
some three dayes after he would see us at our Fort. This greeved
out Captayne very Deeply, for the loving kyndnes of this fellow was such as he trusted himselfe with us out of his owne
Country, intended to come to our Forte, and as wee came he
would make frendship for us, before he would lett us goe a
shore at any place, being (as it seemed) very carefull of our
safety. So our Captayne made all haste home, Determyning
not to stay in any place as fearing some disasterous happ at our
forte. Which fell out as we expected, thus. After our Departure
they seeldome frequented our Fort, but by one or two single
now and then, practising upon oportunity, now in our absence, perceiving there secure Caryadg in the fort; and the
xxvith of May being the Day before our returne, there came
above . 200 . of them with their kyng and gave a very furious
Assault to our fort, endaungering their overthrowe, had not
the Shippes ordinance with their small shott daunted them:
They came up allmost into the Fort, shott through the tentes,
appeared in this Skirmishe (which indured hott about an
hower) a very valiant people: they hurt us . 11 . men (wherof
one dyed after) and killed a Boy, yet perceived they not this
Hurt in us. We killed Dyvers of them, but one wee sawe them
tugg of on ther backes, and how many hurt we knowe not. A
little after they made a huge noyse in the woodes, which our
men surmised was at the burying of their slayne men. Foure of
the Counsell that stood in front were hurt in mayntayning the
Forte, and our president Master Wynckfeild (who shewed
himselfe a valiant Gentleman) had one shott clean through his
bearde, yet scaped hurte.

Thus having ended our Discovery, which we hope may tend
to the glory of God, his Majesties Renowme our Countryes
profytt, our owne advauncing, and fame to all posterity: we

settled our selves to our owne safety, and began to fortefye; Captayne Newport worthely of his owne accord causing his Sea men to ayde us in the best parte therof.

May 28   Thursday We Laboured, pallozadoing our fort.

29   Fryday the Salvages gave on againe, but with more feare, not daring approche scarce within musket shott: they hurt not any of us, but finding one of our dogges they killed him: they shott above . 40 . arrowes into, & about the forte.

30   Satterday, we were quyet.

Sunday they came lurking in the thicketes and long grasse; and a Gentleman one Eustace Clovell unarmed stragling without the Fort, shott . 6 . Arrowes into him, wherwith he came runinge into the Fort, crying Arme Arme, thes stycking still: He lyved . 8 . Dayes, and Dyed. The Salvages stayed not, but run away.

June 1   Monday some . 20 . appeared, shott Dyvers Arrowes at randome which fell short of our Forte, and rann away.

2   Tuesday ⎱ quyet & wrought upon fortification,
3   Wensday ⎰   Clapboord, & setting of Corne.

4   Thursday by breake of Day . 3 . of them had most adverturously stollen under our Bullwark and hidden themselves in the long grasse; spyed a man of ours going out to doe naturall necessity, shott him in the head, and through the Clothes in two places, but missed the skynne.

5   Friday. quyet.

6   Satterday there being among the Gentlemen and all the Company a murmur and grudg against certayne preposterous proceedinges, and inconvenyent Courses, put up a Petytion to the Counsell for reformatyon.

7   Sonday. no accydent.

8   Monday. Master Clovell dyed that was shott with . 6 . Arrowes sticking in him. This afternoone . 2 . salvages presented themselves unarmed a farr of Crying Wingapoh; there were also three more having bowe and arrowes: those we Conjectured came from some of those kinges with whome We had perfect league: but one of our Gentlemen garding in the woodes and having no Comaundement to the Contrary shott at them: at which (as their Custome is) they fell

downe, and after run away: yet farther of we heard them crye Wingapoh notwithstanding.

9   Tuesday in cutting downe a greate oke for Clapboord, there issued out of the hart of the tree the quantity of two barricoes of liquor, in taste as good as any vyneger, save a little smack it tooke of the oke.

10   Wensday the Counsell scanned the Gentlemans Petityon: wherin Captayne Newport shewing himself no lesse Carefull of our Amitye and Combyned frendship, then became him in the deepe Desire he had of our good; vehemently with ardent affectyon wonne our hartes by his fervent perswasyon, to uniformity of Consent, and Callmed that, out of our Love to him, with ease, which I doubt without better satisfactyon had not contentedly ben caryed. Wee confirmed a faythfull Love one to another, and in our hartes subscribed an obedyence to our Superyours this Day. Captaine Smyth was this Day sworne one of the Counsell, who was elected in England.

11   Thursday, Articles and orders for Gentlemen and Soldyers were upon the Court of Garde, & Content was in the Quarter.

12   Fryday, Cutting downe another tree, the like accident of vineger proceeded.

13   Satterday . 8 . salvages lay close among the weedes and long grasse: and spying one or two of our Maryners Master Jhon Cotson and Master Mathew Fitch by themselves, shott Mathew Fytch in the breast somewhat Dangerously, and so rann away this Morning. Our Admiralls men gatt a Sturgeon of . 7 . foote long which Captayne Newport gave us.

14   Sondaye, two salvages presented themselves unarmed, to whome our President and Captaine Newport went out. one of these was that fellow I call in my Relatyon of Discovery our kinde Consort, being hee we mett at Turkye Ile. These certifyed us who were our frendes, and who foes, saying that kyng Pamaunke kyng Arahatec, the kyng of Youghtamong, and the king of Matapoll would either assist us or make us peace with Paspeiouk, Tapahanauk, Wynauk, Apamatecoh, and Chescaik, our Contracted Enemyes: He counselled us to Cutt Downe the long weedes rounde about

our Forte, and to proceede in our sawing: Thus making signes
to be with us shortly agayne, they parted.

15   Monday, we wrought upon Clapborde for England.

16   Tuesday, two salvages without from Salisbury syde
          being Tapahanauks Country, Captayne Newport
went to them in the barge ymagining they had ben our Sonday
frendes: but thes were Tapahanauks and cryed (treacherously)
Wingapoh, saying their king was on the other syde of a point,
where had our Barge gone it was so shold water as they might
have effected their villanous plott: but our Admirall told them
Tapahanauk was matah & chirah, wherat laughing they went
away.

17   Wensdaye. ⎫
18   Thursdaye. ⎪
19   Frydaye.   ⎬ no Accydent
20   Satterday. ⎭

21   Sondaye, we had a Communyon: Captaine
          Newport Dyned a shore with our Dyet, and invyted
many of us to Supper as a farewell.

EDWARD MARIA WINGFIELD

A Discourse of Virginia

RIGHT worshipfull: and more worthy

My due respect to your selves, my allegiance (if I may so terme it) to the Virginean action, my good heede to my poore reputacion, thrust a penne into my handes, so jealous am I to bee missing to any of them; if it wandereth in extravagantes, yet shall they not bee idle to those Phisitions, whose loves have undertaken the saftie and advancement of Virginia.

It is no small comfort that I speake before such gravitie, whose judgement no forrunner can forestall with any opprobrious untruths, whose wisedomes can easily disroabe malice out of her painted garments from the ever reverenced truth.

I did so faithfully betroth my best indeavors to this noble enterprize as my carriage might endure no suspition: I never turned my face from daunger, or hidd my handes from labour, so watchfull a Sentinel stood my self to my self.

I know wel a troope of errors continually beseege mens actions, some of them ceased on by malice, some by ignorance: I doo not hoodwinck my carriage in my self love, but freely and humblie submit it to your grave censures.

I do freely and truely Anatomize the governement and governours that your experience may applie medicines accordinglie, and upon the truth of this journall do pledge my faith, and life, and so do rest.

yours to commaund in all service

Here followeth what happined in James Towne in
Virginia after Captayne Newports departure for England.

Captayne Newport having allwayes his eyes and eares open to the proceedinges of the Collonye, 3. or 4. dayes before his departure, asked the president how he thought himself setled in the government, whose answere was that no disturbaunce could indaunger him of the Collonye, but it must be wrought eyther by Captayne Gosnold, or Master Archer; for the one was strong with freinds and followers, and could if he would; and the other was troubled with an ambitious spirit, and would if he could: The Captayne gave them both knowledg of this the Presidentes opinion, and mooved them with many intreatyes to be myndefull of their dutyes to his Majestie and the Collonye.

June 1607 The 22th Captayne Newport retorned for England, for whose good passadge, and safe retorne wee made many prayers to our allmighty god.

June the 25th an Indian Came to us from the great Poughwaton with the worde of peace, that he desired greatly our freindshipp that the wyroaunces, Paspaheigh, and Tapahanagh should be our freindes, that wee should sowe and reape in peace, or els he would make warrs upon them with us; This message fell out true, for both those wyroaunces have ever since remayned in peace, and trade with us: Wee rewarded the messinger, with many tryfles, which were great wonders to him.

This Powatan dwelleth 10 myles from us upon the River Pamaonche, which lyeth North from us; the Powatan in the former jornall mencioned (a dwellar by Captayn Newports faulls) ys a wyroaunce, and under this great Powaton, which before wee knew not.

July The 3 of July 7 or 8 Indians presented the President a Dear from Pamaonke, a wyroaunce desiring our freindshipp, they enquired after our shipping, which the President said was gon to Croatoon; they feare much our shipps; and therefore he would not have them thinck it farr from us; their wyrounce had a Hatchet sent hym, they wear well Contented with trifles: A litle after this Came a Dear to the President from the great Powatan: he and his messingers were pleased with the like trifles: The President likewise bought divers tymes Dear of the Indyans, beavars and other flesh, which he alwayes caused to be equally devided amongst the Collonye.

About this tyme divers of our men fell sick, wee myssed above Forty before September did see us, amongst whom was the Worthy and Religious gent Captayn Bartholmew Gosnold, upon whose lief stood a great part of good succes, and fortune of our government and Collony: In his sicknes tyme the president did easily fortell his owne deposing from his Comaund, so much differed the president and the other Councellors on mannaging the government of the Collonye.

The 7th of July Tapahanah a wyroaunce dweller on Salisbery side hayled us with the word of peace, the President with a Shallopp well manned went to him, he found him sytting on the ground Crossed legged as is their Custome, with one attending on him, which did often saie this is the wyroance Tapahanah, which he did likewise confirme with stroaking his brest, he was well enough knowne for the President had sene him diverse tymes before, his Countynance was nothing cherefull, for wee had not seene him since he was in the feild against us, but the President would take no knowledg thereof, and used him kindely, giving him a red Wascoat, which he did desire; Tapahanah did enquire after our shipping; he receyved answer as before, he said his ould store was spent, that his new was not at full groath by a foote; That as sone as any was ripe, he would bring it, which promise he truly performed

July

The   of   Master Kendall was put of from beeing of the Counsell, and committed to prison, for that it did manyfestly appeere he did practize to sowe discord betwene the President and Councell.

Sicknes had not now left us vi able men in our Towne, gods onely mercy did now watch and Warde for us, but the President hidd this our weakenes carefully from the salvages, never suffring them in all his tyme to come into our Towne.

The vith of September Paspaheigh sent us a boy that was run from us, this was the first assurance of his peace with us, besides wee found them no Canyballs: The boye observed the men & women to spend the most part of the night in singing, or howling, and that every morning the Women Carryed all the litle Childrenn to the Rivers sides, but what they did there he did not knowe.

Septem:

The rest of the wyroances doe likewise send our men runnagates to us home againe, using them well during their beeing with them; so as now they being well rewarded at home at their retorne, they take litle joye to travell abroad without Pasportes.

The Councell demaunded som larger allowaunce for them selves, and for some sick their favorites, which the President would not yield unto without their Warrantes.

This matter was before propounded by Captayn Martyn, but so nakedly as that he neyther knew the quantity of the stoare to be but for xiii weekes and a half under the Cap Merchauntes hand, he prayed them further to Consider the long tyme before wee expected Captayn Newportes retorne, the incertainty of his retorne, if god did not favour his voyage, the long tyme before our harvest would be ripe, and the doubtfull peace that wee had with the Indyans, which they would keepe no longer then opertunity served to doe us mischeif.

It was then therefore ordered, that every meale of fish or fleshe should excuse the allowance of poridg, both against the sick and hole.

The Counsell therefore sitting again upon this proposition instructed in the former reasons and order, did not thinke it fit to breake the former order by enlarging their allowance, as will appeere by the most voyces reddy to be shewed under their handes.

Now was the Comon store of olye, vinigar, sack, & Aquavite all spent saveing twoe Gallons of each; the sack reserved for the Communion table, the rest for such extreamityes as might fall upon us, which the President had onely made knowe to Captayn Gosnold, of which course he liked well, the vessells wear therefore boonged upp: When Master Gosnold was dead the President did acquaint the rest of the Councell with the said Remnant: but lord how they then longed for to supp up that litle remnant for they had now emptied all their owne bottles, and all other that they could smell out.

A litle wile after this the Councell did againe fall upon the President for some better allowance for themselves and some few of the sick their privates: The President protested he would not be partiall, but if one had any thing of him, every man should have his portion according to their places, Nevertheles that upon their Warrantes he would deliver what pleased them to demaund. Yf the President had at that tyme enlarged the proportion according to their request, without doubt in very short tyme he had starved the whole Company, he would not joyne with them therefore in such an ignorant murder without their owne Warrant.

The President well seeing to what end their ympacience would growe, desired them earnestly & often tymes to bestowe the Presidentshipp amonge themselves, that he could obey, a private man, as well as they could Comaund, but they refused to discharge him of the place, sayeing they mought not doe it, for that hee did his Majestie good service in yt.

In this meane tyme the Indians did daily relieve us with Corne and fleshe, that in three weekes the Presidant had reared upp xx men able to worke, for as his stoare increased he mended the Comon pott; hee had laid up besides provision for 3 . weekes, wheate beforehand.

By this tyme the Councell had fully plotted to depose Wingfeild the then President, and had drawne certeyne Artycles in Wrighting amongst them selves and toke their oathes upon the Evangelistes to observe them, th'effect whereof was first.

To depose the then President

To make Master Ratcliff the next President

Not to depose the one th' other

Not to take the deposed President into Councell againe

Not to take Master Archer into the Councell or any other without the Consent of every one of them; To theis they had subscribed, as out of their owne mouthes, at severall tymes it was easily gathered.

Thus had they forsaken his Majesties government sett us downe in the instruccions, & made it a Triumvirat.

It seemeth Master Archer was nothing acquainted with theis artycles, though all the rest crept out of his noates and Comentaryes that were preferred against the President; yet it pleased god to Cast him into the same disgrace and pitt that he prepared for an other, as will appeere hereafter.

Septem: The 10 of September, Master Ratcliff, Master Smyth, and Master Martynn Came to the Presidentes Tennt with a Warrant subscribed under their handes to depose the President, sayeing they thought him very unworthy to be eyther President or of the Councell, and therefore discharged him of bothe: Hee answered them that they had eased him of a great deale of Care, and trouble; that long since hee had divers tymes profered them the place at an easier rate, and further that the President ought to be removed (as appeereth in his Majesties instruccions for our government) by the greater number of xiii voyces Councellors, that they were but three, and thereofore wished them to proceede advisedly, but they told him if they did him wrong, they must answere it; Then said the deposed President I ame at your pleasure, dispose of me as you will without further Garboile.

I will now wright what followeth in my owne name and give the new President his title, I shalbe the briefer being thus discharged, I was Comytted to a Serjeant, and sent to the Pynnasse: but I was answered with, if they did me wrong, they must answer it.

The 11th of September I was sent for to Come before the President, and Councell upon their Court daie, they had now made Master Archer Recorder for Virginia; The President made a speeche to the Collony that he thought it fitt to acquaint them whie I was deposed. I ame now forced to stuff my Paper with frivilous trifles, that our grave and worthy Councell may the better strike those vaynes where the Corrupt blould lyeth, and that they may see in what manner of government the hope of the Collony now travayleth.

First Master President said that I had denyed him a penny whitle, a Chickyn, a spoonfull of beere, and served him with foule Corne, and with that pulled some graine out of a bagg shewing it to the Company.

Then start up Master Smyth, and said that I had tould him playnly how he lied, and that I said though wee were equall heere, yet if he were in England he would thinck scorne his man should be my Companyon.

Master Martyn followed with, he reporteth that I doe slack the service in the Collonye, and doe nothing but tend my pott, spitt, and oven, but he hath starved my sonne, and denyed him a spoonefull of beere; I have freindes in England shalbe revenged on him, if ever he Come in London.

I asked master President if I should answere theis Complaintes, and whether he had ought els to charge me with all; with that he pulled out a paper booke, loaded full with

Artycles against me, and gave them Master Archar to reade: I
tould Master President and the Councell; that by the instruccions for our government, our proceedinges ought to be verball, and I was there ready to answere: but they said they
would proceede in that order; I desired a Coppie of the Articles, and tyme given me to answere them likewise by wrighting, but that would not be graunted; I badd them then please
themselves; Master Archer then redd some of the Artycles,
when on the suddaine Master President said: staie, staie, wee
knowe not whether he will abide our Judgment, or whether he
will appeale to the King, sayeing to me: how saie you, will you
appeale to the King or no: I apprehended presently that gods
mercy had opened me a Waie through their ignorance, to escape their malice, for I never knewe howe I might demaunde
an appeale, besides I had secret knowledg how they had fore-
judged me to paie five fould for anything that Came to my
handes, whereof I could not discharge my self by wrighting,
and that I should lye in prison untill I had paid it.

The Cape Marchant had delivered me our Marchantdize
without any noat of the pertycularyties under my hand, for
himself had receyved them in grosse; I like wise as occation
mooved me spent them in Trade, or by guift amongst the
Indians, so likewise did Captayn Newport take of them; when
he went up to discover the kinges river, what he thought good,
without any noate of his hand, mentioning the Certainty, and
disposed of them as was fitt for him, of these likewise I could
make no accompt, onely I was well assured I had never bestowed the valewe of three penny Whitles to my owne use, nor
to the private use of any other, for I never carryed any favorite
over with me, or intertayned any thear, I was all one, and one
to all.

Upon theis consideracions I answered Master President and
the Councell that his Majesties handes were full of mercy and
that I did appeale to his Majesties mercy, they then comytted
me prisoner againe to the master of ye Pynnasse with theis
words: looke to him well he is now the kinges prisoner.

Then Master Archer pulled out of his bosome an other paper booke full of Artycles against me, desiring that he might
reade them in the name of the Collony: I said I stood there

ready to answere any mans Complaint whome I had wronged, but no one man spoke one word against me, then was he willed to reade his booke, whereof I complayned; but I was still answered if they doe me wrong they must answere it: I have forgotten the most of the Artycles they were so slight (yet he glorieth much in his penn worke) I knowe well the last, and a speeche that he then made savored well of a mutyny; for he desired that by no meanes, I might lye prysoner in the Towne, least boath he, and others of the Collony, should not give such obedience to their Comaund as they ought to doe, which goodly speech of his they easilye swallowed.

But it was usuall, and naturall to this honest gent Master Archer to be allwayes hatching of some mutany, in my tyme, hee might have appeered an author of 3 severall mutynies.

And hee (as Master Pearsie sent me worde) had bought some Witnesses handes against me to divers artycles with Indian Cakes (which was no great matter to doe after my deposall, and considering their hungar) perswations and threates; at an other tyme he feared not to saie openly, and in the presence of one of the Councell, that if they had not deposed me when they did, he hadd gotten twenty others to him self, which should have deposed me, but this speech of his was likewise easily disjested.

Master Croftes feared not to saie that if others would joyne with him, he would pull me out of my seate, and out of my skynn too; other would saie, (whose names I spare) that unlesse I would amend their allowance, they would be their owne Carvers; for these mutinus speeches, I rebuked them openly, and proceeded no further against them, Considering th'end of mens lives in the kinges service there; one of the Councell was very earnest with me to take a guard aboute me, I answered him I would no guard but gods love, and my owne innocencie. in all theis disorders was Master Archer a Ring leader.

When Master President and Master Archer had made an end of their Artycles above mencioned, I was againe sent prisoner to the Pynnasse, and Master Kendall taken from thence had his liberty, but might not Carry Armes.

All this while the Salvages brought to the Towne suche Corne and flesh as they could spare, Paspaheighe by Tapahanaes mediation was taken into freindshipp with us, the Councellors (Master Smyth especially) traded up and downe the River with the Indyans for Corn, which releved the Colony well.

As I understand by report I ame much charged with starving the Collony; I did allwayes give every man his allowance faithfully, both of Corne, oyle, aquivite &c as was by the Counsell proportioned, neyther was it bettered after my tyme, untill towards th'end of March, a Bisket was allowed to every workeing man for his breake-fast, by meanes of the provision brought us by Captayn Newport, as will appeere here after: It is further said I did much banquit, and Ryot: I never had but one Squirell roasted, whereof I gave part to Master Ratcliff then sick; yet was that Squirell given me; I did never heate a flesh pott, but when the Comon pot was so used likewise; Yet how often Master Presidentes and the Councellors spittes have night & daie bene endaungered to break their backes so laden with swanns, geese, duckes, &c, how many tymes their flesh pottes have swelled, many hungry eies did behold to their great longing: and what great Theeves, and theeving thear hath bene in the Comon stoare since my tyme, I doubt not but is all ready made knowne to his Majesties Councell for Virginia.

The 17th daie of September I was sent for to the Court to answere a Complaint exhibited against me by Jehu Robinson, for that when I was president, I did saie, hee with others had Consented to runn awaye with the Shallop to newfound land, at an other tyme, I must answere Master Smyth, for that I had said hee did conceale an intended mutany; I tould Master Recorder those wordes would beare no actions, that one of the Causes was done without the lymites mencioned in the Patent graunted to us, and therefore prayed Master President that I mought not be thus lugged with theis disgraces and troubles; but hee did weare no other eies or eares then grew on Master Archers head; The Jury gave the one of them 100li, and the other twoe hundred pound damages for slaunder, then Master Recorder did very learnedly comfort me, that if I had wrong, I might bring my writ of error in London, whereat I smiled.

I seeing their lawe so speedie and cheape, desired Justice for a Copper Kettle, which Master Crofts did deteyne from me, hee said I had given it him, I did bid him bringe his proofe for that; he Confessed hee had no proofe, Then Master President did aske me if I would be sworne I did not give it him, and I said I knew no cause whie to sweare for myne owne, hee asked Master Crofts if he would make oath, I did give it him, which oath hee tooke, and wann my Kettle from me, that was in that place and tyme, worth half his waight in gold; yet I did understand afterwards that he would have given John Capper the one half of the Kettle to have taken the oath for him, but hee would no Copper on that price.

I tould Master President I had not knowne the like lawe and prayed they would be more sparing of law, untill wee had more witt, or wealthe, that lawes were goode spies, in a populous, peaceable, and plentifull Cuntry, whear they did make the good men better, & stayed the badd from being worse, y^t wee weare so poore as they did but robb us of tyme that might be better ymployed in service in the Collonye.

The   daie of   the President did beat James Read the Smyth. the Smyth stroake him againe, for this he was condempned to be hanged, but before he was turned of the Lather he desired to speake with the President in private, to whome he accused Master Kendall of a mutiny, and so escaped himself: What Indictment master Recorder framed, against the Smyth I knowe not, but I knowe it is familiar for the President, Counsellors, and other officers to beate men at their pleasures, one lyeth sick till death, an other walketh lame, the third cryeth out of all his boanes, which myseryes they doe take upon their Consciences to Come to them by this their Almes of beating. Wear this whipping, lawing, beating, and hanging in Virginia knowne in England I feare it would drive many well affected myndes from this honorable action of Virginia.

This Smyth Comyng aboord the Pynnasse, with some others, aboute some busines 2 or 3 dayes before his arraignement brought me Comendacions from Master Pearsye, Master Waller, Master Kendall, and some others saieing they would be glad to see me on shoare: I answered him they were honest gentlemen and had carryed themselves very obediently to their governors, I prayed god that they did not thinck of any ill thing unworthie themselves; I added further that upon Sundaie if the weathiar were faire, I would be at the sermon, lastly I said that I was so sickly, starved, lame, and did lye so

could, and wett in the Pynnasse as I would be dragged thithere
before I would goe thither any more, sundaie proved not faire
I went not to the Sermon.

The   daie of   Master Kendall was executed being
shott to death for a mutiny. In th' arrest of his Judgment he alleaged to Master President that his name was Sicklemore, not
Ratcliff: & so had no authority to pronounce Judgment, then
Master Martyn pronounced Judgment.

Some what before this tyme the President, and Councell
had sent for the keyes of my Coffers, supposing that I had
some Wrightinges Concerning the Collony, I requested that
the Clearke of the Councell might see what they tooke out of
my Coffers, but they would not suffer him or any other, under
Cullor heereof they tooke my bookes of Accompt, and all my
noates that concerned the expences of the Collony, and instructions under the Cape Marchantes hande of the stoare of
provision, divers other bookes & trifles of my owne proper
goodes, which I could never recover. Thus was I made good
prise on all sides.

The   daie of   the President Comaunded me to Come
on shore, which I refused as not rightfully deposed and desired
that I mought speake to him and the Councell in the presence
of 10 of the best sorte of the gentry, with much intreaty some
of them wear sent for, then I tould them, I was determined to
goe into England to acquaint our Councell there, with our
weaknes; I said further their lawes, and government was such
as I had no joye to live under them any longer; that I did much
myslike their triumverat, haveing forsaken his Majesties instruccions for our government, and therefore praied there
might be more made of the Councell: I said further I desired
not to goe into England, if eyther Master President, or Master
Archer would goe but was willing to take my fortune with the
Collony, and did also proffer to furnish them with 100^{li}
towards the fetching home the Collonye, if the action was
given over; They did like of none of my proffers, but made
divers shott at mee in the Pynnasse: I seing their resolucions
went a shoare to them, whear after I had staied a while in conference they sent me to the Pynnasse againe.

Decem: The 10th of December Master Smyth went up the

Ryver of the Chechohomynaies to trade for Corne, he was desirous to see the heade of that River, and when it was not passible with the Shallop, he hired a Cannow and an Indian to Carry him up further, the river the higher grew worse and worse then hee went on shoare with his guide, and left Robinson & Emmery, twoe of our men in the Cannow, which were presently slayne by the Indians Pamaonkes men; and hee himself taken prysoner, and by the meanes of his guide his lief was saved, and Pamaonche haveing him prisoner Carryed him to his Neybors wyroances to see if any of them knew him for one of those, which had bene some twoe or three yeeres before us in a River amongst them Northward, and taken awaie some Indians from them, by force, at last he brought him to the great Powaton (of whome before wee had no knowledg) whoe sent him home to owr Towne the viiith of January.

January

During Master Smythes absence the President did swear Master Archer, one of the Councell, contrary to his oath taken in the Artycles agreed upon betweene themselves (before spoken of), and contrary to the kinges instruccions, and without Master Martyns consent, whereas there weare no more but the President and Master Martyn then of the Councell.

Master Archer being setled in his authority sought how to Call Master Smyths lief in question, and had indited him upon a Chapter in Leviticus for the death of his twoe men; hee had hadd his tryall the same daie of his retorne, and I believe his hanging the same, or the next daie, so speedie is our lawe thear, but it pleased god to send Captayn Newport unto us the same eevening to our unspeakable comfortes; whose arryvall saved Master Smyths leif, and myne, because hee tooke me out of the Pynnasse, an gave me leave to lye in the Towne: Also by his comyng was prevented a Parliament, which the newe Counsailor Master Recorder intended thear to summon; Thus error begot error.

Captayne Newport haveing landed, lodged, and refreshed his men, ymploied some of them aboute a faire stoare house, others aboute a stove, and his Maryners aboute a Chruch, all which workes they finished cherefully and in short tyme.

The 7 of January, our Towne was almost quite
January   burnt, with all our apparell and provision; but Cap-

tayn Newport healed our wants to our great Comforts, out of the great plenty sent us by the provident and loving care of our worhtie & most worthie Councell.

This Vigillant Captayne slacking no opertunity that might advaunce the prosperity of the Collony haveing setled the Compnay uppon the former workes, tooke Master Smyth and Master Scrivener (an other Councellor of Virginia, upon whose discretion liveth a great hope of the action) went to discover the Ryver Pamaonche on the further side, whearof dwelleth the great Powaton, and to trade with him for Corne: This River lyeth North from us, and runneth east and West, I have nothing but by relation, of that matter, and therefore dare not make any discourse thereof least I mought wrong the great desart, which Captayn Newports love to the action hath deserved, especially himself being present, and best able to give satisfaccion thereof, I will therefore to his retorne.

The 9th of Marche he retorned to James Towne,
March   with his Pynnasse well loaden with Corne, Wheat,
beanes, and Pease, to our great Comfort & his worthi Comendacions.

By this tyme the Counsell & Captaine haveing intentively looked into the Carryadge bothe of the Councellors, and other officers removed some officers out of the stoare; and Captayn Archer, a Councellor, whose insolency did looke upon that litle in himself with great sighted spectacles, derrogating from other merrites by spueing out his venemous libells, and infamous Chronicles, upon them; as doth appeere in his owne hand wrighting. For which & other worse trickes he had not escaped the halter, but that Captayn Newport interposed his advise to the Contrarye.

Captayne Newport haveing now dispatched all his busines
Aprill   and sett the Clocke in a true course (if so the Councell will keepe it) prepared himself for England upon
Maie   the xth of Aprill, and arryved at Blackwall on Sunday the xxith of Maye 1608.

FINIS

I humbly crave some patience to answere many scandalus imputacions, which malice, more than malice hath scattered upon my name, and those frivolous greevances objected against me by the President and Councell, and though *nil con-scire sibi* be the onely maske that can well cover my blushes; yett doe I not doubt, but this my Appollogie shall easily wipe them awaie.

It is noysed that I Combyned with the Spanniards to the distruccion of the Collony: That I ame an Athiest because I Carryed not a Bible, with me, and because I did forbid the preacher to preache, that I affected a Kindome: That I did hide of the Comon provision in the ground.

I Confesse I have alwayes admyred any noble vertue & prowesse as well in the Spanniards (as in other Nations) but naturally I have alwayes distrusted, and disliked their neighborhoode.

I sorted many bookes in my house to be sent up to me at my goeing to Virginia, a mongst them a bible; They were sent me up in a Trunk to London, with divers fruite, conserves, & preserves, which I did sett in Master Crofts his house in Ratcliff; In my beeing at Virginia I did understand my trunck was thear broken up, much of my sweete meates eaten at his Table, some of my bookes which I missid to be seene in his handes; and whether a mongst them my Bible was so ymbeasiled, or mislayed, by my servauntes; and not sent me I knowe not as yet.

Twoe or three sundayes morninges the Indians gave us allarums at our Towne, by that tymes they were answered, the place aboute us well discovered, and our devyne service ended, the daie was farr spent: The preacher did aske me if it weare my pleasure to have a sermon, hee said hee was prepared for it: I made answere that our men weare weary, and hungry, and that hee did see the tyme of the daie farr past (for at other tymes hee never made such question but the service finished he began his sermon) & that if it pleased him wee would spare him, till some other tyme: I never failed to take such noates by wrighting out of his doctrine as my Capacity could Comprehend, unlesse some raynie day hindred my indeavour.

My mynde never swelled with such ympossible mountebanck humors, as could make me affect any other Kingdome then the kingdome of heaven.

As truly as god liveth I gave an ould man then the keeper of the private stoure, 2 glasses with sallet oyle which I brought with me out of England for my private stoare, and willed him to bury it in the ground, for that I feared the great heate would spoile it, whatsoever was more I did never Consent unto, or knewe of it: And as truly was it protested unto me, that all the remaynder before mencioned of the oyle, wyne &c which the President receyved of me, when I was deposed, theye themselves poored into their owne bellyes.

To the Presidentes and Councelles objections I saie, that I doe knowe Curtesey and Civility became a governor; no penny whitle was asked me but a kniffe, whereof I had none to spare, the Indyans had long before stoallen my knife, of Chickins, I never did eat but one, and that in my sicknes; Master Ratcliff had before that tyme tasted of 4 or 5: I had by my owne huswiferie bred above 37 and the most part of them of my owne Poultrye, of all which at my Comyng awaye I did not see three liveing: I never denyed him (or any other) beare when I had it, the Corne was of the same which wee all lived upon.

Master Smyth in the tyme of our hungar had spred a Rumor in the Collony that I did feast my self and my servauntes, out of the Comon stoare, with entent (as I gathered) to have stirred the discontented Company against me, I tould him privately in Master Gosnolds Tent, that indeede I had caused half a pinte of pease to be sodden, with a peese of porke of my owne provision for a poore old man, which in a sicknes (wherof he died) he much desired, and said that if out of his malice he had given it out otherwise, that hee did tell a lye. It was proved to his face, that he begged in Ireland like a rogue, without lycence, to such I would not my name should be a Companyon.

Master Martins payns during my Comaund never stirred out of our Towne tenn scoare, and how slack hee was in his watching and other dutyes, it is too well knowne: I never defrauded his sonne of anything of his owne allowance, but gave him above it, I believe their disdainefull usage, and threates which they many tymes gave me, would have pulled some distempered speeches out of farr greater Pacyence then myne; yet shall not any revenging humor in me befoule my penn with their base names and lives here and there, I did visit Master Pearsie, master Hunt, Master Brewster, Master Pickasse, Master Allicock, ould short, the Bricklayer and diverse others, at severall tymes, I never miscalled at a gent at any time.

Concerning my deposing from my place, I can well proove

that Master Ratcliff said if I had used him well in his sicknes (wherein I finde not my self guilty of the contrary) I had never bene deposed.

Master Smith said if it had not bene for Master Archers I hadd never bene deposed: since his being heere in this Towne he hath said that he tould the President, and Councell that they were frivolous objections they had Collected against me, and that they had not doone well to depose me; Yet in my Conscience I doe believe him first & onely practizer in theis practises.

Master Archers quarrell to me was, because hee had not the choise of the place for our plantation, because I misliked his leying out of our Towne in the pinnasse, because I would not sware him of the Councell for Virginia, which neyther I could doo or he deserve.

Master Smyths quarrell because his name was mencioned in the entended & Confessed mutiny by Galthropp.

Thomas Wootton the Surjeon, because I would not subscribe to a Warrant (which he had gotten drawne) to the Treasurer of virginia to deliver him mony to furnish him with drugges, and other necessaryes, & because I disallowed his living in the pinnasse, haveing many of our men lyeing sick, & wounded in our Towne to whose dressinges by that meanes he slacked his attendaunce.

Of the same men also Captayn Gosnold gave me warning misliking much their dispositions, and assured me they would ley hold of me if they could, and peradventure many, because I held them, to watching warding, and workeing, and the Collony generally because I would not give my consent to starve them; I cannot rack one word, or thought from my self, touching my Carryadg in Virginia other then is herein sett downe.

If I may now at the last presume upon Your favours; I ame an honourable suitor; that your owne love of truth will vouchsafe to cleare me from all false aspersions happining since I embarked me into this affaire of Virginia, for my first worke (which was to make aright choise of a spirituall Pastor) I appeale to the remembraunce of my Lord of Caunterbury his grace; who gave me very gracious audience in my request. And the world knoweth, whome I tooke with me; truly in my opinion a man not any waie to be touched with the rebellious humors of a popish spirit, nor blemished with the least suspition of a factius scismatick. whereof I had a speciall Care. for other objections if your worthie selves be pleased to sett me free, I have learned to dispise the populer verdict of the vulgar. I ever chered up my self with a confidence in the wisdome of grave judicious Senatours & was never dismayed in all my service by any synister event, though I bethought me of the hard begininges which in former ages betided those worthy spirites, that planted the greatest Monarches in Asia & Europe, wherein I observed rather the troubles of Moses & Aron, with other of like History, then that venom in the mutinous brood of Cadmus or that harmony in the swete consent of Amphion: And when with the former I had considered that even the betheren at their plantacion of the Romaine Empire were not free from mortall hatred, & intestine garboile, likewise that both the Spanish & English Records are guilty of like factions, it made me more vigillant in the avoyding thereof: and I protest my greatest contencion was to prevent contencion, and my chiefest endeavor to preserve the lives of others, though with the great hazard of my own for I never desired to enamell my name with bloude: I rejoyce that my travells & daungers have done somewhat for the behoof of Jerusalem in virginia. If it be objected as my oversight to put my self amongst such men, I can saie for my self there wear not any other for our consort. & I could not forsake the enterprise of opening so glorious a Kingdome unto the king, wherein I shall ever be most ready to bestow the poore remainder of my dayes, as in any other his Heighnes disignes according to my bounden duty with the utmost of my poore Tallent.

HENRY SPELMAN

Relation of Virginea

Beinge in displeasuer of my frendes, and desirous to see other cuntryes, After three moneths sayle we cum with prosperus winds in sight of Virginia wher A storme sodenly arisinge seavered our fleete, (which was of x sayle) every shipp from other, puttinge us all in great daunger for vii or viii dayes to-gither. But the storme then ceasing our shipp called the unitye cam the next morning saffly to an anker at Cape Henry, the daye of October 1609, Wher we found thre other of our fleete, and about a senight after thre more cam thether also. The residew Amongst which was Sir Thomas Gates and Sir George Summers Knights wear not hard of many monthes after our arivall.

From Cape Henry we sayled up the River of Powáhtan & with in 4 or 5 dayes arived at James toune, wher we weare joy-fully welcomed by our cuntrymen beinge at that time about 80 persons under the goverment of Capt Smith, The Præsidant. Havinge heare unladed our goods & bestowed sum senight or fortnight in vieinge of the cuntry, I was caried By Capt Smith our Presidant to the Fales, to the litell Powhatan wher un-knowne to me he sould me to him for a towne caled Powhatan and leavinge me with him the litle Powhatann, He made knowne to Capt weste how he had bought a toune for them to dwell in desireing that captaine West would come & settle himself there, but captaine Weste having bestowed cost to be-gine a toune in another place misliked it: and unkindnesse thereuppon ariseing betweene them Capt Smith at that time repliede litell but afterward conspired with the Pohawtan to kill Capt weste, which Plott tooke but smale effect, for in the meane time Capt Smith was Aprehended, and sent abord for England, my self havenge binn now about vii or viii dayes with the litell Powhatan who though he made very much of me giving me such thinges as he had to winn me to live with him.

Yet I desired to see our english and therfore made signes unto
him to give me leave to goe to our ship to feach such thinges
as I leafte behind me, which he agreed unto and settinge himselfe doune, he clapt his hand on the ground in token he
would stay ther till I returned. But I staying sumwhat to long,
at my cumminge to the place wher I leaft him I found him departed wheruppon I went backe to our shipp beinge still in the
Fales and sayled with them to James toune. wher not beinge
long ther, Before one Thomas Savage with 4 or 5 Indians cam
from the great Powhatan with venison to Capt: Percye who
now was president. After the delivery therof and that he must
returne he was loith to goe with out sum of his cuntrymen
went with him, wher uppon I was apoynted to goe, which I
the more willinglie did, by Reason that vitals were scarse with
us, cariinge with me sum copper and a hatchet which I had
gotten. Cumminge to the Great Powetan I presented to him
such thinges as I had which he took, usinge me very kindly,
And After I had bin with him about 3 weekes he sent me backe
to our English bidding me tell them, that if they would bring
ther ship, and sum copper, he would fraught hir backe with
corne, which I having reported to our English and returning
ther answer to the Kinge, He before ther cumminge layd plotts
to take them, which in sum sort he affected, for xxvi or vii they
killed which cam towards land in ther long boate, and shott
many arrows into the shipp, which our men perseyving and
fearinge the worst, wayed anker and returned. Now whil this
busines was in action the Powhatan sends me and one Samwell
a Dutchman To a toune about xvi miles of, caled Yawtanoone
willinge us ther to stay for him, At his cumminge thether we
understood how althinges had passed by Thomas Savage, as
before is related, the Kinge in shew made still much of us yet
his mind was much declined from us which made us feare the
worst, and having now bin with him about 24 or 25 weekes, it
happned that the Kinge of Patomeck cam to visitt the great
Powetan, wher beinge a while with him, he shewed such
kindnes to Savage Samuell and my self as we determined to
goe away with him, when the daye of his departure was cum,
we did as we agreed and havenge gone a mile or tow on the
way, Savage fayned sum excuss of stay & unknowne to us went
backe to the Powetan and acquaynted him with our departing

with the Patowomeck. The Powetan presenly sends after us comandinge our returne: which we refuseing went still on our way: and thos that weare sent, went still on with us. till one of them findinge oportunity on a sunden strooke Samuell with an axe and killed him, which I seinge ran a way from a monge the cumpany, they after me, the Kinge and his men after them, who overtake them heald them, till I shifted for my self and gott to the Patomeckes cuntry, With this King Patomecke I lived a year and more at a towne of his called Pasptanzie, untill such time as an worthy gentleman named Capt: Argall arived at a toune cald Nacottawtanke, but by our english cald Camocacocke, wher he understood that ther was an english boy named Harry, He desiringe to here further of me cam up the river which the Kinge of Patomeck hearringe sent me to him and I goinge backe agayne brought the kinge to the shipe, wher capt: Argoll gave the Kinge copper for me, which he receyved Thus was I sett at libertye and brought into England.

Xatauahane.

Of ther servis to ther gods

To give sum satisfaction to my frends and contentment unto others, which wish well to this viage, and are desirus to heare the fashions of that cuntrye: I have set doune as well as I can, what I observed in the time I was amonge them. And therfore first concerninge ther gods, yow must understand that for the most part they worship the divell, which the counjurers who are ther preests, can make apeare unto them at ther pleasuer, yet never the less in every cuntry they have a severall Image whom they call ther god. As with the great Pawetan he hath an Image called Cakeres which most comonly standeth at Yaughtawnoone or at Oropikes in a house for that purpose and with him are sett all the Kings goods and presents that are sent him, as the Cornne. But the beades or Crowne & Bedd which the Kinge of England sent him are in the gods house at Oropikes, and in their houses are all the Kinge ancesters and kindred commonly Buried, In the Patomecks cuntry they have an other god whom they call

Caukewis
Manato.
Taukinge
souke
Quiauasack.

Quioquascacke, and unto ther Images they offer Beades and
Copper if at any time they want Rayne or have to much, and
though they observe no day to worshipe ther god: but uppon
necessitye, yet onc in the yeare, ther preests which are ther
conjurers with the men weomen and children doe goe into
the woods, wher ther preests makes a great cirkell of fier in
the which after many observanses in ther conjurations they
make offer of 2 or 3 children to be given to ther god if he will
apeare unto them and shew his mind whome he desier. Uppon
which offringe they heare a noyse out of the Cirkell Nomi-
natinge such as he will have, whome presently they take
bindinge them hand and footte and cast them into the circle of
the fier, for be it the Kinges sonne he must be given if onc
named by ther god, After the bodies which are offered are
consumed in the fier and ther cerimonees performed the men
depart merily, the weamen weaping.

Of the cuntry of Virginia

THE cuntry is full of wood in sum partes, and water they have
plentifull, they have marish ground and smalefields, for corne,
and other grounds wher on ther Deare, goates and
stages feadeth, ther be in this cuntry Lions, Beares,
woulves, foxes, muske catts, Hares [a]fleinge squirells,
and other squirels beinge all graye like conyes, great store of
foule only Peacockes and common hens wanting: fish in
aboundance wher on they live most part of the Summer time.
They have a kind of wheat cald locataunce and Pease and
Beanes, Great store of walnuts growing in every place, They
have no orchard frutes, only tow kind of plumbes the one a
sweet and lussius plumbe long and thicke in forme and liknes
of A Nutt Palme. the other resemblinge a medler But sumwhat
sweeter yet not Ætable till they be rotten as ours are,

[a]caled
assapameek.

Of ther Tounes & buildinges

PLACES of Habitation they have but feaw for the greatest toune
have not above 20 or 30 houses in it, Ther Biuldinge are made

like an oven with a litell hole to cum in at But more spatius with in havinge a hole in the midest of the house for smoke to goe out at, The Kinges houses are both broader and longer then the rest havinge many darke windinges and turnings before any cum wher the Kinge is, But in that time when they goe a Huntinge the weomen goes to a place apoynted before, to biuld houses for ther husbands to lie in att night carienge matts with them to cover ther houses with all, and as the men goes further a huntinge the weomen follows to make houses, always carrienge ther mattes with them. Ther maner of ther Huntinge is thiss: they meett sum 2 or 300 togither and havinge ther bowes and arrows and every one with a fier sticke in ther hand they besett a great thikett round about, which dunn every one sett fier on the ranke grass which the Deare seinge fleeth from the fier, and the menn cumminge in by a litell and litle incloseth ther game in a narrow roome, so as with ther Bowes and arrowes they kill them at ther pleasuer takinge ther skinns which is the greatest thinge they desrie, and sume flesh for ther provision.

Ther maner of mariing

T HE custum of the cuntry is to have many wives and to buye them, so that he which have most copper and Beads may have most wives, for if he taketh likinge of any woman he makes love to hir, and seeketh to hir father or kindsfolke to sett what price he must paye for hir, which beinge one agreed on the kindred meett and make good cheere, and when the sume agreed on be payd she shall be delivered to him for his wife. The cerimony is thus: The parents bringes ther daughter be-twene them (if hir parents be deade then sume of hir kinsfolke, or whom it pleaseth the king to apoynt, for the man goes not unto any place to be maried But the woman is brought to him wher he dwelleth). At hir cumminge to him, hir father or cheefe frends joynes the hands togither and then the father or cheef frend of the man Bringeth a longe stringe of Beades and mea-suringe his armes leangth therof doth breake it over the hands of thos that are to be married while ther handes be joynned together, and gives it unto the womans father or him that brings hir, And so with much mirth and feastinge they goe togither, When the Kinge of the cuntry will have any wives he acquaintes his cheef men that his purpose, who sends into all partes of the cuntry for the fayrest and cumliest mayds out of which the Kinge taketh his choyse given ther parents what he pleaseth. If any of the Kings wives have onc a child by him, he keepes her no longer but puts hir from him givinge hir suffitient Copper and beads to mayntayne hir and the child while it is younge and then is taken from hir and mayntayned by the King, it now beinge lawfull for hir beinge thus put away to marry with any other, The Kinge Poetan havinge many wives when he goeth a Huntinge or to visitt another Kinge under him (for he goeth not out of his owne cuntry) He leaveth them with tow ould men who have the charge on them till his returne.

This Pasptanse was brother to Patoomsk.   It was my happ to be leaft at one of the Kings Pasptanses Howses when we went to visitt another Kinge and two of his wives wear ther also, after the Kings departure, one of them would goe visitt hir father, hir name was Paupauwiske and seigne me, willed me to goe with hir and to take hir child and carye him thether in my armes, beinge a days jouyrnye from the place wher we dwelt, which I refusinge she strook me 3 or 4 blows, but I beinge loith to beare to much gott to hir and puld hir doune giving hir sum blows agayne which the other of the Kings wives perseyvinge, they both fell on me beatinge me so as I thought they had lamd me, Afterwarde when the Kinge cam home: in ther presents I acquainted him how they had used me, The King with out further delay tooke up a *couwascohocan*, which is a kind of paringe Iron, and strooke at one of them with such violenc, as he feld her to the ground in manor deade. I seinge that, fled to a Neyghburs house, for feare of the Kings displeasuer, But his wife cumming againe to hir self: sumwhat apeased his anger so as understandinge wher I was by his brother, he sent me his younge child to still, for none could quiet him so well as my selfe. and about midnight he sent for him againe, The next day morninge the King was erlye upp, and came to the house wher I was: loith I was to see him, yet being cum to him instead of his anger, I found him kind to me, asking me how I did, and whether I was affrayd of him last night, bycause I rann away from him, and hidd my selfe, I being by his speeches sumwhat boulder, Asked him for his Queene, He answerd all was well and that I should goe home with him tellinge me he loved me, and none should hurt me. I thought loith went with him, wher at my cumminge the Queene looked but discontentedly on me, But hoping on the Kinges promise, I cared the less for others frownes, knowinge well that the Kinge made the more of me in hope I should healpe him to sum copper, if at any time our english cam into thos parts. which I often had promised him to doe, and which was by Capt: Argoll Bountifully performed.

How the name ther children

AFTER the mother is delivered of hir child with in sum feaw dayes after the kinsfolke and neyburs beinge intreated ther unto, cums unto the house: wher beinge assembled the father, takes the child in his armes: and declars that his name shall be, as he then calls him, so his name is, which dunn the rest of the day is spent in feastinge, and dauncinge.

Ther maner of visitinge the sicke with the fation of ther buriall if they dye

WHEN any be sicke among them ther preestes cums unto the partye whom he layeth on the ground uppon a matt And having a boule of water, sett betwene him and the sicke partye; and a Rattle by it, The preest kneelinge by the sick mans side dipps his hand into the boule, which takinge up full of watter, he supps into his mouth, spowtinge it out againe, uppon his oune armes, and brest, then takes he the Rattle, and with one hand shakes that, and with the other, he beates his brest, makinge a great noyes, which havinge dunn he easilye Riseth (as loith to wake the sicke bodye, first with one legge, then with the other, And beinge now gott up, he leaysuerly goeth about the sicke man shakinge his Rattle very softly over all his bodye: and with his hand he stroketh the greaved parts of the sicke, then doth he besprinkell him with water mumlinge

certayne words over him, and so for that time leave him, But if
he be wounded after thes cerimonyes dunn unto him he with a
litle flint stone gasheth the wound makinge it to runn and
bleede which he settinge his mouth unto it suckes out, and
then aplies a certayne roote betten to powter unto the Sore. If
he dies his buriall is thus ther is a scaffould built about 3 or 4
yards hye from the ground and the deade bodye wraped in a
matt is brought to the place, wher when he is layd ther on, the
kinsfolke falles a weopinge and make great sorrow, and instead
of a dole for him, (the porer people beinge gott togither)
sum of his kinsfolke flinges Beades amonge them makinge
them to scramble for them, so that many times divers doe
breake ther armes and legges beinge pressed by the cumpany,
this finished they goe to the parties house wher they have meat
given them which beinge Æaten all the rest of the day they
spend in singinge and dauncinge using then as much mirth as
before sorrow more over if any of the kindreds bodies which
have bin layd on the scaffould be so consumed as nothing is
leaft but bonns they take thos bonns from the scaffould and
puttinge them into a new matt, hangs them in ther howses,
wher they continew whille ther house falleth and then they are
buried in the ruinges of the house what goods the partye
leaveth is devided amonge his wives and children. But his
house he giveth to the wife he liketh best for life: after her
death, unto what child he most loveth,

The Justis and government

CONCERNINGE ther lawes my years and understandinge, made
me the less to looke after bycause I thought that Infidels wear
lawless yet when I saw sum put to death I asked the cause of
ther offence, for in the tine I was with the Patomecke I saw 5
executed 4 for murther of a child (id est) the mother and tow
other that did the fact with hir and a 4 for consealing it as he
passed by, beinge bribed to hould his pease. and one for robbinge a traveler of coper and beades for to steale ther neyburs
corne or copper is death, or to lye one with anothers wife is
death if he be taken in the manner,

The manor of execution

Thos that be convicted of capitall offences are brough into a playne place before the Kinges house wher then he laye, which was at Pomunkeye the chefest house he hath wher one or tow apoynted by the Kinge did bind them hand and foote, which being dunn a great fier was made, Then cam the officer to thos that should dye, and with a shell cutt of ther long locke, which they weare on the leaft side of ther heade, and hangeth that on a bowe before the Kings house Then those for murther wear Beaten with staves till ther bonns weare broken and beinge alive weare flounge into the fier, the other for robbinge was knockt on the heade and beinge deade his bodye was burnt

The manor of settinge ther corne
with the gatheringe & Dressing

They make most commonly a place about ther howses to sett ther corne, which if ther be much wood, in that place the cutt doune the great trees sum half a yard above the ground, and the smaller they burne att the roote pullinge a good part of barke from them to make them die, & in this place they digg many holes which before the English brought them scavels and spades they used to make with a crooked peece of woode being scraped on both sides in fation of a gardiners paring Iron. they put in to thes holes ordenarily 4 or 5 curnels of ther wheat and 2 beanes like french beanes, which when the wheat doe growe up havinge a straw as bigg as a canne reede the beanes runn up theron like our hopps on poles, The eare of the wheat is of great bignes in lenght and cumpace and yet for all the greatnes of it every stalke hath most commonly sum fower of five eares on it, Ther corne is sett and gathered about the time we use, but ther maner of ther gatheringe is as we doe our Apells first in a hand basketts emtiinge them as they are filled into other bigger basketts wherof sum are made of the barkes of trees sume of heampe which naturally groweth ther and some of the straw wheron the wheat groweth, Now after the gatheringe, they laye it uppon matts agood thicknes in the sonn to drye & every night they make a great pile of it, coveringe it over with matts to defend it from the dewe, and when it is suffitienly weathered they pile it up in ther howses dayly as occation serveth wringinge the eares in peises betwene ther hands, and so rubbinge out ther corne do put it in to a great Baskett which taketh upp the best parte of sum of ther howses, and all this is cheefly the weomens worke for the men doe only hunt to gett skinns in winter and doe tewe or dress them in summer.

But though now out of order yet let me not altogither for-gett the settinge of the Kings corne for which a day is apoynted wherin great part of the cuntry people meete who with such diligence worketh as for the most part all the Kinges corne is sett on a daye After which setting the Kinge takes the croune which the Kinge of England sent him beinge brought him by tow men, and setts it on his heade which dunn the people goeth about the corne in maner backwardes for they going before, and the king followinge ther faces are always toward the Kinge exspectinge when he should flinge sum beades amonge them which his custum is at that time to doe makinge those which had wrought to scramble for them But to sume he favors he bids thos that carry his Beades to call such and such unto him unto whome he giveth beads into ther hande and this is the greatest curtesey he doth his people, when his corne is ripe the cuntry people cums to him againe and gathers drys and rubbes out all his corne for him, which is layd in howses apoynted for that purpose.

The settinge at meat

THEY sett on matts round about the house the men by them selves and the weomen by ther selves the weomen bringe to every one a dish of meat for the better sort never eates togither in one dish. when he hath eaten what he will, or that which was given him, for he looks for no second corse he setts doune his dish by him and mumleth ceartayne words to himself in maner of givinge thankes, if any leaft the weomen gather it up & ether keeps it till the next meall, or gives it to the porer sort, if any be ther.

The differences amonge them

THE King is not know by any differenc from other of the chefe sort in the cuntry but only when he cums to any of ther howses they present him with copper Beades or Vitall. and shew much reverence to him

The preest are shaven on the right side of ther head close to the scull only a litle locke leaft at the eare and sum of thes have beards But the common people have no beards at all for they pull away ther hares as fast as it growes And they also cutt the heares on the right side of ther heade that it might not hinder them by flappinge about ther bow stringe, when they draw it to shoott, But on the other side they lett it grow and have a long locke hanginge doune ther shoulder,

The Armor and wepon with the dissipline in war

As for Armoure or dissipline in ware the have not any. The weopons they use for offence are Bowes and Arrowes with a weapon like a hammer and ther Tomahaucks for defence which are shilds made of the barke of a tree and hanged on ther leaft shoulder to cover that side as they stand forth to shoote

They never fight in open fields but always ether amonge reede or behind trees takinge ther oportunitie to shoot at ther enimies and till they can nocke another arrow they make the trees ther defence

In the time that I was ther I sawe a Battell fought betwene the Patomecke and the Masomeck, ther place wher they fought was a marish ground full of Reede. Beinge in the cuntry of the Patomecke the peopel of Masomeck weare brought thether in Canoes which is a kind of Boate they have made in the forme of an Hoggs trowgh But sumwhat more hollowed in, On Both sids they scatter them selves sum litle distant one from the other, then they take ther bowes and arrows and havinge made ridie to shoot they softly steale toward ther enimies, Sumtime squattinge doune and priinge if they can spie any to shoot at whom if at any time he so Hurteth that he can not flee they make hast to him to knock him on the heade, And they that kill most of ther enimies are heald the cheefest men amonge them; Drums and Trumpetts they have none, but when they will gather themselves togither they have a kind of Howlinge or Howbabub so differinge in sounde one from the other as both part may very aesely be distinguished. Ther was no great slawter of nether side But the massomecks having shott away most of ther arrows and wantinge Vitall, weare glad to retier;

The Pastimes

WHEN they meet at feasts or otherwise they use sprorts much like to ours heare in England as ther daunsinge, which is like our darbysher Hornepipe a man first and then a woman and so through them all, hanging all in a round, ther is one which stand in the midest with a pipe and a rattell with which when he beginns to make a noyes all the rest Gigetts about wriinge ther neckes and stampinge on the ground

They use beside football play, which wemen and young boyes doe much play at. The men never They make ther Gooles as ours only they never fight nor pull one another doune

The men play with a litel balle lettinge it fall out of ther hand and striketh it with the tope of his foot, and he that can strike the ball furthest winns that they play for.

WILLIAM STRACHEY

A True Reportory

A true reportory of the wracke, and redemption of Sir Thomas
Gates Knight; upon, and from the Ilands of the Bermudas:
his comming to Virginia, and the estate of that Colonie
then, and after, under the government of the
Lord La Warre, July 15. 1610. written by
William Strachy, Esquire.

I.

A most dreadfull Tempest (the manifold deaths whereof are
here to the life described) their wracke on Bermuda,
and the description of those Ilands.

Excellent Lady, know that upon Friday late in the evening, we brake ground out of the Sound of Plymouth, our whole Fleete then consisting of seven good Ships, and two Pinnaces, all which from the said second of June, unto the twenty three of July, kept in friendly consort together not a whole watch at any time, loosing the sight each of other. Our course when we came about the height of betweene 26. and 27. degrees, we declined to the Northward, and according to our Governours instructions altered the trade and ordinary way used heretofore by Dominico, and Mevis, in the West Indies, and found the winde to this course indeede as friendly, as in the judgement of all Sea-men, it is upon a more direct line, and by Sir George Summers our Admirall had bin likewise in former time sailed, being a Gentleman of approved assurednesse, and ready knowledge in Sea-faring actions, having often carried command; and chiefe charge in many Ships Royall of her Majesties, and in sundry Voyages made many defeats and attempts in the time of the Spaniards quarrelling with us; upon the Ilands and Indies, &c. We had

2. June. 1609.

Sea-course altered.

Sir G Summers a good mariner and tried Souldier.

followed this course so long, as now we were within seven or
eight dayes at the most, by Cap, Newports reckoning of making Cape Henry upon the coast of Virginia: When on S. James
his day, July 24. being Monday (preparing for no lesse all the

A terrible
storme
expressed
in a patheti-
call and
retoricall de-
scription.
Black-
darknes.
blacke night before) the cloudes gathering thicke
upon us, and the windes singing, and whistling most
unusually, which made us to cast off our Pinnace
towing the same until then asterne, a dreadfull
storme and hideous began to blow from out the
North-east, which swelling, and roaring as it were by

fits, some houres with more violence then others, at length did
beate all light from heaven; which like an hell of darkenesse
turned blacke upon us, so much the more fuller of horror, as
in such cases horror and feare use to overrunne the troubled,
and overmastered sences of all, which (taken up with amazement) the eares lay so sensible to the terrible cries, and mur-
murs of the windes, and distraction of our Company, as who

Feare of
death at Sea
more
fearefull.
was most armed, and best prepared, was not a little
shaken. For surely (Noble Lady) as death comes not
so sodaine nor apparant, so he comes not so elvish
and painfull (to men especially even then in health and perfect
habitudes of body) as at Sea; who comes at no time so welcome, but our frailty (so weake is the hold of hope in miserable
demonstrations of danger) it makes guilty of many contrary
changes, and conflicts: For indeede death is accompanied at no
time, nor place with circumstances every way so uncapable of
particularities of goodnesse and inward comforts, as at Sea.
For it is most true, there ariseth commonly no such unmercifull tempest, compound of so many contrary and divers Nations, but that it worketh upon the whole frame of the body,
and most loathsomely affecteth all the powers thereof: and the
manner of the sicknesse it laies upon the body, being so unsuf-
ferable, gives not the minde any free and quiet time, to use her
judgement and Empire: which made the Poet say:

> *Hostium uxores, puerique cæcos*
> *Sentiant motus orientis Hædi, &*
> *Æquoris nigri fremitum, & trementes*
> *   Verbere ripas.*

For foure and twenty houres the storme in a rest-
Continuance and increase. lesse tumult, had blowne so exceedingly, as we could
not apprehend in our imaginations any possibility of
greater violence, yet did wee still finde it, not onely more terrible, but more constant, fury added to fury, and one storme
urging a second more outragious then the former; whether it so
wrought upon our feares, or indeede met with new forces:
Sometimes strikes in our Ship amongst women, and passengers,
not used to such hurly and discomforts, made us looke one
upon the other with troubled hearts, and panting bosomes: our
clamours dround in the windes, and the windes in thunder.
Prayers might well be in the heart and lips, but drowned in the
outcries of the Officers: nothing heard that could give comfort,
nothing seene that might incourage hope. It is impossible for
me, had I the voyce of Stentor, and expression of as many
tongues, as his throate of voyces, to express the outcries and
miseries, not languishing, but wasting his spirits, and art constant to his owne principles, not prevailing. Our sailes wound
up lay without their use, and if at any time wee bore but a Hol-
locke, or halfe forecourse, to guide her before the Sea, six and
sometimes eight men were not inough to hold the whipstaffe
in the steerage, and the tiller below in the Gunner roome, by
Swelling Sea set forth in a swelling stile. which may be imagined the strength of the storme: In
which, the Sea swelled above the Clouds, and gave
battell unto Heaven. It could not be said to raine, the
waters like whole Rivers did flood in the ayre. And this I did still
observe, that whereas upon the Land, when a storme hath
powred it selfe forth once in drifts of raine, the winde as beaten
downe, and vanquished therewith, not long after indureth:
here the glut of water (as if throatling the winde ere while) was
no sooner a little emptied and qualified, but instantly the
Compared with the Authors former experiments. windes (as having gotten their mouthes now free, and
at liberty) spake more loud, and grew more tumul-
tuous, and malignant: What shall I say? Windes and
Seas were as mad, as fury and rage could make them;
for mine owne part, I had bin in some stormes before, as well
upon the coast of Barbary and Algeere, in the Levant, and once
more distresfull in the Adriatique gulfe, in a bottome of Candy,
so as I may well say. *Ego quid sit ater Adriæ novi sinus, & quid*

albus Peccet Iapex. Yet all that I had ever suffered gathered together, might not hold comparison with this: there was not a
moment in which the sodaine splitting, or instant over-setting
of the Shippe was not expected.

Leake added to the stormes terrour.   Howbeit this was not all; It pleased God to bring a
greater affliction yet upon us; for in the beginning of
the storme we had received likewise a mighty leake.
And the Ship in every joynt almost, having spued out her
Okam, before we were aware (a casualty more desperate then
any other that a Voyage by Sea draweth with it) was growne
five foote suddenly deepe with water above her ballast, and we
almost drowned within, whilest we sat looking when to perish
from above. This imparting no lesse terrour then danger, ranne
through the whole Ship with much fright and amazement,
startled and turned the bloud, and tooke downe the braves of
the most hardy Marriner of them all, insomuch as he that
before happily felt not the sorrow of others, now began to sorrow for himselfe, when he saw such a pond of water so suddenly broken in, and which he knew could not (without
present avoiding) but instantly sinke him. So as joyning (onely
for his owne sake, not yet worth the saving) in the publique
safety; there might be seene Master, Masters Mate, Boateswaine, Quarter Master. Coopers, Carpenters, and who not,
with candels in their hands, creeping along the ribs viewing
the sides, searching every corner, and listening in every place,
if they could heare the water runne, Many a weeping leake was
this way found, and hastily stopt, and at length one in the
Gunner roome made up with I know not how many peeces
of Beefe: but all was to no purpose, the Leake (if it were but
one) which drunke in our greatest Seas, and tooke in our de-

Leake cannot be found, which cannot but be found.   struction fastest, could not then be found, nor ever
was, by any labour, counsell, or search. The waters
still increasing, and the Pumpes going, which at
length choaked with bringing up whole and continuall Bisket
(and indeede all we had, tenne thousand weight) it was conceived, as most likely, that the Leake might be sprung in the
Breadroome, whereupon the Carpenter went downe, and ript
up all the roome, but could not finde it so.

I am not able to give unto your Ladiship every mans thought
in this perplexity, to which we were now brought; but to me,

this Leakage appeared as a wound given to men that were before dead. The Lord knoweth, I had as little hope, as desire of life in the storme, & in this, it went beyond my will; because beyond my reason, why we should labour to preserve life; yet we did, either because so deare are a few lingring houres of life in all mankinde, or that our Christian knowledges taught us, how much we owed to the rites of Nature, as bound, not to be false to our selves, or to neglect the meanes of our owne preservation; the most despairefull things amongst men, being matters of no wonder nor moment with him, who is the rich Fountaine and admirable Essence of all mercy.

Their labour for life three dayes and foure nights. Our Governour, upon the tuesday morning, (at what time, by such who had bin below in the hold, the Leake was first discovered) had caused the whole Company, about one hundred and forty, besides women, to be equally divided into three parts, and opening the Ship in three places (under the forecastle, in the waste, and hard by the Bitacke) appointed each man where to attend; and there-unto every man came duely upon his watch, tooke the Bucket, or Pumpe for one houre, and rested another. Then men might be seene to labour, I may well say, for life, and the better sort, even our Governour, and Admirall themselves, not refusing their turne, and to spell each the other, to give example to other. The common sort stripped naked, as men in Gallies, the easier both to hold out, and to shrinke from under the salt water, which continually leapt in among them, kept their eyes waking, and their thoughts and hands working, with tyred bodies, and wasted spirits, three dayes and foure nights desti-tute of outward comfort, and desperate of any deliverance, tes-tifying how mutually willing they were, yet by labour to keepe each other from drowning, albeit each one drowned whilest he laboured.

Sea breakes in. Once so huge a Sea brake upon the poope and quarter, upon us, as it covered our Shippe from stearne to stemme, like a garment of a vast cloude, it filled her brimme full for a while within, from the hatches up to the sparre decke. This source or confluence of water was so violent, as it rusht and carried the Helm-man from the Helme, and wrested the Whipstaffe out of his hand, which so flew from side to side, that when he would have ceased the same againe, it so tossed him from Star-boord to Lar-boord, as it was Gods mercy it had not split him: It so beat him from his hold, and so bruised him, as a fresh man hazarding in by chance fell faire with it, and by maine strength bearing somewhat up, made good his place, and with much clamour incouraged and called upon others; who gave her now up, rent in pieces and absolutely lost. Our Governour was at this time below at the Capstone, both by his speech and authoritie heartening every man unto his labour. It strooke him from the place where hee sate, and groveled him, and all us about him on our faces, beating together with our breaths all thoughts from our bosomes, else, then that wee were now sinking. For my part, I thought her alreadie in the bottome of the Sea; and I have heard him say, wading out of the floud thereof, all his ambition was but to climbe up above hatches to dye in *Aperto cælo*, and in the company of his old friends. It so stun'd the ship in her full pace, that shee stirred no more, then if shee had beene caught in a net, or then, as if the fabulous Remora had stucke to her fore-castle. Yet without bearing one inch or saile, even then shee was making her way nine or ten leagues in a watch. One thing, it is not without his wonder (whether it were the feare of death in so great a storme, or that it pleased God to be gracious unto us) there was not a passenger, gentleman, or other, after hee beganne to stirre and labour, but was able to relieve his fellow, and make good his course: And it is most true, such as in all their life times had never done houres worke before (their mindes now helping their bodies) were able twice fortie eight houres together to toile with the best.

The Governours care.

Remero is fabled to be a small fish able to withstand a Shippe in her course.

God inableth whom he will save to save themselves.

During all this time, the heavens look'd so blacke upon us, that it was not possible the elevation of the Pole might be observed: nor a Starre by night, nor Sunne beame by day was to be seene. Onely upon the thursday night Sir George Summers being upon the watch, had an apparition of a little round light, like a faint Starre, trembling, and streaming along with a sparkling blaze, halfe the height upon the Maine Mast, and shooting sometimes from Shroud to Shroud, tempting to settle as it were upon any of the foure Shrouds: and for three or

Utter darknes.

Light on the Shrouds.

foure houres together, or rather more, halfe the night it kept
with us, running sometimes along the Maineyard to the very
end, and then returning. At which, Sir George Summers called
divers about him, and shewed them the same, who observed it
with much wonder, and carefulnesse: but upon a sodaine,
towards the morning watch, they lost the sight of it, and knew
not what way it made. The superstitious Sea-men make many
constructions of this Sea-fire, which neverthelesse is usuall in
stormes: the same (it may be) which the Græcians were wont in
the Mediterranean to call Castor and Pollux, of which, if one
onely appeared without the other, they tooke it for an evill
signe of great tempest. The Italians, and such, who lye open to
the Adriatique and Tyrrene Sea, call it (a sacred
Body) *Corpo Sancto*: the Spaniards call it Saint Elmo,
and have an authentique and miraculous Legend for
it. Be it what it will, we laid other foundations or safety of ruine,
then in the rising or falling of it, could it have served us now
miraculously to have taken our height by, it might have
strucken amazement, and a reverence in our devotions, according to the due of a miracle. But it did not light us any whit
the more to our knowne way, who ran now (as doe hood-
winked men) at all adventures, sometimes North, and North-
east, then North and by West, and in an instant againe varying
two or three points, and sometimes halfe the Compasse. East
and by South we steered away as much as we could to beare
upright, which was no small carefulnesse nor paine to doe, albeit we much unrigged our Ship, threw over-boord much luggage, many a Trunke and Chest (in which I suffered no meane
losse) and staved many a Butt of Beere, Hogsheads of Oyle,
Syder, Wine, and Vinegar, and heaved away all our Ordnance
on the Starboord side, and had now purposed to have cut
downe the Maine Mast, the more to lighten her, for we were
much spent, and our men so weary, as their stengths
together failed them, with their hearts, having travailed now from Tuesday till Friday morning, day
and night, without either sleepe or foode; for the leakeage
taking up all the hold, wee could neither come by Beere nor
fresh water; fire we could keepe none in the Cookeroome to
dresse any meate; and carefulnesse, griefe, and our turne at the
Pumpe or Bucket, were sufficient to hold sleepe from our eyes.

See Tom. 1.
l.9. *c.*12. § 1.

No sleepe or
food from
tuesday till
friday.

And surely Madam, it is most true, there was not any houre (a matter of admiration) all these dayes, in which we freed not twelve hundred Barricos of water, the least whereof contained six gallons, and some eight, besides three deepe Pumpes continually going, two beneath at the Capstone, and the other above in the halfe Decke, and at each Pumpe foure thousand stroakes at the least in a watch; so as I may well say, every foure houres, we quitted one hundred tunnes of water: and from tuesday noone till friday noone, we bailed and pumped two thousand tunne, and yet doe what we could, when our Ship held least in her, after tuesday night second watch, shee bore ten foote deepe, at which stay our extreame working kept her one eight glasses, forbearance whereof had instantly sunke us, and it being now Friday, the fourth morning, it wanted little, but that there had bin a generall determination, to have shut up hatches, and commending our sinfull soules to God, committed the Shippe to the mercy of the Sea: surely, that night we must have done it, and that night had we then perished: but see the goodnesse and sweet introduction of better hope, by our mercifull God given unto us. Sir George Summers, when no man dreamed of such happinesse, had discovered, and cried Land. Indeede the morning now three quarters spent, had wonne a little cleerenesse from the dayes before, and it being better surveyed, the vary trees were seene to move with the winde upon the shoare side: whereupon our Governour commanded the Helme-man to beare up, the Boateswaine sounding at the first, found it thirteene fathome, & when we stood a little in seven fatham; and presently heaving his lead the third time, had ground at foure fathome, and by this, we had got her within a mile under the South-east point of the land, where we had somewhat smooth water. But having no hope to save her by comming to an anker in the same, we were inforced to runne her ashoare, as neere the land as we could, which brought us within three quarters of a mile of shoare, and by the mercy of God unto us, making out our Boates, we had ere night brought all our men, women, and children, about the number of one hundred and fifty, safe into the Iland.

We found it to be the dangerous and dreaded Iland, or

marginal notes:
1200. Barricos an houre, besides 3. Pumps acquitting 100 tuns of water every 4. houres

Summer Ilands descried by Sir George Summers

They go a land

Bermuda
Ilands
supposed the
Divels, &c.

rather Ilands of the Bermuda: whereof let mee give your Ladyship a briefe description before I proceed to my narration. And that the rather, because they be so terrible to all that ever touched on them, and such tempests, thunders, and other fearefull objects are seene and heard about them, that they be called commonly, The Devils Ilands, and are feared and avoyded of all sea travellers alive, above any other place in the world. Yet it pleased our mercifull God, to make even this hideous and hated place, both the place of our safetie, and meanes of our deliverance.

And hereby also, I hope to deliver the world from a foule and generall errour: it being counted of most, that they can be no habitation for Men, but rather given over to Devils and wicked Spirits; whereas indeed wee find them now by experience, to bee as habitable and commodious as most Countries of the same climate and situation: insomuch as if the entrance into them were as easie as the place it self is contenting, it had long ere this beene inhabited, as well as other Ilands. Thus shall we make it appeare, That Truth is the daughter of Time, and that men ought not to deny every thing which is not subject to their owne sense.

Bermuda
Ilands
described.

The Bermudas bee broken Ilands, five hundred of them in manner of an Archipelagus (at least if you may call them all Ilands that lie, how little soever into the Sea, and by themselves) of small compasse, some larger yet then other, as time and the Sea hath wonne from them, and eaten his passage through, and all now lying in the figure of a Croissant, within the circuit of sixe or seven leagues at the most, albeit at first it is said of them that they were thirteene or fourteene leagues; and more in longitude as I have heard. For

Sir George
Summers
diligent
survey: his
draught
which we
have not. M.
Norgate hath
since
published an
exact Map.

no greater distance is it from the Northwest Point to Gates his Bay, as by this Map your Ladyship may see, in which Sir George Summers, who coasted in his Boat about them all, tooke great care to express the same exactly and full, and made his draught perfect for all good occasions, and the benefit of such, who either in distresse might be brought upon them, or make saile this way.

*Orfadams
braccia.

It should seeme by the testimony of Gonzalus Ferdinandus Oviedus, in his Booke intitled, *The Sum-*

In his *Gen. hist. li 2.c.9.* he reciteth the same historie more particularly he saith it hath two names, *Garza*, of the ship which first discovered it, being so called, and *Bermudez* of the Captain of that ship, named John Bermudes. Note that he placeth it more to the North, then that which is by ours inhabited, & say sometime they see it, somtime not as they passe.

mary or Abridgement of his generall History of the West Indies, written to the Emperor Charles the Fift, that they have beene indeed of greater compasse (and I easily beleeve it) then they are now, who thus saith: In the yeere 1515. when I came first to informe your Majesty of the State of the things in India, and was the yeere following in Flanders, in the time of your most fortunate successe in these your kingdomes of Aragony and Casteel, whereas at that voyage I sayled above the Iland Bermudas, otherwise called Gorza, being the farthest of all the Ilands that are yet found at this day in the world, and arriving there at the depth of eight yards of water, and distant from the Land as farre as the shot of a Peece of Ordnance, I determined to send some of the ship to Land, as well to make search of such things as were there, as also to leave in the Iland certaine Hogges for increase, but the time not serving my purpose, by reason of contrary winde I could bring my Ships no neerer: the Iland being twelve leagues in length, and sixteene in breadth, and about thirtie in circuit, lying in the thirtie three degrees of the North side. Thus farre hee.

The Spaniards (as I have heard) which were wracked there in Cap. Butlers time were of opinion that ours are not the Bermudas: Yea some of ours affirme, they have seene such an Iland to the North of ours, and have offered to discover it; *sub judice lis est; veritas temporis filia.*

True it is, the maine Iland, or greatest of them now, may bee some sixteene miles in length East North-east, and West South-west the longest part of it, standing in thirtie two degrees and twentie minutes, in which is a great Bay on the North side, in the North-west end, and many broken Ilands in that Sound or Bay, and a little round Iland at the Southwest end. As occasions were offered, so we gave titles and names to certaine places.

Halo, the circle seen about the Moon, of great compasse.

These Ilands are often afflicted and rent with tempests, great strokes of thunder, lightning and raine in the extreamity of violence: which (and it may well bee) hath so sundred and torne downe the Rockes, and whurried whole quarters of Ilands into the maine Sea (some six, some seven leagues, and is like in time to swallow them all) so as even in that distance from the shoare there is no small danger of them and with them, of the stormes continually raging from them, which once in the full and change commonly of every Moone (Winter or Summer) keeps their unchangeable round, and rather thunder then blow from every corner about them, sometimes fortie eight houres together: especially if the circle, which the Philosophers call *Halo* were (in our being there) seene about the Moone at any season, which bow indeed appeared there often, and would bee of a mightie compasse and breadth. I have not observed it any where one quarter so great, especially about the twentieth of March, I saw the greatest when followed upon the eves eve of the Annuntiation of our Ladie, the mightiest blast of lightning, and most terrible rap of thunder that ever astonied mortall men, I thinke. In August, September, and untill the end of October, wee had very hot and pleasant weather onely (as I say) thunder, lightning, and many scattering showers of Raine (which would passe swiftly over, and yet fall with such force and darknesse for the time as if it would never bee cleere againe) wee wanted not any; and of raine more in Summer then in Winter, and in the beginning of December wee had great store of hayle (the sharpe windes blowing Northerly) but it continued not, and to say truth, it is wintry or summer weather there, according as those North and North-west windes blow. Much taste of this kind of Winter wee had; for those cold windes would suddenly alter the ayre: but when there was no breath of wind to bring the moyst ayre out of the Seas, from the North and North-west, wee were rather weary of the heate, then pinched with extreamitie of cold: Yet the three Winter moneths, December, January, and February, the winds kept in those cold corners, and indeed then it was heavy and melancholy being there, nor were the winds more rough in March, then in the foresaid moneths, and yet even then would the Birds breed. I thinke they bredde there, most monethes in the yeere, in September, and at Christmasse I saw young Birds, and in Februarie, at which time the mornings are there (as in May in England) fresh and sharpe.

Well may the Spaniards, and these Biscani Pilots, with all their Traders into the Indies, passe by these Ilands as afraid (either bound out or homewards) of their very Meridian, and leave the fishing for the Pearle (which some say, and I beleeve well is as good there, as in any of their other Indian Ilands, and whereof we had some triall) to such as will adventure for them. The Seas about them are so ful of breaches, as with those dangers, they may wel be said to be the strongest situate in the world. I have often heard Sir George Summers, and Captaine Newport say, how they have not beene by any chance or discovery upon their like. It is impossible without great and perfect knowledge, and search first made of them to bring in a bable Boat, so much as of ten Tun without apparant ruine, albeit within there are many faire harbours for the greatest English Ship: yea, the *Argasies* of Venice may ride there with water enough, and safe land-lockt. There is one onely side that admits so much as hope of safetie by many a league, on which (as before described) it pleased God to bring us, wee had not come one man of us else ashoare, as the weather was: they have beene ever therefore left desolate and not inhabited.

Experience hath better shewed since, as we after see, both for fruits, wormes, &c. those that dwell there finding more then these, which tooke there Inne or lodging. Yet the dawning & Aurora yeeld a delightsome light, though not all so certaine as the Sun: for which cause I have not omitted these first discoveries.

The soile of the whole Iland is one and the same, the mould, dark, red, sandie, dry, and uncapable I beleeve of any of our commodities or fruits. Sir George Summers in the beginning of August, squared out a Garden by the quarter, the quarter being set downe before a goodly Bay, upon which our Governour did first leape ashore, and therefore called it (as aforesaid) Gates his Bay, which opened into the East, and into which the Sea did ebbe and flow, according to their tides, and sowed Muske Melons, Pease, Onyons, Raddish, Lettice, and many English seeds, and Kitchen Herbes. All which in some ten daies did appeare above ground, but whether by the small Birds, of which there be many kindes, or by Flies (Wormes I never saw any, nor any venomous thing, as Toade, or Snake, or any creeping

Spiders.

beast hurtfull, onely some Spiders, which as many affirme are signes of great store of Gold: but they were long and slender legge Spiders, and whether venomous or no I know not, I beleeve not, since wee should still find them amongst our linnen in our Chests, and drinking Cans; but we never re-

Beetle very sweet.

ceived any danger from them: A kind of Melontha, or blacke Beetell there was, which bruised, gave a savour like many sweet and strong gums punned together) whether, I say, hindred by these, or by the condition or vice of the soyle they came to no proofe, nor thrived. It is like enough that the commodities of the other Westerne Ilands would prosper there, as Vines, Lemmons, Oranges, and Sugar Canes: Our Governour made triall of the later, and buried some two or three in the Garden mould, which were reserved in the wracke amongst many which wee carried to plant here in Virginia, and they beganne to grow, but the Hogs breaking in, both rooted them up and eate them: there is not through the whole Ilands, either Champion ground, Valleys, or fresh Rivers. They are full of Shawes of goodly Cedar, fairer then ours here of Virginia; the Berries, whereof our men seething, straining, and letting stand some three or foure daies, made a kind of pleasant drinke: these Berries are of the same bignesse, and collour of Corynthes, full of little stones, and verie restringent or hard building. Peter Martin saith, That as Alexandria in Egypt there is a kind of Cedar, which the Jewes dwelling there, affirme to be the Cedars of Libanus, which beare old fruite and new all the yeere, being a kinde of Apple which tast like Prunes: but then, neither those there in the Bermudas, nor ours here in Virginia are of that happy kind.

Hogs.

Cedars.
Cedar-drinke.
American Cedars, are not the same kind with those of Libanus, as by the historie of them in our former Tome, pag. 1500, &c.

Likewise there grow great store of Palme Trees, not the right Indian Palmes, such as in Saint John Port-Rico are called Cocos, and are there full of small fruites like Almonds (of the bignesse of the graines in Pomgranates) nor of those kind of Palmes which beares Dates, but a kind of Simerons or wild Palmes in growth, fashion, leaves, and branches, resembling those true Palmes: for the Tree is high, and straight, sappy and spongious, unfirme for any use, no branches but in the uppermost part thereof, and in the top grow leaves about the head of it (the most inmost part whereof they call Palmeto, and it is the heart and pith of the same Trunke, so white and thin, as it will peele off into pleates as smooth and delicate as white Sattin into twentie folds, in which a man may write as in paper) where they spread and fall downward about the Tree like an overblowne Rose, or Saffron flower not early gathered; so broad are the leaves, as an Italian Umbrello, a man may well defend his whole body under one of them, from the greatest

Palmetos.
Many forts of Palmes, the Coco, the Date-Palme, the Wine-Palme, or raddic, &c. besides these Reed-Palmes.
Silke-wormes.

storme raine that falls. For they being stiffe and smooth, as if so many flagges were knit together, the raine easily slideth off. Wee oftentimes found growing to these leaves, many Silkwormes involved therein, like those small wormes which Acosta writeth of, which grew in the leaves of the Tunall Tree, of which being dried, the Indians make their Cochinile so precious and marchantable. With these leaves we thatched our Cabbins, and roasting the Palmito or soft top thereof, they had a taste like fried Melons, and being sod they eate like Cabbedges, but not so offensively thankefull to the stomacke. Many an ancient Burger was therefore heaved at, and fell not for his place, but for his head: for our common people, whose bellies never had eares, made it no breach of Charitie in their hot blouds and tall stomackes to murder thousands of them. They beare a kind of Berry, blacke and round, as bigge as a Damson, which about December were ripe and luscious: being scalded (whilest they are greene) they eate like Bullases. These Trees shed their leaves in the Winter moneths, as withered or burnt with the cold blasts of the North winde, especially those that grow to the Seaward, and in March, there Burgen new in their roome fresh and tender.

Other kindes of high and sweet smelling Woods there bee, and divers colours, blacke, yellow, and red, and one which beares a round blew Berry, much eaten by our owne people, of a stiptick qualitie and rough taste on the tongue like a Slow to stay or binde the Fluxe, which the often eating of the luscious Palme berry would bring them into, for the nature of sweet things is to clense and dissolve. A kinde of Pease of the bignesse and shape of a Katherine Peare, wee found growing upon the Rockes full of many sharpe subtill prickes (as a Thistle) which wee therefore called, The Prickle Peare, the outside greene, but being opened, of a deepe murrie, full of juyce like a Mulberry, and just of the same substance and taste, wee both eate them raw and baked.

Other Trees.

Prickle peare.

Waters. No Springs then found, since Wells have bin there digged which ebbe and flow with the Sea. &c.

Sure it is, that there are no Rivers nor running Springs of fresh water to bee found upon any of them: when wee came first wee digged and found certaine gushings and soft bublings, which being either in bottoms, or on the side of hanging ground, were

onely fed with raine water, which neverthelesse soone sinketh
into the earth and vanisheth away, or emptieth it selfe out of
sight into the Sea, without any channell above or upon the superficies of the earth: for according as their raines fell, we had
our Wels and Pits (which we digged) either halfe full, or absolute exhausted and dry, howbeit some low bottoms (which
the continuall descent from the Hills filled full, and in those
flats could have no passage away) we found to continue as fishing Ponds, or standing Pooles, continually Summer and Winter full of fresh water.

Fish.

The shoare and Bayes round about, when wee
landed first afforded great store of fish, and that of
divers kindes, and good, but it should seeme that
our fiers, which wee maintained on the shoares side drave
them from us, so as wee were in some want, untill wee had
made a flat bottome Gundall of Cedar with which wee put off
farther into the Sea, and then daily hooked great store of many
kindes, as excellent Angell-fish, Salmon Peale, Bonetas, Stingray, Calbally, Scnappers, Hogge-fish, Sharkes, Dogge-fish,
Pilcherds, Mullets, and Rock-fish, of which bee divers kindes:

Salt made
there.

and of these our Governour dryed and salted, and
barrelling them up, brought to sea five hundred, for
he had procured Salt to bee made with some Brine,
which happily was preferred, and once having made a little
quantity, he kept three or four pots boyling, and two or three
men attending else in an house (some little distance from his
Bay) set up on purpose for the same worke.

Likewise in Furbushers building Bay wee had a large Sein, or
Tramell Net, which our Governour caused to be made of the
Deere Toyles, which wee were to carry to Virginia, by drawing
the Masts more straight and narrow with Roape Yarne, and

5000. fishes
taken at a
hale.

which reached from one side of the Dock to the
other: with which (I may boldly say) wee have taken
five thousand of small and great fish at one hale. As
Pilchards, Breames, Mullets, Rocke-fish, &c. and other kindes
for which wee have no names. Wee have taken also from under
the broken Rockes, Crevises oftentimes greater then any of
our best English Lobsters; and likewise abundance of Crabbes,
Oysters, and Wilkes. True it is, for Fish in everie Cove and
Creeke wee found Snaules, and Skulles in that abundance, as

(I thinke) no Iland in the world may have greater store or
Cause of their wholsomnesse. better Fish. For they sucking of the very water, which descendeth from the high Hills mingled with juyce and verdor of the Palmes, Cedars, and other sweet Woods (which likewise make the Herbes, Roots, and Weeds sweet which grow about the Bankes) become thereby both fat and wholsome. As must those Fish needes bee grosse, slimy, and corrupt the bloud, which feed in Fennes, Marishes, Ditches, muddy Pooles, and neere unto places where much
No unscaled fishes. filth is daily cast forth. Unscaled Fishes, such as Junius calleth Molles Pisces, as Trenches, Eele, or Lampries, and such feculent and dangerous Snakes wee never saw any, nor may any River bee invenomed with them (I pray God) where I come. I forbeare to speake what a sort
Whale and Sword-fish. of Whales wee have seene hard aboard the shoare followed sometime by the Sword-fish and the Thresher, the sport whereof was not unpleasant. The Sword-fish, with his sharpe and needle Finne, pricking him into the belly when hee would sinke and fall into the Sea; and when hee startled upward from his wounds, the Thresher with his large Fins (like Flayles) beating him above water. The ex-
Cater-tray beare the bell away. Medio tutissimus ibis. Fowles. amples whereof gives us (saith Oviedus) to understand, that in the selfe same perill and danger doe men live in this mortall life, wherein is no certaine security neither in high estate nor low.

Fowle there is great store, small Birds, Sparrowes fat and plumpe like a Bunting, bigger then ours, Robbins of divers colours greene and yellow, ordinary and familiar in our Cabbins, and other of lesse sort. White and gray Hernshawes, Bitters, Teale, Snites, Crowes, and Hawkes, of which in March wee found divers Ayres, Goshawkes and Tassells, Oxen-birds, Cormorants, Bald-Cootes, Moore-Hennes, Owles, and Battes
Wild Swans. in great store. And upon New-yeeres day in the morning, our Governour being walked foorth with another Gentleman Master James Swift, each of them with their Peeces killed a wild Swanne, in a great Sea-
Web-footed Fowle. They call it of the cry which it maketh a Cohow. water Bay or Pond in our Iland. A kinde of webbe-footed Fowle there is, of the bignesse of an English greene Plover, or Sea-Meawe, which all the Summer wee saw not, and in the darkest nights of November

and December (for in the night they onely feed) they would come forth, but not flye farre from home, and hovering in the ayre, and over the Sea, made a strange hollow and harsh howling. Their colour is inclining to Russet, with white bellies, as are likewise the long Feathers of their wings Russet and White, these gather themselves together and breed in those Ilands which are high, and to farre alone into the Sea, that the Wilde Hogges cannot swimme over them, and there in the ground they have their Burrowes, like Conyes in a Warren, and so brought in the loose Mould, though not so deepe: which Birds with a light bough in a darke night (as in our Low-belling) wee caught. I have beene at the taking of three hundred in an houre, and wee might have laden our Boates. Our men found a prettie way to take them, which was by standing on the Rockes or Sands by the Sea side, and hollowing, laughing, and making the strangest out-cry that possibly they could: with the noyse whereof the Birds would come flocking to that place, and settle upon the very armes and head of him that so cryed, and still creepe neerer and neerer, answering the noyse themselves: by which our men would weigh them with their hand, and which weighed heaviest they tooke for the best and let the others alone, and so our men would take twentie dozen in two houres of the chiefest of them; and they were a good and well relished Fowle, fat and full as a Partridge. In January wee had great store of their Egges, which are as great as an Hennes Egge, and so fashioned and white shelled, and have no difference in yolke nor white from an Hennes Egge. There are thousands of these Birds, and two or three Ilands full of their Burrowes, whether at any time (in two houres warning) wee could send our Cock-boat, and bring home as many as would serve the whole Company: which Birds for their blindnesse (for they see weakly in the day) and for their cry and whooting, wee called the Sea Owle: they will bite cruelly with their crooked Bills.

Wild Hogges how first found out and taken   Wee had knowledge that there were wilde Hogges upon the Iland, at first by our owne Swine preserved from the wrack and brought to shoare: for they straying into the Woods, an huge wilde Boare followed downe to our quarter, which at night was watched and taken in this sort. One of Sir George Summers men went and lay among

the Swine, when the Boare being come and groveled by the
Sowes, hee put over his hand and rubbed the side gently of the
Boare, which then lay still, by which meanes hee fastened a
rope with a sliding knot to the hinder legge and so tooke him,
and after him in this sort two or three more. But in the end (a
little businesse over) our people would goe a hunting with our
Ship Dogge, and sometimes bring home thirtie, sometimes
fiftie Boares, Sowes, and Pigs in a weeke alive: for the Dog
would fasten on them and hold, whilest the Hunts-men made
in: and there bee thousands of them in the Ilands, and at that
time of the yeere, in August, September, October, and November, they were well fed with Berries that dropped from the
Cedars and the Palmes, and in our quarter wee made styes for
them, and gathering of these Berries served them twice a day,
by which meanes we kept them in good plight: and when there
was any fret of weather (for upon every increase of wind the
billow would be so great, as it was no putting out with our Gundall or Canow) that we could not fish nor take Tortoyses, then
wee killed our Hogs. But in February when the Palme Berries
began to be scant or dry, and the Cedar Berries failed two
moneths sooner. True it is the Hogs grew poore, and being
taken so, wee could not raise them to be better, for besides
those Berries, we had nothing wherewith to franke them: but
even then the Tortoyses came in againe, of which wee daily
both turned up great store, finding them on Land, as also
sculling after them in our Boate strooke them with an Iron
goad, and sod, baked, and roasted them. The Tor-
Tortoises   toyse is reasonable toothsom (some say) wholsome
meate. I am sure our Company liked the meate of
them verie well, and one Tortoyse would goe further among
them, then three Hogs. One Turtle (for so we called them)
feasted well a dozen Messes, appointing sixe to every Messe. It
is such a kind of meat, as a man can neither absolutely call Fish
nor Flesh, keeping most what in the water, and feeding upon
Sea-grasse like a Heifer, in the bottome of the Coves and
Bayes, and laying their Egges (of which wee should finde five
hundred at a time in the opening of a shee Turtle) in the Sand
by the shoare side, and so covering them close leave them to
the hatching of the Sunne, like the Manati at Saint Do-
minique, which made the Spanish Friars (at their first arrivall)

make some scruple to eate them on a Friday, because in colour and taste the flesh is like to morsells of Veale. Concerning the laying of their Egges, and hatching of their young, Peter Martyr writeth thus in his Decades of the Ocean: at such time as the heate of Nature moveth them to generation, they came forth of the Sea, and making a deepe pit in the sand, they lay three or foure hundred Egges therein: when they have thus emptied their bag of Conception, they put as much of the same againe into the Pit as may satisfie to cover the Egges, and so resort againe unto the Sea, nothing carefull of their succession. At the day appointed of Nature to the procreation of these creatures, there creepeth out a multitude of Tortoyses, as it were Pismyers out of an Ant-hill, and this only by the heate of the Sunne, without any helpe of their Parents: their Egges are as big as Geese Egges, and themselves growne to perfection, bigger then great round Targets.

II.

Actions and Occurrents whiles they continued in the Ilands:
Ravens sent for Virginia; Divers mutinies; Paine
executed: Two Pinnaces built.

So soone as wee were a little setled after our landing, with all the conveniencie wee might, and as the place, and our many wants would give us leave, wee made up our long Boate (as your Ladyship hath heard) in fashion of a Pinnace, fitting her with a little Deck, made of the Hatches of our ruin'd Ship, so
H. Ravens voyage from Bermuda to Virginia. close that no water could goe in her, gave her Sayles and Oares, and intreating with our Masters Mate Henry Ravens (who was supposed a sufficient Pilot) wee found him easily wonne to make over therewith, as a Barke of Aviso for Virginia, which being in the height of thirtie seven degrees, five degrees from the Iland which we were, might bee some one hundred and fortie leagues from us, or thereabouts (reckoning to every degree that lies North-east, and Westerly twentie eight English leagues) who the twentie eight of August being Munday, with six Saylers, and our Cape Merchant Thomas Whittingham departed from us out of Gates his Bay: but to our much wonder returned againe upon the Wednesday night after, having attempted to have got cleere

of the Iland, from the North North-east to the South-west, but could not as little water as shee drew, which might not bee about twentie inches for shoales and breaches, so as he was faine to go out from Summers Creeks, and the same way we came in on the South South-east of the Ilands, and from thence wee made to Sea the Friday after the first of September, promising if hee lived and arrived safe there, to returne unto us the next new Moone with the Pinnace belonging to the Colony there: according unto which instructions were directed unto the new Leiftenant Governour, and Councell from our Governour here, for which the Ilands were appointed carefully to be watched, and fiers prepared as Beacons to have directed and wafted him in, but two Moones were wafted upon the Promontory before mentioned, and gave many a long and wished looke round about the Horizon, from the North-east to the South-west, but in vaine, discovering nothing all the while, which way soever we turned our eye, but ayre and sea.

You may please, excellent Lady, to know the reason which moved our Governour to dispatch this long Boat, was the care which hee tooke for the estate of the Colony in this his inforced absence: for by a long practised experience, foreseeing and fearing what innovation and tumult might happily arise, amongst the younger and ambitious spirits of the new companies to arrive in Virginia, now comming with him along this same Fleet, hee framed his letters to the Colony, and by a particular Commission confirmed Captaine Peter Win his Lieutenant Governour, with an Assistance of six Counsellours, writing withall to divers and such Gentlemen of qualitie and knowledge of vertue, and to such lovers of goodnesse in this cause whom hee knew, intreating them by giving examples in themselves of duty and obedience, to assist likewise the said Lieutenant Governour, against such as should attempt the innovating of the person (now named by him) or forme of government, which in some Articles hee did likewise prescribe unto them: and had faire hopes all should goe well, if these his letters might arrive there, untill such time as either some Ship there (which hee fairely beleeved) might bee moved presently to adventure for him: or that it should please the right honourable, the Lordes, and the rest of his Majesties Councell in England, to addresse thither the right honourable the Lord

Lawar (one of more eminencie and worthinesse) as the project
was before his comming forth, whilest by their honourable
Cap. Win.
L. Lawarre.
Sir George
Summers
his survay,
and other
industrie. favours, a charitable consideration in like manner
might bee taken of our estates to redeeme us from
hence. For which purpose likewise our Governour directed a particular letter to the Councell in England,
and sent it to the foresaid Captaine Peter Winne (his
now to bee chosen Lieutenant Governour) by him to bee dispatched (which is the first) from thence into England.

In his absence Sir George Summers coasted the Ilands, and
drew the former plat of them, and daily fished, and hunted for
our whole company, untill the seven and twentieth of November, when then well perceiving that we were not likely to heare
from Virginia, and conceiving how the Pinnace which Richard
Frubbusher was a building would not be of burthen sufficient
to transport all our men from thence into Virginia (especially
considering the season of the yeare, wherein we were likely to
put off) he consulted with our Governour, that if hee might
have two Carpenters (for we had foure, such as they were) and
twenty men, over with him into the maine Iland, he would
quickly frame up another little Barke, to second ours, for the
better fitting and conveiance of our people. Our Governour,
with many thankes (as the cause required) cherishing this so
carefull and religious consideration in him (and whose experience likewise was somewhat in these affaires) granted him all
He builds a
Pinnace. things sutable to his desire, and to the furthering of
the worke: who therefore had made ready for him all
such tooles and instruments, as our owne use required not: and for him, were drawne forth twenty of the
ablest and stoutest of the company, and the best of our men,
to hew and square timber, when himselfe then, with daily
paines and labour, wrought upon a small Vessell, which was
soone ready as ours: at which wee leave him a while busied, and
returne to our selves. In the meane space did one Frubbusher,
borne at Graves end, and at his comming forth now dwelling
at Lime House (a painefull and well experienced Shipwright,
F. Frub-
busher
builds
another and skilfull workman) labour the building of a little
Pinnace: for the furtherance of which, the Gov-
ernour dispensed with no travaile of his body, nor
forbare any care or study of minde, perswading as much and

more, an ill qualified parcell of people, by his owne performance, then by authority, thereby to hold them at their worke, namely to fell, carry, and sawe Cedar, fit for the Carpenters purpose (for what was so meane, whereto he would not himselfe set his hand, being therefore up earely and downe late) yet neverthelesse were they hardly drawne to it, as the Tortoise to the inchantment, as the Proverbe is, but his owne presence and hand being set to every meane labour, and imployed so readily to every office, made our people at length more diligent, and willing to be called thereunto, where, they should see him before they came. In which, we may observe how much example prevailes above precepts, and how readier men are to be led by eyes, then eares.

Power of
example.

And sure it was happy for us, who had now runne this fortune, and were fallen into the bottome of this misery, that we both had our Governour with us, and one so solicitous and carefull, whose both example (as I said) and authority, could lay shame, and command upon people: else, I am perswaded, we had most of us finished our dayes there, so willing were the major part of the common sort (especially when they found such a plenty of victuals) to settle a foundation of ever inhabiting there; as well appeared by many practises of theirs (and perhaps of some of the better sort) Loe, what are our affections and passions, if not rightly squared? how irreligious, and irregular they expresse us? not perhaps so ill as we would be, but yet as wee are; some dangerous and secret discontents nourished amongst us, had like to have bin the parents of bloudy issues and mischiefs; they began first in the Sea-men, who in time had fastened unto them (by false baits) many of our land-men likewise, and some of whom (for opinion of their Religion) was carried an extraordinary and good respect. The Angles wherewith chiefly they thus hooked in these disquieted Pooles, were, how that *in Virginia, nothing but wretchednesse and labour must be expected, with many wants, and a churlish intreaty, there being neither that Fish, Flesh, nor Fowle, which here (without wasting on the one part, or watching on theirs, or any threatning, and are of authority) at ease, and pleasure might be injoyed: and since both in the one, and the other place, they were (for the time) to loose the fruition both of their friends and Countrey, as good, and better*

Mutinous
conceptions.

were it for them, to repose and seate them where they should have the least outward wants the while. This, thus preached, and published to each other, though by such who never had bin more onward towards Virginia, then (before this Voyage) a Sculler could happily rowe him (and what hath a more ad-amantive power to draw unto it the consent and attraction of the idle, untoward, and wretched number of the many, then liberty, and fulnesse of sensuality?) begat such a murmur, and such a discontent, and disunion of hearts and hands from this labour, and forwarding the meanes of redeeming us from hence, as each one wrought with his Mate how to divorse him from the same.

And first (and it was the first of September) a con-

Conspiracy. spiracy was discovered, of which six were found prin-
cipals, who had promised each unto the other, not to set their hands to any travaile or endeavour which might ex-pedite or forward this Pinnace: and each of these had severally (according to appointment) sought his opportunity to draw the Smith, and one of our Carpenters, Nicholas Bennit, who made much profession of Scripture, a mutinous and dissembling Im-poster; the Captaine, and one of the chiefe perswaders of others, who afterwards brake from the society of the Colony, and like outlawes retired into the Woods, to make a settlement and habitation there on their party, with whom they purposed to leave our Quarter, and possesse another Iland by themselves: but this happily found out, they were condemned to the same punishment which they would have chosen (but without Smith or Carpenter) and to an Iland farre by it selfe, they were

John Want, Carter, and others exiled and pardoned. carried, and there left. Their names were John Want, the chiefe of them, an Essex man of Newport by Saf-fronwalden, both seditious, and a sectary in points of Religion, in his owne prayers much devout and fre-quent, but hardly drawne to the publique, insomuch as being suspected by our Minister for a Brownist, he was often com-pelled to the common Liturgie and forme of Prayer. The rest of the confederates were Christopher Carter, Francis Peare-point, William Brian, William Martin, Richard Knowles: but soone they missed comfort (who were farre removed from our store) besides, the society of their acquaintance had wrought in some of them, if not a loathsomenesse of their offence, yet a sorrow that their complement was not more full, and therefore a wearinesse of their being thus untimely prescribed; insomuch, as many humble petitions were sent unto our Governour, fraught full of their seeming sorrow and repentance, and earnest vowes to redeeme the former trespasse, with example of dueties in them all, to the common cause, and generall businesse; upon which our Governour (not easie to admit any accusation, and hard to remit an offence, but at all times sorry in the punishment of him, in whom may appeare either shame or contrition) was easily content to reacknowledge them againe.

Yet could not this be any warning to others, who more subtilly began to shake the foundation of our quiet safety, and therein did one Stephen Hopkins commence the first act or overture: A fellow who had much knowledge in the Scriptures, and could reason well therein, whom our Minister therefore chose to be his Clarke, to reade the Psalmes, and Chapters upon Sondayes, at the assembly of the Congregation under him: who in January the twenty foure, brake with one Samuel Sharpe and Humfrey Reede (who presently discovered it to the Governour) and alleaged substantiall arguments, both civill and divine (the Scripture falsly quoted) that it was no breach of honestly, conscience, nor Religion, to decline from the obedience of the Governour, or refuse to goe any further, led by his authority (except it so pleased themselves) since the authority ceased when the wracke was committed, and with it, they were all then freed from the government of any man; and for a matter of Conscience, it was not unknowne to the meanest, how much we were therein bound each one to provide for himselfe, and his owne family: for which were two apparant reasons to stay them even in this place; first, abundance by Gods providence of all manner of good foode: next, some hope in reasonable time, when they might grow weary of the place, to build a small Barke, with the skill and helpe of the aforesaid Nicholas Bennit, whom they insinuated to them, albeit hee was now absent from his quarter, and working in the maine Iland with Sir George Summers upon his Pinnace, to be of the conspiracy, that so might get cleere from hence at their owne pleasures: when in Virginia, the first would be assuredly

[marginal note: Another Mutinie.]

[marginal note: Conscience greatest enemy to conscience.]

wanting, and they might well feare to be detained in that
Countrie by the authority of the Commander thereof, and
their whole life to serve the turnes of the Adventurers, with
their travailes and labours. This being thus laid, and by such a
one, who had gotten an opinion (as I before remembered) of
Religion; when it was declared by those two accusers, not
knowing what further ground it had or complices, it pleased
the Governour to let this his factious offence to have a
publique affront, and contestation by these two witnesses
before the whole Company, who at the toling of a
Bell) assemble before a Corps du guard, where the
Prisoner was brought forth in manacles, and both
accused, and suffered to make at large, to every particular, his answere; which was onely full of sorrow and teares,
pleading simplicity, and deniall. But hee being onely found, at
this time, both the Captaine, and the follower of this Mutinie,
and generally held worthy to satisfie the punishment of his offence, with the sacrifice of his life, our Governour passed the
sentence of a Martiall Court upon him, such as belongs to
Mutinie and Rebellion. But so penitent hee was, and made so
much moane, alleadging the ruine of his Wife and Children in
this his trespasse, as it wrought in the hearts of all the better
sort of the Company, who therefore with humble intreaties,
and earnest supplications, went unto our Governor, whom
they besought (as likewise did Captaine Newport, and my
selfe) and never left him untill we had got his pardon.

Stephen Hopkins condemned and pardoned.

In these dangers and divellish disquiets (whilest the almighty
God wrought for us, and sent us miraculously delivered from
the calamities of the Sea, all blessings upon the shoare, to content and binde us to gratefulnesse) thus inraged amongst our
selves, to the destruction each of other, into what a mischiefe
and misery had wee bin given up, had wee not had a Governour with his authority, to have suppressed the
same? Yet was there a worse practise, faction, and
conjuration a foote, deadly and bloudy, in which the
life of our Governour, with many others were threatned, and
could not but miscarry in his fall. But such is ever the will of
God (who in the execution of his judgements, breaketh the
firebrands upon the head of him, who first kindleth them)
there were, who conceived that our Governour indeede neither

Third Mutiny.

durst, nor had authority to put in execution, or passe the act of Justice upon any one, how treacherous or impious so ever; their owne opinions so much deceiving them for the unlawfulnesse of any act, which they would execute: daring to justifie among themselves, that if they should be apprehended, before the performance, they should happily suffer as Martyrs. They persevered therefore not onely to draw unto them such a number, and associates as they could worke in, to the abandoning of our Governour, and to the inhabiting of this Iland. They had now purposed to have made a surprise of the Store-house, and to have forced from thence, what was therein either of Meale, Cloath, Cables, Armes, Sailes, Oares, or what else it pleased God that we had recovered from the wracke, and was to serve our generall necessity and use, either for the reliefe of us, while wee staied here, or for the carrying of us from this place againe, when our Pinnace should have bin furnished.

But as all giddy and lawlesse attempts, have alwayes something of imperfection, and that as well by the property of the action, which holdeth of disobedience and rebellion (both full of feare) as through the ignorance of the devilers themselves; so in this (besides those defects) there were some of the association, who not strong inough fortified in their owne conceits, brake from the plot it selfe, and (before the time was ripe for the execution thereof) discovered the whole order, and every Agent, and Actor thereof, who neverthelesse were not suddenly apprehended, by reason the confederates were divided and seperated in place, some with us, and the chiefe with Sir Georgs Summers in his Iland (and indeede all his whole company) but good watch passed upon them, every man from thenceforth commanded to weare his weapon, without which before, we freely walked from quarter to quarter, and conversed among our selves, and every man advised to stand upon his guard, his owne life not being in safety, whilest his next neighbour was not to be trusted. The Centinels, and nightwarders doubled, the passages of both the quarters were carefully observed, by which meanes nothing was further attempted; untill a Gentleman amongst them, one Henry Paine, the thirteenth of March, full of mischiefe, and every houre preparing something or

(marginal note, left of second paragraph): Evill, as it hath a deficient cause, so in and before the effects, defects are found.

(marginal note, lower left): H. Paine his Mutinus behaviour.

other, Stealing Swords, Adises, Axes, Hatchets, Sawes, Augers, Planes, Mallets, &c. to make good his owne bad end, his watch night comming about, and being called by the Captaine of the same, to be upon the guard, did not onely give his said Commander evill language, but strucke at him, doubled his blowes, and when hee was not suffered to close with him, went off the Guard, scoffing at the double diligence and attendance of the Watch, appointed by the Governour for much purpose, as he said: upon which, the Watch telling him, if the Governour should understand of this his insolency, it might turne him to much blame, and happily be as much as his life were worth. The said Paine replyed with a setled and bitter violence, and in such unreverent tearmes, as I should offend the modest eare too much to express it in his owne phrase; but the contents were, how *that the Governour had no authoritie of that qualitie, to justifie upon any one (how meane soever in the Colonie) an action of that nature, and therefore let the Governour* (said hee) *kisse, &c.* Which words, being with the omitted additions, brought the next day unto every common and publique discourse, at length they were delivered over to the Governour, who examining well the fact (the transgression so much the more exemplary and odious, as being in a dangerous time, in a Confederate, and the successe of the same wishtly listened after, with a doubtfull conceit, what might be the issue of so notorious a boldnesse and impudency) calling the said Paine before him, and the whole Company, where (being soone convinced both by the witnesse, of the Commander, and many which were upon the watch with him) our Governour, who had now the eyes of the whole Colony fixed upon him, condemned him to be instantly hanged; and the ladder being ready, after he had made many confessions, hee earnestly desired, being a Gentleman, that hee might be shot to death, and towards the evening he had his desire, the Sunne and his life setting together.

His execution.

But for the other which were with Sir George, upon that Sunday following (the Barke beeing now in good forwardnesse) and readie to lanch in short time, from that place (as we supposed) to meet ours at a pond of fresh water, where they were both to bee mored, untill such time as being fully tackled, the wind should serve faire, for our putting to Sea together) being the eighteenth of March, hearing of Paynes death, and fearing hee had appeached them, and discovered the attempt (who poore Gentleman therein, in so bad a cause, was too secret and constant to his owne faith ingaged unto them, and as little needed, as urged thereunto, though somewhat was voluntarily delivered by him) by a mutuall consent forsooke their labour, and Sir George Summers, and like Out-lawes betooke them to the wild Woods: whether meere rage, and greedinesse after some little Pearle (as it was thought) where-

Divers of Sir G. Summers company fled into the woods. with they conceived, they should for ever inrich themselves, and saw how to obtaine the same easily in this place, or whether, the desire for ever to inhabite heere, or what other secret else moved them thereunto, true it is, they sent an audacious and formall Petition to our Governour, subscribed with all their names and Seales: not only intreating him, that they might stay heere, but (with great art) importuned him, that he would performe other conditions with them, and not wave, nor evade from some of his owne promises, as namely to furnish each of them with two Sutes of Apparell, and contribute Meale rateably for one whole yeere, so much among them, as they had weekly now, which was one pound and an halfe a weeke (for such had beene our proportion for nine moneths.) Our Governour answered this their Petition, writing to Sir George Summers to this effect.

Sir T. Gates his letter to Sir G. Summers. That true it was, at their first arrivall upon this Iland, when it was feared how our meanes would not extend to the making of a Vessell, capeable and large enough, to transport all our Countrimen at once, indeed out of his Christian consideration (mourning for such his Countrimen, who comming under his command, he foresaw that for a while, he was like enough to leave here behind, compelled by tyrannie of necessitie) his purpose was not yet to forsake them so, as given up like Savages: but to leave them all things fitting to defend them from want and wretchednesse, as much at least as lay in his power, to spare from the present use (and perhaps necessitie of others, whose fortunes should be to be transported with him) for one whole yeere or more (if so long by any casualtie, the ships which he would send unto them might be staied before their arrivall, so many hazards accompanying the Sea) but

withall intreated Sir George to remember unto his Company (if by
any meanes he could learne where they were) how he had vowed
unto him, that if either his owne meanes, his authoritie in Virginia, or
love with his friends in England, could dispatch for them sooner, how
farre it was from him, to let them remayne abandoned, and neglected
without their redemption so long: and then proceeded, requesting Sir
George Summers againe, to signifie unto them, since now our owne
Pinnasse did arise to that burthen, and that it would sufficiently
transport them all, beside the necessitie of any other Barke: and yet,
that since his Barke was now readie too, that those consultations,
howsoever charitable and most passionate in themselves, might determine, as taken away thereby, and therefore, that he should now bee
pleased to advise them well, how unanswerable this grant or consent
of his should be: first, to his Majestie for so many of his subjects, next
to the Adventurers, and lastly, what an imputation and infamy it
might be, to both their owne proper reputations, and honours,
having each of them authoritie in their places, to compell the adver-
sant and irregular multitude, at any time, to what should bee obedient and honest, which if they should not execute, the blame would
not lye upon the people (at all times wavering and insolent) but upon
themselves so weake and unworthy in their command. And moreover
intreated him by any secret practice to apprehend them, since that the
obstinate, and precipitate many, were no more in such a condition
and state to bee favoured, then the murmuring and mutinie of such
Rebellious and turbulent Humorists, who had not conscience nor
knowledge, to draw in the yoke of goodnesse, and in the businesse
for which they were sent out of England: for which likewise, at the
expence and charge of the Adventurers, they were to him committed,
and that the meanest in the whole Fleet stood the Company in no
lesse then twentie pounds, for his owne personall Transportation, and
things necessary to accompany him. And therefore lovingly conjured
Sir George, by the worthinesse of his (heretofore) well mayntayned
reputation, and by the powers of his owne judgement, and by the
vertue of that ancient love and friendship, which had these many
yeeres beene setled betweene them, to doe his best, to give this revolted Company (if he could send unto them) the consideration of
these particulars, and so worke with them (if he might) that by faire
meanes (the Mutinie reconciled) they would at length survey their
owne errours, which hee would bee as readie, upon their rendring
and comming into pardon, as he did now pittie them; assuring them
in generall and particular, that whatsoever they had sinisterly committed, or practised hitherto against the Lawes of dutie and honestie
should not in any sort be imputed against them.

In which good Office Sir George Summers did so nobly worke, and heartily labour, as hee brought most of them in, and indeed all, but Christopher Carter, and Robert Waters, who (by no meanes) would any more come amongst Sir Georges men, hearing that Sir George had commanded his men indeed (since they would not be intreated by faire meanes) to surprize them (if they could) by any device or force. From which time they grew so cautelous and wary, for their owne ill, as at our comming away, wee were faine to leave them behind. That Waters was a Sayler, who at his first landing upon the Iland (as after you shall heare) killed another fellow Saylor of his, the bodie of the murthered and Murtherer so dwelling, as prescribed now together.

Waters and Carter stand out and are left behind.

During our time of abode upon these Ilands, wee had daily every Sunday two Sermons preached by our Minister, besides every Morning and Evening at the ringing of a Bell, wee repayred all to puplique Prayer, at what time the names of our whole Company were called by Bill, and such as were wanting, were duly punished.

Religious exercises performed by Master Bucke.

The contents (for the most part) of all our Preachers Sermons, were especially of Thankefulnesse and Unitie, &c.

It pleased God also to give us opportunitie, to performe all the other Offices, and Rites of our Christian Profession in this Iland: as Marriage, for the sixe and twentieth of November, we had one of Sir George Summers his men, his Cooke, named Thomas Powell, who married a Maid Servant of one Mistris Horton, whose name was Elizabeth Persons: and upon Christmasse Eve, as also once before, the first of October; our Minister preached a godly Sermon, which being ended, he celebrated a Communion, at the partaking whereof our Governour was, and the greatest part of our Company: and the eleventh of February, wee had the childe of one John Rofe chistened a Daughter, to which Captaine Newport and my selfe were Witnesses, and the aforesaid Mistris Horton and we named it Bermuda, as also the five and twentieth of March, the wife of one Edward Eason, being delivered the weeke before of a Boy, had him then christened, to which Captaine Newport and my selfe, and Master James Swift were Godfathers, and we named it Bermudas.

The most holy; civill and most naturall possession taken of the Bermudas by exercise of Sacraments Marriage, Child-birth, &c. Children named Bermuda and Bermudas.

Likewise, we buried five of our company, Jeffery Briars, Richard Lewis, William Hitchman, and my God-daughter Bermuda Rolfe, and one untimely Edward Samuell a Sayler, being villanously killed by the foresaid Robert Waters, (a Sayler likewise) with a shovell, who strake him therewith under the lift of the Eare, for which he was apprehended, and appointed to be hanged the next day, the fact being done in the twilight (but being bound fast to a Tree all night, with many Ropes, and a Guard of five or six to attend him, his fellow Saylers watching the advantage of the Centinels sleeping) in despight and disdaine that Justice should bee shewed upon a Sayler, and that one of their crue should be an example to others, not taking into consideration, the unmanlinesse of the murther, nor the horror of the sinne, they cut his bands, and conveyed him into the Woods, where they fed him nightly, and closely, who afterward by the mediation of Sir George Summers, upon many conditions, had his tryall respited by our Governour.

Saylers misorder.

Wee had brought our Pinnasse so forward by this time, as the eight and twentieth of August we having laid her Keele. The six and twentieth of February, we now began to calke: old Cables we had preserved unto us, which affoorded Ocam enough: and one barrell of Pitch, and another of Tarre, we likewise saved, which served our use some little way upon the Bilg. wee breamed her otherwise with Lime made of Wilkeshels, and an hard white stone which we burned in a Kill, slaked with fresh water, and tempered with Tortoyses Oyle. The thirtieth of March being Friday, we towed her out in the morning Spring-tyde, from the Wharfe where she was built, boying her with foure Caske in her runne only: which opened into the North-west, and into which when the Breeze stood North and by West with any stiffe gale, and upon the Spring-tydes, the Sea would increase with that violence, especially twice it did so, as at the first time (before our Governour had caused a solid Causey of an hundred load of stone to bee brought from the Hils and Neighbour Rockes, and round about her ribs from stemme to stemme, where it made a pointed Baulke, and thereby brake the violence of the Flowe and Billowe) it indangered her overthrow and ruine, beeing greene as it were upon the Stockes. With much difficultie, diligence, and labour,

we saved her at the first, all her Bases, Shores, and Piles, which
under-set her, being almost carried from her, which was the
second of January, when her knees were not set to, nor one
joynt firme: We launched her unrigged, to carrie her to a little
round the Iland, lying West North-west, and close aboord to
the backe side of our Iland, both neerer the Ponds and Wels of
some fresh water, as also from thence to make our way to the
Sea the better: the Channell being there sufficient and deepe
enough to leade her forth, when her Masts, Sayles, and all her
Trimme should bee about her. Shee was fortie foot by the
Keele, and nineteene foot broad at the Beame, sixe foote
floore, her Rake forward was fourteene foot, her Rake aft from
the top of her Post (which was twelve foot long) was three
foot, shee was eight foot deepe under her Beame, betweene
her Deckes she was foure foot and an halfe, with a rising of
halfe a foot more under her fore Castle, of purpose to scowre
the Decke with small shot, if at any time wee should bee borded
by the Enemie. Shee had a fall of eighteene inches aft, to make
her sterage and her great Cabbin the more large: her sterage
was five foote long, and sixe foote high, with a close Gallerie
right aft, with a window on each side, and two right aft. The
most part of her timber was Cedar, which we found to be bad
for shipping, for that it is wonderous false inward, and besides
it is so spault or brickle, that it will make no good plankes, her
Beames were all Oke of our ruine ship, and some plankes in
her Bow of Oke, and all the rest as is aforesaid. When
shee began to swimme (upon her launching) our
Governour called her *The Deliverance*, and shee
might be some eighty tunnes of burthen.

Cedar ill for shipping.

Before we quitted our old quarter, and dislodged to the
fresh water with our Pinnasse, our Governour set up in Sir
George Summers Garden a faire Mnemosynon in
figure of a Crosse, made of some forme of the timber of our ruined shippe, which was scrued in with
strong and great trunnels to a mightie Cedar, which grew in
the middest of the said Garden, and whose top and upper
branches he caused to be lopped, that the violence of the
winde and weather might have the lesse power over her.

Crosse set up for a memorial.

In the middest of the Cross, our Governour fastened the Picture of his Majestie in a piece of Silver

His Majesties Picture.

of twelve pence, and on each side of the Crosse, hee set an Inscription graven in Copper, in the Latine and English to this purpose.

In memory of our great Deliverance, both from a mightie storme and leake: wee have set up this to the honour of God. It is the spoyle of an English ship (of three hundred tunne) called the Sea Venture, *bound with seven ships more (from which the storme divided us) to Virginia, or Nova Britania, in America. In it were two Knights, Sir Thomas Gates Knight, Governour of the English Forces and Colonie there: and Sir George Summers Knight, Admirall of the Seas. Her Captaine was Christopher Newport, Passengers and Mariners shee had beside (which came all safe to Land) one hundred and fiftie. We were forced to runne her ashore (by reason of her leake) under a Point that bore South-east from the Northerne Point of the Iland, which wee discovered first the eight and twentieth of July 1609.*

About the last of Aprill, Sir George Summers launched his Pinnasse, and brought her from his building Bay, in the Mayne Iland, into the Channell where ours did ride, and shee was by the Keele nine and twentie foot: at the Beame fifteene foot and an halfe: at the Loose fourteene, at the Transam nine, and she was eight foot deepe, and drew sixe foote water, and hee called her the *Patience.*

III.

Their departure from Bermuda and arrivall in Virginia: miseries there, departure and returne upon the Lord La Warres arriving. James Towne described.

FROM this time we only awaited a favourable Westerly wind to carrie us forth, which longer then usuall now kept at the East, and South-east, the way which wee were to goe. The tenth of May early, Sir George Summers and Captaine Newport went off with their long Boates, and with two Canoaes boyed the Channell, which wee were to leade it out in, and which was no broader from Shoales on the one side and Rockes on the other, then about three times the length of our Pinnasse. About ten of the clocke, that day being Thursday, we set sayle an easie gale, the wind at South, and by reason no more winde blew, we were faine to towe her with our long Boate, yet neither with

the helpe of that, were we able to fit our Bowyes, but even
when we came just upon them, we strucke a Rocke on the star-
boord side, over which the Bowye rid, and had it not beene a
soft Rocke, by which meanes she bore it before her, and
crushed it to pieces, God knowes we might have beene like
enough, to have returned anew, and dwelt there, after tenne
monethes of carefulnesse and great labour a longer time: but
God was more mercifull unto us. When shee strucke upon the
Rocke, the Cock-swayne one Walsingham beeing in the Boate
with a quicke spirit (when wee were all amazed, and our hearts
failed) and so by Gods goodnesse wee led it out at three
fadome, and three fadome and an halfe water. The wind served
us easily all that day and the next, when (God be ever praysed
for it) to the no little joy of us all, we got cleere of the Ilands.
After which holding a Southerly course, for seven dayes wee
had the winde sometimes faire, and sometimes scarce and contrarie: in which time we lost Sir George Summers twice, albeit
we still spared him our mayne top-sayle, and sometimes our
fore course too.

      The seventeenth of May we saw change of water,
Signe of
Land.   and had much Rubbish swimme by our ship side,
whereby wee knew wee were not farre from Land.
The eighteenth about midnight wee sounded, with the Dipsing
Lead, and found thirtie seven fadome. The nineteenth in the
morning we sounded, and had nineteene and an halfe fadome,
stonie, and sandie ground. The twentieth about midnight, we
had a marvellous sweet smell from the shoare (as from the
Coast of Spaine, short of the Straits) strong and pleasant,
which did not a little glad us. In the morning by day breake
(so soone as one might well see from the fore-top) one of the
Saylers descryed Land about an houre after, I went up and
might discover two Hummockes to the Southward, from which
(Northward all along) lay the Land, which wee were to Coast
to Cape Henrie. About seven of the clocke we cast forth an
Anchor because the tyde (by reason of the Freshet that set into
the Bay) make a strong Ebbe there, and the winde was but
easie, so as not beeing able to stemme the Tyde, we purposed
to lye at an Anchor untill the next flood, but the wind comming South-west a loome gale about eleven, we set sayle
againe, and having got over the Barre, bore in for the Cape.

This is the famous Chesipiacke Bay, which wee
have called (in honour of our young Prince) Cape
Henrie over against which within the Bay, lyeth another Head-land, which wee called in honour of our Princely
Duke of Yorke Cape Charles; and these lye North-east and by
East, and South-west and by West, and they may bee distant
each from the other in breadth seven leagues, betweene which
the Sea runnes in as broad as betweene Queeneburrough and
Lee. Indeed it is a goodly Bay and a fairer, not easily to be
found.

Chesipiack Bay.

The one and twentieth, beeing Munday in the morning,
wee came up within two miles of Point Comfort, when the
Captaine of the Fort discharged a warning Peece at us, whereupon we came to an Anchor, and sent off our long Boat to the
Fort, to certifie who we were by reason of the shoales which
lye on the South-side, this Fort easily commands the mouth of
the River, albeit it is as broad as betweene Greenwich, and the
Ile of Dogges.

True it is, such who talked with our men from the shoare,
delivered how safely all our ships the last yeere (excepting only
the Admirall, and the little Pinnasse in which one
Michael Philes commanded of some twentie tunne,
which we towed a sterne till the storme blew) arrived, and how our people (well increased) had
therefore builded this Fort; only wee could not learne any
thing of our long Boat, sent from the Bermudas, but what wee
gathered by the Indians themselves, especially from Powhatan,
who would tell our men of such a Boat landed in one of his
Rivers, and would describe the people, and make much scoffing sport thereat: by which wee have gathered, that it is most
likely, how it arrived upon our Coast, and not meeting with
our River were taken at some time or other, at some advantage
by the Savages, and so cut off. When our Skiffe came up
againe, the good newes of our ships, and mens arrivall the last
yeere, did not a little glad our Governour: who went soone
ashoare, and assoone (contrary to all our faire hopes) had new
unexpected, uncomfortable, and heavie newes of a worse condition of our people above at James Towne.

The long Boat sent by Ravens cast away

Upon Point Comfort our men did the last yeere (as you
have heard) rayse a little Fortification, which since hath beene

better perfected, and is likely to proove a strong Fort, and is
now kept by Captaine James Davies with forty men,
and hath to name Algernoone Fort, so called by
Captaine George Percy, whom we found at our arrivall President of the Colony and at this time likewise in the
Fort. When we got into the Point, which was the one and
twentieth of May, being Munday about noone; where riding
before an Indain Towne called Kecoughton, a mightie storme
of Thunder, Lightning, and Raine, gave us a shrewd and fearefull welcome.

Algernoone Fort M. George Percy.

From hence in two dayes (only by the helpe of Tydes, no
winde stirring) wee plyed it sadly up the River, and the three
and twentieth of May we cast Anchor before James Towne,
where we landed, and our much grieved Governour first visiting the Church caused the Bell to be rung, at which
(all such as were able to come forth of their houses)
repayred to Church where our Minister Master
Bucke made a zealous and sorrowfull Prayer, finding all things
so contrary to our expectations, so fully of misery and misgovernment. After Service our Governour caused mee to reade his
Commission, and Captaine Percie (then President)
delivered up unto him his Commission, the old
Patent and the Councell Seale. Viewing the Fort, we
found the Pallisadoes torne downe, the Ports open, the Gates
from off the hinges, and emptie houses (which Owners death
had taken from them) rent up and burnt, rather then the
dwellers would step into the Woods a stones cast off from
them, to fetch other fire-wood: and it is true, the Indian killed as fast without, if our men stirred but
beyond the bounds of their Block-house, as Famine
and Pestilence did within; with many more particularities of
the sufferances (brought upon them by their owne disorders
the last yeere) then I have heart to expresse. In this desolation
and misery our Governour found the condition and state of
the Colonie, and (which added more to his griefe) no hope
how to amend it or save his owne Company, and those yet remayning alive, from falling into the like necessities. For we had
brought from the Bermudas no greater store of provision
(fearing no such accidents possible to befall the Colony here)
then might well serve one hundred and fiftie for a Sea Voyage:

Miserable shewes of welcome.

Old Parens yeelded up.

Their misery invited. Ipsi causa malorum.

and it was not possible, at this time of the yeere to amend it, by any helpe from the Indian. For besides that they (at their best) have little more, then from hand to mouth, it was now likewise but their Seed-time, and all their Corne scarce put into the ground: nor was there at the Fort, as they whom we found related unto us, any meanes to take fish, neither sufficient Seine, nor other convenient Net, and yet if there had, there was not one eye of Sturgeon yet come into the River. All which considered, it pleased our Governour to make a Speech unto the Company, giving them to understand, that what provision he had, they should equally share with him, and if he should find it not possible, and easie to supply them with some thing from the Countrey, by the endevours of his able men, hee would make readie, and transport them all into their Native Countrey (accommodating them the best that he could) at which there was a generall acclamation, and shoute of joy on both sides (for even our owne men began to be disheartened and faint, when they saw this misery amongst the others, and no lesse threatned unto themselves.) In the meane while, our Governour published certaine Orders and Instruc-tions, which hee enjoyned them strictly to observe, the time that hee should stay amongst them, which being written out faire, were set up upon a post in the Church for everyone to take notice of.

Orders established which continued for their short stay: the particulers are here omitted. They contained a Preface and 21. Articles for Pietie, Loyaltie and Politie convenient to the Colonie.

If I should be examined from whence, and by what occasion, all these disasters, and afflictions descended upon our people, I can only referre you (honoured Ladie) to the Booke, which the Adventurers have sent hither intituled, *Advertisements unto the Colony in Virginia*: wherein the ground and causes are favourably abridged, from whence these miserable effects have beene produced, not excusing likewise the forme of government of some errour, which was not powerfull enough among so headie a multitude, especially, as those who arrived here in the supply sent the last yeere with us: with whom the better authoritie and government now changed into an absolute command, came along, and had beene as happily established, had it pleased God, that we with them had reached our wished Harbour.

Unto such calamity can sloath, riot, and vanity, bring the

most setled and plentifull estate. Indeede (right noble Lady)
no story can remember unto us, more woes and anguishes,
then these people, thus governed, have both suffered and puld
upon their owne heads. And yet true it is, some of them,
whose voyces and command might not be heard, may easily be
absolved from the guilt hereof, as standing untouched, and
upright in their innocencies; whilest the privie factionaries shall

Men blamed,
but not all
the Country
free. never find time nor darknesse, to wipe away or cover
their ignoble and irreligious practises, who, it may
be, lay all the discredits, and imputations the while
upon the Countrie. But under pardon, let me speake freely to
them: let them remember that if riot and sloth should both
meet in any one of their best Families, in a Countrey most
stored with abundance and plentie in England; continuall
wasting, no Husbandry, and old store still spent on, no order
for new provisions, what better could befall unto the Inhabitants, Land-lords, and Tenants of that corner, then necessarily
following cleannesse of teeth, famine, and death? Is it not the

Prov. 6. sentence and doome of the Wiseman? *Yet a little
sleepe, a little slumber, and a little folding of the hands
to sleepe: so thy poverty commeth, as one that travelleth
by the way, and thy necessitie like an armed man.* And with this
Idlenesse, when some thing was in store, all wastfull courses
exercised to the heigth, and the headlesse multitude, some
neither of qualitie nor Religion, not imployed to the end for
which they were sent hither, no not compelled (since in themselves unwilling) to sowe Corne for their owne bellies, nor to
put a Roote, Herbe, &c. for their owne particular good in their
Gardens or elsewhere: I say in this neglect and sensuall Surfet,
all things suffered to runne on, to lie sicke and languish; must
it be expected, that health, plentie, and all the goodnesse of a
well ordered State, of necessitie for all this to flow in this
Countrey? You have a right and noble heart (worthy Lady) bee
judge of the truth herein. Then suffer it not bee concluded
unto you, nor beleeve, I beseech you, that the wants and
wretchednesse which they have indured, ascend out of the
povertie and vilenesse of the Countrey, whether bee respected
the Land or Rivers: the one, and the other, having not only
promised, but powred enough in their veines, to convince them
in such calumnies, and to quit those common calamities, which

The
Countrey
commended.

(as the shadow accompanies the body) the precedent neglects touched at, if truely followed, and wrought upon. What England may boast of, having the faire hand of husbandry to manure and dresse it, God, and Nature have favourably bestowed upon this Country, and as it hath given unto it, both by situation, height, and soyle, all those (past hopes) assurances which follow our well planted native Countrie, and others, lying under the same influence: if, as ours, the Countrey and soyle might be improved, and drawne forth: so hath it indowed it, as is most certaine, with many more, which England fetcheth farre unto her from elsewhere. For first wee have experience, and even our eyes witnesse (how yong so ever wee are to the Countrie) that no Countrey yeeldeth good her Corne, nor more manifold increase: large Fields wee have, as prospects of the same, and not farre from our Pallisado. Besides, wee have thousands of goodly Vines in every hedge, and Boske running along the ground, which yeelde a plentifull Grape in their kinde. Let mee appeale then to knowledge, if these naturall Vines were planted, dressed, and ordered by skilfull Vinearoones, whether wee might not make a perfect Grape, and fruitefull Vintage in short time? And we have made triall of our owne English seedes, kitchen Hearbs, and Rootes, and finde them to prosper as speedily as in England.

*Rem acu
tetigit.* True
cause of
misery in
Virginia.

Onely let me truely acknowledge, they are not an hundred or two of deboist hands, dropt forth by yeare after yeare, with penury, and leisure, ill provided for before they come, and worse to be governed when they are here, men of such distempered bodies, and infected mindes, whom no examples daily before their eyes, either of goodnesse or punishment, can deterre from their habituall impieties, or terrifie from a shamefull death, that must be the Carpenters, and workemen in this so glorious a building.

Then let no rumour of the poverty of the Country (as if in the wombe thereof there lay not those elementall seedes, which could produce as many faire births of plenty, and increase, and better hopes, then any land under the heaven, to which the Sunne is no neerer a neighbour) I say, let no imposture rumour, nor any fame of some one, or a few more changeable actions, interposing by the way, or at home, wave any mans faire purpose hitherward, or wrest them to a declining and falling off from the businesse.

I will acknowledge, deere Lady, I have seene much propensnesse already towards the unity, and generall endeavours: how contentedly doe such as labour with us, goe forth, when men of ranke and quality, assist, and set on their labours: I have seene it, and I protest it, I have heard the inferiour people, with alacrity of spirit professe, that they should never refuse to

doe their best in the practise of their sciences and knowledges, when such worthy, and Noble Gentlemen goe in and out before them, and not onely so, but as the occasion shall be offered, no lesse helpe them with their hand, then defend them with their Sword. And it is to be understood, that such as labour, are not yet so taxed, but that easily they performe the same, and ever by tenne of the clocke have done their Mornings worke: at what time, they have their allowances set out ready for them, and untill it be three of the clocke againe, they take their owne pleasure, and afterwards with the Sunne set, their dayes labour is finished. In all which courses, if the businesse be continued, I doubt nothing, with Gods favour towards us, but to see it in time, a Countrie, an Haven, and a Staple, fitted for such a trade, as shall advance

assureder increase, both to the Adventurers, and free Burgers thereof, then any Trade in Christendome, or then that (even in her earely dayes, when Michael Cavacco the Greeke, did first discover it to our English Factor in Poland) which extends it selfe now from Calpe and Abila, to the bottome of Sidon, and so wide as Alexandria, and all the Ports and Havens North and South, through the Arches to Cio, Smyrna, Troy, the Hellespont, and up to Pompeys Pillar, which as a Pharos, or watch Tower, stands upon the wondrous opening into the Euxine Sea.

From the three and twentieth of May, unto the seventh of June, our Governour attempted, and made triall of all the wayes, that both his owne judgement could prompe him in, and the advise of Captaine George Percy, and those Gentlemen whom hee found of the Counsell, when hee came in, as of others; whom hee caused to deliver their knowledges, concerning the State and Condition

[marginal notes:]
Times of labour under Sir T. Gates.

Note. The hopes of Virginia.

Sir T. Gates his care.

of the Countrey: but after much debating, it could not appeare, how possibly they might preserve themselves (reserving that little which wee brought from the Bermudas in our Shippes, and was upon all occasions to stand good by us) tenne dayes from starving. For besides, that the Indians were of themselves poore, they were forbidden likewise (by their subtile King Powhatan) at all to trade with us;

Pohatans policy.

and not onely so, but to indanger and assault any Boate upon the River, or stragler out of the Fort by Land, by which (not long before our arrivall) our people had a large Boate cut off, and divers of our men killed, even within command of our Blocke-house; as likewise, they shot two of our people to death, after we had bin foure and five dayes come in: and yet would they dare then to enter our Ports, and trucke with us (as they counterfeited underhand) when indeede, they came but as Spies to discover our strength, trucking with us upon such hard conditions, that our Governour might very well see their subtiltie, and therefore neither could well indure, nor would continue it. And I may truely say beside, so had our men abased, and to such a contempt, had they brought the value of our Copper, that a peece which would have bought a bushell of their Corne in former time, would not now buy a little Cade or Basket of a Pottle. And for this misgovernment, chiefely our Colony is much bound to the Mariners, who never yet in any Voyage hither, but have made a prey of our poore people in want; insomuch, as unlesse they might advance foure or five for one (how assured soever of the payments of their Bils of Exchange) they would not spare them a dust of Corne, nor a pinte of Beere, to give unto them the least comfort or reliefe, although that Beere purloyned, and stolne perhaps; either from some particular supply, or from the generall store: so uncharitable a parcell of people they be, and ill conditioned. I my selfe have heard the Master of a Shippe say (even upon the arrivall of this Fleete, with the Lord Governour and Captaine Generall, when the said Master was treated with for such Commodities as hee brought to sell) that unlesse hee might have an East Indian increase, foure for one, all charges cleered, hee would not part with a Can of Beere. Besides, to doe us more villany and mis-

Savage Spies.

Basenesse of our people.

Mischiefes of Mariners.

chiefe, they would send of their long Boates still by night, and (well guarded) make out to the neighbour Villages, and Townes, and there (contrary to the Articles of the Fort, which now pronounce death for a trespasse of that qualitie) trucke with the Indians, giving for their trifles Otter skinnes, Bevers, Rokoone Furres, Beares skinnes, &c. so large a quantity, and measure of Copper, as when the Trucke-Master for the Colony, in the day time offered trade, the Indians would laugh and scorne the same, telling what bargains they met withall by night, from our Mangot Quintons (so calling our great Shippes) by which meanes, the Market with them forestalled thus by these dishonest men, I may boldly say, they have bin a consequent cause (this last yeare) to the death and starving of many a worthy spirit; but I hope to see a true amendment and reformation, as well of those as of divers other intollerable abuses, thrust upon the Colony by these shamelesse people, as also for the transportation of such provisions and supplies as are sent hither, and come under the charge of pursers (a parcell, fragment, and odde ends of fellowes dependancies to the others) a better course thought upon: of which supplies, never yet came into the Store, or to the Parties, unto whom such supplies were sent, by relation hitherto, a moitie or third part: for the speedy redresse of this, being so soveraigne a point, I understand how the Lord Governour and Captaine Generall, hath advised unto the Counsell, that there may be no more provisions at all delivered unto Pursers, but hath intreated to have the provision thus ordered. He would have a Commassary Generall of the Victuals to be appointed, who (receiving the store for the Colony, by Indenture from the Treasurer, and Victuallers in England) may keepe a just accompt, what the grosse amounteth unto and what is transported every Voyage, in severall kindes, as of Bread, Meate, Beere, Wine, &c. which said Commissary shall deliver over the same, to the Master of every Ship, and take an Indenture from the said Master, of what he hath in charge, and what he is to deliver to the Treasurer of the store in Virginia: of which, if any be wanting, he the said Master shall make it good, out of his owne intertainment, otherwise the Pursers, Stewards, Coopers, and quarter Masters, will be sure still, not onely to give themselves and

Pursers fraud.

Remedy.

their friends double allowances, but thinke it all well gotten that they can purloine and steale away.

Besides that the Indian thus evill intreated us, the River (which were wont before this time of the yeare to be plentifull of Sturgion) had not now a Fish to be seene in it, and albeit we laboured, and hold our Net twenty times day and night, yet we tooke not so much as would content halfe the Fishermen. Our Governour therefore sent away his long Boate to coast the River downward, as farre as Point Comfort, and from thence to Cape Henry, and Cape Charles, and all within the Bay: which after a seven nights triall and travaile, returned without any fruites of their labours, scarse getting so much Fish as served their owne Company.

The Colony when they came within foure dayes of starving. And to take any thing from the Indian by force, we never used, nor willingly ever will: and though they had well deserved it, yet it was not now time, for they did (as I said before) but then set their Corne, and at their best, they had but from hand to mouth; so as what now remained such as we found in the Fort, had wee staid but foure dayes, and doubtlesse bin the most part of them starved, for their best reliefe was onely Mushrums, and some hearbes, which sod together, made but a thin and unsavory broath, and swelled them much. The pitty hereof moved our Governour to draw forth such provision as he had brought, proportioning a measure equally to every one a like. But then our Governor began to examine how long this his store would hold out, and found it (husbanded to the best advantage) not possible to serve longer then sixteene dayes: after which, nothing was to be possibly supposed out of the Countrey (as before remembred) nor remained there then any meanes to transport him elsewhere. Whereupon hee then entred into the consultation with Sir George Summers, and Captaine Newport, calling unto the same the Gentlemen and Counsell of the former Government, intreating both the one and the other to advise with him what was best to be done. The provision which they both had aboord himselfe and Sir George Summers, was examined, and delivered, how it, being rackt to the uttermost, extended not above, as I said, sixteene dayes, after two Cakes a day. The Gentlemen of the Town, who knew better of the Country, could not give him any hope, or wayes, how to improve it from the Indian. It soone then appeared most fit, by a generall approbation, that to preserve and save all from starving, there could be no readier course thought on, then to abandon the Country, and accommodating themselves the best that they might, in the present Pinnaces then in the road, namely in the *Discovery* and the *Virginia*, and in the two, brought from, and builded at the Bermudas, the *Deliverance*, and the *Patience*, with all speede convenient to make for the New found Land, where (being the fishing time) they might meete with many English Ships into which happily they might disperse most of the Company.

Purpose to leav the Country.

This Consultation taking effect, our Governor having caused to be carried aboord all the Armes, and all the best things in the store, which might to the Adventurers make some commodity upon the sale thereof at home, and burying our Ordnances before the Fort gate, which looked into the River. The seventh of June having appointed to every Pinnace likewise his complement and number, also delivered thereunto a proportionable rate or provision, hee commanded every man at the beating of the Drum to repaire aboord. And because hee would preserve the Towne (albeit now to be quitted) unburned, which some intemperate and malicious people threatned, his owne Company he caused to be last ashoare, and was himselfe the last of them, when about noone giving a farewell, with a peale of small shot, wee set saile, and that night, with the tide, fell downe to an Iland in the River, which our people have called Hogge Iland; and the morning tide brought us to another Iland, which we have called Mulberry Iland; where lying at an ancor, in the afternoone stemming the tide, wee discovered a long Boate making towards us, from Point Comfort: much descant we made thereof, about an houre it came up; by which, to our no little joyes, we had intelligence of the honorable my Lord La Warr his arrivall before Algarnoone Fort the sixt of June, at what time, true it is, his Lordship having understood of our Governours resolution to depart the Country, with all expedition caused his Skiffe to be manned, and in it dispatched his letters by Captain Edward Bruster (who commandeth his Lordships

The highest pitch & lowest depth in the Colonies miseries fearsly escaping the jawes of devouring desperation. Hopes morning. L. La Warrs arrivall.

Company) to our Governour, which preventing us before the aforesaid Mulberry Iland, the eight of June aforesaid, upon the receipt of his honours letters, our Governour bore up the helme, with the winde comming Easterly, and that night (the winde so favourable) relanded all his men at the Fort againe: before which (the tenth of June, being Sunday) his Lordship had likewise brought his Ships, and in the afternoone, came a shoare with Sir Ferdinando Weinman, and all his Lordships followers.

Here (worthy Lady) let mee have a little your pardon, for having now a better heart, then when I first landed, I will briefely describe unto you, the situation and forme of our Fort. When Captain Newport in his first Voyage, did not like to inhabit upon so open a roade, as Cape Henry, nor Point Comfort he plied it up to the River, still looking out for the most apt and securest place, as well for his Company to sit downe in, as which might give the least cause of offence, or distast in his judgement, to the Inhabitants. At length, after much and weary search (with their Barge coasting still before, as Virgill writeth Æneas did, arriving in the region of Italy called Latium, upon the bankes of the River Tyber) in the Country of a *Werowance* called Wowinchapuncke (aditionary to Powhatan) within this faire River of Paspiheigh, which wee have called the Kings River, a Country least inhabited by the Indian, as they all the way observed, and threescore miles & better up the fresh Channell, from Cape Henry they had sight of an extended plaine & spot of earth, which thrust out into the depth, & middest of the channell, making a kinde of Chersonesus or Peninsula, for it was fastened onely to the Land with a slender necke, no broader then a man may well quaite a tile shard, & no inhabitants by seven or six miles neere it. The Trumpets sounding, the Admirall strooke saile, and before the same, the rest of the Fleete came to an ancor, and here (as the best yet offered unto their view, supposed so much the more convenient, by how much with their small Company, they were like inough the better to assure it) to loose no further time, the Colony disimbarked, and every man brought his particular store and furniture, together with the generall provision ashoare: for the safety of which, as

[marginal note: Description of the seate and site of James Towne.]

likewise for their owne security, ease, and better accommodating, a certaine Canton and quantity, of that little halfe Iland of ground, was measured, which they began to fortifie, and thereon in the name of God, to raise a Fortresse, with the ablest and speediest meanes they could: which Fort, growing since to more perfection, is now at this present in this manner.

A low levell of ground about halfe an Acre, or (so much as Queene Dido might buy of King Hyarbas, which she compassed about with the thongs cut out of one Bull hide, and therein built her Castle of Byrza) on the North side of the River, is cast almost into the forme of a Triangle, and so Pallizadoed. The South side next the River (howbeit extended in a line, or Curtaine six score foote more in length, then the other two, by reason the advantage of the ground doth so require) contains one hundred and forty yards: the West and East sides a hundred onely. At every Angle or corner, where the lines meete, a Bulwarke or Watchtower is raised, and in each Bulwarke a peece of Ordnance or two well mounted. To every side, a proportioned distance from the Pallisado, is a setled streete of houses, that runs along, so as each line of the Angle hath his streete. In the middest is a market place, a Store house, and a Corps du guard, as likewise a pretty Chappell, though at this time when wee came in, as ruined and unfrequented: but the Lord Governour, and Captaine Generall, hath given order for the repairing of it, and at this instant, many hands are about it. It is in length threescore foote, in breadth twenty foure, and shall have a Chancell in it of Cedar, and a Communion Table of the Blake Walnut, and all the Pewes of Cedar, with faire broad windowes, to shut and open, as the weather shall occasion, of the same wood, a Pulpet of the same, with a Font hewen hollow, like a Canoa, with two Bels at the West end. It is so cast, as it be very light within, and the Lord Governour and Captaine Generall doth cause it to be kept passing sweete, and trimmed up with divers flowers, with a Sexton belonging to it, and in it every Sonday wee have Sermons twice a day, and every Thursday a Sermon, having true preachers, which take their weekely turnes, and every morning at the ringing of a Bell, about ten of the clocke, each man addresseth himselfe to prayers, and so at foure of the

The Fort, &c. described.

clocke before Supper. Every Sunday, when the Lord Governour, and Captaine Generall goeth to Church, hee is accompanied with all the Counsailers, Captaines, other Officers, and
all the Gentlemen, and with a Guard of Holberdiers, in his
Lordships Livery, faire red cloakes, to the number of fifty both
on each side, and behinde him: and being in the Church, his
Lordship hath his seate in the Quier, in a greene Velvet Chaire,
with a Cloath, with a Velvet Cushion spread on a Table before
him, on which he kneeleth, and on each side sit the Counsell,
Captaines, and Officers, each in their place, and when he re-
turneth home againe, he is waited on to his house in the same
manner.

And thus inclosed, as I said, round with a Pallizado of
Planckes and strong Posts, foure foote deepe in the ground, of
yong Oakes, Walnuts, &c. The Fort is called in honour of his
Majesties name, James Towne; the principall Gate from the
Towne, through the Pallizado, opens to the River, as at each
Bulwarke there is a Gate likewise to goe forth, and at every
Gate a Demi-Culverin, and so in the Market Place.
The houses first raised, were all burnt, by a casualty
of fire, the beginning of the second yeare of their
seate, and in the second Voyage of Captain Newport, which
since have bin better rebuilded, though as yet in no great uniformity, either for the fashion, or beauty of the streete. A delicate wrought fine kinde of Mat the Indians make, with which
(as they can be trucked for, or snatched up) our people do
dresse their chambers, and inward roomes, which make their
houses so much more handsome. The houses have wide and
large Country Chimnies in the which is to be supposed (in such plenty of wood) what fires are maintained: and they have found the way to cover their
houses: now (as the Indians) with barkes of Trees, as durable,
and as good proofe against stormes, and winter weather, as the
best Tyle defending likewise the piercing Sunbeames of Summer, and keeping the inner lodgings coole enough, which
before in sultry weather would be like Stoves, whilest they
were, as at first, pargetted and plaistered with Bitumen or
tough Clay: and thus armed for the injury of changing times,
and seasons of the yeare, we hold our selves well apaid, though

The Houses.

Barke Roofes.

wanting Arras Hangings, Tapistry, and guilded Venetian Cordovan, or more spruse houshold garniture, and wanton City ornaments, remembring the old Epigraph:

> *We dwell not here to build us Bowers,*
> *And Hals for pleasure and good cheere:*
> *But Hals we build for us and ours,*
> *To dwell in them whilst we live here.*

Unhealthfulnesse of James Towne.

True it is, I may not excuse this our Fort, or James Towne, as yet seated in some what an unwholesome and sickly ayre, by reason it is in a marish ground, low, flat to the River, and hath no fresh water Springs serving the Towne, but what wee drew from a Well sixe or seven fathom deepe, fed by the brackish River owzing into it, from whence I verily beleeve, the chiefe causes have proceeded of many diseases and sicknesses which have happened to our people, who are indeede strangely afflicted with Fluxes and Agues; and every particular season (by the relation of the old inhabitants) hath his particular infirmity too, all which (if it had bin our fortunes, to have seated upon some hill, accommodated with fresh Springs and cleere ayre, as doe the Natives of the Country) we might have, I beleeve, well escaped: and some experience we have to perswade our selves that it may be so; for of foure hundred and odde men, which were seated at the Fals the last yeere when the Fleete came in with fresh and yong able spirits, under the government of Captain Francis West, and of one hundred to the Seawards (on the South side of our River) in the Country of the Nansamundes, under the charge of Captaine John Martin, there did not so much as one man miscarry, and but very few or none fall sicke, whereas at James Towne, the same time, and the same moneths, one hundred sickned, & halfe the number died: howbeit, as we condemne not Kent in England, for a small Towne called Plumsted, continually assaulting the dwellers there (especially new commers) with Agues and Fevers; no more let us lay scandall, and imputation upon the Country of Virginia, because the little Quarter wherein we are set downe (unadvisedly so chosed) appeares to be unwholesome, and subject to many ill ayres, which accompany the like marish places.

IIII.

The Lord La Warres beginnings and proceedings in
James Towne. Sir Thomas Gates sent into England;
his and the Companies testimony of Virginia,
and cause of the late miseries.

UPON his Lordships landing at the South gate of the Pallizado (which lookes into the River) our Governour caused his
Company in armes to stand in order, and make a Guard: It
pleased him, that I should beare his Colours for that time: his
Lordship landing, fell upon his knees, and before us
all, made a long and silent Prayer to himselfe, and
after, marched up into the Towne, where at the Gate,
I bowed with the Colours, and let them fall at his
Lordships feete, who passed on into the Chappell,
where he heard a Sermon by Master Bucke, our Governours
Preacher; and after that, caused a Gentleman, one of his owne
followers, Master Anthony Scot his Ancient, to reade his Commission, which intitled him Lord Governour, and Captaine
Generall during his life, of the Colony and Plantation in Virginia (Sir Thomas Gates our Governour hitherto, being now
stiled therein Lieutenant Generall.)

His speech After the reading of his Lordships Commission,
Sir Thomas Gates rendred up unto his Lordship his
owne Commission, both Patents, and the Counsell
Seale: after which, the Lord Governour, and Captaine Generall, delivered some few words unto the Company, laying many
blames upon them for many vanities, and their Idlenesse,
earnestly wishing, that he might no more finde it so, least he
should be compelled to draw the sword of Justice, to cut off
such delinquents, which he had much rather, he protested,
draw in their defence, to protect them from injuries; hartening
them with the knowledge of what store of provisions
he had brought for them, *viz.* sufficient to serve
foure hundred men for one whole yeare.

The twelfth of June, being Tuesday, the Lord Governour and Captaine Generall, did constitute, and give places
of Office, and charge to divers Captaines and Gentlemen, and
elected unto him a Counsell, unto whom he did administer an

Marginal notes:
Commission
red. Lord La
Warrs title.
Sir T. Gates
Lieutenant
Generall.

Provisions
brought.
Counsell
chosen &
sworne.

Oath, mixed with the oath of Allegiance, and Supremacy to his Majestie: which oath likewise he caused to be administered the next day after to every particular member of the Colony, of Faith, Assistance, and Secrecy. The Counsaile which he elected were. Sir Thomas Gates Knight, Lieutenant Generall.

Colony sworn.

Sir George Summers Knight, Admirall. Captaine George Percy Esquire, and in the Fort Captaine of fifty. Sir Ferdinando Weinman Knight, Master of the Ordnance. Captaine Christopher Newport, Vice-admirall. William Strachei Esquire, Secretary, and Recorder.

Officers appointed.

As likewise the Lord Governour and Captaine Generall, nominated Captaine John Martin, Master of the Battery workes for Steele and Iron: and Captaine George Webb Sergeant Major of the Fort: and especiall Captaines over Companies, were these appointed; Captaine Edward Bruster, who hath the command of his Honours owne Company. Captaine Thomas Lawson. Captain Thomas Holecroft. Captaine Samuell Argoll. Captaine George Yardley, who commandeth the Lieutenant Generals Company. Divers other Officers were likewise made, as Master Ralph Hamer, and Master Browne, Clarkes of the Counsell, and Master Daniell Tucker, and Master Robert Wilde, Clarkes of the Store, &c.

The first businesse which the Lord Governour and Captaine Generall (after the setling of these Officers) thought upon, was to advise with his Counsell, for the obtaining of such provisions of victuals for store, and quality, as the Countrey afforded. It did not appeare, that any kinde of Flesh, Deere, or what else, of that kinde, could be recovered from the Indian, or to be sought in the Countrey, by the travaile or search of his people, and the old dwellers in the Fort (together with the Indians not to friend) who had the last winter, destroyed and killed up all the Hogges, insomuch, as of five or sixe hundred (as it is supposed) there was not one left alive; nor an Henne, nor Chicke in the Fort; and our Horses and Mares, they had eaten with the first, and the provision which the Lord Governour, and Captaine Generall had brought, concerning any kinde of flesh, was little or nothing; in respect it was not drempt of by the Adventurers in England, that the Swine were destroyed.

In Counsell therefore the thirteenth of June, it pleased Sir George Summers Knight, Admirall, to propose a Voyage, which

Sir G.
Summers
undertaketh
to bring the
provisions
from
Bermudas.
for the better reliefe, and good of the Colony, he would performe into the Bermudas, from whence he would fetch six moneths provision of Fleshe and Fish, and some live Hogges to store our Colony againe: and had a Commission given unto him the fifteenth of June, 1610. who in his owne Bermuda Pinnace, the *Patience*, consorted with Captaine Samuell Argoll, in the *Discovery* (whom the Lord Governour, and Captaine Generall, made of the counsell before his departure) the nineteenth of June, fell with the Tyde from before our Towne, and the twenty two left the Bay, or Cape Henry a sterne.

And likewise, because at the Lord Governous, and Captaine Generals first comming, there was found in our owne River no store of Fish; after many trials, the Lord Governour, and Captaine Generall, dispatched in the *Virginia*, with instructions, the seventeenth of June, 1610. Robert Tyndall, Master of the *De la Warre*, to fish unto, all along, and betweene Cape Henry, and Cape Charles, within the Bay; who the last of the said moneth returned unto us againe, but as ill speeding as the former, whom our Governour (now Lieutenant Generall) had addressed thither before for the same purpose. Nor was the Lord Governour, and Captaine Generall in the meane while idle at the Fort; but every day and night hee caused the Nets to be hawled, sometimes a dosen times one after another. But it pleased not God so to blesse our labours, that we did at any time take one quarter so much, as would give unto our people one pound at a meale a peece, by which we might have better husbanded our Pease and Oatemeale, notwithstanding the great store we now saw daily in our River: but let the blame of this lye where it is, both upon our Nets, and the unskilfulnesse of our men to lay them.

The sixth of July Sir Thomas Gates Lieutenant Generall, comming downe to Point Comfort, the North wind (blowing rough) he found had forced the long Boate belonging to Algernoone Fort, to the other shoare upon Nansamund side, somewhat short of Weroscoick: which to recover againe, one of the Lieutenant Generals men Humfrey Blunt, in an old Canow made over, but the wind driving him upon the Strand, certaine Indians (watching the occasion) seised the poore fellow, and led him up into the Woods, and sacrificed him. It did not a little trouble the Lieutenant Governour, who since his first landing in the Countrey (how justly soever provoked) would not by any meanes be wrought to a violent proceeding against them, for all the practises of villany, with which they daily indangered our men, thinking it possible,* by a more tractable course, to winne them to a better condition: but now being startled by this, he well perceived, how little a faire and noble intreatie, workes upon a barbarous disposition, and therefore in some measure purposed to be revenged.

* Ad Grœcas Calendas. Can a Leopard change his spots? Can a Savage remayning a Savage be civill? Were not wee our selves made and not borne civill in our Progenitors dayes? and were not Cœsars Britaines as brutish as Virginians? The Romane swords were best teachers of civilitie to this & other Countries neere us. Grassesilke.

The ninth of July, he prepared his forces, and early in the morning set upon a Towne of theirs, some foure miles from Algernoone Fort, called Kecoughtan, and had soone taken it, without losse or hurt of any of his men. The Governour and his women fled (the young King Powhatans Sonne not being there) but left his poore baggage, and treasure to the spoyle of our Souldiers, which was only a few Baskets of old Wheate, and some other of Pease and Beanes, a little Tobacco, and some few womens Girdles of Silke, of the Grasse-silke, not without art, and much neatnesse finely wrought; of which I have sent divers into England, (beeing at the taking of the Towne) and would have sent your Ladiship some of them, had they beene a Present so worthy.

We purposed to set a Frenchman heere a worke to plant Vines, which grew naturally in great plentie. Some few Corne fields it hath, and the Corne in good forwardnesse, and wee despaire not but to bee (able if our men stand in health) to make it good against the Indian.

The continuall practises of the subtle King Powhatan, doth not meanely awaken all the powers and workings of vertue and knowledge, in our Lord Governour and Captaine Generall, how to prevent not only his mischiefes, but to draw him upon some better termes, and acknowledgemen of our forces and spirits, both able and daring to quit him in any valiant and martiall course whatsoever, he shall dare to runne with us, which hee doth yet scarsly beleeve. For this therfore, since first, and that so lately, he hath set on his people, to attempt us with private Conspiracies and actuall violence, into the one drawing his Neighbour Confederates and under Princes, and by the other working the losse and death of divers of our men, and by such their losse seising their Armes, Swords, Peeces, &c. of which he hath gathered into his store a great quantitie and number by Intelligence above two hundred Swords, besides Axes, and Pollaxes, Chissels, Howes, to paire and clense their ground, with an infinite treasure of Copper, our Lord Governour and Captaine Generall sent two Gentlemen with an Ambassie unto him, letting him to understand of his practises and outrage, hitherto used toward our people, not only abroad but at our Fort also: yet flattering him withall how the Lord Governour and Captaine Generall did not suppose, that these mischiefes were contrived by him, or with his knowledge, but conceived them rather to be the acts of his worst and unruly people, his Lordship therefore now complayning unto him required, that hee (being so great and wise a King) would give an universall order to his Subjects, that it might bee no more so, left the Lord Governour and Captaine Generall should be compelled (by defending him and his) to offend him, which he would be loath to do: withall he willed the Messengers to demand of him the said Powhatan, that he would either punish or send unto his Lordship such of his people whom Powhatan knew well not long before, had assaulted our men at the Blockhouse, and but newly killed foure of them, as also to demaund of Powhatan, willing him to returne unto the English Fort, both such men as hee detayned of ours, and such Armes as he had of theirs in his possession, and those conditions he performed, hee willed them to assure unto Powhatan that then their great *Werowance*, the Lord Governour and Captaine Generall would hold faire quarter, and enter friendship with him, as a friend to King James and his Subjects. But refusing to submit to these demands, the Lord Governour and Captaine Generall gave in charge to the Messengers, so sent to signifie unto Powhatan that his Lordship would by all meanes publike and private, seeke to recover from him such of the English as he had, being Subjects to his King and Master, unto whom even Powhatan himselfe had formerly vowed, not only friendship but homage, receiving from his Majestie therefore many gifts, and upon his knees a Crowne and Scepter with other

English Armes treasured by Powhatan.
Message to Powhatan.

Ornaments, the Symbols of Civill State and Christian Soveraigntie, thereby obliging himselfe to Offices of dutie to his Majestie. Unto all which Powhatan returned no other answere, but that either we should depart his Country, or confine our selves to James Towne only, without searching further up into his Land, or Rivers, or otherwise, hee would give in command to his people to kill us, and doe unto us all the mischiefe, which they at their pleasure could and we feared: withall forewarning the said Messengers, not to returne any more unto him, unlesse they brought him a Coach and three Horses, for hee had understood by the Indians which were in England, how such was the state of great *Werowances*, and Lords in England, to ride and visit other great men.

After this divers times, and daily hee sent sometimes two, sometimes three, unto our Fort, to understand our strength, and to observe our Watch & Guard, and how our people stood in health, and what numbers were arrived with this new *Weroance*: which being soone perceived our Lord Governour and Captaine Generall forewarned such his Spies, upon their owne perill, to resort no more unto our Fort. Howbeit, they would daily presse into our Blocke-house, and come up to our Pallizado gates, supposing the government as well now, as fantasticall and negligent in the former times, the whilest some quarter of a mile short of the Block-house, the greatest number of them would make assault, and lye in ambush about our Glasse-house, whether. Divers times indeed our men would make out either to gather Strawberries, or to fetch fresh water, any one of which so stragled, if they could with conveniencie, they would assault and charge with their Bowes and Arrowes, in which manner they killed many of our men: two of which being Paspaheans, who were ever our deadliest enemies, and not to be reconciled; at length being apprehended (and one of them a notable villaine, who had attempted upon many in our Fort) the Lord Governour caused them to be manacled, and convented before him and his Counsell, where it was determined that hee that had done so much mischiefe should have his right hand strooke off, sending him away withall, with a message to Powhatan, that unlesse hee would yet returne such Englishmen as he detayned, together with all such their Armes (as before spoken of) that not only the other (now Prisoner) should die, but all such of his Savages (as the Lord Governour and Captaine Generall, could by any meanes surprize) should runne the same course: as likewise the Lord Governour and Captaine Generall would fire all his Neighbour Corne Fieldes, Townes, and Villages, and that suddenly, if Powhatan sent not to contract with him the sooner.

What this will worke with him, wee know not as yet, for this was but the day before our ships were now falling to Point Comfort, and so to set sayle for England: which ships riding before Werosciock to take in their fraight of Cedar, Clap-boord, Blacke Wal-nut, and Iron Oare, tooke Pris-oners likewise the chiefe King of Werosciock, called Sasenticum, with his Sonne Kainta, and one of his chiefe men. And the fifteenth day of July, in the Blessing Cap-taine Adams brought them to Point Comfort, where at that time (as well to take his leave of the Lieutenant Gen-erall Sir Thomas Gates, now bound for England, as to dispatch the ships) the Lord Governour and Cap-taine Generall had pitched his Tent in Algernoone Fort.

King of Weroscoick taken Prisoner.

Sir T. Gates bound for England.

The Kings Sonne Kainta the Lord Governour and Captaine Generall, hath sent now into England, untill the ships arrive here againe the next Spring, dismissing the old *Werowance*, and the other with all tearmes of kindnesse, and friendship, prom-ising further designes to bee effected by him, to which hee hath bound himselfe, by divers Savage Ceremonies, and admirations.

And thus (right Noble Ladie) once more this famous busi-nesse, as recreated, and dipped a new into life and spirit, hath raysed it (I hope) from infamy, and shall redeeme the straines and losse under which she hath suffered, since her first Con-ception: your Graces still accompany the least appearance of her, and vouchsafe her to bee limmed out, with the beautie which wee will begge, and borrow from the faire lips: nor feare you, that shee will returne blushes to your cheekes for praysing her, since (more then most excellent Ladie) like your selfe (were all tongues dumbe and envious) shee will prayse her selfe in her most silence: may shee once bee but seene, or but her shadow lively by a skilfull Workman set out indeed, which heere (bungerly as I am) I have presumed (though defacing it) in these Papers to present unto your Ladiship.

After Sir Thomas Gates his arrivall, a Booke called *A true Declaration of Virginia*, was published by the Company, out of which I have heere inserted this their publike testimonie of the causes of their former evils, and Sir Thomas Gates his Report upon Oath of Virginia.

The ground of all those miseries, was the permissive Providence of God, who, in the fore-mentioned violent storme, seperated the head from the bodie, all the vitall powers of Regiment being exiled with Sir Thomas Gates in those infortunate (yet fortunate) Ilands. The broken remainder of those supplyes made a greater shipwracke in the Continent of Virginia, by the tempest of Dissention: every man over-valuing his owne worth, would be a Commander: every man underprizing anothers value, denied to be commanded.

The next Fountaine of woes was secure negligence, and improvidence, when every man sharked for his present bootie, but was altogether carelesse of succeeding penurie. Now, I demand whether Sicilie, or Sardinia (sometimes the Barnes of Rome) could hope for increase without manuring? A Colony is therefore denominated, because they should be Coloni, the Tillers of the Earth, and Stewards of fertilitie: our mutinous Loyterers would not sow with providence, and therefore they reaped the fruits of too deere bought Repentance. An incredible example of their idlenesse, is the report of Sir Thomas Gates, who affirmeth, that after his first comming thither, he hath seene some of them eat their fish raw, rather then they would goe a stones cast to fetch wood and dresse it. *Dei laboribus omnia vendunt*, God sels us all things for our labour, when Adam himselfe might not live in Paradice without dressing the Garden.

Unto idlenesse you may joyne Treasons, wrought by those unhallowed creatures that forsooke the Colonie, and exposed their desolate Brethren to extreame miserie, You shall know that eight and twentie or thirtie of the Company, were appointed (in the ship called the *Swallow*) to trucke for Corne with the Indians, and having obtained a great quantitie by trading, the most seditious of them, conspired together, perswaded some, and enforced others, to this barbarous project. They stole away the ship, they made a league amongst themselves to be professed Pirats, with dreames of Mountaines of Gold, and happie Robberies: thus at one instant, they wronged the hopes, and subverted the cares of the Colonie, who depending upon their returne, fore-slowed to looke out for further provision: they created the Indians our implacable enemies by some violence they had offered: they carried away the best ship (which should have beene a refuge in extremities:) they weakened our forces, by substraction of their armes and succours. These are that scumme of men that fayling in their Piracie, that being pinched with famine and penurie, after their wilde roving upon the Sea, when all their lawlesse hopes failed, some re-mayned with other Pirates, they met upon the Sea, the others resolved to returne to England, bound themselves by mutuall Oath, to agree all in one report to discredit the Land, to deplore the famine, and to protest that this their comming away, proceeded from desperate ne-cessitie: These are they, that roared out the Tragicall Historie of the man eating of his dead Wife in Virginia; when the Master of this ship willingly confessed before for the witnesses, that at their comming away, they left three monethes victuals, and all the Cattell living in the Fort: sometimes they reported that they saw this horrible action, sometimes that Captain Davies said so, sometimes that one Beadle the Lieutenant of Captaine Davies did relate it, varying this report into diversitie of false colours, which hold no likenesse and proportion: But to cleere all doubts, Sir Thomas Gates thus relateth the Tragedie.

There was one of the Company who mortally hated his Wife, and therefore secretly killed her, then cut her in pieces and hid her in divers parts of his House: when the woman was missing, the man sus-pected, his House searched, and parts of her mangled bodie were dis-covered, to excuse himselfe he said that his Wife died, that he hid her to satisfie his hunger, and that hee fed daily upon her. Upon this, his House was againe searched, where they found a good quantitie of Meale, Oat-meale, Beanes and Pease. He thereupon was arraigned, confessed the Murder, and was burned for his horrible villany.

Now shall the scandalous reports of a viperous generation, prepon-derate the testimonies of worthy Leaders? Shall their venemous tongues, blast the reputation of an ancient and worthy Peere, who upon the ocular certainty of future blessings, hath protested in his Letters, that he will sacrifice himselfe for his Countrie in this service, if he may be seconded: and if the Com-pany doe give it over, hee will yet lay all his fortunes upon the prose-cution of the Plantation?

Lord Lawarre.

Unto Treasons, you may joyne covetousnesse in the Mariners, who for their private-lucre partly imbezeled the provisions, partly pre-vented our Trade with the Indians making the Matches in the night, and forestalling our Market in the day: whereby the Virginians were glutted with our Trifles, and inbaunced the voices of their Corne and Victuall. That Copper which before would have provided a bushell would not now obtaine so much as a Pottle.

Joyne unto these another evill: there is great store of Fish in the
River, especially of Sturgeon; but our men provided no more of them
then for present necessitie, not barrelling up any store against that
season the Sturgeon returned to the Sea. And not to dissemble their
folly, they suffered fourteene nets (which was all they had) to rot and
spoyle, which by orderly drying and mending might have beene preserved: but being lost, all helpe of fishing perished.

The State of the Colony, by these accidents began to finde a sensible declining: which Powhatan (as a greedy Vulture) observing, and
boyling with desire of revenge, hee invited Captaine Ratcliffe, and
about thirty others to trade for Corne, and under the colour of fairest
friendship, hee brought them within the compasse of his ambush,
whereby they were cruelly murthered and massacred. For upon confidence of his fidelitie, they went one and one into severall houses,
which caused their severall destructions, when if but any sixe had remained together, they would have beene a Bulwarke for the generall
preservation. After this, Powhatan in the night cut off some of our
Boats, he drove away all the Deere into the farther part of the Country, hee and his people destroyed our Hogs (to the number of about
sixe hundred) hee sent one of his Indians to trade with us, but layed
secret ambushes in the Woods, that if one or two dropped out of the
Fort alone, they were indangered.

Cast up the reckoning together: want of government, store of idlenesse, their expectations frustrated by the Traytos, their market
spoyled by the Mariners, our Nets broken, the Deere chased, our
Boats lost, our Hogs killed, our trade with the Indians forbidden,
some of our men fled, some murthered, and most by drinking of the
brackish water of James Fort weakened and indangered, famine and
sicknesse by all these meanes increased, here at home the monyes
came in so slowly, that the Lord Laware could not bee dispatched till
the Colony was worne and spent with difficulties: Above all, having
neither Ruler, nor Preacher, they neither feared God, nor man, which
provoked the wrath of the Lord of Hosts, and pulled downe his
judgements upon them. *Discite justitiam moniti.*

The Councell of Virginia (finding the smalnesse of that returne,
which they hoped should have defrayed the charge of a new supply)
entred into a deepe consultation, and propounded amongst themselves, whether it were fit to enter into a new contribution, or in time
to send for home the Lord La-ware, and to abandon the action. They
resolved to send for Sir Thomas Gates, who being come, they adjured
him to deale plainly with them, and to make a true relation of those
things which were presently to be had, or hereafter to be hoped for in
Virginia. Sir Thomas Gates with a solemne and sacred oath replied,

that all things before reported were true: that the Countrey yeelded abundance of Wood, as Oake, Wainscot, Walnut Trees, Bay Trees, Ashe, Sarsafrase, live Oake, greene all the yeere, Cedar and Fir; which are the materialls, of Soape ashes, and Pot ashes, of Oyles of Walnuts, and Bayes, of Pitch and Tar, of Clap-boards, Pipe-staves, Masts and excellent boards of fortie, fiftie, and sixtie length, and three foot breadth, when one Firre tree is able to make the maine Mast of the greatest Ship in England. He avouched that there are incredible varietie of sweet woods, especially of the Balsamum tree, which distilleth a precious Gumme; that there are innumerable white Mulberry trees, which in so warme a climate may cherish and feede millions of Silke-wormes, and returne us in a very short time, as great a plenty of Silke as is vented into the whole world from all the parts of Italy: that there are divers sorts of Minerals, especially of Iron oare lying upon the ground for ten Miles sircuite; of which wee have made a triall at home, that it maketh as good Iron as any is in Europe: that a kinde of Hempe or Flaxe, and Silke Grasse doe grow there naturally, which will affoord stuffe for all manner of excellent Cordage: That the River swarmeth with all manner of Sturgeon: the Land aboundeth with Vines; the Woods doe harbour exceeding store of Beavers, Foxes, and Squirrels; the Waters doe nourish a great encrease of Otters, all which are covered with precious Furres: that there are in present discovered the Dyes and Drugges of sundry qualities; that the Orenges which have been planted, did prosper in the winter, which is an infallible argument, that Lemmons, Sugar Canes, Almonds, Rice, Anniseede, and all other commodities which wee have from the Straights, may be supplied to us in our owne Countrey, and by our owne industry: that the Corne yeeldeth a terrible encrease more then ours: and lastly, that it is one of the goodliest Countries under the Sunne; enterveined with five maine Rivers, and promising as rich entrals as any Kingdome of the earth, to whom the Sunne is no neerer a neighbour.

WILLIAM STRACHEY

FROM

The Historie of Travell into Virginia Britania

CAPUT 3. DE ORIGINE, POPULI.

*1. Of the first beginning of this Salvag People, from whom, and
Whence. 2. How the Inhabitaunts call this portion or Tract
of Land which we call Virginia. 3. Their great kings
Name, 4. the Bowndes of his Empire. 5. wher he keepes
his Courte. 6. His personall Discription. 7. His
Jelosy of us, and Policy to temporize with us.
8. His Multiplicity of Weomen, and som
of their Names. 9. How he bestowes
them. 10. His Treasury.*

1. It were not perhappes too curyous a thing to demaund, how these people might come first, and from whome, and whence, to enhabite these so far remote westerly partes of the world, having no entercourse with Africa, Asia nor Europe, and considering the whole world, so many yeares, by all knowledg receaved, was supposed to be only conteyned and circumscrybed in the discovered and travelled Bowndes of those three: according to that old Conclusion in the Scholes *Quicquid præter Africam, et Europam est, Asia est.* Whatsoever Land doth neither appertayne unto Africk, nor to Europe, is part of Asia: as also to question how yt should be, that they (if descended from the people of the first creation) should maynteyne so generall and grosse a defection from the true knowledg of God, with one kynd, as yt were of rude and savadge life, Customes, manners, and Religion,? yt being to be graunted, that with us (infallably) they had one, and the same discent and begynning from the univer-

sall Deluge, in the scattering of Noah his children and Nephewes, with their famelies (as little Colonies) some to one, some to other borders of the Earth to dwell? as in Egipt (so wryting Berosus) Esenius, and his howshold, tooke up their Inhabitacion: In Libia, and Cyrene, Tritames: and in all the rest of Africa, Japetus Priscus; Attalaas in East-Asia; Ganges, with some of Comerus Gallus children, in Arabia-Fælix, within the confines of Sabaea, called the Frankincense bearer; Canaan in Damascus, unto the utmost bowndes of Palestyne; etc.

But, yt is observed that Cham, and his famely, were the only far Travellors, and Straglers into divers and unknowne countries, searching, exploring and sitting downe in the same: as also yt is said of his famely, that what country soever the Children of Cham happened to possesse, there beganne both the Ignorance of true godliness, and a kynd of bondage and slavery to be taxed one upon another, and that no inhabited Countryes cast forth greater multytudes, to raunge and stray into divers remote Regions, then that part of Arabia in which Cham himselfe (constrayned to fly with wife and Children by reason of the mocking that he had done to his father) tooke into possession; so great a misery (saith Boem of Auba) brought to mankynd, the unsatisfyed wandring of that one man: for first from him, the Ignoraunce of the true worship of god took beginning, the Inventions of Hethenisme, and adoration of falce godes, and the Devill, for he himself, not applying him to learne from his father, the knowledge and prescrybed worship of the eternall god, the god of his fathers, yet by a fearefull and superstitious instinct of nature, carryed to ascribe unto some supernaturall power, a kynd of honour and reverence, not divout to knowe the essence, and quality of that power, taught his successors new and devised manner of Gods, sacryfices, and Ceremonies; and which he might the easier ympresse into the Children, by reason they were carryed with him so young away from the Elders, not instructed, nor seasoned first, in their true Customes, and religion: In so much as then we may conclude, that from Cham, and his tooke byrth and begynning the first universall Confusion and diversity, which ensued afterwardes throughout the whole world, especially in divine and sacred matters, whilst yt is said agayne of the Children of Sem, and Japhet, how they being taught by their elders, and content with their owne lymitts and confynes, not travelling beyond them into new Countryes as the other, retayned still (untill the comming of the Messias,) the only knowledge of the eternall, and never chaungeable triuth.

By all which yt is very probable likewise, that both in the travells and Idolatry of the famely of Cham, this portion of the world (west-ward from Africa, upon the Atlantique Sea) became both peopled, and instructed in the forme of prophane worshippe, and of an unknowne Diety: nor is yt to be wondred at, where the abused truith of Religion is suffred to perish, yf men in their owne Inventions, and lives, become so grosse and barbarous as by reading the processe of this history will hardly be perceaved, what difference may be betweene them and bruit beasts, sometymes worshipping bruit beasts, nay things more vyle, and abhorring the inbredd motions of Nature yt self, with such headlong, and bloudy Ceremonies, of Will, and Act.

But how the vagabond Race of Cham might discend into this new world, without furniture (as may be questioned) of shipping, and meanes to tempt the Seas, togither how this great Continent (devided from the other three) should become stoared with beasts, and some Fowle, of one, and the same kynd with the other partes, especially with Lions, Beares, Deare, Wolves, and such like, as from the first Creation tooke begynning in their kynd, and after the generall floud were not anew created, nor have their being or generation (as some other) *ex putredine, et sole*, by corruption and Heate. Lett me referre the reader to the search of Acosta in his　　booke, Chap:　　of his morall and naturall History of the West-Indies, who hath so officiously laboured herein, as he should but bring Owles to Athens, who should study for more strayned, or new Aucthority Concerning the same.

Thus much then may in brief be sayd, and allowed, Concerning their originall, or first begynning in generall, and which may well reach even downe unto the particuler Inhabitants of this particuler Region, by us discovered, who cannot be any other, then parcell of the same, and first mankynd.

2.　　　Concerning themselves more especially and their division as we fynd them in these provinces where we are; we may well say how this Tract or Portion of Land, which wee call Virginia Britania, by the Inhabitans as aforesaid

Tsenacommacah, is governed in chief by a great king, by them called by sondry names, according to his divers places, qualityes or honours by himself obteyned, either for his valour his government, or some such like goodnes, which they use to admire and Commend to succeeding tymes, with memorable Tytles, and so Commonly they of greatest merritt amongst them aspire to many names.

3.   The great Emperour at this tyme amongest them we Commonly call Powhatan for by that name true yt is, he was made known unto us, when we arryved in the Country first, and so indeed he was generally called when he was a young man, as taking his denomynacion from the Country Powhatan, wherein he was borne, which is above at the Falls as before mencioned, right over aneinst the Islands, at the head of our river, and which place or birth-right of his, he sold Anno 1609. about Sempemter, unto Captain Francis West, our Lord Generalls brother, who therefore erected there a Fort, calling yt Wests-Fort, and sate himself downe there with 120. English: the Inhabitants themselves especially his frontier neighbour princes, call him still Powhatan, his owne people sometymes call him Ottaniack, sometymes Mamanatowick, which last signifyes great Kinge, but his proper right name which they salute him with (himself in presence) is Wahunsenacawh.

4.   The greatnes and bowndes of whose Empire by reason of his Powerfulnes, and ambition in his youth, hath lardger lymittes then ever had any of his Prediccessors in former tymes: for he seemes to comaund South and North from the Mangoags, and Chawonookes, bordering upon Roanoak or South-Virginia, to Tockwogh, a towne pallisado'de, standing at the North-end of our Bay in 40. degrees or thereaboutes: South-west to Anoeg (not expressed in the Mappe) whose howses are buylt as ours, 10. dayes journye distant from us, from whence those inhabiting Weroances sent unto him of their Commodityes, as Weionock (a servaunt in whom Powhatan reposed much trust) would tell our elder Planters, and could repeat many wordes of their language which he had learned amongst them, in his imployment thither for his king, and whence he often retourned full of Presents to Powhatan; and west-ward, he Commaundes to Monahassanugh, which standes at the foot of the mountaynes, from Chesapeak or the

mouth of our Bay 200. myles: Nor-west, to the bordures of Massawomeck, and Bocootawwonough: Nor-east and by east to Accohanock, Accowmack, and some other petty Nations, lying on the East syde of our Bay.

5.   He hath divers seates or howses, his Chief when we came into the Country was upon Pamunky-River, on the North side which we call Pembrook-side, called Werowoco-maco, which by interpretacion signifyes Kings-howse. howbeit not lyking to neighbour so neere us, that howse being within some 15. or 16. myles, where he saw we purposed to hold our-selves, and from whence in 6. or 7. howres we were able to visitt him, he removed and ever synce hath most what kept, at a place in the desartes called Orapaks, at the top of the river Chickahamania, betweene Youghtamund, and Powhatan.

Powhatans Discription 6.   He is a goodly old-man, not yet shrincking, though well beaten with many cold and stormy wyn-ters, in which he hath bene patient of many necessi-tyes and attempts of his fortune, to make his name and famely great, he is supposed to be little lesse than 80. yeares old, (I dare not say how much more, others say he is). Of a tall stature, and cleane lymbes, of a sad aspect, rownd fat visag'd with gray haires, but playne and thyn hanging upon his broad showlders, some few haires upon his Chynne, and so on his upper lippe. He hath bene a strong and able salvadge, synowie, active, and of a daring spiritt, vigilant, ambitious, subtile to enlarge his dominions, for but the Countryes Powhatan, Arrohateck, Ap-pamatuck, Pamunky, Youghtamond, and Mattapanient which are said to come unto him by Inheritaunce, all the rest of the Territoryes before named and expressed in the Mappe, and which are all adjoyning to that River, whereon we are seated, they report (as is likewise before mencioned) to have bene either by force subdued unto him, or through feare yeilded: Cruell he hath bene, and quarrellous, as well with his owne Weroances for triffles, and that to stryke a terrour and awe into them of his power and condicion, as also with his neighbours in his younger dayes, though now delighted in security, and pleasure, and therefore standes upon reasonable condicions of peace, with all the great and absolute Weroances about him, and is likewise more quietly setteled amongest his owne.

Watchful he is over us, and keeps good espiall upon our pro-

7.

ceedings, Concerning which he hath his Sentinells, that at what tyme soever any of our boates, pinaces or shippes, come in, fall downe, or make up the River, give the Alarum, and take yt quickly the one from the other, untill yt reach and come even to the Court, or hunting howse, wheresoever he, and his *Cronoccoes*, i. Councellors, and Priests, are; and then he calls to advise, and gives out directions, what is to be done, as more fearing, then harmed at any tyme, with the danger and mischief, which he saith wee intended unto him, by taking away his land from him, and conspiring to surprize him, which we never yet ymagined nor attempted, and yet albeyt the Conceipt of as much strongly possesseth him, he doth often send unto us to temporize with us, awayting perhapps but a fitt opportunity (inflamed by his bloudy and furious priests) to offer us a tast of the same Cuppe which he made our poore Countrymen drinck off at Roanoak not yet seeming willing to hold any open quarrell or hostility with us, but in all advantages, which he sometymes takes against or credulous and beguyled people, he hath yt alwaies so carryed, as upon our Complaynt to him, yt is rather layd upon some of his worst and unruly people, of which he tells us even our King James, (comaunding so many divers men) must have some irreguler and unruly people, or ells upon some of his pettye Weroances, whome peradventure we have attempted (saith he) with offences of the like nature, then that yt is any act of his, or done by his commaund, or according to his will, often flattering us, that he will take order, that yt shalbe no more so, but that the *Tassantasses*, that is the straungers, Kinge James his people, and his people, shalbe all one, brothers, and freindes, and thus he served us at what tyme he wrought the Chickahamanias (a Nation as we have learned, before the comming in of us, so far from being his subjectes, as they were ever his enemyes) into a hatred of us (being indeed a mighty people, and our neighbours, within some 10. or 12. myles of James-towne) and us into the suspicion of them, by telling us that they were naught, and not to be trusted by us, attending but opportunity to do us a mischief; and by urging them to betray such of our men as should come at any tyme to trade with them for corne, and true yt is, upon an advantage at such a tyme they slew three of our men without Cause or offence given, only put into this

Jelousy of our faire dealing with them by Powhatan, and they had done as much for all the rest of ours at that tyme, with them in the Bardg, had not their owne feare and Cowardize more withheld them, then the readines of our people to stand upon their guard, and when this was complayn'd of unto Powhatan, he wholly lay'd the blame upon the unrulines, and force of so mightie a people, excusing himself to us by their nomber, and insolence; yea so far he will herein go sometyme, that when some of his people have done us wrong, (and by his provoaking too) he will not fayle underhand, after the fact, to tell us the Authors of our wronge, giving us leave, and bydding us revenge us upon them, of such subtile understanding and politique carriage is hee.

In all his ancient Inheritaunces, he hath howses built after their manner, and at every howse provision for his entertayne-ment, according to the tyme: about his person ordinarily at-tendeth a guard of 40. or 50. of the tallest men his Country doe affourd. every night upon the 4 quarters of his howse, are 4. Sentinells drawne forth, each standing from other a flight shot, and at every half howre, one from the *Corps du guard*, doth hollow, unto whome every Sentinell returns answere, rownd from his stand, yf any faile, an officer is presently sent forth, that beateth him extreamely.

The word Weroance, which wee call and conster for a king, is a Common word, whereby they call all Comaunders, for they have but few wordes in their language, and but few occa-sions to use any officers, more then one Commaunder, which comonly they call Weroance.

It is straung to see with what great feare and adoration all these people doe obey this Powhatan, for at his feet they pre-sent whatsoever he Commaundeth, and at the least frowne of his brow, the greatest with tremble, yt may be because he is very terryble, and inexorable in punishing such as offend him: for example, he caused certayne Malefactors (at what tyme Capt Smith was Prysoner with them, and to the sight whereof, Capt Smith for some purpose was brought) to be bound hand and foot, when certayne officers appointed thereunto, having from many fires gathered great store of burning Coales, raked the Coales rownd in forme of a Cockpit, and in the middst they cast the offenders to broyle to death: sometymes he causeth the heades of them that offend to be layed upon the Aulter or sacryficing stone, and one or twoo with Clubbs beat out their braynes; when he would punish any notorious enemy or Tres-passer, he causeth him to be tyed to a tree, and with muscle-shells or Reedes, the Executioner cutteth off his Joyntes one after another, ever casting what is cut off into the Fier, then doth he proceed with shells and reedes to case the skyn from his head and face, after which they rippe up his belly, teare out his bowells, and so burne him with the tree and all. Thus them-selves reported, that they executed an englishman one George Cawson, whom the women enticed up from the barge unto their howses at a place called Appocant. Howbeit his ordinary correction is, to have an offendor whome he will only punish, and not put to death, to be beaten with Cudgells as the Turks doe, wee have seene a man kneeling on his knees, and at Pow-hatans comaund, twoo men have beat him on the bare skynn, till the skynne hath bene all bollen, and blistered, and all on a goare blood, and till he hath fallen senceles in a swound, and yet never cryed, complayned, nor seemed to aske pardon, for that they seldome doe.

And sure yt is to be wondered at, how such a barbarous and uncivill Prynce, should take into him (adorned and set forth with no greater outward ornament and munificence) a forme and ostentacion of such Majestie as he expresseth, which often-times strykes awe and sufficient wonder into our people, pre-senting themselves before him, but such is (I believe) the Impression of the divine nature, and howsoever these (as other) heathens forsaken by the true light, have not that portion of the knowing blessed Christian-spirit, yet I am perswaded there is an infused kynd of divinenes, and extraordinary (appointed that it shalbe so by the king of kings) to such who are his ymediate Instruments on earth (how wretched soever other-wise under the Course of misbelief and Infidelity, as it is in the Psalme. *Dixi vos sicut Dii estis*, to governe and dwell in the eyes and Countenaunces of Princes, somwhat may this Catagraph, or Portrayture following, serve to expresse the presentement of this great king Powhatan.

8.   According to the order and custome of sensuall Hethenisme in the Allowaunce of Poligamy, he may have as many women as he will, and hath (as is supposed)

many more then one hundred, All which he doth not keepe, yet as the Turke in one Saraglia or howse, but hath an appointed number, which reside still in every their severall places, amongest whome when he lyeth on his bedd, one sitteth at his head, and another at his feet, but when he sitteth at meat, or in presenting himself to any Straungers, one sitteth on his right hand, and another on his leaft, as is here expressed.

Of his women there are said to be about some dozen at this present, in whose Company he takes more delight then in the rest, being for the most parte very young women, and these Commonly remove with him from howse to howse, either in his tyme of hunting, or visitation of his severall howses; I obteyned their names from one Kempes an Indian, who died the last yeare of the Scurvye at James towne, after he had dwelt with us almost one whole yeare, much made of by our Lord Generall, and who could speake a pretty deale of English, and came orderly to Church every day to prayers, and observed with us the keeping of the Sabaoth, both by ceassing from Labour, and repayring to church, the names of the women I have not thought altogither amisse to set downe as he gave them unto me, and as they stood formost in his Kings affection, for they observe certayne degrees of greatnes, according to the neerenes they stand in their Princes love, and amourous entertaynment.

Winganuske.	Attossocomiske.	Ortoughnoiske.
Ashetoiske.	Ponnoiske.	Oweroughwough.
Amopotoiske.	Appomosiscut.	Ottermiske.
Ottopomtacke.	Appimmonoiske.	Memeoughquiske.

He was reported by the said Kemps, as also by the Indian Machumps, who was sometyme in England, and comes to and fro amongest us, as he dares, and as Powhatan gives him leave, for yt is not otherwise safe for him, no more then yt was for one Amarice, who had his braynes knock't out for selling but a baskett of Corne, and lying in the English fort 2. or 3. daies without Powhatans leave, I say, they often reported unto us that Powhatan had then lyving twenty sonnes and ten daughters besydes a young one by Winganuske, Machumps his sister and a great Dearling of the kings, and besydes younge Pocohunta a daughter of his, using sometyme to our Fort in tymes past, now marryed to a pryvate Captayne called Kocoum some 2. yeares synce.

9.   As he is weary of his women, he bestowes them on those that best deserve them at his handes, when he dyneth or suppeth, one of his women before and after meat, bringeth him water in a woodden platter, to wash his handes, another wayting with a bunch of feathers to wipe them in steed of a towell, and the Feathers, when he hath wyped, are washed and dryed agayne.

10.   A myle from Oropaks in a Thickett of wood he hath a principall howse, in which he keepeth his kind of Treasure, as Skins copper, Pearle, and Beads, which he storeth up against the tyme of his Death and buryall, here is also his store of redd paint for oyntment, and bowes and arrowes, this howse is 50. or 60. yards in length, frequented only by Priests, at the 4 corners of this howse stand 4 Imadges, not as Atlantes or Telamones, supporters to beare up Pillers, Posts or somewhat ells in the stately building, nor as in the auncyent tymes, the Imadges and Pedegrees of the whole Stock or Famely were wont to be sett in Portches, or the first entraunce into howses, with a Porter of speciall trust, who had the Charge of keeping and looking unto them, called Atrienses: but these, are meerly sett, as carefull Sentinells (forsooth) to defend, and protect the howse: (for so they believe of them:) one is like a Dragon, another like a Beare, the third like a Leopard, and the fourth a Giant-Like man, all made evill favoured ynough, according to their best workmanshippe.

CAPUT 4.

A Catalogue of the severall petty Weroaunces Names within the precincts of Tsenacommacoh, under the commaund of the great King Powhaton, with the Denomination of the perticuler shyre (as it were) wherin they governe, togither with what forces for the present they ar hable to furnish Powhatan in his Warrs. by the way toutching at the takeing in of Kecoughtan by Sir Tho: Gates, Lifetenaunt Generall, and the erecting ther of the two Princes Fortes, Forte Henry, and Charles Fort, upon Sowthampton River.

THE great king Powhatan hath devided his Country into many provinces, or Shiers (as yt were) and over every one placed a severall absolute Commaunder, or Weroance to him contributory, to governe the people there to inhabite, and his petty Weroances in all, may be in nomber, about three or fower and thirty, all which have their precincts, and bowndes, proper, and Commodiously appointed out, that no one intrude upon the other, of severall forces, and for the grownd wherein each one soweth his corne, plants his Apoke, and gardeyn fruicts, he tythes to the great king of all the Commodityes growing in the same, or of what ells his shiere brings forth apperteyning to the Land or Rivers, Corne, beasts, Pearle, Fowle, Fish, Hides, Furrs, Copper, beades, by what meanes soever obteyned, a peremptory rate sett downe, as shalbe mentioned in the sixth Chapter, nor have I thought yt altogether amisse to remember here, and offer to consideracion (for all after occasions) a Cathologue, of the several Weroances names, with the denomynation of the particuler shier (as aforesaid) wherein they governe, togither with what forces for the present they are able to send unto the warrs.

Upon Powhatan, or the kinges River, are seated as followeth.

1. Parahunt one of Powhatans sonnes, whome we therefore call Tanxpowatan, which is as much as to say Litte Powhatan, and is Weroance of the Country which hath his owne name called Powhatan, lying (as is before mencioned) close under the Falls, bordering the Monacans, and he may at the present be furnished with 50. fighting and ready men

2. Ashuaquid Weroance of Arrohateck—60. men.

3. Coquonasum Weroance of Appamatuck 100. men.

4. Opossunoquonuske sister to Coquonasum, a Weroancqua, or Queene of a little Mussaran, or smale village of Appamatuck, not unlike an ancyent Episcata Villatica, and she was of power to have spared upon Commaund, some 20. able fighting men, howbeit her Towne we burnt, and killed some of her people (her self miscarying with smale Shott, in pursuit in the woods in winter 1610.) for a trecherous Massacre, which she practized upon 14 of our men, whome she caused her people to envite up into her Towne, to feast and make merry,

entreating our men before hand, to leave their Armes in their boat, because they said how their women would be afrayd ells of their pieces.

5. Kaquothocun Weroance of Weanock—100. men.

6. Ohoroquoh another petty Weroance in the province of Weonock called Cecocomake, upon a By-river to the southward of Weonock—50. men.

7. Oholasc Queene of Coiacohhanauke, which we comonly (though corruptly) call Tapahanock, and is the same, which Capt Smith in his Mappe calls Quiyoughcohanock on the south-shoare or Sallisbury side, whose sonne being yet young, shalbe by Powhatans appointment Weroance of the said Quiyoughcohanock, his name is Tatahcoope. The Weroance Pepiscunimah (whome by construction as well the Indians, as we, call Pipsco) was sometyme possessed in right of this part, as by birth and possession descended the true and lawfull Weroance of the same: but upon a displeasure which Powhatan conceaved against him (in that the said Pipsco, and that not many yeares synce, had stollen away a Chief woman from Opechankeno, one of Powhatans brothers) he was deposed from that Regiment, and the aforesaid Tatacoope (a supposed sonne of Powhatans by this said Queene Oholasc) made Weroance, who being yet young (as is said) is for the most parte in the governement of Chopoke at Chawopo one of Pipscoes brothers, yet is Pipsco suffered to retayne in this his Country a little smale Kaasun or village, upon the rivadge of the streame, with some fewe people about him, keeping the said woman still, whome he makes his best beloved, and she travells with him upon any remove in hunting tyme, or in his visitacion of us, by which meanes twice or thrice in a Sommer, she hath come unto our Towne; nor is so handsome a savadge woman, as I have seene amongest them, yet with a kynd of pride can take upon her a shew of greatnes: For, we have seene her forbeare to come out of her Quintan or Boat, through the water, as the other both maydes and marryed women usuallye doe, unles she were carryed forth betweene twoo of her servants, I was once earely at her howse (yt being Sommer tyme) when she was layd without dores under the shadow of a broad leav'd tree, upon a Pallett of Osiers spredd over with 4. or 5. fyne grey matts, her self

Covered with a faire white drest deare-skyn or towe, and when she rose, she had a Mayde who fetch't her a frontall of white Corrall, and pendants of great (but imperfect coulored, and worse drilled) pearles, which she putt into her eares, and a Chayne with long lynckes of Copper, which they call *Tapaan-taminais* and which came twice or thrice double about her neck, and they accompt a jolly Ornament, and sure, thus attyred with some variety of feathers, and flowers stuck in their hayres, they seeme as debonayre, quaynt, and well pleased, as (I wis) a daughter of the howse of Austria behoung with all her Jewells, Likewise her Mayd fetch't her a Mantell, which they call Puttawus, which is like a side cloak, made of blew feathers, so arteficially and thick sowed togither, that yt showes like a deepe purple Satten, and is very smooth and sleek, and after she brought her water for her handes, and then a bunch or towe of fresh greene ashen leaves, as for a towell to wipe them; I offend in this digression the willinger, synce these were Ceremonies which I did little looke for carrying so much presentment of Civility, and which are not ordynarily perfourmed to any other amongst them, and the Quiyoughcohanocks may be able to make for the warrs—60. fighting men.

8. Tackonekintaco an old Weroance of Warraskoyack, whome Cap: Newport brought prisoner with his sonne Tangoit about 1610. to our Lord Generall, lying then at Point Comfort and whome againe his Lordship released upon promises and a soleme Contract made by the old man, to exchaung with his Lordshippe (after he should have gathered in his harvest in August following) 500. bushells of wheat, beanes and peas, for Copper, beades, and hatchetts, and for the better coulour, carrying away his Sonne, he left a nephew (as he sayd) of his, with his Lordship as a Pawne or hostage untill the perfourmaunce; howbeit the imposture nephew, privy before hand to the falcehood of the old man, watching his opportunity, leapt over bourd one night (being kept in the Delawarre) and (to be more sure of him at that tyme) fettered both leggs togither with a Sea gowne upon him, yet I say he adventured to gett from us by swymming and sure either he recovered the South shoare, or sunck in the attempt, which of either was his fortune we know not, only (if he miscaryed) we never fownd his body nor gowne, and the Indyans of Warraskoyack would oftentymes

afterwards mock us, and call to us for him, and at length make a great laughter, and tell us he was come home, how true or falce is no great matter, but indeed the old king after that tyme refused to perfourme the former bargayne, for which his Lordship, to give them to understand, how he would not be so dealt with all, sent forth 2. Companies, the   of   : his Lordships owne Companie, under the Commaund of Captayne Brewster, and some Seamen under Capt. Argoll, who fell upon 2. townes of his, and burnt them to the Grownd, with all their goodly furniture of Matts, and dishes, woodden potts, and platters, for of this sort is all their goodly Epitrapezia, or vessells belonging to their use for the table, or what ells, And these Warraskoyacks may make 60. men.

9. Weyhohomo a great Weroance of Nansamund.

10. Annapetough another lesse Weroance of Nansamund.

11. Weywingopo a third Weroance of Nansamund.

12. Tirchtough a fourth Weroance of Nansamund; and these 4 togither may make of sturdy and bold Salvages 200.

13. Wowinchopunck Weroance of Paspahegh whome the 9. of February 1610. whilst he with a Company of his people, were attempting some practize upon our old block-House, at James towne, and had bene for the same skulking about there, some 2. or 3. dayes and nightes, Capt George Percy Governour of the Towne, sent forth Ensigne Powell and Ensigne Walker to make surprize of him, yf they could possebly, and bring him alive into the towne. But they not fynding him at any such advantage, yet lothe to loose him, or lett him escape altogither, set upon him, (he being one of the mightiest and strongest Salvadges that Powhatan had under him, and was therefore one of his Champions, and one who had killed trecherously many of our men, as he could beguyle them, or as he at any tyme found them, by Chaunce single in the woodes, strayed beyond the Comaund of the Block-howse) and Powell runing upon him thrust him twice through the body with an arming Sword, howbeit his people came in so fast, and shott their arrowes so thick, as our men being unarmed in their dublett and hose only, and without pieces, were fayne to retyre, whilest the Indians recovered the Weroances body, and carryed yt away with a mightie quicknes and speed of foot, and with a horrible yell and howling, howbeit the Lieutenaunt of the Block-howse,

one Puttock followed hard, and overreached one of the Cronockoes or Chief men, and closing with him overthrew him, and with his dagger sent him to accompany his Master in the other world, And the Paspaheghes may make in number for the Warrs—40.

14. Pochins one of Powhatans sonnes at Kecough-
Kechoughtan a goodly Seate. tan, and was the young Weroance there, at the same tyme when Sir Thomas Gates Lieutenant Generall tooke possession of yt, yt is an ample and faire Country indeed, an admirable portion of Land comparatively high, wholsome and fruictfull, the Seat sometymes of a thowsand Indians and 300. Indian howses, and those Indians, as yt may well appeare, better husbands then in any parte ells, that we have observed, which is the reason that so much grownd is there Cleered and open, ynough with little Labour alreddy prepared, to receave Corne or make Vyneyards of 2. or 3000. Acres, and where besyde we fynd many fruict-trees, a kynd of Gooseberry, Cherries, and other Plombes, the Mariock-apple, and many pretty Copsies, or Boskes, as yt were, of Mulberry trees:
Great store of Mulberry Trees at Kecoughtan. and is indeed a delicate and necessary seat for a Citty, or Chief fortefication, being so neere (within 3. myles by water) the mouth of our Bay, and is well appointed a fitt Seat for one of our Chief Comaunders, synce Point Comfort being (out of our dispute) to be fortefyed, to secure our Townes above, to keepe open the mouth of our River, by which our Shipping may be lett in, yt will require the faith and Judgement of a worthy Commaunder, to be there alwaies present: besydes there wilbe good Fishing, and upon one of the Capes may be placed a Garrison to attend the furnaces and boyling Potts for the making of salt, which without question there (as in the Bermudas) may be made, for all occasions to serve the Colony, and the fishing Voyages for the same: likewise upon Point-Comfort a greate quantety of one kynd of silke grasse growes, there as yett disorderly, which having the grownd prepared and fitted for yt, would retribute a Commodity, worthy the paynes, yf not going beyond the expectacion of the good which is hoped of yt: our Lord Generall and Lieutenant Generall, have erected here 2. fortes as is before remembred, the one called Fort-Henry, the other Charles-Fort, as the River which runs in and serves both his Lordshippe hath

called Southampton-River: Upon the death of an old

Weroance of this place some 15. or 16. yeares synce (being too powerfull neighbours to syde the great Powhatan) yt is said Powhatan taking the advantage subtilly stepped in, and conquered the People killing the Chief and most of them, and the reserved he transported over the River, craftely chaunging their seat, and quartering them amongst his owne people, untill now at length the remayne of those lyving have with much sute obteyned of him Payan-

katank, which he not long since (as you have heard likewise) dispeopled; they might have made of able men for the warres—30.

15. Upon the river of Chickahamania some 8. or 12. miles from James-towne, which falls from the North-side unto our kinges river ar the Chickahamaniaes, who being a warlick and free people, albeyt they pay certayne dutyes to Powhatan, and for Copper wilbe waged to serve and helpe him in his Warrs, yet they will not admitt of any Weroance from him to governe over them, but suffer themselves to be regulated, and guyded by their Priests, with the Assistaunce of their Elders whome they call *Cawcawwassoughs*, and they may make—300. men.

Upon Pamunkey or the Princes River.

16. Opechancheno   All three Powhatans brethren, and
17. Kequotaugh   are the Trium-viri as yt were, or 3.
18. Taughaiten   kings of a Country called Opechan-
                     cheno upon the Head of Pamunky
                     river, and these may make 300. men.

19. Ottahotin Weroance of Kiskiack—50.

At Werowocomaco Powhatan himself hath a principall Residence, and there may be of able men—40.

20. Ohonnamo Weroance of Cantaunkack—100.
21. Ottondeacommoc Weroance of Mummapacun—100.
22. Essenetaugh Weroance of Pataunck—100.
23. Uropaack Weroance of Ochahannauke—40.
24. Keyghaughton Weroance of Cassapecock—100.
25. Weyamat Weroance of Caposepock—300.
26. Attasquintan Weroance of Pamareke—400.
27. Nansuapunck Weroance of Shamapa—100.
28. At Orapaks Powhatan himself comaundes with 50.
29. Opopohcumunk Weroance of Chepeco—300.

30. Attossamunck A Tanx Weroance of Baraconos—10.
31. Pomiscutuck Weroance of Youghtamund—70.
32. Werowough Weroance of Mattapanient—140.

In all: 3,220.

And thus yt may appeare how they are a people who have their severall division, Provinces and Princes, to live in, and to comaund over, and doe differ likewise (as amongst Christians) both in stature, language, and Condicion, Some being great people, as the Sasquesahanoughs, some very little as the Wicocomocoes, some speaking likewise, more articulate and plaine, and some more inward and hollow, as is before remembred, some curteous and more civill, others cruell and bloudy. Pawhatan having large Territories, and many petty kings under him; as some have fewer.

CAPUT 5.

A true Description of the People; of their Collour, Constitution and Disposition; their Apparrell.

THEY are generally of a Coulour browne, or rather

Their
Collour.
tawnye which the Mothers cast them into with a kynd of Arsenick-stone (like redd Patise, or Orpement,) or rather with redd tempered oyntementes of earth, and the juyce of certayne scrused rootes, so sone as they ar borne, and this they doe (keeping themselves still so smudged and besmeered) either for the Custome of the Country, or the better to defend them (synce they goe most what naked) from the stinging of Muskeetoes, (kyndes of Flyes, or byting Gnatts, such as the Greeks called Scynipes, as yet in great swarmes within the Arches,) and which heere breed aboundantly, amongst the marish whorts, and fenburies; and of the same hue are their women, howbeit yt is supposed neither of them naturally borne so discoulored, for Captayne Smith (living sometyme amongst them) affirmeth, how they are from the woumb indifferent white, but as the men so doe the women, dye and disguise themselves, into this tawny coulour, esteeming yt the best beauty, to be neerest such a kynd of Murrey, as a sodden

Quince is of, (to lyken yt to the neerest coulour I can) for which they daylie annoynt both face and bodyes all over, with such a kynd of fucus or unguent, as can cast them into that stayne, as is sayd of the Greek-women, how they colloured their faces all over with certayne rootes called Brenthyna; and as the Britaynes died themselves redd with woad: howbeit he, or shee, that hath obteyned the perfectest art in the tempering of this Coulour with any better kynd of earth, hearb, or roote, preserves yt not yet so secrett, and pretious unto her self, as doe our great Ladies their oyle of Talchum, or other Paynting white and redd, but they freindly comunicate the secrett, and teach yt one another: after their annoynting (which is dailye) they drie them in the Sun, and thereby make their skynnes (besyde the Coulour more black and spotted, which the Sun kissing oft, and hard, addes to their paynting) the more rough and rugged.

Their heades and showlders they paynt oftennest, and those red, with the roote Pochone, brayed to poulder mixed with oyle of the walnut, or Beares grease, this they hold in Summer doth check the heat, and in winter armes them (in some measure) against the Cold, many other formes of payntings they use; but he is the most gallant who is the most monstrous and ugly to behold.

Their hayre is black, grosse, longe and thick, the men have no beardes, their noses are broad flatt and full at the end, great bigge Lippes, and wyde mouthes, (yet nothing so unsightly as the Moores,) they are generally tall of stature, and streight, of comely proportion, and the women have handsome lymbes, slender armes, and pretty handes, and when they sing they have a delightful and pleasant tang in their voyces.

For their apparrell, they are sometymes covered with the skynns of wild beasts, which in winter are dressed with the haire, but in the Sommer without, the better sort use large mantells of divers skyns, not much differing from the Irish falinges; some ymbroydered with white Beads, some with copper, other paynted after their manner, but the Comon sort have scarse wherewithall to cover their nakednes, but stick long blades of grasse, the leaves of Trees or such like under broad Baudricks of Leather which covers them behind and before.

The better sort of women cover them (for the most parte)

all over with skyn mantells, fynely drest, shagged and fringed at the skirt, carved and coulored, with some pretty worke or the proportion of beasts, fowle, tortoyses, or other such like Imagery as shall best please or expresse the fancy of the wearer, their younger women goe not shadowed amongest their owne company untill they be nigh eleaven or twelve returnes of the Leafe old (for so they accompt and bring about the yeare, calling the fall of the leafe *Taquitock*) nor are they much ashamed thereof, and therefore would the before remembered Pochohuntas, a well featured but wanton young girle Powhatans daughter, sometymes resorting to our Fort, of the age then of 11. or 12. yeares, gett the boyes forth with her into the markett place and make them wheele, falling on their handes turning their heeles upwardes, whome she would follow, and wheele so her self naked as she was all the Fort over, but being past once 12. yeres they put on a kynd of semicinctum leathren apron (as doe our artificers or handicrafts men) before their bellies and are very shamefac'd to be seene bare: we have seene some use mantells, made both of Turkey feathers and other fowle so prettely wrought and woven with threeds that nothing could be discerned but the feathers, which were exceeding warme and very handsome: *Nuda mulier erat pulchra*, (saith Plautus) *quam purpurata pulchrior?* Indeed the ornament of that Sexe, who receave an addicion of delicacy, by their garments true yt is sometymes in cold weather, or when they goe a hunting, or seeking the fruicts of the woodes, or gathering bents for their matts, both men and women, to defend them from the bushes, put on a kynd of leather breeches and stockings, all fastened togither, made of deere skynes, which they tye and wrappe about the loynes after the fashion of the Turkes or Irish Trouses.

They adorne themselves most with Copper beades and paynting, of the men there be some, who will paint their bodies black and some yellow, and being oyled over, they will stick therein the soft downe of sondry Coloured birdes, of blew birdes, white herneshews, and the feathers of the Carnation byrd, which they call *Ahshowcutteis*, as if so many variety of laces were stitched to their skyns, which makes a wonderous shew, the men being angry and prepared to fight paint and Crosse their foreheades, cheekes, and the right syde of their heades diversly, either with *terra-sigillata*, or with their root Pochone.

The women have their armes, breasts, thighes, showlders and faces, cunningly imbroydered with divers workes, for pouncing and searing their skyns with a kynd of Instrument heated in the fire, they figure therein flowers and fruicts of sondry lively kyndes, as also Snakes, Serpents, Efts, etc., and this they doe by dropping upon the seared flesh, sondry Colours, which rub'd into the stampe will never be taken away agayne because yt will not only be dryed into the flesh, but grow therein.

The men shave their hayre on the right syde very Close keeping a ridge commonly on the toppe or Crowne like a Coxcomb; for their women with twoo shells will grate away the haire into any fashion they please; on the leaft syde they weare their haire at full length with a lock of an ell long, which they annoynt often with walnut oyle, whereby yt is very sleeke, and shynes like a Ravens wing: sometymes they tye up their lock with an arteficiall and well laboured knott (in the same fashion, as I have seene the Carazzaies of Scio, and Pera:) stuck with many coloured Gewgawes, as the cast head or Browantle of a deare, the hand of their Enemy dryed, Croisetts of bright and shyning Copper, like the new Moone, many weare the whole skyn of a hawke stuffed, with the winges abroad, and Buzzardes or other fowles whole wings, and to the feathers they will fasten a little Rattle about the bignes of the Chape of a rapier, which they take from the taile of a Snake, and sometymes divers kyndes of shells hanginge loose by smale purfleets or threedes, that, being shaken as they move, they will make a Certayne murmering or whistling noyse by gathering wynd, in which they seeme to take great jollety, and hold yt a kynd of bravery.

Their eares they boare with wyde holes comonly twoo or three, and in the same they doe hang chaynes of stayned perle, braceletts of white bone, or shredds of Copper, beaten thin and bright, and would up hollow, with a great pride certayne Fowles leggs, Eagles, Hawkes, Turkeys, etc., with Beasts Clawes, Beares, Arrahacounes, Squirrells, etc. the clawes thrust through, they lett hang upon the Cheeke to the full view; and some of their men there be, who will weare in those holes, a smale greene and yellow couloured live Snake neere half a yard in length, which Crawling and lapping himself about his neck oftentymes familiarly he suffers to kisse his lipps, others weare a dead ratt tyed by the Taile, and such like Conundrums.

The women are in themselves so modest, as in the tyme of their sicknes, they have great care to be seene abroad, at what tyme they goe apart, and keepe from the men in a severall roome, which they have for themselves as a kynd of Gynæceum, nor will the men at such a tyme presse into the nursery where they are.

The men are very strong of able bodies, and full of agility, accustoming themselves to endure hardnes, to lye in the woodes under a tree, by a smale fire in the worst of winter in Frost and Snow, or in the weedes and grasse, as in Ambuscado to accomplish their purposes in the Sommer.

They are inconstant in every thing, but what feare constrayneth them to keepe, Craftye tymerous, quick of apprehension, ingenious ynough in their owne workes, as may testefy the weeres, in which they take their Fish, which are certayne inclosures made of Reedes and framed in the fashion of a Labourinth or Maze, sett a fathome deepe in the water, with divers Chambers or bedds, out of which the entangled Fish cannot retourne or gett out being once in well may a great one by chaunce break the Reedes and so escape, otherwise he remaynes a pray to the Fisher-man the next low water, which they fish with a nett tyed at the end of a pole; as likewise may speake for them their Netts, their arteficiall dressing of Leather, their Cordage, which they make of their naturall hemp and flax togither with their Cunning dressing of that and preserving the whole yeare great Litches or bundells of the same to be used upon any occasion; and of their girdells, which they make of silke grasse, much like St. Francis Cordon, their Cloakes of feathers their bowes and Bowstrings, their Arrowes, their Crownetts, which their Weroances weare; and their Queenes *fasciae crinales*, Borders, or Frontalls, of white Beades Currall and Copper, especially their boates, which they call Quintans and are very shapefull, made of one piece of Tymber like the auncyent *Monoxylum Navigium*, their Matts and all their howshold Implements and such like.

Some of them are of disposicion fearefull (as I said) and not easely wrought therefore to trust us, or Come into our Forts, others agayne of them are so bould and audatious as they dare come unto our forts, truck, and trade with us and looke us in the face, crying all freindes, when they have but new done us a mischief, and when they intend presently againe, if yt lye in their power to doe the like, they are generally Covetous of our Comodities, as Copper, white beades for their women, Hatchetts, of which we make them poore ones of Iron, Howes to pare their Corne grownd, knyves and such like.

They are soone moved to anger, and so malitious that they seldome forgett an Injury; they are very thievish, and will as closely as they can convey any thing away from us, howbeit they seldome steale one from another, lest their Conjurers should reveale yt, and so they be pursued and punished: that they are thus feared yt is certayne; nor let any man doubt but that the devill cann reveale an offence actually committed.

CAPUT 6.

The manner of the Government of the People of
Virginia, their townes, Howses, Dyet, Fishing,
Fowling, Hunting. Etc.

ALTHOUGH the Country people be vary barbarous, yet have they amongest them such governement, as that their Magistrates for good Comaunding, and their people for due subjection and obeying excell many places that would be accompted Civile, the forme of their comon wealth by what hath bene alreddy delivered, you may well gather to be a Monarchall governement, where one as Emperour ruleth over many kings: their Chief ruler likewise for the present you have heard before how named and from whence; as also you have heard the nomber of his Weroances, their forces, and his owne description, you shall now understand, how his kingdome descendeth not to his sonnes, nor Children, but first to his breathren, whereof he hath (as you have heard) three, and after their deceasse to his sisters; first to the eldest sister, then to the rest, and after them to the heires male and Feemale of the eldest sister, but never to the heires of the male.

He nor any of his people understand howe to expresse their

myndes by any kyndes of Letters, or any kind of ingraving which necessity or invention, might have instructed them in, as doe other Barbarians in these new Discoveries; nor have they posetive lawes, only the law whereby he ruleth is custome; yet when he pleaseth his will is lawe, and must be obeyed, not only as a king, but as half a god, his People esteeme him so. His inferiour kings are tyed likewise to rule by like Customes, and have permitted them power of life and death over their people as their Comaund in that nature.

Theire habitations or Townes, are for the most parte by the Rivers; or not far distant from fresh Springes comonly upon the Rice of a hill, that they maie overlooke the River and take every smale thing into view which sturrs upon the same, their howses are not manie in one towne, and those that are stand dissite and scattered, without forme of a street, far and wyde asunder.

As for their howses, who knoweth one of them knoweth them all, even the Chief kings house yt self, for they be all alike builded one to another, they are like gardein arbours, (at best like our sheppardes Cottages,) made yet handsomely enough, though without strength or gaynes; of such young plants as they can pluck up, bow, and make the greene toppes meete togither in fashion of a rownd roofe, which they thatch with mattes, throwne over, the walls are made with barkes of trees, but then those be principall howses, for so many barkes which goe to the making up of a howse, are long tyme of purchasing, in the middst of the howse there is a lover, out of which the smoake yssueth, the fire being kept right under, every howse commonly hath twoo doores, one before and a Posterne, the doores be hung with matts, never locked nor bolted, but only those matts be to turne up, or lett fall at pleasure, and their howses are Comonly so placed under Covert of Trees, that the Violence of fowle weather, snow or rayne cannot assault them, nor the Sun in Somer annoy them, and the roofe being covered, as I say, the wynd is easely kept out, in so much as they are as warme as stoaves albeit very smoakye, wyndoes they have none, but the light comes in at the doare, and at the Lover, for should they have broad open wyndowes in the quarters of their howses, they knew not well, how upon any occasion, to make them close to lett in the light too; for glasse they know not (though the Country wants not Salsodiack enough to make glasse off, and of which we have made some store in a goodlie howse, sett up for the same purpose, with all offices and furnaces thereto belonging, a little without the Island where James towne standes) nor have they lynnen Cloth (albeyt they want not neither naturally the Materialls for that) paper, or such like to dippe in oyle to convey in as a Diaphanick body the light, or to keepe out the weather.

By their howses, they have sometymes A Scæne or high Stage raised like a Scaffold, of smale Spelts, Reedes or dryed Osiers covered with Matts, which both gives a shadowe, and is a Shelter and serves for such a Covered place, where men used in old tyme to sitt and talke for recreation or pleasure which they called *Prœstega*, and where on a loft of hurdells they laie forth their Corne, and fish to dry, they eate, sleepe and dresse their meate all under one roofe, and in one Chamber as yt were.

Rownd about the howse on both sydes are their bedsteedes, which are thick short posts, stak't into the grownd, a foote highe and somewhat more, and for the sydes smale poles layd along, with a hurdell of reedes cast over, whereon they rowle downe a fyne white Matt or twoo (as for beddes) when they goe to sleepe the which they fould up agayne in the Morning when they rise, as we doe our Pallatts, and upon these, rownd about the howse, they lye, heades and points one by the other, especially making a fier before them in the middest of the howse, as they doe usually every night, and some one of them by agreement maynteynes the fier for all that night long. Some of them when they lye downe to sleepe, Cover them with matts, some with skynns, and some lye stark naked on the grownd from six to twentye in a howse, as do the Irish.

About their howses, they have commonly square plotts of cleered grownd, which serve them for gardeins, some 100. some 200. foote square, wherein they sowe their Tobacco, pumpeons, and a fruit like unto a musk-million; but lesse and worse, which they call *Macocks*. Gourds and such like, which fruicts encrease exceedingly and ripen in the begynning of July, and contynue untill September, they plant also the Field-apple, the Maracock a wilde fruict like a Pomgranet, which encreaseth infinitely and ripens in August, Contynuing untill the end of October, when all the other fruicts be geathered, but they sowe neither herb, Flower, nor any other kynd of fruict.

They neither doe empale for deare, nor breed Cattell nor bring up tame poultry, albeit they have great store of Turkeys nor keepe byrds, squirrells, nor tame Partridges, Swan, duck, nor Geese. In March and April they live much upon their Weeres, and feed on Fish, Turkeys, and Squirrells and then as also sometymes in May they plant their Feilds and sett their Corne, and live after those Monethes most of Acrons, Wallnuts, Chesnutts, Chechinquamyns and Fish, but to mend their dyett, some disperse themselves in smale Companies, and live upon such beasts as they can kill, with their bowes and arrowes. Upon Crabbs, Oysters, Land Tortoyses, Strawberries, Mulberries and such like; In June, July, and August they feed upon the rootes of Tockohowberryes, Grownd-nuts, Fish, and greene Wheat, and sometyme upon a kynd of Serpent, or great snake of which our people likewise use to eate.

It is straunge to see how their bodies alter with their dyett even as the deare and wylde beasts, they seeme fatt and leane, strong and weake, Powhatan and some others that are provident roast their fish and flesh upon hurdells and reserve of the same untill the scarse tymes, Commonly their Fish and Flesh they boyle, either very tenderly, or broyle yt long on hurdells over the fire, or ells (after the Spanish Fashion) putting yt on a spitt, they turne first the one syde, then the other till yt be as dry as their Jerkyn-beef in the West Indies, and so they may keepe yt a moneth or more, without putryfying. The broath of Fish or Flesh they sup up as ordinarily, as they eate the meate.

Their Corne they eate in the eares greene, rosted, and sometymes, brusing yt in a morter of wood with a like pestell they lappe yt in Rolls within the leaves of the Corne, and so boyle yt for a dayntie, they also reserve that Corne late planted that will not ripe, by rosting yt in hott ashes, the which in wynter (being boyled with beanes) they esteeme for a rare dish calling yt *Pausarawmena.* their old wheat they first steepe a night in hott water, and in the Morning pownding yt in a Morter, they use a smale baskett for the Boulter or Searser, and when they have sifted forth the fynest they pownd againe the great, and so separating yt by dashing their hand in the baskett, receave the flower in a platter of wood, which blending with water, they make into flatt broad cakes (much like the sacryficing bread which the Grecians offred to their godes called *Popanum*) and these they call *Apones*, which Covering with Ashes till they be baked (as was the ancyent *Escharites panis* raked within the Imbers) and then washing them in faire water, they lett dry with their owne heate, or ells boyle them with water, eating the broath with the bread which they call *Ponepope*, the growtes and broken pieces of the Corne remayning, they likewise reserve, and by fannyng away the Brann, or huskes in a Platter or in the wynd, they lett boyle in an earthen pott three or fower howres, and thereof make a straunge thick pottage, which they call *Usketehamun* and is their kynd of Frumentry, and indeed is like our Ptisane husked Barley, sodden in water, yt may be not much unlike that homely *Ius nigrum*, which the Lacedemonians used to eate and which Dionisius could not abyde to tast of, albeyt he bought a Cooke from thence, only to make him that broath, for which the Cooke told him, he must have a Lacedemonians stomach indeed to eate of the Lacedemonian diett. And some of them more thriftye then Cleanely, doe burne the Coare of the eare to poulder which they call *Pungnough* mingling that in their meale, but yt never tasted well in bread or broath.

Their drinck is (as the Turkes) cleere water; for, albeyt they have Grapes, and those good store, yet they have not falne upon the use of them, nor advised how to presse them into wyne. Peares and Apples they have none to make Cider or Perry of, nor hony to make meath, nor Lycoris to seeth in their water, they call all things that have a spicy tast *Wassacan*, which leaves a supposicion, that they may have some kynd of spice trees, though not perhapps such as ellswhere.

The men bestowe their tymes in fishing, hunting, wars, and such man-like exercises without the doores, scorning to be seen in any effemynate labour, which is the Cause that the women be very paynefull, and the men often idle.

Their fishing is much in Boates, these they call *Quintans*, as the West-Indians call their Canoas, they make them with one Tree, by burning and scraping away the Coales with stones and Shells till they have made in forme of a Trough, some of them

are an ell deepe and 40. or 50. foote in length, and some will
transport 40. men, but the most ordinary are smaller, and will
ferry 10. or 20. with some luggage, in steed of oares they use
paddles and sticks with which they will row faster than we in
our bardges.

They have netts for fishing, for the quantety as formally
brayed and mashed as ours, and these are made of barkes of
certayne trees, deere synewes, for a kynd of grasse, which they
call *Pemmenaw*, of which their women betweene their handes
and thighes spin a threed very even and readely, and this threed
serveth for many uses, as about their howsing, their mantells
of feathers, and their Trowses and they make also with yt lynes
for Angells.

Their Angells are long smale rodds, at the end whereof they
have a Clift, to the which the lyne is fastened, and at the lyne
they hang a hooke, made either of a boane grated (as they nock
their arrowes) in the forme of a crooked pynne or fishooke, or
of the Splinter of a bone, and with a threed of the lyne, they
tye on the bayt, they use also long arrowes tyed in a lyne, wherewith they shoote at fish in the Rivers. those of Accowmack use
Staves like unto Javelyns headed with bone, with these they
dart Fish, swymming in the water, they have also many arteficiall weeres (before descrybed) in which they take aboundance
of Fish.

In the tyme of their huntings, they leave their habitations
and gather themselves into Companies as doe the Tartars, and
goe to the most desart places with their famelyes, where they
passe the tyme with hunting and fowling up towards the
mountaynes by the heades of their Rivers, where indeed there
is plenty of game, for betwixt the Rivers the land is not so large
below, that therein breed sufficient to give them all content,
considering especially how at all tymes and seasons they de-
story them, yt may seeme a Marvayle how they can so directly
passe and wander in those desartes, sometimes three or fower
dayes Journyes, meeting with no habitations, and by reason of
the woodes not having sight of the Sun, whereby to direct
them to coast yt.

Their hunting howses are not so laboured, substanciall nor
arteficiall as their other, but are like our Soldiers Cabyns the
frame sett up in twoo or three howres, cast over head with

Matts, which the women beare after them, as they carry likewise Corne, Acrons, Morters, and all bag and baggage to use
when they come to the place where they purpose for the tyme
to hunt.

In the tyme of hunting every man will stryve to doe his best
to shew his fortune and dexterity, for by their excelling therein,
they obteyne the favour of the women.

At their hunting in the desartes, they are Comonly twoo or
three hundred togither, with the Sun-rysing they call up one
another and goe forth, searching after the heard, which when
they have found, they envyron and circle with many fires, and
betwixt the Fires they place themselves, and there take up their
Standes making the most terriblest noyse that they can. The
deare being thus feared by the fires and their voyces, betake
them to their heeles whome they chase so long within that
Circle, that manie tymes they kill 6. 8. 10. or 15. in a morning,
they use also to drive them into some narrow point of Land,
when they fynd that advantage, and so force them into the
River, where with their boates they have the Ambuscadoes to
kill them, when they have shott a deare by Land, they follow
him (like blood Howndes) by the blood and strayne, and oftentymes so take him. Hares, Partridges, Turkeys, fatt or leane,
young or old in eggs in breeding tyme, or however, they de-
vowre, at no tyme sparing any that they can katch in their
power.

One Savadge hunting alone useth the skyn of a deare, slitt
on the one syde, and so put upon his arme through the neck,
in that sort that the hand comes to the head, which is stuffed,
and the Hornes, Head, Eyes, Eares and every part as arteficially
Countourfeyted as they can devise; thus shrowding his body in
the skyn, by stalking he approacheth the deare, creeping on
the grownd from one tree to another, yf the deare chaunce to
fynd fault or stand at gaze, he turneth the head with his hand
to the best advantage to wyn his shoot, having shott him, he
chaseth him by his blood and strayne till he gett him.

In these hunting and fishing-exercises, they take extreame
paynes, yet they being their ordinary labours from their Infancy, they place them among their sports and pleasures, and
are very prowde to be expert therein, for thereby (as before
remembered, they wyn the loves of their women who wilbe

the sooner contented to live with such a man, by the readiness and fortune of whose bow and dilligence such provision they perceave they are likely to be fedd with well especially of fish and flesh as the place where they are to dwell can affourd; for indeed, they be all of them huge Eaters, as of whome we may saie with Plautus *Noctes diesque estur*; for which we ourselves doe give unto every Indian, that labours with us in our Forts, dowble the allowaunce of one of our owne men, and these active hunters, by their contynuall ranging and travayle, doe know all the advantages, and places most frequented, and best stored with deare or other Beasts, Fish, Fowle, Roots, Fruicts and Berryes.

A kynd of Excercise they have often amongest them much like that which boyes call Bandy in English and may be an auncyent game as yt seemeth in Virgill, for when Æneas came into Italy at his Marriage with Lavinia King Latinus daughter, yt is said the Trojans taught the Latins scipping and frisking at the Ball: likewise they have the excercise of Footeball, in which yet they only forceably encounter with the foote to carry the Ball the one from the other, and spurne yt to the goale with a kynd of dexterity and swift footmanshippe, which is the honour of yt, but they never strike up one anothers heeles as we doe, not accompting that praise worthy to purchase a goale by such advantage.

Dice plaie or cardes or lotts they knowe not, howbeit they use a game upon rushes much like Primero, wherein they card and discard and lay a stake too, and so wyn and loose, they will play at this for their bowes and arrowes, their Copper beads, hatchetts, and their leather Coates.

If a great Commaunder arrive at the habitation of a Weroaunce, they spredd a Matt (as the Turks doe a carpett) for him to sitt upon, upon another right opposite they sitt themselves, then doe they all with a tunable voice of showting byd him welcome: after this doe 2. or more of their chief men make severall orations testefying their love, which they doe with such vehemency and so great earnestnes of passion, that they sweat till they droppe, and are so out of breath, that they can scarse speake, in so much as a Straunger would take them to be exceeding angry or stark mad: after this verbal Entertaynement, they cause such victuall as they have or can provide to be brought forthe with which they feast him fully and freely, and at night they bring him to the lodging appointed for him, whither upon their departure, they send a young woman fresh paynted redd with *Pochone* and oyle to be his bedfellow.

The voyd tyme betweene their sleepe and meat, they commonly bestowe in revelling dauncing and singing, and in their kynd of Musique, and have sondry Instrumentes for the same; they have a kynd of Cane, on which they pipe as on a Recorder and are like the Greeke Pips which they call *Bombices*, being hardly to be sounded without great strayning of the breath, upon which they observe certain rude tunes, but their chief Instruments are Rattles made of smale Gourdes or Pumpeon shells, of these they have Base, Tenor, Countortenor, Meane, and Treble, these mingled with their voices sometymes 20. or 30. togither make such a terrible howling as would rather affright then give pleasure to any man.

They have likewise their *errotica carmina*, or amorous dittyes in their language, some numerous and some not, which they will sing tunable ynough: they have contryved a kynd of angry song against us in their homely rymes, which concludeth with a kynd of Petition unto their Okeus, and to all the host of their Idolls, to plague the Tassantasses (for so they call us) and their posterityes, as likewise another scornefull song they made of us the last yeare at the Falls in manner of Tryumph at what tyme they killed Capt. William West our Lord Generalls nephew, and 2. or 3. more, and tooke one Symon Score a saylor and one Cob a boy prisoners, that song goes thus

1. Mattanerew shashashewaw crawango pechecoma
   Whe Tassantassa inoshashaw yehockan pocosack
   Whe, whe, yah, ha, ha, ne, he, wittowa, wittowa.
2. Mattanerew shashashewaw, erawango pechecoma
   Capt. Newport inoshashaw neir in hoc nantion matassan
   Whe whe, yah, ha, ha, etc.
3. Mattanerew shashashewaw erowango pechecoma
   Thom. Newport inoshashaw neir in hoc nantion monocock
   Whe whe etc.
4. Mattanerew shushashewaw erowango pechecoma
   Pockin Simon moshasha mingon nantian Tamahuck.
   Whe whe, etc.

Which may signifie how that they killed us for all our

Poccasacks, that is our Guns, and for all Capt Newport
brought them Copper and could hurt Thomas Newport (a
boy whose name indeed is Thomas Savadge, whome Capt
Newport leaving with Powhatan to learne the Language, at
what tyme he presented the said Powhatan with a copper
Crowne and other guifts from his Majestie, sayd he was his
sonne) for all his *Monnacock* that is his bright Sword, and how
they could take Symon (for they seldome said our Sirname)
Prysoner for all his Tamahauke, that is his Hatchett, adding as
for a burthen unto their song what lamentation our people
made when they kild him, namely saying how they would cry
whe whe, etc., which they mock't us for and cryed agayne to
us Yah, ha ha, Tewittaw, Tewittawa, Tewittawa: for yt is true
they never bemoane themselves, nor cry out, giving up so
much as a groane for any death how cruell soever and full of
Torment.

As for their dauncing the sport seemes unto them, and the
use almost as frequent and necessary as their meat and drinck
in which they consume much tyme, and for which they appoint
many and often meetings, and have therefore, as yt were sett
Orgies or Festivalls for the same Pastime, as have at this day
the merry Greekes within the Arches; at our Colonies first
sitting downe amongest them, when any of our people repayred
unto their Townes, the Indians would not thinck they had expressed their welcome unto them sufficiently ynough untill
they had shewed them a daunce: the manner of which is thus:
one of them standeth by with some furre or leather thing in his
left hand, upon which he beates with his right, and sings withall, as if he began the Quier, and kept unto the rest their just
tyme, when upon a certayne stroke or word (as upon his Cue
or tyme to come in) one riseth up and begynns the daunce;
after he hath daunced a while steppes forth an other, as if he
came in just upon his rest, and in this order all of them so many
as there be one after another who then daunce an equall distance
from each other in a ring, showting, howling and stamping
their feet against the grownd with such force and payne, that
they sweat againe, and with all variety of straung minick-trickes
and distorted faces, making so confused a Yell and noise, as so
many frantique and disquieted Bacchanalls, and sure they will
keepe stroake just one with another, but with the handes, head,

face, and body every one hath a severall gesture, as who have seene the Darvises in their holy daunces in the Moschas upon Wednesdayes and Frydayes in Turkey many resemble these unto them, you shall fynd the manner expressed in the figure in the second booke Chapt.

Every Weroance knowes his owne Meeres and lymitts to fish fowle or hunt in (as before said) but they hold all of their great Weroance Powhatan, unto whome they paie 8. parts of 10. tribute of all the Commodities which their Country yeildeth, as of wheat, pease, beanes, 8. measure of 10. (and these measured out in little Cades or Basketts which the great king appoints) of the dying roots 8. measures of ten; of all sorts of skyns and furrs 8. of tenne, and so he robbes the poore in effect of all they have even to the deares Skyn wherewith they cover them from Could, in so much as they dare not dresse yt and put yt on untill he have seene yt and refused yt; for what he Comaundeth they dare not disobey in the least thing.

So well observed by Sir W. R.

CAPUT 7.

Of the Religion amongst the Inhabitaunts; their God: their Temples: their opinion of the Creation of the World: of their belif concerning the Immortallity of the Sowle; of their Conjurations, and sacrafising of Children.

THERE is as yet in Virginia no place discovered to be so savage and simple, in which the Inhabitants have not a Religion, and the use of Bow and Arrowes, all thinges they conceave able to doe them hurt, beyond their prevention they adore with their kynd of divyne worship, as the fier, water, Lightening, Thunder our Ordinaunce Pieces, Horses etc. but their chief god they worship is no other indeed then the devill, whome they make presentements of and shadow under the forme of an Idoll which they entitle *Okeus* and whome they worship as the Romaynes did their hurtfull god Vejovis more for feare of harme then of hope of any good, they say they have Conference with him and fashion themselves (in their disguisements) as neere to his shape as they ymagyne.

In every Territory of a Weroance is a Temple and a Priest peradventure 2. or 3. yet happie doth that Weroance accompt himself who can deteyne with him a *Quiyoughquisock* of the best grave luckye well instructed in their misteryes, and beloved of their god and such a one is no lesse honoured then was Dianaes priests at Ephesus for whome they have their more pryvate Temples with Oratories and Chauncells therein according as is the dignity and reverence of the *Quiyoughquisock*, which the Weroane wilbe at charge to build upon purpose, sometyme 20. foote broad, and a hundred in length, fashioned arbour wise, after their building, having Commonly the dore opening into the east, and at the west end a Spence or Chauncell separated from the body of the Temple with hollow windynges and pillers, whereon stand divers black Images fashioned to the Showlders, with their faces looking downe the Church, and where within their Weroances upon a kynd of Beare of Reedes lye buryed, and under them apart in a vault, low in the grownd (as a more secrett thing) vayled with a Matt sitts their Okeus an Image ill-favouredly carved, all black, dressed with Chaynes of Pearle the presentment and figure of that god (saye the Priests unto the Laytie, and who religiously beleeve what the priests saie) which doth them all the harme they suffer, be yt in their bodies, or goodes, within dores or abroad, and true yt is many of them are divers tymes (especially offenders) shrewdly scratched as they walke alone in the woodes, yt maie well be by the subtile Spirritt the malitious enemy to mankind whome therefore to pacefie and worke to doe them good (at lest no harme) the priests tell them doe these and these Sacrifices unto, of these and these things, and thus and thus often, by which meanes not only their owne children but Straungers are sometymes sacryficed unto him; whilst the great god (the priests tell them) who governes all the world, and makes the Sun to shine, creating the Moone and Starres his Companions, great powers, and which dwell with him, and by whose vertues and Influences, the under earth is tempered and brings forth her fruictes according to her seasons, they calling Ahone, the good and peaceable god, requires no such dutyes, nor needes be sacryficed unto, for he entendeth all good unto them, and will doe

no harme, only the displeased Okeus looking into all mens ac-
cions and examyning the same according to the severe Scale of
Justice, punisheth them with sicknesses, beates them, and
strikes their ripe Corne with blastings, stormes, and thunder-
clappes, stirres up warre and makes their women falce unto
them, such is the misery and thraldome under which Sathan
hath bound these wretched Miscreants.

Sir W. R.   Indeed their Priests being the ministers of Sathan
obser: and (who is very likely visibly conversant amongest them)
Advi: feare and tremble, lest the knowledge of god and of
our Saviour Jesus Christ should be taught in those parts, doe
now with the more vehemency perswade, the people to hold
on their wonted Ceremonyes, and every yeare to sacryfice still
their owne Children, to the auncyent god of their fathers, and
yt is supposed, gayne double oblations this waie, by reason they
doe at all tymes so absolutely governe and direct the Weroances or Lords of Countryes in all their accions and this Custome he hath politiquely maynteyned and doth yet universally,
a few places excepted over all the Indies: In Florida they sacrifice the first borne Male child: in Mexico they forebeare their
owne, and offer up such Prisoners as they take in the warres,
whome they torture with a most barbarous Cruelty, that the
Devill hath obteyned the use of the like offering in many other
parts of America, Acosta hath observed and related in his mor-
rall and naturall History of the West Indies: the same honour
the Devill obteyned from all Antiquity in effect, even from the
Israelites and their borderers, from the Carthaginians Persians
and the first Planters of Italy and other Nations: to have suffered still therefore, methincks these Priests of Baal or Belzebub
were greatly offensive to the Majestie of god, as most perillous
for the English to inhabite within those parts for these their
Quiyoughquisocks or Prophetts be they that perswade their
Weroances to resist our settlement and tell them how much
their Okeus wilbe offended with them, and that he will not be
appeased with a sacrifice of a thowsand, nay a Hecatomb of
their children, yf they permitt a Nation despising the auncyent
Religion of their forfathers to inhabite among them, synce
their own godes have hitherto preserved them, and given
them victory over their enemies from age to age.

It is true that hitherto our Colony hath consisted (as yt were) but of a handfull of men, and not stored with desired victualls fytt for such Eaters as the English are, nor untill Anno 1610. Hath yt bene the best governed to undertake this service to god; but now, the Commodityes of our owne Country being thither in some good quantety transported, and those there thryving and growing daily into good Increase, as kyne, Goates, Swyne, Horses, Mares, etc. and the first ragged government nowe likewise prudently chaunged into an absolute Comaund, and over the same many learned and juditious Gentlemen of his Majesties Councell, as a body politique resident in England, and they also enlightened from the supreme understanding of his Majesties privy Counsaile, and the Lord Generall, now to goe agayne is a very worthie valiant noble man and well instructed in the busines, who hath Sir Thomas Gates Lieutenaunt Generall (whose Commendation lyeth in his name) Sir Thomas Dale Marshall both there at this present informing themselves of the Country and people, both excellent old soldiers, and well knowing all Circumstances of warre and advantages of grownd, yt cannot be doubted but that all things shalbe so forseene, that the best Courses shalbe taken and the surreption of these Priests more seriously thought on then heretofore, and by whose Apprehension wilbe wrought the saffety of such of our people, as shalbe ymployed herein for his Majesties honour and the enlargement of his dominion, for whose sake god will prosper all our lawfull and Christian attempts yet noe Spanish Intention shalbe entertayned by us neither, hereby to roote out the Naturalls as the Spaniards have done in Hispaniola and other parts, but only to take from them these Seducers, untill when they will never knowe god nor obey the kings Majestie and by which meanes we shall by degrees chaung their barbarous natures, make them ashamed the sooner of their savadge nakednes, informe them of the true god, and of the waie to their salvation, and fynally teach them obedience to the kings Majestie and to his Governours in those parts, declaring (in the Attempt thereof) unto the several weroances, and making the comon people likewise to understand, how that his Majestie hath bene acquainted, that the men women, and Children of the first plantation at Roanoak were by practize and Comaundement of Powhatan (he himself perswaded thereunto by his Priests) miserably slaughtered without any offence given him either by the first planted (who 20. and od yeares had peaceably lyved and inter-mixed with those Savadges, and were out of his Territory) or by those who now are come to inhabite some parte of his desart landes, and to trade with him for some Commodityes of ours, which he and his people stand in want of, notwithstanding be-cause his Majestie is of all the world, the most just and most mercifull Prynce, he hath given order that Powhatan himself with his Weroances, and all his people shalbe spared, and re-venge only taken upon his *Quiyoughquisocks*, by whose advise and perswasions was exercised that bloudy Cruelty, and only how that Powhatan himself, and the Weroances must depend on his Majestie both acknowledging him for their superior Lord, and whereunto the inferiour Weroances sure will most willingly condiscend, when yt shalbe tould them that whereas Powhatan doth at his pleasure, dispoyle them both of their lyves and goodes, without yeilding them any reason, or alleadging or proving any just cause against them, they shall for hereafter be delivered from his Tyranny, and shall enjoy freely the fruictes of their owne Territoryes, so shall they the fish and the Fowle thereof of which the most rare and delicate of the one, and the best and wholsommest of the other are now forbidden them and reserved and preserved to Powhatan, and that they shalbe freed likewise from delivering of their Children for sac-rifice, and the poore womens songs of lamentation converted into rejoycings, the true God and his Governour king James comaunding that the Children of men be preserved and not slaughtered without offence given, as the devill and his Quiy-oughquisocks have ordayned; against which Sathanicall Inven-tion, may yt please his Majestie to make an Ordinaunce, that the fathers of those Children, and all that consent unto the sacrifices hereafter shalbe put to death as Traytors to god and his Majestie as also when they shall understand how the try-bute which they shall pay unto his Majestie shalbe far lesse then that which Powhatan exacteth from them, who robbes them as you have heard of all they have: but after such tyme as they shall submitt themselves to the kings Majestie and con-sent to paie him a Trybute to be agreed upon, Powhatan shall lay no more his exactions upon them, but they shall freely en-joy all they can geather and have a peaceable and franck trade

with the English for the Commodityes they can make of their
owne exchaunging them for ours and that the English will take
of their poorest into their famelies as their better sort shall by
pattents and Proclamations hold their landes as free burgers
and Cittizens with the English and Subjectes to king James,
who will give them Justice and defend them against all their
enemyes, whereas now they live in miserable Slavery, and have
no assuraunce either of their lives or of their goodes: and indeed hereby these double and mixed commodities will arrise,
namely the English Garrisons shall not only be provided of
Corne, and their storehowses of marchandizes, but the Naturalls being thus constrayned to paye duly this their Tribute will
Clense double as much grownd as they doe, whereby the
Country will not only be made the more passeable for horse
and Foote, but the people themselves who are now for the
most parte of the yeare idle, and doe little ells then sharpen
their arrowes against the English, shall fynd by the geathering
togither of their severall sortes of Tribute somewhat els to entertaine themselves withall. and although (peradventure) this
may seeme a burthen at the first, untill they have acquainted
themselves with another kynd of life, and perceave themselves
indeed to become thereby the more civill, as likewise to enjoy
the rest of their owne more freely then under Powhatan, they
will fynd themselves in far better estate, then now they are; for
the Cassiques or Comaunders of Indian Townes in Peru,
whome the Virginians call Weroances, although they paie unto
the king of Spayne great Tribute, yet because they make exchaunge with the Spaniards for what remaynes, they doe not
only keepe great Hospitality and are rich in their furniture
horses and Cattell, but as Capt Ellis vowes, who lived
amongst them some few yeares, their diett is served to them
in silver vessells and many of them have naturall Spaniardes,
that attend them in their howses; when on the other syde, the
Spaniards were not able to make the Twenteth parte of proffitt
which they now doe but by the helpe of those Cassiques, for
they furnish out of their severall Territoryes, not so few as
50000. people to worke in the mines of Potosi, who after so
many monethes travaile are returned into their Countryes, and
50000. others by another Company of Cassiques provided to
supplie them: in new Spayne they doe the like, for the naturall

people gather all the Schuchinella which the Spaniards have and receave no more for a weekes labour then so much money as will buy them a pott of wyne to drinck drunck the Satterday night.

In Guiana 30. of the people with their Conoa wilbe hired for one hatchett to row whither they are Commaunded for a whole monethe, and sell a hundred weight of good biskett for a three penny kniffe, and if our Copper had bene well ordered in Virginia, as may be hereafter I am assured that lesse then one ounce will serve to entertayne the labour of a whole howshould for ten dayes.

And surely all this being delivered in fitt termes, by some perfect Interpreter, and to men that are Capable ynough of understanding, yt may begett a faire conceipt in them, of us and our proceedinges, and leave them well satisffyed, and indeed be yt beleeved, that when so just an occasion shall after these Priests of Asmodius or the devill into the handes of the Lord Generall, a better tyme then that will not be found to performe the same acceptable service to god, that Jehu king of Israell did when he assembled all the priests of Baal, and slue them to the last man in their owne Temple, of this maie every vulgar Sence be well assured, that seeing these Monsters doe offer up unto the Devill their owne Children, and being hardened against all Compassion naturall and divine enforce their owne mothers to deliver them to the Executioner with their owne handes, they will easely Condiscend unto, and assist the destruccion and extirpation of all Straungers knowing or acknowledging the true god.

Within the Chauncell of the Temple by the Okeus are the *Cenotaphies* or the monuments of their kings, whose bodyes so soone as they be dead, they embowell, and scraping the flesh from off the bones, they dry the same upon hurdells into asshes, which they put into little potts (like the ancyent urnes) the Annotamye of the bones they bynd togither, or case up in Leather, hanging braceletts or Chaynes of Copper, beades, pearle, and such like, as they used to weare about most of their Joynts and neck, and so repose the body upon a little Scaffold (as upon a tomb) laying by the dead bodyes feet all his ritches in severall basketts his Apooke and Pipe, and any one toy which in his life, he held most deere in his fancy. Their Inwards they stuff with pearle, Copper, beades, and such Trash sowed in a skynne, which they overlappe againe very Carefully in white skynnes one or twoe, and the bodyes thus dressed, lastly they rowle in mattes, as for wynding sheetes and so lay them orderly one by one, as they dye in their turnes upon an Arch standing (as aforesaid) for the Tomb; and these are all the Ceremonies we yet can learne, that they give unto their dead, we heare of no sweet oyles or oyntments that they use to dresse or Chest their dead bodies with albeyt they want not of the pretious Rozzin running out of the great Cedar, wherewith in the old tyme they used to embalme dead bodyes, washing them in the oyle and liquor thereof, only to the Priests the care of these Temples are to them as solitary Asceteria, Colledges or Mynsters to exercise themselves in Contemplacion, for they are seldome out of them, and therefore often lye in them, and maynteyne contynuall Fire in the same upon a Harth somwhat neere to the East end.

For their ordinary buryalls, they digge a deepe hole in the earth with sharpe stakes, and the Corps being lapped in Skyns and Mattes with their Jewells, they laye them upon stickes in the grownd, and so Cover them with earth the buryall ended, the women (being paynted all their faces with black Coale and oyle) do sytt 24. howres in their howses mourning and lamenteing by turnes with such yelling and howling, as may expresse their great passions.

Their principall Temple, or place of superstition is at Uttamussack at Pamunky, nere unto which towne within the woodes is a chief holie howse proper to Powhatan upon the toppe of Certayne red sandy hills, and yt is accompanied with 2. other 60. foote in length filled with Images of their kinges and devills, and tombes of their predicessors: this place they count so holie, as that none but the Priestes and kings dare come therein; in this as the Grecian Nigromancers in their Psychomantie did use to call up spiritts either the Priests have conference and consult indeed with the Devill and receave verball answeres, and so saith Acoste he spake to the Boitii or Chaplyns of the West Indies in their Guacas or Oratories, or at lest these Conjurers make the simple laytie so to believe, who therefore (so much are the people at the Priests divotion) are ready to execute any thing how desperate soever which they shall Comaund. The Salvadges dare not goe up the river in boates by yt, but that they solemnely Cast, some piece of Copper, white beades or Pocones into the River, for feare their Okeus should be offended and revenged of them: in this place commonly are resident 7. Priests, the chief differing from the rest in his ornament, whilst the inferiour Priests can hardly be knowne from the Comon people save that they had not (yt may be, may not have) so many holes in their eares, to hang their Jewells at: the Ornamentes of the Chief Priests, was upon his showlders a middle seised Cloke of feathers, much like the old sacrificing garment, which Isodorus calls Casiola, and the Burlett or attire of his head, was thus made: some 12. or 16. or more Snakes Sloughes, or skyns, were stuffed with Mosse, and of weasells and other vermyne, were skyns perhappes as manie, all these were tyed by the tayles, so as their Tayles mett in the toppe of the head, like a great Tassell, and rownd about the Tassell was Circled a Crownet (as yt were) of feathers, the Skyns hanging rownd about his head, neck, and showlders and in a manner Covering his face. The faces of all their Priests are paynted as ugly as they can devise, in their handes they carry every one his rattle for the most parte as a Symbale of his place and profession, some base some smaller, their divotion is most in songes, which the Chief Priest begyns, and the rest follow him, sometymes he makes invocation with broken Sentences by starts and straunge passions, and at every pawse, the rest of the priests give a short groane.

We have not yet hitherto perceaved that any solemne *fasti*, or *feriæ præcidaniæ, vigelli*, or any one daie more holye then other is amongest them, but only in some great distresse of want, feare of enemyes, tymes of Tryumphes, and gathering togither their fruictes, the whole Country men women and Children, come togither to their Solemnityes, the manner of which jolly divotion is sometymes to make a great fier in the howse or feildes, and all to sing and daunce about yt in a ring (like so many Fayries) with rattles and showtes, 4. or 5. howers togither, sometymes fashioning themselves in twoo Companies, keeping a great Cercuyt, one Company daunceth one waie and the other the Contrary, (all very fynely paynted,) certayne men going before with either of them a Rattle, other following in the midst, and the rest of the trayne of both wings in order 4. and 4. and in the Reare certayne of the Chiefest young men with long Switches in their handes to keepe them in their places: after all which followes the Governour or Weroance himself in a more slowe or sollemne measure, stopping, and dauncing, and all singing very tunable.

They have also divers Conjurations, one they made at what tyme they had taken Captayne Smith Prisoner, to knowe as they reported, yf any more of his Countrymen would arrive there and what they intended, the manner of yt Captayne Smith observed to be as followeth: first so soone as day was shutt in, they kyndled a faire greater Fier in a loue house, about which assembled 7: priests, taking Captayne Smith by the hand, and appointing him his seat, about the fier they made a kynd of enchaunted Circle of Meale, that done the Chief Priest (attyred as is expressed) gravely began to sing and shake his rattle, solemnely marching and rownding about the fier, the rest followed him sylently, untill his song was done, which they all shutt up with a groane; at the end of the first song the chief Priest layd downe certayne graynes of wheat, and so contynued howling and invoking their Okeus to stand firme and powerfull unto them, in divers varietyes of songes still compting the songes by the graynes, untill they had Circled the fier three tymes, then they devided the graynes by certayne nombers with little stickes all the while uttering some impious thing unto themselves, oftentymes looking upon Capt Smith: in this manner they contynued 10. or 12. howres without any other Ceremonies or Intermission with such violent stretching of their armes and various passions, Jestures, and Symptoms as might well seeme straunge to him before whome they so conjured, and who every hower expected to be the Hoast and end of their Sacrifice: not any meat did they eate untill yt was very late and the night far spent, about the rising of the morning-star they seemed to have fynished their worke of darkenes, and then drew forth such Provision as was in the said howse and feasted themselves and him with much mirth three or fower daies they Contynued these elvish Ceremonies: now besydes these manner of Conjurations thus within dores (as we read) the Augurers in the old tyme of the like Superstition did ascend or goe up into certayne Towers or high places, called therefore *Auguracula* to devyne of matters so do they goe forth, and either upon some rock standing alone, or upon some desolate promontory-Toppe, or ells into the midst of thick and solitary woodes, they call out upon their Okeus, and ymportune their other Quiyoughquisocks with most impetious and intermynate Clamours, and howling and with such paines and strayned accions as the neighbour places eccoe agayne of the same, and themselves are all in a sweat and over wearyed.

They have also certain aulter stones which they call *Paw-corances*, but those stand from their Temples, some by their howses, others in the woodes and wildernes, upon these they offer bloud, deare suet, and Tobacco, and that when they re-turne safe from the warres, luckely from hunting, and upon many other occasions.

We understand they give great reverance to the Sun for which both at his early rysing and late sytting they Couch themselves downe, and lift up their handes and eyes, and at certayne tymes make a rownd Circle on the grownd with To-bacco, into which they reverently enter and murmure certayne unhallowed wordes with manie a deformed gesture.

They have also another kynd of Sorcery which they use in Stormes a kynd of *Botanomantia* with herbes when the waters are rough in the Rivers and Sea-coasts, their Conjurers run to the water-syde, or passing in their Quintans, after many hellish outcryes, and Invocacions they cast whesican Tobacco, Copper, Pocones or such trash into the water to pacefy that god, whome they thinck to be very angry in those stormes.

Before their dynners and supperes (as Heliodorus remembers the Egiptians were wont to doe when they sate to meate or at Candle light) the better sort will doe a kynd of Sacrifice taking the first bitt, and casting yt into the fier, and to yt repeat cer-tayne wordes. I have heard Machumps at Sir Thos. Dales table, once or Twice upon our request, repeat the said grace as yt were, howbeyt I forgott to take yt from him in wryting.

In some parte of the Country, they have yearely a Sacrifice of Children, such a one was at Quiyoughcohanock some 10. myles from James Towne, as also at Kecoughtan, which Cap-tayne George Percey was at and observed, the manner of yt was: 15. of the properest young boys betweene 10. and 15. yeares of age, they paynted white, having brought them forth the people spent the forenoone in dauncing and singing about them with

rattles: in the afternoone they solemnely led those Children to
a certayne tree appointed for the same purpose, at the roote
whereof round about they made the Children to sitt downe,
and by them stood the most and the ablest of the men, and
some of them the fathers of the Children, as a watchfull Guard
every one having a Bastinado in his hand of Reedes, and these
openedd a lane betweene all along, through which were appointed 5. young men to fetch those Children, and accordingly
every one of the 5. tooke his turne and passed through the
Guard to fetch a child, the Guard fiercely beating them the
while with their Bastinadoes, and shewing much anger and displeasure, to have the Children so ravisht from them, all which
the young men patiently endured, receaving the blowes and
defending the Children with their naked bodies from the unmercifull stroakes that payd them soundly, though the Children escaped: all the while sate the mothers and kynswomen a
far off, looking on weeping and crying out very passionately,
and some in pretty wayementing tunes singing (as yt were)
their dirge or funerall songe provided with Matts Skynnes
Mosse and dry wood by them as things fitting their Childrens
funeralls: after the Children were thus forceably taken from
the Guard, the Guard possessed as yt were with a violent fury
entred upon the tree and tore yt downe bowes and braunches
with such a terrible fiercenes and strength, that they rent the
very body of yt and shivered yt in a hundred pieces, whereof
some of them made them garlandes for their heades and some
stuck of the braunches and leaves in their haire wreathing
them in the same, and so went up and downe as mourners,
with heavy and sad downe cast lookes, what ells was done with
the Children might not be seene by our people, further then
that they were all cast on a heape in a vallye, where was made
a great and solemne feast for all the Company, at the going
whereunto the night now approaching, the Indians desired
our people that they would withdrawe themselves and leave
them to their further Proceedings, the which they did, only
some of the Weroances being demaunded the meaning of this
Sacrifice, made answere, that the Children did not all of them
suffer death; but that the Okeus did suck the blood from the
left breast of that Child, whose chaunce yt was to be his by Lott,

till he were dead, and the remayne were kept in the wildernes by the said young men till 9. monethes were expired, during which tyme they must not Converse with any, and of these were made their Priests and Conjurers, to be instructed by tradition from the elder Priests: these Sacryfices or Catharmata, they hold to be so necessary, that yf they should omitt them they suppose their Okeus and all the other *Quioughcosoughes*, which are their other godds would let them have no deare, Turkeis, Corne, nor Fish, and yet besydes he would make a great slaughter amongest them in so much as if ever the auncyent Superstitious tymes feared the Devills *postularia fulgara* lightenings that signified Religion of Sacrifices and voyces to bee neglected, these people are dreadfully afflicted with the Terror of the like in so much, as I may truly saye therefore the like thunder and lightening is seldome agayne either seene or heard in Europe as is here.

Concerning the ymortality of the Sowle, they suppose that the Comon people shall not live after death, but they thinck that their Weroances and Priests indeed, whome they esteeme also, half Quioughcosoughes, when their bodies are layd in the Earth that that which is within shall goe beyond the Mountaines and travell as far as where the Sun setts into most pleasant feildes, growndes and pastures, where yt shall doe no labour, but stuck fynely with feathers, and paynted with oyle and Pocones rest in all quiet and peace, and eate delicious fruicts, and have store of Copper, beades, and hatchetts, sing, daunce and have all variety of delights and merryments till that waxe ould there as the body did on earth, and then yt shall dissoulve and dye, and come into a womans womb againe, and so be a new borne unto the world not unlike the heathen Pythagoras his opinion and fable of Metempsychosis: nor is this opinion more ridiculous or Savage, then was the Epicures long synce in tyme too of morality, who taught that the sowle of man, as of bruit beasts, was nothing ells but lief or the vitall power, arrysing of the temperature and perfeccion of the body and therefore dyed and extinguished togither with the body, the Sowle so being a meere quality in the body, and when the bodye was to dissolve, the sowle must likewise become nothing: nor is yt more Hethenous then our Athists, who

would (even out of Scripture) prophanely conclude no ymortality of the sowle to be, wresting that of Solomon who saith,
"The condicion of men and beasts are even as one," not acknowledging their impious reasoning by fallacies, concluding
that which is in some respects so, to be symply so, as because
their bodyes dye alyke, therefore the Sowle of man must perish
too; but, (alas) well may these poore Heathen be pytied and
pardoned untill they shalbe taught better, neither borne under
grace nor of the Seed of promise, when such as professe themselves in their great places to be our Saviour Christs chief vicars
here upon earth, dare be far more dissolute, as yt is written of
Paule the 3. Pope of Rome, when he was breathing out his
sowle, and ready to dye, sayd, that now at length he should try
and know three things, whereof in his whole tyme he much
doubted (viz.) first, whether there was a god, secondly
whether Sowles were ymmortall, and lastly whether there was
any Hell: and Stephanus upon Herodotus, remembers us the
Pope Leo the 10. answeared Cardinall Bembo that alleadged
some parte of the Ghospell unto him: "Lord Cardinall, what a
wealth this fable of Jesus Christ hath gotten us?" I say therefore yt maie well seeme lesse straunge, yf among these Infidells
both the knowledg of our Saviour be questioned and the ym-
mortality of the sowle not rightly understood: howbeit to divert them from this blyndnesse many of our people have used
their best endeavours Chiefely with Pepiscuminah weroance of
Quiyoughcohanock whose apprehension and good disposicion towardes us hath hitherto much exceeded any in those
countries, with whome though as yet we have not prevayled to
forsake his falce godes, yet this he was wonne to say, that he
beleeved or god as much exceeded theires as our guns did their
bow and arrowes, and many tymes upon our peoples first comming into the Country did send to the President at James
Towne men with Presents entreating him to pray to his god
for rayne, for his gods would not send him any: and in this
lamentable Ignoraunce doe these poore sowles live.

I will conclude these points with opinion of the Indians of
Patawomeck-river the last yeare 1610. about Christmas when
Capt Argoll was there trading with Jopassus the great kings
brother, after many daies of acquaintaunce with him as the

Pynnace road before the Towne Mattchipongo, Jopassus comming abourd and sitting (the weather being very Cold) by the
fire upon a harth in the Hold with the Captayne, one of our
men was reading of a Bible, to which the Indian gave a very at-
tent eare and looked with a very wish't eye upon him as if he
desired to understand what he read, whereupon the Captayne
tooke the booke, and turned to the Picture of the Creation of
the world, in the beginning of the book, and caused a Boy one
Spilman, who had lived a whole yeare with this Indian-King
and spake his language, to shew yt unto him, and to enterprett
yt in his language, which the boy did, and which the king
seemed to like well of: howbeit he bade the boy tell the Capt,
yf he would heare, he would tell him the manner of their begynning, which was a pretty fabulous tale indeed: "We have
(said he) 5. godes in all our chief god appeares often unto us in
the likewise of a mightie great Hare, the other 4. have no visible shape, but are (indeed) the 4. wyndes, which keepe the 4.
Corners of the earth (and then with his hand he seemed to
quarter out the scytuation of the world) our god who takes
upon this shape of a Hare conceaved with himself how to
people this great world, and with what kynd of Creatures, and
yt is true (said he) that at length he divised and made divers
men and women and made provision for them to be kept up
yet for a while in a great bag, now there were certayne spirritts,
which he described to be like great Giants, which came to the
Hares dwelling place, being towards the rising of the Sun and
hadd perseveraunce of the men and women, which he had
put into that great bag, and they would have had them to eate,
but the godlike Hare reproved those Caniball Spirritts and
drove them awaie. Nowe yf the boy had asked him of what he
made those men and women and what those spirritts more particularly had bene and so had proceeded in some order, they
should have made yt hang togither the better, but the boy was
unwilling to question him so many things lest he should offend
him, only the old man went on, and said, how that godlike hare
made the water and the fish therein and the land and a great
deare, which should feed upon the land, at which assembled
the other 4. gods envious hereat, from the east the west from
the north and sowth and with hunting poles kild this deare

drest him, and after they had feasted with him departed againe east west north and sowth, at which the other god in despight of this their mallice to him, tooke all the haires of the slayne deare and spredd them upon the earth with many powerfull wordes and charmes whereby every haire became a deare and then he opened the great bag, wherein the men and the women were, and placed them upon the earth, a man and a woman in one Country and a man and a woman in another country, and so the world tooke his first begynning of mankynd, the Captayne bade the boy aske him, what he thought became of them after their death, to which he answered somwhat like as is expressed before of the Inhabitants about us, howe that after they are dead here, they goe up to the toppe of a highe tree, and there they espie a faire plaine broad pathe waye, on both sydes whereof doth grow all manner of pleasant fruicts, as Mulberryes, Strawberryes, Plombes etc. In this pleasant path they run toward the rysing of the sun, where the godlike hares howse is, and in the midd waie they come to a howse, where a woman goddesse doth dwell, who hath alwaies her doores open for hospitality and hath at all tymes ready drest greene *Uskatahomen* and *Pokahichary* (which is greene Corne bruysed and boyld, and walnutts beatten smale, then washed from the Shells, with a quantety of water, which makes a kynd of Milke and which they esteeme an extraordinary dainty dish) togither with all manner of pleasant fruicts in a readines to entertayne all such as do travell to the great hares howse, and when they are well refreshed, they run in this pleasant path to the rysing of the Sun, where they fynd their forefathers living in great pleasure in a goodly feild, where they doe nothing but daunce and sing, and feed on delicious fruicts with that great Hare, who is their great god, and when they have lived there, untill they be starke old men, they saie they dye there likewise by turnes and come into the world againe.

Concerning further of the religion, we have not yet learned, nor indeed shall we ever knowe all the Certaynty either of these their unhallowed misteryes or of their further orders and pollicyes untill we can make surprize of some of their *Quiyoughquisocks.*

CAPUT 8.

Their manner of Warrs, and consultations therin; of cer-
tayne Prophycyes amongst them; of Powhatons auntient
Ennimyes, and how they may be turned against
him by joyning in League with us: and how
his best Freindes may be wonne from him,
wherby we may bring him likewise to
be in Freindship with us: their
Armes, and weopens.

WHEN they intend any warrs, the Weroances usually advise
with their Priests or Conjurers, their Allies and best trusted
Councellors and Freindes, but commonly the Priests have the
resulting voice, and determyne therefore their resolucions
either a Weroance or some lusty fellow is appointed Captayne
over a Nation or Regiment to be led forth, and when they
would presse a number of Soldiers to be ready by a daie, an
officer is dispatcht away, who comming into the Townes, or
otherwise meeting such whome he hath order to warne, he
strykes them over the back a sound blow with a bastynado,
and byds them be ready to serve the great king, and tells them
the Randivous, from whence they dare not at the tyme appointed be absent: they seldome make warrs for landes or
goodes, but for women and Children, and principally for
revendge, so vindicative and jelous they be, to be made a diri-
sion of, and to be insulted upon by an enemy.

There be at this tyme certayne Prophesies afoote amongst the
people enhabiting about us, of which Powhatan is not meanely
jelous and carefull to divert the constraccion and daunger,
which his priests contynually put him in feare of. Not long
synce yt was that his Priests told him, how that from the Chesapeack Bay a Nation should arise, which should dissolve and give
end to his Empier, for which not many years synce (perplex't
with this divelish Oracle, and divers understanding thereof) according to the auncyent and gentile Custome, he destroyed and
put to sword, all such who might lye under any doubtfull con-
struccion of the said prophesie, as all the Inhabitants, the
weroance and his Subjects of that province and so remayne all
the Chessiopeians at this daie, and for this cause extinct.

Some of the Inhabitants againe, have not spared to give us
to understand, how they have a second Prophesy likewise
amongest them, that twice they should give overthrowe and
dishearten the Attempters, and such Straungers as should en-
vade their Territoryes, or laboure to settell a plantation
amongest them, but the third tyme they themselves should fall
into their Subjection and under their Conquest, and sure in
the observation of our Settlement, and the manner thereof
hitherto we maye well suppose, that this their apprehension
may fully touch at us, I leave to expresse the particulers unto another place, albeit, lett me say here straunge whispers (indeed)
and secrett at this hower run among these people and possesse
them with amazement what maie be the yssue of these straung
preparations, landed in their Coasts, and yearely supplyed with
fresher troupes: every newes and blast of rumour strykes them,
to which they open their eares wyde, and keepe their eyes
waking, with good espiall upon every thing that sturrs, the
noyse of our drumms of our shrill Trumpetts and great Ordinance terrefyes them so as they startle at the Report of them,
how far soever from the reach of daunger, suspicions have
bredd straung feares amongest them, and those feares create as
straunge Construccions, therefore begett strong watch and
guard, especially about their great king, who thrusts forth
trustye Skowtes and carefull Sentynells as before mentioned,
which reach even from his owne Courte downe almost even to
our Palisado-gates which answere one another duly: many
things (whilst they observe us) are suffred amisse amongest
themselves, who were wont to be so servilye fearefull to trespasse against their Customes as yt was a chief point of their Religion not to break in any, and all this and more then this is
thus with them whilst the great Tirant himself nor his priests
are now confident in their wonted courses: Judge all men
whether these maie not be Forerunners of an Alteration of the
devills Empire there? I hope they be now I dare prognosticate,
that they ussher great accidents, and that wee shall effect them:
the divine Power assist us in this worke which begun for heavenly endes may have as heavenly a Period.

Powhatan had manie enemies, especially in the westerly
Countryes, before we made our Forts and habitacions so neere
the Falls, but now the generall Cause hath united them, and

the poore power of their Mallice they contend to powre upon
us; beyond the Mountaynes and at the heades of the Rivers
upon the head of the Powhatans are the Monacans whose Chief
habitation is at Rassawek unto whome the Mowhemenchuges
the Massinnacacks the Monahassanughs and other Nations
paie Trybute, and those Monacans, (as I said) have been
deadly enemyes ever unto Powhatan, and may easely be joyned
freindshippe with by us to be so againe, untill when we shall
ever have Powhatan at these prowd and insolent termes at
which he now standes, and therefore yt was most considerately
and directly advised, by one of a good place, and great knowledge, and by long experyence trayned in the managing of
busines of this nature, when Sir Thomas Gates went over sole
Governour May 1609. that we should endeavour what all En-
vadors and Planters seeke out namely to knowe and entertayne
the bordering Enemy of that Nation, whome we shalbe forced
by our sitting downe amongest them; out of many offred occasions to offend and constrayne; for, who can be ignorant
(saith he) that there was never any Invasion, Conquest, or Far
off-plantacion that had successe without some partie in the
place ytself or neere it? witnes all the Conquests made in these
our partes of the world, and all that the Spaniards have perfourmed in America, yt cannot but appeare to all men of
Judgement essentially necessary for our Colony to get knowledg or make Freindshippe (as Conveniently as yt may with as
many of the Weroances which border and make warre with
Powhatan as yt can) against whome, or against whose people,
yf wee should fynd cause nowe or hereafter to use violence,
there is no man among themselves so savadge, or not Capable
of so much Sence, but that he will approve our Cause, when
he shalbe made to understand, that Powhatan hath slaughtered so many of our Nation without offence given, and such
as were seated far from him, and in the Territory of those
Weroances which did in no sort depend on him, or acknowledge him: But yt hath bene Powhatans great care, to keepe us
by all meanes from the acquaintaunce of those nations that
bordure and Confront him, for besydes his knowledge how
easely and willingly his enemyes wilbe drawne upon him by the
least Countenance and encouragement from us, he doth by
keeping us from trading with them monopolize all the Copper

brought into Virginia by the English: and whereas the English are now content, to receave in Exchaunge a few measures of Corne for a great deale of that mettell (valuing yt according to the extreeme price yt beares with them, not to the estymacion which yt hath with us) Powhatan doth againe vent some smale quantety thereof to his neighbour Nations for 100. tymes the value, reserving notwithstanding for himself a plentiful quantety to levy men withall, when he shall fynd cause to use them against us; for, the before remembred Weroance of Paspahegh, did once wage 14. or 15. Weroances to assist him in the attempt upon the Fort of James Towne for one Copper-plate promised to each Weroance.

Beyond the Springs of the river Toppahanock (the second from Powhatan) is a people called Mannahoucks, to these are Contrybutary the Tanxsnitanians the Shackaconias the Outpankas the Tegoneas the Whonketias the Stegaras the Hassniugas and divers others all Confederates with the Monacans, though many of them different in language and very barbarous, lyving for the most parte upon wild beasts and fruictes, and have likewise assisted the Monacans in tymes past against Powhatan, and may also by us be dealt with all, and taken into freindshippe as opportunity and meanes shall afford.

Beyond the Mountaines, from whence is the head of the River Pattawomeck, do enhabite the Massawomecks (Powhatans yet mortall Enemyes) upon a great salt water which by all likelyhoods may either be some parte of Caneda some great lake, or some Inlet of some Sea, that may fall into the West Ocean, or Mar del zur: these Massawomecks are a great Nation and very populous, for the Inhabitants of the heades of all those Rivers especially the Pattawomecks the Patuxunts the Sasquesahanoughs the Tockwoghs are contynually harrowed and frighted by them of whose cruelty the said people generally complayned, and were very importunate with Captayne Smith and his Company in the tyme of their discovery to free them from those Tormentors, to which purpose they offredd food, Conduct, Assistaunce, and Contynuall subjection, which were motives sufficient for Captayne Smith to promise to returne with sufficient forces to constrayne the said Massawomecks: but there were in the Colony at that tyme such Factions and base Envyes, as Mallice in some, in some Ignoraunce and

Cowardize in others, made that opportunity to be lost: Seaven boatesfull of the Massawomecks, the discoverers before mencioned encountred at the head of the Bay, whose Targetts, Basketts, Swordes, Tobacco-pipes, Platters, Bowes, and arrowes and everything shewed they much exceeded them of our partes, and their dexterity in their smale boats, made of the Barkes of trees sowed togither and well luted with gum and Rosyn of the Pine-tree argueth that they are seated upon some great water, of these likewise yt may please the Lord Generall againe to enforme himself, as Circumstances and occasion shall serve, to turne against Powhatan.

I graunt that such new Inhabitants that now people Chessapeak again (the old extinguished as you have heard upon the Conceipt of a prophesye) togither with the Weroances of Nandsamund Warraskoyack and Weanock are now at peace with him, howbeit they maie peradventure be drawne from him for some rownd Rewardes and a plentifull promise of Copper thus much (and not unnecessarily) digressed.

Their weapons for offence are Bowes and arrowes and woodden swordes: for defence Targetts, their bowes are of some young plant, either of the locust-tree or of witch which they bring to the forme of ours by the scraping of a Shell and give them strings of a Staggs gutt, or thong of a deares Hide twisted, their arrowes are made some of streight young Spriggs, which they head with bone twoo or three Inches long, and these they use to shoot at Squirrells and all kind of Fowle, another sort of arrowes they use made of Reedes, these are pieced with wood, headded with Splinters of Cristall, or some sharpe stone, with the spurrs of a Turkye Cock, or the bill of some bird, feathered with a Turkyes feather, which with a knife (made with the Splinter of a Reed which he will make as sharpe as a Surgeons Gammot,) he cutts him into forme and with which knife also he will joynt a deare or any Beast, shape his sandalls, Buskins, mantell etc., to make the notch of his arrow he hath the tooth of a Bever sett in a stick, wherewith he grateth yt by degrees; his arrow head he quickly maketh with a little bone (which he ever weareth at his Bracer, and which Bracer is Commonly of some beasts skynne, either of the Woolf, Badger, or black Fox, etc.) of any Splint of a stone or piece of a deares bone, of an oysters-shell, or of Cristall in the forme of a heart

barb'd and jagged, and these they glue to the end of their arrowes with the synewes of deare and the Toppes of deares
horne boyld into a Jelly, of which they make a glewe that will
not dissolve in cold water. 40. yardes will they shoot levell, or
very neere the Marke, and 120. is their best at Random.

Their Swoardes be made of a kynd of heavy wood which
they have, much like such woodden Instruments, as our English women swingle their Flaxe withall, and which they call
Monacocks as the Salvages in Dariena in the West Indies call
their Macanas, and be alike made, but oftentymes they use for
swordes, the horne of a deare, put through a piece of wood in
forme of a Pickaxe; some use a long stone sharpened at both
endes, thrust through a handell of wood in the same manner,
and these last they were wont to use in steed of hatchetts to
fell a tree, or cut any massy thing in sunder but now by
trucking with us, they have thowsandes of our Iron hatchetts
such as they be.

Targetts they have, though not many, nor every wheare but
those they have are made of the barkes of Trees rownd and thick
ynough to keepe out an arrowe.

For their drums they have a great deepe platter of wood, the
Mouth whereof, Covering with a skynne at each Corner they
tye a walnut which meeting on the backsyde nere the bottome
with a smale Cord they twitch them togither untill they be so
tought and stiff, that they maie beat upon them as doe wee
upon a drum, and they yeild a reasonable ratteling sownd.

Their chief Attempts are by Stratagems, surprizes and Trech-
eryes, yet the Weroances, women or Children they put not to
death, but keep them Captives, they have a method in warre,
and for a pleasure Powhatan would needes have it shewed
once to our people and yt was in this manner performed at
Mattapanient.

Having paynted and disguised themselves in the fayrest
manner they could devise, they devided themselves into twoo
Companies, well neere 100. in a Companie, the one Company
they called Monacans, the other Powhatans, either army had
their Captayne: these (as Enemyes) tooke their Standes a Mus-
kett shott one from another rancking themselves 15. a breast,
and each ranck from other 4. or 5. Yardes, not in file, but in the
opening betwixt their files so as the Reare Could shoot as

Conveniently as the Front: having thus pitched the Feild from either went a Messenger with Condicions, that whosoever were vanquished, such as escaped, upon their submission or Comming in, though two daies after, should live, but their wives and Children should be prize for the Conquerors, the Messengers were no sooner returned but they approached in their Orders on each flanck a Sergeant and in the Reare an officer for Liuetenaunt, all duly keeping their Ranckes yet leaping and singing after their Customed tune, which they use only in warrs, upon the first flight of Arrowes, they gave such horrible Showtes and Scritches as so many infernall Hellhowndes: when they had spent their arrowes, they joyned togither, prettely Chardging and retyring, every ranck seconding other: as they gott advantage they Catched their Enemies by the haire of their Head, and downe he came that was taken, his enemy with a woodden sword seemed to beat out his braynes, and still they Crept to the Reare to maynteyne the skirmish, the Monacans decreassing, the Powhatans chardged them in forme of a halfe Moone, they unwilling to be enclosed fled all in a troupe to their Ambuscadoes, on whome they led them very Cunningly, the Monocans disperst themselves among the Fresh men, whereupon the Powhatans retyred with all speed to their Secondes, which the Monacans seeing tooke that advantage to retire againe to their owne Battaile, and so each returned to theire owne quarter; all their Accion, voyces, and gestures both in Chardging and retyring were so strayned to the height of their quality and nature: that the Straungenes thereof made yt seeme very delightfull.

Concerninge a greene Wound, caused either by the stroake of an Axe, or Sword, or such sharpe thinge, they have present remedy, for of the Juyce of Certayne herbes howbeit, a compound wound, as the Surgeons call yt, where besyde the opening, and Cutting of the Flesh, any rupture is, or bone broken, such as our smale shott make amongest them, they know not easely how to cure, and therefore languish in the misery of the payne thereof: old Ulcers likewise and putrifyed hurts, are seldome seene cured amongest them: howbeit, to scarrefye a swelling or make incision, they have a kynd of Instrument of some splinted stone.

Every Spring thay make themselves sick with drincking the

Juyce of a Roote, which they call *Wighsacan* and water whereof they take so great a quantety, that yt purgeth them in a very violent manner, that in 3. or 4. daies after, they scarse recover their former health; sometymes they are sore troubled with dropseyes, Swellings, Aches, and such like diseases, by reason of their uncleannes and fowle feeding, for cure whereof they buyld a Stove in the forme of a dovehowse with matts so Close, that a few Coales therein Covered with a pott will make the patient sweat extreamely.

For swellings also, they use smale pieces of tutchwood in the forme of Cloves, which pricking on the grief, they burne Close to the flesh, and from thence drawe the Corruption with their Mouth: they have manie professed Phisitians, who with their Charmes and Rattells, with an infernal rowt of wordes and ac-cions, will seeme to suck their inward grief from their Navells, or their affected places, but concerning our Surgeons, they are generally so conceyted of them, that they beleeve that their plaisters will heale any hurt.

GEORGE PERCY

A Trewe Relacyon

To the right honorable the Lorde Percy

My Lorde

This Relacyon I have here sente your Lordshipp is for Towe respectts. The one to Sheowe howe mutche I honnor yow, and desyre to doe yow service. The other in Regard thatt many untrewthes concerneinge Theis procedeings have bene formerly published, wherein The author hathe nott Spared to apropriate many desertts to him selfe which he never performed and stuffed his Relacyons with so many falseties and malicyous detractyons nott onely of this parte and Tyme which I have selected to Treate of, Butt of former ocurrentts also: So thatt I coulde nott conteine my selfe butt expresse the Trewthe unto your Lordshipp concerninge Theis affayers. And all which I ayme att is to manyfeste my selfe in all my actyons bothe now and alwayes To be,

Your Lordshipps humble and faithfull Servante.
G. P.

———

A Trewe Relacyon of the procedeings and ocurrentes of Momente
which have hapned in Virginia from the Tyme Sir Thomas
Gates was Shippwrackte uppon the Bermudes Anno
1609 untill my departure owtt of the Cowntry
which was in Anno Domini 1612

If we Trewly Consider the diversety of miseries mutenies and famishmentts which have attended upon discoveries and plantacyons in theis our moderne Tymes, we shall nott fynde our plantacyon in Virgina to have Suffered aloane.

 La doniere had his share thereof in Florida nextt neighbour

unto Virginia where his sowldiers did fall into mutenies, and in the ende weare allmoste all Starved for wante of foode.

The Spanyards plantacyon in the River of Plate and the streightes of Magelane Suffered also in so mutche thatt haveinge eaten upp all those horses to susteine themselves withal, Mutenies did aryse and growe amongste them, for the which the generall Diego Mendosa cawsed some of them to be executed, Extremety of hunger inforceinge others secrettly in the night to Cutt downe Their deade fellowes from of the gallowes and to bury them in their hungry Bowelles.

The plantacyon in Carthagena was also Lamentable that wante of wholesome foode wherewith for to mainteyne Lyfe, weare inforced to eat Toades Snakes and sutche lyke venemous wormes sutche is the sharpnes of hunger.

To this purpose many other examples mighte be recyted butt the Relacyon itt selfe beinge briefe I have noe intente to be Tedyous butt to delyver the Trewthe briefly and plainely the which I dowtt nott butt will rather Lyke then Loathe the Reader, nor doe I purpose to use any elloquentt style or phrase, The which indede in me is wanteinge, Butt to delyver thatt trewly which my selfe and many others have had bitter experyence of: Many other woes & miseries have hapned unto our Collonie in Virginia bothe before and since thatt Tyme which now I doe intende to Treate of, Haveinge selected this parte from the reste for towe Respectts, firste in regard I was moste frequente and acquaynted with theis procedeings beinge moste parte of the tyme presydentt and governour, nextt in respectt the leaste parte hereof hathe nott bene formerly published.

In the yere of our Lorde 1609 Sir Thomas Gates and Sir George Somers acompanyed with dyvers gentlemen Sowldiers and seamen in nyne good Shippes did begine their voyage for Virginia the towe knightes beinge in the Admirall whereof Christopher Newport was Captayne and haveinge sayled with prosperous wyndes many Leagues, att Lenghte did fall upon the Bermudes where meteinge with a vyoelentt storme the Admirall wherein the towe knightes were inbarqued Suffred wracke. neverthelesse hoyseinge outt their boate Safely Landed the 2 knightes and the Reste of thatt Company upon the

Bermudes, of whome I will forebeare to Treate of further un-till their arryvall in Virginia.

The other 8 shippes shorttly after aryved in Virginia where the passengers beinge noe soener well Landed butt presenttly a discencyon did growe betwine them and Capteyne Smithe then presydentt butt after some debate all was quyeted and pacifyed. Yett Capteyne Smithe feareinge the worste and thatt the seamen and thatt factyon mighte growe too stronge and by a meanes to depose him of his govermentt So Jugled with them by the way of feasteinges Expense of mutche powder and other unnecessary Tryumphes, Thatt mutche was Spente to noe other purpose butt to Insinewate with his Reconcyled en-emyes and for his owne vayne glory for the which we all after Suffred And thatt which was intollerabe did geve leave unto the Seamen to Carry away whatt victewalls and other neces-saryes they wolde doeinge the same more safly in Regard the Contentts thereof was in the Admirall which was Caste away.

Nott Longe after Capteyne Smithe sentt Capteyne Martin and my selfe with threskore people to goe for Nansemunde, Capteyne Martin's Lefetenantt leadinge moste of the men overland and we towe with the Reste followed them by water, where being aryved we inquyred of the Indyans of our men butt they acordinge to their Subtelltyes wold nott acquaynte us therewith. Whereupon I requested Capteyne Martin thatt I mightt goe a shoare to discover the trewthe to the which he wolde nott Condiscende. Neverthelesse the nighte beinge Stormy and wette, I wente on Lande with my Company where I fownde our men by goode fyers in saffety whereof I adver-tyzed Capteyne Martin the nextt morneinge who presently with his company did Come ashoare unto us. Where after some Consultacyon helde we sentte 2 messengers to the kinge of Nancemonde To Barter with him for an Island righte opposite ageinste the mayne we weare uppon for Copper hatches and other Comodeties. Butt our messengers stayeinge Longer then we expected we feared thatt which after hapned. So Capteyne Martin did apointe me with halfe of our men to take the Island perforce and beinge upon the waye we espyed a Canoe wherein we weare perswaded our messengers to be, butt they perceaveinge us Retourned backe from whense they came and

we never sett eye upon our messengers after, Butt understood
from the Indyans themselves thatt they weare sacrifysed and
thatt their Braynes weare Cutt and skraped outt of their heades
with Mussell shelles. beinge Landed and acquaynted with their
trechery we Beate the Salvages outt of the Island burned their
howses ransaked their Temples, Tooke downe the Corpes of
their deade kings from their Toambes, and Caryed away their
pearles Copper and braceletts wherewith they doe decore their
kings funeralles.

   In the meane Tyme the Salvages upon the mayne did fall into
discencyon with Capteyne Martin who Seised the Kings sonne
and one other Indyand and broughte them bownde unto the
Island where I was, where a shipp Boye takeinge upp a Pistoll
accidentyallie nott meaneinge any harme The pistoll suddenly
fyered and shotte the salvage prisoner into the Breste. And
thereupon whatt with his passyon and feare he broake the
Cordes asunder wherewith he was Tyed and did Swimme over
unto the mayne, with his wownd bleedinge. And there beinge
greate store of maize upon the mayne I cowncelled Captyne
Martin to take possesyon thereof the which he Refused pretendinge thatt he wolde nott putt his men into hassard and
danger. So haveinge seene Capteyne Martin well settled I Retourned with Capteyne Nellson to James Towne ageine
acoringe to apoyntementte.

   Shortly after Capteyne Smithe sente Capteyne Francis West
with one hundrethe and fortye men upp to the falles with six
monthes victewells to inhabitt there. Where being Reasonable
well settled dyvers of his men stragled from their foarte, some
of them Comeinge hoame wownded, others never retourned
to bringe any Tydeings butt weare Cutt of and slayne by the
Salvages. So thatt in small processe of Tyme Capteyne Smithe
did take his jorney upp to the falles to understand how things
weare there ordered, when presenttly after his comeinge
thether, a greate devisyon did growe amongste them. Capteyne
Smithe perceaveinge bothe his authorety and person neglected, incensed and animated the Salvages ageinste Capteyne
West and his company, Reporteinge unto them thatt our men
had noe more powder lefte them then wolde serve for one volley of shott. And so Capteyne Smithe Retourninge to James
Towne ageine fownd to have too mutche powder aboutt him,

The which beinge in his pockett where the sparke of a matche Lighted, very shreawdly burned him. And comeinge in thatt case to James towne Capteynes Rattliefe, Archer, and Martin practysed ageinste him and deposed him of his govermentt Smithe beinge an ambityous unworthy and vayneglorious fellowe, attempteinge to take all mens authoreties from them. For bothe Ratliefe Archer and Martin beinge formerly of the Cowncell Smithe wolde Rule all and ingrose all authorety into his owne hands, althoughe indede there was noe other certeine apointed govermentt then Sir Thomas Gates had comissyon for who was then in the Bermudes, onely a yerely presidenttshipp to governe by the advyse of the Cowncell. Butt Smithe aymeinge att a sovereigne Rule withoutt the assistance of the cowncell was justely depryved of all.

The place of govermentt beinge voyde the thre busy instrumentts in the plantacyon profered the same unto me, the which att firste I refused in Regard of my sicknes. Butt by their importunetie promiseinge to undergoe the Chefeste offices and Burthen of govermentt for me untill I weare Recovered, att lenghte I accepted thereof and then was Smithe presenttly sentt for England.

After I had bene presydentt some fowertene dayes I sentt Capteyne Rattliefe to pointe Comforte for to Buylde a foarte there. The which I did for towe Respects. The one for the plenty of the place for fisheinge The other for the Comodious discovery of any Shippeinge which sholde come uppon the Coaste. And for the honnor of your Lordshippes name and howse I named the same Algernowns Foarte.

Nott Longe after Capteyne Martin whome I lefte att the Island did come to James towne pretendinge some occassions of busynes butt indede his owne Saffety moved him thereunto, feareinge to be Surprysed by the Indyans, who had made dyvers excursions ageinste him, so thatt haveinge lefte Lieftenantt Sicklemore to Camawnd in his absence, amongste whose company shorttly after did growe a dangerous mutenie in so mutche Thatt dyvers of his men to the number of seaventene did take away a Boate from him perforce and wente therein to Kekowhaton pretendinge they wolde trade there for victwelles Butt they were served acordinge to their desertts for nott any of them weare heard of after and in all lykelyhood weare Cutt of and slayne by the Salvages And within fewe dayes after Lieftenantt Sickelmore and dyvers others weare fownd also slayne with their mowthes stopped full of Breade, beinge donn as itt seamethe in Contempte and skorne, thatt others mighte expectt the Lyke when they shold come to seeke for breade and reliefe amongste them.

Baldivia a Spanishe generall beinge served somewhatt answerable hereunto in Chily in the Weste Indies who beinge Surprised by the Indyans inforced him to drincke upp a certeine quantety of melted gowlde useinge theis words unto him now glutt thy selfe with gowlde, Baldivia haveinge there sowghte for gowlde as Sickelmore did here for foode. And all the reste of Sickelmors Company which weare liveinge Retourned to us to James towne to feede upon the poore store we had lefte us.

Also within a shorte Tyme after Capteyne Weste did Come downe to us from the Falles haveinge loste eleaven men and a Boate at Arsetocke besydes those men he loste att the Falles so our number at James towne increaseinge and our store decreaseinge for in Charety we cold nott deny them to participate with us. Whereupon I apointed Capteyne Tucker to Calculate and caste upp our store. The which att a poore alowanse of halfe a Cann of meale for a man a day, amownted unto thre monthes provissyon. Yett Capteyne Tucker by his industry and Care caused the same to howlde outt fowere monthes. Butt haveinge noe expectacyon of Reliefe to Come in so shorte a Tyme I sentt Capteyne Ratliefe to Powhatan to procure victewalls and corne by the way of comerce and trade the which the Subtell owlde foxe att firste made good semblanse of althoughe his intente was otherwayes onely wayteinge a fitteinge tyme for their destruction as after plainely appered. The which was partly ocasyoned by Capteyne Ratliefes Creduletie for Haveinge Powhatans sonne and dowghter aboard his pinesse freely suffred them to departe ageine on shoare, whome if he had deteyned mighte have bene a Sufficyentt pledge for his saffety. And after, nott kepeinge a proper and fitteinge Courte of guarde, butt Suffreinge his men by towe and thre and small numbers in a Company to straggle into the Salvages howses when the slye owlde kinge espyed a fitteinge Tyme Cutt them all of, onely Surprysed Capteyne

Ratliefe alyve who he caused to be bownd unto a tree naked with a fyer before, and by woemen his fleshe was skraped from his bones with Mussell shelles and before his face throwne into the fyer. And so for wantt of Circumspection miserably perished.

In the meane Tyme Capteyne William Phetiplace Remayned in the pinnesse with some fewe men and was dyvers tymes assawlted by the Indyans butt after dyvers Conflictts with them with the losse of some of his men hardly escaped, and att lengthe aryved att James Towne, onely with sixtene men the Remaynder of fifty Capteyne Ratliefe hathe Chardge of att his goeinge forthe And so he related unto us the Tragaedie of Capteyne Ratlife nott bringeinge any Reliefe with them either for them selves or us

Upon which defeate I sentt Capteyne James Davis to Algernowe foarte to Comawnd there in Capteyne Ratliefes place and Capteyne West I sentt To Potoamack with aboutt thirty six men to trade for maize and grayne, where he in shorte tyme Loaded his pinesse Sufficyently yett used some harshe and Crewell dealinge by Cutteinge of towe of the Salvages heads and other extremetyes. And Comeinge by Algernowns foarte Capteine Davis did Call unto them acquainteinge them with our greate wantts exhortinge them to make all the Spede they cowlde to Releve us upon which reporte Capteyne Weste by the perswasion or rather by the inforcement of his company hoysed upp Sayles and shaped their Course directtly for England and lefte us in thatt extreme misery and wantte.

Now all of us att James Towne beginneinge to feele the sharpe pricke of hunger which noe man trewly descrybe butt he which hathe Tasted the bitternesse thereof. A worlde of miseries ensewed as the Sequell will expresse unto yow, in so mutche thatt some to satisfye their hunger have Robbed the store for the which I Caused them to be executed. Then haveinge fedd upour horses and other beastes as longe as they Lasted, we weare gladd to make shifte with vermin as doggs Catts Ratts and myce all was fishe thatt Came to Nett to satisfye Crewell hunger, as to eate Bootes shoes or any other leather some Colde come by and those beinge Spente and devoured some weare inforced to searche the woodes and to feede upon Serpentts and snakes and to digge the earthe for wylde and unknowne Rootes, where many of our men weare Cutt of and

slayne by the Salvages. And now famin beginneinge to Looke
gastely and pale in every face, thatt notheinge was Spared to
mainteyne Lyfe and to doe those things which seame incredible, as to digge upp deade corpes outt of graves and to eate
them. And some have Licked upp the Bloode which hathe
fallen from their weake fellowes. And amongste the reste this
was moste lamentable. Thatt one of our Colline murdered his
wyfe Ripped the Childe outt of her woambe and threwe itt
into the River and after Chopped the Mother in pieces and
sallted her for his foode, The same not beinge discovered
before he had eaten parte thereof. For the which Crewell and
unhumane factt I adjudged him to be executed the acknowl-
edgment of the dede beinge inforced from him by torture
haveinge hunge by the Thumbes with weightes att his feete a
quarter of an howere before he wolde Confesse the same.

Upon theis Calameties haveinge one boate and a Canoe
Lefte us, our Boate did accidentyally breake Loose and did
dryve fower myles downe the River before she was espyed.
Whereupon Capteyne Martin apointeinge some to follow her
the which beinge neglected and acquaynteinge me therewith I
stepped outt of my howse with my Sworde drawne and what
with my Threates and their feares happy was he Colde shipp
himselfe into the Canoe firste And so our Boate thatt nighte
was ageine Recovered Yett wanteinge more Boates for
fisheinge and other nedfull ocassions Capteyne Daniell Tucker
by his greate industry and paines buylded a Large Boate with
his owne hands The which was some helpe and a little Reliefe
unto us and did kepe us from killeinge one of an other To eate.
Many of our men this starveinge Tyme did Runn away unto
the Salvages whome we never heard of after.

By this Tyme beinge Reasonable well recovered of my Sicknes I did undertake a Jorney unto Algernowns foarte bothe to
understand how things weare there ordered as also to have
bene Revenged of the Salvages att Kekowhatan who had
trecheously Slayne dyvers of our men. Our people I fownd in
good case and well lykeinge haveinge concealed their plenty
from us above att James Towne, Beinge so well stored thatt
the Crabb fishes wherewith they had fedd their hoggs wold
have bene a greate relefe unto us and saved many of our Lyves.
Butt their intente was for to have keptt some of the better

sorte alyve and with their towe pinnesses to have Retourned
for England nott Regardinge our miseries and wantts att all.
Wherewith I taxed Capteyne Davis and tolde him thatt I had a
full intente to bringe halfe of our men from James Towne to
be there Releved and after to Retourne them backe ageine and
bringe the reste to bee Susteyned there also. And if all this
wolde nott serve to save our mens Lyves I purposed to bringe
them all unto Algernowns foarte Telleinge Capteyne Davis
thatt another towne or foarte mighte be erected and Buylded
butt mens lyves onse Loste colde never be recovered.

Our miseries now beinge att the hygheste and intendinge as
I formerly Related unto yow to Remove some of our men to
Algernowns foarte the very nextt Tyde, we espyed towe pinnesses Comeinge into the Baye nott knoweinge as yett whatt
they weare, butt kepinge a Courte of guard and watche all
thatt nighte. The nextt morneinge we espyed a Boate
Comeinge of from one of the pinnesses So standeinge upon
our guard we haled them and understood thatt Sir Thomas
Gates and Sir George: Somes weare Come in these pinnesses
which by their greate industry they had buylded in the Bur-
mudes, with the remaynder of their wracktt shipp and other
woode they fownde in the Cowntry. Upon which newes we
Receved noe small joye, Requesteinge them in the Boate to
Come ashoare the which they refused, and Retourned aboard
ageine for Sir Thomas Gates haveinge noe knowledge of any
foarte to be Builded there, was dowtfull whether we weare
frends or noe butt beinge possesed of the trewthe he and Sir
George Somers with dyvers others did Come ashoare at Alger-
nownes foarte and the nextt Tyde wente upp to James Towne
where they mighte Reade a lecture of miserie in our peoples
faces and perceve the skarsety of victewalles and understande
the mallice of the Salvages, who knoweinge our weaknes had
dyvers Tymes assawlted us withoutt the foarte. Fyndeinge of
fyve hundrethe men we had onely Lefte aboutt sixty, The reste
beinge either sterved throwe famin or Cutt of by the salvages.
And those which weare Liveinge weare so maugre and Leane
thatt itt was Lamentable to behowlde them, for many throwe
extreme hunger have Runne outt of their naked bedds beinge
so Leane thatt they Looked lyke anotannes, Cryeinge owtt
we are starved. We are starved. others goeinge to bedd as we

imagined in healthe weare fownd deade the next morneinge
and amongste the Reste one thinge hapned which was very
Remarkable wherein god sheowed his juste Judgement. For
one Hughe Pryse beinge pinched with extreme famin, In a furious distracted moode did Come openly into the markett place
Blaspheameinge exclameinge and Creyinge outt thatt there
was noe god, alledgeinge thatt if there were a god he wolde
nott Suffer his Creatures whome he had made and framed to
indure those miseries and to perishe for wante of food and
Sustenance Butt itt appeared the same day thatt the Almighty
was displeased with him, for goeinge thatt afternoene with a
Butcher a Corpulentt fatt man into the woods to seke for some
Reliefe, bothe of them weare slaine by the Salvages. And after
beinge fownde gods Indignacyon was sheowed upon Pryses
Corpes which was Rente in pieces with wolves or other wylde
Beastes and his Bowles Torne outt of his boddy beinge a Leane
spare man. And the fatt Butcher nott lyeinge above six yardes
from him was fownd altogether untouched onely by the salvages arrowes whereby he Receaved his deathe.

Theis miseries Considered itt was Resolved uppon By Sir
Thomas Gates and the whole Collonie with all Spede to Retourne for England. whereupon moste of our men weare sett
to worke some to make pitche and Tar for Trimmeinge of our
shoppes others to Bake breade and fewe or noene nott imployed in one occasyon or another. So thatt in a small Space of
Tyme fowere pinnesses weare fitted and made Reddy all pre-
pareinge to goe aboarde. And if Sir Thomas Gates had nott
Laboured with our men they had sett the Towne on fyer,
useinge theis or the lyke words unto them. My masters lett the
towne Stande we knowe nott butt thatt as honeste men as our
selves may come and inhabitt here. Then all of us enbar-
queinge our selves, Sir Thomas Gates in the Deliveranse with
his company Sir George Somers in the patience my selfe in the
discoverie and Capteyne Davis in the Virginia, all of us
sayleinge downe the River with a full intente to have proceded
upon our voyadge for England, when Suddenlye we espyed a
boate makeinge towards us. wherein we fownde to be Capteyne
Bruster sentt from my Lorde La Ware, who was come unto us
with many gentlemen of quallety and thre hundrethe men
besydes great store of victewles municyon and other provis-

syon. Whereupon we all Retourned to James Towne ageine where my Lorde shorttly after Landed and sett all things in good order selecteinge a Cowncell and makeinge Capteines over fifty men apiece.

Then Sir Thomas Gates beinge desyreous for to be Revendged upon the Indyans att Kekowhatan did goe thither by water with a certeine number of men, and amongste the reste a Taborer with him. beinge Landed he cawsed the Taborer to play and dawnse thereby to allure the Indyans to come unto him the which prevayled. And then espyeinge a fitteinge oportunety fell in upon them putt fyve to the sworde wownded many others some of them beinge after fownde in the woods with suche extreordinary Lardge and mortall wownds thatt itt seamed strange they cold flye so fur. The rest of the Salvages he putt to flighte. And so posseseinge himselfe of the Towne and the fertill grownd thereunto adjacentt haveinge well ordered all things he lefte his liefetenantt Eareley to comawnd his company and then Retourned to James Towne ageine and Shorttly after did take his voyadge for England.

My Lord generall aboutt this Tyme sentt Capteine Howldcrofte to buylde a foarte in the woods, neare unto Kekowhatan. The which beinge finished my Lord named the same Charles foarte in honnor of our kings majestie thatt now is.

Also my Lorde sentt Sir George Somers and Capteyne Argoll in towe shippes into the Bermudes to make provissyon of hoggs and fishe for us. Sir George aryved there, where shorttly after he dyed, his men makeinge good profitt of amber griese and other comodeties Retourned for England. Butt Capteyne Argoll fayleinge of the place fell to the northward where he hapned upon some fishe the which haveinge Sallted and dryed Retourned therewith to us to James Towne ageine.

Sir Ferdinando Wayman aboutt this Tyme dyed whose deathe was mutche Lamented beinge bothe an honeste and valyantt gentleman. My Lord generall nott forgetteing oulde Powhatans Subtell Trecherie sentt a messenger unto him to demawnde Certeine armes and dyvers men which we supposed mighte be liveinge in his country Butt he Retourned noe other then prowde and Disdaynefull answers.

Whereupon my Lord beinge mutche incensed Cawsed a comission to be drawne, wherein he apointed me Chiefe

Comawnder over seaventie men and sentt me to take Revendge upon the Paspaheans and Chiconamians and so shippeinge my selfe and my Sowldiers in towe boates I departed from James Towne the 9th of August 1610 and the same nighte Landed within thre myles of paspahas towne. Then draweinge my sowldiers into Battalio placeinge a Capteyne or Leftenante att every fyle, we marched towards the Towne haveinge an Indyan guyde with me named Kempes whome the provoste marshall ledd in a hande locke This Subtill salvage was Leadinge us outt of the Way the which I misdowteinge Bastinaded him with my Truncheon and threatned to Cutt of his heade whereupon the slave alltered his Cowrse and browghte us the righte way neare unto the towne So thatt then I comawnded every Leader to drawe away his fyle before me to besett the salvages howses thatt noene mighte escape, with a Chardge nott to geve the allarume untill I weare come upp unto them with the Cullers. Att my comeinge I apointed Capteyne William Weste to geve the allarume, the which he performed by shooteinge of a pistoll. And then we fell in upon them putt some fiftene or sixtene to the Sworde and almoste all the reste to flyghte. Whereupon I cawsed my drume to beate and drewe all my sowldiers to the Cullers, my Lieftenantt bringeinge with him the Quene and her Children and one Indyann prisoners for the which I taxed him becawse he had Spared them. his answer was, thatt haveinge them now in my Custodie I mighte doe with them whatt I pleased. Upon the same I cawsed the Indians heade to be Cutt of, and then dispersed my fyles apointeinge my Sowldiers to burne their howses and to Cutt downe their Corne groweing aboutt the Towne. And after we marched with the quene and her Children to our Boates ageine. Where beinge noe soener well shipped my sowldiers did begin to murmer becawse the quene and her Children weare spared. So upon the same a Cowncell beinge called itt was agreed upon to putt the children to deathe the which was effected by Throweinge them overboard and shoteinge owtt their Braynes in the water. Yett for all this Crewellty the Sowldiers weare nott well pleased and I had mutche to doe To save the quenes lyfe for thatt Tyme.

Then sayleinge some towe myles downe the River I sentt Capteyne Davis ashoare with most of my Sowldiers my selfe beinge wearyed before and for my owne parte butt an easie footeman Capteyne Davis att his landeinge was affronted by some Indyans who spared nott to send their arrowes amongste our men butt within a shorte Tyme he putt them to flighte and landed without further opposityon marcheinge aboutt fowrtene myles into the Cowntry Cutt downe their Corne burned their howses Temples and Idolles. and amongste the rest a Spacyous Temple Cleane and neattly keptt, a thinge strange and seldome sene amongste the Indyans in those partes So haveinge performed all the spoyle he cowlde, Retourned aboarde to me ageine and then we sayled downe the River to James Towne.

My Lord generall nott beinge well did lye a Shippboard. to whome we Rowed, he beinge joyfull of our safe Retourne yett seamed to be Discontente becawse the quene was Spared as Capteyne Davis towlde me, and thatt itt was my Lords pleasure thatt we sholde see her dispatched The way he thowghte beste to Burne her. To the firste I replyed thatt haveinge seene so mutche Blood shedd thatt day, now in my Cowld bloode I desyred to see noe more, and for to Burne her I did nott howlde itt fitteinge butt either by shott or Sworde to geve her a quicker dispatche. So Turninge my selfe from Capteyne Davis he did take the quene with towe sowldiers a shoare and in the woods putt her to the Sworde and althoughe Capteyne Davis towlde me itt was my Lords direction yett I ame perswaded to the Contrary.

Nott longe after our Retourne to James Towne Capteyne Argoll was sentt with the lyke Comission ageinste the Wariscoyans. The salvages beinge warned by their neighbours harmes weare very vigilante and Carefull and all of them fledd and escaped. So thatt Capteyne Argoll Cowlde have no other Revendge then by Cutteinge downe ther Corne burneinge their howses and Sutche lyke. The which beinge performed he Retourned to James Towne ageine.

The Salvages still Contineweinge their mallice ageinst us sentt some as Spyes to our foarte who beinge apprehended my Lord Cawsed one to have his hande Cutt of, and so sentte unto his fellowes to geve them warneinge for attemptinge the lyke.

Aboutt this Tyme there was a Conspiracy plotteinge amongste

some of our men which wrought in Iron mynes, To Runn away with a barkque. The same beinge discovered my Lord for an example adjudged one of them by marshall lawe to be executed. The execution proveinge strange and seldome heard of I thowghtt nott to omit, for the party beinge throwen of the Lather whatt with the Swindge and weighte of his body the Roape did breake and he fell upon the grownde and in Regard of the accidentt my Lord pardoned him althowghe itt nothinge avayled him haveinge Receved his deathe with the gerde of the Roape and extremety of the fall so thatt within 2 dayes after he dyed.

My Lord intendeinge to searche for mineralls and to make further proofe of the Iron mynes sentt dyvers men in a barkque upp to the falles and goeinge by Apoamatake they weare Called ashoare by the Salvages and beinge to fill their Baricoes with water weare easely thereunto induced and after intysed by the Salvages upp to their howses pretendeinge to feaste them. butt our men forgetteinge their Subtellties lyke greedy fooles accepted thereof more esteameinge of a Little foode then their owne lyves and saffety for when the Indyans had them in their howses and fownd a fitteinge Tyme, when they Leaste dreaded any dawnger did fall upon them Slewe dyvers and wownded all the reste who within towe dayes after also dyed onely Dowse the Taborer who flyeinge to their boate was hardly pursewed. butt gayneinge the same he made a vertewe of necessety useinge the Rudder in steade of a Targett to kepe their arrowes outt of his body, and so skulleinge of by little and little gott outt of their Reache and freed himselfe. The Salvages be nott soe Simple as many Imagin who be not acquaynted with their Subtellties for they had nott forgotten how their neighbours att Kekowhatan were alured and defeated by Sir Thomas Gates when he had the Same Taborer with him.

Presenttly after Capteyne Bruster was sentte upp to the falles with a Certeine number of men To attende there for my Lords Comeinge who purposed to procede in the Searche of mineralles In his jorney he had dyvers encownters & skirmishes with the Indyans, att Lenthe aryveinge att the Falles, where my Lord did shorttly after Come unto him Leaveinge the Chardge and Comawnd of James Towne with me.

Now my Lorde beinge att the Falles and winter Comeinge on, he Cawsed a foarte to be buylded there, bothe for their defence and shellter and named the same Lawares foarte Intendinge to have Reposed himselfe there all the winter and to have proceded upon the discovery of mineralls the nextt Springe where for a Tyme we will Leave him and Retourne to our procedeings att James Towne ageine.

The govermentt whereof beinge lefte to me Paspahe with a small Troope of Indyans in sheowe did Come unto our Blockhowse thinkeinge by some pollecy either to have Surprysed the same or some of our men. The which Comeinge to my hearinge I presenttly sentt Capteyne Powell then my antyentt with a Certeine number of men to surprise Paspahe allyve if possible they cowlde for the same wolde have bene to good purpose if itt Cowld have bene effected. Whereupon our men draweinge neare unto him where he stoode upon the ende of a Banke, when presenttly Mr John Waller stepped unto him and Cawghtt howlde of him and gave the watche worde for the Reste to Come to assiste him The which the Salvages perceveinge dyvers of them appeared which before weare nott seene, sendeinge their arrowes frely amongste our men. The which Capteyne Powell seeinge did apprehend thatt their was small hope to bringe in Paspahe alyve for he Strugled maynely. Whereupon he Thruste him twyse throwghe the boddy with his Sworde and for all thatt the stowte Indyan Lived and was Caryed away upon Rafters by the Salvages. And liefetenantt Puttocke encowntringe with one of the Salvages hande to fiste grapled with him and stabbed him to deathe with his ponnyard.

My Lord generall all this Tyme Remayneinge att the Falles where nether sicknes nor skarsety was wanteinge had dyvers encownters with the Indyans some of his men beinge slayne amonge the Rest his Kinsman Capteyne William Weste and Capteine Bruster narrowly escaped.

And now my Lorde groweinge very Sicke he was inforced to allter his former determinacyon and to retourne to James towne ageine where his Sicknes nothinge abated butt rather increased So thatt for the Recovery of his healthe he did Take his voyadge for the bathe att Mevis in the Weste Indies. Butt the

wyndes nott favoreinge them they weare inforced to shape their
Cowrse directtly for England, my Lorde haveinge lefte and
apointed me deputy governour in his absence, To execute
marshall lawe or any other power and authorety as absolute as
himselfe.

After my Lords departure the Indyans did fall to their
wonted practyses ageine, Comeinge one eaveninge Late, and
Called att our blocke howse. The which when I understood I
presently sentt to Lieftenantt Puttocke who Comawnded
there thatt he sholde by noe meanes Stur owtt of the Blocke
howse, butt to kepe an excedinge Carefull guarde and watche,
and to strengthen him I sentt him more men to double his
guard ageine expresly geveinge him Chardge thatt he shold
nott goe outt of the blockhowse upon any Tearmes whattso-
ever promisseinge him thatt the nextt morneinge I wolde send
him a Convenyentt number of men to discover whatt they
weare and of whatt strenght which had soe Called them.

But Liefetenantt Puttocke beinge Called ageine early the
nextt morneinge, before our watche was dischardged in the
foarte, Contrary to my Comawnde and moste unadvysedly did
goe outt of the Blockehowse with the small number of men he
had Sheowinge more vallour then witt, more fury then Judge-
mentt. And some fewe Indyans beinge in Sheowe he followed
them withoutt apprehensyon of thatt which ensewed. For the
Salvages still Retyreinge he followed them untill they broughte
him into their ambuskado, where beinge fyve or sixe hundrethe of Salvages lett flye their arrowes as thicke as hayle
amongste our handfull of men and defeated and Cutt them all
of in a moment The arrowes which they had shott beinge so
many in Number thatt the grownd thereaboutts was allmoste
Covered with them. Upon which defeate the Salvages did so
aclamate Showte and hallowe in Tryumphe of their gayned
victory thatt the Ecchoe thereof made bothe the ayere and
woods to Ringe. The which filleinge our eares in the Foarte
presenttly with all spede I sentt lieftenantt Abbott with fifty
men to assiste Puttocke nott knoweinge derecttly whatt had
befallen them althoughe we feared thatt which had alereddy
hapned. Neverthelesse Lieftenantt Abbott encowntred with
the salvages, They then Changeinge their noate Cryeinge Paspahe. Paspahe. Thereby importeinge as mutche as thatt they

had Revendged his wrongs. Att lenghtt Abbott putt the Indyans to flight Recovered the deade bodyes of our men
whome he broughte to our foarte where they weare Buryed.

Upon this disaster I sentt a messenger unto Algernowns
foarte Supposeinge my Lorde, Laware had bene noe further on
his voydge to have informed him hereof butt the messenger
Loste his Labour my Lord beinge before departed In shorte
Tyme after Capteyne Addames did come into our Bay in a
shipped called the blessinge with freshe Supply bothe of men
and victewells geveinge us notice thatt Sir Thomas Dale was to
come shorttly after with a greater supply the which proved
Trewe for within towe monthes after he aryved in Virginia and
browghtt with him thre hundrethe men besydes greatt store of
armour, municyon victewalls and other provissyon. And beinge
Landed he ordeyned newe Lawes sette downe good articles
which weare well observed. All our men beinge setto worcke
some to plante some to sowe Corne and others to buyld boates
and howses moste men inployed in one thinge or an other all
things in Tyme beinge well settled and ordered Sir Thomas
Dale made preperacyon and wentt ageinste the Nancemondies
with a hundrethe men in armour where he had dyvers encownters and skirmishes with the Salvages bothe by Lande and water,
dyvers of his company beinge wownded. Amongste the Reste
Capteyne Francis Weste was shottt into the Thyghe and
Capteine Martin into the arme. Sir Thomas Dale himselfe narrowly eskapeinge for an arrow lightt just upon the edge or
Brimme of his heade piece The which if itt had fallen a thowghtt
Lower mightt have shott him into the Braynes and indangered
his Lyfe. In theis Conflictts many Indyans beinge also slayne
and wownded, and nott beinge acquainted nor acustomed to
encownter with men in armour mutche wondered thereatt especyally thatt they did nott see any of our men fall as they had
donne in other Conflictts. Whereupon they did fall into their
exorcismes Conjuracyons and Charmes throweinge fyer upp
into the skyes Runneinge up and downe with Rattles and
makeinge many dyabolicall gestures with Many nigramantcke
Spelles and incantacions Imageininge thereby to cawse Raine to
fall from the Clowdes to extinguishe and putt outt our mens
matches and to wett and Spoyle their powder. Butt nether the
dievell whome they adore nor all their Sorceries did any thinge

avayle them for our men Cutt downe their Corne Burned their howses and besydes those which they had slayne broughtt some of them prissoners to our foarte.

Sir Thomas Dale makeinge more invaysons & excursions upon the Salvages had many Conflictts with them and one thinge amongste the reste was very remarkable The which may be Supposed to have bene ocasyoned by the salvages Sorceries and Charmes, for Sir Thomas Dale with some of the better sorte sitteinge in an Indyans howse a fantasy possesed them, thatt they imagined the Salvages were sett upon them eache man Takeinge one an other for an Indyan and so did fall pell mell one upon an other beateinge one an other Downe and breakeinge one of an others heades, thatt mutche mischiefe mighte have bene donn butt thatt itt pleased god the fantasy was taken away whereby they had bene deluded and every man understood his errour.

Aboutt this tyme a Spanishe Caravell aryved upon the Coaste and did Come into the Bay withowtt comaund Of Shotte. Thre principall of the Spanyards comeinge a shoare in their Boate nott furr of Algernowns foarte. The which Capteyne Davis espyeinge layd in ambushe for them they not knoweinge of any foarte to be theare and so Surprysed them the chefeste of them beinge one Diego Malinos a comawnder of some foarte or houlde in the Weste Indies the other Antonio Pereos his companyon. The thirde a pylott who wentt under the name and habbitt of a Spanyard butt was after fownde and discovered to be Inglishe man his name beinge Limbrecke haveinge lived many yeres amongste the Spanyards and Reputed to be a goode Pylott After the surpryseinge of theis thre the boate wherein they did Come putt from the shoare the men therein being questyoned pretended to seke for one of the Kinge of Spaynes shippes loaden with municyon bownd for the Weste Indies Requesteinge Capteyne Davis to lett them have a pylott to bringe their shipp into the harbour the which was grawnted Butt haveinge the pylott noe soener aboard hoysed upp their Sayles and Caryed the pylott quyte away with them. Leaveinge the thre which weare Surprysed in his steade behynd them who weare thereupon broughtt to James Towne and sentt as prissoners aboard severall Shippes. And shorttly after Sir Thomas Dale sentt my selfe Capteyne Newport and Mr Stracy secretary to the Collonie to examin them and so acuseinge them to have Come for Spyes they utterly denyed the same, butt still urgeinge them therewith Antonio Pereos answered thatt we had noe Cawse att all to feare any thinge this yere butt whatt mightt happen the nextt he coulde nott tell and as itt after appeared their intente was as eavell as we imagined, for the Spannishe ambassadour shorttly after gayned a Comissyon from the Kings Majestie Kinge James Thatt we shold sent the princypall Diego Malinos into England the which with all spede was effected Capteyne Martin beinge his conductt. Don Diego stayed nott longe in England, Butt was sentt hoame where he was made generall of sixe tall Shippes in all lykeliehoode and as we weare after Certenly informed sett outt of purpose to Supplantt us. Butt haveinge bene att Sea aboutt a monthe a mutenie did growe amongste them in so mutche thatt one of Diegoes company stabbed him to Deathe whereupon their Course was alltered and their former determinacyon Ceased. Antonio Pereos he dyed before in Virginia. and Sir Thomas Dale att his goeinge for England did take our hispanyolated Inglisheman Limbrecke with him, and acordinge to some pryvate Comissyon when he did Come within sighte of the Inglishe Shoare he cawsed him to be hanged upp att the yardes arme as afterwards itt was trewly reported.

Before Sir Thomas Dales departure Capteyne Davis att Algernowns foarte espyed nyne shippes upon the coaste Supposeinge them to be Spanishe. And sendeinge notice thereof to Sir Thomas Dale he presenttly sentt Capteyne Bruster and Lieftenantt Abbott with forty men to discover whatt they weare and they nott Retourneinge acordinge to Sir Thomas expectacyon he feared thatt they weare either Surprysed or defeated. Whereupon he drewe all his forces into forme and order reddy for encownter Calleinge a Cowncell to Resolve whether itt weare beste to mete with them aboard our shippes or for to maynteine the foarte. My opinyon I delyvered to Sir Thomas Dale and the Reste, Thatt it was dowttfull whether our men wolde stande unto itt ashoare and abyde the Brunte, butt a shippboard of necessety they muste for there was noe runneinge away. So makeinge preperacyon to goe aboard. Capteyne Bruster and Lieftenantt Abbott retourned and broughte us certeine newes thatt itt was Sir Thomas Gates

flete who was come now to be governour And aryved there
thatt eaveninge with a freshe Supply bothe of men and provissyon haveinge unladen the shippes & ordered other necessary
ocassyons Sir Thomas Gates apointed Sir Thomas Dale then
marshall of the collonie as itt was agreed upon in England to
passe upp into the Cowntry neare unto the Falles with aboutt
towe hundrethe men to inhabitt there Capteyne Bruster Lead-
einge moste of his men overland and himselfe and a small
company goeinge by water Capteyne Bruster in his martche
was dyvers tymes assawlted and encowntered by the salvages
beinge sentt from Powhatan haveinge for their Leader one
Munetute Comonly called amongste us Jacke of the feathers
By Reason thatt he used to come into the felde all Covered
over with feathers and Swans wings fastened unto his
showlders as thowghe he meante to flye. Capteyne Bruster
comeinge to the place apointed where Sir Thomas Dale did
also mete with him. And after dyvers encownter and skirmishes
with the Salvages gayned a convenyentt place for fortificatyon
where presenttly they did begin to buylde a foarte and Sir
Thomas Dale named the same Henericus foarte in honnor of
prinse Henry. The Salvages weare nott Idle all this Tyme butt
hindred their designes as muche as they colde shoteinge arrowes into the foarte wherewith dyvers of our men weare
wownded & others indangered and some haveinge inploy-
mentt withoutt The foarte did Come shorte hoame and weare
slayne by the Salvages.

Sir Thomas Dale haveinge allmoste finished the foarte and
settled a plantacyon in thatt parte, dyvers of his men beinge
Idell and nott willeinge to take paynes did Runne away unto
the Indyans many of them beinge taken ageine Sir Thomas in
a moste severe mannor cawsed to be executed. Some he
apointed to be hanged some burned some to be broken upon
wheles others to be Staked and some to be shott to deathe all
theis extreme and crewell tortures he used and inflicted upon
them To terrefy the reste for attempteinge the Lyke, And
some which Robbed the store he cawsed them to be bownd
faste unto Trees and so sterved them to deathe.

So leaveinge Sir Thomas busely inployed in finisheinge the
Foarte and settleinge their habitacyons lett us Retourne to
James Towne ageine where our governour Sir Thomas Gates

was resydentt. Onely by the waye Toutche a little att Alger-
nownes foarte the which was accidentially burned downe to
the grownd exceptt Capteyne Davis howse and the store howse,
whereupon Capteyne Davis feareinge to Receve some displeasure and to be Removed from thense the same beinge the
moste plentifulleste place for food, he used sutche expedityon
In the Rebuyldeinge of the same ageine thatt itt is allmoste incredible.

Dyvers Indyans used to come to our foarte att James Towne
bringeinge victewalls with them Butt indede did Rather come
as Spyes then any good affectyon they did beare unto us. Some
of them Sir Thomas Gates Cawsed to be apprehended and executed for a Terrour to the Reste to cawse them to desiste
from their Subtell practyses.

Thus haveinge Related unto your Lordshipp the Trewe procedeings in Virginia from Sir Thomas Gates Shippwracke upon
the Bermudes untill my departure outt of the Cowntry which
was the 22th Aprell 1612, The which day I sett sayle in a shipp
named the Tryall and haveinge by computacyon sayled aboutt
200 leagues with a Reasonable good wynde and fayere weather,
upon a Sudden a greate storme did aryse In so mutche thatt
the mission maste did Springe with the vyolence of the wyndes
and lyeinge in the greate Cabbin where the mission stoode I
was thereby muche indawngered and in perrill of my Lyfe, for
the same with greate force did grate upon my Cabbin and narrowly missed me and a barrell full with bere Beinge in the
Cabbin the mission Strucke the same to pieces thatt all the
bere did Runne abowtt the Cabbin.

The Storme Ceaseinge and our mission amended we Recovered flores Corves and St Michells nott towcheing att any
of theis Islands, Butt shaped our Course Northewarde, where
falleinge becallmed our dawnger was greater then the former for
feare of famin and wante of foode haveinge butt a poore small
quantetie of freshe water and thatt was so stencheous thatt
onely washeinge my hands therewith I cold nott endure the
sentt thereof. Our greateste store of foode was pease, and those
weare so Corrupted mowldie Rotten and worme eaten thatt
there was noe Substance lefte in them butt beinge stirred wolde
Crumbell into Duste, so thatt for wante of foode we weare lyke
to perishe. Butt god lookeinge mercyfully upon us when we

leaste expected to see our native Cowntry ageine, we happely mett with a shipp of London bownde for new fownd lande one Baker beinge master thereof who Releved us with Befe fishe Breade bere and Tobaco which greattly comforted us and saved our lyves for itt was above Thirty dayes after before we made lande Which was Ireland So after a longe and dangereous voyage we did fall with the Lande and putt into Crooke Haven, where we Remayned some fowretene dayes, in which Tyme we Refreshed our selves and Revicteweled our ship, and then sett sayle ageine and within eightt dayes after aryved in England and anchored in Dover Roade where we did mete with Sir Samuell Argall bownde for newe England To displante the Frenche collonie there. The which as I after hearde he valliantly performed. Butt how juste the Cawse was I refer the same to a Judityous Censure. So stayeinge some fewe dayes att Dover to acompany Sir Samuell I toake poaste horse and from thense Roade to London.

RALPH HAMOR

A True Discourse of the Present Estate of Virginia, and the success of the affaires there till the 18 of June 1614.

Together with a relation of the severall English Townes and forts, the assured hopes of that countrie and the peace concluded with the Indians.

The Christening of Powhatans daughter and her marriage with an English-man.

Written by Raphe Hamor the yonger, late Secretarie in that Colony.

Alget, qui non ardet.

To the truly Honorable, and right worthy Knight, Sir Thomas Smith, Governour of the East India, Muscovia, North-west passages, Somer Islands Companies, and Treasurer for the first Colony in VIRGINIA.

Honourable Sir:

Having in the time of my residence in Virginia (as it is true my imployment then invited mee hereunto) collected for my owne use and benefit, some few occurrents and accidents, which are obvious in all new imployments, a thing which perhaps but few regard there to busie themselves with, and fewer heer to peruse: I resolved indeed only to delight my selfe, and som who I am bound to be thankefull unto in that kinde, with the unworthy view of them, the rather, because I have seen many publications & impressions of those affaires, by those, whose books I should be proud to beare after them: but such is the perversenes of mankinde, such their incredulity of every thing, save what their eies tell them to be true: yea, such their backwardnes in the persuit of honorable enterprises, that though there should bee no end of writing, but every day should drawe foorth his line, and every line his reall encouragement, as mine may in the state of the Colony, as it now standeth, it were hard to say whether one of so many thousands as abound in England, might be thereby moved to joine with others right worthyly disposed, to become a harty and devoted furtherer of an action so noble, as is this, which thing if I faile in effecting, I shall not lose much labour, since when I undertook this taske, I imagined no such thing: but meerly my owne delight and content. It shall be reward enough for me to expresse my indeavours there, though not equall with the best, yet not idly mispent.

I labor not to seduce or betray any into an action or imployment, wherein once personally ingaged, they should have any cause to blame me, neither would I force the helpe of any mans purse, more then voluntary, if I could beyond my art, use such effectuall perswasions.

There are enough in my opinion, and those the worthyest of England already united, as the way is now laid downe, to perfect this businesse, whose indevours, if they proceed without back slyding, and therein persist some fewe yeers longer, shall be requited and paid with such treble interest, as it shall not repent him that is now most cold in the pursuit, to have refused more Competitors to be sharers in the returnd profit.

Your noble selfe Sir, ever emulous of vertue, and honourable Enterprises, should shine to the world more noble in the upholding of this imployment, though it apeared, as in the beginning, full of discouragement, which neverthelesse, I know your selfe rests so assured is now more neer, then ever to perfection. Your innate and habituall vertue needs no spurre, your honourable indeavours well witnesse the same: would God (as is yours) al mens offrings, though not so ample, were so free, so hartily sacrificed: then could they not thus long have wanted their rewards, perhaps for no other end detained, but to make others, a thing which God professeth to love and delight in, more cheerful givers. Accept (worthy Sir) this unworthy Treatise, the best testimony of my gratuity, which as yet my disabilities may render. Trueth shall shroud and patronize it, from the malevolent detracting multitude; whose blame though it incurre their shame and imputation, it scorns, and returns unto them.

My zeale to the Action, though I may seeme to have forsaken it, gives mee the heart to publish, what I know, to the world: To your selfe particularly your own worth, and deserts to me, irrequitable, graunt but that favourable acceptation, which ever accompanies your worth; and I shal ever acknowledge my selfe wholy yours, in hope wherof I conclude with my service: & rest.

At your commaund to be disposed off;
RALPH HAMOR.

———

To the Reader.

Ignorant, or envious, if you be Readers: it is not to satisfie the best of you that I now wright, a more seasonable time I must take to imbarque my selfe in so rough a Sea and come off safe: onely his authoritie (who hath power to compell my selfe and duety) hath commaunded me to satisfie his affections (covetous of the dignitie and truth of this pious Plantation) with these particulars: that they are got abroad, and become publike, was no purpose in their first conception, though some respect have made them so now: A naked and unstudied discourse, I acknowledge, without notes reserved (but in Memorie) to helpe it: yet thus much I doe avow, that it hath duety and truth to make good all other the wants, and imperfections of it: I will labour in no further excuse.

Concerning the Virginie pious worke it selfe, how it hath thrived under the commaund both of Sir Thomas Gates Knight, Governnour, and Sir Thomas Dale Knight, and Marshall of the Collonie, these three yeeres and more: let me say, if (setting aside thine owne overweening and singularity) thy unhoodded eye, can now at length looke upon it (after so many yeeres of her patience and passions) thou wilt easily acknowledge, whose finger hath the alone guidance of it, and then (I doubt nothing) be pleased to here thy selfe intreated (out of those great plenties and havings which God hath lent thee) to spare a little little portion to the full setling and finishing up a *Sanctum Sanctorum* an holy house, a Sanctuary to him, the

God of the Spirits, of all flesh, amongst such poore and innocent seduced Savages as we treate off, on whome let our hopes
be, that it hath vouch safed him now to be sufficiently revenged for their forefathers Ingratitude and treasons, and now
in his appointed time to descend in mercie, to lighten them
that sit in darknes, and in the shaddow of death, and to direct
their feete in the waies of peace.

Sure yong though in yeeres and knowledge I may be said to
be, yet let me remember, to thee perhaps much knowledge
Reader, what the wisest man that ever writ or speake (excepting
him that was both God and man) hath said, that such who
bring others unto righteousnesse shal themselves shine as the
stars in the firmament. And doubtlesse I doe beleeve, even
amongst the rest of my Articles, when these poore Heathens
shall be brought to entertaine the honour of the name, and
glory of the Gospell of our blessed Saviour, when they shall
testifie of the true and everliving God, and Jesus Christ to be
their Salvation, their knowledge so inlarged and sanctified,
that without him they confesse their eternal death: I do
beleeve I say (and how can it be otherwise?) that they shal
breake out and cry with rapture of so inexplicable mercie:
Blessed be the King and Prince of England, and blessed be the
English Nation, and blessed for ever be the most high God
possessor of Heaven and earth, that sent these English as
Angels to bring such glad tidings amongst us. These will be
doubtlesse the empaticke effects and exultation of this so
Christian worke, and may these nothing move? Alas let Sanballat and Tobiah, Papists and Plairis, Ammonites and Horonites,
the scumme and dregges of the people, let them mocke at this
holy Businesse, that they be filthie, let them be filthie still, and
let such swine wallow in the mire, but let not the rod of the
wicked fall upon the lot of the righteous, let not them shrinke
backe, and call in their helpes from this so glorious enterprise,
which the Prophet Isaiah cals, the declaring of God to the left
hand, but let them that know the worke, rejoice and be glad in
the happie successe of it, proclaiming that it is the everliving
God that raigneth in England, and unto the ends of the world.

Excuse me (curteous Reader) if caried beyond my purpose,
I declaime passionately in this passive and innocently despised
worke, which I am sure is so full of goodnesse, and have bin

almost six yeeres a Sufferer and eye witnes of his now well nigh atchieved happinesse, the full and unstaind reportory of every accident whereof even from his beginning, together with the causes of the backwardnes, in prosperity thus long, touching at the miraculous delivery of the scattered company, cast upon the Bermudas, when those fortunate Islands like so many faire Neriades which received our wrackt company, with the death of that pure and noble hearted Gentleman Sir George Sumers diing there, my purpose is shortly at large to publish, that at length some one escaped Leaper, amongst so many saved, may returne backe and pay his vowes of thanks giving unto that ever to be praised mercifull providence that brought us thither, until when I with thy zealous and fervent thoughts indevours to a businesse so full of piety, as is this our Virginie Plantation.

RAPHE HAMOR.

THE many publications and impressions of Virginia, an imployment wherein to this day my selfe with many other unstaid heads & thirstie after new designes, have bin to unprofitably ingaged, might justly excuse my silence, did not the filiall duty whereby in all things to the utmost of my power I am bound to obey my Father, compell me unwillingly thereunto: A taske I know by himselfe and others, meerely because I have bin *Oculatus testis*, thus imposed upon me, in the undertaking and performance whereof, I hartily wish that my poore relation, rich onely in truth (as I shall cleerely justifie my selfe by eie witnesses also) may give any credit or incouragement to proceede in a businesse so full of honour, and worth, whereunto (if there were no secondary causes) the already publisht ends, I meane the glory of God in the conversion of those Infidels, and the honour of our King and country (which by right may claime at the least their superfluities, from those whom God hath in this world made his dispensors and purse-bearers) might be a sufficient spurre to resolved Christians, especially the state and condition of our collonie, so standing when I left it, and I assure my selfe in this time growne more mature, that an honest hart would even relent, and mourne to thinke how poorely, I dare not say unworthily it is prosecuted. It being true that now after five yeeres intestine warre with the revengefull

implacable Indians, a firme peace (not againe easily to be broken) hath bin lately concluded, not onely with the nighbour,
and bordering Indians, as on Pataomecke, Topahanah, and
other Rivers, but even with that subtill old revengefull Powhatan and all the people under his subjection, for all whom
Powhatan himselfe stands firmely ingaged, by which meanes
we shall not onely be furnished with what commodities their
countrie yeeldeth, and have all the helpes they may afforde us
in our indevours (as they are easily taught, and may by lenitie
and faire usage, as Sir Thomas Dale now principall commander
there, and most worthy the honour he houlds, is well experienced in their dispositions, and accordingly makes use of them)
be brought, being naturally though ingenious, yet idely given,
to be no lesse industrious, nay to exceede our English, especially those which we hitherto and as yet are furnished with,
who for the most part no more sensible then beasts, would
rather starve in idlenesse (witnesse their former proceedings)
then feast in labour, did not the law compell them thereunto,
but also which will be most for our benefit, our owne men may
without hazard, I might say with security (by selfe-experience)
follow their severall labours, whereby twentie shall now bee
able to performe more then heretofore hath bin fortie.

Though I conjecture and assure my selfe that yee cannot be
ignorant by what meanes this peace hath bin thus happily both
for our proceedings and the welfare of the Naturals concluded,
yet for the honour of Captain Argol whose indevours in the
action intituled him most worthy, I judge it no whit impertinent in my discourse to insert them, which with as much
brevity as I may, not omitting the circumstances most pertinent and materiall, I shall indevour.

The general letters upon my knowledge, directed and sent
to the honourable Virginia Councell, being most of them
(though my selfe most unworthy) by me penned have inti-
mated, how that the everworthy gentleman Captain Argall in
the heate of our home furies & disagreements by his best experience of the disposition of those poeple, partly by gentle
usage & partly by the composition & mixture of threats hath
ever kept faire & friendly quarter with our neighbours bordering on other rivers of affinity, yea consanguinity, no lesse
neere then brothers to Powhatan, such is his well knowne tem-

per and discretion, yea to this passe hath he brought them, that they assuredly trust upon what he promiseth, and are as carefull in performing their mutuall promises, as though they contended to make that Maxim, that there is no faith to be held with Infidels, a meere and absurd Paradox: Nay as I have heard himselfe relate, who is *fide dignus*, they have even bin pensive and discontented with themselves, because they knew not how to doe him some acceptable good turne, which might not onely pleasure him, but even be profitable to our whole Collonie, and Plantation, yea ever assuring him that when the times should present occasion, they would take hold of her forelocke, and be the instruments to worke him content, and even thus they proved themselves as honest performers, as liberall promisers. It chaunced Powhatans delight and darling, his daughter Pocahuntas, (whose fame hath even bin spred in England by the title of Nonparells of Virginia) in her princely progresse, if I may so terme it, tooke some pleasure (in the absence of Captaine Argall) to be among her friends at Pataomecke (as it seemeth by the relation I had) imploied thither, as shopkeepers to a Fare, to exchange some of her fathers commodities for theirs, where residing some three months or longer, it fortuned upon occasion either of promise or profit, Captaine Argall to arrive there, whom Pocahuntas, desirous to renue hir familiaritie with the English, and delighting to see them, as unknowne, fearefull perhaps to be surprised, would gladly visit, as she did, of whom no sooner had Captaine Argall intelligence, but he delt with an old friend, and adopted brother of his Japazeus, how and by what meanes he might procure hir captive, assuring him, that now or never, was the time to pleasure him, if he entended indeede that love which he had made profession of, that in ransome of hir he might redeeme some of our English men and armes, now in the possession of her Father, promising to use her withall faire, and gentle entreaty: Japazeus well assured that his brother, as he promised would use her curteously promised his best indevours and secresie to accomplish his desire, and thus wrought it, making his wife an instrument (which sex have ever bin most powerfull in beguiling inticements) to effect his plot which hee had thus laid, he agreed that himselfe, his wife, and Pocahuntas, would accompanie his brother to the water side,

whether come, his wife should faine a great and longing desire
to goe aboorde, and see the shippe, which being there three or
four times, before she had never seene, and should bee earnest
with her husband to permit her: he seemed angry with her,
making as he pretended so unnecessary a request, especially
being without the company of women, which deniall she
taking unkindely, must faine to weepe, (as who knows not that
women can command teares) whereupon her husband seeming
to pitty those counterfeit teares, gave her leave to goe aboord,
so that it would please Pochahuntas to accompany her: now
was the greatest labour to win her, guilty perhaps of her fathers
wrongs, though not knowne as she supposed to goe with her,
yet by her earnest perswasions, she assented: so forthwith
aboord they went, the best cheere that could be made was seasonably provided, to supper they went, merry on all hands,
especially Japazeus and his wife, who to expres their joy, would
ere be treading upon Captain Argals foot, as who should say tis
don, she is your own. Supper ended, Pochahuntas was lodged
in the Gunners roome, but Japazeus and his wife desired to
have some conference with their brother, which was onely to
acquaint him by what strategem they had betraied his prisoner,
as I have already related: after which discourse to sleepe they
went, Pochahuntas nothing mistrusting this policy, who nevertheles being most possessed with feare, and desire of returne,
was first up, and hastened Japazeus to be gon. Captain Argall
having secretly well rewarded him, with a small Copper kettle,
and some other les valuable toies so highly by him esteemed,
that doubtlesse he would have betraied his owne father
for them, permitted both him and his wife to returne, but told
him, that for divers considerations, as for that hir father had
then eigh of our English men, many swords, peeces, and other
tooles, which he had at severall times by trecherous murdering
our men, taken from them, though of no use to him, he would
not redeliver, he would reserve Pocahuntas, whereat she began
to be exceeding pensive, and discontented, yet ignorant of the
dealing of Japazeus, who in outward appearance was no les
discontented that he should be the meanes of her captivity,
much a doe there was to perswade her to be patient, which
with extraordinary curteous usage, by little and little was
wrought in her, and so to James towne she was brought, a

messenger to her father forthwith dispached to advertise him, that his only daughter was in the hands & possession of the English: ther to be kept til such time as he would ransom her with our men, swords, peeces, & other tools treacherously taken from us: the news was unwelcome, and troublesom unto him, partly for the love he bare to his daughter, and partly for the love he bare to our men his prisoners, of whom though with us they were unapt for any imployment he made great use: and those swords, and peeces of ours, (which though of no use to him) it delighted him to view, and looke upon.

He could not without long advise & delibertion with his Councell, resolve upon any thing, and it is true, we heard nothing of him till three moneths after, by perswasions of others he returned us seaven of our men, with each of them a Musket unserviceable, and by them sent us word, that whensoever wee pleased to deliver his daughter, he would give us in satisfaction of his injuries done to us, and for the rest of our peeces broken and stolne from him, 500 Bushells of Corne, and be for ever friends with us, the men, and Peeces in part of payment we received: and returned him answere, that his daughter was very well, and kindely intreated, and so should be howsoever he dealt with us: but we could not beleeve that the rest of our Armes were either lost, or stolne from him, and therefore till he returned them all we would not by any meanes deliver his daughter, and then it should be at his choice, whether he would establish peace, or continue enemies with us. This answere as it seemed, pleased him not very wel, for we heard no more from him till in March last, when with Captaine Argalls Shippe, and some other Vessells belonging to the Colony, Sir Thomas Dale with an hundred and fifty men well appointed, went up into his owne River, where his chiefest habitations were, and carried with us his daughter, either to move them to fight for her, if such were their courage and boldnesse, as hath been reported, or to restore the residue of our demands, which were our peeces, swords, tooles. Some of the same men which he returned (as they promised) ran to him again, and because he had put us to the trouble to fetch them five hundred bushels of Corne: A great bravado all the way as we went up the River they made, demaunding the cause of our comming thither, which wee tould them was to deliver

Pocahuntas, whom purposely we had brought with us, and to receive our Armes, men, & corn, or else to fight with them, burn their howses, take away their Canoas, breake downe their fishing Weares, and doe them what other damages we could: Some of them to set a good face on the matter, replied, that if wee came to fight with them we were welcome, for they were provided for us, councelling us rather to retire (if wee loved our safeties) then proceed, bragging, as well they might, that wee had ever had the worst of them in that River, instancing by Captain Ratliefe (not worthy remembring, but to his dishonor) who, with most of his company they betrayed and murthered: we told them since they durst remember us of that mischief, unlesse they made the better and more speedy agreement, we would now revenge that trechery, and with this discourse by the way as we went, we proceeded, and had no sooner entred the narrow of the river, the channell there lying within shot of the shoare, but they let their arrowes flie amongst us in the shippe, themselves unseene to us, and in the forehead hurt one of our men, which might have hazarded his life without the present helpe of a skilfull Chirurgion.

Being thus justly provoked, we presently manned our boates, went ashoare, and burned in that verie place some forty houses, and of the things we found therein, made free boote and pillage, and as themselves afterward confest unto us, hurt and killed five or sixe of their men, with this revenge satisfying our selves, for that their presumption in shooting at us, and so the next day proceeded higher up the River, the Indians calling unto us, and demaunding why we went a shoare, burnt their houses, killed and hurt their men, and tooke away their goods. We replied that though we came to them in peaceable manner, and would have beene glad to have received our demaunds with love and peace, yet we had hearts and power to take revenge, and punish where wrongs shold be offered, which having now don, though not so severely as we might, we rested content therewith and are ready to imbrace peace with them if they pleased. Many excuses they seemed to pretend, that they shot not at us, but (if any such abuse were offered) it was some stragled Indian, ignorant of our pretence in comming to them, affirming that they themselves would be right glad of our love, and would indeavour to helpe us to what we came for, which

being in the possession of Powhatan their King, they would
without delay dispatch messengers to him, to know his purpose and pleasure, desiring faire quarter some 24 howers, for
so long they pretended it would be before their messengers
might returne: this wee graunted, and what we promised, we
ever exactly performed, the time now come, we inquired what
Powhatan would doe, and had for answere, that our Englishmen lately with him, fearefull to be put to death by us, were
runne away, and some of Powhatans men sent abroade in
quest of them, but our swords and peeces so many as he had
should be brought the next day, which meerely to delay time,
they bare us in hand the next day they came not, higher up the
river we went, and ancored neere unto the chiefest residencie
Powhatan had, at a towne called Matchcot where were assembled (which we saw) about 400 men, well appointed with their
bowes and arrowes to welcome us, here they dared us to come
a shoare, a thing which we purposed before, so a shoare we
went, our best landing being up a high steepe hill which might
have given the enemy much advantage against us, but it seemed
they as we were unwilling to begin, and yet would gladly have
bin at blowes, being landed as if they had no shew of feare, they
stirred not from us, but walked up and downe, by and amongst
us, the best of them inquiring for our Weroance or king, with
whom they would gladly consult to know the occasion of our
comming thither, wherof when they were informed, they made
answere that they were there ready to defend themselves, if we
pleased to assault them, desiring neverthelesse some small time
to dispatch two or three men once more to their king, to know
his resolution, which if not answerable to our requests, in the
morning if nothing else but blood would then satisfie us, they
would fight with us, and thereby determine our quarrell, which
was but a further delay to procure time to carrie away their provisions, neverthelesse we agreed to this their request, assuring
them till the next day by noone we would not molest, hurt,
nor detaine any of them, and then before we fought, our
Drum and Trumpets should give them warning: upon which
promise of ours, two of Powhatans sonnes being very desirous
to see their sister who was there present ashoare with us, came
unto us, at the sight of whom, and her well fare, whom they
suspected to be worse intreated, though they had often heard

the contrary, they much rejoyced, and promised that they would undoubtedly perswade their father to redeeme her, and to conclude a firme peace forever with us, and upon this resolution the two brothers with us retired aboarde, we having first dispatched two English men, Maister John Rolfe and maister Sparkes to acquaint their Father with the businesse in hand, the next day being kindly intreated, they returned, not at all admitted Powhatans presence, but spake with his brother Opechankano, his successor, one who hath already the commaund of all the people, who likewise promised us his best indeavors to further our just requests, and we because the time of the yeere being then Aprill, called us to our businesse at home to prepare ground, and set corne for our winters provision, upon these termes departed, giving them respite till harvest to resolve what was best for them to doe, with this Proviso, that if finall agreement were not made betwixt us before that time, we would thither returne againe and destroy and take away all their corne, burne all the houses upon that river, leave not afishing Weere standing, nor a Canoa in any creeke therabout, and destroy and kill as many of them as we could.

Long before this time a gentleman of approved behaviour and honest cariage, maister John Rolfe had bin in love with Pocahuntas and she with him, which thing at the instant that we were in parlee with them, my selfe made known to Sir Thomas Dale by a letter from him, whereby he intreated his advise and furtherance in his love, if so it seemed fit to him for the good of the Plantation, and Pocahuntas her selfe, acquainted her brethren therewith: which resolution Sir Thomas Dale wel approving, was the onely cause: hee was so milde amongst them, who otherwise would not have departed their river without other conditions.

The bruite of this pretended marriage came soone to Powhatans knowledge, a thing acceptable to him, as appeared by his sudden consent thereunto, who some ten daies after sent an olde uncle of hirs, named Opachisco, to give her as his deputy in the Church, and two of his sonnes to see the mariage solemnized, which was accordingly done about the fift of Aprill, and ever since we have had friendly commerce and trade, not onely with Powhatan himselfe, but also with his subjects round about us; so as now I see no reason why the Collonie should not thrive a pace.

Besides this love by this meanes with Powhatan concluded, it will be worth my paines to run over our friendship with our next neighbours, the Chicohominies lately confirmed, a lustie and daring people, who have long time lived free from Powhatans subjection, having lawes and governors within themselves: these people hearing of our concluded peace with Powhatan, as the noise thereof was soone bruted abroad, sent two of their men unto us, and two fat Bucks for present to our king (for so Sir Thomas Dale is generally reputed and termed amongst them) and offered themselves and service unto him, alleadging that albeit in former times they had bin our enemies, and we theirs, yet they would now if we pleased become not onely our trustie friends, but even King James his subjects and tributaries, and relinquish their old name of Chicohominies, and take upon them, as they call us the name of *Tossantessas*, and because they have no principall commander or Weroance, they would intreate Sir Thomas Dale as King James his deputie to be their supreme head, King and governor, and in all just causes and quarrels to defend them, as they would be ready at all times to aide him, onely their desire was to injoy their owne lawes and liberties, and because himselfe, by reason of his many other imployments, beside the charge he hath of his owne people, may not be alwaies present amongst them, to be governed as formerly by eight of the elders and principall men amongst them, as his substitutes and councellers, and even this was the summe and effect of their embassie. Sir Thomas Dale appointed a day to send some men into their river, to propose certaine conditions unto them, whereunto if they assented he would gladly accept of their proffered friendship, and be himselfe their Weroance: and with this answere offering them copper for their venison, which they refused to take, dismissed them.

When the appointed day came, Sir Thomas Dale himselfe and Captain Argall with 50 men in a barge and frigot, well appointed, least any trecherie might be intended, set forward to Chicohominie, an arme of our river some seaven miles from James Town, where we found the people according to promise expecting our comming, assembled and met together, who after their best and most friendly manner, bad us welcome, and because our businesse at home would permit us but small time of stay with them, they presently sent for their principal men, some of whom were then absent, which hastned unto us, & the next morning very early assembled, and sat in counsell about this businesse, Captaine Argall (supplying Sir Thomas Dales place amongst them, who though there present for some respects, concealed himselfe, and kept aboarde his barge) after long discourse of their former proceedings, Captaine Argall tould them, that now since they had intreated peace and promised their love and friendship, hee was sent unto them from the great Weroance to conclude the same, all former injuries on both sides, set apartt and forgotten, which he would doe upon these conditions.

First that they should take upon them, as they promised, the name of *Tassantasses* or English men, and be King James his subjects, and be forever honest, faithfull and trustie unto his deputie in their countrie.

Secondly, that they should never kill any of our men or cattell, but if either our men or cattle should offend them or runne to them, they should bring them home again, and should receive satisfaction for the trespasse done them.

Thirdly, they should at all times be ready and willing to furnish us with three or foure hundred bowmen to aide us against the Spaniards, whose name is odious amongst them, for Powhatans father was driven by them from the west-Indies into those parts, or against any other Indians which should, contrary to the established peace offer us any injurie.

Fourthly, they shall not upon any occasion whatsoever breake downe any of our pales, or come into any of our Townes or forts by any other waies, issues or ports then ordinary, but first call, and say the *Tossantessas* are there, and so comming they shall at all times be let in, and kindely entertained.

Fifthly, so many fighting men as they have which may be at the least five hundred should yeerely bring into our store house, at the beginning of their harvest two bushels of corne a man, as tribute of their obedience to his Majestie, and to his deputy there, for which they should receive so many Iron Tomahawkes or small hatchets.

Lastly, the eight chiefe men which governe as substitutes

and Councellors under Sir Thomas Dale, shall at all times see these Articles and conditions duly performed, for which they shall receive a red coat, or livery from our King yeerely, and each of them the picture of his Majesty, ingraven in Copper, with a chaine of Copper to hang it about his necke, wherby they shall be knowne to be King James his noble Men: so as if these conditions, or any of them be broken, the offenders themselves shall not onely be punished, but also those Commaunders, because they stand ingaged for them.

After these Articles were thus proposed, the whole assembly assenting thereunto, answered with a great shout, and noise, that they would readily and willingly performe them all: and immediately began the chiefe of the eight to make an oration to the rest, bending his speech first to the old men, then to the yong men, and in conclusion to the women and children, giving them thereby to understand the summe of the proposed conditions: and how strictly they were to observe them: in consideration whereof, he further declared what wee have promised to doe for them, not onely to defend and keepe them from the fury & danger of Powhatan, which thing they most feared, but even from all other enemies, domesticke, or forraigne, and that we would yeerely by trade furnish them with Copper, Beades, Hatchets, and many other necessaries, yea, which liked them best, that we would permit them to enjoy their owne liberties, freedoms, and lawes, and to be governed as formerly, by eight of their chiefest men.

It shall not be unnecessarie to insert the occasion (as we imagine) of this their much desired, unexpected friendship, which was questionlesse some sodaine feare of Powhatans displeasure, being united with us, now able to revenge their disobedience done unto him for you must imagine, these people presuming upon their owne strength and number (in no one place in those parts, which we know, so many togeather) to have a long time neglected Powhatan, and refused, which the place hath been formerly accustomed, and as his right may challenge the homage and duty of subjects, which they ought to have performed: to which obedience, fearing our power might compell them, they chose rather to subject themselves to us, then being enemies to both, to expose & lay themselves open to Powhatans tiranny, & oppression: for this they did chiefely insist upon, that he was an ill Weroance, full of cruelty, and injustice, covetous of those things they had, and implacable if they denyed him whatsoever he demaunded, and for these reasons, desired to be made one people with us, to curbe the pride and ambition of Powhatan, from whom to defend them they tould us it would be no breach of peace on our parts, since now they were no longer Chicohomimes, or Naturalls, of that place, but *Tossantessars*, and King James his subjects, whom we are bound to defend.

So soone as there was an end of speaking, and the peace firmely concluded, and assented unto, Captaine Argall by the guift of eight great peeces of Copper, and eight great Tomahawkes, bound the eight great men, or Councellors to the exact performance, and keeping of the same, according to the conditions proclaimed, which they very gladly and thankefully accepted, and returned him, as testimonies of their loves, Venison, Turkies, Fresh fish, baskets, Mats, and such like things as they were then furnished with, and so the Councell brooke up, and then every man brought to sell to our men Skinnes, boules, mats, baskets, tobacco, &c. and became as familiar amongst us, as if they had been English men indeede.

Thus have I briefely as the matter would permit, discoursed our established friendship with the Naturalls, and the occasions thereof, which I hope will continue so long betweene us, till they shall have the understanding to acknowledge how much they are bound to God for sending us amongst them (then which) what worke would be more acceptable to God, more honourable to our King and country?

The greatest, and many enemies and disturbers of our proceedings, and that which hath hitherto detered our people to addresse themselves into these parts have been onely two; emnity with the Naturalls, and the bruit of famine: one of these two (and that indeede, which was some cause of the other) I have already removed, and shall as easily take away the other: howbeit it were too great folly (I might say impudency in men) to aver that there hath raigned no such infection in the Colony, occasioned, meerly by misgovernment, idlenesse, and faction, and chiefely by the absence of the ever worthy Commaunders, Sir Thomas Gates, and Sir George Summers by the providence of God, miraculously wract and saved upon the hopefull Sumer Islands, since my selfe cannot but witnesse (of which I had some tast) in what a miserable condition, we found the Colony at our arivall there, from the Bermudas, not living above threescore persons therein, and those scarse able to goe alone, of welnigh six hundred, not full ten moneths before: yet now I dare and will boldly affirme to the greatest adversary of the Plantation, that shall aver the contrary, that there is that plenty of foode, which every man by his owne industry may easily, & doth procure that the poorest there, & most in want, hath not bin so much pinched with hunger this 4 yeers that if he would take any pains, he knew not wher to fetch a good meales meate: and true it is, that every day by the providence, and blessing of God, and their owne industry, they have more plenty then other, the reason hereof is at hand, for formerly, when our people were fedde out of the common store and laboured jointly in the manuring of the ground, and planting corne, glad was that man that could slippe from his labour, nay the most honest of them in a generall businesse, would not take so much faithfull and true paines, in a weeke, as now he will doe in a day, neither cared they for the increase, presuming that howsoever their harvest prospered, the generall store must maintain them, by which meanes we reaped not so much corne from the labours of 30 men, as three men have done for themselves: to prevent which mischiefe heerafter Sir Thomas Dale hath taken a new course, throughout the whole Colony, by which meanes, the generall store (apparrell onely excepted) shall not be charged with any thing: and this it is, he hath allotted to every man in the Colony, three English Acres of cleere Corne ground, which every man is to manure and tend, being in the nature of Farmers, (the Bermuda undertakers onely excepted) and they are not called unto any service or labor belonging to the Colony, more then one moneth in the yeere, which shall neither be in seede time, or in Harvest, for which, doeing no other duty to the Colony, they are yeerly to pay into the store two barrells and a halfe of Corne: there to be reserved to keep new men, which shall be sent over, the first yeere after their arrivall: and even by this meanes I dare say, our store will be bountifully furnished, to maintain three or foure hundred men, whensoever they shall be sent thither to us, that mony which hitherto hath bin disbursed, to

provide a twelvemoneths victualls, if there were but now halfe
so much bestowed in clothes, and bedding, will be such comfort to the men, as even thereby the lives of many shall not
onely be preserved, but also themselves kept in strength and
heart, able to performe such businesses, as shall be imposed
upon them: and thus shall also the former charge be well saved,
and yet more businesse effected, the action renowned, and
more commodity returned to the Merchant, as yet faint for
want of encouragement.

Concerning the undertaking of the Bermuda Citty, a businesse of greatest hope, ever begunne in our Territories there,
their Pattent, which I purpose in this Treatise to insert, doth
apparantly demonstrate, upon what termes and conditions they
voluntarily have undertaken that imployment, how forward
that businesse is, in his due place shall bee expressed, onely give
me leave with as much brevity as I may, least any man should
divert his minde, and be fearefull to adventure his person
thither, for feare of famine and penury, to amplifie a little the
plenty there, for if it be true, as most certaine it is, that those
whome I have described under the title of Farmers, can pay
into our Store, two barrels and a halfe of Corne yeerely, and
others who labour eleaven moneths in the generall businesse
of the Colony, and but one to provide themselves victualls, why
should any man (if he be industrious) mistrust starving? if
otherwise for any part, and I thinke all that are ingaged in the
Action, and understand the businesse, accord with me heerein,
and would not with his company there, nay they shall much
wrong themselves, and the Action, if they doe not withstand
such, and deny them passage: for even they and none else have
been the occasions of the manifould imputations, & disgraces,
which Virginia hath innocently undergon, through their de-
faults: I would therefore by these relations not onely encourage honest and industrious: but also deterre all lasie, impotent,
and ill livers from addressing themselves thither, as being a
Country too worthy for them, and altogeather disconsonant to
their natures, which must either brooke labour or hazard, and
undergoe much displeasure, punishment, and penury, if they
escape a thing which few idlers have don, the scurvy disease,
with which few, or none once infected, have recovered.

To proceed therefore in my incouragement to painefull

people, such as either through crosses in this world, or wract rents, or else great charge of children and family live heer, and that not without much care and sweat, into extreame poverty: for those this Countrey hath present remedy: Everie such person, so well disposed to adventure thither, shal soon find the difference between their own, and that Country. The affaires in the Colony, being so well ordered, and the hardest taskes already overpast, that whosoever (now, or heerafter) shall happily arrive there, shall finde a hansome howse of some foure roomes or more, if he have a family, to repose himselfe in rent free, and twelve English Acres of ground, adjoyning thereunto, very strongly impailed, which ground is onely allotted unto him for Roots, Gardaine hearbs, and Corne: neither shall hee need to provide himselfe, as were wont the first planters, of a yeers provision of victualls, for that the store there will bee able to affoord him, & upon these conditions he shall be entertained; He shall have for himselfe & family, a competent 12 months provision delivered unto him, in which time it must bee his care to provide for himselfe and family ever after, as those already there, to this end he shall be furnished with necessary tooles of all sorts, and for his better subsistance he shall have Poultry, and swine, and if he deserve it, a Goate or two, perhaps a Cow given him, which once compast, how happily he may live, as doe many there, who I am sure will never returne, I submit to their own future well experienced judgements.

Now, least any man should yet rest discouraged because as yet no mention is made of any other provision of victualls, save onely of bread-corne, which graunt, it may with labour be competently procured, will affoord but a bare, and miserable living, I thinke there is no man so ignorant to conceive, that such a main continent as is Virginia, boundlesse, for ought we have discovered, and so goodly Rivers, no where else to be parralled, should be more barraine of Cattell, Fish, and Foule, then other Lands, assuredly they are not: for true it is, that the Land is stored with plenty and variety of wilde beasts, Lions, Bears, Deere of all sorts, onely differing from ours in their increase, having usuall, three or foure Fawnes at a time, none that I have seen or heard off under two: the reason whereof som of our people ascribe to the vertue of some grasse or hearb which they eate, because our Goats often times bring foorth three, and most of them two: for my part I rather impute their fecundity to the providence of God, who for every mouth provideth meate, and if this increase were not, the Naturalls would assuredly starve: for of the Deere (they kill as doe wee Beefes in England all the yeer long, neither sparing yong nor olde, no not the Does readie to fawne, nor the yong fawnes, if but two daies ould) Beavers, Otters, Foxes, Racounes, almost as big as a Fox, as good meat as a lamb, hares, wild Cats, muske rats, Squirills flying, and other of three or foure sorts, Apossumes, of the bignesse and likenesse of a Pigge, of a moneth ould, a beast of as strange as incredible nature, she hath commonly seaven yong ones, sometimes more and sometimes lesse which at her pleasure till they be a moneth olde or more she taketh up into her belly, and putteth forth againe without hurt to her selfe or them.

Of each of these beasts, the Lion excepted, my selfe have many times eaten, and can testifie that they are not onely tastefull, but also wholesome and nourishing foode.

There are foule of diverse sorts, Eagles, wilde Turkeis, much bigger then our English, Cranes, Herons white and russet, Hawkes, wilde Pigeons (in winter beyond number or imagination, my selfe have seene three or foure houres together flockes in the aire, so thicke that even they have shaddowed the skie from us) Turckie Bussards, Partridge, Snipes, Owles, Swans, Geese, Brants, Ducke and Mallard, Droeis, Shel Drakes Cormorants, Teale, Widgeon, Curlewes, Puits, besides other small birds, as Blacke-birde, hedge sparrowes, Oxeies, wood peckers, and in winter about Christmas many flockes of Parakertoths.

For fish the Rivers are plentifully stored, with Sturgion, Porpasse, Base, Rockfish, Carpe, Shad, Herring, Ele, Catfish, Perch, Flat-fish, Troute, Sheepes-head, Drummers, Jarfish, Crevises, Crabbes, Oisters and diverse other kindes, of all which my selfe have seene great quantity taken, especially the last summer at Smiths Island, at one hale, a frigots lading of Sturgion, Base and other great fish in Captaine Argals Saine: and even at that very place which is not above fifteene miles from Point comfort, if we had beene furnished with salt, to have saved it, wee might have taken as much fish as would have served us that whole yeere.

Nor are these provicion of bread, flesh, and fish, al we have for sustentation of mans life, behold more change and variety of foode, which our soile and climate affordeth, Carrats, Parsneps, Turneps, Raddish, Pumpions (of the west Indie kinde in great abundance, of one feede I have seen an hundreth, much bigger then ours and lasting all the yeere), Cabbadge, Parsley, all manner of pothearbs and other hearbes, Margerum, Time, winter-Savory, Lettice, Purslaine, &c, and besides the naturall graine of that Country, as wheate pease and beanes, it did me much good to view our English wheate how forward it was, full eard, of one graine fortie eares or more, a span long, and onely wanting ripening in mid June, our English pease then ripe, and beanes very forward, and English barly very hopefull, such as mine eies never beheld better in England: And if that soile bring forth these things (as can those which have bin there with me affirme and witnesse) as plentifull and unchangeable for taste and quantity as England or any other country, why shold any man that hath his limbes, in a peaceable state as is that, so much as dreame of starving?

To goe yet a little further, I my selfe know no one Country yeelding without art or industry so manie fruites, sure I am England doth not: wilde grapes in abundance al the woods over, their juice sweete and pleasant in taste, some of them wee have replanted in a vineyard adjoyning to Henrico, the quantity of three or foure Akers which were this yeere very plentifully laden, to what perfection they will come, the next returne will advertise: Cherries little inferior to ours, which if replanted may proove as much better as now they are worse, Pissmien plums in bygnes and fashion like a Medlar of a slipticke quality, other sorts of plummes like to our wheat plums, and in goodnes answerable: great fields and woods abounding with Strawberies much fairer and more sweete then ours, Mulberries of great bignesse, and about the Bermuda Cittie and Hundirds thereunto belonging great store thereof, Maricocks of the fashion of a Lemmon whose blossome may admit comparison with our most delightsome and bewtifull flowers, and the fruite exceeding pleasant and tastfull: Chestnut-trees towards the fals as many as oakes, and as fertile, many goodly grovers of Chincomen trees with a huske like unto a Chesnut, raw or boyled, luscious and harty meate: Walnuts of three or foure sorts, whereof there might be yeerely made great quantity of oyles, as usefull and good as that of Olives: some filberds I have seene, Crabbes great store, lesse, but not so sower as ours, which grafted with the Siens of English aple trees, without question would beare very good fruite, and we doubt not but to have the Siens enough the next yeere, there being in Sir Thomas Gates his garden at James town, many forward apple & peare trees come up, of the kernels set the yeere before.

If all this be not sufficient, loe further incouragement, the collony is already furnished with two hundred neate cattell, as many goates, infinite hogges in heards all over the woods, besides those to everie towne belonging in generall, and every private man, some Mares, Horses & Colts, Poultry great store, besides tame Turkeis, Peacockes and Pigeons plentifully increasing and thriving there, in no Countrie better.

Of our yong Steeres the next winter we doubt not to have three or foure Ploughes going, which once compast, we shall in short time be able to repay England the corne they have lent us.

If I knew yet any further impediments which might seeme to give discouragement to adventure thither, I should as easily remove them.

Object that pleaseth the want of cloathes, so long as there are wilde beasts there, and the beasts have skinnes on their backes (if the necessity were such) why should not we as doe the naturals, cloath our selves therewith, it is no worse then our fore-fathers have worne before us, and such as will save us from the colde in winter, and heate in summer: but admit there were no skinnes or being there, our people disdaine to weare them. If there be any man that hath beene so ill an husband here that he cannot furnish himselfe with a yeeres provision of apparrell; if I might counsell he should not be suffered to goe thither, for that country is not for him, as for others who can provide apparrell for the first yeere, I holde him a worse husband then the former, that shall at any time after be worse cloathed then he went over: the valuable commoditie of Tobacco of such esteeme in England (if there were nothing else) which every man may plant, and with the least part of his labour, tend and cure will returne him both cloathes and other necessaries. For the goodnesse whereof, an answerable to west-Indie Trinidado or Crasus (admit there hath no such bin returned) let no man doubt. Into the discourse wherof, since I am obviously entred, I may not forget the gentleman, worthie of much commendations, which first tooke the pains to make triall thereof, his name Mr John Rolfe, *Anno Domini* 1612. partly for the love he hath a long time borne unto it, and partly to raise commodity to the adventurers, in whose behalfe I witnesse and vouchsafe to holde my testimony in beleefe, that during the time of his aboade there, which draweth neere upon sixe yeeres, no man hath laboured to his power, by good example there and worthy incouragement into England by his letters, then he hath done, witnes his mariage with Powhatans daughter, one of rude education, manners barbarous and cursed generation, meerely for the good and honour of the Plantation: And least any man should conceive that some sinister respects allured him hereunto, I have made bold contrary to his knowledge in the end of my treatise to insert the true coppie of his letter, written to Sir Thomas Dale to acquaint him with his proceedings, and purpose therein, the rather to give testimony to the misconstruing and ill censuring multitude of his integritie, in the undertaking a matter of so great a consequent, who in my hearing have not spared to speak their pleasures; his owne letter hits them home, and the better sort, who know to censure judiciously cannot but highly commend and approve so worthy an undertaking.

Thus farre I have applied my selfe to incourage personall Adventurers: I would gladly now by worthy motives, allure the heavie undertakers to persist with alacritie and cheerefulnesse, both for their owne reputations, the honour of God, and their King and Country. The worthier sort, I meane those Nobles and others of that honourable counsell interessed therein, neede no spurre, their owne innate vertues drives them a pace. The Merchant onely wants some feeling and present returne of those commodities which he is perswaded the country affordeth: to them therefore I will addresse my speech, and if I may perswade them to be constant in their proceedings, some small time longer, the benefit will be the greater and the more welcome when it commeth.

It is not for nothing Sir Thomas Dale, so noblie without respect to his living, to his Lady here in England, past the prefixed time of his resolved returne, yet remaineth there; I am sure if he pleased he might returne with as much honour as any man from thence, I say not more.

I shall little neede, and indeede it were but wast and Idle for me to repeate and mention the commodities, which with onely labour may bee there procured: many Treatises hath them at full. Samples have beene sent home, and no man disputeth the goodnes, or the quantitie there to be had: take therefore double courage to your selves, and let those two yeeres neglect be restored by a cheerefull and new onset, and for your incouragement reade yet a little further, and view the face of the Colony, even superficially portraide: see what effects these three yeeres have wrought.

In May 1611 Sir Thomas Dale, with a prosperous passage, not full eight weekes arrived there, with him about three hundred people, such as for the present speede, and dispatch could then be provided, of worse condition then those formerly there, who I sorrow to speake it, were not so provident, though once before bittten with hunger and pennury, as to put corne into the ground for their winters bread, but trusted to the store, then furnished but with eight months provision. His first care therefore was to imploy al hands about setting of Corne at the two Forts, seated upon Kecoughtan, Henry and Charles, whereby the season then not fully past, thogh about the end of May, we had there an indifferent Crop of good corn.

This businesse taken order for, and the care and trust of it committed to his under officers, to James Towne he hastened, where the most company were, and their daily and usuall workes, bowling in the streetes, these he imployed about necessary workes, as felling of Timber, repairing their houses ready to fall upon their heads, and providing pales, posts and railes to impaile his purposed new Towne, which by reason of his ignorance in those parts, but newly arrived there, he had not resolved where to seate. For his better knowledge therefore of those parts, himselfe with an hundreth men, spent some time in discovery, first Nansamund River, which in dispight of the Indians, then our enemies, he discovered to the head, after that, our owne River, to the fals, whereupon a high land inviroñed with the mayn River, som sixteene or twentie miles, from the head of the Fals, neere to an Indian Towne called

Arsahattocke, he resolved to plant his new Towne, and so did whereof in his due place I shall make a briefe relation.

It was no meane trouble to him, to reduce his people, so timely to good order, being of so il a condition as may well witnesse his severe and strict imprinted booke of Articles, then needefull with all severity and extremity to be executed, now much mitigated, for more deserved death in those daies, then do now the least punishment, so as if the law should not have restrained by execution, I see not how the utter subversion and ruine of the Colony should have bin prevented, witnesse Webbes and Prises designe the first yeere, since that Abbots and others more daungerous then the former, and even this summer, Coles and Kitchins Plot, with three more, bending their course towards the Southward, to a Spanish Plantation, reported to be there, who had travelled (it being now a time of peace) some five daies jorney to Ocanahoen, there cut off by certaine Indians, hired by us to bring them home to receive their deserts. So as Sir Thomas Dale hath not bin tyranous, nor severe at all; Indeede the offences have bin capitall, and the offenders dangerous, incurable members, for no use so fit as to make examples to others, but the manner of their death may some object, hath bin cruell, unusuall and barbarous, which indeede they have not bin, witnesse France, and other Countries for lesse offences: what if they have bin more severe then usuall in England, there was just cause for it, we were rather to have regard to those whom we would have terrified, and made fearefull to commit the like offences, then to the offenders justly condemned. It being true that amongst those people (who for the most part are sencible onely of the bodies torment) the feare of a cruell, painefull and unusuall death, more restrains them then death it selfe.

Thus much obviously, I proceede in his indevours untill Sir Thomas Gates his happie arrivall, which was onely in preparing timber, pales, posts and railes for the present impaling this new Towne to secure himselfe and men from the mallice and trechery of the Indians, in the midst and hart of whom, he was resolved to set downe, but before he could make himselfe ready for that businesse, Sir Thomas Gates though his passage more long then usuall, to second him herein, happily arrived about the second of August, with six good Shippes, men, provisions and cattle, whom as yet not fully discovered, we supposed to be a Spanish fleete, thus induced the rather to beleeve, because in company with him were three Carvals, vessels which never before had bin sent thither, and now onely for the transportation of the Cattle. It did mee much good, and gave great courage to the whole company to see the resolution of Sir Thomas Dale, now wholy busied (our land fortifications to weake to withstand a forraigne Enemy) in lading our provisions aboard the two good Shippes, the Starre and Prosperous, and our own Deliverance, then riding before James town, aboarde which Shippes, he had resolved to encounter the supposed Enemy, animating his people, not onely with the hope of victory if they readily obeied his direction, but also assuring them that if by these meanes God had ordained to set a period to their lives, they could never be sacrificed in a more acceptable service, himselfe promising, rather to fire the Spanish Shippes with his owne, then either basely to yeelde, or to be taken: and in nothing he seemed to much discontent as that we could not possibly lade aboarde all our provisions before (the winde being then very faire) they might have bin with us, whilest therefore the rest were labouring their utmost to lade aboarde our provisions, hee caused a small shallop to be manned with thirty readie and good shot to discover directly what Shippes they might be, and withall speede to returne him certaine word, which within three houres they did, assuring him that it was an English fleete, Sir Thomas Gates Generall thereof: which newes how welcome it was unto him, principally because now he doubted not the happie progression of the affaires in hand, let any man (equally with him affected to the good and welfare of the action) judge and determine.

The worthies being met, after salutation and welcome given, and received, Sir Thomas Dale acquainted Sir Thomas Gates both with such businesses as he had affected since his arrivall, and also of his resolution to builde a new Towne, at the Fales, which designe and purpose of his, Sir Thomas Gates then principall Governour in Virginia, well approving, furnished him with three hundred and fiftie men, such as himselfe made choise of, and the beginning of September 1611 he set from James town, and in a day & a halfe, landed at a place where he purposed to seate & builde, where he had not bin ten daies before

he had very strongly impaled seven English Acres of ground
for a towne, which in honour of the noble Prince Henrie (of
ever happie and blessed memory, whose royall heart was ever
strongly affected to that action) he called by the name of Henrico. No sooner was he thus fenced, and in a manner secured
from the Indians, but his next worke (without respect to his
owne health or particular welfare) was building at each corner
of the towne, very strong and high commanders or watch-
towers, a faire and handsome Church, and storehouses, which
finished he began to thinke upon convenient houses, and
lodgings for himselfe and men, which with as much speede as
was possible, were more strongly and more handsome then any
formerly in Virginia, contrived and finished, and even in foure
moneths space, he had made Henrico much better and of more
worth then all the worke ever since the Colonie began, therein
done.

I should be to tedious if I should give up the accompt of
every daies labour, which therefore I purposly omit, and will
onely describe the towne, in the very state and perfection wich
I left it, and first for the situation, it standes upon a neck of a
very high land, 3 parts thereof invironed with the main River,
and cut over betweene the two Rivers, with a strong pale, which
maketh the neck of land an Island. There is in this towne 3
streets of well framed howses, a hansom Church, and the foundation of a more stately one laid, of Brick, in length, an hundred foote, and fifty foot wide, beside Store houses, watch
houses, and such like: there are also, as ornaments belonging
to this Town, upon the verge of this River, five faire Block
houses, or commaunders, wherein live the honester sort of
people, as in Farmes in England, and there keepe continuall
centinell for the townes security, and about two miles from the
towne into the Main, a Pale of two miles in length, cut over
from river to river, garded likewise with severall Commanders,
with a great quantity of corne ground impaled, sufficient if
there were no more in the Colony secured, to maintain with
but easiy manuring, and husbandry, more men, then I suppose, will be addressed thither, (the more is the pitty) these 3
yeeres.

For the further enlargement yet of this Town, on the other
side of the River, by impaling likewise: for we make no other

fence, is secured to our use, especially for our hogges to feede in, about twelve English miles of ground, by name, Coxen-Dale, secured by five Forts, called, Hope in faith, Charity Fort, Mount malado, a retreat, or guest house for sick people, a high seat, and wholsome aire, Elzabeth Fort, and Fort patience: and heere hath Mr. Whitacres chosen his Parsonage, or Church land, som hundred Acres impaled, and a faire framed parsonage house built thereupon, called Rocke Hall of this Towne, and all the Forts thereunto belonging, hath Captaine James Davis, the principall Commaunde, and Government.

I proceed to our next and most hopefull habitation, whether we respect commodity, or security, (which we principally aime at) against forraigne designes, and invasions, I meane the Bermuda Citty, begun about Christmas last, which because it is the neerest adjoyning to Henrico, though the last undertaken, I hould it pertinent to handle in the next place. This Towne, or plantation is seated by land, some 5 miles from Henrico, by water fourteene, being the yeer before the habitation of the Appamatucks, to revenge the trecherous injurie of those people, done unto us, taken from them, besides all their Corne, the Somer before without the losse of any, save onely some few of those Indians, pretending our hurt, at what time Sir Thomas Dale, being himself upon that service, and duly considering how commodious a habitation and seat it might be for us, tooke resolution to possesse and plant it, and at that very instant, gave it the name of the new Bermudas, whereunto he hath laid out, and annexed to be belonging to the freedome, and corporation forever, many miles of Champion, and woodland, in severall Hundreds, as the upper and nether Hundreds, Rochdale hundred, Wests Sherly hundred, and Digges his hundred. In the nether hundred he first began to plant, and inhabite for that there lyeth the most convenient quantity of Corne ground, and with a Pale cut over from River to River, about two miles long, wee have securd some eight miles circuit of ground, the most part champion, and exceeding good Corne ground, upon which pale, and round about, upon the verge of the River in this Hundred, halfe a mile distant from each other, are very faire houses, already builded, besides divers other particular mens houses, not so few as fifty, according to the conditions of the pattent graunted them, which whoso pleaseth to peruse shall in the end of my discourse finde it inserted. In this Plantation next to Sir Thomas Dale is principal, in the Commaund, Captaine Georg Yardley, Sir Thomas Gates his lieftenaunt, whose endeavours have ever deserved worthy commendations in that imployment. Rochdale Hundred by a crosse pale, well nigh foure miles long, is also already impaled, with bordering houses all along the pale, in which Hundred our hogges, and other cattell have twenty miles circuit to graze in securely. The undertaking of the chiefe Citty deferred till their Harvest be in, which once reaped, all hands shall be imployed thereon, which Sir Thomas Dale purposeth, and he may with some labour effect his designes, to make an impregnable retreat, against any forraign invasion, how powrefull so ever.

About fifty miles from this seat, on the other side of the Rivers, is James towne situate, upon a goodly and fertile Island: which although formerly scandoled with unhealthfull aire, we have since approved as healthfull as any other place in the country: and this I can say by mine own experience, that that corn and gardaine ground (which with much labour beeing when we first seated upon it, a thick wood) wee have cleered, and impaled, is as fertile as any other we have had experience and triall off. The Towne it selfe by the care and providence of Sir Thomas Gates, who for the most part had his chiefest residence there, is reduced into a hansome forme, and hath in it two faire rowes of howses, all of framed Timber, two stories, and an upper Garrret, or Corne loft high, besides three large, and substantiall Storehowses, joyned togeather in length some hundred and twenty foot, and in breadth forty, and this town hath been lately newly, and strongly impaled, and a faire platforme for Ordenance in the west Bulwarke raised: there are also without this towne in the Island, some very pleasant, and beutifull howses, two Blockhouses, to observe and watch least the Indians at any time should swim over the back river, and come into the Island, and certain other farme howses. The commaund and government of this town, hath master John Scarpe, Liftenant to Captain Francis West, Brother to the right Honourable, the Lord Lawarre.

From James towne downewards, some forty and odde miles at the mouth of the river, neer Point Comfort, upon Kecoughtan, are two pleasant and commodious Forts, Henrie and

Charles, goodly seats, and much corne ground about them, abounding with the commodities of fish, fowle, Deere, and fruits, where by the men live there, with halfe that maintenaunce out of the Store, which in other places is allowed: certainly this habitation would bee no whit inferiour to the best we have there, save, as yet, with the poore meanes we have; we cannot secure it, if a forraigne enemy, as we have just cause to expect daily should attempt it. And of these Forts, Captain Georg Web was lately establishd the principall Commander.

It hath been our greatest care, and labour hitherto, and yet but these three yeers, the former foure meerely mispent, to compasse these businesses, which being thus setled, and brought to such perfections, as I have described, now doth the time approch, that commodity may be expected, and if meanes bee sent over, will assuredly be returned. What honest spirit, having hitherto laboured herein, would at the upshot (as I may so term it) be discouraged or desist? I hope none, rather more will be animated, (if need require) to put too their helping hands and purses.

And even thus I have shaddowed I hope, without the guilt of tedious, or prolix discourses (as I have been able) the true condition (though many circumstances omitted) of Virginia, what may the substance be, when the externall shew is so forward, so glorious.

I have purposely omitted the relation of the Contry commodities, which every former treatise hath abundantly, the hope of the better mines, the more base, as Iron, Allom, and such like, Perfectly discovered, and made traill off, and surely of these things I cannot make so ample relation, as others, who in the discovery of those affaires, have bin, then my selfe more often conversant, onely of the hopefull, and marchantable commodities of tobacco, silke grasse, and silke wormes: I dare thus much affirme, and first of Tobacco, whose goodnesse mine own experience and triall induces me to be such, that no country under the Sunne, may, or doth affoord more pleasant, sweet, and strong Tobacco, then I have tasted there, even of mine owne planting, which, howsoever being then the first yeer of our tirall thereof, wee had not the knowledge to cure, and make up, yet are ther some now resident there, out of the last yeers well observed experience, which both know, and I doubt not will make, and returne such Tobacco this yeere, that even England shall acknowledge the goodnesse thereof.

Now I proceed to the silke grasse which groweth like unto our flax, I meane not, of that kinde formerly sent over, I have seen, even of the naturall, and wilde plants, which Captaine Martin, who much delighteth in those businesses, hath made, exceeding fine, and exceeding strong silke, and himselfe hath replanted many of the wilde plants this yeere, the silke whereof he purposeth to returne for triall.

The silke wormes sent thither from England, in seeds the last winter, came foorth many of them the beginning of March, others in Aprill, Maye, and June, thousands of them grown to great bignesse, and a spinning, and the rest well thriving of their increase, and commodity well knowne to be reaped by them, we have all most assurance (since sure I am) no Country affoordeth more store of Mulbery trees, or a kind with whose leafe they more delight, or thrive better.

It may be heere happily expected, that I should give up the relation of Captaine Argalls particular voyages and indeavours, and even as in a Plat, demonstrate his Norward discoveries, from which businesse I desire to be excused, partly, because himselfe is best able to make his owne relations, and partly, because my home imployments would not permit me leisure to accompany him, though my selfe desirous, in any of his voyages, whose indeavours, if I should indeavour to make knowne, and publish, could receive no honour at all by my commendations, or descriptions: much might they be impaired, through my ignorance, or unskillfullnes to set them foorth: yet cannot I omit to publish to the world, what present reliefe he hath don to the Colony, furnishing us by two trading voyages, with three and twenty hundred bushels of Corne, into our store delivered: beside, what he reserved for his mens provision, what he bestowed upon well deservers, and what his men appropriated.

I passe by the benefit of peace in those parts, by reason of his Captive Pochahuntas, concluded established, and will onely name the commoditie by his meanes done unto us, in repairing of our weatherbeten boats, and furnishing us with new, both strong, and usefull without whose assistance heerin, unlesse wee should have omitted other necessary imployments, I see not how we should have had passage one to another.

His Norward discoveries towards Sacadehoc, and beyond to Portroyall, Sancta Crux, and thereabout may not be concealed: In which his adventures, if he had brought home no commodity to the Colony, (which yet he did very much, both of apparrell, victualls, and many other necessaries) the honour which he hath done unto our Nation, by displanting the French, there beginning to seate & fortifie within our limits, and taking of their Ship and Pinnas, which he brought to James Towne, would have been reward enough for his paines, and will ever speake loud his honour, and approved valour.

I have heard it credibly reported, even from the mouth of Captaine Argall, that in one small Shippe, and in one voyage, the French have cleered eight thousand pounds by trade with the Indians, for furs, which benefit wil be as easily by us procured.

It is true the Salvadges there inhabiting (before Captaine Argalls arrivall) esteemed the French as Demy-Gods, and had them in great estimation: but seeing them vanquished and overcom by us, forsook them, yea, which is no meane point of pollicy, desired our friendship, telling Captaine Argall, that hee had undone them for ever, for that the French by yeerely trade with them for Furres, furnished them with many necessaries, whereof they had great want, which trade by this meanes might happily be hindered. But Captaine Argall hath agreed with them to reserve their Furres for him, and promised them, once a yeere to come thither, and truck with them: they seemed very well content, assuring him, that though the French should at any time arrive there, and proffer them trade, they would reserve all their Furs for him, and what profit by this meanes onely, may be returned to the Virginia adventurers, I submit to Captaine Argalls owne opinion and judgement.

I purposely omitted one thing in the Treatise of our concluded peace, wherewith I intend to conclud my discourse, which already I have drawne to a longer period then I purposed, whereby wee have gathered the better assurance, of their honest inward intentions, and this it is.

It pleased Sir Thomas Dale (my selfe being much desirous before my returne for England, to visit Powhatan, & his Court, because I would be able to speak somwhat thereof by mine own knowledge) to imploy my selfe, and an english boy for my

Interpreter on Thomas Salvage (who had lived three yeers with Powhatan, and speakes the language naturally, one whom Powhatan much affecteth) upon a message unto him, which was to deale with him, if by any meanes I might procure a daughter of his, who (Pochahuntas being already in our possession) is generally reported to be his delight, and darling, and surely he esteemeth her as his owne soule, for surer pledge of peace.

I departed the fifteenth of May early in the morning, with the English Boy, and two Indian guides, from the Bermudas, and came to his court or residence (as I judge some three score miles distant from us, being seated at the head almost of Pamaunkie River, at a towne called Match Cot) the next night after, about twelve of the clocke, the former night lodging in the open woods, feareles and without daunger: when we were come opposite to his Towne, the maine river betweene him and us, least at any time we should martch by land unto him undiscovered: my Indian guides called for a Canoa (a boate made onely of one tree, after the fashion of a hollow trough) to transport us, giving them to know that there was two English sent upon businesse to Powhatan from the English Weroance, which once knowne, a Canoa was presently sent, and we ferried over, Powhatan himselfe attending at the landing place to welcome us. His first salutation was to the Boy, whom he very wel remembred, after this manner: my childe you are welcome, you have bin a straunger to me these foure yeeres, at what time I gave you leave to goe to Paspahae (for so was James towne called before our seating there) to see your friends, and till now you never returned: you (said he) are my child, by the donative of Captaine Newport, in lieu of one of my subjects Namontacke, who I purposely sent to King James his land, to see him and his country, and to returne me the true report thereof, he as yet is not returned, though many ships have arrived here from thence, since that time, how ye have delt with him I know not. Having thus ended his speech to him, he addressed himself to me, and his first salutation without any words at all, was about my necke, and with his hand he feeled round about it, so as I might have imagined he would have cut my throate, but that I knew he durstnot, he asked me where the chaine of pearle was, I demaunded what chaine: that, said he,

which I sent my Brother Sir Thomas Dale for a present, at his
first arrivall; which chaine, since the peace concluded, he sent
me word, if he sent any Englishman upon occasion of busines
to me, he should weare about his necke, otherwise I had order
from him to binde him and send him home againe. It is true
Sir Thomas Dale had sent him such word (which till then my
selfe never heard of) and for this purpose had given his Page
order to deliver me the said chaine, who forgot it: I was doubtfull at the first how to answere him, yet presently I replied that
I was not ignorant of that message from his brother, formerly
sent unto him, whereby he onely entended that if upon extraordinary and sudden occasion, he should be constrained to
send an English man unto him without an Indian guide, then
in testimonie that he sent him hee should weare the chaine
about his necke: but in case any of his owne people should
conduct any English unto him, as did me, two of his owne
men, one of them a Counceller unto him, who was acquainted
with my businesse, their testimony should be sufficient, and
the chaine then needelesse to be worne, which answere pleased
him well, and fourthwith he brought us to his house, not full a
stones cast from the waterside, whereinto being come, himselfe sat downe on his bedsteade side, bed there was none more
then a single mat, on each hand of him was placed a comely
and personable young woman, not twenty yeeres old the eldest,
which they call his Queenes, the house with in round about
bee set with them, the outside guarded with an hundred bow-
men, with their quivers of arrowes at their backes, which at all
times, & places attend his person.

The first thing hee offered us was a pipe of Tobacco, which
they call *Pissimore*, whereof himselfe first dranke, and then gave
it me, and when I had drank what I pleased, I returned his
pipe, which with his owne hands he vouchsafed to take
from me: then began he to inquire how his Brother Sir
Thomas Dale fared, after that of his daughters welfare, her
mariage, his unknowne sonne, and how they liked, lived and
loved together: I resolved him that his brother was very well,
and his daughter so well content that she would not change
her life to returne and live with him, whereat he laughed
heartily, and said he was very glad of it. Now proceede (said
he) to deliver the cause of your unexpected comming; I certi-

fied him my message was private, to be delivered to himselfe, without the presence of any, save one of his Councellers, by name Pepaschicher, one of my guides, who was acquainted with my businesse, he instantly commanded all, both men and women out of the house, his two Queenes onely excepted, who upon no occasion whatsoever, may sequester themselves. Now (said he) speake on, and my selfe by my interpreter thus begun. Sir Thomas Dale your Brother, the principal commander of the English men, sends you greeting of love and peace, on his part inviolable, and hath in testimonie thereof by me sent you a worthie present, *vid.* two large peeces of copper, five strings of white and blew beades, five wodden combes, ten fish-hookes, and a paire of knives, all which I delivered him, one thing after another, that he might have time to view each particular: He willed me also to certifie you, that when you pleased to send men, he would give you a great grinding stone: my message and gift hitherto pleased him, I proceeded thus. The bruite of the exquisite perfection of your yongest daughter, being famous through all your territories, hath come to the hearing of your Brother Sir Thomas Dale, who for this purpose hath addressed me hither, to intreate you by that brotherly friendship you make profession of, to permit her (with me) to returne unto him, partly for the desire which himselfe hath, and partly for the desire her sister hath to see her of whom, if fame hath not bin prodigall, as like enough it hath not, your brother (by your favour) would gladly make his neerest companion, wife and bedfellow (many times he would have interrupted my speech, which I intreated him to heare out, and then if he pleased to returne me an answere) and the reason hereof is, because being now friendly and firmely united together, and made one people (as he supposeth and beleeves) in the band of love, he would make a naturall union betweene us, principally because himselfe hath taken resolution to dwel in your country so long as he liveth, and would therefore not only have the firmest assurance hee may, of perpetuall friendship from you, but also hereby binde himselfe thereunto.

When I had thus made an ende of speaking; the sooner by his often interruption, I had no neede to require his answere; which readily, and with no lesse gravity he returned thus.

I gladly accept your Kings salute of love & peace, which while

I live I shall exactly, both my selfe and subjects maintaine and conserve: his pledges thereof I receive with no lesse thankes, albeit they are not so ample; howbeit himselfe a greater Weroance, as formerly Captaine Newport, whom I very well love, was accustomed to gratefie me with. But to the purpose, my daughter whom my brother desireth, I should within these few daies to be wife to a great Weroance for two bushels of Roanoake (a small kinde of beades) made of oystershels, which they use and passe one to another, as we doe money (a cubites length valuing sixe pence) and it is true she is already gone with him, three daies jorney from me. I replied that I knew his greatnesse and power to be such, that if he pleased heerein to gratifie his Brother hee might, restoring the Roanoake without the imputation of Injustice, take hoame his daughter againe, the rather because she was not full twelve yeeres old, and therefore not marriageable: assuring him beside the band of peace, so much the firmer he should have treble the prise of his daughter, in beades, Copper, Hatchets and many other things more usefull for him. His answere hereunto was, that he loved his daughter as deere as his owne life, and though he had many Children, he delighted in none so much as in her, whom if he should not often beholde, he could not possibly live, which she living with us he knew he could not, having with himselfe resolved upon no termes whatsoever to put himselfe into our hands, or come amongst us, and therefore intreated me to urge that suite no further, but returne his brother this answer.

I desire no firmer assurance of his friendship, then his promise which he hath already made unto mee; from me, he hath a pledge, one of my daughters, which so long as she lives shall be sufficient, when she dieth he shall have another childe of mine, but she yet liveth: I holde it not a brotherly part of your King, to desire to bereave me of two of my children at once; further give him to understand, that if he had no pledge at all he should not neede to distrust any injurie from me, or any under my subjection, there have bin too many of his men and my killed, and by my occasion there shall never bee more, I which have power to performe it, have said it: no not though I should have just occasion offered, for I am now olde, and would gladly end my daies in peace, so as if the English offer me injury, my country is large enough, I will remove my selfe farther from you. Thus much I hope will satisfie my brother. Now because your selves are wearie, and I sleepie, we will thus end the discourse of this businesse. Then called he one of his men, and willed him to get some bread for us, himselfe the meane while telling us that they not expecting our comming, as usually they doe eate up all their other victuals, presently the bread was brought in two great wodden bouls, the quantity of a bushel sod breade made up round, of the bignesse of a tenise ball, where of we eate some few, and disposed the rest to many of his hungrie guarde which attended about us: when we had eaten he caused to be fetched a great glasse of sacke, some three quarts or better, which Captain Newport had given him sixe or seaven yeeres since, carefully preserved by him, not much above a pint in all this time spent, and gave each of us in a great oister shell some three spoonefuls; and so giving order to one of his people to appoint us a house to lodge in, tooke his leave for that night, and we departed. We had not bin halfe an houre in the house before the fleas began so to torment us that wee could not rest there, but went forth, and under a broade oake, upon a mat reposed our selves that night no sooner were we awake and up in the morning, but Powhatan himselfe came to us, and asked us how we fared, and immediatly led us to his howse, where was provided for our breakefast a great bole of Indian pease and beanes boyled together, and as much bread as might have sufficed a dosen hungry men, about an houer after boyled fresh fish, and not long after that roasted Oysters, Crevises and Crabbes: his men in this time being abroade a hunting some venison, others Turkeis and such like beasts and foule as their woods afforde, who returned before ten of the clocke with three does and a bucke, very good and fat venison, and two great cocke Turkeis, all which were dressed that day, and supper ended, scarce a bone to be seene.

Whiles I yet remained there, by great chaunce came an English man thither, almost three yeeres before that time surprised, as he was at worke neere Fort Henrie, one William Parker growen so like both in complexion and habite to the Indians, that I onely knew him by his tongue to be an Englishman, he seemed very joyfull so happily to meete me there. Of him when we often inquired, the Indians ever tolde us that he

fell sicke and died, which till now we beleeved: he intreated me
to use my best indevours to procure his returne, which thing I
was purposed so soone as I knew him, and immediately went
with him to Powhatan, and tolde him that we credibly beleeved
that he was dead, but since it was otherwise I must needes
have him home, for my selfe of necessitie must acquaint his
brother that I had seene him there: who if he returned not,
would make another voyage thither purposely for him:
Powhatan seemed very much discontent, and thus replied.
You have one of my daughters with you, and I am therewith
well content, but you can no sooner see or know of any English mans being with me, but you must have him away, or else
breake peace and friendship: If you must needes have him, he
shal goe with you, but I will send no guides along with you, so
as if any ill befall you by the way, thanke your selves. I answered, that rather then I would goe without him, I would
goe alone, the way I knew well enough, and other daungers I
feared not, since if I returned not safely, he must expect our revenge upon him and his people, giving him further to know,
that his brother our king might have just occasion to distrust
his love to him, by his slight respect of me, if he returned mee
home without guides. He replied not hereunto, but in passion
and discontentment went from me, not till suppertime speaking any more unto me: when sending for me, he gave me share
of such eates as were for himselfe provided, and as good aspect
and countenance as before; but not a word concerning my returne, till himselfe at midnight comming to me, and the boy
where we lay awaked us, and tolde me that Pepaschechar and
another of his men, in the morning should accompany us
home, earnestly requesting me to remember his brother to send
him these particulars. Ten peeces of Copper, a shaving knife,
an iron frow to cleave bordes, a grinding stone, not so bigge
but four or five men may carry it, which would be bigge
enough for his use, two bone combes, such as Captaine Newport had given him; the wodden ones his own men can make:
an hundred fish-hookes or if he could spare it, rather a fishing
saine, and a cat, and a dogge, with which things if his brother
would furnish him, he would requite his love with the returne
of skinnes: wherewith he was now altogether unfurnished (as
he tolde me) which yet I knew hee was well stored with, but

his disposition mistrustfull and jelous, loves to be on the surer hand.

When he had delivered this his message, he asked me if I will remember every particular, which I must repeat to him for his assurance, & yet still doubtful that I might forget any of them, he bade me write them downe in such a Table book as he shewed me, which was a very fair one, I desired him, it being of no use to him, to give it mee: but he tolde me, it did him much good to shew it to strangers which came unto him: so in mine owne Table booke, I wrot downe each particular, and he departed.

In the morning, himselfe and wee were timely stirring to be gone: to breakefast first we went, with a good boyled Turkie, which ended, he gave us a whole Turkie, besides that we left, and three baskets of bread to carry us home, and when we were ready to depart, hee gave each of us an excellent Bucks skin, very well dressed, and white as snow, and sent his sonne and daughter each of them one, demaunding if I well remembred his answer to his brother, which I repeated to him: I hope (said he) this will give him good satisfaction, if it doe not, I will goe three daies journy farther from him, and never see English man more: if upon any other occasion hee send to me again, I will gladly entertain his messengers, and to my powre accomplish his just requests: and even thus himselfe conducting us to the water side, he tooke leave of us, and we of him: and about ten of the clock the next night after, we were come to the Bermudas. This discourse I have briefely as I could, and as the matter would permit, the rather related, to make knowne, how charie Powhatan is, of the conservation of peace, a thing much desired, and I doubt not right welcom newes, to the undertakers heer, as may appeare by his answeres to my requests, and also by my safe passage thither, & homewards, without the lest shew of injury offred unto us, though divers times by the way, many stragling Indians met us, which in former times, would gladly have taken so faire occasion to worke their mischiefe and bloody designes upon us. By all which, as likewise by our forward progression in our affaires, I hope such good successe and benefit to bee speedily reaped, that my selfe, though I blesse God for it, who hath so provided for me, that I may live more happily heere, then many who are fearefull to adventure thither) could even willingly make a third voyage thither if by my poore endeavours the businesse might receive the least furtherance. God, (I hope) will raise up meanes beyond mans imagination, to perfect his owne glory and honour, in the conversion of those people, of whom undoubtedly, (as in all other parts in the world, he hath predestinated some to eternall salvation, and blessed shall those be that are the instruments thereof) I hope this poor Narration will move every honest heart, to put his helping hand thereunto. For my part, as I have been five yeers a personall workeman in that building, so shall I ever, as my meanes may permit me, be ready to offer my mite towards the furnishing of others, and againe (if need require) personally labor therein.

———

To the Reader.

There be two properties especially remarkeable, which should move all men earnestly and constantly, with all their meanes and endevour, to desire the atcheiving of any thing, and bringing of the same unto perfection: first the worth and excellencie: secondly the durablenesse and continuance thereof. For as that thing which is not durable, by reason of fragilitie and fugacitie, is not usually esteemed of men, though it be excellent: so that likewise which is not precious, is worthely little regarded, though it be never so durable. Now the Virginian plantation hath both these notable properties, if at the least we will, and impeach them not our selves; for what is more excellent, more precious and more glorious, then to convert a heathen Nation from worshipping the divell, to the saving knowledge, and true worship of God in Christ Jesus? what more praiseworthy and charitable, then to bring a savage people from barbarisme unto civillitie? what more honourable unto our countrey, then to reduce a farre disjoyned forraigne nation, under the due obedience of our dread Soveraigne the Kings Majestie? what more convenient then to have good seates abroad for our ever flowing multitudes of people at home? what more profitable then to purchase great wealth, which most now adaies gape after over-greedily? All which benefits are assuredly to bee had and obtained, by well and plentifully upholding of the plantation in Virginia. And for the durablenesse of all these great and singular blessings, there can (by Gods assistance) be no doubt at all made, if mens hearts unto whom God hath lent abilitie, were but inlarged cheerefully to adventure and send good companies of honest industrious men thither with a mind to inlarge Christs kingdome: for then will God assuredly maintaine his owne cause. But alas, as there was never yet any action so good, so honourable, so glorious, so pious and so profitable, but hath had checkes and discouragements, both by open enemies abroade, and intestine adversaries at home with in it owne bowels: even so may I truely say, hath this most glorious, most honourable most pious and most profitable enterprise had. For as of old, when Zerubbabell, Ezra and Nehemia returned from Babell, by allowance of the king of Persia to Jerusalem, and began to repaire the walles thereof, and to restore Gods service, there wanted not a Sanballat and others to say: what doe these weake Jewes? will they fortifie themselves? will they sacrifice? will they finish it in a day? Noe, for although they builde, yet if a fox goe up, he shall even breake downe that stony wall, Even so deale many Sanballates and Tobiahes, forraigne and domestic all enemies of this most religious worke: yea there be many who will not seeme enemies thereunto, but yet will neither further the businesse themselves, no not according to their owne ingagements which in conscience and credite they ought, nor quietly suffer others that otherwise wold, but discourage them therin all they may som saying as Judah once did. The strength of the bearers is weakened, and there is much earth, so as we are not able to builde the wall. Som saying with the unfaithfull Spies, sent forth to search the land of Canaan: The land wee went through to search it out is a land that eateth up the inhabitants thereof, for all the people we saw in it are strong, and men of great stature: yea and some others say, there is much already expended, and yet no profit ariseth, neither is there victuals to be had, for the preserving of life and soule together. But oh my deere countriemen, be not so farre bewitched herewith as to be still discouraged thereat for those that bring a vilde slaunder upon this action, may die by a plague before the Lord, as those men did: but rather remembring your auncient worth, renowne, valour and bounty, harken unto Caleb and Josua, who stilled

the peoples mourning: saying, Let us goe up at once and possesse it, for undoubtedly we shall overcome it; yet not so much
now by force of armes as the Israelites did then by warrant
from God (nor by utterly destroying of them, as some have
cruelly done since) as by gentlenesse, love, amity and Religion.
As for profit it shall come abundantly, if we can with the hus-
band-man, but freely cast our corne into the ground, and with
patience waite for a blessing. And of victuals, there is now no
complaint at all, and that which was hapned by the meere lasie
negligense of our owne people.

Now to the end that you may the better perceive these things
to be true, & be thereby the more animated cheerefully to goe
forward in the upholding of this holy worke, I will no longer
detaine you from the perusall of some Calebs and Josuahs
faithfull reports (writ there in June last this present yeere 1614.
and sent hither by the last shippe that came thence) for further
incouragement to put hereunto speedily & plentifully your
helping hands with al alacrity: As for them that are able, & yet
wil not further but indaunger the utter ruining of this so glorious a cause by their miserablenesse (being without love and
charitie) to the great dishonour of God, and our Countries
perpetuall shame should it now sinke, and fall to the gound: I
leave them to him that made them, to dispose of them according to his infinite wisdome. And so come to the letters
themselves: the first and chiefest whereof is from Sir Thomas
Dale, Marshall and Governour of Virginia, unto a Minister of
London.

To the R. and my most esteemed friend Mr. D.M.
at his house at F. Ch. in London.

Right Reverend Sr. by Sr. Thomas Gates I wrot unto you of
such occasions as then presented themselves, and now again by
this worthy Gentleman Captaine Argall I salute you: for such is
the reverend regard I have of you, as I can not omit any occasion to expres the sincere affection I beare you. You have ever
given me encouragements to persever in this religious Warfare,
untill your last Letters; not for that you are now lesse well affected thereunto: but because you see the Action to bee in

danger by many of their non performances who under tooke
the businesse. I have undertaken, and have as faithfully, & with
all my might indeavored the prosecution with all allacrity, as
God that knoweth the heart, can beare me record, what recompence, or what rewards, by whom, or when I know not
where to expect; but from him in whose vineyard I
Prince Henry   labor, whose Church with greedy appetite I desire to
erect. My glorious master is gone, that would have
ennamelled with his favours the labours I undertake, for Gods
cause, and his immortall honour. He was the great Captaine of
our Israell, the hope to have builded up this heavenly new
Jerusalem he interred (I think) the whole frame of this businesse, fell into his grave: for most mens forward (at least seeming so) desires are quenched, and Virginia stands in desperate
hazard. You there doe your duties, I will no way omit mine, the
time I promised to labour, is expired: it is not a yoke of Oxen
hath drawn me from this feast: it is not the marriage of a wife
maks me hast home, though that sallat give an appetite to cause
me returne. But I have more care of the Stock, then to set it
upon a die, and rather put my selfe to the curtesie of noble &
worthy censures then ruine this worke; and have a jury (nay a
million) of foule mouthed detracters, scan upon my endeavours, the ends whereof they cannot dive into. You shall briefely
understand, what hath betide since my last, and how we now
stand, and are likely to grow to perfection, if we be not altogeather neglected, my stay grounded upon such reason, as had
I now returned, it would have hazarded the ruine of all.

Sir Thomas Gates having imbarqued himselfe for England, I
put my selfe into Captaine Argalls ship, with a hundred and
fifty men in my frigot, and other boats went into Pamaunkie
river, where Powhatan hath his residence, and can in two or
three daies, draw a thousand men togeather, with me I carried
his daughter, who had been long prisoner with us, it was a day
or two before we heard of them: At length they demaunded
why we came; I gave for answere that I came to bring him his
daughter, conditionally he would (as had been agreed upon
for her ransome) render all the armes, tooles, swords, and men
that had runne away, and give me a ship full of corne, for the
wrong he had done unto us: if they would doe this, we would
be friends, if not burne all. They demaunded time to send to

their King; I assented, I taking, they receiving two pledges, to carrie my message to Powhatan. All night my two men lay not far from the water side, about noon the next day they told them the great King was three daies journey off, that Opochankano was hard by, to whom they would have had them deliver their message, saying, that what he agreed upon and did, the great King would confirme. This Opocankano is brother to Powhatan, and is his and their chiefe Captaine: and one that can as soone (if not sooner) as Powhatan commaund the men. But my men refused to doe my message unto any save Powhatan, so they were brought back, and I sent theirs to them, they tould me that they would fetch Simons to me, who had thrice plaid the runnagate, whose lies and villany much hindred our trade for corne: But they delayed us, so as we went a shore they shot at us, we were not behinde hand with them, killed some, hurt others, marched into the land, burnt their houses, tooke their corne, and quartered all night ashore.

The next day we went further up the river, they dogged us, and called to know whither we went; wee answered, to burne all, if they would not doe as we demaunded, and had been agreed upon. They would they said, bring all the next day so wee forbare all hostility, went a shore, their men in good numbers comming amongst us. But we were very cautious, & stood to our arms. The Kings daughter went ashore, but would not talke to any of them scarce to them of the best sort, and to them onely, that if her father had loved her, he would not value her lesse then olde swords, peeces, or axes: wherefore she would stil dwel with the English men, who loved her. At last came one from Powhatan, who tould us, that Simons was run away, to Nonsowhaticond, which was a truth, as afterwards appeared, but that the other English man was dead, that proved a lie: for since, Mr. Hamor, whom I employed to Powhatan brought him to me, our peeces, swords, and tooles within fifteen daies, should be sent to James towne, with some corne, and that his daughter should be my childe, and ever dwell with mee, desiring to be ever friends, and named such of his people, and neighbour Kings, as he desired to be included, and have the benefit of the peace, promising if any of our men came to him, without leave from me, he would send them back: and that if any of his men stole from us, or killed our cattel, he would send them to us to bee punished as we thought fit. With these conditions we returned, and within the time limited, part of our Arms were sent, and 20. men with corne, and promised more, which he hath also sent. Opachankano desired I would call him friend, and that he might call me so, saying he was a great Captaine, and did alwaies fight: that I was also a great Captaine, and therefore he loved mee; and that my friends should be his friends. So the bargain was made, and every eight or ten daies, I have messages and presents from him, with many apparances that he much desireth to continue friendshippe.

Now may you judge Sir, if the God of battailes have not a helping hand in this, that having our swords, drawn, killing their men, burning their houses, and taking their corne: yet they tendred us peace, and strive with all allacrity to keep us in good oppinion of them; by which many benefits arise unto us. First, part of our Armes, disgracefully lost long agoe, (kept by the Savages as Monuments and Trophies of our shames) redelivered, some repaire to our honor. Our catle to increase, without danger of destroying, our men at liberty, to hunt freely for venison, to fish, to doe any thing else, or goe any whither, without danger; to follow the husbanding of their corne securely, whereof we have about five hundred Acres set, and God be praised, in more forwardnesse, then any of the Indians, that I have seene, or heard off this yeere, roots, and hearbs we have in abundance; all doubt of want is by Gods blessing quite vanished, and much plenty expected. And which is not the least materiall, we may by this peace, come to discover the countrey better, both by our own travells, and by the relation of the Savages, as we grow in familiarity with them.

Powhatans daughter I caused to be carefully instructed in Christian Religion, who after shee had made some good progresse therein, renounced publickly her countrey Idolatry, openly confessed her Christian faith, was, as she desired, baptised, and is since married to an English Gentleman of good understanding, (as by his letter unto me, containing the reasons for his marriage of her you may perceive) an other knot to binde this peace the stronger. Her Father, and friends gave approbation to it, and her Uncle gave her to him in the Church: she lives civilly and lovingly with him, and I trust will increase in goodnesse, as the knowledge of God increaseth in her. She will goe into England with me, and were it but the gayning of this one soule, I will thinke my time, toile, and present stay well spent.

Since this accident the Governours and people of Checka-homanies, who are five hundred bow-men, and better, a stout and warlike Nation, have made meanes to have us come unto them, and conclude a peace, where all the Governours would meete me. They having thus three or foure times importuned mee, I resolved to goe; so taking Captaine Argall, with fifty men in my frigot, and barge I went thither: Captaine Argall with forty men landed, I kept aboord for some reasons. Upon the meeting they tould Captain Argall they had longed to be friends, that they had no King, but eight great men, who governd them. He tould them that we came to be friends, asked them if they would have King James to be their King, & whether they would be his men? They after som conference between themselves, seemed willing of both, demaunding if we would fight against their enemies, he tould them that if any did them injurie, they should send me word, and I would agree them, or if their adversaries would not, then I would let them have as many men as they would to help them: they liked well of that, and tould him that all their men should helpe us. All this being agreed upon, Captaine Argall gave every Councellor a Tamahawk, and a peece of Copper, which was kindly taken; they requested further, that if their boats should happen to meet with our boats, and that they said they were the Chika-hominy Englishmen, and King James his men, we would let them passe: we agreed unto it, so that they pronounced them-selves English men, and King James his men, promising within fifteen daies to come unto James town to see me, and conclude these conditions; every bowman being to give me as a Tribute to King James two measures of Corne every harvest, the two measures contayning two bushells and a halfe, and I to give every bowman a small Tamahawke, and to every Counseller a suit of red cloath, which did much please them. This people never acknowledged any King, before; no nor ever would ac-knowledge Powhatan for their King, a stout people they be, and a delicate seat they have.

Now Sir you see our conditions, you, and al worthy men may judge, whether it would not be a griefe to see these faire hopes frostbitten and these fresh budding plants to wither? which had I returned, had assuredly followed: for heer is no one that the people would have to govern them, but my selfe: for I had now come away, had I not found a generall desire in the best sort to returne for England: letter upon letter, request upon request from their friends to returne, so as I knew not upon whom to conferre the care of this busines in my absence whom I thought fitte was generally distasted, so as seeing the eminent ensuing danger, should I have left this multitude, not yet fully resined, I am resolved to stay till harvest be got in, and then settle things according to my poor understanding, and returne: if in the interim there come no authorised Governour from England.

Consider I pray you since things be brought to this passe, as you see, and that I should have come away, if then through their factions, humors, mutinies, or indiscretion of the Chiefs I had left behind, this should fall to ruine: I then should receive the imputation; I incurre the blame, for quitting the Plantation, although I might doe it, both with my honour, my promised stay of time being expired, and having warrant from my Soveraigne, the Kings Majesty: but the precedent reasons moved me and that this action of such price, such excellency, and assured profit to mine own knowledge should not die to the scorne of our Nation, and to give cause of laughter to the Papists that desire our ruine. I can assure you, no countrey of the world affoordes more assured hopes of infinit riches, which both by mine own peoples discovery, & the relation of such Savages, whose fidelity we have often found assureth me.

Oh why should so many Princes, and noble men ingage themselves and therby intermedling herein, have caused a number of soules transport themselves, and be transported hither? why should they (I say) relinquish this so glorious an Action: for if their ends bee to build Gods Church, they ought to persever: if otherwise, yet their honour ingageth them to be constant, Howsoever they stand affected, heer is enough to content them, let their ends be either for God, or Mammon.

These things have animated me to stay for a little season, to leave those, I am tied in conscience to returne unto, to leave the assured benefits of my other fortunes, the sweete society of my friends, and acquaintance, with all mundall delightes, and reside heer with much turmoile, which I will constantly doe,

rather then see Gods glorie diminished, my King and Countrey dishonoured, and these poore people, I have the charge or
ruined. And so I beseech you to answere for me, if you heare
me taxed for my staying, as some may justly do, and that these
are my chiefe motives God I take to witnesse. Remember me,
and the cause I have in hand, in your daily meditations, and
reckon me in the number of those that doe sincerely love you
and yours, and will ever rest in all offices of a friend, to doe
you service.

From James towne in Virginia the 18 of June, 1614.

Thomas Dale.

————

To my verie deere and loving Cosen M. G.
Minister of the B. F. in London.

Sir the Colony here is much better. Sir Thomas Dale our religious and valiant Governour, hath now brought that to passe,
which never before could be effected. For by warre upon our
enemies, and kinde usage of our friends, he hath brought them
to seeke for peace of us, which is made, and they dare not
breake. But that which is best, one Pocahuntas or Matoa the
daughter of Powhatan, is married to an honest and discreete
English Gentleman Master Rolfe, and that after she had openly
renounced her countrey Idolatry, confessed the faith of Jesus
Christ, and was baptised; which thing Sir Thomas Dale had
laboured along time to ground in her.

Yet not withstanding, are the vertuous deeds of this worthy
Knight, much debased, by the letters which some wicked men
have written from hence, and especially by one C.L. If you
heare any condemne this noble Knight, or doe feare to come
hither, for those slaunderous letters, you may upon my word
bouldly reprove them. You know that no malefactors can abide
the face of the Judge, but themselves scorning to be reproved,
doe prosecute withall hatred, all those that labour their amendment. I marvaile much that any men of honest life, should
feare the sword of the magistrate, which is unsheathed onely in
their defence.

But I much more muse, that so few of our English Ministers
that were so hot against the Surplis and subscription: come

hither where neither spoken of. Doe they not either wilfully hide their Tallents, or keepe themselves at home for feare of loosing a few pleasures? Be there not any amongst them of Moses his minde, and of the Apostles, that forsooke all to follow Christ? But I referre them to the Judge of all hearts, and to the King that shall reward every one according to the gaine of his Talent. But you my cosen, holde fast that which you have, and I though my promise of 3 yeers service to my country be expired, will abide in my vocation here untill I be lawfully called from hence. And so betaking us all unto the mercies of God in Christ Jesus, I rest for ever.

Virginia June 18. 1614.

Your most deere and loving cosen
Alex. Whitakers.

———

The coppie of the Gentle-mans letters to
Sir Thomas Dale, that after maried Powhatans daughter,
containing the reasons moving him thereunto.

Honourable Sir, and most worthy Governor: when your leasure shall best serve you to peruse these lines, I trust in God, the beginning will not strike you into a greater admiration, then the end will give you good content. It is a matter of no small moment, concerning my own particular which here I impart unto you, and which toucheth mee so neerely, as the tendernesse of my saluation. Howbeit I freely subject my selfe to your grave and mature judgement, deliberation, approbation and determination; assuring my selfe of your zealous admonitions, and godly comforts, either perswading me to desist, or incouraging me to persist ther in, with a religious feare and godly care, for which (from the very instant, that this began to roote it selfe, within the secret bosome of my brest) my daily and earnest praiers have bin, still are, and ever shall bee proved forthwith, as sincere, a godly zeale, as I possiblely may to be directed, aided and governed in all my thoughts, words and deedes, to the glory of God, and for my eternal consolation. To persevere wherein I never had more neede, nor (till now) could ever imagine to have bin moved with the like occasion.

But (my case standing as it doth) what better worldly refuge can I here seeke, then to shelter my selfe under the safety of your favourable protection? And did not my ease proceede from an unspotted conscience, I should not dare to offer to your view and aprroved judgement, these passions of my troubled soule, so full of feare and trembling is hypocrisie and dissimulation. But knowing my owne innocency & godly fervor, in the whole prosecution hereof, I doubt not of your benigne acceptance, and clement construction. As for malicious depravers, & turbulent spirits, to whom nothing is tastful, but what pleaseth their unsavory pallat, I passe not for them being well assured in my perswasion (by the often triall and proving of my selfe, in my holiest meditations and praiers) that I am called hereunto by the spirit of God; and it shall be sufficient for me to be protected by your selfe in all vertuous and pious indevours. And for my more happie proceeding herein, my daily oblations shall ever be addressed to bring to passe so good effects, that your selfe, and all the world may truely say: This is the worke of God, and it is marvelous in our eies.

But to avoide tedious preambles, and to come neerer the matter: first suffer me with your patience, to sweepe and make cleane the way wherein I walke, from all suspicions and doubts, which may be covered therein, and faithfully to reveale unto you, what should move me hereunto.

Let therefore this my well advised protestation, which here I make betweene God and my own conscience, be a sufficient witnesse, at the dreadfull day of judgement (when the secret of all mens harts shall be opened) to condemne me herein, if my chiefest intent and purpose be not, to strive with all my power of body and minde, in the undertaking of so mightie a matter, no way led (so farre forth as mans weakenesse may permit) with the unbridled desire of carnall affection: but for the good of this plantation for the honour of our countrie, for the glory of God, for my owne salvation, and for the converting to the true knowledge of God and Jesus Christ, an unbeleeving creature, namely Pokahuntas. To whom my hartie and best thoughts are, and have a long time bin so intangled, and inthralled in so intricate a laborinth, that I was even awearied to unwinde my selfe thereout. But almighty God, who never faileth his, that truely invocate his holy name, hath opened the gate, and led me by the hand that I might plainely see and discerne the safe paths wherein to treade.

To you therefore (most noble Sir) the patron and Father of us in this countrey doe I utter the effects of this my setled and long continued affection (which hath made a mightie warre in my meditations) and here I doe truely relate, to what issue this dangerous combate is come unto, wherein I have not onely examined, but throughle tried and pared my thoughts even to the quicke, before I could finde any fit wholesome and apt applications to cure so daungerous an ulcer. I never failed to offer my daily and faithfull praiers to God, for his sacred and holy assistance. I forgot not to set before mine eies the frailty of mankinde, his prones to evill, his indulgencie of wicked thoughts, with many other imperfections wherein man is daily insnared, and oftentimes overthrowne, and them compared to my present estate. Nor was I ignorant of the heavie displeasure which almightie God conceived against the sonnes of Levie and Israel for marrying strange wives, nor of the inconveniences which may therefore arise, with other the like good motions which made me looke about warily and with good circumspection, into the grounds and principall agitations, which thus shauld provoke me to be in love with one whose education hath bin rude, her manners barbarous, her generation accursed, and so discrepant in all nurtriture from my selfe, that oftentimes with feare and trembling, I have ended my private controversie with this: surely these are wicked instigations, hatched by him who seeketh and delighteth in mans destruction; and so with fervent praiers to be ever preserved from such diabolical assaults (as I tooke those to be) I have taken some rest.

Thus when I had thought I had obtained my peace and quietnesse, beholde another, but more gracious tentation hath made breaches into my holiest and strangest meditations; with which I have bin put to a new triall, in a straighter manner then the former: for besides the many passions and sufferings, which I have daily, hourely, yea and in my sleepe indured, even awaking mee to astonishment, taxing me with remisnesse, and carelesnesse, refusing and neglecting to performe the duetie of a good Christian, pulling me by the eare, and crying: why dost not thou indeavor to make her a Christian? And these have happened to my greater wonder, even when she hath bin furthest seperated from me, which in common reason (were it not an undoubted worke of God) might breede forgetfulnesse of a farre more worthie creature. Besides, I say the holy spirit of God hath often demaunded of me, why I was created? If not for transatory pleasures and worldly vanities, but to labour in the Lords vineyard; there to sow and plant, to nourish and increase the fruites thereof, daily adding with the good husband in the Gospell, somewhat to the tallent, that in the end the fruites may be reaped, to the comfort of the laborer in this life, and his salvation in the world to come? And if this be, as undoubtedly this is, the service Jesus Christ requireth of his best servant; wo unto him that hath these instruments of pietie put into his hands, and wilfully despiseth to work with them. Likewise, adding hereunto her great appearance of love to me, her desire to be taught and instructed in the knowledge of God, her capablenesse of understanding, her aptnesse and willingnesse to receive anie good impression, and also the spirituall, besides her owne incitements stirring me up hereunto.

What should I doe? Shall I be of so untoward a disposition, as to refuse to leade the blind into the right way? Shall I be so unnaturall, as not to give bread to the hungrie? or uncharitable, as not to cover the naked? Shall I despise to actuate these pious dueties of a Christian? Shall the base feare of displeasing the world, overpower and with-holde mee from revealing unto man these spirituall workes of the Lord, which in my meditations and praiers, I have daily made knowne unto him? God forbid. I assuredly trust hee hath thus delt with me for my eternall felicitie, and for his glorie: and I hope so to be guided by his heavenly grace, that in the end by my faithfull paines, and christianlike labour, I shall attaine to that blessed promise, Pronounced by that holy Prophet Daniell unto the righteous that bring many unto the knowledge of God. Namely, that they shall shine like the starres forever and ever. A sweeter comfort cannot be to a true Christian, nor a greater incouragement for him to labour all the daies of his life, in the performance thereof, nor a greater gain of consolation, to be desired at the hower of death, and in the day of judgement.

Againe by my reading, and conference with honest and religious persons, have I received no small encouragement, besides *serena mea conscientia*, the cleerenesse of my conscience, clean from the filth of impurity, *quæ est instar muri ahenei*, which is unto me, as a brasen wall. If I should set down at large, the perturbations & godly motions, which have striven within mee, I should but make a tedious & unnecessary volume. But I doubt not these shall be sufficient both to certifie you of my tru intents, in discharging of my dutie to God, & to your selfe, to whose gracious providence I humbly submit my selfe, for his glory, your honour, our Countreys good, the benefit of the Plantation, and for the converting of one unregenerate, to regeneration; which I beseech God to graunt, for his deere Sonne Christ Jesus his sake.

Now if the vulgar sort, who square all mens actions by the base rule of their owne filthinesse, shall taxe or taunt me in this my godly labour: let them know, it is not any hungry appetite, to gorge my selfe with incontinency; sure (if I would, and were so sensually inclined) I might satisfie such desire, though not without a seared conscience, yet with Christians more pleasing to the eie, and lesse fearefull in the offence unlawfully committed. Nor am I in so desperate an estate, that I regard not what becommeth of mee; nor am I out of hope but one day to see my Country, nor so void of friends, nor mean in birth, but there to obtain a mach to my great content: nor have I ignorantly passed over my hopes there, or regardlesly seek to loose the love of my friends, by taking this course: I know them all, and have not rashly overslipped any.

But shal it please God thus to dispose of me (which I earnestly desire to fullfill my ends before sette down) I will heartely accept of it as a godly taxe appointed me, and I will never cease, (God assisting me) untill I have accomplished, & brought to perfection so holy a worke, in which I will daily pray God to blesse me, to mine, and her eternall happines. And thus desiring no longer to live, to enjoy the blessings of God, then this my resolution doth tend to such godly ends, as are by me before declared: not doubting of your favourable acceptance, I take my leave, beseeching Almighty God to raine downe upon you, such plentitude of his heavenly graces as your heart can with and desire, and so I rest,

At your commaund most willing to be disposed off

John Rolfe.

Virginia therefore standing now in such a goodly proportion, and faire forwardnesse of thriving, as it was never yet hitherto seen in, since it began to be first planted: cannot but soone come to perfection, to the exceeding great comfort of all well affected Christians, and no small profit of the planters, and adventurers: if it be well seconded and supplyed, with a good number of able men: Wherefore, let none bee heerafter unwilling all they may to further this most honourable Action, and be forward to uphold and support it from falling, by their speech, and countenance, and freely adventuring thither, both in their persons, & also by their purses, as God hath inabled them. To conclude, as Azariah sayd once to King Azah, Juda, and Benjamin, so say I unto all. Bee yee strong therefore, and let not your hands be weake, for your worke shall have a reward. And as the holy Apostle said to the Corinthians, Be ye therefore stedfast, unmoveable, abundant alwaies in the workes of the Lord, for as much as ye know your labour is not in vaine in the Lord, let us not therefore bee wearie of welldoing: for in due season, wee shall reape, if wee faint not as the Apostle tolde the Galations. Farewell.

LORD DE LA WARRE

A Short Relation

*Made by the Lord De-La-Warre, to the
Lords and others of the Counsell of
Virginea, touching his unexpected returne home,
and afterwards delivered to the generall Assembly
of the said Company, at the court holden
the twenty five of June, 1611.*

My Lords, &c.

Being now by accident returned from my Charge at Virginea, contrary either to my owne desire, or other mens expectations, who spare not to censure me, in point of duty, and to discourse and question the reason, though they apprehend not the true cause of my returne, I am forced, (out of a willingnesse to satisfie every man) to deliver unto your Lordships, and the rest of this Assembly, briefely, (but truely) in what state I have lived, ever since my arrivall to the Colonie; what hath beene the just occasion of my sudden departure thence; and in what termes I have left the same: The rather because I perceive, that since my comming into England, such a coldnesse and irresolution is bred, in many of the Adventurers, that some of them seeke to withdraw those paiments, which they have subscribed towards the Charge of the Plantation, and by which that Action must bee supported and maintained; making this my returne, the colour of their needlesse backwardnes and unjust protraction. Which, that you may the better understand, I must informe your Lordships, that presently after my arrival in James Towne, I was welcommed by a hote and violent Ague, which held mee a time, till by the advice of my Physition, Doctor Laurence Bohun, (by blood letting) I was recovered, as in my first Letters by Sir Thomas Gates I have informed you.

That disease had not long left me, til (within three weekes after I had gotten a little strength) I began to be distempered with other greevous sicknesses, which successively & severally assailed me: for besides a relapse into the former disease, which with much more violence held me more then a moneth, and brought me to great weakenesse, the Flux surprised me, and kept me many daies; then the Crampe assaulted my weake body, with strong paines; & afterwards the Gout (with which I had heeretofore beene sometime troubled) afflicted mee in such sort, that making my body through weakenesse unable to stirre, or to use any maner of exercise, drew upon me the disease called the Scurvy; which though in others it be a sicknesse of slothfulnesse, yet was in me an effect of weaknesse, which never left me, till I was upon the point to leave the world.

These severall maladies and calamities, I am the more desirous to particularise unto your Lordships (although they were too notorious to the whole Colonie) lest any man should misdeeme that under the general name and the comon excuse of sicknes, I went about to cloke either sloth, or feare, or anie other base apprehension, unworthy the high and Honourable charge, which you had entrusted to my Fidelitie.

In these extremities I resolved to consult my friends, who (finding Nature spent in mee, and my body almost consumed, my paines likewise daily encreasing) gave me advise to preferre a hopefull recovery, before an assured ruine, which must necessarily have ensued, had I lived, but twenty dayes longer, in Virginia: wanting at that instant, both food and Physicke, fit to remedy such extraordinary diseases, and restore that strength so desperately decayed.

Whereupon, after a long consultation held, I resolved by generall consent and perswasion, to shippe my selfe for Mevis, an Island in the West Indies, famous for wholesome Bathes, there to try what help the Heavenly Providence would afford mee, by the benefit of the hot Bath: But GOD, who guideth all things, according to his good will and pleasure, so provided, that after wee had sailed an hundred Leagues, wee met with Southerly windes which forced mee to change my purpose, (my body being altogether unable to endure the tediousnesse of a long voyage) and so sterne my course for the Western Islands, which I no sooner recovered, then I found help for my health, and my sickenesse asswaged, by meanes of fresh diet, and especially of Orenges and Lemonds, an undoubted remedy and medicine for that disease, which lastly, and so long, had afflicted mee: which ease as soone as I found, I resolved, although my body remained still feeble and weake, to returne backe to my charge in Virginia againe, but I was advised not to hazard my selfe before I had perfectly recovered my strength, which by counsell I was perswaded to seeke in the naturall Ayre of my Countrey, and so I came for England. In which Accident, I doubt not but men of reason, and of judgement will imagine, there would more danger and prejudice have hapned by my death there, then I hope can doe by my returne.

In the next place, I am to give accompt in what estate I left the Collony for government in my absence. It may please your Lordships therefore to understand, that upon my departure thence, I made choise of Captaine George Pearcie, a Gentleman of honour and resolution, and of no small experience in that place, to remaine Deputie Governour, untill the comming of the Marshall Sir Thomas Dale, whose Commission was likewise to be determined, upon the arrivall of Sir Thomas Gates, according to the intent and order of your Lordships, and the Councill here.

The number of men I have left there, were upward of two hundred, the most in health, and provided of at least tenne moneths victuals, in their store-house, (which is daily issued unto them) besides other helps in the Countrey, lately found out by Captiane Argoll by trading with pettie Kings in those parts, who for a small returne of a piece of Iron, Copper, &c. have consented to trucke great quantities of Corne, and willingly imbrace the intercourse of Traffique, shewing unto our people certaine signes of amitie and affection.

And for the better strengthening and securing of the Collony, in the time of my weaknesse there, I tooke order for the building of three severall Forts, two of where are seated neere Poynt Comfort, to which adjoyneth a large Circuit of ground, open, and fit for Corne: the third Fort is at the Falles, upon an Iland invironed also with Corne ground. These are not all manned, for I wanted the commoditie of Boates, having but two, and one Bardge, in all the Countrey, which hath beene cause that our fishing hath beene (in some sort) hindered, for want of those provisions, which easily will be remedied when wee can gaine sufficient men to be imployed about those businesses, which in Virginia I found not: but since meeting with Sir Thomas Gates at the Cowes neere Portsmouth (to whom I gave a perticular accompt of all my proceedings, and of the present estate of the Collony as I left it) I understood those wants are supplyed in his Fleete.

The Countrey is wonderfull fertile and very rich, and makes good whatsoever heretofore hath beene reported of it, the Cattell already there, are much encreased, and thrive exceedingly with the pasture of that Countrey: The Kine all this last Winter, though the ground was covered most with Snow, and the season sharpe, lived without other feeding then the grasse they found, with which they prospered well, and many of them readie to fall with Calve: Milke being a great nourishment and refreshing to our people, serving also (in occasion) as well for Physicke as for food, so that it is no way to be doubted, but when it shall please God that Sir Thomas Dale, and Sir Thomas Gates, shall arrive in Virginia with their extraordinary supply of one hundred Kine, and two hundred Swine, besides store of all manner of other provisions for the sustenance and maintenance of the Collony, there will appeare that successe in the Action as shall give no man cause of distrust that hath already adventured, but encourage every good minde to further so worthy a worke, as well redound both to the Glory of GOD, to the Credit of our Nation, and to the Comfort of all those that have beene Instruments in the furthering of it.

The last discovery, during my continuall sicknesse, was by Captaine Argoll, who hath found a trade with Patamack (a King as great as Powhatan, who still remaines our enemie, though not able to doe us hurt.) This is in a goodly River called Patomack, upon the borders whereof there are growne the goodliest Trees for Masts, that may be found elsewhere in the World: Hempe better then English, growing wilde in aboundance: Mines of Antimonie and Leade.

There is also found without our Bay to the Northward an excellent fishing Bancke for Codde, and Ling, as good as can be eaten, and of a kinde that will keepe a whole yeare, in Shippes hould, with little care; a tryall whereof I now have brought over with mee. Other Islands there are upon our

Coasts, that doe promise rich merchandise, and will further exceedingly the establishing of the Plantation, by supply of many helpes, and will speedily afford a returne of many worthie Commodities.

I have left much ground in part manured to receive Corne, having caused it the last Winter to be sowed for rootes, with which our people were greatly releeved.

There are many Vines planted in divers places, and doe prosper well, there is no want of anything, if the action can be upheld with constancy and resolution.

Lastly, concerning my selfe, and my course, though the World may imagine that this Countrey and Climate, will (by that which I have suffered beyond any other of that Plantation) ill agree, with the state of my body, yet I am so farre from shrinking or giving over this honourable enterprise, as that I am willing and ready to lay all I am worth upon the adventure of the Action, rather then so Honourable a worke should faile, and to returne with all the convenient expedition I may, beseeching your Lordships, and the rest, not onely to excuse my former wants, happened by the Almighty hand: but to second my resolutions with your friendly indeavours: that both the State may receive Honour, your selves Profit, and I future Comfort, by being imployed (though but as a weake Instrument) in so great an Action.

And thus having plainely, truely, and briefely, delivered the cause of my returne, with the state of our affayres, as wee now stand, I hope every worthy and indifferent hearer, will by comparing my present resolution of returne, with the necessitie of my comming home, rest satisfied with this true and short Declaration.

JOHN ROLFE

A True Relation of the State of Virginia

lefte by Sir Thomas Dale Knight
in May last 1616.

To ye right Honorable the Earle of Pembroke Knight of the most noble order of the garter, one of his Majesties most Honorable pryvy Councell

RIGHT HONORABLE

THERE have bene of late divulged manie ympressions, judiciallie and trulie penned; partlie to take awaie the ignomynie, skandales and maledictions wherewith this Action hath bene branded: and partlie to satisfie all (especially the best) with the manner of the late proceedinges, and the prosperitie lykely to ensue. How happilie and plenteousely the good Blessinges of God, have fallen upon the people and Colony since the last ympression (faithfully wryten by a gentleman of good merit Mr Ralph Hamor, sometyme an actuall Member in the Plantation, even then departing when the groundworke was newlaied of their now thrift and happynes) of the earthie and worldly man is scarsely beleived: but, of heavenlyer myndes, they are most easyly discerned, for they daily attend and marke how those Blessinges (though sometymes restrayned for a tyme) in the end are powred upon the servauntes of the Lord at his due pleasure. Shall your Honor with piety and pittie: with piety being zealous for Godes glory: and with pittie mourning the defectes, vouchsafe the reading thus much of the estate of this Colony, as it remayned in May last when Sir Thomas Dale left the same, I shall deeme myself most happie in your noble acceptance, and most readylie offer to your approved judgement; whether this Cause, so much dispised and disgraced, doe not wrongfully suffer many ymputacions.

First to meete with an objection commonly used amongst manie men, who search truthes no farther then by common

reportes, namely: How is it possible Virginia can now be so
good? so fertile a Country? so plentifully stoored with food and
other commodities? is it not the same still it was, when men
pined with famyne? can the earth now bring forth such a plentifull increase? were there not Governors, Men and Meanes to
have wrought this heretofore? and can it now on the suddayne
be so fruitfull? surly (saie they) these are rather baites to catch
and intrapp more men into woe and mysery, then otherwise
can by ymagined. These with many as frivolous I have harde
instigated, and even reproachfully spooken agaynst Virginia.
To aunswere whom (the most part of them incredulous
worldlinges, such as beleive not, unles they feele the goodnes
of the Lord sensibly to touche them) though it be not much
materiall, yet lett them know. Tis true, Virginia is the same it
was, I meane for the goodnes of the Seate and fertilenes of the
land, and will no doubt so contynue to the worldes end. A
Country as worthy of good report, as can be declared by the
penn of the best wryter. A Country spacious and wide, capable
for many hundred thousandes of inhabitans. For the Soyle
most fertile to plant in. For Ayre, freshe and temperate: somewhat hotter in sommer, and not alltogether so cold in wynter
as in England. yet so agreeable it is to our constitucions that
now it is more rare to heare of a mans death, then in England
amongst so many people as are there resident. For Water, most
wholesom and verie plentyfull: and for faire navigable ryvers,
and good harbors, no Country in Christendom in so smale a
circuit, so well stoored. For Matter fitt for buildinges and for-
tifacions: and for building of shipping with everything thereto
apperteyning: I maie boldly avouch, scarce anie or no Country
knowen to man of itself more aboundantly furnished. These
things (maie some saie) are of greate consequence towardes the
settling of a Plantation: but where are the beastes and Cattle to
feed and clothe the people? I confess this is a mayne want. yet

The Horses
and Bullocks
are ymployed
to goe to
Cart: and to
plough
ground for
English
Corne.

some there are alreadie, as Neate cattle, horses,
Mares, and Goates, which are carefully preserved for
increase both males and females, the one for the
plough, thother for mylke butter and cheese: the
number whereof hereafter shalbe sett downe in a particular noate by themselves There are also great
stoore of Hogges both wilde and tame, the nomber uncertayne,

and Powltry greate plenty: which all men, if they will themselves maie keepe. But the greatest want of all is least thought
on; which is good and sufficient men, as well of birth and qual-
lyty to command: souldiers to march, discover and defend the
Country from Invasions: as artificers, Laborers, and husbond-
men: with whom were the Colony well provided; then might
triall be made, what lieth hidden in the womb of the Land: the
Land might yerely abound with corne and other provisions
for mans sustenaunce: buildinges, fortifications and shipping
might be reared, wrought and framed: commodyties of divers
kindes might be reaped yerely, and sought after: and many
thinges (Godes blessinges contynuing) might come with ease
to establishe a firme and perfect Common-weale. But to come
agayne to my matter from which I have a little straied, and to
give a more full aunswere to the Objectors. Maie you please to
take notice; that the begynning of this Plantacion was governed
by a President & Councell Aristocratycallie. The President
yerely chosen out of the Councell, which consisted of twelve
persons. This goverment lasted above two yeres: in which tyme
such envie, dissentions and jarrs were daily sowen amongst
them, that they choaked the seedes and blasted the fruits of all
mens labors. If one were well disposed and gave good advise-
ment to proceed in the Busines: others out of the malice of
their hartes would contradict, interdict withstand and dashe
all. Some rung out and sent home to loud prayses of the riches
& fertilenes of the Country, before they assaied to plant, to
reape or search the same. Others sayd nothing; nor did any
thing thereunto. All would be Keisars, none inferior to other.
Some drew forward, more backward. The vulgar sort looked
for Supplies out of England, neglected husbandry. Som wrote
home, there was no want of food, yet sought for none. Others
that would have sought could not be suffered: in which confusion, much confusion yerely befell them, and in this goverment happened all the mysery. Afterward a more absolute
goverment was graunted Monarchally, wherein it still contynueth. And although for some few yeres it stood at a staie,
especially in the manuring and tilling of ground: yet men spent
not their tyme idely nor ymprofitably. For they were daily ymployed in pallazadoing and building of Townes, ympaling
groundes, and other needfull busynesses, which now is both

benficiall to keepe the Cattle from ranging and preserveth the corne safe from their spoile. Being thus fitted and prepared to sow corne, and to plant other seedes and fruites in all the places of our habitacions: one thing notwithstanding much troubled our Governor, namely Enmytie with the Indians. For howsoever wee could well defend ourselves, Townes and Seates from anie assault of the Natives: yet our Cattle and Corne laie too open to their courtysies, and too subject to their mercies. Whereupon a Peace was concluded, which still contynueth so firme, that the people yerely plant and reape quyetly; and travaile in the woodes a fowling and a hunting as freely and securely from feare of danger or treachery as in England. The greate Blessinges of God have followed this Peace; and it next under him hath bredd our plenty: every man sitting under his figtree in safety, gathering and reaping the fruites of their labors with much joy and comfort. But a question maie be demaunded what those fruites are? For such as the Countrie affordeth naturally (for variety and goodnes comparable to the best in Christendom, growing wilde as they doe) I pass them over: other Discourses having lardgly manifested them to the veiwe of the world. But for the peoples present labors, they have Indian Wheate called Mays in the West Indies, Pease and Beanes: English Wheate, Pease, Barley, Turnips, Cabbages, Pumpions West-Indian and others, Caretts, Parsnips and such lyke, besides hearbes and flowers all of our Englishe seedes, both for pleasure and for the kitchin so good, so fruitfull, so pleasant and profitable, as the best made ground in England can yeild. And that you maie know what twoe mens labors only with a spade and sholve can manure in one yere: fiftie poundes of monny was offered for their Cropp, which they refused to take. For Hemp, and Flax, none better in England or Holland. Silk-wormes some of their labors, and tastes of other good and vendible commodities were now brought home. Lykewise Tobacco (though an esteemed weed) verie commodyous, which there thriveth so well, that (no doubt) after a little more triall, and experience in the curing thereof, it will compare with the best in the West Indies. For fishe, fowle, Deere and other beastes, reportes and wrytinges have rather bene too sparing then prodigall. About two yeres since Sir Thomas Dale (whose worth and Name in concluding this

Peace, and mannaging of the affayres of the Colony, will outlast
the standing of the Plantation) found out two seasons of the
yere to catch fishe, namely the Spring, and the Fall. He himself
tooke no smale paines in the triall, and at one hale with a Sayne
coought five thousand fishe, three hundred of them as bigg as
Codd, the least of the residue a kind of Salmon Trout two foote
long: yet durst he not adventure on the mayne [   ] for
breaking his nett. Lykewise twoe men with axes, and such lyke
weapons have taken and kild neere the shoare and brought
home forty as greate as Codd in two or three howers space. So
that now there is not so greate plenty of victualles in anie of the
forenamed kind yerely with smale paynes to be gotten in any
part of England amongst so few people. And whereas heretofore we were costrayned yerely to seeke after the Indians, and
intreate them to sell us Corne, which made them esteeme very
basely of us: now the case is altered, they sue to us, come to
our Townes, sell the skins from their shouldiers which are their
best garmentes to buy corne: yea som of their petty Kinges
have borrowed this last yere, 4. or 500, bushelles of wheate, for
payment whereof this harvest, they have mortgaged their wholl
Countries, som of them not much less in quantytie then a Sheir
in England. By this meanes plenty and prosperitie dwelleth
amongst them, and the feare and danger of famyne is cleane
taken awaie, wherewith the Accion hath a long tyme suffered
injurious defamacions.

Now that your Honor maie with the more ease understand
in what Condycion the Colony standeth, I have breiflie sett
downe the manner of all mens severall ymploymentes, the
nomber of them, and the severall places of their abode: which
places or seates are all our owne ground, not so much by conquest, which the Indyans hold a just & lawfull title but purchased of them freely, and they verie willingly selling it.

The places which are now possessed and inhabited are sixe.
1. Henrico and the lymittes
2. Bermuda Nether ⎫ Hundreds ⎫ Members belonging to
3. West and Sherley ⎭   ⎬ the Bermuda towne: a
4. James Towne.   ⎪ place so called there, by
5. Kequoughtan.   ⎪ reason of the strength,
6. Dales Gifte.   ⎪ of the scytuation, were
                            ⎭ it indifferently fortified.

The generall and mayne Bodie of the Planters are divided into

Officers.

Laborers.

Farmors.

The Officers have the chardge & care aswell over the Farmors as Laborers generally that they watch and ward for their preservations: and that both the one and the others labors and busynes maie be dailie followed, to the performance of those ymploymentes which from the one are requyred, and the other by Covenaunte are bound unto. These Officers are tied to mayntayne themselves and famylies with food and rayment by their owne and their servauntes industry.

The Laborers are of twoe sortes. Some ymployed onlie in the generall workes, who are fedd and clothed out of the stoore: others especyally Artyficers, as Smithes, Carpenters, Shoemakers, Tailors, Tanners &c doe worke in their professions for the Colony, and mayntayne themselves with food and apparrell, having tyme lymytted them to till and manure their ground.

The Farmors live at most ease, yet by their good indeavors bring yerely much plenty to the Plantation. They are bound by Covenaunte for themselves and servauntes to mayntayne his Majesties right and title in that Kingdom agaynst all forraigne and domestick enemyes. To watch and ward in the Townes where they are resident. To doe 31. daies service for the Colony, when they shalbe called thereunto, yet not at all tymes, but when their owne busynes can best spare them. To mayntayne themselves and famylies with food and rayment. And every Farmor to paie yerely into the Magazin for himself and every manservaunt two barrelles and a half apeece of their best Indian wheate, which amounteth to twelve bushelles and a half of Englishe measure. Thus breifly have I sett downe everie mans particuler ymployment, and manner of lyving. Albeit least the People (who genrally are bent to covet after gayne, especially having tasted of the sweetes of their labors) should spend too much of their tyme and labor in planting Tobacco, knowen to them to be verie vendible in England, and so neglect their tillage of Corne and fall into want thereof. It is provided for by the providence and care of Sir Thomas Dale, That no Farmor nor other who must mayntayne themselves, shall plant anie Tobacco, unles he shall yerely manure, sett and mayntayne for himself and every manservaunt, twoe acres of ground with Corne: which doing they may plant as much Tobacco as they will, elles all their Tobacco shalbe forfeyte to the Colony. By which meanes the Magazin shalbe sure yerely to receyve their Rent of Corne, to mayntayne those who are fedd thereout, being but a few, and many others if need be, They themselves wilbe well stored to keepe their famylies with overplus: and reape Tobacco enough to buy clothes, and such necessaries as are needfull for themselves and household. For an easy Laborer will keepe and tend two acres of corne; and cure good stoore of Tobacco, being yet the Principall commodytie the Colony for the present yeildeth. For which as for other comodyties the Councell and Company for Virginia have allready sent a Shipp furnished with all manner of clothing, household stuff and such necessaries to establishe a Magazin there: which the people shall buy at easy rates for their Commodyties, they selling them at such prizes, that the Adventurers maie be no loosers. This Magazin shalbe yerely supplied to furnish them, if they will indeavor by their labors to mayntayne it: which wilbe much beneficiall to the Planters, and Adventurers, by interchanging their Commodyties: and will add much incorragement to them and others to persever and follow the Accion, with a constant resolution to uphold the same.

The people which inhabite the sayd 6. severall places are disposed as followeth.

At Henrico and in the precinctes (which is seated on the No: side the ryver 90 odd myles from the mouth thereof, and within 15. or 16. myles of the Falles or head of the ryver, being our furthest habitacion into the Land) are 38. men and boyes, whereof 22. are Farmors, the rest Officers and others, all which mayntayne themselves with food and apparrell. Of this Towne Captaine Smalley hath the commaund, in the absence of Captaine James Davis. Mr William Wickham Mynister there, who in his lyfe and doctrine give good examples, and godlie instructions to the people.

At Bermuda Nether Hundred (seated on the south side the ryver, crossing it and going by land five miles lower then Henrico, by water 10.) are 119. Which seate conteyneth a good circuit of ground the ryver wynding round, so that a pale runnyng cross a neck of land, from one part of the ryver to the other, maketh it (as it were) an Isleland. The houses and dwellinges of the people are sett round about by the ryver, and all along the pale so farr distant one from the other, that upon anie All-arme they can second and succor one the other. These people are injoyned by a Charter (being incorporated to the Bermuda towne, which is made a Corporation) to effect and performe such duties and services, whereunto they are bound for a certeyne tyme, before they have their freedom. This Corporation admytt no Farmors, unles they procure from the Governor four of the Colonies men to be their servauntes, for whom (being no Members of the Corporation) they paie Rent Corne as other Farmors. Of this kind there are about 17. Others also (comprehended in the said nomber of 119) there are resident, who labor generally for the Colony, amongst whom, some make pitch and Tarr, Pott-ashes, Charkcoale, and other workes, and are mayntayned by the Magazin, but are not of the Corporation. At this place for the most part liveth Captaine Yeardley Deputy Marshall, and Deputy Governor. Mr Allexander Whitaker (sonn to that reverend and famous Divine Doctor Whitaker) a good Divine hath the mynisteriall chardge there.

At West and Sherley Hundred (seated on the North side the ryver lower then the Bermuda 3. or 4 myles) there are 25. commaunded by Captaine Maddeson who are ymployed only in planting and curing Tobacco, with the profitt thereof to cloth themselves, and all those who labor about the generall Busynes.

At James Towne (seated on the North side the ryver, from the West and Sherley Hundred lower downe about 37. myles) are 50. under the commaund of Leiftenaunte Sharpe, in the absence of Captaine Francis West Esquire, Brother to the right Honorable the Lord Lawarre, whereof 32. are Farmors. All these mayntayne themselves with food and rayment. Mr Richard Buck Mynister there a verie good Preacher.

At Kequoughtan (being not farr from the mouth of the ryver, 37 miles below James Towne on the same side) are 20. whereof

11. are Farmors. All these also mayntayne themselves as the former. Captaine George Webb Commander. Mr William Mays Mynister there.

At Dales Gifte (lieng upon the sea neere unto Cape Charles, about 30. myles from Kequoughtan) are 17. under the commaund of one Leiftenaunte Cradock: all these are fedd and mayntayned by the Colony. Their labor is to make salte; and to catch fishe at the 2. seasons aforemencioned.

So the nomber of Officers and Laborers are .205. The Farmors .81. besides 65 woemen and chilldren in every place some, which in all amounteth to 351. persons: a smale nomber to advaunce so greate a Worke.

These severall places are not thus weakely mannd, as capable of no greater nomber for they will mayntayne many 100:s more: but because no one can be forsaken without loss and detryment to all. If then so few people thus united, ordered and governed doe live so happilie: every one partaking of the others Labors: can keepe in possession so much ground as will feed a farr greater nomber, in the same or better condycion. And seeng to too many poore Farmors in England worke all the yere, rysing early, and going to bedd late, live penuriousely, and much adoe to paie their Land-Lordes Rent, besides a daily karking and care to feed themselves and families: what happynes might they injoy in Virginia, were men sensible of these thinges? where they maie have ground for nothing more then they can manure: reape more fruites and profittes with half the labor: void of many cares and vexations, and for their Rent a matter of smale or no moment, I leave to your mature judgement and consideracion: nothing doubting but He (who by his infinite goodnes, with so smale meanes, hath settled these poore and weake begynnynges so happilie) will animate, stirr up and incourrage many others cheerefully to undertake this Worke: and will assuredly add a daily strength, to uphold and mayntayne what he hath allready begunn.

Seeng then this languishing Action is now brought to this forwardnes: no person but is provided for, either by his owne or others labors to subsist themselves for food: and be able to rayse commodyties for clothing and other necessaries. Envy it self poysoned with venom of Aspes cannot wound yt.

Now to draw a Conclusion of this my poore Oblation, I

would crave your Honorable patience a little longer, and that yow would turne your hart to a more heavenly meditacion, wherein much joy and comfort is to be reaped and found of all such, who shall truly, sinceerely and unfaynedlie seeke to advaunce the Honor of God, and to propagate his Gospell. There is no smale hope by piety, clemency, courtysie and civill demeanor (by which meanes som are wonn to us already) to convert and bring to the knowledge and true worshipp of Jesus Christ 1000:s of poore, wretched and mysbeleiving people: on whose faces a good Christian cannot looke, without sorrow, pittie and commyseracion; seeng they beare the Image of our heavenly Creator, & wee and they come from one and the same moulde: especially wee knowyng, that they meerly through ingorance of God and Christ, doe runn headlong, yea with joy into distruccion and perpetuall damnation. For which Knowledge we are the more bound and indebted to Allmighty God (for what were we before the Gospell of Christ shined amongst us?) and cannot better express our Duties and thankfullnes for so greate mercies; then by using such meanes to them, as it pleased him to lend unto others, to bring our forefathers and us into the waies of truth. It is much to be mourned and lamented, how lightly the workes of God are now-adayes generally regarded, and less sought after: but the workes of the World as though they were eternall hungred for and thirsted after with unsatiable greedines. But should we well consider, examyne and search into ourselves what we were and now are: there can be no hart (if not hardned as the nether Millstone) but would even breake itself too peices, and distribute to many poore soules som part thereof to purge them from their lees of synn, and to settle them in the right pathes of holynes and righteousnes to serve the King of heaven. By which meanes, and Godes holy assistance, no doubt they will sone be brought to abandon their old supersticions and idolatries, wherein they have bene nursed and traynned from their infancies, and our greatest Adversaires shall not taunt us with this reproach: Which of them have you Wonn to Christianity? What a Crowne of glory shalbe sett upon their heades, who shall faithfully labor herein, I leave to the injoying of them who shall indeavor unfaynedly to merit the same. Finally as Caleb and Josuah in the very heate of the grudgings, murmors and assemblies of the chilldren of Israell, stood stoutly for the Lordes Cause, commending the goodnes of the Land they discovered, to the faces of their Opposers, and the easines to obtayne it, even to the perill of their lives. So many right Honorable and worthy personages both here and in Virginia, amongst whom yourself not the least protector, (when generally the greatest part withdrew themselves, that this Action was allmost sunck downe in forgettfullnes) have mightyly upheld this Christian Cause, and God even our owne God did helpe them. For neither evill reports, nor slaunders, nor murmors, nor backslidinges of others, nor any disaster did once dismay or hinder them from upholding thereof, with their good reportes, incorragements and meanes yerely sent to the Planters to nourish life and being in this zealous Worke. I beseech God to rayse up many more such, so zealous for godes glory to forward the same. We have tasted of some fruites thereof. There are no great nor strong Castles, nor men lyke the Sonnes of Anack to hinder our quyete possession of that Land. Godes hand hath bene mighty in the preservation thereof hetherto. What need wee then to feare, but to goe up at once as a peculier people marked and chosen by the finger of God to possess it? for undoubtedly he is with us. And as to murmerors, slanderors, and backsliders, a due porcion for their reward shalbe given them: so the blessings of Caleb and Josuah shall fall upon all those, that constantly persever to the end. Thus craving your Honorable patience for my boldnes, beseechinge God to send you the fullnes of his Blessings in this world, and in the life to come I rest

> At your Honors service
> and command in all duty
> Jo: ROLF

The nomber of Neate Cattle Horses and Goates which were alive in Virginia at Sir Thomas Dale his departure thence.

Cowes		
Heifers	83.	
Cow calves		in all . . . . 144.
Steeres . . . . 41.		
Bulles . . . . 20.		

Memorandum] 20 of the Cowes were greate with calfe at his departure.

Horses . . . .   3. ⎤
Mares . . . .   3. ⎦ in all . . . . . .   6.

Goates ⎤
and   ⎬   male & female in all . . . .   216.
Kiddes ⎦

        ⎤ wilde ⎤
Hoggs ⎬ and   ⎬   not to be nombered.
        ⎦ tame ⎦

Powltry great plenty . . . .

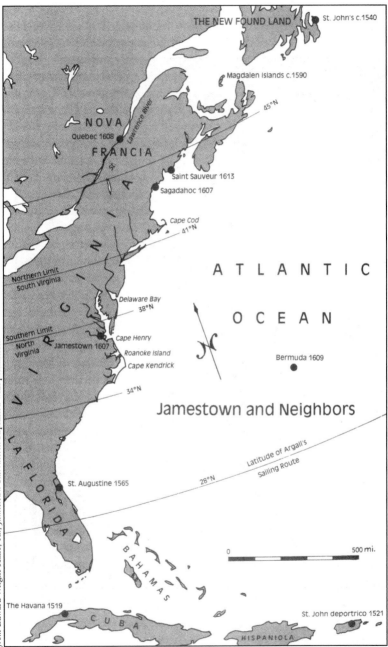

THE NEW FOUND LAND

St. John's c.1540

Magdalen Islands c.1590

45°N

NOVA

Quebec 1608

FRANCIA

Saint Sauveur 1613

Sagadahoc 1607

V

Cape Cod
41°N

I

R

ATLANTIC

Northern Limit
South Virginia

G

OCEAN

Delaware Bay
38°N

I

Southern Limit
North Virginia

N

Jamestown 1607

Cape Henry

Roanoke Island

Bermuda 1609

I

Cape Kendrick

A

34°N

Jamestown and Neighbors

LA FLORIDA

Latitude of Argall's
Sailing Route

St. Augustine 1565

28°N

0   500 mi.

BAHAMAS

The Havana 1519

St. John deportrico 1521

CUBA

HISPANIOLA

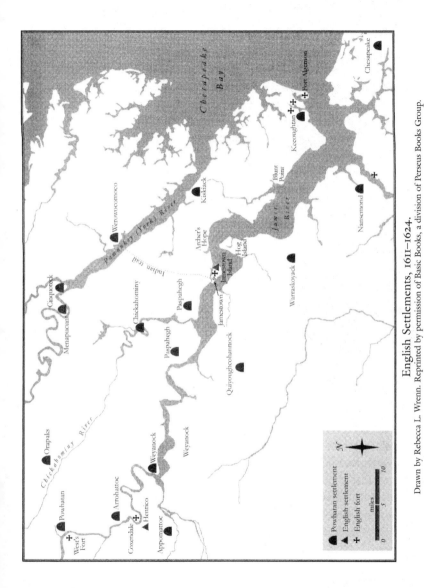

English Settlements, 1611–1624.

Drawn by Rebecca L. Wrenn. Reprinted by permission of Basic Books, a division of Perseus Books Group.

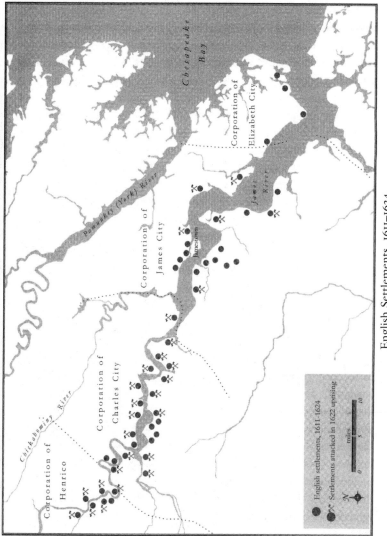

English Settlements, 1611–1624.

Drawn by Rebecca L. Wrenn. Reprinted by permission of Basic Books, a division of Perseus Books Group.

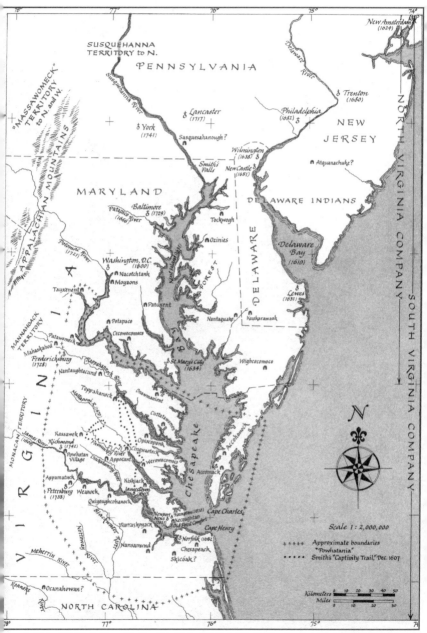

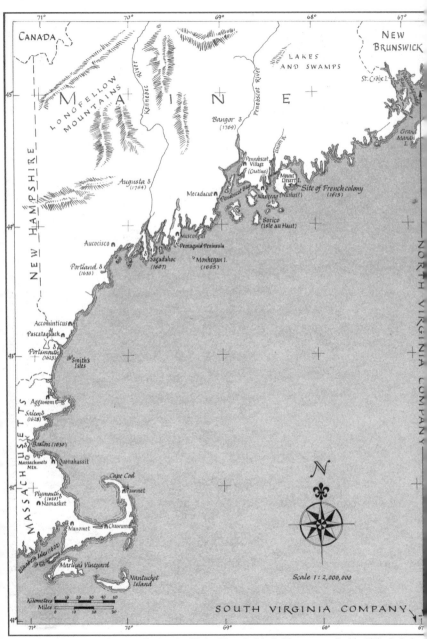

Drawn by Richard J. Stinely. From *The Complete Works of Captain John Smith, 1580–1631*, edited by Philip L. Barbou with a foreword by Thad W. Tate. Published for the Omohundro Institute of Early American History and Culture Copyright © 1986 by the University of North Carolina Press. Used by permission of the publisher.

Chronology

1580   John Smith is baptized January 9 at St. Helen's Church, Willoughby, Lincolnshire, the first child of George Smith and Alice Rickard Smith. Father's family is from Cuerdley, Lancashire, near Liverpool; mother's family is from Great Heck in Yorkshire. Father is a tenant farmer on the estate of Lord Willoughby de Eresby and also owns property in Lough and farmland at Great Carlton, two nearby towns in Lincolnshire.

1581   Brother Francis is baptized on November 6.

1583   Sir Humphrey Gilbert, half-brother of Walter Ralegh, is lost at sea while returning from an expedition to Newfoundland.

1584   Ralegh receives the royal patent, previously held by Gilbert, for the exploration and settlement of North America. He sends two ships, commanded by Philip Amadas and Arthur Barlowe, on an expedition across the Atlantic. They explore the Outer Banks of North Carolina in July and August before returning to England.

1585   Ralegh sends seven ships and about 600 men under the command of Sir Richard Grenville to establish a colony on the Outer Banks. Grenville builds a fort on Roanoke Island and leaves behind a garrison of 100 men under the command of Ralph Lane before sailing for England in late summer. Lane sends a scouting expedition northward along the coast.

           War begins between England and Spain as an English army under the command of the Earl of Leicester is sent to the Netherlands to fight with the Dutch against the Spanish. In September Sir Francis Drake sails with a large fleet to attack Spanish possessions in the Caribbean.

1586   Scouting expedition sent by Lane returns to Roanoke in late winter after exploring Chesapeake Bay. Lane leads expeditions up the Chowan and Roanoke rivers and hears stories of "Chaunis Temoatan," a distant region where copper, and possibly gold, is abundant and where a passage to the South Sea (Pacific Ocean) may be found. Drake anchors off the Outer Banks in June. Hostilities with Indians and a lack of supplies force Lane to abandon Roanoke, and the colonists return to England with Drake's fleet. An expedition led by Grenville reaches the Outer Banks in the summer and leaves 15 men at Roanoke before returning to England.

Smith's sister Alice is baptized on July 16; her twin, Richard, dies ten days after birth.

1587   Smith begins attending Queen Elizabeth's Grammar School in Alford, two miles from Willoughby.

John White leads attempt to found a colony on the southern shore of Chesapeake Bay. Expedition stops at the Outer Banks and finds the fort at Roanoke abandoned. Simon Fernandes, the expedition pilot, refuses to sail farther northward, and the colonists land on Roanoke Island. White sails for England in late summer to obtain supplies and recruit more settlers, leaving behind 114 men, women, and children.

1588   White makes unsuccessful attempt to return to Roanoke. The Spanish Armada is defeated in the Channel by the English, but continuing naval war prevents White from mounting another relief expedition. Thomas Hariot publishes *A Briefe and True Report of the New Found Land of Virginia*.

1589   Richard Hakluyt publishes *The Principal Navigations, Voyages, Traffiques and Discoveries of the English Nation*.

1590   White returns to Roanoke with two English privateers and finds the settlement abandoned.

1592   Smith is sent to King Edward VI's Grammar School in Louth, 12 miles from Willoughby.

1595   Smith is apprenticed to Thomas Sendall, a wealthy merchant in King's Lynn, a port in Norfolk.

1596–98 Smith's father dies in April 1596. Mother marries Martin Johnson sometime before February 1597. Smith ends his apprenticeship, then joins company of soldiers commanded by Captain Joseph Duxbury fighting the Spanish in the Low Countries.

1599–1600 Smith returns to England, then accompanies Peregrine Bertie, a son of Lord Willoughby, on a tour of France.

Leaves Bertie and sails for Scotland from Holland. After being shipwrecked on the island of Lindisfarne off the coast of Northumberland, Smith visits Edinburgh and unsuccessfully attempts to gain an audience with James VI. Returns to Willoughby and secludes himself in the countryside, studying Machiavelli's *The Art of War* and writings of Marcus Aurelius. Practices horsemanship with Theodore Paleologue, the Greek-Italian riding master of Henry Clinton, earl of Lincoln. Decides to join the Hapsburg armies fighting the Ottoman Empire in southeastern Europe. Travels to the south of France, then sails on a French ship through the eastern Mediterranean. After his ship captures a Venetian merchant vessel in the Adriatic, Smith uses his share of the prize to travel through Italy.

1601   Spends Easter in Rome. Continues travels in Italy, then goes to Graz, Austria, where he enlists in a Hungarian regiment commanded by Henry Volda. Sees action against the Turks at Lendava, Slovenia, and in Hungary at the siege of Székesfehérvár ("Alba Regalis") and in battle near Adony. Promoted to captain of cavalry.

1602   In February his regiment joins the army of Zsigmond Báthory, prince of Transylvania, and begins fighting the Hadjus, mercenaries dismissed from the Hapsburg army who are ravaging the countryside. While besieging a city in Transylvania, Smith kills three Turkish champions in individual duels (many of the Hadjus are of Turkish background). After the campaign against the mercenaries ends, Smith's regiment rejoins the imperial Hapsburg army and marches through the Transylvanian Alps into Walachia, a tributary of the Ottoman Empire. Smith is wounded during a battle at the Turnu Roşu (Red Tower) Pass on November 18 and is captured by battlefield looters.

1603   Smith is taken to the slave market at Axiopolis (Cernavodă, Romania) on the Danube River and is sold to a Turkish trader, who sends him to Constantinople. Becomes the slave of a young woman, who sends him to her brother, an Ottoman pasha in the Tartar lands on the eastern coast of the Black Sea. Travels to Varna, then sails across the Black Sea and through the Sea of Azov to what is now southern Russia. Treated harshly by the pasha, Smith kills him and escapes on horseback to a Russian garrison on the Don

River. Travels through Russia (Muscovy), Ukraine (then part of the Polish-Lithuanian Commonwealth), Poland, Transylvania, and Hungary before reaching Prague late in the year. Continues on to Leipzig, where Zsigmond Báthory grants him 1,500 ducats in gold (about £500) and the right to a coat of arms displaying three Turkish heads.

Elizabeth I dies March 24 and is succeeded by James I (James VI of Scotland). Walter Ralegh is convicted of treason and imprisoned in the Tower of London (he is executed in 1618).

1604   Smith travels through Germany, France, and Spain. He joins the crew of a French privateer, visits Morocco, and survives a battle with two Spanish warships that leaves his ship badly damaged before returning to England late in the year.

England and Spain conclude a peace treaty in August, ending war that began in 1585.

1605   Smith considers joining an expedition to bring supplies to the English colony in Guiana. Meets Bartholomew Gosnold, who had led a successful expedition to New England in 1602. Gosnold and his cousin, Edward Maria Wingfield, begin promoting a new plan for founding a colony in Virginia.

The French establish a settlement at Port Royal, Nova Scotia.

1606   Royal patent issued on April 10 grants North American settlement rights to the London Company, formed by merchants and investors in London, and the Plymouth Company, formed by merchants and investors from Plymouth, Bristol, Exeter, and other West Country ports. The London Company is granted the right to establish colonies between latitudes 34° and 41° North (from Cape Fear, North Carolina, to present-day New York City), while the Plymouth Colony is granted rights between latitudes 38° and 45° North (from Chesapeake Bay to present-day Bangor, Maine). Both companies are to be governed by a council in London appointed by the king.

In August an expedition sent by the Plymouth group to explore the coast of Maine is captured by the Spanish off Puerto Rico. The London Company issues detailed instructions for the establishment of its colony. On December 20, the *Susan Constant*, *Godspeed*, and *Discovery* leave Blackwall Docks in London with 144 colonists and mariners on board. Smith sails on board the *Susan Constant* along with Wingfield and Captain Christopher Newport, the commander of the fleet.

1607   The fleet spends several weeks off the English coast waiting for favorable winds, then begins crossing the Atlantic. Smith is arrested in mid-February and accused of plotting to murder the leaders of the expedition and "make himself king." In late March the fleet reaches the West Indies and stops to take on water and provisions. A gallows is built on Nevis and Smith is almost hanged, but is then reprieved. The expedition enters Chesapeake Bay on April 26 and sends a party onshore, where they fight a skirmish with a group of Indians. Newport opens sealed orders from the London Company appointing a resident council to govern the colony; its members are Newport, Wingfield, Gosnold, Smith, John Ratcliffe, John Martin, and George Kendall. Wingfield is elected president of the council, while Smith is released from arrest but is not allowed to take his seat. The expedition spends the next three weeks exploring the James River, and encounters Nansemonds, Kecoughtans, Paspaheghs, Quiyoughcohannocks, Appomattocs, and other Indian groups.

On May 13 Wingfield selects Jamestown Island, which was part of the Paspahegh hunting grounds, as the site of the English settlement, and the expedition begins unloading the ships the next day. Newport leads a party of men, including Smith, up the James River on May 21 in an attempt to find a passage into the interior. They reach the falls of the James (near present-day Richmond) on May 23 and meet Parahunt, whom they mistake for Wahunsonacock, the paramount chief of the Powhatans. (Wahunsonacock became known to the English as "Powhatan," after the village of his birth, located near the falls of the James River. By 1607 he ruled, or had influence over, about 30 Algonquin-speaking groups, living in coastal Virginia between the James and Potomac rivers, who have become collectively known as the "Powhatans.") Newport erects a cross and claims all the lands from Cape Henry to the falls for James I. On their return downriver the English feast with the Arrohattocs, visit Opossunoquonuske, the female chief of the Appomattocs, and meet with a leader of the Pamunkeys, possibly Opechancanough, a

brother of Wahunsonacock. An attack on Jamestown on
May 26 by about 200 warriors from several groups kills
two settlers and wounds ten before being repulsed by the
ships' cannons. Newport's expedition returns on May 27
and the colonists begin building a triangular palisaded
fort with cannons mounted in three bulwarks. Sporadic
attacks by Indians continue. Newport sails for England on
June 22 with the *Susan Constant* and *Godspeed*, leaving
about 100 settlers at Jamestown.

An expedition sent by the Plymouth Company reaches
the coast of Maine in early July, and in August a colony
of 65 settlers is founded at the mouth of the Kennebec
River. (Colony is abandoned in September 1608.)

Between July and September typhoid, dysentery, and
other diseases kill almost half of the Jamestown colonists,
including Bartholomew Gosnold on August 22. George
Kendall is removed from the council in late August and
on September 10 Wingfield is deposed as president and
replaced by John Ratcliffe. As food supplies dwindle,
Smith begins trading with Indians for provisions, sometimes forcing them to make exchanges. Kendall is shot on
orders of the council for fomenting rebellion.

In December Smith travels up the Chickahominy River
and encounters a large Pamunkey hunting party led by
Opechancanough. Smith is captured and his two companions are killed. After being marched back and forth
between the Chickahominy and Rappahannock rivers and
witnessing a divination ritual conducted by Pamunkey
priests, he is taken to Werowocomoco, the paramount
chief's principal residence, where he questioned by Wahunsonacock. Smith learns of the possible survival of
some of the Roanoke colonists and is told of a great sea
beyond the mountains in the interior. Wahunsonacock
offers to let the colonists live in peace in the territory of
Capahowasicke, downriver from Werowocomoco, in return for copper, iron goods, and their acceptance of
Powhatan supremacy. Smith would later write that he was
then saved from execution by the intervention of Pocahontas, Wahunsonacock's young daughter, although it is
more likely that he underwent a Powhatan adoption ritual in which he was symbolically killed and reborn. Two
days later Smith meets with Wahunsonacock, who adopts
him as a son, gives him the name Nantaquoud, and makes

him a Powhatan chief, then instructs him to supply the Powhatans with cannon and a grindstone in return for food.

1608   Smith is released on January 1 and returns to Jamestown as its leaders are planning to abandon the colony. Accused of responsibility for the death of the two companions killed during his capture, Smith is tried and sentenced to death. He is saved by the arrival on January 2 of Newport and about 80 settlers on the *John and Francis* (the "first supply"). An accidental fire on January 7 destroys the houses at the fort, leaving the settlers to endure the cold until new quarters can be built. Two colonists are sent to the south with the Paspahegh chief, Wowinchopunck, to look for surviving Roanoke colonists.

In February, Newport, Smith, and an escort of about 30 men visit Werowocomoco, where they meet with Wahunsonacock, trade copper pots for corn, and gather information about possible mines in the interior. The trading party returns to Jamestown in March as the colonists discover what they incorrectly believe to be gold on the banks of the James River. Newport sails for England on April 10, carrying samples of the supposed gold and accompanied by Namontack, a Powhatan sent by Wahunsonacock to report on England. Smith explores the Nansemond River and is impressed by the fertility of the region.

Captain Francis Nelson of the *Phoenix* arrives on April 20, bringing provisions and two dozen settlers. When Nelson sails in early June, Smith sends to England a long letter describing events from December 1606 to May 1608 and a sketch map of the region from North Carolina to the Potomac River that includes information about the Roanoke colonists and the possible location of the South Sea. (The letter is published in London as *A True Relation*; the map later becomes known as the "Zúñiga map" after the Spanish ambassador in London, Pedro de Zúñiga, who sent a copy to Philip III in September 1608.)

In early June, Smith and 14 men leave Jamestown in an open barge to search for gold and a river passage to the South Sea. During a voyage of seven weeks they explore the eastern and western shores of Chesapeake Bay and sail up the Potomac River. During their return voyage Smith is badly hurt by a stingray near the mouth of the Rappahannock River. The exploring party returns to Jamestown on July 21.

Smith and 12 men set out on a second expedition on July 24 and sail to the head of Chesapeake Bay, where they encounter a large group of Massawomecks, an Iroquoian-speaking people (the Powhatans are Algonquian speakers). After trading with the warriors, they travel to a Tockwough town on the eastern shore, where they meet a large group of Susquehannocks, another Iroquoian people. Smith concludes from his conversations with the Susquehannocks that reports of a sea beyond the mountains probably refer to the Great Lakes and not the Pacific Ocean. The expedition explores the lower reaches of the Susquehanna River, then surveys the Patuxent, Rappahannock, Piankatank, and Nansemond rivers and skirmishes with several Indian groups before returning to Jamestown on September 7.

Smith assumes the presidency of the council on September 10, and organizes the enlargement of the fort and the regular drilling of the colonists. In early October the "second supply" arrives at Jamestown when Newport returns with Namontack and 70 settlers, including eight German and Polish craftsmen and two women. Instructions from the London Company direct Newport and the council to continue the search for gold mines, a passage to the South Sea, and survivors of the Roanoke colony, and to crown Wahunsonacock as a king under the authority of James I. Smith and Newport travel to Werowocomoco to present Wahunsonacock with gifts and conduct the coronation ceremony. Newport then leads an expedition of 120 men about 40 miles past the falls of the James into the lands of the Monacans, a Siouan-speaking people who are bitter enemies of the Powhatans. Smith remains at Jamestown to load Newport's ship with timber, glass, soap, potashes, pitch, tar, and other products. He writes a letter to the Company criticizing their plans for the colony, and encloses a manuscript describing the surrounding country and its potential for settlement.

Newport sails for England in early December with Namontack and Machumps, another Powhatan. With the weather worsening and food supplies running low, Smith seeks to trade with local Indians and discovers that Wahunsonacock has ordered an embargo. On his way to Werowocomoco to confront Wahunsonacock, Smith obtains the services of Warrascoyack guides and sends them with Michael Sicklemore to the Chowan River to search for news of the Roanoke colonists.

1609   Wahunsonacock refuses to provide the settlers with corn unless he receives swords and guns in return. He tells Smith that he believes the English have come to Virginia not to trade, but to invade and possess the Powhatan lands. After two days of tense discussions, Wahunsonacock leaves and warriors surround Smith and his men, but the English brandish their weapons and are able to leave Werowocomoco. Smith then goes upriver to negotiate with Opechancanough; when Pamunkey warriors surround him, Smith grabs Opechancanough by his scalp lock and holds him hostage until the Indians fill the English boats with corn. After gathering more corn along the York River, Smith and his party return to Jamestown in mid-February. When Sicklemore finds no news of the lost colonists, Smith sends Anas Todkill and Nathaniel Powell to search for Roanoke survivors among the Mangoag Indians in the interior of North Carolina. Smith assembles the colonists at the fort and tells them that those who refuse to work will not receive food.

Nova Britannia, a promotional work written by Robert Johnson, deputy treasurer of the London Company, is published in England in February. During the spring Company leaders are told, possibly by Machumps, that the surviving Roanoke colonists were killed by Powhatan warriors about the time the first English settlers arrived in the James River in 1607. The Company decides to depose Wahunsonacock, destroy the Powhatan priesthood, and begin the conversion of the Indians to Christianity. In May the Company sends Captain Samuel Argall in the Mary and John to find a shorter route to Chesapeake Bay that avoids the West Indies. A new charter, drafted by Sir Edwin Sandys, is granted to the London Virginia Company in late May, under which Sir Thomas Smythe, a powerful merchant, becomes treasurer (principal officer) of the Company. Sir Thomas West, Baron De La Warr, is appointed governor of the Jamestown colony, and Sir Thomas Gates is named to act as interim governor until De La Warr's arrival. In confidential instructions the Company orders Gates to continue the search for gold mines and a passage to the South Sea, employ settlers in the production of goods needed in England, make alliances with Indians hostile to the Powhatans, and eventually to overthrow Wahunsonacock. A fleet of eight ships carrying Gates and about 500 colonists leaves Plymouth in June.

A shortage of provisions at Jamestown causes Smith to disperse the colonists, sending some downriver to fish and gather oysters and others upriver to live off the land at the falls. Argall reaches Virginia on July 13 and prevents a small Spanish ship from entering the James River the following day. A storm scatters Gates's fleet on July 24, and the *Sea Venture* is shipwrecked four days later, stranding Gates, Newport, and Sir George Somers in Bermuda. Six ships from the fleet reach Jamestown in August and report the disappearance of the *Sea Venture*.

In Gates's absence Smith continues to serve as president as about 400 colonists are billeted in and around the Jamestown fort. Smith sends John Martin, George Percy, and about 60 men downriver to found a settlement on the Nansemond and Francis West and 120 men upriver to establish a settlement at the falls. In September Smith is badly burned while returning from the falls when his powder bag catches fire. He is removed from office by Martin, Ratcliffe, and Gabriel Archer, who choose Percy as his successor, place him under guard on a ship, and draw up a list of his alleged abuses in office to discredit him with the Company. Smith sails for England in early October. The settlements on the Nansemond and at the falls are abandoned as dozens of colonists, including Michael Sicklemore, are killed in fighting with the Indians. Ratcliffe is captured and killed by the Powhatans while attempting to trade for food. Smith arrives in London in late November, several weeks after Samuel Argall had brought news of the disappearance of the *Sea Venture*. In December the Company publishes *A True and Sincere Declaration* in an effort to reassure investors and publicize the planned departure of De La Warr.

1610   Through the winter and spring Indian warriors besiege Jamestown and cut off food supplies. Hundreds of colonists are killed in Indian attacks or die from hunger and disease during the "starving time," and some settlers resort to cannibalism. In late May Gates, Newport,

Somers, and about 140 other survivors arrive in two small boats built on Bermuda after the wreck of the *Sea Venture*. They find about 60 settlers still alive at the fort. Gates decides to abandon Jamestown, but as the surviving colonists sail down the James River they meet three ships carrying De La Warr and 150 new settlers. De La Warr assumes command on June 10 and reorganizes the colony along military lines, implementing a strict code of discipline that becomes known as the "Lawes Divine, Morall, and Martiall." After repairing the fort, the English launch offensives during the summer against the Kecoughtans, Paspaheghs, Chickahominies, and Warraskoyacks. De La Warr establishes two small forts, Charles and Henry, at the entrance to the Hampton River, and reinforces Fort Algernon at Point Comfort. Gates and Newport return to London in September. The Company publishes *A True Declaration of the Estate of the Colony in Virginia* later in the year to celebrate the survival of Gates and the colony.

1611   De La Warr sails for England in late March to recover his health. Sir Thomas Dale arrives in May with 300 settlers and takes command of the colony. In June a Spanish ship briefly anchors off Point Comfort, hastening plans to move the main seat of the colony farther up the James River. Gates arrives in August with 300 settlers. Dale and 350 men establish Henrico, a fortified settlement near the falls, and use it as a base for raids against the Appomattocs.

    In England Smith works with the engraver William Hole on a map of Virginia, and with Richard Pots, the former clerk of the council in Virginia, on compiling a history of the colony.

1612   In March the London Company secures a new charter that extends its jurisdiction to Bermuda. John Rolfe begins experimenting with the cultivation of tobacco on his plantation along the James River, using seeds from Trinidad and Venezuela. *A Map of Virginia with a Description of the Countrey*, written by Smith and featuring Hole's map, and *The Proceedings of the English Colonie in Virginia*, a collection of accounts by Pots and several other colonists, are published together in Oxford by Joseph Barnes.

1613   While trading along the Potomac River Captain Samuel

Argall abducts Pocahontas, who had been visiting with the Patawomecks, and returns with her to Jamestown. The English begin negotiations with Wahunsonacock to exchange her for corn and weapons taken from the colonists. Dale sends Argall to Maine and Nova Scotia, where he destroys the small French settlements at Mount Desert Island, St. Croix, and Port Royal.

1614   Negotiations involving Dale, Opechancanough, and Wahunsonacock result in a truce between the English and the Powhatans. Pocahontas marries John Rolfe after converting to Christianity and taking the baptismal name Rebecca.

Unable to return to Jamestown because of his criticisms of the Company, Smith sails for "North Virginia" in March with two small ships to seek gold and copper and hunt whales. He arrives off Penobscot Bay, Maine, in late April and surveys the coast and rivers of Massachusetts and Maine while fishing and trading for furs. After returning to England in August Smith secures support from Sir Ferdinando Gorges and merchants of the Plymouth Company for colonizing the region Smith names "New England."

1615   Smith sails from Plymouth in March seeking to found a colony in Maine. After one of his ships is damaged in a storm, he returns to Plymouth and then sails again in June. On his second voyage Smith is captured by a French privateer and is unable to return to England until December.

1616   In the spring John Rolfe conducts a survey of the Virginia colony that records 351 men, women, and children living in six settlements (about 1,500 settlers were sent from England to Jamestown between 1609 and 1616). Smith seeks backing from London investors for his New England colonization plan and publishes *A Description of New England*, which includes a detailed map of the region, in June. Dale returns to England accompanied by Pocahontas, Rolfe, and their infant son, Thomas, as well as about 12 other Powhatans; George Yeardley assumes command of the colony. Smith writes a letter to Queen Anne, consort of James I, extolling Pocahontas's virtues, and visits her at her lodgings in Brentford, the first time they had

met since 1609. Pocahontas and the Powhatans are intro-
duced to London society while Rolfe markets his tobacco
to English merchants.

1617   Rolfe and Pocahontas are received by James I and Anne
at their Twelfth Night revels. Pocahantas dies at Gravesend in March, and their son remains in England while
Rolfe returns to Virginia. Smith attempts to sail to New
England with three ships but is prevented by contrary
winds from clearing the English coast. Argall returns to
Jamestown in May and succeeds Yeardley.

1618   Wahunsonacock dies and is formally succeeded as paramount chief by his brother Opitchapam, although
Opechancanough becomes the de facto leader of the
Powhatans. Under the leadership of Sir Edwin Sandys,
the Company reforms the laws, government, and land
policies of the colony in an effort to attract more settlers
and investors. The Virginia settlements are divided into
four boroughs, and a general assembly is created, consisting of an appointed council of state and an elected
house of burgesses. New settlers who paid their own passage would receive 50 acres of land, and another 50 acres
for each additional person they paid to have transported.
Large numbers of poor people, including destitute children, are shipped to the colony to work as indentured
servants on plantations owned by the Company and by
private landowners. (About 3,750 new settlers arrive between 1618 and 1621, although most of them die from
disease within a year of their arrival.) English settlements
spread rapidly along the James River as tobacco cultivation increases, forcing Indians off their lands.
        Smith sends a long letter about New England to Sir
Francis Bacon, the Lord Chancellor, in an unsuccessful
bid for his patronage.

1619   In April Sir Edwin Sandys succeeds Sir Thomas Smythe as
treasurer of the Company, and George Yeardley assumes
his position as the new governor of the colony. Yeardley
repeals the "Lawes Divine, Morall, and Martiall" and pre-
sides over the first meeting of the general assembly in late
July. The Company grants the Separatists of Leiden (the
Pilgrims) permission to settle in the northern part of its
Virginia claim. In August a Dutch privateer arrives at

Jamestown and sells 20 Angolans seized from a Portuguese slave ship into servitude. (It is not known whether the Africans became slaves or indentured servants.)

1620   The Pilgrims land on Cape Cod and decide to establish a colony at Plymouth, outside the London Virginia Company's northern boundary at 41° N. Smith publishes *New Englands Trials*.

1621   Smith unsuccessfully petitions the London Company to reward him for his services in Virginia. Sir Francis Wyatt succeeds Yeardley as governor of the Virginia colony.

1622   Hundreds of warriors sent by Opechancanough attack over two dozen English settlements and plantations on March 22 and kill more than 300 colonists. After news of the uprising reaches London in July, Smith offers his services as a military commander to the Company, which declines to employ him. Wyatt launches a series of raids against Indian villages. In the fall Smith publishes a revised edition of *New Englands Trials*.

1623   Hundreds of settlers die in Virginia from hunger and disease during the winter and spring. A royal commission is established in May to investigate the London Virginia Company and conditions in Virginia; it hears testimony from Smith and other critics of the Sandys regime. Hostilities between the English and Powhatans continue throughout the year.

1624   The London Company's charter is revoked on May 24 and jurisdiction over the Virginia colony reverts to the crown. In July the English defeat hundreds of Pamunkey warriors in a two-day battle and win a decisive victory over the Powhatans (sporadic hostilities continue until 1632). Smith publishes *The Generall Historie of Virginia, New-England, and the Summer Isles* during the summer. George Percy writes, but does not publish, "A Trewe Relacyon" as a rebuttal of Smith's version of events. The English establish their first colony in the West Indies on St. Christopher (St. Kitts).

1625   A muster conducted during the winter lists 1,218 men, women, and children living in the Virginia settlements. James I dies on March 27 and is succeeded by his son, Charles I. On May 13 the new king declares Virginia a royal colony.

1626   Smith publishes *An Accidence, or The Pathway to Experience*, a manual for seamen and privateers. (An "accidence" is a treatment of the rudiments or first principles of a subject.)

1627   The success of *An Accidence* leads Smith to publish a revised edition as *A Sea Grammar, With the plain Exposition of Smith's Accidence for young Seamen, enlarged*. An English settlement is founded on Barbados.

1628   An English colony is established on Nevis.

1629   The Massachusetts Bay Company is chartered in March. Encouraged by Sir Robert Bruce Cotton, a wealthy scholar and manuscript collector, Smith begins work on his autobiography.

1630   *The True Travels, Adventures, and Observations of Captaine John Smith* is published. English Puritans begin their migration to the Massachusetts Bay colony.

1631   Smith publishes *Advertisements for the unexperienced Planters of New England, or anywhere* in the spring. He dies in London on June 21, possibly at the home of Sir Samuel Saltonstall, and is buried in St. Sepulchres in the City of London.

Biographical Notes

Gabriel Archer (c. 1575–?1610) Born in Mountnessing, Essex. Educated at Cambridge, then studied law at Gray's Inn in London. Sailed with Bartholomew Gosnold to the coast of New England in 1602, and wrote "The Relations of Captain Gosnold's Voyage to the North part of Virginia," subsequently published by Samuel Purchas in *Hakluytus Posthumus, or Purchas his Pilgrimes* (1625). Sailed for Virginia in 1606 and was a member of the expedition's first landing at Cape Henry on April 26, 1607, where he was wounded by an arrow in an Indian attack. Proposed a location for settlement ("Archer's Hope"), but it lacked deep-water mooring sites and Jamestown was chosen instead. Joined expedition up the James River, May 21–June 21, 1607, and is probably the author of an account of the expedition, "A relatyon . . . written . . . by a gent. of ye Colony." Named a councilor after John Smith's capture by the Powhatans in December 1607, and during the winter tried to persuade the council to abandon the colony. Led calls for Smith's trial and execution after Smith's return to Jamestown in January 1608. Sailed for England on April 10, 1608. Returned to Jamestown on August 11, 1609, and again led the opposition to Smith. Wrote letter on August 31, 1609, to an unidentified correspondent that was later published in *Purchas his Pilgrimes* as "A Letter of M. Gabriel Archar." Died in the winter of 1609–10 during the "starving time."

Arthur Barlowe May have served with Walter Ralegh in Ireland in the early 1580s. Commanded a pinnace, possibly the *Dorothy*, on an exploratory voyage with Philip Amadas to the Outer Banks of North Carolina in 1584, and wrote "Discourse of the First Voyage," a highly favorable account of the region. May have been in command of a privateer in 1590.

Sir Thomas West, Baron De La Warr (July 9, 1577–June 7, 1618) Son of Thomas West, eleventh Baron De La Warr, and Ann, daughter of Sir Francis Knollys. Entered Queen's College, Oxford, in 1592. Traveled in Italy, 1595. Married Cecilia Shirley, the daughter of his godfather, Sir Thomas Shirley, in 1596. Served as Member of Parliament for Lymington in 1597. Fought in the Netherlands and in Ireland, 1598–99, under Robert Devereux, the second Earl of Essex. Knighted in 1599. Briefly imprisoned in 1601 after Essex's failed rebellion, but was exonerated. Succeeded father as twelfth Baron De La Warr and was admitted to the Privy Council in 1602. Became a member of the London Virginia Company in 1609, and the following year was appointed the first governor and captain-general of Virginia. Arrived in Virginia with three ships, 150 settlers, and supplies on June 8, 1610, intercepting the departing colonists who had decided to abandon Jamestown. Named a new council, consisting of Sir Thomas Gates (lieutenant governor), Sir George Somers, Christopher Newport, Sir Ferdinando Wainman (master of ordnance), William Strachey (secretary), and George Percy (captain of the fort). Ordered the construction of two small forts at the mouth of the Hampton River and established military standards of discipline at Jamestown that were codified in the "Lawes Divine, Morall and Martiall." Led colony during series of skirmishes with the Powhatans while suffering from deteriorating health. Sailed for England on March 28, 1611. At the request of the London Virginia Company, published *The Relation of the Right Honourable the Lord De-La-Warre* (1611), an account of his time in Virginia. Along with his wife, provided introductions to London society in June 1616 for John Rolfe and his wife, Rebecca (Pocahontas). Sailed for Virginia in May 1618 after receiving word of discord in the colony under the rule of his deputy, Samuel Argall. Died en route; his body may have been brought to Jamestown for burial. The Delaware River was named in his honor by Argall in 1610.

Ralph Hamor (1589–1626) Born in February 1589, the son of Ralph Hamor, the elder, a founding director of the East India Company. Sailed for Virginia aboard the *Sea Venture*, on June 2, 1609, and was shipwrecked off Bermuda on July 28. Left Bermuda in a pinnace built from salvaged material on May 10, 1610, and arrived in Virginia on May 21. Named to the Virginia Council in 1611 and served as its secretary. Began experimenting with the cultivation of tobacco around 1613. Sent by deputy governor Sir Thomas Dale as an emissary to the Powhatan leader Wahunsonacock in May 1614 in an unsuccessful attempt to negotiate the betrothal of Dale to Wahunsonacock's youngest daughter. Sailed for England with Samuel Argall in June 1614. Invested most of his inheritance in the London Virginia Company, eventually underwriting the transport of 16 colonists to Virginia, including his brother, Thomas Hamor, in 1615. Published *A True Discourse of the Present State of Virginia* (1615). Returned to Virginia in March 1617 as part of the first major infusion of new settlers in nearly six years, and again served on the Council. Fought during the Indian attack of March 22, 1622, and was placed in charge of the plantation at Martin's Hundred. Died in Virginia.

Thomas Hariot (1560–July 2, 1621) Born in the parish of St. Mary, Oxford. Educated at St. Mary Hall, Oxford, receiving a B.A. in 1580. Joined the household of Sir Walter Ralegh, offering instruction in astronomy, navigation, and mathematics to both Ralegh and his half-brother and fellow adventurer, Sir Humphrey Gilbert. Joined the expedition sent to the Outer Banks of North Carolina by Ralegh in 1585, becoming the first Englishman to undertake a systematic examination of the flora and fauna of North America. Published *A Briefe and True Report of the New Found Land of Virginia* (1588), which appeared in four languages within two years. Wrote a work on navigation, the "Arcticon," now lost. After Ralegh's fall from favor at the court of Elizabeth I, Hariot was sponsored by Henry Percy, ninth Earl of Northumberland, and resided at Syon House, Northumberland's estate near London. Studied optics, comets, and sunspots, which he discovered almost simultaneously with Galileo. Imprisoned for three weeks after the discovery of the Gunpowder Plot in 1605. Corresponded with Johannes Kepler regarding experiments with refraction of light, 1606–8. Wrote *Artes Analyticae Praxis*, an influential study of algebraic equations (published posthumously in 1631). Died in London.

Ralph Lane (c. 1530–1603) Born in Lympstone, in Devon, the second son of Sir Ralph Lane of Orlingbury and his wife, Maud, daughter of William, Lord Parr. Became an equerry in the service of Queen Elizabeth I in 1563. Served as sheriff of County Kerry in Ireland, 1583–85. Sailed to the Outer Banks of North Carolina in 1585 as an officer aboard the *Tiger* under the command of Sir Richard Grenville (a cousin of Sir Walter Ralegh). Became governor of the first settlement at Roanoke, commanding 107 men. Abandoned Roanoke and returned to England with Sir Francis Drake and all but three of the colonists in June 1586. Wrote "Discourse on the First Colony" and sent it to Ralegh; it was later published by Richard Hakluyt in *The Principal Navigations, Voyages, Traffiques and Discoveries of the English Nation* (1589). Served as governor of Guernsey and of the Isle of Wight in 1588 as part of the defense against the Spanish Armada, and as a colonel under Drake during an expedition to Spain and Portugal in 1589. Later served as a government paymaster in Ireland and was knighted in 1593. Severely wounded while fighting Irish rebels in 1594. Died in Ireland.

George Percy (September 4, 1580–1633) Born at Petworth House, in West Sussex, the eighth and youngest son of Henry Percy, eighth Earl of Northumberland. Educated at Eton College, 1591–93, and Gloucester Hall, Oxford, before being admitted to study law at the

Middle Temple in London in 1597. Traveled to the West Indies, 1602–3, Ireland, and the Netherlands. After his eldest brother, the ninth Earl of Northumberland, was imprisoned in the Tower of London in connection with the Gunpowder Plot of November 1605, Percy became involved in plans for colonizing Virginia. Sailed from England on December 20, 1606. Named president of the resident Virginia council on September 10, 1609, replacing John Smith, who returned to England. Endured the winter of 1609–10, a period of Indian attacks, internal conflict, and famine that became known as the "starving time." Served as acting governor between the departure of Baron De La Warr on March 28, 1611, and the arrival of deputy governor Thomas Dale on May 12, 1611. Sailed for England on April 22, 1612. Considered joining an expedition to the Amazon delta in 1615. Extracts from his Virginia diary, now lost, were published by Samuel Purchas in *Hakluytus Posthumus, or Purchas his Pilgrimes* (1625) as "Observations gathered out of a Discourse of the Plantation of the Southerne Colonie in Virginia." Wrote, but did not publish, "A Trewe Relacyon" in response to the publication in 1624 of John Smith's *Generall Historie*. Died in early 1633.

John Rolfe (1585–1622) Born in Heacham, Norfolk, the son of John Rolfe and his wife, Dorothea Mason, and baptized with his twin brother Eustacius, on May 6, 1585. Married his first wife in 1608. Sailed for Virginia aboard the *Sea Venture* on June 2, 1609, and was shipwrecked on Bermuda on July 28. A daughter, Bermuda, was born and died on the island. Sailed with his wife for Virginia in a pinnace built from salvaged material on May 10, 1610, and reached Virginia on May 21; his wife died shortly after their arrival. Established Varina, a plantation about 25 miles upriver from Jamestown, where he used seeds from Trinidad and Venezuela to create a stronger and sweeter strain of *Nicotiana tabacum* for the English market, 1611–13. (This strain of tobacco would become the mainstay of the colonial economy in Virginia.) Married Pocahontas (who took the name Rebecca), daughter of the Powhatan leader Wahunsonacock, at Jamestown on April 5, 1614; their son, Thomas, was born in 1615. Sailed with Rebecca and Thomas to England in 1616, where they attracted considerable attention. Shortly after the family left London for their return voyage, Rebecca died and was buried at Gravesend on March 21, 1617. Rolfe returned to Virginia, leaving Thomas behind in the care of his brother, Henry Rolfe. Named secretary and recorder of the colony, serving until 1619. Married Jane Pierce in 1619, who gave birth to a daughter in 1621. Appointed to the new Council of State established by the London Virginia Company in 1621. Died shortly before the Indian attack of March 22, 1622.

Henry Spelman (1595–March 23, 1623) Born in Norfolk, son of Erasmus Spelman, and a nephew of Sir Henry Spelman, treasurer of the Guiana Company, member of the Council of New England, and a well-known antiquary. Sailed for Virginia in 1609 and was sent by John Smith shortly after arriving to live with the Powhatans to learn their language. Returned in December 1610 to Jamestown, where he was recognized as a skilled interpreter and named a captain of the Virginia militia. Sailed for England on March 28, 1611. Wrote "Relation of Virginia, 1609" (first published in 1872). Returned to Virginia aboard the *Treasurer* in 1618. Tried by the House of Burgesses in 1619 for allegedly maligning Governor George Yeardley before the Powhatan leader Opechancanough and was punished with the loss of his militia commission. With the colony short of food, volunteered in 1623 to lead an expedition north to the Potomac River to barter with Indians, but was killed by Patawomecks near present-day Washington, D.C.

William Strachey (1572–June 1621) Born in Saffron Walden, Essex, the son of William Strachey. Educated at Emmanuel College, Cambridge, and studied law at Gray's Inn, London. Married Frances Forster, daughter of William Forster, lord of the manor at Chellows, Surrey, on June 9, 1595; their son William was baptized on March 30, 1596. Became a stockholder in the Blackfriars Theatre, where he met William Shakespeare and many of the players. Served in Constantinople as secretary to Thomas Glover, English ambassador to the Ottoman sultan and agent of the Levant Company, 1606–8. Purchased stock in the London Virginia Company and sailed for Virginia aboard the *Sea Venture* on June 2, 1609. Shipwrecked on Bermuda in a hurricane on July 28. Reached Virginia on May 21, 1610, having sailed from Bermuda in a pinnace constructed of salvage material. Named secretary of the colony. Wrote "A True Reportory of the wrack and redemption of Sir Thomas Gates, knight" shortly after his arrival and sent it to an unnamed "Excellent Lady" in England. (It is believed to have been one of the sources used by Shakespeare in writing *The Tempest*.) Returned to England in the early fall of 1611, where he published *For the Colony in Virginea Britannia: Lawes Divine, Morall and Martiall* (1612), the legal code first promulgated in Virginia in 1610. Compiled "Historie of Travell into Virginia Britannia," but was unsuccessful in arranging its publication (the work was first printed in 1849). Lived in poverty in London. Buried at Camberwell, Surrey, on June 21, 1621. (A signet ring bearing the Strachey family crest was unearthed at Jamestown in 1996.)

John White Voyaged with Martin Frobisher's expedition to Meta

Incognita (Baffin Island) in 1577, and was a member of the 1584 expedition to the Outer Banks of North Carolina led by Arthur Barlowe and Philip Amadas. Joined the 1585 expedition to North Carolina commanded by Sir Richard Grenville, and painted a series of watercolors of Indians and flora and fauna; the paintings served as the basis for engravings by Theodore de Bry that were published in 1590. Named governor of the planned colony on Chesapeake Bay in January 1587, he sailed from England on May 8 in command of three ships carrying 117 colonists and two returning Indians. Instead of reaching the Chesapeake, they landed on Roanoke Island, where his daughter, Elinor Dare, gave birth on August 18 to Virginia Dare, the first English child born in America. Departed for England on August 27, 1587, to obtain supplies for the colony, but was unable to return until August 18, 1590, when he found the settlement deserted. Moved to Newtown, Kilmore, in County Cork, Ireland, sometime after 1591. Wrote to Richard Hakluyt in 1593, enclosing his narrative of the 1590 voyage and expressing grief for the men and women of the lost colony of Roanoke.

Edward Maria Wingfield (c. 1550–?1619) Born at Stonely Priory, in Huntingdonshire, son of Thomas Maria Wingfield, the godson of Mary of France, youngest sister of Henry VIII. Studied law at the Inns of Chancery in London in 1576, then left after three years to serve as a soldier in Ireland and the Netherlands. Captured by the Spanish in 1588 along with Ferdinando Gorges and held at Lille until the following year, when he returned to England in a prisoner exchange. Became involved with Gorges, Bartholomew Gosnold, and Sir John Popham, the Lord Chief Justice, in efforts to secure a charter from James I to settle Virginia. Mortgaged his estate to raise capital for the venture. Named as one of eight patentees in the charter granted on April 10, 1606, along with Sir Thomas Gates, Sir George Somers, Richard Hakluyt, Thomas Hanham, Ralegh Gilbert, William Parker, and George Popham, and was the only patentee to sail for Virginia in December 1606. Became the first president of the resident Virginia council on April 26, 1607. Removed from office on September 10 after being accused of mismanagement, arbitrariness, and favoritism, and was briefly imprisoned. Sailed for England on April 10, 1608. Wrote "Discourse of Virginia" (first published in 1860). Died sometime after 1619.

Note on the Texts

This volume collects seven works by, or closely associated with, Captain John Smith, *A True Relation* (1608), *The Proceedings of the English Colonie in Virginia* (1612), *A Description of New England* (1616), *New Englands Trials* (1622), *The Generall Historie of Virginia, New-England, and the Summer Isles* (1624), *The True Travels* (1630), and *Advertisements for the Unexperienced Planters of New-England* (1631), as well as 16 additional narratives by 13 other writers describing the English exploration and settlement of North Carolina and Virginia between 1584 and 1616. The texts of the works by Smith are taken from *The Complete Works of Captain John Smith*, edited by Philip L. Barbour (3 volumes, Chapel Hill: The University of North Carolina Press, 1986), the most recent edition of his writings to appear. This edition, prepared with the assistance of the Institute of Early American History and Culture, prints the texts of Smith's works with very few alterations in spelling and punctuation. (An earlier edition, *Capt. John Smith, President of Virginia, and Admiral of New England: Works, 1608–1631*, edited by Edward Arber, was published in two volumes in Birmingham, England, in 1884.) Of the 16 additional narratives, eight were published during the lifetime of the writers, five of them in general histories of exploration, and three in pamphlet form; the remaining eight were first published posthumously. The texts of the additional narratives included in this volume are presented in the approximate chronological order of the events they describe and are taken from the best printed sources available.

John Smith helped found the Jamestown colony in 1607 and the following year sent a long letter describing events in Virginia to an unidentified correspondent in England. Smith's letter was published as a pamphlet, *A True Relation of such occurances and accidents of note, as hath hapned in Virginia*, that was printed in London by John Tappe for sale by William Welby and registered with the Company of Stationers on August 13, 1608. In the first issue of *A True Relation* its authorship was attributed to "Thomas Watson," who may have been the recipient of Smith's letter, and in the second issue to "a Gentleman." The third issue of the pamphlet correctly identified Smith as the author of the work, but incorrectly described him as "Coronell" (colonel) of the colony. It also included a preface signed by "I.H.," who apparently helped prepare Smith's letter for publication ("I.H." may have been John Healey, a translator). The text printed in this volume is of the fourth issue, which includes the preface and a corrected identification of Smith, and is taken from *The Complete Works of Captain John Smith* (hereafter *Complete Works*), volume I, pp. 23–97.

In 1609 Smith was removed from power in Jamestown and forced to return to England. He subsequently wrote *A Map of Virginia, With a Description of the Countrey, the Commodities, People, Government and Religion*, which was printed at Oxford by Joseph Barnes in 1612 along with a companion volume, *The Proceedings of the English Colonie in Virginia*, a collection of accounts compiled by Richard Pots and William Symonds. The preface of *The Proceedings* was signed by Thomas Abbay, and its individual chapters were signed by Thomas Studley, Anas Todkill, Walter Russell, Nathaniel Powell, Richard Wiffin, William Phettiplace, and Pots, with the first and second chapters attributed to Studley and the third and fourth to Studley and Todkill. However, much of what was attributed to Studley in *The Proceedings* could not have been written by him, since it describes events that took place after his death in Virginia on August 28, 1607. When Smith published an expanded version of *The Proceedings* as Book III of *The Generall Historie of Virginia, New-England, and the Summer Isles* in 1624, he added the initials "J.S." to the signature for the first two chapters. It is possible that Smith wrote some of the portions of the 1612 edition of *The Proceedings*, perhaps using notes made by Studley before his death; it is also likely that Smith helped Pots, his friend and ally during their time in Virginia, compile *The Proceedings*. For these reasons, this volume includes the 1612 edition of *The Proceedings* among its selection of the works of Captain John Smith. The text printed here is taken from *Complete Works*, volume I, pp. 199–279.

Prevented from returning to Jamestown by his criticisms of the company that ruled the colony, Smith turned his attention to the exploration and possible settlement of the region he named "New England," making a successful voyage to Maine and Massachusetts in 1614 and two unsuccessful attempts to return the following year. *A Description of New England*, printed in London by Humfrey Lownes for sale by Robert Clerke, was entered in the Stationers' Register on June 3, 1616. The text printed here is taken from *Complete Works*, volume I, pp. 305–61.

In 1618 Smith sent a letter to Sir Francis Bacon, who recently had been appointed Lord Chancellor of England, in an unsuccessful attempt to obtain his patronage for efforts to colonize New England. Smith published *New Englands Trials*, a revised version of his letter to Bacon, in 1620; a revised and expanded second edition appeared in 1622. Both editions of *New Englands Trials* were printed in London by William Jones. The present volume prints the text of the 1622 edition, taken from *Complete Works*, volume I, pp. 419–41.

Smith circulated a broadside in 1623 to promote the publication of his forthcoming *Generall Historie* and to outline its contents. *The Generall Historie of Virginia, New-England, and the Summer Isles* was printed in London by John Dawson and John Haviland for sale by Michael Sparkes, and was entered in the Stationers' Register on July 12, 1624. *The Generall Historie* is divided into six books, each of which is based on existing sources. For the first book Smith drew primarily on *The Principal Navigations, Voyages, Traffiques and Discoveries of the English Nation* by Richard Hakluyt (1589) and on the materials Samuel Purchas would publish in *Hakluytus Posthumus, or Purchas his Pilgrimes* (1625). The second book of *The Generall Historie* is a revised version of Smith's own *A Map of Virginia* (1612), and the third book is a revised and expanded version of *The Proceedings of the English Colonie in Virginia* (1612). Book IV is based on a variety of accounts of the Virginia colony, while Book V draws on manuscripts by Nathaniel Butler and Richard Norwood, as well as a published work, *A Plaine Description of the Barmudas* (1613) by Silvester Jourdain. The sixth book of *The Generall Historie* is based on two of Smith's previous works, *A Description of New England* (1616) and the second edition of *New Englands Trials* (1622). The text of *The Generall Historie* printed here is taken from *Complete Works*, volume II, pp. 33–475.

In 1625 Samuel Purchas included "The Travels and Adventures of Captain John Smith," an autobiographical narrative, in *Hakluytus Posthumus, or Purchas his Pilgrimes*. Smith then published two books on seamanship, *An Accidence* (1626) and *A Sea Grammar* (1627), before expanding "The Travels and Adventures" into a longer work. *The True Travels, Adventures, and Observations of Captaine John Smith* was entered in the Stationers' Register on August 29, 1629, but did not appear until 1630, when it was printed in London by John Haviland for sale by Thomas Slater. The text printed here is taken from *Complete Works*, volume III, pp. 137–241.

Smith's final published work, *Advertisements for the Unexperienced Planters of New-England, or Any Where*, was printed in London in 1631 by John Haviland for sale by Robert Milbourne. The text here is taken from *Complete Works*, volume III, pp. 259–302.

"Discourse of the First Voyage" by Arthur Barlowe was first published in 1589 by Richard Hakluyt in *The Principal Navigations, Voyages, Traffiques and Discoveries of the English Nation* (hereafter *Principal Navigations*). The text printed in the present volume is taken from *The Roanoke Voyages, 1584–1590* (hereafter *Roanoke Voy-*

ages), edited by David Beers Quinn (2 vols., London: The Hakluyt Society, 1955), volume I, pp. 91–116.

"The Journal of the *Tiger*" was first published anonymously in 1589 in *Principal Navigations*; the text printed here is taken from *Roanoke Voyages*, volume I, pp. 178–93.

"Discourse on the First Colony" by Ralph Lane first appeared in 1589 in *Principal Navigations*. The text printed here is taken from *Roanoke Voyages*, volume I, pp. 255–94.

"Narrative of His Voyage" by John White was first published in *Principal Navigations*. The text printed here is taken from *Roanoke Voyages*, volume II, pp. 515–38.

"A Briefe and True Report" by Thomas Hariot first appeared as a pamphlet printed in London by Robert Robinson in 1588. The text printed here is taken from *Roanoke Voyages*, volume I, pp. 318–87.

"Narrative of the 1590 Voyage" by John White was first published in the 1600 edition of *Principal Navigations*. The text printed here is taken from *Roanoke Voyages*, volume II, pp. 598–622.

"Discourse" by George Percy was first published in 1625 by Samuel Purchas in *Hakluytus Posthumus, or Purchas his Pilgrimes*. The text printed in the present volume is taken from *The Jamestown Voyages under the First Charter, 1606–1609* (hereafter *Jamestown Voyages*), edited by Philip L. Barbour (2 vols., London: Cambridge University Press for the Hakluyt Society, 1969), volume I, pp. 129–46.

"A Relatyon of the Discovery of Our River" by Gabriel Archer was first published in 1860 by the American Antiquarian Society in *Archaelogia Americana*. The text printed here is taken from *Jamestown Voyages*, volume I, pp. 80–98, which uses the manuscript in the Public Record Office, Kew, England, as its source.

"A Discourse of Virginia" by Edward Maria Wingfield was first published in 1845. The text printed in the present volume is taken from *Jamestown Voyages*, volume I, pp. 213–34, which uses the manuscript in the Lambeth Palace Library in London as its source.

"Relation of Virginea" by Henry Spelman was first published in *Relation of Virginia by Henry Spelman*, edited by James F. Hunnewell (London: The Chiswick Press, 1872), pp. 15–58. The text printed here is taken from the Hunnewell edition.

"A True Reportory" by William Strachey was first published by Samuel Purchas in *Hakluytus Posthumus, or Purchas His Pilgrimes*, printed in London in 1625 by William Stansby for sale by Henry Fetherstone. The text printed here is taken from the Library of Congress, Kraus Collection of Sir Francis Drake copy of *Purchas His Pilgrimes*, volume IV, pp. 1734–58.

The Historie of Travell into Virginia Britania, also by William Strachey, was first published in 1849 in an edition prepared by R. H.

Major from a manuscript in the British Museum. The text of the selection from the *Historie* printed in the present volume is taken from *Historie of Travell into Virginia Britania*, edited by Louis B. Wright and Virginia Freund (London: The Hakluyt Society, 1953), pp. 53–111; this edition is based on a manuscript in the Princeton University Library.

"A Trewe Relacyon" by George Percy was first published in 1922 by Lyon G. Tyler in *Tyler's Quarterly Historical and Genealogical Magazine*. The text printed here is taken from Mark Nicholls, "George Percy's 'Trewe Relacyon': A Primary Source for the Jamestown Settlement," *Virginia Magazine of History and Biography*, vol. 113, no. 3 (2005), pp. 242–63, and is based on the manuscript in the Free Library of Philadelphia.

"A True Discourse of the Present Estate of Virginia" by Ralph Hamor first appeared as a pamphlet printed in London in 1615 by John Beale for sale by William Welby. The text presented here is taken from the Huntington Library copy, as printed in facsimile in *A True Discourse of the Present State of Virginia* (Richmond: The Virginia State Library, 1957).

"A Short Relation" by Thomas West, Baron De La Warre, was first published as a pamphlet in London in 1611, printed by William Hall for sale by William Welby. The text printed here is taken from the copy of *The Relation of the Right Honourable the Lord De-La-Warre* in the New York Public Library.

"A True Relation of the State of Virginia" by John Rolfe was first published in paraphrased form by Samuel Purchas in the 1617 edition of *Purchas his Pilgrimage*. The text printed here is taken from *A True Relation of the State of Virginia lefte by Sir Thomas Dale Knight in May last 1616* (New Haven: 1951), printed for Henry C. Taylor and based on the manuscript in his private collection.

Texts are printed here as they appeared in the sources from which they were taken, with a few alterations. Errata that were listed in the original sources have now been incorporated into the texts, and some marginalia in the source texts have been printed in this volume in "windows" (indented spaces within the texts). In cases where the source texts print contractions using superscript letters, the present volume expands the contractions, so that "w^t" becomes "what," "w^{ch}" becomes "which," "y^e" becomes "the," and "y^t" becomes "that." Contractions that are expanded in the source texts using bracketed or italic letters are printed in this volume in their expanded form without brackets or italics. In cases where the source texts printed within brackets material that was canceled in a manuscript, this volume omits the canceled material. Bracketed editorial emendations used to supply letters or words omitted from the source texts by an obvious slip of the pen or printer's error are accepted in this volume and printed without brackets, but bracketed editorial insertions used to clarify meaning have been deleted. The editors of *The Complete Works of Captain John Smith* used bracketed ellipses in their text of *A True Relation* to indicate where material in Smith's original letter may have been omitted in the published version; the present volume deletes these editorial insertions. The manuscript of *The Historie of Travell into Virginia Britania* contains numerous instances where an opening or closing parenthetical mark appears without a corresponding closing or opening mark; these single parenthetical marks are printed in the Wright and Freund edition of *The Historie of Travell into Virginia Britania*, but the present volume omits them. In the text of "A True Relation of the State of Virginia" presented in *A True Relation of the State of Virginia lefte by Sir Thomas Dale Knight in May last 1616*, a bracketed asterisk is used to indicate an illegible passage, but in this volume the passage is indicated by a bracketed two-em space, i.e., [   ]. Some of the source texts printed in this volume use bracketed numerals to record the page leaf numbers of earlier printings or manuscripts; these numbers are deleted in the present volume, as are the symbols used in some source texts to mark page and paragraph breaks. Italics in the source texts have been set in roman in the present volume except in cases where they were used for poetry, ship's names, Indian words other than proper nouns, and other foreign words, or in cases, such as lists, where they have been retained for the sake of typographic clarity.

This volume presents the texts of the original printings chosen for inclusion here without change, except for the alterations previously discussed and for the correction of typographical errors. It does not attempt to reproduce nontextual features of their typographical design or features of 16th- and 17th-century typography such as the long "s" and the use of "u" for "v" (for example, "haue" for "have"), "v" for "u" (for example, "vppon" for "uppon"), or "i" for "j" (for example, "adioyning" for "adjoyning"). Spelling, punctuation, and capitalization are often expressive features, and they are not altered, even when inconsistent or irregular. The following is a list of typographical errors corrected in modern printings, cited by page and line number: 875.26, have not done; 898.1, on; 945.1, comes also comes also; 1086.17, sturrrs.

Note on the Plates

The plates in this volume have been published with support from Furthermore, the publication program of The J. M. Kaplan Fund.

This volume reproduces all of the images that originally accompanied the works printed here, including maps (see pages 120–21 and 304–5), a portrait frontispiece (page 202), seals and coats of arms (pages 672, 708, 709, 772, and 779), and illustrations of narrative incidents and scenes (pages 262–63 and 524–25). In addition, it presents a portfolio of 29 plates, in two sections of 14 and 15 plates respectively. Among these plates are 15 drawings by John White, who traveled with Sir Richard Grenville's expedition to Roanoke in 1585; 8 enlarged details from illustrations in the works of John Smith; 4 engravings by Theodor de Bry, first published in *A Briefe and True Report of the New Found Land of Virginia* (Frankfurt am Main, 1590), after drawings by John White, now lost; a 1608 sketch map, probably copied from an original by John Smith, of Jamestown and its environs (the "Zúñiga map," so called because the only surviving contemporary version of the map was discovered in the correspondence of Pedro de Zúñiga, the Spanish ambassador in London); and an engraving, published separately in 1617, of Pocahontas.

The list below gives the original title or caption for each image, the name of the artist and date of composition (when known) and the engraver and date of engraving (where applicable), and the name of the work or institution from which the image has been obtained. It also reprints, after images by John White and Theodor de Bry, Thomas Hariot's commentary on the scenes depicted, as published in *A Briefe and True Report*, where it follows de Bry's engraved versions of White's drawings. At a few points, Hariot's commentary is keyed to letters, or refers to details, that appear in de Bry's engravings but not in White's drawings; these differences are explained within Hariot's commentary in square bracketed italics.

For additional information about the works and artists included and references to other studies, see: Philip L. Barbour, ed. *The Jamestown Voyages under the First Charter, 1606–1609* (London: The Hakluyt Society/Cambridge: Cambridge University Press, 1969), vol. I; Philip L. Barbour, ed., *The Complete Works of Captain John Smith* (Chapel Hill: University of North Carolina Press, 1986); Thomas Hariot (Paul Hulton, intro.), *A Briefe and True Report of the New Found*

Land of Virginia: The Complete 1590 Theodor de Bry Edition (New York: Dover, 1972); Paul Hulton and David Beers Quinn, eds., *The American Drawings of John White, 1577–1590* (London: Trustees of the British Museum/Chapel Hill: University of North Carolina Press, 1964); and David Beers Quinn, ed., *The Roanoke Voyages, 1584–1590* (London: The Hakluyt Society, 1955), vol. I.

Sources are indicated by the following abbreviations:

Beinecke   Beinecke Rare Book and Manuscript Library, Yale University. Reprinted by permission.

BM   The British Museum, London. Reproduced by permission. Copyright © The Trustees of the British Museum.

Brown   The John Carter Brown Library at Brown University. Reprinted by permission.

Hariot   Thomas Hariot, *A Briefe and True Report of the New Found Land of Virginia* (Frankfurt am Main, 1590).

PLATE 1

The Portraictuer of Captayne John Smith, Admirall of New England
Simon van de Passe, engraved by Robert Clerke (1616–17)
Detail from the map of New England associated with *A Description of New England* (1616), upper left compartment (see page 120 in this volume)
Beinecke

PLATE 2

His Combat with Grualgo, Capt of Three Hundred Horsemen
John Payne, engraved by Martin Droeshout (1630)
Detail from an illustration in *The True Travels*, center compartment (see pages 686–87 in this volume)
Brown

PLATE 3

Capt Smith Led Captive to the Bashaw of Nalbrits in Tartaria
John Payne, engraved by Martin Droeshout (1630)
Detail from an illustration in *The True Travels*, lower left compartment (see page 686 in this volume)
Brown

PLATE 4

The arrival of the Englishemen in Virginia
Theodor de Bry, after John White (1590/1585–86)
Hariot

    The sea coasts of Virginia arre full of Ilands, wehr by the entrance

into the mayne land is hard to finde. For although they bee separated with divers and sundrie large Division, which seeme to
yeeld convenient entrance, yet to our great perill we proved that
they wear shallowe, and full of dangerous flatts, and could never
perce opp into the mayne land, until wee made trialls in many
places with or small pinness. At lengthe wee fownd an entrance
uppon our mens diligent serche thereof. Affter that wee had
passed opp, and sayled ther in for a short space we discovered a
mightye river fallinge downe in to the sownde over against
those Ilands, which nevertheless wee could not saile opp any
thinge far by Reason of the shallewnes, the mouth ther of
beinge annoyed with sands driven in with the tyde therefore
saylinge further, wee came unto a Good bigg yland, the Inhab-
itante thereof as soone as they saw us began to make a great and
horrible crye, as people which never befoer had seene men apparelled like us, and camme a way makinge out crys like wild
beasts or men out of their wyts. But beenge gentlye called
backe, we offred them of our wares, as glasses, knives, babies,
and other trifles, which wee thougt they deligted in. Soe they
stood still, and percevinge our Good will and courtesie came
fawninge uppon us, and bade us welcome. Then they brougt us
to their village in the iland called, Roanoac, and unto their
Weroans or Prince, which entertained us with Reasonable curtesie, althoug the wear amased at the first sight of us. Suche was
our arrivall into the parte of the world, which we call Virginia,
the stature of bodee of wich people, theyr attire, and maneer of
lyvinge, their feasts, and banketts, I will particullerlye declare
unto yow. (*Hariot, plate II*)

PLATE 5

Americæ pars, Nunc Virginia dicta (The carte of all the coast of
  Virginia)
Theodor de Bry, after John White (1590/1585–86)
Hariot

PLATE 6
Ther Idol Kiwasa
Theodor de Bry, after a watercolor by John White now lost (1590/
  1585–86)
Hariot

> The people of this cuntrie have an Idol, which they call KIWASA:
> yt is carved of woode in lengthe 4. foote whose heade is like the
> heades of the people of Florida, the face is of a flesh colour, the
> brest white, the rest is all blacke, the thighes are also spottet

with whitte. He hath a chayne abowt his necke of white beades, betweene which are other Rownde beades of copper which they esteeme more then golde or silver. This Idol is placed in the temple of the towne of Secotam, as the keper of the kings dead corpes. Somtyme they have two of thes idoles in theyr churches, and somtine 3. but never above, which they place in a darke corner wher they shew tetrible. Thes poore soules have none other knowledge of god although I thinke them verye Desirous to know the truthe. For when as wee kneeled downe on our knees to make our prayers unto god, they went abowt to imitate us, and when they saw we moved our lipps, they also dyd the like. Wherfore that is verye like that they might easelye be brought to the knowledge of the gospel. God of his mercie grant them this grace. (*Hariot, plate XXI*)

PLATE 7
The Marckes of sundrye of the Cheif mene of Virginia
Theodor de Bry, after John White (1590/1585–86)
Hariot

The inhabitants of all the cuntrie for the most parte have marks rased on their backs, wherby yt may be knowen what Princes subjects they bee, or of what place they have their originall. For which cause we have set downe those marks in this figure, and have annexed the names of the places, that they might more easelye be discerned. Which industrie hath god indued them withal although they be verye sinple, and rude. And to confesse a truthe I cannot remember, that ever I saw a better or quietter people then they.

The marks which I observed amonge them, are here put downe in order folowinge.

The marke which is expressed by A. belongeth tho Wingino, the cheefe lorde of Roanoac.

That which hath B. is the marke of Wingino his sisters husbande.

Those which be noted with the letters, of C. and D. belonge unto diverse chefe lordes in Secotam.

Those which have the letters E. F. G. are certaine cheefe men of Pomeiooc, and Aquascogoc. (*Hariot, plate XXIII*)

PLATE 8
How they tooke him prisoner in the Oaze 1607 . . . Smith bindeth a salvage to his arme, fighteth with the King of Pamaunkee and all his company, and slew 3 of them
Robert Vaughan (1624)

Detail from "Ould Virginia," an illustration published in *The Generall Historie*, middle left (see page 262 in this volume)
Beinecke

PLATE 9

Their triumph about him . . . Smith bound to a tree to be shott to death 1607

Robert Vaughan, based on Theodor de Bry and John White (1624/1590/1585–86)

Detail from "Ould Virginia," an illustration published in *The Generall Historie* (see page 262 in this volume)
Beinecke

PLATE 10

King Powhatan commands C. Smith to be slayne, his daughter Pokahontas beggs his life his thankfullness and how he subjected 39 of their kings, reade yn historie

Robert Vaughan (1624)

Detail from "Ould Virginia," an illustration published in *The Generall Historie*, bottom right (see page 263 in this volume)
Beinecke

PLATE 11

Map of James Fort and Its Environs [inset detail: James Fort]
Unknown copyist after John Smith (1608)

Philip L. Barbour, ed., *The Jamestown Voyages under the First Charter, 1606–1609*, vol. I, pp. 238–40, after a contemporary copy in the Archivo General de Simancas, Valladolid, Spain (M.P.D., IV–66, XIX–163)

PLATE 12

C: Smith taketh the King of Pamaunkee prisoner 1608

Robert Vaughan, based on Theodor de Bry and John White (1624/1590/1585–86)

Detail from "Ould Virginia," an illustration published in *The Generall Historie*, top right (see page 263 in this volume)
Beinecke

PLATE 13

C: Smith takes the King of Paspahegh prisoner. Ao 1609.

Robert Vaughan (1624)

Detail from "Ould Virginia," an illustration published in *The Generall Historie*, top right (see page 263 in this volume)
Beinecke

PLATE 14
Matoaka als Rebecca [Pocahontas]
Simon van de Passe, engraved by Compton Holland (1616–17)
Single folio engraving
Brown

PLATE 15
La Virginea Pars [Map of Eastern North America from Cape Look-
    out to Chesapeake Bay]
John White, 1585–86
BM

PLATE 16
*The towne of Pomeiock and true forme of their howses, covered and en-
    closed some with matts, and some with barcks of trees. All compassed
    about with smale poles stock thick together in stedd of a wall.*
John White, 1585–86
BM

> The townes of this contrie are in a maner like unto those which
> are in Florida, yet they are not so stronge nor yet preserved with
> soe great care. They are compassed abowt with poles starcke
> faste in the grownd, but they are not verye stronge. The entrance
> is verye narrowe as may be seene by this picture, which is made
> accordinge to the forme of the towne of Pomeiooc. Ther are but
> few howses therin, save those whiche belonge to the kinge and
> his nobles. On the one side is their tempel separated from the
> other howses, and marked with the letter A. [*the temple is at the
> upper right in White's watercolor, with the slightly pointed roof*] yt
> is builded rownde, and covered with skynne matts, and as yt
> wear compassed abowt. With cortynes without windowes, and
> hath noe ligthe but by the doore. On the other side is the kings
> lodginge marked with the letter B. [*the lodging is the open long-
> house at the upper left in White's watercolor*] Their dwellinges are
> builded with certaine potes fastened together, and covered with
> matts which they turne op as high as they thinke good, and soe
> receve in the lighte and other. Some are also covered with
> boughes of trees, as every man lusteth or liketh best. They
> keepe their feasts and make good cheer together in the midds
> of the towne as yt is described in the 17. Figure [*see* PLATE 21].
> When the towne standeth fare from the water they digg a great
> poude noted with the letter C. [*not in White's watercolor*]
> wherhence they fetche as muche water as they neede. (*Hariot,
> plate XIX*)

PLATE 17
A Chiefe Herowans wyfe of Pomeoc and her daughter of the age of .8. or 10 yeares.
John White, 1585–86
BM

About 20. milles from that Iland, neere the lake of Paquippe, ther is another towne called Pomeioock hard by the sea. The apparell of the cheefe ladyes of dat towne differeth but litle from the attyre of those which lyve in Roanoac. For they weare their haire trussed opp in a knott, as the maiden doe which we spake of before, and have their skinnes pownced in the same manner, yet they wear a chaine of great pearles, or beades of copper, or smoothe bones 5. or 6. fold obout their necks, bearinge one arme in the same, in the other hand they carye a gourde full of some kinde of pleasant liquor. They tye deers skinne doubled about them crochinge hygher about their breasts, which hange downe before almost to their knees, and are almost altogither naked behinde. Commonlye their yonge daugters of 7. or 8. yeares olde do waigt upon them wearinge abowt them a girdle of skinne, which hangeth downe behinde, and is drawen under neath betwene their twiste, and bownde above their navel with mose of trees betwene that and their skinnes to cover their priviliers withall. After they be once past 10. yeares of age, they wear deer skinnes as the older sorte do. They are greatlye Diligted with puppetts, and babes which wear brought oute of England. (*Hariot, plate VIII*)

PLATE 18
The aged man in his wynter garment
John White, 1585–86
BM

The aged men of Pommeioocke are covered with a large skinne which is tyed uppon their shoulders on one side and hangeth downe beneath their knees wearinge their other arme naked out of the skinne, that they maye bee at more libertie. Those skynnes are Dressed with hair on, and lyned with other furred skinnes. The yonnge men suffer noe hairr at all to growe uppon their faces but as soone as they growe they put them away, but when thy are come to yeeres they suffer them to growe although to say truthe they come opp verye thinne. They also weare their haire bownde op behynde, and, have a creste on their heads like the - others. The contrye abowt this plase is soe fruit full and good, that England is not to bee compared to yt. (*Hariot, plate IX*)

PLATE 19
Secoton
John White, 1585–86
BM

Their townes that are not inclosed with poles aire commonlye fayrer. Then suche as are inclosed, as appereth in this figure which livelye expresseth the towne of Secotam. For the howses are Scattered heer and ther, and they have gardein expressed by the letter E. [*not in White's watercolor*] wherin groweth Tobacco which the inhabitants call Uppowoc. They have also groaves wherin thei take deer, and fields wherin they sowe their corne. In their corne fields they builde as yt weare a scaffolde wher on they sett a cottage like to a rownde chaire, signiffied by F. [*the scaffold is at upper right, under caption "Their rype corne"*] wherin they place one to watche. for there are suche number of fowles, and beasts, that unles they keepe the better watche, they would soone devoure all their corne. For which cause the watcheman maketh continual cryes and noyse. They sowe their corne with a certaine distance noted by H. [*at center right, with caption "Corne newly sprong"*] other wise one stalke would choke the growthe of another and the corne would not come unto his rypeurs G. [*above center right, with caption "Their greene corne"*] For the leaves thereof are large, like unto the leaves of great reedes. They have also a severall broade plotte C. [*lower right, with caption "A Ceremony in their prayers with strange jesturs and songs dansing about posts carved on the topps lyke mens faces"*] whear they meete with their neighbours, to celebrate their cheefe solemne feastes as the 18. picture [*see* PLATE 22] doth declare: and a place D. [*just below center, with caption "Their sitting at meate"; see also* PLATE 23] whear after they have ended their feaste they make merrie togither. Over against this place they have a rownd plot B. [*above building in lower left corner, with caption "The place of solemne prayer"*] wher they assemble themselves to make their solemne prayers. Not far from which place ther is a lardge buildinge A. [*at lower left, with caption "The house wherin the Tombe of their Herounds standeth"*] wherin are the tombes of their kings and princes, as will appere by the 22. figure [*see also* PLATE 20] likewise they have garden notted bey the letter I. [*not depicted in White*] wherin they use to sowe pompions. Also a place marked with K. [*the fire to the left of "Their greene corne"*] wherin the make a fyre att their solemne feasts, and hard without the towne a river L. [*top center*] from whence they fetche their water. This people therfore voyde of all covetousnes lyve cherfullye and att their harts ease. Butt they solemnise their feasts in the nigt, and therfore they keepe verye great fyres to avoyde darkenes, and to testifie their Joye. (*Hariot, plate XX*)

PLATE 20

The Tombe of their Cherounes or cheife personages, their flesh taken of from the bones save the skynn and heare of their heads, which flesh is dried and enfolded in matts laide at theire feete. their bones also being made dry, are covered with deare skynns not altering their forme or proportion. With theire Kywash, which is an Image of woode keeping the deade.

John White, 1585–86

BM

The builde a Scaffolde 9. or 10. foote hihe as is expressed in this figure under the tombs of their Weroans, or cheefe lordes which they cover with matts, and lai the dead corpses of their weroans theruppon in manner followinge. first the bowells are taken forthe. Then layinge downe the skinne, they cutt all the flesh cleane from the bones, which they drye in the sonne, and well dryed they inclose in Matts, and place at their feete. Then their bones (remaininge still fastened together with the ligaments whole and uncorrupted) are covered a gayne with leather, and their carcase fashioned as yf their flesh wear not taken away. They lapp eache corps in his owne skinne after thesame is thus handled, and lay yt in his order by the corpses of the other cheef lordes. By the dead bodies they sett their Idol Kiwasa, wherof we spake in the former chapiter: For they are persuaded that thesame doth kepe the dead bodyes of their cheefe lords that nothinge may hurt them. Moreover under the foresaid scaffolde some on of their priests hath has lodginge, which Mumbleth his prayers nighte and day, and hath charge of the corpses. For his bedd he hath two deares skinnes spredd on the grownde, yf the wether bee cold hee maketh a fyre to warme by withal. Thes poore soules are thus instructed by nature to reverence their princes even after their death. (*Hariot, plate XXII*)

PLATE 21

Their manner of prainge with Rattels abowt te fyer

John White, 1585–86

BM

When they have escaped any great danger by sea or lande, or be returned from warr in token of Joye they make a great fyre abowt which the men, and woemen sitt together, holding a certaine fruite in their hands like unto a rownde pompion or a gourde, which after they have taken out the fruits, and the seedes, then fill with small stons or certayne bigg kernellt to make the more noise, and fasten that uppon a sticke, and singinge after their manner, they make merrie: as myselfe observed and noted downe at my being amonge them. For it is a strange custome, and worth the observation. (*Hariot, plate XVII*)

PLATE 22
Their danses which they use att their hyghe feastes.
John White, 1585–86
BM

At a Certayne tyme of the yere they make a great, and solemne feaste wherunto their neighbours of the townes adjoninge re-payre from all parts, every man attyred in the most strange fash-ion they can devise havinge certayne marks on the backs to declare of what place they bee. The place where they meet is a broade playne, abowt the which are planted in the grownde cer-tayne posts carved with heads like to the faces of Nonnes covered with theyr vayles. Then beeing sett in order they dance, singe, and use the strangest gestures that they can possiblye devise. Three of the fairest Virgins, of the companie are in the mydds, which imbrassinge one another doe as yt wear turne abowt in their dancinge. All this is donne after the sunne is sett for avoyd-inge of heate. When they are weerye of dancinge, they goe oute of the circle, and come in until their dances be ended, and they goe to make merrye as is expressed in the 16. figure [*see* PLATE 23]. (*Hariot, plate XVIII*)

PLATE 23
Theire sitting at meate
John White, 1585–86
BM

Their manner of feeding is in this wise. They lay a matt made of bents on the grownde and sett their meate on the mids therof, and then sit downe Rownde, the men uppon one side, and the woemen on the other. Their Meate is Mayz sodden, in suche sorte as I described yt in the former treatise of verye good taste, deers flesche, or of some other beaste, and fishe. They are verye sober in their eatinge, and trinkinge, and consequentlye verye longe lived because they doe not oppress nature. (*Hariot, plate XVI*)

PLATE 24
One of their Religious men
John White, 1585–86
BM

    The Priests of the aforesaid Towne of Secota are well stricken in yeers, and as yt seemeth of more experience then the comon sorte. They weare their heare cutt like a creste, on the topps of thier heades as other doe, but the rest are cutt shorte, savinge those which growe about their foreheads in manner of a perriwigge. They also have somwhat hanginge in their ears. They weare a shorte clocke made of fine hares skinnes quilted with the hayre outwarde. The rest of thier bodie is naked. They are notable enchaunters, and for their pleasure they frequent the rivers, to kill with their bowes, and catche wilde ducks, swannes, and other fowles. (*Hariot, plate V*)

PLATE 25
The manner of their fishing
John White, 1585–86
BM

    They have likewise a notable way to catche fishe in their Rivers. for whear as they lacke both yron, and steele, they faste unto their Reedes or longe Rodds, the hollowe tayle of a certaine fishe like to a sea crabb in steede of a poynte, wehr with by nighte or day they stricke fishes, and take them opp into their boates. They also know how to use the prickles, and pricks of other fishes. They also make weares, with settinge opp reedes or twigges in the water, which they soe plant one within a nother, that they growe still narrower, and narrower, as appeareth by this figure. Ther was never seen amonge us soe cunninge a way to take fish withall, wherof sondrie sortes as they fownde in their Rivers unlike unto ours. which are also of a verye good taste. Dowbtless yt is a pleasant sighte to see the people, somtymes wadinge, and goinge somtymes sailinge in those Rivers, which are shallowe and not deepe, free from all care of heapinge opp Riches for their posterite, content with their state, and livinge frendlye together of those thinges which god of his bountye hath given unto them, yet without givinge hym any thankes according to his desarte. So savage is this people, and deprived of the true knowledge of god. For they have none other then is mentionned before in this worke. (*Hariot, plate XIII*)

PLATE 26
The broyling of their fish over the flame of fier
John White, 1585–86
BM

> After they have taken store of fishe, they gett them unto a place
> fitt to dress yt. Ther they sticke upp in the grownde 4. stakes in
> a square roome, and lay 4 potes uppon them, and others over
> thwart thesame like unto an hurdle, of sufficient heigthe. and
> layinge their fishe upon this hurdle, they make a fyre under-
> neathe to broile the same, not after the manner of the people of
> Florida, which doe but schorte, and harden their meate in the
> smoke onlye to Reserve thesame duringe all the winter. For this
> people reservinge nothinge for store, they do broile, and spend
> away all att once and when they have further neede, they roste
> or seethe fresh, as wee shall see heraffter. And when as the hur-
> dle can not holde all the fishes, they hange the Rest by the fyrres
> on sticks sett upp in the grounde against the fyre, and than they
> finishe the rest of their cookerye. They take good heede that
> they bee not burnt. When the first are broiled they lay others
> on, that weare newlye broughte, continuinge the dressinge of
> their meate in this sorte, until they thincke they have sufficient.
> (*Hariot, plate XIIII*)

PLATE 27
A chiefe Herowan
John White, 1585–86
BM

> The cheefe men of the yland and towne of Roanoac reace the
> haire of their crounes of theyr heades cutt like a cokes combe,
> as the others doe. The rest they wear longe as woemen and truss
> them opp in a knott in the nape of their necks. They hange
> pearles stringe oppon a threed att their eares, and weare brace-
> lets on their armes of pearles, or small beades of copper or of
> smoothe bone called minsal, nether paintinge nor powncings of
> them selves, but in token of authoritye, and honor, they wear a
> chaine of great pearles, or copper beades or smoothe bones
> abowt their necks, and a plate of copper hinge upon a stringe,
> from the navel unto the midds of their thighs. They cover them-
> selves before and behynde as the woemen doe with a deers
> skynne handsomley dressed, and fringed, More over they fold
> their armes together as they walke, or as they talke one with an-
> other in signe of wisdome. The yle of Roanoac is verye pleisant,

ond hath plaintie of fishe by reason of the Water that environeth thesame. (*Hariot, plate VII*)

PLATE 28
The manner of their attire and painting them selves when they goe to their generall huntings or at theire Solemne feasts
John White, 1585–86
BM

The Princes of Virginia are attyred in suche manner as is expressed in this figure. They weare the haire of their heades long and bynde opp the ende of thesame in a knot under thier eares. Yet they cutt the topp of their heades from the forehead to the nape of the necke in manner of a cokscombe, stirkinge a faier longe pecher of some berd att the Begininge of the creste uppun their foreheads, and another short one on bothe seides about their eares. They hange at their eares ether thicke pearles, or somwhat els, as the clawe of some great birde, as cometh in to their fansye. Moreover They ether pownes, or paynt their forehead, cheeks, chynne, bodye, armes, and leggs, yet in another sorte then the inhabitantz of Florida. They weare a chaine about their necks of pearles or beades of copper, wich they muche esteeme, and ther of wear they also braselets ohn their armes. Under their brests about their bellyes appeir certayne spotts, whear they use to lett them selves bloode, when they are sicke. They hange before them the skinne of some beaste verye feinelye dresset in such sorte, that the tayle hangeth downe behynde. They carye a quiver made of small rushes holding their bowe readie bent in on hand, and an arrowe in the other, radie to defend themselves. In this manner they goe to warr, or tho their solemne feasts and banquetts. They take muche pleasure in huntinge of deer wher of theris great store in the contrye, for yt is fruit full, pleasant, and full of Goodly woods. Yt hathe also store of rivers full of divers sorts of fishe. When they go to battel they paynt their bodyes in the most terrible manner that thei can devise. (*Hariot, plate III*)

PLATE 29
The flyer
John White, 1585–86
BM

> They have comonlye conjurers or juglers which use strange
> gestures, and often contrarie to nature in their enchantments:
> For they be verye familiar with devils, of whome they enquier
> what their enemys doe, or other suche thinges. They shave all
> their heads savinge their creste which they weare as other doe,
> and fasten a small black birde above one of their ears as a badge
> of their office. They weare nothinge but a skinne which hangeth
> downe from their gyrdle, and covereth their privityes. They
> weare a bagg by their side as is expressed in the figure. The In-
> habitants give great credit unto their speeche, which oftentymes
> they finde to bee true. (*Hariot, plate XI*)

Notes

In the notes below, the reference numbers denote page and line of this volume. (The line count includes headings, and the reference numbers for material printed in "windows"—indented spaces within the texts—contain the italic letter *n*.) No note is made for material included in the eleventh edition of *Merriam-Webster's Collegiate Dictionary*. For further historical and biographical background, references to other studies, and more detailed notes, see James Horn, *A Land As God Made It: Jamestown and the Birth of America* (New York: Basic Books, 2005); Philip L. Barbour, *The Three Worlds of Captain John Smith* (Boston: Houghton Mifflin Company, 1964); *The Complete Works of Captain John Smith*, edited by Philip L. Barbour (3 vols., Chapel Hill: The University of North Carolina Press, 1986); David Beers Quinn, *Set Fair for Roanoke: Voyages and Colonies, 1584–1606* (Chapel Hill: The University of North Carolina Press, 1985); *The Roanoke Voyages, 1584–1590*, edited by David Beers Quinn (2 vols, London: The Hakluyt Society, 1955); *Jamestown Narratives*, edited by Edward Wright Haile (Champlain, Virginia: RoundHouse, 1998); Helen C. Rountree, *The Powhatan Indians of Virginia* (Norman: University of Oklahoma Press, 1989); *The Jamestown Voyages Under the First Charter, 1606–1609*, edited by Philip L. Barbour (2 vols., London: Cambridge University Press for the Hakluyt Society, 1969); William Strachey, *The Historie of Travell into Virginia Britania*, edited by Louis B. Wright and Virginia Freund (London: The Hakluyt Society, 1953); Mark Nicholls, "George Percy's 'Trewe Relacyon': A Primary Source for the Jamestown Settlement," *Virginia Magazine of History and Biography*, vol. 113, no. 3 (2005); Ralph Hamor, *A True Discourse of the Present State of Virginia* (Richmond: The Virginia State Library, 1957); and John Rolfe, *A True Relation of the State of Virginia lefte by Sir Thomas Dale Knight in May last 1616* (New Haven: Printed for Henry C. Taylor, 1951).

A TRUE RELATION

3.29   Thomas Watson] Watson may have been the recipient of John Smith's letter, published without Smith's knowledge as *A True Relation*. It is likely that some words and phrases in the letter were omitted or transposed in the printed version.

4.36   *I.H.*]   Possibly John Healey, who translated *Mundus alter et idem* (1609), Bishop Joseph Hall's satire on America, and who later went to Virginia, where he died sometime before the end of 1610.

5.9   downes]   A roadstead for shipping off the north coast of Kent where the fleet was confined throughout January 1607 by unfavorable winds.

5.16   Captain]   Captain Christopher Newport (1560–1617) of Limehouse, London, was the commander of the fleet. An experienced mariner in American waters, he was involved in numerous privateering ventures in the Spanish West Indies throughout the 1590s.

5.18–19   Captaine Archer]   See Biographical Notes.

5.22   the Box opened]   The sponsors of the colony, the Virginia Company of London, had kept the identity of the ruling council of the colony secret by placing the names of the councilors in a sealed box that was to be opened only when the fleet reached its destination.

5.25–26   Edward Maria Wingfield]   See Biographical Notes.

5.28–29   Captaine Gosnold]   Captain Bartholomew Gosnold (c. 1572–1607), a cousin of Wingfield, was a privateer, explorer, and member of the council in Virginia.

5.32   two and twenty day of Aprill]   May 21, 1607.

6.11   Arsatecke]   Arrohateck, principal settlement of the Arrohateck Indians.

6.12   hee whom we supposed to be the chiefe King]   The English mistook Parahunt for Wahunsonacock, the paramount chief of the Powhatans.

6.28   Whitsunday]   The holiday fell on May 24 in 1607.

6.35–36   observe the height]   Take measurements to determine the latitude.

6.37   Queene of Apamatuck]   Opussonoquonuske of the Appomattocs.

7.8   Hinde]   Servant.

7.13   Tappahanocke]   Lands of the Quiyoughcohannock people.

7.18   Ordinances]   Cannon.

7.21   drie-fats]   Cases or casks.

7.30   King of Pamaunke]   The chief of the Pamunkeys was Opitchapam and the man he sent was Navirans. The English also referred to his brother Opechancanough as a Pamunkey chief.

8.3   Captaine Martin]   Captain John Martin (c. 1567–1632?), son of Richard Martin (1534–1617), master of the mint, 1581–1617, and lord mayor of London.

8.15 Captaine Ratcliffe] Captain John Ratcliffe, possibly an alias for Sicklemore. He was killed by Indians in 1609.

8.35 Cape Marchant] The officer responsible for the purchase, sale, or barter of goods and provisions.

9.20 foure shot] Four men armed with muskets.

10.28 country of Chikhamania] The lands along the Chickahominy River. Its inhabitants, the Chickahominies, were allies of Wahunsonacock, the paramount chief of the Powhatans, but did not recognize him as their ruler.

12.18 osey] Muddy, oozy.

13.18 lacke] Lake.

13.30 boughts] Bends.

14.8 Opeckankenough] This was the first meeting between Smith and Opechancanough (1550s?–1644), a brother of Wahunsonacock. In 1618 he succeeded Wahunsonacock as the paramount chief of the Powhatans. After organizing an attack against the English settlements in 1644, Opechancanough was imprisoned at Jamestown, where he was shot and killed by a guard.

15.13 King of Paspahegh] Wowinchopunck.

15.14 the King] Opechancanough.

15.18 Ocanahonan] Ocanahowan, in the interior of North Carolina.

15.21 Paspahegh] Jamestown, which was built on Paspahegh hunting grounds.

15.29–30 incerted the fort . . . the back sea] It is possible that "incerted" is a misprint for "incensed" (informed), and that some words were omitted in the printed version of this passage.

16.1 Youghtanan] Youghtanund, on the Pamunkey (York) River.

16.2 Mattapanient] The Mattaponi River.

16.29 Topahanocke] Rappahannock.

17.1 Topmanahocks] Mannahoacs.

17.3–4 Werowocomoco . . . great king is resident] Werowocomoco was the principal residence of Wahunsonacock, the paramount chief of the Powhatans, until 1609.

17.9 their Emperour] Wahunsonacock (1540s?–1618), also known as Powhatan, paramount chief of the Powhatans.

17.12 *Rahaughcums*] Raccoon skins.

17.36   Monocan] The Monacans, a powerful Siouan-speaking people who lived in the Virginia Piedmont; they were enemies of the Powhatans.

18.5   Anchanachuck] Possibly the Atquanachukes, who lived about 75 miles south of the Hudson River.

18.8   Pocoughtronack] Also known to the English as the Bocootawonauk.

18.9   Moyaoncer, and Pataromerke] The Moyaone and the Patawomecks were Indian groups who lived along the Potomac River.

18.21   Chawwonock] Chowanoc, on the Chowan River in North Carolina, principal residence of the Chowanoc Indians.

18.23   Anone] Possibly the Eno, who lived in the interior of North Carolina.

18.31   Meworames] Weroance, chief or head of a village.

18.35   Capahowasicke] An area a few miles downriver from Werowocomoco.

19.18–19   Terra Sigillata] A reddish astringent clay used as medicine.

19.22   Kiskirk] Kiskiack, capital town of the Kiskiack people.

20.38   Nuport, who arriving there the same night] Newport arrived at Jamestown with additional settlers and provisions on January 2, 1608.

21.1–2   maister Scrivener] Matthew Scrivener (1580–1609).

21.24   Panawicke] An Indian village on the coast of North Carolina south of Roanoke Island.

21.32–33   20. shot armed in Jacks] Twenty soldiers armed with muskets and wearing leather quilted jackets.

22.38   Demy Culverings] Cannon weighing between 3,000 and 4,000 pounds that fired nine-pound solid shot.

24.17   over the Baye] To the eastern shore of Chesapeake Bay.

24.23   Thomas Salvage] Thomas Savage (c. 1594–c. 1633) was originally from Cheshire. He learned Algonquian and served as an interpreter in Anglo-Powhatan meetings.

26.17   Seaman Mantiuas] Possibly a misprint for "son Nantaquaus."

27.16   his Daughter] This is Smith's first reference to Pocahontas.

27.25   Katatough] Kekataugh.

28.2   *Panasarowmana*] A stew of green corn and beans; succotash.

29.27   Kings river]   James River.

30.21–22   Maister Nelson . . . tempests passed]   Captain Francis Nelson had sailed from England with Newport in October 1607, but had become separated from the flagship in fog in December and spent the winter in the West Indies before continuing on to Virginia.

31.5   Thicks]   Thickets, undergrowth.

31.28   randevous]   Rendezvous, i.e., a store of provisions.

33.5   Muskets with match in the cockes]   Muskets that had been made ready to fire.

33.7   Comouodos]   Comrade.

33.37   extraordinary resort]   Frequent meetings.

34.3   loaded]   This is possibly a misprinting of "lodged."

34.25   his Daughter]   Pocahontas.

35.2   Bracer]   Wrist guard.

THE PROCEEDINGS OF THE ENGLISH COLONIE IN VIRGINIA

39.12   Richard Pots]   Pots arrived in Virginia with the first supply on January 2, 1608, and became a friend and supporter of John Smith.

40.14   T. Abbay]   Thomas Abbay arrived in Jamestown in October 1608.

41.4–6   Thomas Studly . . . William Phetiplace]   Thomas Studley, Nathaniel Powell, and Anas Todkill, a carpenter, were members of the first expedition. Walter Russell, a "Doctour of Physicke," and William Phettiplace arrived with the first supply in January 1608.

41.15   defailement]   Failure.

41.31–32   one of 100 Tonns . . . a Pinnace of 20]   The *Susan Constant* was rated at 120 tons, the *Godspeed* at 40 tons, and the *Discovery* at 20 tons.

42.6   Master Hunt]   Reverend Robert Hunt, M.A. (c. 1569–1608), formerly of Reculver, Kent.

42.22   Gwardalupa]   Guadeloupe.

42.24   Monica]   Monito, a small island off the western coast of Puerto Rico.

42.26   Mevis, Mona]   Nevis; Mona is also a small island off western Puerto Rico.

42.28   Gwayn]   Iguana.

48.40   Weraskoyks]   Warraskoyack Indians, who lived on the south bank of the James River.

49.18   fauken]   Falcon, a cannon weighing about 700 pounds and firing two or three pound solid shot.

49.33–34   pumpions, and putchamins]   Pumpkins and persimmons.

49.35   Tuftaffaty humorists]   Dressed foolishly in tufts of taffeta.

53.6–7   conceipt]   Knowledge of, understanding of.

53.25   an Irish mantle]   A large cloak.

54.38   in the winter . . . 1607]   The fire that burned the fort occurred in early January 1608.

55.24   our gilded refiners . . . golden promises]   Two ore refiners and two goldsmiths had arrived with Newport in January 1608.

56.5   plaies]   Underhanded tricks.

57.29–30   composition]   Terms.

58.10   falling to the Cedar Ile]   Sailed downriver to Cedar Island.

61.23   this king]   The chief of the Accomacs was Esmy Shichans, called the "Laughing King" by the English.

62.29   Massawomekes]   A powerful group of Iroquoian-speaking Indians who lived north of the Powhatans.

62.40   inlet . . . Bolus]   Probably the Patapsco River.

63.1   Bole-Armoniacke]   *Bole armeniac*, an astringent red clay used as an antidote for poison.

63.10–11   Sir Ralfe Lane, . . . discoverie of Morattico]   Ralph Lane, commander of the Roanoke colony of 1585–86, led an expedition up the Roanoke River in the spring of 1586 in a search for gold mines in the interior.

70.17–19n reduced to the forme of this figure . . . *QUERE*, 8]   The diagram of the fort was not inserted into the text, hence the printer's query.

70.25–26   lost company of Sir Walter Rawley]   The Virginia Company believed that survivors of the lost Roanoke colony sponsored by Sir Walter Ralegh were still alive somewhere in the interior of North Carolina.

73.6–7   redelivered him Namontack]   Namontack had accompanied Newport to England in April 1608 and returned with the second supply in October.

75.30   Master Persey]   George Percy; see Biographical Notes.

79.4   provided for Nansamund]   Made preparations to go to Nansemond.

79.15   Chawopo]   In the lands of the Quiyoughcohannocks.

81.15 Anthony Baggly *Serg.*] An error for Anthony Bagnall, Surgeon.

81.18 Dutchmen] Germans.

81.35 silke grasse] Fibrous plants.

84.18 brute from Nansamund] In *The Historie of Travell into Virginia Britania*, William Strachey wrote that the rumor originating among the Nansemonds was that "from the *Chesapeack* Bay a Nation should arise, which should dissolve and give end" to the Powhatan "Empier."

85.17–18 we shall so unadvisedly starve] This is probably a setting error for "we shall not so unadvisedly starve."

90.10 vambrace] Armor worn on the forearm.

91.21–22 to second his occasions] To be ready to support him.

93.12 Master West] Francis West (1586–1633), younger brother of Sir Thomas West, Baron De La Warr.

95.38–39 Spanish Decades, and relations of Master Hacklut] *The Decades of the newe worlde or west India* (1555), a translation by Richard Eden of *De orbe novo* by Pietro Martire d'Anghiera; Richard Hakluyt, *The Principal Navigations, Voyages, Traffiques and Discoveries of the English Nation* (1598–1600).

96.16 When the shippes departed] In late November or early December 1608.

97.35 the king of Paspaheigh] Wowinchopunck.

98.2–3 two of the Poles] Three or four Polish artisans arrived at Jamestown in October 1608 to help with the production of potashes, soap ashes, pitch, and tar.

98.16 went by the heeles] Placed in leg irons.

98.30 Kinsock] Tassore.

101.6 last of pitch] A last was 12–14 barrels.

106.24 Lord De-la-ware] See Biographical Notes.

106.25–26 Sir George Somers] George Somers (1554–1610), one of the first sponsors of the Virginia Company, sailed with Sir Thomas Gates on the *Sea Venture* as Admiral of Virginia. The Somers Isles (Bermuda), where he died, were named in his honor.

106.27 catch] Ketch, a small two-masted vessel.

106.28 Admirall] The flagship, the *Sea Venture*.

108.4 the Presidents yeare being neere expired] Smith's term of office expired on September 10, 1609.

108.8–9   The people being contributers]   The Nansemonds supplied corn to the English.

112.17   curats . . . moryons]   Cuirasses; helmets without visors.

114.12   *W.P.*]   William Phettiplace.

115.23–24   Berondoes]   Bermuda.

115.29   cuning the ship]   Conning (steering) the ship.

118.8–9   sonnes of Anak]   See Numbers 13:33.

118.13   *W.S.*]   William Symonds.

A DESCRIPTION OF NEW ENGLAND

124.28   sacring]   Dedicating.

128.23   Pelias]   The half-brother of Jason's father.

133.3   two Ships]   One of the ships was commanded by Smith and the other by Master Thomas Hunt; they carried a crew of 45 men and boys.

133.11   Jubartes]   Finback whales.

133.13   the Masters]   Thomas Hunt.

133.22   Cor fish]   Salted fish.

134.1   Traine]   Train oil (oil from marine animals).

134.8   ryalls the quintall]   A Spanish real was worth about six pence in early 17th-century English currency; a quintal was the equivalent of one hundredweight (112 lbs.).

134.11   Nova Albyon]   New Albion, the western coast of North America.

134.12–13   Sir Francis Drake . . . the worlde]   Drake circumnavigated the globe between 1577 and 1580.

134.13–14   stiled New England]   Smith was the first to coin the phrase.

134.24–25   unprosperously . . . by the French]   French Huguenots established a settlement at Fort Caroline, near present-day Jacksonville, Florida, in 1564. The colony was destroyed in 1565 by the Spanish.

134.40   a Booke and Map]   *A Map of Virginia, With a Description of the Countrey* (1612).

136.12   Terra Incognita]   Baffin Island, explored by Martin Frobisher in three voyages between 1576 and 1578, and subsequently by other English navigators seeking a Northwest Passage to China.

136.20–21   Master Hutson]   Henry Hudson, who explored New York

Bay and the Hudson River in 1609 on behalf of the Dutch. He was set adrift by his crew in Hudson Bay in 1611.

139.21   Easterlings]   Citizens of the Hanse towns of the Baltic.

140.11   Busses, Flat bottomes, Sword pinks, Todes]   Types of fishing vessels.

140.21   Biskaines]   Inhabitants of the Biscay region of northern Spain.

140.22   Cape-blank]   Cap Blanc (Ras Nouadhibou) in northwestern Mauritania.

140.22–23   Porgos . . . Puttargo]   Sea bream; botargo, a relish made from mullet or tuna roe.

140.25   Poore-John]   Salted and dried cod or hake.

141.30   Bononia]   The Latin name for Bologna.

142.1   Chily and Baldivia]   Chile was conquered by Pedro de Valdivia (c. 1498–1554), the founder of Santiago.

142.27   Polonia]   Poland.

142.28   Sweathland]   Sweden.

143.36–37   Avera, Porta port]   Aveiro, Port Oporta.

143.38   Ilanders]   Mariners fishing off Newfoundland.

144.21   serve a stage . . . turne Poor John]   Processes in the preparation of train oil and fish.

145.15   red berries . . . Alkermes]   A source of red dye, the dried bodies of female insects of the genus *Kermes* were mistaken for berries until the 18th century.

146.40   Straits commodities]   Goods from the Mediterranean.

148.35–36   Tragabigzanda . . . the three Turks heads]   Charatza Tragabigzanda was a young woman who treated Smith kindly while he was a slave in Constantinople. Smith's coat of arms displayed three heads to commemorate his exploits in defeating three Turkish champions in Transylvania in 1602; see Chronology.

149.25   hurts]   Huckleberries.

149.38   Capawack]   Martha's Vineyard.

150.19   Sorico]   Isle au Haut.

150.38   respices]   Raspberries.

151.6   saxefrage]   Sassafras.

151.7   Gripes]   Vultures.

151.9   Dive-doppers] Grebes.

151.11   Porkpisces] Porpoises.

151.12   Cole] Pollock.

151.14   Cunners] Blue perch.

151.14   Wilkes] Whelks.

151.18   Aroughconds] Raccoons.

151.19   Musquassus] Muskrats.

151.24   Clampes] Clams.

158.8   Spinsters] Spinners.

161.19   Dohannida] Tahanedo was kidnapped and taken to England in 1605 by George Waymouth but was returned to Maine the following year. He assisted the unsuccessful colony established by English settlers at Sagadahoc, Maine, in 1607–08.

161.22–23   alliants] Allies.

163.2–3   Michaell Cooper the Master] Cooper was master of one of the ships on the voyage.

163.34–35   Sir Ferdinando Gorge, and Master Doctor Sutliffe] Sir Ferdinando Gorges (1568–1647), a major sponsor of the colonization of New England; Dr. Matthew Sutcliffe, Dean of Exeter Cathedral, was also an important backer of colonization projects in North America.

165.5–6   Iles of Flowers] Flores, westernmost island in the Azores.

165.7   Fyall] Fayal or Faial, a small island in the Azores.

165.14*n*   murderers] Small cannon or mortars.

165.18   close fights] Barricades that allowed men to take cover while loading and firing their weapons.

166.34–35   the Bank] The Newfoundland Banks, fishing waters that extend about 300 miles off Newfoundland.

167.27   Saint Michaels] Largest of the islands in the Azores.

167.29   suckets] Candied fruit.

167.32   English red crosses] The English flag of St. George.

167.36   Carvell] Caravel, a small ship.

168.1   cutchanell] Cochineal, a red dye.

168.2   ryalls of 8] Pieces of eight, Spanish coins worth eight reals.

168.7   Iles] Azores.

168.15   Gulion]   Aiguillon.

168.18–19   him that burnt their Colony in New France]   In 1613 Captain
Samuel Argall was sent by Sir Thomas Dale, the acting governor of Virginia,
to destroy French settlements in Maine and Nova Scotia.

168.26   Rat Ile]   Ile de Ré.

168.32   Charowne]   Charente River.

169.7   English Ambassador then at Burdeaux]   Sir Thomas Edmondes.

169.8–9   the Kings great mariage brought from Spaine]   Louis XIII married Anne of Austria, the daughter of Philip III of Spain, at Bordeaux in late
November 1615.

169.33–34   desperate]   Risky or doubtful.

170.14   hants and feedings]   Haunts and feeding grounds.

170.29   travell]   Travail, work or labor.

NEW ENGLANDS TRIALS

179.22   Master Dee]   John Dee (1527–1608), *General and Rare Memorials
pertayning to the Perfect Arte of Navigation* (1577). Dee's interests included
navigation, mathematics, geography, alchemy, astrology, and magic. He
served as Elizabeth I's royal astrologer and played an influential role in English exploration in the late 16th century.

179.31   Ireland at Baltemore]   Baltimore on the south coast of Ireland.

179.34   Blacke Rocke]   Achill Island, County Mayo, Ireland.

180.1   Master Gentleman]   Tobias Gentleman was the author of *England's way to win wealth* (1614).

180.7   Hambrough and the Sound]   Hamburg and the strait between
Denmark and Sweden.

180.20–22   Doggers . . . Busses]   Types of fishing boats.

180.28   Pumerland, Sprussia]   Pomerania and East Prussia.

180.29   Lefland]   Latvia.

181.20   Terceras, Mederas]   Azores, Madeira.

183.25   Admirall of that Country]   New England.

183.36   Bilbow]   Bilbao, Spain.

184.16–17   at the first penie]   At the best rate.

184.38–39   Pembrocks bay to Harrintons bay]   Penobscot Bay to Casco
Bay.

184.40   Taulbuts bay]   Salem Harbor.

185.26   Cape James]   Cape Cod.

185.36   another of 55 Tunnes]   The *Fortune*.

187.16   the plantation]   Thomas Weston's settlement at Wessagusset (Weymouth), on the southern shore of Massachusetts Bay.

187.24–25   Piccaroun]   Privateer.

187.25   Argere]   Algiers.

187.28   massacre in Virginia]   The Powhatan uprising of March 22, 1622; see Chronology.

189.4–5   the honorable Company . . . to go thither]   Under the leadership of Sir Edwin Sandys, in 1618 the Virginia Company began recruiting felons and destitute children for settlement in the colony.

189.20   your West country men]   An expedition sent by Gorges in 1614.

189.23–24   Master Hunt . . . stealing some savages]   Hunt kidnapped two dozen Indians to sell as slaves in Spain.

190.34   Billings gate]   A London dock.

190.35–36   Greenwich, . . . and Margit]   Greenwich, Gravesend, Tilbury, and Leigh were ports along the Thames, Queenborough was on the Medway, and Margate was on the coast of Kent.

192.28–31   Master Hackluts . . . infidell]   The quotation is from George Chapman, *De Guiana Carmen Epicurum* (1596), reprinted by the younger Richard Hakluyt in *The Principal Navigations, Voyages, Traffiques, and Discoveries of the English Nation* (3 vols., 1598–1600).

193.23   Island]   Iceland.

194.12–13   King Edgar]   English king who ruled from 959 to 975.

196.17   Master Pierce]   Smith credits John Pierce of London with obtaining the patent from the Virginia Company in 1620 that allowed the Pilgrims to settle in North America.

196.39   Prince Sigimundus Bather]   Zsigmond Báthory (1572–1613), prince of Transylvania.

THE GENERALL HISTORIE OF VIRGINIA, NEW-ENGLAND, AND THE SUMMER ISLES

199.3   Summer Isles]   Bermuda.

199.15   sometymes Governour]   Smith served as president of the resident council in Virginia but not as governor.

203.3–4   the Lady Francis, Duchesse of Richmond and Lennox]   The daughter of Thomas, Lord Howard of Bindon, she was married to Ludovick Stuart, the Duke of Richmond.

203.33–34   Bashaw of Nalbrits]   The Tymor Bashaw, brother of Charatza Trabigandza, lived east of the Black Sea. After being treated harshly by him, Smith killed the Bashaw and made his escape from slavery in 1603. (A timor was a small fiefdom within the Ottoman Empire.)

203.34   the Lady Callamata]   The Lady Callamata, named by Smith for a port in southern Greece, was the wife of the commander of an outpost in Muscovy who was kind to Smith after his escape from the Tymor Bashaw.

204.1   the good Lady Madam Chanoyes]   Madam Chanoyes of La Rochelle, France, may have been the wife of a lawyer, Chaurroy, who assisted Smith in his efforts to gain compensation for the loss of a bark of 60 tons taken by French pirates in the summer of 1615.

208.34–37   S.M. . . . T.T.]   Neither S.M. nor T.T. have been positively identified, although T.T may have been Thomas Thorpe, the publisher of Shakespeare's sonnets.

210.6   *Cælum non animum mutant]   Horace, *Epistles*, I, xi, 27: "Cælum non animum mutant, qui trans mare currunt" (they who go across the sea change their climate, not their mind).

212.20   Ro: Norton]   Robert Norton (d. 1625), gunner and engineer at the Tower of London.

214.10   David Wiffin]   Wiffin arrived in Virginia in January 1608.

214.31   William Grent]   Educated at Cambridge University and Middle Temple, Grent was a writer and explorer.

222.37–38   A Proclamation, . . . from Virginia]   Domestic production of tobacco in England was banned by James I in 1619.

223.16   The rent]   Rule.

227.8   Stories of Arthur, Malgo, and Brandon]   King Arthur and Malgo were legendary 6th-century British monarchs who ruled over the British Isles, Iceland, Norway, and Denmark. St. Brendan was an Irish monk who made several voyages into the Atlantic in the 6th century, perhaps as far as Iceland or the Azores.

227.10   the Fryer of Linn]   Nicholas of Kings Lynn, a Franciscan friar, is described in Hakluyt's *The Principal Navigations, Voyages, Traffiques, and Discoveries of the English Nation* as using magic to explore regions near the North Pole.

228.15–16   Meta incognita]   Baffin Island.

228.26   he perished in his returne] Sir Humphrey Gilbert (1537–1583) was lost at sea returning from Newfoundland in September 1583.

229.7   Captaine Barlowe] Smith's description of the 1584 voyage is derived from a narrative by Arthur Barlowe; see pp. 819–30 in this volume.

234.3–235.7   *Sir Richard Grenvills . . . the number of 108*] This passage is taken from the journal of the 1585 voyage published in Hakluyt's *The Principal Navigations*, vol. 3 (1600); see pp. 831–37 in this volume.

234.28   the 18. of September. 1585] October 18, 1585.

235.8–242.6   Touching the most remarkeable . . . the same yeare] This passage is taken from Ralph Lane's account of the colony of 1585–86; see pp. 838–59 in this volume.

242.8–11   *To reason lend . . . ere understood.*] From Bishop Martin Fotherby, *Atheomastix; clearing foure truthes, against atheists* (1622), derived from Lucretius.

242.13–247.40   *The Observations of Master Thomas Heriot . . .* Civilitie and Christianitie] This passage is derived from Thomas Hariot, *A briefe and true report of the new found land of Virginia* (1588); see pp. 874–905 in this volume.

248.2–7   *Nature her selfe . . . better grace.*] A translation of Marcellus Palingenius, *Zodiacus Humanae Vitae*, from Fotherby, *Atheomastix.*

248.9   *How Sir Richard Grenvill*] Smith's account of Grenville's relief expedition is taken from Hakluyt's *The Principal Navigations*, vol. 3 (1600).

248.13   Easter] April 3.

248.24   fiftie men] Grenville left 15 men.

248.31   *Who broacheth . . . good for naught.*] Fotherby, *Atheomastix.*

249.1–251.34   *Three Ships more . . . of about 115.*] Smith's account of the 1587 voyage is based on John White's narrative; see pp. 860–73 in this volume.

249.16   George How] George Howe was killed on July 28.

252.1–254.6   *The fift Voyage . . .* September 1590.] Smith's account of the 1590 voyage is based on a narrative by John White; see pp. 906–19.

254.11–12   *Not all . . . upon men.*] Fotherby, *Atheomastix*, derived from Homer.

254.14–257.22   *A briefe Relation . . .* 23 of July] This passage is based on John Brereton, *A Briefe and true Relation of the Discoverie of the North part of Virginia* (1602).

254.26   heretofore by 500. leagues] Brereton has the "better part of a thousand leagues."

254.30   11. of May]   May 14.

255.28   Martha's Vineyard]   The island was named by Bartholomew Gosnold.

257.23–27   *But yet . . . doth onely give.*]   Fotherby, *Atheomastix*, derived from Plutarch and Homer.

258.1   Bristow]   Bristol.

258.4–5   Robert Salterne]   Chief agent of the principal backers of the voyage.

258.20–21   *Lay hands unto . . . and perfit it.*]   Fotherby, *Atheomastix*.

258.23–264.12   *A relation of a Discovery . . . they went forth.*]   This passage is derived from James Rosier, *A True Relation of the most prosperous voyage made this present yeere 1605, by Captaine George Waymouth . . .* (London, 1605).

258.31   24 of Aprill]   In the Rosier text, April 14.

260.32   cirke]   A creek.

261.2–3   three which we kept . . . on shore]   The five Indians were Tahánedo (a chief), Amóret, Skicowáros, Maneddo, and Sassacomoit, a servant.

261.12   houle]   Hold of a ship.

261.27   Oranoque]   Orinoco River.

261.27–28   Reogrande, Loyer]   Amazon, Loire.

264.14–16   *God hath not . . . in none.*]   Fotherby, *Atheomastix*.

265.1   *The second Booke.*]   This book is substantially a reprint of Smith's *A Map of Virginia* (1612).

265.2   The Sixt Voyage]   The previous five voyages, all to Roanoke, were in 1584, 1585, 1586, 1587, and 1590.

266.17   a very goodly Bay]   The Chesapeake Bay.

267.20   bole Armoniac, terra sigillata]   *Bole armeniac*, a red clay used along with *terra sigillata* as an antidote for poison and as an astringent.

267.38   Powhatan]   King's River or James River.

268.1   Sacre]   Saker, a cannon weighing about 1,900 pounds that fired five-pound shot.

269.24   their great King]   Wahunsonacock, also known as Powhatan, the paramount chief of the Powhatans.

269.35   Toppahanock]   Rappahannock.

272.16–17   in their Barge] This is probably a setting error for "in our barge."

273.4–5   Master White] John White.

273.21–24   *Thus have I walkt . . . eyes doe finde.*] Fotherby, *Atheomastix*, derived from Lucretius and Horace.

274.27   *Putchamins*] Persimmons.

274.33   Crabs] Crab apples.

274.40   French Brittish wine] Breton wine.

275.7   *Chechinquamins*] Chinquapin, dwarf chestnut.

275.36–37   *Mattoum* growthe as our Bents] Cane grass (bent is an English term for reedy grass).

276.2   Raspises, hurts] Raspberries, hurtleberries (huckleberries).

276.8–9   *Tockawhoughe.*] Tuckahoe, green arrow arum.

276.20–21   *Wighsacan*] Milkweed.

276.23   *Pocones*] Puccoon, a red vegetable dye used by the Indians as a balm and for body painting.

276.28   *Musquaspen*] Bloodroot.

276.32   Pellitory of Spain] Pyrethrum, a medicine or remedy.

277.2   *Aroughcun*] Raccoon.

277.14   *Mussascus*] Muskrat.

278.2   Lanerets] Lanneret, a male lanner.

278.15   Bretts] Turbots.

278.18   Crevises] Crayfish.

278.27   moskered] Crumbled.

279.35   *Garnasses*] Chickpeas.

279.39   a Polt] A pestle.

280.6   Temmes] Siever.

280.13   *Ponap*] Pone or corn pone.

280.28   *Pumpeons*] Pumpkins.

280.29   *Macocks*] Gourds.

282.10   surprised mee at Pamaunkee] During his final encounter with Opechancanough; see Chronology, 1609.

283.28 chape] Metal cap covering the tip of a scabbard.

284.39 fishing wires] Fishing weirs.

287.19 tooke me prisoner] Smith was captured by Opechancanough in December 1607; see Chronology.

291.11–14 *But 'tis not . . . Phisicians art.*] Fotherby, *Atheomastix*, derived from Ovid.

292.28–29 *Fear was . . . Gods were not.*] Fotherby, *Atheomastix*.

293.10–11 *Thus seeke . . . of happinesse.*] Fotherby, *Atheomastix*, from Horace.

293.24–19 *Through God . . . create all these.*] Fotherby, *Atheomastix*, 124.

294.14–15 they have yearely a sacrifice of children] Referring to the *huskanaw* ritual in which Indian boys attained their manhood.

295.35–38 *Religion 'tis . . . cannot doe so.*] Fotherby, *Atheomastix*, from Juvenal.

306.6 WILLIAM SIMONS] The Rev. William Symonds (1556–1616?) preached at St. Saviours, Southwark, London.

307.4 Blackwall] Blackwall Docks in London.

310.9–14 *Good men . . . rest and ease.*] Fotherby, *Atheomastix*.

312.35 common Kettell] Common storehouse.

315.15–16 *Thus God . . . would us devour.*] Fotherby, *Atheomastix*.

317.9 King of Pamaunkee] Opechancanough.

317.14 gauld] Injured.

319.5 Table booke] Notebook.

319.29–30 *As if neare . . . Devils to dwell.*] Fotherby, *Atheomastix*, derived from Seneca.

320.7 Mutchato's] Moustaches.

321.1–3 *But his waking . . . of stupendious makes.*] Fotherby, *Atheomastix*, derived from Lucretius.

321.4 Merononomoco] Werowocomoco.

321.10 Rarowcun] Raccoon.

321.34–39 *They say he bore . . . suspected lead.*] Fotherby, *Atheomastix*, from Euripedes.

323.3–4 *Thus from numbe . . . all other griefe.*] Fotherby, *Atheomastix*.

324.1–5 *We men imagine . . . a mourning vaine.*] Fotherby, *Atheomastix*.

325.3–4 *Thus the Almightie . . . was God alone.*] Fotherby, *Atheomastix*, derived from Boethius.

326.4 cratches] Wooden frames or timbers.

329.16–19 *Oh cursed gold . . . an av'ritious man.*] Fotherby, *Atheomastix*, derived from Virgil and Juvenal.

330.19–24 *The God of Heav'n . . . and with shame.*] Fotherby, *Atheomastix*, from Homer.

332.3–4 *He hath not . . . hold it oap.*] Fotherby, *Atheomastix*, from Juvenal.

332.8n Sir Thomas Smith] Sir Thomas Smythe (1558–1625) was a leading London merchant and treasurer of the Virginia Company.

335.35 barricoes] Casks.

335.40–336.1 Ployer . . . Brittane] The lordship of Plouer in Brittany.

336.3 Isles of Morap] Isles of Morase (morass).

338.31–32 three or foure thousand] In the 1612 edition of *The Proceedings*, the Indians are described as numbering between 300 to 400.

339.16 skurfe] Deposit.

342.2–3 Callenture] Fever.

342.30 rackets] Rockets.

345.3 Ocean Sea] Atlantic.

345.4–5 we called Perigrines mount] Named for Peregrine Bertie, Lord Willoughby.

346.18 offering] Attempting.

347.4 thoules] Thole pins, pegs for keeping oars in place.

347.40n Manahaacks] Mannahoacs, a Siouan-speaking people who lived in the Virginia Piedmont.

354.1–10 *But to this place . . . a greater Barke.*] Fotherby, *Atheomastix*.

357.16 Mascarado] Masque or play.

357.28–29 *Thus did they shew . . . others voices chanting.*] Fotherby, *Atheomastix*.

358.36 Gentlewoman and woman-servant] Mistress Forrest and Anne Burras.

359.23–28 *But those that hunger . . . a thing so infinite.*] Fotherby, *Atheomastix*, from Seneca.

360.10–11   *For he who scornes . . . nor man, but both.*]   Fotherby, *Atheomastix*, from Antiphanes.

360.13   haggers]   Hackers, cutters.

362.9   *Peccavi*]   I have erred.

362.17   *Pocones*]   Puccoon.

362.39–40   Lord of Salisbury]   Robert Cecil, earl of Salisbury (1563?–1612), the Lord Treasurer and a leading figure in the Virginia Company.

362.40   President]   John Ratcliffe.

368.30   Chawwonock]   Chowanoc, on the Chowan River in North Carolina, principal residence of the Chowanoc Indians.

368.35–38   *So this Kings . . . against his Gods.*]   Fotherby, *Atheomastix.*

374.13   cocking of our matches]   Preparing to open fire.

374.19   brusting]   Bursting.

374.39–40   put out our matches]   Putting out the slow-burning matches in the firing locks of their muskets.

375.17–18   *Is any free . . . as the best.*]   Fotherby, *Atheomastix.*

377.5   bewrayed]   Betrayed.

381.39   Potauncak]   On the north bank of the Pamunkey River.

382.6   Wecuttanow]   Son of Opitchapam.

386.17   King of Paspahegh]   Wowinchopunck.

386.19   faucheon]   Falchion, a short broad sword.

387.12   Tussore]   Tassore.

387.27   fishing wires]   Fishing weirs.

389.31   Last of Tarre . . .]   A last was 12–14 barrels.

389.35   Wires]   Weirs.

391.6   *nolens, volens*]   Whether unwilling or willing.

392.13–16   *I know those things . . . yet finds none.*]   Fotherby, *Atheomastix*, derived from Seneca.

393.36–37   William Volday, a Zwitzar]   William Faldoe, a Swiss mineral expert.

394.38   Captaine Argall]   Captain Samuel Argall (1580–1626), a mariner and explorer who would later serve as acting governor of Virginia, was hired by the Virginia Company in 1609 to find a more direct route across the Atlantic that avoided the West Indies.

394.39   Master Cornelius] John Cornelius, a goldsmith, merchant, and member of the Virginia Company, who had sponsored Argall's voyage.

395.4   heard] Hard.

395.5   fraughted] Freighted.

396.27–28   their owne publication] The Virginia Company published two pamphlets, *A True and Sincere Declaration* and *A True Declaration*, in 1610.

396.32   Sir Thomas Dale] Dale (d. 1619) arrived in Jamestown in 1611 as deputy governor and marshal of Virginia. Like his friend Sir Thomas Gates, Dale had fought in the Netherlands against the Spanish.

397.12   Catch] Ketch, a small two-masted vessel.

398.11–16   *When ratling Thunder . . . that vengeance cryes.*] Fotherby, *Atheomastix*, derived from Lucretius.

399.5   Martin] Captain John Martin (c. 1567–1632), one of the original settlers.

401.9–11   *Thus oft we see . . . rest play'd theefe.*] Fotherby, *Atheomastix.*

403.18–21   *Strange violent forces . . . imbrace the worst.*] Fotherby, *Atheomastix*, derived from Ovid.

405.8   dyed most miserably.] Faldoe died of a fever in 1610.

406.19   G.P.] The identity of G.P. is uncertain, but it is possibly a misprint for W.P., William Phettiplace.

410.32   Henry Spilman] Henry Spelman (1595–1623) arrived in Virginia in August 1609, lived among the Patawomecks, and became an interpreter; see pp. 967–78 in this volume.

411.25   carbonado'd] Barbequed.

411.26   powdered] Salted.

413.9–38   Hee that shall . . . land of Canaan:] This passage is derived from the pamphlet *A True Declaration* (1610), published in London by the Virginia Company in 1610.

414.4–8   *That neither . . . all this whatsoever.*] Fotherby, *Atheomastix*, derived from Manilius.

416.39   *Out of a Declaration*] *A True Declaration* (1610).

418.31   *Lord La Wares discourse*] *A Short Relation made by the Lord De-La-Ware* (1611).

419.3   *out of Master Hamors Booke.*] Ralph Hamor, *A True Discourse* (1615).

419.30   Arsahattock . . . his new towne] Arrohattoc. The new town was Henrico, built near present-day Richmond, Virginia.

419.33   booke of Articles] *The Lawes Divine, Morall and Martiall*, published in London in 1612.

421.19–20   maine River] James River.

421.38   Master Whitaker] The Rev. Alexander Whitaker (1585–1617) arrived in Virginia in 1611 to serve as a missionary.

422.12   Champian] Champaign, open hilly country.

422.13   hundreds] An English administrative district below the county level.

423.5   Patawomeake] Potomac River.

423.9   Iapazaws] Iopassus.

425.10   Matchcot] At the head of the Pamunkey River, approximately 60 miles from Jamestown.

425.29   Master John Rolfe] Rolfe (1585–1622) arrived in Virginia in 1610 with Gates. He pioneered the cultivation of profitable tobacco in the colony.

428.17–18   Port Royall and Sancta Crux] Port Royal and St. Croix, Bay of Fundy, Nova Scotia.

430.8   *Rawrenoke*] Roanoke, small beads made of oyster shells that Indians used in barter.

431.14   Frowe] Froe, a tool for splitting staves, shingles, etc.

433.1–2   *The Contents . . . by the Counsell*] A summary of *A Declaration for the certaine time of drawing the great standing Lottery*, published by the Virginia Company in 1615.

433.17   losing] Lessening.

435.38   Pilot for England in 88.] In 1588, the year of the Spanish Armada.

436.9   the English Pilot] John Clarke.

436.13   Master George Yearly] Captain George Yeardley (c. 1577–1627) had fought in the Netherlands before arriving in Virginia with Gates in 1610. He served as deputy governor from April 1616 to May 1617, and later as governor from November 1618 to November 1621.

439.23   During this time] Pocahontas, who took the name Rebecca, married John Rolfe at Jamestown on April 5, 1614. They traveled to England with their young son, Thomas, in 1616. Pocahontas died at Gravesend in March 1617 while returning to Virginia.

439.34–35   Queenes most excellent Majestie] Queen Anne of Denmark, wife of James I.

441.10   might have line] Might have lain.

442.10   Branford] Brentford, Middlesex, a village near London.

442.28   Uttamatomakkin] A priest who served as a trusted counselor to Wahunsonacock, Uttamatomakkin was married to one of the chief's daughters, Matachanna. On his return to Virginia, he gave a very unfavorable report of his experiences in England to Opechancanough.

443.19–20   deserved] Requited.

443.32   March] April.

444.24   Companies companie] Company servants.

446.13   Richard Killingbeck] Killingbeck arrived in Virginia in January 1608.

446.26–27   *Machacomocko* house] Temple or treasure house.

446.29   Farfax] William Fairfax.

447.16   Itopatin] Although Opitchapam formally succeeded Wahunsonacock, Opechancanough became the de facto paramount chief.

447.28   Captaine Bruster] Edward Brewster.

448.11–12   Sir Edwin Sands] Sir Edwin Sandys (1561–1629), a leading figure in the House of Commons and a prominent member of the Virginia Company, succeeded Sir Thomas Smythe as Company treasurer in 1619. He was responsible for instituting wide-ranging reforms in the colony between 1618 and 1624.

448.23   generall assembly] The first general assembly met from July 30–August 4, 1619, in the church at Jamestown.

448.25   Captaine Lownes] Captain Christopher Lawne, a Puritan, promoted a large Puritan settlement at Lawne's Creek, Warrascoyack, on the south side of the James River.

449.16   Verinas] Varinas, a high quality tobacco from Venezuala.

449.27   Monahigan] Monhegan Island off the coast of Maine.

449.32   sold us twenty Negars] This remark by John Rolfe describes the arrival of the first Africans in English North America. Originally from Angola, they had been put on board a Portuguese slave ship, *St. John the Baptist,* bound for Vera Cruz in the Gulf of Mexico. The slaver was attacked by two privateers in American waters; one of the privateers, the *White Lion,* then went to Virginia, where the Africans were bartered for provisions.

449.38–39   foure Corporations] Elizabeth City, James City, Charles City, and Henrico. The Company laid out 3,000 acres for the governor's use near Jamestown and 10,000 acres near Henrico for a school intended to educate

Indian youths in English ways. In each of the four boroughs, 3,000 acres was set aside for the Virginia Company where servants sent at Company expense would work.

450.2–3   ancient Planters being set free]   In return for their service to the Company, ancient planters (those who arrived before April 1616) were granted 100 acres of land for their own use.

451.4–26   There went this yeare . . . the Plantations.]   This passage is derived from *A Declaration of the Colonie and Affairs in Virginia* published by the Virginia Company in 1620.

451.27   *A deperat Sea-fight*]   The description of the battle is taken from *A True Relation of a Wonderfull Sea Fight* (1621).

451.31*n*   Earle of Southampton]   Southampton was elected treasurer of the Virginia Company in June 1620.

452.5   Mettalina]   Martinique.

455.23   *The Names of the Adventurers*]   The names are taken from *A Declaration of the Colonie and Affairs in Virginia* (1620).

468.12   Sir Francis Wyat]   Wyatt (c. 1588–1644) from Boxley, Kent, was married to one of Sir Edwin Sandys' nieces. He succeeded Yeardley as governor in January 1621.

469.17   Master Jonas Stockam]   Stockham became the minister of Elizabeth City parish in May 1621.

469.33   decree of Darius]   See Ezra 6:11.

470.22–25   Master George Sands]   George Sandys, the youngest brother of Sir Edwin, served as treasurer of the Company in Virginia from 1621 until 1624.

472.21–30   *See'st not the world . . . leaves the same.*]   Fotherby, *Atheomastix.*

473.17   Kiptopeke]   Chief of the Accohannocks.

474.34   laughing Kings]   Esmy Shichans, chief of the Accomacs, was known to the English as the "Laughing King" because of his friendliness toward the settlers.

475.33   in making black Boyes]   During the *huskanaw* initiation ceremony.

476.4   February]   February 1622.

476.11–13   companies . . . Plantation of themselves]   Private or "particular" plantations, largely independent of the Virginia Company, developed in the colony after 1616 as a means of attracting settlers and investment.

477.16   *The massacre upon the two and twentieth of March.*]   Smith's account is based on *A Declaration of the State of the Colony and Affaires in Virginia* (1622), written by Edward Waterhouse on behalf of the Virginia Company.

479.35   guelt]   Gelded.

480.35   Thomas Hamer]   Thomas Hamor, older brother of Ralph Hamor.

486.22   Contraction house]   The Contraction House in Seville, Spain, regulated trade to the Americas.

488.11–15   *Men in this taking . . . fained Arts.*]   Fotherby, *Atheomastix*, derived from Lucretius.

489.14   Chiskact]   Kiskiack on the York River.

489.38–490.4   *Even as the wind . . . againe have roused.*]   Fotherby, *Atheomastix.*

490.25   Captaine Spilman]   Captain Henry Spelman.

491.28   by next Michaelmas]   By September 29, 1623.

492.23   custome of Virginia]   Revenues from duties on imports into England from Virginia.

497.2   Vineyetours]   Vintners, wine-growers.

497.23   Taber and a Pipe]   Drum and fife.

498.10   pety Magazines]   Small ships carrying stores and provisions.

498.36–37   9. of September]   September 9, 1622.

500.7   King and the great Conjuror]   The chief of the Patawomecks and his priest.

501.12–13   *But, alas the cause . . . what was amisse.*]   Fotherby, *Atheomastix.*

503.35   Lope Skonce]   Entrenchment, from the Dutch "loopschans."

505.26–29   *For the great . . . not be contented.*]   Fotherby, *Atheomastix.*

505.31   Barnestable]   Barnstaple, Devon.

505.32   Captaine Nathaniel Butler]   Butler remained in Virginia until January 1623. On his return to London he wrote a severe critique of the condition of the colony and mismanagement of the Virginia Company.

508.37–38   *Thus things proceed . . . we know them not.*]   Fotherby, *Atheomastix.*

509.1   *A particular of such necessaries*]   The list is taken from a broadside, *The Inconveniences That Have happened to Some Persons* (1622).

511.28   Eriffe and Chelsey] Erith, Kent, and Chelsea, London, both along the Thames.

515.20   *Out of these Observations*] Smith testified before the royal commission established in 1623 to investigate the alleged mismanagement of the colony by the Virginia Company.

516.1   stinted] Fixed or regulated.

521.37   the Court] The governing body of the Virginia Company.

522.4   Sir Thomas Smiths] Sir Thomas Smythe, a former treasurer of the Virginia Company, was a leading critic of the Sandys and Southampton administrations.

523.2–3   GENERALL HISTORIE OF THE BERMUDAS] Smith's account is based principally on two manuscripts, Nathaniel Butler's "Historye of the Bermudaes or Somers Isles" and Richard Norwood's "A Plott or Mappe of Bermudas or the summer Islands . . ."

526.4   pumish-like] Like pumice stone.

527.38   red weed] Castor-oil plant.

529.38   Pemblyco] Pimlico, north of London.

531.26   Madar] Madder.

531.36   Norrod] Norwood.

532.1   *A briefe relation*] This account is taken from "A Briefe Note of a Voyage to the East Indies," published by Hakluyt in *The Principal Navigations.*

532.26   Wine of hight] Wine drunk to mark reaching a certain latitude.

534.1   *The first English ship*] This account is based on material in Silvester Jourdain, *A Discovery of the Bermudas* (1610).

536.1   fis-gigs] Fishgigs, harpoons.

536.23   Master Raven] Henry Ravens, a ship's master.

537.17   Namuntack . . . Matchumps] Namontack and Machumps were sent to England in 1608 by Wahunsonacock to find out more about the English.

537.39   North parts of Virginia] Maine.

539.3   repairing] Preparing.

539.28   Matachin] Sword-dancer.

544.27   Tribes] Eight tribes were established and named for leading investors. Each tribe was represented by a bailiff (later councilor) and, from 1620, by two burgesses.

549.40   Dollars]   Spanish silver pesos.

553.33   pynes]   Pineapples.

554.6   Westerne Iles]   West Indies.

554.6–7   Brasile man]   Portuguese ship trading to Brazil.

556.5   wained]   Weaned.

556.16   garbish]   Gut.

557.9   fitters]   Pieces.

564.13   Lewes]   Lewis Hughes.

565.16   N.B.]   Probably Nathaniel Butler.

566.20   a Preacher]   Master Lang.

567.13   Redout]   Redoubt, fortification.

568.9   January]   About January 23, 1620.

568.24   rommy for the Sea]   Roomy, meaning to sail away.

569.28   Garnsey and Jarse]   Guernsey and Jersey, Channel Islands.

570.29   *In the yeere 1611*]   Somers died on November 9, 1610.

573.39   crasie]   Weakened in health.

574.7   Newgate . . . Bridewell]]   Newgate and Bridewell were London
prisons.

575.22   party cast]   Losing party.

576.24   Plait]   Silver bullion from Peru and Mexico.

577.29   two Virginian Women]   Two of the Powhatan women who had
accompanied Pocahontas to England in 1616.

577.38   the damnable plot]   The Gunpowder Plot to blow up James I and
Parliament on November 5, 1605.

578.18   Cassado roots]   Cassava.

578.24   Sacars]   See note 268.1.

578.32   Murderers]   See note 165.14*n*.

578.35–36   Curtaines, . . . Ravilings]   Curtains are walls between bas-
tions, and ravelins are earthworks thrown up in front of the curtains.

581.10   time of Captain Butlers government]   Butler's term as governor
ended in October 1622.

581.23–24   not allowed them the benefit of their booke]   The benefits of
established legal procedure.

581.33   Heriot]   Thomas Harriott.

582.16–18   Captaine Felgat . . . Ginner]   Captain Robert Felgate, lieutenant general, Captain Thomas Stokes, sheriff, Master Lewis Hughes,
preacher, George Needham, an old planter, and Anthony Jenner, an overseer.

583.2–7   *Till trechery and faction . . . have power to save.*]   Fotherby,
Atheomastix, from Plautus.

583.23   *Master John Harrison*]   Captain Harrison served from late December 1622 until October 1623.

585.9–587.28   *To his friend Captaine Smith . . . Carlton.*]   These verses
were first published in Smith's *Description of New England* (1616).

588.2–3   THE GENERALL HISTORIE OF NEW-ENGLAND]   The
sixth book draws heavily upon Smith's *Description of New-England* and *New
Englands Trials* but also includes material from *A Relation or Journall of the
English Plantation Setled at Plimoth* (1622), Edward Winslow, *Good Newes
from New-England* (1624), and Richard Whitbourne, *A Discourse Containing
a Loving Invitation to Adventurers in the New-Found-Land* (1622).

589.30   Capawe]   Capawack, which the English called Martha's Vineyard.

589.34   core fish]   Wet salt-fish.

591.1   Maligo]   Málaga, Spain.

596.24   Master Hutson]   Captain Henry Hudson.

596.40–597.1   Pitzara . . . Magilanus]   Pizarro, de Soto, Magellan.

602.1   Natolia]   Anatolia.

602.27   Podolia, Sagovia]   Regions of modern day Ukraine and Bulgaria.

605.29   Kermes]   See note 145.15.

611.24–36   Grips . . . Musquassus]   See notes 151.7–24.

622.12   Tantum]   Probably Squantum (Tisquantum).

624.33   together by the eares]   Fighting.

624.38   Rochilers]   From La Rochelle.

628.38–39   Master Crampton]   Samuel Crampton had sailed to New England with Smith in 1614.

631.25–27   *Its want of reason . . . not to grant.*]   Fotherby, *Atheomastix*.

632.20   thirty thousand pounds]   In previous versions, Smith gives two
to three million pounds.

634.20–22   Bastable . . . Tattnesse]   Barnstaple (Devon), Bodmin, Pen-
ryn, Fowey (all in Cornwall), Marlborough (Devon), Abson, near Bristol
(Gloucestershire), and Totnes (Devon).

636.6–7   *They say this plague . . . pleas'd not* Tantum *well.*]   Fotherby, *Atheomastix*, from Ovid.

636.22–23   *A due desert, . . . of base condition.*]   Smith wrote this couplet.

637.12   Cape James]   Cape Cod.

638.18   Gins]   Traps.

640.14   an Ile]   Clarks Island, Duxbury Bay.

640.15–16   a good Harbour]   The site of Plymouth.

641.35   a tall Salvage]   Samoset.

641.36–37   a Sagamo]   Chief.

642.3   Massasoyts]   Massasoit was chief of the Wampanoag people.

642.4   Nawsits]   Nausets.

643.15*n*   Pakanoki]   Pokanocket.

643.24   Namascet]   Namaskett.

645.2   Counacus]   Conanacus.

645.35   Coubatant]   Corbitant, chief of the Pocasset people.

646.34   naked]   Unarmed.

646.37   the next morning]   August 15, 1621.

648.40   Bases]   Bass.

649.8   beginning of July]   In 1622.

649.9   Master Westons]   Thomas Weston founded a settlement at Wessagusset (Weymouth), on the southern shore of Massachusetts Bay.

649.13   Wichaguscusset]   Wessagusset.

649.23   death of their Governor]   Weston's brother-in-law, Richard Green.

650.21   Massasowat]   Probably Massasoit's village, Sowams.

651.32   Wassapinewat]   Brother of the chief of the Massachusetts, Obtakiest.

652.18   these two Roarers]   Pecksuot and Wittawamat.

652.30   The Towne]   Wessagusset.

653.1   Barty Iles]   Monhegan.

654.3–4   two ships]   The *Anne* arrived at the end of July 1623 and the *Little James* at the end of August.

654.11–14   *Thus all men . . . is Author.*] Fotherby, *Atheomastix.*

660.5   *Master Dee*] See note 179.22.

662.17   Master Cherley] Probably James Sherley, treasurer of the adventurers of Plymouth.

663.9–10   Captaine Charles Whitbourne] Captain Richard Whitbourne, author of *A Discourse and Discovery of New-Found-Land* (1620) and *A Discourse Containing a Loving Invitation to Adventurers in the New-Found-Land* (1622).

664.12   Boriers] Borers.

664.16   dinnage] Dunnage, brushwood placed under salt to keep it dry.

664.31   Ocome] Oakum, used for cauking the seams of ships.

664.32   Maps] Mops.

664.33   Bolls] Bowls.

664.37   rode Ropes] Ropes for riding at anchor.

664.42   maunds.] Wicker baskets

665.3   kipnets] Hook and net used in fishing.

665.3–4   gagging hooks.] Probably gaffing hooks.

665.9   Saynes] Seine nets.

665.15   Deale Bourds.] Thin boards of fir or pine.

665.23   poore John] Salted and dried fish.

666.26   Toloune and Merselus] Toulon and Marseilles.

666.27   Kintall] Quintal, a hundredweight (112 lbs.).

670.2–3   Mines of Guiana or Potassie,] The legendary mines of Guiana unsuccessfully sought by Sir Walter Ralegh; the rich silver mines of Potosí, in the high Andes, discovered by the Spanish in 1546.

THE TRUE TRAVELS

673.2   William *Earle of Pembroke*] William Herbert (1580–1630), earl of Pembroke, a prominent investor in the Virginia and Bermuda companies.

673.5   Robert *Earle of Lindsey*] Robert Bertie (1582–1642), Baron Willoughby of Eresby, first earl of Lindsey, friend and patron of Smith.

673.7   Henrie *Lord Hunsdon*] Henry Cary, fourth Baron Hunsdon, Viscount Rochford, and first earl of Dover, a cousin of Thomas West, Baron De La Warr.

673.12   Sir Robert Cotton] Sir Robert Bruce Cotton (1571–1631), antiquarian, collector of manuscripts, and politician. In his later years, Smith had access to Sir Robert's library.

673.30   Sea Grammar] Smith published *A Sea Grammar* in 1627.

673.31   Sir Samuel Saltonstall] Sir Samuel Saltonstall (1580s?–1641), draper and son of Sir Richard Saltonstall, Lord Mayor of London, was a friend and patron of Smith. In his last years, Smith may have lived at Saltonstall's London house.

682.3   du'le] Duel.

683.5   Ithacan] Odysseus.

683.30   Nulla fides pietasque, qui castra sequuantur.] Marcus Annaeus Lucan: "There is no faith or piety in men who follow camps."

683.31   πολλῶν . . . ἔγνω] Homer, *Odyssey*: "He saw the cities and came to know the minds of many men."

684.2–3   Quisque . . . usque suæ?] Based on Sallust quoting Appius: "Everyone is the maker of his own destiny: has any smith ever more truly forged his own fortune than you, Smith?"

689.19   His parents dying] Smith's father died in 1596; his mother, who soon remarried, lived until at least 1609.

690.10   Master David Hume] A poet and scholar, Hume was a distant cousin of a Scottish nobleman who was a friend of the Berties.

690.12   Roane] Rouen.

690.15   Peace being concluded] Scholars believe Smith confused the sequence of events at the beginning of his military career; see Chronology, 1596–1600.

690.19   Ancusan] Enkhuizen, in the Netherlands.

690.21   holy Ile . . . neere Barwicke] Isle of Lindisfarne. Near Barwicke refers to Berwick-upon-Tweed, an English garrison on the border with Scotland.

690.23–34   Ripweth] Redpath

690.36   Seignior Theadora Polaloga] Theodore Paleologue, riding master to Henry Clinton, earl of Lincoln.

691.17   Dutchesse of Mercury] Duchess of Mercoeur.

691.33   Carralue] French quart d'ecu, worth one shilling, six pence.

692.2   Mortaigne] Possibly Mortain in Normandy, near the border with Brittany.

692.6–7   Deepe . . . Cane] Dieppe, Caudebec, Honfleur, Pont-Audemer, and Caen.

692.26   Pounterson and Dina]   Pontorson and Dinan.

693.2–3   Simbreack]   Saint-Brieuc.

693.3   Tuncadeck]   Tonquédec.

693.3–4   Gingan]   Guingamp.

693.35–36   Cape Rosata]   Cape Ras et Tin, near Derna, Libya.

693.37   Scandaroone]   Alexandretta, now Iskenderun.

693.40   Candia]   Crete.

694.1   Isle of Zaffalonia]   Cephalonia, now Kefallinia.

694.10   the Britaine]   The Breton.

694.26   Pyasters, Chicqueenes and Sultanies]   Forms of currency: piasters (pieces of eight), zecchini, and sultanons.

694.36–695.1   Antibo in Peamon]   Antibes in Piedmont, a territory of the dukes of Savoy.

695.1–2   five hundred chicqueenes]   Worth about £200.

695.36   Slavonia . . . in Steria]   Slovenia, Ljubljana, Graz, and Styria.

695.37–38   Almania]   Germany.

695.40   Lord Ebersbaught]   Eibiswald, a prominent family of Slovenia.

696.2   Baron Kisell]   Lieutenant Colonel Hanns Jakob Khissl, chief of artillery at Graz.

696.3   the Earle of Meldritch]   Count of Modrusch.

696.7   *Olumpagh*]   Lendava, Slovenia.

696.9   Caniza]   Nagykanizsa (Great Kanizsa), a major fort.

696.18   this strange invention]   Smith probably learned the code and system from an appendix to Machiavelli's *Arte of Warre* added by the translator, Peter Whitehorne.

697.2   linke]   Torch.

697.19   Hysnaburg]   Eisenburg (Vasvar).

697.35   Kerment]   Kormend.

698.2   *Stowlle-wesenburg*]   Székesfehérvár (Alba Regalis), an ancient capital and burial place of the kings of Hungary, was captured by the Ottoman Turks in 1543.

698.4   *Earle Rosworme*]   Hermann Christoff, Graf von Russworm.

698.9   the Emperour]   Holy Roman Emperor Rudolph II.

698.11–12   Duke Mercury]   Philippe-Emmanuel, Duke of Mercoeur.

698.14   Gonzago]   Ferrante II Gonzaga, count of Guastella.

698.15   Georgio Busca]   Giorgio Basta.

698.24   Bemers]   Bohemians.

698.38   Earle Von Sulch]   Karl Ludwig Graf zu Sultz, imperial chief of artillery.

698.36   Comora]   Smith spent the winter of 1600–1 at Kormaron, at the confluence of the rivers Danube and Vah.

699.18   Segeth]   A suburb of Székesfehérvár.

699.22   bavins]   Light brushwood.

700.7   *Assan Bashaw*]   Hasan Pasha, grand vizier and commander in chief in Hungary.

700.10   Mahomet, the great Turke]   Mehemed III, the Ottoman Sultan.

701.15   Zanzacks]   Cavalry.

701.29   Zigetum]   Szigetvar.

701.39   Strigonium]   Esztergom.

702.14   *Prince Sigismundus*]   Zsigmond Báthory, prince of Transylvania (1572–1613).

702.27   Michael]   Mihail Viteazul, voivode (prince) of Walachia was assassinated in August 1601 on the orders of Giorgio Basta.

703.37   Skonces]   A small fort or earthwork.

704.8   Zachel Moyses]   Mózes Székely.

704.23   Turbashaw]   The name probably means Turkish captain.

704.30–31   Howboyes]   Hautboy, a wind instrument.

704.34   Janizary]   Janissaries were elite infantry troops.

704.39   Beaver]   Face guard on a helmet.

705.14   placard]   Armor.

705.35   bils]   Bills, hooked blades.

706.5   Cutlets]   Armor protecting the back.

706.14   *Prince Rodoll*]   Radul Serban, appointed voivode of Walachia by Rudolph.

707.9   composition]   Surrender terms.

707.31   three hundred Ducats]   About £150.

712.16	Temesware] Temesvár.
712.33	Jeremie] Jeremia Movila, appointed voivode of Walachia by the Turks.
713.12	Rebrinke] Ramnicu-Valcea.
713.13	Argish] Curtea-de-Arges.
713.14	Peteske] Pitesti.
713.16	Crym-Tartar] Gazi Giray II, (1554–1608), khan of the Crimean Tartars.
713.19	Porters] Officers commanding the gates.
713.23	*Rotenton*] Rotenturm (Verestorony).
714.1	Hydukes] Hajduks, irregulars, mercernaries.
715.1	Langanaw] Campulung (Langenau).
717.40	Axopolis] Axiopolis (Cernavoda, Romania).
718.4–5	Adrinopolis] Modern Edirne.
718.8	Charatza Tragabigzanda] The name means "girl from Trebizond."
718.11	*Dissabacca Sea*] Sea of Azov.
719.10	Osie-shoulds] Muddy, oozy shallows.
719.40	*Drub-man*] Dragoman, interpreter, guide.
720.3	Ulgries] Big-horned sheep.
720.5	*Forsades*] Galley slaves.
720.16	Garnances] Garbanzos, chickpeas.
721.6	bases] Skirts reaching to the knee.
721.16	*Burracho's*] Leather bottles.
721.18	Hordias] Hordes, large groups.
721.23	lome] Loam, caulk.
721.25	*Murse*] Mirza, prince.
721.30	*Stroggs*] Sailing vessel.
723.16	*Cossmos*] Kumiss, fermented milk.
724.40	Taurica, or Osow] Crimea, Azov.
725.1	Tanais] Don River.
725.24	Bezer] Bezoar-stone was prized as a medicine.

725.33   Chan] Khan.

726.16   Sultaines . . . Marhies] Sultans were younger sons of the khan, tuians and ulans were nobles, and mirzas were princes' sons.

727.6   cruds] Curds.

728.37   cavarine] Javelin.

729.23–24   Saberya, Yaick, and Yem] Siberia, the Ural River and Yema.

730.25   Castragan] The road to Astrakhan.

731.16   Meotis] Another name for the Sea of Azov.

732.8   rampiers] Ramparts.

732.16   calievers] Arquebuses.

732.23–24   curious] Finely crafted.

732.33–34   Lipswick . . . Misenland] Leipzig, Meissen.

732.40   Hama . . . Mentz] Hanau, Mainz.

733.6   Cheryes, Cales] Jerez, Cádiz.

733.12   Guta] Ceuta.

733.21   brouch] Rod or pole.

733.33   Alfantica] Customhouse.

734.9   Larbes] Berbers.

734.17   Mully Hamet] Mulai Ahmed IV. His three sons were Mulai Es-Sheikh (the crown prince), Mulai Zidan, and Mulai Abd-el-Aziz.

734.39   Plummers] Craftsmen in metals, especially lead.

737.5   John de Leo] Leo Africanus (1488?–1554?), Moorish traveler and writer whose *Description of Africa* was translated into English in 1600. He converted to Christianity while enslaved in Italy.

737.6–7   Ginny and Binne] Guinea and Benin.

737.14   Gago or Tumbatu] Gao and Timbuktu.

737.29   Cape of Bone Esperance] Cape of Good Hope.

739.5   Anchicos] Anzichi.

739.15   *Lamache*] Lumache, snails.

740.4   Presbiter John] The legendary Christian kingdom in Africa founded by Prester John.

740.37   Saffe]   Safi.

741.3   *Captaine Merham*]   Smith had traveled from Spain to Morocco with Merham, a French privateer.

741.18   Boyadora]   Cape Bojador.

741.19   Cape Noa]   Cape Nun or Noun.

741.24–25   sprung his loufe]   Brought the ship's head closer to the wind.

742.3   yare]   Quick.

743.5–6   Sancta Cruse, Cape Goa]   Agadir, Cape Ghir.

745.29–30   Master Abraham Perce]   Pierce, or Piersey, was the head merchant of the colony and one of its wealthiest planters.

746.30   Doctor Poot]   Dr. John Pott was temporary governor, 1629–1630.

748.32   Parmacitty]   Spermacetti, used in medicines and for making candles.

748.34   byle]   Boil.

748.35   snuffe]   Wick.

749.9   too much custome]   Too many tolls.

749.19   much beating it]   Over fishing.

749.29   Turbay]   Tor Bay, or Torbay, Devon.

752.1   no other nation]   The Dutch established their colony of New Amsterdam on the Hudson River in 1625.

753.14   Mano]   Manoa.

753.17   Francis Sparrow]   Francis Sparrey.

753.26   Captaine Ley]   Captain Charles Leigh, brother of Oliph Leigh, sailed for Guiana (the region between the Orinoco and Amazon) in 1604.

753.28   River Weapoco]   Oyapock River.

753.31   Sir Thomas Roe]   Roe visited Guiana around 1610. He was later ambassador to the Great Mogul Jahangir, 1613–19, and to the Sublime Porte in Istanbul from 1621 to 1628.

755.15   Lord Gundamore]   Don Diego de Acuña, Conde de Gondomar.

756.22   This great River]   Amazon.

758.2   Guanes]   Iguanas.

758.11   Monsieur de Nombe]   Pierre Belain, sieur d'Esnambuc.

758.13   Charybes]   Caribs.

758.35–36   Tortels]   Marine tortoises.

758.40–759.1   Earle of Carlile]   James Hay, earl of Carlisle, was made lord proprietor of the Caribbean in July 1627.

760.5   It]   St. Christopher (St. Kitts).

760.13   Saint Mattalin]   Martinique

760.16   Deceado]   Déserade, off Guadeloupe.

760.17   Bernardo]   Barbuda.

762.3   Mayes]   Maize, corn.

762.9   cods]   Pods.

762.32   poudered]   Salted.

763.7   Captaine Henry Powel]   Powell arrived with 80 colonists in February 1627.

763.8   Disacuba]   Essequibo River, Guyana.

763.10   Arawacos]   Arawaks.

763.22   Mancinell apple]   Manchineel.

763.34   Gwane]   Guava.

763.37   Fusticke trees]   The fustic tree yields a yellow dye.

764.4   Ginni wheat]   Guinea wheat, another name for maize.

764.26   Sir William Curtine]   Sir William Courteen, a wealthy Anglo-Dutch merchant who vied with the earl of Carlisle to settle Barbados.

765.2   *Mevis*]   Nevis.

765.32   Master Littleton]   Thomas Littleton, a merchant.

765.34   Barbados]   Smith probably means Barbuda.

766.36   vast]   Waste land.

768.8   Callis]   John Callice, cousin of Henry Herbert, earl of Pembroke.

768.11   Flemming]   Captain Thomas Flemyng.

769.6   Sally]   Salé near Rabat, Morocco, an infamous pirate haunt.

769.8   Massalqueber]   Mers-el-Kebir, Algeria.

769.10   Arzella]   Arcila, near Tangier.

770.4   purchase]   Booty, plunder.

ADVERTISEMENTS FOR THE UNEXPERIENCED PLANTERS

771.1   ADVERTISEMENTS] Advice.

773.3   GEORGE] George Abbot.

773.8   SAMUEL] Samuel Harsnett.

780.3   Brownists] Followers of Robert Browne who advocated separating themselves from the Anglican Church. The Pilgrims of Leiden and Plymouth were Brownists, as were some of the early Puritan settlers in Virginia.

781.7   bravery] Luxury.

784.4   a roarer] A profane, unruly gallant.

784.23   seven or eight thousand] Smith is confusing the number of English settlers sent to the colony between 1607 and 1622 with the actual English population before the Indian uprising.

787.4   the Author] William Bradford.

787.24–25   culturate] Cultivate.

787.25   coyle] Turmoil.

791.1   *Chapter 6.*] A condensed version of Book IV of *The Generall Historie* (1624).

793.8   bottoms] Skeins.

793.12   *Chapter 7.*] This chapter is drawn from *New Englands Trials* (1622).

793.25   Colonels Seale] Colony's seal.

794.13–14   humorists] Enthusiasts, fanatics.

794.28   naked] Mere.

794.30   Bayses] Bass.

797.10   couzened] Cheated.

798.4   mart] Marque.

799.3   procured new Letters Patent] Smith refers to Sir William Alexander's patent of 1621 to settle Nova Scotia and part of Canada.

803.18   the marble harbour] Marblehead. The "marble" is gray granite.

806.38   this October] October 1630.

806.38   for toies] Trinkets, small trade goods.

809.10   Cratchets] Poles with forks at the top.

809.30   mundall] Mundane.

812.7   chiefe undertaker]   Chief investor.

812.38   Cicilia]   Sicily.

814.19–20   literall Captaines]   Captains in name only.

814.23   Port Riall]   Port Royal, Bay of Fundy in Nova Scotia.

816.7   Captaine Candish]   Captain Thomas Cavendish.

816.7–8   Sir Richard Luson]   Sir Richard Leveson.

OTHER NARRATIVES OF ROANOKE, JAMESTOWN, AND THE FIRST ENGLISH SETTLEMENT OF AMERICA

819.31   disbogging]   Disemboguing, flowing out.

820.15   The first that appeared unto us]   An inlet between capes Lookout and Hatteras.

821.9   Conies]   Rabbits.

821.12   Hyrcania]   A region of Persia located southeast of the Caspian Sea.

821.17–18   Master Winter . . . the Streights of Magellane]   On December 13, 1577, John Winter (d. 1581) sailed in command of the *Elizabeth* as part of Sir Francis Drake's expedition to circumnavigate the globe. After passing through the Strait of Magellan the *Elizabeth* became separated from the rest of the fleet. It repassed the Strait and returned to England on June 2, 1579, with, among other exotic articles, some cinnamon.

822.1   Pinnesse]   Pinnace. A small boat with oars and sails.

822.8   Wingina]   A chief of the Indians living on and near Roanoke Island.

822.30–32   the King himself . . . called Wingina]   The identification of Wingina's enemy as Wingina is probably the result of a printer's error.

823.4   Buffe]   Possibly bison skins.

824.8   these men, which we brought home]   Manteo and Wanchese, Indians who returned to England with Amadas and Barlow.

825.36   very artificially]   Very artfully.

825.40–826.1   for the beating of the billoe]   So as to avoid the tide.

826.13   furmentie]   Frumenty, wheat boiled in milk and seasoned.

826.13   sodden Venison]   Stewed with corn and beans.

827.31   Menatoan]   Chief of the Chowanoac tribe.

829.31–32   this inclosed Sea]   Pamlico Sound.

829.33   one is sixeteene miles long]   Roanoke Island.

829.36 Currans] Small grapes.

831.3 Sir Richard Greenvile] Grenville (1542–1591) was a cousin of Sir Walter Ralegh and led Ralegh's second expedition to Virginia when Elizabeth I denied Ralegh permission to lead it in person.

831.5 The 19. daye of Maye] The text printed here is taken from the first edition of Richard Hakluyt, *The Principal Navigations, Voyages, Traffiques and discoveries of the English Nation* (1589). In the 1600 edition, Hakluyt corrected this date to "The 9. day of April."

831.8 Flie boate] A flat-bottomed Dutch vessel with a high stern and either one or two masts.

831.12 Master Ralfe Lane] Ralph Lane, see Biographical Notes.

831.12–13 Master Thomas Candishe] Thomas Cavendish (c. 1555–1592), captain of the *Elizabeth.* Cavendish later successfully circumnavigated the globe, 1586–88, but died off the coast of South America while attempting a second circumnavigation.

831.13 Master Raimund] George Raymond (d. 1591), captain of the *Lyon.* In 1591, he commanded the *Penelope* as part of the first English expedition to the East Indies, and was lost.

831.23 the Island of S. John] Puerto Rico.

831.25 The 15. day of Maye] Corrected by Hakluyt to "The 12. day of Maye" in the 1600 edition.

831.31 a new pinnesse] A pinnace belonging to the *Tiger* had been lost when the fleet was scattered by bad weather off Portugal.

831.33 fet] Fetched.

833.5 The 29. day] This is probably a printer's error.

833.6 stoong] Stung.

833.23 mauger] Despite.

833.28 Isabella] Near Puerto Plata, Dominican Republic.

834.24 kyne] Cows.

835.4–5 then Master John Hawkins . . . saint John de Ullua] In 1567 John Hawkins (1532–1595) commanded a fleet of six ships engaged in illicit trade and piracy along the coast of Spanish America. Putting in to the Mexican port of San Juan de Ulúa, Mexico, for provisions and repairs, the English were surprised by a flotilla of 13 Spanish ships, with the new Viceroy of Mexico, Don Martín Enríquez, on board. Although negotiations produced an agreement allowing the English to leave, Don Martín ordered an attack. Only two English ships, the *Minion*, captained by Hawkins, and the *Judith*, commanded by Hawkins's kinsman Francis Drake, escaped.

835.5–6   John Oxnam . . . streights of Dariene]   After earlier successful forays in Spanish America, John Oxenham (d. 1580) led an expedition to Panama in 1575 that crossed the Isthmus of Darien, built a boat, and began attacking Spanish shipping in the Pacific. Oxenham and his crew became the first Englishmen to sail the Pacific, but when they attempted to return across the isthmus with their plunder, they were captured and Oxenham and the other leaders of the expedition were hanged.

835.13   the Admirall]   *The Tiger*, the flagship of the fleet.

835.16   Portingall]   A Portuguese.

835.19   Guanema]   An island in the Bahamas, probably Cat Island.

835.20   Sygateo]   An island in the Bahamas, probably Eleuthera.

835.27   Wocokon]   On the Outer Banks.

836.3   Tilt boate]   A small transport.

836.5   Master Harriot]   Thomas Hariot, see Biographical Notes.

836.7–8   John White]   See Biographical Notes.

836.8–9   Ococon]   Wococon.

836.11–12   the great lake . . . Paquype]   The present Lake Mattamuskeet, in Hyde County, North Carolina.

836.14   Pomeioke]   See Plate 16.

836.16   Secotan]   See Plate 19.

836.19   the Admirall]   Philip Amadas.

836.32   The Admirall was sent to Weapemeoke]   Amadas was being sent to explore Albermarle Sound.

838.6   Ralfe Lane]   Ralph Lane, see Biographical Notes.

839.2   kenning]   Sight.

839.12   Chesepians]   A tribe living near the mouth of the Chesapeake Bay, near present-day Virginia Beach, Virginia.

839.20   beares]   Berries.

839.29   Choanoke]   On the Chowan River, in present-day Hertford County, North Carolina.

842.20   the River of Morotico]   The Roanoke River.

842.31   vale water]   Ebb-tide.

844.19   weares . . . womans Towne]   The fish weirs of the Weapemeoc villages on Albermarle Sound.

844.33 mastives] Bull mastiffs.

846.29–30 light horseman] A long, light boat or wherry.

847.22 Easter eve] Saturday, April 2, 1586.

847.33 perfited] Accomplished.

848.16 Master Yougham] Joachim Ganz, the expedition's specialist in minerals.

852.1 Cassada, and Chyna] Cassada is a bread made from starchy roots, and chyna is made from prickly vines; both foods were a regular part of the Indians' winter diet.

852.10 in ure] Into effect.

852.25 moneths minde] A month's mind, a traditional Roman Catholic mass for the soul of the deceased, celebrated a month after death.

853.30–31 Croatoan my lord Admirals Island] Lane had named Croatoan, a barrier island near Cape Hatteras, in honor of Admiral Charles Howard, Lord Effingham (1536–1624).

855.21 Canuisado] Camisado, a surprise attack by night.

856.18 Petronell] A large pistol.

857.30 caliever] Arquebus.

858.7 experimented] Experienced.

858.8 gings] Troops.

859.16–17 considering the doings . . . and also for America] A reference to the ongoing war with the Spain.

861.1 Santa Cruz] St. Croix, U.S. Virgin Islands.

862.2 Beake] Vieques Island.

862.2 S. Johns] San Juan, Puerto Rico.

862.7 Cottea] A small island off the south coast of Puerto Rico.

862.10 Musketas Bay] Guayanilla Harbor, Puerto Rico.

862.19 Rosse Baye] Either Sucia Bay to the east or Salinas Bay to the west.

863.1–2 S. Germans Baye] Boqueron Bay.

863.2 Pines] Pineapples.

863.3 Mameas] Mamey, a tropical fruit related to the mango.

863.3 Platonos] Plantains.

863.27–28   the French Ambassador . . . Alanson into Spaine] Alanson was a French trader who, along with other French merchants, had been removed from Hispaniola by the order of Philip II of Spain.

863.33   the Islande Caycos] Probably East Caicos.

864.30   the Summer was farre spent] For privateering directed at Spanish treasure ships.

867.3   Winchese] Wanchese.

868.16   differre] Defer.

871.33   Capestone] Capstan.

872.33–34   Smewicke . . . of Ireland] Smerwick Harbor, on the northwest coast of the Dingle peninsula in County Kerry.

872.36   Dingen Cushe] Dingle.

873.13   Martasew] Marazion.

876.10   chiefe enterpriser . . . of her Majestie] Ralegh.

878.31   Grogran] Grosgrain.

878.32   silke wormes] Probably tent caterpillars, since silkworms are not native to North America.

879.26   Wapeih] The Indian word for a white clay believed to have medicinal qualities.

879.27   terra Sigillata] See note 19.18–19.

880.3–4   the booke of Monardes . . . from the West Indies] Nicholas Monardes, *Joyful newes out of the new founde worlde* (1577).

880.28   Marterne] Marten.

880.31   Luzarnes] Bobcats or lynx.

880.38   Civet cattes] Skunks.

881.21   Testrone] Teston.

881.29   pide] Pied.

882.21   Oade] Woad.

883.16   *Pagatowr*] An Indian word for "things put in a kettle to boil."

884.23   *Melden*] *Melde* is Dutch for members of the spinach and beet family. The plant was likely a kind of orarch, of the genus *Atriplex*.

884.33   Planta Solis] A sunflower.

886.37   fleame] Phlegm.

889.28   *Metaquesúnnauk*]   An Indian word possibly meaning "eaten un-cooked" and referring here to the prickly pear, genus *Opuntia*.

889.33   Cochinile]   Cochineal, a red dye made from crushed bodies of the insect *Dactylopius coccus*, which is found on several species of cactus in Mexico. It was at first commonly supposed to be made from the berry or grain of a plant.

891.38   Stockdoves]   Mourning doves.

892.11   Parats]   The Carolina paroquet (*Conuropsis carolinensis carolinensis*), now extinct.

892.28–34   The inhabitants use . . . for this purpose.]   See Plate 25.

893.3   Crevises]   Crayfish.

893.36   a kinde of trees]   Probably a tulip tree or a cypress.

894.25   Cassia Lignea]   Lignum vitae.

895.7   wot]   Know.

895.14   Tenet and Shepy]   Thanet and Sheppey, both in Kent.

897.35–39   They think . . . *Machicómuck*]   See Plate 6.

899.4   priestes]   See Plate 24.

902.32   conclude]   Hakluyt altered this to "exclude" in the 1600 edition.

903.30   pollicie]   Polity.

904.5   Jury]   Judea.

904.5   Candy]   Crete.

904.12   unknowne]   Hakluyt altered this to "knowen" in the 1600 edition.

904.27   speciall]   Hakluyt altered this to "specially" in the 1600 edition.

906.12   East of Cape Cantyn, and the Bay of Asaphi]   Cape Beddouza and the Bay of Safiff, in Morocco.

906.13   Ile of Mogador]   Off Essaouira, Morocco.

907.9   Los Santos]   Îles des Saintes.

908.28–29   Master Lane, Captaine of the Pinnesse]   William Lane, captain of the *John Evangelist*.

908.38   Whitsunday Even]   June 6.

910.5n   Iland of Navaza]   Located approximately 100 miles south of Guantanamo Bay, Cuba.

910.15   Captaine Cooke]   Abraham Cocke, captain of the *Hopewell*.

911.20   the Mooneshine]   The *Moonlight*.

911.19   disbocked]   Disembogued, passed through the straits.

912.33   2 Minions and a Falkon]   Small cannons.

913.2   Kindirkers mountes]   Prominent sand dunes near Cape Kenrick.

916.28   apecke]   Apeak, vertical, i.e., when a ship is directly above its anchor.

917.37   lye atry]   Lying to, i.e., turning the bow to the wind to keep the ship from moving forward.

920.9   the Downes]   See note 5.9.

920.11   the Captaine]   See note 5.16.

920.15–16   Mattanenio]   Martinique.

921.25   Mevis]   Nevis.

922.18   Castutia]   Probably a reference to St. Eustatius.

922.34   Mona]   An island off the western coast of Puerto Rico.

923.2   Guanas]   Iguanas.

924.7   Captaine Gabrill Archer]   See Biographical Notes.

925.11   Cape Henry]   The cape was named after Prince Henry (1594–1612), the eldest son of James I.

926.33   Targatiers]   Men armed with swords and carrying targets (round shields).

928.2   Watchet . . . Murray]   Wachet is a light blue, murray a dark purple.

929.2   pace]   Forest path.

929.36   Hasell]   Hazel.

931.37   Mountaines]   Elevations.

933.13   Cape Merchant]   See note 8.35.

937.10   Popham syde]   The northern side of the James River.

938.14   greate kyng Pawatah]   Pawatah was also known as Tanx (Little) Powhatan.

942.32   tewed]   Exhausted.

944.34   a Loofe]   Aloof.

945.10   400.^li]   £400.

945.17   pompions]   Pumpkins.

945.21   Salisbury syde]   The southern side of the James River.

950.5   your selves]   This manuscript was probably addressed to the Virginia Company of London.

950.9   Phisitions]   Physicians, i.e., students of natural science.

950.32   the president]   Wingfield; see Chronology.

951.29   Croatoon]   Croatan Sound in North Carolina.

952.37–38   runnagates]   Renegades, deserters.

959.19   Lather]   Ladder.

961.24   Chapter in Leviticus]   Leviticus 24.

962.34   Blackwall]   Blackwall Docks in London.

963.1–2   *nil conscire sibi*]   To be conscious of no wrongdoing.

965.17   Galthropp]   Stephen Calthorp, a Jamestown settler who died from disease on August 15, 1607. It is not clear whether the "Confessed mutiny" Wingfield refers to was involved in John Smith's arrest and detention during the voyage to Virginia in 1607 (see Chronology).

967.22   litell Powhatan]   See note 938.14.

969.10   Capt: Argall]   See note 394.38.

969.22   viage]   Voyage.

976.7   tewe]   Make into leather.

977.4   Vitall]   Victual.

979.14   EXCELLENT Lady]   The recipient of Strachey's letter has not been identified. It was first published by Samuel Purchas in *Hakluytus Posthumus, or Purchas His Pilgrimes* (1625).

980.35–38   *Hostium . . . ripas.*]   Horace, *Odes*, III, 27, ll. 21–24: "May the wives and children of our foes alone be the victims of the rising South Wind and the roaring of the dark waters, and the beaches shaken by the blast." (Translated Richard M. Gummere.)

981.38   a bottome of Candy]   A ship from Crete.

981.39–982.1   *Ego . . . Iapex.*]   Horace, *Odes*, III, 27, ll. 18–20: "I know the murky waves of the Adriatic and the ominous signs of the clear West Wind." (Translated Richard M. Gummere.)

983.18   Bitacke]   Binnacle.

984.7   Our Governour]   Sir Thomas Gates.

984.16   *Aperto cœlo*]   The open sky.

986.3   Barricos]   Small barrels.

987.39–988.2   Gonzalus . . . *West Indies*]   Gonzalo Fernández de Oviedo y Valdés (1478–1557), *La Historia general de las Indias* (1535).

988.26*n*   Cap. Butlers]   Nathaniel Butler was governor of Bermuda, 1619–22.

988.35–36*n*   *sub judice . . . filia.*]   The controversy is before the court; truth is the daughter of time.

989.36   Biscani]   Biscay.

992.5   Acosta]   José de Acosta (1540–1600), author of *Historia natural y moral de las Indias* (1590).

993.16   Gundall]   Gondola.

994.10–11   Junius]   Hadrianus Junius, Latin name of the Dutch physician and naturalist Adriaan de Jong (1511–1575).

994.24*n*   *Medio tutissimus ibis.*]   You will go most safely in the middle.

994.22   Oviedus]   See note 987.39–988.2.

997.3–4   Peter Martyr . . . Ocean]   Peter Martyr d'Anghiera (1457–1526) began publishing reports of Spanish exploration of the New World in 1511. Organized into "decades" (series of ten chapters), they appeared as *De orbe novo* in 1530 and were translated into English by Ricard Eden in 1555.

997.30   Barke of Aviso]   A boat carrying news, dispatches, or intelligence.

1000.23   Loe]   Low.

1000.33   Pooles]   Heads.

1001.34   Brownist]   A follower of the separatist preacher Robert Brown (c. 1550–1633).

1013.5   Duke of Yorke Cape Charles]   Charles I (1600–1649) was Duke of York from 1605 until his ascension to the throne in 1625.

1013.8–9   Queeneburrough and Lee]   Queenborough, on the Isle of Steppey in Kent, is on the south side of the mouth of the Thames, and Leigh, Essex, is on the north side.

1013.18   Ile of Dogges]   The Isle of Dogs is a peninsula on the north bank of the Thames in London, opposite Greenwich.

1014.3–4   Algernoone Fort . . . George Percy]   Percy named the fort after his nephew Algernon Percy (1602–1668), the eldest son of his brother Henry Percy, ninth earl of Northumberland.

1014.29*n*   *Ipsi causa malorum*]   They created their own misfortune.

1016.19–22   *Yet a little . . . armed man.*]   Proverbs 6:10–11.

1017.26*n*   *Rem acu tetigit*]   You have touched the matter with a needle; you have accurately described it.

1017.26   deboist]   Debauched.

1018.33   the Euxine Sea]   The Black Sea.

1019.24   Cade]   Cask.

1023.37   quaite]   Throw.

1024.10   Byrza]   Byrsa, the hill on which was built the citadel of the city of Carthage.

1024.22   Corps du guard]   Guardhouse.

1025.4   Holberdiers]   Men armed with halberds.

1025.19   Demi-Culverin]   See note 22.38.

1030.5*n*   *Ad Græcas Calendas*]   To the Greek Calends, a Roman expression meaning "never."

1036.34   *Discite justitiam moniti.*]   Be advised and learn justice.

1038.4–5   *The Historie . . . Britania*]   Strachey probably completed writing *The Historie* by 1612; it remained unpublished until 1849.

1039.3–4   so wryting Berosus]   Strachey draws upon a history published in 1545 by the Italian writer Annius of Viterbo (c. 1432–1502), which Annius falsely attributed to Berosus, a Hellenistic Babylonian historian of the 4th and 3rd centuries B.C.E.

1039.21   Boem of Auba]   German humanist Johannes Böhm (c. 1485–c. 1535), also known as Bohemus Aubanus.

1040.27   Acosta]   See note 992.5.

1041.16–17   Francis West, our Lord Generalls brother]   West (1586–1633?) was a younger brother of Baron De La Warr.

1045.34   Psalme. *Dixi vos sicut Dii estis*]   See Psalm 82:6: "I have said, ye are gods."

1045.35   Catagraph]   Outline, first delineation.

1048.9   Apoke]   Tobacco.

1049.26   rivadge]   Bank.

1050.36   Sea gowne]   A short-sleeved gown worn by mariners.

1051.34–35   arming Sword]   A single-handed, double-edged sword.

1054.22   scrused]   Squeezed.

1054.28   the Arches]   The Aegean archipelago.

1055.39   Baudricks]   Baldrics.

1056.16   semicinctum]   Half-encircling.

1056.22–23   *Nuda . . . pulchrior?*]   Plautus, *Mostellaria*, I, iii: "A beautiful woman will be more beautiful naked than dressed in purple."

1057.19   Carazzaies of Scio, and Pera]   "Carazzaies" is derived from a Greek word for girls. Scio (Khíos) is an island in the Aegean; Pera was the name used for the section of Istanbul located in Europe.

1057.25   Chape]   The metal tip of a scabbard.

1058.33   *fasciae crinales*]   Hair bands.

1060.21   gaynes]   Notches made to receive timbers.

1060.27   lover]   Louver.

1061.2   Salsodiack]   Sodium carbonate.

1062.5   empale]   Create a fenced enclosure.

1062.39   Boulter or Searser]   Sieve.

1063.16   *Ius nigrum*]   A black broth made from hare's blood.

1065.21   strayne]   Tracks.

1066.6   *Noctes diesque estur*]   Night and day he eats.

1069.13*n*   W.R.]   Walter Ralegh.

1072.6   kyne]   Cows.

1075.1   Schuchinella]   Cochineal.

1075.17   Asmodius]   Asmodeus, a demon that appears in the Book of Tobit.

1075.19–21   Jehu . . . Temple]   See 2 Kings 10:19–27.

1076.13   Asceteria]   Hermitages.

1077.12   Burlett]   Coif, hood.

1077.27–28   *fasti . . . vigelli*]   Festivals, holidays, vigils.

1082.2–3   Solomon . . . as one,"]   Cf. Ecclesiastes 3:18–21.

1089.32   Gammot]   Incision knife.

1090.9   Dariena]   A Spanish colony on the northern coast of the Isthmus of Panama.

1093.3–4   *A Trewe Relaycon* . . . Lorde Percy]   Percy wrote this account sometime after the publication of John Smith's *Generall Historie* in 1624 and dedicated the work to his nephew, Algernon Percy (see note 1014.3–4). The manuscript was first published in 1922.

1093.30   La doniere]   René de Laudonnière founded a Huguenot colony at the mouth of the St. Johns River in Florida in 1564. The colony was destroyed by the Spanish the following year.

1098.7–8   Baldivia . . . Chily]   Pedro de Valdivia (c. 1498–1554), Spanish conqueror and governor of Chile.

1101.39   anotannes]   Anatomies, i.e., shriveled, emaciated bodies.

1104.18   William Weste]   A nephew of Baron De La Warre, West was killed by Indians during the winter of 1610–11.

1107.39   Mevis]   Nevis.

1113.30   flores Corves and St Michells]   Islands in the Azores.

1115.13   *Alget, qui non ardet*]   He grows cold who does not burn.

1115.16   Somer Islands]   Bermuda.

1118.5–7   to lighten them . . . of peace.]   Luke 1:79.

1118.10–13   the wisest man . . . the firmament.]   See Daniel 12:3.

1118.27–28   Sanballat . . . Horonites]   Sanballat the Horonite and Tobiah the Ammonite opposed the efforts of Nehemiah to rebuild the walls of Jerusalem and reform its laws. "Plairis" is probably a variant spelling of "players."

1118.31–32   the rod . . . the righteous]   Psalm 125:3.

1119.22–23   *Oculatus testis*]   An eyewitness.

1121.6   *fide dignus*]   Trustworthy.

1139.5   booke of Articles]   See note 419.33.

1153.6   Table book]   Notebook.

1155.17–20   what doe these . . . stony wall]   Cf. Nehemiah 4:2–3.

1155.27–29   as Judah once . . . the wall.]   Cf. Nehemiah 4:10.

1155.30–32   The land wee . . . great stature:]   Cf. Numbers 13:32.

1156.1–2   Let us goe . . . overcome it]   Cf. Numbers 13:30.

1157.16–17   it is not a yoke . . . a wife]   See Luke 14:16–20.

1157.18   sallat]   Salad.

1162.12–13   M.G. . . . B.F.]   Master Gouge; Black Friars.

1162.37   subscription]   A declaration of assent to the 39 Articles of the Church of England.

1168.12–20   Azariah sayd . . . the Galations]   See 2 Chronicles 15:7; 1 Corinthians 15:58; Galatians 6:9.

1170.39   the Western Islands]   The Azores.

1184.17   Sonnes of Anack]   See Numbers 13:33.

Index

Library of Congress Cataloging-in-Publication Data

Smith, John, 1580–1631.
  [Selections. 2007]
  Writings / Captain John Smith ; with other narratives of
    Roanoke, Jamestown, and the first English settlements of
    America ; edited by James Horn.
      p. cm. — (The Library of America ; 171)
  Includes bibliographical references and index.
  ISBN-13: 978-1-59853-001-8 (alk. paper)
  ISBN-10: 1-59853-001-1 (alk. paper)
      1. Virginia—History—Colonial period, ca. 1600–1775.
2. New England—History—Colonial period, ca. 1600–1775.
3. America—Discovery and exploration—English—Early works
to 1800. I. Horn, James P. P. II. Title. III. Title: Other narratives of Roanoke, Jamestown, and the first English settlements
of America. IV. Title: Captain John Smith : writings, with
other narratives of Roanoke, Jamestown, and the first English
settlement of America.

F229.S592   2007
975.5′02—dc22   2006050239

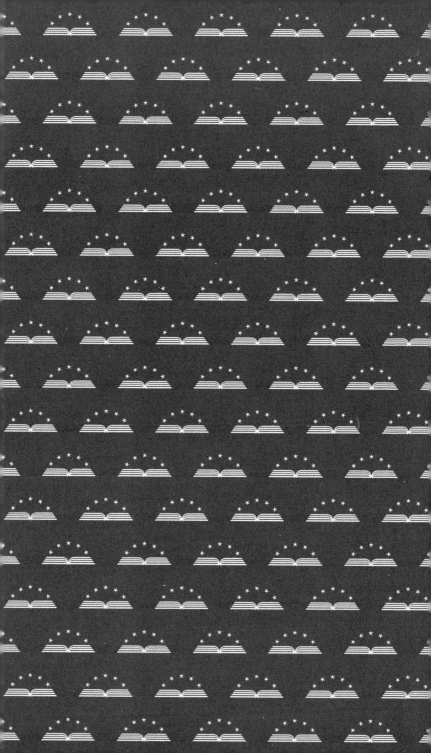